The Wash
The Fens
Great Wood and Beeches
Aylmerton
Sedgeford
Hindringham
Thursford Common
Edgefield Woods
Swanton Novers Woods
Melton Constable
Bacton Wood
Hindolveston Woods
Thurning
Blickling
Cawston
Reffley Wood
KING'S LYNN
Foxley Park
Haveringland Park
Barton Turf
Gressenhall
Hockering Wood
Horsham St Faith
Sporle Wood
E. DEREHAM
Mousehold Heath
Thorpe Wood
Bradenham
Shipdham
Earlham Park
NORWICH
Bedford Purlieus
Castor Hanglands
PETERBOROUGH
Saham Toney
Watton
Kimberley
Hethel
Langley
GREAT YARMOUTH
Whittlesey
Wayland Wood
Fritton Common
Hedenham Wood
Great Hockham
Long Stratton
Tindall Wood
Holme Fen
Doddington
Sexton Wood
Ditchingham
Mettingham
Kenninghall
Pulham
Bungay
Sotterley Park
Little Gidding
Monks' Wood
Moorend Wood
Shippea Hill
Brandon
ELY
Lakenheath
Gawdy Hall Wood
The Saints
Harleston
Wrentham Great Wood
Redenhall
Abbot's Ripton
Holland Wood
Somersham
Breckland
Hinderclay Wood
Redgrave Park
Sapley
Earith
Wicken Fen
Westhall Wood
Ubbeston Wood
Heveningham
Chippenham Fen
West Stow
Stanton
Kimbolton
Overhall Grove
Boxworth
Sibton
Knapwell Wood
Bruisyard Wood
BURY ST EDMUND'S
Barrow
Hardwick W.
Swaffham Prior
Norton W.
Kelsale
Papworth Wood
Swaffham Bulbeck
Horringer
Mendlesham
Framlingham
Madingley W.
Ickworth P.
Link Wood
Kingston Wood
CAMBRIDGE
STOWMARKET
Sandlings
Waresley Wood
Cherry Hinton
Lawshall Frith
Bradfield Woods
Iken Wood
Gamlingay Wood
Alpheton Wood
Felsham
Bull's W. (Cockfield)
Wandlebury
Eversden W.
Thorpe Morieux
Hartest
White Wood
Cobb's Wood
Hitcham
Barking Woods
Sheerhatch W.
Weston Colville
Lineage Wood
Staverton Park
Lavenham
Offton Middle W.
Abington
Rivey W.
Easty Wood
Wimpole
Milden Thicks
Elmsett Park
E. Hatley
Lit. Gransden
Hadstock
Kentwell
Castle Camps
IPSWICH
Long Melford
Wolve's Wood
Hayley Wood
Groton W.
Hintlesham Woods
Tadlow
Emanuel W.
Brundon W.
Buff Wood
Shadwell W.
Raydon
SUDBURY
Shelley
Holbrook Park
SAFFRON WALDEN
Hempstead W.
Gt Waldingfield
Polstead
Flatford
Dodnash Wood
Sampford West Wood
Arger-fen Wood
R. Stour
Boxted
Thaxted
Great W.
Dedham Heath
Stour Wood
Dovercourt
Parkhall W.
Earl's Colne
Bovingdon-Bassingbourn W.
Chalkney Wood
Soane W.
Wymondley
Dunmow High Wood
Markshall Woods
Takeley
Alsa W.
Little Bentley
Dunmow
COLCHESTER
Birchanger Wood
Frating
LUTON
BISHOPS STORTFORD
Felsted
Black Notley
Coggeshall
Brooklands (Weeley-Hall) Wood
Chest W.
Thorley W.
Welshwood Park
Bladder Wood
Sherrard's Park W.
Hatfield Forest
Lynderswood
Rivenhall
Pod's W.
St Osyth
Terling
Tiptree
Rothamsted
Garnett's Wood
Witham
Kingswood Forest
Essendon
Leaden Roding Woods
New Hall
Toppinghoe Hall Wood
Colchester High Woods
Hatfield (Herts)
Broxbourne
Nazeing
Skreens Park
CHELMSFORD
Birch Wood
Wormley Wood
Galley Wood
Wintry Forest
Writtle Forest
Gt Baddow
Woodham Walter Common
Northaw Gt Wood and Common
Ongar Great P.
Pheasant-house Wood
Lingwood Common
Enfield Chase
Waltham Abbey
Ingatestone
South Weald
Mountnessing
Ingrave
Meepshole Wood
Epping Forest
Havering Park
Norsey Wood
Thorndon P.
Eastwood
Hampstead Heath
Ken Wood
Leyton
Hainault Forest
Langdon Hills Woods
Basildon
SOUTHEND
LONDON
Northlands Wood
Belfairs Wood
Aveley
Jackwatts Wood
Hadleigh Great Wood
Thundersley West Wood
Lessness Woods
Thanet
Ellenden Wood
Chesnut Woods
Otford
CANTERBURY

Ancient Woodland

its history, vegetation and uses in England

NEW EDITION

A woodland scene attributed to Simon Benninck, the late-medieval Flemish artist. The figures are somewhat conventionalized[440] but the scenery is probably the most convincing picture of the interior of a wood ever painted. It is recognizable as a limewood. The underwood in the foreground was felled last year, leaving standing most of the scattered and variable timber trees of elm and oak. The felled stools are sprouting to form the next underwood crop; among them are 'coppicing plants' which include broom, male-fern, bramble, and the honeysuckle *Lonicera xylosteum*. The toadstool *Oudemansiella radicata* is parasitizing the roots of an elm. In the background tall lime underwood on big stools awaits the next felling. Except for *L. xylosteum*, all these features – even the pig-sticking – could have been paralleled in Chalkney Wood, North Essex, at the time. (I am indebted to Mr John Hunter for drawing my attention to this picture.) British Library: Add. 18855 f.108v

Ancient Woodland

its history, vegetation and uses in England

NEW EDITION

Oliver Rackham

CASTLEPOINT PRESS

First published in Great Britain in 1980

New edition published in 2003 by
Castlepoint Press
Colvend, Dalbeattie, Kirkcudbrightshire, DG5 4QB

Typeset in Minion and Cerigo by
Pioneer Associates, Camserney, Perthshire and
printed and bound under supervision
by M.R.M. Graphics Ltd, Buckinghamshire

British Library Cataloguing-in-Publication Data

A cataloguing record for this book is available from
the British Library

ISBN 0–897604–27–0 (hardback)

Castlepoint Press wishes to acknowledge the financial support
of English Nature, the Forestry Commission, England and
the International Tree Foundation.

We also acknowledge support from the Tree Council,
the Woodland Trust, the Arboricultural Association and
the British Ecological Society.

Contents

Chapters Added in 2003

In tribute to
DAVID EDWIN COOMBE
1927–1999

For 41 years my friend and teacher, he first introduced me to the Cambridgeshire woods, in which he made observations for some 50 years.

In memory also of colleagues who helped so much with the original book and have not lived to see it reissued: especially Len Cram, J Evans, George Heygate, Nan and Jack Litchfield, William Palmer, Colin Ranson, John Rishbeth, and Harold Whitehouse.

Preface to the 1980 Edition

Why write yet another book about British woods? Many authors have written (or copied from earlier authors) on woods for their beauty, as the home of much of our wild life, or as an approach – to some degree – to our vanished natural vegetation. But there is more to woods than this. The complex variety of native woodlands, which should be the basis both of their romance and of their scientific interest, has been strangely neglected: rarely do writers try to convey the richness of detail to be found within many apparently ordinary woods. Only recently have we begun to understand woods as the antiquities which many of them are and to appreciate how they have been an integral part of our civilization from its beginnings. The questions of where woods come from and what they are for, confused by three centuries of misleading forestry propaganda, are now being reopened as energy and transport cease to be cheap.

Scope of this book

Woods are both natural and artificial. Some are largely natural – a direct link with the prehistoric landscape – others almost wholly artificial. They are the outcome of centuries of interaction between men and trees. They are difficult things to understand or classify: how many authors get right even the fundamental distinction between woods and plantations?

This book is about woods that have been in existence for at least 200, and usually at least 500, years, and which therefore have a substantial natural element. It includes the trees of parks, commons, and places like Epping Forest, but excludes orchards and forestry plantations. I have written elsewhere on the history of hedgerow trees[846] and say little about hedges here. The book is complementary to works on forestry, which deal mainly with modern plantations, and to the many studies of prehistoric vegetation which are based on pollen analysis.

I have already written two books in this field, one dealing chiefly with woods as archaeological features,[122] the other being a monograph of Hayley Wood in Cambridgeshire.[120] Here I am concerned both with the biology of woods and with the part that they have played in human affairs. This is a first attempt to consider why ancient woods should be of so many kinds and what is the separate history of each type.

Historical ecology seeks to interpret the natural and artificial factors that have influenced the development of an area of vegetation to its present state. It is the history of particular woods, especially of those that are still extant, rather than the history of generalizations about woodland. The science of historical ecology began in 1769–72 with a debate in the Royal Society on whether or not the sweet-chestnut was an exotic tree. The controversy, which anticipated some of the arguments used in this book, is summarized in Chapter 21. It was forgotten, and the next work to combine field observation with written and archaeological records was *The Making of the* [*Norfolk*] *Broads* in 1960.[768]

Ecological writing

Although historical ecology combines the specialized techniques of the field, the archives, and the laboratory, most of the results are not too remote from ordinary experience. My object has been to write for both botanists and historians and for amateurs as well as professionals. The occasional technicalities necessary to satisfy some specialist readers will, I hope, be skipped by those whose interests lie elsewhere without unduly interrupting the argument.

An ecological book can be written at three levels of generality. It may analyse vegetation as a whole and the effects of factors such as soil differences, grazing, or shade. Or it may deal with particular kinds of vegetation e.g. limewoods, chestnut-woods, or ashwoods. Or it may describe particular sites such as Chalkney Wood or Hayley Wood. Much modern ecological writing neglects the last of these levels. Many analyses of some aspects of the vegetation of a site fail to tell the reader what the site looks like as a whole, much as if a learned writer on art were to concern himself exclusively with the pigments and brushwork of sample areas of paintings. By not considering his sites as a whole an investigator runs the risks of improperly selecting his data and of making his observations non-reproducible: it becomes difficult to recognize comparable sites elsewhere or to go back in fifty years and see how the site has changed. In our subject it is essential to pursue all three levels of generality. Chalkney Wood, for instance, is partly a limewood, partly a hornbeam-wood, and partly an ashwood; we

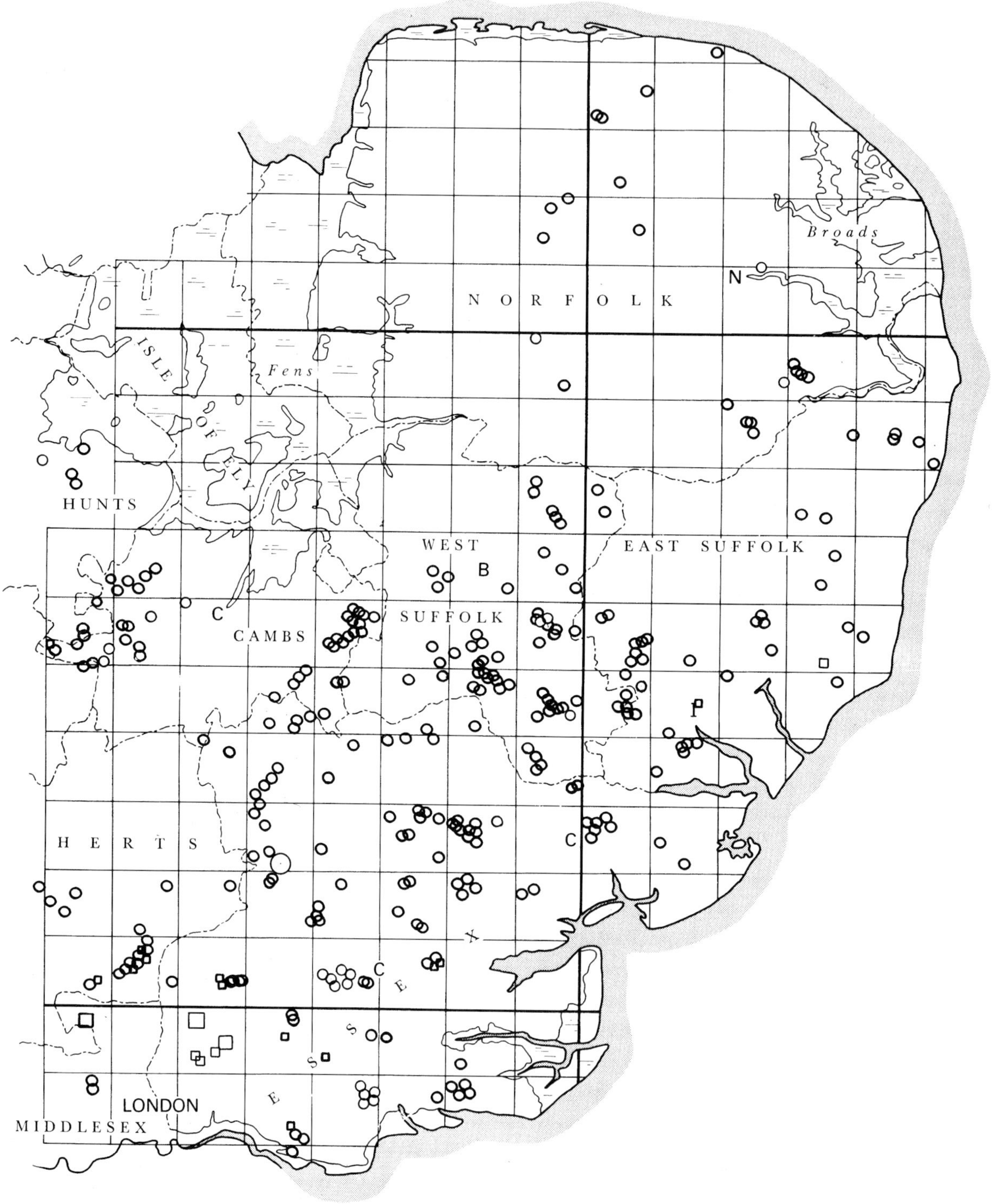

Fig. 0.1 Eastern England, showing the location of the woods providing the main body of evidence on which this book is based. □: sites which are wholly wood-pasture. This and other distribution maps give the National Grid (10-km squares), county boundaries, and the extent of marshland and fen. Norwich, Cambridge, Bury St Edmunds, Ipswich, Colchester, and Chelmsford are shown by their initial letters.

learn more about these three types from their interactions in the same wood than we could hope to discover by studying them in isolation in different woods. In this book, woods are described each as a whole, with its earthworks and documentation; aspects relevant to other parts of the book are dealt with by cross-references rather than by splitting the description among several chapters.

English and Botanical Latin names of plants are a problem: is the author to risk imprecision with the former or pedantry with the latter? I shall generally use English names for trees and the commoner herbs; in lists, the need for precision and conciseness often dictate the use of Latin. With rare exceptions, Latin names are in accordance with the *Excursion Flora of the British Isles* (1968 edition).[632]

Geographical scope and general methods

Although knowledge is rapidly accumulating, a book on British woods as a whole would be too ambitious an undertaking at present. This book contains examples from many parts of Britain and from the Continent, but is based mainly on my own studies in Eastern England, which are partly a general survey and partly a detailed investigation of particular areas.

Woods covered in my general survey are shown in Fig. 0.1. They represent about a quarter of the ancient woods in the region, but more of the large and medium-sized woods have been included than of the small ones. Sampling was not random but was intended to cover all types of woodland, giving greater prominence to the rarer or more interesting ones. The only areas wholly neglected are those which appear not to have ancient woods. A record card (Fig. 0.2) was used to collect the minimum information about a wood; from most woods extra information was recorded in order to construct maps of earthworks, trees, and ground vegetation. In woods of particular interest other aspects have been studied in much more detail.

Documentary studies have covered the same woods as those seen in the field, plus others not extant or not visited. The amount of material varies enormously with accidents of recording and preservation. My book *Hayley Wood* includes the complete documentation for a moderately well-recorded wood.

Eastern England combines an unusual variety of native woods with excellent documentation. There has been a strong symbiosis between men and trees: for over a thousand years there has been relatively little woodland, which, being particularly important to the inhabitants, has been systematically conserved. The region is still rich in the fabric and traditions of medieval woodland. Recent destruction has been at work here as in every region, but has been less thorough than in most, and some areas have largely escaped.

Similar studies could be done in many parts of the country. Areas with more woodland tend to be less conservative in its management. In some well-wooded regions much of the work would consist of rescuing scraps of evidence from amid conifer plantations rather than recording ancient woods in a recognizable state. In Wales, Scotland, and Ireland the archives are usually poor: woodland histories, unless they can be supplemented by pollen analysis, are likely to be shorter and less detailed than in most of England.

It has recently been estimated that a third of the total area of woodland and plantation in Britain is on sites that have been continuously covered with trees since at least the Middle Ages.[101] Of this area more than half has been replanted at some time, so that at most a sixth of what is green on the map (i.e. a little over 1% of the total land area) survives as ancient woodland. This is still too much to be completely catalogued on a national scale, though much could be done with a series of regional studies.

The constant spring: past and future

The main theme of this book is the self-renewal typical of English woodland history: the quiet, usually unremarked regrowth of the young shoots, known as ***spring***, automatically replacing the woods every time they were cut down, decade after decade and century after century. During the last hundred years this stable relationship between men and trees has gone out of fashion. Men have ceased to use the native woods, which at first fell into neglect but latterly have been destroyed and replaced by arable or by plantations. Neglect is much less destructive of the character of a wood than are most forms of replanting. From 1945 to 1975 a greater percentage of ancient woodland disappeared through grubbing or replanting than in any thirty years since the Norman Conquest. My previous cautious estimate of a third of the total lost in this period[122] is almost certainly too low.

The destruction of woods costs money and is less prevalent now than a few years ago; people have come to value ancient woods for various reasons, and to restore them to their proper functions. But we still hear growls from the faction that maintains that the mere production of timber – of however poor quality and at however great an expense – is the only proper function of the sites of woods, and that neither knows nor cares what is destroyed in the hope of achieving this end. Most large woods have already been thus sacrificed, and the recording of what is left is an urgent priority. To protect the middle-sized and small woods we need to know what woods we still have, which are worth preserving, and how the features which we value originated and were maintained.

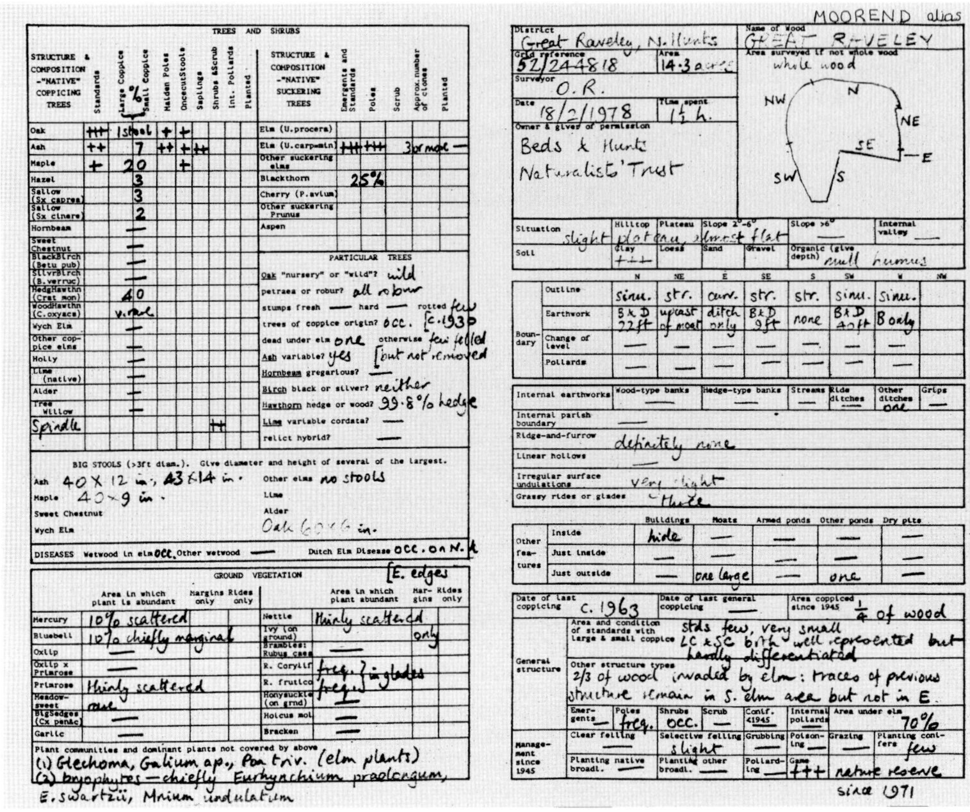

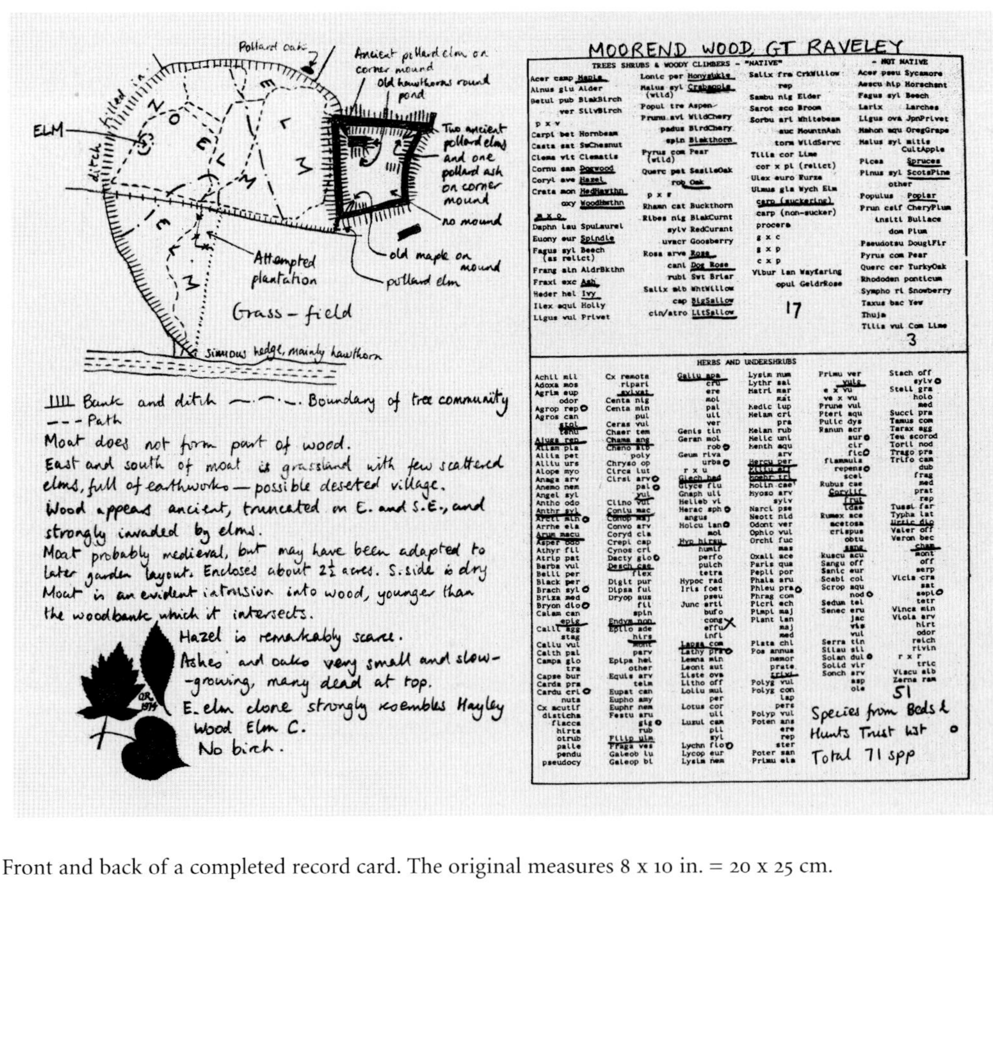

Fig. 0.2 Front and back of a completed record card. The original measures 8 x 10 in. = 20 x 25 cm.

Conventions

The counties in this book are the geographical counties (e.g. Worcestershire, Middlesex, Huntingdonshire) and take no account of the administrative rearrangements of 1974.

The terms ***Middle Ages*** and ***medieval*** cover the years 1066–1536 and thus exclude the Anglo-Saxon period.

Soil characteristics (e.g. pH), unless otherwise stated, are measured at a depth of 15 cm below the surface of the mineral soil.

'Woodland' does not normally include wood-pasture or plantations (Chapter 1).

Dates B.C. or A.D. are in actual calendar years; b.c. or a.d. are in radiocarbon years (p. 97).

English Measures

1 in.	=	25 mm
1 ft = 12 in.	=	0.30 m
1 yard = 3 ft	=	0.91 m
1 mile = 1,760 yards	=	1.6 km
1 modern acre	=	0.40 ha
1,000 modern acres	=	4.0 km^2
1 cubic ft	=	0.028 m^3
1 ton	=	1.0 t
1*d*	=	£0.0042
1*s* = 12*d*	=	£0.050

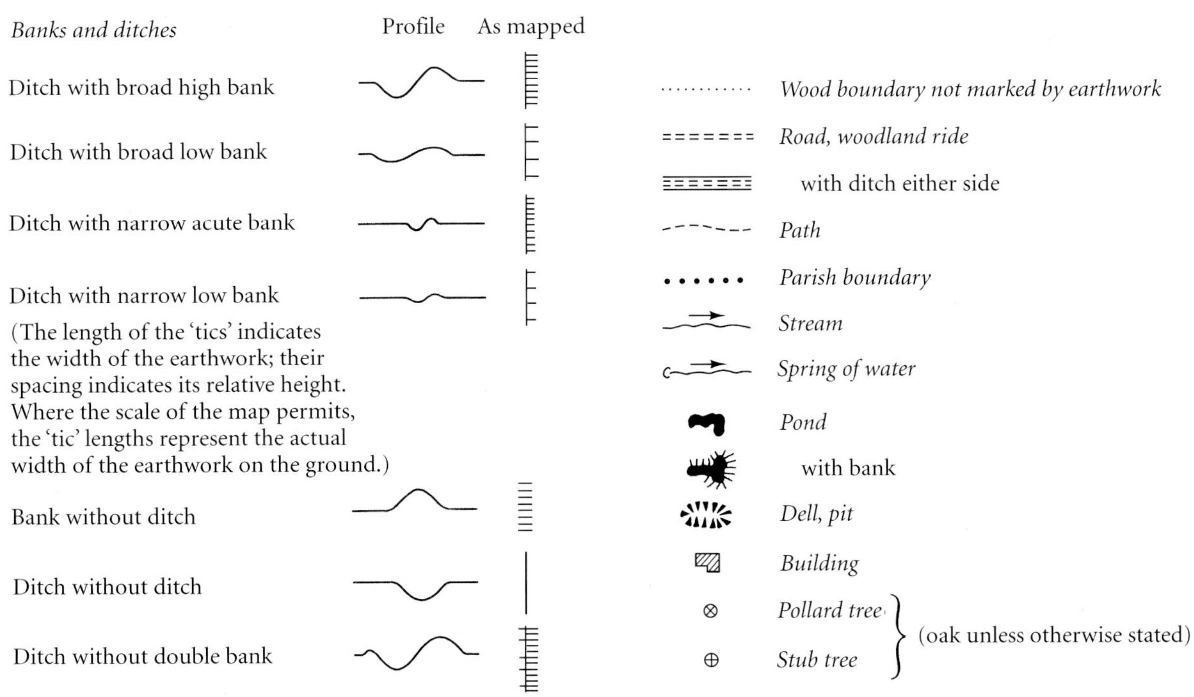

Fig. 0.3 Conventional signs on maps

Acknowledgements

I was brought up in a medieval East Anglian town and owe my interest in topographical history to my father, Mr G. H. Rackham. I had the further good fortune to be instructed in the Cambridge ecological tradition by Dr A. S. Watt, Professor Sir Harry Godwin, Dr G. C. Evans, Dr D. E. Coombe, Professor R. G. West, and Professor C. D. Pigott. I am grateful to all of these but especially to Dr Coombe for his deep interest in vegetation as part of the historic landscape, and to Dr Evans for his insights into the physiological basis of plant ecology; both have given me constant help and encouragement over many years.

For the work recorded in this book I am indebted to many landowners who have allowed me to visit their woods and to the owners and custodians of archives listed in the references. In both field and documentary studies I have been most ably helped by Mrs Susan Ranson and Mrs Hildegard Heygate. The soil analyses were done by Miss Pat Maher. This research was supported by generous grants from the Natural Environment Research Council to Cambridge University Botany School and from Corpus Christi College, Cambridge. I thank also Dr R. M. S. Perrin and Mr M. D. Fysh (advice about soils); Dr H. J. B. Birks and Mr B. Huntley (help with phytosociology); Dr Birks and Dr R. Bradshaw (pollen analysis); Dr Birks, Dr J. Rishbeth, Dr J. N. Gibbs, and Dr C. M. Brasier (tree pathology); Professor J. K. S. St Joseph and Cambridge Committee for Aerial Photography; Professor C. Cheney, Mr A. Davison, Dr D. W. Dewhirst, the late Professor B. Dickins, Mr D. P. Dymond, Mr J. Hunter, the late Rev J. T. Munday, and Dr R. I. Page (historical documents); Dr J. M. Coles (prehistoric woodmanship); and Dr J. M. Fletcher and Mr C. A. Hewett (medieval carpentry). The help of others is specifically acknowledged in the text. Mr. L. Cram, Mr J. Davis, Mrs A. Hart, the late Professor C. McBurney, Miss J. Manning, Mr W. H. Palmer, Mr M. Stratton, and Professor P. M. Warren have generously helped me in various ways with fieldwork.

The text of this book was kindly read by Mrs J. Evans, whose advice I greatly value. I am similarly indebted to Dr Coombe and to Mr Palmer for reading particular chapters.

My particular thanks are due to Colin and Susan Ranson for their hospitality, their constant encouragement, and their many valuable suggestions. I have visited many places in their company or at their instigation. Much of this book was written, and the whole of it typed and corrected, in their house, within sight of limewoods and black poplars. Without Colin's persuasion and enthusiasm the woodland survey would not have begun; without Susan's determination and persistence its results would not have seen the light of day.

OLIVER RACKHAM

Corpus Christi College,
Cambridge, 1979

Preface to the 2003 Edition

This book was the published outcome of research done by the author for the then Natural Environment Research Council. Appearing in 1980, it almost coincided with George Peterken's *Woodland Conservation and Management*. It was kindly, indeed generously, received by reviewers, although they seldom went into any depth of response to the ideas put forward.

By the 1970s woods had been interpreted in terms of factors such as light and waterlogging, matters within the scope of current observation and ultimately depending on plant physiology, which had been my first field of research. In a separate area of science, much had been ascertained through pollen analysis about the precursor of woodland in the wildwood of prehistoric times. In both of these Cambridge University Botany School then had a supreme reputation. My object was to bridge the gap between them by giving a time-dimension to woodland ecology. At the same time I sought to put woodland history on a scientific basis by making it the sum of what could be ascertained about the separate histories of hundreds of individual woods.

Twenty-two years have gone by, and research into woodland history and ecology has not stood still. Among regional studies I would mention those of Professor Mel Jones and the Sheffield school of woodland history, Dr Richard Gulliver and Dr Margaret Atherden in Yorkshire, Dr David Morfitt and Dr Sarah Wager in Warwickshire, Leslie Hepple and Alison Doggett in the Chilterns, Ursula Broughton and Brian Wright on the ancient woods near Chalkney Wood, George Roberts in

Kent, Anne Horsfall and Dennis Seaward in Dorset. Also in Kent, Alexander Wheaten and the Blean Research Group have just published an historical and ecological account of the Blean Woods north of Canterbury. Dr Della Hooke has extended the interpretation of place-names and other Anglo-Saxon evidence.

Research into woodland history and ecology has widened to include Wales, Scotland, and Ireland, Belgium and Spain and Sardinia, Japan and Tasmania, Texas and West Africa. Its scope has enlarged to embrace many other aspects of landscape. There remains the problem of combining different disciplines. Few professional historians fully understand what trees are and how they behave, and how one tree behaves differently from another. Few professional ecologists fully grasp the nature of historical or archaeological evidence and what it can or cannot do. Writers who confine themselves to written documents cut themselves off from knowing what was happening at times when people were not writing things down. Those who do no fieldwork, or never study historic buildings, will never appreciate that archives do not tell the whole story. In this field many amateurs perform at least as well as professionals.

Others in Britain (as well as myself) have uncovered vastly more detail than was available in the 1970s. The great importance of seed-bank plants, not visible every year, has come to light (Chapter 26). Two additional classifications of woodland have been published (Chapter 31), and a remarkable study of the relations between ancient woodland and wildwood (Chapter 32). There have been many regional and local studies of woodland outside Britain: I particularly commend the magnificent book by Tack, van den Bremt, and Hermy on the woods of Flanders. A recent, brilliantly argued study of Hungary by Peter Szabó shows that much of what is known about the woodland history of England has its parallels in that country as well and, by implication, in much of central Europe.

There have been many physical changes in woodland and the landscape. The conservation scene has changed out of recognition. My original work was written during 'the years that the locust hath eaten' – the period when ancient woods were thought of as mere vacant land and were casually destroyed in order to grow a few more pine-trees or a little more wheat. But those years were drawing to an end. Almost all the woods that I wrote about in 1979 are still there, and most of them are appreciated and valued. Conservation bodies like the Woodland Trust and the county Wildlife Trusts are large woodland owners. The National Trust, which down the years did not always guard ancient woodland as vigorously as one would expect from its objectives (p. 325), has made full amends. Hatfield Forest, its most important historic tree-land property, is now managed with the precise attention to detail that the Trust displays with historic buildings. It has been studied by specialists in many fields, and its management plan descends to the level of caring, one by one, for several hundred notable trees. This is the National Trust at its best, and it is due to the enthusiasm and scholarship of Vikki Forbes, the Warden, and her staff and her predecessors Lawrence Sisitka and Nigel Hester (to whom I am greatly indebted).

The Forestry Commission, which until the 1980s was the single most active enchroacher on ancient woodland, is now one of the most active conservers. This is partly from force of circumstances, but also results from a genuine change of ethos. Its earlier attempts to convert ancient woods into plantations often proved to be a fiasco (an expensive fiasco, but who remembers the money spent?), as native trees recover from attempts to kill them and overtake the planted trees. Forestry itself has been through hard times, and has had to diversify from its former main objective of producing ordinary coniferous timber – which, once grown, has to be sold in competition with Britain's traditional, well-organized overseas suppliers. From 1990 the Commission has actively sought to 'de-coniferize' many of its ancient woods. Chalkney Wood, for example (pp. 246–51), is now once again a magnificent lime- and hornbeam-wood almost throughout. The nearby Markshall estate (p. 251) is at last being rehabilitated with energy and panache by the Thomas Phillips Price Trust – just as the historic structures shown in Figs 10.7 and 10.8 (pp. 146–7) were, at long last, acquired and rehabilitated by the Cambridge Preservation Society and the National Trust.

One aspect in which I am gratified to be proved wrong is the compilation of a register of ancient woodland: a formidable task which I thought impossible in 1980 (p. xiii). Within ten years, the Nature Conservancy Council (predecessor of English Nature) had compiled a provisional Inventory of Ancient Woodland (Kirby and others 1998). Besides helping to link ancient woodland into the planning process the Inventory was to form the practical basis of the Forestry Commission's new policy after 1985.

Interest in ancient trees has revived after a period of being out of fashion. The English have always valued them as objects of wonder and beauty and historical association, as celebrated (for example) by Shakespeare, by Strutt the artist in 1822 and Menzies the photographer in 1864, and again after a gap by another great photographer, Thomas Pakenham, in *Meetings with Remarkable Trees*. It is now realized that 'veteran trees', like the great oaks of Sherwood and Windsor Forests (Fig. 17.7, p. 302), or the pollards of Hatfield Forest and Staverton Park, are of scientific importance too, being the unique habitat of very many specialized insects, spiders, and lichens. Much of the wildlife associated with trees depends on ancient trees. Ted Green and

Helen Read, among others, have re-established public interest in Veteran Trees (p. 524).

Deer – native red and roe, anciently-introduced fallow, and modern introductions – relentlessly increase. In 1980 the word *muntjac* did not appear in the index; it is now the commonest deer. The effects especially on ground vegetation can be dramatic. For example, the experiment shown in Fig. 5.2 has been abruptly terminated by increased deer activity (Fig. 25.25). Artificially large numbers of deer replaced crude destruction as the top conservation problem of the 1990s. They are an international problem which is still unsolved.

A complete revision of this book would be a formidable task; but it would mostly involve adding new material and details, rather than unsaying things that I said. In response to many requests, I have reissued the text as it stood, with a few corrections of mistakes, amendments of statements that are time-dependent ('in the last ten years') or out of date, and some additions at the ends of chapters. The photographs, whose original reproduction left much to be desired, have been re-scanned and extra ones added. Radiocarbon dates have been calibrated into approximate actual years B.C. I have also chosen nine areas of physical change or of changes in knowledge which are sufficiently coherent to form supplementary chapters.

When adding to an existing book there is the problem of nomenclature. The original objective of Botanical Latin names – to set up a permanent system of naming plants which everyone will understand – has never been achieved: it has been subverted by the secondary objective of displaying successive taxonomists' theories of evolutionary relationship.[1] The names which I used in the original book, and which I shall have to use in the additions, are now old-fashioned. Bluebell was called by Linnaeus *Hyacinthus non-scriptus* because it was unwritten (it did not have the letters AI written on its petals as the Ancient Greek plant *hyakínthos* did). In later Floras this was altered to *Scilla non-scripta*. By 1980 the fashionable genus-name was *Endymion*, which I used in *Ancient Woodland* – thereby, by implication, signing up to Garcke's theory of the subdivision of the genus *Scilla*, even though I did not understand it. The name in vogue for the present is *Hyacinthoides*. What can I do but fall back on the name Bluebell?

The nature of historical ecology

Woodland history is a branch of historical ecology, which is both a science and a part of history. As I have pointed out at length elsewhere,[2] it is all too easy for scientists to create a pseudo-history, and for historians to create a pseudo-ecology, through each not understanding the other half of the story. This gives rise to the common fallacy of treating plants and animals as mere Environment, as if they were part of the scenery of the theatre of landscape, rather than actors in the play.

Ecology is not a hard science like physics, with well-defined, highly quantitative laws to which there are no exceptions. Ecological history is mainly an observational science like astronomy, although (as in this book) there is some scope for experimentation. Although data have accumulated over the years, there is not yet a body of theory of historical development of ecosystems. Historical ecology is still at the stage of discovery and interpretation: it 'lags behind' (as some would put it) branches of science such as evolution, where most new research is intended to exemplify or elaborate pre-existing theory rather than taking its departure from observation. I leave it to readers whether to rejoice or lament over this state of affairs.

New data have strengthened my conviction that ancient woods are all different, and each has its own unique development. In the supplementary chapters I show that woods close together, and which on any rational scheme of classification have very similar characteristics, have nevertheless followed different trajectories of change for reasons that still defy explanation. Far less is known about the populations and demography of plants than of animals, and still less about those of wild trees.

Ancient woods are more complex than anything else that scientists study, with the possible exception of the genome itself. A scientist by inclination and training, I reflect in pessimistic moments on the words of C. S. Lewis:

> What cannot be trusted to recur is not material for science: that is why history is not one of the sciences. You cannot find out what Napoleon did at the battle of Austerlitz by asking him to come and fight it again in a laboratory with the same combatants, the same *terrain*, the same weather, and in the same age. You have to go to the records.[3]

As I shall explain in Chapter 33, conservation is really applied historical ecology. Conservationists need to combine the mind-sets of scientists and historians in an age which discourages dialogue between the two.

[1] For further discussion see: Iliff, J. (2003). New names, genera, families and their 'natural orders' – a plea. *Botanical Society of the British Isles News* **92** 29–31.

[2] For example in Grove & Rackham *The Nature of Mediterranean Europe.*

[3] Lewis, C. S. (1946). Phoenix Quarterly **1**, no. L.

Acknowledgements

I mourn the death of David Coombe, who first introduced me to the Cambridgeshire woods (in which he made observations for some 50 years) and encouraged me to develop the records and ideas in this book.

I am indebted to the many owners, past and present, who have allowed me to visit their woods. I have made use of data collected by David Briggs, Chris Preston, and their students on hybridization in Buff Wood.[4] In Hayley Wood I have used data collected long ago by W. H. Palmer, I. Hepburn, F. H. Perring, and J. E. Dobson. Charles Turner and Mark Powell have helped over many years in the West Cambridgeshire woods, Michael Astor in Buff Wood, and Alexander Wheaten and the Blean Research Group in the Canterbury area. Information about deer numbers comes from Ray Symonds and his many helpers at the annual deer count in and around Hayley Wood. James and Ann Hart have helped me over many years in the Bradfield Woods. Simon Leatherdale has instructed and encouraged me in the Forestry Commission's woods in Suffolk and Essex. Many of his colleagues in other areas have gone out of their way to help me with Forest Enterprise properties. I have had useful discussions about conservation objectives with Nicholas Hammond and Simon Pryor. Margaret Slee has helped me at Hempstead Wood. At Staverton I have enjoyed the friendship of three generations of the Kemball family. Over the years I have derived much profit from the staff and students of Flatford Mill Field Study Centre in Suffolk, and of the Kingcombe Centre in Dorset. Michael Martin and Rob Jarman have been with me in the field in Gloucestershire; Stephen Bott and Oliver Padel in Cornwall. Many people, especially John Bloomfield of Hadleigh (Suffolk), have introduced me to ancient buildings.

In Europe I acknowledge the hospitality, friendship, and help of Mr A. T. Grove and the late Dr Jean Grove, and Dr Jennifer Moody. I have learnt much from Professor Diego Moreno, friend for many years in Italy. In Sweden I am indebted to Professor Björn Berglund, Professor Richard Bradshaw, and Dr Tommy Knutsson, in France to Alain Desbrosse, and in Austria to Hermann Margl and Andreas Schreckeneder. In Greece I have touched on the work of the archaeological surveys of Grevená (director, Nancy Wilkie); Sphakiá, Crete (Lucia Nixon, Jennifer Moody, and Simon Price); and Kythera (Cyprian Broodbank). In America, I am indebted to Henry Art, Kathy Biddick, Susan Bratton, Richard Brewer, Wick Dossett, Ernie Gould, David Houston, Jennifer Moody, Hugh Raup, David Smith, Peter White, Stephen Wingate, and Vickie Ziegler. My studies in Japan have been at the invitation and with the help of Dr Katsue Fukamachi, Dr Tomohiko Kamitani, Professor Jun-ichi Ogura, Professor Toru Nakashizuka, Dr Hiroshi Tanaka, and Dr Toshiya Yoshida. For guidance, hospitality, and inspiration in Australia I am indebted to Dr Daniel Lunney, Mrs Jenny Mills, and Dr Tim Nevard.

I thank Lesley Beaney and Janet Dunn for their skill and patience in re-designing and preparing this very complex book.

Through decades of study I have enjoyed the friendship and support, formal and informal, of successive Masters, Fellows, and Scholars of Corpus Christi College, Cambridge: a particularly valued and productive privilege for a general practitioner of science like myself.

OLIVER RACKHAM

Corpus Christi College, Cambridge
St Etheldreda's Day, 2002

[4] MS in Plant Sciences Library, Cambridge.

ENGLISH NATURE

English Nature

Oliver Rackham has transformed the way that we look at the countryside. His deep scholarship, clear prose and sharp insight challenge our tendencies towards broad and often bland generalisations of what was or should be the state of our ancient woodland. He stresses that each wood is different, the product of hundreds of years of a unique interaction between the climate, soil and treatment of a particular site. This expanded edition of his classic book has enabled him to develop some of the themes present in the original edition, but also to comment on issues and ideas that have emerged over the last 20 years: the impact of the severe storms of 1987 and 1990; the turnaround in forestry policy; the recent debates on the role of large herbivores in the wildwood and the increasing impact of deer on current woodland communities.

We are pleased that he is able to report some progress in the conservation of ancient woodland since 1980: English Nature is proud of the role that it and its predecessor, the Nature Conservancy Council, have played in developing ancient woodland inventories and in promoting policy shifts that have encouraged the removal of conifers from many replanted ancient woodland sites. Oliver does not however allow us any room for complacency: he rightly criticises the tendency for formulaic descriptions of woodland and unreadable management plans; for too much time spent on committees and not enough recording the plants and animals of individual woods. He fears that woods will increase in quantity, but decline in quality, 'their guts eaten out . . . by sheep and deer'. We must accept his challenge and use the wealth of knowledge presented here to ensure that in this one aspect he is proved wrong.

Dr Andrew Brown
Chief Executive, English Nature

Forestry Commission
England

Forestry Commission

The first edition of Ancient Woodland was universally recognised as a seminal work, which profoundly changed our appreciation of woodland. The fact that a few years after publication the Forestry Commission changed its policy to provide much greater protection to ancient woodland was no coincidence.

Foresters are used to working with trees inherited from the previous generation, and growing trees which will be valued by the next. However, this book made foresters realise that they needed to look back over many generations, if not several millennia, to really understand the woodlands they were managing. It opened our eyes to features, such as banks and pollards, which we had taken for granted, and gave them new significance. Managing with an awareness of such a long time-line has certainly made woodland management more complex, but also more rewarding.

Oliver pulls no punches in these pages over the impact of the Forestry Commission's utilitarian post-war policy. We may not always agree with his perspective, but we do now acknowledge that ancient woods in England are far too valuable and diverse to be used for the single-minded growing of timber crops. We are keen to put right the wrongs of the past by actively pursuing and encouraging the restoration of such 'coniferised' ancient woodland.

Ancient woods are effectively irreplaceable and each is individual, but they are not rare or remote. One third of England's woodland is ancient, and such woods are familiar features of most landscapes and parishes. We are proud to have nearly 70,000 hectares of ancient woodland and Royal Forest on the Forestry Commission estate, and the vast majority of this is open for free public access. Ancient woodland is a piece of our heritage which you can stroll around in, not peer at in a glass cabinet.

We are more optimistic than Oliver about the outlook for ancient woodland in England. Subtle decline and attrition, particularly browsing by deer and sheep, are serious threats, but ones which we are prepared to tackle. Indeed, we believe that this book itself is part of the solution: raising public understanding of woodland and inspiring owners to cherish their rich inheritance is a critical contribution.

Lord Clark
Chairman, Forestry Commission

Foreword

by S. M. Walters, Sc. D., V.M.H.,
sometime Director of Cambridge University Botanic Garden and instigator of the *Atlas of the British Flora* and *Flora Europaea*

I was very pleased to accept Oliver Rackham's request that I might contribute this short foreword to one of his most remarkable books, now happily to appear with colour photographs and nine new Chapters in a brand new edition. It is just over forty years since the then infant Cambridgeshire and Isle of Ely Naturalist Trust (now the Wildlife Trust for Cambridgeshire) launched a successful appeal to buy its first nature reserve, Hayley Wood, which began its 'new life' in 1963. Since I, along with several other friends and colleagues, was much involved in the purchase and early management of this most valuable reserve, it is a real pleasure to recall the part played by Oliver, then a young research student in the Botany School of the University, in the development, not just of our knowledge of Hayley itself, but also of the whole subject we now call 'historical ecology'. Indeed it is not too much to claim that the book *Hayley Wood: its History and Ecology*, published by the Trust in 1975 and reprinted in 1990, which rightly bears Oliver's name as author, did much to convince, not just Cambridge botanists, but a wider world of ecologists, that here was a rising star indeed!

In commending to you, the reader, this handsome new edition of one of Oliver's later books, I can assume that you will already be aware that we have in our midst, happily still in his prime, one of the really outstanding botanical writers of our times, with a unique, direct and often marvellously witty style like no-one else. May you long continue to delight us, Oliver, with your talks illustrated with pieces of, say, Ely Cathedral, and your writings which we all so much admire. Could I dare conclude 'Vivant Bosci Antiqui', to commemorate that extraordinary expertise of Oliver's with the deciphering and translation of Church documents in Medieval Latin, a skill that throws such light on the ancient woodlands of our land?

Max Walters
4 July 2003

International Tree Foundation

The original edition of this book has been a force for good in the world of woodland conservation and in shaping new relationships between people and their environments. Oliver Rackham writes persuasively and powerfully. His love of trees is as evident as his intellectual understanding of their presence and purpose in ecosystems.

ITF has been caring for trees since 1922, for us, the relationship between people and trees is a vital part of the human experience. To be deprived of trees is to be enfeebled, to be able to enjoy them is to be enriched. The experts among us will find the revised edition a scholarly tour de force, updated to include many new areas of concern and research. For those of us who are amateurs, this text is both a teacher and a friend, from which we can learn more about our favourite subject. We are also reminded constantly that human interactions with the landscape are the most profound force in shaping the world, for good or ill. Oliver Rackham does not just teach or please, he also challenges. ITF members who have met him speak of his ardent call to preserve the best and reject the mediocre, as well as his desire to manage woodlands in reality, not just on paper.

For all of us, trees are a constant, often unremarked presence. This book reminds us that we must be vigilant to preserve the woodlands that are at once our heritage and our future. We are delighted to be associated with the revised edition and hope that the messages it carries will become a part of woodland management across Europe and beyond.

PETER RAPSON
Chair, International Tree Foundation

The Woodland Trust

Ancient Woodland is an outstanding book about one of the great glories of our natural heritage. Ancient woods are our richest habitat for wildlife, places of inordinate beauty, reservoirs of evidence for environmental change, archaeology and economic history, and a source of inspiration.

Our remaining ancient woodland only covers two per cent of the UK, so what remains is infinitely precious. Despite wide appreciation that nearly half the ancient woodland remaining in the 1930s was either cleared for agriculture or converted to plantations last century, ancient woodland continues to be lost to development, while overgrazing and the continued presence of non-native conifer plantations still damage ancient woods.

Almost half of the sites included in the ancient woodland inventories across Great Britain are less than five hectares and there are just 46 sites larger than 300 hectares. Only 15 per cent of ancient woodland is designated for its scientific and conservation importance and even this lacks full protection.

The greatest long-term threat is posed by rapid climate change, which will disrupt and disturb natural systems. Immediate action is needed to tackle its causes and to implement strategies to place ancient woodland on a more robust footing and help its associated wildlife to adapt.

The Woodland Trust believes that there should be no further loss of ancient woodland. We are proud to be associated with Oliver Rackham's seminal work and hope that it will fill people with wonder and inspire them to take action before it is too late.

MIKE TOWNSEND OBE
Chief Executive, The Woodland Trust

The Tree Council

It is no coincidence that Oliver Rackham was featured in the first issue of the Tree Council's re-launched 'Tree News' magazine and has been a regular contributor ever since. To make trees matter to everyone, we wanted independently minded, well-informed and well written features that would inspire interest in trees.

Oliver's track record speaks for itself. He has probably done more than any other single writer to increase understanding and appreciation of the history of trees and woodlands – and thus save many of them and influence their management for the good. His books are scholarly, meticulously researched, backed up by all-important field work and observation, peppered with polemic and tell a fascinating story with passion. It is these qualities which have given them such wide appeal.

This new edition is no exception. But it is the final chapter, 'Conservation and the Future', on which all who value this unique heritage should particularly focus. Here Oliver has set out the many factors which are a threat to ancient woodlands expressed with clarity and frankness. Coming from a man who has dedicated his life's work to this subject they deserve to be taken very seriously and acted upon. We will play our part as the lead UK tree campaigning charity with the help of our member organisations and many dedicated supporters.

CAROLINE DAVIS MBE
Chairman, The Tree Council

Plate 1 The consequences of felling a tree.

(a) Small-leaved lime: new shoots arise from dormant buds and bore their way out through the bark.

(b) Lineage elm (p. 257): a callus forms at the junction between bark and wood, and new shoots organize themselves within it.

(c) East Anglian elm: suckers arise from shallow roots.

(d) Sallow near the end of the first season's regrowth, having grown at least 2 inches a day. Such growth-rates are not uncommon in sallow and chestnut in hot wet summers. Bradfield Woods. 15 August 1986

Plate 2 Woodbank, probably of Anglo-Saxon date, exposed by coppicing (Chapter 1). Felshamhall Wood, Bradfield Woods. February 1973

Plate 3 Woodbank constructed in 1297–8 (pp. 5, 158). Hindolveston Wood (anciently Eastwood), Norfolk. September 1994

Plate 4 A very late woodbank, constructed in the nineteenth century when the wood was partly grubbed out. Note the straight, weak bank and the hedge of a single row of hawthorns. North Elmham Wood, Norfolk. October 1969

Plate 5 Crab, an anti-gregarious tree, nearly always solitary (pp. 65, 355). Hayley Wood. May 1968

Plate 6 (a– h) Vegetation zones in relation to flooding, Hayley Wood (Chapters 7, 25).

(a) Zone 1: wet hollow with *Carex acutiformis.* April 2001

(b) Zone 2: oxlip, *Primula elatior*, after coppicing, Hayley Wood. Such densities of oxlip used to be common but are now rare. April 1974

(c) Zone 3: oxlip-bluebell. April 1972

(d) Zone 4: bluebell. Bluebell is now seldom so dense as this. May 1997

Plate 6 (continued)

(e) Zone 5: bluebell-mercury. April 2002

(f) Zone 6a: mercury with occasional bluebell. May 1997

(g) Zone 6: dog's-mercury, *Mercurialis perennis*. This continuous carpet of near-evergreen foliage – not so common in the 2000s as it was in the 1960s – excludes most other herbs and ash seedlings. May 1966

(h) Primrose and bluebell confined to slightly higher patches on plateau in a wet spring. Buff Wood, May 1983

Plate 7 (a–q) Views from the same point, year by year, through a 14-year coppice cycle and part of the next cycle, Hayley Wood. This area (one-acre plot no.7, p.413) was felled early in 1986 for the third time under the present regime. It is fenced against fallow deer.

(a) Just felled. Oxlip plants (yellow) flowering sparsely. 30 April 1986

(b) 1 year's growth: regrowth of hazel and other underwood; prodigious flowering of oxlip; beginnings of *Deschampsia* tussocks. 23 April 1987

Plate 7 (continued)

(c) 2 years' growth: oxlip eclipsed by *Deschampsia*. 21 March 1988

(d) 3 years' growth: 25 March 1989

(e) 4 years' growth: underwood canopy nearly closed. 14 March 1990

Plate 7 (continued)

(f) 5 years' growth. 13 April 1991

(g) 6 years' growth. 5 April 1992

(h) 7 years' growth. 17 April 1993. Shade increases and *Deschampsia* declines.

(i) 8 years' growth: oxlip again becoming visible. 31 March 1994

(j) 9 years' growth. 29 March 1995

(k) 10 years' growth. This is Ash–Hazel-wood; most of the regrowth is from stools, but one birch (reddish bark) has come from seed. 15 April 1996

Plate 7 (continued)

(l) 11 years' growth. 31 March 1997

(m) 12 years' growth. Oxlip again prominent as most of the *Deschampsia* has been shaded out. 20 April 1998

(n) 13 years' growth. 22 April 1999

Plate 7 (continued)

(o) 0 years' growth in the next cycle. 7 April 2000

(p) 1 year's growth. This time round, enough *Deschampsia* survived the shade phase to get off to a quicker start than in the previous cycle; less of an oxlip response than in 1987. 17 April 2001

(q) 2 years' growth. Most of the oxlip plants are still there, hidden by *Deschampsia* tussocks. 1 April 2002

Plate 8 Bradfield Woods, $1\frac{1}{2}$ years after coppicing. Underwood mainly ash. The dense scatter of small oaks, now exceptional, would have been typical in the middle ages, as witness the hundreds of such trees that went into each ordinary building (pp. 145–7). July 1976

Plate 9 (a –b)

(a) The stuff of woodland history: ash stool, estimated at 400 years old (p. 15). Hayley Wood. February 1967

(b) This ash stool is all one individual, estimated at 800 years old. Paynsden Wood (Quendon, Essex). May 1971

Plate 10 A large 'two-band faggot' (p. 142). Bradfield Woods, March 1984.

Plate 11 Internal woodbank marking medieval property boundary. The pollard oak is a sign either of wood-pasture or (as here) of a boundary marker. Eversden Wood (p. 138). April 1971

Plate 12 Wood-pasture in operation. The cattle congregate in an area of scrub-clearance where leafy boughs of hawthorn and of pollarded hornbeams have been put at their disposal. In the foreground is an ancient hornbeam which rooted down through its own hollow bolling into the ground, and is now sustained by those roots after the bolling has rotted away and disappeared. Hatfield Forest. September 2002

Plate 13 Ancient Trees. (a–f)

(a) The Cavalier Oak, Stock-Gaylard Park, Dorset: a named tree incorporated into a later park. May 1998

(b) One of the few pollard oaks left in Savernake Forest, Wiltshire, where pollarding seems to have been terminated in c. 1600. April 1994

(c) Savanna landscape of wonderful ancient trees: Grimsthorpe Park, Lincolnshire. February 1998

Plate 13 (continued)

(d) Ancient pollard hawthorn, Grimsthorpe. February 1998

(e) Pollard hornbeam, originally free-standing in a grassy plain. Ancient, hollow hornbeams are a particularly good habitat for specialized invertebrates. Hatfield Forest. November 2001

(f) Ancient hawthorn with mistletoe, Hatfield Forest. Mistletoe, particularly abundant on pollard maples and hawthorns at Hatfield, is one of the few creatures of ancient trees that lend themselves to photography. September 1998

Plate 14 (a–b)

(a) Fantastic savanna: ancient oaks, Staverton Park. April 2003

(b) Advancing rainforest?: Staverton Thicks, oak savanna which became infilled with hollies *c.* 200 years ago. Note hollies rooted in rings round bases of oaks, and (in foreground) remains of oak overtopped and killed in the 19th century. May 2003

Plate 15 Wood-pasture at the ends of the earth: pollard eucalypts in Tasmania, the combined management effect of Aboriginal savanna and English colonial wood-pasture. July 2001

1

Introduction to woods and their history

Until recently it was widely believed that the history of British woodland was a story of unrelieved decline, neglect, and destruction. In *Trees and woodland in the British landscape* I sought to establish that this traditional view is mistaken. For a thousand years England, at least, has had less woodland than most European countries and has taken correspondingly more care of its woods. By the thirteenth century A.D. woodland management was a fully-developed art with conservation as its chief objective; its success is measured by the many medieval woods known to have lasted, often with the same boundaries, for 700 years or more. In many areas more than half the woods named in medieval documents survived into the twentieth century and are either still there or have only recently succumbed to the less conservative land-uses of our own period (Figs. 1.1, 2.1, 2.2).

The trees of Britain

Native and introduced trees

The British flora contains between fifty and seventy ***native*** tree and shrub species, which arrived here in prehistoric times. Some elms and conceivably other trees may have been imported by prehistoric men. These, together with sweet-chestnut (an introduction by the Romans which has persisted), form the historic woody flora and are the main subject of this book.

A few species are ***naturalized***: originally introduced in gardens and parks, they maintain themselves without human intervention and have invaded native vegetation. Sycamore, imported perhaps in the late Middle Ages (p. 203), and *Rhododendron ponticum*, a nineteenth-century introduction,[639a] are widespread; more local are cherry-plum (*Prunus cerasifera*) (p. 352) and acacia (*Robinia pseudacacia*). Scots pine survives as a native tree only in the Scottish Highlands and beech in parts of England; both have been widely planted and naturalized outside their native ranges.

All other trees and shrubs – e.g. pines, spruces, and larches, horse-chestnut and London plane, snowberry (*Symphoricarpos rivularis*) and cherry-laurel – are non-naturalized exotics: they predominate in plantations and gardens and a few may be locally self-sown, but they do not invade native woodland and seldom grow except where men have put them.

How trees are replaced

Poets and writers on forestry tell us that trees reproduce their kind by sexual methods, by acorns and other seeds. This may be true over much of Europe, but in Britain it happens more often when trees colonize new ground than in maintaining existing woods. The history and causes of this lack of seed reproduction will be examined for different trees in later chapters. One important factor is that all our trees are near their climatic limit, which lies somewhere within these islands for every species. Many trees produce seed irregularly and chiefly after hot summers. Trees, however, are long-lived creatures, and most species do in fact produce enough seedlings from time to time: the obstacle to reproduction comes in the second or third year, when the young trees perish for reasons which are still little known. The term ***establishment*** will be used to cover the whole process from the seed to the sapling ten years old which has survived the perils of infancy.

As every gardener who has cut down an ash or elm will know, most British trees possess vegetative means of regeneration. By exploiting these, woods have traditionally been maintained with little need for seedlings. Most species ***coppice***: the stump sends up shoots and becomes a ***stool*** (called a ***moot*** if it is of oak) from which an indefinite succession of crops of poles or ***slop*** can be cut at intervals of years (Figs. 1.2, 1.3). Aspen, cherry, service, and most elms ***sucker***: the stump dies but the root system remains alive indefinitely and sends up successive crops of poles, forming a patch of genetically-identical trees called a ***clone***.

If repeatedly cut, stools remain alive and vigorous for many centuries (Plate 9, p. 14). The phrase 'worn-out coppice stools', repeated in some books, has no ascertainable meaning, although stools of any age are weakened or killed if shaded by taller trees.

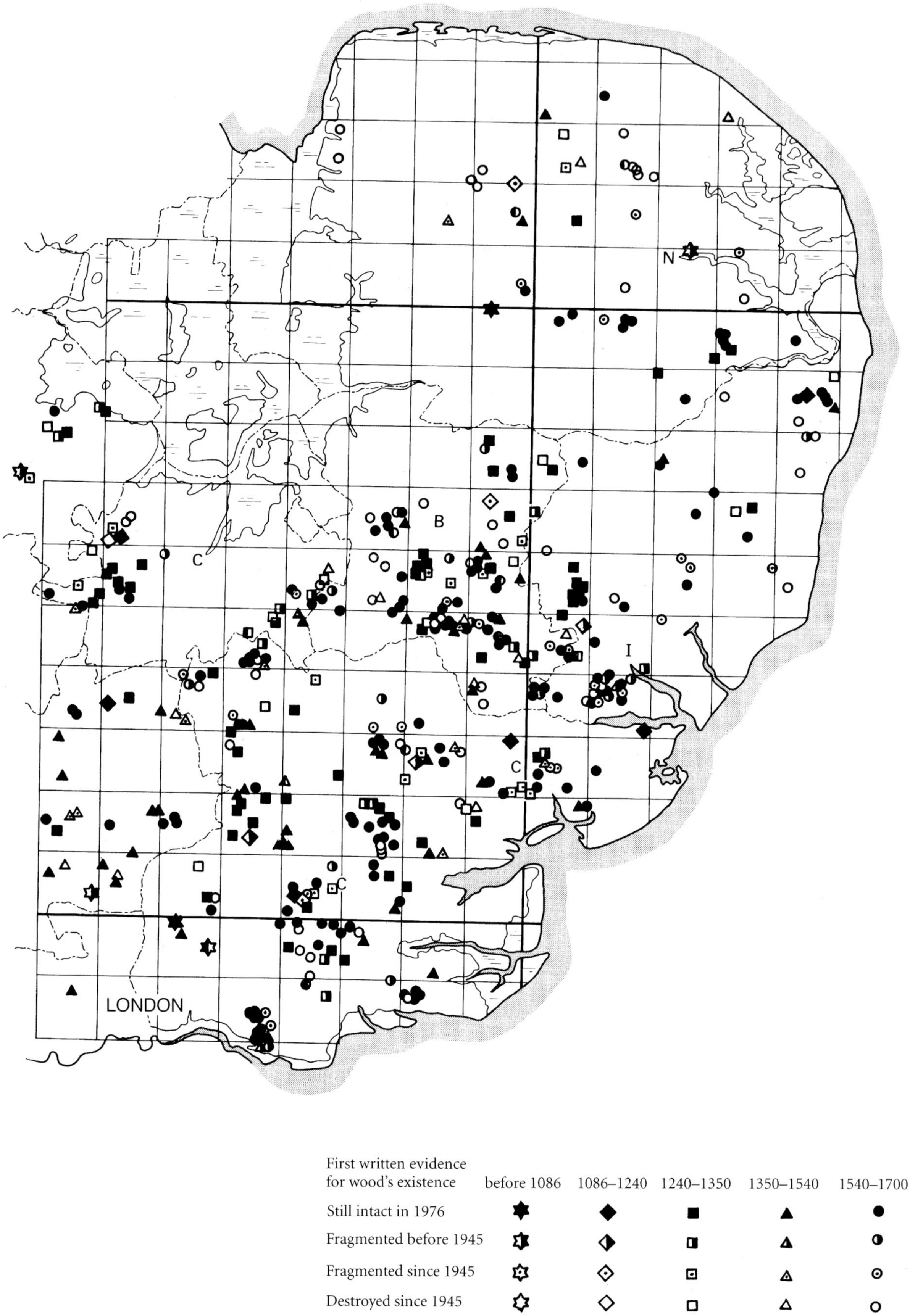
N
B
C
C
I
C
LONDON
First written evidence for wood's existence
before 1086
1086–1240
1240–1350
1350–1540
1540–1700
Still intact in 1976
Fragmented before 1945
Fragmented since 1945
Destroyed since 1945

The management of trees

Trees form part of four quite different and independent traditions of land-use:

(1) ***plantations***, where the trees are all of one age and often of one species, and have been deliberately planted;
(2) ***woods***, where the trees are of different ages, or different species, or both, and have not (or not all) been intentionally planted;
(3) ***wood-pastures***, where the growing of trees is combined with grazing animals;
(4) ***non-woodland***, hedgerow trees and trees standing about in fields (plus orchard, town, and garden trees, which are outside the scope of this book).

Plantations

Although Continental foresters take a wider view of their art, in Britain forestry is usually synonymous with the growing of trees in plantations, like an arable crop. The ground is cleared and the trees planted, grown, and finally harvested at about a third of their natural life-span; the stumps are then intended to die, and the ground is either replanted or put to some other use.

This is the junior of the four methods of managing trees. Orchards and free-standing trees have been planted in Britain from Anglo-Saxon times, but plantations of *areas* of trees hardly existed before 1580. With one possible thirteenth-century exception (pp. 290–1), the earliest example known to me appears to be in Gressenhall (Norfolk), where a survey of 1610 records 'A planting in the common called West Carre';[412] an earlier survey, dated 1495, suggests that this plantation already existed and had recently been formed out of a sheep-walk.[421–2] Sixteenth-century instances are rare and include an oak plantation, possibly still recognizable, in Windsor Great Park, attributed to Lord Burghley in 1580.[37, 90] Plantations were few and small before 1700 and most were imitations of existing woods rather than early examples of modern forestry: they had underwood as well as timber trees, and were intended to be self-perpetuating once established.

During the eighteenth century forestry diverged from woodmanship, with a tendency to plant only one or two species and an increasing emphasis on conifers. Usually new plantations were on former farmland or heathland. In the mid-nineteenth century the practice began of 'replanting', i.e. of destroying existing woods in order to establish plantations on the site.

Woods

The tradition of ***woodmanship*** is the art of getting produce from a wood without destroying the existing vegetation. The practice was already widespread and ancient by the time of Domesday Book (1086); it changed remarkably little down the centuries; in 1900 many woods differed only in detail from what they had been in 1200, and an increasing minority are still managed in the same way today.

A normal wood consists of two kinds of trees, ***timber*** or ***standard*** trees and ***underwood*** or ***coppice***. The timber trees are usually oak, less often ash or some other species; the underwood may also be oak but is more often of a wide range of different species, depending on the kind of woodland. Every year an area or ***panel*** of underwood poles is felled and harvested as a crop. The stools remain, and from them sprout coppice shoots or ***spring*** which regenerate the underwood with great speed and reliability. Sallow (*Salix caprea* and *S. cinerea*) commonly grows over 2 in. (5 cm) a day and reaches a height of 10–13 ft (3–4 m) in one season [Plate 1d]. The ***coppice cycle*** – the interval between successive cuttings of the underwood – is sometimes regular but more often irregular; it can vary between four and thirty years, although most trees will coppice after at least 100 years.

Timber trees are allowed to stand for several rotations of the underwood and then felled to yield larger material. They are replaced by ***promoting*** – leaving uncut when coppicing – saplings or selected underwood poles known as ***wavers*** or ***staddles*** to grow on to form the next timber crop.

Timber and ***wood*** traditionally mean different things. Timber (Latin *meremium*) is the trunks of timber trees suitable for beams, planks, and gateposts. Wood (Latin *boscus*) is poles, brushwood, and similar small stuff suitable for fencing and light construction, firewood, or charcoal-burning. This is an important legal, social, and practical distinction – we still talk of 'timber' buildings but 'wood' fires – and exact definitions, such as that wood is anything less than 2 ft in girth, have been laid down. Wood is produced not only by coppicing but also by pollarding (see p. 5) and from hedge-trimmings and the branches of felled trees.

The word ***coppice*** and its spelling variant ***copse***, supposedly of Norman-French origin (my earliest

Fig. 1.1 Ancient woods in Eastern England: woods, having a written history extending from before 1700, which were still extant in 1945. Woods entirely destroyed before 1945, and woods regarded as ancient on other evidence but having no surviving documentation, are not shown. Parks and Forests (Fig. 12.10) are not mapped as such but some woods within them are shown.

The historical evidence is a compilation from all the sources used in this book. It is by no means exhaustive and could easily be extended. Dates of first mention are nearly always determined by the survival of the records rather than by the actual origin of the wood. Information about the present state of preservation is sometimes derived from aerial photographs, maps, etc. rather than from my own visits: in a few woods I have probably underestimated the extent of recent destruction; in others attempts at destruction have been less complete or less successful than I have supposed.

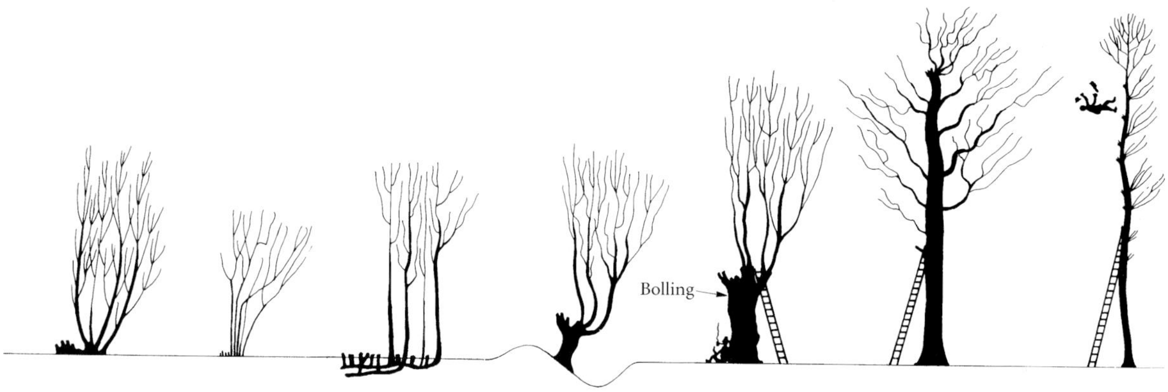

Fig. 1.2 Methods of producing wood from trees. Left to right: coppice stool above ground (e.g. ash); coppice stool below ground (e.g. hazel); clone of suckers (e.g. elm); stub on boundary-bank; pollard; high pollard; shredded tree. The left-hand half of each has just been cut; the right-hand half is fully regenerated and is about to be cut again.

Fig. 1.3 A coppicing scene in the Bradfield Woods near Bury St Edmund's. The wood consists of underwood, of a great variety of species, with scattered timber trees of oak and ash. In the foreground the underwood has just been felled to produce the poles which form the principal crop, leaving the timber trees standing. Note that several poles have been cut from each underwood stool. On the left is an area which was felled a year ago and in which, without further treatment, the underwood has grown up to be now 5–6 ft high. In the background the underwood has grown up for about fifteen years and is ready to be cut again.

Such a scene has been repeated on this site every few years since at least the thirteenth century. The only serious anachronism in this picture is the bonfire, consuming *spray* and *brushwood* – the tops and branches of underwood poles (p. 142) – which would formerly have been taken away and put to use. January 1970

record, as the Latinized *copicium*, is at Lavenham (Suffolk) in 1331),[448] means a wood managed by this method. The earlier words are ***underwood*** (still a common surname), its Latin equivalent *subboscus*, and ***spring***. The actual Norman-French word, tailz (cf. Modern French *taillis*), is occasionally found in place-names.

The proportion of timber trees to underwood varies from wood to wood and from time to time. Timber trees come and go; the continuity of the wood is maintained by the long-lived underwood stools and by the herbaceous plants which constitute the ***ground vegetation***. As a result of some big felling a wood might temporarily lose its timber trees, but the distinction which books often make between 'simple coppice' and 'coppice-with-standards'[154] is not supported by historical records.

In most kinds of woodland underwood was the main and regular product; since underwood grows poorly in shade, the timber trees were kept to a minority and not allowed to form a continuous canopy. Woods with timber trees only, without underwood, appear occasionally in the documents, but most were of only a few acres. The name 'high forest', by which woods of timber trees only are known to the academic world, is a translation of the German *Hochwald*; the common place-name High Wood (Latin *boscus altus*) in England apparently means merely a wood on high ground, and woods so named were coppiced (e.g. Dunmow High Wood, Essex, in 1336),[449] or occasionally pollarded, just like other woods.

Young spring is very palatable to cattle, sheep, and deer, and from the earliest times great importance was attached to keeping animals out of woods after felling. Woods were surrounded by ***woodbanks***, massive earthworks which are still a typical feature of ancient woods. The woodbank, with its external ditch, supported a hedge or a fence and often a row of pollard trees.

Wood-pasture

Wood-pasture goes back as a separate tradition of handling trees at least to Anglo-Saxon times; *silua pastilis* is extensively recorded in Domesday Book. There are three variants:

(1) ***Commons***, unfenced pieces of land on which groups of people called ***commoners*** have the right to graze cattle, sheep, and other animals. If there are trees, as often on the bigger commons, the commoners may have rights in the wood as well, but the timber and surplus wood generally belong to the lord of the manor.

(2) ***Parks***, private land on which the owner keeps deer – usually fallow deer, *Dama dama* – and often cattle and sheep as well. The deer are confined by a ***pale***, a deer-proof ring-fence often made of special cleft-oak stakes.

(3) ***Forests***, meaning Royal Forests, which in the practical sense of the word are commons, with or without trees, grazed by commoners' livestock and also by deer put there by the Crown and originally intended for the King's table. Forests differ from parks in having no ring-fence.

It was appreciated very early that grazing conflicts with trees: grass does not grow well in shade, and cattle, sheep, and deer eat saplings and especially spring. The more trees there are, the less abundant and the worse will be the pasture, and the more animals graze the pasture, the more difficult it becomes to replace the trees. The conflict is not as severe as is often supposed; it was successfully dealt with by several different methods, and many wood-pastures, such as Epping Forest (pp. 187–8), were hardly less stable than woods.

Wood-pastures differ widely in appearance according to the amount of grazing and the method chosen to control it: they can vary from almost open grassland to a close approximation to woodland. Many wood-pastures involve ***pollarding***, otherwise ***lopping*** or ***cobbing***, the practice of cutting a tree at 7–18 ft (2–5 m) above ground, leaving a permanent base called a ***bolling*** (Fig. 1.2). This sprouts in the same way as a coppice stool, but at a height where animals cannot reach the shoots, and yields an indefinite succession of crops of poles. Examples are the pollards of Epping Forest, Burnham Beeches (a common) and many ancient parks. The ancient oaks of Windsor and Sherwood Forests display a curious variant, dating from many centuries ago, in which the tree is beheaded at some 40 ft above ground, as though to defeat giraffes. An alternative to pollarding is the practice of ***shredding*** or ***shrouding***, cutting off the branches of a tree, leaving a tuft at the top, in the expectation that they will grow again. Shredding is often mentioned in documents up to *c.* 1600, and is still to be seen in parts of France and Germany; it has long been extinct in Britain, but I have seen a few ashes in Gloucestershire which retain traces of the practice.

Non-woodland trees

Hedges and hedgerow trees are largely outside the scope of this book (p. vii). Despite the popular myth that they are a recent addition to the landscape, they are of comparable antiquity to the woodland and wood-pasture traditions. Many hedges, some with hedgerow trees, were described in Anglo-Saxon charters before Domesday Book, and some of them can be shown to be still in existence. Hedges increased in numbers, especially in those English counties that adjoin the sea or the Welsh Border, and by the later Middle Ages were often an important source of timber and underwood.

Hedges may contain underwood – the shrubs of the hedge itself –, timber trees, and pollards. Their management involves some techniques of woodland or wood-pasture as well as others peculiar to hedges. It was the practice to plant hedges and hedgerow trees long before planting was usual in woodland or wood-pasture.

Hedges are sometimes regarded as linear woods, but the analogy must not be taken too far. Even an ancient hedge with many species[837] rarely resembles the tree composition of the local native woodland, and hedges seldom contain the more specialized woodland plants.

The decline of tree management

Despite popular beliefs to the contrary, the decay and destruction of the tree-management systems of medieval England is chiefly the work of the last 200 years, and especially of the period 1950–1980. Forests and commons were the first to become unfashionable and were destroyed on a large scale between 1770 and 1860. The decline of woodmanship followed in the next hundred years, and hedges have been widely destroyed since 1945. Each of these was a more rapid and severe change than any since the Conquest. It became customary to regard timber production – despite its poor economic record in Britain after 1860 – as the only proper function of woods. Foresters increasingly laid claim to ancient woodland as one of the kinds of land on which to form plantations. Replanting, followed by grubbing out for agriculture, are by far the chief causes of disappearance of ancient woodland. Such destruction continued into the 1970s. In the remaining woods, however, there has been much revival of traditional management since 1970 (pp. 168–9 and Chapter 35).

The Highland and Lowland Zones

The two main types of woodland history in Britain correspond to the geographers' Highland and Lowland Zones. The Lowland Zone comprises the greater part of England, including for this purpose Devon and Cornwall. The Highland Zone comprises the Pennines and Lake District, the Welsh Border, Wales, Scotland, and Ireland.

My summary of tree management was written with Eastern England in mind, but applies with small modifications to most of Lowland England and with larger modifications to parts of France. The Highland Zone has a different history. Its inhabitants, having plenty of stone to build with and of peat or coal to burn, have been less inclined to conserve trees. Woodlands have been less intensively used and less stable.

In Scotland woodmanship arrived late – mainly in the sixteenth century – and declined early. Formal wood-pasture systems seem never to have become established, though many woods (as also in Wales) are used as shelter for stock. Modern forestry began earlier and was more influential in Scotland and Ireland than in England. In the Scottish Highlands there are many pockets of native woodland – the Caledonian pinewoods are a famous example which has no parallel in England – but they survive in remote places and are less the result of centuries of deliberate conservation as are the ancient woods of Lowland England.

Ancient and recent woods

The wildwood

There have been trees in Britain for hundreds of millions of years, but they are not directly relevant to our purpose because the ecological continuity of the vegetation has been broken by the Ice Ages. Woodland history effectively begins about 10,000 B.C. when the return of a hospitable climate enabled trees to recolonize these islands and to reestablish the prehistoric forests, the ***wildwood***, which came to cover almost the whole of Britain (Chapters 8, 32). The destruction of the wildwood to form our present farmland and moorland began in the Neolithic period, was well advanced by Roman times, and was almost completed by the Anglo-Saxons.

Ancient woods and their variation

Woods and wood-pastures may have been formed from fragments of the prehistoric forest that have been brought under management without ever having been cleared of trees. These will be termed ***primary***, in contrast to the ***secondary*** woodland and wood-pasture which have been formed on areas that at some time in the historical period have been farmland, moorland, etc.

Some secondary woods are ancient. A few newly-formed woods are recorded in Domesday Book. In the middle of Epping Forest, which has been wood-pasture for at least a thousand years, there are two Iron Age hill-forts whose existence presupposes that their immediate surroundings, and perhaps also their distant views, were not then obstructed by trees which might cover an enemy. These are exceptions: the destruction of woods has at most times outweighed their creation, and few secondary woods are known to be more than 300 years old. There can be little doubt that many woods which existed in 1500, and even in 1800, are on primary woodland sites. It is difficult to prove that any particular wood is primary and it is more useful to discuss ***ancient*** woods, in existence before some date such as A.D. 1700, as opposed to those which are more recent.

It has long been conjectured that the present native woods of Britain are in some way related to the wildwood; but only recently has enough knowledge been gained of the details of wildwood, of management history, and even of present woodland for this relation to be explored. For a long time the matter was obscured by a belief in a particular form of the doctrine of the ***climax***. Ecologists traditionally suppose that there is a particular type of vegetation which will eventually

2

Sources for woodland history

Pollen analysis

The pollen grains of trees and other plants are preserved in vast numbers in the stratified deposits of peat-bogs and lake muds, in some archaeological deposits, and in some types of acid soil. They can be identified to the genus and sometimes the species which produced them, and together with the bits of leaves, flowers, tree-trunks, etc. that sometimes accompany them can be used to document the prehistory of vegetation, especially the wildwood and the earlier stages of its destruction. The textbooks of Godwin,[710] Pennington,[824] and others explain how this is done.

Pollen analysis has been less used in the historical period or for the history of individual woods still existing. Many deposits have lost their upper layers by erosion or peat-cutting. The remaining peat may be difficult to date with sufficient precision. Because of the fragmented structure of the historic countryside it may be difficult to sort out pollen coming from the immediate surroundings of a deposit from that contributed by crops, woods, hedgerow trees, plantations, etc. at varying distances away. Recently some progress has been made towards solving this problem and working out the history of individual plant communities rather than of the landscape as a whole. Cores have been taken from woodland ponds and small basins rather than from lakes which average the pollen fall-out over a wide catchment. Use has been made of pollen in mor (p. 36) and in acid soils, although the stratification is often obscured by rain-wash. We are finding out how to compensate pollen counts for the fact that some tree species produce more pollen than others, and that some pollens blow further from the tree or are more readily preserved.

We still know little about types of woodland that grow away from the kind of places where deposits form. For instance, the prehistory of hornbeam and maple is much less well known than that of hazel and lime.

Written evidence

Place-names form the earliest useful documentation; many of them date from well before the Norman Conquest. Their interpretation involves many pitfalls. Few commentators resist the temptation to read into place-names more than they actually say. *Oakley*, 'oak-clearing', gets mistranslated as 'clearing in the oakwoods' and *Brentwood*, 'burnt wood', as 'woodland cleared by burning'. The unwarranted assumption that place-names in *cat* refer to the wildcat, rather than to the mere wandering pussy, has been compounded by the further assumption that the wildcat was a beast of woodland. Scholars have been known to credit the Anglo-Saxons, against all other evidence, with having had fir-trees (*Sapley*, Hunts, rendered 'fir-clearing') and even olives. Rightly used, place-names tell us something about the presence of the rarer kinds of tree and about some aspects of the development of the landscape. Cornwall, Wales, Scotland, and Ireland are served by Celtic place-names, but these, like many English names, are often indefinite as to date.

Anglo-Saxon charters describe in detail what some particular piece of country was like in the ninth to eleventh centuries. They record many hedgerow and free-standing trees, often by species, and are our earliest record of woods in precisely identifiable places.

Domesday Book attempts to provide a comprehensive survey of woodland in England in the year 1086. It is even now [1980] a much-neglected document; one of the problems of interpretation is the lack of a comparable modern survey. It is useful chiefly on a broad scale rather than for the history of particular woods.

The practice of record-keeping suddenly advanced about the year 1250 (Figs. 2.1 and 2.2). From this time onwards there is a continuous stream of documentation for some woods. Surveys give names, areas, ownerships, locations, and management; estate accounts record what woods produced year by year and what was spent on management; customals set out local by-laws and the duties of tenants in respect of woods and trees; and court rolls record how the by-laws were broken and whether the offences were condoned or punished. These documents are most copious for lands belonging to the Crown, religious houses, or Oxford colleges. Their quality gradually declines as the Middle Ages progress, and some classes disappear altogether.

In the sixteenth century record-keeping was reinvigorated. From this period we have a few surveys explicitly stating what species underwood consisted of, information that at other times has to be pieced together from records of sales. Woodland leases, often with

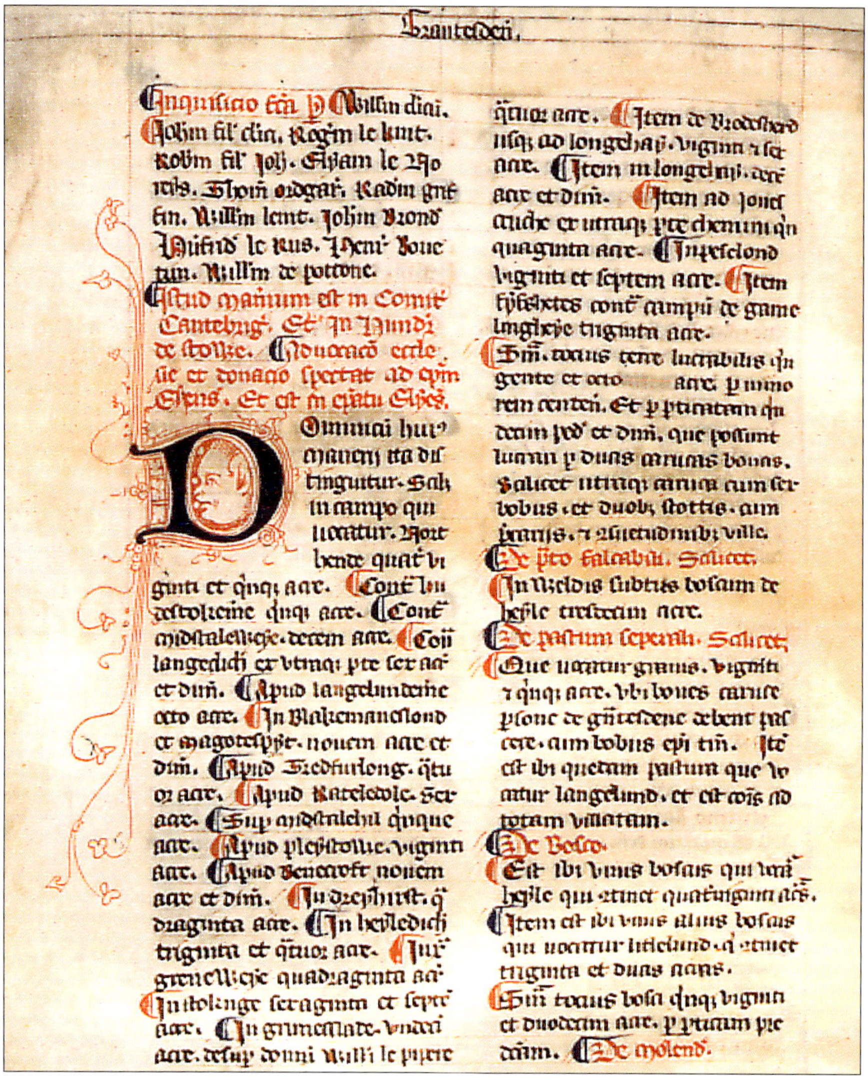

Fig. 2.1 A page from the *Old Coucher Book of Ely*,[270] one of the earliest surviving detailed topographical surveys, dated 1251. This entry describes the estate of the Bishop of Ely at 'Grantesden' (Little Gransden, Cambs) field by field. This is a translation of the woodland entry:

The Wood. There is there one wood which is called Heyle which contains fourscore acres.

Item, there is there one other wood which is called Litlelund, which contains thirty-two acres.

The total of all the wood is fivescore and twelve acres, by the aforesaid perch [of 15½ ft].

Later pages deal with the boundaries and uses of the wood. 'Heyle' is the present Hayley Wood; 'Litlelund' was destroyed *c.* 1650.[120] (Reproduced, by kind permission of the Master and Fellows, from Gonville and Caius College copy fol. 149 v.)

detailed conditions, give an insight into management. We now begin to get generalizations about woods: descriptions by travellers; complaints of destruction; legislation and propaganda; and eventually the famous and much-plagiarized textbook, Evelyn's *Sylva* (1664),[335] and its successor, Duhamel du Monceau's *De l'exploitation des bois* (1764).[269]

Early maps at large scales, usually of a single estate, begin about 1580; some are of excellent quality, showing hedges and hedgerow trees and wood boundaries with great detail and accuracy. Estate maps increase in frequency during the seventeenth and eighteenth centuries. The large-scale county maps (1 or 2 inches to the mile), such as Chapman and André's Essex (1778) (Fig. 12.9), attempt to record all woodland but are not wholly reliable: the object was not accomplished until the post-1830 Ordnance Survey. Maps at larger scales continue with the enclosure or tithe maps of almost all English parishes in the eighteenth and nineteenth centuries; the 6-in. Irish Survey of the 1820s and 1830s; and the earlier editions of the 6-in. English Ordnance Survey. Some of these show individual trees in hedges and pastures. The mapmaker's art reached its zenith in the 1880s and standards have steadily declined since then (Fig. 1.4). Maps can now be supplemented by aerial photographs: most of the kingdom has been photographed in the 1940s and more than once since then.

Fig. 2.2 Hayley Wood in 1969. The coppicing has been revived.

Records of surveys, sales, and woodland management continue through the seventeenth, eighteenth, and early nineteenth centuries. The decline in woodmanship was accompanied by a rapid decline in the number and quality of the records: 1890 to 1950, as far as written evidence is concerned, is the darkest period in the woodland history of Eastern England since the twelfth century.

Earthworks and surface features

Elsewhere I have reviewed the many earthworks and surface features that can exist in woods.[122] Some of them tell us the history of the wood; others record land-uses or natural processes occurring before the site was a wood.

Medieval woods have a characteristic irregular shape; the boundary is either ***sinuous***, changing in direction every few yards, or is a series of zigzags. The perimeter is usually surrounded by a ***woodbank***, a massive bank and ditch typically about 35 ft (10 m) in total width, with the bank on the *wood* side [Plates 2, 3]. Many banks are older than 1250 but there are occasional records of new ones being made (p. 158). The woodbank stabilizes the outline: many woods shown on sixteenth-century maps are still exactly the same shape today, with the same sinuosities and zigzags [Figs 25.2, 25.3]. When a wood is enlarged, the old woodbank is left behind as a witness of its former extent; when a wood is truncated or grubbed out, the '***ghost***' of its old perimeter sometimes remains as a hedge or a soil mark. Post-medieval wood boundaries tend to be straight or regularly curved, and their woodbanks become less massive in succeeding centuries. A wood with a complex history (Fig. 10.1) may have many kinds of earthwork recording its changes of outline.

The boundaries of parks and Forests (Chapter 12) differ in shape and embanking from those of woods.

Other earthworks must be interpreted individually: we have already argued from the hillforts in Epping Forest. ***Ridge-and-furrow***, the undulations created by past, usually medieval, ploughing, can only occur in secondary woodland [Fig. 25.24].

Woods also contain features for which it is difficult to invent an artificial explanation and which were presumably created by wind and ice in the days before the wildwood. Some of these are described in Chapter 4. Here I draw attention to the remarkable prevalence of depressions, both dry (dells) and wet (ponds), in ancient woods, only a few of which have any obvious explanation as artefacts [Fig. 2.6]. Wolve's Wood near Ipswich contains at least 43 ponds in 92 acres (over one pond per hectare). Ponds have a curious habit of occurring in pairs or chains (Fig. 2.3). Presumably they represent the natural surface topography; outside woods they have either been ploughed out or are difficult to distinguish from other kinds of field pond.[842]

Vegetation

The annual rings of living trees, or in the stumps and tops of felled trees, tell how old the tree is (and thus normally set a lower limit to the age of the wood) and also form a record of good and bad seasons, disease, and practices such as pollarding and coppicing.[120, 122] (The tree-rings of small-leaved lime are treacherous: see Chapter 15.)

Bollings and the bases of coppice stools are usually hollow, so that rings cannot be counted all the way to

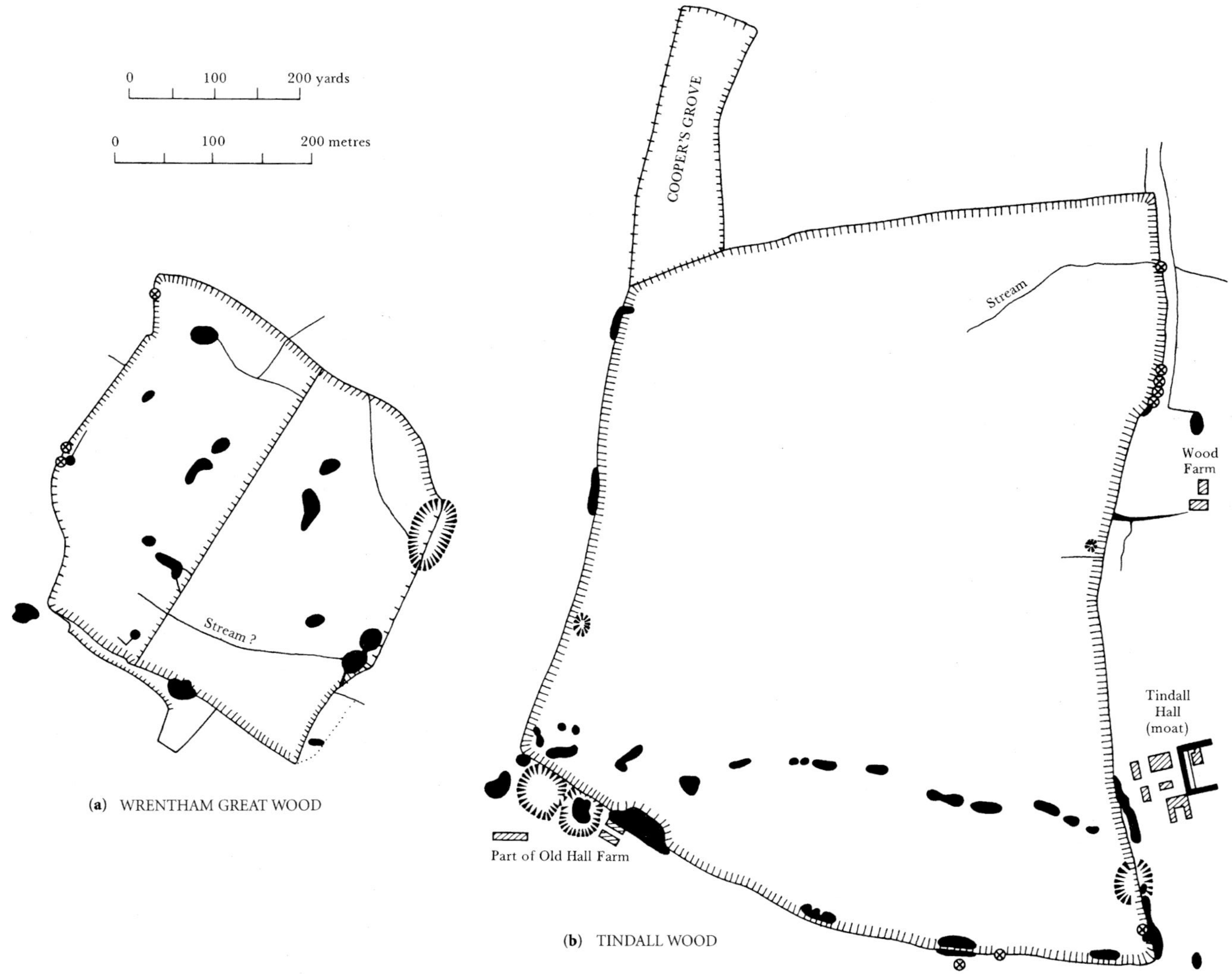

Fig. 2.3 Ponds and dells in two ancient woods. (**a**) Great Wood, Wrentham (E. Suffolk). 35-acre wood with thirteen internal ponds (including four pairs); another pond and a dell are bisected by the wood-boundary; two more ponds lie just outside. Some of the ponds have been incorporated in a rudimentary drainage system. (**b**) Tindall Wood, Ditchingham (E. Norfolk). 105-acre wood with a chain of sixteen ponds. Nine other depressions (excluding those associated with farmsteads) lie on the boundary; two of these are bisected by the woodbank. This wood is documented back to the thirteenth century (p. 232) and its perimeter appears not to have been altered for at least 700 years.

Both woods are on almost perfectly level ground with no geological discontinuity to account for the ponds. Ponds and dells are depressions in the flat surface with no corresponding spoil-heaps or other evidence of artificial excavation.

the centre, but their age can often be estimated from partial sections. Ash, maple, wych-elm, oak, chestnut, lime, and occasionally alder form ***giant stools*** more than 6 ft (2 m) across [Plate 9]. These are certainly of great age. From sections I estimate that a stool 6 ft in diameter will seldom be less than 400 years old on a good site, except for elm and sweet-chestnut, which can reach this size in 250–300 years. Stools on waterlogged or infertile sites may grow much more slowly, and I have seen ash, elm, and lime exceed 20 ft (6 m) in diameter; it is probable that some coppice stools are over a thousand years old, and are witnesses to a wood's history more powerful than any document.

Ancient stools are often high as well as broad [Fig. 3.0b]. Ash and lime in some woods may be cut at up to 4 ft above ground; elm and oak are lower; maple, hazel, and sallow are nearly always cut at ground level. I have never seen this distinction mentioned in writing and have no evidence as to its meaning. (High coppicing is the mark of a beginner, until he discovers that it is more laborious; it is frowned upon by academic writers, who claim that it is bad for the regrowth. In my experience it does not matter at what height or with what tool the underwood is cut.)

In Chapter 5 I review the plant species observed to be correlated with woods having a particular kind of history: with primary woods, secondary woods, or woods on sites that have been inhabited.

Archaeological artefacts

In medieval buildings it is possible to examine the timbers and to determine the species of tree, the ages of the trees at felling, their height, girth, branching, etc. This tells us something of the conditions in which the trees were grown. We can determine the number of trees that would have gone into, let us say, Norwich Cathedral or the town of Lavenham, and what effect this would have had on timber supplies.[845, 847] Similar evidence for underwood comes from ***wattle-and-daub*** (pp. 144, 465), but is not so representative because building was the chief use for timber but only a minor user of underwood.

Evidence for earlier periods is scanty but is growing rapidly: for instance from the charcoal found at Roman and Iron Age industrial sites, and above all from the great quantity of timber and underwood recently excavated in the Somerset Levels (Chapter 8).

Iconography

Paintings are disappointing sources. Few artists paint woodlands: most 'wooded landscapes' are really farmland with trees. Non-woodland scenes are better served, but it is curious how few artists ever portray a recognizable oak or ash tree. This is a technical problem. No man (and no camera) can ever record naturalistically the complexity of a big tree. It is a rare accomplishment to know what are the distinctive details that give a tree its individuality; most artists – even the famous – tend to pick out non-distinctive details and so depict trees with all the anonymity of a bad portrait.

The chief exceptions are the late-medieval Flemings, who show convincing hedgerow, farm, and occasionally woodland trees. A particularly fine example, showing the recognizable interior of a real wood comparable with Chalkney or Groton, is reproduced as the Frontispiece.

Sixteenth- and seventeenth-century English landscapes, from Cuningham's view of Norwich (1558) to Kip's illustrations of country houses around 1700, tell us about hedges and farmland trees. There are pollards in the old Italian and Dutch masters, shredded trees (p. 5) in Meyndert Hobbema's *Avenue at Middelharnis* (1689), and suspicions of Dutch Elm Disease in Italian landscapes of *c.* 1500 (p. 263). Constable and Stubbs often record very convincing trees in sketches, even if the trees lapse into anonymity in their finished paintings.[861] The Pre-Raphaelites sometimes managed by attention to detail to convey what a mid-nineteenth-century wood looked like: for instance the stages of felling and regrowth in Arthur Hughes's *The Woodman's Child* and J. E. Millais's *The Woodman's Daughter*.

Practical experience and oral tradition

As G. E. Evans reminds us in his books, the testimony of aged men can be a valuable source of evidence for the history of the countryside. For woodland I have found it disappointing. Woodmanship is a specialized craft; it is not familiar to the whole population, as ploughing and sowing used to be; and it has been in decline since well before living memory.

To understand woodmanship one has to practise it oneself: a little experience, such as many people are now acquiring through the growth of interest in woodland conservation, is worth any amount of book-learning. Where specialized crafts still exist, as with the Bradfield Woods (p. 27), they tell us much about working with trees. Where the crafts have gone it is remarkable how soon the traditions die out too. Occasionally an old countryman remembers the curious knot for tying a faggot (Fig. 10.5), or uses the ancient measure for underwood, the ***rindge***, $^1/_8$ or $^1/_{10}$ acre, which has rarely appeared in print. These genuine traditions are difficult to separate from what has been picked up from books. Often one marvels at how little people observe and how short memories are. More than once I have been told by someone familiar with a wood that nothing had been done to it in his time; yet the tree-rings have shown incontrovertibly that it must have been felled well within my informant's recollection!

The interpretation of historical evidence

Different kinds of evidence are complementary. A study based on documents, however scholarly, is bound to be weak unless related to what the land itself has to tell; but it is rash to infer the history of a wood solely from vegetation without support from earthworks or written evidence.

Medieval documents are usually precise as to date but vague in topography. Earthworks are difficult to date closely but tell of topographical changes that are too early to be recorded in maps. For instance, at Rivenhall (mid Essex) there are two woods which are remnants of a large and complex wood surrounding enclaves of farmland, shown on a map of *c.* 1716.[285] The banks and ditches of the present woods are only partly explained by the *c.* 1716 outline; they evidently result from some yet earlier group of woods, enlarged at some unknown date to form the eighteenth-century wood (Fig. 2.4).

The use of documents

Historical ecology is, to a large extent, history and not pure science. Few of the data come from experiments or observations performed to answer specific questions.

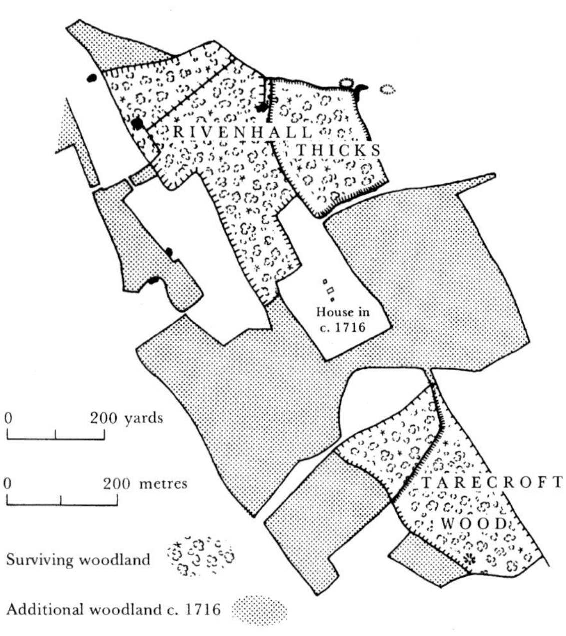

Fig. 2.4 Two of the surviving woods of Rivenhall (Essex), together with the outline of the complex eighteenth-century wood from which they have been reduced. The boundary banks suggest that only the eastern third of Rivenhall Thicks and the south-eastern two-thirds of Tarecroft may be primary woodland. Much of the eighteenth-century wood was probably secondary; the enclaves of farmland were survivors of agricultural decline rather than pioneers of agricultural expansion.

Usually we have to make do with information which exists and has survived for reasons unconnected with its usefulness to us, and whose quality needs to be critically assessed. The most useful documents are workaday records of actual topographies or specific events: names and sizes of woods, sales year by year of trees or of acreages of underwood, prosecutions for particular offences, etc. Slightly less reliable are records which state what area of underwood *ought* to be cut each year or what actions *ought not* to be done under the manorial customs. Historians of woods have tended to pass over these humbler documents in favour of more generalized sources of dubious reliability. Forest Law is quoted as if it were evidence of what actions did not take place within Royal Forests, whereas records of Forest courts show clearly that many technically illegal activities were treated as a source of revenue from fines rather than as crimes to be prevented.[124, 214] The Statute of Woods of 1543, purporting to regulate woodland management, is often quoted without any supporting evidence of what prosecutions, if any, were brought under it. Complaints of destruction of woodland, for instance for industrial fuel, are taken at face value without evidence from maps of what woods were destroyed or from rentals of what happened to the former woodland.

Some events are more likely to be recorded than others. Felling or planting trees attracts attention and sometimes protest; their natural regrowth, which costs nothing, is too commonplace to be recorded. Planting trees appears as an expense; their death in a subsequent drought is overlooked. Records are kept of agricultural expansion but not of agricultural decline: grubbing out woodland, which is a capital investment, may be recorded, but the formation of secondary woodland goes unnoticed.

Generalized sources such as legislation and complaints are evidence of public attitudes to woodland rather than of woods themselves. Travellers and general writers rarely understand trees; the general public, in former centuries as now, regarded all trees as irreplaceable and the harvesting of them as the destruction of a resource. Even Evelyn's *Sylva*, the fruit of a lifetime's interest in trees, is a generalized book: it is for us to form our own opinion of whether Evelyn was right in his generalizations.

The shortcomings of historical evidence: the history of oak

By combining several kinds of evidence we reduce the risk of bias in any one source. Bias is liable to arise when documents are used for a different purpose from that for which they were compiled, but it is not confined to written records.

There is far more evidence about oak than about any other tree. Allusions to it abound in documents from

Anglo-Saxon charters to *Sylva* and from the accounts of Henry III's Forests to those of eighteenth-century farms (Table 2.1). It is the chief timber in historic buildings, furniture, and ships. It is well represented in prehistoric archaeology and in pollen deposits. Many authors, taking this evidence at face value, suppose that the history of British trees and woodlands is almost entirely the history of oak. It is widely assumed that oak-dominated forest would be the natural vegetation of almost the whole of Britain, and that it is nowadays represented, not only by oak coppice, but also by the oak standard trees in maple-woods, hazel-woods, lime-woods, etc. To many ecologists nearly every wood is a more or less modified oakwood. Although oak is one of our least endangered species a great deal of work has been done on its conservation. The attitude of scientists accords with popular affection for the oak as the embodiment of British (or French or German) national dignity, associated with those parts of our history that we look back on with pride.

No civilized man can be unmoved by the legends, poetry, and song that celebrate the oak – by Abraham's Oak, the oaks of Dodona, the Druids, the Gospel Oaks, Herne's Oak, the Major Oak, the Oaks of Reformation, the Oak of Guernica – but these reflect people's attitudes to oaks and not the place of oak in vegetation. Many factors have conspired to over-represent oak in the record. It is a non-woodland as well as a woodland tree and hence is familiar to artists, poets, and the public as well as to woodmen; the tree, its leaves, acorns, timber, and pollen are easily identified; it is variable, and individual trees can be recognized and named (pp. 283–4); it has more specific uses, for which other species will not serve, than any other tree; its timber is costly and durable and tends to be used in structures that survive; by custom it belongs to landlords, who leave documents behind them, rather than to tenants, who do not; and its felling is a matter of ceremony and profit rather than an unrecorded annual routine. The special relations between oaks and

Table 2.1 The notice which people take of trees. Percentage frequency with which tree species are mentioned in: (*a*) two samples of Anglo-Saxon charters;[122] (*b*) the names of English towns, villages, and hamlets;[669, 882] (*c*) the works of Shakespeare;[887] (*d*) a sample of well-known British literature other than Shakespeare.[815] Literary references to introduced trees or to trees outside Britain are excluded.

	(*a*) Charters	(*b*) Place-names	(*c*) Shakespeare	(*d*) Other literature
Total number of occurrences	121	812	115	77
Frequency of:				
Thorn (including hawthorn and blackthorn)	38	18.0	28	16
Oak	19	11.8	26	31
Sallow, willow, withy	7	15.5	8	12
Ash	3	17.7	0	5
Hazel, nut	0	7.5	13	4
Apple (wild), crab, wilding	9	0.5*	10*	1*
Elder	4	1.4	5	3
Elm, wych	0	4.9	2	6
Birch	2	3.6	2	5
Holly	1	3.1	2	4
Lime, linden	4	3.1	1	1
Beech	0	1.8	1	6
Aspen	1	1.6	2	4
Alder	0	6.9	0	0
Pear (wild)	6	—†	—†	—†
Maple	4	1.8	0	0
Chestnut (sweet)	0	0.4	2	1
Service	1	0	0	0
Cherry (wild)	1	0.1	—†	—†
Rowan	0	0.1	0	0
Hornbeam	0	0	0	0
	100	100	100	100

* 'Crab' only. † Omitted because impossible to distinguish from cultivated trees.

men – or between oaks and the sorts of men and activities that create historical records – ensure that we hear more about oaks than about the same numbers of hornbeams or maples. Moreover the present abundance of oak is partly the result of centuries of various activities which, deliberately or accidentally, have favoured it at the expense of other trees. Oaks in woodland are prominent even if few, because they are standard trees; they reflect the decision of past woodmen to treat oak as timber and not as underwood. Other species, by custom, have been coppiced and are thus less prominent than oak; but they are usually more numerous and on them depend most of the biological character and historical continuity of a wood. The over-representation of oak continues back into prehistory, both in peat deposits – for it produces more pollen per tree than most other species – and because its rot-resistant timber is more likely to be preserved in archaeological contexts. We must avoid assuming that abundant evidence for oak means that the tree itself was proportionately abundant; greater weight must often be given to less abundant evidence of other trees.

Words

Woodmanship records are full of obscure technical words in English, Latin, and Norman-French, all of which had precise meanings. Sometimes a former distinction

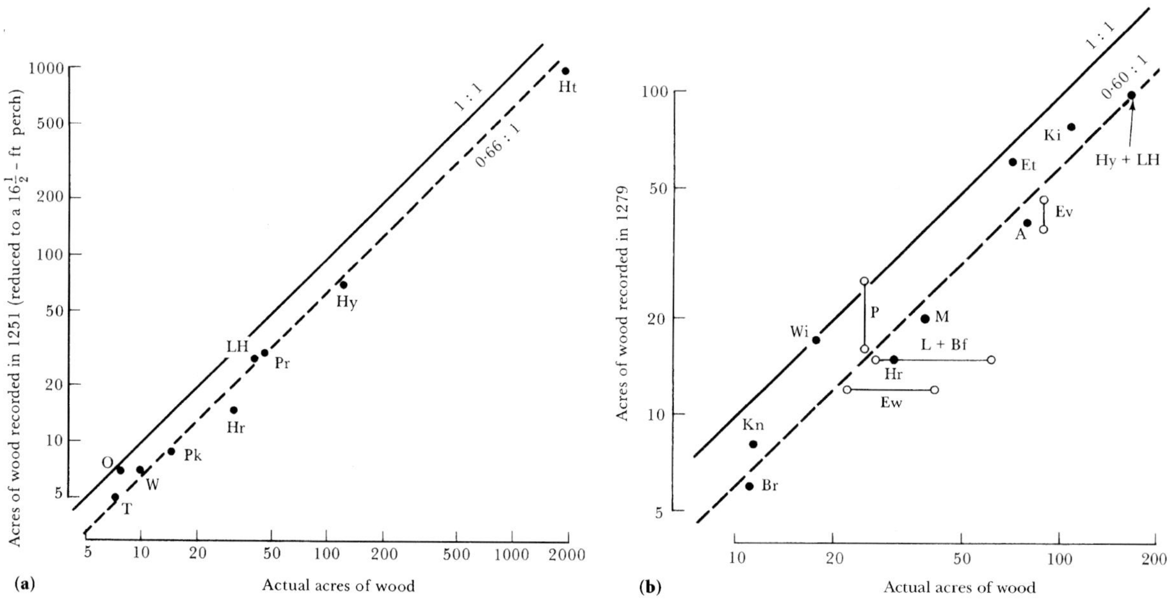

Fig. 2.5 Acres of wood recorded (**a**) in the Ely Coucher Book of 1251[270] and (**b**) in the Hundred Rolls of 1279,[474] compared with the known sizes of the woods at the time in terms of modern acres. Changes in the boundaries of the woods and variations in the length of the perch have been allowed for. Pairs of white points connected by a line represent the limits of an uncertainty in either the ancient area or its modern equivalent. Both scales are logarithmic. Woods used:

West Cambridgeshire

A	Avenelles (part of Gamlingay Wood)
Bf	Buff
Br	Bourn
Et	Eltisley
Ev	Eversden
Ew	Elsworth
Hr	Hardwick
Hy	Hayley
L	Longstowe
LH	Littlehound (near Hayley Wood)[120]
Ki	Kingston
Kn	Knapwell
M	Mertonage (part of Gamlingay Wood)
P	Papworth Everard
Wi	Wimpole (part of Eversden Wood)

Suffolk

Pk	Park (in Barking)[122]
Pr	Priestley (in Barking)
T	Titley (in Barking)
W	Wetheresheg (Swingen's Wood in Barking)
O	Oxenholt (Lumpit Wood in Glemsford)

Hertfordshire

Ht	Hatfield Great Wood

of meaning has become disused, as with ***timber*** and ***wood*** or the Latin *quercus* and *robur* (p. 182). With other words a former exact meaning has lost its precision, as with ***coppice*** (alias ***copse***) and ***spinney*** (Latin *spinetum*, a place of thorns). Many words, e.g. *bletro* and *wrangelon*, are still uncertain. We must be cautious in assuming that any two words in the same language are exact synonyms.

Areas

To estimate the area of an irregularly-shaped wood is more difficult than for a field. It is rarely possible to see the whole at a glance, and trees interfere with measuring chains and with lines of sight. Medieval estimates of wood-areas, nevertheless, are often surprisingly close to the actual area and must be taken seriously.

An acre is a rectangle of 40 x 4 perches, but the perch did not always have its present length of 16½ ft; it could vary from parish to parish between 15½ and 22 ft, giving an acre of between 0.88 and 1.78 times the modern acre (4,047 m^2). Surveys (e.g. Fig. 2.1) usually give the length of the perch and can be amended accordingly. As late as 1675 it was stated 'of Coppice-wood eighteen foot to the Perch is the usual allowance'.[519]

Medieval estimates of area, compared with the actual area within the woodbank – allowing both for the length of the perch and for known alterations to the wood – usually turn out too low. Figure 2.5 illustrates this tendency for two thirteenth-century surveys.

The surveyor's art advanced in the fourteenth century. The earliest accurate survey to include woods that are still extant is that of Leaden Roding (Essex) in 1439:[288] a description, field by field, of lands in the parish, each defined by reference to four or more properties which it adjoined. Four woods are mentioned, and though the names are different it is certain, from their relation to roads, greens, and the parish boundary, that they are the same as the four woods in or adjoining Leaden Roding today. The areas of three of the woods are given in acres, roods, perches, and fractions and can be compared with the modern acreages (Table 2.2). Both the 1439 surveyors and the Ordnance Survey make a preposterous show of accuracy; to determine the area to within ¼ square perch or 0.001 acre involves defining the boundaries to within about an inch on the ground. The two surveys agree to within the practical limits of reproducibility set by the width of woodbanks. A survey of Sibton (E. Suffolk) in 1325[261] claims equal accuracy, but the woods which it measures appear not to survive.

How the accuracy of these surveys was achieved is a mystery. Later maps of woods are sometimes divided into pencilled triangles for computing areas, but maps of sufficient accuracy are first heard of 140 years after the Leaden Roding survey.

Table 2.2 The Leaden Roding woods in 1439.

1439 name	1439 acreage	Decimal equivalent acres	Modern name	Area in 1897 (Ordnance Survey) acres	Percentage difference of area
Filolleswode	12a. 1r. 3¼p.	12.270	Stiles Wood	12.762	– 3.9%
Walramswode	13a. 2r. 15p.	13.594	Parsonage Wood	13.735	– 1.0%
Blunteswood	15a 2½r. 15¼p.	15.720	Poorhouse Wood	15.837	– 0.7%
Weston Wood	(not given)		Lord's Wood		

Fig. 2.6 Pond in Great Monk Wood, Coggeshall, Essex. Like many woodland ponds this has no corresponding bank or mound. June 1979

Fig. 3.0 (a–f) Bradfield Woods, west Suffolk, now managed by Suffolk Wildlife Trust.

(a) Internal ditch of Monks' Park, resulting from its deer-park history. April 2001

(b) Giant stool of ash, which probably dates from the time of the monks; it still produces a good crop of poles. June 1981

(c) Woodstack at the end of the coppicing season, to be processed during the summer. Peter Fordham has organized the large-scale coppicing and marketing of the Bradfield Woods for many years with especial skill and efficiency. May 1987

(d) Plants characteristic of the non-acid parts of the wood (GV1 negative): oxlip, primrose-oxlip hybrid, anemone, violet, dog's-mercury. *Primulas* now seldom appear on this scale. April 1985

(e) Wild garlic, *Allium ursinum*, an extremely gregarious plant, highly dominant for a brief period in spring, and one of the main determinants of ground vegetation (GV2). May 1974

(f) Bracken glade on a sand-lens (p. 42); broom is also highly characteristic.

3

The variation of woods [See also Chapter 31]

Ancient woods are highly individual and unpredictable. No two are the same, and it is not uncommon to find three or four types of woodland in a wood of 50 acres. They come in comparatively small samples: there are not many semi-natural woods bigger than 250 acres, and the larger a wood the more likely it is to have suffered recent alterations which make its natural and historical elements difficult to reconstruct. They are stratified: a typical wood contains timber trees, one or more layers of underwood, herbaceous vegetation, the bryophytes (mosses and liverworts) that grow on the ground, and the ***epiphytes*** – bryophytes, lichens, algae, etc. – that grow on tree-trunks. They change with time, but for a variety of reasons, and some much more slowly than others.

These complexities are particularly severe in woods with the long history of management that is the peculiar characteristic of British, and especially English, woodland. It is a mistake to argue, as some ecologists do [p. 520], that woodland management is a minor and relatively recent disturbing influence whose effects are not an integral part of woods as we now know them. For practical purposes, the history of woods in Britain goes back some 12,000 years. For nearly half that time (Chapter 8), some woodland appears to have been deliberately managed to grow particular sizes of wood. The management of game animals may go back much further into the prehistoric period. Even the written records of individual woods sometimes date back for a thousand years.

We must avoid also the opposite error, to which forestry writers are prone, of supposing that woods are almost wholly artificial, the product, in the main, of tree-planting over the last 300 years. This impression may be given by the more generalized silvicultural literature, but workaday documents – the records of what actually happened in particular places – tell a different story. Planting has been a less widespread and influential factor in woodland than is often supposed. Plantations were generally formed on new sites and were distinguished, and are still distinguishable, from native woodland. Tree-planting within, or on the site of, ancient woods was relatively rare before the nineteenth century; even now there are many woods that have totally escaped planting.

Human activities are such a long-standing and continuous ecological factor that it is now hardly profitable to speculate on what woods would be like without them. Until quite recently they have been of a symbiotic nature: people have influenced the ***structure*** of woods – the sizes, ages, and shapes of individual trees and their relations to one another – rather than the composition. Changes in the tree species composing a wood, or in what grows under them, have usually been indirect rather than intended consequences of management. It is only after 1860, and especially after 1950, that this symbiosis broke down and it became customary to replace woods with plantations.

Methods of classifying woodland

It is possible to classify woods on purely historical or structural criteria which take little or no account of their vegetation: such were the Forestry Commission census categories of 'Broadleaved High Forest', 'Simple Coppice', 'Unutilizable Scrub', etc. The subject-matter of this book calls for a mainly biological classification. In practice this means a classification by flora or vegetation, and especially by trees and other flowering-plants. Animals, though an essential element in any wood, seldom comprise any large part of the woodland itself, and are more elusive and harder to assess than plants. Even with the easier animals (e.g. birds, butterflies, snails, and slugs) the collecting of information is slow and is unlikely ever to be completed for more than a few woods. Hence, with the important exception of woodland versus wood-pasture, the classification of woods will be based on plants rather than animals.

Botanists sometimes study the ***flora*** of a wood, i.e. what plant species are present, and sometimes its ***vegetation***, the abundance of each species and its relationship to other species. (For example, a single oxlip plant in a wood may be a highly significant part of its flora although insignificant in terms of vegetation.) The rest of this chapter deals with vegetation; we shall return to flora in Chapter 5.

Any wood consists of one or more ***plant communities***, assemblages of plants which are more or less closely integrated with each other, can be recognized in other woods, and can be described and named. It is conventional to treat the trees, shrubs, herbaceous plants, and the bryophytes growing on the ground at any one point as forming a single community; the bryophytes and lichens growing on trees are often regarded as one or more separate communities.[611]

There are several independent schools of plant ecology, which present the investigator with a vast choice of systems for separating, describing, and organizing plant communities.[876] Which system to select depends on the purpose of the investigation and the nature of the vegetation, and on the investigator's views on the nature and interrelations of plant communities. Systems differing widely in philosophy often produce broadly similar results.[614]

The British tradition classifies plant communities principally according to their ***dominant*** species – the one, or a few, species which are so abundant or so large as to impose their character on the community as a whole – and to the soil types on which they occur. Sir Arthur Tansley, for instance, described 'damp oakwoods', 'dry oakwoods', 'beechwoods on loam', etc.[150]

Continental ecologists, particularly the 'Zürich-Montpellier' school of phytosociology,[621] characterize plant communities by ***floristic*** methods. An area or a plot of vegetation is chosen as being uniform and representative of its community. A list is prepared of the plants in it, usually with some record of their abundance. By collating such lists, plant ***associations*** are set up, defined mainly by the presence of species of narrow ecological preferences which are peculiar to one association. The defining species are often quite rare, even in their own associations, and dominants are given little weight. The art is highly developed and formalized; associations are supposed to have the same kind of reality as that possessed by plant and animal species; they are given Latin names, e.g. Querco-Carpinetum stachyetosum, derived from those of plants characteristic of them; and they are grouped into higher units of classification – alliances, orders, and classes – much as species are grouped into genera, families, and orders. The advantages and limitations of the method, are discussed by M. E. D. Poore[838] and H. J. B. Birks.[614] The Scandinavian tradition of phytosociology gives greater weight to dominants and other common species.[641]

Methods have been developed for expressing affinities and differences between species lists in numerical form and thus comparing them by more rigid, and supposedly more objective, criteria than was previously possible. Sample plots can thus be sited systematically or at random, avoiding the ill-defined procedure of choosing uniform and representative vegetation. Many different arithmetical procedures have been described, and it can be argued that the technique, while eliminating subjectivity in collecting the data, reintroduces it in choosing the computer programme.

All forms of classification are open to the objection that vegetation and environment vary continuously; that plant communities often intergrade gradually where they meet, and the sharp boundaries presupposed by classification are sometimes artificial. The techniques of ***ordination***[622] have been devised to meet this difficulty. Let us consider a wood consisting of ash and maple in some places and of oak and hazel in others. To divide it simply into oak–hazel and ash–maple woodland might be unsatisfactory if there was a gradual transition between the two communities. Ordination would assign any small area in the wood, according to its composition, to some point on an ***axis*** defined at one end by a high proportion of oak and hazel and at the other end by ash and maple. This is a one-dimensional illustration of a problem that usually has several dimensions. The computer programme commonly produces two, three, or more independent axes of variation, each related more or less closely to particular positive and negative groups of species. This is a powerful technique but often gives Sibylline answers. It may be difficult to interpret the axes in terms of actual plant communities or to relate them to variation in the environment. Our oak–hazel versus ash–maple axis might be correlated with acid versus calcareous soil, or with sandy versus clayey soil, but it could also turn out to be related to some rather vague combination of the two variables.

Describing British woods

For our purpose we need a system that shall embrace nearly all ancient woodland, describing it in terms which can be related to historical records, and, preferably, will be understood by the less botanically-trained reader of this book. These considerations rule out a simple extension of Continental phytosociology, based as it is on carefully selected sites, with units often defined by species too insignificant to be recorded in historical documents and producing too little pollen to appear in prehistoric deposits.

Floristic classifications of any kind are not well suited to British woods for two fundamental reasons. The first concerns the size of the recording plot. Many of our woods are intimately-mixed mosaics of plant communities, and the 'minimal area' needed to ensure representation of all the plants characteristic of one community may be so large that an actual plot of such an area runs into the territory of a different community [p. 488]. For instance, alder-buckthorn (*Frangula alnus*) is a highly characteristic species of oak–hornbeam woods (Chapter 14); yet it is so infrequent that even with a plot as large as 1 ha one would not always include it. Such a plot is much too large for many woods. In the Bradfield Woods study (see p. 28), plots as small as 0.008 ha often crossed obvious boundaries between communities. The requirements for inclusiveness and homogeneity may be irreconcilable, however acute the investigator's judgement of his plot size.

The other difficulty is that woods undergo cycles of change over periods longer than a year. The regular succession of felling and regrowth, at intervals of a few years, is as inherent a feature of woodland as grazing or mowing are of grassland, and we dare not regard any one phase – certainly not the neglected state in which many woods now are – as more typical than any other. Many herbaceous plants are not visible every year. For instance, the spurges *Euphorbia amygdaloides*, etc. and the St John's-wort *Hypericum humifusum*, characteristic of particular kinds of woodland, often appear for only a year or two after felling; for the rest of the time they wait as buried seed [Chapter 26]. A species list may therefore be unduly influenced by what phase of the plant community happens to be represented at the time of recording.

An early attempt at a floristic classification of woods in the whole of Britain was that of R. G. H. Bunce.[17] The unit of recording was normally the whole of a wood. A computer programme was devised to select significant species whose presence or absence was used to classify species-lists for 2,463 woods into a hierarchy of types. Although to some extent the classification corresponds to actual vegetation types, particularly in Highland regions, the very principle of classifying entire woods is open to the objection that differences between parts of the same wood are often at least as great as those between one wood and another. Moreover some of the discriminant species, such as maple, wood-sorrel (*Oxalis acetosella*), and *Sphagnum*, are present but rare in many woods and are often confined to wood-margins or pockets of different soil not representative of the rest of the wood; it is a matter of chance whether they happen to survive and whether the person collecting the data happens to find them.

A further complication in classifying British woodland vegetation, particularly in the eastern counties from which much of the material for this book is drawn, is the lack of correspondence between trees and ground vegetation. This is a matter of common observation and is analysed in detail in later chapters. For example in Hayley Wood (Chapter 4) the striking and often abrupt transition between the bluebell (*Endymion nonscriptus*) and dog's-mercury (*Mercurialis perennis*) herbaceous communities does not exactly correspond to a difference in the ash–maple–hazel woodland under which both of them grow [but see pp. 488–91]. Conversely, in Chalkney Wood (Chapter 15), lime woodland adjoins hornbeam woodland without any systematic difference in the ground vegetation. Where tree and herb communities both vary, as in descending into a valley, the two transitions may not occur at the same point on the gradient.

Lack of integration seems not to be a problem over much of Europe. There can be little doubt that in the environs of Zürich or of Montpellier trees and ground vegetation tend to vary together and can justifiably be treated as forming a single plant community. This may be because, in the rugged topography of much semi-natural vegetation there, differences of soil, slope, and climate are so abrupt and overwhelming as to affect all layers in the vegetation together. In Lowland England, on the other hand, the topography is more subdued and the geology and glaciological history are exceptionally complex. Paradoxes such as acid soils on chalk-lands are the rule rather than the exception. Vegetation boundaries are often determined by slight and subtle influences – a slope of less than one degree, or a small change in the depth of the topsoil – and there is no reason why these should affect all layers of the vegetation equally. Another feature of Britain is the infrequent establishment of seedlings by many tree species. Whether a tree occupies a particular site may depend not so much on whether it is well-adapted to that environment as on whether it happened to have a good seedling year immediately after the site became available for colonization. The abundance and permanence of birch, an arctic tree and a very poor competitor, in southern England (Chapter 19), reminds us that ability to colonize, in which birch excels, makes up for much ill-adaptedness in other respects.

Methods used in this book

These arguments show that the Tansleyan tradition is, after all, the most practical way of classifying British woods. The procedure is simple and direct and depends mainly on trees, which are well represented in the historical and sub-fossil record. It also avoids having to explain to the non-botanical reader why, for instance, the ashwoods of Skye are properly assigned to the phytosociological Alliance Fagion sylvaticae,[614] even though there is no indigenous beech (*Fagus sylvatica*) within 400 miles.

This book departs from Tansley's system in four important details.

(1) Wood-pasture will be recognized as a distinct kind of vegetation from woodland; it has a distinct structure and flora and at least a thousand years of separate history. Plantations and hedges, in so far as they appear in this book, are also distinguished from woodland.

(2) Tansley, while to some extent appreciating the artificial prominence of timber trees, continued to regard them as the most significant element in a wood. In this book tree communities are defined mainly in terms of underwood, as being the less artificial and less arbitrary component of the trees (Chapter 1).

(3) Trees and ground vegetation will be treated as separate plant communities, the former providing part of the environment in which the latter operates. In this way it becomes feasible to discuss all the possible combinations without unduly multiplying the number of types recognized. A historically-based book must necessarily say more about trees since there is less evidence for the ground vegetation in the past.

(4) The earlier British ecological philosophy was much influenced by the concept of determinate successions proceeding in ordered sequence to a predictable climax plant community (pp. 6–7). We now know that the last occasion on which there was a sufficiently long period of stability of climate

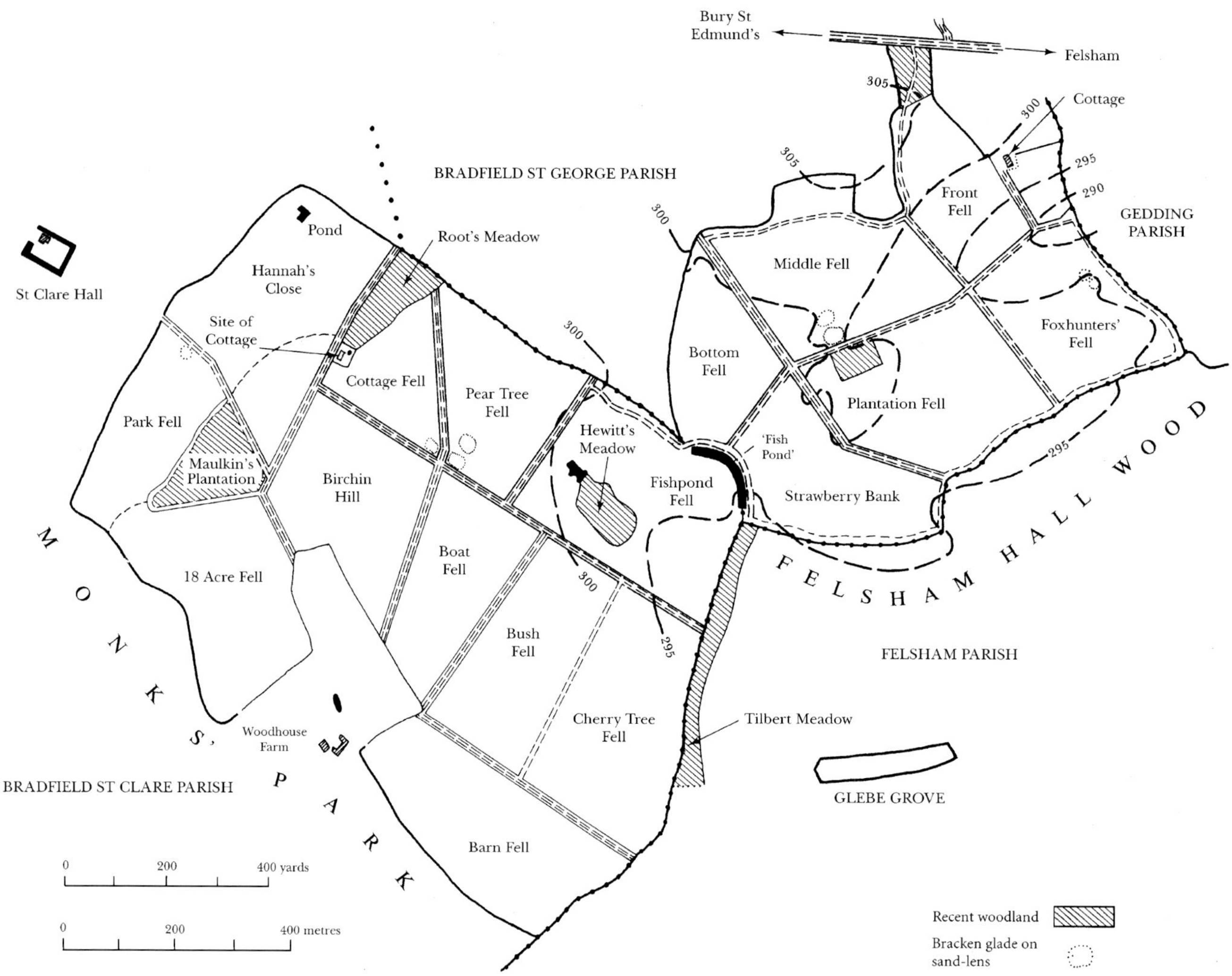

Fig. 3.1 The Bradfield Woods: modern topography. Contours at 5-ft intervals are given for the Bradfield Woods Reserve. Features destroyed since 1966 are shown by thin lines.

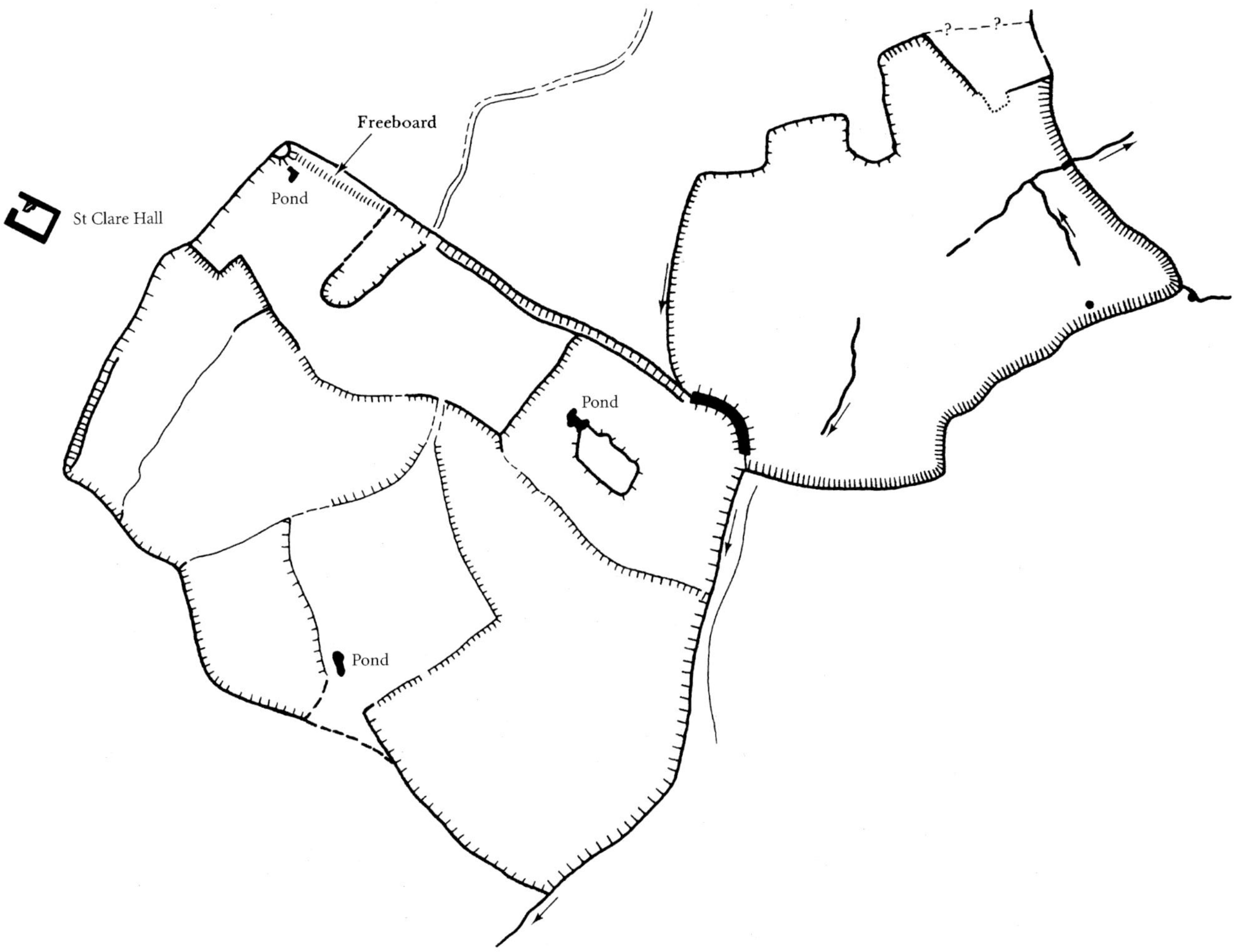

Fig. 3.2 The Bradfield Woods: ancient earthworks. Features shown by thin lines have been destroyed, mostly since 1966, but are visible from the air as soil-marks.

and freedom from human interference for this process to approach completion was in the Middle Stone Age, and that the climax forest then attained was not as simple as we used to suppose. Successions and sub-climaxes of one kind and another play an important part in British woodland, but the determinism of the grander aspects of the theory has little relation to present reality.

I shall draw parallels where possible between English woodland types and Continental phytosociology. Even as close as Belgium[772] it seems that there are few exact equivalents. English woods are not just an extension of Central European ones. The climate and topography are different, and we have a prevalence of odd geological materials like Chalky Boulder-clay. Our seasonally-wet woods tend to be on hilltops and are not associated with extra fertility as they are in Europe where waterlogging occurs in valleys. Several of our principal trees – ash, maple, hazel, birch, lime – play only subordinate parts in Continental phytosociology. Similar problems arise between different Continental countries; the systems devised for Poland[891] and S.W. Germany[809] by no means agree in detail. Categories, terminologies, and classifications devised for plant communities hundreds of miles away are more of an encumbrance than a help. To describe English woods in phytosociological terms would be a new task and is not an objective of this book.

The Bradfield Woods and their plant communities

Felsham Hall Wood in Bradfield St George and the adjoining Monks' Park Wood in Bradfield St Clare, West Suffolk (Fig. 3.1), appear in many contexts in this

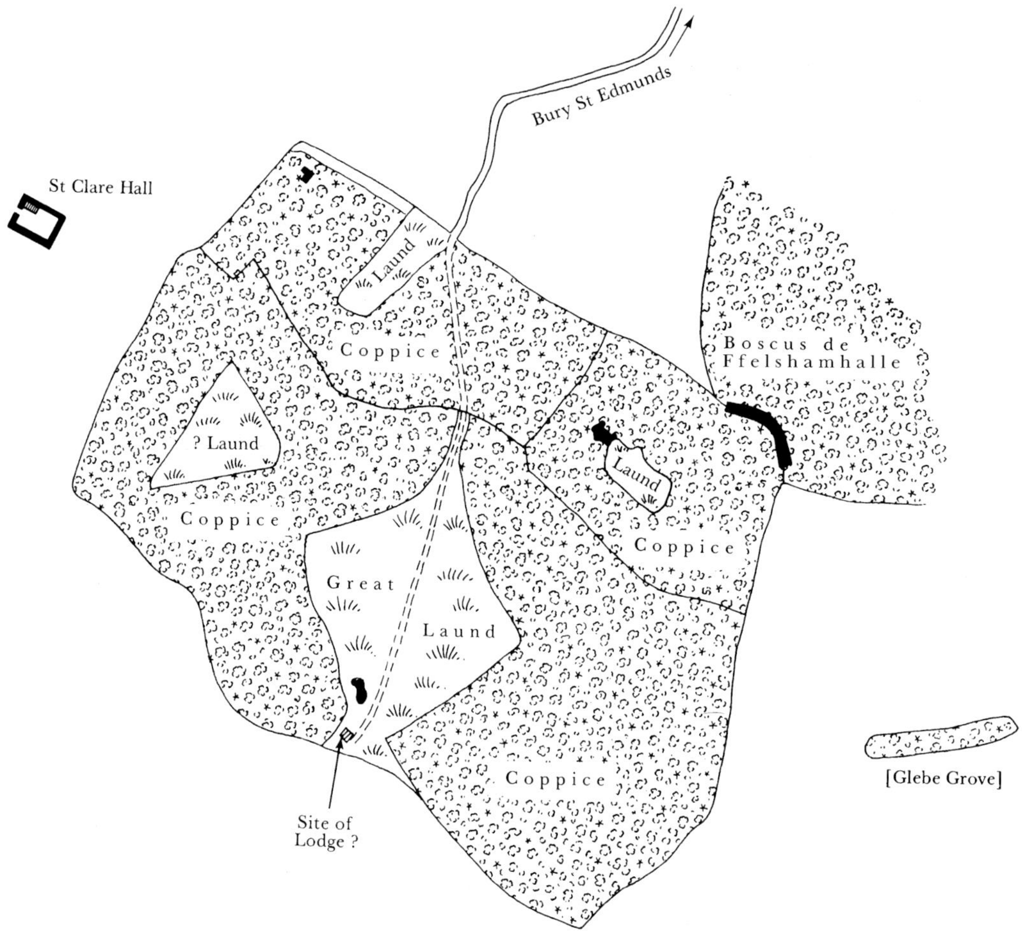

Fig. 3.3 The Bradfield Woods: reconstruction of the medieval topography showing the coppices and launds (p. 173) of Monks' Park.

book, for they are a microcosm ot the ancient woods of England: they combine many aspects of vegetation and history that elsewhere have to be observed in separate woods.

In the Middle Ages the woods belonged to different departments of the great Abbey of Bury St Edmund's; Felsham Hall (103 acres) was a normal coppice, but Monk's Park (220 acres) was a compartmented deer-park (Chapter 12). The name *Ffelshamhalle*, 'at the Felsham corner', preserves the Anglo-Saxon dative case of *halh*, a corner (the wood is at the corner nearest Felsham of Bradfield St George parish). *Munces park* – a spelling which persisted into the last century – preserves the genitive case of *munuc*, a monk. Coppicing dates from before 1252;[446] in 1540 a detailed survey lists the acreages of underwood of from one to thirty years' growth;[459] management records continue to the present day. Felsham Hall is bounded by a massive woodbank with pollard trees; Monks' Park has more complex earthworks related to its history as a deer-park probably of the twelfth century (Figs. 3.0a, 3.2 and 3.3).

Despite their large size, both woods continued intact, coppiced on an average cycle of 10–11 years, until the 1960s. In 1929 Monks' Park, which had a considerable entomological reputation,[502–3, 903] had been proposed as a national nature reserve,[875] but the plan was shelved and the wood forgotten. In 1966 this wood began to be grubbed out for agricultural land, and the woods would doubtless have disappeared unrecorded, as had many other historic Suffolk woods, but for the opposition of local residents who valued them. Attempts to arouse a wider interest among public authorities and conservation bodies were at first met with a remarkable variety of excuses for inaction. Eventually, after two-thirds of Monks' Park had gone, the remainder was protected by a Tree Preservation Order. In 1970 the then Society for the Promotion of Nature Reserves, through the generosity of many benefactors, was able to acquire the whole of Felsham Hall Wood and about one-ninth of the original Monks' Park. The case was something of a turning-point in woodland conservation, for it was one of the few instances outside Essex where the destruction of a wood had been successfully resisted. [Twenty years on, the woods (by then including most of what was left of Monks' Park) were declared a National Nature Reserve.[850]]

The Bradfield Woods are noted for their variety of tree communities and of flowering plants and for such animals as the dormouse, nightingale, and White Admiral butterfly; also for fungi and for bush-crickets and other invertebrates.

The Reserve is a working wood, yielding most of the products described in Chapter 11 and retaining its social links. Particular sizes of underwood used to be used by a factory that made rakes, scythe-sticks, and articles of turnery.[116, 880] The woods yield poles and stakes, and thatching wood of various kinds, and supply the neighbourhood with fuel. Even the twigs are not wasted, for the ashes of bonfires are collected and sold to potters for glazing.

Vegetation and its analysis

The list of flowering plants and ferns stands [in 1980] at some 370 species, a total which appears to be exceeded for a British wood only by Bedford Purlieus near Peterborough.[129] There are forty-two native trees and shrubs, about two-thirds of the whole British list.

The woods consist almost entirely of ancient woodland. The underwood varies from newly-cut to about thirty years' growth; the panels are irregular and not planned in advance. The timber trees – chiefly oak, ash, birch, and alder – are mostly less than seventy years old and are thinly and evenly scattered.

The site is a plateau with shallow valleys and sandy hillocks. The soils are derived from Chalky Boulder-clay overlain by varying thicknesses of sand and loess mixed to differing degrees (pp. 47–50); the apparently simple topography – slopes never exceeding $2\frac{1}{2}°$ – conceals a most complex range of soils. Acidity varies from pH 3.1 to 7.4, almost the entire range that is possible

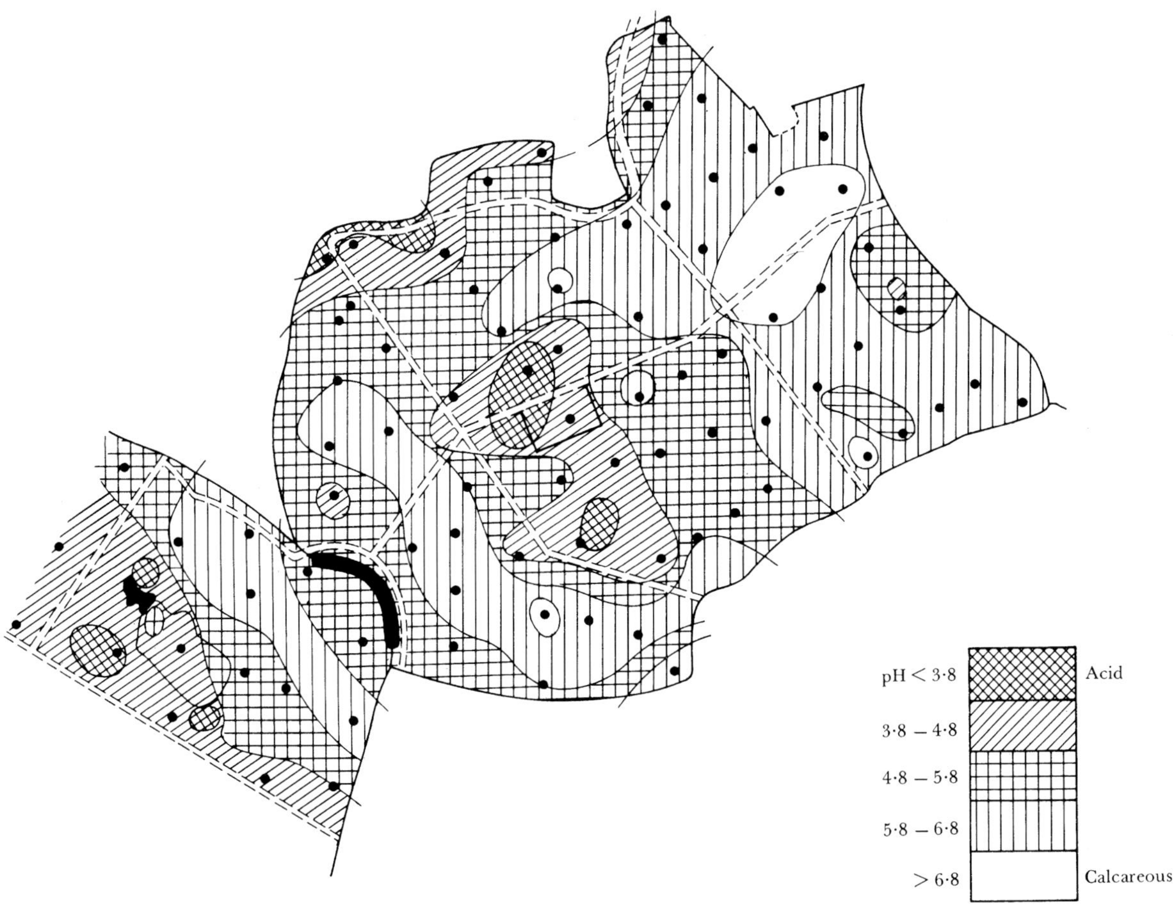

Fig. 3.4 Felsham Hall Wood and part of Monks' Park: sample plots (●) and distribution of topsoil pH.

in British soils, and places a few yards apart may differ by as much as two pH units (Fig. 3.4). A full description of Bradfield soils, including the effects of slope, changes in composition down the profile, variations in fertility, and sub-surface drainage would require a major research project and might even then miss some aspects of importance.

The plant communities of the Bradfield Woods merge gradually into one another to a degree unusual in Eastern England. Three to six trees usually are co-dominant, and the proportions change continuously: it is hardly possible to define areas of alder-wood, birchwood, ash–hazel wood, etc. This reflects the subtle soil changes, but also the unbroken history of coppicing, which allows more species to coexist than would otherwise be possible (p. 208).

We have rejected numerical classification and ordination of plot records as techniques for exploring the variation of woods in general. For the circumscribed problem of the Bradfield Woods the objections are less strong. Recording can be more intensive and more disciplined for one site than for a wider survey. The large number of species, indefinite vegetation boundaries, and soils whose complexity defies adequate description encourage the hope that a numerical analysis might yield insights into plant communities that could not be got in any other way.

The procedure is in four stages. Plant records are collected, in this case from 84 plots. A computer programme arranges the plots in such a way as to bring out relationships between them based on the plant records. These relationships are then interpreted in terms of actual assemblages of species. They are also correlated, as far as possible, with measurements of environmental factors.

1. Collection of records

Records were collected from 1970 to 1974, at similar times of year (late May) to avoid seasonal differences. The 84 plots were sited at points determined on the map and then found on the ground (Fig. 3.4). The survey was restricted to the general woodland, excluding the special habitats of rides or woodbanks, and was designed to give uniform coverage. The plot size – a circle of radius 5 m – was a compromise between the requirements of inclusiveness and homogeneity previously mentioned. Within each plot all trees and other flowering plants and ferns were recorded; their abundance was scaled by a version of Domin's method[876] in order that rare as well as abundant species should make their due contribution to the analysis.

2. Ordination

The data for analysis comprised underwood (including shrubs) and ground vegetation (herbs and undershrubs, cf. p. 74); timber trees were too few, and their occurrence too haphazard, to be included. Underwood and ground vegetation were the subject of separate analyses; we shall not assume that trees and herbs should vary together.

An attempt at classifying the plots by the computation known as multivariate cluster analysis[813, 843] produced little better than chance groupings of plots. Classification methods in general are unlikely to be suited to the gradual transitions and many-sided affinities of Bradfield vegetation, and this approach was not pursued.

The ordination programme, devised by Dr John Birks, is based on that of J. C. Gower.[720] The computer selects a number of independent axes or dimensions of variation, each expressing a particular gradient of relationship between the plot records, and assigns each plot to a numerical position on each axis. The first axis expresses the strongest relationships, those most likely to correspond to some ecological reality. How far to take the process is a matter of taste; in the present instance I can assign a meaning to the first three dimensions of the underwood analysis and the first four of the ground vegetation.

3. The axes interpreted in terms of plant species

Ordination axes are presented by the computer as mere abstractions. To determine what actual variation in plant communities is represented by, say, underwood Axis 1 we arrange the plot records in the order in which the 84 plots are placed on the axis, and we observe which plants appear particularly in plots placed high or low. Dogwood, for instance, is associated with the positive end of this axis, birch (*Betula pubescens*) and sallow (*Salix caprea*) with the negative end. (The labelling of one end as 'positive' and the other as 'negative' is arbitrary.)

Species associated with the first three underwood axes are given in Table 3.1. This includes not only trees and shrubs, in terms of which the axes were originally computed, but also herbs and undershrubs. Species associated with the ground vegetation axes are given in Table 3.2.

4. Underwood and ground vegetation axes related to environmental variables and to each other

At each of the eighty-four sampling points measurements were made of slope; soil pH; clay, silt, and sand content of the soil; distance from the wood edge; and age since last felling. Other records include the number of tree and shrub species in the plot, the total number of plant species, and the percentage of the ground covered by ground vegetation. Each of the seven ordination axes can be tested for correlation with each of these external variables; the three underwood axes can also be tested against the four ground vegetation axes (Tables 3.1, 3.2).

The ground vegetation axes have well-defined ecological meanings. Axis GV1 is strongly correlated with soil acidity and also with the proportions of clay and sand which are closely linked to acidity (Table 3.3): it involves brambles, bracken, honeysuckle, bluebell etc. (plants of acid sandy soils) versus oxlip, meadowsweet, twayblade, etc. (plants of calcareous clayey soils). The next most important axis, GV2, involves garlic (*Allium ursinum*) standing almost alone against a large number of other species;

Table 3.1 Bradfield Woods: dimensions of variation in the underwood as determined by ordination from 84 plots.

Axis	Underwood species (including shrubs)		Associated herbs and undershrubs	Correlations with other variables	
UW1	+ + + Dogwood	*Cornus sanguinea*	+ + *Mercurialis perennis*	Clay content	0.45
	+ + Hawthorn	*Crataegus laevigata*	+ *Conopodium majus*	% cover of herbs	0.39
		x *monogyna*	+ *Tamus communis*	Slope	0.27
	+ + Spindle	*Euonymus europaeus*	+ (2 other species)	pH	0.22
	+ + Blackthorn	*Prunus spinosa*	– *Holcus mollis*	Tree and	–0.25
	+ + Elder	*Sambucus nigra*	– *Poa trivialis*	shrub species	
	– – Alder	*Frangula alnus*	– *Rubus fruticosus* agg.	Distance from	–0.33
	buckthorn		– (10 other species)	wood edge	
	– – – Birch	*Betula pubescens*	– – *Oxalis acetosella*	Sand content	–0.33
	– – – Honeysuckle	*Lonicera periclymenum*	– – – *Lonicera periclymenum*	GV2	–0.49
	– – – Oak	*Quercus robur*	– – – *Lysimachia nemorum*	GV3	–0.23
	– – – Sallow	*Salix caprea*			
	– – – Guelder-rose	*Viburnum opulus*			
UW2	+ + + Alder	*Alnus glutinosa*	– *Anemone nemorosa*	Distance from	0.46
	+ Oak	*Quercus robur*	– *Carex riparia*	wood edge	
	+ Sallow	*Salix cinerea*	– *Deschampsia caespitosa*	Sand content	0.23
	+ Elder	*Sambucus nigra*	– (16 other species)	Clay content	–0.27
	– Ash	*Fraxinus excelsior*	– – *Arum maculatum*	Tree and	–0.58
	– Holly	*Ilex aquifolium*	– – *Brachypodium sylvaticum*	shrub species	
	– Rose	*Rosa arvensis*	– – *Carex sylvatica*	Total species	–0.66
	– Rose	*R. canina*	– – *Geum rivale*	GV3	0.54
	– Elm	*Ulmus minor*	– – *Poa trivialis*	GV1	0.34
	– – Hawthorn	*Crataegus monogyna*	– – *Primula elatior*	GV2	–0.26
	– – Blackthorn	*Prunus spinosa*	– – *Rubus caesius*		
	– – – Maple	*Acer campestre*	– – *Tamus communis*		
	– – – Hawthorn	*C. laevigata*			
UW3	+ + + Honeysuckle	*Lonicera periclymenum*	+ + + *Rubus Corylifolii*	Sand content	0.43
	+ + + Rose	*Rosa arvensis*	+ + *Urtica dioica*	% cover of herbs	0.23
	+ + Oak	*Quercus robur*	+ *Endymion nonscriptus*	Clay content	–0.39
	+ + Elder	*Sambucus nigra*	+ *Holcus mollis*	pH	–0.45
	+ Alder	*Frangula alnus*	+ *Pteridium aquilinum*	GV1	0.41
	buckthorn		+ (6 other species)		
	+ Red-	*Ribes sylvestre*	– *Filipendula ulmaria*		
	currant		– *Primula elatior*		
	– Alder	*Alnus glutinosa*	– (5 other species)		
	– Spindle	*Euonymus europaeus*	– – *Carex sylvatica*		
	– Rose	*Rosa canina*	– – *Geum rivale*		
	– Sallow	*Salix caprea*	– – – *Rubus caesius*		
	– Wych-elm	*Ulmus glabra*			
	– Guelder-rose	*Viburnum opulus*			
	– – Maple	*Acer campestre*			
	– – Ash	*Fraxinus excelsior*			

Notes

The symbols + + +, + +, + and – – –, – –, – indicate species with stronger or weaker affinities with the positive or negative ends of the ordination axes.

Oak is counted only when it consists of saplings or coppice stools.

Honeysuckle (*Lonicera*) is sometimes a shrub or climber, recorded as underwood, and sometimes an undershrub, recorded as ground vegetation.

The figures in the last column are correlation coefficients, which can range from +1 (perfect positive correlation) to –1 (perfect negative correlation). With 82 degrees of freedom, as here, correlations stronger than ±0.28 are statistically significant at the 1% level of probability; those stronger than ±0.35 are significant at the 0.1% level.

Correlations weaker than ±0.22 are non-significant and are omitted.

Table 3.2 Bradfield Woods: dimensions of variation in the ground vegetation as determined by ordination from 84 plots.

Axis	Herbs and undershrubs	Associated underwood and shrubs		Correlations with other variables	
GV1	+ + + *Lonicera periclymenum*	+ + Alder buckthorn	*Frangula alnus*	Sand content	0.43
	+ + + *Rubus Corylifolii*	+ + Elder	*Sambucus nigra*	Distance from	0.27
(+ end acid,	+ + *Dryopteris dilatata*	+ Honeysuckle	*Lonicera periclymenum*	wood edge	
– end calcareous)	+ + *D. spinulosa*	+ Oak	*Quercus robur*	Total species	–0.32
	+ + *Endymion nonscriptus*	– Dogwood	*Cornus sanguinea*	% cover of herbs	–0.38
	+ + *Holcus mollis*	– Spindle	*Euonymus europaeus*	Clay content	–0.55
	+ + *Pteridium aquilinum*	– Ash	*Fraxinus excelsior*	pH	–0.72
	+ + *Urtica dioica*	– Rose	*Rosa canina*	UW2	0.34
	+ *Rubus fruticosus*	– – Maple	*Acer campestre*	UW3	0.41
	+ (3 other species)	– – Hawthorn	*Crataegus monogyna*		
	– *Anemone nemorosa*	– – Wych-elm	*Ulmus glabra*		
	– (2 other species)				
	– – *Carex pendula*				
	– – *C. sylvatica*				
	– – *Deschampsia caespitosa*				
	– – *Geum rivale x urbanum*				
	– – *Mercurialis perennis*				
	– – *Paris quadrifolia*				
	– – *Taraxacum* spp.				
	– – – *Filipendula ulmaria*				
	– – – *Geum rivale*				
	– – – *Listera ovata*				
	– – – *Orchis mascula*				
	– – – *Primula elatior*				
	– – – *Ranunculus ficaria*				
	– – – *Rubus caesius*				
GV2	+ + + *Lonicera periclymenum*	+ + Birch	*Betula pubescens*	Total species	0.46
	+ + + *Potentilla sterilis*	+ + Hawthorn	*Crataegus monogyna*	Tree and	0.31
(the garlic	+ + + *Viola riviniana*	+ + Guelder-rose	*Viburnum opulus*	shrub species	
factor)	or *reichenbachiana*	+ Sallow	*Salix caprea*	Clay content	0.25
	+ + *Ajuga reptans*	– Alder	*Alnus glutinosa*	Sand content	–0.25
	+ + *Carex sylvatica*	– Dogwood	*Cornus sanguinea*	% cover of herbs	–0.33
	+ + *Deschampsia caespitosa*	– Elder	*Sambucus nigra*	UW2	–0.26
	+ + *Dryopteris spinulosa*			UW1	–0.49
	+ + *Luzula pilosa*				
	+ + *Lysimachia nemorum*				
	+ *Poa trivialis*				
	+ *Rubus Corylifolii*				
	+ (11 other species)				
	– *Filipendula ulmaria*				
	– *Mercurialis perennis*				
	– *Stachys sylvatica*				
	– – – *Allium ursinum* (garlic)				
GV3	+ + *Filipendula ulmaria*	+ Alder	*Alnus glutinosa*	Distance from	0.43
	+ *Holcus mollis*	– Hazel	*Corylus avellana*	wood edge	
(+ end interior,	+ (4 other species)	– Holly	*Ilex aquifolium*	Total species	–0.50
– end margins)	– *Mercurialis perennis*	– Honeysuckle	*Lonicera periclymenum*	UW2	0.54
	– *Poa trivialis*	– Blackthorn	*Prunus spinosa*	UW1	–0.23
	– *Rubus Corylifolii*	– Elm	*Ulmus minor*		
	– (13 other species)	– – Maple	*Acer campestre*		
	– – *Anemone nemorosa*	– – Hawthorn	*Crataegus monogyna*		
	– – *Brachypodium sylvaticum*	– – Rose	*Rosa arvensis*		
	– – *Conopodium majus*				
	– – *Primula elatior*				
	– – *Tamus communis*				
	– – – *Arum maculatum*				

Axis	Herbs and undershrubs	Associated underwood and shrubs	Correlations with other variables
GV4	+ *Anemone nemorosa*	None	Age of underwood 0.67
	+ *Luzula pilosa*		% cover of herbs –0.26
old (+)	+ *Rubus Corylifolii*		Total species –0.40
versus	– *Cardamine pratensis*		
young (–)	– *Chamaenerion angustifolium*		
underwood)	– *Hypericum hirsutum*		
	– *Poa trivialis*		
	– (3 other species)		
	– – *Arctium* spp.		
	– – *Cirsium palustre*		
	– – *Filipendula ulmaria*		
	– – *Juncus effusus*		
	– – *Lysimachia nemorum*		
	– – *Stachys sylvatica*		
	– – – *Cirsium palustre*		

Notes as for Table 3.1.

it is hardly correlated with any of the factors measured, but the general behaviour of garlic (p. 95) suggests that sub-surface movement of water may be important. Axis GV3 is correlated with wood-margins versus the interior: marginal species, *Arum*, *Conopodium*, maple, hedgerow hawthorn, etc., are opposed to internal species such as meadowsweet and alder. Axis GV4 gives expression to the age of the underwood.

The three underwood axes are correlated with the first three ground vegetation axes; they evidently express the same set of environmental variables but in a different order of importance and do not disentangle them so neatly. UW1 is correlated with GV2; UW2 is correlated with GV3 and weakly with GV1; UW3 is also correlated with GV1. Acidity, distance from the edge, and sand versus clay are all involved, but each underwood axis is influenced by at least two of these factors. Age of the underwood has no detectable influence, which is not surprising since little underwood has reached the age at which the less competitive species start to die out.

Conclusions

This is an application of a somewhat fashionable [in 1980] technique to a problem chosen as being specially suitable. It involved collecting and processing data on a scale suitable to intensive study of a particular group of woods; it could not lightly be extended to the woods of a whole region.

For ground vegetation the results are clear-cut and provide insights into plant distribution and plant communities that might not otherwise have been possible. The procedure devised for interpreting the ordination axes, by looking for species characteristic of groups of plots at one end or other of each axis, enables us to use records of uncommon plants which do not appear in every plot in the community of which they are typical.

The effects of pH (GV1) and of coppicing (GV4) are to be expected. The 'garlic factor' (GV2) is not wholly surprising, but may not be easy to define by an environmental measurement. The edge effect (GV3) is most interesting, especially to a historian of woods. It cannot

Table 3.3 Bradfield Woods: correlation coefficients of environmental and structural variables with each other.

	Total number of species	Tree and shrub species	% cover	Age of underwood	Distance from edge	Slope	Clay	Silt	Sand
Soil:									
pH	—	—	–0.31	—	—	—	0.70	–0.30	–0.55
sand content (106–212 μm)	—	—	–0.37	—	0.39	—	–0.88	–0.25	
silt content (20–63 μm)	0.22	—	—	—	—	–0.23	—		
clay content (<2 μm)	—	—	0.40	—	–0.37				
Slope	—	—	—	—	—				
Distance from edge	—	—	–0.23	—					
Age of underwood	–0.29	—	–0.30						
% cover of herbs	—	—							
Number of tree and shrub species	0.69								

See notes to Table 3.1. Non-significant correlations are omitted.

be a matter of microclimate, for it extends some distance in, is equally present on north and south edges, and is unrelated to coppicing. Woodbanks were expressly excluded from the samples. GV3 is evidently related to some difference between the geology and soils of the wood and of the surrounding fields, and is thus connected with the question of why this piece of land should have been left as woodland in Anglo-Saxon times.

The four ground vegetation axes are correlated with the structure of plant communities as well as with particular species. The number of herbaceous species present and the degree of cover are both greater in the more calcareous soils (GV1) and beneath the younger underwood (GV4). The garlic factor (GV2) is associated with increased cover but with fewer species, both of trees and shrubs and of herbs. The edge effect (GV3) increases the total number of species but has no effect on cover.

For underwood, similar factors are at work but the method is less successful at disentangling them. Each axis is weakly correlated with two or three soil factors rather than strongly influenced by a single factor. It may be partly by chance that the trees happen to turn out this way, but this Bradfield analysis bears out the general conclusion that factors influencing tree distribution are more subtle than those affecting ground vegetation and are not so easily accessible to measurement, at least from the soil surface. Herbs are of more value as indicators of pH, drainage, and other surface factors.

The results probably depend to some extent on the sampling method. The records were taken at a time when there was relatively little recent coppicing in the woods; had the work been done five years earlier or later there would have been a more balanced distribution of ages, and age of underwood would almost certainly have been more than the fourth most important influence on ground vegetation. Had the sampling been designed to take special account of areas of lime or elm, on the grounds that these are major woodland trees elsewhere though little represented at Bradfield, the underwood results might well have been different. Ordination has proved a useful method for Bradfield, but we should not claim any special accuracy or objectivity for its results, nor can we easily extrapolate them to interpret woodland in general.

Fig. 3.5 (a–c) Bradfield Woods.

(a) Bracken glade on the largest sand-lens. Bracken is so strongly dominant as to keep out most trees. The coppiced oak is characteristic (in lowland England) of specially acid and infertile places (Chapter 17). March 2002

(b) The waterlogging effect (here due to rainwater ponded up by the woodbank).

(c) Small-scale example of the gradient GV1. Bracken (on sand-lens) to left; anemone in middle; dog's-mercury to right. April 1997

4

Woodland soils

Relationships between soils and vegetation work in both directions: the soil influences what grows on it, and plants exert some influence on the composition of the soil and on the animals and micro-organisms that live in it.

The soils of ancient woods are not a random sample of all soils nor a mere extension of those of the surrounding farmland. Woods tend to have survived on sites that were of little use for anything else, on areas of poor soil according to medieval or earlier ideas of land capability. To the medieval farmer, fertility was much more important than it is now,[839] but slopes and poor drainage were less severe obstacles to cultivation than in our mechanized age. Woodland soils differ in development as well as in origin from those of farmland: they have been influenced by trees and have escaped ploughing, draining, liming, and fertilizing. Wood-pastures can have a wider range of soils, influenced by the pasture vegetation as well as the trees. Plantations can inherit almost any soil from the previous land-use.

For soils in general the reader should consult a standard textbook such as that by L. F. Curtis and others.[640] The Soil Survey of Great Britain,[608] in its monographs and maps, uses a rather more advanced treatment than the one I adopt; although concerned chiefly with agricultural soils it is well worth consulting. The Survey uses a taxonomy of soils with many named soil series; these are too numerous to describe here, but in later chapters I shall refer in passing to some of the names.

The parent materials of soils

Every schoolboy is taught that soils are formed by the weathering of the underlying rocks; yet in much of Britain there is little correlation between solid geology and soils. Half of Eastern England is mapped as Chalk, which here very rarely enters directly into the soils of ancient woods and can usually be ignored. Woods over variable solid geology, such as Castor Hanglands near Peterborough, are often relatively uniform in their vegetation.

Most of the stuff of woodland soils is derived from the ***drift*** geology – the upper layers, from 1 to 70 m thick, of Boulder-clay, sands and gravels, etc. laid down over the bedrock chiefly by the action of glaciers and their meltwater. This is mapped by the drift editions of the Geological Survey, but even these are a poor guide to woodland soils. For example Boulder-clay, the most abundant drift of Eastern England, is normally a heavy clay containing lumps of chalk; yet woodland soils on it are often sandy or silty and include some of the most acid soils anywhere in Britain.

Drift geology corresponds poorly to woodland soils, partly because the drifts themselves vary, and partly because they are overlain by thinner and more recent deposits still. It is a most important discovery of recent years that much of England is overlain by thin deposits of silt and fine sand (particles from 0.02 to 0.06 mm in diameter). This uppermost skin of the earth's crust is rarely as much as 1 m thick and hence is not recorded by the Geological Survey. Thin silty deposits were first separately recognized in seminatural vegetation, such as heathlands on chalk,[826] the heaths of the Lizard Peninsula,[636] and the grasslands of the Derbyshire limestone plateau.[834] Dr R. M. S. Perrin has shown that they have a definite geographical distribution covering most of eastern and southern England;[828] in some regions they are associated with similar thin surface layers of coarser sand. On farmland such surface deposits have often been removed by sheet-erosion or mixed in by ploughing, yet a careful analysis of soil-particle sizes from plateau sites will generally reveal their presence. In many places the minerals which they contain have been proved not to come from the underlying drift or bedrock.

It is widely believed that both the sand and the silt are wind-blown, the result of great dust-storms in late-glacial times. The sand was carried in short jumps like blown sand on a beach; the silt was borne for longer distances and forms indeed an attenuated tail of the great ***loess*** deposits familiar in Germany and extending as far as China. I shall, for short, refer to the 0.02–0.06 mm surface deposits as loess.

Disturbance, mixing, and separation

Roots may penetrate to a depth of 3 m or more and may encounter surface deposits, drift, and bedrock, often more than one variant of each. Usually these parent materials are not neatly superimposed but have been disturbed in various ways.

Periglacial action

When Britain was an arctic land, covered by tundra, the top metre or two of the soil froze and thawed each year over a permanently frozen subsoil. The pressures generated by this ***periglacial action*** disturbed the stratification in ways which have left their mark all over the landscape. Although regular periglacial soil patterns, such as the 'stripes and polygons'[635, 827] of the East Anglian Breckland, seldom extend into ancient woods, less regular disturbances are very widespread.[886] An example is the convoluted transition often seen where sand overlies Boulder-clay (Fig. 4.12f). Other periglacial relicts are the shoals of ponds and wet hollows common on the Breckland-Fen margin, produced apparently by the melting of huge lenses of ice known as ***pingos***. These rarely extend into ancient woods; but other kinds of ice-action may be responsible for many of the other ponds in the countryside, particularly the large numbers of ponds and dells in some woods (Chapter 2).

On slopes (sometimes as little as 1°), periglacial action often acted as a lubricant, allowing the surface layers to slither downhill. Slope soils often consist of more or less mixed-up debris, rather than of the regular geological sequence which might be expected to crop out. Soils are often deeper at the foot of the slope.

Historical and modern processes

Ploughing has a simplifying influence. The layer reached by the plough is thoroughly mixed and may also be moved sideways. The thinner surface layers may disappear, exposing drift or bedrock. The extent of the disturbance is illustrated by the lynchets which form at the edges of woods on slopes. The downhill edge of an ancient wood often stands up to 1 m above the surrounding farmland (Fig. 4.1); this ***negative lynchet*** – which may be deep enough to destroy the wood-boundary ditch and leave the woodbank standing at the top of a low cliff – results from the whole field creeping away downhill under the influence of ploughing and sheet erosion. In the less common situations where an ancient wood has an uphill edge a ***positive lynchet*** may be formed by soil piling against the uphill bank.

Ancient woods escape such drastic disturbance and may be expected to have a more stratified soil than ploughland, but they can be mixed in other ways. When a big tree is uprooted in a storm its root-mat may overturn several tons of soil. This is most often seen in fen and plantation trees. Woodland trees more usually rot above ground and fall to pieces leaving a stump, or else rot at the bigger roots (especially if damaged by drought or waterlogging or the fungus *Armillaria mellea*) and topple making only a small hole.

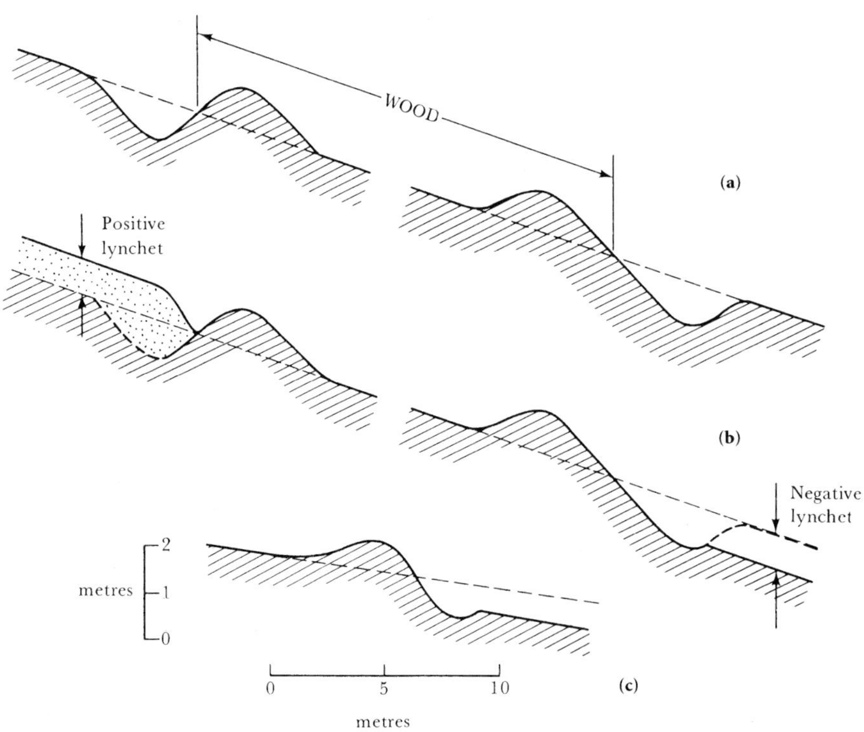

Fig. 4.1 Lynchets at sloping edges of woods.
(**a**) Theoretical profile of top and bottom margins of wood soon after making of woodbanks. (**b**) The same woodbanks now, assuming soil erosion in adjacent fields but none in wood. (**c**) Actual measured profile at downslope edge of medieval wood (Chalkney Wood).

Uprooting is thus an uncommon fate for a woodland tree, even if it is not cut down first. However, with the giant trees of Epping Forest, successive uprootings in the past have helped to create a complex mosaic of disturbed patches.[600] Gentler but more widespread mixing agents are the displacement of soil by growing roots, the worm-casting action of some species of earthworms, and the tunnelling of moles. Mixing may be expected to be least under deep-rooted earth-fast trees and in soils too acid to support many worms – although even if worms are few there may still be moles.[788] The soils of the wooded parts of the New Forest, which meet these conditions, appear to be highly stratified and have great archaeological potential.[45]

Lessivage is the action of rain-water trickling down through the more permeable soils and taking with it some of the clay in the upper layers, forming eventually a clay-depleted ***sol lessivé***.

Surface acidity

In the relatively wet climate of Britain most soils are affected by ***leaching***. Rain-water percolates through the soil or through cracks or worm-burrows, taking dissolved substances and clay particles with it; these materials may be redeposited deeper in the profile or, particularly in efficiently-drained farmland, washed away into the nearest river.

Most woodland soils belong to the class of Brown Earths or to waterlogged or *lessivé* variants of it. In Brown Earths, leaching is moderate and does not produce the strong redistribution horizons which some other soils have. The humus content and the soil micro-organisms retard the downward movement of minerals, and the loss of minerals is partly counteracted by the addition of minerals brought up by tree roots and released from rotten leaves. The breakdown of leaves, however, produces acidic organic chemicals, and the surface layers of woodland soils tend to become acid and to dissolve any calcium carbonate which they may contain.

Acidification and lessivage vary widely from soil to soil and are influenced by the vegetation, the type of humus which it produces, and the extent of mixing. In E,astern England, the commonest woodland soils are derived from a thin layer of sand or loess overlying London Clay or Boulder-clay. Such soils are more acid and usually less clayey towards the surface, but it is not always obvious how much of the difference was there in the geology and how much has been produced by acidification and lessivage.

Acidity of parent materials

The alkalinity of soils, which is the most useful single index of their ecological properties, is measured in terms of their pH; this varies from 3.1 in the most acid woodland soils to about 8.0 in the most alkaline. The pH of undisturbed Boulder-clay containing fragments of chalk is about 7.8. Woodland soils more alkaline than pH 7.0 are produced where Boulder-clay (or chalk or limestone itself) reaches the surface and where mixing outweighs acidification. They also arise where Boulder-clay has been artificially brought to the surface on woodbanks and rides. On waterlogged sites, where mixing is weak, acidification may bring the pH down to about 5.0. More acid soils are generally associated with considerable amounts of silt or sand.

London Clay, which underlies many of the woods of south Essex and Herts, starts at a pH of about 6.5 or less; it sometimes acidifies spontaneously when aerated by the oxidation of pyrites to sulphuric acid.

Surface sand and loess both start from a pH of about 5.5 (cf. Fig. 4.12). Acidification of this already rather acid material can bring the pH down to 3.5 or occasionally below. Similar values are sometimes recorded for the Tertiary or glacial sands and gravels which form the bedrock of many ancient woods.

Humus

Mull and mor

Organic material in soils is derived mainly from ***litter*** – the dead leaves, acorn-cups, twigs, caterpillar frass, and other things that fall from trees and plants – but also from within the soil, from dead roots, root exudations, and the excretions and carcasses of soil animals and micro-organisms. Much the largest input is from dead tree-leaves, which add minerals as well as organic matter to the topsoil. The behaviour of organic matter in soil is very complex: the reader is referred to the work of W. L. Kubiëna.[766] For our purpose a simple treatment is sufficient, recognizing only the two general classes of humus and passing over the many variations that have been described.

What happens to fallen leaves depends largely on the gastronomy of earthworms, a subject for which Charles Darwin is celebrated.[651, 667] Worms emerge at night, seize dead leaves and drag them down for consumption below. They start with soft leaves such as elm and ash and leave tough bitter leaves like oak and sweet-chestnut until last. Dr D. E. Coombe tells me that worms can distinguish even between different elms.

In a mixed-coppice wood on a reasonably calcareous soil, worms are abundant and take most of the litter within a few months; even oak-leaves disappear in about a year. In this type of soil, known by the Danish term ***mull***, the litter rots quickly and becomes intimately associated with the clay particles in the soil, and the resulting clay-humus complex gives the topsoil a characteristic crumb structure.

On acid soils worms are fewer and do not behave in this way. Dead leaves pile up on the soil surface from year to year and rot slowly to form a layer of ***mor*** humus which, if incorporated at all, disappears only slowly as a result of the activities of fungi, mites, and animals other than worms.

The boundary between mull and mor is usually quite sharp. The presence and amount of mor depend chiefly on the soil but are also influenced by the trees. Table 4.1 gives the characteristic pH for each tree below which it usually forms mor. In general the mor-forming tendency of a tree is correlated with its tolerance of acid soils: mor is very common under chestnut and beech, but very rare under elm or maple which seldom grow on the extremely acid topsoils which they need to form mor.

On rare occasions, with a particularly suitable soil and climate, mor may build up for thousands of years and the pollen in it may form a record of woodland history.[75, 752] In Britain only the tough tannin-containing leaves of sweet-chestnut, beech, and sometimes holly accumulate more than a few centimetres deep.

Podzolization

On some types of mor soil, known by the Russian name of ***podzol***, the decay of mor generates soluble organic acids which have the property of leaching iron and aluminium compounds out of the top of the mineral soil and redepositing them, often in the form of concretions, lower in the profile. Podzols are characteristic of heathland and some conifer plantations, and their absence from woods or wood-pasture has been used as an argument (e.g. at Staverton Park, E. Suffolk)[97] that there has never been heath on the site. But beech and occasionally even oak can form podzols when growing on very acid soils.[45] Although true podzols are rare in woods in Eastern England, the top horizons of many sandy woods have the bleached sand grains, shorn of their coating of dark humus-iron materials, which mark the first stage of the process.

Table 4.1 pH at the mull to mor transition beneath different trees.

Sweet-chestnut	at least 4.6
Beech	4.6
Oak (as underwood)	about 4.4
Hornbeam	4.4 (4.2–4.7)
Birch	4.2
Lime	4.1 (4.0–4.2)
Ash	4.1 (3.7–4.4)
Hazel	4.0 (3.5–4.4)
Elm (non-invasive)	3.9 (3.7–4.2)
Elm (invasive)	3.6
Maple	3.5 (3.4–4.3)

Figures are the average soil pH below which mor, and above which mull, forms. Figures in brackets indicate the range over which the two humus types overlap. From my own observations in Eastern England, except for beech.[150, 167]

Drainage and waterlogging

The majority of ancient woods, except on steep slopes, are seasonally wet to some degree. They may seem bone-dry in summer, but a soil pit usually reveals the tell-tale orange or yellow and grey mottling that indicates a ***gley*** – the Russian word by which periodically-waterlogged soils are known. Wet periods are most likely in April and May, when the soil is saturated by winter and spring rains and the trees are not sufficiently in leaf to be capable of much transpiration. Actual flooding can be quite dramatic in unexpected places [Fig. 3.4b]. Hayley Wood (W. Cambs), for instance, is on high ground in the driest part of Britain, yet in springs like 1975 [and 2001] much of the wood is under water for weeks on end [Plate 6h, Figs 4.13 and 25.24].

Types of waterlogged soil

Clay soils form ***surface-water gleys***. Rain-water cannot easily percolate through the impermeable clay and has to drain away over the surface. On level ground, especially on plateaux and flat hilltops, it drains with difficulty and is ponded up by the slightest irregularity. Sloping ground is less often waterlogged – a slope of as little as ½° makes all the difference – as are banks and the neighbourhood of ditches. Clay soils shrink when dry and form semi-permanent cracks which act as drains until they eventually heal as the clay swells in wet winters. Surface-water gleys occur on loess soils for much the same reason; but loess is less liable to crack and can flood briefly after a heavy shower even in summer. Walkers in South Essex will know the dangerously slippery state of loess woodland paths!

Waterlogging on sandy soils occurs if, as in most sandy ancient woods, there is an underlying impervious layer that holds up the water. Such soils are a transition to the ***ground-water gleys*** created by the rise and fall of a water-table imposed on the soil from below. Slow sideways trickles of water beneath the surface of sandy soils have not been widely investigated, but are probably important in plateau alder-woods (cf. pp. 308–10). More typical ground-water gleys are found in small patches in alder slades (Chapter 18).

Effects of waterlogging

When waterlogged a soil is ill-aerated because the water displaces nearly all the air in the soil pore spaces and cuts off the exchange of oxygen between the atmosphere and the remaining air (oxygen diffuses through water some 10,000 times more slowly than through air). Micro-organisms and plant roots deplete the oxygen dissolved in the soil water; the former then continue to live by reducing oxidized iron and manganese compounds which act for them as a substitute for oxygen. These compounds are responsible for most of the reddish and yellowish colours in normal oxidized soils; in their reduced state the soil becomes greyish. Since oxidation and reduction are not uniform – they are affected by cracks and old root holes which act as sources of air – gley soils have a distinctive mottling by which they can be recognized. Another characteristic is the presence of 'manganese nodules' – small, rather soft, concretions coloured purplish-black by manganese dioxide – which accumulate in the more oxidized parts of most kinds of gley soils.[88]

Waterlogging is bad for almost all agricultural crops, as the sums spent by farmers and taxpayers on drainage testify, but its effects on natural vegetation vary. Most native trees are not obviously affected – even beech and birch will stand slight waterlogging – and some, such as aspen and lime, are positively associated with winter-wet woods. The main effect appears to be by restricting the rooting depth and thus reducing the volume of soil which the roots can exploit for water and nutrients. For this reason waterlogged woods are particularly liable to summer drought – to a transition from a flooded May to a parched June, as in Hayley in 1975.

The ground flora varies from plants such as *Carex acutiformis* and other sedges, which flourish under permanent flooding, to dog's mercury and bracken, which are quickly damaged by even slight waterlogging. The experiments of M. H. Martin[87] show that for many plants the damage is not a direct consequence of poor aeration, of lack of oxygen in the soil or of accumulation of carbon dioxide, but is due to the reduction of iron compounds, which are harmless in the ferric (oxidized) but toxic in the ferrous (reduced) state. The relative ability of woodland herbs to withstand poisoning by ferrous iron closely reflects the positions in which they grow. Dog's mercury, for instance, is very sensitive and grows only on the better-drained soils; in dry springs it creeps down into less well-drained hollows, particularly in ridge-and-furrow, but is killed back as soon as there is a wet spring, the dying stems wilting and turning blue. Oxlip (*Primula elatior*), at the other extreme, is very tolerant of ferrous iron; it grows chiefly in the worse-drained woods, not because it prefers bad drainage, but because it cannot compete with mercury.

The drainage factor in Hayley Wood

Hayley Wood has existed continuously with little alteration since before 1251 (Figs. 2.1, 2.2) and is almost certainly a primary wood. It belonged to the medieval Bishops of Ely and now to Cambridgeshire and Isle of Ely Naturalists' Trust. It is the subject of a book.[120] Most of Hayley is an ash–maple–hazel wood (Chapter 13) with standard oaks.

The soils are very uniform in composition, derived from Chalky Boulder-clay with a small admixture of loess. The main ecological variable is the slope. A flat central plateau is surrounded by slopes of gradually increasing angle (Fig. 4.2). Waterlogging is frequent and severe in spring on the plateau, especially in slight hollows, and relatively slight on the steeper slopes (which however never exceed 4°).

On the winter-wet plateau there are many clones of aspen, which is locally dominant. Apart from this, drainage subtly affects the tree composition [pp. 488–92], and it influences growth rates, particularly of ash. Ash trees on the plateau are notably slow-growing, have small crowns, and are long-lived. This is the result of drought rather than a direct consequence of flooding. In any dry summer the plants of the plateau wilt more than those of the slope, and in severe droughts such as that of 1976 the ash-trees too are hard-hit. Widths of annual rings are correlated with summer rainfall – wet summers producing wide rings – except that dry late summers (e.g. 1915 and 1930) tend to produce narrow rings the next year.[120]

The ground vegetation forms a series of zones ranging from Zone 1, dominated by the big sedges *Carex acutiformis* and *C. riparia*, in hollows on the plateau, through Zone 2, dominated by meadowsweet (*Filipendula ulmaria*) and oxlip, on the rest of the plateau, to Zone 4, dominated by bluebell on the gentler slopes, and to the dog's-mercury Zone 6 on the steeper slopes [Plate 6]. These plant communities form a series related both to the general topography and to local anomalies of drainage. The degree of resistance to ferrous iron of the dominants and other common species agrees very well with their place in the sequence[87] (see also p. 77).

The uniform parent materials of Hayley Wood make it possible to explore the relation between drainage and surface acidification. Measurements of pH at different depths (Fig. 4.3) show that acidification is greater, and extends deeper, on the ill-drained plateau than on the slopes. Waterlogging discourages worms and moles and reduces the amount of mixing which, on the slopes, counteracts the tendency of calcium to be leached out of the topsoil.

Fertility

This section is concerned with mineral nutrients, particularly with nitrogen, phosphorus, and potassium, the 'macro-nutrients' whose presence, in a chemical form which plants can assimilate, largely determines the inherent fertility of a soil.

Nowadays fertility is bought in a sack, but in pre-1800 agriculture it was a valuable inherent property of the soil. Not surprisingly, ancient woods tend to be on relatively infertile soils. Their fertility will have been further reduced by the removal of produce, particularly underwood which is relatively rich in minerals

Fig. 4.2 Contour map of Hayley Wood, drawn by the author from a levelling survey by Dr R. M. S. Perrin. Contours are at 1-ft intervals. Earthworks are omitted.

(particularly phosphate).[114] Since 1800 nearly all farmland has been artificially fertilized but woods have not. There is not much systematic information about the available nutrients of woodland soils, but there can be little doubt that most ancient woods are very low in phosphate and often in nitrate also.[88, 807] Woodland vegetation in general is adapted to a low level of fertility; the more fertile types of wildwood vanished long ago.

Places in woods where, for some reason, nutrients (particularly phosphate) have accumulated tend to be marked by plants which need plenty of minerals or are inefficient at extracting them from the ground. The stinging-nettle (*Urtica dioica*) is the best known of such 'phosphate plants', whose significance is discussed further in Chapter 7. They grow mainly in places which have been lived in (or buried in) in the past, although phosphate and other minerals can accumulate from other causes. Some trees, notably elms (p. 96) and alder (p. 310), may have the power of increasing the fertility of soils on which they grow.

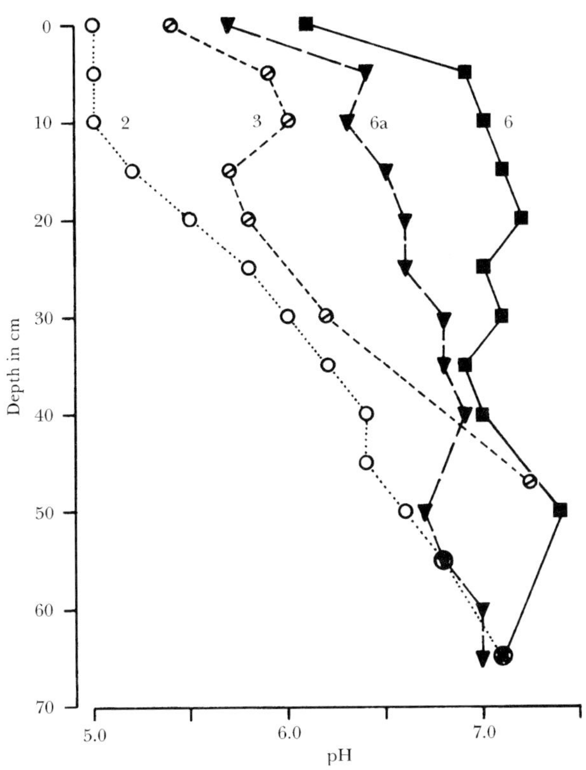

Fig. 4.3 Soil pH profiles in Hayley Wood, from pits dug in ground vegetation Zones 2 (plateau), 3 (slight slope), 6a (greater slope), and 6 (greatest slope).

A survey of woodland soils in Eastern England

Any survey of woodland soils must inevitably be superficial: a full investigation of even a single wood is a lengthy piece of research. The minimum of factors for a general survey are pH, humus type, slope and topography, and range of particle sizes. In Eastern England a further important factor is the depth of soil down to the Boulder-clay, London Clay, etc.; but this is often variable and ill-defined – especially where wind-blown sand or silt has levelled up a previously uneven surface – and little systematic information is yet available. A boring or even a pit is often not enough to define the depth and variation of the horizons: occasionally their full complexity is exposed in a newly-dug ditch.

This study was intended as a general exploration of woodland soils in Eastern England combined with an investigation of their variation within individual woods. The number of samples taken varies from wood to wood; but all the main woodland areas and types are included in realistic proportions, so that the result should be representative of the ancient woods of the region.

Samples were normally collected from 15 cm below the surface of the mineral soil. Ideally, several depths should have been sampled, but to do so systematically would have required an impracticably large number of analyses.

Method of mechanical analysis

The method is almost identical to that of C. L. Bascomb.[609] The sample, its pH measured, was air-dried and riddled to remove stones (> 2 mm diameter) and plant debris. A 30 g subsample was treated with hydrogen peroxide and then acetic acid to remove organic matter and calcium carbonate if any. It was then gently ground and mechanically shaken in a series of sieves to separate the particle-size fractions down to 63 μm. The fractions from 63 to 2 μm were separated by sedimentation in an aqueous solution. All fractions were weighed in an oven-dry state.

Results – general

The analysis separated the material into categories at particle sizes 2, 6, 20, 40, 63, 106, 212, 500, 1000, and 2,000 μm, which form a roughly exponential series. In Fig. 4.4 examples are given including two contrasting materials, Boulder-clay from a deep pit and blown sand from a fossil dune. The former is unsorted material, almost as it was dumped by a glacier; a third of it is clay and the rest is geological debris of various kinds evenly distributed through the size-classes. The latter has been sorted by wind into a narrow range of sizes centring on 160 μm.

Woodland soils in Eastern England typically have three peaks corresponding to clay from Boulder-clay or London Clay (particles smaller than 2 μm), loess (particles centring on 40 μm), and sand (particles centring on 300 μm). Occasionally in the south there are particles of around 80 μm, but otherwise there is little material in the ranges 2–20, 60–100, or 500–2,000 μm. The chief parent materials are thus quite distinct.

Variation within woods

Figure 4.5 illustrates the variations encountered in a wood in which Boulder-clay, sand, and loess are all well represented. The plateau and gentle slopes are reasonably constant in composition (e.g. samples 1, 9, 21, 22), except in one area (7 and 15) where there is more clay, probably because the surface deposits are thinner and more of the underlying Boulder-clay has been brought up by mixing; this corresponds to a higher pH and to less calcifuge vegetation. Samples 3 and 26 are from a steeper slope where there is also more incorporated clay. Samples 14, 17, and 18 are from steep-sided valleys deeply cut into the clay, with a much higher clay fraction and strongly calcareous soil. These are all typical variations common in other woods.

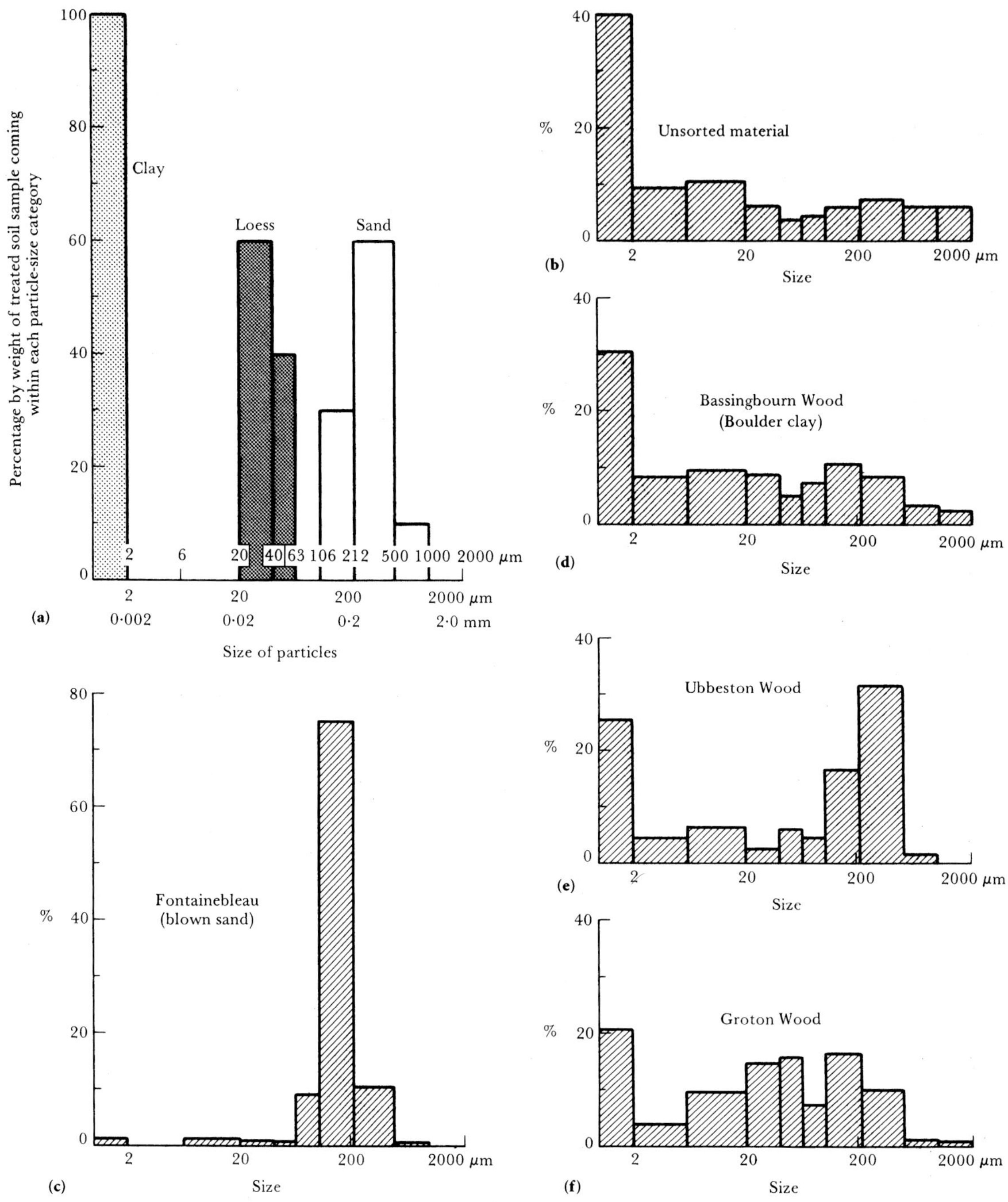

Fig. 4.4 Particle-size distribution in soils. (**a**) Theoretical compositions for soils derived from pure clay (light grey), pure loess (dark grey), and pure sand (white). Numbers above the bottom axis indicate the size-classes into which soils were sorted in the analysis. (**b**) Theoretical composition for a completely unsorted soil with 40% clay. Had it been practicable to sort the soils into a perfectly exponential series of size-classes (e.g. 2, $2\sqrt{10}$, 20, $20\sqrt{10}$, 200 μm, etc.) the proportions in each size-class above 2 μm would have been equal; the differences between proportions are due to the fact that some size-classes are narrower than others. (**c**) Actual composition of blown sand from topsoil in the Forêt de Fontainebleau, S.E. of Paris. (**d**) Actual composition of Boulder-clay beneath Bassingbourn Wood in Bocking, N. Essex. 30% is clay; the remainder conforms very closely to the theoretical composition of unsorted material up to 500 μm. (**e**) Actual composition of topsoil, Ubbeston Wood, N. E. Suffolk. Clay and sand. (**f**) Actual composition of topsoil, Groton Wood, S. Suffolk. Clay, loess, and sand; little material in the 2–6 μm and 63–106 μm categories.

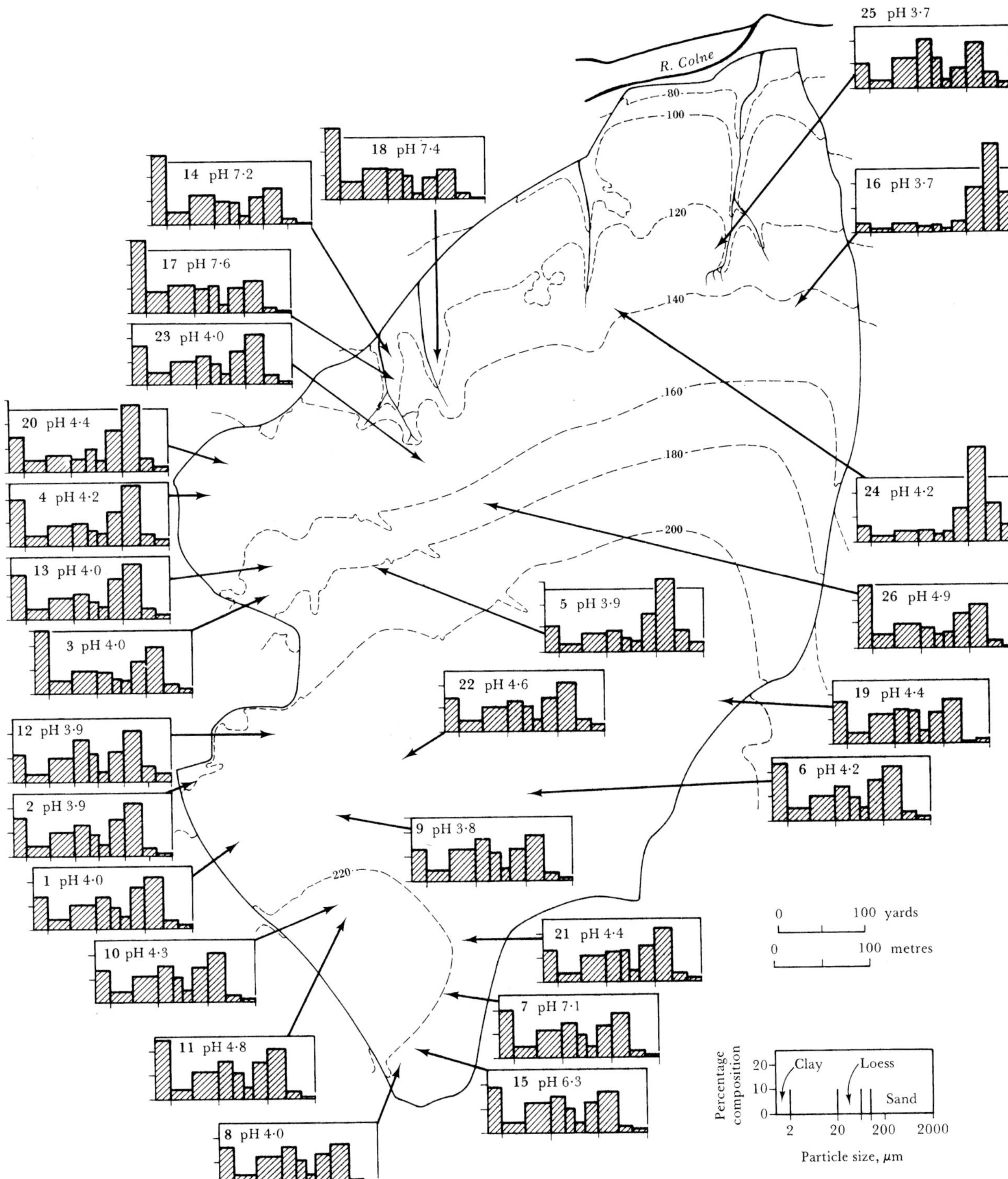

Fig. 4.5 Particle-size distribution of topsoils (15 cm depth) in Chalkney Wood, Essex, plotted according to the conventions of Fig. 4.4. The southern plateau is officially mapped as Boulder-clay, overlying London Clay which is supposed to be exposed on the northern slope. Both materials are thickly or thinly overlain by sand and loess, with at least two pockets of almost pure sand.

Contours are in feet. Further details of the topography are shown in Figs. 15.6 and 15.8.

Sample 16 illustrates a sudden change to a very different kind of material, more than two-thirds of it sand. Sandy patches, usually 50–100 m across, slightly raised above their surroundings and often forming bracken glades (p. 85) occur in many ancient woods on various soils (e.g. Figs. 3.0, 3.1, 13.6b, 14.5). They are somewhat mysterious structures, apparently undescribed but reminiscent of certain fossil sand-dunes near York.[783] At least sometimes they are biconvex, extending below the surface more than they project above it (Fig. 4.12f, 4.14), and accordingly I shall call them ***sand-lenses***.

Variation in acidity is usually correlated with soil composition – positively with sand and loess, negatively with clay (whether from Boulder-clay or London Clay). The relationship is not very close and its parameters – i.e. the proportion of clay needed to produce a given pH – vary from wood to wood and even, slightly, between different parts of the same wood (Fig. 4.6).

Variation throughout Eastern England

Figures 4.7 to 4.10 are based on soils from about sixty ancient woods, sampled from plateau sites or gentle slopes in order to avoid the local variations of steep slopes, valleys, or sand-lenses. Such samples might be expected to preserve the large-scale variation of parent materials as it was after the end of periglacial action and before it had been disturbed by erosion, downwash, and ploughing. The distribution of materials, particularly of loess, agrees very well with Perrin's distribution for plateau soils in general.[828]

Sand, represented chiefly by the 106–500 μm fraction (Fig. 4.7), forms the bulk of the topsoil in the woods of Norfolk and N.E. Suffolk and decreases towards the south. Much of it probably came from close at hand, from local outcrops of sandy drift or occasionally sandstone. There is much local variation in its amount and fineness. For instance, in West Cambridgeshire there is an outcrop of Lower Greensand, from which coarse sand (around 400 μm particle-size) has blown up on to the adjoining Boulder-clay plateau to create acid areas in Gamlingay and Waresley Woods;[1] yet in Hayley and Buff Woods, only 4 km away to the east, the sand can hardly be detected.

Loess (Fig. 4.8) is limited to two well-defined regions, one in N.E. Norfolk and the other in Essex and S.E. Suffolk. It has presumably been blown for longer distances and shows much less local variation. Clay (Fig. 4.9) has a less regular distribution with a general east–west trend; it reflects the presence of Boulder-clay or London Clay and their nearness to the surface and degree of incorporation.

Types of woodland soil and relation to agricultural soils

Figure 4.10 summarizes the topsoil textures encountered

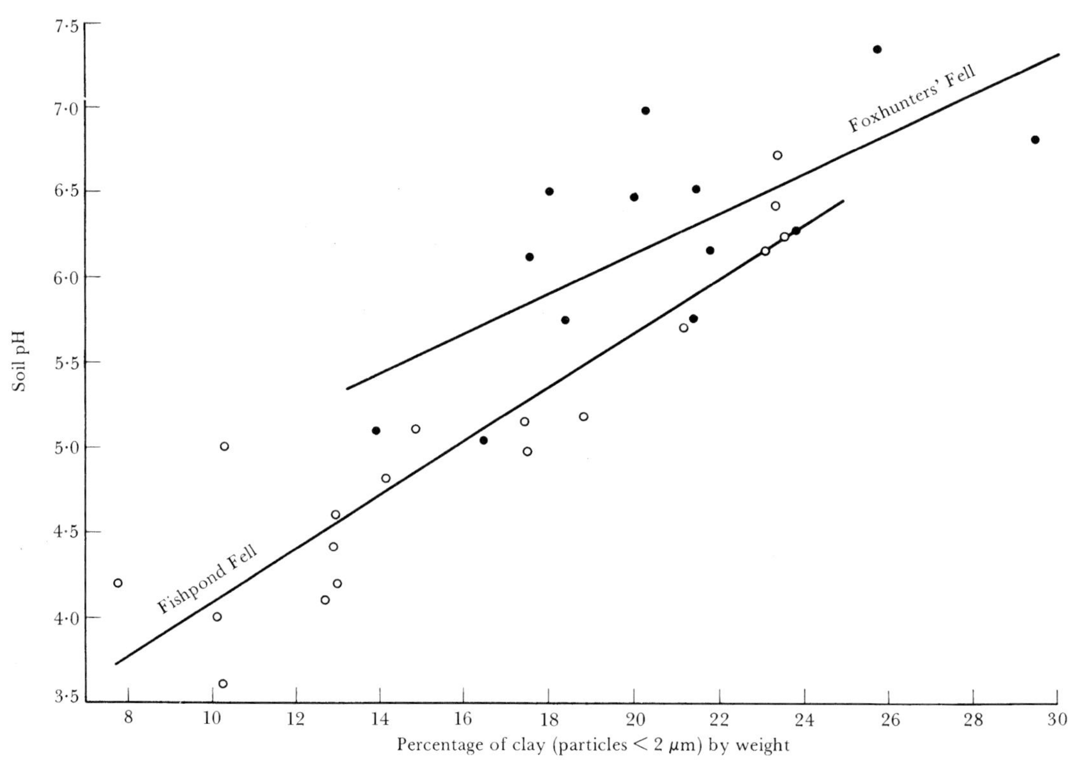

Fig 4.6 Relationship between pH and clay content for soil samples collected, each at 15 cm depth, in different places in each of two compartments of the Bradfield Woods (Fig. 3.1). (●) Foxhunters' Fell ($y = 3.80 + 0.117x$); (o) Fishpond Fell (including Hewitt's and Pear-tree) ($y = 2.50 + 0.159x$).

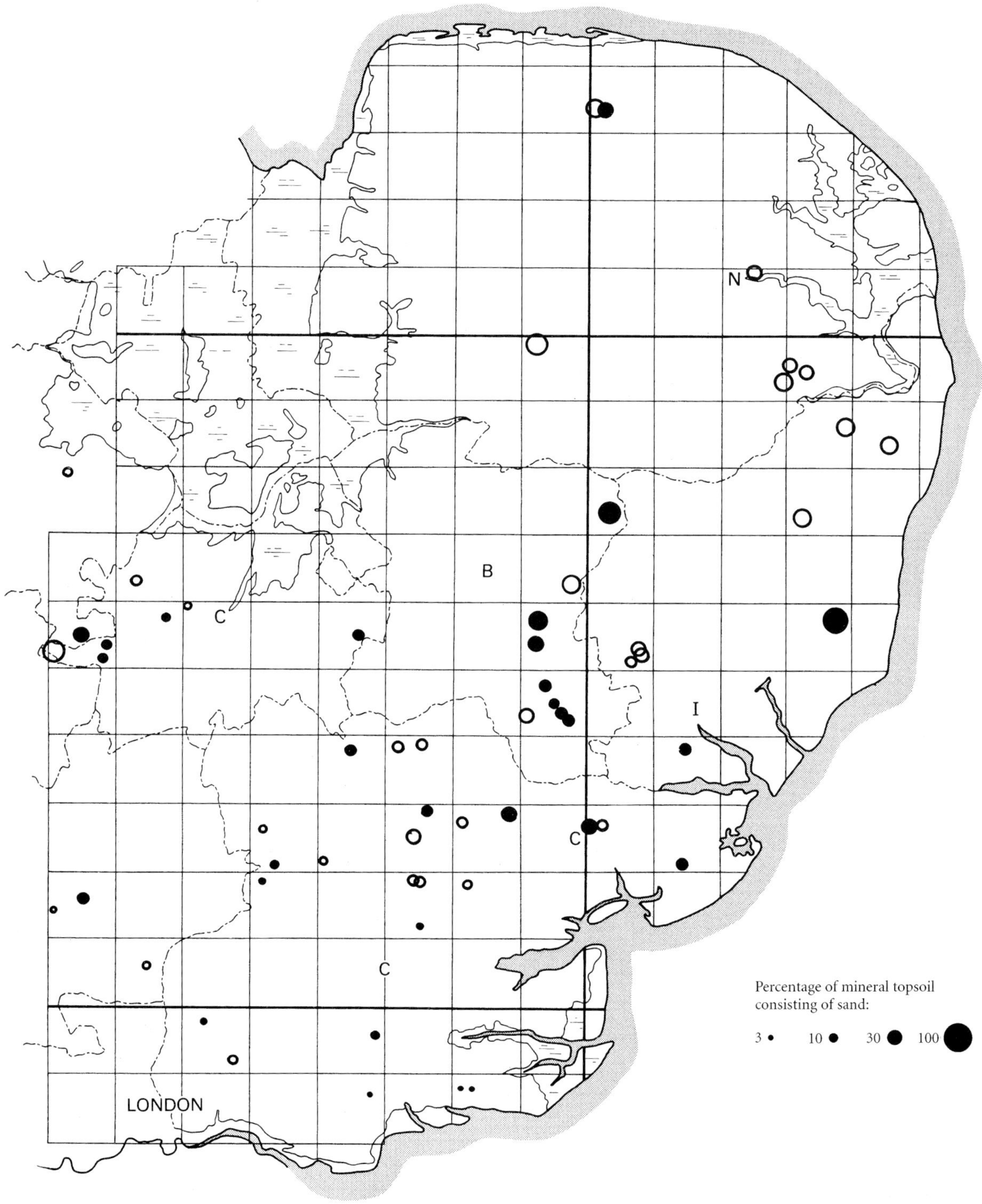

Fig 4.7 Sand content of woodland topsoils in Eastern England. The size of each spot is proportional to the percentage by weight of sand (particles 106–500 μm diameter). Samples are confined to ancient woods; in calculating the means for each wood, samples from sand-lenses or from sites with strong downwash were ignored. (●) based on at least four samples per wood; (○) on fewer than four samples.

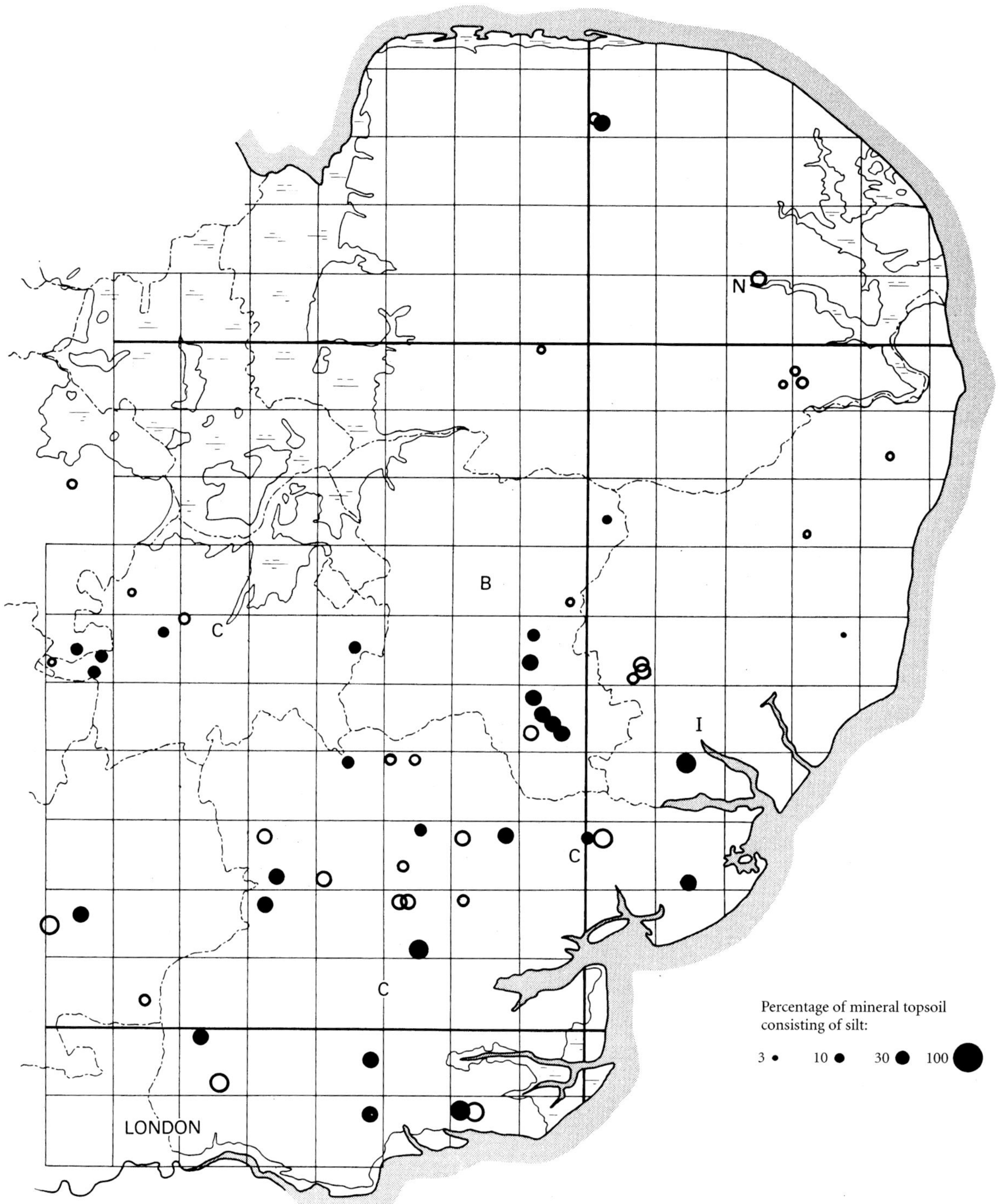

Fig. 4.8 Silt or loess content of woodland topsoils (particles 20–63 µm diameter). Conventions as for Fig. 4.7.

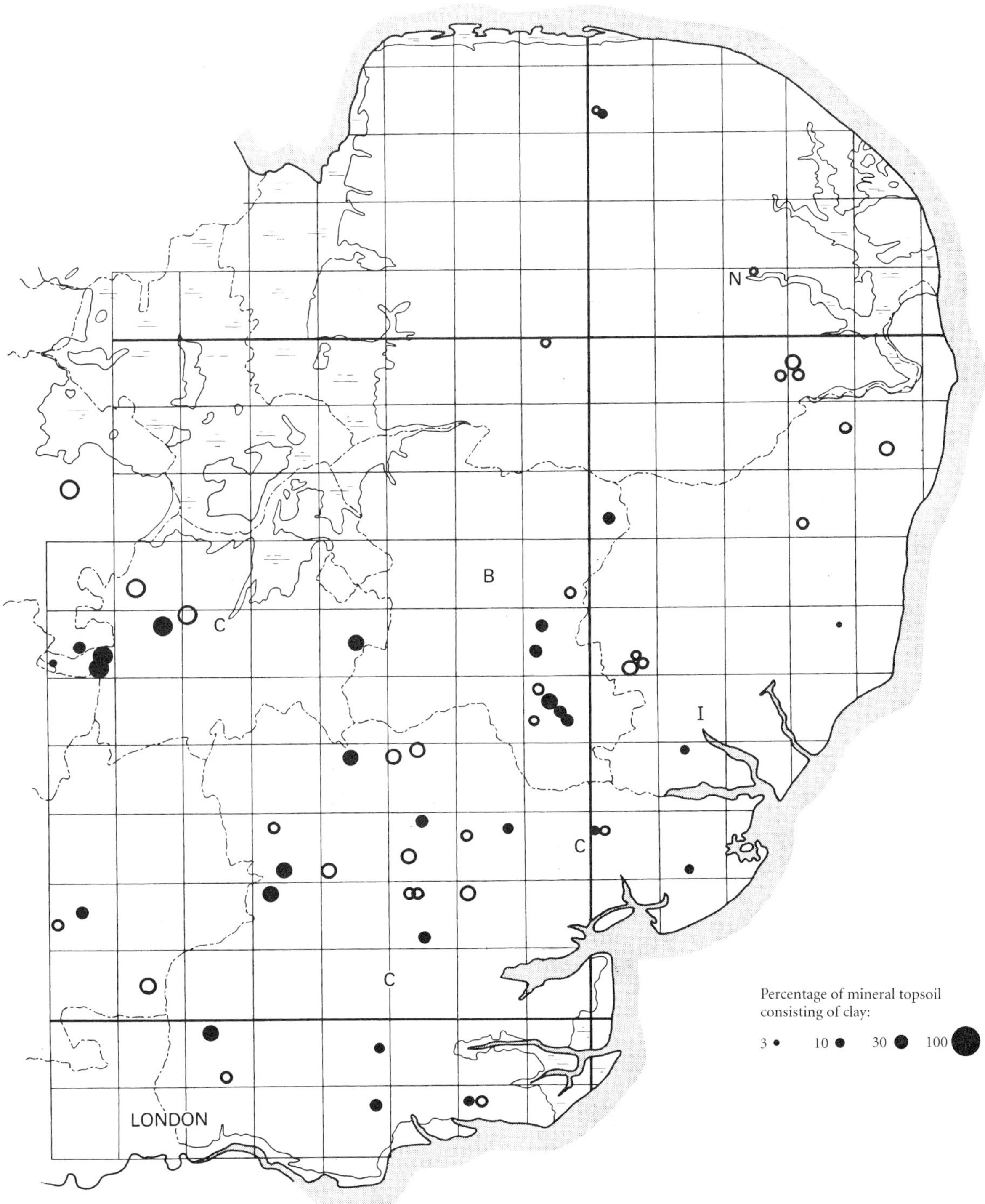

Fig. 4.9 Clay content of woodland topsoils (particles < 2 μm diameter). Conventions as for Fig. 4.7.

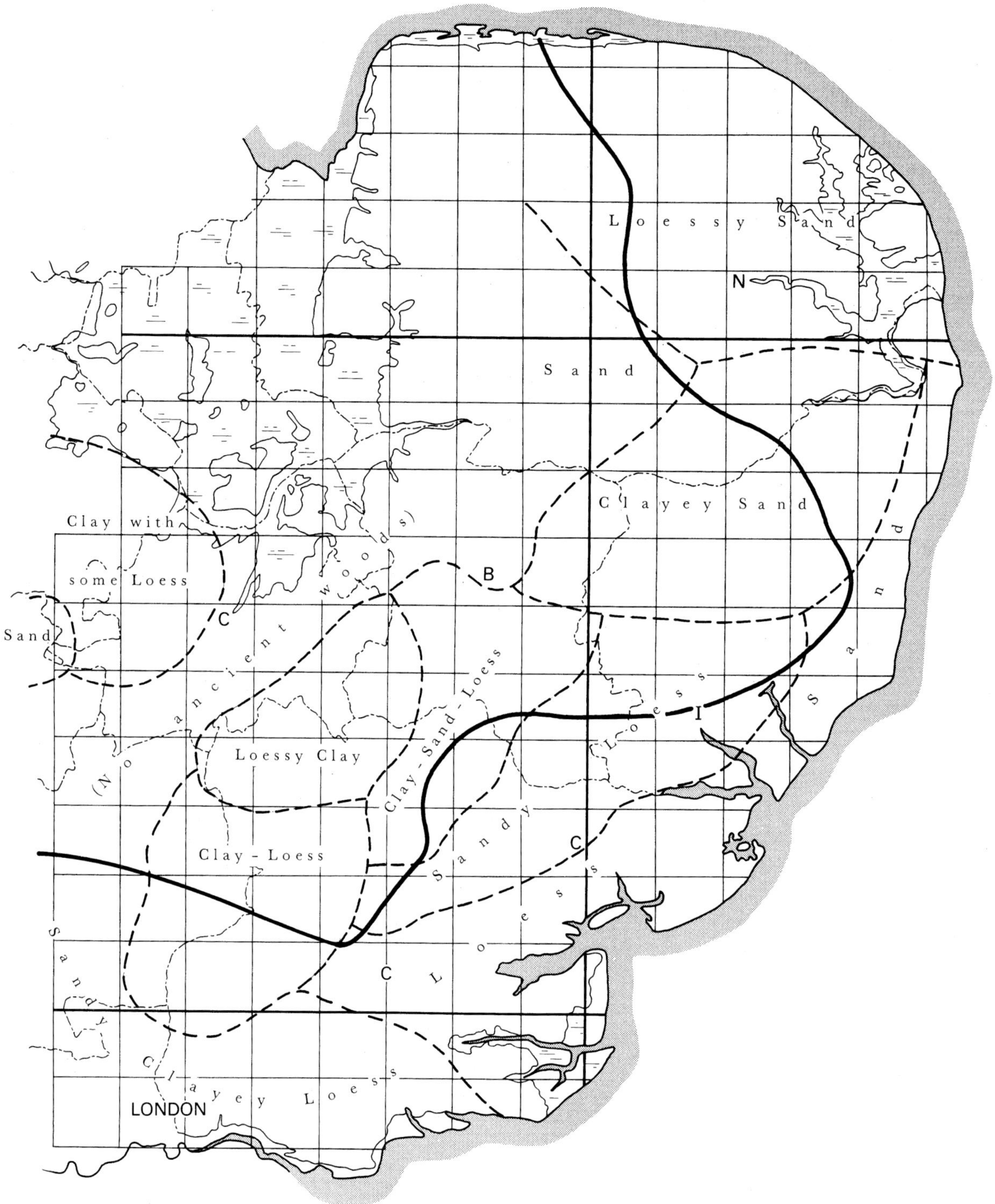

Fig. 4.10 Summary of the regional variation of topsoil textures in ancient woods (excluding valleys, dells, and sand-lenses). The thick black line separates the Acid Soil Province (to the east and south) from the Calcareous Province (north and west). These soil characteristics should not be extrapolated to agricultural soils.

in ancient woods. They range from the blown sands, with practically no clay or loess within reach, of Iken Wood and Staverton Park in East Suffolk, to the loess woods of east Essex and the Boulder-clay, slightly mixed with loess, of West Cambridgeshire. The most complex and varied mixtures are in S.W. Suffolk and mid-north Essex.

The distribution of soil textures in ancient woods, when compared with that in the countryside as a whole (e.g. with Fig. 15 in *Flora of Essex*),[600] suggests in part why such sites should have remained as woodland. With few exceptions, ancient woods are in areas where at least some of the soils are heavy, but within those areas the woods themselves tend to have lighter soils than their surroundings. At the time the sites of the woods were determined the lesser fertility of pockets of lighter soil made them more likely to be left as woodland. In West Cambridgeshire and N.E. Essex, however, the woods are on soils no lighter than their surroundings, and here some other obstacle to agriculture, e.g. waterlogging, is likely to have prevailed; in both these areas the abundance of *-ley* place-names (pp. 127–8) suggests a late survival of wildwood.

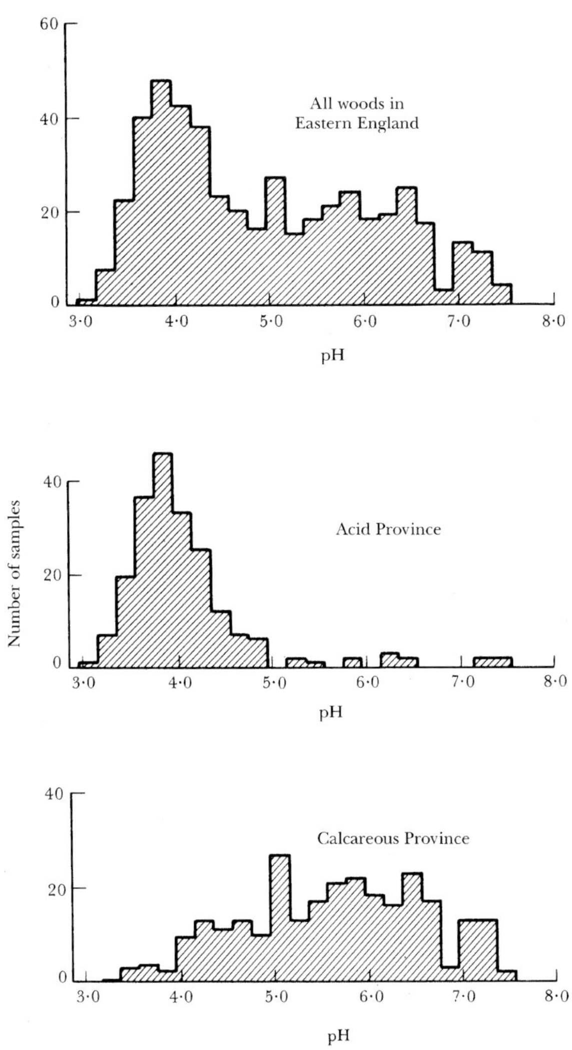

Fig. 4.11 Distribution of soil pH at 15 cm depth in ancient woods. All kinds of topography are included.

Soil acidity

In Eastern England soil pHs (at 15 cm depth) range from 3.0 to 7.6, with a concentration around 4.0 (Fig. 4.11). But there is a remarkable geographical discontinuity. It is possible to draw a line on the map (Fig. 4.10) which separates almost all the strongly acid woods from the weakly acid to alkaline ones. Superimposed on this distinction are local variations of the kinds shown in Fig. 4.5; but nevertheless in the ***Acid Province*** (east and south of the line) 84% of the woodland soils are more acid than pH 4.5, while in the ***Calcareous Province*** (north and west of the line) 85% of the soils are less acid than pH 4.5. The boundary agrees very roughly with the eastward extent of the underlying chalky Boulder-clay.

Some specimen soil profiles

Boulder-clay soils with slight loess component

Figure 4.12a shows a typical surface-water gley from nearly the most waterlogged part of Hayley Wood, in a plant community dominated by *Primula elatior* and *Filipendula ulmaria* and flooded in wet springs. It is gleyed to within 18 cm of the surface and the mixing action of earthworms is weak. The surface is moderately acid, attributable almost entirely to surface acidification.

Figure 4.12b is a clayey Brown Earth from a part of Hayley Wood where a slope of a couple of degrees permits surface water to run away. The ground vegetation is well-developed dog's-mercury. Gleying does not begin until over 50 cm depth; the rooting depth is greater and mixing processes are very active. Surface acidification is much less.

Soils derived from sand and loess overlying clay

In the Bradfield Woods Boulder-clay is overlain by very variable amounts of sand and a rather more constant layer of loess. The junctions between these materials are very irregular and convoluted. In Fig. 4.12c the Boulder-clay begins about 38 cm down; the transition is obscured by mixing. The profile is well-drained (gleying begins at 61 cm down) and mixing is sufficiently active to reduce surface acidification to the minimum expected of this combination of materials.

Figure 4.12d is similar in composition, but the sand and loess are somewhat thicker – the transition to Boulder-clay is about 52 cm deep. The site is much wetter – gleyed to within 16 cm of the surface. For both

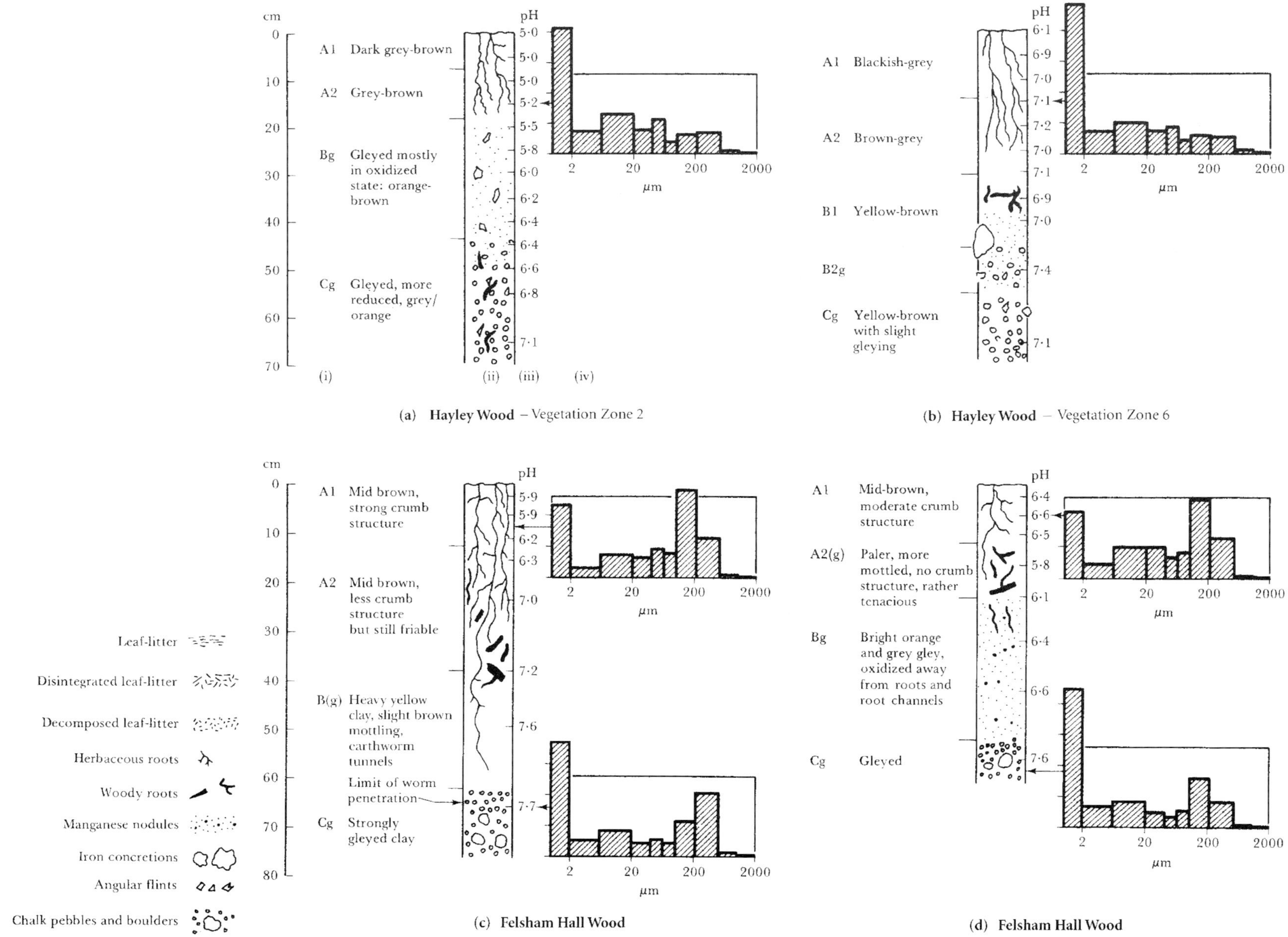

(a) **Hayley Wood** – Vegetation Zone 2

(b) **Hayley Wood** – Vegetation Zone 6

(c) **Felsham Hall Wood**

(d) **Felsham Hall Wood**

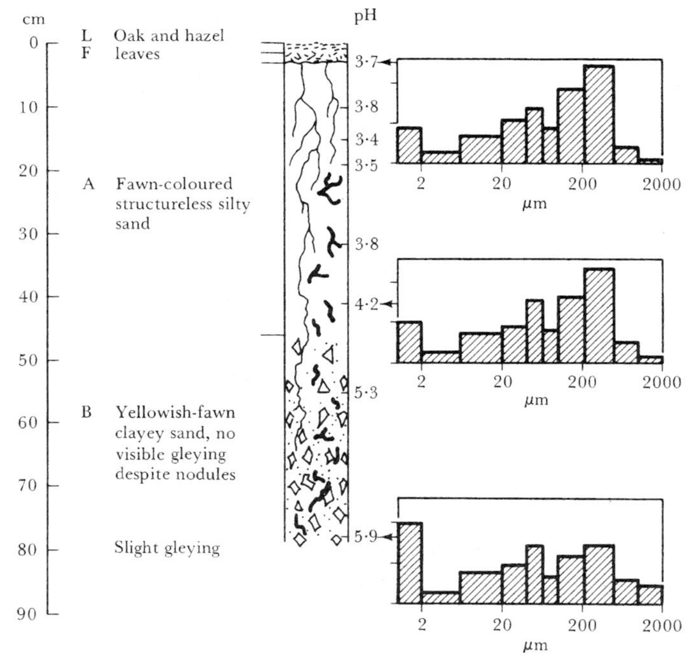

(e) **Swanton Novers Great Wood**

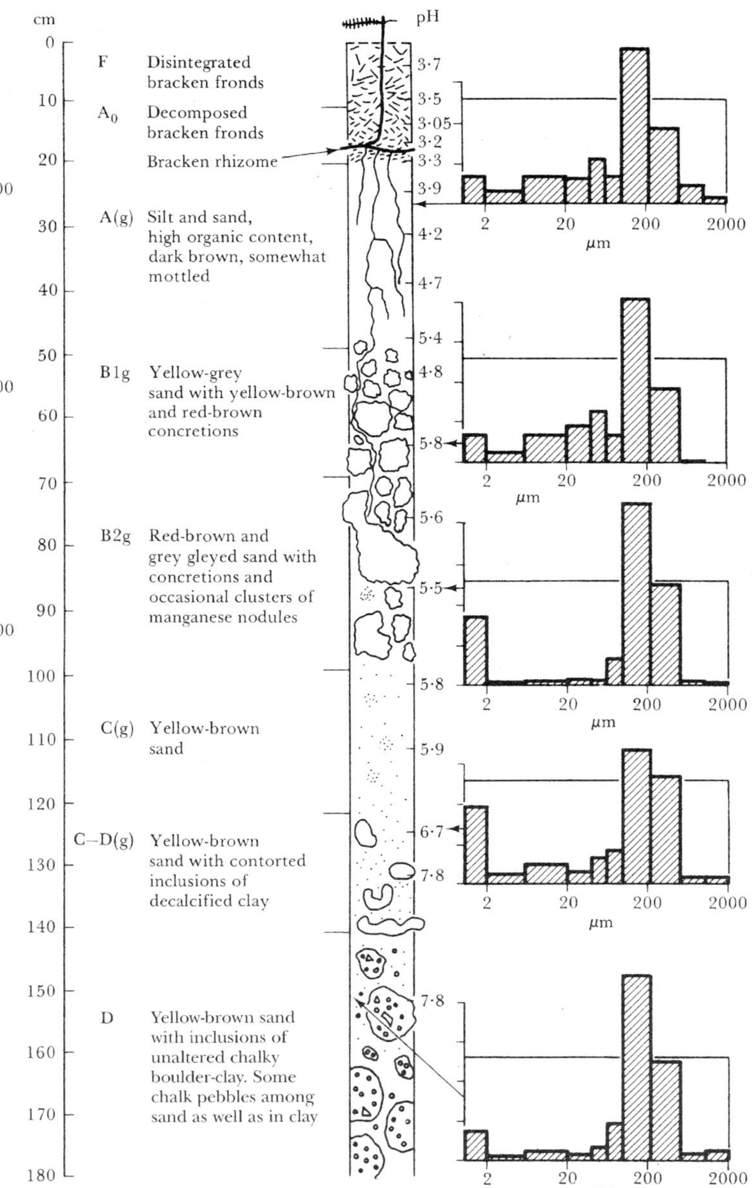

(f) **Felsham Hall Wood** – sand-lens

Fig. 4.12 Six woodland soil profiles. Each profile has four columns showing:

(**i**) Description of the horizons, designated by the following letters:[766]

- L Leaf litter
- F Disintegrated leaf litter
- A_0 Decomposed leaf litter

(L, F and A_0: shown only where these form distinct layers)

- A Mineral soil much enriched in humus
- B Mineral soil altered by movement of iron compounds and other minerals
- C Parent material little altered by weathering
- D Unaltered bedrock playing little or no part in soil chemistry

Where there are two visibly distinct A or B horizons these are distinguished A1, A2, etc. Gleying is indicated by g; weak gleying by (g).

(**ii**) Appearance of profile in diagrammatic form.

(**iii**) pH.

(**iv**) Particle-size composition diagrams, using the conventions of Fig. 4.4. The *y*-axes are graduated at intervals of 10%.

Profiles (**a**) and (**b**) are partly after M. H. Martin.[88]

these reasons the topsoil is more acid. The reversal of acidity near the surface is due to the release of calcium and other minerals from the wood burnt on a coppicing bonfire $9^1/_2$ years previously.

Figure 4.12e shows a similar profile from Swanton Novers Great Wood, on the north Norfolk loess. This site has more sand and is very well drained (only slightly gleyed at 75 cm depth); mixing processes have been active, despite the extreme acidity; the loess has been well mixed with the sand, and the sand-clay transition is very gradual.

Section through a sand-lens

Figure 4.12f is a profile of one of the sand-lenses in the Bradfield Woods. The general surface sand is of an unusual thickness – nearly 2 m – and fills a hollow in the Boulder-clay; the surface rises about 0.4 m above the surrounding level. The top 70 cm of sand are mixed with loess.

The site is a bracken glade (p. 85); the absence of any trace of old tree-roots suggests that it is a glade of great antiquity. It is flooded by capillary action right to the surface in wet winters, and this is reflected in the gleying depth. By the book[836] this should be a most unsuitable site for bracken, yet bracken flourishes as it does perhaps nowhere else in England; it is sometimes more than 4 m high. Litter and mor derived from bracken lie 23 cm deep on the surface. The rhizomes of the bracken take root in its own humus and thus escape the flooding of the mineral soil. Bracken humus is strongly acidifying – its own pH goes as low as 3.05 – and surface acidification takes the soil pH down to 3.3.

This soil has a definite water-table, the up-and-down movement of which is probably responsible for the massive iron-cemented concretions – a deposit of bog iron ore – at 50–100 cm. Although of very different composition from the soils previously considered, this profile too has a strong development of manganese nodules. The degree of gleying decreases at depth, probably because of a sideways seepage of oxygenated ground-water through the sand.

The transition from sand to Boulder-clay is gradual and convoluted, probably a relic of periglacial action; gobbets of clay, gradually increasing in number, are dispersed among the sand. The acid sand has dissolved out the chalk from the upper gobbets, leaving lumps of decalcified clay.

Added in 2003 edition

Over England as a whole, ancient woods have more of a tendency to be on uncultivably steep slopes. Waterlogging is less frequent than in eastern England, and flushing (when slopes are irrigated from spring-lines, as in Chalkney Wood, p. 248ff) more common. Characteristic of chalkland are strips of wood on the steepest slopes, strewn with sharp flints. Woods occur on cliffs and rock outcrops all over the world, including north and west England (e.g. the Avon Gorge, Bristol). A feature of Dorset are woods on landslips, coastal and inland, with their alder-grown pits of bottomless black ooze.

Fig. 4.13 Waterlogging: the plateau of Hayley Wood under ice. February 2003

Fig. 4.14 Soil pit in sand-lens, Felsham Hall Wood, dug by Alex and Annie Watt and the author (cf Fig. 4.12f). The cane is marked in 1-foot (30 cm) intervals. May 1971

5

Flowering plants and ferns in ancient woods

The historical study of the floras of woods – i.e. of the plant species present, as opposed to the vegetation, the plant communities which are dealt with in Chapters 6 and 7 – is hampered by the poor historical documentation and scanty sub-fossil record of woodland herbs other than bracken. The prehistoric evidence will be reviewed in Chapter 8. This chapter explores three aspects of the history of woodland floras, two based on their present composition, the third on historical records.

The flora of an ancient wood normally consists of trees and shrubs; shade-bearing plants; plants which appear after coppicing; 'woodland grassland' plants of rides, glades, and tracks within, around, or sometimes near the wood; and casuals and agricultural weeds which come into the wood from outside after felling gives them an opportunity. All of these except the last contribute to the character of the wood. Woodland grassland may be important not only as an element in the wood but also as a distinctive type of grassland, especially in areas where most ancient meadow and pasture have been destroyed or fertilized .

The floras of ancient and modern woods

The flora of ancient woodland

When a new wood is formed, whether by accident or design, it does not suddenly acquire a full woodland flora. The plants previously on the site decline, though some may persist for many decades in glades or gaps.[173] They are replaced by woodland plants arriving from existing woods or other sources (cf. p. 8). The rate at which these arrive depends on the distance of the new wood from existing woods, on the ability of different species to colonize new sites, and on the effects which the previous land-use may have had on the soil. Some plants appear to have poor colonizing abilities: they may be reluctant even to invade an extension to an existing wood (an ***attached secondary wood***); they may be absent, after several centuries, from a secondary wood surrounded by farmland. Many instances are known of the 'inertia of vegetation', of uncommon plants still to be found in the exact spot where they were recorded 300 or even 1,000 years ago (pp. 239, 241).[104, 110]

The use of the flora of a wood as a guide to its history is complicated by problems of alternative habitats. Plants typical of ancient woods, for the most part, are those woodland species which do not normally grow in hedges. For example oxlip (*Primula elatior*) grows in none of the hedges abutting on Hayley Wood, most of which are at least 400 years old, though there used to be four million plants in the wood itself.[120] In the Midlands, dog's-mercury spreads into hedges from ancient woods at the rate of less than one metre a year.[837] But if a wood is grubbed out, leaving its perimeter as a ghost hedge, several woodland herbs – including mercury, bluebell, and *Anemone nemorosa* – can survive indefinitely in the hedge.[111] If a wood is converted to grassland, woodland species may persist as long as it is kept mowed and not grazed or ploughed. This is documented for Hayley Wood, where a railway destroyed a corner of the wood, but for over a century oxlips (as well as bluebells, anemones, etc.) persisted in the verges and delimited, to within a few feet, where the wood had been.[120]

Many plants of ancient woods do not require shade: they require freedom from grazing, ploughing, and the competition of tall herbs, and may live under the protection of the scythe as well as of the axe. Oxlip grows almost entirely in woods, but meadows are a rare alternative habitat;[19] the one Norfolk locality was even in a reed-bed! Several species, such as *Ophioglossum vulgatum* and *Conopodium majus*, grow equally in old woodland and old grassland but have little ability to colonize in either.

These points are illustrated by a group of three Cambridgeshire woods (Fig. 5.1). Knapwell Wood is documented back to the twelfth century and has many ancient-woodland plants including oxlip, bluebell, and mercury.[115] The hedges around the wood, which are probably ghosts from a greater wood of before 1100, have mercury. Overhall Grove and Boxworth Grange contain moated sites and other earthworks and are certainly secondary; they are known to be between 350[356] and 600 years old. Both have rather poor floras and in particular lack mercury. Overhall has oxlip, derived probably from streamside meadows, but Grange has none. Bluebell occurs in both Overhall and Grange but is missing from more recent secondary woods in the area.

The performance of these three plants agrees with measurements in attached secondary woodland at Hayley, which show oxlip migrating from the adjoining

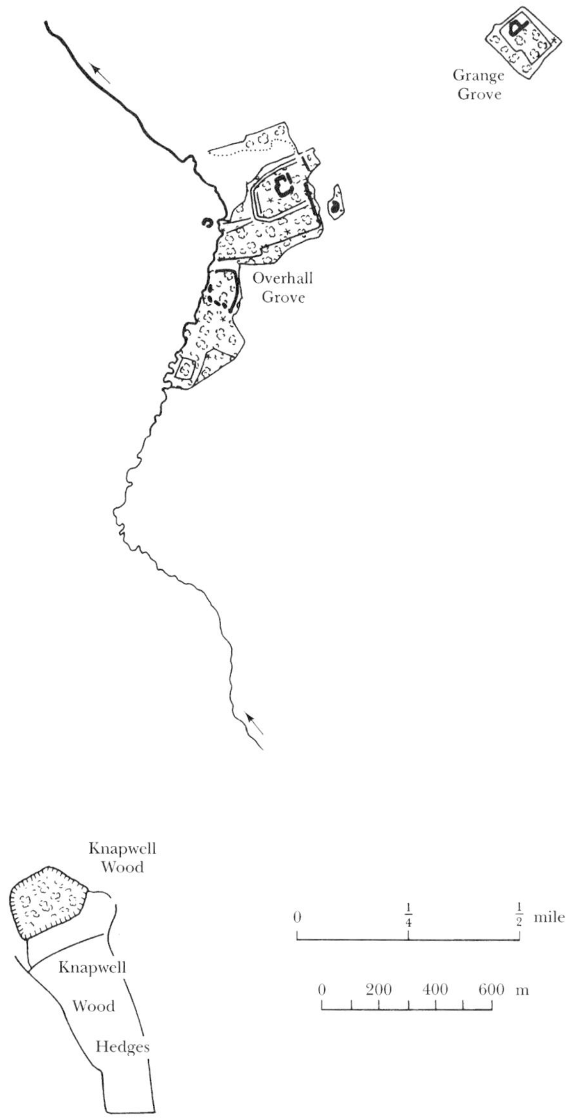

Fig. 5.1 Knapwell Wood, Overhall Grove, and Boxworth Grange Grove, West Cambs. The extent, but not the detail, of the earthworks is shown.

ancient wood at just over one metre a year, but mercury and especially bluebell moving faster (Fig. 5.2).

Lists of ancient-woodland plants

To infer woodland history from the behaviour of plants we need a list of indicator species, for a suite of plants is a more reliable guide than a single species. Plants vary from region to region in this as in other ecological characters. *Luzula sylvatica* in East Anglia is a rare plant of ancient woods; in Northern England it is common and is not confined to woods at all. Mercury is strongly associated with ancient woods in Huntingdonshire; in Suffolk it is common in ancient hedges and is less informative for woods.

The plants characteristic of ancient woodland in Derbyshire are discussed by C. D. Pigott.[106] The most extensive study so far is that of mid Lincolnshire by G. F. Peterken,[98] using the floras of 85 woods which, on documentary and archaeological evidence, he regards as primary, together with over 150 secondary woods and many hundreds of hedges and other habitats. By collating the lists and taking account of survival and colonization he has produced a provisional schedule of 50 species characteristic of primary woodland.

In Table 5.1 I give an abstract of Peterken's Lincolnshire data and discuss the performance of each of his species in Eastern England, as derived from my own observation supplemented by the county Floras. There is much correspondence between the two regions. Of the 50 species in Peterken's list, 38 also have some affinity with ancient woodland in Eastern England, and most of the exceptions are plants so rare in Lincolnshire that their ecology is difficult to determine. Within Eastern England five species are more mobile in the south than the north or vice versa. There are a further twenty species having some affinity with ancient woodland which either do not occur in Lincolnshire or do not there satisfy Peterken's criteria for primary woodland plants (Table 5.2).

The flora of secondary woodland

Secondary woods are usually first colonized by plants such as *Arum maculatum*, *Brachypodium sylvaticum*, *Poa trivialis*, and *Stachys sylvatica*, which are equally common in woods and hedges. There are also plants that have a definite affinity for secondary woodland, occurring in ancient woods only rarely and near the margins. In Eastern England these include *Anthriscus sylvestris*, *Alliaria petiolata*, *Daphne laureola*, and *Viola odorata*, all more typical of hedges or scrub than of woodland. Ivy is also a characteristic plant of wood-margins and secondary woods; it is rarely abundant in ancient woods, and in some such (e.g. Hardwick Wood, Cambs) it may have been allowed to colonize by a past replanting or have spread from adjacent secondary woodland. Black poplar is a strictly non-woodland tree,[122] and if (as at Groton, Suffolk) there is one in a wood it is evidence that the tree was there before the wood.

Cowslip (*Primula veris*) is a plant of grassland (including woodland grassland); in secondary woodland cowslips and primrose-cowslip hybrids can persist for up to a century. Juniper is a light-demanding shrub

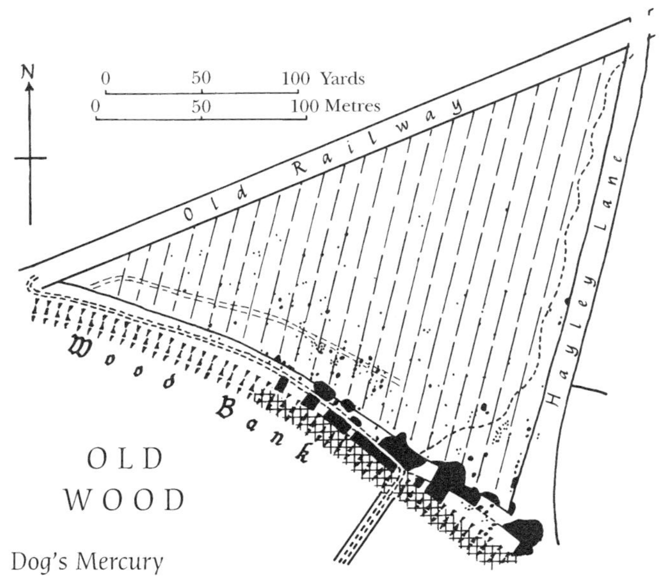

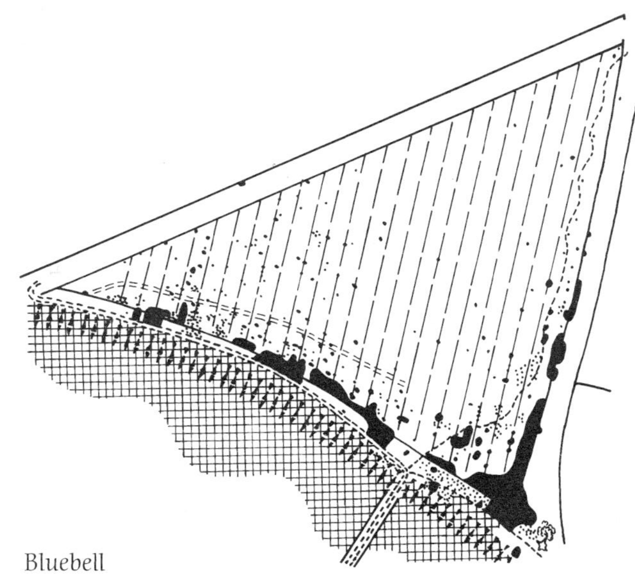

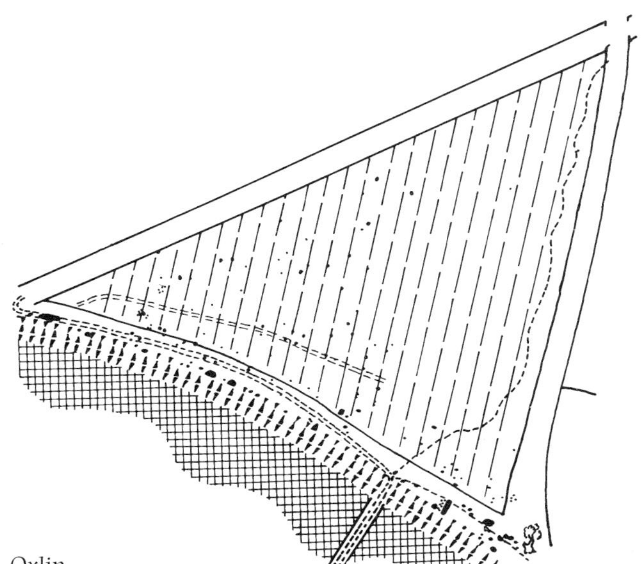

Fig. 5.2 Invasion of the Triangle, Hayley Wood, by oxlip, bluebell, and dog's-mercury. Dots and patches indicate the position of individual plants and colonies in 1973.
Cross-hatching shows in which adjoining areas of the old wood the species are abundant. The broken lines are the ridge-and-furrow of seventeenth-century ploughing.[120]
[For continuation see Fig. 25.25].

Table 5.1 Plants provisionally associated with ancient woodland in central Lincolnshire, and their behaviour in Eastern England. The Lincolnshire data are due to G. F. Peterken.[98] 'Common' means present in at least a quarter of the Lincs woods; 'rare' means present in fewer than a tenth.

Behaviour in Lincs		Species	Behaviour in Eastern England		
Group	Frequency		Frequency	Affinity with ancient woodland	Notes
1. Confined to primary woodland	(*a*) Common	*Carex pallescens*	Uncommon	Strict	
		Milium effusum	Rather common	Strong	Widely believed to have been sown by gamekeepers;[746] this is not substantiated by its actual distribution
		Oxalis acetosella	Rather common	Strong	
	(*b*) Uncommon	*Carex pendula*	Rather common	Strong	In Essex it is commoner and grows in other habitats
		Melampyrum pratense	Uncommon	Strong	In several wood-pastures and one fen
		Neottia nidus-avis	Uncommon	Moderate	Some colonizing ability as in the Triangle of Hayley Wood (Fig. 5.2)
		Paris quadrifolia	Uncommon	Very strong	Sometimes in pre-1700 secondary woodland
	(*c*) Rare	*Agropyron caninum*	Rather common	None	Also in hedges
		Aquilegia vulgaris	Rare	Doubtful	Mainly a garden escape or in fens
		Campanula trachelium	Uncommon	Strong	Also circumboscal
		Carex laevigata	Rare	Strong	Also on wood-pasture commons
		C. strigosa	Rare	Strong	A few park and common records
		Chrysosplenium alternifolium	Rare	None	Wet shaded places in general
		Equisetum sylvaticum	Rare	Weak	Chiefly in wood-pasture (but see Table 5.4)
		Lathraea squamaria	Rare	Doubtful	
		Lathyrus montanus	Rare	Strong	Also in wood-pasture
		Maianthemum bifolium	One site		In an ancient wood
		Polystichum aculeatum	Rather rare	None	Ditches and shaded places in general
		Scutellaria galericulata	Rather common	None	Not a woodland plant
		Vicia sylvatica	Extinct		Lost with the destruction of the ancient Ditton Hall Wood (E. Cambs)
2. Almost confined to primary woodland. All localities outside primary woods explicable by survival on site, or (rarely) by planting	(*a*) Common	*Carex remota*	Common	Moderate	Has some colonizing ability
		Galeobdolon luteum	Common	Strong	Rarely in hedges, etc.
		Asperula odorata	Rare	Very strong	
		Luzula pilosa	Common	Very strong	Rarely in hedges, etc.
		Melica uniflora	Common	Strong	Characteristic grass of medieval woodbanks; in S. Essex common in interiors of woods
	(*b*) Uncommon	*Luzula sylvatica*	Rare	Very strong	A few wood-pasture records
	(*c*) Rare	*Chrysosplenium oppositifolium*	Rather rare	Weak	Wet shaded places in general

3. Almost confined to primary woodland. May colonize secondary woodland very rarely	(*a*) Common	*Anemone nemorosa*	Common	Strong	Rarely in grassland (sometimes on former woodland) or isolated secondary woods
		Convallaria majalis	Rather rare	Strong	Some wood-pasture records; occasionally introduced
		Hypericum hirsutum	Common	Strong	In Essex it is less associated with ancient woods
		Platanthera chlorantha	Uncommon	Strong	
	(*b*) Uncommon	*Lysimachia nemorum*	Uncommon	Strong	In Essex it is commoner and grows in other habitats
		Ranunculus auricomus	Rather common	Weak	Also in old grassland and old hedges
		Viola reichenbachiana	Common	Weak	Shaded habitats in general
4. Most localities in primary woodland. Colonization definite but rare	(*a*) Common	*Allium ursinum*	Uncommon	Weak	Wet shaded places in general
	(*b*) Uncommon	*Adoxa moschatellina*	Rather rare	None	Wet shaded places in general
		Campanula latifolia	Very rare	Probably none	
		Sanicula europaea	Common	None	
		Veronica montana	Locally common	Probably weak	
	(*c*) Rare	*Cardamine flexuosa*	Rather common	None	Wet shaded places in general
		Dipsacus pilosus	Rather rare	None	Mainly river-banks and hedges
5. Most localities in primary woodland, but also in other long-established habitats. No evidence of colonizing ability	(*a*) Common	*Calamagrostis canescens*	Local	Weak	Mainly in fens, but also ancient woods
		Conopodium majus	Rather common	Moderate	Old grassland and ancient woods
		Geum rivale	Rather rare	Moderate	Also in grassland and fens, in which it is commoner in Norfolk
		Orchis mascula	Common	Moderate	Almost confined to woods; has some colonizing ability
		Primula vulgaris	Common	Weak	Alternative but declining habitat in hedges and old grassland
6. Native tree and shrubs confined to primary woods and ancient hedges, except where (rarely) planted	(*a*) Common	*Euonymus europaeus*	Common	Weak	Ancient hedges and ancient woods
		Sorbus torminalis	Rather rare	Very strong	Weak colonizing ability on Essex; very rarely planted
		Tilia cordata	Locally common	Strong	Weak colonizing ability (Chapter 15)
	(*b*) Rare	*Quercus petraea*	Very local	Strong	Rare in wood-pasture (Chapter 17); very rarely planted

Table 5.2 Provisional list of other plants which in Eastern England have some association with ancient woodland.

Species	Frequency	Degree of association	Notes
Alchemilla vestita	Rare	Strong	Also in old grassland
Corydalis claviculata	Uncommon	Moderate	Also on heaths
Crataegus laevigata	Common	Strong	Widely associated with ancient woodland; rare hedgerow occurrences perhaps due to practice of getting thorn-plants from woods
Dryopteris borreri	Uncommon	Moderate	Also in wood-pasture; less characteristic in the north
Endymion nonscriptus	Common	Moderate	In old secondary woods, occasionally in bracken outside woods
Epipactis helleborine	Rare	Strong	Also in wood-pasture
E. purpurata	Rare	Strong	Also in wood-pasture
Euphorbia amygdaloides	Uncommon	Strong	Also circumboscal
Helleborus viridis	Rare	Strong	
Hordelymus europaeus	Rare	Very strong	I have recently discovered this grass in Suffolk on the medieval woodbanks of Thorpe Morieux and Offton Middle Woods
Mercurialis perennis	Common	Variable	Moderate affinity in Cambs; weak in areas with many ancient hedges
Moehringia trinervia	Common	Variable	Less characteristic in Norfolk and Essex
Myosotis sylvatica	Rare as native	Moderate	Confused by introductions
Narcissus pseudo-narcissus	Rare as native	Weak	Also in old grassland; garden-escapes seldom prosper
Ophioglossum vulgatum	Rare	Moderate	Also in old grassland
Peplis portula	Rare	Strong	Commoner and less characteristic in Norfolk
Primula elatior	Locally common	Strong	
Pyrus communis	Very rare as native	Strong	See Chapter 24
Ruscus aculeatus	Rare as native	Strong	Native only in coastal Essex and Suffolk
Sedum telephium	Rare	Moderate	Also rare in hedges, perhaps as garden-escape

whose dead remains may long persist as witnesses of a former non-woodland environment.

Changes in woodland floras

Losses

It is only botanists who keep systematic records of woodland plants. There are three seventeenth-century plant lists from woods that still exist. In 1629 Thomas Johnson, the herbalist, listed plants observed in a wood adjoining Hampstead Heath,[377] which, as Rocque's London map of 1746 shows,[472] was almost certainly Ken Wood. In 1660 John Ray, in his Flora of Cambridgeshire,[466–7] published many plant records for Madingley and Kingston Woods. All these records make no pretence of completeness, only the more striking plants being included, but they are supplemented by other observations in the eighteenth and nineteenth centuries.[200a, 237, 395–6, 761] We have also a shorter but more complete series of plant records for Hayley Wood begun by C. C. Babington and W. W. Newbould in the 1850s.[237]

A record of the last few centuries comes from a pollen core, 70 cm long, from the mud of a pond forming part of the medieval system of launds (Fig. 3.3) in Monks' Park in the Bradfield Woods. I am indebted to Dr John Birks for identifying no less than ninety-four kinds of pollen in it.

The woods are of different kinds and have changed to varying degrees. In Monks' Park the area near the pond is mainly acid, with birch, hazel, oak, and lime, but there is more calcareous woodland close at hand. It is still a coppice-wood; it changed hardly at all from the Middle Ages to 1967, except that the laund, originally rough grazing, became a meadow by 1664[229] and then arable[231] before reverting to woodland about 1890.

The three Cambridgeshire woods are mainly ash–maple–hazel woodland. Hayley is the wettest and has the richest flora; Madingley is comparatively well drained. Since the seventeenth century Kingston has changed the least; part of it was coppiced in the 1970s [but see p. 396]. At Hayley, coppicing declined in the 1880s and ceased in the 1920s; the wood was then largely neglected until 1964, when the Cambridgeshire Naturalists' Trust resumed management including coppicing. Madingley (Fig. 5.3) is the most altered. Soon after Ray's time, half the wood was grubbed out to make four small arable fields. They gradually reverted to woodland, the last open land (by then grassland) disappearing in the 1920s. The wood has thus returned to almost

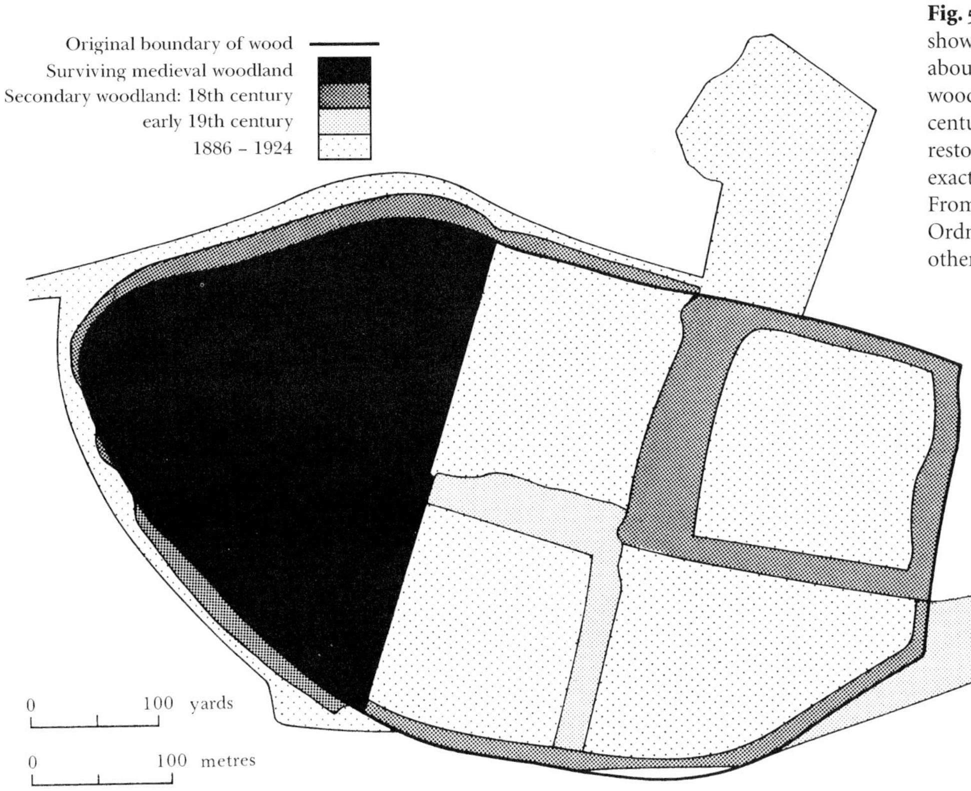

Fig. 5.3 Madingley Wood, showing the destruction of about two-thirds of the wood in the seventeenth century and its gradual restoration to almost exactly the original outline. From earthworks and Ordnance Survey and other maps.[242, 246]

its medieval outline, but has a complex internal structure. It has not been coppiced for about a hundred years, and more of it has been invaded by elms than of the other woods.

Ken Wood is an oakwood on very infertile acid soil. It appears not to have been coppiced for about 250 years and consists of giant timber trees with a thin understorey of holly and hornbeam. It has undergone slight changes of outline. Parts of it have been much altered by planting of beech and invasion by birch and rhododendron.

Many plants have disappeared from all these woods (Table 5.3). Some of these, by their nature, were only a temporary part of the flora: planted trees, arable crops grown in the Monks' Park laund, and casual and ruderal species that appear from outside and grow for a year or so in felled areas. Omitting these, and allowing for thc possible reappearance of a few other species, all five woods have lost much of their original permanent flora. The losses have been most severe in Ken and Madingley, the two most altered woods, but are appreciable even in the apparently unaltered Monks' Park.

Losses of plants that will grow in permanent shade (Table 5.4) are few except in Madingley Wood, which lost part of its area and with it the oxlip among other plants. Losses of plants dependent on coppicing are also few and are related to the length of time since coppicing ceased.

Most losses are of grassland and scrub plants requiring permanent light and growing in rides, launds, and especially wood-margins. With declining woodland management internal clearings become overgrown and the wood-margin becomes more abrupt. For instance, by 1860 the extensive medieval grasslands which had adjoined Hayley Wood had been ploughed up; the grassland flora survived chiefly on lanes and tracks, one of which ran round the wood outside the woodbank. This boundary track has now either been ploughed away or overgrown by bushes; but some of the plants survive in the later refuge provided by the *Arrhenatherum*-dominated grassland of the verges of a railway, especially at the points where the railway crosses the course of the lane. The railway is in turn disused and would be bushed over but for the intervention of Cambridgeshire Wildlife Trust.[120]

The Bradfield Woods are among the richest sites in Britain in native trees and shrubs, but nevertheless have lost four species. Juniper, along with the heathland plants, evidently went with the ploughing or bushing-over of the laund. *Viburnum lantana* is at its northern climatic limit and apparently retreating; it was thought extinct in Norfolk until recently re-found in Gawdy Hall Wood. *Prunus padus* is at its southern climatic limit. All these and rowan (*Sorbus aucuparia*) are rare in Suffolk.

If these five woods are representative, there has been a general decline in the flora, not only of neglected or replanted woods, but even of the better-managed ones.

Table 5.3 Changes in the floras of five woods.

Wood	Original records	Number of these species still there*	Number of species not recently recorded	Number of extinctions
Ken	24 spp. in 1629	12[761]	12	12 out of 24 spp.
Madingley	27 spp. in 1660 + 20 in 18th cent.	23[237]	24	24 out of 47 spp.
Kingston	23 spp. in 1660 + 18 in 18th cent.	30[237]	11	11 out of 41 spp.
Hayley	*c.* 285 spp. (total recorded since *c.* 1855)	*c.* 239[120]	46 including 14 casuals	32 out of *c.* 271 spp.
Monks' Park	91 spp. (+ 3 from outside wood) in sediment core	73	18 including 5 crops and 1 casual	12 out of 85 spp.

* My own observations, together with those of D. E. Coombe (for Madingley) and Mrs Ann Hart and others (for Monks' Park) and of the authorities cited.

The losses, apart from those few possibly due to climatic change, are almost entirely attributable to increasing shade. Coppicing has declined and woodland grassland, where not ploughed away, has become overshadowed or overgrown. Some losses are of relatively widespread plants, such as *Succisa*, which once were in almost every wood but are now in smaller numbers in few woods. Others, such as *Lathyrus sylvestris* and *Melampyrum cristatum*, have become nationally quite rare. Dr D. E. Coombe tells me that the disappearance of *Euphorbia pilosa*, now apparently extinct in Britain, is almost certainly due to lack of felling in those few woods in which it grew.

The decline of woodland and wood-margin grassland is particularly regrettable because in some areas, especially of East Anglia, it forms much of the total ancient grassland now remaining. Some plants, such as *Serratula tinctoria*, are now largely restricted to this habitat over much of Britain.

Gains

It is more difficult to detect the appearance of new species in individual woods. Only very recently have a few woods been surveyed in sufficient detail to establish that a particular species was not present before a certain date.

We are best informed about plants which are not indigenous to Britain as a whole, a handful of which are now regular members of the floras of native woods. Sweet-chestnut and probably some elms, introduced in Roman times or the Iron Age, are dealt with in their respective chapters. Sycamore and *Rhododendron ponticum*, more recent introductions, apparently did not invade woodlands before the nineteenth century. Among herbs, *Epilobium adenocaulon* appeared in 1891 from America and, with its hybrids, is now the commonest willow-herb in many woods. The Central Asian *Impatiens parviflora* is well established but slow to spread. The moss *Orthodontium lineare* from South Africa was first recorded in 1920 and is now on nearly every surface-rotted oak stump.

A few apparently native woodland plants are known to have become more widespread. Rosebay (*Chamaenerion angustifolium*) is now common on bonfire sites and gravel tracks. A century ago it was rare and not particularly a woodland plant. Its spread was probably due to the introduction from America of an indistinguishable but more aggressive plant [p. 436],[900] rather than to the new habitats provided by the practices of burning lop-and-top (Fig. 1.3) and of making gravel roads. The spread of the ferns *Dryopteris dilatata* and *D. carthusiana* into the drier parts of the country has bcen ascribed to the neglect of woodland,[829] though both are common in the Bradfield Woods, especially on alder stools, and survive coppicing. A mystery is the appearance of *Nowellia curvifolia*, a rare liverwort of strongly western distribution, in Hayley Wood [p. 410] and more recently in a wood at Chippenham (Cambs). It grows on a non-historic substrate, fallen oaks dead for about forty years; its nearest known locality is in Derbyshire, and since it rarely produces spores it is difficult to see how it arrived.

The floras of woods of different sizes

It is commonly observed that larger woods are richer in plants and animals than smaller ones; in selecting a nature reserve or Site of Special Scientific Interest size is often thought to outweigh lack of suitability in some other respect. The question is occasionally discussed in terms of 'species per km^2' as though (other things being equal) the number of species should be proportional to the area. In practice there is a law of diminishing returns: doubling the size of the wood usually less than doubles the number of species.

Table 5.4 Ecological classification of missing woodland plants. **Bold**: plants first recorded in 17th century. ***Italic bold***: first recorded in 18th century.

	Ken Wood	Madingley Wood*	Kingston Wood	Hayley Wood	Monks' Park
Crops					*Fagopyrum* *Larix* *Onobrychis* *Picea* *Secale*
Casuals				*Anthemis cotula* *Picris echioides* and twelve others	*Silene diocia*
Trees and Shrubs	**Frangula alnus** **Populus tremula**	**Rhamnus cathartica**		*Prunus domestica* *Rosa rubiginosa* *Salix aurita*	*Juniperus communis* (pollen and fruit) *Prunus padus* *Sorbus aucuparia* *Viburnum lantana*
Relicts of old cultivation		***Vinca major***	**Inula helenium**	*Aegopodium podagraria*	
Shade-bearing plants	**Mercurialis perennis** **Oxalis acetosella**	**Campanula trachelium** ***Equisetum sylvaticum*** ***Neottia nidus-avis*** **Platanthera chlorantha** ***Poa nemoralis*** **Primula elatior**	***Orchis fuscsii*** ***Platanthera chlorantha***	*Allium ursinum* *Epipactis helleborine*	
Coppicing plants	**Euphorbia amygdaloides** **Hypericum tetrapterum** **Lysimachia nemorum** **Solidago virgaurea**	***Calamagrostis epigejos*** ***C. canescens*** ***Galium palustre*** **Malva moschata**	**Chenopodium polyspermum** ***Holcus mollis***	*Calamagrostis canescens*	
Ride, margin, and circumboscal plants	**Gnaphalium sylvaticum** **Lathyrus montanus** **Lysimachia nummularia** **Serratula tinctoria**	***Campanula glomerata*** ***Cartex spicata*** **Lathyrus pratensis** **L. sylvestris** **Melampyrum cristatum** ***Serratula tinctoria*** **Stachys betonica** ***Vicia hirsuta***	**Lithospermum officinale** ***Stachys betonica*** ***Veronica montana*** ***Vicia hirsuta***	*Carex otrubae* *Lathyrus sylvestris* *Lysimachia vulgaris* *Phalaris arundinacea* *Potentilla anglica* *P. erecta* *Serratula tinctoria* *Succisa pratensis* *Trifolium medium* *Viola odorata*	*Humulus* *Rumex acetosella*
Grassland and heath plants		**Cirsium eriophorum** ***Filipendula vulgaris*** **Galium cruciata** ***Ophrys apifera*** ***Veronica officinalis***	***Ophrys apifera***	*Briza media* *Carlina vulgaris* *Cynosurus cristatus* *Daucus carota* *Festuca pratensis* *Gentiana amarella* *Lotus tenuis* *L. uliginosus* *Phleum pratense* *Pimpimella saxifraga* *Ranunculus acris* *Rhinanthus minor* *Sherardia arvensis* *Trifolium ochroleucon*	*Calluna* *Jasione* *Pedicularis* *Thymus*
Aquatics				*Iris pseudacorus*	*Bidens cernua* *Nymphaea*

* For a more recent account see Rackham & Coombe (1996) in new bibliography.

Hayley and Knapwell Woods in West Cambridgeshire are as near as we are likely to get to two woods identical in all respects except size: they are similar in shape, history, plant communities, soils, and management. The numbers of plant species recorded are:

	Acres	Native trees, shrubs, and woody climbers	Total vascular plants
Hayley (omitting old records and associated tracks and railway)	122	33	*c.*200
Knapwell	11.4	20	72

Hayley thus has less than three times the flora in more than ten times the area.

With simple plant communities it is sometimes found that there is a point beyond which an increase in the size of the sample area adds few or no further species. This concept of the ***minimal area***, which underlies much ecological practice, is rather unrealistic for ancient woods with their complex mosaics of plant communities. For inhomogeneous vegetation or for the countryside as a whole, it is more often found that the number of species, *S*, is related to the area, *A*, by an exponential formula:

$$S = aA^{b} \quad \text{or} \quad \log S = \log a + b \log A$$

where *a* and *b* are parameters. There is some theoretical justification for this expression and for expecting *b* to be constant at about 0.27.[841] It is sometimes found in practice that *b* varies with the degree of isolation of sites: contiguous sample areas have *b* values of 0.18–0.21, but isolated islands have values of 0.3 or above.[742]

Dr Max Hooper finds that *b*, as calculated from species lists for the several woods of Rockingham Forest (Northants), turn out to be 0.19; for the West Cambridgeshire woods it is 0.5.[742] This means that in the latter woods there is more difference in the number of species between small and large woods than there is in the former. He claims that this is due to the greater isolation of the Cambridgeshire woods, separated by an average of 0.8 km since at least the thirteenth century, than of the Rockingham woods, which were almost contiguous until the eighteenth century and are still only 0.4 km apart. Species have been dying out at random through time in all woods; a given species is more likely to die out in a smaller wood because its numbers are likely to be fewer; and whether or not it later returns depends on how far away the nearest surviving population is in another wood.

It is not easy to apply the method more widely, because the number of species in a wood is difficult and elusive to define, depending on how much recording is done and over how long a period.[117] For Hayley and Knapwell Woods, where the recording is reasonably thorough, the trees etc. give a *b* value of 0.21 and the total flowering-plant flora gives *b* = 0.55 (close to Hooper's value). In the examples that follow, the species counts are not meant to be complete but are based on a recording procedure intended to cover evenly the woods within each group.

The highest *b* value, 0.47 (Fig. 5.4a), is for the Ditchingham woods in S.E. Norfolk, which are broadly similar to one another and separated by distances of about 1 km. The more isolated Gawdy Hall Wood is no poorer in species than the others of comparable size.

The next highest value, 0.35 (Fig. 5.4b), is for the Milden Thicks group of woods in S.W. Suffolk. These woods have a complex history and are a tight mosaic of many plant communities, several of which are represented in all but the smallest wood. They are separated by about 0.3 km; the more distant Camps and Groton Woods are no poorer.

A lower *b* value, 0.32, is that of a group of ancient woods in and near Long Melford, S.W. Suffolk (Figs. 5.4d, 16.10). The woods are very diverse one from another and are separated by about 0.1 km. Again, three more isolated woods are no poorer, but a secondary wood originating *c.* 1600 has distinctly fewer species.

The Rivenhall woods in Essex (Fig. 5.4c), although very well separated, fail to produce a significant *b* value at all. They have the same kind of internal diversity as the Milden Thicks woods.

There is no indication of any correlation at all between species and area for the woods in and around Hatfield Forest, west Essex (Fig. 5.4e), which are almost contiguous and which vary internally more than they vary from wood to wood.

For native trees and shrubs alone, the *b* values are smaller and more consistent, lying between 0.17 and 0.22.

A log-log correlation between area and number of species, similar to that for the floras and faunas of islands, can thus be demonstrated in four out of these six groups of woods carefully selected for comparability. The correlation is readily disturbed by factors other than area and must not be assumed for woods in general. Some very large ancient woods have poor floras: for instance, Glebe Grove in Felsham (W. Suffolk), 2.4 acres, is just as rich as Holbrook Park (E. Suffolk), about a hundred times its size.

Where there is a correlation between size and species, the parameter *b* – a measure of the extent to which large woods are richer than small – lies around 0.2 for trees and shrubs but is larger and more variable for the total vascular flora. The variation in *b* gives little support for Hooper's theory of the effects of isolation. The more isolated woods in each group do not consistently have fewer species. Hooper's argument is, indeed, inherently somewhat improbable for plants. Species often become extinct in particular woods, but we have no evidence that they return from

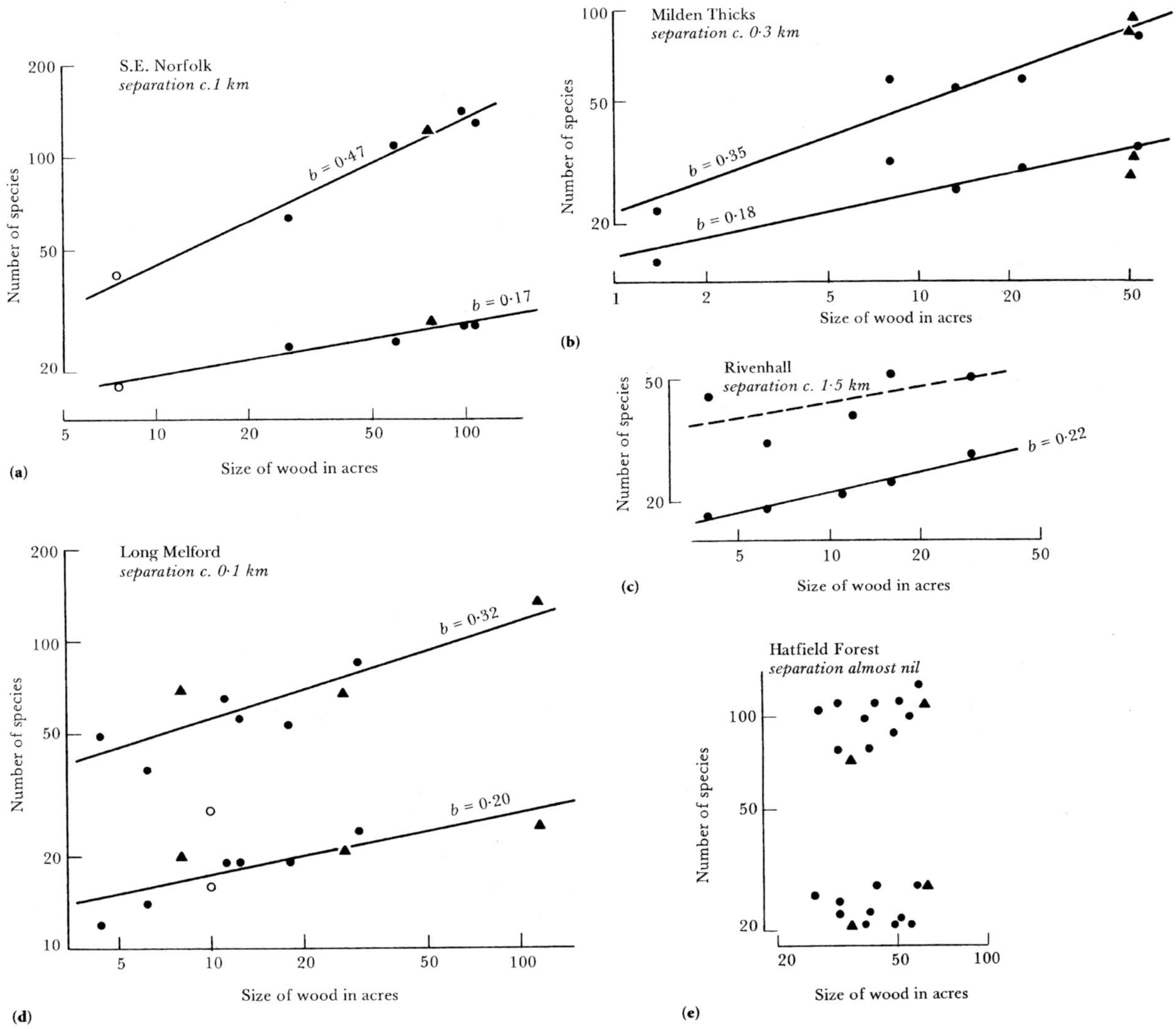

Fig. 5.4 Relationships between numbers of species (recorded by a standard procedure, omitting planted trees) and area of wood for five groups of ancient woods. On each graph the bottom set of points is for trees and shrubs only; the top set of points is for all flowering-plants and ferns; each set has its own regression line. Both axes are logarithmic. (**a**) Five woods in and near Ditchingham (Norfolk) plus Gawdy Hall Wood (▲) which is 8 km distant from the others. (o) is for Round Grove, Hedenham, known to be a pre-1617 secondary wood.[435] (**b**) Five woods in and near Milden (Suffolk) plus Camps and Groton Woods (▲) which are 1.8 km distant from the others (in different directions). (**c**) The woods of Rivenhall (Essex). (**d**) Seven woods in Kentwell and Shimpling, near Long Melford (Suffolk), plus Lineage, Spelthorne, and Alpheton Woods (▲) which are about 1.5 km distant from the others. (o) is for Hospital Grove in Shimpling, a secondary wood of *c.* 1580.[221] (**e**) The woods of Hatfield Forest (Essex), plus two purlieu woods (▲) which are not quite contiguous to the others. The regression statistics are as follows:

	Total flora		Trees and shrubs	
	Correlation coefficient	Regression equation	Correlation coefficient	Regression equation
(**a**)	0.990	$\log S = 1.18 + 0.47 \log A$	0.980	$\log S = 1.12 + 0.167 \log A$
(**b**)	0.964	$\log S = 1.34 + 0.35 \log A$	0.851	$\log S = 1.22 + 0.181 \log A$
(**c**)	0.871	$\log S = 1.43 + 0.32 \log A$	0.853	$\log S = 1.04 + 0.202 \log A$
(**d**)	0.593 (not significant)	($\log S = 1.46 + 0.17 \log A$)	0.975	$\log S = 1.11 + 0.217 \log A$
(**e**)	0.313 (not significant)		(not significant)	

neighbouring woods. Extinction is not a random process but is the result of changing circumstances which will generally not be confined to one wood and will affect both large and small woods. The changes which wipe out a plant in one wood will usually render survival in the next wood precarious and recolonization impossible. *Serratula tinctoria*, for instance, which appears three times in Table 5.4, disappeared [by 1990] from all its West Cambridgeshire woods.

Variation in *b* is more likely to reflect the differing nature of woodland plant communities. In West Cambridgeshire, for instance, the woods have few, extensive, and individually-rich communities; in Rivenhall or Milden, the communities are many and intricate, and some are individually rather poor. With such differences in the scale of ecological variation we can hardly expect the relations between species and area to have the same parameters.

A similar calculation for birds in British woods by N. W. Moore and Hooper[93] shows size to be a much more important factor than for plants. A correlation for 433 plantations and woods approximates closely to the log-log formula, with *b* equal to its theoretical value of 0.27. This is partly because a wider range of sizes was taken, including many groves of less than one acre. But birds are territorial and individually independent, unlike plants, and many species are common only in woods of over twenty or even over a hundred acres.

Added in 2003 edition

Real changes in the last 24 years are discussed in Chapter 25. The revival of coppicing has given new life to many buried-seed plants and others of intermittently-shaded woodland, but plants of edges and permanently-open habitats continue to decline. Deer continue to impoverish the woodland flora, as shown by Fig. 25.25, which brings up to date Fig. 5.2.

The belief that large areas of habitat are better than small, and need to be joined up to create larger areas still, has persisted and become somewhat of a dogma among conservationists. In Chapter 30 I argue that for woods it is, at best, over-stated and does little to solve the real conservation problems.

Fig. 5.5 (a–b) Two plants that have suffered from increasing shade and the decline in wood-edge habitats, photographed in 1969 in Hayley Wood where both are now extinct.

(**a**) Dyer's Greenweed, *Genista tinctoria*.

(**b**) The cow-wheat *Melampyrum cristatum*, now reduced to a handful of sites.

from some 70 cm of a fine sand overlying soft limestone and varying in pH from 4.1 to 6.4 according to their clay content. At Rivenhall the surface geology and soils change every few yards with a complexity unusual even for Essex.

The mosaic of woodland types may be altered by historical influences, both artificial (e.g. the compartmentation of Forests (Chapter 12)) and natural. Patterns generated by the trees themselves include the circular patches formed by the suckering of invasive elm, aspen, and cherry.

The pattern size of the woodland mosaic is best visualized as an answer to the question: if you go to a random point in a wood and walk in a random direction, how far on average will you go before you come to a different kind of woodland? For practical purposes it is more easily measured by the ratio

$$\frac{\text{Area of the wood}}{\text{Number of stands in the wood}}.$$

A ***stand*** is defined, here and throughout this book, as an area of a particular plant community, bounded by other communities or by the edge of the wood. A community that occurs in two separate parts of the same wood counts as two stands. In some woods the number of stands is large and ill-defined because of elm invasions, particularly round the edges, or of small aspen and cherry clones. To avoid allowing the mosaic size to be unduly influenced by these species I shall not count any stands of invasive elm, or any cherry or aspen of less than 1/4 acre (0.1 ha); nor shall I count more than one stand of aspen in a wood even if it is dispersed among several clones.

By these rules, Tarecroft Wood has eight stands (counting two lime and two hornbeam and omitting the two elm invasions). The mosaic size is thus 2.0 acres. Chantilly also has eight stands, with a mosaic size of some 900 acres.

The mosaic sizes of about 190 ancient woods are plotted in Fig. 6.3. The procedure has no pretension to accuracy: many stands, particularly in small woods, are truncated by reaching the edge of the wood; it is often possible to quibble about whether a group of trees is large or distinct enough to be counted as a stand. But the variation in mosaic size is so great that accuracy is hardly needed. All the woods in any one district tend to have roughly the same mosaic size, but the size varies widely from district to district. In West Cambridgeshire the mosaic size, save in a few small woods, is around fifty acres; in mid Essex it tends to be about three acres. This does not correspond to any differences of ownership or management. Areas with a particularly small-scale mosaic have an unusual number of possible dominant trees, including lime, hornbeam, and non-invasive elm; they lie close to the border between the Acid and Calcareous Soil Provinces (Fig. 4.10) and have complex soil compositions in which clay, sand, and loess are all prominent.

Relations of tree communities with one another

Why should part of a wood consist of one tree rather than another? What are the relationships between communities? The ranges which trees occupy can to some extent be defined in terms of history and environment. The environmental measurements most used in this book are topsoil pH and particle-size composition, but – given sufficient resources – many more factors could be taken into account.[51] Sometimes, as with alder and beech, it is possible to define quite narrowly where a tree will be dominant; more often the best we can do is to estimate the probability that it will occur in a given place. Even with many more measurements there is no assurance that we would be able to predict what a wood would consist of. The problem is too complex and may involve factors almost inaccessible to measurement, such as the weather following a particular felling in history.

Relations between tree communities can be expressed in terms of their ***contiguity***, of how often one community abuts on or intermingles with another. This can be approximately measured by making a map of the tree communities in a wood and observing what fraction of the perimeter of a stand of Community *A* adjoins Communities *B*, *C*, and *D* (Fig. 6.4a). In practice it is simpler to estimate the contribution of the various dominant and co-dominant trees to the perimeter,

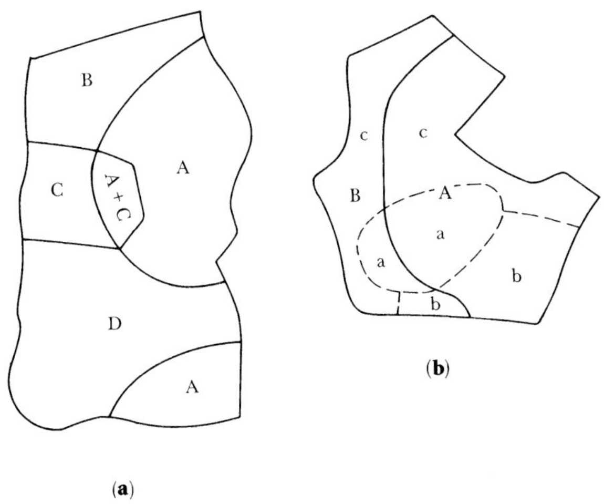

Fig. 6.4 (**a**) Map of an imaginary wood containing five stands of four tree communities, A, B, C, D, two of which (A and C) intermingle. The perimeter of Community A abuts approximately 30% on B, 20% on C, and 50% on D. B abuts 70% on A and 30% on C. (**b**) An imaginary wood with tree communities A and B and ground vegetation communities a, b, c. Community A grows approximately 20% over a, 30% over b, and 50% over c; B grows 15% over a, 10% over b, and 75% over c.

Table 6.2 Frequency of abuttals and associations between tree communities and other tree species. The table gives an approximat measure of the frequency with which each type of woodland comes into contact with trees other than those dominant in it. This h been done mainly in terms of what trees are most often dominant or co-dominant in woodland adjacent to the tree community under consideration (List A: see text for details). Allowance has been made for trees which intermingle with other types of woodla rather than forming tree communities themselves (Lists B and C).

The information comes from ancient woods (including old secondary woodland) throughout Eastern England. Trees known o suspected to have been planted are ignored.

TR

	Ash–maple–hazel woods							Hornbeam-woods				Limewoods[a]		
	Pure hazel	Pure ash	Mixed hazel	Mixed ash	Ash–hazel	Maple–hazel	Maple	Maple–hornbeam	Hornbeam–ash	Pure hornbeam	Oak–hornbeam	Large stands	Small stands	Clusters and single stools
Number of woods studied	15	17	37	34	42	58	16	33	97	41	17	21	23	19
LIST A TREES DOMINANT IN ADJACENT WOODLAND														
Ash								18	**34**	11	*6*	24	21	20
Maple								**32**	8	*4.8*	*0.6*	6	12	8
Hazel								23	22	*5*	*7*	*7*	*10*	*13*
Hornbeam	21	**49**	22	**56**	22	29	29					31	23	21
Lime	7	**15**	6	*1.2*	6	6	**8**	*1.4*	**9**	*0.5*	—			
Elm: invasive	**17**	8	**22**	**14**	**20**	**32**	**25**	8	8	5	*1.2*	*1.0*	*2.6*	*3.2*
Lineage	*0.7*	*3.2*	**13**	**4.4**	**5**	**7**	**17**	**4.7**	**6**	2.4	1.8	1.2	**8**	**13**
wych[f]	**2.7**	**1.2**	0.4	0.7	**1.0**	—	—	—	**1.6**	0.5	—	—	**2.1**	—
Oak[c]	**16**	1.2	1.4	*0.6*	*0.1*	*0.4*	2.8	2.3	—	*0.6*	**10**	**4.8**	—	2.6
Alder	**4.0**	**2.9**	2.4	2.4	**3.6**	1.4	—	—	*0.5*	2.1	—	**3.0**	—	1.1
Birch	8	8	10	9	13	6	*3.4*	*2.9*	*3.4*	**31**	15	*6*	*4.8*	10
Chestnut	7	5	7	*0.1*	*1.7*	*1.5*	*0.3*	*0.6*	*0.9*	**24**	**45**	10	10	*3.9*
LIST B TREES OCCASIONALLY DOMINANT, MORE OFTEN INTERMINGLING														
Aspen	3.7	3.2	**6**	2.2	**12**	4.1	**6**	2.4	**4.5**	**8**	**9**	**4.5**	**6**	2.9
Holly	1.3	*0.6*	0.8	—	1.1	1.1	—	—	*0.2*	0.8	*0.6*	—	—	—
Cherry	**2.0**	*0.3*	**2.5**	**3.8**	**6**	1.7	—	*0.3*	1.3	0.8	—	*0.2*	—	1.1
Hawthorn	**3.3**	0.6	1.8	**2.1**	**3.2**	**6**	**7**	**2.9**	0.5	0.5	**2.1**	—	—	—
Sycamore	**2.0**	0.3	**1.7**	—	—	**2.2**	1.2	—	*0.2*	—	—	—	—	—
LIST C OTHER INTERMINGLING SPECIES														
Sallow	**4.0**	1.8	0.9	1.2	**5**	1.7	0.6	1.4	0.9	1.2	—	*0.2*	—	—
Blackthorn	—	—	**1.6**	0.6	0.7	—	—	—	—	*0.2*	—	—	—	—
Rowan	—	—	—	—	—	—	—	—	—	0.2	—	—	—	—
Service	—	—	—	0.1	—	—	—	—	—	—	**1.2**	—	—	—
Prunus padus	—	—	—	—	0.3	—	—	0.3	—	—	—	0.2	—	—
Others	—	—	0.3	0.9	—	0.3	—	—	0.6	0.7	—	—	—	—

Bold figures: woodland types with which a particular tree species comes into contact markedly more often than would be expected from chance association.

Italic figures: woodland types which a tree species meets markedly less often than would be expected by chance. (These distinctions are not statis cally precise but are intended merely to draw attention to positive and negative associations.)

a 'Large' stands of lime are defined as those of >4 acres (>1.6 ha) of *Tilia cordata*; 'clusters' as stands of <¼ acres (0.1 ha).

b Only the more substantial elm invasions (p. 273) are taken into account. Small stands of Lineage elm and single stools of wych-elm are included.

c Defined as on p. 283. Oak timber trees over underwood of other species are not included.

Woodland types follow the list of Table 6.1, somewhat modified because of the practical difficulty of drawing boundaries etween some tree communities on the ground. With ash–maple–hazel woodland each individual wood contributes only once to ne table; no attempt has been made to separate different kinds of ash–maple–hazel woodland where more than one kind occurs in ne same wood. Limewoods and (in part) chestnut-woods are subdivided by size of stand rather than by vegetation. Aspen-, holly-, herry-, hawthorn-, and sycamore-woods, which are of small extent and are not sharply differentiated from other kinds of wood-nd in which these trees are intermingled, are not tabulated as separate woodland types.

The figures are percentages for each woodland type: each column adds up to 100 (apart from rounding errors).

OMMUNITY

Elmwoods[b]				Oakwoods			Alder-woods		Birchwoods	Chestnut-woods[e]		
vasive *Jlmus inor)*	Invasive *(U. procera)*	Lineage Elm	Wych-elm	Coppice oak	Non-coppice[c]	Hatfield Forest	Valley	Plateau	Birch[d]	With *Quercus petraea*	Large stands	Small stands
82	17	76	67	17	3	4	22	13	30	11	35	19
24	23	19	17	—	—	14	18	14	17	*1.8*	9	*11*
18	10	12	8	—	—	**24**	*3*	*2*	*2.0*	—	*1.1*	*4.7*
31	**31**	24	23	*11*	17	15	24	14	14	*0.5*	*13*	*6*
12	27	24	20	21	*2*	*6*	18	*6*	26	**60**	32	35
1.7	—	**8**	**9**	7	—	—	2.5	**24**	4.3	5.0	7	**14**
———	———	*3.4*	*3.3*	*1.5*	—	15	*2.5*	*1.5*	—	*0.5*	*1.4*	*1.6*
0.8	—	———	**9**	—	—	—	3.5	1.5	1.2	—	1.1	**6**
0.1	0.6	—	———	—	—	—	—	—	—	—	0.6	—
1.9	—	1.3	—	———	———	———	2	**4.5**	2.7	**9**	1.4	**6**
0.1	—	1.4	*0.4*	0.9	**5**	—	———	———	2.3	2.3	**3.1**	—
2.2	—	*1.4*	*2.7*	**24**	17	22	8	20	———	19	21	3.9
1.4	—	3.3	*3.4*	**22**	—	—	**19**	8	**28**	———	———	———
0.9	—	*0.5*	*0.2*	2.1	—	—	*0.5*	1	1.5	0.9	1.1	3.2
0.8	2.9	—	0.9	3.8	**38**	—	—	—	0.7	1.4	—	1.8
1.1	—	0.8	1.5	—	—	—	—	—	—	—	1.3	1.6
1.9	**2.4**	*0.1*	—	—	—	4	—	—	—	—	—	1.3
0.1	**1.8**	—	*0.1*	1.2	—	—	—	—	—	—	**2.9**	0.5
0.2	—	—	0.5	—	—	—	—	—	—	—	0.6	0.5
0.4	**1.2**	—	0.6	—	—	—	—	—	—	—	—	
—	—	—	—	**2.6**	**8**	—	—	—	—	—	—	—
—	—	—	—	0.3	—	—	—	—	—	**0.5**	—	—
—	—	—	0.4	0.6	**5**	—	—	—	—	—	—	—
1.1	—	—	—	2.7	8[g]	—	—	—	—	—	3.1	3.2

nly long-established birchwoods, as defined on p. 316, are included.
hestnut-woods are divided into those with *Quercus petraea* (i.e. chestnut-oak woods, Table 6.1 and p. 332) and those with only . *robur*. The latter are subdivided into stands larger or smaller than 2½ acres (1 ha).
operly belongs in List B but is placed here for comparison with other elms.
ainly *Rhododendron ponticum*.

Table 6.3 Frequency of different dominant herbs and undershrubs beneath each tree community. The table summarizes the relationship between the different tree and ground vegetation communities. It shows which of the commoner dominant and co-dominant herbs and undershrubs occur under each type of woodland and approximately how often. It is derived from almost the same woods, classified in the same way, as those used in Table 6.2.

No account is taken of how dense or sparse the ground vegetation is. Bare ground, rides, and recently-felled areas are excluded. No account is taken of plants dominant in one community when they occur as scattered individuals in another community.

		Ash–maple–hazel woods							Hornbeam-woods			
		Pure hazel	Pure ash	Mixed hazel	Mixed ash	Ash–hazel	Maple–hazel	Maple	Maple–hornbeam	Hornbeam ash	Pure hornbeam	Oak–hornbeam
Number of woods studied		15	11	42	34	58	66	16	31	92	37	17
LIST A												
Deschampsia flexuosa		—	—	—	—	—	—	—	—	—	—	0.3
Pteridium aquilinum	Bracken	8	*0.9*	6	*3.4*	*2.2*	*2.5*	—	*0.2*	*1.0*	**30**	**48**
Corydalis claviculata		—	—	—	—	—	—	—	—	—	0.8	—
Teucrium scorodonia	Wood-sage	—	—	—	—	0.3	—	—	—	—	—	—
Holcus mollis		—	1.8	2.7	1.2	*0.6*	*0.2*	—	*0.6*	*0.1*	**9**	**7**
Endymion nonscriptus	Bluebell	**19**	15	12	**18**	14[g]	14[g]	6	11	16	**23**	6
Oxalis acetosella	Wood-sorrel	—	—	0.2	—	0.2	—	0.6	**1.1**	*0.1*	—	—
Anemone nemorosa	Wood anemone	—	—	*0.2*	0.6	0.5	—	—	—	**1.1**	—	**1.2**
Lonicera periclymenum	Honeysuckle[i]	1.3	—	*0.2*	1.9	1.0	0.5	—	*0.3*	0.9	0.7	**4.4**
Dryopteris spp[h]	Male fern, etc.	—	—	—	—	—	—	—	—	*0.1*	—	—
Rubus fruticosus and **Corylifolii**	Brambles	30	**45**	18	26	17	*9*	*7*	*7*	23	**32**	**31**
Primula vulgaris	Primrose	8	**20**	3.7	6	5	5	7	**10**	**8**	*0.1*	—
Geum rivale	Water avens	—	—	—	—	0.3	0.2	—	—	—	—	—
Galeobdolon luteum	Archangel	—	0.9	—	0.3	—	0.5	—	**1.6**	*0.1*	0.4	—
Deschampsia caespitosa		2.0	—	2.1	1.8	5	5	**8**	**13**	*1.0*	—	—
Mercurialis perennis	Dog's-mercury	22	*10*	26	28	34	**47**	**57**	**42**	37	*2.8*	—
Primula elatior	Oxlip	*0.3*	—	**14**	1.0	**9**	**5.0**	1.2	1.1	2.9	—	—
Rubus caesius	Dewberry (bramble)	—	—	0.1	—	**0.9**	**0.6**	—	—	—	—	—
Filipendula ulmaria	Meadowsweet	—	—	**3.6**	0.6	**2.6**	0.8	0.6	0.6	0.4	—	—
Hedera helix	Ivy[i]	7	—	4.5	**8**	1.6	2.6	3.8	**8**	5	0.4	0.9
LIST B												
Allium ursinum	Wild garlic	—	—	*0.1*	—	0.2	—	—	—	0.3	—	—
Carex pendula etc.[j]	Big sedges	**0.7**	—	—	—	0.5	0.5	—	—	0.1	—	—
LIST C												
Urtica dioica	Nettle	1.3	**6**	0.8	2.2	3.4	3.5	**9**	3.2	1.7	1.2	—
Galium aparine	Goosegrass	—	—	—	—	—	0.2	—	—	0.3	—	—
Digitalis purpurea	Foxglove	—	—	—	—	—	—	—	—	—	—	—
Silene dioica	Red campion	—	—	**5**	0.9	—	0.6	—	—	*0.3*	—	—
LIST D												
Poa trivialis		—	—	1.2	1.0	*0.1*	1.1	—	—	—	—	—
Glechoma hederacea	Ground-ivy	—	—	—	—	—	0.3	—	—	—	—	—
Anthriscus sylvestris	Cow parsley	—	—	—	—	—	—	—	—	—	—	—
OTHER PLANTS		—	—	—	—	1.2	0.1	—	0.6	—	—	2.4

Bold figures: woodland types under which a particular plant was most often recorded.
Italic figures: woodland types under which a particular plant was least often recorded.
a–e See Table 6.2.
f Valley alder-wood has a peculiar set of herbaceous communities found under no other tree community (p. 308). The ground vegetation tabula[ted]
here is that under the 'dry-land' woodland – of whatever type – which immediately adjoins the valley alder-wood.

Plants in List A are general woodland species arranged in approximate order of their tendency to occur on acid or calcareous ils. (*Deschampsia flexuosa* being the most calcifuge). List B is of plants almost indifferent to pH but characteristic of wet places. st C is of indicators of unusual fertility including 'phosphate plants' (pp. 95–6). List D is of 'elm plants' (p. 96). Species named in **ld** are further discussed in Chapter 7.
The figures in each column total 100.

OMMUNITY

Limewoods[a]			**Elmwoods**[b]				**Oakwoods**			**Alder-woods**		**Birch-woods**	**Chestnut-woods**[e]		
ge nds	Small stands	Clusters and single stools	Invasive (*Ulmus minor*)	Invasive (*U. procera*)	Lineage Elm	Wych-elm	Coppice oak	Non-coppice[c]	Hatfield Forest	Valley[f]	Plateau	Birch[d]	With *Quercus petraea*	Large stands	Small stands
	21	18	72	14	72	52	18	4	4	14	11	27	11	34	16
	—	—	—	—	—	—	**1.7**	**2**	—	—	—	—	**2.3**	—	—
	—	5	*1.9*	*2.9*	*1.0*	*0.2*	**45**	**55**	—	**27**	11	**26**	**42**	**26**	12
	—	—	—	—	—	—	**0.6**	—	—	—	—	—	—	**1.0**	—
	—	—	—	—	—	—	**1.1**	—	—	**1**	**2**	**1.3**	—	0.3	—
	6	—	—	3.6	—	*0.8*	**4.0**	2	—	**11**	**5**	3.5	**6**	**7**	—
	12	**17**	14[g]	7	14	**21**	8	—	—	**24**	*5*	*3.9*	7	**18**	*4.1*
	—	—	0.6	—	—	—	—	—	—	—	—	—	—	—	—
	2.6	—	0.4	—	0.9	0.8	—	—	—	**2**	—	—	0.9	—	**3.1**
	—	—	—	—	—	—	**3.6**	—	—	—	**9**	2.2	**3.2**	1.6	—
	—	—	*0.1*	—	—	—	—	—	—	1	**8**	—	—	—	—
	31	24	*7*	*3.6*	*11*	*11*	**32**	**41**	*3*	26	26	**46**	**34**	**33**	**48**
	12	**11**	6	2.9	8	*1.8*	—	—	—	—	**9**	6	3.6	*1.5*	6.2
	4.8	**1.1**	*0.1*	—	0.3	0.6	—	—	—	—	**3**	—	—	—	—
	—	—	0.6	**3.9**	—	—	—	—	—	—	**4**	—	—	—	—
	—	6	4.1	—	2.4	—	—	—	**39**	—	**8**	1.9	—	1.6	—
	20	25	**38**	**42**	**41**	**45**	—	—	**56**	—	*5*	6	—	*3.2*	23
	—	0.6	**4.5**	0.7	**7**	**8**	—	—	—	3	1	1.7	—	—	—
	1.0	—	—	—	—	—	—	—	—	—	—	—	—	—	—
	—	—	—	—	0.4	**2.5**	—	—	—	**2**	**4**	—	—	1.8	—
	6	**10**	2.4	5.0	4.2	0.6	2.8	—	—	—	—	—	—	3.7	—
	—	—	*0.1*	—	**1.1**	**0.6**	—	—	—	—	**2**	—	—	—	—
	—	—	—	—	—	—	—	—	—	—	0.5	—	—	—	—
	—	0.6	**12**	**16**	4.2	3.5	—	—	3	3	—	0.7	—	*0.9*	—
	—	—	0.5	**1.1**	—	—	—	—	—	—	—	—	—	—	—
	1.9	—	—	—	—	—	—	—	—	—	—	—	—	—	—
	3.8	—	1.2	0.7	1.2	—	—	—	—	—	—	—	—	—	—
	—	—	**7**	**7**	3.6	3.1	—	—	—	—	—	—	—	*0.4*	—
	—	—	0.3	—	—	0.3	—	—	—	—	—	—	—	—	—
	—	—	—	**1.4**	—	—	—	—	—	—	—	—	—	—	—
	—	—	0.6	—	0.3	0.2	2.3	—	—	—	0.5	—	1.4	—	3.1

hese tree communities are associated mainly with the less calcifuge bluebell of Cambs and Hunts.
. *filix-mas*, *dilatata*, and *carthusiana*
undershrub; records when a climber are not included.
so *C. acutiformis*, *riparia*, and *pseudocyperus*.

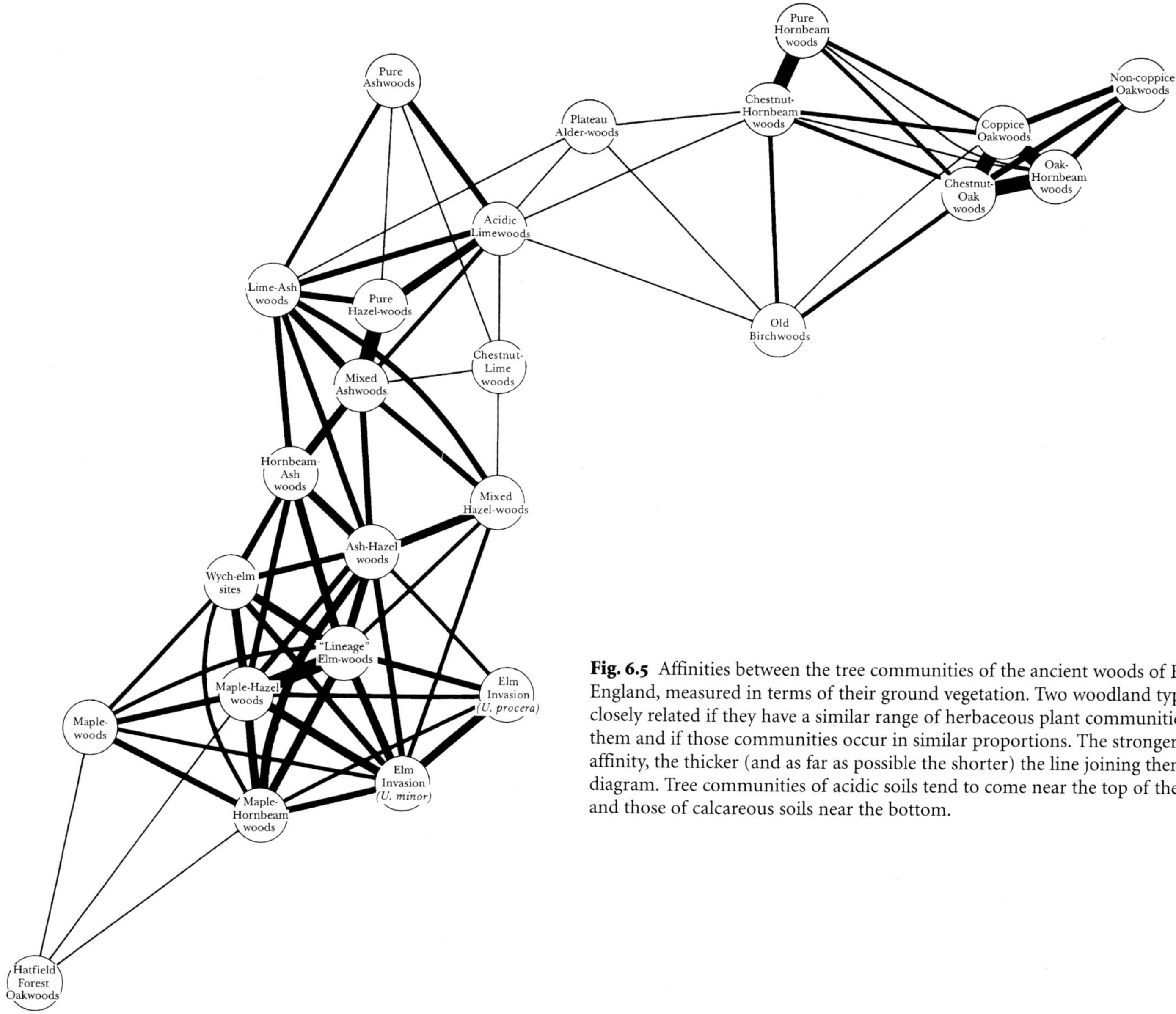

Fig. 6.5 Affinities between the tree communities of the ancient woods of Eastern England, measured in terms of their ground vegetation. Two woodland types are closely related if they have a similar range of herbaceous plant communities beneath them and if those communities occur in similar proportions. The stronger this affinity, the thicker (and as far as possible the shorter) the line joining them in the diagram. Tree communities of acidic soils tend to come near the top of the diagram and those of calcareous soils near the bottom.

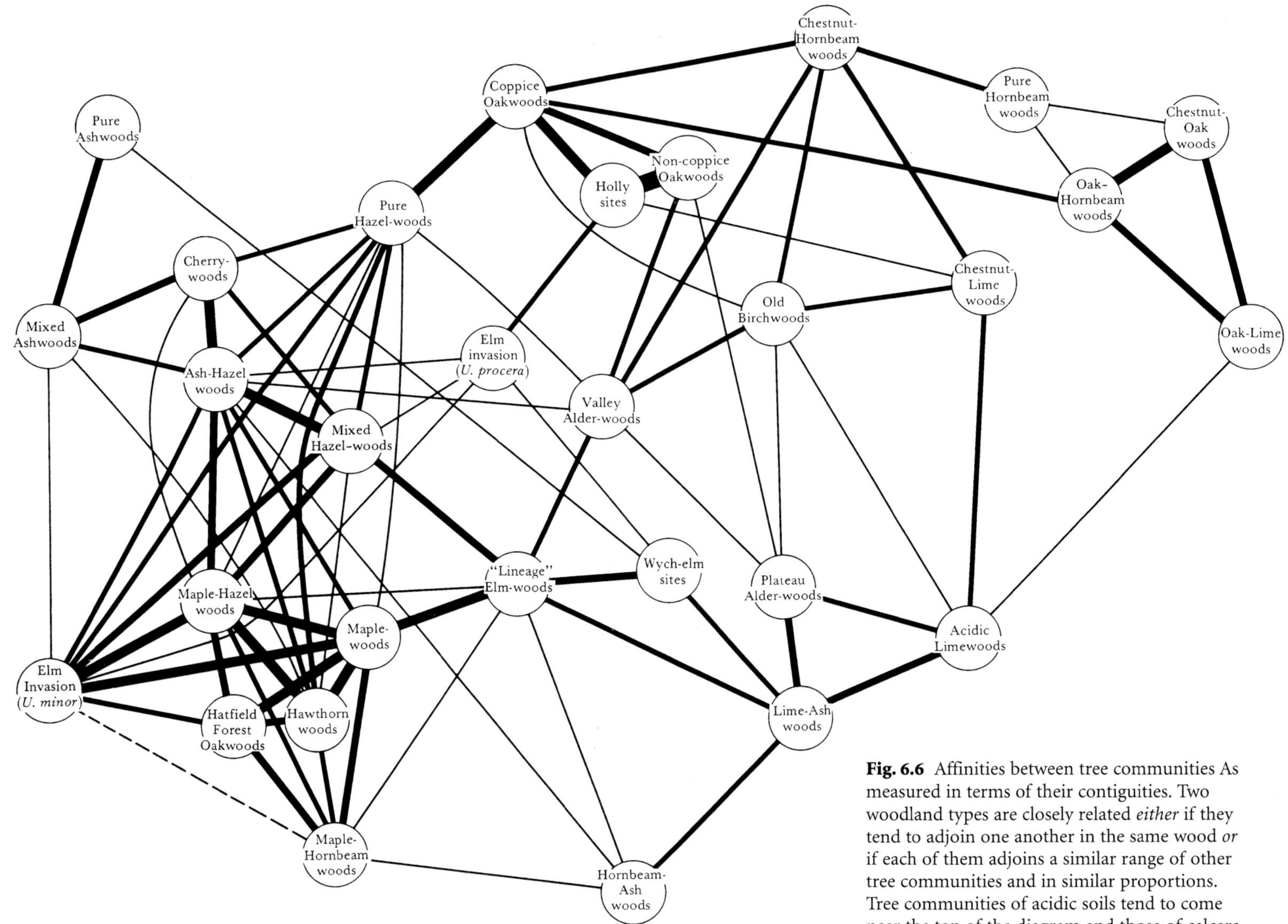

Fig. 6.6 Affinities between tree communities As measured in terms of their contiguities. Two woodland types are closely related *either* if they tend to adjoin one another in the same wood *or* if each of them adjoins a similar range of other tree communities and in similar proportions. Tree communities of acidic soils tend to come near the top of the diagram and those of calcareous soils near the bottom.

rather than to specify Communities *B*, *C*, and *D* in detail, especially as this enables allowance to be made for trees that intermingle with no sharp boundary. If Community *A* occurs more than once in a wood the stands are combined according to the lengths of their perimeters. Figures from different woods are treated as independent samples of the local woodland mosaic; they are added up giving each wood an equal weight regardless of its total area or of the area of Community *A* represented.

The results of this analysis, reduced to percentages, form ***tree contiguity tables*** of which Table 6.2 is a general summary. The column for plateau alder-wood, for instance, indicates that this woodland type abuts on lime 24% of the time, on chestnut 8%, and on hornbeam 6%. Since lime forms only 4.2% of thc total area of woods sampled, this is strong evidence that plateau alder-wood tends to grade into limewood; indeed there is no other woodland type which is so often adjacent to lime. Conversely hornbeam-woods occupy 23.6% of the area sampled, and although they are not all pure hornbeam there is strong evidence that hornbeam tends to avoid the vicinity of plateau alder. Chestnut is dominant in 8.8% of the woodland area sampled: the 8% contiguity with plateau alder-wood may reasonably be attributed – since this is not a precise calculation – to chance association.

A third method of measuring the interrelations of tree communities is in terms of their ground vegetation. We estimate what proportion of the area of Tree Community *A* in a given wood is occupied by ground vegetation communities *a*, *b*, and *c* (Fig. 6.4b). The process is repeated for other woods and the results are added up, giving each wood equal weight, to form a grand estimate of how often Community *A* grows over communities *a*, *b*, or *c*. This is the basis of ***ground vegetation tables*** of which Table 6.3 is a general summary. In it we see, for instance, that in plateau alder-woods 26% of the area is taken up by stands of brambles, 11% by bracken, 5% by dog's-mercury, etc.

Table 6.3 enables us, by a simple form of the ordination procedure described on p. 22, to measure how far any two tree communities differ in their vegetation. For instance, non-invasive elmwoods have much the same range of ground vegetation communities as hazel–maple woods and in almost the same proportions; the oakwoods of Hatfield Forest, however, differ very strongly from all other oakwoods. A measure of the difference between Tree Communities *A* and *B* is obtained by working out, for all ground vegetation communites *a*, *b*, . . . *z*, the quantity

$$\sqrt{\{(p_{A,a}-p_{B,a})^2+(p_{A,b}-p_{B,b})^2+\ldots+(p_{A,z}-p_{B,z})^2\}}$$

where $p_{A,a}$ etc. are the percentages entered in the appropriate columns and rows of the table. This is the distance between the points which would represent *A* and *B* on a many-dimensioned graph in which each dimension corresponded to one ground vegetation community. Non-invasive elmwoods turn out to be nine units distant from maple–hazel woods; Hatfield Forest oakwoods are ninety units from the other oakwoods. Figure 6.5 is an attempt to portray this network of relationships in two dimensions, keeping, as far as possible, the stronger affinities undistorted.

A similar but independent network of relationships can be derived from an analysis of the abuttals of tree communities on each other (Table 6.2) and is portrayed in Fig. 6.6.

The two affinity diagrams are broadly similar, with maple-woods, elmwoods (*U. minor*), etc. at one extreme, chestnut–oak and oak–hornbeam woods at the other, and ashwoods, limewoods, birchwoods, etc. between. There are suffficient discrepancies of detail to remind us that this type of diagram, despite its seeming objectivity, is not a definitive description of the subtle relationships between tree communities. Both diagrams, however, clearly show that those relationships take the form of a network; they do not encourage us to try to organize tree communities into a hierarchy of classes and orders on the model of Continental phytosociology.

Shrubs

In ancient woods it is seldom possible to define a prominent shrub layer. Hazel and sallow form part of the underwood and thus count as trees; undershrubs such as brambles are counted with the ground vegetation. Shrubs are defined as woody plants larger than undershrubs but too small to make any appreciable contribution to the underwood.

Shrubs are more easily affected by management than are trees or shade-bearing herbs and are of limited value in characterizing plant communities. In a coppiced wood shrubs may be abundant in gaps between the stools; when the same wood is neglected they are overtopped by the underwood and often perish except near margins and rides.

The absence of shrubs tells us little, but if present they often go with particular soils and particular types of woodland, as follows:

Calcicolous shrubs In most ash–maple–hazel and elm woods, even if these have moderately acid topsoil:

- Hedgerow hawthorn *Crataegus monogyna* (more often a tree and dealt with in Chapter 24)
- Woodland hawthorn *C. laevigata*
- Dogwood *Cornus sanguinea*
- Spindle *Euonymus europaeus*

Shrubs of wet places

- Guelder-rose *Viburnum opulus*
- Woody nightshade *Solanum dulcamara* (chiefly by ponds)

Alder-buckthorn *Frangula alnus* (on the most acid soils, especially oak–hornbeam woods, though not particularly calcifuge when it occurs outside woods)

Indicators of ancient woodland

Woodland hawthorn
Spindle (also in ancient hedges)

Indicator of soils rich in phosphate (or ? nitrate)

Elder *Sambucus nigra*

Other shrubs such as juniper and buckthorn are characteristic of scrub and not of woodland. Wayfaring-tree *Viburnum lantana* sometimes occurs in wood-margins and the edges of woodland grassland.

Added in 2003 edition

Since 1980 this subject has been developed further by Dr George Peterken, and (and largely independently) by the National Vegetation Classification. This results in three systems, including the one in this book. Although their objectives and methods are not the same, the time has come to attempt a synthesis to which each shall contribute. This I have begun in Chapter 31.

Fig. 6.7 Oakwood on blown sand. In eastern England ancient oakwoods are almost confined to very acid and infertile sites. Iken Wood, Suffolk. May 1975

Fig. 6.8 Patch of oak coppice, Dorset. Going westward, ancient oakwoods, though still infrequent, are less specialized, forming a transition to the Highland Zone where oakwoods predominate. High Stoy, Hillfield. April 1980

Fig. 7.0 (a–c)

(**a**) Recording shade, using the method devised by D. E. Coombe (p. 376). A camera with with a fish-eye lens lies on its back on a cradle with two white arrows to mark north and south. Note compass for orientation, spirit-level and wedges for levelling, and disc mounted on a cane to prevent the sun from shining directly on the lens.

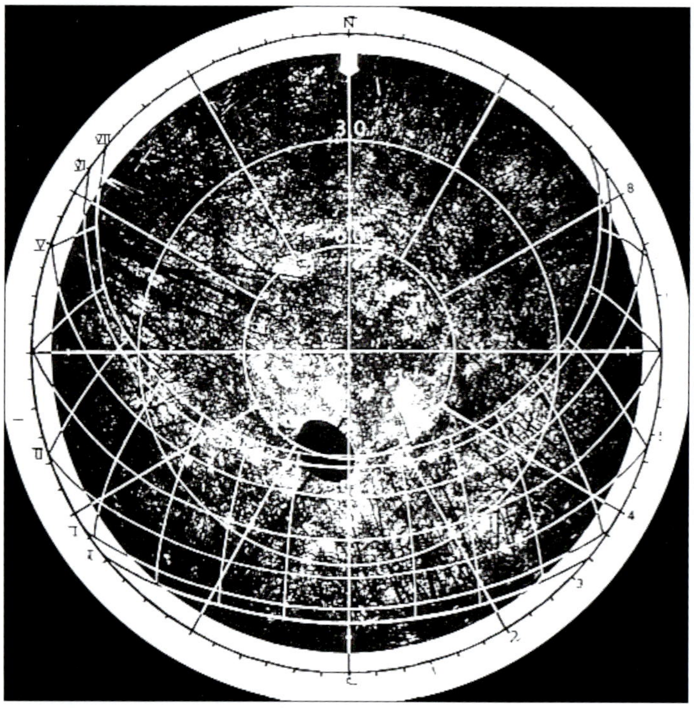

(**b**) Photograph taken with this apparatus. The seven curved solar tracks, computed for the 21st of December, January or November, February or October, March or September, April or August, May or July, and June indicate whether the sun is obscured by trees at any hour in the year. Such images are further discussed in Chapter 25. Seven-year-old underwood, Bradfield Woods.

(**c**) Patch of primrose in an otherwise mercury-dominated area, Buff Wood. Waterlogging in a small hollow has kept out mercury and allowed the more resistant primrose to flourish (p. 90). April 1978

7

Ground vegetation

The ground vegetation of an ancient wood usually consists of areas of different 'societies', as the older ecologists called them – assemblages of plants each dominated by one or a few species. They form a mosaic resembling that of the tree communities, although usually independent of them and often on a smaller scale.

Environmental factors and competition

The distribution of woodland plants can often be related to some definite external factor such as history, soil composition, drainage, soil fertility, or shade. The matter is complicated by competition. There are three reasons why a plant *X* may grow in place *A* rather than place *B*:

(1) because *X* requires some feature of *A* – shade, say, or waterlogging – which B does not afford;
(2) because *X* has not reached *B*;
(3) because X cannot compete with stronger-growing plants, *Y* and *Z*, which grow well in *B* but cannot withstand the shade or waterlogging which they encounter in *A*.

The relations between oxlip, bluebell, and dog's-mercury in the West Cambridgeshire woods such as Hayley Wood, as investigated by B. A. Abeywickrama and by M. H. Martin, are an example.[0, 120] Oxlip grows in poorly-drained areas, bluebell is intermediate, and mercury grows on better-drained sites. Mercury will not grow in oxlip or bluebell areas because it is poisoned by ferrous iron (p. 37). Oxlip will grow at least as well in mercury areas as it does in oxlip areas, provided that the mercury is damaged by picking or trampling: the rarity of oxlip in such areas results from the presence of the mercury. The latter is a highly competitive plant because it carpets the ground for most of the year and subjects oxlip and other shorter-growing plants to heavy shade. Bluebell will invade mercury areas provided that the mercury shoots are regularly picked. It is probable that the shade of the mercury operates against the bluebell seedling. Full-grown bluebells are at least as tall as mercury and can hold their own but may not be able to renew themselves from seed.[78]

A full account of ground-vegetation ecology is beyond the scope of this book. Although this is an active field of research, it is only in one or two woods such as Hayley, which is unusually simple (there are only three important variables, drainage, shade, and grazing) and unusually well studied, that anything like a full story can be told. Shade will particularly be discussed because it is an important historical factor, largely determined by woodmanship practices.

Shade and the effects of coppicing

What is meant by shade?

The measurement of light in woods is one of the most difficult technical problems in ecology. Anyone can take a few readings with a light meter, but simple measurements are generally useless. Measurements of woodland light to which a biological meaning is to be attributed have to take into account its enormous variation from place to place, from minute to minute of the day, and from month to month, and its changes in colour and direction – to which plants often respond in a quite different way from measuring instruments.

Much of the work on woodland light climates has been done by B. A. Abeywickrama, G. C. Evans, D. E. Coombe, M. C. Anderson, and D. P. Edwards[0, 5, 6, 34, 50, 53–4] in Hayley and Madingley Woods, ash–maple–hazel woods with standard oak trees and invasion by elm. This summary is adapted from their work. I shall consider an idealized wood containing areas of four shade variants. Variant B is the moderate degree of shade encountered under, for instance, a mixture of ash, maple, and hazel not recently coppiced. Variant A is dense shade as under long-uncoppiced hornbeam or lime, or locally under thick hazel or hawthorn. Variant C is the light shade of places where the underwood is sparse or consists entirely of ash. Variant D occurs in canopy gaps, glades, and other places where the woodland floor is open to the sky.

In the open, taking one day with another, about half our total light energy is ***sunlight*** coming straight from the sun, and half is ***skylight*** diffused from clouds or blue sky.

During that half of the year when the trees are bare, the interception of light by twigs and branches is more or less neutral as regards colour: the light reaching the ground is weaker than it would be in the open, but differs little in colour composition. Moreover most of the wood has much the same light climate, irrespective of local differences of shading. Most of the ground in a bare wood receives a quarter to a third of the *skylight* that it would get in the open; this ratio does not vary much with the time of year as long as the trees are leafless, nor is it likely to vary much from wood to wood. In addition, the ground receives *sunlight* varying from almost nothing in December (when the sun's rays do not often reach the woodland floor except in large glades) to not much less than skylight by April.

When leaves are on the trees, the light climate depends very much on local differences of shading. *Skylight* in glades continues at about a quarter of what it would be in the open (the proportion varies with the size of the glade). With increasing shade, skylight is severely reduced, down to a fraction of 1% under the densest shade. The leafy wood is not a neutral filter: the light inside it is green (red and blue wavelengths have been partly absorbed by tree leaves) and for this reason less useful to plants in photosynthesis. The denser the shade, the weaker and greener the light that gets through. *Sunlight* occurs regularly only in Variant D. Elsewhere, when the sun is shining, there is an irregular pattern of dappled shade as parts of its rays penetrate through small holes in the leafy canopy. In addition, in Variants B and C, once in a while (in some places perhaps only once a season) the sun may get in line with a bigger gap in the canopy and produce a big sun-fleck; for seconds or minutes the woodland floor receives full sunlight at perhaps several hundred times the intensity that it normally encounters. It is doubtful whether woodland plants can make use of these short bursts of intense light, and there is evidence that they are harmful, probably by overheating.[76, 119–20]

Figure 7.1 gives the yearly march of light intensity in the open and at sites characteristic of Variants A to D. In early spring, most parts of most woods receive roughly the same light, which increases to reach a

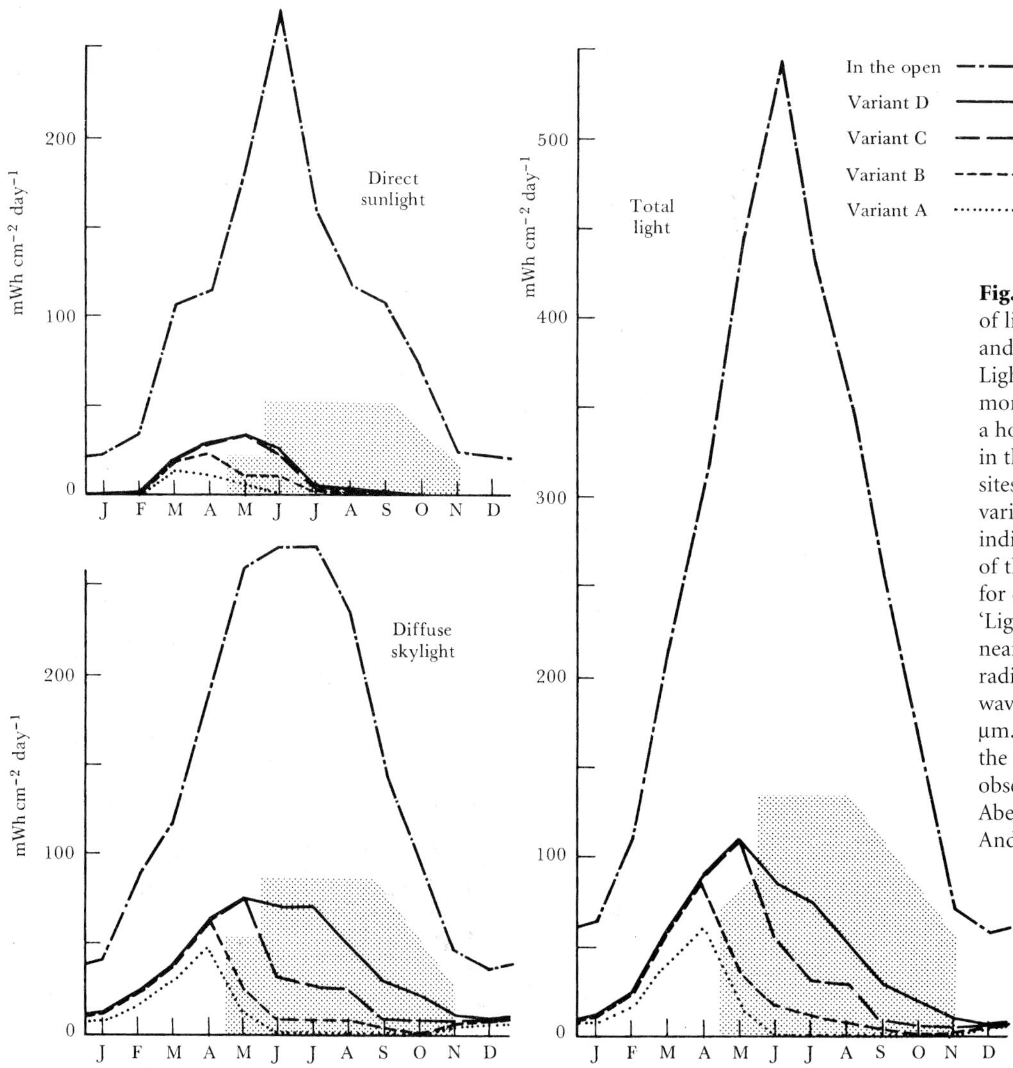

Fig. 7.1 Yearly march of light in the open and in woodland. Light energy received month by month on a horizontal surface in the open and at sites characteristic of variants A to D. Tint indicates the length of the leafy half-year for each variant. 'Light' includes near-infra-red radiation of wavelengths up to 3 µm. Estimated by the author from the observations of Abeywickrama and Anderson.

maximum just before the tree leaves open. At all but the least shaded variant, light then decreases rapidly to an extent which varies widely from one place to another. The light year is asymmetrical; the spring maximum is not balanced by an autumn maximum, because the leaves remain on the trees until within a few weeks of the winter solstice.

The light climate at any point in a wood is characterized chiefly by three variables: the intensity of shade in summer, the frequency of sun-flecks in summer, and the time at which the trees come into leaf. The last is important: a month's delay in tree-leafing means four weeks' extra growing weather for the ground vegetation at the most favourable time of year (compare Variants B and C of Fig. 7.1).

Woodland plants and shade

Continuous shade is not a normal feature of deciduous woods. Most places in a wood get about a third of full daylight in spring, and any managed wood is suddenly exposed to almost complete daylight every time it is felled or coppiced. Comparatively few woodland plants appear to require shade; plants that do not occur outside woods often need some other feature of the environment (e.g. humidity for the ferns and bryophytes of woodland ditches and ravines) rather than low light as such.

Competition applies to the shade factor. Species characteristic of Variant D or dominant in Variant C are light-demanding plants which if given the chance form a closed community and partly suppress the species of shaded variants. To do this they need light in summer and autumn, without which they perish or fail to achieve dominance. Plants found under shade, however, *tolerate* shade but for the most part do not *demand* it. If given light but no competition, as immediately after coppicing, they grow better than in shade. Some of them occasionally grow in mown grassland (pp. 51, 90), where they get light but reasonable protection from competition. It is probably competition rather than light which keeps many of these plants out of hedges adjacent to woods.

The plants that leaf and flower in spring, which are so characteristic of ancient woods, are best regarded as ***shade-evaders***. Bluebell, for instance, usually appears in late February and its leaves last three and a half months. It does most of its photosynthesis on the third of full daylight that gets through while the trees are bare. Wood-anemone and *Ranunculus ficaria* have an even shorter and earlier leafing season. In contrast, plants such as *Rubus caesius* and *Circaea lutetiana* are ***shade-resisters***; they do most of their photosynthesis on the much lower light intensity when the trees are in leaf. Some of them have the power to make up for a shortage of useful light by producing larger and thinner leaves,[172] a characteristic most extensively studied in *Impatiens parviflora*.[33, 55] Other plants, such as oxlip and primrose, are both spring- and summer-leafing and presumably combine both mechanisms. Many more or less evergreen woodland herbs, such as violets, ground-ivy, and dog's mercury, are perhaps best regarded as shade-evaders which make the best of opportunities for photosynthesis in winter as well as in spring.

Spring-leafers occur in almost all native woodland and are relatively independent of the degree of shade. Summer-leafers and plants with long leafing seasons vary from place to place. In glades and rides they are luxuriant; in moderate shade they may still be dominant but relatively weak and not flowering; in the deepest shade only a few widely-separated bracken fronds or primrose plants may stay alive. They vary from year to year: in 1977, for instance, when the ashes and elms of the West Cambridgeshire woods produced abnormally few and small leaves as a result of the previous years' droughts, plants such as meadowsweet (*Filipendula ulmaria*) and ground-ivy (*Glechoma hederacea*) were unusually vigorous, to the detriment of the bryophytes which form an even lower layer in the vegetation.

The most densely-shading kind of native woodland is pure hornbeam, lime, or beech. Any interruption to its continuity introduces more summer light and increases the ground vegetation. Even a single stool of ash, for instance, being late-leafing and lightly-shading, results in a patch of reduced shade around as well as underneath its own canopy. Standard oak trees amid densely-shading underwood usually improve the ground vegetation, whereas their presence has little effect if the underwood is lightly-shading. A single oak tree in a hornbeam-wood makes a gap in the hornbeam directly beneath it and thus admits more light to the ground in the weeks which elapse between the leafing of the hornbeam and that of the oak; even in summer, some light may penetrate obliquely through the space between the canopies of oak and hornbeam.

Coppicing

A regular feature of managed woodland is the change in the ground vegetation which follows every time the underwood is felled. This cycle, often of spectacular beauty in its effects on the spring flowers, was long familiar to our ancestors, but until recently was fading from public memory over much of England. This decline, rather than the depredations of visitors, is responsible for many complaints that primroses or violets are not what they used to be.

A coppicing effect is first recorded by Benninck, who depicts broom and other plants in his woodland scene of *c.* 1500 (Frontispiece). Ray noted in 1660 that '*Blitum album minus*' (i.e. *Chenopodium polyspermum*) was 'found in Kingston Wood [W. Cambs] after it had been new felled'.[466] Broom and *Chenopodium* still behave as coppicing plants (Fig. 26.7). When commercial coppicing was still widespread, classic papers were written by R. S. Adamson on Gamlingay Wood (W. Cambs)[1] and by E. J. Salisbury on the Hertfordshire hornbeam-woods.[136–7, 139]

In the years after felling the underwood, much of the ground vegetation increases in vigour and flowering, and light-demanding species appear which were not previously visible. As the underwood grows up again to form a new canopy, the light-demanding plants disappear, while the permanent ground vegetation returns to its previous shaded state. In the Bradfield Woods, where the underwood is particularly vigorous, the canopy is often largely closed by the fourth autumn after felling and the light-demanding plants have almost vanished by the sixth season. A newly-closed canopy, especially of hornbeam, may be more densely-shading than it was before coppicing.

Even in well-known woods such as Hayley and Bradfield, the sequence is unpredictable: adjacent coppice panels, cut in successive years, may behave quite differently. The most important factor is probably the weather in May and June after felling. A wet season such as 1968 allows seedlings, e.g. of rushes (*Juncus* spp.) and *Deschampsia caespitosa*, to become established and often to become dominant for years to come.[120] Should May and June be dry, the seedlings perish and the plant community is formed instead by the perennials already there. Other influences include small differences in the previous ground vegetation, the positions of standard trees and of bonfires, and the activities of deer and other grazing animals. Table 14.2 illustrates the range of variation.

Fig. 7.2 Oxlips (*Primula elatior*) flowering in Hayley Wood after coppicing inside a deer-proof fence. (Photograph by W. H. Palmer.)

Effects of coppicing on different classes of plants

(1) The best-known effect is the increase in spring flowers. For instance, in Hayley Wood, the number of oxlip flowers in sample plots (protected from deer) increases at least ten-fold in the second, or less often the third, year after coppicing (Figs. 7.2, 7.3). The difference is mainly in the number of inflorescences per plant, and to a lesser extent in the number of flowers in an inflorescence; the plants increase slightly in size but not in numbers. A 23-fold increase has been found in the flowering of anemones in the second year, and a 40-fold increase in violets (*Viola riviniana* and *V. reichenbachiana*).[120] Other shade-tolerant plants which respond spectacularly to coppicing include bluebells, ground-ivy, primroses (p. 90) and water-avens (*Geum rivale*). Usually the increased flowering comes from an increase in vigour rather than in numbers of plants. The flowering season may also be prolonged: at Bradfield violets, primroses, and water-avens regularly flower in November after coppicing.

Spring-flowering plants spend their first season after coppicing in accumulating reserves and in laying down flower-buds. Flowering does not increase until the second season, and generally declines in the third season, although this is sometimes the peak year.

(2) Other herbs with some shade tolerance, already present, such as meadowsweet, *Carex riparia*, and bracken, increase from the first summer; they may become dominant – unless forestalled by some other class of plant – and commonly flower after coppicing where they did not in shade.

(3) Buried seeds of light-demanding plants are stimulated into germination. For instance rushes come up in Hayley Wood in vast quantities in some years and may become dominant. Not a single plant normally grows in uncoppiced woodland, and there is no means of transporting such abundance of seed from elsewhere. The genus is noted for long-lived seed[799] and it is almost certain that coppicing awakens buried seed produced by rushes that grew up after the last coppicing 50–90 years ago. In the Bradfield Woods wood-spurge (*Euphorbia amygdaloides*), a light-demanding plant, appears in many thousands every time a moderately acidic part of the wood is felled. In the district it is a rare and strictly woodland plant, and we are forced to suppose that its heavy fruits have been lying buried since the last coppicing. A similar profusion of raspberry (*Rubus idaeus*) has suddenly arisen after the coppicing of lime in Chalkney Wood (N. Essex).

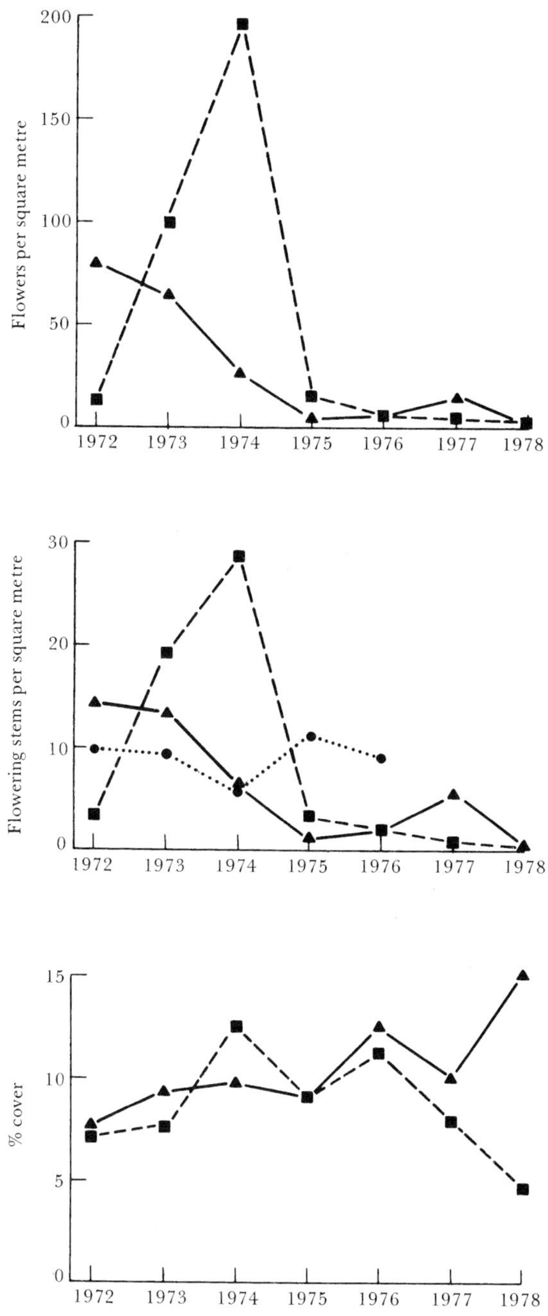

Fig. 7.3 Changes in oxlip (*Primula elatior*) populations after coppicing: in numbers of flowers, numbers of inflorescences, and size of plants (as measured by percentage of the ground covered by leaves). Hayley Wood. (▲) area coppiced in winter 1970–1; peak flowering in second spring (i.e. 1972). Mean of five plots. (■) adjacent area on similar terrain, coppiced in winter 1971–2; bigger response with peak in third spring (i.e. 1974). Mean of five plots. (●) flowering stems per square metre in another, uncoppiced, part of the wood with a higher density of oxlip plants. All records are from permanently-marked plots in which the same plants were observed year after year. All areas were fenced against deer; a correction has been made for inflorescences removed by other animals.[120]

There is little published information on the seed content of woodland soils, and it is difficult to separate this class of plants from those that follow; but there are many coppicing plants for which the absence of either a source of fresh seed or a sufficient means of dispersal strongly indicates a buried-seed origin. These include Benninck's broom and Ray's *Chenopodium polyspermum*, as well as centaury (*Centaurium erythraea*), St John's-worts (especially *Hypericum humifusum*), purple loosestrife (*Lythrum salicaria*), the mallow *Malva moschata*, the tiny sedge *Isolepis setacea*, and the grass *Holcus mollis*.

(4) Newly-coppiced areas are invaded by light-demanding plants that move round the wood, from a permanent home in rides or glades or from one coppice panel to the next, by an efficient dispersal mechanism. Examples are thistles (*Cirsium palustre*, *C. vulgare*), willowherbs (*Epilobium hirsutum*, *E. parviflorum*, *E. adenocaulon*, and *Chamaenerion angustifolium*), and probably some grasses. Most are biennials or short-lived perennials.

(5) 'Casual' species, mostly arable weeds, appear from outside the wood. *Cirsium arvense* and *Picris echioides* are regular members of this class.

(6 A few shade-tolerant or perhaps shade-demanding plants decline after felling. Dog's-mercury suffers a definite setback after coppicing.[139] In the Bradfield Woods, wild garlic (*Allium ursinum*) withers early and often loses its inflorescences in newly-cut panels, except directly under oak standard trees. *Paris quadrifolia* also reaches its greatest vigour beneath older underwood.

The environment of coppiced areas

The most obvious effect is on shade. Felling the coppice suddenly changes what had previously been areas of Variants A, B, or C into the equivalent of Variant D. At a typical site coppicing increases summer light at least twenty-fold; increases winter and spring light three- or four-fold; and in many woods extends the period of spring light by about three weeks, because the remaining shade is provided by timber trees which come into leaf later than the underwood.

Increased summer light explains the invasion by light-demanding plants and the increased flowering of some shade-tolerant evergreens (e.g. violets), summer-leafers (e.g. meadowsweet), and spring-and-summer-leafers (e.g. oxlip). More surprising is the effect on spring-leafers like bluebell and anemone, whose extra flowering may be quite disproportionate to the modest increase in light during their growing season. The balance between light and flowering is sensitive: spring-leafers do not evade the effects of shade altogether.

Adamson and Salisbury mention higher temperatures and increased evaporation of water among the lesser effects of coppicing. At Bradfield, the surface temperature of vegetation, as more recently measured by infra-red pyrometry,[119] depends chiefly on its position in the woodland structure rather than on the species of plant. In recently-coppiced areas, on a sunny day, herbs growing in the wind-sheltered gaps among the growing stools are for much of the time 6°–9°C warmer than similar plants in shade; such a rise in temperature is experienced by shaded plants only on the rare occasion of a big sun-fleck. Higher temperatures are likely to be beneficial to some species and detrimental to others.

In recently-coppiced woods both the timber trees and the ground vegetation often show more severe drought symptoms in summer than do those of the uncoppiced wood. This seems paradoxical: a wood loses moisture mainly through the transpiration of the trees, and if some of the trees are felled we might expect their share of the moisture to remain in the ground. What evidently happens is that the total transpiration of a wood is determined mainly by the energy available from light (much more of which goes into evaporating water than into photosynthesis) and is not much altered by changing the woodland structure. Much of the water saved by felling the underwood is lost by increased transpiration from the timber trees, new underwood, and ground vegetation, which as a result of the felling are more exposed to the sun's rays and to wind eddies which carry moisture away from the air around them. Drought, as well as determining whether a particular coppice panel shall be dominated by the existing shade-tolerant plants or by light-demanders, may also affect those plants which decline after coppicing, although mercury is also damaged by the trampling and disturbance of the coppicing operation.

The historical significance of coppicing

Coppicing has been a relatively constant factor for so long that much of the woodland flora now consists of species more or less dependent on it: of plants which need the extra light following coppicing to build up their resources, yet need the shaded phase of the coppice cycle to avoid competition from species of permanent clearings. Some of these are strictly woodland plants, such as *Euphorbia amygdaloides*; others, such as ragged robin (*Lychnis flos-cuculi*), have other habitats but are becoming limited to woodland by the destruction of fens and old grassland. Other plants, such as anemone (p. 90), grow in a wider range of woods under coppicing than without it. Coppicing provides some of the largest concentrations of plant species in woods, such as 101 vascular plants recorded by Mrs Ann Hart in 1.7 acres of the Bradfield Woods felled in 1970.

The decline of coppicing, after destruction of woodland and the disappearance of woodland grassland (p. 57), is the third most important of the changes impoverishing the flora of woods. It happens that one of the few plants which flourish in the absence of coppicing is dog's-mercury, which is then one of the strongest competitors. In many woods it is increased mercury shade as well as increased tree shade which reduces or eliminates the other herbs after coppicing ceases. C. D. Pigott has shown that in long-uncoppiced wood the removal of mercury shade without altering the shade of the trees, was followed by marked increase in bluebells, primroses, and other plants.[835]

The decline of coppicing does not have the finality of the other two changes. Experience in Hayley shows that even after an eighty-year lapse it is possible to recover much of the coppicing flora. It is likely that in future most coppicing will be on long rotations (p. 169). Although, because of the variability, it is difficult to get precise information on the effect of the interval between coppicings and the quality of the subsequent flora, there is no reason to doubt that a rotation of twenty or even thirty years will be adequate to maintain most of the ground vegetation.

The specification of woodland plant communities

To reduce the intricate variety of ground vegetation to summary suitable for a chapter in a historical book I shall make two simplifications: the first concerned with shade, the second with describing communities in terms of the dominant species.

Disentangling the effects of shade

In rides and glades, open to the sky all the time (Variant D), the absence of top shade is usually an overriding influence. The plant communities are not closely related to those of the body of the wood. At the other extreme, parts of woods that are heavily shaded all the time, particularly where the shade comes from the topography rather than the trees, may also have special plant communities. Woodland gorges, the north sides of rock outcrops, and grundles and gulls (broad and narrow ravines incised in the Boulder-clay of Eastern England) are of great interest, particularly for ferns and bryophytes, but since they are small in area and lack a historical dimension I shall say no more about them here.

Between these two extremes lies the vegetation of the general woodland floor, more than 95% of most woods. There is some shade nearly all the time, but the degree of shade is difficult to define. It varies from yard to yard – from under a hornbeam to under an ash – and from year to year as the trees change. Many woods happen now to be in a phase of neglect in which they do not change rapidly. In Madingley Wood, for instance, D. E. Coombe took photographs of the canopy with a 'fish-eye' lens in 1951.[54] In 1976 he and I re-located the spots and repeated the pictures. Although this appears to be a dynamic wood – it is being invaded by elm – three out of four sites showed no significant change in twenty-five years. In history, however, this is a long time to elapse without something happening; shade has normally been less stable.

I propose to treat shade, over most of its range, as a secondary ecological variable. Apart from the extremes of glades and gulls, I shall not deal in terms of separate plant communities characteristic of different degrees of shade, but of more or less shaded variants of communities determined by other factors. This has the practical advantage of reducing the communities to a manageable number and avoiding the difficulties of measuring shade at many points. It is justified by the observation that many communities can exist over a wide range of degrees of shade; they respond to changing shade by becoming more or less dense rather than by turning into a different community. In the long term, shade waxes and wanes, but the plant communities beneath it appear to be more permanent (cf. the Bradfield ordination (pp. 28–32)).

Defining plant communities in terms of the dominant species

Most shaded communities in British woods have one or a few dominant species whose behaviour largely determines the character of the vegetation. Each of these plants can be dominant on its own, though they often form mixtures or mosaics such as the oxlip–bluebell and bluebell–mercury intermediate communities of Hayley Wood; the widely-occurring mixtures of bluebells and bracken;[150] and the mixtures which occasionally form even between such ecologically dissimilar plants as bracken and mercury.

The number and abundance of other species depends partly on the structure of the dominant. Bracken and mercury, when growing strongly, are aggressive plants which tolerate few or no associates, but weak and gappy stands of these plants, near the limits of their ranges, can have many other species. Oxlip and primrose are weak dominants, growing sparsely with much bare ground between them, and are associated with many other plants. The richest plant communities in the shaded parts of woods are those which avoid extreme shade, waterlogging, or infertility, but are too ill-drained for the growth of mercury and not fertile enough for stinging-nettles. The oxlip–bluebell transitional zone in Hayley Wood (p. 37) is an example.

Woodland grassland

Long-established rides, glades, and lanes round the edges of woods often carry a great part of the flora of a wood. They may resemble one form or another of old grassland or may have communities of their own. The rides of Hayley Wood, for instance, are often a close and tussocky turf of *Carex remota*, resembling the plant community called Caricetum strigosae, described from wet woodland rides in the Île-de-France.[758]

The disappearance of woodland grassland has been mentioned as the second most important loss to the flora of woods (p. 57). Rides are at risk from becoming overgrown, from attempts to adapt them to the use of tractors, or from grading, re-seeding, or making up with gravel. Tidy-minded gamekeepers even spray rides with weedkiller to produce a 'lawn-like' appearance!

The history of woodland grassland

From the lack of medieval references to woodland rides I conclude that there were then merely temporary tracks winding among the stools (Fig. 15.7). Lanes around and between woods, however, were commonplace: surviving examples – some of them very overgrown – include the Shire Rack between the coppices of Cranborne Chase on the Wilts–Dorset border and the lanes which dissect the woods of Eversden (W. Cambs) (Fig. 10.1). Such lanes, or ***chases***, are bordered by woodbanks on both sides and are not part of the wood.

Most woodland rides are straight and are likely to be post-medieval. The oldest that I know are in Norsey Wood, which are shown on a map of 1593.[327] We may conjecture that the sixteenth-century introduction of sporting guns, replacing the medieval nets, made a straight field of fire desirable.

Rides, chases, the bracken glades shortly to be described, and a few other openings are the remnants of a long tradition of permanent clearings in woods. The ancient use of woods for grazing implies that there was something for cattle to eat other than the almost worthless leaves of shade-bearing grasses. With the formalization of wood-pasture systems the grassland came either to supplant most of the shade-bearing plants altogether, as in uncompartmented parks and Forests, or to occupy definite compartments – the launds of parks and the plains of Forests (Chapter 12).

In coppice-woods, although grazing was prohibited or severely curtailed, we find frequent references to a grassland element: small payments for *herbagium* or apologies for its absence. In Bocking Park Wood (Braintree, Essex) in 1309, for instance, the herbage of the 480 acres was worth 12*d* per annum, 'and not more because it does not grow except in a few places'.[329] At Aldham (Suffolk) the pasture in a wood in 1331 was worth nothing 'because of the shade'.[448] As late as 1794, in St Osyth (Essex) hay was made in the 'avenues' of Hartley Wood, and in 1846 £3 was spent on 'gathering Grass seeds in the woods.[283, 324]

Occasional surveys measure gaps in woods. A survey of Grovely Forest (Wilts) in 1566 details 1011 acres of copses (p. 185), of which 87 acres were 'empty' (*vacue*).[493] An Essex example is given on p. 253. Modern examples are the irregular glades in Hatfield Forest and Hayley

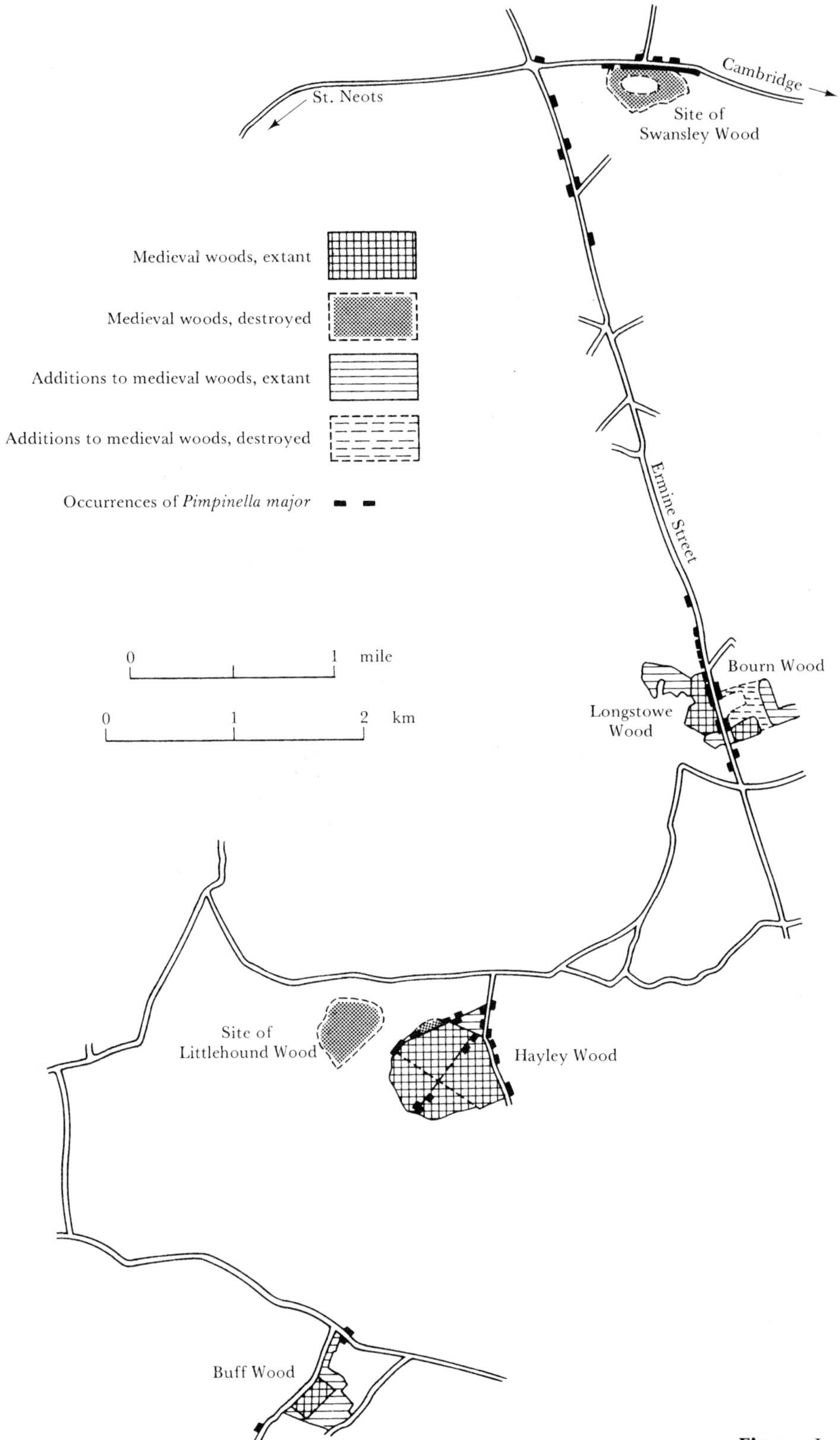

Fig. 7.4 Localities for *Pimpinella major* ('Greater Burnet-saxifrage') in part of West Cambridgeshire in relation to ancient woods. From observations by Dr D. E. Coombe and the author.

Wood, the result of the depredations of cattle and deer after coppicing.

Circumboscal plants

I create this word to describe species which grow in the vicinity of ancient woods rather than in the woods themselves. A well-documented example is *Melampyrum cristatum*, a rare plant whose British localities are in tall grass near the edges of woods or of places where woods have been, but rarely within woods.[745] Another is *Pimpinella major*, whose West Cambridgeshire localities (Fig. 7.4) are on ancient roads and tracks close to woodland. The same pattern is repeated in East Cambridgeshire and N.W. Essex; for instance, in Weston Colville this plant grows on just that stretch of roadside which once bordered Moyns Wood, last recorded on a map of 1612.[245] *P. saxifraga*, in contrast, grows on verges irrespective of the presence of woodland.

Other circumboscal plants in Eastern England include *Lathyrus sylvestris*, *Stachys officinalis*, and to some extent *Serratula tinctoria* and the cherry-tree (Chapter 24).

The chief dominant herbs of shaded woodland vegetation in Eastern England

Plants of very acid soils

Bracken, Pteridium aquilinum

This is the only woodland herb to have a well-documented history; it is called *brake* or *fern*, Medieval Latin *fugerium* or *feugera* (cf. French *fougère*).

Modern ecology

Bracken is the commonest dominant herb on the most acid well-drained soils. It is the most calcifuge of common woodland herbs: in Eastern England (Fig. 7.5) I have only once recorded it outside the pH range 3.2–4.3, and it is commonest around pH 3.7. It grows equally on soils derived from sand or silt, but avoids those with more than 20% clay.

Bracken has an extensive creeping rhizome which probably lives for hundreds of years;[810] it rarely reproduces by spores. Fronds are produced on short-shoots of the underground system. Bracken will tolerate almost any shade except the very densest lime or hornbeam, but the fronds are sparse and small in dense shade.

The plant is common outside woods and may, as in the Breckland, be independent of a previous history of woodland; its reputation as a woodland relict is hardly justified. It is well known as calcifuge and intolerant of waterlogging, but a thin skin of acid or well-drained soil or even of its own litter (p. 50, Fig. 4.12f over an unsuitable sub-soil suffices to support it. It is very sensitive to late frosts, but this affects mainly its behaviour outside woods.[907]

After felling or coppicing, bracken, if previously present, produces a full complement of fronds. A light cover of bracken on soils that are marginal for it may protect the regrowth of trees, but if well grown it is the most aggressive of coppicing plants. The tall fronds not only cast a dense shade but, when dead and heavy with rain, collapse and drag down anything growing among them. They rot slowly and build up mor humus. Vigorous bracken can kill tree seedlings and can even interfere with the regrowth of underwood, especially if this is damaged by rabbits or deer. Soils suitable for bracken therefore tend to develop permanently treeless ***bracken glades***. These glades may be very extensive in woods on light soils, e.g. Holbrook Park (p. 337); in woods with more clay they are confined to sand-lenses, as at Bradfield (p. 50).

No other herbs will coexist with a strong stand of bracken, but where it is not too dense it mingles with bluebell, anemone, *Oxalis acetosella*, or *Holcus mollis*. As pointed out long ago by T. W. Woodhead,[172] these perennials leaf and flower sufficiently early to avoid the shade of the living bracken, which does not emerge until late May. Brambles also mingle with bracken of moderate density.

Bracken is particularly associated with oakwoods and oak–hornbeam woods (Chapters 14, 17). In Eastern England it is common in chestnut and pure hornbeam woods. Limewoods, on the whole, are too ill-drained for it. It also grows in the most acidic ash and hazel woods.

Prehistory

The spores of bracken are often found in pollen deposits. As we should expect from its frost-sensitivity, it appeared late in the development of the wildwood, at the same time as alder. It increased rapidly, particularly from Neolithic times onwards.[710]

Bracken, although a native plant, owes its prominence to human activities. Even the modest clearing and burning of Mesolithic times (pp. 103–4) may have given it a foothold. During and after the Neolithic, tree-felling, woodland management, and abandoned arable increased its habitats, particularly since the light soils favoured by early farmers are also favoured by bracken. Felling, bracken, and grazing animals may have been a potent combination of agents converting wildwood to heath.

History

Bracken is a common element in place-names from Anglo-Saxon times to the present. It was a commercial product, used for litter in stables and cowsheds, and was burnt to make ash for glass-making.[762] It came mostly from non-woodland sources – even, as at Staverton (E. Suffolk),[463] winkled out of the lord's corn – but there are some records for woodland. At East Dereham (Norfolk) in 1251 the Bishop of Ely had two woods: one of 130 acres which brought in annually 30*s* from underwood (about half the usual rate), 30*s* from herbage, and 15*s* from fern; the other of 100 acres, worth only 16*s* a year in underwood and 3*s* in fern.[270]

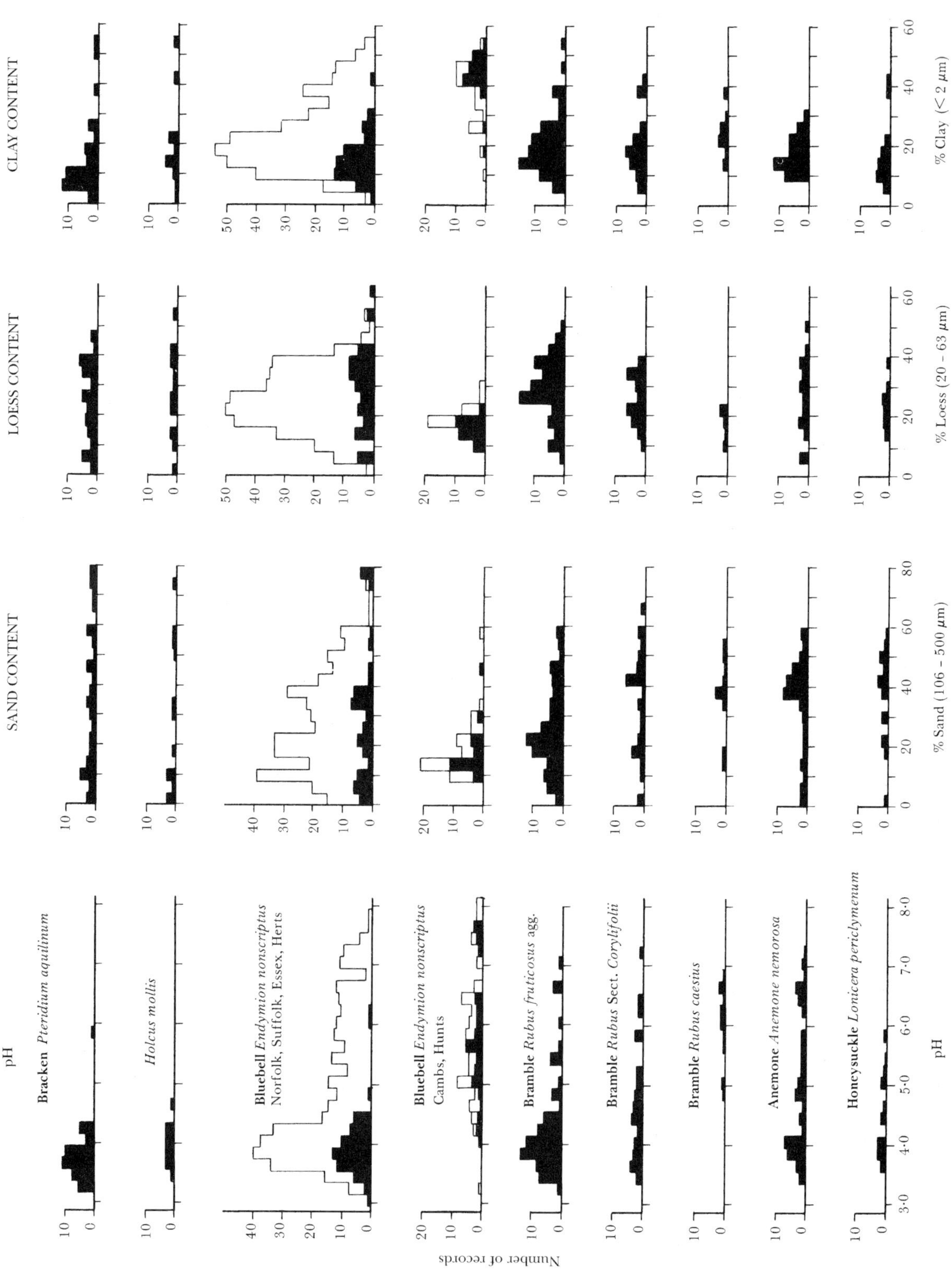
pH
SAND CONTENT
LOESS CONTENT
CLAY CONTENT
Bracken *Pteridium aquilinum*
Holcus mollis
Bluebell *Endymion nonscriptus*
Norfolk, Suffolk, Essex, Herts
Bluebell *Endymion nonscriptus*
Cambs, Hunts
Bramble *Rubus fruticosus* agg.
Bramble *Rubus* Sect. *Corylifolii*
Bramble *Rubus caesius*
Anemone *Anemone nemorosa*
Honeysuckle *Lonicera periclymenum*
Number of records
pH
% Sand (106 - 500 μm)
% Loess (20 - 63 μm)
% Clay (< 2 μm)

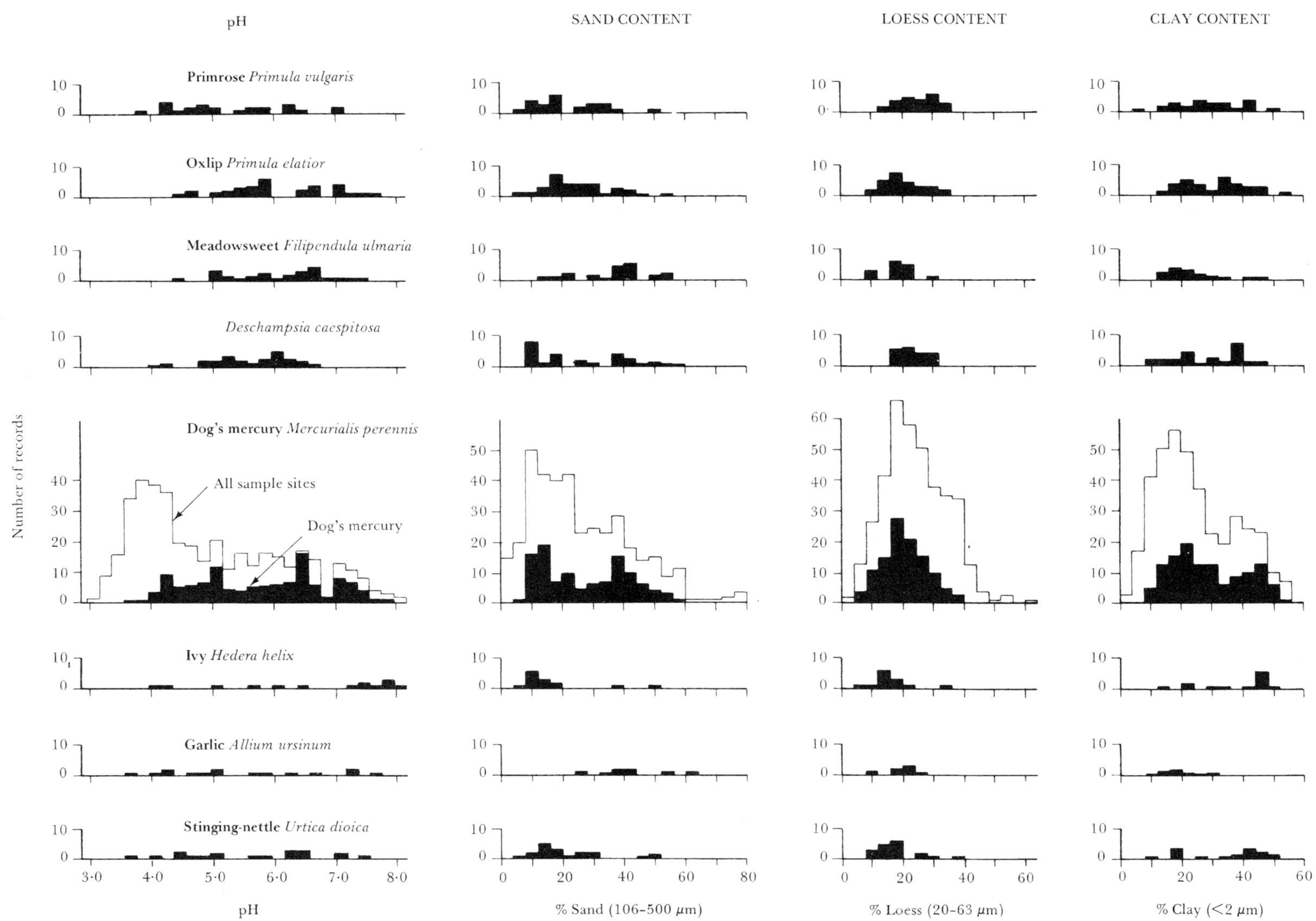

Fig. 7.5 Distribution of the commoner woodland herbs and undershrubs in relation to soil acidity and texture. The topsoil was sampled at some 400 points in ancient woods (cf. Fig. 4.7) and the tree communities and ground vegetation were noted at each point.

The left-hand column of diagrams shows how often each plant was recorded, as dominant or co-dominant, at different values of soil pH. These should be compared with the diagram (in outline, attached to the dog's-mercury diagram) giving the distribution of soil pH at all the sites sampled. (This differs slightly from the equivalent distribution diagram in Fig. 4.11, which is based on a somewhat different set of samples.) The eastern and western bluebell populations are plotted separately, each with its own comparison diagram (outline).

The other three columns of diagrams show how often each plant was recorded at different sand, silt, or clay contents.

Wood-pasture records include thirteenth-century sales from Staverton Park (p. 294). In Sherwood Forest (Notts), at some time probably in the thirteenth century, the authorities were ordered to inquire

> who may have caused waste or destruction of the heather or fern in the Forest or may have burnt them to get better pasture for his animals, because they are the chief refuge (*recettamentum*) for the Lord King's beasts . . .[214]

Another item of inquiry concerned illicit sales of heather and bracken

> which the Lord King's beasts habitually frequent and where the does habitually fawn and take shelter (*deffencionem*) with their fawns.

These records strongly suggest that bracken, then as now, was common in wood-pasture and less dense woods on light and infertile soils. Staverton Park is still dominated by bracken. At Sherwood, although most of the vast heathlands in the Forest were destroyed in the eighteenth century, the surviving wood, Birkland, still consists, as the terms of inquiry imply, of great trees without underwood and having little or no low cover apart from bracken.

The grass Holcus mollis

This creeping grass is sometimes dominant in woods on silty acid soils (Fig. 7.5) particularly under hornbeam or chestnut. It is probably tolerant of waterlogging, and is particularly extensive in South Essex woods such as Norsey (p. 335). It persists in moderately dense shade; it responds for a while to coppicing, but may then be overrun by brambles. It can sometimes spread at the expense of other vegetation.[96]

Plants mainly of acid soils but having a wider range

Bluebell, Endymion nonscriptus

Bluebell woods are one of the most glorious and distinctive types of British vegetation; no other country has them on so large a scale. The bluebell has a strongly 'Atlantic' distribution, limited to the western seaboard of Europe. In Britain it is recorded in almost every 10 km grid square that has any woodland, but this apparent ubiquity conceals a distinctive distribution pattern.

In Eastern England the bluebell is common in Cambridgeshire, west Norfolk, and N.W. Essex, and again within 10–15 miles of the Essex and Suffolk coasts: it is present in almost every ancient wood and is widely dominant. Between these two regions is a tract, from London to Norwich, in which bluebells are about a hundred-fold less common; they grow in only a few woods and in small quantities (Fig. 7.6).

The bluebell of Norfolk, Suffolk, and Essex is a calcifuge, growing mainly in pH 3.4–4.6, in sandy or silty soils with a low clay content; its requirements are almost as extreme as those of bracken (Fig. 7.5). It is typical of woods of hornbeam, chestnut, or lime and of some oakwoods. It is somewhat characteristic of ancient woods and of the sites of former woods. It withstands all degrees of shade but flowers more freely in the less-shaded woods (or under bracken in the open) and responds to coppicing.

In Cambridgeshire and Huntingdonshire bluebell behaves very differently. It grows on all the available soils, typically on heavy calcareous Boulder-clays of intermediate drainage (p. 37) ranging in pH from 5.0 to 7.7, under ash, maple, and hazel. It occurs in ancient woods and the older secondary woods. It is dominant in a well-characterized plant community overlapping with oxlip on the one hand and with mercury on the other (p. 77). It also especially prefers woodbanks. It may be abundant in any degree of shade but flowers more freely after coppicing. These bluebells behave so differently from those further east that they seem hardly to be the same plant. The possibility of a genetic difference should be followed up.

The scarcity of bluebells in parts of Eastern England does not follow any obvious soil boundaries. Although it includes the environs of London, there is no reason to suspect human depredation: bluebells are little affected by picking – thousands may be taken, but millions remain – and vast numbers survive in the public woods of S.E. Essex. A possible explanation may lie in the climate. Bluebell may be missing from the part of England remote from the Atlantic, as it is from the interior of Europe, and may reappear in the extreme east under the weaker maritime influence of the North Sea. What aspect of the Atlantic climate may be involved, and whether it is a historical influence or still active, can only be conjectured. The exceptional summers of 1975 and 1976 had no evident effect.

Brambles

Brambles form the greater part of the genus *Rubus* and are well known for their taxonomic complexity. They comprise one well-defined species, *R. caesius*, the dewberry, and several hundred microspecies most conveniently grouped in twelve sections.[630, 906] One section, *Corylifolii*, consists of hybrids between *caesius* and the other eleven sections. *R. caesius*, *Corylifolii*, and at least five of the eleven sections (*Vestiti*, *Radulae*, *Apiculati*, *Silvatici*, *Clandulosi*) are common in ancient woods; but I have little evidence of the ecology of the microspecies and am compelled to treat them all together under the aggregate name of *R. fruticosus*.

Fruticosus woodland brambles have a strong calcifuge tendency, growing chiefly on soils with pH 3.5–4.5. I have recorded them as most often dominant on soils with middle to high silt contents, middle to low clay, and middle sand; they form the typical ground vegetation of acid ashwoods and are also very common under lime,

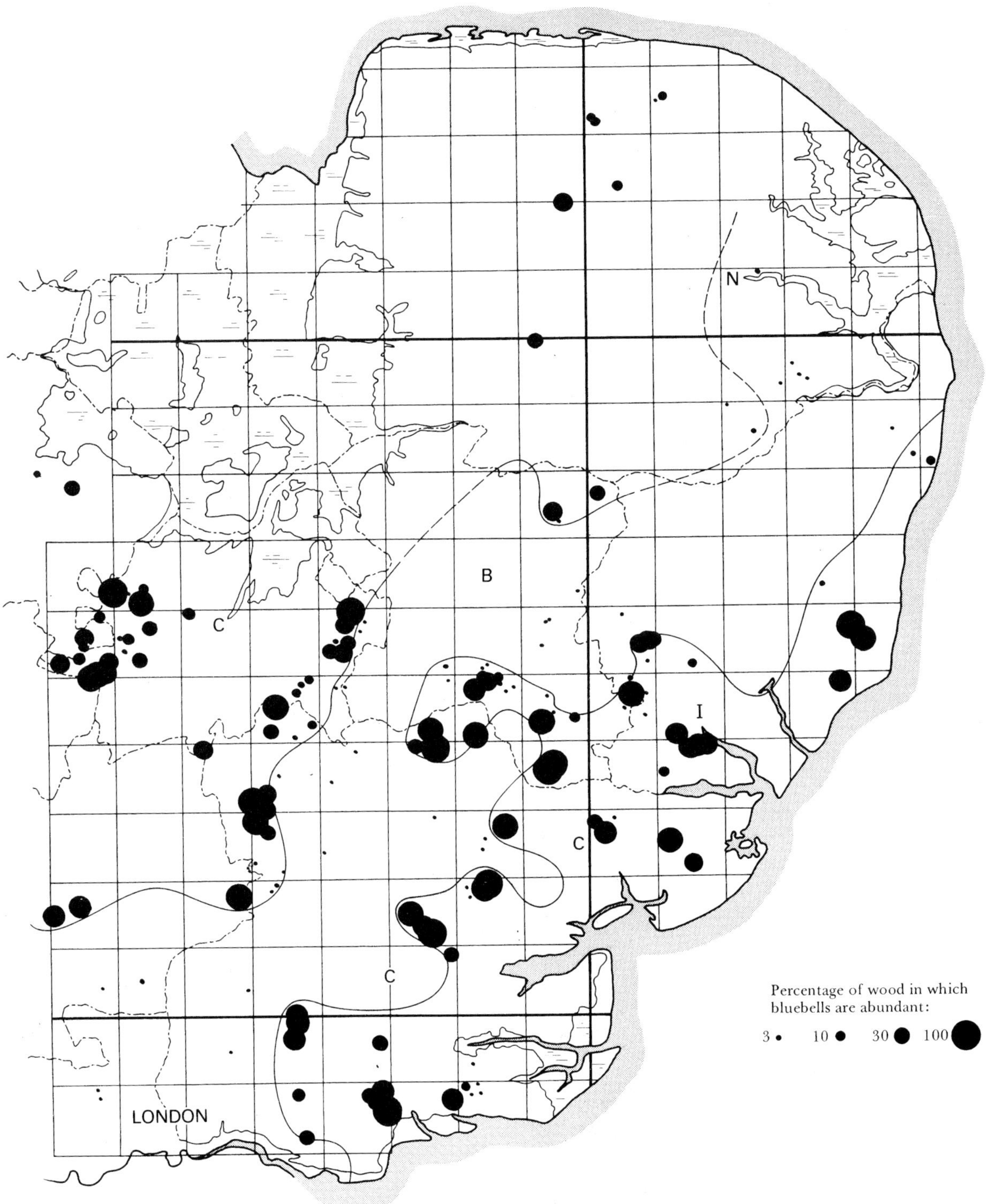

Fig. 7.6 Relative abundance of bluebell (*Endymion nonscriptus*) in ancient woods in Eastern England. The curving lines define areas within which bluebell occurs, usually in abundance, in all the ancient woods visited.

hornbeam, chestnut, and oak. They survive moderately dense shade. Some brambles will grow on almost any woodland soil, but those of less acid soils are light-demanding.

Rubus caesius is moderately calcicole (pH 5.0–6.8), chiefly on soils with moderate to high sand, low silt, and middle clay contents. *Corylifolii* brambles are intermediate in soil preferences as well as taxonomy.

Brambles are quite sensitive to waterlogging and are very responsive to light. On acid soils coppicing stimulates any brambles that may be there already. On less acid or calcareous soils where they are less shade-tolerant, it often produces a dense stand of brambles where there were none before; presumably they come from buried seed. Bramble thickets are often regarded by naturalists as a nuisance, but are a normal part of woodland vegetation and are especially useful to birds and insects. In public woods they are to be welcomed as a living fence that effectively and unobtrusively protects the fauna and flora from children and dogs. If underwood shoots are browsed, brambles may cause trouble by shading their regrowth.

Wood-anemone, Anemone nemorosa

Anemone grows in small quantities in almost any ancient wood, but distinctly prefers *either* acidity *or* waterlogging *or* regular coppicing. In permanent shade it is abundant chiefly in acid woods (pH 3.7–4.4), as in Birchanger Wood (N.W. Essex) where clonal carpets of flowering anemones beneath hornbeam and elm are a beautiful spectacle. On less acid soils it persists in shade but flowers fully only after felling. In the Bradfield Woods it is abundant on all but the most calcareous soils, though distinctly commoner on soils more acid than pH 5.5. In Hayley Wood, on heavy, moderately calcareous soils, anemone is characteristic of the most waterlogged parts of the wood, those in which oxlip is dominant; but it is not as common as in the acid woods, and responds strongly to coppicing.

Anemone is a plant of wide-ranging ecology whose abundance may be determined chiefly by the limitations of its competitors. Being low-growing with a short leafing season, it is easily out-competed and is abundant chiefly in places too acid or too waterlogged for plants such as *Mercurialis*. It responds rapidly to coppicing but is soon overtaken by stronger slower-developing coppice plants. When protected by mowing it can persist even in grassland (as on the Hayley Wood railway, p. 57).

Honeysuckle, Lonicera periclymenum

As a woody climber, honeysuckle enters into both the tree community and the ground vegetation. In the latter capacity it is less ubiquitous than when growing up trees; sometimes it carpets the ground, alone or with brambles, in moderately acid woods (pH 3.6–5.9).

Primrose, Primula vulgaris

This is a familiar plant of woodland and also of old grassland with some protection from drought. In Eastern England it is less common than in the rest of the country and is less often found outside woods. It is abundant and locally dominant in ancient woods in a belt running from Norfolk across mid-Suffolk into mid-Essex, and also in the peripheral woods of West Cambridgeshire. Outside these areas, especially in South Essex, primroses are rare – though recorded from nearly every 10-km square – and many woods have none (Fig. 7.7). They are seldom found in quantity with either bluebell or oxlip. As long ago as *c.* 1820 Rebecca Ribbans, the poetastress, noticed their absence from Cockfield in the Suffolk oxlip country, which she ascribed to a curse.[470]

Primrose grows on a wide range of soil acidity (Fig. 7.5). The soils tend to be low in sand, low to middle in silt, and medium in clay. In the West Cambridgeshire woods primroses are intermediate in the waterlogging and competition scale between bluebells and oxlips.

Primrose grows mainly under ash, lime, plateau alder, and coppicing elm; it is seldom in chestnut-woods, oak-woods or pure hornbeam-woods; sometimes it is associated with elm plants (p. 96). These indications strongly suggest that it requires more mineral nutrients than average for ancient woodland. Where primroses are rare in a wood they are often in hollows and valleys of slightly greater fertility owing to downwashing.

Primroses withstand shade, all but the densest, but are sparse and seldom flower. They respond to coppicing with great vigour. In Buff Wood a panel was felled in 1968 for the first time for over sixty years; primroses, which had been inconspicuous, began to flower in the following November and produced at least a hundred times their usual output of flowers, continuing round the year for the next eighteen months (Fig. 25.32).

There is some evidence that primroses were once more widespread; for instance, E. J. Salisbury in 1918 recorded them as scarce but typical in the oak–hornbeam woods of S.E. Hertfordshire, which is hardly so now.[137] There is no evidence that they have ever been abundant on the acid and infertile woodland soils of south and east Essex.

It is often supposed, following a suggestion of R. W. Robbins in 1915,[130] that primroses suffer from the depredations of the public and that this is why they are rare in the environs of London. It is difficult to establish how far this is true. These depredations were probably more serious in Robbins's time – when it seems to have been the practice to dig up primroses for sale – than now. Primroses are long-lived; it is hardly conceivable that picking the flowers should have an appreciable effect in comparison with the many other hazards to which they are liable, but digging up the roots could have exterminated small populations. We must remember also that coppicing was then declining;

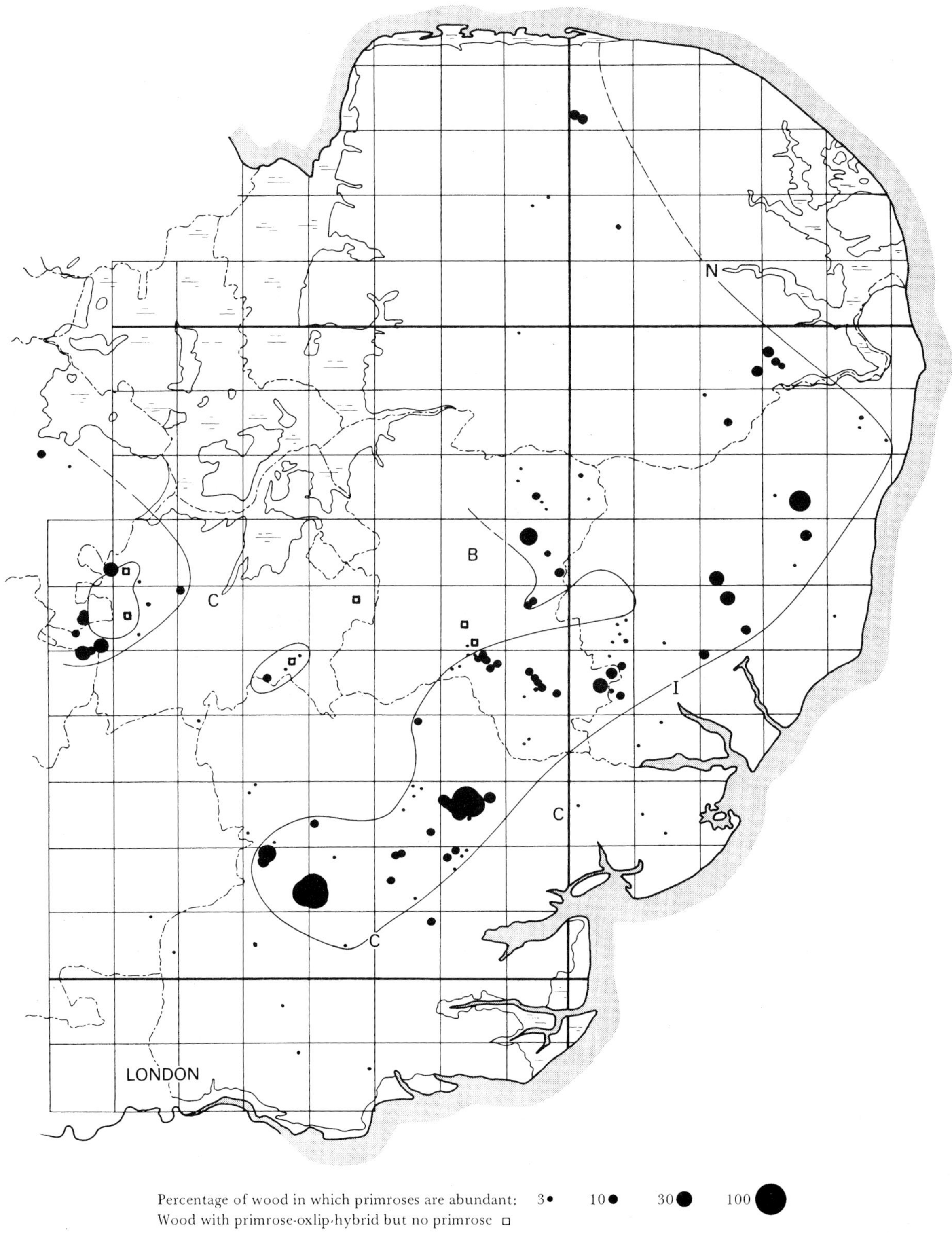

Fig. 7.7 Relative abundance of primrose (*Primula vulgaris*) in ancient woods in Eastern England. No account is taken of primroses in other habitats. The curving lines define areas within which primrose occurs in almost all ancient woods. Note the enclave of absence in West Cambridgeshire.

this would certainly have caused a general decrease in primroses, in private woods as well as those open to the public, and could easily have eliminated the sparser populations on the poorer soils.

The *Atlas of the British Flora* shows that London, Birmingham, Manchester, Liverpool, Sheffield, Leeds, and Glasgow are each surrounded by a few 10-km squares without primroses; these are significant gaps, but not the only ones in the distribution. I have been unable to find any definite correlation between the extent to which a wood is visited by the public and the abundance of primroses. Of the top twenty primrose woods in Eastern England, three are among the most public of all rural woods; one is both closed to the public and well away from roads; the others are intermediate in their degree of privacy. Primroses are rare in woods that abut on towns, but most such are in south or east Essex where primroses are rare in remote woods also.

The evidence strongly suggests that primroses were never common around London. The decline of coppicing caused them to become less numerous, to disappear from some places, and to set much less seed, so that plants dug up would not be replaced. In some of the more public woods these reduced populations were probably exterminated by visitors, but this was not the primary cause of the decline. In Epping Forest the decline of pollarding, resulting in increasingly permanent shade,[124] coincided with growing numbers of visitors. The last few primroses may have been taken by visitors, but it is unlikely that they would have survived the shade for much longer had there been no visitors; had pollarding continued the primrose population would have remained in good health and might have withstood the depredation.

Plants of poorly-drained calcareous soils

Oxlip, Primula elatior

This plant appeals to the imagination by its beauty, its combination of spectacular abundance and national rarity, and its remarkable distribution. It is closely related to cowslip (*P. veris*) and primrose. Superficially it looks more like cowslip, but it is genetically and ecologically more like primrose. The cowslip grows almost entirely outside woods and the oxlip in woods, the primrose being intermediate. The primrose hybridizes freely with both oxlip and cowslip, while the oxlip–cowslip hybrid is difficult to produce.[160]

Distribution

The oxlip is widespread in Europe. In Britain it is strictly confined to two small inland areas (Fig. 7.8), within which it grows in every ancient wood and is often very abundant and locally dominant. These two areas correspond to gaps in the distribution of primrose (Fig. 7.7), so that many woods have oxlips but no primroses.

Modern ecology

Oxlip grows on less acid and more clayey soils than primrose, but there is much overlap between their ranges; in Bull's Wood, Cockfield (W. Suffolk) one of the densest of all stands of oxlip is accompanied by the calcifuge *Oxalis acetosella* on a soil about equal in sand, silt, and clay with pH 4.6–5.4. Oxlip is sensitive to competition but very tolerant of flooding and ferrous-iron poisoning.[87] The largest populations, as in Hayley Wood, are on the worst-drained sites. In well-drained woods it is often limited to the edges of paths, being less damaged by trampling than mercury. It can persist in old meadows (p. 51) but is reluctant to invade secondary woodland (Fig. 5.2). Oxlip responds strongly to coppicing (p. 81) but probably persists in shade better than primrose.

Where oxlip and primrose both grow in a wood, the primroses are not usually intermingled but are often on sand-lenses or other acid patches (e.g. Gamlingay Wood, W. Cambs),[1] or on slopes (Waresley Wood, Hunts), or around the wood margin (Knapwell Wood, W. Cambs), or on areas of secondary woodland (Hardwick Wood, W. Cambs). Hybrids are abundant at junctions between the two species.

Oxlip is a favourite food of fallow deer, which destroy leaves and flowers with great efficiency. At Hayley Wood the population has declined at least four-fold since 1948, and ten years of fencing experiments show that this is almost entirely due to deer.[120] Drought apparently kills some plants: at Hayley 24% of the oxlips died after the drought of 1947,[0, 120] and a high proportion of those weakened by deer damage succumbed to the 1975–6 drought. But oxlip withstands regular drought on the Continent, and such deaths, followed by replacement from seed, probably form part of its normal life-cycle; they matter only where seed is not produced because of excessive grazing or shade.

History

Early references to oxlip are uncertain because of confusion between *Primula elatior* and the widespread but uncommon *P. veris* x *vulgaris*. We cannot be sure that the 'cuslyppan & oxanslyppan' of the Anglo-Saxon *Leechdoms* mean *P. veris* and *P. elatior*. Of the two 'oxlips' in Shakespeare, one is clearly a garden plant, while the other:

> I know a banke where the wilde time blowes,
> Where Oxslips and the nodding Violet grows . . .[481]

is some wild plant, presumably one more familiar than *veris* x *vulgaris*. Shakespeare seems never to have visited *P. elatior* territory, so it is unlikely that he had it in mind – unless we are to believe those critics who claim that the plays were written by Christopher Marlowe, who as a Cambridge undergraduate might have known it.

Sixteenth-century herbalists such as Turner were vaguely aware of a large pale 'petie Mulleyn' in

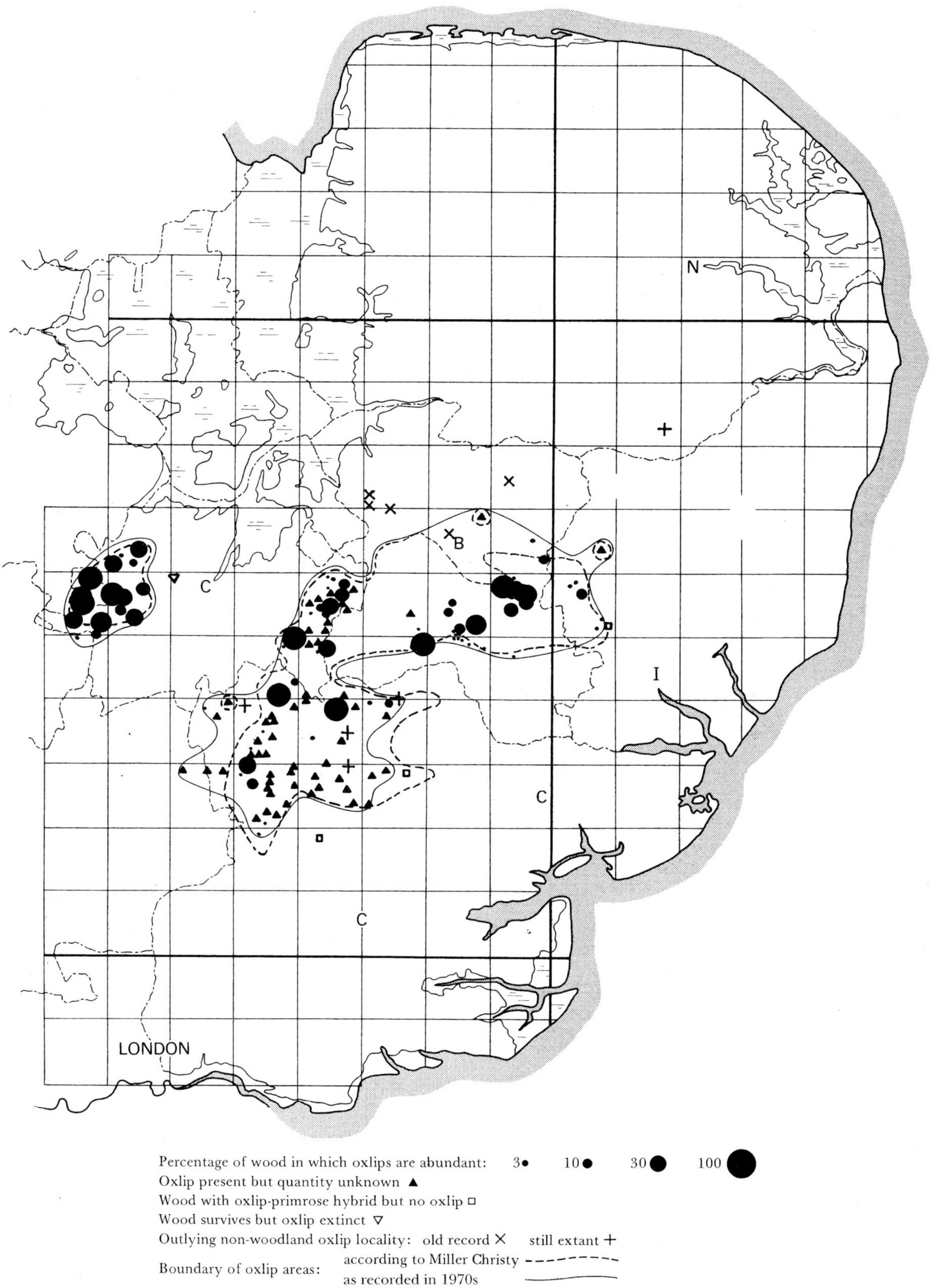

Fig. 7.8 Relative abundance of oxlip (*Primula elatior*) in ancient woods in Eastern England. Oxlips in habitats away from woods are shown separately. Continuous lines define areas within which oxlip occurs in all ancient woods. Broken lines are the boundaries of oxlip areas as known *c.* 1920.[19, 20, 69, 738] From county Floras, etc.[171, 662, 755, 918] and my own observations.

Cambridgeshire. The first certain record is that of Ray in 1660:[466] 'in Kingston and Madingley woods abundantly and elsewhere'. He correctly equated the local oxlip with the Continental plant later known as *Primula elatior*. Writers up to the mid-nineteenth century often reverted to the old confusion, although the identity of *P. elatior* was never wholly forgotten.

A distribution map of the oxlip was published by Miller Christy in 1897,[19, 20] unfortunately in a form in which few individual sites can be identified. Christy was the first to appreciate the connection between oxlip and ancient woods. He also proposed that oxlip was being hybridized out of existence by the more 'aggressive' primrose. Since Christy's time the known distribution has been slightly extended by the discovery of outlying sites. The oxlip is declining, but for reasons unconnected with the primrose: grubbing-out of woods, coniferization (as at Hempstead Wood (N.W. Essex), the largest population), increase of deer, and neglect of coppicing. Madingley Wood is the only wood from which it is known to have disappeared, but grubbing may have been responsible (p. 56). The largest remaining population is probably in Waresley Wood (Hunts) on the extreme edge of its range.

D. H. Valentine[159–60] and S. R. J. Woodell[171] have studied primrose–oxlip hybridization in the field and by experiments and have found no evidence to support Christy's theory that it should favour primrose more than oxlip. Hybrids seldom spread far from the boundary of the primrose and oxlip populations at which they arise. There is no evidence that oxlips are declining faster than primroses. In Knapwell Wood the primrose minority is now smaller than it is reported to have been in the 1930s.[92, 115] The primroses which Christy put into an Essex oxlip wood have disappeared.[171]

In the 69 oxlip woods known to me, the proportions of oxlip and primrose are as follows:

	Woods
Oxlip only, or oxlip and doubtful hybrids	36
Oxlips and hybrids, no pure primroses	5
Oxlips more than three times as many as primroses	9
Oxlips and primroses roughly equal	8
Primroses more than three times as many as oxlips	9
Primroses and hybrids, no pure oxlips	2

Had the oxlip areas been the last stronghold of a species being diluted away by hybridization, we might expect to find many more woods with only traces of an oxlip population than we do. Woods with a primrose minority are no less numerous than those with an oxlip minority, and several woods have only traces of a primrose population. The oxlip–primrose relationship is stable and symmetrical: small numbers of either species may be absorbed by the other, but there is no evidence for a progressive expansion of primrose.

Conclusions

Why one species should replace the other in two geographical areas remains a mystery. Habitat differences, although definite in individual woods, are insufficient to account in general for the strangely sharp separation of the two plants. There may not be much good oxlip habitat in the generally more acid and less clayey woods of East Suffolk and South Essex, but amid their great ecological variety there should be some niches for the plant.

It is possible that a plant so sensitive to deer-grazing may have been reduced by this agency in the past. In the two oxlip areas there were slightly fewer medieval parks than in most of Eastern England (Fig. 12.10), although the plant does survive in at least six former parks and (just) in one Forest. However, it is unlikely that fallow deer have ever been ubiquitous even in Essex. In default of some convincing explanation in present ecology or recent history, we must suppose that the distribution of oxlip and primrose was determined by their ecology in the conditions of the wildwood, and has been frozen in the state which it had reached when woods became isolated from each other more than a thousand years ago.

Meadowsweet, Filipendula ulmaria

This is a plant of all kinds of calcareous seasonally-wet places. In woods it frequents weakly calcareous soils with a wide range of compositions. Meadowsweet and oxlip have much the same degree of tolerance to waterlogging and are often alternate dominants. Meadowsweet is more light-demanding; it flowers only in light shade, and then only weakly; in heavy shade the stems are sparse. Oxlip thus predominates under heavy shade, or after coppicing following heavy shade; meadowsweet flourishes after coppicing following light shade. Meadowsweet has a much wider geographical range than oxlip. The events of 1975–6 show that it is remarkably tolerant of drought.

The grass Deschampsia caespitosa

This coarse tussocky grass is a plant of seasonally-wet places. In woods it usually grows on ill-drained clayey soils in the pH range 4.8–6.4, and thus overlaps widely with oxlip and meadowsweet. It is more light-demanding even than meadowsweet. After coppicing it comes up from seed – whether buried or transported is not known – very abundantly but only in some years. Once established it sometimes persists indefinitely under light shade.

Although not an appetizing grass – it tastes like a bundle of hacksaw blades – it can be eaten by deer, and was probably the chief component of the *herbagium* of woods. In Hatfield Forest in 1612 the commoners were said to enter the enclosed coppices for the purpose of

> reaping the Grass & carrying it away in Baggs . . . a great hindrance to them in neglect of Business of greater Weight . . . Except it be a poor Body that hath nothing else to do . . . and he perhaps may lye in a coppice reaping grass a whole day together.[276]

In *c.*1630 'one Thomas Clark a wandering fellowe' was 'Imployed to cutt grasse in the coppices' at 1*d* a bundle.[289] *Deschampsia* is the only grass likely to have grown in the coppices in sufficient quantity. Even now – despite the decline of coppicing – it is the second most abundant woodland herb in the Forest.

Plants of better-drained calcareous soils

Dog's-mercury, Mercurialis perennis

This is a most important plant in a negative way; it determines where other species will not grow. It is chiefly abundant in soils of pH 6.0 and above, though quite common down to pH 4.2, and I have even found it in pH 3.7. It favours soils low in silt and high to moderate in clay; the sand content is immaterial. In the Calcareous Province it is abundant in almost every ancient wood; in the Acid Province it is more local, often only in hollows and valleys or on woodbanks.

Mercury is very sensitive to waterlogging (p. 37) but tolerant of shade. In moderate shade it forms a continuous carpet of foliage which lasts longer than the growing seasons of most other plants. The double shade of trees and mercury is largely responsible for the poor floras of well-drained calcareous woods; it even interferes seriously with the regeneration of ash.[161] Mercury spreads underground rhizomes and forms extensive clonal patches, all the stems of which are of the same sex and often share some genetic peculiarity of foliage. Clones usually occupy definite territories without intermingling. Their history and extent would form an interesting long-term study.

Mercury is damaged by coppicing (p. 81). Although present since prehistoric times (Table 8.1) and associated with ancicnt woodland (Ch. 5), its extreme abundance and the influence which it exerts on woodland ecology are probably the result of declining management.

Ivy, Hedera helix

Ivy, as well as being a woody climber, carpets the ground in all kinds of secondary woodland,[16] of which it is highly characteristic. The earliest record of it in a hedge is the ivy-tod (*ifihtan stoc*) in the twelfth-century poem *The Owl and the Nightingale*.

Ivy grew in the wildwood, but in surviving ancient woodland is remarkably local; where it does occur it is chiefly on calcareous soils near the edges of woods, along rides, in or near an addition to the wood, or in a wood with a history of replanting (p. 283). A typical distribution in a wood of complex history is given in Fig. 16.8b.

Ivy has profited from human activities, despite men's hands being against it because of the superstition that it strangles the tree it grows up. It gets into secondary woods, possibly associated with a hawthorn succession, and persists for centuries, but has little power of spreading into existing woodland. It was collected for fodder from Neolithic times[751] to the sixteenth century (p. 174).

Plants of wet places in general

Wild garlic, Allium ursinum

This is a local plant in Eastern England and grows in similar sites to those of alder (Chapter 18): in valley bottoms, around springs, and rarely on plateau sites. (The largest plateau alder-wood, in the Bradfield Woods, also has the largest stand of garlic.) Garlic frequents somewhat sandy soils of almost any pH (Fig. 7.5). In most sites there is some evidence of moving water in the form of springs or flushes. Seasonal waterlogging will not suffice: its few Boulder-clay localities (e.g. in Hardwick and Eversden Woods, W. Cambs) are not particularly wet, and at Bradfield it is often mixed with *Mercurialis*.

Although it is not always with alder, garlic is often associated with other plants of springs, such as giant horsetail (*Equisetum telmateja*) and golden saxifrage (*Chrysosplenium* spp.).

Garlic often grows in great abundance; its leaves (a welcome addition to peanut-butter sandwiches) cover the ground and give the impression that it is a strong dominant. But it has curiously little effect on the associated flora, possibly because the cover lasts only a short time. At Bradfield, at the end of May, its leaves deliquesce and after a few stinking days have gone, leaving the fruiting stems in an apparently normal community of *Filipendula* and *Geum rivale*.

In other parts of the country it behaves differently. At Brackenbury Ditches, near Wotton-under-Edge (Glos), for instance, it grows under ash and wych-elm on dry limestone scree and even reaches the top of the ramparts of an overgrown hill-fort. In Western England it is said to be less tolerant of shade.[901]

Big sedges, Carex pendula, riparia, acutiformis, pseudocyperus

These sedges are characteristic of wet hollows in woods and of the wettest parts of plateaux. They are highly competitive, forming tall dense stands which once established resist drought. *C. riparia* and *acutiformis* form a permanent community in depressions in Boulder-clay woods.[120] *C. pendula* is sensitive to shade and waxes and wanes with the coppice cycle; it often overruns a wood during an attempt at coniferization. *C. pseudocyperus* is a plant of woodland ponds, and probably survives between coppicings as buried seed.

Phosphate plants

The stinging-nettle (*Urtica dioica*) is one of a group of plants that indicate unusual fertility. As C. D. Pigott and K. Taylor showed,[109] it specifically requires phosphate, and its roots are inefficient at getting it. Soils that have enough phosphate to support nettles rarely remain as woodland. The presence of stinging-nettles in ancient woods therefore indicates an accumulation of phosphate.

Phosphate may accumulate from geological causes or bird roosts, but the most common cause is from human activities. Phosphate from the countryside as a whole is collected into bones, ashes, and household rubbish and goes to feed nettles in gardens and churchyards, provided the soil is not too acid it stays there for centuries, much of it being taken up by the nettles and recycled each year. Among many examples, now woodland, are the deserted medieval manors of Overhall in Boxworth (Fig. 5.1)[356] and Wratworth (now Cobb's Wood) in Wimpole,[869] West Cambs, both of them forgotten and wooded-over by the seventeenth century, and the deserted village of Little Gidding (Hunts), of whose existence Nicholas Ferrar the ascetic, who lived on the spot in the 1640s, seems to have been unaware;[784] all of these are marked by extensive man-high nettles, accompanied by goosegrass (*Galium aparine*) and elderberry. Even the Romano-British villages on the Grovely Ridge near Salisbury, where overgrown by woodland, are marked by dense nettles and other phosphate plants, living on the debris of an occupation that ended 1600 years ago.

On acid soils phosphate is not so persistent, but plants such as foxglove (*Digitalis purpurea*) and red campion (*Silene dioica*) may mark areas of enhanced fertility.

Elm plants

The vegetation under elm, particularly invasive elm (Chapter 16), is often different from that under other trees adjacent. Nettles, red campion, and goosegrass are frequently present, and there are more specific elm plants such as the grass *Poa trivialis* and ground-ivy (*Glechoma hederacea*). These may be dominant, often mixed with sparse bluebells or mercury. The moss *Eurhynchium swartzii* is also abundant under elm. The elm plants are most striking when elm is invading into acid woodland, as at Galley Wood (S.W. Essex); at the edge of the elms there is an abrupt change to a type of vegetation in which elm plants are totally lacking.

Elm and alder (Chapter 18) are the only trees that are accompanied by specific suites of herbs. Elms tend to invade on the more fertile soils (Chapter 16), but it is possible that they change the local environment in some way which favours these plants. It may be that elms, more than other trees, extract mineral nutrients from the subsoil and add them to the topsoil in drips or leaf-litter, fertilizing and deacidifying the soil.

Fig. 8.0 Bog oaks, Wicken Fen. The massive, columnar, unbranched trunks are very unlike English oaks of the historic period – but they grew in a peculiar environment. Bog trees, the last tangible remains of wildwood, are embedded in peat in many parts of England and Scotland.

8

The prehistory of woodland

This chapter recounts the development of woodland in Britain, as ascertained from pollen analysis, stratigraphy, and archaeology, up to the Anglo-Saxon period, for which written evidence first becomes important. From the nature of the evidence it is, as yet, the history of the countryside in general rather than of particular woods; most prehistoric deposits have been described from sites that have long ceased to be woodland and are not readily comparable with surviving woods. I summarize here an extensive and well-known field of study; the full story is told in the textbooks of Godwin,[710] West,[912] and Pennington.[824]

[The original book, written when radiocarbon dates were still not fully calibrated, expressed prehistoric dates in 'radiocarbon years'. Here they are converted into an approximation to true years B.C.]

The development of the wildwood

All trace of the Tertiary forests of Britain, which were not unlike those now in the S.E. United States, was swept away by a succession of cold periods, loosely called ***glaciations***, in the last million years. The history of British woodland is confined to the warm period which we now enjoy, called the ***post-glacial*** (the ***Flandrian*** by those who remember learned names). It begins at the end of the last (***Weichselian***) glaciation, roughly 12,000 B.C., when the climate once again became suitable for the growth of trees. The Late Weichselian and Flandrian are customarily divided into nine periods or 'zones'. The first seven zones (I–VIIa) cover the end of the Palaeolithic and the Mesolithic periods of human prehistory and thus precede agriculture. Zones VIIb and VIII involve civilization as we know it and are described later.

Zones I–III (Late-Glacial) [12,000–10,000 B.C.]

At the end of the Weichselian Britain gradually ceased to be an arctic land. Plants could easily re-enter the British Isles since at this time, and for long after, land extended across the English Channel and Irish Sea; of course there was no agricultural land to impede colonization.

The first trees to colonize the tundra were birch, aspen, and probably sallow. These spread throughout the country. Pine probably invaded Kent and Hampshire. The trees sometimes formed continuous woodland; more typically they grew as groves (the books misleadingly call them 'copses') in favoured spots amid the tundra. The one or more temporary returns of a cold climate did not interrupt the recolonization.

Zone IV (Pre-Boreal) [10,000–8700 B.C.]

The climate rapidly became warmer and woods became continuous over almost the whole of Britain except at high altitudes. Birch was generally the commonest tree. Pine was widespread but abundant only in the south. Hazel became remarkably abundant in the north-west. There are also records of aspen and alder and a few probable records of lime.

Zone V (Early Boreal) [8700–8000 B.C.]

Hazel increased further in abundance and extended southwards in England and Ireland. Pine increased northwards. Both changes were at the expense of birch which remained, however, generally common. The Highland Zone was thus predominantly a mixture of hazel and birch and the Lowland Zone of pine and birch.

This period yields the first definite records of oak and elm, which were rare but widespread. Lime continued to be rare.

Zone VI (Mid and Late Boreal) [8000–6200 B.C.]

This was particularly the age of hazel, whose pollen was extremely abundant almost throughout the British Isles. Pine became common in Scotland, Ireland, and Wales as well as England. Oak increased in England, Wales, and Ireland but remained rare in Scotland. Elm increased everywhere, especially in Ireland. Lime became common in the southern half of England. Alder shows a modest increase throughout Britain but was still uncommon even in the vicinity of places where deposits were forming. Birch declined and became uncommon in much of England and Ireland.

At this time we find the first definite records of ash (very widespread but rare), holly (widespread, abundant in Ireland, Wales, and W. England), beech (only in S. England), and possibly hornbeam.

Changes at the beginning of Zone VIIa [*6200* B.C.]

The beginning of the Atlantic Period is characterized by a rapid increase in alder pollen throughout Britain; in many deposits it became the commonest pollen type. Lime became a very common tree in England (except the extreme north) and Wales, but never reached Ireland and doubtfully Scotland. There was a modest increase in oak. Pine declined considerably except in the Scottish Highlands and parts of Ireland. There were moderate decreases of hazel and birch. Elm was almost unaltered.

Interpretation

The warming of the climate set off the successive return of species with different tolerances of cold and different powers of colonization. At first the wildwood consisted of a few relatively arctic tree species; later it became more complex as less tolerant trees arrived. The newcomers did not wholly displace the trees already present; even birch, the most arctic and least shade-tolerant tree, remained in Zone VIIa.

The various trees did not, in general, roll up from the south in successive waves of massive invasion. Each crept in in small numbers and became widespread but rare long before it increased to its full abundance. Both the date of a tree's first known presence and the date at which it achieved full abundance are, to some extent, correlated with its 'arcticity' as measured by its present northern limit in Europe (Fig. 8.1). In general the lag between the two dates was longer for the later arrivals such as ash and beech which had to displace existing trees and not merely to occupy vacant ground. The details of invasion are not always easy to reconcile with the trees' present ecological behaviour. Why should hazel, which is only a moderately arctic species and does not readily form secondary woodland, have been so prominent at such an early date? Why should pine, much more arctic and more efficiently dispersed, have arrived no earlier than hazel and have expanded somewhat more slowly? Why should alder, nowadays easily dispersed, have waited so long to become abundant?

The climatic changes were evidently more than a mere increase of mean annual temperature. Rainfall undoubtedly changed, and there may have been more subtle changes in summer and winter temperatures independently, in evaporation rates, and in frost (particularly important for hazel). Experience of recent extreme seasons (Chapter 20) suggests that one or a few exceptional years, of which we can hardly now expect to find any direct record, may have encouraged particular species more effectively than many decades of average weather. It is also possible that prehistoric trees may have had a different range of genetic make-up from that selection of the same species which survives today, or that they may have had to wait for the arrival of their mycorrhizal fungi.

The Boreal Period is supposed to have been at least as warm as the present climate and comparatively dry. In the Atlantic Period the climate suddenly became wetter, as shown by the growth of peat-bogs and the rising level of some lakes. This change is usually regarded as the cause of the sudden increase in alder, a tree of sites liable to periodic flooding and seepage. Such an explanation is hardly adequate for so universal an increase in a country so diverse in rainfall and topography as Britain. If East Anglia was wet enough in the Atlantic for extensive alder-woods, then Wales ought to have been wet enough in the Boreal. A rising water-table would have increased the width of the alder fringes round some lakes and bogs, but around others – depending on the shape of the basin – the fringes would have been unaltered or might even have shrunk. The ecology of alder is complex (Chapter 18) and it is difficult to explain all aspects of its increase by a simple

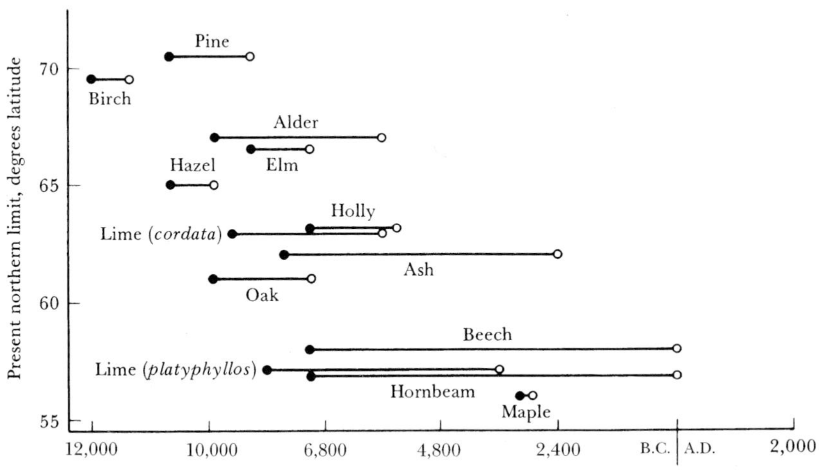

Fig. 8.1 Correlation between the present northern limits of trees in N.W. Europe[750] and the dates at which they colonized Britain in the post-glacial.[710] (●) date at which pollen is first recorded in sufficient quantity to indicate local presence of tree. (○) date at which tree first became abundant over the whole of its range.

Northern limits take no account of isolated occurrences or artificial introductions.

hypothesis, still less to include in the explanation the parallel rise of lime.

The fully-developed wildwood: Zone VIIa (Atlantic) [6200–3800 B.C.]

As far as we know this was a long period of relatively stable climate. Human activities were inconsiderable compared with what was to come later. At the end of the Boreal Period a rise in sea-level had cut off first Ireland and then Great Britain, so that few if any more species could enter these islands. Circumstances were therefore suitable, as they have never been since, for plants that had already got here to produce a series of ***climax*** plant communities (pp. 6–7) by prolonged competition and succession.

Regional and local variation

A picture of the plant communities at the end of this golden age has been compiled by Dr John Birks and his colleagues.[12] In 145 pollen diagrams they noted the proportions of the principal tree pollens at a time just before the decline in elm which ends the Atlantic Period. Their sites cover most of the British Isles, although Lowland England (other than East Anglia), extreme N.E. Scotland, and the islands are poorly represented.

The figures were examined by principal-component ordination (p. 22). The first axis of variation selected by the computer program differentiated the pine and birch woods of the Scottish Highlands from all less arctic communities. The second most important axis distinguished mid Ireland, where elm and hazel were dominant, from the rest of the British Isles. The third axis differentiated the woods of Lowland England, with their abundant lime, from the others. The fourth and fifth axes appear to be more concerned with local than with regional variation.

Combining this analysis with what is known of the pollen productivity of different trees (see later), we conclude that the fully-developed wildwood contained at least the following plant communities:

(1) Pinewoods in the central Scottish Highlands and on certain mountains in Ireland. Pine had retreated from the rest of Britain but survived locally in the Lake District and the Fens.
(2) Birchwoods in the Scottish Highlands, on other Irish mountains, and locally in southern Scotland, the Lake District, Wales, and S.W. England. Small amounts of birch still grew throughout the country.
(3) Woods of hazel and elm, predominating in most of Ireland and locally in Wales and S.W. England.
(4) Woods of oak and hazel, predominating in W. Ireland and in the rest of the Highland Zone of Great Britain. A variant in northern England included ash.
(5) Woods in which lime was the commonest tree, pre-dominating throughout Lowland England – as far as the evidence goes – and north into Lancashire. The second commonest tree varied irregularly; it could be oak, hazel, or ash.
(6) Woods of alder, occurring throughout Britain but rare in the Scottish Highlands, W. Ireland, and S.W. England. They presumably fringed lakes and peat- basins.

The natural successions of the Atlantic Period had thus produced, not the uniform 'mixed oak forest' once supposed to have been the natural vegetation of almost the whole of Britain, but a great diversity of regional and probably of local plant communities. All these, unlike the tree communities of the earlier ages of instability, are immediately familiar to us as the wildwood equivalents of existing types of woodland. Some Scottish pinewoods and birchwoods have been proved by pollen analysis to be derived from their Atlantic predecessors.[11] The continuity of the other types, though seldom so directly proven, can hardly be doubted. Lime-woods, although now greatly reduced and disjunct, still have the same broad geographical distribution as 5,000 years ago. Oakwoods, then as now, were predominantly the woodland type of the Highland Zone. Hazel-woods, now so peculiar a feature of Britain that many plant-geographers have refused to believe that they are natural, were equally prominent in the Mesolithic.

The story is still incomplete. We do not know whether the hazel–elm wildwood of Ireland or the oak–hazel wildwood of northern England consisted of mixtures of the two trees or of a patchwork of the two growing separately. Lack of suitable deposits in much of Lowland England deprives us of knowledge of the origins of hornbeam-woods, maple-woods, beechwoods, and many others.

The wildwood of Eastern England

For this region I shall try to go beyond the pollen counts to reconstruct in more detail the tree communities that produced the pollen. The late Atlantic Period is represented in twenty-six published pollen diagrams; for further analysis I have selected, where possible, the mean pollen counts for the few centuries immediately before the Elm Decline.

As conventionally plotted (Fig. 8.2) these indicate a 'mixed oak forest' of dry-land trees with variable amounts of hazel (which by pollen-analytical tradition is deemed not to be a tree). Alder varies from a few per cent of the pollen at Hampstead to more than double the total of the dry-land trees in east Norfolk; these differences are not systematic and presumably reflect merely the widths of the alder fringes to different peat-basins.

In Denmark, S. P. Andersen has shown that pollen counts should be multiplied by the following coefficients

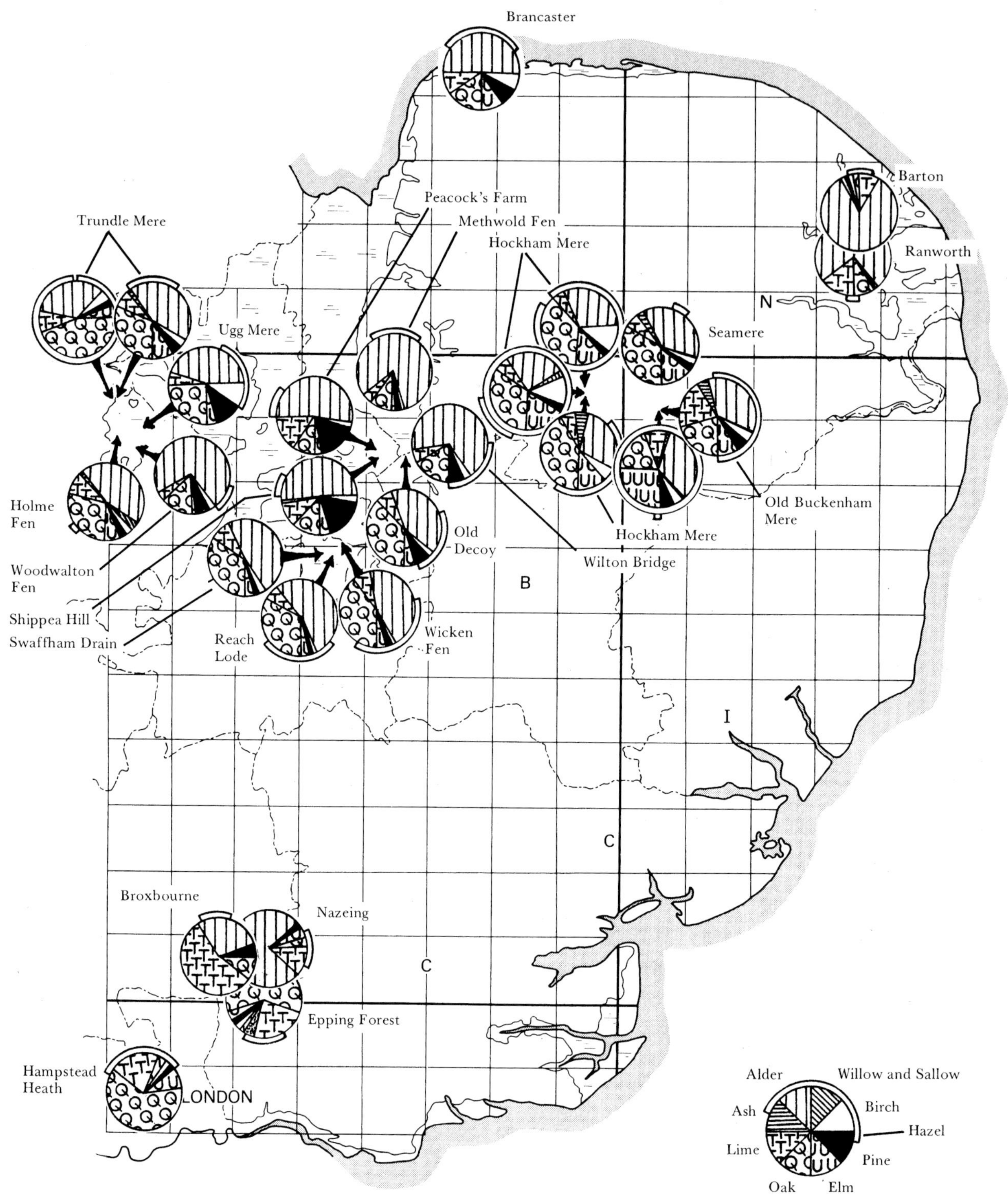
Brancaster
Barton
Ranworth
Peacock's Farm
Methwold Fen
Hockham Mere
Trundle Mere
Ugg Mere
Seamere
N
Holme Fen
Woodwalton Fen
Shippea Hill
Swaffham Drain
Reach Lode
Old Decoy
Wicken Fen
B
Wilton Bridge
Hockham Mere
Old Buckenham Mere
I
C
Broxbourne
Nazeing
C
Epping Forest
Hampstead Heath
LONDON
Alder
Willow and Sallow
Birch
Ash
Hazel
Lime
Pine
Oak
Elm

to compensate for differences in the amounts of pollen produced by different trees:[4]

Pine, oak, birch, alder (copious producers)	x 1
Hornbeam	x $1\frac{1}{3}$
Elm	x 2
Beech	x 4
Lime, ash, maple (poor producers)	x 8

The adjustment of pollen counts for this and other factors is a technique in which further advances are shortly to be expected.[15] Andersen's coefficients are not unreasonable for England and I shall use them until better figures become available. Unfortunately he gives no coefficient for hazel. Casual observation suggests that hazel is very productive, probably comparable to oak, provided it is not shaded; it seems reasonable to give it a coefficient of x 1 in estimating its contribution to the wildwood canopy.

In order to reconstruct the general wildwood composition, uncomplicated by the special tree communities of the fringes of peat-basins, I shall omit from the calculation alder and the small amount of *Salix* pollen sometimes found with it. This is an imperfect discrimination between dry-land and wet-land trees but is the best we can do at present.

The contribution of each tree to the wildwood is calculated by multiplying its pollen count by its productivity coefficient and expressing the result as a percentage of the total of tree pollens (including hazel but not alder or *Salix*) so multiplied:

$$\text{Weighted pollen percentage for species } S = 100 \times \frac{n_s P_s}{\Sigma n P}$$

where n is the pollen count for any species and P is the coefficient for that species.

The dry-land wildwood composition, thus estimated for each of the twenty-six profiles, is plotted in Fig. 8.3. The trees, in decreasing order of abundance, are:

(1) Lime, the commonest tree at twenty-two sites, overtaken by hazel at the other four.
(2) Oak, never the commonest tree (although at Hockham and Seamere the excess of lime is slight and could be reversed by a revision of the productivity coefficients) but the second commonest tree at half the sites and the third commonest at one site in three.
(3) Hazel, the commonest species at four sites, the second commonest at 7–8 and the third commonest at 9–10 sites.
(4) Elm, typically the third or fourth commonest tree.
(5) Pine, rare except in the Fens, where it is sometimes in second place.
(6) Ash, chiefly prominent in Norfolk, where it is occasionally in second place.
(7) Birch, consistently present in fifth or sixth place.
(8) Beech, in third place in Epping Forest, otherwise rare (though it had reached Norfolk).
(9) Hornbeam, always rare.

Despite the imperfections of the calculation, and especially the guesswork that has to be applied to hazel, it is clear that the general predominance of lime overlay much local variation (e.g. between Hockham and Old Buckenham) similar to the mosaic of tree communities that still exists in ancient woods. We can see the wildwood beginnings of the existing limewoods, hazel-woods, ashwoods, alder-woods (whether valley or plateau we cannot tell), and perhaps some elmwoods. Oak, then as now, was present in all types of woodland though seldom the most numerous tree.

A close comparison with existing ancient woodlands is difficult because these are mainly on upland sites and represent a different sample of the wildwood from that collected by peat-basins. I shall later produce evidence that not merely alder but to some extent lime (p. 310) and hazel (p. 214) may be involved in the zonation at the edges of peat deposits. Compared with the figures just discussed, surviving ancient woods have a vastly smaller proportion of lime; a much greater proportion of hornbeam; rather more oak, though much of this is a very recent increase (p. 148); considerably more ash;

Fig. 8.2 Tree pollen composition of the Atlantic wildwood at twenty-six sites in Eastern England at, or as near as possible to, a date just before the Elm Decline. The proportions of the pollen species are shown without any adjustment for productivity. Hazel is deemed not to be a tree: its pollen proportion is represented by an outer ring.

Norfolk: Barton,[768] Brancaster,[712] Hockham,[713, 878] Methwold Fen,[705] Old Buckenham,[709] Old Decoy,[705] Ranworth,[768] Seamere,[878] Wilton Bridge.[705]

Cambridgeshire: Peacock's Farm,[705] Reach Lode,[705] Shippea Hill,[633] Swaffham Drain,[705] Wicken Fen.[705]

Huntingdonshire: Holme Fen,[714] Trundle Mere,[705] Ugg Mere,[705] Woodwalton Fen.[705]

Essex: Epping Forest,[8] Nazein.[603]

Hertfordshire: Broxbourne.[905]

Middlesex: Hampstead Heath.[701]

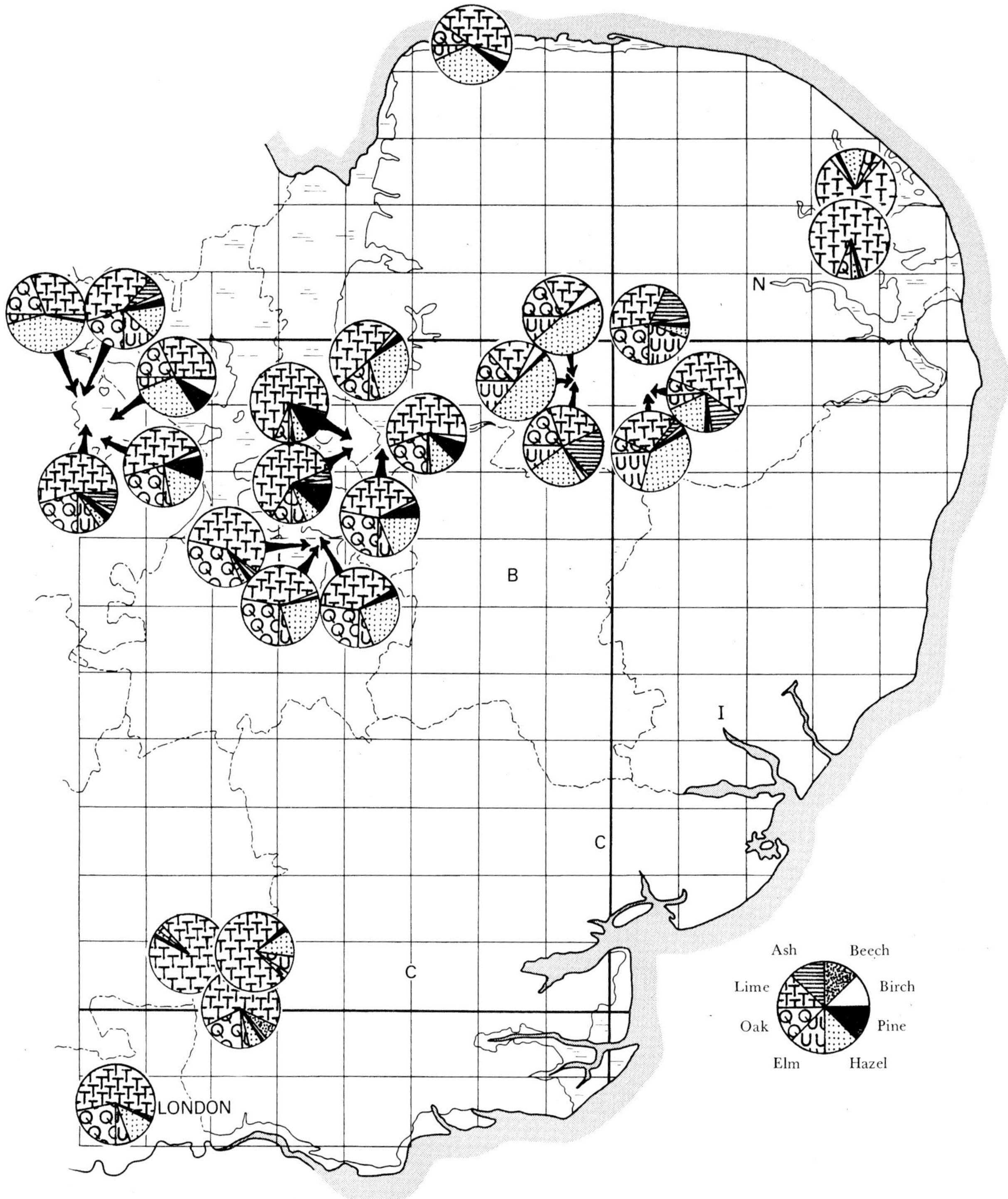

Fig. 8.3 Tree composition of the Atlantic wildwood. Same data as for Fig. 8.2, but adjusted for pollen productivities. Hazel is included with the other trees; alder and willow are excluded as being wet-land trees. [For more recent data see Fig. 32.11.]

Fig. 8.4 Excavation of the Neolithic trackway at Walton Heath in the Somerset Levels. It is made of wattle hurdles. (Photograph by the Somerset Levels Project, reproduced by kind permission of Dr J. M. Coles.)

fewer sails were used than in a modern hurdle and the ethers were seldom bent back into the hurdle at its end.

The woodmanship of the Neolithic hurdles and trackways turns out to be surprisingly elaborate.[123] Rods – the Walton Track contained at least 5,000 – were produced mainly by coppicing with occasional indications of pollarding. They were nearly all hazel, though I have recorded ash (including one pollarded rod) and birch. Rods used as ethers varied from four to ten years' growth; evidently a stand of hazel was worked by ***drawing***, selecting stems of suitable size for the purpose in hand and leaving the others to grow on, rather than by felling a whole area at once as is now the custom. At least half the stems have a narrow last annual ring indicating cutting in summer. Many of them had the leading shoot cut off two, three, or four years before being felled.

The wood in which the rods were grown consisted of hazel with a little ash (cf. Chapter 13). It was a mixture of stools and parts of stools in different stages of regrowth (including old rods with the tops cut off and growing new leading shoots) and of small pollards. This complex system appears to be determined partly by a need to select rods of the exact size for the work in hand, for they could not be adjusted by splitting the thick ones. Cutting off the tops and cutting in summer both suggest that a main product was green foliage, presumably for feeding cattle. Each rod would yield one crop of foliage when it was topped and a second crop when it was felled. It is quite possible that the men of the Somerset Levels regarded wood as a by-product of coppices whose main function was growing leaves. This is still the purpose of pollarded (less often coppiced) trees in many foreign countries[70] (p. 265).

Woodmanship in Roman times

Regrettably little is known of the growing of timber and underwood in Roman Britain: the material probably survives but has not yet been examined with this in mind. Roman and medieval civilizations operated on a similar scale and with a similar range of technologies, and we might expect the Romans to have had systematic woodmanship like that of the medievals, indeed, with their interests in things like baths,[866a] bricks, hypocausts, and corn-driers, the Romans would have had a stronger incentive to maintain regular fuel supplies. Columella, the first century B.C. agricultural writer, describes the coppicing of oak and chestnut and the making of parks for exotic animals by empaling existing woods.[253] He refers to Italy and Gaul, but it is likely that such practices, the predecessors of medieval woods and parks, were later transferred to Britain. Emparking died out in the Anglo-Saxon period, but there is no reason why woodmanship, and even the management of particular woods, should not have continued; in Chalkney Wood (Essex) a Romano-British road is lined by traces of what may be woodbanks (Fig. 8.5).

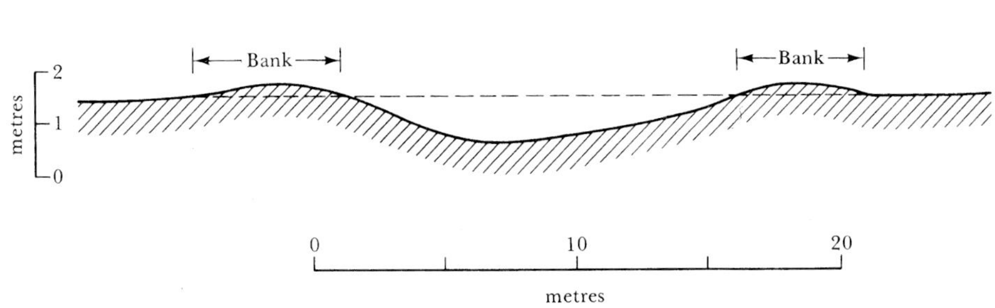

Fig. 8.5 Profile of a Romano-British holloway in Chalkney Wood, Essex; for further details see Fig. 15.6.

The extent of Roman wood-using activity is illustrated by the calculations of H. Cleere on the Roman iron industry of the Weald, and in particular on that part of it which was operated in the neighbourhood of Battle (Sussex) by the provincial navy (*Classis Britannica*), a 'military-industrial complex' supplying iron to the army as well.[23–4] The output of the six main works (estimated from the volume of the slag-heaps) totalled some 90,000 tons of iron, most of it produced at the rate of 550 tons per year in the period A.D. 120–240. Cleere estimates that it took 84 tons of wood to make the charcoal needed to make a ton of iron, so that the industry used in all 7½ million tons of wood. He further estimates that it would have consumed the standing crop on 300 sq. km, i.e. 75,000 acres, of wildwood, about 9% of the whole of the Weald.

In practice it is unlikely that the ironworks lived by destroying wildwood. There was nothing to prevent the woodland felled in the early years of the industry from growing again. The regrowth would have been easier to use than the remaining wildwood and would have been situated nearer the works. There can be little doubt that the industry eventually settled down to some kind of stable coppice system. On this basis I estimate that the 550 tons of iron produced annually would have needed 46,000 tons of wood, the annual yield from very roughly 23,000 acres (93 sq. km) of woodland. To this must be added whatever land was needed to support the labour force – beginning with 400–500 woodcutters – their animals, families, and camp-followers.

We must not suppose that the Roman iron industry, any more than its successors (pp. 153–4), caused wide tracts of woodland to disappear from the map. But its impact was very considerable even on this, supposedly the least settled part of England. My estimate of 23,000 acres of managed woodland is the total for six out of the thirty-six Roman ironworking sites so far identified in the Weald. The Romans later established ironworks

Table 8.1 Woodland plants (other than the principal trees) known to have a prehistoric record.[710]

Present behaviour in woodland	Known before the Atlantic Period [before 6200 B.C.]		First known during the Atlantic Period [6200–3900 B.C.]	First known from Neolithic to Roman [after 3900 B.C.]
Shrubs and less prominent trees	*Cornus sanguinea* *Crataegus* sp. *Frangula alnus* *Hedera helix* *Lonicera periclymenum* *Prunus padus*	*Salix caprea* *S. cinerea* *Sambucus nigra* *Sorbus aucuparia* *Viburnum opulus*	*Clematis vitalba* *Euonymus europaeus* *Prunus spinosa* *Rhamnus cathartica*	*Malus sylvestris* *Prunus avium* *Pyrus pyraster* *Sorbus torminalis*
Shade-bearing herbs	*Carex strigosa* *Circaea lutetiana* *Dryopteris* sp. *Filipendula ulmaria* *Luzula sylvatica?*	*Mercurialis perennis* *Moehringia trinervia* *Ophioglossum vulgatum* *Rubus fruticosus* agg. *Vaccinium myrtillus*	*Chrysosplenium oppositifolium* *Endymion nonscriptus* *Oxalis acetosella* *Potentilla sterilis* *Silene dioica*	*Cardamine flexuosa?* *Scirpus sylvaticus* *Viola riviniana* or *reichenbachiana*
Herbs associated with coppicing	*Cardamine pratensis* *Carex pendula* *Chamaenerion angustifolium* *Digitalis purpurea* *Galeopsis tetrahit*	*Geum* sp. *Lychnis flos-cuculi* *Lythrum salicaria* *Melampyrum* sp.	*Ajuga reptans* *Fragaria vesca*	*Conopodium majus* *Euphorbia amygdaloides* *Isolepis setacea*
Herbs of rides and margins	*Angelica sylvestris* *Heracleum sphondylium* *Potentilla erecta* *Prunella vulgaris* *Rumex sanguineus*	*Sanguisorba officinalis* *Solanum dulcamara* *Stachys sylvatica* *Succisa pratensis* *Valeriana officinalis*	*Hypericum tetrapterum*	*Agrimonia eupatoria* *Betonica officinalis* *Hypericum dubium* *Lysimachia nemorum* or *nummularia* *Serratula tinctoria*
Mainly in glades	*Pteridium aquilinum*	*Rubus idaeus* *Teucrium scorodonia*		
On trees	*Viscum album*	*Polypodium* sp.		

of unknown extent in the Forest of Dean.[23] Roman ironworking was on a larger scale than medieval: the thirteenth-century ironworks in Dean had at most 30,000 acres of woodland at their disposal. It is doubtful whether the scale of Roman ironworking in the Weald was much surpassed even in the seventeenth century, when, as has been estimated, the largest single ironworks could have been sustained permanently by 13,000 acres of woodland.[67]

The prehistory of shrubs and herbs

Table 8.1 is a list of woodland plants, other than the principal trees, which can be proved from pollen or other remains to have grown in Britain in the pre-Neolithic period. Remains of shrubs and herbs are meagre compared to those of most trees, and many species could hardly be preserved at all; yet the list includes not only shrubs and shade-bearing plants but also species now associated with coppicing and woodland grassland. Some of the latter presumably grew in different habitats in prehistory: for instance, *Valeriana officinalis*, *Succisa pratensis*, *Melampyrum*, and *Galeopsis* were common plants in the tundra that preceded the wildwood, for which their present association with rides or coppicing happens to provide a substitute.

Many other plants are first known from the Neolithic period or later. This partly reflects the tendency of archaeologists to spend more time looking for plant remains in Neolithic and later archaeological deposits, but to some extent it may represent a real change: the increasingly felled and managed woodland of civilization was probably a better habitat for shrubs and herbs than the original wildwood.

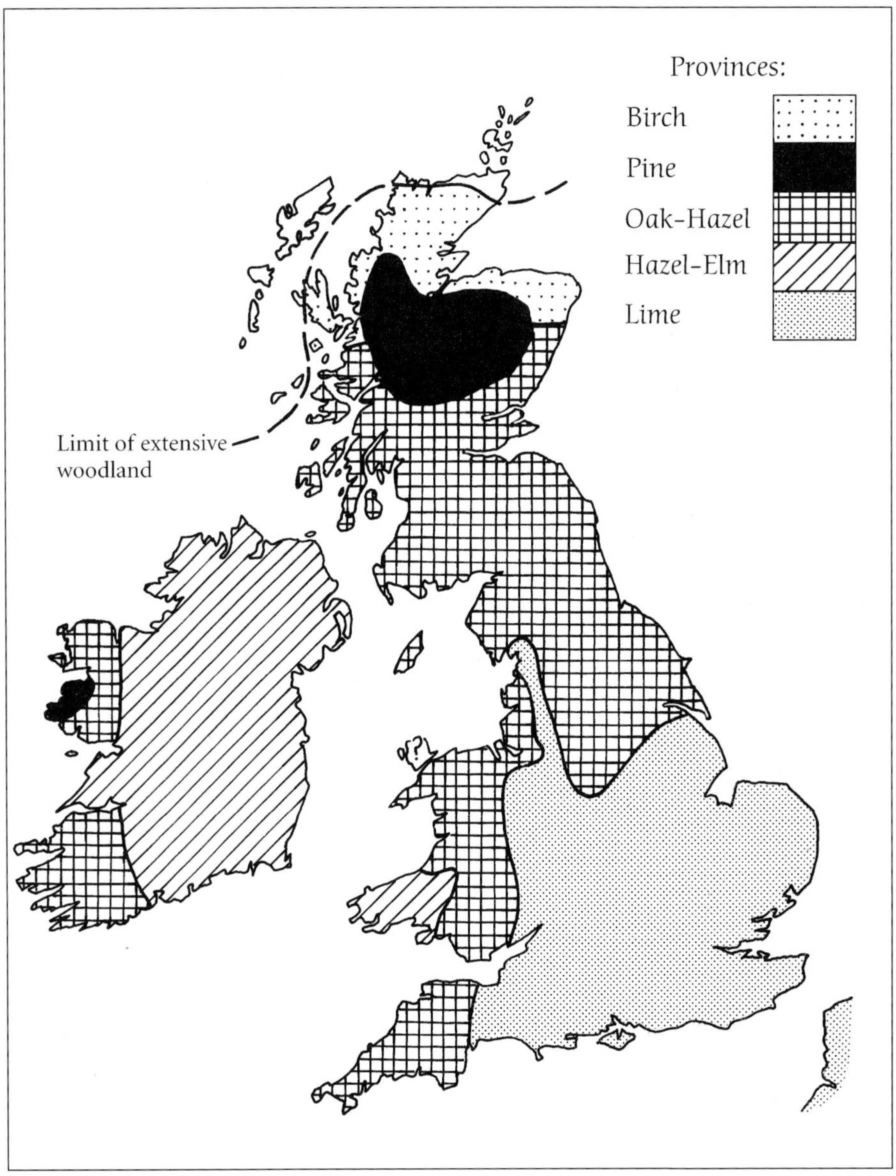

Fig. 8.6 Provinces of the fully developed wildwood, just before the Neolithic period, compiled from the work of Birks and others. Each province covered many local types of woodland, including outliers from other provinces.

Added in 2003 edition

Much detail has been added to the development of wildwood and the early development of agriculture. Some of this is discussed in Chapter 32. Archaeological research has extended and back-dated the range of early human activity to the point of questioning whether there ever was 'real' wildwood, undisturbed by human activity, this side of the last glaciation (p. 520). Otherwise, most of what is said in this chapter still stands.

Additional pollen diagrams, especially from Norfolk, reveal rather more local complexity than was shown in Fig. 8.2. As well as limewoods, hazel-woods, oakwoods, and elmwoods, there is now evidence for areas dominated by ash in south Norfolk.

However, a very different theory of how woodland developed out of wildwood has been proposed by Franciscus Vera, and this is discussed in Chapter 33.

More is known, though still rather sporadically, about prehistoric timber structures and their materials. The Brigg and Hasholme dugout boats from the Humber estuary, each some 50 feet long and 5 feet in diameter at the small end, are the biggest single timbers of any period.* But such giants were exceptional: as in most of the world's cultures, people preferred to fell, and by implication to grow, the smallest tree that would serve the purpose. (Cutting up forest giants is a job for power saws.) The Bronze Age crannog or artificial island excavated at Flag Fen, Peterborough is the biggest timber structure that there has ever been in Britain; it is made from small oaks, typically less than a foot in diameter.

Roman timber-framed buildings, from what little is known of them, seem to have been comparable with medieval in their materials, though the details of construction are different.** Timber frames were made from small, fast-grown oaks. The preferred infill seems to have been laths, although there is plenty of evidence for prehistoric wattle.

Fig. 8.7 Wattle hurdle, made to a Neolithic pattern under the Somerset Levels Project in the Bradfield Woods using stone tools.

Fig. 8.8 Portingbury Rings, an Iron Age site (farmstead?) in the middle of Hatfield Forest, Essex. Most of the big wooded areas of medieval England were not just wildwood but contained sites of prehistoric or Roman activity. May 1995

* Millett, M. and McGrail, S. (1987) Archaeology of the Hasholme logboat. *Archaeol. J.* **144**, 69–155.

** Milne, G. (1995) *Book of Roman London*. English Heritage (Chapter 9).

9

The making of the woods

Many readers in 1980 were brought up on the view that Norman England was still a primitive land, a temperate jungle of boundless wildwoods broken occasionally by clearings in which smoke rose from a handful of settlers' huts, more like the Amazon Basin of 1970 than the England of 1980. This belief supposes either that the Romans had made little impression on the wilderness or that their agriculture, as well as their institutions and themselves, had perished in the barbarian invasions. The invaders had taken over a ruined land; elm and thorn grew over the heaps of bricks and occasionally a skull gleamed in the bushes. They had begun afresh the making of their own agricultural institutions, but being supposedly few and barbarous they had not got far with this task by the end of the Anglo-Saxon period.

This chapter examines the place of woodland in Anglo-Saxon England, whether the landscape of those days was really so unlike our own, and how the pre-Conquest woods developed into the ordered and managed woodland of the thirteenth century. I begin by squeezing the juice from Domesday Book, compare this with other evidence to work backwards towards the twilight of Rome, and finally work forwards into the thirteenth century.

It used to be thought that the existence and even the character of woodland could be inferred from the local geology. On this basis the supposed distribution of woodland was plotted on earlier editions of the Ordnance Survey antiquities maps, and it has often been alleged that settlers were repelled from certain areas on account of the 'heavy forest cover'. This argument is ill-founded. When we do know the distribution of woodland, as in Norman Lincolnshire, it often seems illogical and could not have been inferred *a priori*.

In this chapter I shall usually take 'woodland' as including wood-pasture; the distinction existed but we cannot often tell how much of the woodland was pastured. The terms 'dense' or 'sparse' woodland refer to the proportion of the land surface – so many acres out of every thousand – that was woodland as opposed to non-woodland; I do *not* refer to the numbers or sizes of trees on each wooded acre, about which we have almost no information.

Domesday Book

In 1085, according to the Anglo-Saxon Chronicle, William I instituted a great survey of his kingdom. Census techniques were more efficient then than now and the work was done within a year. Domesday Book was not a mere fiscal survey but was intended and used as a definitive record of land tenure. It records many things, such as woods, that were not taxable assets.

All students of Domesday are immensely indebted to those who have done much of the hard work of identifying the places, determining the units of measurement, and interpreting and mapping the data: to F. W. Maitland[781] and more recently to Professor H. C. Darby and his colleagues for their regional and national volumes.[643, 645–50] Apart from C. S. Taylor[893] and G. B. Grundy,[723] who attempted calculations somewhat on the lines of those in this chapter, there has not been a systematic translation of Domesday woodland entries into actual acreages. Commentators often assume that the entries are too vague or uncertain to be treated quantitatively. To some extent they are uncertain if we limit ourselves to arguments *a priori* about what they mean; but there are ways in which the results can be independently checked. We must not be too ambitious about accuracy. In eleventh-century history there is no point in distinguishing, as a modern census can with difficulty, between a tract of country that is 60% woodland and one that is 62% wooded; we shall be quite satisfied with being able to discriminate between 60% and 50%, or even 60% and 40%, woodland. Indeed even rough evidence which allows us to decide whether a region was 60% woodland (woods adjoining continuously over long distances) or 6% (a 'modern' landscape with islands of wood amid farmland) is well worth having, although I shall seldom do as badly as this.

Domesday Book appears to have been compiled by the filling up of forms.[358] As with modern surveys, the form did not always prove adequate to its purpose and information of kinds not expected in advance was somewhat neglected. With woodland, the form was changed at least twice in the course of the survey.

The Domesday commissioners had peculiar notions of what was England. They did not venture into the four northern counties and did not record woodland in the Craven district of Yorkshire, but they did include Flintshire and a small part of Denbigh. In the Forest of Dean, Herefordshire, Shropshire, Lancashire, and the North Riding the woodland records are unsatisfactory and will be treated under the heading of ***marginal counties***. The rest of England was divided into three. North and west of a line from the Wash to Poole Harbour the records tell us the size of woods; these I call the ***area counties***. From East Anglia to Buckinghamshire most of the records tell us how many pigs each wood was supposed to feed; these are the ***swine counties***. In the south-east, in the ***swine-rent counties***, we are usually told how many swine the users of each wood were supposed to render annually to their lord. The form of the record changes abruptly at county boundaries and results from a change in the method of survey.

Domesday Book is a record of eleventh-century land ownership and tenure, about which much has been written.[645,781] To summarize, the unit of recording is the ***estate***, the land of a particular owner in a particular place. Woodland usually formed part of an estate and was rarely owned separately. The unit of location is the ***settlement*** (*villa*), referred to by name, which could be anything from a city to a single farm. Most estates consisted each of one ***manor*** (*manerium*), the administrative unit of much of medieval England, but some were too small to be proper manors, and some were what I shall call ***giant manors***, estates extending over many settlements and administered as a unit. In the Midlands each *villa* or settlement was often in a single ownership, forming one manor and one estate and later one parish and one modern village. In Devon or Essex, where many settlements were smaller than villages, the *villa* usually consisted of a group of hamlets or farms and was named after one of them; it forms a fraction of a parish. In Cambridgeshire the *villa* often consisted of a large village [or what was later to be a village] divided into two or more manors in different ownerships.

Woodland was normally recorded as a single entry for each estate. In counting the number of woods I shall take each such entry to be one wood, although in practice it must on many estates have been divided among two or more woods. Occasionally Domesday Book says that an estate had more than one wood; I then count the woods separately. Then as now, many woods must have adjoined one another. In recording whether or not a settlement had any woodland I take no account of the number of woods assigned to it: thus a *villa* divided into six estates, two of which had woods, is regarded as a settlement possessing woodland. It is often uncertain whether two estates of the same name count as two settlements or as parts of one; in doubtful cases I have been guided by Darby's maps.

In this analysis I go back to published versions of the original text, mainly those in the *Victoria County History*. For a modern comparison I shall use the Board of Agriculture returns of 1895, the best we can do for a record of what area of woodland there was before the main impact of modern plantations. The counties are also those of 1895, and are the historic counties in a slightly rationalized form without most of their detached portions. I divide Yorkshire and Lincolnshire into their three divisions, separate the Isle of Ely from Cambridgeshire, and assign Greater London to its three historic counties.

Settlements and woodland

Almost the whole of the eleventh-century England was densely settled. Domesday names nearly every modern village, many villages that have disappeared, and thousands of hamlets and isolated farms. Recorded settlements are spaced from one to four miles apart throughout England; yet the actual number of settlements was larger still, for as we know from other documents many settlements existed but are not recorded separately by Domesday because they formed part of a larger estate.

Most of the gaps in the settlement pattern are attributable to mountain, fen, and moorland rather than to large tracts of woodland. One large and apparently uninhabited area is formed by the Weald, but, as we shall see, this is mainly due to an anomaly of recording. With this exception there is no gap between settlements more than about eight miles across that can be attributed to woodland.

Domesday Book gives particulars of some 7,800 woods. If we count the places on Darby's maps that are recorded as having at least one wood and make a small correction for giant manors which aggregate the wood of several settlements into one entry, we find (omitting Lancashire and Craven) that 6,208 out of a total of 12,580 settlements, i.e. 49.5%, possessed woodland. This may seem a low proportion, but there is no doubt that it is genuine: as we shall see, there may be some under-recording of woodland in East Anglia, but in the area counties very small woods are meticulously recorded. The woodless settlements, though they occur almost throughout England, are concentrated in particular areas such as the Midland vales, the Fens and Breckland, and east and N.W. Yorkshire (Fig. 9.1). Although there is no simple relation to topography the woodless areas were mainly on low ground or on lighter soils, especially on chalk, limestone, and sand; they were either highly agricultural and densely peopled or seem to have been largely grassland, fen, or heathland; all of them were conspicuously lacking in woodland up to the nineteenth century and often to the present day. Terrain where every settlement possessed woodland was mainly in the Home Counties.

We have already enough evidence to dispel the notion that Norman England was a very wooded land. On the contrary, it was a land in which nearly half the

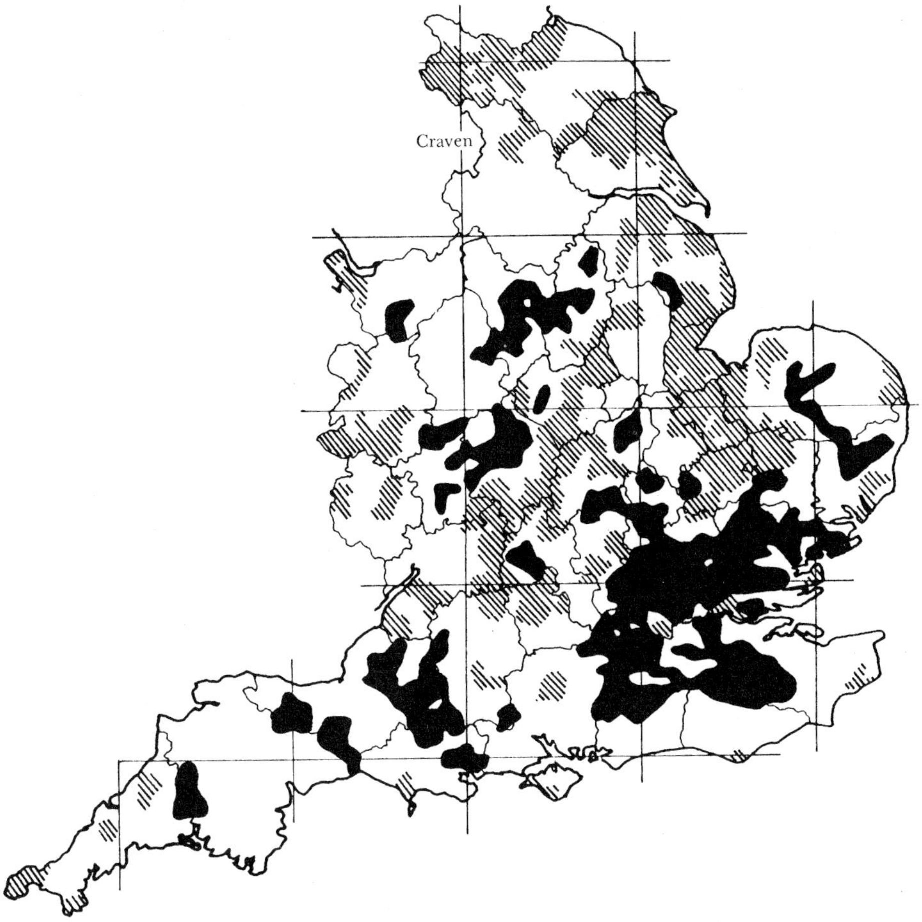

Fig. 9.1 Presence of woodland in Domesday Book England in 1086. Hatched areas: no woodland recorded at all. White areas: woodland possessed by some settlements but not others. Black areas: woodland possessed by every settlement. No account is taken of the amount of woodland. There are no usable returns for counties north of Cheshire and Yorkshire, nor for Craven.

settlements had no wood, and in which it was nowhere possible to penetrate into woodland further than one and a half hours' walk from some habitation. Tracts of uninhabited woodland six miles across – on the scale of the modern New Forest – were few, and eight miles across – on the scale of the Forêt de Fontainebleau – were almost unknown. Many villages were over four miles from any wood, and a day's journey from any substantial woodland: we may well ask why and when such an apparently essential resource had been allowed to disappear.

The area counties

Method of computation

The sizes of woods are expressed sometimes as so many acres; sometimes by length and breadth given in leagues (*leuue* or *leuce*), furlongs (*quarentene*), or occasionally perches; and infrequently by a single dimension. Usually they are in round numbers but in some counties, particularly Lincolnshire, they are more precise. The smaller woods tend to be measured in acres and the larger as length and breadth, but the change-over varies from county to county. I assume that where one dimension is given it represents both the length and the breadth, except for the rare phrase x *leuce inter longitudinem et latitudinem* which I interpret as meaning the sum of the length and breadth.

As Maitland showed, the size of the acre probably varied from place to place; within our limits of accuracy this uncertainty does not greatly matter. I multiply Domesday acreages by 1.2 to allow for the probability that the average acre, particularly for measuring woodland, was larger than ours, and for the possibility that Domesday surveyors, like their thirteenth-century successors (p. 19), may have underestimated the areas of woods. The acre is a rectangle of 40 perches by 4, which explains the occasional woods given as so many acres long or wide.

The Domesday league is well established as the equivalent of twelve furlongs,[781] and I assume that it represents one and a half modern miles. Shorter lengths are given as fractions of leagues or as furlongs according to local custom.

Given the length and breadth of a number of woods, how do we compute their area? The influence on area of variations in shape is not as great as we might suppose. The area of a piece of land is given by its length times breadth multiplied by a ***form factor*** which varies with its shape. For a rectangle (measured along its sides) the form factor is 1; for a circle or ellipse it is $\frac{1}{4}\pi = 0.785$; for a triangle it is $\frac{1}{2}$. It is clearly impossible for an area to have a form factor of more than 1; although a very straggling shape may have a factor of less than $\frac{1}{2}$, this will be offset by a tendency of whoever is making the estimate to leave out any outlying peninsulas. Already we see that if we take a form factor of 0.7 we are most unlikely to be more than 30% in error for any one wood, an error which diminishes for the average of a number of woods.

I have found a sample of fifteen woods in Eastern England, whose thirteenth-century boundaries are known, to have form factors ranging from 0.44 to 0.98, with an average of 0.78. These are all coppice-woods. Much 'woodland' in 1086 consisted of wood-pasture. Wooded commons, including wooded Royal Forests, had rambling and predominantly concave outlines (Fig. 12.1, 12.9), with peninsulas and enclaves, having form factors less than the average for woods. Parks, which usually had a more compact shape than woodland, are a mainly post-Domesday development and can be ignored.

These considerations confirm our choice of an average form factor of 0.7. For instance, a wood stated to measure 10 x 10 (or 20 x 5) *quarentene* will be set down as having an area of 70 square *quarentene*, i.e. 700 modern acres. Even though we cannot tell how strong was the informants' tendency to omit peninsulas of woodland, and though we may suspect that what purports to be the length and breadth of a wood is sometimes a composite pair of measurements somehow derived from two or more woods, these uncertainties can be accepted within the limits of accuracy we have set ourselves.

Table 9.1 gives the woodland areas, computed by this method, county by county. A more precise distribution

Table 9.1 Domesday woodland areas in the area-counties.

	Area (000 acres)	Woodland in 1086 (000 acres)	%	'Woodland' in 1895 (000 acres)	%	Ratio 1086/1895	Number of woods 1086	% of settlements with wood 1086	Median size of wood in 1086 (acres)	Smallest wood recorded in 1086 (acres)
West Yorkshire (without Craven)	1,302	207	16	63	4.8	3.3	263	50	320	2.8
East Yorkshire	754	34	4.4	17	2.3	2.0	43	8	320	14
Flint (plus three places in Denbigh)	167	27	16	8.3	5.0	3.2	30	—	550	1.2
Cheshire	654	175	27	25	3.8	7.0	143	51	470	1.2
Stafford	745	238	32	39	5.3	6.1	178	54	470	2.4
Derby	650	170	26	26	4.0	6.6	168	60	500	7
Nottingham	540	68	12	29	5.3	2.4	188	56	105	0.07
Lincoln (Lindsey plus Kesteven)	1,434	58	4.0	43	3.0	1.3	432	37	65	1.2
Lincoln (Holland)	263	2 woods almost nil		0	0.0	—	2	6	—	—
Worcester	455	181	40	19	4.2	9.4	127	56	240	3.6
Warwick	605	117	19	21	3.5	5.5	120	43	240	3.5
Leicester	533	18	3.3	14	2.7	1.2	90	31	55	2.4
Rutland	97	9.3	9.6	3.8	4.0	2.4	24	55	42	1.8
Northampton	639	56	8.8	28	4.4	2.0	163	50	30	0.10
Huntingdon	234	17	7.4	4.7	2.0	3.7	69	76	70	1.2
Gloucester (without Forest of Dean)	728	70	9.6	35	4.7	2.0	77	25	500	7
Wiltshire	864	114	13	52	6.0	2.2	254	65	28	1.2
Oxford	481	77	16	27	5.5	2.9	122	43	55	3.5
Somerset	1,038	111	11	46	4.4	2.4	518	70	35	1.2
Dorset	626	83	13	38	6.0	2.2	261	63	55	0.6
Devon	1,671	64	3.8	86	5.2	0.74	767	68	17	0.6
Cornwall	868	28	3.2	31	3.6	0.91	184	54	14	1.2
Total	15,348	1,919	12.5	655	4.3	2.9	4,223	50.6		

is shown in Fig. 9.2, where the woodland is assigned to 10-km squares of the National Grid. Each square usually contains the woodland (if any) of from eight to twenty settlements; the woodland of settlements whose parish boundaries overlap square boundaries has, where appropriate, been divided between squares.

Checks of accuracy

Many readers will be surprised that the woodland area in 1086 should have been so small. I shall therefore be chiefly concerned with the possibility that these arguments have under-estimated the actual area.

Occasionally it is possible to compare a Domesday wood with the wood as known in later centuries. For Sawtry Judith (Hunts), for instance, the wood is given as 18 x 4 *quarantene*, which should be 18 x 4 x 0.7 x 10 = 504 acres. The wood can be positively identified as the present Monks' Wood; an exact comparison is not possible because of boundary changes at unknown dates, but the area of Monks' Wood has fluctuated around 500 acres throughout the intervening centuries, and 18 x 4 furlongs is not a bad estimate of its dimensions up to 1855. In this county, indeed, the figure of one and a half miles for the 'league' is, if anything, rather too great.[72] In central Lincolnshire, Dr G. F. Peterken's studies show that the places having woodland in 1086 match very closely the parishes having ancient woods now; in many of them the area is roughly the same. I have found a similar agreement in area for the Lizard Peninsula (Cornwall), where in 1086 the woods were evidently confined (as they still are) to sheltered valleys.

A larger-scale comparison is possible in S.W. Somerset. The 10-km square around Castle Neroche (31/21) is curiously blank in the Domesday record: the settlements are few and small and have little territory assigned to them. Immediately to the east, around Ilminster (square 31/31), there is an apparent excess of land-recording. Settlements are closely spaced and well-provided with farmland, and many of them are given large areas of woodland for which there could not possibly have been room amid the close-packed landscape of the surrounding villages. The anomaly is resolved by the fact, which we learn from later sources, that most of the territory around Castle Neroche, later known as the Forest of Neroche, consisted of exclaves of manors lying to the east; until recently much of the evidence was preserved by the parish boundaries. Most of the woodland was in the exclaves and most of the farmland around the parent settlements, and this was probably so to an even greater degree in 1086. There were seven settlements having exclaves and six on the edge of the blank area. The woodland of these thirteen places – a mixture of acres, leagues and furlongs – adds up to 17,600 acres, and the area around Castle Neroche not accounted for by other land-uses is about 15,000 acres. The calculated acreage of woodland thus agrees well with the space available in which to put it.[125]

Another check comes from the fact that Worcestershire, the most wooded of the area counties, had (by our calculations) 40% of woodland, two and a half times the average. If we are in error by as much as a factor of 2, so that Leicestershire, at the other extreme, had as much as 7% instead of 3½% of woodland, the woods of Worcestershire must have covered 80% of the county, leaving little room for other land-uses. Indeed, if the woods of Leicester covered as much as 10% of the land surface, those of Worcester must have begun to cover the land twice over. Worcester was certainly not a much less agricultural county than Leicester. The south-east of Worcester, including one whole 10-km square, had no woodland at all. The ploughs of Worcestershire in 1086 numbered 2,120; and if, as generally supposed, a plough implies roughly 120 acres of land this means that nearly half the county was under the plough. The figure of 40% for woodland thus leaves only 15% for pasture and other land-uses and is most unlikely to be an under-estimate.

How much woodland was there in the most wooded parts of the country? In 1086 no 10-km square could have had 100% of woodland – for none was totally devoid of agriculture – but it is very likely that a few squares were more than 90% wooded; even in 1895 there were some squares with over 60% woodland. If, therefore, we never get a 10-km square for which the Domesday woodland adds up to nearly the whole area of the square, we shall suspect that woodland areas as a whole have been underestimated. In practice, out of some 600 squares in the areas counties, one has more than 90% of woodland and a further five appear to have more woodland than the area of the square. This is precisely as we should expect, for errors are bound to be made in assigning woodland to particular squares, and in well-wooded country occasional squares will unavoidably be given more than they have room for.

These checks of different kinds, applicable to woodland of different sizes and different densities, prove that Domesday woodland areas are generally reliable and that our estimates are more likely to be too great than too little. The figures for counties are more reliable than those for single squares. Errors of the Neroche type, where the wood of a settlement was in a well-wooded exclave at some distance away, exist in other places (e.g. Warwickshire[683] and the Oxfordshire Chilterns[672]) but seldom involve more than two adjoining squares. Because of such anomalies the contrast between the wooded and woodless parts of England in 1086 was even more remarkable than Fig. 9.2 shows it to be.

Numbers and sizes of woods

The largest single wood recorded in Domesday, apart from aggregate woods assigned to giant manors, appears

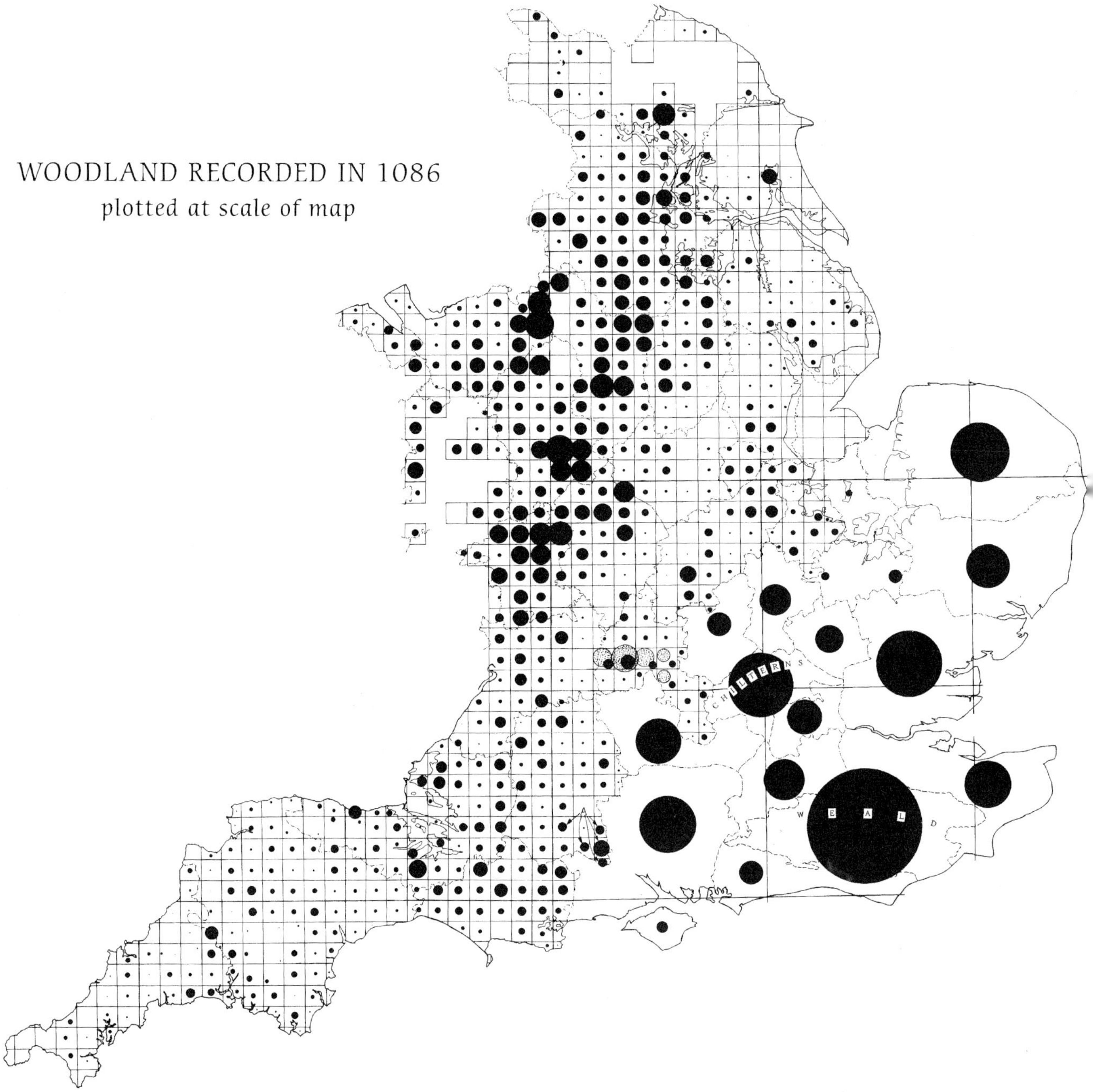

Fig. 9.2 Areas of woodland recorded in Domesday England. The size of the black circles represents the estimated area covered by woodland in 1086 at the scale of the map. In area counties woodland is mapped by 10-km National Grid squares: each black circle represents the total woodland area assigned to places located within the square. In swine- and swine-rent counties woodland is mapped county by county, the Weald and Chilterns being treated separately. No distinction is made between kinds of woodland.

Stippled circles in Oxfordshire represent Forests (see text). In Wiltshire the woodland assigned to Amesbury (A) has been redistributed as explained in text. The Neroche square is immediately west of the large black circle in south Somerset.

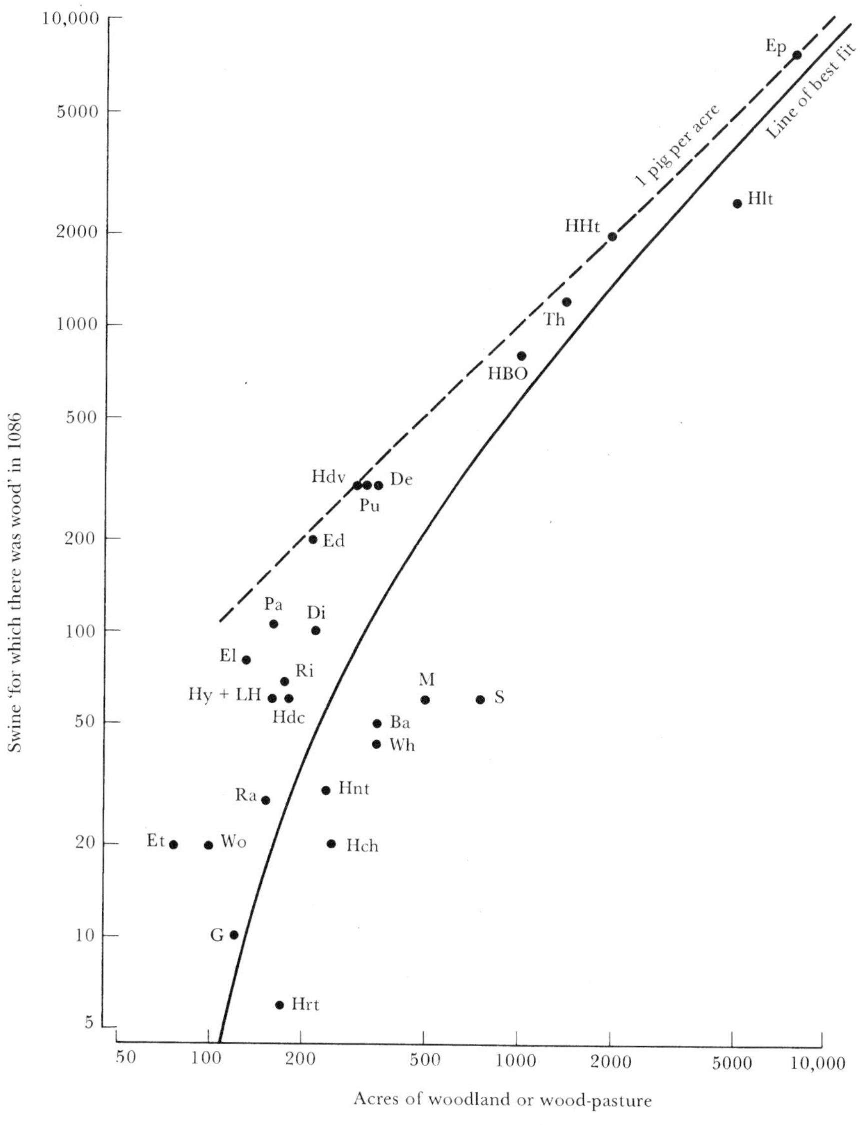

Fig. 9.4 Numbers of swine at which the woodland of certain places was assessed in 1086, compared with the known area of woodland chiefly in the thirteenth century (corrected for under-estimation, p. 19). Both scales are logarithmic.

Norfolk: Dereham (De),[270] Ditchingham (Di) (p. 232), Edgefield (Ed), [213, 387] Hindolveston (Hdv) (p. 157), Pulham (Pu),[270] Shipdham (S),[270] Thorpe-next-Norwich (Th).[122]

Suffolk: Barking (Ba),[270] Elmswell (El),[345] Hartest (Hrt),[270] Hinderclay (Hdc),[345] Hintlesham (Hnt),[234–11 Ed 1] Hitcham (Hch),[270] Long Melford (M),[819] Pakenham (Pa),[345] Rattlesden (Ra),[270] Rickinghall (Ri),[345] Whepstead (Wh),[345] Woolpit (Wo).[345]

Essex: Epping Forest (Ep),[124] Hainault Forest (Hlt),[124] Hatfield Forest (HBO).[122]

Cambs: Eltisley (Et),[474] Gamlingay (G),[474] Hayley and Littlehound Wood (Hy + LH).[270]

Herts: Hatfield (HHt).[270]

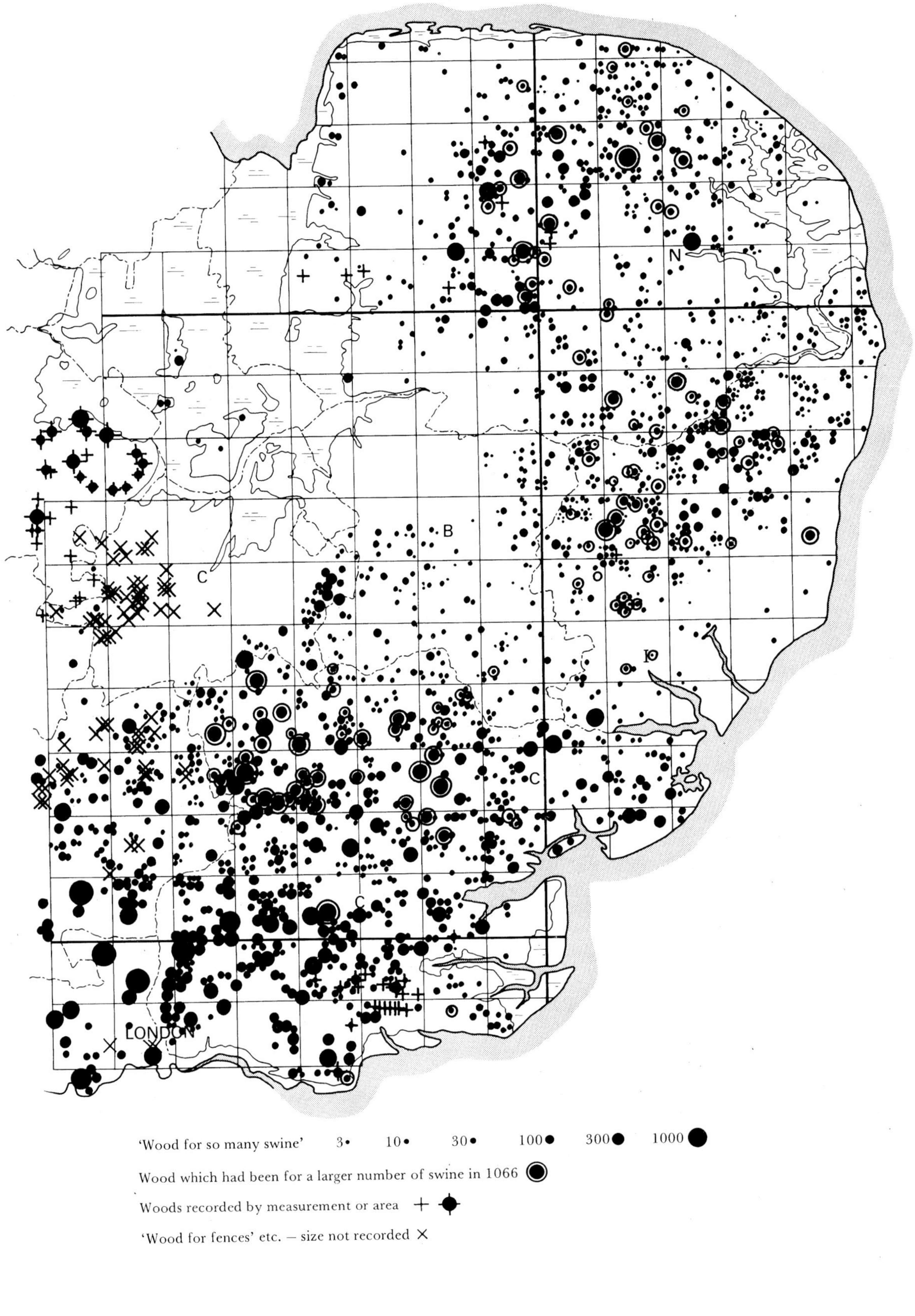
N
B
C
C
C
C
LONDON
'Wood for so many swine' 3 10 30 100 300 1000
Wood which had been for a larger number of swine in 1066
Woods recorded by measurement or area
'Wood for fences' etc. – size not recorded

Norfolk (Fig. 9.5)
Norfolk had a denser population than Suffolk (twenty recorded persons per square mile) and thus probably more underwood; it had more of the larger swine-entries and thus presumably more wood-pasture. Let us say 4% for the underwood and 8% for the wood-pasture, making a total of 12%. This may seem unduly high compared with Lincolnshire, but nearly half the settlements in Norfolk had recorded woodland, compared with little more than a third of those in Lincoln, and the majority of the Lincoln woods were so small that they would probably not have been recorded in terms of swine.

Cambridgeshire (Fig. 9.5)
The woods of this county are divided into an eastern and a western group. The western woods, apart from a few very small swine ratings, are given 'miscellaneous' entries which imply coppicing but tell us nothing of their size. Their area in the thirteenth century is known accurately from records and field evidence and totals 830 acres. In 1086 thirty-two parishes had woodland, as against fourteen two centuries later, so I shall enter the total area of the woods at 1,900 acres. In East Cambridgeshire there is a total of thirty-four swine-woods which, by the first arithmetical process used for Suffolk, add up to 8,600 acres.

Cambridgeshire closely resembles Lincolnshire in its woodland history: it had only 3.3% of woodland in 1086, but the two groups of woods are still prominent in the landscape.

The Isle of Ely had very little woodland: seven swine-entries on the fen islands indicate a total of 1,850 acres. The last of these woods, at Doddington (Fig. 12.12), was not destroyed until 1942.

Essex (Fig. 9.5)
Domesday records woodland for three-quarters of the settlements in Essex, more than any other county except Hertfordshire. Six hundred and thirty-five woods were supposed to feed 94,000 pigs, and a further twenty-three woods are recorded by area. Essex appears to have been about five times as wooded as Suffolk, but this is partly because of the sparser population: with only nine recorded inhabitants per square mile, it is probable that less of the woodland had been encoppiced and more could be recorded in terms of swine. Small swine-entries, of a kind that we have been associating with coppicing, occur chiefly in the north-west, north-east, south-east, and in a belt across the middle; in the rest of the county the entries are mainly for large numbers of swine.

Under the first arithmetical procedure used for Suffolk the swine-woods add up to 237,000 acres: the area-woods amount to 3,000 modern acres and we should add some 2,000 acres for unrecorded coppices. Another approach is to start from the swine-entries given for places involved in what were later to be Epping and Hainault Forests, which add up to 10,182 pigs, about a ninth of the total for the county. The area of the Forests is known, from the position of settlements that surrounded them and from records of encroachments,[124] to have been about 13,000 acres. If the Forests were representative the total woodland and wood-pasture in Essex should have been some 120,000 acres. The second of these estimates is probably too low because it fails to allow for the under-recording of coppice-woods; the first is likely to be too high because, with woodland so abundant in Essex, some of the smaller woods would have been contiguous to other woods and should really be treated as parts of larger units. I select 200,000 acres as a reasonable compromise.

The Chiltern counties
One of the largest wooded areas in England extended from the Chiltern escarpment down the dip-slope almost to the gates of London. It inspired a famous passage in the description of London by the twelfth-century writer Fitzstephen:

> On the north are fields and pastures and a pleasant stretch of meadows . . . Nearby lie a huge Forest (*ingens foresta*), wooded glades, and the lairs of wild beasts: harts, does, boars, and bulls [*or, in other MSS*, bears].[338]

Although the beasts are magnified in Fitzstephen's timorous imagination, Domesday confirms the existence of a very wooded area some 40 miles by 25, extending into four counties. In the south-west half of Hertfordshire, south Buckinghamshire, north Middlesex, and the southern tip of Bedfordshire the settlements were fewer and more widely spaced than anywhere in Essex; nearly every one had wood, usually for at least 500 swine. Although not lacking in ploughland the landscape evidently had so much wood as to restrict other activities. By analogy with the more wooded parts of the west Midlands I shall give it a density of 50%. The Oxfordshire Chilterns and the extreme south-western edge of Buckinghamshire had much less woodland.

Fig. 9.5 Woodland in Eastern England as recorded in Domesday Book in 1086. Each point represents one mention of woodland. The records are mostly in terms of swine, and are represented hy dots whose sizes are chosen, on the basis of Fig. 9.4, to give a rough impression of the areas that the woods are likely to have occupied at the scale of the map; but as explained in the text the relation between swine and acres must be treated with the utmost caution.

Woods whose swine-assessment decreased between 1066 and 1086 are shown as points with rings round them. The diameter of the rings is arbitrary; in most instances the decrease was too small to be shown at thc scale of the map.

The map also includes woods recorded in terms of length and breadth, and woods recorded only in qualitative terms.

Usually it has only been possible to assign woods to the area of the settlement for which they are recorded, although where the precise location of a wood is known from later evidence it has been used.

The north-eastern half of Hertfordshire (Fig. 9.5) has many small swine-entries and a handful of big ones, plus a scatter of 'wood for fences' entries. This suggests a state intermediate between Essex and Suffolk, with something like 15% of woodland, much of it coppiced.

The south of Middlesex was much less wooded than the Chiltern portion, with several woodless places. A reasonable guess for the whole county is 30%.

Non-Chiltern Buckinghamshire closely resembled adjoining Northamptonshire; there was a concentration of woodland (including the later Whaddon Chase) along the border, but in the Vale of Aylesbury the swine-entries are small and many places had none. Like Northamptonshire, north Buckingham would have been about 9% woodland.

Bedfordshire has woodland recorded for a high proportion – 71% – of its settlements; most of the entries are middle-sized. It was clearly more wooded than Northamptonshire but less than Essex: 15% is a reasonable estimate.

All these estimates are collected together in Table 9.3. There was much the same range of variation in the swine-counties as in the area-counties, but on average the proportion of woodland seems to have been a little greater.

The swine-rent counties

In S.E. England we are even less in touch with the real world. Woods, with rare exceptions, are entered as 'wood rendering *x* swine annually for pannage' or some variant of this formula (occasionally herbage is mentioned). We have to reckon, not only with the uncertain connection between pigs and the size of the wood, but with the relation between the swine-rent and the number of animals and with the general tendency of rents to reflect obsolete rather than current land-uses. Usually the owner of the wood is supposed to have had one pig in every ten, but there is some evidence for a rent of one pig in seven.[646] These estimates of woodland area are therefore even more uncertain than those of the swine-counties. I hope that somebody with detailed knowledge of the area and its documentation can improve on them.

The Weald

By far the biggest concentration of woodland in Norman England was the Weald of Kent, Sussex, and Surrey. The Weald appears on the Domesday map as a vast, almost blank area some 70 miles by 25, and until recently it has been popularly thought that long after the eleventh century it was still an untrodden desert of primaeval wildwood. We now know that its apparent emptiness was due to a peculiar social structure which generated a series of 'Neroche' anomalies of recording. Settlements grew up in the Weald as offshoots of places outside it, and by 1086 many of them, with their woodland, were still regarded as dependencies of their parent manors and are not separately recorded. Tonbridge, for instance, though a quite important place, is hidden in the entry for Otford, ten miles away.[170] Only those few Wealden settlements which had declared independence are specifically described.

The economy and settlement history of the Weald of Kent are well documented in other early sources and have been thoroughly and ingeniously investigated by K. P. Witney.[170] The Sussex Weald has been studied by P. Brandon.[616] The Weald was a stronghold of pannage, pigs being brought from the parent manors to seasonal settlements called ***denns***, many of which developed into permanent agricultural hamlets and eventually into towns like Tenter*den*. Witney lists 117 manors with pannage in the Kentish Weald; their swine-rents totalled about 6,000 pigs, which at the rate of one in ten implies that 60,000 animals fed in the woods each autumn. By East Anglian standards this would mean

Table 9.3 Estimated woodland areas in the swine-counties.

	Area (000 acres)	Woodland in 1086 (000 acres)	Woodland in 1086 %	'Woodland' in 1895 (000 acres)	'Woodland' in 1895 %	Ratio 1086/1895	% of places with recorded woodland in 1086
Norfolk	1,315	158	12	54	4.1	2.9	48
Suffolk	949	84	9	35	3.7	2.4	43
Essex	980	200	20	31	3.2	6.5	76
Isle of Ely	238	1.8	0.8	nil	0	—	44 (Isle of Ely and Cambridgeshire)
Cambridgeshire	315	11	3.5	6.1	1.9	1.7	
Herts: north-east	234	35	15	25 (north-east and south-west)	6.1	4.9	89
Herts: south-west	170	85	50				
Middlesex	181	54	30	3.8	2.1	14	66
Bedfordshire	303	45	15	12.5	4.1	3.6	71
Buckinghamshire: north	279	25	9	32 (north and south)	6.7	3.9	58
Buckinghamshire: south	200	100	50				
Total	5,164	799	15.5	199	3.9	4.0	

that only about half the 850,000 acres of the Weald of Kent were woodland, but a swine-rent implies an obligation to produce the actual animals and is likely to be more realistic than a mere estimate of a capacity that was seldom fully used. In Sussex pannage was less important, the swine-rents totalling only 3,400 pigs,[79] although there was more than twice as much Weald.

We cannot persuade Domesday to tell us directly how much of the Weald was woodland. Witney shows that even in Kent pannage was in decline by 1086 and was rapidly being replaced by conventional agriculture. The fabric and institutions of a settled countryside had spread to every part of the Weald of Kent, although they were still thin on the ground. In Sussex, as Brandon shows, the process had apparently gone further: in the Low Weald of the west the better soils were widely cultivated, and in the High Weald even Domesday records many independent settlements and appreciable arable land.

According to Brandon, the grubbing-out of the woods of the Sussex Weald was very actively pursued for 250 years after Domesday: by 1349 – the Black Death – the landscape had been reduced almost to its modern state. In Kent the woods may have survived a little longer. We are given the impression that something like 30% of the woodland of the Weald was destroyed before 1086 and 50% after 1086; 18% is still wooded. This implies that roughly 70% of the area, some 600,000 acres, was woodland in Domesday times.

Non-Wealden Kent, Sussex, and Surrey

In Kent the Weald evidently accounted for much more of the total woodland than it does now. Witney shows that ninety manors not known to have had Wealden colonies received a total of 1,523 rent-swine, a quarter of those received from the Weald. There are many references to woods in other terms and a few to underwood; but only 65% of the places in the county as a whole had woodland. This suggests that woods outside the Weald amounted to little more than half the acreage of those within it – let us say 100,000 acres – but, being more accessible, were mainly used for purposes other than pannage.

For Sussex, although we do not have Witney's analysis of *denns*, the evidence suggests that there was even less woodland outside the Weald. The coast was one of the most highly-farmed parts of England, and in the whole county only 48% of settlements had any woodland. A possible figure for the woodland of non-Wealden Sussex is 25,000 acres.

Non-Wealden Surrey seems to have been more wooded than Kent, with many large swine-rents accruing to places well away from the Weald. The density of population and of agriculture suggest an analogy with Essex. Pending more information on the development of the Surrey heaths, I shall assume that this part of Surrey was 20% woodland.

Other swine-rent counties

Berkshire had woodland recorded for four places out of ten. The north-western third was almost devoid of recorded wood and was densely settled, but in the east, already designated as Windsor Forest, settlements were widely-spaced and had very large swine-rents. The county was probably more wooded than Wiltshire but less than Buckinghamshire, which suggests a proportion of 20%.

Hampshire had woodland recorded for 55% of its places, with large swine-rents in the east and south-west, a general scatter of small swine-rents, and many 'miscellaneous' entries. The impression is of a county a little more wooded than Wiltshire – let us say 15%. The Isle of Wight had woodland recorded for only a quarter of its settlements, mainly as very small swine-rents or as 'miscellaneous' entries. By analogy with the less-wooded parts of East Anglia I set it down as 6%.

These estimates for the swine-rent counties are collected into Table 9.4. The modern, as well as the Domesday, figures are less reliable than for other counties, because they have been inflated by secondary woodland springing up on heaths in the nineteenth century; particularly in Surrey, which in 1793 had practically no woodland outside the Weald.[388]

The marginal counties (Table 9.5)

The North Riding of Yorkshire appears to be a normal area county until we come to the statement that the woods of the giant manor of Pickering measured 16 x 4 leagues. This is much the largest woodland entry in Domesday Book, and the only place where there is room to put it is the North York Moors. There are several other very large entries for N.E. Yorkshire, which if taken literally mean that the plateau of the Moors, as well as the valleys, was woodland. This is at variance with the strong archaeological and pollen evidence that the plateau has been woodless since the Bronze or Iron Age.[605a, b, 658–9, 887a] Probably the woods did extend throughout the areas recorded, but only in the valleys (much as in the thirteenth century[914]), and thus occupied a small and unknown proportion of the 16 x 4 leagues. In the two-thirds of the North Riding which do not involve this difficulty (Fig. 9.2) we find some 54,000 acres of woodland, 6.1% of the land area. At least 2% of the land area was underwood. The north-east appears to have been much more wooded, but the woodland of the whole subcounty is unlikely to have exceeded 12%.

Woodland is recorded for the southern half of Lancashire, but mostly in the form of large aggregated entries, some of them in mountainous terrain; with the Pickering anomaly in mind, we dare not guess how much they amount to.

Shropshire has a curious mixture of swine-entries

Table 9.4 Estimated woodland areas in the swine-rent counties.

	Area (000 acres)	Woodland in 1086 (000 acres)	%	'Woodland in 1895 (000 acres)	%	Ratio 1086/1895	% of places with recorded woodland in 1086
The Weald	859	601	70	155 (in 1930)*	18.1	3.9	—
Kent (outside Weald)	765	100	13	*c.* 65	*c.* 8.5	1.5?	65 (for all Kent)
Sussex (outside Weald)	415	*c.* 25	6	*c.* 21	*c.* 5.1	1.2?	48 (for all Sussex)
Surrey (outside Weald)	376	*c.* 75	20	*c.* 36	9.6	2.1?	69 (for all Surrey)
Berkshire	462	92	20	36	7.7	2.6	40
Hampshire	959	144	15	121	12.6	1.2	55
Isle of Wight	94	5.6	6	4.8	5.1	1.2	25
Total	3,930	1,043	26.5	439	11.2	2.4	

*The comparison date for the Weald is 1930, the survey date of the first gridded edifion of the Ordnance Survey which affords the earliest reliable means of estimating the modern area. The 1895 area is unlikely to have been very different.

and single dimensions. The wood-entries are thinly scattered and much of the south had none. The dimensions suggest an area of about 40,000 acres, and the mostly small swine-entries suggest something like a further 30,000: a total of about 8% of the county.

Herefordshire is vague. There is one large aggregate entry (for Leominster), several small measurements, a variety of other kinds of entry, and a number of woods not set down on the pretext that they had been included in Forests. The Conqueror's Commissioners hardly showed their faces in the Welsh districts of Herefordshire at all. They give the impression that the county was no more wooded than Shropshire; it had some of the most intensive agriculture in England. I shall put it down for 8%.

West Gloucestershire is recorded with similar vagueness. It was dominated by Dean, already designated a Forest. The pattern of settlements strongly suggests that not more than 40,000 out of the 77,000 acres were woodland.

General conclusions

In Table 9.6 the total woodland area of Domesday England (omitting five northern counties but including Welsh Flintshire) comes to 4 million acres, 15% of the land area. These figures involve a good deal of guesswork, particularly in the swine-rent counties, but our guesses have been generous; the swine-rent counties come out with twice as much woodland as the area counties where there has been least guesswork. The figure of 15% is unlikely to be far from the truth and is more likely to be an over-estimate than an under-estimate.

Some scholars, aware of the discrepancy between the traditional picture of Norman England – the jungle with clearings – and what Domesday Book says England was like, have sought to explain it away by accusing the Domesday surveyors of under-recording woodland: they are supposed to have missed woods that had no economic use. No evidence has been produced to support this charge, and I have not found any in this

Table 9.5 Estimated woodland areas in the marginal counties

	Area (000 acres)	Woodland in 1086 (000 acres)	%	'Woodland in 1895 (000 acres)	%	Ratio 1086/1895	% of places with recorded woodland in 1086
North Yorkshire	1,362	163	12	53	3.9	3.1	18
Shropshire	862	69	8	50	5.9	1.4	31
Herefordshire	539	43	8	42	7.8	1.0	21
West Gloucestershire	77	40	52	24	31.2	1.7	—
Total	2,840	316	11.1	169	6.0	1.9	

certain records of grubbing are a few 'assarts' in Herefordshire. Possibly the process had been interrupted by the Conquest: for some time it had been easier to claim the fields of men slain with the sword than to hew out new fields.

We might expect that Domesday would record a stage in the development of a landscape which, at least up to 1066, had been rapidly changing: that place-names would reveal former woodland in areas which in 1086 had little or none. This turns out not to be so. Areas such as the Cambridgeshire Wilds are few and small, and even if we include parts of Devon they amount to only a few per cent of England. As far back as the place-names go – and some of them date from heathen times – they reveal a distribution of woodland not very different from that in 1086. For about 500 years the well-wooded areas had been eaten away from within by leys and hursts; but there is no reason to suppose that the poorly-wooded areas had been appreciably less extensive in the seventh or even the sixth century than they were in the eleventh.

Norse names reinforce this argument. Many examples from the Lake District to Derbyshire show that the Vikings could hew out hamlets in the woods and call them thwaites (Fig. 9.6). But in Lincolnshire, East Anglia, and Leicestershire there are hardly any Danish settlement-names related to clearings, although Viking village-names of other kinds are very common, and Viking names for woods (e.g. Way*land* Wood, anciently Wanelund (S.W. Norfolk) and Hol*land* Wood, anciently Havelund (Hunts), both from *lúndr*, a grove) are frequent. This can only mean that by the ninth century there was little superfluous woodland in these counties and few opportunities for making thwaites; indeed some of the present woods were already recognizable.

Another remarkable correlation is between open-field agriculture – the cultivation of strips in common fields – and lack of evidence for wildwood. From 1730 to 1880 Enclosure Acts dealing with open-fields covered about a fifth of England. This was almost entirely limited (Fig. 9.7) to precisely that part of the country – the East Yorkshire–Norfolk–Dorset triangle – that had had little woodland in 1086 and few woodland place-names. The Acts did not, of course, cover the whole former extent of open-field,[814] but they are a good record of a *strong* open-field tradition, suppressible only by Act of Parliament. Other areas known to have had extensive open-field, such as non-Wealden Sussex,[616] also have little evidence for woodland.

The classic Midland open-field village rarely had more than 5% woodland; more than half had none at all. Settlements in well-wooded areas usually took the form of hamlets and scattered farms and either never had an open-field system or lost it early.

It is possible to find counter-examples to this thesis. The group of hamlets called The Saints, near Bungay (Suffolk), has a very ancient – perhaps pre-Roman – regular system of enclosed rectangular fields, and has no evidence of ever having possessed woodland. Conversely the Cambridgeshire Wilds show that it was possible for an open-field village to develop out of a clearing in the woods. But these are somewhat exceptional. We do not havc any parallel to the German *Waldhufendörfer*,[785] large and regularly-planned forest villages. In general, the cooperative agriculture which gave rise to medieval open-field villages developed chiefly on land already cleared by someone else. Where men had to make their fields before they could till them they created an individualistic landscape of hamlets and isolated farms; in such areas open-field systems, where they existed at all, were weakly established and faded away before the period of the main enclosures.

The woodland left by the Romans

These arguments suggest that the distribution of wooded and non-wooded areas in Anglo-Saxon England was, in the main, not the work of the Anglo-Saxons. The tribes took over a land that was already more than half farmland and in which the wooded areas, though denser, were little more extensive than they were to be in 1086.

The woodland evidence strongly favours that school of opinion which holds that the Anglo-Saxon takeover of England was gradual and not always violent. Had Roman Britain gone down in a cataclysm of battle, murder, and sudden death most of its area would have been secondary woodland within thirty years; we should expect to find evidence of woodland and woodland clearance almost uniformly distributed through Anglo-Saxon England. In fact there is very little evidence of extension of woodland at the time of the transition. Such pollen diagrams as cover this period suggest that forest clearance sometimes ceased for a time (as at Old Buckenham, Norfolk)[709] but in northern England and southern Scotland it actually continued during the fifth and sixth centuries (as at Bloak Moss, Ayrshire).[899] The invaders may merely have settled on lands that, with the collapse of the Roman Empire, were no longer needed for growing crops for export. Although there was some retreat of agriculture from marginal land, the Anglo-Saxons continued to cultivate even the poorer Roman sites. At Shakenoak in North *Leigh* (Oxfordshire) the site of a Roman villa tumbled down to woodland, but not until long after the legions left; Saxons took it over and farmed it for three centuries before finally giving it up.[623]

The less-wooded areas of Roman England, which we have concluded covered nearly half the country, passed into Anglo-Saxon hands and were covered by the new regime with open-field villages. How long this took and how it was done we cannot yet say. The other half of England was by no means all wooded – it had contained cities, such as Colchester and St Albans, and

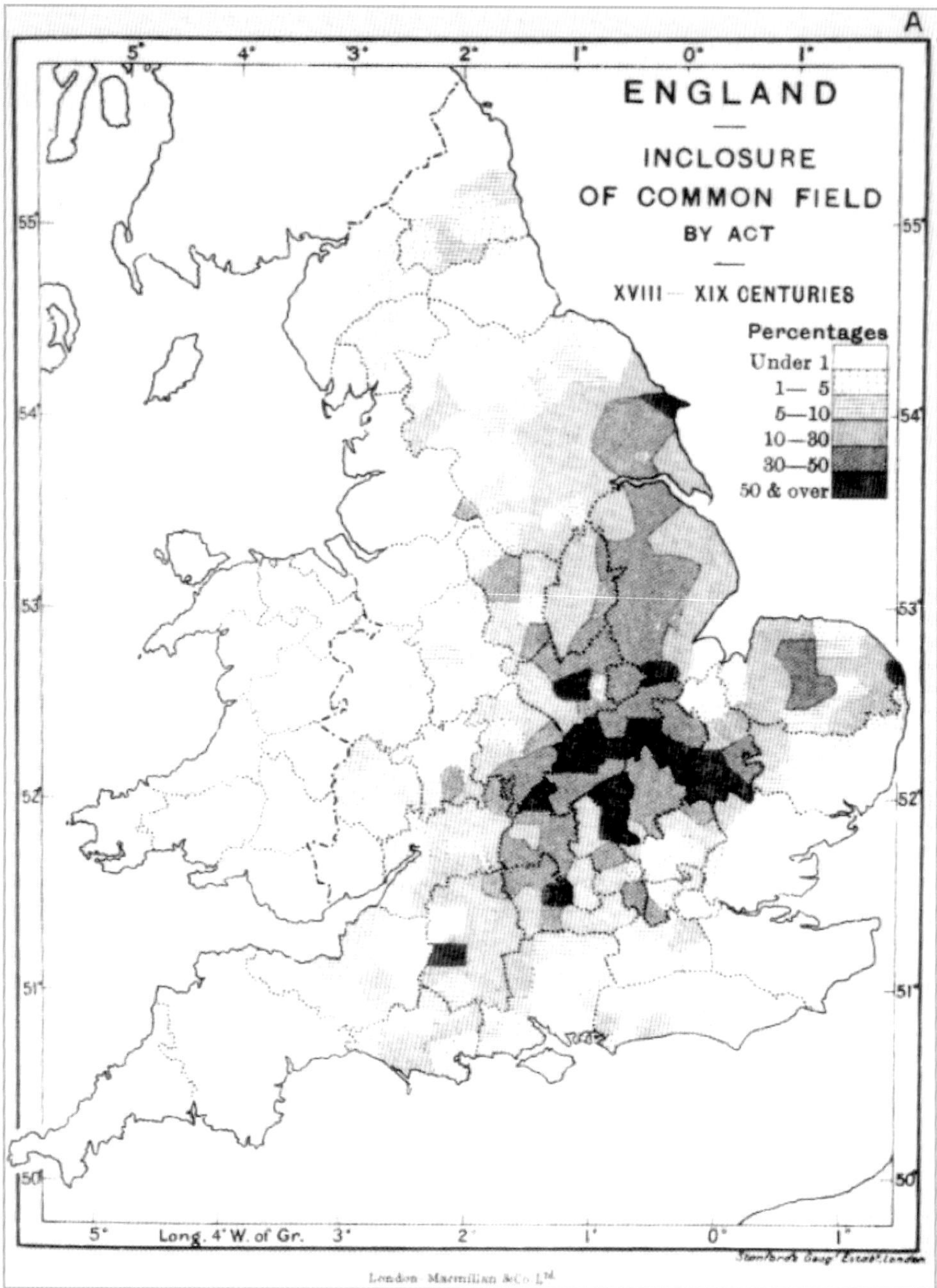

Fig. 9.7 The extent of parliamentary enclosure of common arable fields. From E. C. K. Gonner's book[715] published by Macmillan in 1912.

many villas – and afforded some areas of farmland large enough for Anglo-Saxon villages: the parish-names ending in -field in N.E. Herefordshire, east Berkshire, Essex, and Suffolk are examples. The distribution of heathen cemeteries and barrows, although only a very rough guide to early Anglo-Saxon settlement, is indeed strongly and inversely related to what we have supposed to be the distribution of woodland.[811] By the seventh century at latest the inhabitants were finding the Roman farmland too small for them and were hewing out new settlements in the wooded parts of the country. Such woodland as survived in the less-wooded areas was too valuable as a resource to be treated as vacant land, and there are few records of its destruction.

We know a few of the Celtic wood-names in England, although inevitably they are those of wooded areas rather than of specific woods. Selwood on the Wiltshire–Somerset border – prominent on the Domesday map, and even now still recognizable though largely coniferized – is the Anglo-Saxon name for what the Britons called Coit Maur, the Great Wood (cf. Welsh *coed mawr*),[606] a name which suggests that the surrounding country did not have much woodland. The great wood of S.E. Staffordshire, later Cannock Chase, gave rise to the town name of *Letocetum*, Greywood (Welsh *coed llwyd*, later transferred to near-by *Lich*field.[882] Another Greywood, in S.E. Dorset, gave rise to *Lytchett* Matravers. *Coit* is generally anglicized to *chet*, as in the wooded area of S.E. Wiltshire later known as the Forests of Mel*chet*, Pen*chet* alis Clarendon,[63] and *Chute*. Penchet means Woodhead or Woodend (Welsh *pen + coed*), and turns up again in the early spellings of *Penk*hill in Stoke-on-Trent, *Penge* (Surrey), and *Pans*hill in Boarstall (Oxford–Bucks border). There are *Chat*hams in Kent and Essex and a parish of *Chetw*ode near Buckingham. All these are in or on the edge of what were still wooded areas in 1086. The name of a specific wood is preserved in the sub-county of *Ke*steven, in which *chet* has been combined with Old Norse *stefna*, meeting. Presumably the county administration grew out of a meeting first held, as such assemblies sometimes were, in one of the woods of what was already a little-wooded area; the wood may well still exist, although we can no longer identify it. The Celtic namcs (Fig. 9.8) can be supplemented by a few very early Anglo-Saxon names for wooded tracts, e.g. *Derawudu* and *Elmete*, recorded by Bede in the eighth century.[203]

The non-wooded and wooded areas which the Romans left were to remain for about 800 years. Although only fragments of the distribution are now directly discernible, it has left behind it one of the most fundamental distinctions in the English landscape, that between the 'Planned Countryside' of the parliamentary enclosures and the 'Ancient Countryside' whose roads, fields, hedges, etc. were created piecemeal before 1700.[122] The fabric of the former is modern, but it occupies the sites of open-fields which, in turn, in large part occupied the site of Roman farmland. The latter, occupying the more wooded areas of Anglo-Saxon times, involves smaller blocks of Roman farmland, together with fields hewn singly from thc intervening woods by farmers from prehistoric to Stuart times. The contrast between the intimate complexity of the Ancient Countryside and the sweeping sameness of enclosure-act country – between thc Semley country (S.W. Wilts) and the nearby chalklands, or between the Chiltern plateau and the Vale of Aylesbury, or between most of Suffolk and most of Cambridgeshire – is due more to history than to geography and apparently is determined by events of some 1,500 years ago.

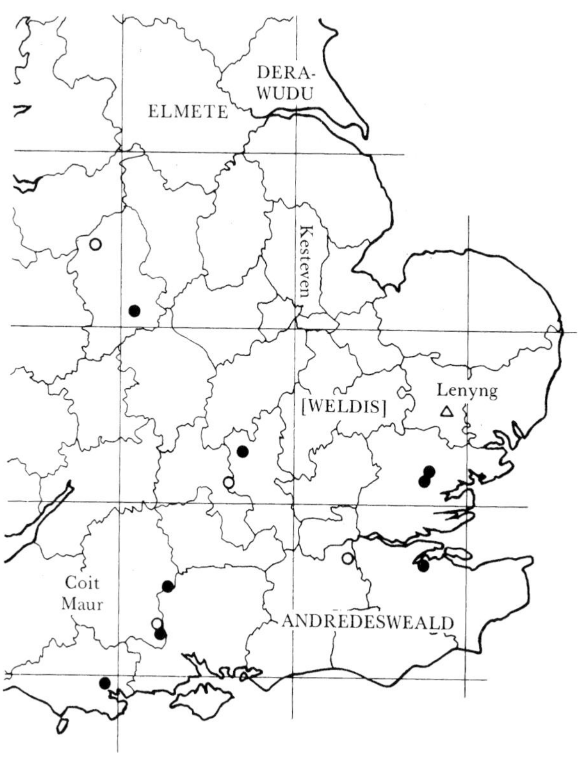

Fig. 9.8 Celtic and early Anglo-Saxon wood-names in non-Celtic parts of England. (●) *coit* place-namcs. (○) *pen + coit* place-names. Capitals: Anglo-Saxon names of wooded districts. For the wood-name Lenyng, see p. 277.

Changes in the twelfth and thirteenth centuries

England as a poorly-wooded country

Many peculiarities of the Anglo-Saxon and medieval history of England are traceable to an unexpectedly small proportion of woodland. This explains our strong tradition of woodland conservation; the early importance of hedgerows and non-woodland trees as a substitute for woodland; the development of timber transport, beginning with St Cuthbert's monks rafting timber down the Tyne in the seventh century[202] and fully established, inland and overseas, by the thirteenth century (Chapter 10); and the continuance in use of so many Roman roads. Mammals depending on large remote woodland areas disappeared early. The wild swine is last heard of in England, except as a beast of the park, around 1260 (p. 181); it flourishes to this day in much of France and Germany, which now have at least twice as much woodland, in relation to their area, as thirteenth-century England. The roe-deer is heard of by the thirteenth century only in a few places where woodland or fen was particularly abundant; it is still very common on the Continent. Beaver, bear, and lynx, extinct in England well before the Conquest, still survive in parts of Europe. Less directly, even the civilization and prosperity of Anglo-Saxon England, its attractiveness to invaders, and its early development of strong government may in part be seen as marks of a country that has passed out of the pioneering stage of human existence.

The further grubbing of woodland

Fifteen per cent of woodland was still more than the Norman population had a use for. Soon after 1086 the rising population asserted itself in the expansion both of agriculture and of woodland management. Almost all the expansion of agriculture had to come from extending the farmed area. Much of this was in the Fens[702] or on moorland or heath; but in almost every county there is some evidence of encroachment on the woods. Some leys and hursts are almost certainly post-Conquest: when documentation becomes abundant in the thirteenth century we are told of many ***assarts***, newly-won fields, although assarts were not always from woodland, were not always recent, and were usually very small.[849] There was also unintentional destruction of woodland through over-grazing, as with Thorpe Wood, Norwich, in the twelfth century, despite efforts to preserve it.[122]

This phase in the making of the landscape needs to be studied individually in different areas. In general it lasted about 250 years. It was brought to an end either by running out of woodland or by the calamities of famine in the 1310s and plague in 1348–9. In general it is the larger wooded areas that were attacked. Counties which had more woodland in 1086 lost more of it in the centuries that followed (Tables 9.1, 9.3, 9.4); but destruction is correlated with the mean size of the woods of a county as well as with the proportion of woodland (Fig. 9.9). Within counties the bigger woods usually disappeared while the smaller remained: examples are the N.W. Lincolnshire woods, Thorpe Wood (the largest in Norfolk), the big swine-woods of N.E. Suffolk, and the Neroche woods of Somerset.

The two largest wooded areas were too big to be completely destroyed in the time available. In the Weald the woods were reduced to something like their present form and extent by 1350, 'an achievement without parallel in medieval England' (P. Brandon).[616] The men of the Weald grubbed out some 450,000 acres of woodland in at most 260 years, which is not surpassed even by the contemporary draining of the Fens. Doubtless the Wealden woods would have disappeared almost completely but for the Black Death. By the time the population had recovered, the revival of an iron industry had provided a reason for not destroying any more woodland: a petitioner of *c.* 1660 claimed that there were then no fewer than 200,000 acres of coppices in Sussex.[820] The Chilterns tell a similar story of rapid destruction in the twelfth and thirteenth centuries: the remaining woods were saved by famine and pestilence and later became valuable as a source of fuel for London.[131, 802]

All the second-rank concentrations of woodland in Domesday, of from 50,000 to 200,000 acres, fared worse. Arden with north Worcestershire,[683] the Lyme, the Surrey–Berkshire area, and the wooded areas of Yorkshire, Derbyshire, and Staffordshire became no more wooded than the rest of the country. The same applied to third-rank wooded areas (10,000–30,000 acres) in Neroche, north Dorset, and N.E. Suffolk, although those in the New Forest and its environs, the Forest of Dean, S.W. Essex, and the two Northamptonshire concentrations survived.

Assuming, as is probable, that the time-scale for the Weald applied to these other areas, woodland was reduced to at most 10% of England by 1350; this is equivalent to the destruction of 17½ acres a day (5 acres in the Weald and 12½ in the rest of England) for 250 years.

The attack on the larger remaining woods has been repeated in later centuries as farmers, and latterly foresters, have claimed successively smaller woods as vacant land for their activities. The largest *continuous* area of tree-land to retain some semblance of its state under the Normans is probably 5,000 acres in Epping Forest.[124] In recent years the survival intact of an ancient wood as large as 200 acres has become quite rare. The woods least affected both by medieval and later destruction are the isolated woods and small aggregations, of Anglo-Saxon and possibly even Roman origin, in areas which by 1086 had little woodland. Eight of the nine Domesday aggregations in Lincolnshire, Leicestershire, and Cambridgeshire still exist. West Suffolk and probably Devon are also rich in small woods of great antiquity.

Anglo-Saxon woodmanship and its expansion

The Anglo-Saxons, like their predecessors, were large users not only of timber but of underwood for fencing, wattle-work, and light structures of many kinds and presumably also for fuel. The evidence comes from many excavations (e.g. at West Stow (Suffolk), where Early Anglo-Saxon buildings have been reconstructed using underwood from the Bradfield Woods) and occasionally from standing buildings (Fig. 9.10).

Few pre-Conquest documents dealing with woodland management are preserved. We get a vivid glimpse from a charter, dated 866, of Burgred, king of Mercia, granting a regular supply of

> pasture for 70 pigs in that wooded common . . . which the country-folk call Wulfferdinleh [Wolverley, Worcs] and 5 wagons full of good rods (*virgis*) and every year one oak for building . . . and wood . . . for the fire as necessary . . . [206]

Wolverley was in one of the most wooded parts of England, where woodland management should have been slow to penetrate. Yet the regular large-scale supply of rods (p. 142), as well as timber and firewood, from a wooded common presupposes not merely coppicing but compartmented wood-pasture (Chapter 12). The importance of woodmanship is eloquently illustrated by the fact that such a highly-organized variant of it should have reached this backward place by the ninth century.

In the eleventh century woodland management was still concerned more with growing material for partic-

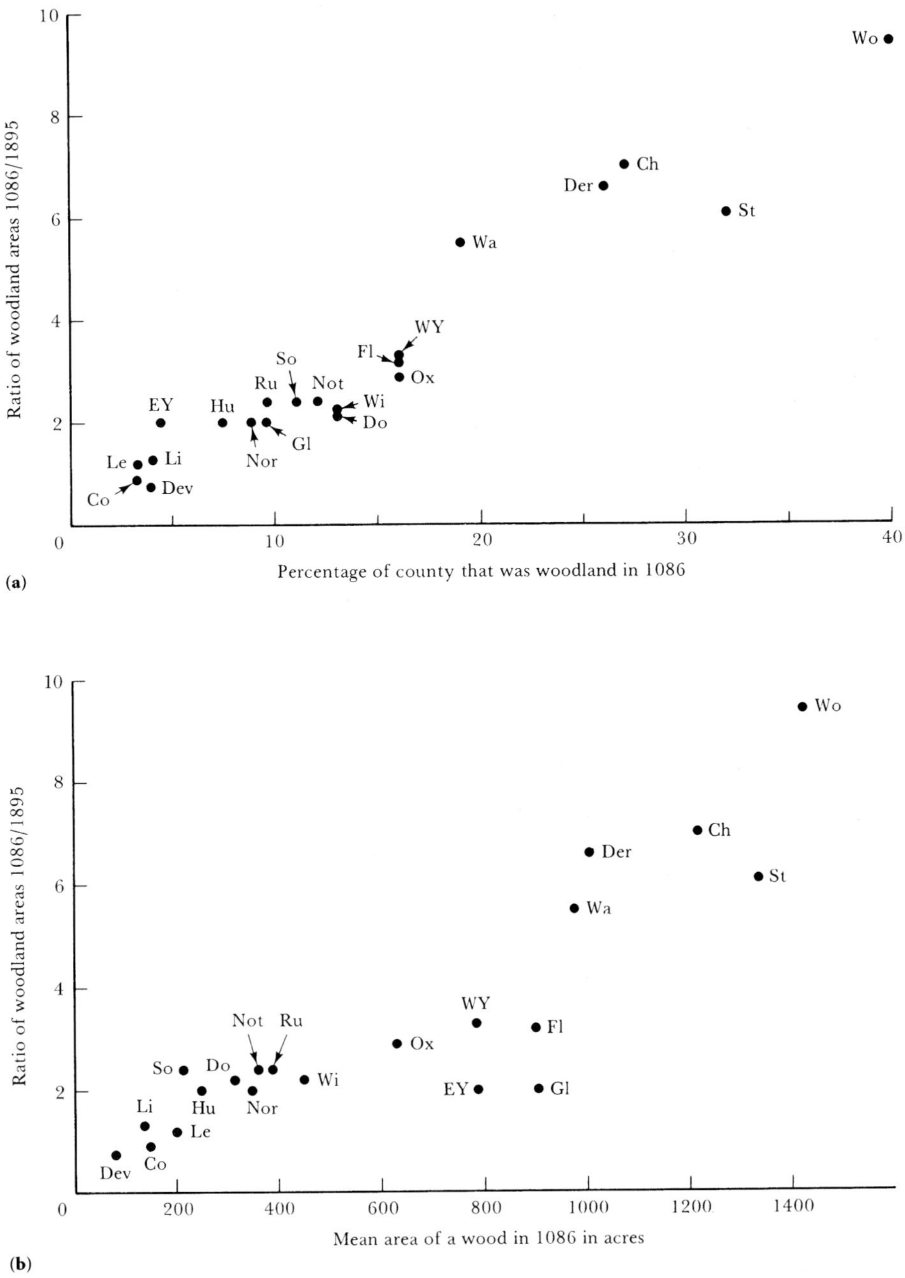

Fig. 9.9 Net destruction of woodland between 1086 and 1895 by counties as related to (**a**) the proportion of each county that was woodland in 1086; (***b***) the mean size of woods in each county in 1086. Statistics are for the area counties (Table 9.1), identified by their initial letters.

ular uses than with conservation. Some of the larger woods were still used merely for pannage and were shortly to disappear. Wood-pasture – the phrase is first recorded in 935 (p. 130) – was probably the predominant woodland land-use. Underwood, the most valuable kind of woodland, predominated in poorly-wooded areas but was not confined to them (Table 9.2).

By 1250 the various uses of woods were more sharply defined and conservation was taken for granted. Pannage had become an unimportant by-product. Wood-pasture, where it survived, had crystallized into the three forms of commons, parks, and Forests. Coppicing was almost universal, had spread even to such large wooded areas as the Forest of Dean,[69] and overlapped widely with wood-pasture. A scene had been set that was to change little in the next 600 years.

Woodland management continued to expand by the conversion of wood-pasture to underwood long after 1350, as in the New Forest in the fifteenth century[155] and in Scotland in the seventeenth.[152] In West Cambridgeshire almost all the woods appear to have been encoppiced by 1086, yet half of them had disappeared by 1300; the pressure on land was so exceptional as to

Fig. 9.10 Anglo-Saxon work in timber and underwood. One of the pre-Conquest windows of Hadstock church, Essex, with a double-splayed arched head formed entirely in concrete-like rubble masonry without the use of dressed stone. The massive oak window-frame – set deep in the thickness of the wall and therefore original – has a row of holes round its head, about which there has been much speculation. When re-examining this window I was able to show that the holes, which are oblique, served to hold the ends of stakes interwoven with ethers to form a semi-conical wattlework basket which formed the shuttering for the concrete 'arch'. Impressions of the ethers remain on the underside of the splay. On the inside of the frame similar holes, for the wattle shuttering of the inner splay, have been shown to exist.

outweigh the disadvantage of having to import wood and timber. After 1350 its population and the demands of agriculture declined, as shown by the many shrunken or deserted settlements.[869] The woods of the area are now about twice as extensive as they were in 1300, and comprise primary woods such as Hayley and Knapwell (pp. 13, 51); medieval secondary woods, all of them coppiced, such as Overhall Grove (p. 51) and parts of Buff and Eversden Woods (p. 273; Fig. 10.1); and secondary woods, some of them coppiced, of various later periods.

Added in 2003 edition

The calculation of woodland area in Domesday Book, now 25 years old, has not been seriously challenged. The figure of 15% of England could be a little too high, being over twice that known for any subsequent period. However, it is unrealistic to expect to measure woodland area to an accuracy of 1%, because of problems of definition: are the trees big enough or close enough to count as woodland? There are not many countries in the world today where the forest area can be confidently said to be, for example, 15% and not 14%.

More examples have come to light of places in woodless areas possessing woodland at a distance. For example, much of the woodland later known as Blackmoor Forest in Dorset belonged to Fordington by Dorchester, eleven miles away. Such anomalies have the effect of making the distinction between wooded and woodless areas sharper in reality than it is shown in Fig. 9.2.

The incidence of woodland among boundary features in Anglo-Saxon charters is now quantified, and correlates strongly with that in Domesday Book and from place-names. This supports the view that the broad distribution of more-wooded and less-wooded regions was laid down in Roman times and persisted into the Norman period; and that open-field strip-cultivation was a feature of the less-wooded regions.*

Della Hooke has given much attention to Anglo-Saxon landscape and woodland.

* *History of the Countryside* chapters 5, 8.

10

Woodland management, products, and uses since 1250

Woods are very stable features of the landscape; like roads and churches, they have outlasted many changes in the societies which they serve. Woodland conservation is first specifically recorded in *c.* 1100 in the orders of Herbert de Losinga, first Bishop of Norwich, concerning Thorpe Wood near Norwich,[122] but there is no reason to suppose that the idea was then new. By the thirteenth century woods were run as a permanent self-renewing asset with a regular sustained yield; whenever a tree was felled another would grow in its place. A survey of Hayley Wood in 1356 makes this particularly clear:

> A certain Wood called Heylewode which contains 80 acres by estimate. Of whose underwood there can be sold every year, without causing waste or destruction, 11 acres of underwood which are worth 55*s* at 5*s* the acre . . . There is another Wood called Litlelond which contains 26 acres by estimate. Whose underwood can be sold as a whole every seventh year. And it is then worth in all £6 10*s* at 5*s* the acre.[456]

Ownership and organization

Throughout recorded history most woods have been privately owned, although woodland could also form part of a Forest or other wood-pasture common (Chapter 12). Woodland usually formed part of an estate and until recently was seldom owned separately. The woods that we chiefly hear about are those of twenty acres or more belonging to religious houses, colleges, and the larger gentry. Small landowners and tenants had groves sometimes as small as a fraction of an acre, but these are difficult to trace and those of less than two acres seem rarely to survive. Sometimes a wood was divided among many owners, as in thirteenth-century Hethel (Norfolk):

> . . . four acres and one rod [i.e. 4¼ acres] of wood in Haþlle lying between the wood of the said Master and Brethren on the south and the wood which used to belong to Sir Bartholomew son of William to the north, and abutting on the free wood of the church of Haþlle to the east and the wood of the aforesaid Eglentine and William to the west . . .[410]

A similar elaborate subdivision is recorded by the labyrinth of woodbanks in Eversden Wood, Cambridgeshire (Fig. 10.1).

Woodland management varied in detail from owner to owner and from time to time: it is rare to find evidence of differences in the management of woods of different tree species. The surviving records probably have some bias towards the more commercial and better organized woods. Norwich Cathedral Priory and Beaulieu Abbey set standards of woodmanship which have never been surpassed; not every owner of a few acres of woodland had such a skill.

Some writers fall into the error of looking back on the Middle Ages as a time of self-sufficiency when every village lived on what grew within its own boundaries. For the woodland economy, however, trade and transport were essential. From Anglo-Saxon times many parishes had no woodland and others had more than they could use. Even places with plenty of woodland regularly bought special kinds of timber and factory-made articles like boards, hurdles, and wheels.

Underwood

Coppice cycles

There are three methods of organizing the felling of underwood. A wood may be divided into a number of ***fells***, one being cut every year according to a predetermined plan. Or the whole wood may be felled every so many years. Or the area cut year by year may be allowed to fluctuate according to variations in growth-rate and demand.

Surveys of woods, as for Hayley in 1356, are usually cast in the form of a predetermined plan of the first or second kind. Where annual statistics survive they show that the plan is really the estimated average of a more flexible procedure. The 1356 survey says that Hardwick Wood (W. Cambs) was cut on a five-year cycle: the manorial accounts show that the actual fall varied from none in three years to a third of the wood in one year, five years being a good estimate of the average.[120] In medieval *post-mortem* surveys it is surprisingly common to find woods not valued because all the underwood had just been cut: possibly the first action of the

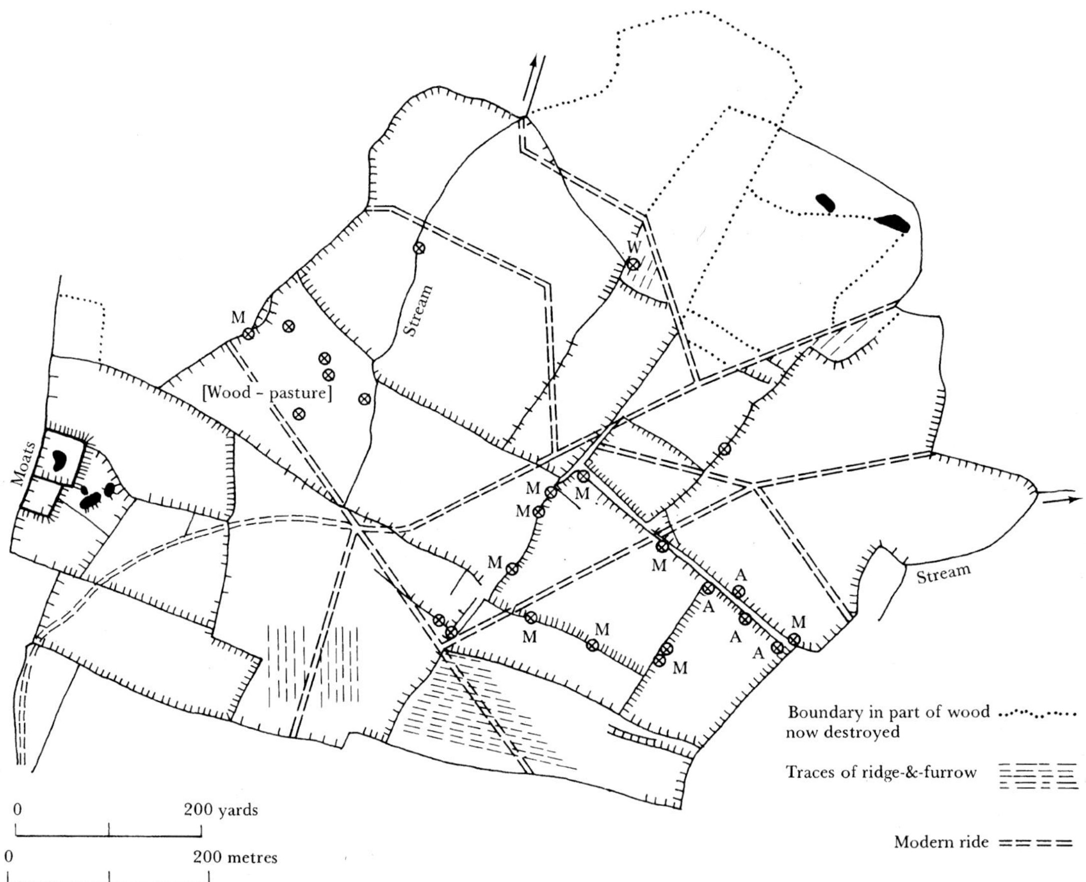
Stream
[Wood - pasture]
Moats
M
W
A
Stream
Boundary in part of wood now destroyed
Traces of ridge-&-furrow
Modern ride
0
200 yards
0
200 metres

(a)

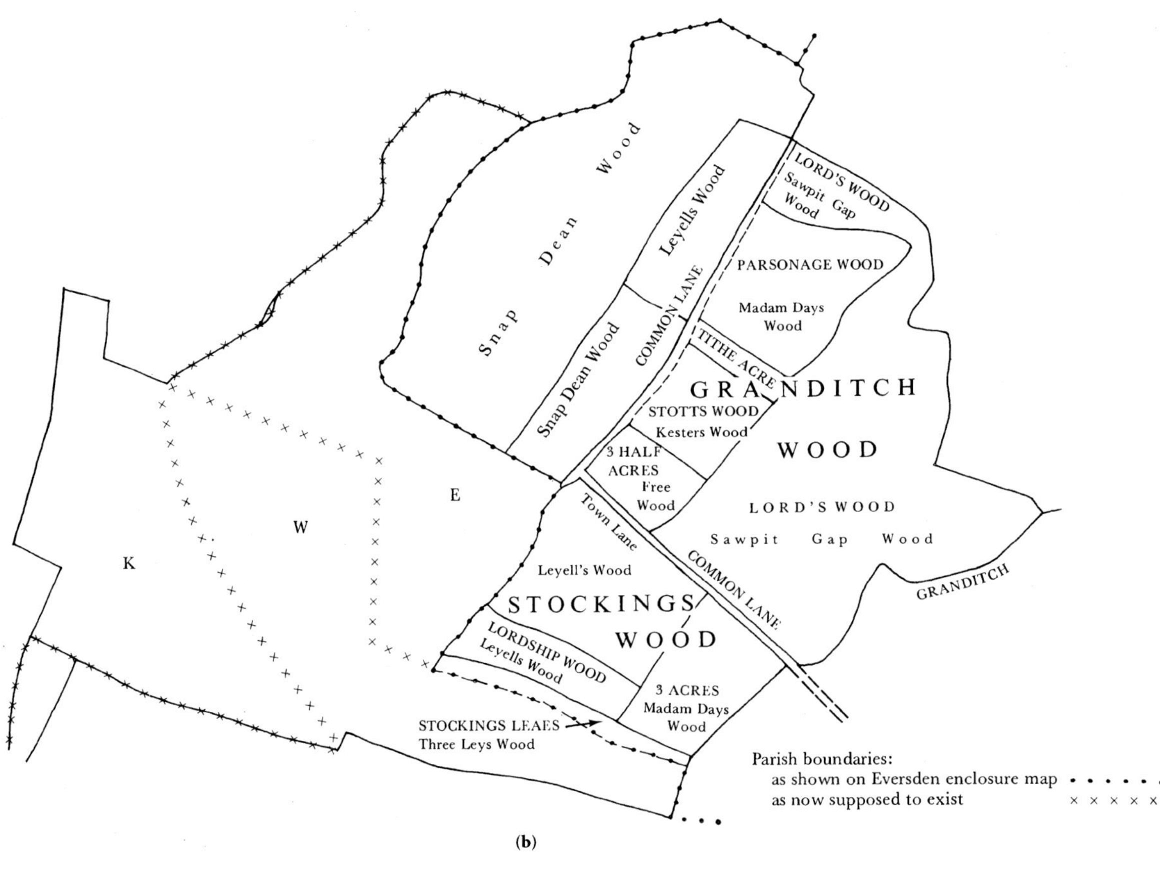
Snap Dean Wood
Leyells Wood
LORD'S WOOD
Sawpit Gap Wood
PARSONAGE WOOD
Madam Days Wood
COMMON LANE
Snap Dean Wood
TITHE ACRE
GRANDITCH WOOD
STOTTS WOOD
Kesters Wood
3 HALF ACRES
Free Wood
LORD'S WOOD
Sawpit Gap Wood
Town Lane
COMMON LANE
GRANDITCH
K
W
E
Leyell's Wood
STOCKINGS WOOD
LORDSHIP WOOD
Leyells Wood
3 ACRES
Madam Days Wood
STOCKINGS LEAES
Three Leys Wood
Parish boundaries:
as shown on Eversden enclosure map
as now supposed to exist

(b)

Fig. 10.1 Eversden Wood, Cambridgeshire. An ancient wood with a complex history, extending into three parishes (Great Eversden, Wimpole, Kingston) and formerly in many ownerships. (**a**) Earthworks and other surface features. Note the pollard trees on banks, defining property boundaries; the scattered pollards indicating a small area of former wood-pasture; the faint ridge-and-furrow indicating that at least four of the parcels have been ploughed; the pair of lanes forming a T-junction; and the double moat with associated 'fish-ponds' representing a deserted and undocumented settlement. Pollards: A = ash; M = maple; W = willow; otherwise oak. (**b**) Interpretation with the help of the Great Eversden glebe terrier (i.e. a verbal description of the church lands and their abuttals) of 1638[271] and the Eversden enclosure map of 1811.[238] Names of 1638 are in capitals; names of 1811 are in lower-case. In 1638 the Great Eversden portion was regarded as two woods, Granditch and Stockings Woods, each in several ownerships. The S.E. corner, Stockings Leaes, was still not woodland in 1638 (the word *lea* is here used in its special Cambridgeshire sense of 'one unit of ridge-and-furrow in pasture on former arable').[453] By 1811 the names and ownerships had all changed and 'Stockings Leaes' had become woodland. Similar subdivisions presumably existed in the Wimpole and Kingston portions but no documentation for them is known.

Shortly after 1811 the ownerships were amalgamated and a system of rides was set out (Fig. 10.1a) ignoring the old boundaries, although the boundary pollards as well as the earthworks remain. By the time of the large-scale Ordnance Surveys, from 1887 onwards, the true course of the parish boundaries had been forgotten. Modern maps misassign the area marked E (Fig. 10.1b) to Great Eversden; areas W and K are supposed to belong to Kingston and Wimpole. Presumably the Kingston–Wimpole boundary is a corruption of a parish boundary that originally followed one of the earthworks.

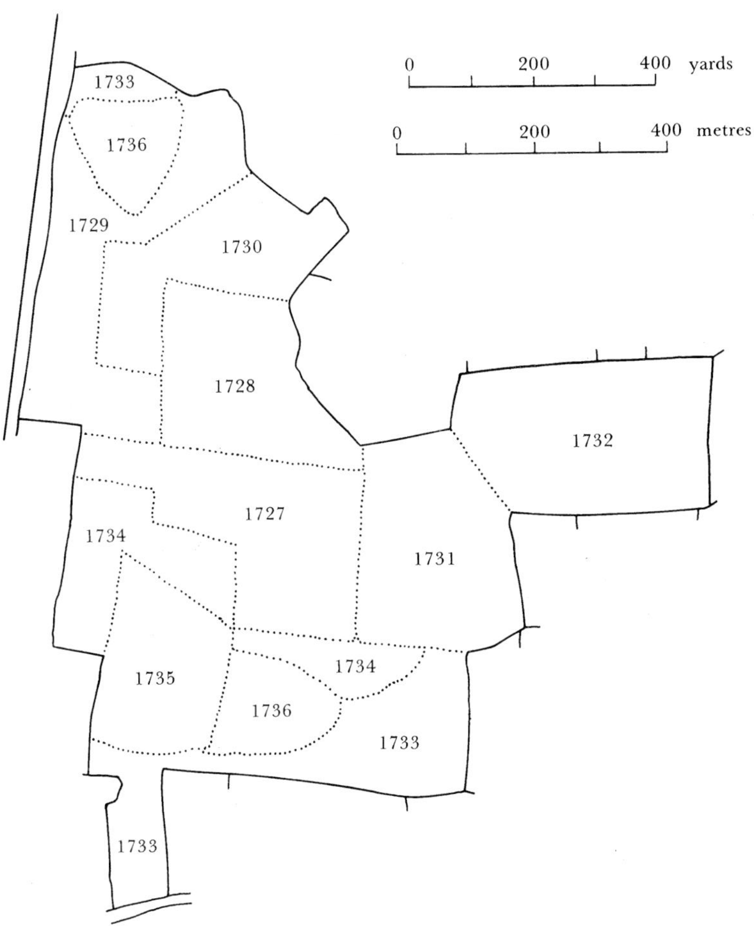

Fig. 10.2 Link Wood (W. Suffolk) coppiced in the traditional irregular manner. The whole wood was felled in the ten years from 1727 to 1736. In some years (e.g. 1732) twice as much was cut as in others (e.g. 1736). Note the very irregular shapes of the 1729 and 1734 panels and the two panels for 1733 and again for 1736. After a contemporary large-scale map.[217]

deceased's executors was to sell the underwood lest it fall into the wrong hands.

In later centuries some woods continued to be cut irregularly (Fig. 10.2). Others were managed with strict regularity, each fell within a wood, or the whole of a wood on an estate with many woods, being cut every twelve or fifteen years. As anyone who manages a wood will know, such inflexibility works better on paper than it does on the ground. Growth rates vary from one cycle to the next, markets fluctuate, and woodmen fall ill. Underwood is none the worse for being cut a year or two early or late, and before the days of deposit accounts a wood often formed a convenient temporary store of capital.

For Eastern England, records or estimates of coppice rotations range from 4 to 28 years (Fig. 10.3). In the Middle Ages coppice cycles were usually short or very short (4–8 years); about 20% of woods had longer cycles (12–20 years), but anything over 20 years is unknown. From the sixteenth to the eighteenth century most woods ranged from 10 to 20 years, with a few longer and a few shorter cycles, but rotations of less than 6 years had disappeared. After 1850 the short rotations of less than 10 years disappear and there is some decline in the very long rotations.

This lengthening of the rotation from an average of 6 years in the thirteenth century to 14 or 15 years in the nineteenth can be shown in some woods to be a gradual process (Fig. 10.4). In the region as a whole the evidence strongly suggests a rapid change between 1420 and 1540. This might be due to a change in demand from faggots to burn on an open hearth to billets and logs for chimneys (pp. 167–8); it might also involve the rising cost of labour or a decline in woodland fertility, owing to the removal of phosphate in successive crops of underwood,[114] and consequently falling growth-rates. The poor documentation of this period does not allow us to decide.

The earliest formal account of wood production

This is to be found in the account-book of Beaulieu Abbey (Hants), written in 1269–70. (From the Camden Society edition,[347] by permission; my translation; prices originally expressed in Paris money, worth a third of sterling, and here converted.)

THE FORESTER'S TABLE

Bundles

From one arpent or one acre of grove, of the age of twenty years and of average value, are usually collected 400 dozen bundles of small burning wood, of which each bundle contains five pieces of wood a little less thick than the thickness of a lance and three feet long. And pieces of wood, found among the others, thicker than this amount are split into two, three, or four as their thickness requires.

100 dozen of the said burning wood are cut, tied, and made ready for 1*s* 4*d*.

A four-wheeled cart with two horses can usually carry 20 dozen of the said bundles, and 2 bundles of the said wood are sold for 1/3*d*. And one dozen of the said bundles is sold in the grove for 1*d*.

Furthermore, from the same arpent or acre there can be collected 500 bundles of vine-stakes (*paxillorum ad vineas*) or rods for fencing, of which 100 are cut and made ready for 8*d*. And in each bundle there are 40 *paxilli* at least 6 ft long. And 100 of the said bundles are worth 2*s* in the grove.

Faggots

In addition there are made from the same arpent or acre 4,000 oven-faggots (*fagatorum furnille*) of which a thousand are cut and made ready for 1*s* 4*d*. And 100 of the said faggots are worth 4*d* in the grove.

Coti

If, however, the grove is too young, so that the wood cannot be split, it should be cut and made ready for a lower price according to age.

But if the grove is sited in a difficult place full of stones, the wood can then be cut at a height of a foot. And then there remain *coti* which afterwards are cut close to the ground and are made into charcoal, whose quantity and value are not fixed, because of the variable quality of the *coti*.

Measurement

The *modulus* is a certain round or square iron hoop two feet wide and long and 6 ft in circumference. The wood to be measured in this hoop is as thick as a man's thigh, round or split as its thickness requires, and 2½ ft long. And the said hoop, full of the said wood, is cut and prepared for 1/3*d*. And it is worth 2 2/3*d* in the grove and is sold for 6 2/3*d*. One cart with two horses can carry 8 measures, i.e. eight of the said hoops filled. And this wood is called measure-wood.

This is an abstract description, but is linked to reality by an account of the felling of a particular parcel of woodland, from which it can be worked out that these yields of wood and money were actually obtained.

The main product of this, as of many woods, was firewood. Large underwood was cut to length as billets and measured by packing into the *modulus*; smaller sizes were sold as sticks; slender straight rods made the small stakes called *paxilli*; twigs and branches were tied up as faggots. Nothing was wasted; odds and ends were burnt to charcoal and sold.

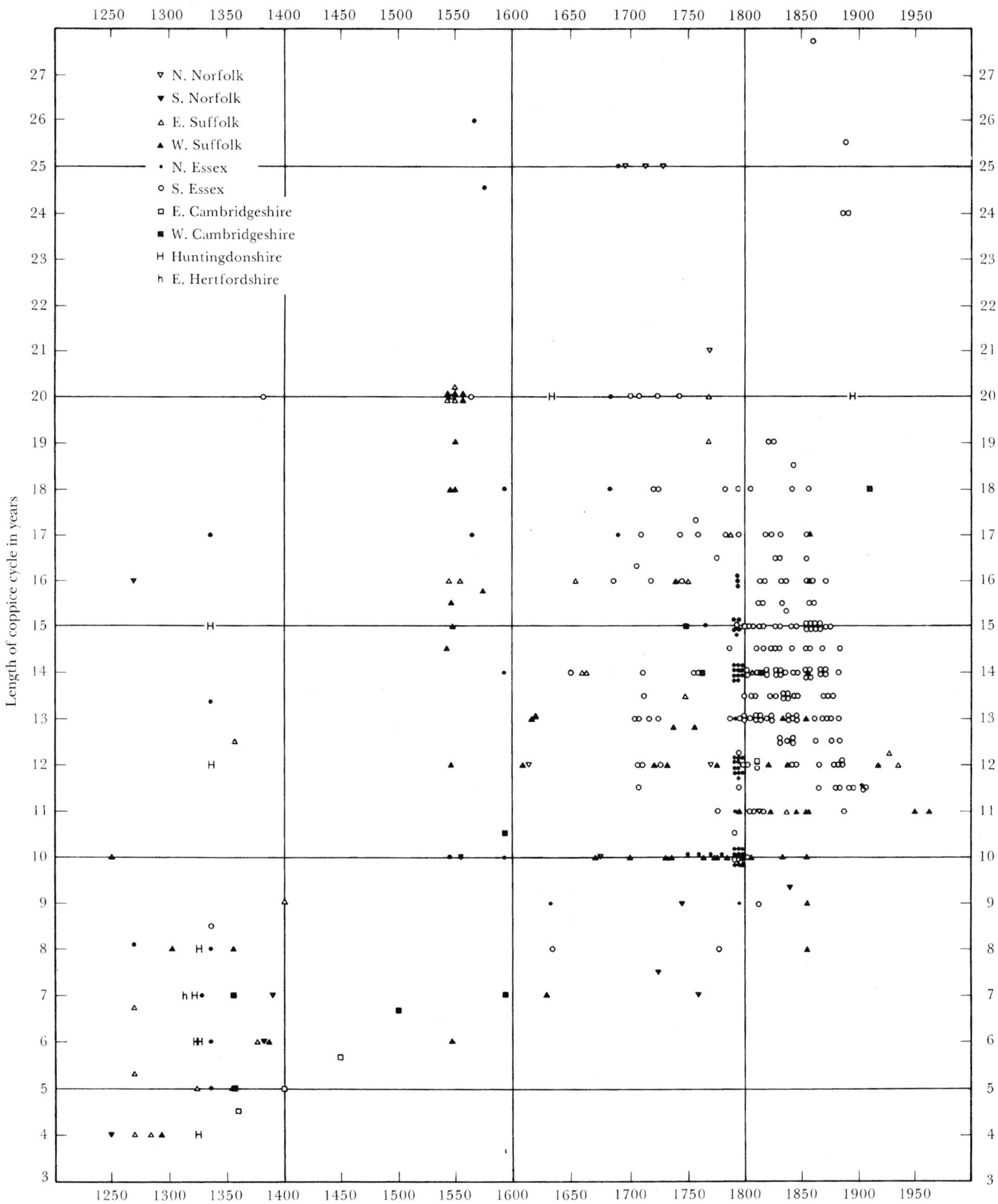

Fig. 10.3 Coppice cycles in woods in Eastern England from the thirteenth to the twentieth century. Each point is one estimate of the length of a coppicing rotation (often of the average length of an irregular rotation). From sources[270, 315a, 446a, 449, 456] and other surveys, accounts, etc. too numerous to specify in detail.

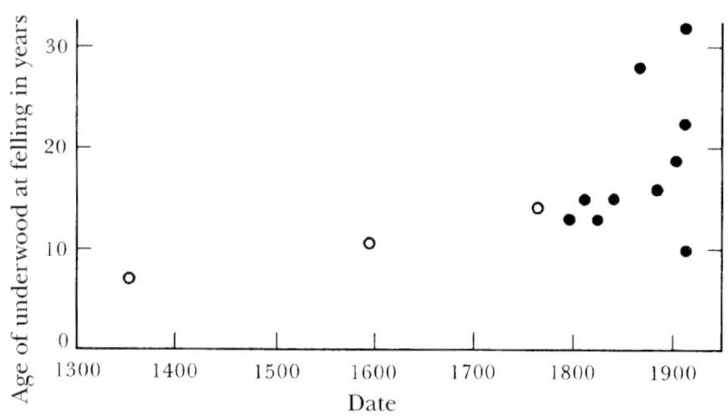

Fig. 10.4 The lengthening coppice cycle at Hayley Wood. Derived from management records (○) and the annual rings in stool bases (●).[120]

Both the twenty-year-old underwood envisaged in the Table and the wood actually sold in the account were of hazel or some other species too slender to sell by the *modulus*. The yields per acre were identical:

	Value standing	Cost of felling, etc.	Value in bundles	Value as delivered
24,000 firewood sticks	28*s*	5*s* 4*d*	33*s* 4*d*	66*s* 8*d*
20,000 small stakes	6*s* 8*d*	3*s* 4*d*	10*s*	
4,000 faggots	8*s*	5*s* 4*d*	13*s* 4*d*	
Total per acre	42*s* 8*d*	14*s*	56*s* 8*d*	

These amounted to some thirty cartloads, probably 40–50 tons, i.e. over two tons per acre per annum, which seems a high yield, even if nothing was wasted. The expected return of 2*s* 1½*d* per acre per annum is over twice the maximum recorded for Eastern England, even though wood was plentiful in Hampshire. It was probably a big acre (p. 19): the manuscript is damaged at the point where it gave the length of the perch.

This was not the whole operation of the woodland. The annual account includes £40 from the sale of timber by the acre, apparently from another part of the wood; among the expenses are £3 for the stipend of the 'forester' – this term is explained later – and £2 on maintenance.

This is an elaborate example of a procedure found in most sufficiently-recorded woods. It is unusual to find a wood in which timber production predominated over underwood, and the separation of timber and wood into different parts of the woodland, as the sale of timber by the acre suggests, is a particularly rare refinement. But the division into *large* and *small* underwood, the latter being either of hazel or on a shorter coppice cycle, is frequent.

Underwood products

In the early twentieth century there was a vast range of underwood trades, whose techniques and social relations are described by H. E. Fitzrandolph and M. D. Hay[57] and H. L. Edlin.[49] Most of these crafts, often curious and sometimes ancient, used only small quantities or particular species of wood. At this point we are more concerned with bulk underwood for general purposes, which in medieval (as in Neolithic) woodland centred on the production of ***rods***, Latin *virge*. Samples preserved in the wattle-and-daub of buildings show the *virga* to have been a hazel or sallow stem, 1–2 in. in diameter at the base, 3–6 ft high to the end of the first season's growth (2.5–5 x 90–180 cm), with 5–8 annual rings.

Fuelwood

Faggots are bundles of rods or twigs too small to burn separately. They are made from small underwood, branches (called ***brushwood*** or ***spray***) from large underwood, or the lop-and-top of timber trees, tightly tied with a special twisted rod called a ***bond*** or ***band*** (Fig. 10.5). They produce a short hot blaze suitable for heating bread-ovens or burning heretics or bricks. Common names for particular kinds, from the largest to the smallest, are *two-band faggot* [Plate 10], *one-band faggot*, *kid*, *bavin*, and *ostrey* (the last being a firelighter). Faggots are laborious to make – in the Middle Ages the cost of making was usually about a quarter of the selling price – but use up waste products. They appear continuously from the 1250s. They were used for baking at Long Melford (Suffolk) into the 1970s. Other uses for faggots include land-drains – the predecessors of tile-drains – and marshland sea-defences, the chief surviving use (Fig. 10.6).

'Log' is a word first recorded in the Latinized phrase *schredinghe logarum de I acr'* di' 'de-branching the logs from 1½ acres' at Tindall Wood, Ditchingham (Norfolk) in 1271.[462] This was a long-rotation wood – it is now of hornbeam (pp. 233–4) and logs were evidently the main product. Terms for various kinds of logs are *shide*, *billet*, *talwood* (apparently from Norman-French *boys de tailz*, 'coppice-wood'), and *astell*. Pollard poles, like

Fig. 10.5 A traditional faggot, held together with a hazel band tied with a peculiar knot. Made in the Bradfield Woods by Mr R. Last, 1971.

large coppice, were made into a combination of billets and faggots (for details, see p. 323).

From the fifteenth century, attempts were made to standardize the sizes of firewood. A statute of 1542[487] prescribed that faggots for sale had to be 3 ft long and ¾ yard in girth (0.9 x 0.7 m). There were five permitted sizes for shides, all of the same length but of different girths:

> Every shyde of talwood to conteyne in lengthe foure fote . . . at the least besyde the carfe,* and every tall shyde of oone to be in greatnes in the myddes twentie Inches . . . at the leaste . . .
> And everye tall shyde named of fyve, to conteyne in greatnes . . . 44 ynches . . .

**Kerf*, the oblique face produced by cross-cutting with an axe.

Billets were to be 3½ ft long and either 9 or 12 inches in girth.

Billets were the commonest kind of log, and andirons of the period are designed to take them. Shides could be much larger, up to 14 in. in diameter. These evidently came from the branches of timber trees or the trunks of standard trees unsuitable for timber. Later the billet sizes were elaborated so that billets could be sold cleft into two or four with corresponding adjustments in the permitted girths.[489]

Charcoal

Charcoal, a common industrial and urban fuel, came mainly from well-wooded areas, where its convenience of handling and light weight outweighed the energy wasted in making it. Records in Eastern England are thinly scattered; they include place-names such as Colierscroft, Collier Row, and Carbonel. At Abbot's Ripton (Hunts) in 1252 the tenants were required to transport the lord's underwood products, including charcoal, as a labour service.[247]

Charcoal is made by burning wood in an insufficient supply of air: usually in pits, but later in the more familiar earth-covered stacks, and later still in iron retorts and kilns. Wood-leases, as at Long Stratton (Norfolk) in 1581,[424] occasionally specify that charcoal-pits must be filled up afterwards; it is doubtful whether any survive. Some South Essex wood-leases forbid charcoal-burning.[275, 296]

Gunpowder charcoal is further dealt with in Chapter 18.

Fig. 10.6 Faggots made of the spray of *Tilia cordata*, tied with wire, to be used for preventing erosion in salt-marshes. Brundon Wood, north Essex, 1978.

Hurdles and fencing-stuff

Hurdles are of two kinds: one made of small underwood rods interwoven; the other of large underwood, like a small seven-barred gate, incorporating at least ten nails. Wattle hurdles were the commoner kind in the Middle Ages. At Gamlingay in 1333 hurdles had to be bought, 'for lack of *virge* in the Wood', and yet in the following season there was a record production of kids.[399] Wattle hurdles were used, and are sometimes depicted, as fencing, for sheepfolds, for conveying traitors to the gallows, and in sea-defences.[328] Gate-hurdles also existed: at Takeley (Essex) in 1325 there were eighteen hurdles of which four were wattle,[337] and at Hatfield Broadoak nearby in 1377–8 hurdles were made of cleft sapwood of oak (*cost' querc'*).[316] Hurdles are rarely mentioned in large numbers.

Fencing-stuff ranged from stakes and thorns for mending gaps in hedges to complete fences of stakes interwoven with thin rods called ***ethers***. Stakes and ethers are still used in some forms of the craft of 'laying', anciently ***plashing***, a hedge.

Wattle-and-daub [see also p. 465]

Underwood is often preserved in the wattle-and-daub of timber-framed buildings. There are many regional variants. In East Anglia the panels are tall and narrow; each has three ***splints***, horizontal bars wedged into mortices and grooves cut in the timber frame, which hold in place several vertical rods, the whole being buried in daub. The splints are usually oak (records often specify ash), the rods hazel or sallow. In southern England the splints are often vertical. Sometimes the upright *virge* are replaced by oak laths, and I have seen more or less elaborate interweavings of laths instead of underwood. Wattle-and-daub of a more flimsy kind continued to be made long after the Middle Ages. Splints were sold from Wayland Wood (Norfolk) as late as 1856[514] and I know a Suffolk example which is almost certainly twentieth century.

Some other products

Thatching wood is an essential small use of underwood. In the Middle Ages, as now, ***sways***, ***spars***, and ***broaches*** were constantly bought for the *arundinator* (Latin for reed thatcher) or *coopertor* (straw thatcher).

Poles of various kinds were made from large underwood. Hop-gardens were big consumers in some areas. Hops were grown in medieval and perhaps Anglo-Saxon Kent,[917] but elsewhere are probably later. Hop-poles, or poles so called, appear at Ingrave (Essex) *c.* 1575[303] and from Wayland Wood (Norfolk) in 1594.[510] Nineteenth-century wood-books on some large estates record sales of poles in minute, though often unilluminating, detail.

Underwood organization

Some woods had residual common-rights. At Hayley Wood in 1251 certain villagers had rights to specified allocations of fencing-stuff for which they paid 68 hens annually.[270] At Hardwick nearby a similar right persisted; by 1587 the allocation had become 'one Rindge of woode' at what was then seven years' growth.[441] This measure for woodland, $^1/_8$ acre, is found also in N.W. Essex in the eighteenth and nineteenth centuries[302] and still survives in West Cambridgeshire in a decimalized form ($^1/_{10}$ acre). Hardwick Wood, which is long and narrow, was allotted to the villagers in one-rindge strips across its width.[442] Such a 'dole' allocation is common in meadows; in woodland it would result in disputes over the ownership of stools on rindge boundaries, and I know of no other example.

With these exceptions, underwood was used, or more often sold, by the owner of the wood. Sales were often of standing underwood to a bulk purchaser, presumably a woodmonger. From 1550 to 1800 woods were sometimes leased; examples of wood-leases are given later. At all times some wood was sold, either standing or in the form of faggots or logs, direct to the consumer. A typical sale was in 1787–8 of £80 worth of wood from Kingston and Eversden woods (W. Cambs) to 125 different customers, like 'Widow Prat – 4*s*', some poor cottager buying her ton or two of winter logs.[239]

Underwood is difficult to transport because of its weight and bulk in relation to its value. Small purchasers seldom lived more than two parishes away from the wood. Wood could be sent to other estates in the same ownership: the Hardwick accounts for 1412 record the cutting of underwood 'in the Lord's wood of Heylee [Hayley]',[443] apparently because Hardwick Wood had temporarily run out. Woodmongers conveyed wood to places, particularly towns like Cambridge, which had no local supply. Wood was sent by water from coastal South Essex to London.[274] At Mettingham (N.E. Suffolk) in 1562 it was claimed that the woods 'are sold at highe prises because ye same may be conveyed to London by walter [water]',[403] although the distance is well over 100 miles! Wood was rarely used more than twenty miles from where it grew; only in recent years, because there is no organized underwood trade, has it become usual to go 100 miles or more (e.g. from Essex to Somerset) to get thatching wood, etc.

Hurdles were sometimes made locally; in some woods such as Hayley hurdle-making was, in theory, one of the labour services which the medieval tenant owed his lord.[270] But from the thirteenth century the skill to make a good hurdle was uncommon; some hurdles were made in the wood but most were bought from specialists anticipating the modern wattle-hurdle makers in Cranborne Chase (Dorset) or the gate-hurdle factory which operated until the 1970s at Barrow (W. Suffolk).

Timber [see also Chapter 29]

It is difficult to generalize about timber trees in woods. Unlike underwood, they are almost entirely the direct result of management – of deciding which trees to treat as timber – and reflect the attitudes, fortunes, and whims of particular owners. Timber has often been regarded, not only as a source of regular income like wood, but as a long-term reserve of material or capital for use in emergency: it was the one emergency reserve of the average landowner whose realization would not damage – indeed it would often enhance – the productivity of the estate. Numbers and sizes of timber trees were often determined by how long had elapsed since the last building project or financial crisis.

The competition between timber trees and underwood particularly for light, was widely recognized:

> The tymber & decaying trees mencioned . . . may be taken when the coppices shalbe sold, for that they stand to the spoile of the vnderwoods therin.
>
> (Northamptonshire, 1604)[464]

> A great part of the timber trees growing upon . . . Munsces Park were felled in or about 1656 and 1657 and on the fall of the same the underwood of . . . Munsces Park is become of a greater value by a third part than it was when the timber was standing.
>
> (Bradfield Woods, W. Suffolk, 1669)[454]

> The Timber if not taken down would howse your underwood and spoil its growth.
>
> (Raydon near Hadleigh, Suffolk, eighteenth century)[364]

Species

By far the commonest timber tree in nearly all kinds of woodland is oak. The second commonest in the records and in woods as they are now is usually ash. In ancient buildings at least 97% of the timber is oak, most of the rest is elm, and other species including ash are rare. I shall assume that timber is oak unless otherwise stated. Examples of elm are:

(i) Grundle House, Stanton (W. Suffolk),[845] a slightly larger than average all-timber farmhouse of about 1500. Eighty per cent of the timbers are oak and 20% elm. The species are largely interchangeable but elm tends to be used in places well away from the weather and for very long timbers such as the collar-purlin.

(ii) Long Lane Farm, East Hatley (W. Cambs), an unusually small and humble late-medieval farmhouse extended in the nineteenth century. Both the solid original structure and the flimsy additions are entirely elm. Elm was then mainly a hedgerow tree in the district, but oak should have been the commonest local woodland timber.

(iii) Blackfriars, Gloucester, a Dominican friary converted into a house in the 1540s.[847] The heavy principal-joists of the floors then inserted are elm – *Ulmus procera* being the common hedgerow tree of the area – whereas those of the original thirteenth-century floor are oak brought from a distance (p. 153).

Numbers and sizes of trees

The Middle Ages

Medieval documents rarely tell us directly about sizes of trees; the evidence comes chiefly from building timbers. There was a close link between carpentry, woodmanship, and the design of buildings; the carpenter often chose and felled the trees himself. Medieval carpentry characteristically used large numbers of small oaks. The timbers are whole logs squared with the adze, a process called ***scappling*** (Latin *scapulatio*). Each timber, large or small, is made out of the smallest tree that will serve the purpose; the timbers are usually ***waney***, i.e. rounded at the corners through reaching the outside of the log; the sapwood is almost always left on. In the fifteenth century it was sometimes the practice to saw a log lengthwise into two, but lengthwise sawing (apart from boards) was avoided if possible. This is obvious in most medieval buildings in Eastern England (Fig. 10.7), except for some of the grander church roofs, and in many other places including Sussex and Oxford; my chief exception, Gloucester Blackfriars, has a special explanation (p. 153). Carpenters made ingenious use of oaks that were not straight, and deliberately selected curved trees for crucks or braces, but the latter were used in small numbers and there is no reason to suppose them specially grown.

Table 10.1 is an analysis of the numbers of trees contained in various representative buildings. Grundle House has just been described; I ignore the difference between oak and elm. Corpus Christi College is an unostentatious two-storeyed community house built round a single court; its outer walls are of stone. Norwich Cathedral roofs were typical of the great utilitarian roofs above the vaults of cathedrals, many of which (e.g. at Wells and Lincoln) date from the thirteenth century.[735] King's College Chapel roof,[868] though later concealed by a vault, is typical of the more ostentatious Perpendicular church roofs. The Swaffham Prior house is a small three-celled house of *c.* 1600 in an area without woodland.

Except for King's College Chapel, a sumptuous royal building of great span, all these structures use quite slender oaks. Class 4, a usual size for a 'mature' oak nowadays, is hardly represented at all. Rafters are commonly made from whole oak trees no more than 6 in. in diameter; their straightness rules out the possibility of branches or top-lengths. Latin documents call these *quercus de cheverons*, 'rafter-oaks' (Fig. 10.7). In one very small Suffolk house – a rare survival of a very humble dwelling – the rafters are smaller even than Class 0. Oaks used in buildings were usually felled at from twenty to seventy years' growth.

The timbers of ordinary buildings are usually up to

Fig. 10.7 The Tadlow Granary (Cambs), a small utilitarian building of the early fifteenth century. All the timbers except planks are squared from whole lengths of oak-tree. Each original rafter represents an entire oak 25–30 years old and no more than 6 in (15 cm) in diameter.
[Now moved to Wandlebury Country Park near Cambridge. The special planks that fit between the uprights are Baltic oak (p. 462).]

20 ft (6 m) long; any that are longer are usually crooked, knotty, and tapering where they reach into the crown of a tree that was not really long enough. This results from woodland structure. An oak in a wood usually has a bole of this length because the underwood prevents it from branching; above the underwood canopy it branches out and the trunk is lost. This is illustrated, for a later century, by Fig. 10.10a, which shows a wood that could easily provide beams 20 ft long, that had a few oaks from which 28-ft beams could just be cut provided the quality did not matter, but in which anything longer was impossible. The span of buildings is limited by this property of oaks. The great barns – those largest and earliest of extant timber buildings, a witness to the enterprise of the monks (Fig. 10.8) – are divided up by posts but sometimes manage a span of 30 ft.

Cathedral roofs, with their wide span and steep pitch, each called for several hundred oaks with a reasonably straight length of about 35 ft (11 m). These come into the class of outsize timber to be discussed later. The Norman cathedrals of England are rarely

Table 10.1 Numbers and sizes of trees contained in various buildings. Trees arc classified by basal diameter under bark, each class corresponding to twice the cross-section area of the previous class.

Class of tree	Basal diameter in	(cm)	House at Swaffham Prior, Cambs	Grundle House, Stanton, W. Suffolk	Corpus Christi College, Cambridge	Norwich Cathedral (main roofs)	King's College Chapel Cambridge main roof
0	4½–6	(11–)	—	32	—	—	—
1	6½–8½	(16–)	38	140	1,249	—	—
2	9–12½	(22–)	34	121	91	—	336
3	13–17½	(32–)	7	36½	60	675	48
4	18–25½	(45–)	—	3	—	—	107
5	26–36½	(65–)	—	—	—	—	42
Total trees			79	332½	1,400	675	533
Length and width of frame: ft			40 x 16	67 x 20	402 x 24	505 x 36	289 x 46
(m)			(12 x 5)	(20½ x 6)	(123 x 7½)	(154½ x 11)	(88 x 14)

Dimensions given, in the case of buildings with more than one range, are the combined length and mean width of the ranges.
The method of analysis and other details have been published elsewhere.[845]

more than 36 ft in span. The Norman cathedrals of Sicily, which are up to twice as wide, and Old St Peter's, Rome, spanning about 80 ft (24 m), depended on finding great conifers, to be used as tie-beams bridging the span; these were not available in England. Not until the fourteenth century, when timber engineering had reached its zenith and roofs could be made to span nearly twice the length of the available timbers, did a few buildings in England (e.g. Westminster Hall) have unsupported widths approaching those of Sicily.

Woodland accounts record the felling, sale, and transport of oaks. At Gamlingay and Hardwick (W. Cambs) the prices of oaks ranged from 0.30*d* to 20*d* each; there were also sales of oak stakes at from 0.23*d* to 0.30*d*.[118] Allowing for fluctuations in the value of money, there was at least a ninety-fold range in the values of oaks in ordinary woodland; but, as we shall see, outsize oaks could change hands for much larger sums. Numbers of timber trees were variable but often large. At Gamlingay 40 acres (16 ha) of woodland supplied at least 561 trees of various sizes in 1333–7, and about 180 trees, mainly oaks in 1358–9.[399, 400] Various Norfolk woods had from five to forty timber trees to the acre in the fifteenth century,[10] which is a fair estimate of the range.

To summarize, in a typical medieval wood the oaks were of various sizes and ages but mainly very young; what we would regard as 'mature' oaks were rather few. There was a rapid and irregular turnover, trees being felled as occasion demanded and replaced without difficulty.

Sixteenth and seventeenth centuries

In this period the modern practice spread of making building timbers out of oaks grown to a larger size and sawn lengthwise into many pieces. This is a technical retrogression, for it is wasteful (especially with crooked trees) and weakens the timbers if the grain is not straight. As a result of this change it becomes difficult to tell how many or how large trees went into a building, but surveys of woods and sales of timber begin to record the sizes of trees, usually measured by the *cubic foot* (pp. 161–2). The oaks of medieval buildings (Table 10.1) usually contain less than 12 cu. ft; a good-sized modern oak contains about 40 cu. ft and a big one 100 cu. ft; exceptional oaks can grow much larger still (e.g. the Golanos Oak, Monmouthshire, felled in 1810, measured 2,426 cu. ft).[389]

There was a very wide variation in the number of timber trees; for instance, at Barking (Suffolk) in 1607, Bonny Wood had 20.0 timber trees to the acre while the neighbouring Swingen's Wood had none.[362] The maximum recorded is about 40 to the acre (100 per ha). Sizes were similarly variable but there is a distinct tendency towards larger oaks; for instance, half the trees in Bonny Wood in 1609 averaged 34.2 cu. ft each.[457] From 1540 to 1580 it was the custom for surveys to state that woods were 'sett with okes of [*x*] yeres groweth': see p. 223 for an example. Estimates of age range from thirty to 200 years but there is no hint as to how or with what confidence they were arrived at. Even a century later it was unsettled whether growth rings were annual or not.[335]

From 1483 onward, attempts were made to control woodland management by legislation. The most important statute, the 'Acte for the preservacion of woods' in 1543, required woods to contain a minimum of twelve standard trees per acre, 'not felled . . . till they . . . shalbe of tenne ynches square within thre fote of the ground'.[487] Other provisions required woods to be fenced after felling to protect the spring, forbade woods to be grubbed out, and tried to regulate wood-pasture. It is unlikely that the statute had much effect,

Fig. 10.8 The great barn of *c.* 1200 at Coggeshall Abbey, Essex, measuring 121 x 43 ft (37 x 13 m).
[It has been completely and skilfully repaired and now belongs to the National Trust. For the nearby, similar barns at Cressing Temple and their timber content, see p. 461.]

for it enjoined what were already long-established practices which owners had a strong economic interest in observing. The Act had many loopholes and, as regards timber trees, the penalty of 3*s* 4*d* per tree was soon rendered useless by inflation. I know of only two prosecutions (both in Essex)[673] and no applications for exemption. The relative prices of timber and wood (Chapter 11) encouraged owners to grow timber. Leases and contracts for the sale of underwood specify how many staddles (young timber trees) the purchaser shall leave standing. The statutory figure of twelve to the acre is sometimes mentioned – I have seen it as late as 1871 – but most wood-leases specify twenty or more staddles to the acre: for an extreme example see p. 336.

Eighteenth century

Surveys of woods in Eastern England show that the timber trees averaged around 22 per acre (55 per ha). The range varies from five to thirty-five trees per acre: we rarely if ever hear of timber-less woods, nor did woods ever have as many timber trees as we should expect from the number of staddles supposed to have been promoted.

Most surveys are imprecise because they fail to state how big a staddle had to get before it counted as a timber tree. Surveys recording staddles as well as timber show that usually there was an ample supply of staddles, but the ratio of staddles to timber trees could vary greatly even between adjacent woods: a survey of trees in eight woods in Little Cornard (Suffolk) in 1774 gives ratios ranging from 3 : 1 to 1 : 2.[511]

Some surveys give details of individual trees, as in Figs. 10.9 and 10.10. Dunmow High Wood was a survival of what would have been a typical distribution in the Middle Ages; all sizes were present, with a preponderance of young trees and very few that would nowadays be 'mature'; there had evidently been a rapid turnover of small oaks. Dunmow New Wood shows the distribution in what was then a newly-formed secondary wood. Toppinghoe Hall, in contrast, is an early example of a 'modern' age-distribution, with a preponderance of big oaks, hardly any young ones (though many small ashes), and evidently no turnover; it foreshadows events to come.

For Shadwell Wood, Ashdon (Fig. 10.10a), we are given the distribution of height and girth in a wood still having the 'medieval' age-distribution recorded at Dunmow. 'Height' here means the length of the trunk up to the point at which it becomes too slender to be timber. An oak reached, early in life, a maximum height, 20–26 ft, determined largely by the competition of the underwood, and thereafter increased in girth but not in effective height. Figure 10.10b shows a much less common growth-pattern in which the oaks went on growing in height as well as in girth; this may be characteristic of *Quercus petraea*, the less common of the two oaks (Chapter 17), with its greater tendency to apical dominance. In the adjacent Pheasant-house Wood I recorded a very similar height-girth distribution in 1974 (Fig. 10.10c).

Woodland oaks in the eighteenth century were still quite small. In 1787, at Coggeshall (Essex), oaks averaging less than 13 cu. ft were described as having 'done growing'.[291] Although most oaks sold, being the bigger ones from their woods, were larger than this, anything over 40 cu. ft usually had to be got from parks, hedges, or Forests. The biggest woodland oaks which have come to my notice from this period were 205 trees sold from Dodnash Wood, East Suffolk, in 1760, which averaged 54 cu. ft and included one of 126 cu. ft.[360] There is some evidence for an increase in average size in the course of the century.

Nineteenth and twentieth centuries

After 1800 surveys of woods become rare but are replaced by the evidence of existing trees. Many woods now have, or have recently had, more and bigger oaks than at any time previously. Hayley Wood, for instance, has nearly twenty oaks to the acre which now average some 35 cu. ft per tree; stumps and felled tops show that in 1900 it had twice as many.

Many of these oaks date from the period 1790–1850, when the abnormally high price of oak-trees tempted many owners to shift the traditional woodland balance in favour of timber. The boom in oak was then followed by a slump, so that oaks, except on the most highly-organized estates, were not felled when they normally would have been. At the same time the supply of new oaks ceased in one wood after another (Chapter 17).

For these reasons, woods entered the twentieth century with an unusually large stock of timber. Some of this was felled because of the high prices generated by World War I, the social upheavals between the wars – when much of England changed hands and owners often found themselves in need of capital – and the sudden demands of World War II. These fellings are often regarded as a disaster, but their impact on ancient woods was neither as extensive nor as unprecedented as is supposed. A proper function of timber in woods, with precedents going back at least to the thirteenth century, is to act as a reserve for just such crises. The damaging effects, where there were any, were due not to the felling itself but to the decline in woodmanship at the same time, and in many woods the failure of new oaks to replace those cut down.

In Eastern England I have examined 246 woods for stumps and other evidence of timber-felling between 1910 and 1945, with these results:

Most or all of the timber trees cut down	59 woods (24%)
Heavy felling but many timber trees remain	57 woods (23%)
No unusual felling or no felling of timber at all	130 woods (53%)

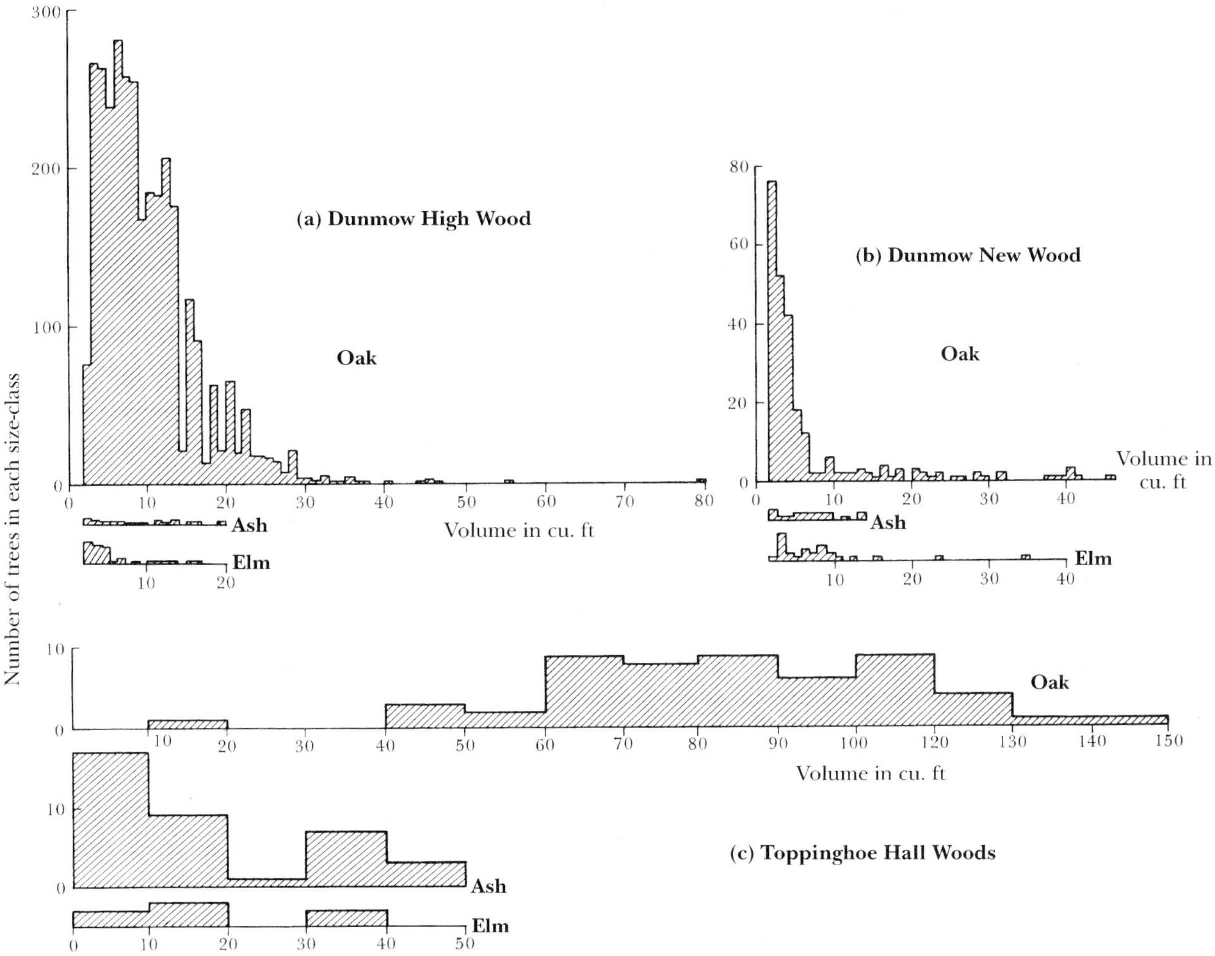

Fig. 10.9 Distribution of sizes of timber trees in three woods. The trees were measured standing and their sizes are expressed as volume of usable timber in cubic feet. (**a**) High Wood, Great Dunmow, Essex, from a survey of 1801.[299] About 100 acres of already ancient woodland with 33 timber trees per acre; a very skew distribution with a preponderance of smaller trees. (**b**) New Wood, Great Dunmow, also in 1801.[299] 29 acres which had recently become woodland with 10.3 timber trees per acre. Even smaller trees predominate; the few bigger ones are probably hedgerow trees dating from before the wood. (**c**) Toppinghoe Hall, Hatfield Peverel, Essex, *c.* 1700.[298] About 25 acres of woodland with 2.6 oaks and 2.5 other timber trees per acre. Oake were few and large, as in many woods today; the smaller trees were ash or elm.

There is some correlation between felling and size; 74% of the woods below 10 acres, but only 39% of those above 100 acres, escaped unusual felling.

This survey may slightly under-estimate the extent of pre-1945 felling because it includes few woods destroyed since 1945, a fate which probably happened more often to woods that had already lost their timber trees. Allowing for this factor, at least a third of woods escaped wartime and inter-war fellings altogether and in another third the fellings roughly restored the historic balance of timber trees. Even in the third of woods that were clear-felled little permanent harm was done. Monks' Wood (Hunts), of which in *c.* 1920 'more than half its area was a desert of grey ashes',[72] has grown again from the stools and has recovered much of its former structure; 33 years later it was declared a National Nature Reserve.

At present, some ancient woods still have abnormally many and large oaks. Others have, to varying degrees, replaced the oaks felled between 1914 and 1945; many of the then smaller oaks escaped the fellings and are now big trees. In the Bradfield Woods a great felling in 1927,[225] followed by unusually successful regeneration, has resulted in the best extant example of the 'medieval' kind of age-structure shown in Figs. 10.9a and 10.10a.

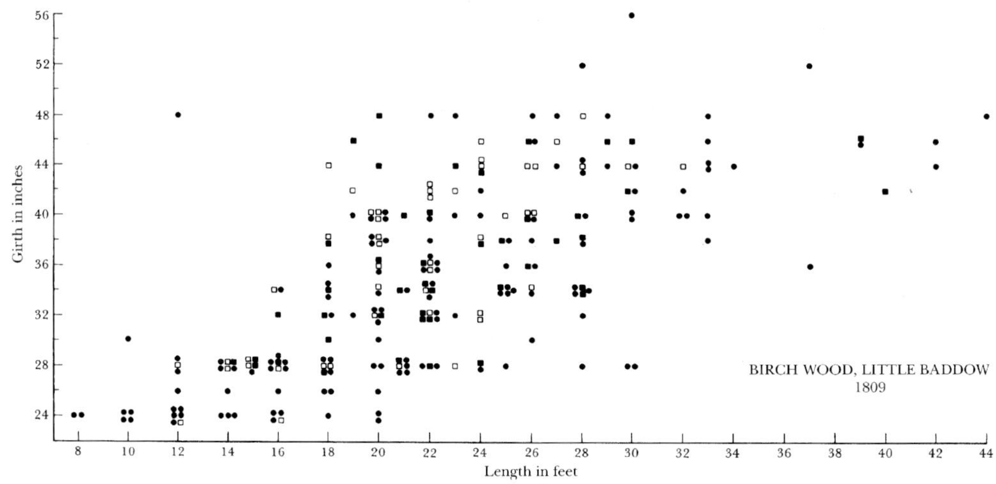
Girth in inches
Length in feet
BIRCH WOOD, LITTLE BADDOW
1809
24 28 32 36 40 44 48 52 56
8 10 12 14 16 18 20 22 24 26 28 30 32 34 36 38 40 42 44

(b)

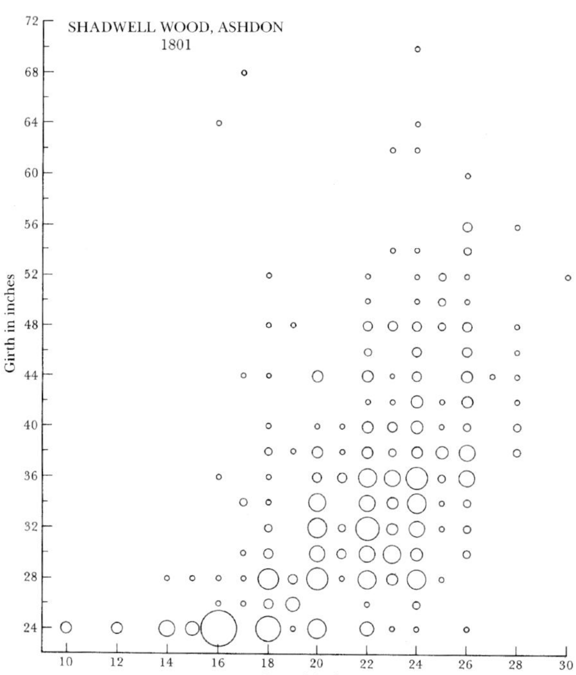
SHADWELL WOOD, ASHDON
1801
Girth in inches
Length in feet
24 28 32 36 40 44 48 52 56 60 64 68 72
10 12 14 16 18 20 22 24 26 28 30

(a)

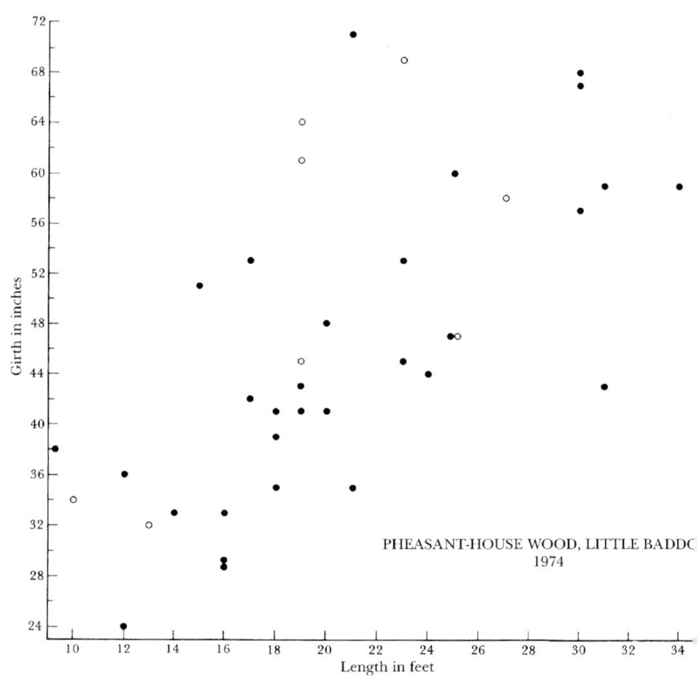
PHEASANT-HOUSE WOOD, LITTLE BADDC
1974
Girth in inches
Length in feet
24 28 32 36 40 44 48 52 56 60 64 68 72
10 12 14 16 18 20 22 24 26 28 30 32 34

(c)

In most other woods there is a shortage of young oaks; but, in the short term, the conservation problem of having too many oaks is at least as common as that of having too few.

Transport

Timber is much easier to transport than wood, and even seventh-century records (p. 133) show it being moved about the country. In 1224 the customal of Felsted (Essex) laid on tenants the duty of providing vehicles to transport their lady's timber from the woods.[320] A landlord used timber on the buildings and equipment of the demesne farm and on public facilities – mills, bridges, gallows, etc. – which he provided. Tenants usually had rights, called ***botes*** (p. 174), to take timber (often from hedges round their fields) for their buildings and equipment. Timber was also sent from one estate to another in the same ownership.[120]

Some manors of the Bishops of Ely illustrate transfers from estate to estate. Brandon (Suffolk) was a woodless Breckland manor. In the 1390s it lived partly on white and black poplar (*abel'* and *popeler*), non-woodland trees still to be seen on the margins of the Breckland fens. It also drew timber from the Bishop's woods at Shipdham (18 miles away), East Dereham (21 miles), and Hitcham (28 miles, much of it over the worst lanes of the Suffolk Boulder-clay). In 1396–7 timber was sent from Hitcham to Brandon, shipped round the Fenland waterways (then about 50 miles)[687] to Earith, and taken two miles more by land to be used at Somersham (Hunts),[252, 373] Somersham had extensive woods of its own,[270] but woods did not guarantee timber as and when needed.

Medieval transport was relatively cheap, and many journeys seem to us unnecessary. People often used timber from distant rather than nearby sources, and the location of sawyers could be as important as that of trees. From 1222 onwards Henry III regularly drew timber for Dover Castle from a wood that he owned in the Forest of Kingswood near Colchester,[233] rather than buying it from private suppliers in Kent. Some examples of long-distance transport are shown in Fig. 10.11. Many of them are of royal gifts, which were always of the king's own timber and therefore determined by the location of Crown lands, or of outsize trees.

The main sources of timber from overseas were the Baltic countries. The trade was well established in the thirteenth century.[477, 770] The common names ***Estrychbord*** and ***bord de Rygold*** refer to boards shipped from Estonia and Riga; timber also came via Danzig and Hamburg and from Norway. Much of this was softwood. Coniferous softwoods did not, of course, grow at this time in England; the pines of Scotland were rare and apparently not exploited commercially. Softwoods were less used then than they are now, and much use was made (as in modern Italy) of local supplies of broadleaved softwoods such as black and white poplar; but any large building work such as the Octagon of Ely Cathedral (1322–40)[476] involved purchases of fir-trees for scaffolding-poles and of Rygold boards for falsework. Ships' masts came from Norway.[840]

The late Rev. J. T. Munday, to whom I am indebted for the Brandon accounts, drew my attention to a thirteenth-century door in the tower of the church at Lakenheath (Suffolk), remote from any native timber supplies. It has an oak diagonal-braced frame and pine boards, which are an integral and original part of the door and have typical medieval V-section tongue-and-grooving; they are up to 9 ft 8 in. long, vary in width from 7¼ to 10¼ in., and are ¾ in. thick. These are the only surviving Rygoldbord that I know of. Some of the medieval houses of King's Lynn are framed in deal.[818]

Oak was also imported. There can be little doubt that many of the oak beams bought, like Rygold and Estrych, at King's Lynn or Stourbridge Fair in Cambridge came from overseas [p. 462]. Better documented are the oak ***wainscot*** boards made chiefly in Poland and brought in very large quantities from the Baltic ports. Wainscots were used – often in places which had plenty of local timber – for panelling and vehicles (their original purpose) and also for general use; even, as at Hindolveston in 1361–3, for making sheds (*tiguria*). The exporting countries had straight knot-free oak – difficult to get in Britain – and power-driven saws which would cut boards more cheaply and accurately than the trestle-saws and pit-saws used here. Ships and boats were also imported ready-made.[840]

Timber transport has an important bearing on the practice of dating artefacts by sequences of wide and narrow rings. Much tree-ring dating in England is done on the oak boards of furniture and panel-paintings. These are seldom of known provenance and it is not always sufficiently realized that such boards are particularly likely to be imported. Fortunately much of the

Fig. 10.10 Distribution of sizes of oak timber trees in three woods. The trees were measured standing and their sizes are expressed as the useful length of each tree and its girth half-way along that length. Trees smaller than 8 ft in useful length or 24 in. in girth are omitted as not being timber. (**a**) Shadwell Wood, Ashdon, Essex, in 1801.[300] 34 timber trees per acre, all *Quercus robur*. The smallest circles each represent one tree; each larger circle represents a number of trees proportional to the area of the circle. Note the sharply-defined maximum length, which is almost independent of girth. (**b**) Birch Wood, Little Baddow, Essex, in 1809.[317a] 23 timber trees per acre; *Quercus petraea* present. Note the much wider range of lengths than at Shadwell, despite the narrower range of girths. Each point represents one tree. White points: oaks dead in the top. Square points: oaks taken at the next felling of timber, in 1811–12. (**c**) Pheasant-house Wood, next to Birch Wood, in 1974. Mixed *Quercus robur* and *Q. petraea* population. Trees were measured by Mrs S. Ranson and the author using, as far as possible, the same methods as in 1801 and with much the same result. Note the trees dead in the top.

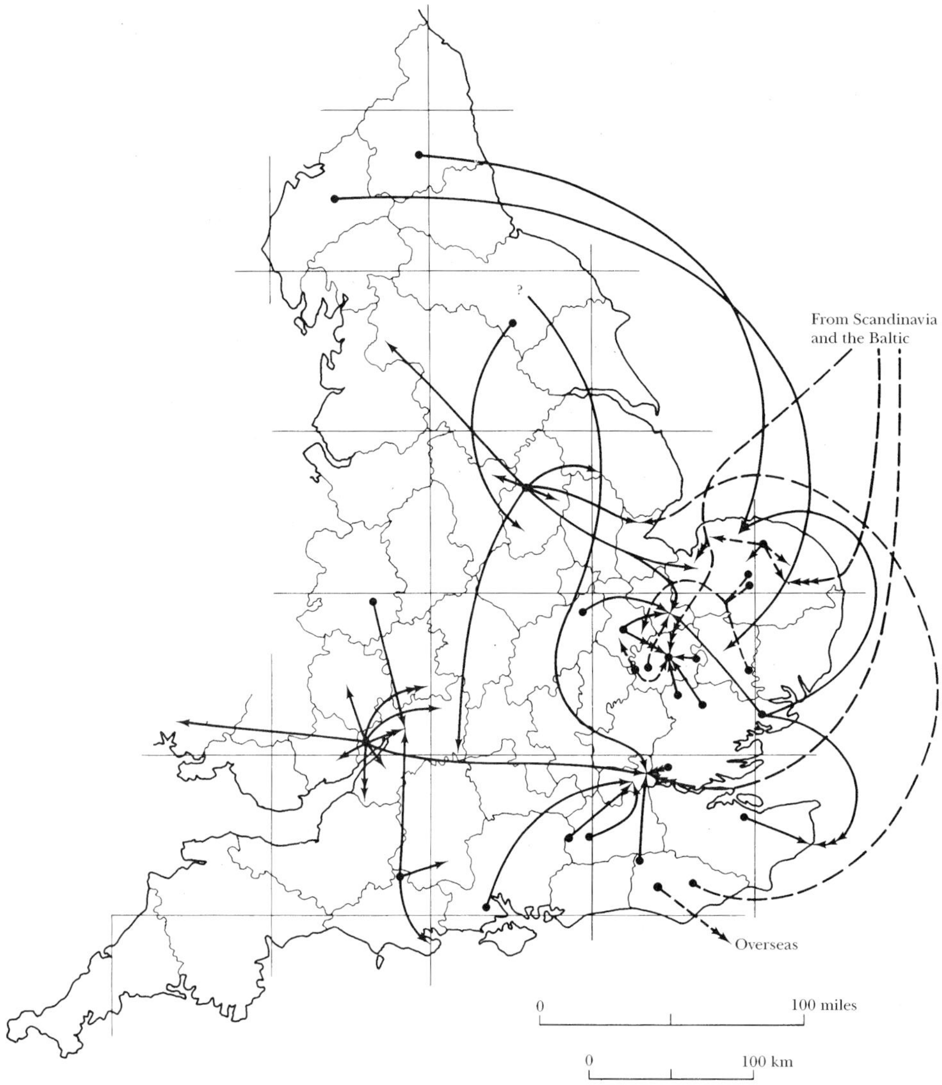

Fig. 10.11 Some examples of the long-distance transport of timber in the Middle Ages. The arrows show sources and destinations but not the routes by which timber was conveyed. These instances are an almost random selection from the extensive, though scattered, documentation on the subject; they are not intended to give a complete or quantitative picture of medieval timber transport, although single, occasional, or frequent consignments have been roughly distinguished by arrows with one, two, or three heads. Solid arrows: the king's timber. Broken arrows: timber of private persons or corporate bodies. Principal sources [39, 43, 69, 373, 415] also Close and Liberate Rolls *passim*.

early work in this science was done in Germany, not very far from the likely origin of the boards, and ring-width sequences in oak agree reasonably well over a large part of Europe.[680–1]

Outsize trees

The average estate imported boards because these were troublesome and expensive to make in small quantities or at short notice. There was also one timber that the local wood could seldom produce at all, namely the post on which the windmill stood. Some early pictures of mills[204] show the body of the mill perched on a very tall post set in the ground like a gate-post. It was difficult to get and instal these great timbers:

> 8 men hired for 6 days for digging a pit round the mill, 4*s*. 10 men hired for 2 days for removing the old post out of the ground, 20*d*. 14 men hired for two days for ramming the new mill-post and other jobs . . . 2*s* 4*d*.
> (Gamlingay 1295–6)[398]

> For mending 1 cart which broke with the great mill- post, 7½*d*
> (Gamlingay 1298–9)[398]

> 4 men brought for 8 days installing a new post and filling the pit round the post, ramming & compacting the same, 6*s* 8*d* . . . 2 men brought for 3 days carrying water for the clay to ram the said post, 12*d* . . .
> (Gamlingay 1333–4)[399]

Mill-posts for Gamlingay cost (excluding transport) from 18*s* to 25*s* 1*d*, more than ten times the price of the largest oak sold in Gamlingay Wood. We must have in mind a post at least 40 ft long and something like 2 ft thick (12 x 0.6 m), weighing 3–4 tons.

Timbers like mill-posts, of unusual length or girth, were rare and very expensive in cost per cubic foot, and were transported long distances. They came chiefly from parks and Forests rather than woods. At Hatfield Broadoak (Essex) in 1328, the local blacksmith (lucky man) had the right, as a perquisite of his office, to go into Hatfield Forest every year and take the second-best oak tree:

> . . . The lord shall choose the best one and the said John shall have the second-best. And this concession to the smith is worth 13*s*. 4*d*.[280]

Such oaks were kingly gifts. In 1251 Henry III gave thirty oaks from the Forest of Inglewood (Cumberland) to the monks of Bury St Edmund's, over 250 miles away; no less than 18*s* per tree was provided for the cost of transport.[235] In 1260 he gave the Abbess of Wilton (Wilts) two oaks from the Forest of Gillingham (Dorset) 'to make two long beams' for repairs. In 1251 he presented Salisbury Cathedral with twenty oaks, scraped together from four different Forests, 'to make 10 couples' (i.e. twenty rafters).[233] They are still there, reused in the present roof, and, as the king's order implies, each rafter is a whole tree; in this case the length was unusual.

The Forest of Dean was a noted source of outsize oaks. By the thirteenth century, Dean was being intensively exploited for timber, wood, and minerals. Even in this remote place the price of an oak often exceeded 5*s* and once was as much as 13*s* 4*d*,[69] which suggests unusual size. Among the many recipients of Dean oaks were the Black Friars of Gloucester, who received 61 (plus 21 from other Forests) between 1241 and 1265. Examination of the thirteenth-century fabric of the Gloucester Blackfriars shows that each tree was about 50 ft in usable length and 2 ft 2 in. in diameter (14½ x 0.7 m) and was sawn lengthwise into four or six rafters, etc. The 82 oaks of the king's gift account for about half the timber used in the original building.[847] On this one occasion, large and costly oaks were sawn up into ordinary timbers, but this is explained by the fact that the Friars did not buy their own oaks – they were not supposed to have any money – but had to use those that the king gave them.

In 1257 Henry III suspended such benefactions in many Forests 'because of the destruction caused'.[233] In the following century, great oaks seem to have been harder to get. In the Octagon of Ely Cathedral, some eighty years after Gloucester Blackfriars, the fabric shows that, having all England to draw on for the timber, the carpenter had to get the utmost length out of trees that were not quite big enough.[122] Timbers 50 ft long, however, are recorded in stock at Westminster in 1329,[477] and at the end of the century the roof of Westminster Hall, which uses nearly this length, was prefabricated at Farnham (Surrey), probably from timber out of Alice Holt Forest.[477]

Fifteenth- and sixteenth-century structures involving outsize oaks include the roof of King's College Chapel, Cambridge (Table 10.1) – for which, as the late Mr John Saltmarsh told me, the timber came from eight parks and one wood, chiefly in Essex – and the reconstruction of the nave roof of Salisbury Cathedral. In later centuries such trees became less rare: the naval dockyards of the eighteenth century regularly ordered oaks of 200 cu. ft per tree.

Trees of this size are probably less rare now than at any time since 1300; they even occur in some woods, owing to lack of recent felling, as well as in parks and hedges [Fig. 29.10]. If they are now said to be unobtainable, this reflects more on some timber merchants than on the trees. Also the modern carpenter, by insisting on perfectly straight timber lacking sapwood, large knots, and pockets of rot, uses an oak less efficiently than his predecessors and needs a bigger tree for a timber of given size.

Woods and industry

Fuel-using industries

Economic historians, forgetting that trees grow again, have many times told us that felling for fuel, particularly by the iron and glass industries from 1550 to 1700, has been a chief cause of destruction of British woodland. On this allegation, seldom if ever supported by evidence of what actually happened to any particular wood, is built an inverted pyramid of argument: woods felled are supposed to have ceased to be woodland, leading to a 'timber famine', high prices, restrictive legislation, industries moving further afield, and even an impetus to technical invention in order to find substitutes for wood.

The work of M. W. Flinn[58] and G. Hammersley[67] has exploded this general thesis. I have reviewed the arguments elsewhere[122] and shall give only a brief summary here. Industrialists, no less than other wood-users, had a strong interest in conserving fuel supplies; many of them were also landowners and did in fact run their woods as a renewable resource. The 'timber famine' and the high prices prove to be largely an illusion (cf. Chapter 11). Legislation was intended, not to restrict the ironworks and glassworks, but to prevent them from taking over those woods already fully exploited for domestic fuel; moreover it was half-hearted and was soon abandoned. The cost of standing trees never rose high enough to be an important restraint on industries; their fortunes rose and fell as determined by other costs or by foreign competition. Industries that moved into more remote places, as did the iron industry into Ireland, were expanding their production, not abandoning their existing sites. Coal was substituted for wood, in different industries over a long period, not because wood was scarce but because coal was cheap and falling in price, its labour costs being less.

Industries undoubtedly had a protective effect on woodland. Woods disappear if people do not burn them: it is farmers who grub out the stools, and cattle that eat the spring. Wherever there is now a concentration of woodland above what the local population could reasonably have exploited, the historian should look for an industrial use to explain its preservation. During the heyday of the wood-burning industries, it was not the industrial Weald, the Forests of Dean and Wyre, nor Furness but agricultural Norfolk that lost most of its medieval woods.

Shipbuilding

Another popular belief is that the history of woodlands has been everywhere dominated by the influence of the sea. Dockyards are alleged to have been chronically short of timber and in their search for suitable trees to have destroyed our ancient forests or, in another version, to have maintained our ancient woods. It is even supposed that coppice-with-standards woodland was invented in order to produce crooked branchy trees specially needed for the curved shapes of hulls.

Here I summarize the arguments in my earlier book. The influence of shipbuilding was neither steady nor all-pervasive. As a major consumer of timber the industry was short-lived: the output of timber shipping in Britain from 1800 to 1860 was probably equal to that in all the rest of history put together. The entire fleet that defeated the Armada could have been built in a few months by the naval dockyards in the days of Trafalgar; the entire merchant fleet in 1629, 115,000 tons, already the result of a considerable expansion,[654] was no more than the amount built in some single years of the nineteenth century.[394]

Complaints of shortage of oak are almost wholly attributable to lack of funds, organization, and transport rather than to lack of trees. They come mainly from the naval dockyards rather than from commercial shipbuilders. The Navy, inheriting the parsimonious habits of medieval kings, preferred to scrounge timber from the Royal Forests (which existed mainly for other purposes) rather than to buy it. When purchase could not be avoided, the Navy expected to get the large sizes and special shapes for building warships at no more than the average price for ordinary oak. It was very reluctant to buy timber (other than masts) from overseas, to use other materials, or to practise the most obvious and harmless economies. The contract price for oak was not put up in step with inflation, so that by 1795 the dockyards were paying for very large straight oak, 100 cubic feet to the tree, less than the average price for ordinary oak in an Essex wood: the Navy was getting the felling and transport and the extra value of big oak in exchange for nothing more than the value of the bark and branches (cf. Fig. 11.4). Dockyards drew their supplies from limited areas and preferred park or hedgerow timber; few woodland oaks would have been big enough for naval shipping.

During the heyday of timber shipbuilding, from 1780 to 1850, the price of oak-trees, probably throughout Britain, was abnormally high, though not as high as is often alleged; this boom in oak and the subsequent slump have had a considerable effect on woods as they are now. In the next chapter we shall examine how far the price-changes can really be attributed to this industry.

Tanning

Until the mid-nineteenth century the bark of oak was a raw material for tanning leather. From the thirteenth century onwards, accounts record small sums from sales of bark. Trees were normally felled in late spring in order that the bark could be peeled; occasionally a note says that no bark could be sold because the oaks were wanted at the wrong time of year. But the timbers of many medieval buildings still have some of the bark on: evidently it was a minor by-product and carpenters did not always trouble to peel it.

During the Industrial Revolution there was a boom in the tan-bark trade almost as great as the near-contemporary expansion of shipbuilding. This is documented by L. A. Clarkson,[22] who uses the Excise statistics of leather production to calculate the amount of bark needed year by year. In the 1810s, at the peak of its output, the trade in England and Wales was about three times as large as it had been a century earlier and used 90,000 tons of bark a year.

Oak bark, if stripped from timber trees, corresponds to at least four times its weight of timber, so that if we make a modest allowance for Scotland and Ireland the total bark consumption in 1810 would have involved the felling of at least 500,000 tons of timber a year. By comparison, the naval dockyards appear only once to have used more than 45,000 loads – at roughly one ton per load – of British oak a year.[3, 353] Merchant shipbuilders in the 1820s turned out an average of 85,000 registered tons of shipping annually, the building of which, at a generous estimate, cannot have used more than 200,000 tons of British oak.

The tanyards in their heyday were no mere users-up of by-products but a gigantic industry, a much bigger consumer of oak-trees than the naval dockyards and almost certainly a bigger consumer than the merchant shipyards. Tanning had a greater direct influence on woods than shipbuilding, and not merely because tanyards, unlike shipyards, drew supplies from almost every wood and hedge in the land. In practice, bark was not only a by-product of timber but also the main product of oak underwood. There were thousands of acres of oak coppice (Chapter 17), in which timber production was deliberately sacrificed for an increased yield of bark; their remains are still one of the most widespread British woodland types.

Minor uses of woodland

Pannage

A well-known figure of romance is the swineherd driving pigs into the woods to fatten on the acorns and beechmast which fall in the autumn. The term ***pannage*** properly means a payment by the pigs' owners to the owner of the wood; it was extended to the activity itself and later to other activities of pigs.

Pannage is widely if airily recorded by Domesday Book. In medieval customals it is the subject of detailed and curious regulations. At Felsted (Essex) in 1224 a tenant

> If he has swine shall give reasonable pannage, as the custom is, if they are in the Lady's wood and it is a full mast-year (*plenum peisson*): 2*d* for a pig a year old or more; one penny if it is half a year old; less if it is younger. If he has 10 swine of the same age the Lady is allowed to take the best one out of ten. If the mast-year in the Lady's wood is not full he shall give only half the pannage as the custom is. If he keeps his pigs from going into the wood in a full mast-year he shall give half the pannage. He cannot sell or kill them until the pannage is paid. From Michaelmas to Martinmas [Sept. 30 to Nov. 11 – equivalent to Oct. 7 to Nov. 18 in the modern calendar]. If he has a sow he shall give pannage once for her and then is quit as long as she lives . . .[320]

At Hatfield Broadoak (Essex) in 1328, for the related custom of ***avesage***, the tenant had to give two pigs to the lord; if he had only one pig he had to buy another identical one and give both; if he had no pigs he was excused.[280]

The trouble with pannage is that the *peisson* or acorn crop varies enormously and unpredictably from year to year. At best it lasts only a few weeks, but it often fails completely. This was certainly so from Anglo-Saxon times onwards: surveys value pannage *cum acciderit*, 'when it happens' (a phrase used of grapes and other erratic crops), and accounts state 'none this year because there were no acorns' (e.g. Hindolveston 1362–3).[415] Some particular fluctuations are shown in Fig. 10.12. Pannage was apparently important in Anglo-Saxon Kent:[170] with so many oaks and beeches it might usually be possible to find a few that were bearing mast, but even in the Weald the pigs must have fed for much of the time on things other than acorns. By the fourteenth century surveys contain phrases like 'No pannage because the oaklings (*querculi*) are few',[280] 'None because it grows in only a few spots',[330] or 'None because it has just been felled'.[330]

In Eastern England, post-Domesday records of pannage are thinly scattered, mainly in North Essex and the Suffolk border. The sums paid are mostly trivial. As the practice declines it becomes diffficult to separate from other porcine customs. At Writtle (Essex) in 1398, 37 pigs (belonging to eleven owners) were pannaged in

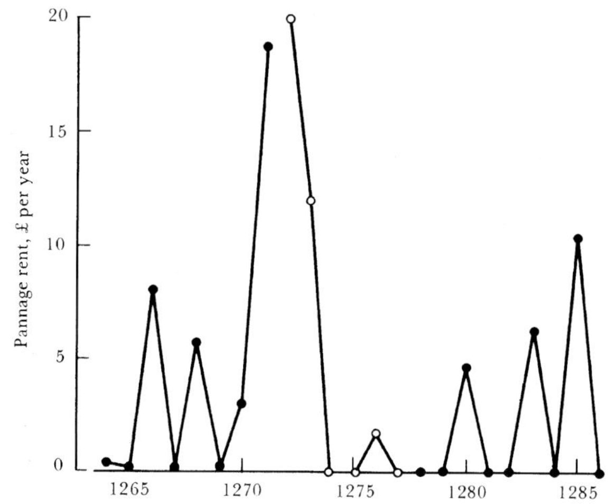

Fig. 10.12 Monies received for pannage each year in part of Nottinghamshire, 1264–86. (●) Clipston Park plus parts of Sherwood Forest. (○) Clipston Park only.[214]

Forest, but 41 under oak-trees in the warren.[311] Elsewhere we hear of pannage in parks, fields, stubble, and even, as at Bocking (Essex) in 1309, in a garden.[329] The last record of regular pannage in this region appears to be in Hatfield Forest in 1446,[295] although fees described as pannage appear up to 1483 in Little Bentley (N.E. Essex).[278] The practice still survives in the New Forest and possibly the Forest of Dean.

Pasture and herbage

Woods regularly used for grazing are discussed in Chapter 12. Keeping stock out of ordinary woods was an important part of their maintenance, though wood-sale contracts (see later) sometimes allowed the purchaser to graze a few beasts of the cart. Woodland herbage is described in Chapter 7.

Crime

Although Robin Hood's Sherwood Forest was mainly heathland, the medieval traveller expected to be murdered or hijacked when he approached a wood. To discourage highwaymen, clearings called ***trenches*** were made alongside main roads where they passed woods: a practice begun before the Conquest on the roads through the Chilterns by the piety of Leofstan, Abbot of St Alban's[817a] and widespread in the thirteenth century. In 1285 a statute required underwood and woodbanks to be destroyed within 200 ft of a highway. Although this was not always observed, trenches can still be seen, notably along the A1 in Huntingdonshire,[72] Ermine Street in Cambridgeshire [Fig. 25.27],[122] and the roads out of Canterbury.

These measures reflect the prevalence of crime rather than of woodland. The perils of medieval

England were more like those of 1980s Central Park, New York, than of the Orinoco jungle. Even in our own times, malefactors are not unknown in woods and Forests. Did not masked men in 1976 hold up the Paris to Moscow express in the Forêt de Chantilly, paint it all over with anti-Soviet graffiti, and vanish into the limewoods leaving the train to proceed to Moscow in its redecorated state?[498]

Other uses

Hazel-nuts and chestnuts are dealt with in Chapters 13 and 21. Acorns were sometimes collected, presumably to be given to pigs outside the pannage season: at Writtle in 1397 seven people were fined a total of 3*s* 7*d* for gathering acorns without permission.[311]

Specific references to game in woods are surprisingly few. Before firearms, woodcock were caught in nets strung across re-entrant angles, and a specially-shaped cockshoot-wood appears on the Kentwell (Long Melford, Suffolk) map of 1613.[122, 222] An early shooting agreement with detailed provisions (e.g. no ringdoves to be shot at night) exists for Wayland Wood in 1768.[512] There are eighteenth-century particulars for Bedford Purlieus (Peterborough).[128] Systematic gamekeeping and pheasant-rearing, however, do not become common till the late-Victorian period and are too late to be well recorded.

Bast is referred to in Chapter 15.

Ashes of wood (as well as of seaweed or bracken) were a raw material of the glass and other industries. They were a product of wood-burning industries more often than of woodland, but in Avening (Glos) in the twelfth century ash-men were blamed for reducing the value of the woods for pannage.[205] Wood-ash was imported in the fifteenth century.[840] It is now a valuable raw material for potteries (p. 27).

Finally let us mention the '10 Sacks of Moss tyed at ye Neck' gathered in Pod's Wood (Messing, Essex) in 1750,[287] and the fish stolen from a woodland pond in Bradenham (Norfolk) in 1226.[257]

Woodland maintenance

Staff

Throughout most of history a wood was managed by a ***woodward***, usually a part-time employee, in the Middle Ages often a tenant excused from his other customary works. Most of the actual work was done by purchasers of standing wood or timber or by hired labourers. The tenants on many medieval estates were supposed to cut the lord's underwood as a labour service, but this was seldom demanded in practice.

The owner of a wood lying within an area subject to Forest Law (Chapter 12) was required to appoint a woodward as his representative in matters concerning the Forest jurisdiction. By the thirteenth century the use of the Latin word *forestarius* to translate 'woodward' had been extended even to areas with no connection with a Forest, e.g. in 1277–8 at Hindolveston (Norfolk).[415] This usage appears to be peculiar to the thirteenth century and not to be the origin of the modern wood 'forester'; after 1300 the Forest jurisdiction was curtailed and the official reverts to being a *wodewardus* or *prepositus silve*.

Boundaries and security

Most land adjoining woods was pastured at least some of the time, and it was important to maintain a stock-proof boundary in the form of a woodbank with external ditch plus a hedge or a fence. Perimeter earthworks are mentioned in many medieval documents, e.g. 'the underwood growing on the woodbank' (*subboscus crescens super le Wodebank*) in Norton Wood (W. Suffolk) in 1410–11.[219] Usually they were already ancient, but sometimes we hear of new ones being made, as at Hindolveston (see below). Repair of fences and ditches was usually the chief or only maintenance expense of a wood. Purchasers of underwood were often required to do the work.

It is difficult to maintain a hedge under the eaves of a wood. The shade-resistant hornbeam and holly are best, and hornbeam seems to have been introduced to some woods in the Chilterns for hedging (p. 227).

'Thefts' of wood often came before manorial courts; often, we suspect, merely as a means of collecting payment from casual 'cut-it-yourself' woodsales, but sometimes as a genuine offence: in 1385 a fine of 9*d* was imposed at East Donyland (Essex) for stealing ¼*d* worth of the lord's faggots.[293] Woods had padlocked gates to prevent thieves from driving vehicles in. After 1550 punishments for woodstealing become more severe (p. 168). At Horsham St Faith's (Norfolk) a wood-lease of 1611 requires the lessee to prevent theft;[433] and in 1765 at Thorndon (Essex) there is a payment for 'stacking fagotts in ye wood to prevent 'em being stole'.[306] To this day cut underwood has a habit of disappearing.

Planting

Records of planting trees in existing woods are rare before the mid-eighteenth century, and then occur only on some of the larger estates. Planting was usually on a very small scale, and much of it consisted merely of setting acorns.

During the decline of woodland management planting becomes more frequent. Some woods were converted to close-set stands of genetically uniform oaks (p. 283). Such may be seen in some Royal Forests such as Windsor (p. 303) and Alice Holt. On a smaller scale, the ancient Hardwick Wood near Cambridge is partly occupied by uniform oaks dating from *c.* 1840, too close for each other's good, which have suppressed the original underwood. Occasional groups of conifers, beeches, and horse-chestnuts in some woods result from the Victorian forester's habit of trying everything.

Both the records and the trees themselves show that planting is a small, recent, and for the most part readily-detected influence on native woodland. That this is not due to deficient documentation is shown by the many records of trees planted in situations other than woodland.[846] On occasion, woods were used as sources of plants for other places, as at Gamlingay in 1333–4:

> 1 boy pulling (*evellat*') thorns for 4 days in the Wood for the [hedge on the] ditch of Stocking [Field, Fig. 25.2].[399]

Pruning

It is not infrequent in medieval timbers to find the stump of a branch, cut off with a saw while the tree was young and subsequently grown over (Fig. 10.13). My earliest example is in a board of the twelfth-century church door at Haresfield (Glos).

Pruning branches is most often recorded with hedgerow trees; it was a common source of dispute between neighbours. The Hindolveston records show that it occasionally happened in woods.

Fig. 10.13 Medieval oak timber containing the sawn-off stump of a branch embedded by further growth of the tree. A great post in the Perpendicular-style gatehouse of the Dominican Friars in Sudbury, Suffolk.

Some management records

Hindolveston, Norfolk

On the estate of Norwich Cathedral Priory at Hindolveston, seventeen miles north-west of Norwich, were two woods, Eastwood of 123 modern acres and Westwood of 172. These were a very important asset in one of the most populous and least wooded counties. Unusually detailed annual account rolls survive from 1255 to 1390[415, 478] and reveal many aspects of the organization. They include our clearest example of a deliberate change in management policy during the Middle Ages.

Westwood was grubbed in the seventeenth and eighteenth centuries[414] but its ghost still haunts the map; Eastwood survives in a partly replanted state.

General ecology and management

Hindolveston is on a wet plateau with shallow fenny valleys in the loess country of north Norfolk (p. 42). The woods were evidently of ash–maple–hazel with standard oaks (Chapter 13) and with a transition to plateau alder-wood (p. 308); all five species are regularly mentioned, together with thorn. [The surviving wood is now mixed hazel-wood with patches of alder.] There were also non-woodland trees, chiefly ash, around the manor-house and elsewhere; willows by ponds; small fen alder-carrs, one of which adjoined the wood; and occasional hedges and patches of thorns. There were small alternative sources of fuel from 'Wynn' (i.e. furze) on heaths, and from peat.

The woods produced timber, underwood, and various minor products. In most years there were sales of underwood; timber was taken mainly for the Priory's own purposes and is usually recorded only through sales of branchwood, bark, etc. There were frequent sales of windfallen trees and of dead ashes and maples, both of which suggest that the root-rotting fungus *Armillaria mellea* (p. 208) was more than usually active. Income from non-woodland trees and second-hand timber was never more than a tenth of that from the wood and was nil in many years.

The period up to 1272

The woods may have been part of a park mentioned in 1261–2[416] and commemorated in the name of Le Launde given to an adjoining pasture. By 1255 the park was defunct and the woods encoppiced. Sales of underwood are sometimes differentiated into '*virge* & hazel', i.e. small coppice, and 'ash maple & alder', i.e. large coppice. Probably there were simultaneous long and short coppice rotations. Underwood realized about £4 per annum, roughly an eighth of the manor's gross income; in relation to the area of woodland this was about average for the time. Smaller sums arose from branchwood, bark, etc.

The events of 1272–3

On the back of the otherwise normal account-roll of

this year there appears, as an afterthought, the following astonishing entry:

> Wood sold at Thuringe [Thurning] 110*s* . . .
> Received £213 16*s* 8*d* from the wood sold at Hindolveston . . .

These sums exceed the gross income for the whole estate for seven years. The Priory had just been sacked and burnt in a riot and urgently needed funds for repairs. So great an amount could hardly have been raised from underwood on 300 acres; it must represent the sale of timber. As we shall see, the Priory took particular care of its timber trees, and up to 1272 the woods may have been managed in order to build up reserves of timber to meet this kind of emergency.

We are not told how the Priory contrived to sell so much timber in this remote place; evidently they solved the problem of organization efficiently and at very short notice.

1273–1326

The great sale had little immediate effect: for at least fifteen years production continued much as before. But after 1294 the income rapidly increased. In 1309–10 the sale of underwood brought in £39, and in the following decade it averaged £24, nearly half the income from the estate. Underwood was sold in plots mostly to unnamed purchasers. There were still some timber trees, for considerable sales of branchwood took place in 1287–8 and 1320–1.

The rise in income cannot be accounted for by a general rise in prices. It suggests a decision by the monks to take advantage of the great felling to reorganize their woods so as to produce underwood instead of timber as the main product: in effect, to convert the woods from a capital-growth to a high-income investment. This would have made sense, especially as peat-digging in what are now the Broads, which had provided much of Norfolk with fuel, was in a bad way because of flooding due to rising sea-level,[768] and the price of wood could have been expected to rise. The Priory had a large stake in the peat industry and would have been well aware of its difficulties.

The change could not have taken effect at once: the stools would need to recover from the shade of the former timber trees, and new stools would have to be formed from saplings in gaps. A time-lag of fifteen years is not unreasonable.

Several other changes are connected with this more intensive use. Between 1274 and 1277 a woodward was appointed at a salary of £1 7*s* 5*d* a year – something like half a full-time job. Much more attention was paid to the boundaries. Previously only small sums had been spent on ditching round the woods, but in 1277–8 £1 10*s* was paid for major fencing and ditching works, and in 1297–8 a new woodbank [Plate 3] was made round both woods at a cost of £10 10*s* and a hedge was planted on it. Regular sums were spent thereafter on repairing the ditch and the bridges over it and on the gates. There were apparently eight gates each with a 'feterlok'; the purchase of twenty-six padlocks in eleven years shows that the average life of a lock was three and a half years.

When the woods consisted chiefly of timber trees their organization and security had not been very important. When they were expected to produce a large income from underwood it was worthwhile to pay a man to look after them and to secure them against cattle and thieves. Some attention may even have been paid to drainage, for in 1324–5 10*s* was spent on making a 'grope', i.e. a grip or internal drainage ditch – an item not heard of again in a wood for 400 years.

The making of the new woodbank in 1297–8 is described in detail. The operation was financed out of the 'branches of trees and underwood' growing on the line of the new ditch. These were sold for £10 12*s*, two-thirds to a syndicate of buyers and the rest in small amounts to twenty local people. The ditch was dug by five named contractors at 2*d* a perch-length. The total length was 1058½ perches; assuming a 16½-ft perch and including 128 perches dug in 1277–8, this comes to 3.7 miles. (I estimate the actual combined perimeter of the woods at 4.3 miles.) The account ends with 5*s* spent on 'drawing thorns and briars', presumably to make a hedge. In the next surviving account, for 1299–1300, there is an entry for 33 man-days 'repairing the wood-ditches in places, with planting little plants and thorns'.

1358–1389

After a period of incomplete accounts we find a different arrangement. As often in the later Middle Ages, lands were leased out, and this evidently happened to the small underwood. The 'underwood called Heselwond' was bought for a regular sum each year, sometimes four years at a time, by a syndicate of unfree tenants, known as 'le Wondmen', organized by one John Robynes. (Eastwood was called Robins Wood into the nineteenth century.) They usually paid £13 16*s* 8*d*, and sometimes also bought part of the branchwood. The hazelwands could be used for wattle-and-daub and, as in 1385–6, for making hurdles for scaffolding. Probably the Wondmen were, in effect, a firm of hurdle-makers.

Underwood other than hazel was made into faggots tied with bands bought back from the Wondmen. There were also ***astell***, billets cleft from large coppice.

Less appears to have been spent on maintenance at this time, though in 1385–6 3*s* 4*d* was spent on 'heightening the woodbanks' (*exaltando fossata bosci*).

Pruning timber trees

An apparently unique feature of these accounts is the regular occurrence of items like the following:

> 60*s* from *schragg'* & *paryng* young oaks, together with [sales of] thorns in various places on the woodbanks etc. (1362–3)

The word *schraggyng* is evidently a variant of *shredding*, cutting the lower branches from a tree (p. 5). *Paryng* and the Latin *mundura*, 'cleaning', appear to have a similar meaning. The treatment was applied to young trees, not always oaks, and sometimes even to alders. It produced rods which could, on occasion, be used for binding faggots. These yielded a considerable income, usually around £2 a year and once as much as £5, though not every year.

It appears that the trees were regularly pruned to yield wood from epicormic shoots and probably also to improve the timber. The practice is first recorded in the 1260s. After the great sale there is a gap until 1309–10. It then reappears – doubtless on the next generation of timber trees – in most years until 1328 and at longer intervals thereafter.

Other matters

The estate was by no means self-sufficient: it could seldom manufacture articles requiring special skills or costly labour. There were frequent purchases of hurdles; less often of wheels, and of hardwood and softwood boards – *Waynskot*, *Estrissh*, and *Rygolt* – brought from overseas via King's Lynn and used, for instance, on the mill in 1362–3.

Hindolveston sent timber to Norwich and to all the Priory manors in N.W. Norfolk. For instance in 1384–5 eight carts with four carters came three times from Sedgeford, 22 miles away, to collect timber.

For about forty years after the felling, sales of herbage (sometimes including bracken) brought in about 16*s* a year. Usually it was 'to be reaped in bundles'; it often remained unsold for lack of buyers. Occasionally horses were pastured in the wood in winter, presumably tethered; one was 'stolen out of the wood' in 1311–12. Pannage brought in a few shillings in some years between 1311 and 1360. Possibly the appointment of a woodward made it possible to organize this activity as soon as the oaks were fruiting again after the great sale.

The woods were a source of young trees:

> Stipend of 2 men pulling ashes to plant at Hyndringham and Gateli for 6 days, 2*s*. (1312–13)

The parallel account for Hindringham records the planting of them, apparently in non-woodland sites.[417]

Hazards arose from the presence of Westwood near the manor-house, as we see in the stock account for 1309–10:

> *Swans* . . . 5, of which 2 devoured by a fox (*gupill'*) . . .
> *Peafowl* . . . 4, of which 2 lost in the wood . . .
> *Young peafowl* . . . 4, of which 2 devoured by the polecat (*le fulmerd*) . . .

There is one reference to pheasants.

Castle-Camps, S.E. Cambridgeshire 1411

In 1411 Richard de Veer, Earl of Oxford, contracted with William Selong for the sale of fifty acres of standing wood called Colyers Tayles (meaning 'charcoal-man's coppice') in the Earl's park at Castle-Camps. This is an unusually early example of the contract with a woodmonger by which woods were often sold. The care taken with the season of cutting, access, the repair of fences, and the protection of the regrowth are typical of such contracts. The inclusion of timber in the sale is unusual. The contract is in Norman-French, as remarkable then as a similar document in Latin would be now.

> . . . The said William may have full entry and exit by three gates . . . (one gate near Hauerhill, the second gate near John Turnor's of Campes, and gate three called the Colyers Gate) to carry and cut the said wood and timber from [2 February] next following . . . for the next ensuing 6 years. And the said William shall cut all the said wood and timber at seasonable times during the said term; and shall carry away the said wood and timber thus cut out of the said Colyers Tayles as speedily as he can well do, so that the new *plauntz & burgeonnez & espringgs* may not be destroyed nor oppressed by the said cut timber and underwood. And the said William shall cause to be sufficiently closed all the gateways and all the places by which he shall have his entrances . . . for the protection of the spring of the said Colyers Tayles. And the said Earl . . . grants to the said William in the said Colyers Tailes pasture for his own Horses in the time of carrying the said wood and timber . . . [282]

Cawston (Norfolk) 1612

This is a fourteen-year lease of the twenty-four-acre South Hawe Wood. The terms are typical, except for the references to planting sallows – my earliest record, by about a century, of planting trees in an existing wood. Note also the promotion of twelve new timber trees to the acre, the repair of boundaries, and the protection of regrowth from cattle.

> . . . [The lessee shall fell two acres of underwood a year] in the seasonablest & best tyme . . . in February Marche or Aprell . . . [and shall] leave standing . . . ffower and twentye of the ffynest . . . stands [i.e. staddles] of Oake and Ashe or one of them in amongst the said two acres of underwood . . . together with all the olde standes nowe . . . growing . . . [He] shall yearely and everie yere of the 14 yeres putt a good number of Sallowes in the vacant emptie places of the . . . two acres of underwood . . . so that the sayd vacant and emptye places may be well planted and supplied with wood . . . [He shall] at his own costs . . . [maintain] all the dykes in

and about the . . . wood . . . and keep the dytches gates styles and ffences . . . in good and suffficient repairings . . . And the sprynge in and about the said wood . . . shall with all diligent care and respect protecte from the bytinge & brusinge of cattle . . .[409]

Lawshall (W. Suffolk) 1621

This is a lease of woods including Lawshall Frith, now Frithy Wood. Note the care taken with measurement; the details of haulage; and the prohibition of ***drawing***, the practice of cutting only the best poles on a stool or the best stools in a wood, leaving the others standing to interfere with their regrowth.

> . . . [Ten acres are to be felled annually] the Measure thereof to be accounted according to the Statute de Terris mensurandis . . . to be taken from the Stantye or Stake in the fences . . . Every yeares fall . . . in places together and not scatteringly . . . whereby the Slopp and Springe . . . may renew most orderly and proply . . .
>
> They shall . . . carry awaie all the same wood . . . before the last daie of June yearely, Except it be in such yeares as by reason of abundance of raine or weat weather [carts cannot get into the wood, in which case it may be delayed until 1 August].[368]

Sporle (Norfolk) 1745

This is a lease of Sporle Wood on a nine-year rotation, at a time when detailed leases were becoming rare. Note the promotion of as many as forty new timber trees to the acre, to be maidens if possible but otherwise by promoting coppice poles; the provision that coppicing shall be finished by an unusually early date; and the extraction date of 24 June. The grazing allowance and the stiff penalty clause are unusual in such leases.

> . . . Christopher Gapp [the lessee] shall . . . cut down and fall in an Husbandly manner between the first day of November . . . and the second day of February . . . One ninth part of the Underwood . . . after the rate of three pounds the Acre . . . He carrying out and clearing such Wood . . . on or before the twenty fourth day of June . . . leaving . . . all such Stands of Oake Ash and Elm as were left in the fall or at any time before. And also forty Wavers of Oak at least on every Acre . . . if the same are there to be found in Convenient Places for Stock and Store of Timber and if not so to be found then so many as are . . . there. And the Defeciency to be made up with so many Shoots of Oakes from Stubbs . . . Preserving the Shoots and Slopps of such Wood from being bitt by the Horses fetching out the same . . . doing as little Damage to the Stubbs [i.e. stools] as can be . . .
>
> [The owner shall maintain the boundaries] . . . Christopher Gapp [may] keep . . . in the said Underwood Yearly . . . between the first day of Novr. and the second day of February . . . Ten Year Old Budds [i.e. heifers] of the Cow kind And as many Year of the Horse kind . . . [If he] shall cutt down or damage any of the Timber in the said Wood . . . He . . . shall for every such foot of Timber damaged or cut down forfeit . . . five Shillings . . .[430]

Added in 2003 edition

Studies in other parts of England show that the treatment of woods did not vary as much as might have been expected, given the great differences in the proportion of the landscape that was wooded and in the composition of the woods. Examples from northern England can be found in *Woodland in the Landscape* (see Atherden in additional bibliography), especially the article by Jennifer Kaner on the work of the Woodland History Group of Yorkshire Philosophical Society. There is a history of coppicing in Ireland, and (probably to a smaller degree) in Scotland. Wales too has coppice-woods and ancient woodland, but there is also a mysterious tradition of patches of woodland forming parts of fields, rather than being separate plots of land on their own. The tradition of woodland in Cornwall resembles England rather than Wales; some woods had names of their own in the Cornish language.

The distinction between woodland and wood-pasture also exists in Continental countries, most of which had strong traditions of coppicing and pollarding, even if they had a much higher ratio of woodland to population than England. In some countries, like Germany and Sweden, the ancient woods are less well preserved, having been transformed by the earlier growth and wider practice of modern forestry.

Coppicing exists in countries with different trees as well as different people, even in some tropical countries. In Japan a strong and ancient practice of woodmanship coexisted for centuries both with wood-pasture (Figs 11.9, 11.10) and with an early, independent tradition of plantation forestry. North American Indians seem not to have practised coppicing, but it was introduced by European settlers, and its remains can be seen spreading across the continent from the maples of New England in the seventeenth century to the live-oaks of remote west Texas in the late nineteenth. There was a phase of coppicing of eucalypts in Australia in the nineteenth century, especially species that yielded eucalyptus oil.

Timber and underwood in English buildings are discussed at length in Chapter 29.

11

The economic and social history of woods

Economics are one of the keys to the social function of woods. We must avoid the trap of supposing that people are always moved by, or correctly aware of, considerations of monetary profit. An owner may preserve a wood because it pays better, or he thinks it pays better, than other land-uses; because he lacks the capital to grub it out or is legally restrained from doing so; because he appreciates it as a pheasant-covert or an ancient monument; because he likes woods, or has forgotten he owns it, etc. Such imponderables defy cost-benefit analysis, especially in individual cases. However, the changing prices of wood and timber down the centuries, averaged over many woods, do illuminate our appreciation of owners' attitudes to woods and their management.

Traditionally woods are accounted for, like other land, on a steady-state basis. Each year a wood yields produce and incurs expenses. Products and expenses are of the same kind year after year but vary in amount. The cost of establishing one crop – usually a matter merely of maintaining the boundaries – is charged against the value of the previous crop and often paid for by the purchaser. The cash flow, averaged over a number of years, thus tells us the value of the wood.

The products of importance are underwood, timber, and bark. Herbage, pannage, nuts, etc. rarely yield large sums, and shooting becomes a financial asset only after 1850 and is thus poorly documented.

This section is mainly concerned with Eastern England but I shall give some indications of variations in other areas. It is useless to compare figures taken haphazardly from different parts of the country. Eastern England was the richest, most populous, and most urbanized part of medieval England. It demonstrates well the influence of town uses of woodland products; but it does not give the effect of heavy industry, which remains to be investigated elsewhere. In later centuries the population rose (except in London) less than in other regions.

Economic and social value of timber

Measurement

Early sales are given as so many trees, usually of unspecified size. My earliest evidence for the measurement of timber by volume is a fifteenth-century set of tables *A boke to mete tymber by*.[256] From 1500 onwards squared timber was sold at so much the cubic foot. The measurement of standing trees begins a little later and by 1604 had developed into a regular practice of computing volumes in cubic feet.[465]

There are several ways of coping with the cylindrical shape of logs and with the fact that some of the log is inevitably lost in conversion. Early measurements, describing trees as so many inches square, apparently reckoned the useful volume of a log to be that of the largest square beam that can be hewn from it. This 'inscribed-square rule', if strictly applied, gives a volume of $2/\pi = 64\%$ of the actual volume of the cylinder. The later 'Hoppus' formula reckons the volume of a log to be $(^1/_4 \times \text{girth})^2 \times \text{length}$, which amounts to $\pi/4 = 79\%$ of the true volume of the cylinder. This rule, known to Evelyn in 1664,[335] was publicized by the architectural writer E. Hoppus in 1736,[744] became generally adopted and is still widely used. Actual ancient beams, being waney at the corners, often have a section slightly

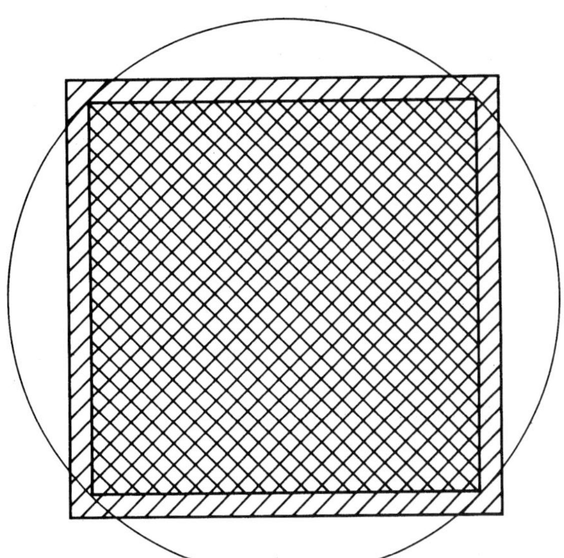

Fig. 11.1 Cross-section of a cylinder showing (double-hatched) the inscribed-square volume and (single-hatched) the extra volume by the Hoppus rule.

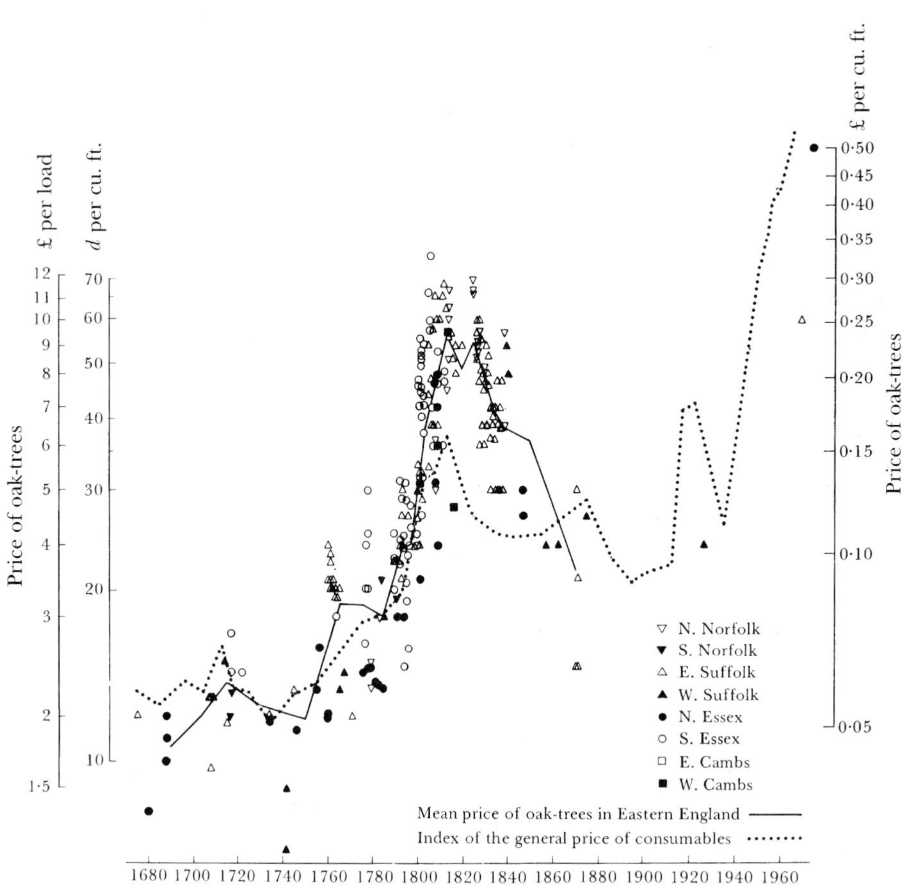

Fig. 11.2 Prices of oak-trees in Eastern England, 1675–1976. The average values are calculated for five- to twenty-year intervals depending on the amount of information.

Logarithmic scale.

The data for this and for Figs. 11.4 to 11.6 come from mainly unpublished sources, chiefly in the Norfolk, Suffolk, Essex, and Cambridgeshire Record Offices. These include the Petre (Essex Record Office) and Ashburnham (Ipswich Record Office) archives; the Tollemache muniments at Helmingham; the Court of Augmentation records (Public Record Office); medieval Inquisitions Post-mortem;[234] the Hardwick (Cambridge) records in Pembroke College, Cambridge; the Ely Coucher Book;[270] and others too numerous to specify.

The price-index consists of five- or ten-year averages from Brown and Hopkins,[624] plotted to the same logarithmic scale from an arbitrary origin.

larger than the inscribed square, so that the difference between the 'Hoppus' and square volumes (Fig. 11.1) is probably not significant.

The larger unit is the ***load***, usually of 40 cubic feet, sometimes of 50. Theoretically the 50-ft load should be used for squared timber, measured in true cubic feet, and the 40-ft load for round timber measured in 'Hoppus feet' which are about a quarter larger. In practice both loads are used at all periods and seem to be merely local variants of usage.

In this discussion I ignore the difference between the 'Hoppus' and the inscribed-square volumes; I assume that a 'cubic foot' of tree, measured by either rule, yields a true cubic foot of useful timber; and I adopt a 40-ft load (equivalent to 1.13 cu. m.)

Evidence for prices of timber

The vast majority of records are of oak, the commonest and usually the most expensive timber (but see ash later). Its value was determined mainly by the size of tree, large oaks being about twice as expensive per cubic foot as small ones,[118] and outsize trees being costlier still. At any one time the price of different batches of oak varies by about 25% either side of the average. My figures show no evidence of consistent differences in price from place to place within Eastern England. Statistics for the whole country might show some variation, although long-distance transport would tend to even out prices.

Evidence of sales of trees from woods and hedges is copious from 1680 to 1840 (Fig. 11.2). From 1500 to 1680 we have to fall back on the prices paid for squared oak by builders, of which there is a good series for Cambridge (Fig. 11.3). Successive editions of *Laxton's Builders' Price-book* tell us what builders have expected to pay for oak year by year since 1840.[384]

In the late seventeenth century the average price of oak in Cambridge was 11½*d* a cubic foot, £1 18*s* a 40-ft load. The selling price of oak-trees averaged £1 14*s* a load. The price of oak in Cambridge was evidently determined mainly by the cost of the tree rather than of labour or transport: although there were no nearby woods communications were good. I shall suppose that the same was true throughout the sixteenth and seventeenth centuries. As a reasonable approximation I assume that the *lower* prices paid for timber by Cambridge builders equalled the *average* prices

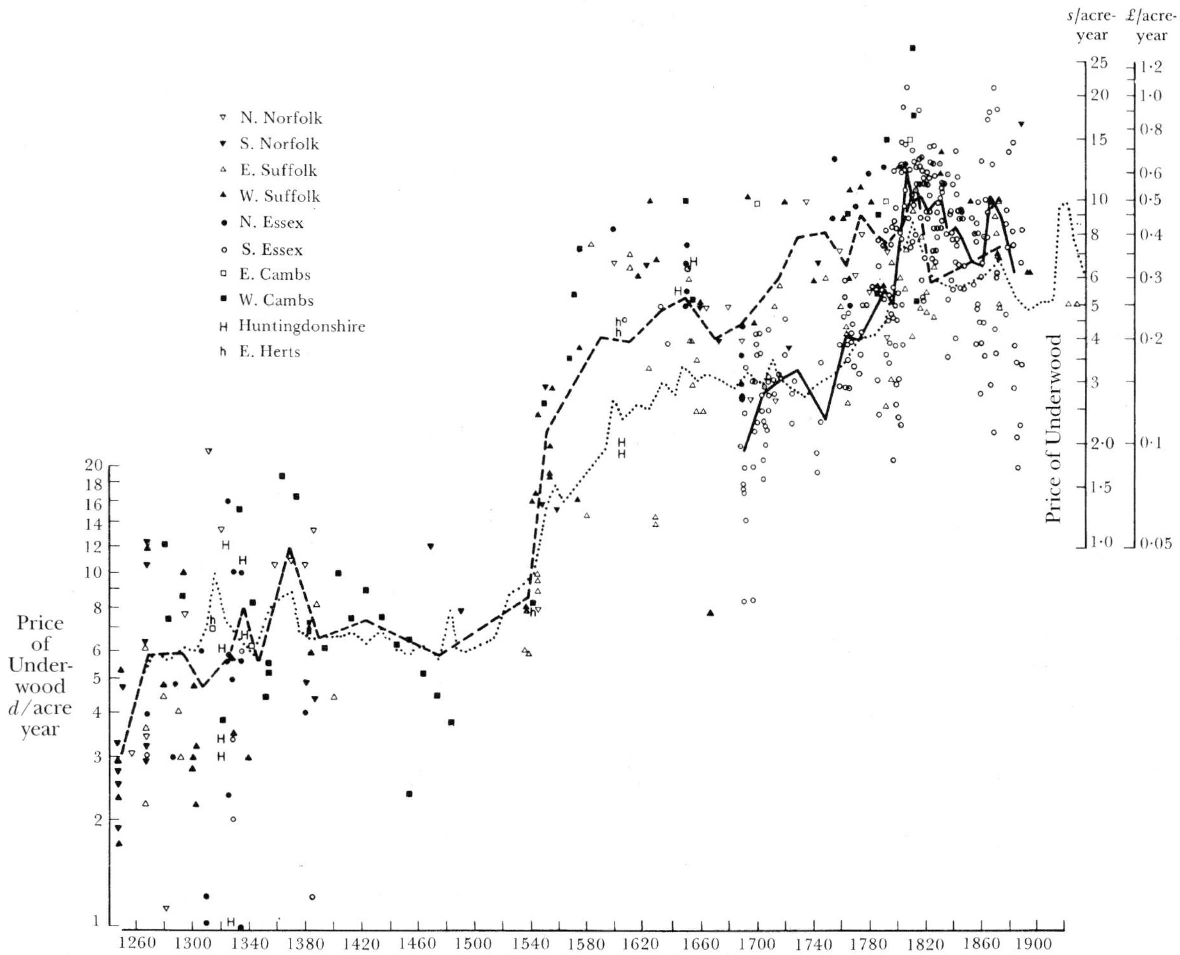

Fig. 11.6 Prices of underwood in Eastern England, 1251–1931. Details as for Fig. 11.2. Mean value of underwood in south Essex (———) and in the rest of Eastern England (-------). Index of general price of consumables (·············). Logarithmic scale.

as with timber, most of the rise results from general inflation.

In real terms there was only one price-rise in the value of underwood as sold in the wood. This was an increase of 75% between 1540 and 1553. It is possible that the rise was not quite as fast as this, for the 1540 figures come from Augmentation Office surveys and could possibly be systematically under-estimated; but even if this is so, it remains certain that underwood became nearly twice as valuable, in relation to the value of money, during the first half of the sixteenth century. The rise was not sustained; prices followed very closely the general course of inflation until 1650, when there was a fall.

Retail prices may well have risen faster owing to increasing complexity in the woodmongering trade. As we are well aware, in times of inflation rises in the retail price of produce have a habit of not being proportionately passed on to the grower. Wholesalers were prohibited in 1553 by a bluntly-worded statute:

> Forasmuche as by the gredye appetite and covetousness of divers persons, Fuell Coles and Woodd runnethe many times throughe foure or fyve severall hands or mo[r]e before it comethe to thandes of them that for their necessitie doo burne or retaile the same . . .[489]

This was an age not only of rising population but of rising expectations of domestic heating. In the Middle Ages most people heated their houses, if at all, by a bonfire on the floor. The sixteenth century was the time of a Great Chimney-building, and not only in new houses: in my Cambridge college, as in thousands of buildings, holes were cut in medieval roofs for the insertion of chimney-stacks. A chimney is more comfortable than an open hearth and probably less efficient, so its owner will be tempted to use it more often and to keep a larger fire. Considering also the hard winters of the Little Ice Age,[767] it is not surprising that wood should have become clear and frequently stolen. In the 1590s and 1600s – those terrible years of cold and poverty – 'hedge-stealers' did time in the stocks or even, at Ingatestone (Essex), were whipped till they 'bleed well'. Householders were sometimes required by manorial courts to lay in stocks of wood lest they steal their neighbours'.[674]

In other parts of the country there was a conflict between industrial and domestic users of wood, which I have discussed elsewhere.[122] It is surprising that the value of wood should have risen so little. The reason probably lies in competition from coal. Shipments of coal from Newcastle increased from 35,300 tons in 1549–50 to 409,300 tons in 1633–4;[805] wood was losing some of its urban markets, especially in London, though still used in most of the countryside.

Underwood from 1700 to 1820

In the eighteenth century the records at hand shift to South Essex. Underwood there began much cheaper than in the rest of Eastern England, probably because South Essex records are for areas with much woodland in relation to the population and also conveniently sited for importing coal. The price in South Essex rose faster than inflation, especially after 1795, reaching 12*s* an acre-year in 1807, which in real terms was double what it had been in 1700. Possibly the growth of London increased the market for uses such as baking for which coal was not an alternative.

In the rest of Eastern England the records are few but suggest that the price of underwood rose earlier and to a lesser degree. In the mid-eighteenth century prices were higher in real terms than ever before, but by the 1800s they were no higher than in South Essex.

Underwood after 1820

In the mid-nineteenth century the documentation, though incomplete, suggests that prices of underwood fell but not to the same extent as timber trees. The railways introduced cheap coal to the countryside, but this was partly balanced by an expansion in specialized coppice crafts (Fig. 11.7). Some of the last records, from 1870 to 1890, give unexpectedly high prices for underwood.

Coppicing steadily retreated from the north of Britain, surviving chiefly south of the Thames. In Eastern England some woods, particularly those in which there is evidence of planting, ceased to be felled in the nineteenth century, but coppicing usually continued until 1939 and often into the 1950s.

Like other declines, that of coppicing is ill-documented and it is uncertain which of the possible causes had most influence. Fitzrandolph and Hay, reporting on the underwood *trades* in 1925,[57] described a welter of tiny and inflexible businesses cutting each other's throats and not cooperating either to control their supplies and their markets, to enforce a fair price for their products, or to introducc machinery. Some crafts were affected by foreign competition or by the invention of substitutes for things like hay-rakes and barrel-hoops, and all suffered from the general depression in agriculture and industry at the time; but the general cause of the decline was disorganization among the producers rather than lack of demand for the products. The decline in woodland management preceded, and partly caused, the decline in the specialized trades.

Woodmanship probably suffered from much the same influences. Wood-prices in the 1920s and 1930s seem to have been very low, and the fuel shortage of World War II did not arrest the decline for long. The chief economic factor was probably the rising cost of labour, but social and political factors were more potent still. The popularity of modern forestry, stimulated by the founding of the Forestry Commission in 1919, absorbed all the capital and skill available for trees. No attempt was made to modernize the organization and equipment of woodmanship, or to introduce to ancient woodland the capital, mechanization, subsidies, and research which were applied to modern forestry to offset its labour costs.

The revival of underwood [see also p. 518]

By 1965 coppicing survived in Eastern England chiefly in South and East Essex, in the Bradfield Woods near Bury St Edmund's, and in S.E. Norfolk. It was maintained to support small industries or on shooting estates to provide a suitable woodland structure for pheasants.

Since 1970 there has been an increasing revival. By 1980 there were at least fifty active coppice-woods in Essex alone. The remaining specialized trades have shown considerable vitality: for instance, the demand for thatching wood often exceeds the material available. With the rising price of energy woods are again being used for their traditional purpose of growing fuel. D. E. Earl pointed out the absurdity of the nation simultaneously spending money on poisoning ancient woods and on importing, as in 1971, some 13,000 tons of charcoal a year.[666]

A chief objective of the ecological conservation movement has been, not so much to preserve woods in an unused state, as to prevent coppicing and the woodland structures and habitats linked with it from dying out. This began before there was any hope of an economic return:[113] for instance, the 'conservation coppicing' of Buff Wood (pp. 90, 273–5, 426–32) was begun by Cambridge University in 1954 for purposes of teaching and research. The influence of organizations such as the Nature Conservancy[90, 273–5] Council [later English Nature]and the county Naturalists' Trusts has rapidly grown. They maintain underwood for ecological

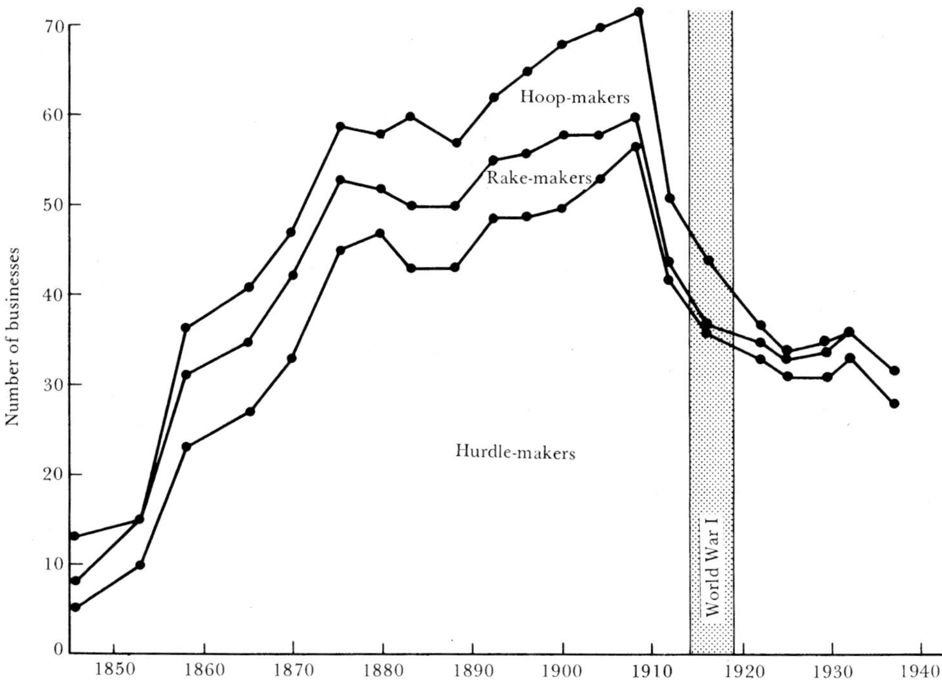

Fig. 11.7 Specialized underwood trades in Norfolk, Suffolk, and Cambridgeshire: numbers of makers of hurdles, rakes, and wooden barrel-hoops listed in successive editions of *Kelly's Directory* and its predecessors. The first two editions may not be comprehensive. An account of how to start up in these trades in the late 1870s is given in *The Rabbit-skin Cap*.[610]

reasons often with the help of volunteer labourers; but they are also in touch with many owners of woods and are beginning to be able to provide the coordination – the means for somebody wanting a particular kind of underwood to find out where to get it – that the industry has never had.

Coppicing can usually be revived after at least 100 years of neglect.

Future coppicing is likely to tend to longer rotations, perhaps thirty years, for logs rather than faggot and hurdle sizes. The woods will not, by themselves, solve our energy problems, but the remarkable popularity of wood-burning stoves since 1973 demonstrates their potential.

The balance of woodland uses: wood *versus* timber

The relative prices of timber and underwood give us some insight into how a woodland owner struck a balance between the two products.

In the later Middle Ages underwood was worth an average of about 6*d* an acre-year. If oak-trees were worth about 1¼*d* a cubic foot, it follows that an acre-year of wood was worth about 4.8 cu. ft of timber. An acre of woodland, managed to produce timber only, ought to yield several times this amount a year. Unless we have grossly over-estimated its value, timber was therefore a more profitable use of the land than wood; it is surprising that medieval landowners did not grow more timber. The monks of Beaulieu in 1269 sold five acres of woodland for timber for £40 (pp. 140, 142); this would have been equal in value to 75 years' growth of underwood, even at the exceptionally high price which they got for wood, and the timber could probably have been felled at no more than 50 years of age. As we have seen, the monks of Norwich took particular care of their timber, but this was very unusual even among corporate bodies.

The modern practice of forest 'economics', invented in the early nineteenth century,[405] and used from 1930 to 1980 to estimate in advance the expected profitability of plantations, sought to solve the problems of setting off present against future costs and returns by a discounting procedure. Owing to the long time-span the outcome of the estimate depended very sensitively on what rate of discount is chosen: the accuracy of the calculation may be seriously affected by a change from 3.1% to 3.2% per annum, and a change from 3% to 4% may give quite a different answer.[872] Since it was difficult to give a rational basis for choosing, say, even a 3% rate rather than 1% or 7%, it was unfortunate that this arithmetical procedure should have acquired the respectability, and the influence on planting policy, which it had. Nevertheless the procedure tried to cope, in however clumsy and sophistical a fashion, with the genuine problem of equating long-term and short-term benefits. The medievals did not know the method and – lacking our uncritical respect for figures – would not have believed it if they had; but their preference for a steady income from underwood rather than the apparently greater capital accumulation of timber was their own answer to the problem. They may also have been influenced by the greater transportability of timber: it was less important than with wood to avoid a local shortage.

After 1540 the value of underwood rose faster than that of timber (Fig. 11.8), so that from 1550 to 1650 an acre-year of underwood was worth from 6 to 9 cu. ft of standing timber. This tended to keep the balance at least as much in favour of underwood as it had previously been. The fall in underwood values around 1660 brought the ratio back to what it had been in the Middle Ages, at which it remained, with fluctuations, until late in the eighteenth century.

From 1790 inwards, the rising value of oak-trees tipped the balance strongly in favour of timber; an acre-year of wood fell to the equivalent of less than 2½ cu. ft of timber. This goes far to explain why many woods still have large numbers of oaks dating from the early nineteenth century. After 1860 many landowners must have regretted the change but were too committed to timber to reverse it.

At this point the gamekeeper replaces the woodward in such records as were still kept. In many woods the timber and underwood began to be subordinated to the shooting interest. This change, although often detrimental to birds of prey and other wild-life, gave a purpose to the existence of woods in a time of depression; it sometimes perpetuated the woodland grassland (Chapter 7) and the coppicing.

This brought us to the mad world of the 1970s, in which the price of ordinary oak-*trees* was as low, in relation to the value of money, as at any time since the fifteenth century; the price of oak *timber* was higher, again in relative terms, than at any time in history; and prices paid for underwood, provided the seller knows where to find the buyer were roughly equal to the previous all-time maximum in the eighteenth century.

Woods *versus* other land-uses

In general terms, the economic trends shown in Fig. 11.8 go far to explain why woodland should have been such a stable land-use. For at least 600 years prices of trees, both timber and underwood, remained steady or rose in real terms; falls were rare and were not sustained until 1850. Any wood that was profitable in 1250 is likely to have remained so. Woodland (unlike modern forestry) brought in a good income with practically no expenditure; maintenance costs were low and could easily be passed on to the purchaser.

Presumably there had been a time when woodland, apart from areas specially set aside for coppicing, had been less valuable than any other land-use. In Eastern England this phase had drawn to an end about the time of the Conquest if not before; in some regions with plenty of woodland it was to persist well into the Middle Ages. The low values of 1251 (Fig. 11.8) possibly represent the tail-end of this phase, though as they are all derived from the Ely Coucher Book it is conceivable that they may be systematically under-estimated.

By 1270 woods were no longer the cheapest land-use: the average return, 6*d* per acre-year in underwood, plus timber and other products, was greater than for arable (about 4*d* per acre per year) and comparable with enclosed pasture. A well-placed or well-run wood like Hindolveston might easily yield more. Landowners had little incentive to turn woods into farmland. Meadow, however, was worth about four times as much as woodland, and ancient woods avoid well-watered sites that could otherwise be meadow.

In Eastern England one sometimes finds tiny 'wood-closes', often reverted to woodland, within the woodbank of an ancient wood; these represent the very last encroachment of medieval agriculture on the woods. Datable records of major destruction fall mainly into four phases: 1550 to 1650, 1700 to 1770, the 1850s and 1860s, and after 1945.

The 1550–1650 grubbings came at a time of high prices for wood and timber, but also of rising land values. On some Wiltshire estates agricultural rents went up about four-and-a-half-fold between 1540 and 1620.[763] If it applied to Eastern England this rise would have been roughly equal to that in the prices of wood and timber. There is some evidence that rents went up faster in Eastern England.[763] The economic climate thus seems to have been slightly unfavourable to woodland.

The fall in the value of woodland after 1660 seems not to have led to any grubbings. The next phase of destruction, 1700–70, came at a time of high prices for woodland products and, for much of the time, of agricultural depression.[795] The nineteenth-century grubbings were in a period of woodland depression and were cut short by the agricultural depression that followed.

Although economic influences can to some extent be correlated with the destruction of woodland, many grubbings took place at times when they were not particularly strong. But the ground occupied by woodland had more than a merely economic value. It was *land unencumbered by manorial regulations or common-rights*, on which the owner could do as he pleased, and as such was very attractive in counties such as Huntingdonshire with its extensive open-field arable and Norfolk with its extensive common pasture. Outside Hayley Wood successive seventeenth-century lords of the manor tried to escape from the open-field system by annexing part of the common against the determined opposition of their tenants. When, after fifty years of litigation, William Power wrested just enough land from the villagers to set up a new farm, he added to its acreage by destroying Littlehound, the companion wood to Hayley (Fig. 2.1).[120] Many medieval woods may have come to a similar end in Norfolk, a county with a long record of agricultural innovation.

The fourth and greatest phase of destruction, after 1945, came at a time of stronger pressures than any

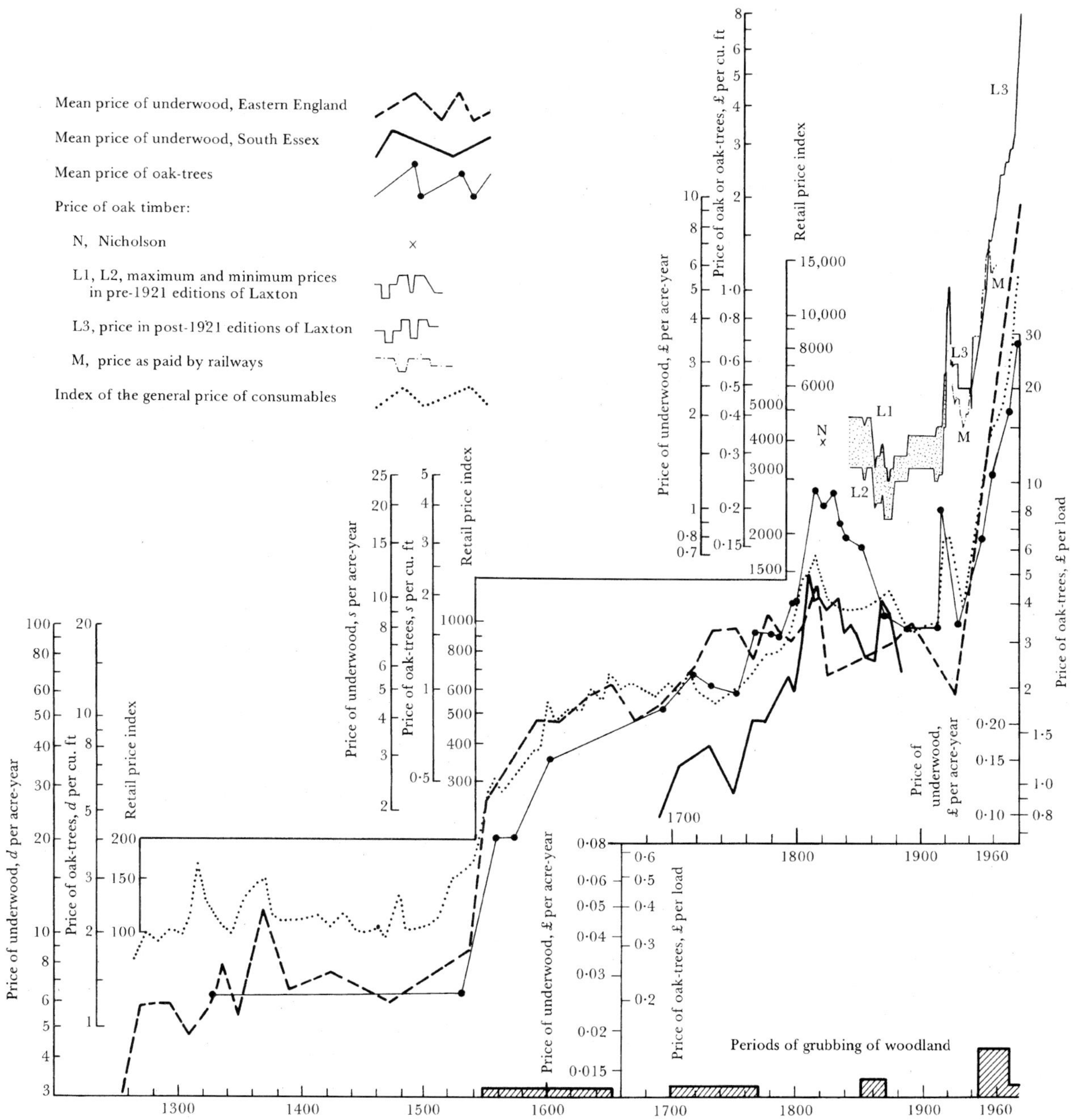

Fig. 11.8 Comparison of price movements in underwood and oak, 1251–1976. Logarithmic scale.
Underwood: (**a**) Eastern England, continuous series of average values, 1251–1830 (from Fig. 11.6), extended by isolated figures since 1830. (**b**) South Essex, series of average values, 1690–1890.
Oak trees: Eastern England, continuous series of average values, 1690–1870 (from Fig. 11.2); extended before 1690 by estimation from values of timber (Fig. 11.3); extended since 1870 by isolated figures from Eastern England and a few from elsewhere.[728, 737]
Oak timber: England 1823–1976.[384, 407, 776]
Price index: as Fig. 11.2, extended to 1976 by the Index of Retail Prices.
Periods when woodland is known to have been destroyed are shown by shaded rectangles.

since 1250: very high land values, economic pressures to grub out woods, and political pressures to turn them into plantations despite the expense. Yet it is obvious that many owners either resisted these pressures or did not have the capital still needed to destroy their woods; even secondary woodland was occasionally still formed (pp. 8–10). In the 1970s political pressures were less and capital was harder to acquire, yet some woods were still destroyed, often after a change of ownership. The survival of woods depends not only on the economic climate but on changing fashions and politics and on the interests and resources of individual people.

Added in 2003 edition

One reason why naval shipbuilding has a disproportionate prominence in accounts of woodland history is that timber was used not only to build the ship but to pay the shipwrights, who insisted on wages in kind. In consequence the stack of logs 'needed' to build a 74-gun warship might come to more than the entire volume of the hull.*

Charcoal-making is almost impossible to detect in level woods, but on a slope it leaves a characteristic platform, a circle some 30 feet in diameter, scooped into the hillside. Under the leaf-mould can be found pieces of charcoal from which the wood used can be identified and its growth-rate ascertained. Occasionally the wood no longer exists, leaving the platforms in moorland.

The story is continued, with the economic collapse of modern forestry, the varying fortunes of woodmanship, and the intervention of deer, in Chapter 33.

Fig. 11.9 Japanese woodland: an old coppice-stool of *Quercus mongolica* near Chino. November 1998

Fig. 11.10 Japanese wood-pasture: pollard horsechestnut (*Aesculus turbinata*) in grassland, now getting invaded by birch. Norikura. October 1998

*Guillery, P. and Herman, B. (1999). Deptford houses: 1650 to 1800. *Vernac. Archit.* **30**, 58–84. I am indebted to Geoffrey Roberts for valuable correspondence on this point.

12

Wood-pasture systems and products

Introduction

It is more difficult to give a balanced ecological account of wood-pasture than of woodland. With grazing as well as trees, there is more room for variation in management. The multiple land-uses of wood-pasture are usually documented unevenly – for it was rarely anybody's business to record every aspect of a system – and we can easily overlook some important activity. Wood-pasture is less inherently stable than woodland and fluctuations in one land-use react on the others. Economic analysis is difficult and uncertain – even such an important product as venison cannot be valued because it was thought improper to sell it – and misleading, because economics formed only a small part of the variety of motives from which people developed or upheld the systems. The products of wood-pasture are seldom recognizable in archaeology. The systems have declined more than woodland and can very rarely be observed in working order. The surviving Continental wood-pastures, e.g. the *Lärchenwiesen* (larch-meadows) of the Alps, are so different from ours as to be of little help in interpreting them.

Wood-pasture is an important part of our social history. There have been many studies of parks and Forests, more often of their legal aspects than of their practical operations or what is there on the ground. In a single chapter I can do no more than present some new evidence and draw what will inevitably be broad generalizations.

Trees and grazing

Wood-pasture necessarily involves grassland as well as trees. Cattle, sheep, and deer will eat bark and foliage, often in preference to grass [Plate 173] – I have seen a large poplar on a common blow down in a summer storm, and within seconds of its fall a herd of bullocks arrive at the gallop to devour the leaves – but in a wood they soon consume all the vegetation within reach, and it does not easily grow again at a height at which they can get it. Most of the plant material in a wood is produced in the canopies of the trees; the productivity of shrubs and ground vegetation is insufficient to sustain a worthwhile number of animals.

Wooded commons, parks, and Forests were of two kinds: ***uncompartmented***, with trees and grassland irregularly mixed, and ***compartmented***, where certain areas were set aside as woodland and other areas as grassland (with or without trees). The distinction is first expressly recorded in the thirteenth century but could be much older (cf. pp. 134–5).

In an uncompartmented wood-pasture grazing animals had access to the whole area at all times. The wildwood with occasional glades, the natural precursor of such wood-pastures, had in most instances been opened out into grassland (or heath) with a denser or sparser scatter of trees, usually of the less edible species such as oak, beech, or holly (pp. 7, 345). The trees, being difficult to replace, were seldom felled; they were generally treated either as pollards, to yield wood and to protect its regrowth, or as large and long-lived timber trees. Hawthorn or holly bushes were a natural and essential feature of uncompartmented wood-pastures; they protected new oaks growing up in their midst, as is well known, for instance, in the New Forest.[832] Under a statute of 1768 it was possible to get up to three months' hard labour with a whipping in each month for damaging hollies or thorns.[491]

In compartmented wood-pastures each wooded compartment was fenced after felling until the regrowth had grown sufficiently not to be damaged by livestock. The fences would then be removed and animals admitted for the rest of the coppice cycle. Presumably they ate the remains of brambles and other coppicing plants, grass in gaps in the underwood, and the lower twigs and foliage of the underwood itself; but such sustenance would be meagre and non-renewable, and most wood-pastures also had permanent grassy areas called ***plains***, ***lawns***, or ***launds***. Coppicing in wood-pasture, requiring as it did a formal reconciliation of the wood and grazing interests, tended to be more regularly programmed than in woods; the cutting procedure and period of fencing might be laid down in manorial by-laws, and the compartments were defined by ***copse-banks***.

Compartmentation benefits the owner of the trees. Continuous coppice produces more wood than scattered pollards and is much easier to harvest: pollarding is difficult and tiring work – as I know from experience – involving ladders or trestles. Compartmentation is very detrimental to the grazing, because livestock are excluded in those years in which the ground vegetation is most productive. It was introduced at various times in wood-pastures where the wood-interests prevailed, but was successfully resisted in those, like Epping Forest, with a strong grazing interest. In theory it should have been encouraged by the Statute of Woods (1543), which provided under a quite heavy though rarely imposed fine (13*s* 4*d* per acre per month) that woods should be fenced for seven years after felling.[488]

Browse-wood

The prehistoric practice of feeding livestock on the twigs or foliage of pollarded or shredded trees (p. 5) continued into the historical period; it is recorded by Thomas Tusser in sixteenth-century Essex:

> If frost doo continue, this lesson doth well
> For comfort* of cattel the fewell to fell:
> From euerie tree the superfluous bows
> now prune for thy neat† therevpon to go brows.
>
> . . . . . .
>
> If snow doo continue, sheepe hardly that fare
> craue Mistle and Iuie‡ for them to spare.[506]

This is possibly the function of the ancient pollard elms of Cambridgeshire villages.[122] The practice still occasionally continues in northern England, especially on holly (p. 345). In many Alpine valleys I have seen ash-trees pollarded or shredded in late summer, on a one- or two-year cycle, to feed goats.

In parks and Forests wood was cut to sustain deer, either regularly or in a hard winter. For instance in the Essex parks of Newhall (Boreham) and Havering in 1565, oak, ash, hornbeam, hawthorn, and maple were customarily shredded for browse-wood, and the parkers had the wood for fuel when the deer had finished with it.[460] Holly is still cut for the purpose in the New Forest.[156]

Trees on commons

In the eleventh century there were still parts of England where woods were so extensive as to provide merely casual grazing with an irregular bonus of acorns for pigs. The many small *silue pastiles* recorded in less-wooded areas presumably imply some more formalized kind of wood-pasture such as became general later in the Middle Ages. Wood-pasture commons are expressly recorded in some Anglo-Saxon charters (p. 130).

There is no sharp distinction between wood-pasture and other kinds of common-land. A common might have only a few trees – like the handful of pollard oaks still to be seen on Fritton Common (Norfolk) – or only bushes, like Langland Common in Little Gransden (Cambs) in the sixteenth century.[120] The trees on a common could disappear altogether (cf. p. 326). A previously woodless common could acquire trees in a period of slack grazing: this has been claimed for the famous beech pollards of Burnham Beeches (Bucks), said to have originated on heathland about 1600.[83] Neither process is likely to appear in contemporary records, so the continuity of trees on commons is more difficult to establish than the continuity of woods.

I have elsewhere drawn attention to the peculiar straggling shapes of commons, with concave outlines funnelling out into roads and often enclaves of private land in the interior.[122] This is partly because commons were residues of unenclosed land, left over after a succession of encroachments, and partly because the owner of the soil of a common was not responsible for fencing it and had no incentive to shorten the perimeter. In this respect wood-pasture commons resemble other commons and differ from woods (Fig. 12.1); they have no perimeter earthworks apart from the hedgebanks of the fields and the woodbanks of the woods on which they happen to abut.

Commons were regulated by local customs administered by the manor courts. Usually the grazing belonged to the commoners and the soil and timber (including the bollings of pollards) to the lord of the manor. The wood might belong to either. Reffley Wood (W. Norfolk; now coniferized) exemplifies a less usual arrangement whereby a third party had all the right to the trees. This was already so in the sixteenth century.[425] In 1751 it was set down that

> The Pasturage . . . belongs to the Inhabitants of certain Houses . . . the Timber & Underwood . . . to Mr Folkes. The Game . . . to my Lord Andover who is presumed to be Lord of the Soil . . . To whom does belong the Right of killing . . . Rabbets?[420]

The wood's owner evidently had no right to compartment the wood, sales from which included thorns and tops of pollards.[428]

Sometimes tenants had specific quotas of wood for fuel and fencing (***firebote***, ***hedgebote***) and were allowed timber when needed for repairing buildings and equipment (***housebote***, ***cartbote***, etc.); but these rights do not imply the existence of a common wood, for they were more often exercised on hedgerow trees and occasionally in private woods (p. 144).

Usually only the large commons had trees, and only a few of the very largest were compartmented. Sometimes the trees were allowed to disappear, as often in the Chilterns (e.g. most of Berkhamsted Frith (p. 326)). But courts often succeeded in protecting the trees as well as the grazing, as with the compartmented commons of Minchinhampton (Glos).[122, 515] The ecological sensitivity of some manorial courts is illustrated by the preservation orders made for pollard limes on Dedham Heath (Essex) (p. 248).

Two examples of commons with trees are given below;

* strengthening † cattle ‡ mistletoe and ivy

others are Childerditch Common in Thorndon Park (p. 199) and Frithsden Beeches (p. 326).

Tiptree Heath, Essex

This was a vast inter-manorial common ramifying into seventeen parishes, like a Forest but without deer. Part of it was compartmented into woods and part was heathland with pollards and scattered trees. Very little of it survives.

The elaborate by-laws were re-codified in *c.* 1523.[406] The woods belonged to the lords of the manors, who might fell any trees in them that the commoners did not require for repairing their own buildings. For cartbote, ploughbote, and hedgebote the commoners might lop or shred (p. 5) suitable trees in their lords' woods; if there were not enough of these they might cut others 'by the grounde'. For fuel and other general purposes they were allowed to cut broom, furze, and thorns at any time, but other species only between 2 February and 1 April. By preference these other species were to be 'bircheses, willowghes, sallowghes, and alders, to be felled and cutte downe by grounde'; if there were not enough of these the commoners were allowed to 'loppe and croppe [i.e. pollard] Mapull and Beche'; and if these were still insufficient they might 'loppe suche trees of Oke as hathe ben before lopped, and . . . shredde suche as hath not ben before lopped'.

The Mens (Kirdford and Fittleworth, W. Sussex)

This is one of the best surviving wooded commons – though the common-rights have fallen into disuse – and belongs to the Sussex Wildlife Trust. Dr Ruth Tittensor has written an account of its history[153] to which I am indebted for some of the following particulars.

The common has a splendidly irregular outline (Fig. 12.1). It straggles across the Wealden soil sequence, most of the soils being very heavy. It is compartmented by small, relatively straight banks, established probably no earlier than the eighteenth century, apart from Idehurst Hurst, a wood which may have been defined much earlier.

The name Mens, first recorded in 1300, is apparently from Anglo-Saxon *gemǣne*, 'common', presumably implying a contrast with what were already private woods surrounding it (a parallel is Swingfield *Minnis*, a common near Dover). The common has apparently always had trees, though a map of 1650 shows it less wooded than it is now.

Woodcutting and grazing ceased at least a century ago. Grassland has vanished, save for the small Strood Green, and almost the whole area is now dominated by beech and oak. Most of these have grown up since management declined, but there are some pollards and other old trees dating from before the compartmentation. Holly, hazel, and hornbeam are widespread. Compartmentation was presumably followed by coppicing, but the stools (chiefly oak) are small and infrequent, which confirms that this phase lasted not more than 100 years.

Invasion by oak with a holly understorey, followed by beech – which in places is overtopping and killing the oak – appears to bc characteristic of wood-pasture, particularly declining wood-pasture, on almost any soil within the native range of beech. Other examples appear in Chapters 17 and 20. But the flora of The Mens is richer than that of most wood-pastures. Hazel and hornbeam probably survive from an earlier phase in its history, while service and woodland hawthorn are diagnostic of ancient woodland (Chapter 5).

Tittensor's researches show The Mens, like many wood-pastures, to have had a less stable history than most ancient woods; fragments of evidence from several phases survive on the ground. It is a pity that so little should remain of the historic grassland, scrub, and pollards, but in this case recent neglect has produced one important habitat, rotten wood, in which The Mens excels.

Forests

Legal and physical Forests

In this book I use Forest in the original sense of a place inhabited by the king's (or some other lord's) deer. The word has been transmuted in many strange ways: in the thirteenth century *forestarius* sometimes translated 'woodward' (p. 140); from the sixteenth to the eighteenth century 'forest' could mean 'heath' (e.g. 'the forest (*forrestum*) called Hula Heath' in Sotterley (E. Suffolk) many miles from any genuine Forest);[366] and from 1650 onwards it gradually developed its modern meanings of 'plantation' and 'large wood'. With these later senses we are not concerned.

The word Forest was originally a purely legal term – a tract of land governed by special laws, ostensibly concerned with protecting deer, and a special administration; a modern parallel is a National Park in the British sense. Each Forest normally contained a tract of uncultivated land in which the deer lived and to which the Forest name eventually came to be transferred. The remainder of the Forest consisted of ordinary farmland, private woodland, villages and towns. It is important not to confuse, as many writers have done, the legal with the physical Forest. The legal jurisdiction included not only the land on which the deer lived but any land on to which they might stray. Land could be afforested or disafforested for political reasons without any effect on the ground. These administrative changes were an important political and fiscal device[612, 740] but are of little ecological interest. Normally the legal Forest covered at least five times the area of the physical Forest; confusion between the two areas is largely responsible for the popular myth that the Forests were continually shrinking.

Fig. 12.1 A complex wood-pasture common: The Mens, Sussex. Note the concave boundary, funnelling out into roads and joining up with another common in the next parish, and the many enclaves of private woodland and of other land.

The Forestal rights – the rights to keep deer, to appoint Forest officials, to hold Forest courts and to pocket the fines levied therein – were distinct from the ownership of the Forest land. In Hatfield Forest (Essex) the king happened to own the land on which he kept his deer; in Epping Forest he kept deer on other people's land and had no right to cut down trees or to graze any other animals. When in 1238 the king disposed of his Hatfield estate he retained the Forestal rights and continued to take deer.[233]

Deer

Medieval parks and Forests could contain three species of deer, red, roe, and fallow, which are carefully distinguished by the Latin words *cervus* and *bissa* (hart and hind), *capreolus* or *cheverellus* (roe), and *damus* and *dama* (buck and doe). The wild swine (*aper* and *laya*, boar and sow) was treated as if it were a deer. In one Forest – Somerton (Somerset) – the hare was an honorary deer and was, for instance, supposed to be the subject of an inquest whenever one was found dead.[42]

The Anglo-Saxons and their Welsh contemporaries[508] knew the high or red deer (*heah deor*) and the roe; the fallow deer is an exotic species. Fallow may have been briefly introduced by the Romans but did not persist; supposed pre-Conquest evidence for them turns out to rest on mistaken identification or translation.[629] There can be no doubt that the Normans deliberately introduced fallow from the Levant or the Near East as a means of producing meat from poor agricultural land. The rabbit[874] and the pheasant, which have comparable histories and provenances, are other relics of the Normans' enterprise in seeking alternatives to agriculture. The fallow deer is not mentioned among William the Conqueror's favourite animals in the Anglo-Saxon Chronicle's obituary of him in 1087, and it is possible that it was first introduced in the early twelfth century as part of the second phase of making parks and Forests. A conceivable source would be through the Sicilian-Norman connection; their conquest of Sicily after 1060 brought the Normans into contact with Classical and Islamic traditions of emparking and of keeping oriental beasts. Fallow are still much more abundant in Great Britain than in the rest of Europe.

Fallow deer were an immediate success, probably because they are easier to manage than the other species; their habit of staying in one area[628] would be a particular advantage in small Forests. Whatever their natural habitat may have been, they fitted well into medieval wood-pasture. They are mainly grass-feeders.[629] Although they get some sustenance from dead leaves, brambles, fruits and nuts (if any), a habitat consisting entirely of woodland would support deer only precariously and in small numbers. They attack saplings and coppice regrowth no less destructively than cattle or goats.[121] In continuous woodland, especially in underwood, they would have been very hard to capture. Accordingly, although the medievals believed that fallow deer needed access to trees, most parks and Forests had at least some grassland as well, and there were many in which grassland predominated.

Red deer, although widespread in Lowland England, appear to have been most abundant in mountain and moorland areas with little or no woodland, much as in modern Scotland. Roe could also be non-woodland deer: in 1254 there was a poaching case concerning forty roe in the fens of Whittlesey (Hunts).[504]

Numbers and nature of physical Forests

I have some record of 142 Forests (Fig. 12.2). This number, though higher than any previously published figure, is a minimum estimate of the total. Some Forests had a shadowy existence: for instance we might think the 'Forest' of Arden (Warwick) to have originated in the antiquarian imagination of Michael Drayton, the poet,[663] but for a single twelfth-century record that it really was a Forest.[716] There is sometimes uncertainty as to whether to treat two nearby Forests as one. Most of the records are of the twelfth and thirteenth centuries; it is doubtful whether any new Forests were formed in England after 1250.

The king had more Forests than all his subjects: 86 of the 142 were predominantly royal. (The word 'Chase' is sometimes, though inconsistently, used to distinguish the Forest of a subject.) A Forest was the supreme status symbol for the noblest families, such as the multi-Forest Earls of Richmond. Among princes of the Church, only the Bishops of Durham, Winchester, and Ely aspired to Forests. Besides Forests, the king had many woods but only about twenty parks.

Forests are not well correlated with woodland. They were comparatively few in the biggest concentrations of woodland – the Weald, the Chilterns, Arden; they were most numerous in moderately-wooded counties such as Hampshire, Wiltshire, and Shropshire. Counties without Forests were either very well-wooded (Kent, Herts) or rather poorly-wooded (E. Yorks, Suffolk, Cambs). The mountain and moorland Forests, such as Dartmoor, Exmoor, and many in the Pennines and Lake District, were almost woodless, like the red-deer Forests of the modern Scottish Highlands. Other Forests were all fenland, like Kesteven (Lincs) and Hatfield Chase near Doncaster; others all heath, like Wolmer (Hants) and Rudheath (Cheshire);[660] others appear to have been ordinary countryside, like Wirral (Cheshire) and Corfe (Dorset).

The largest physical Forests that were not moorland were probably the New Forest, with *c.* 80,000 acres of heath and woodland,[156] and Sherwood, with *c.* 50,000 acres.[249] Several, such as Weybridge (Hunts) or Hatfield (Essex), had as little as 1,000 acres of wood-pasture; others, such as Chute (Wilts), appear to have been

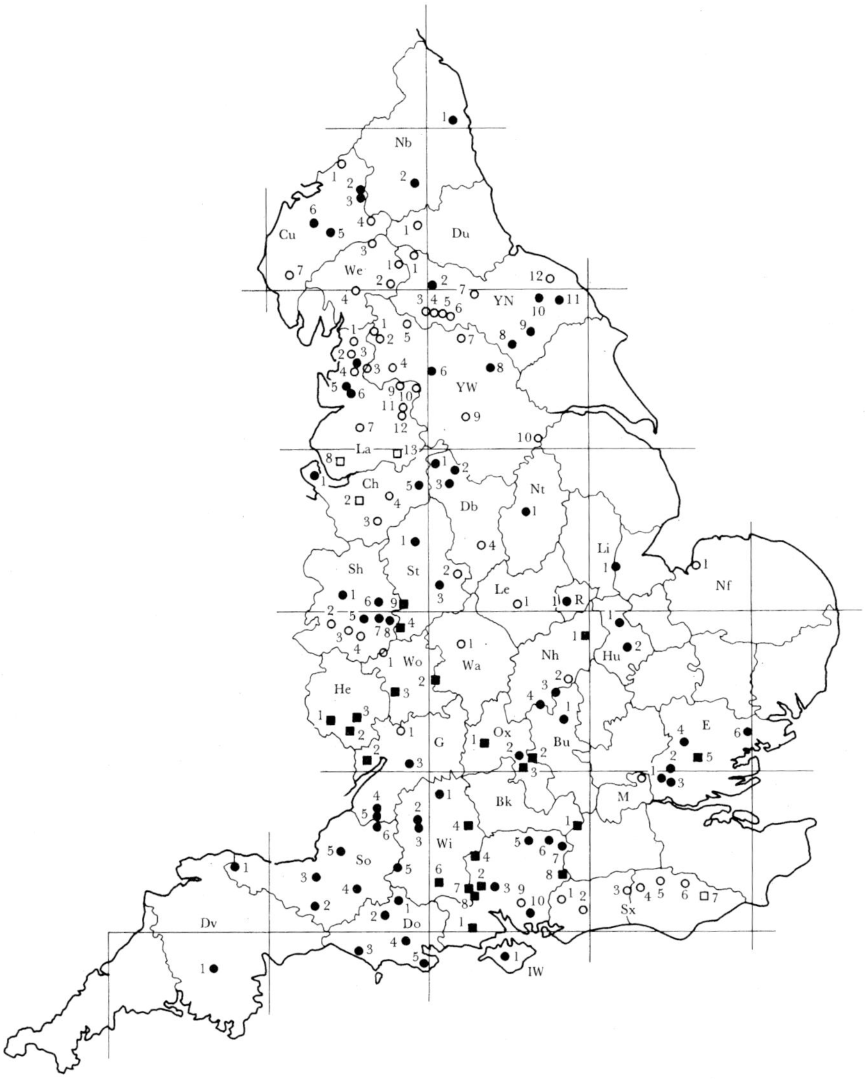

Fig. 12.2 Forests. Black: Royal Forests (i.e. Forests whose Forestal rights belonged to the Crown for all or most of the time up to 1300). White: private Forests. Squares: Forests mentioned or implied in Domesday Book. Circles: Forests first recorded after 1086 (nearly all are recorded by 1300).

The size of individual Forests is not shown because the legal boundaries had no ecological significance and the size of the physical Forests cannot often be ascertained. The circles have an area (at the scale of the map) of 19 sq. km or 4,800 acres; the average size of a physical Forest was probably something like 5,000 acres.

There was a 'Forest of Cornwall' up to 1204[444] but it appears to have been only a fiscal device.

General sources[741] and articles on 'Forestry' in *Victoria County Histories.*

Berkshire
1 Windsor
Buckinghamshire
1 Whaddon Chase
2 Bernwood
Cheshire
1 Wirral
2 Delamere
3 Mondrum
4 Rudheath
5 Macclesfield
Cumberland
1 Nichol
2 Brathwaite
3 Geltsdale
4 Gilderdale
5 Inglewood
6 Allerdale
7 Copeland

Derbyshire
1 Longdendale
2 Hope
3 Campana
(1–3 collectively called Peak)
4 Duffield Frith
Devon
1 Dartmoor
Dorset
1 Gillingham
2 Blackmore
3 Powerstock
4 Bere Regis
5 Corfe
Durham
1 Weardale
Essex
1 Waltham (Epping)
2 Wintry
3 Hainault
4 Hatfield Broadoak
5 Writtle
6 Kingswood (Colchester)
Gloucestershire
1 Corse
2 Dean
3 Cirencester
4 Horwood
5 Kingswood
Hampshire
1 New
2 Buckholt
3 Bere Ashley
4 Chute (partly Wilts)
5 Pamber
6 Eversley
7 Alice Holt
8 Wolmer
9 Waltham Chase
10 Bere Porchester

merely a scattered group of woods with no recognizable nucleus.[63] At a rough estimate there were eighty wooded Forests with an average of 5,000 acres of wood-pasture each, amounting in all to some 400,000 acres of wood-pasture, a tenth of the Domesday Book 'woodland' in England. The total area of *physical* Forests would have been nearly a million acres, about 3% of England, but the *legal* area of Forest jurisdiction – royal and private – covered at least a third of the country.[612]

The growth of the Forest system

The idea of Forests probably originated in Continental game laws and was introduced to Britain by the Normans. Anglo-Saxon kings were fond of venison and had a high regard for professional hunters. In a very few places (e.g. Writtle, Essex) they even had an official whom the Domesday Commissioners chose to set down retrospectively as a *forestarius*, but there is no reason to suppose that kings before 1066 exceeded the ordinary sporting rights of any landowner. The Anglo-Saxons had no word for Forest; the supposed pre-Conquest evidence turns out to rest either on medieval forgeries such as the 'Laws of Pseudo-Canute', seeking to invest Forests with respectable antiquity,[124, 773] or on modern mistranslation.

William the Conqueror saw deer, not merely as a royal hobby, but as a business – a kind of subsistence farming for the support of the court – and introduced special laws for their protection. The Anglo-Saxon Chronicle for 1087 says:

> The king W[illiam] set up great protection for deer

Herefordshire
1 Trivel
2 Archenfield
3 Hereford Hay
Huntingdonshire
1 Huntingdon (including Sapley)
2 Weybridge
Isle of Wight
1 Parkhurst
Lancashire
1 Hornby
2 Quernmore
3 Over Wyresdale
4 Bleasdale
5 Myerscough
6 Fulwood
7 Horswood
8 Simonswood
9 Pendle
10 Trawden
11 Rossendale
12 Tottington
13 Burtonwood
Leicestershire
1 Leicester
Lincolnshire
1 Kesteven
Middlesex
1 Enfield Chase
Norfolk
1 Castle Rising[413]
Northamptonshire
1 Rockingham (including Geddington and Cliffe)
2 Yardley Chase
3 Salcey
4 Whittlewood
Northumberland
Number and location of Forests not certain
Nottinghamshire
1 Sherwood
Oxfordshire
1 Wychwood
2 Stowood
3 Shotover
Rutland
1 Leighfield
Shropshire
1 Lythewood
2 Stiperstones
3 Corve
4 Clee
5 Long
6 Wrekin
7 Shirlett
8 Morfe
9 Brewood (partly Staffs)
Somerset
1 Exmoor
2 Neroche
3 North Petherton
4 Somerton
5 Mendip
6 Filwood
Staffordshire
1 New
2 Needwood
3 Cannock
4 Kinver
Sussex
1 Stanstead
2 Arundel
3 St Leonard's
4 Worth
5 Ashdown
6 Waterdown
7 Ballington
Warwickshire
1 Arden
Westmorland
1 Stainmore
2 Mallerstang
3 Milburn
4 Whinfell
Wiltshire
1 Braydon
2 Chippenham
3 Melksham (including Pewsham)
4 Savernake
5 Selwood (partly Somerset)
6 Grovely
7 Clarendon
8 Melchet
Worcestershire
1 Wyre (partly Shropshire)
2 Feckenham
3 Malvern
Yorkshire (North Riding)
1 Lune
2 Langthwaite
3 Raydale
4 Bishopsdale
5 Waldale
6 Coverdale
7 New
8 Galtres
9 Spaunton
10 Farndale
11 Pickering
12 Danby
Yorkshire (West Riding)
1 Burton
2 Mewith
3 Bowland
4 Gisburn
5 Langstrothdale Chase
6 Skipton
7 Kirby Malzeard
8 Knaresborough
9 Sowerby

> (*deorfrip*), and legislated to that intent, that whosoever should slay hart or hind should be blinded . . . he loved the high-deer as if he were their father.

This indicates that Forest Law (not that it is known ever to have exacted such a penalty) was first introduced to conserve the existing red deer. At first the laws were confined to large estates over which thc Crown had complete control, such as the king's 'demesne Forests' in Oxfordshire (p. 117). William later began to impose the jurisdiction on other men's lands. The New Forest was doubtless called 'new' because it was at the time an unprecedented extension of Forest jurisdiction: it is possible that an area was depopulated for the benefit of the deer, though this is disputed by modern scholars.[156] Domesday Book mentions about 25 Forests, sometimes directly – a piece of land had declined in value because it had been scheduled as a Forest – but more often obliquely. Most of these were in areas which had red deer in later centuries (Fig. 12.4). It is often alleged that all the Royal Forests existed in 1086 but that the Commissioners did not trouble to record them systematically. This view appears to be unfounded. There is no evidence that the Forests of subjects were recorded more fully than those of the king (only four private Forests are mentioned) nor that the account of Crown lands is deficient in any respect other than that of Forests. Nor is it reasonable that the record should have neglected an aspect of the king's rights particularly liable to come into dispute with the rights of others. Domesday gives unusually full particulars of some forty manors having shares in what were to be Epping and Hainault Forests; it is inconceivable that it should have failed to mention the Forests had they had a legal existence at the time. The system was in its infancy at the Conqueror's death: about a quarter of the eventual tally of Royal Forests had been declared, and a few magnates such as the Earl of Chester were venturing to declare Forests of their own.

Afforestment was continued by Henry I (1100–35). We are tempted to associate this second period with the introduction of fallow deer, which would have been more advantageous than red deer in existing lowland Forests and would have made it easier to establish Forests in places where there were not deer already. Many Forests are first heard of about this time (e.g. Sherwood in 1154,[43] Epping in the 1130s)[134] and the legal bounds of others were enlarged. There was a third phase of afforestment under Richard I (1189–99) which probably included Neroche Forest (Somerset), first mentioned in 1221.[42] The increase in Forests and their corrupt bureaucracy was one of the chief sources of friction between the king and the nobility and was one of the abuses curtailed by Magna Carta (1216).[740] After this date the system began to decline and changes were largely limited to tinkering with the legal boundaries.

Establishing a Forest

No proper record survives of the operation of declaring a Forest. Besides defining the boundaries and appointing justices, wardens, Foresters-of-fee, verderers, regarders, etc. there would usually have been the one practical matter of introducing some deer. In 1279 a Forest was held to have been established inadvertently by allowing deer to escape from a park,[612] but this was exceptional. These extracts from the Liberate Rolls for 1238, concerned apparently with starting a Forest in what is now Belgium, suggest the more normal procedure.

> 3 Dec. 1238. To Richard de Muntfichet . . . to cause to be taken . . . within and without the king's park of Havering [i.e. in Havering Park and Hainault Forest] 80 live does and 40 live bucks for the use of the count of Flanders, and to deliver them to Reynold Ruffus, the king's yeoman, and to have made . . . such cages as shall be needed to put them in.[235]
>
> 2 Dec. 1238. To the Sheriff of Essex . . . to cause 120 bucks and does that the king ordered to be taken alive in the Forest of Essex for the use of the count of Flanders to be carried in carts to the Thames and to cause Reynold Ruffus . . . to have a ship to carry them to Flanders.[235]

The uses of medieval Forests

The heyday of Forests before 1216, when to a large extent they actually sustained the king and his court, has been extensively studied by Dr Clifford Owen. The more easily accessible records of the thirteenth century form the basis of major studies of the Forests of Dean[69] and Sherwood,[214] and I have used them in Epping,[124] Hatfield, Blackmore and Neroche.[125]

Nearly every Forest was also a common; it involved landowners and commoners as well as the Crown. The Close and Liberate Rolls, particularly for the reign of Henry III (1216–72), tell the story of the Crown's exploitation of the Forests. The activities of other parties are more difficult to establish in full, but much can be learnt from the records of Forest courts. The Sherwood and Dean studies reveal a vast range of technically illegal activities; the judicial system was used not only to punish genuine offences but also as a means to collect money from ordinary sales and lettings. Forest Law may have been oppressive to the nobility and gentry, but to the ordinary man Forests afforded many opportunities of enterprise and profit. Illicit woodcutting or grazing, or even appropriating part of the Forest land, were usually condoned for a modest fine; horses and carts or livestock, sometimes confiscated for such offences, were redeemed by the culprit for about a third of their value.[124] The curious custom of *expeditating* dogs living within the Forest – cutting off part of one of the animal's feet lest it run after the deer, or, rather, collecting a fee from the dog's owner for not doing so – contrasted with that of *expeditating* trees, cutting off part of the tree's roots to induce it to fall down, a malpractice on the part of persons having windfallen trees as a perquisite.[214]

Deer

Records of the king's hunting in person are surprisingly few; it is possible that he hunted as a guest in other people's Forests more often than he did in his own. Usually he ordered his professional huntsmen to take specified deer from particular Forests, as for example:

> 8 Nov. 1251. Order to the king's constable of St Briavel's to let Sibyl de Clifford have two [wild] sows in the Forest of Dean, of the king's gift.[233]
>
> 4 Sept. 1251. Order to William Luvel and Henry de Candour, the king's huntsmen, that when they have taken 60 bucks in the king's Forest of Dean, as the king ordered, they should go to the king's New Forest and take another 60 bucks there, and when these have been taken deliver them to the king's lieutenant of Hampshire, whom the king ordered to receive them and to cause them to be salted and transported to London for the forthcoming feast of St Edward [13 October].[233]

Males were taken from April to September and females from October to March.

By this time deer were associated more with festivity than with subsistence. They were eaten on the greater feasts of the Church or to celebrate weddings, graduations, pregnancies, consecrations, etc. The king's feasts were not inconsiderable. For his Christmas dinner in 1251 Henry III had 180 harts, 250 hinds, 200 fallow bucks, 100 roedeer, 200 wild swine (from the last remaining population, which never recovered), 1,300 hares, 395 swans, 115 cranes, etc., etc.[233] He gave smaller numbers of deer to his friends or to statesmen and prelates, and also supplied live deer for stocking parks.

The cropping of deer was very irregular[124] but a sample of six years gives us some idea of where the deer lived (Figs. 12.3–12.5) and what use was made of them. In an average year Henry III took 607 fallow deer (325 bucks and 282 does), of which 526 came from Forests; the remainder were got from royal parks or by raiding the parks of bishoprics which happened to be vacant. 47% of these he ate himself; 37% went to the tables of his friends; 16% were given away live for stocking parks. Of red deer the annual consumption was very irregular but averaged 159 head (83 harts and 76 hinds), almost all for the king's own use. The average consumption of roe was about 45 head. Wild swine averaged 88 a year until 1260, apparently the last year in which they are recorded.

Fallow were the common deer of the lowlands, present in nearly all the fifty or so Forests appearing in the records. Their numbers bear little relation to the size of the physical Forest: the small Braydon (Wilts) yielded more deer than the vast Forest of Sherwood. Red deer were present in about thirty Forests but came chiefly from the northern ones, especially Inglewood; the largest southern source was the small Forest of Grovely. Roe appear in significant numbers only in Yorkshire. Wild swine are recorded up to 1231 in the Forest of Pickering (Yorks) and thereafter only in Dean.

Deer were also consumed by the local inhabitants; this was an imprisonable offence, but the chance of detection was so remote as to be little deterrent. In Sherwood prosecutions for poaching averaged nine a year,[214] some of which involved several animals; illicit cropping of deer must at least have equalled the thirty head a year ordered by the king. Even if we multiply the official figures by three to allow for royal hunts, poaching, unrecorded orders, and orders not specifying the numbers of animals, the Forest deer were not an intensive use of the land. Hatfield Forest (Essex), one of the biggest producers of venison in relation to its size, officially yielded thirteen fallow a year (average for all years from 1234 to 1263) on 1,000 acres; even if the actual yield was forty a year, this is only one animal from 25 acres. [The problem of how the medievals kept deer down to reasonable numbers is discussed on p. 513.]

The Forests had been superimposed on existing wood-pasture ecosystems but can rarely have had much effect on them. Usually the grazing of cattle and sheep and the cutting of timber and wood continued. Most of the productivity of the ecosystem, as on other wooded commons, went either into trees or into farm livestock; except in a few of the small Forests, little was diverted into venison.

Timber

The king owned trees on only about half of his Forests. The chief sources of timber mentioned in the Close Rolls are the Forests of Dean, Windsor, and Sherwood; Gillingham (Dorset) and Kingswood (Essex) yielded large numbers of oaks despite their small area. The following is a typical order for timber.

> 29 May 1250. Order to Wilfred de Langele, justiciar of the Forest, that he should let Bertram de Crioll, warden of the king's castle of Dover, have 60 oaks in the king's Forest of Kingswood outside Colchester for repairing the buildings of the said castle; Mr John, carpenter of the said castle, wants to choose them for that work.[233]

Although the orders were often for only one or two oaks and rarely for as many as 100, they appear to exploit a scarce resource, *outsize* trees (p. 153). The ability to bestow great oaks on one's subjects was one of the privileges of being a king. The trees were transported long distances (p. 153). It was appreciated that this resource was difficult to renew and unsuccessful attempts were made to conserve it (p. 153).

Ordinary timber trees were used by the local inhabitants. Forest courts imposed fines for 'illicit' felling, but these probably had no punitive intention and were merely a means of collecting money from casual sales.

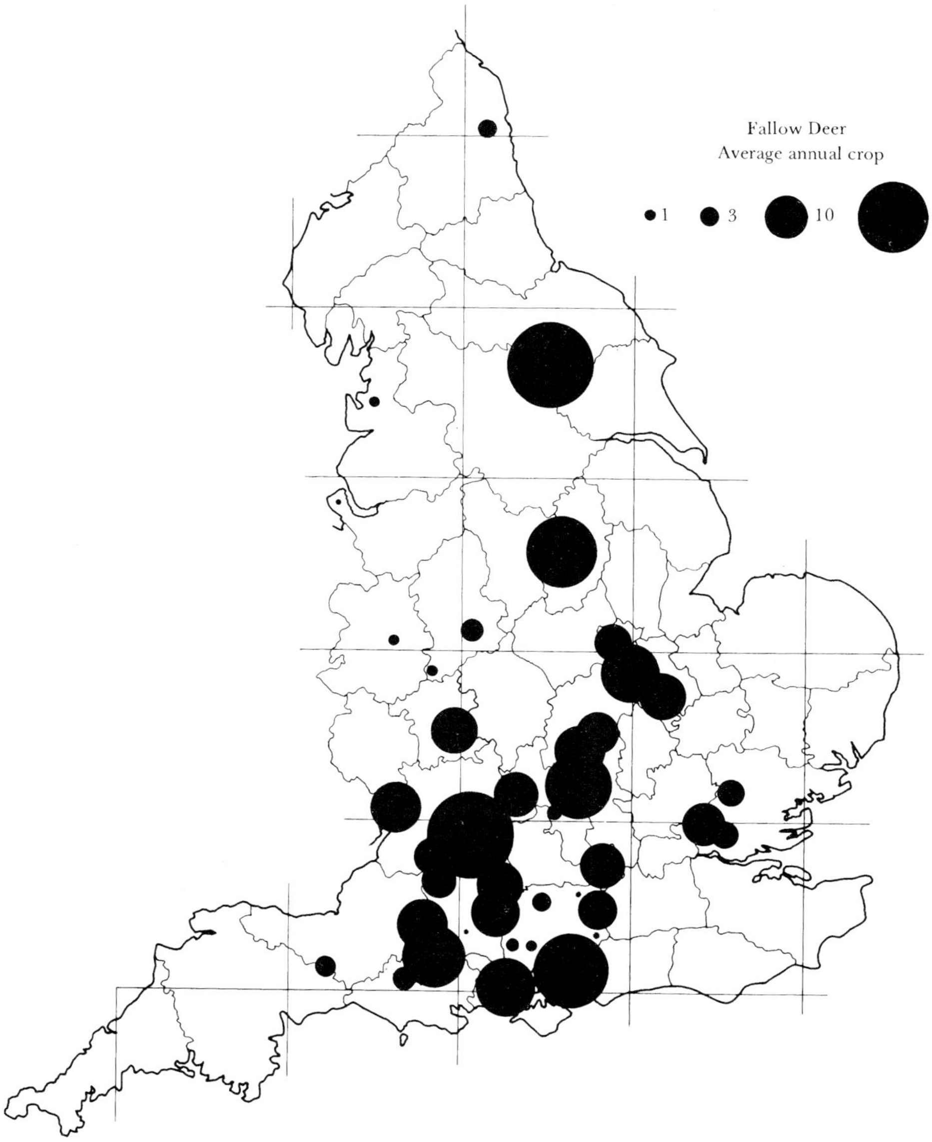

Fig. 12.3 Fallow deer ordered by Henry III from his Forests. The size of each spot is proportional to the average annual consumption of deer in the sample years 1231, 1242, 1251, 1258, 1265, and 1272.[233, 235] Private Forests, such as those in Sussex and most of the Pennines, are not included.

Wood

Wood appears in two forms in Forest archives. There are single trees called *robora*, a word of uncertain meaning. The Rolls distinguish consistently between *quercus*, which is not oak in general, but an oak suitable for timber (*quercus apta ad meremium*), and *robur*, which is a firewood tree (*robur ad focum*), not necessarily an oak. Often 'a dry *robur*' or 'an old *robur* not bearing leaves' is specified. I have argued that *robur* means a pollard; that pollards were normally cut by commoners with woodcutting rights and thus do not appear in the Rolls; and if pollards died they ceased to be of use to the commoners and became the perquisite of the landowner.[124] *Robora* are mentioned, usually in small numbers, in uncompartmented Forests where the king was landowner, notably Windsor and Hainault (Essex). They might be used for the king's own purposes or given to others, e.g.:

> 12 Dec. 1228. The king to the Forester . . . of Havering. We order you to let the constable of the Tower of London have 30 *robora* in the outwood of Havering [*forinseco bosco de H.*, i.e. Hainault Forest] to make a certain lime-kiln (*rogum*) for the works of the said Tower of London.[233]
>
> 13 June 1231. Order to Richard de Muntfichet to let Helen of Winchester, once the king's nurse, have two old *robora* in the outwood of Havering for her fire, of the king's gift.[233]

In other Forests there are references to underwood (*subboscus*). In 1229, 3,000 hurdles were ordered for Portsmouth Dockyard from Grovely and other Forests for some purpose connected with the invasion of France the following year.[233] The Rolls do not record the beginnings of coppicing in Forests – hurdles could not have been provided unless there had been underwood already grown with which to make them – but they show its extension into remote places and the spread of compartmentation. Henry III, who was in constant trouble with his creditors, appreciated the money to be made out of underwood if properly managed and sold. An example illustrates the industrialization of the Forest of Dean, which was doubtless responsible – more than the excesses of the king's table – for the extinction of wild swine. In 1237 the Constable of St Briavel's was ordered

> to cause to be erected 9 mobile underwood forges (*forgias itinerantes ad subboscum*) . . . and to sustain those forges . . . with thorn, maple, hazel, and other underwood; so that no oak, chestnut, or beech be cut down; and to cause the area felled and allocated . . . to be well and sufficiently fenced lest any deer or other beast be able to get in to browse there.[233]

The exploitation of the king's underwood was well organized but was restricted by existing rights. Henry III scrupulously respected manorial laws, which prevailed over the Forest Law or the Crown's interests. For instance, in 1252 he ordered Wilfrid le Chamberleng and

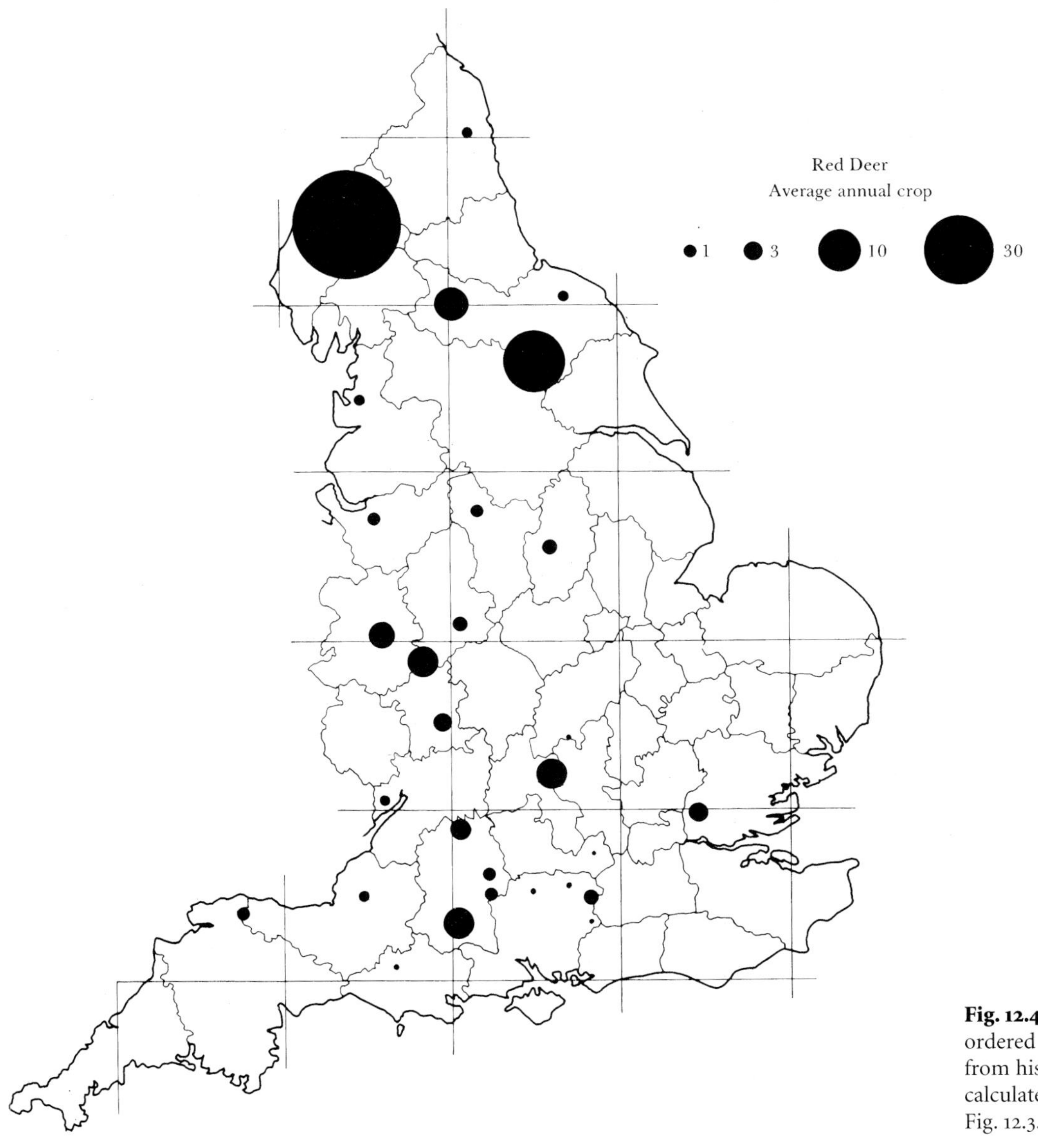

Fig. 12.4 Red deer ordered by Henry III from his Forests, calculated as for Fig. 12.3.

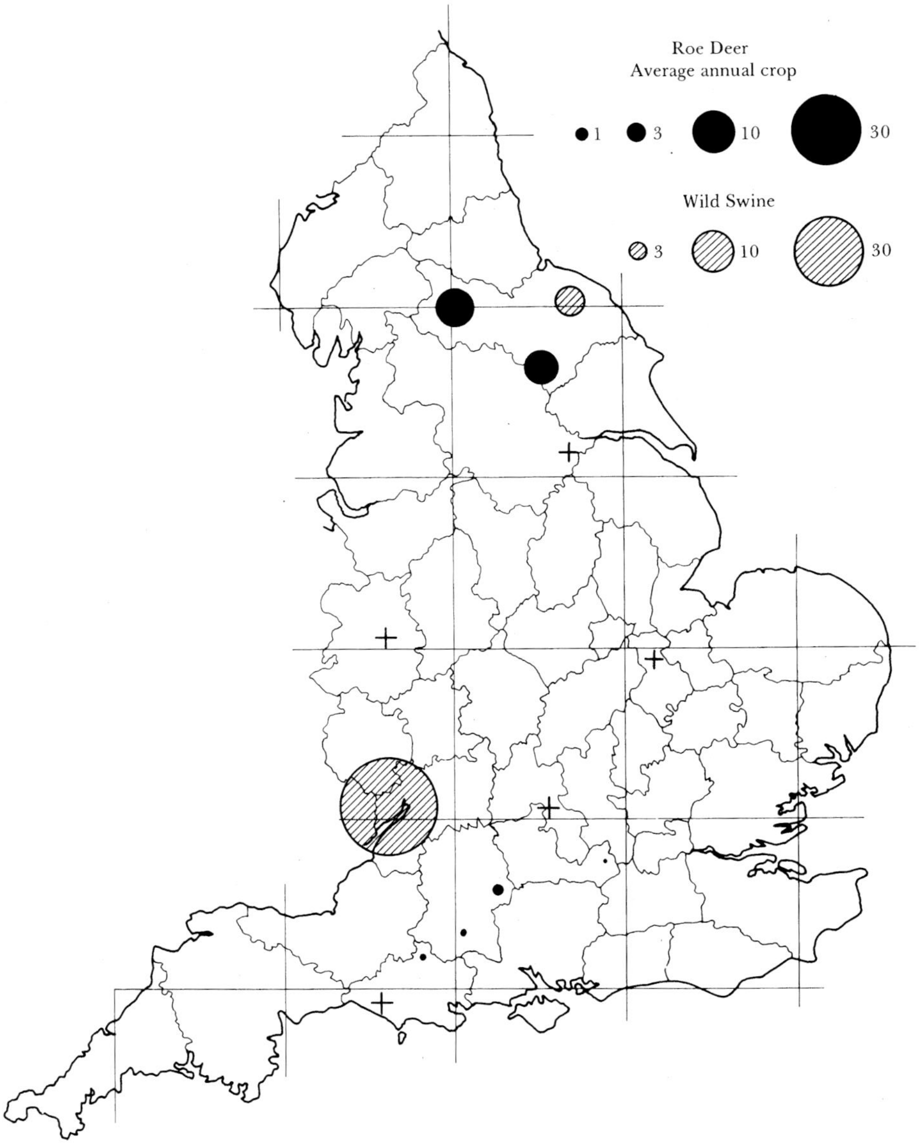

Fig. 12.5 Roe deer and wild swine ordered by Henry III from his Forests, calculated as for Fig. 12.3 Crosses indicate Forests in which roe are known to have existed but were not taken by the king in the sample years.

his colleagues, 'sellers of the king's underwood in Wiltshire', who had just sold £20 worth (probably some 1,600 acre-years, cf. Fig. 11.6) in Grovely Forest

> to fence in all the places in the king's wood of Grovely, from which they have sold underwood by the king's order, so that the king may not suffer damage, nor the men of Barford and Wishford [who had the common-rights] be inconvenienced by having their beasts shut into the enclosure . . . And the king orders that when the said underwood shall have grown up, the said men may have their common-rights there, as they used to have earlier.[233]

The compartments necessary for coppicing existed only on local sufferance and sometimes could not be made at all:

> 12 April 1397. Licence for the . . . provost of the cathedral church of Wells, to cut down 100 acres of wood within the metes of the Forest of Nerechych [i.e. Neroche], . . . and cart it away, provided that he enclose the said acres according to the assize of the Forest . . .
>
> 22 Nov. 1398. Licence renewed to the . . . provost of . . . Wells . . . releasing him from the condition of the former licence, viz. that he should enclose the said 100 acres according to the assize of the Forest; because he cannot rightly do so, as the ground is and from time immemorial has been common of pasture of the adjacent country . . .[236]

Conclusions

From the Crown's point of view the Forests were very

different from one another. Kingswood (Essex), for instance, yielded timber; Braydon (Wilts) fallow deer; Grovely (Wilts) red deer and underwood; Inglewood (Cumberland) red deer and timber; and Dean minerals, underwood, timber, and wild swine. The total annual yield to the king was less than a thousand deer, a few hundred big oaks and *robora*, and a few thousand acre-years of underwood.[806] This is a poor return from at least 500,000 acres of physical Forest, but there was also indirect exploitation through the Forest courts. At Sherwood in 1287 a court, dealing with 23 years' accumulated cases (for Forest justice moved at its leisure), fined 209 'trespassers against the venison' a total of £418 and collected smaller sums from 725 offenders against the vert (i.e. trees and bracken).[214] These were useful amounts, though no greater than the income from a single large agricultural estate. For a short time King John had exacted much larger sums through the Forest courts,[740] but this was by using the system as a tax-collecting machine rather than from exploiting the land itself.

The chief value of Forests to the king was probably social rather than economic. They were a source of prestige, of gifts of a kind that money could not buy, and of honorific jobs in the Forest hierarchy.

In most Forests the king's land-uses, although well documented, were a minor addition to the common-land grazing and woodcutting which remained the chief uses of the Forests. For example, in the 6,000 acres of Epping Forest there were:

(*a*) the king's deer, estimated at 300 fallow and a few dozen red;
(*b*) grazing rights of commoners and landowners – at least 2,000 sheep and probably over 1,000 cattle;
(*c*) large numbers of goats and other animals illicitly grazed;
(*d*) commoners' and landowners' woodcutting rights on some tens of thousands of pollard trees;
(*e*) a few timber trees belonging to landowners.[124]

Other studies, such as that of the Forest of Dean,[69] suggest a similar degree of exploitation. Forests were not under-used, considering that they were mostly land unsuitable for agriculture. Where the king's rights were extensive, as in Dean, he used them fully. Where he derived little benefit from a Forest, as in Epping, this was because his rights were limited and the land was exploited by other people.

The later history of Forests

The Crown lost interest in the deer in one Forest after another, though in Epping, Windsor, and the New Forest not until the nineteenth century. The woodland management of Henry III was not kept up: despite an attempt to revive woodmanship in the sixteenth century, woods in Crown-owned Forests were very ineffectively managed.[66] The New Forest, for example, was extensively encoppiced in the Middle Ages but later reverted to an uncompartmented state.[155]

Charles I revived the Forest Laws, chiefly for the money that might be raised by enforcing or extinguishing them. From the mid-seventeenth century onwards the Crown became interested in growing timber, chiefly for sale to the Navy; large areas of Dean, the New Forest, Alice Holt (Hants) and Bere (near Portsmouth), where the Crown still owned the soil, were enclosed and planted with oak. Most of the plantations were not properly looked after, and these measures often damaged the traditional land-uses without producing worthwhile timber: an example is the prohibition of pollarding in the New Forest in 1698.[490] The Crown did get some useful oak from Hainault Forest (Essex) in the late eighteenth century, but this had grown naturally and had cost nothing.[124]

Most Forests continued to exist as commons and played an important part in social history down to the nineteenth century. Agricultural improvers such as Vancouver[507] disapproved of Forests, which they failed to understand. The reputation of Forests for lawlessness was one factor in the tightening of the criminal law in the eighteenth century, under which, for instance, it again became a hanging matter – as it had been for short periods in the twelfth and sixteenth centuries – to steal a deer.[896] The chief destruction of Forests was by Enclosure Acts: Enfield Chase (Middx) went in 1777, Needwood (Staffs) in 1801,[95] Windsor in 1817 (but see p. 303), Neroche (Somerset) in 1830, Hainault (Essex) in 1851, and Wychwood (Oxon) in 1857.

Management of trees in Forests

Compartmented Forests

Coppices in Forests differed from ordinary woods in having longer and more rigidly defined felling cycles: this was necessary in order to accommodate the intermittent grazing.

A survey of Grovely Forest (Wilts) in 1566[493, 517] shows it divided into fifteen compartments: fourteen 'copses' ranging from 46 to 116 acres, and a sixty-acre pasture, the total area being 1,071 acres (all apparently measured with an 18-ft perch (p. 19)). The system suggests a fourteen-year coppice cycle. There was insufficient grassland to sustain the grazing, for even the sixty-acre plain was reserved for the deer and the landlord's cattle; but part of each copse was described as 'empty' (*vacua*), these informal glades amounting to 87 acres. The copses are first named *c.* 1330[718] but may already have existed in the thirteenth century (p. 184). Since 1800 they have been replanted almost beyond recognition (but see p. 321).

At Hatfield (Essex)[122] about three-quarters of the 1,000-acre Forest was supposed to be coppiced on an

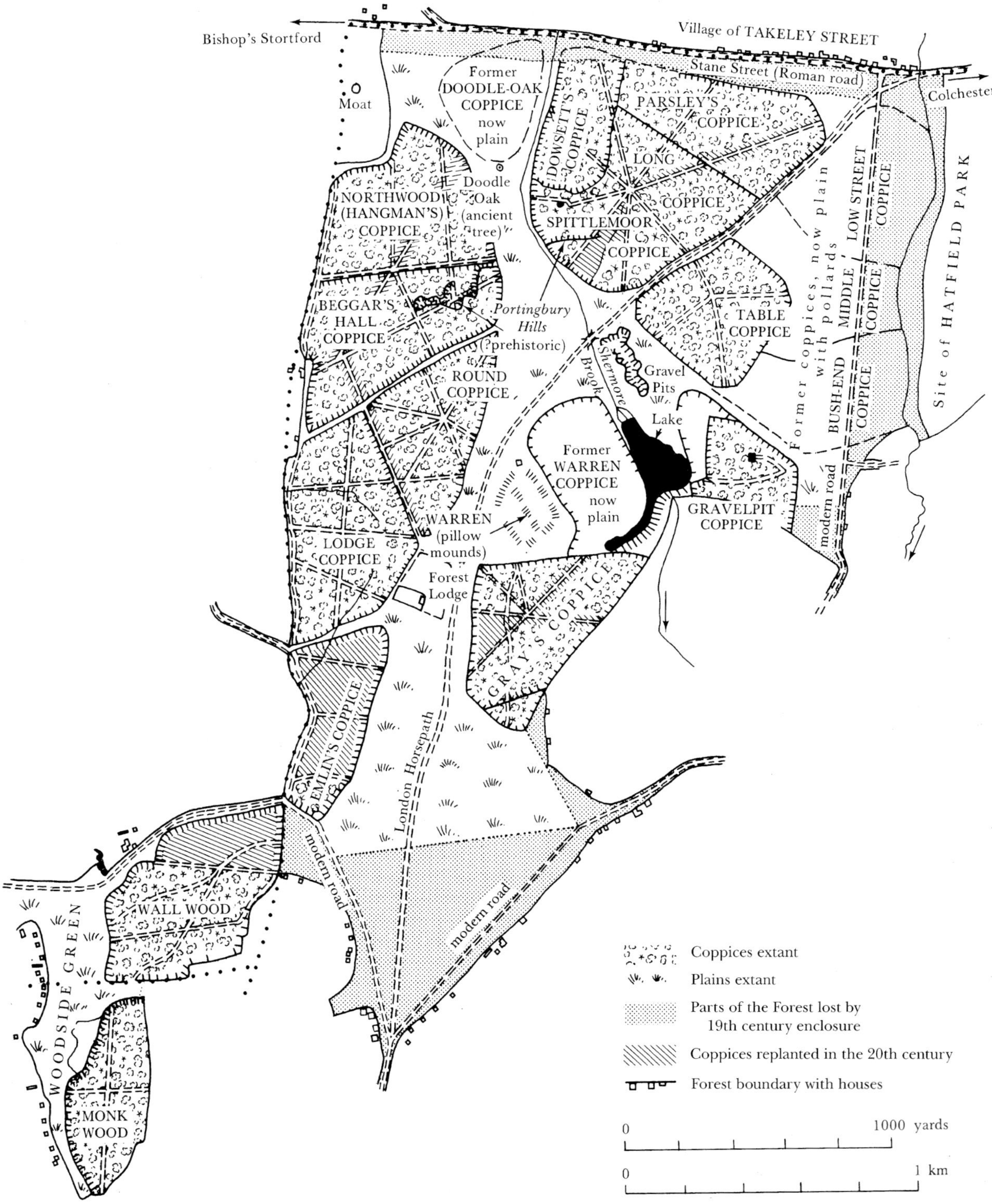

Fig. 12.6 Hatfield Forest, Essex. A compartmented Forest divided into coppices and plains. The seventeen coppices are given their traditional names.[278a] Note the originally concave perimeter (cf. Fig. 12.1) with houses facing on to the Forest.

Wall and Monk Woods were *purlieu woods* – outside the legal Forest but subject to some provisions of Forest Law. Woodside Green is a wood-pasture common resembling the Forest plains but not part of the Forest.

eighteen-year cycle by its two landowners, the remainder being plains with scrubs and pollard trees (Fig. 12.6). The coppices were to be fenced against all livestock after felling; after six years deer-leaps were to be made to admit deer but no other animals; and after a further three years all animals were to be admitted.[279] The arrangement was less regular in practice than in theory; despite the larger proportion of plains, stock sometimes got into the coppices and damaged the spring (p. 291).

Shotover and Stowood Forests (Oxon), each of about 900 acres, were in the seventeenth century run together on an 18-year cycle with nine coppices in each.[730, 731] Wychwood (Oxon) was cut on an 18- to 21-year cycle with seven years' fencing; in 1809 there were 34 coppice compartments and many plains.[38]

Uncompartmented Forests

Pollarding cycles are rarely given in documents but can be inferred from the cycles of narrow and wide annual rings in cross-sections of bollings.[122] In Epping Forest these indicate a rotation of about 13 years; in the surviving part of Hainault Forest there was a variable cycle of 18 to 25 years.

Grazing did not prevent the regeneration of trees, which sprang up infrequently but in great numbers. This is implied by a Parliamentary inquiry in 1701 into the alleged mismanagement by Lord Stamford of Enfield Chase (Middx), a Crown Forest.[348] The Chase, unusually, had neither pollards nor underwood but only timber trees. Some fifty years before, in the Civil War, all the timber had been felled. By 1701 there were said to be 160 oaks and other trees to the acre, 'the most Part 30 Foot high'; it was claimed on Lord Stamford's behalf to be 'necessary some should be cut down, in order to the better growth of the rest'. Beech, hornbeam, ash, and elm – all present today in the surviving fragment of the Chase – are mentioned. Similar phases of regeneration occurred in Hainault[124] and other Forests; the Crown's early attempts at planting in Forests probably yielded less timber than would have been got by doing nothing. In the New Forest it has been possible to correlate such phases with periods of slack grazing.[156]

Some examples of Forests

Most Forests are now little more than names on the map, and even where they appear to survive, as with Grovely, Dean, Alice Holt, and about a quarter of Wychwood, they may have been transformed by replanting, often more than once. Except in Windsor Forest (p. 303) with its independent management and in the New Forest with its strong common-rights and public interest the Crown has a deplorable record as a guardian of native woodland over the last 250 years. Those few Forests that retain something of their historical character are mostly in private ownership.

Hatfield and Writtle Forests (Essex)

These small compartmented Forests have very similar histories: both passed into private ownership – to the family of Robert the Bruce – in 1238. I have elsewhere drawn attention[122] to Hatfield (which now belongs to the National Trust) as the supreme example of a surviving medieval Forest with all its features and most of its uses still functioning: the coppices – with their boundary banks – and plains; the mosaic of native woodland types in the coppices; the pollards, scrubs, and ancient thorns in the plains (Fig. 12.7); the cattle and deer; and the seventeenth-century lodge and rabbit warren (Fig. 12.6). The soils are derived from chalky Boulder-clay mixed with loess – this is one of the few calcareous Forests – and variants of ash–maple–hazel are the commonest woodland types. Although the Forest bears some witness to the eighteenth- and nineteenth-century love of geometrical rides and specimen trees and to the twentieth-century love of bulldozers and plantations, only small areas have been sacrificed. In recent years coppicing has been resumed on a large scale and even some of the pollards have been cut [pp. xvii, 514, 524].

At Writtle (Fig. 12.8) there is a similar system on a very different site: very acid loessy soils overlying Eocene gravels on hilltops, with hornbeam and oak–hornbeam as the commonest woodland types and alder and willow slades (Chapter 18) along the streams. The compartmentation may be later than in Hatfield; it was still not fully developed in the sixteenth century.[808] The plains or commons were peripheral to the coppices and not central as at Hatfield. The Forest was cut in two by Writtle Park, founded before 1237.[233] It is less well-preserved than Hatfield Forest: all but one of the commons have gone and with them the beech pollards (Chapter 20); parts of the coppices were grubbed in the 1960s. But a lonely cottage still marks the site of Bedemansberg, a hermitage founded over 800 years ago by King Stephen wherein a monk might have solitude to pray for the king's health and the souls of his predecessors. It stands at the heart of the Forest, on a possible Roman site,[749] and is still surrounded by the assart with its 'great ditch to the north' given to the hermit for his support.[248]

Epping Forest

No uncompartmented Forest is as well preserved as Hatfield. The best we can do is probably Epping, which escaped serious changes of management until about 1860; although its medieval features have rapidly declined since then, owing to the breakdown of the wood-pasture system, enough remains to tell the imaginative visitor what the Forest looked like when

Fig. 12.7 The central plain of Hatfield Forest, still in its medieval state with grassland, pollard oak and ash trees, and tracts of thorn scrub. Behind the scrub, and clearly demarcated from it, is one of the coppices. February 1977.

its pollards, grasslands, and heaths were fully used. This is a summary of what I have written elsewhere.[122, 124]

The Forest was created in the twelfth century out of a wood-pasture not much greater than its present size. It was not a Crown estate – which is why it survives – but belonged to many private landowners in different parishes. Woodcutting and grazing were both shared between the commoners and the landlords: the Forest courts provided the necessary co-regulation between manors. The trees were almost all pollards; there was very little coppice and not much timber; the woodcutting rights becamc carefully defined.

The Forest had the typical shape of a wood-pasture common (Fig. 12.9), which changed little until the nineteenth century and still survives unaltered in the northern, less urbanized, half. The distribution of plains and tracts of pollards was also remarkably stable, although they were not demarcated in any way. Among treeless areas, Wanstead and Leyton Flats in the south were already heathland in 1199;[232] Honeylane Green in the north-west and the two 'Fairmaids' in the middle can be traced to the sixteenth century. Although no measures were taken to maintain it, the ratio of trees to grassland changed very little in 700 years of wood-pasture history; only in the last hundred years have the trees greatly increased at the expense of the plains.

Recent pollen studies show that lime was dominant in the Forest-to-be as late as the Anglo-Saxon period (p. 242). Lime gave way to hornbeam, oak, and beech. The change from lime to hornbeam and oak is probably associated with the setting-up of the wood-pasture system; the further rise of oak, colonizing the plains, and the increasing dominance of beech are associated with its decline (pp 201–2).

Parks

A park differs from a physical Forest in having a perimeter fence to retain the deer, in being wholly private property, and in not having any special laws or administration.

The deer of parks were almost exclusively fallow but other species are occasionally noted. In 1232, for instance, a park at Bere Regis (Dorset) was stocked with roe from another park and from Powerstock Forest.[233] In 1223 two of the king's wild swine were put into his park at Havering (Essex), establishing a population on which he drew at intervals until 1260;[233] other medieval swine-parks existed at Chalkney Wood (Essex) (p. 250) and Knepp (Sussex).[79] There were red deer in Guildford Park in 1251.[233] James I even established a hare-park at Swaffham Bulbeck (Cambs) in *c.* 1605.[870]

The origin of parks

There were probably a few parks before the coming of fallow deer. Domesday lists about 35 'parks of woodland beasts' (*parci ferarum siluaticarum*), a phrase which does not suggest a newly-introduced exotic animal.

A puzzling word is Anglo-Saxon *haga* or *hege*, from which the two forms 'hay' and 'hedge' have diverged. Normally it means just a hedge; the many wood-names ending in -hay or -y (e.g. Eas*ty* Wood, Cavendish (Est*hey* 1453)[218] imply a wood with a hedge or fence round it. When we are told in 1251 that Birkland in Sherwood Forest (pp. 313, 316) was a *haya* of the king's in which nobody had common-rights[214] we suspect that the word means an 'anti-park', a wood in a poorly-wooded Forest fenced to keep out deer and

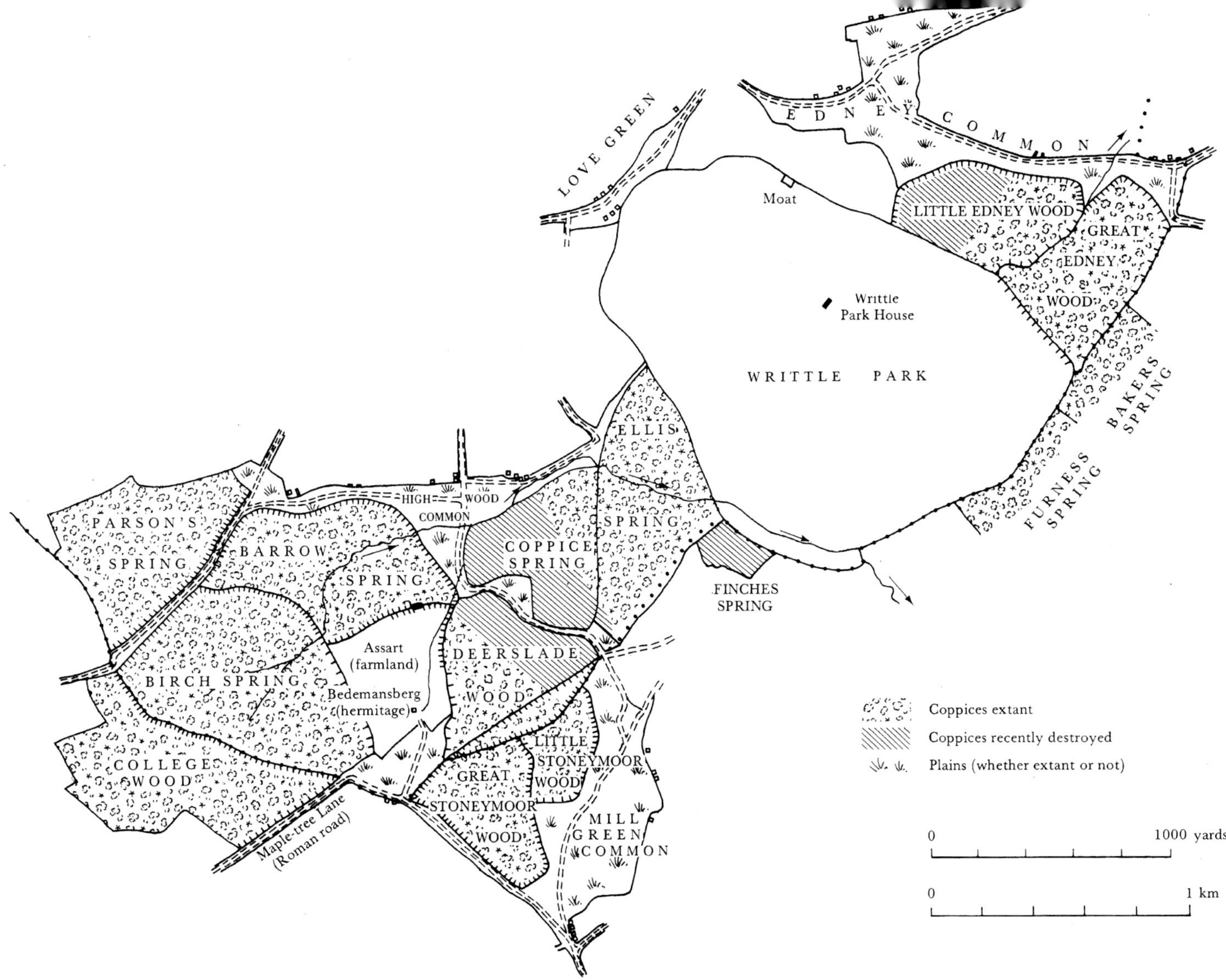

Fig. 12.8 Writtle Forest, Essex. A compartmented Forest, much like Hatfield but 'inside-out' with the plains arranged round the periphery. Note the boundary houses as at Hatfield. Only some of the woodbanks are shown.

The woods and plains south of the Writtle parish boundary, e.g. the Stoneymoor Woods and Mill Green Common, resembled the Forest but were not part of it. Writtle Park was uncompartmented up to the eighteenth century.

Most of the plains except Mill Green Common have been destroyed. Those that remain have lost their pollards (which survive only in the assart) and are much overgrown with secondary woodland.

Fig. 12.9 'Waltham' and 'Henhault', i.e. Epping and Hainault, Forests as surveyed in 1772–4 by Chapman and André. The map differentiates the Forests and other wood-pasture from nearby or adjacent woodland. Within the Forests there were no coppices and no demarcated woods, but the map distinguishes accurately between treeless plains and tracts of pollards. Note the concave perimeters, which dated from the Middle Ages, with hundreds of boundary houses. The southern tip of Waltham Forest is omitted.

The outline of Epping Forest north of Chingford is still almost unchanged, but only small parts of Hainault survive. Published originally at 2 in. to the mile (1 : 32,000) and here reproduced at a scale of 1 : 96,000.

cattle which might damage it. In Domesday there are over seventy *haye*, chiefly along the Welsh Border; the occasional explanatory note 'hays for taking roedeer' indicates that these were not parks but corrals or other devices for catching wild deer. However, at Ongar (Essex) an Anglo-Saxon will of 1045 refers to 'the wood . . . outside the deerhay (*derhage*)'[516] in the very place where later there was a *parcus*; so the existence of at least one park before the Conquest seems established.

The rise of parks was slower than that of Forests. Many were established in the twelfth century when they needed no 'planning permission', but the thirteenth-century Pipe and Close Rolls abound with licences to empark or to enlarge parks and with gifts of deer from the king's Forests to stock or restock parks.

Numbers and distribution of parks

In Eastern England there is documentary evidence for the following number of parks before 1535 (Fig. 12.10):

Norfolk	59	(one park to 35 square miles)
Suffolk	96	(one to 15.5 square miles)
Essex	159	(one to 9.6 square miles)
Cambridgeshire and Isle of Ely	16	(one to 54 square miles)
Hertfordshire	90	(one to 7.0 square miles)

Except in Hertfordshire,[802] where there is some evidence of late emparking, a large majority date from before 1330 and most of them were in existence at the same time. Other studies of parks reveal a similar range of densities, for instance:

Dorset	90	(one to 10.9 square miles)[892]
Sussex	112	(one to 13.0 square miles)[616]
Northants	52	(one to 19.2 square miles)[145]

In estimating the total number of parks I shall assume that the eastern counties are representative of England, and also that the number of parks formed after the main period of emparking is balanced by the number that were formed early but of which no record has yet come to light. On these assumptions there were about 3,200 parks in England in the heyday of parks around 1300. The average area was something like 200 acres, so that the total area of parks came to roughly 640,000 acres, roughly 2% of England – not far from our rough estimate of the total area of physical Forests.

The owners of parks were the nobility and gentry, bishops, and religious houses. Anyone could have a park who could afford it. The greater nobles and prelates had ten or more parks each, but the Crown had only about twenty. A park usually formed part of a large or medium-sized manor.

Parks are much more strongly correlated with woodland than are Forests. Figures 9.5 and 12.10 show that parks occurred in areas where Domesday had had large swine-entries: many of the less intensively-used woods of 1086 had become parks by 1300. Where woods had been absent or intensively used there were few or no parks. Emparking licences often specify the nature of the ground, which was usually at least half woodland, though there are frequent exceptions (e.g. sixty acres of heath at Great Baddow (Essex) in 1247).[142] Later-medieval and post-medieval emparking was often of grassland and arable. L. Munby regards emparking in Herts as a sign of agricultural decline and cites complaints by the clergy of the consequent loss of tithes.[802]

Management of parks

Parks varied in size from the 4,000 acres of Clarendon Park near Salisbury – bigger than many Forests – to the fourteen acres of Barking Park (Suffolk)[270] (Fig. 12.11). They varied widely in function. Some large parks, as at Enfield (Middx) in 1336[449] and Hatfield (Herts) in 1251,[270] had common rights, but usually a park was in the absolute control of its owner. The four land-uses of deer, other livestock, wood, and timber could be combined in almost any proportion. There may also have been anti-parks: a dweller in a legal Forest might find himself obliged under Forest Law to apply for a 'licence to empark' his property, not to enclose his own deer, but to keep out the king's, as suggested by this example:

> 14 Nov. 1281. Licence for Reginald de Gynges to empark 20 ac. wood, 10 ac. laund, 1 ac. garden in Ingrave [Essex] round his court there, notwithstanding that the deer repair there by reason of the density of his wood . . .[236]

Park boundaries

The only indispensable feature of a park is a deerproof perimeter, usually a ***park pale***, a special palisade of cleft-oak pales set in the ground and fastened to a rail so that the decay of one pale did not make a gap. Walls, in or near stone-wall country, and hedges are also heard of. Sometimes the pale was provided with ***deer-leaps***, devices to allow deer to get in but not out.

The pale was very expensive in timber and labour; it required high-quality oak that did not grow everywhere. Henry III, giving twenty does to Hugo de Nevill to restock his park at Great Hallingbury (Essex) in 1221, accompanied them with two oaks to make pales, but this was unusual.[475] Nazeing Wood (Essex) was emparked in 1542 at a cost of £132, of which the paling cost £26, the transport of 'posts, pales, and rayles' – which could not be made locally – cost £38, the 'makyng of a launde' by grubbing out trees (see later) came to £54, while two buildings – a park lodge and a 'standing', i.e. an observation tower – cost only £14.[142]

Empaling needed to be repeated as the pales rotted. In a few of the older parks this was supposed to be done

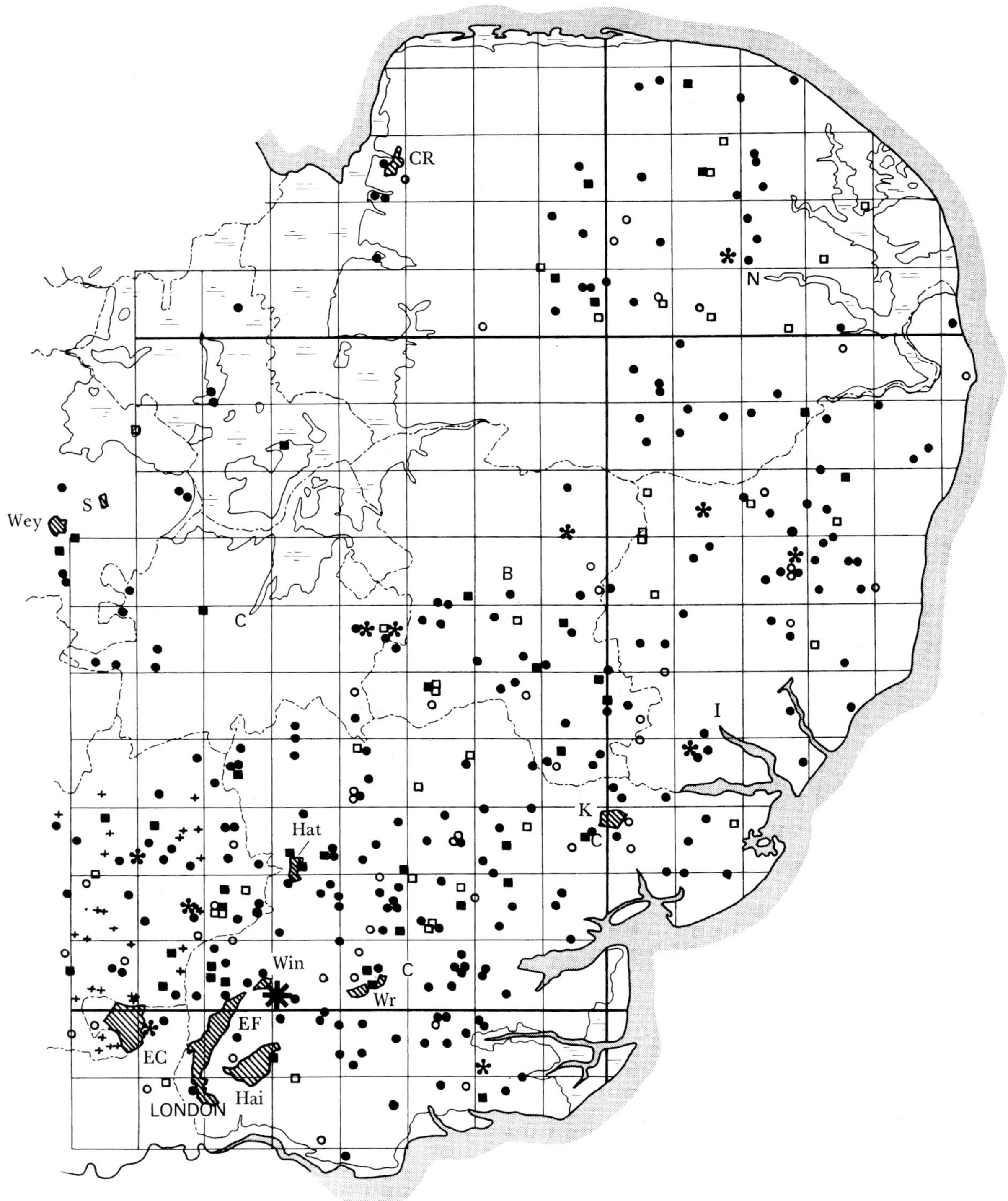

Parks, date of earliest record 1045 ✱ 1087 – 1230 ■ 1351 – 1450 ○

1086 * 1231 – 1350 ● 1451 – 1530 □

Undated parks

Forests (physical extent)

by the lord's tenants as a labour service. The customal of Hatfield Broadoak (Essex) in 1328 says that a particular tenant

> shall make and keep 32 perches of pale round the park of Hatfield from the lord's timber in the park, and shall have the old timber of the said pale when it is not worth putting back in the pale. And this concession [of the old pales] is worth 7½*d* per annum.[280]

In all, 49 manorial tenants had to maintain 151 perches of pale and 119 perches of hedge round Hatfield Park,[277] a total of nearly a mile. Not that they did this in practice. At least from the late fourteenth century, as the accounts and court rolls relate, the perimeter was inspected year by year; a note was made of whose sections needed repair, whether they were pale or hedge, and whether they abutted on Hatfield Forest, the road, or farmland; the appropriate tenants were fined; and a contractor was hired to do the actual work.[316] In 1444, for instance, the contractor's bill came to

> 25 perches of new fence and 48 perches of old fence re-pointed [*noui barbati*, i.e. the rotten base cut off and a new point made for driving into the ground] at 4*d* the perch of new fence and 2*d* the perch of old fence re-pointed, total 16*s* 4*d*.[295]

The high cost of fencing is doubtless the reason for the characteristic shape of many of the oldest parks, a rectangle with rounded corners (Fig. 12.11). (The same shape has been re-invented for the expensive security fences round prisons.)

Park perimeters often have a bank with a ditch on the inside, the reverse of the orientation of woodbanks, for park-banks are intended to keep animals in while woodbanks keep them out. Not every site of a park has a recognizable reversed bank, for many have been woods either before or after their history as parks and thus may have normal woodbanks.

The pale was sometimes set back from the boundary of the property. The interval – usually one perch wide – was called the ***freeboard***; it was apparently used for access to the pale for inspection and repair. Most of my references to freeboards are comparatively late: e.g. Framlingham (Suffolk) in 1589[372] and Windsor Great Park in 1864.[90]

Deer and other livestock

A well-managed park was a much more efficient producer of venison than a Forest. From the royal park of Havering (Essex), 1,100 acres, Henry III ordered an average of 44 fallow deer annually from 1234 to 1263; from the Forests of S.W. Essex, ten times the area, he got only 40 fallow and 4 red deer a year[124] – and these were among the more important venison Forests. Havering Park also yielded grazing for the king's own cattle and pigs, grazing rents and pannage from local farmers, and timber.

Deer in a park were more easily managed than in a Forest. Their owner knew where to find and catch them and did not have to persuade the local inhabitants that animals which wandered about and ate their crops were his and not theirs. But park deer were liable to starvation and disease. In 1251 the bailiff of Havering was ordered to remove 'the bodies of dead beasts and swine which are rotting in the park' and hay was to be provided for feeding the deer.[233]

E. P. Shirley, the nineteenth-century authority on parks, recommends one fallow deer per acre (two bucks and one doe to three acres). The actual numbers of deer in parks in his day ranged from about a half to two head per acre; these are low estimates because in some cases woodland, from which deer get little sustenance, was included in the acreage.[142]

Statistics exist for a herd of deer in Framlingham Park (E. Suffolk) for four and a half years from 1515 to 1519.[142] The park was of 600 acres,[255] probably all grassland. The average annual yield was 192 deer (86 bucks, 57 does, 49 young or unspecified) of which 137 were slaughtered, 54 sent to other parks, and one taken by poachers. But there was an average annual wastage of 321 deer (97 males, 63 females, 158 fawns, two unspecified); of these 34 fawns died at birth, 58 deer died of disease ('Garget', 'Rotte', and 'Wyppys'), 224 died 'in winter' (presumably of starvation), and six were killed by stray dogs. The total turnover of 514 implies a population of at least 1,500 animals, which even Shirley would have regarded as gross overstocking.

A deer-park was a troublesome and precarious enterprise; it involved special fencing, often feeding in winter, a high risk of animals dying, and the difficulty of maintaining trees. The lack of a value for venison makes it difficult to compare with conventional farming, but the advantage would lie with the bigger parks, in which the cost of the pale per head of deer would be less and in which starvation would be less of a risk. The

Fig. 12.10 Medieval parks and Forests in Eastern England. Forests are shown with their actual physical boundaries as in *c.* 1300. The sizes of parks cannot be shown individually, but each of the circular dots represents an area of 300 acres, which is a little larger than the average size of a medieval park, so the dots give a rough indication of how much of the landscape would have been occupied by parks.

CR	Castle Rising Forest or Chase[413]	Hat	Hatfield Forest	Wey	Weybridge Forest
EC	Enfield Chase	K	Kingswood Forest	Win	Wintry Forest
EF	Epping Forest	S	Sapley Forest	Wr	Writtle Forest
Hai	Hainault Forest				

Compiled from the Close Rolls[233] and from surveys and other documents too numerous to list. Professor L. M. Cantor, Mr W. H. Liddell, Mr J. Hatherly, and Mr J. Hunter have generously allowed me to incorporate their unpublished lists. I have also made use of the parks listed by E. P. Shirley,[142] E. Farrar,[423, 436] and L. M. Munby.[802]

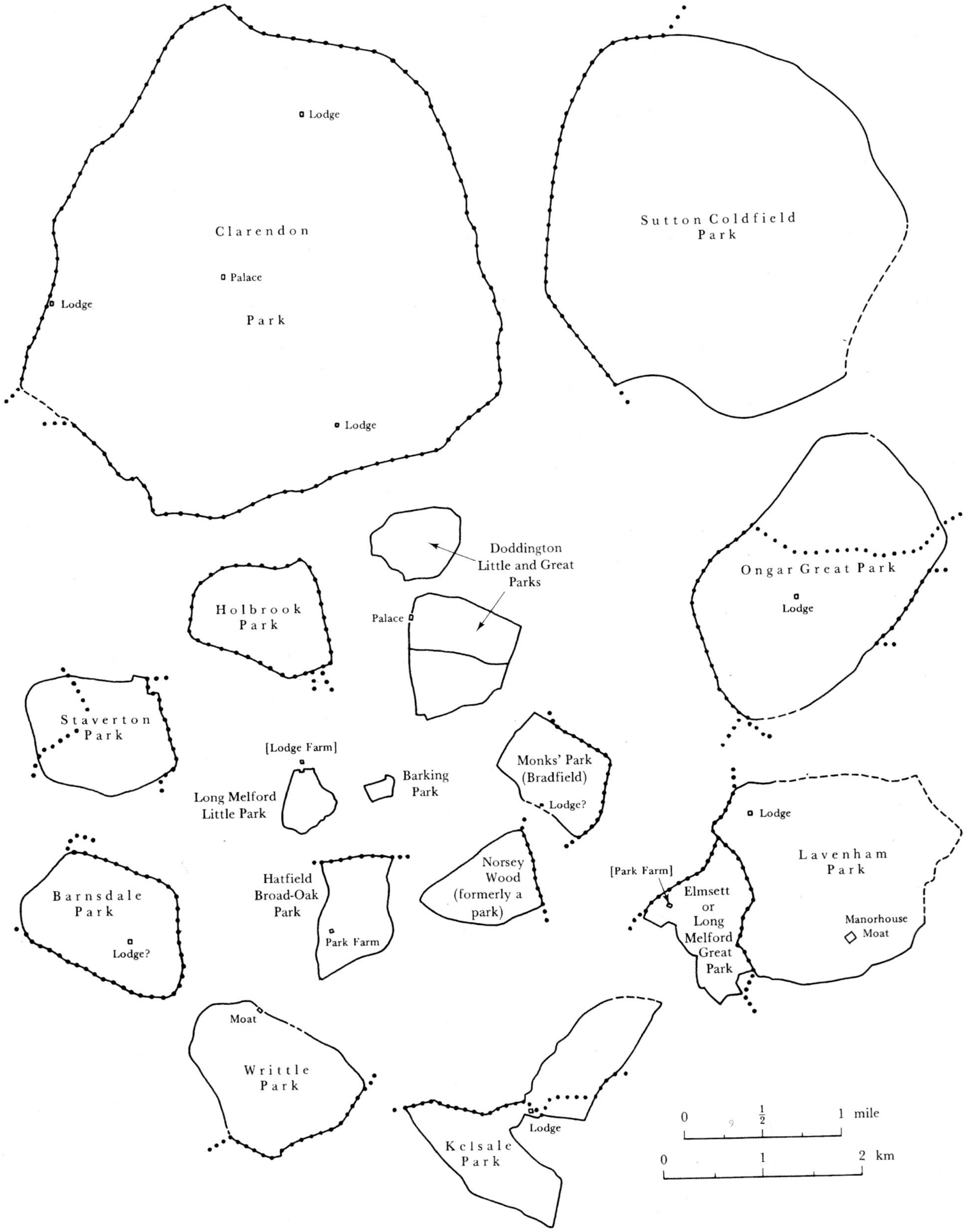
Clarendon
Park
Lodge
Palace
Lodge
Lodge
Sutton Coldfield
Park
Doddington
Little and Great
Parks
Palace
Ongar Great Park
Lodge
Holbrook
Park
Staverton
Park
[Lodge Farm]
Long Melford
Little Park
Barking
Park
Monks' Park
(Bradfield)
Lodge?
Lodge
Lavenham
Park
Manorhouse
Moat
[Park Farm]
Elmsett
or
Long
Melford
Great
Park
Barnsdale
Park
Lodge?
Hatfield
Broad-Oak
Park
Park Farm
Norsey
Wood
(formerly a
park)
Moat
Writtle
Park
Kelsale
Park
Lodge
0
½
1 mile
0
1
2 km

many parks of less than fifty acres would have been of value chiefly as status symbols. Some medieval parks were repeatedly restocked, and others contained no deer at the time they were surveyed; for example, as early as 1251 half the sixty-acre park at Pulham (Norfolk) was arable,[270] and in 1309 Bocking Park (Essex) was an ordinary coppice of 480 acres with little grass (p. 83).[329]

Trees in uncompartmented parks

Parks, like Forests and commons, could be uncompartmented, with pollards and big timber trees, or compartmented, with near-normal coppice-woods protected by internal fences during their regrowth.

The severe grazing pressure in uncompartmented parks often turned them into 'parkland' in the modern sense, i.e. grassland with only scattered big trees. Woodland is less prominent in surveys of established parks than in specifications for licences to empark; and since something like a sixth of the woodland in England in 1300 was, or had at some time been, within a park emparking must be regarded as one of the causes of disappearance of woodland. One of the two parks in Long Melford (Suffolk), though called the Great Wood, yielded in 1386 from its 260 acres £2 per annum in grazing rents but only 600 faggots, worth 8*s*, of wood.[397, 819] At Writtle (Essex) in 1336 the park of the de Bohuns (probably not the Writtle Park of Fig. 12.8 or p. 323) was said to have pasture 'which would be worth £7 3*s* 8*d* per annum if the deer and other beasts were not there', pannage worth 13*s* 4*d* 'when it happens', fallen wood (*cablicium*) worth 3*s* 4*d*, but no underwood.[449] The park at Kimbolton (Hunts) in 1336 had £1 worth of pasture and pannage worth 5*s* 'when it happens'; but 'the underwood there is hardly enough to fence it'.[449]

Hatfield Broadoak Park (p. 193), although uncompartmented, maintained a small turnover of timber trees. Ashes, a few oaks, and the occasional aspen were felled for local use, and in 1441 there was a big sale of large ash-trees (p. 166). The underwood was valued in 1328 at only 6*s* 8*d* per annum 'apart from maintaining the fences'; actual woodsales were small and were chiefly in the form of faggots, suggesting pollarding, rather than underwood sold by the acre, as sometimes in Hatfield Forest. This park yielded hay as well as grazing, and tenants of the manor were supposed to mow it as a labour service.[280, 295, 316]

Parks were particularly important in the supply of outsize trees (Chapter 10), a function which continued into the shipbuilding period.[122]

Compartmentation and underwood

Many surveys of parks mention some separation between livestock and trees. The commonest is a reference to one or more ***launds***, definite acreages of grassland (very rarely arable) separate from the woods: for instance in 1251 in the Bishop of Ely's parks at Barking and Glemsford (Suffolk) and Pulham (Norfolk).[270] A laund usually arose from a piece of non-woodland that happened to be included in the park or from an informal glade in the woods.

An elaborate system of coppice compartments without grassland is exemplified by the park of John de Bohun in Walden (Saffron or Little Walden, Essex), in 1336:

> There is a park containing 2 leagues in circuit, and it is divided into 17 quarters in which 10 acres of underwood can be sold every year, worth £4 at 8*s* an acre. The pasture is worth nothing because of the multitude of beasts. The nuts . . . when they happen are worth 12*d*.[449]

This is a rare instance of a park producing a full yield of underwood as well as deer. The cycle is long for the period but the value is reasonable (cf. Fig. 11.6). Presumably the deer were fenced out from the newly-felled 'quarters' and lived on whatever they could find in those whose regrowth was more advanced.

The records suggest that about one medieval park in two had some kind of compartmentation. Figure 12.12 illustrates their variation from early maps. At Haveringland there were three wooded compartments and a chain of launds later used as meadows. Doddington Great Park had five 'quarters', and an elaborate system of launds. Doddington Little Park had scattered trees and only one wooded compartment, called significantly 'The Heute' – *hewet* or 'hewing-wood' (Anglo-Saxon *hēawan* + *-ett*) i.e. coppice. A wood (or a common on the site of a wood) excluded from the park was called Outwood (cf. p. 337).

Fig. 12.11 Outlines of some representative medieval parks, mostly of the thirteenth century. The position of the great house, if any, is shown, and of the park lodge where known. The lodge, where the parker lived and did his business, was usually on a hilltop overlooking as much as possible of the park.

Dotted lines are parish boundaries.

Essex: Hatfield Broad-oak (p. 193), Norsey (pp. 335–7), Ongar (p. 197), Writtle (p. 323).

Isle of Ely: Doddington (Fig. 12.12).

Rutland: Barnsdale.[122]

Suffolk: Barking (p. 191), Bradfield St Clare (p. 197, Fig. 3.1), Kelsale, Holbrook (pp. 337–8), Lavenham,[122] Long Melford,[221] Staverton (pp. 293–4).

Warwickshire: Sutton Coldfield (p. 292).

Wiltshire: Clarendon.

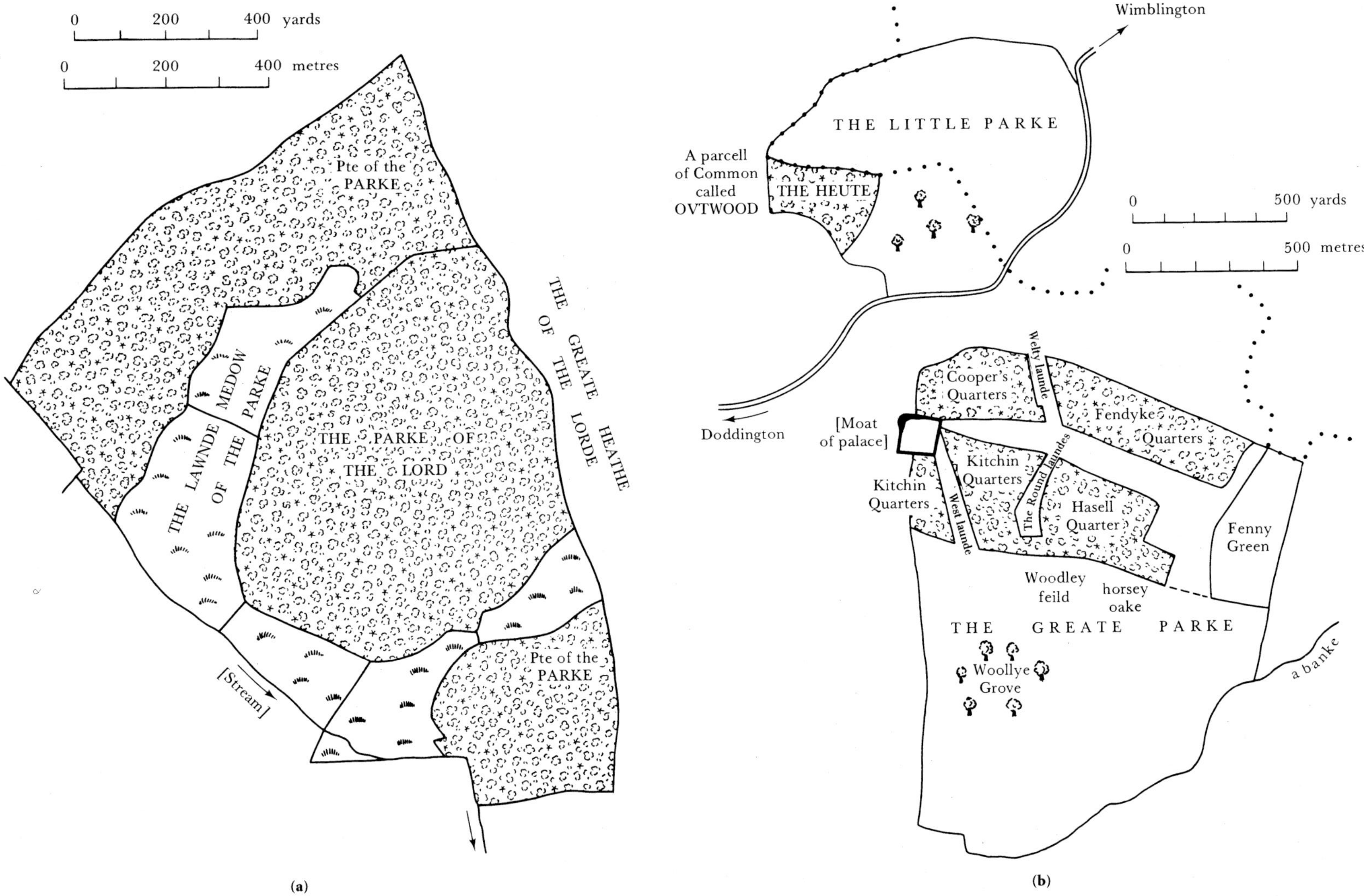

Fig. 12.12 (**a**) Haveringland Park, Norfolk, from a sixteenth-century map.[431] [Now replanted, but retains a patch of pollard oaks in 'THE PARKE OF TH E LORD' and a few lime stools.] (**b**) The two parks at Doddington, Isle of Ely, slightly adapted from a seventeenth-century map.[393] They were made by the Bishops of Ely in the thirteenth century.[909] Now destroyed; 'The Heute' survived until 1942.

The later history of parks

The post-medieval history of parks is well known[112, 725] and I have reviewed it elsewhere.[122] Parks less often have a continuous history than woods; they often went out of use or were deliberately destroyed. New parks were created when emparking returned to fashion in the sixteenth, eighteenth, and nineteenth centuries.

The function of parks changed. In principle the medieval park – a utilitarian enterprise producing meat – gave way successively to the hunting park of Henry VIII and Queen Elizabeth, the landscape park forming the setting for a country mansion, the municipal park for public recreation, and the country park set up by local authorities. The five kinds of park often passed from one function to another. The idea of the landscape park is almost as old as that of the deer-park: the Norman kings would have known about it from their Sicilian colleagues, and the great parks associated with the twelfth-century palaces of Havering (Essex) and Clarendon (Wilts) represent the earliest introduction of this Oriental idea which has become so firmly adopted by England. Early deer-parks had often been in remote places, but in the later Middle Ages it became increasingly common to establish parks next to country houses or vice versa, as at Kenninghall and Kimberley (Norfolk);[213, 423] in the map of Doddington Great Park (Fig. 12.12), with its launds converging on the site of the medieval bishop's palace, we see the remains of an early landscape design. The works of 'Capability' Brown (1716–83) were the culmination of a 600-year tradition of ornamental landscaping. For the origin of municipal and country parks we go to Sutton Coldfield Park (Warwicks), which has had both functions since the sixteenth century.[613]

Parks never regained the importance in the landscape that they had had in the fourteenth century, but all their earlier functions still exist. Landscape parks and many country parks have cattle and sometimes even deer;[775] in 1975 there were fallow deer in 94 English parks.[629] The Queen still bestows venison and live deer on favoured subjects: in 1978 she sent some to start a park in Canada.[494] Parks are preservers of early landscapes with their trees, woods, and earthworks. Blenheim Park (Oxon) is one of the grandest works of Capability Brown, yet Brown did not obliterate its royal predecessor, Woodstock Park, whose ancient oaks still cover much of the area. Christchurch Park (Ipswich), with pollard oaks and ancient chestnuts, is the municipalized but still-recognizable park of a sixteenth-century mansion. The country park of Bradgate (Leics) is a genuine medieval park.

Examples of parks

Ongar Great Park (Essex)

This was probably the earliest park recognizable in England. Much of it survived until 1945, and its destruction was one of the most grievous losses to the South Essex landscape in the last hundred years. It was one of a group of early parks around Wintry Forest, in a dispersed-settlement landscape of hamlets, greens, and lanes, close to the supposedly Anglo-Saxon timber church at Greensted.

The park in Ongar can be traced back to a 'deerhay' of 1045 (p. 191). The 'great park of Aungre' appears in the Close Rolls for 1243. By *c.* 1640 'Vnger Parke' had ceased to be a functional park.[331]

Almost the whole park perimeter survived until recently as field boundaries. It was a rectangle with rounded corners (Fig. 12.13), enclosing about 1,200 acres, a very large park in which red deer might well have been kept before fallow were available. Its antiquity is corroborated by the way in which the settlement pattern and the parishes have developed round it. Some of the surrounding greens abut on it but none intrudes. Much of the perimeter has been used as a parish boundary. The park interrupts the Roman road from London to Great Dunmow. Evidently the emparking took place before the settlements and land ownerships had fully crystallized; even by 1086 it would have been difficult to acquire so large and regular a piece of land in this tightly-knit part of Essex.

The site is a wet plateau of acid soils overlying London Clay and Boulder-clay. The surviving woodlands are pure hornbeam, oak–hornbeam, valley alder-wood, and aspen-wood; they contain fragments of a system of compartment-banks. Most of the western boundary of the park survives, separating Ongar Park Wood from Stapleford Tawney High Wood; it is a very massive woodbank with a ditch on the High Wood side and also a ditch on the Ongar side in places; at one point it makes a deviation in order to bisect a pond, evidently a pre-existing feature which had to be shared between two estates.

Monks' Park (Bradfield St Clare, W. Suffolk)

This forms part of the Bradfield Woods (Chapter 3). It is almost certainly the park at 'Bradefelde' given to Bury St Edmund's Abbey by Abbot Anselm (1121–35),[266] which makes it one of the earliest fallow-deer parks. It is similar in shape to Ongar and also has a parish boundary conforming to its perimeter; it encloses 216 acres. It has an Anglo-Saxon name (p. 26). The Abbey leased the estate to the St Clare family who although important people made it their chief seat. In 1269 John de St Clare was allowed by the Abbey to empark, or rather to re-empark, his wood at Bradfield St Clare 'where the Abbot's predecessors used to have their chase' and to put beasts there, provided that the Abbot might take two does each winter.[243] By the fifteenth century the wood had reverted to the Abbey and had evidently ceased to be a park.[241, 436]

The Bradfield Woods are among those omitted from Domesday because, as we have supposed, they were already encoppiced and not used for swine. Coppicing

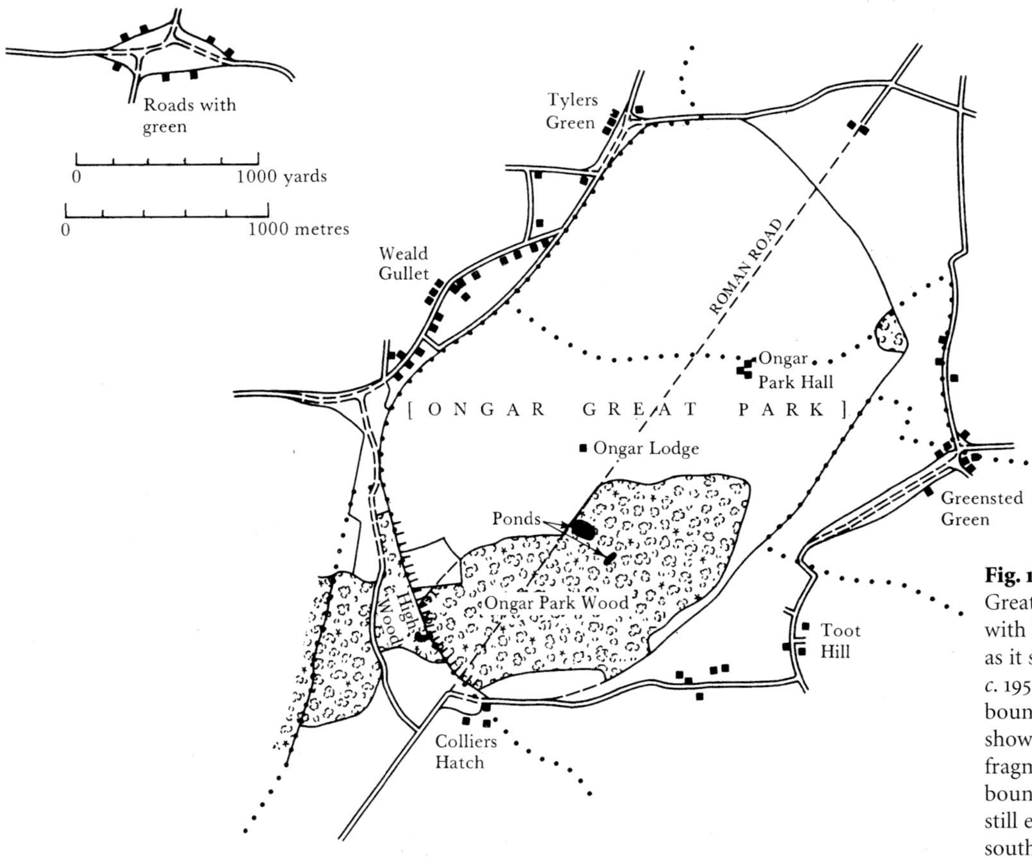

Fig. 12.13 Ongar Great Park, Essex, with its surroundings as it survived until *c.* 1950. The parish boundaries are shown, as is the fragment of park boundary which still exists in the south-west.

before the re-emparking is attested in 1252.[446] After re-emparking there is an account roll of 1283–4 which says that the underwood of 200 acres was ordinarily worth £5 but 'nothing can be felled this year because almost the whole wood has been coppiced (*subboscatus*) in the last two years'.[461] The co-existence of deer and intensive woodland management thus seems well established.

The internal glades are first recorded in a survey of 1664 which includes

> Munces parke together with severall inclosures called the Wood Close and one meadow called Roots Meadowe and one other meadowe called Hewits meadowe conteyning together . . . two hundred and twenty acres.[229]

Root's Meadow and Hewitt's Meadow existed as glades until the late nineteenth century. Although they are called meadows, the pollen in the pond attached to Hewitt's (Table 5.4) shows that that enclave was once heathland; later it was ploughed and sown with rye and buckwheat. In recent decades the glades became overgrown with trees.

Until latterly, Monks' Park seemed to be an ordinary wood with a rectangular grid of rides (Fig. 3.1); only the enclaves and some slight anomalies of the ride system suggested that anything might underlie it. Between 1967 and 1972 about two-thirds of the Park was destroyed. Since then a complete system of internal divisions has come to light (Figs. 3.2, 3.3), either as earthworks within the surviving wood or as soil-marks visible from the air in the grubbed-out part. The perimeter of Monks' Park is marked by a flat-topped woodbank with a distinct inside ditch for much of its length; one stretch is set back to form a freeboard. Most of the internal boundaries are normal woodbanks, up to 30 ft in total width. They define four coppices and three or four launds. There are three ponds, two of them related to launds. A double soil-mark indicates a winding lane as the chief access, leading off towards Bury St Edmund's; this route is perpetuated as an oblique ride with a bend. A seventeenth-century farmhouse at one end of the principal laund may be on the site of the park lodge.

The system shows some signs of planning, though its details depend on the exigencies of particular years' operations and the positions of pre-existing ponds. To have as many embanked and fenced 'quarters' as there were years in the felling cycle would have been impractical in a park of this size. Instead, each coppice would have enclosed up to five years' felling. At any one time deer would have been admitted to two coppices with their launds and excluded from the two that contained young underwood.

Pseudo-medieval parks

Ongar, Monks' Park, Staverton (p. 293), and Holbrook (p. 337) are examples of the well-documented, if sometimes fragmentary, survival of a medieval park. Sometimes history is not so simple and appearances deceive.

Thorndon Park (S. Essex)

Near Brentwood are the spectacularly ruined mansion [recently restored] and park of the Petre family. The Georgian mansion went up in a blaze of glory in 1878. Since this conflagration the park has tumbled down to birchwood, among which are giant pollard oaks and hornbeams from its earlier history. The area is now rehabilitated as Thorndon North Country Park. The visitor, musing on scenes of Piranesian decay and succession, and noting from sections that some of the trees are over 400 years old, would have supposed this to be the park for which Thomas Tyrrell got a licence in 1363.[236]

But this would be wrong. A fine series of early maps[268, 272] proves that there have been at least four successive parks on different sites; the old Hall and the first two parks were over a mile away, and their remains are to be seen in Thorndon South Country Park. The present North Country Park is the youngest of the four and was not taken in until after 1774.[250] Previously it had been Childerditch Common, on which a survey in 1774 records 2,080 oak pollards and 1,323 'hornbine' trees.[309]

Sotterley Park (E. Suffolk) (Fig. 12.14)

This magnificent park (which is private) also has splendid pollards and other ancient trees. It is (for East Anglia) particularly rich in lichen species[132] and has often been interpreted as a medieval park, despite the lack of documentary evidence, the suspiciously perfect elliptical outline, the parish boundary that wanders aimlessly across one side, and the medieval church at its centre (an infallible sign of late emparking).

Close examination shows that many of the ancient trees are in rows and stand on faint banks. They originated not as wood-pasture but as hedgerow trees, preserved by emparking a piece of ordinary countryside. The date is not recorded but it may have been associated with the building of the present Hall *c.* 1744. There is no mention of a park in a Sotterley account-book of 1598–1608.[366]

Corroboration comes from the details of Sotterley Wood, a hornbeam–ash wood which on the park side has a succession of woodbanks indicating early subdivisions and alterations. The wood is certainly older than the park. A map of *c.* 1800 shows the park boundary cutting off part of the wood, which remained as an awkwardly-shaped field. At one point the park perimeter incorporated a short length of wood-boundary which happened to follow its intended course, and here the map deliberately shows the sinuosities of the wood-outline as distinct from the smooth curves of the rest of the park outline. These details are still visible on the ground. The wood is recorded as supplying loads of billets from 1598 to 1608 and could be the 'boscus de Soterlee' about which there was a dispute in 1214.[264]

Making parks involved adapting existing features as much as creating new ones. Park designers did not always plant trees and wait for them to grow; where possible, they made 'instant parks' by emparking existing trees and woods. Occasionally, as at Thorndon, this merely transferred land from one wood-pasture use to another. Parallels to Sotterley, where trees that had begun life on farmland were converted to wood-pasture, are more common. A well-documented example is at Ickworth Park (W. Suffolk), where a survey of 1665 – within the lifetime of many of the present trees (Fig. 12.15) – proves the absence of a park.[357] The seventeenth-century park at Earlham (Norwich) incorporates the trees of a deserted village and its fields.

Plants and animals of wood-pasture

Some wood-pastures differ little in history or vegetation from ordinary woodland. These include the more efficiently-compartmented parks and the many Park Woods that were parks for only a short period. But long-continued wood-pasture tends to impoverish the tree flora, eliminating the more edible species. Although some wood-pastures are on the least fertile soils, there is often historical or pollen evidence that they once had more tree species than they have now; the New Forest, for instance, has lost lime and hazel (p. 241). Wood-pasture also impoverishes the ground flora and has an effect opposite to that of coppicing. Many woodland herbs, e.g. oxlip (p. 92), are sensitive to grazing. As glades enlarge and trees become more widely scattered, the herbs are subjected to the permanent competition of light-demanding species; the wood-pasture often turns into grassland or heath with trees, having no specifically woodland herbs at all.

On the other hand, wood-pasture is an essential environment for the lichens and invertebrate animals which inhabit pollards or other ancient trees. These often require specific habitats such as old dry bark (especially under the overhangs of pollards) or large red-rotted trunk cavities. They are said also to depend on continuity of such habitats from the wildwood, in much the same way as some flowering plants do on ancient woodland (Chapter 5). They are often referred to as 'old forest organisms', an inexpert translation of German *Urwaldtiere* (animals of the prehistoric forest). They are not usually to be found in woodlands (except sometimes on boundary pollards) because of the

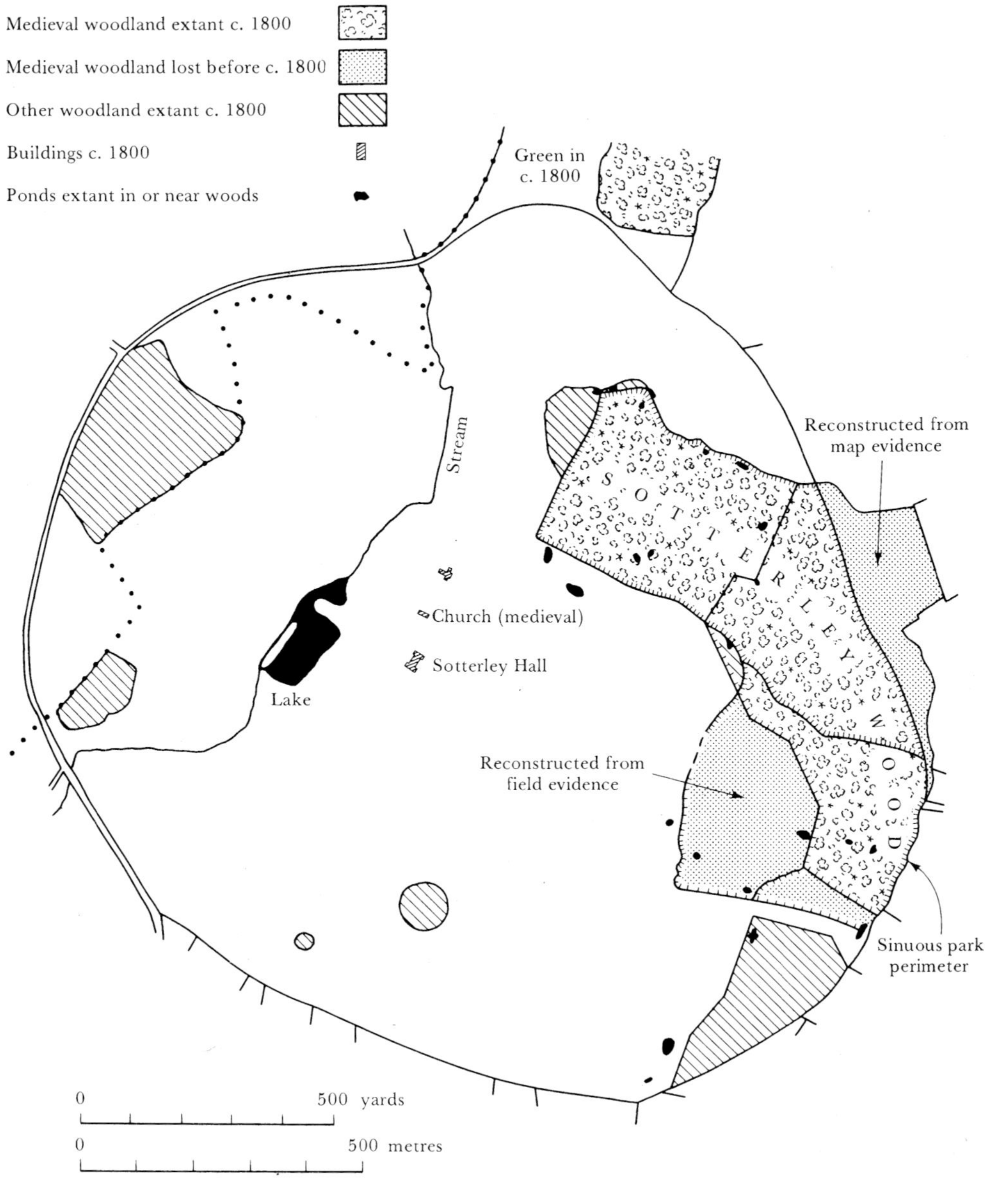

Fig. 12.14 The park at Sotterley, N.E. Suffolk, in relation to the medieval Sotterley Wood. The park perimeter and the distribution of woodland are derived from a map of *c.* 1800;[427] almost all these features are still extant. The earthworks are derived from field observation. Note the many ponds (p. 13).

frequency of coppicing and lack of old timber trees and dead wood; nor are they usually on hedgerow trees.

The lichens in this category are discussed by F. Rose.[132–3] The New Forest is probably the supreme site for such plants in western Europe; parks such as Eridge (Sussex) and Boconnoc (Cornwall) run it close. The requirements for many lichens include old acid bark, high humidity but not much shade, freedom from air pollution and from contamination by fertilizers and animal excreta, and lack of disturbance. Many beetles[168, 727] and some spiders[665] are also associated with specific parts of the interiors of old or dead trees; molluscs[821, 884] appear to depend more on continuity of woodland.

The connection of certain organisms with ancient trees is well established, but little has been published so far on their requirement for ancient trees in a specific environment. The possibility remains that some of them may be relicts, not directly from the wildwood, but from earlier agricultural history: when the whole country was less contaminated by pollutants and fertilizers, and when – as often in the seventeenth century – hedgerow trees were more abundant than they are now,[846] these organisms might have been more widespread, able to colonize younger trees, and less restricted to wood-pasture. How far are environmental requirements, such as that for lack of disturbance, borne out by the detailed history of particular parks and Forests? Are pseudo-medieval parks of the Sotterley type distinguishable from real medieval parks?

Fig. 12.15 The Tea-Party Oak, a pollard in Ickworth Park (W. Suffolk); its annual rings suggest an age of about 700 years. It started life in farmland and was already an ancient tree when the park was made in 1701.

Conservation

The modern proliferation of deer [see also pp. 511–17]

In one sense the long decline of wood-pasture has been reversed in recent decades by a remarkable increase of deer. Roe deer are now much more widespread than they have been since the twelfth century; red deer have returned to areas, such as East Anglia, where they had been extinct for a thousand years or more, and feral fallow have been reported from every county of England.[629] Studies in Essex show both red and fallow to have been as widespread and probably at least as numerous in the county in the 1960s as in the heyday of the Forest of Essex.[628] Since World War II the countryside has become peculiarly favourable for deer, partly because fewer people work on the land and it is easier for them to avoid human contact. The change is comparable to that in the ecology of the rabbit, which from being semi-domesticated turned into a ubiquitous pest some 250 years ago.[874]

With so much of the country now effectively Forest, the medieval arts of living with deer need to be revived. Deer are the only important agents of failure of coppicing: the spring is either eaten right down or nibbled at the tip and caused to grow crooked. In Hayley Wood, where the problem is very severe, both the traditional methods have been tried. Pollarding (Fig. 12.16) is a highly effective means of protecting the regrowth of trees, but is very hard work and protects nothing else. Compartmentation protects all the vegetation but even with modern fencing materials is expensive.[120–1] Deer are a resource that should be used: it is a pity that so much excellent meat should be running round the countryside and often nobody using it, the numbers being limited only by starvation and poaching.

Management of ancient wood-pastures

Wood-pasture is an immensely important habitat, partly because of the specific value of old trees, and partly because of its variety of structures – trees, scrub, long and short grass – and the interfaces between them, which are diminishing in other land-uses and are particularly valuable for birds and insects. It is also much loved and appreciated as terrain of public resort, as the popularity of the New Forest, Epping, and Burnham Beeches exemplifies. Like ancient woodland, wood-pasture can withstand a good deal of public use without much loss to its ecological value, although ancient trees are damaged or polluted by fires,[133] dead wood tends to disappear, and dogs can cause trouble. Thorndon Park has been successfully used for three quite different purposes in its history. It is a tragedy that the Georgians and Victorians should have foreseen no further use for wood-pastures and should have taken it upon themselves to destroy so many. There was less destruction in the mid-twentieth century, though this included the coniferization of much of the remaining Sherwood Forest (pp. 302, 315). Beginning with the Epping Forest Act in 1878, many wood-pastures have been managed by public and semi-public bodies for public recreation. The Country Park movement has given a new lease of life to many ancient sites and started new wood-pastures in the 'pseudo-medieval' tradition: Langdon Hills (pp. 8–10) is a modern 'instant park' as Sotterley once was.

A lesson of the last 120 years is that wood-pasture authorities, while rightly rejecting the techniques of modern forestry or of municipal parks, are often insufficiently appreciative of the stability and virtues of traditional grazing and woodcutting practices and are too solicitous about young trees. The Epping Forest Act set forth admirably detailed objectives: the Conser-vators of the Forest are obliged to 'protect the timber and other trees, pollards, shrubs, underwood, heather, gorse, turf, and herbage growing on the Forest'.[492] Unfortunately the authorities pursued their duty of protecting timber trees with more enthusiasm than the other requirements of the Act, despite the lack of evidence that the Forest had ever been threatened by a shortage of trees. They promptly exercised their option to terminate the woodcutting rights, forgetting that pollards can only be effectively protected by continuing

Fig. 12.16 Ash-trees in Hayley Wood, originally coppiced but now made into pollards and photographed in the first year of regrowth. New shoots have appeared all the way up the bollings, but have been completely eaten back up to the height which a fallow deer can reach; only those at the top of the bollings have escaped.

to pollard them; they felled many pollards and manipulated the Forest so as to encourage an unnecessary amount of regeneration from seed. In the 1970s the Forest was on the way to becoming undistinguished secondary woodland. Its distinctive features, the pollards, non-timber trees, shrubs, and underwood were declining through neglect or excessive shade. The decline of grazing and lack of effective action to replace it had resulted in many of the plains being overgrown, with the loss of much of the turf and herbage and nearly all the heather and gorse.[124, 126] Apart from lichens, which may have been more affected by air pollution, the decline in the Forest's flora and fauna was largely attributable to these structural changes. It was often claimed that the Forest was returning to a 'natural aspect' of which it had been deprived by centuries of misuse, but this was an illusion: it was tending to a closed canopy of beech or hornbeam unlike anything in its history. [Since 1980 the Conservators have made great efforts to recover the distinctive character of the Forest, but the task is immense.]

Planting or encouraging young trees is a well-defined objective which commends itself to officialdom and to the public and attracts funds and helpers. This easy political option is often pursued in wood-pasture, whether or not there is a demonstrable need for it, to the neglect of more urgent problems and at the sacrifice of glades and ancient trees.

Young and middle-aged trees are the most robust element in many wood-pastures; there is as often an excess as a shortage, and they are well capable of looking after themselves. A tree needs to be at least 300 years old and preferably a pollard before it will harbour many of the more distinctive wood-pasture organisms. The historical character and biological importance of wood-pastures reside in grassland, heath, and scrub, and in old and dead trees.[18] These are often fragile, though the protection which they need may be unglamorous and inexpensive. Often it is a matter of not tidying up 'diseased' or 'unsightly' trees; in other instances the uprooting of young birches (Chapter 19) may suffice. The two general remedies are the resumption of grazing[775] and of pollarding. Existing pollards should be re-pollarded cautiously and experimentally and we should also start many new pollards, for this is the only reliable way of ensuring that there shall be ancient trees in the future to replace those of today. The conservation of old trees is further discussed in Chapters 17 and 33.

13

The woods of ash, maple, and hazel

Ash (*Fraxinus excelsior*), maple (*Acer campestre*), and hazel (*Corylus avellana*) are among the commonest woodland trees in England. Hazel, although technically a shrub (and neglected by many ecological writers for that reason), is no less a woodland-forming tree than are ash and maple. Between them the three trees are the dominant underwood of some 40% of the native woodland area of Eastern England; they also form the usual woodland of most of the Midlands and on clayey or calcareous soils elsewhere. In the Highland Zone they are less abundant, but ash and hazel are woodland-forming trees in Wales and as far north as Wester Ross, and hazel-woods are well known in western Ireland.[753] Maple hardly extends outside England. All three trees are common in hedges and other non-woodland sites.

There is only one native species of each tree. All three are very variable; there are garden varieties of hazel, and some botanists recognize a hairless variety of maple, but there is no problem of taxonomy. The name '*field* maple' exemplifies the academic habit of not using one word where two will do.

Sycamore (*Acer pseudoplatanus*) is an exotic tree from central Europe. It is first definitely recorded in England in 1578 as a rare planted tree,[390] though there are some alleged earlier plantings in Scotland in the fifteenth century and it is said to be represented on a thirteenth-century carving at Oxford.[756] It was not extensively planted until the late eighteenth century.[756] As a recent invader of native woodland it just comes within the scope of this book.

Ash, maple, and hazel are dealt with together, not because they define a homogeneous plant community, but because they are so intermingled as to defy rigid classification. They can be mixed in almost any proportion (Fig. 13.1). Extreme variants, such as limestone ashwoods and maple-woods on clay, may be as dissimilar as woodlands can be, but they are connected by intermediates among which no objective boundaries can be drawn.

Many ash–maple–hazel woods have standard oak-trees and are traditionally regarded as variants of 'damp oak-wood' or 'ash-oakwood'.[150] But they seldom have oak as underwood and (apart from some extreme forms) are very different from oakwoods in the more restricted sense used in this book.

The prehistoric record

Hazel

Hazel is identifiable from pollen, nuts, and occasionally wood. It is difficult to compare with other species because we do not know what part it played in the wildwood structure. Early pollen analysts thought it was an understorey shrub and established a convention of not including hazel in the total of tree pollen. This was a mistake: as anyone can see in a neglected coppice-wood, hazel is not very tolerant of shade; if overtopped by neighbouring trees it may linger for many years but flowers poorly if at all. The abundance of hazel pollen in most prehistoric deposits implies that the tree was not shaded; we do not know whether it grew taller than it does now or whether the wildwood as a whole was less tall than is usually supposed. The magnificent canopy hazels in, for instance, Spittlemoor Coppice in Hatfield Forest (Fig. 13.10) are a possible modern parallel.

Hazel was an early post-glacial invader, beginning mysteriously from the north-west. In Zone VI it was exceedingly common: in Ireland its pollen is up to seventeen times, and in England up to four times, as abundant as all other trees put together. Even allowing for the mild winters of Ireland, which would favour pollen production by this early-flowering tree, such frequencies imply that it was dominant over wide areas.

In the Atlantic Period hazel declined slightly but it remained, along with elm or oak, one of the two commonest trees in Wales, northern England, southern Scotland, and Ireland. In the Scottish Highlands and Lowland England hazel may have been the third, fourth, or fifth commonest tree.[12] From the Neolithic onwards it fluctuated considerably but its distribution pattern remained the same.

The pollen record for Eastern England shows much local variation (Figs. 8.2, 8.3). In the late Atlantic Period in some places, hazel pollen is about one and a half times as abundant as that of all other 'dry-land' trees. Elsewhere, especially in the Norfolk Broads, it is comparatively scarce. Hazel was evidently as variable in its occurrence as it is in ancient woods today.

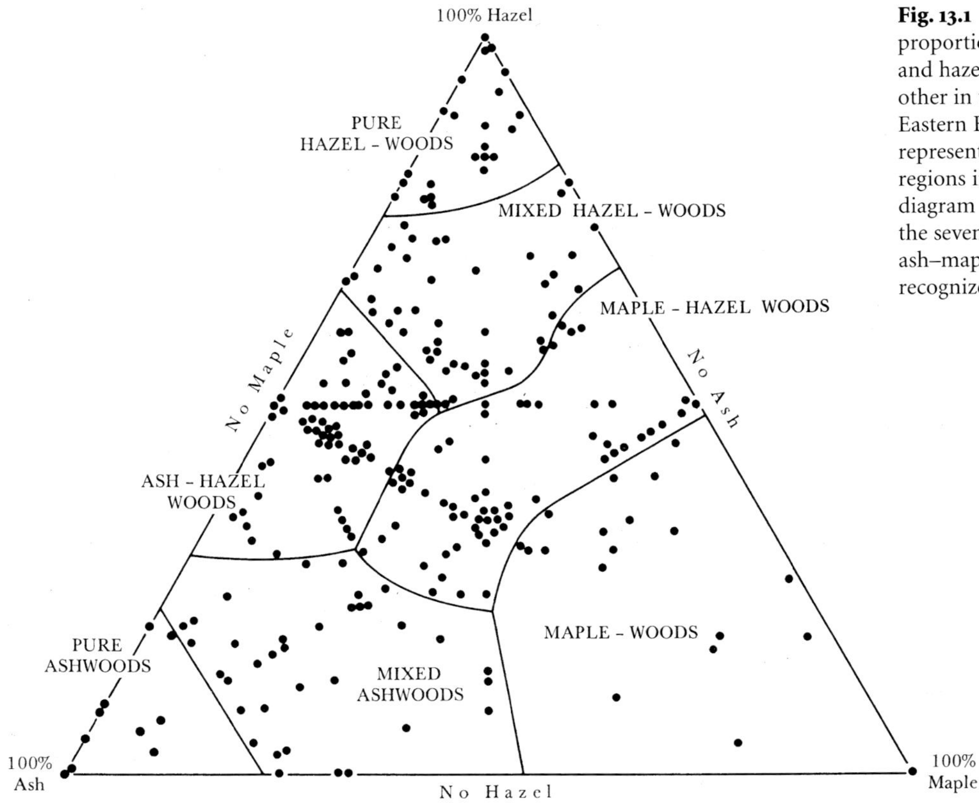

Fig. 13.1 Approximate proportions of ash, maple, and hazel relative to each other in the ancient woods of Eastern England. Each point represents one wood. The regions into which this diagram is divided define the seven types of ash–maple–hazel woodland recognized in this book.

Ash

Ash invaded Britain much later than hazel. It is first extensively recorded in Zone VI. By the end of the Atlantic Period it occurred throughout Great Britain, especially in northern England, but was rare in Ireland. It rarely forms as much as 5% of the total tree pollen. Although wind-pollinated, ash is reckoned to be a poor producer of pollen, and the figures imply that it was widespread in the Atlantic wildwood but only locally common.

The Elm Decline was accompanied or immediately followed by a rapid and systematic increase of ash, which often reaches 10% of the total tree pollen in Zones VIIb and VIII. This is most obvious in northern England, where ash was already well established, but has been observed almost everywhere south of Glasgow and also in Ireland. Neolithic activities in some way favoured ash, which replaced some of the elm and possibly lime that had been destroyed. Why it should have been ash that profited from this interference is not clear. Ash is unlikely to have been deliberately favoured: if the decline of elm was due to pollarding for fodder (Chapter 16), then ash (which is equally suitable) ought also to have been affected. If secondary woodland was being formed on abandoned clearings, it is surprising that it should have been widely dominated by ash rather than by oak, which is nowadays in general a more effective pioneer tree and would have been more readily available as a seed source. However, ash often forms secondary woodland, especially on chalk (p. 324) or limestone[106] soils and on old gardens (p. 8). It is possible that it was the most effective colonizer of the particular sites – e.g. very fertile calcareous soils which cannot now be observed under woodland – from which the elms had disappeared. Alternatively there may have been some more subtle change like the present conversion of many limestone hazel-woods into ashwoods (p. 219).

In Eastern England ash behaves in the same general way and does not usually become prominent until after the Elm Decline. However, some profiles from mid Norfolk show up to 8% of ash pollen (implying, in its context, about 40% of ash trees) considerably before any appreciable decline in elm (Figs. 8.2, 8.3, 32.11).

Maple

The record for maple is very unsatisfactory. In this interglacial its remains are known only from the Neolithic onward and are limited to single pollen grains and occasional finds of wood.[710] Maple might be under-represented for several reasons. It is rare or absent in the northern and western regions from which much of the pollen evidence comes. It is insect-pollinated and a poor pollen producer, though rated no worse than ash or lime.[4] It grows mainly on clay soils away from pollen-collecting basins. Nevertheless, it is remarkable that even in East Anglia, the present stronghold of maple, it should have so little prehistoric record.

Conclusions

The record of hazel is amply sufficient to account for its present abundance: it has certainly been widespread as a dominant or co-dominant tree since well before the Atlantic Period.

The record of ash is less certain. After the introduction of agriculture it may have formed secondary woods some of which may be the predecessors of the present limestone ashwoods. It is doubtful whether this process has anything to do with the main body of surviving ashwoods on clayey or acid soils. The Norfolk pollen diagrams indicate that there may have been ash-containing variants of wildwood well represented by surviving woods but rarely sampled in deposits.

The pollen record of maple, taken at face value, indicates that the tree has greatly increased, or could even have been introduced, since the development of agriculture. This is difficult to reconcile with its modern ecology: maple is a non-aggressive tree which does not easily form secondary woodland. As a colonizer of clearings in woodland or of abandoned farmland it is less effective than ash or even hazel. The question must be left unanswered: the lack of evidence tells us less about the prehistory of maple than about the limitations of palaeobotanical techniques.

The historical record

Pre-Conquest evidence

All three trees are well represented in English place-names and Anglo-Saxon charters. Ash and thorn are the commonest trees as place-name elements (Table 2.1); the evidence tells us merely that ash was ubiquitous and universally noticed.

Hazel is less conspicuous and has been confused with elm and hornbeam (p. 221); nevertheless it is the fifth commonest tree in place-names (e.g. *Hasle*mere). The former place-name *Haslett*[882] implies a wood consisting of hazel (*hæsel* + *-ett*, cf. Birchet, p. 312). Charters refer frequently to hazel-groves and also to a hazel-hedge (*hæselrǣwe*)[379] and, surprisingly often, to single trees like 'the white hazel'[382] and 'the great hazel-stool' (*hæselwrið*, from *wridian*, to sprout).[381] Evidently free-standing hazels, recognizable as individuals, were commoner than they are now. The nuts are referred to in place-names such as *Nut*hampstead. Although common, hazel could be valuable private property; in South Wales as early as the tenth century a single stool was valued for compensation at 3¾ sheep[508] (cf. p. 319).

For maple the place-name evidence is also abundant – the tree is easily recognized, although I have known it confused with service – and corresponds remarkably well with the modern distribution: north to *Mapple*well in Darton (S. Yorks),[883] south-west to *Maper*ton (Somerset) and *Mappowder* (from the Old English form *mapuldor*) in Dorset. It is significant that ash (*uinnseann*) and hazel (*calltuinn, coll*) are frequent in Gaelic but there is apparently no word for maple, which evidently did not grow in Gaelic territory. The Welsh *masarnen* looks suspiciously like a derivative of English *mazer* (p. 207). Charters often mention maple and sometimes refer to its genetic variation, as with the mention of a 'red-leaf maple'[380] which, then as now, was a striking peculiarity of certain individual trees.

Medieval and post-medieval evidence

The woodland trees most commonly recorded in the Middle Ages, after oak, are ash, maple, hazel, and thorn. Ash appears in Latin as *fraxinus* and hazel as *corulus*; maple may be *acer*, *arabilis* (cf. Modern French *érable*), or just *mapel*. For instance, the thirteenth- and fourteenth-century accounts of Hindolveston (Norfolk) (Chapter 10) mention all three, and those of Gamlingay (Cambs) mention maple, now somewhat local in Gamlingay Wood, and ash. Hazel is implied by the many medieval references to nuts and thatching wood. Ash, maple, and less often hazel are also mentioned as non-woodland trees, and ash was planted as such (p. 159).

Hazel, ash, and maple are among the commonest underwood species in sixteenth-century surveys of woods. At White Notley (Essex) in 1574, for instance, a wood was 'verie well sett with yonge asshes for the most parte'.[281] At New Hall (Boreham, Essex) in 1565 (p. 223) we find a coppice of hornbeam, maple, and ash and another of beech, maple, and hornbeam (a combination which I have seen surviving only at Frithsden (Berkhamsted, Herts) (p. 223)). At Little Easton (Essex) the same survey reports underwood of hornbeam, maple, and aspen in the park.[460] Hazel was associated with oak in Stockton Wood (Wilts) in 1566 (p. 292).[493] Hazel, ash, and maple are three of the five commonest underwood trees recorded in surveys of the coppice compartments of Rockingham Forest (Northants), in 1564–5 (Table 13.1). The extreme abundance of maple is noteworthy.

Hazel, as the second commonest material for wattle-and-daub, is well represented in medieval buildings; ash and maple were less used.

This evidence shows that ash–maple–hazel woods were abundant before the era of plantations and that some of their present variants could already be distinguished.

From the seventeenth century onwards ash, either alone or in a mixture, was one of the commonest trees for plantations. Hazel was occasionally used; for instance in 1804–5 three acres, probably at Horringer (W. Suffolk), were sown with acorns, hazel-nuts, and ash-keys.[227] I

Table 13.1 Composition of Crown coppices in Rockingham Forest as recorded by Houghton (1564) and Taverner (1565). (From the analysis of G. F. Peterken.[100])

	1564 survey	1565 survey
Number of coppices for which underwood species is given	81	106
Number of coppices containing underwood of:		
Thorn	81	101
Maple	40	103
Hazel	21	67
Sallow or withy	5	26
Ash	6	22
Oak	—	15
Beech	1	—
'Poplar'	—	1

have one reference to the sowing of maple in a new wood, at Felbrigg (Norfolk) in 1676.[764]

Historic uses and management of ash, maple, and hazel

All three trees have specific uses; but, as with most trees, these uses seldom accounted for all the available wood, and there was usually a large excess for firewood and other general purposes. The uses go back well into pre-history (Chapter 8); in the Somerset Levels, ash and hazel were much used in Neolithic trackways and maple was used in the Bronze Age.

Ash

In ancient woods most ash-trees are, and have been, coppiced but a large minority are treated as timber. Throughout history ash has generally been the second commonest recorded timber tree, and there is just enough information to reconstruct the history of its value (Fig. 11.5).

Ash is best known as the traditional material, chosen for its elasticity, for the handles of all kinds of tools and for the frames and shafts of vehicles – from chariots to the Morris Traveller car – and aircraft. In Anglo-Saxon literature, *æsc* is a poetic word for 'spear', and ash has indeed been the commonest wood for all kinds of spears down to the modern cavalry lance. (But *æsc* is also a word for 'ship', although it was not a shipbuilding timber.) For most of these purposes, ash would be best grown as large underwood, and in the Bradfield Woods ash poles were grown in the 1970s to be steam-bent into the three-dimensional curves of scythe-sticks. Ash is now more often used as timber but like all sawn timber may break if the grain is not parallel to the length. Ash should be fast-grown to develop its special qualities; good ash timber is more difficult to grow, and demands a more fertile site, than good ash underwood.

There is a prejudice against ash as a building timber, but it is successfully used in the heavy frames of a seventeenth-century house at Felsham (Suffolk) and of the modern library of Christ's College, Cambridge. Ash-trees were chopped up for splints in wattle-and-daub at Ditchingham (Norfolk) in 1272.[462] Barrel-hoops, although usually of hazel, could be cleft and bent from ash;[49] my first record of this trade, which flourished until World War I (Fig. 11.7), is from Writtle (Essex) in 1406–7,[312] and mentions small timber ash-trees as the raw material. Ash, unexpectedly, is mentioned as *staves* for herring-barrels at Mettingham (Suffolk) in 1562.[403] Ash has been much used as hop-poles, but there is a prejudice against using it for bean-poles.

Hazel

Although hazel will just grow to timber size I have never heard of it used except as underwood. From Neolithic times onwards it has been the normal tree for wattle-work – hurdles, wattle-and-daub, woven fences – and for thatching wood. Its specific advantage is that it can be twisted to separate the fibres and then bent at a sharp angle without breaking: thatching broaches and the rods at the ends of hurdles need to be bent through 180°, and faggot-bands (Fig. 10.5) are tied in knots. Hazel-rods can be split to compensate for differences in their thickness, though the earliest wattle-work does not use this property (p. 107). For these purposes hazel is best coppiced on a short rotation; after twelve to fifteen years' growth it becomes difficult to work.

For many uses hazel is not essential. Wattle-and-daub and thatching wood are often of sallow, and modern woven hurdles are often of osier. There is a parallel technology which uses very thinly-split oak laths.[49] But hazel is so abundant that these alternatives have seldom been used on a large scale.

Hazel, though seldom named, presumably provided most of the rods (*virge*), woven hurdles, and thatching wood whose history is given in Chapter 10. At Hindolveston in the fourteenth century the existence of a stand of hazel appears to have given rise to a hurdle-making business; presumably the same happened, at different times, in other hazel-rich areas such as Cranborne Chase.

Before walnuts and chestnuts became common, and before there were marauding grey squirrels, wild hazelnuts were a crop worth having. In the twelfth century the hermit of Writtle Forest (Essex) was allowed to have men in the Forest gathering nuts in season.[248] In Barking (Suffolk) in 1251 each of the tenants owing labour services

> shall gather nuts, namely one full measure which is called a *pibot* of which four make up one bushel.[270]

A pibot or peck would have contained something like 2,300 nuts; by analogy with other labour services it may represent about half a day's work, i.e. 7–8 nuts a minute. At Kimbolton (Hunts) the nuts in the park and its associated woods were valued in 1337 at 6*s* 8*d* per annum 'when they happen'.[449]

Nutting was a social occasion. In 1826 the owner of Hatfield Forest (Essex) complained that

> as soon as the Nuts begin to get ripe . . . the idle and disorderly Men and Women of bad Character from [Bishop's] Stortford . . . come . . . in large parties to gather the Nuts or under pretence of gathering Nuts to loiter about in Crowds . . . and in the Evening . . . take Beer and Spirits and Drink in the Forest which affords them an opportunity for all sorts of Debauchery. . .[326]

In 1865 we find a man paid for 'Watching Nuts in Wayland Wood [Norfolk]'.[513]

Maple

Books claim that maple is nearly always coppiced, but in fact it is often a standard tree, sometimes of large size. Timber maples are recorded in the Gamlingay accounts for 1334, where the bailiff claimed that he had been overcharged by 2*s* 7*d* 'for maples which they made out as oaks in the previous account'.[399] There was a sale of maple as timber at Haveringland (Norfolk) in 1814 (no price given).[408]

The specific uses of maple are on a very small scale, for musical instruments, furniture, and the like. Graeme Lawson tells me that it is the wood most often identified in archaeological remains of Anglo-Saxon musical instruments. The art of making decorative spoons, bowls, etc. of sycamore, which was highly developed in nineteenth-century Wales, has been conjectured to be a development of an earlier maple craft.[49] A famous, once large-scale, use is for the medieval drinking-bowls called *mazers*.[835a] In my Cambridge college we treasure the Swan Mazer, described in an inventory of *c.* 1380 as

> one maser with lid . . . with broad silver bindings on the circumference and base of the bowl . . . and in the middle of the bowl there is a silver-gilt column on which sits a gilded swan . . .[374]

The wooden bowl measures about 5 x 2½ in., and is made from a rare variant of maple-wood with a beautiful feathery grain. [For an account of Anglo-Saxon and medieval mazers, their manufacture, and the derivation of the word see Rackham (2002) *Treasures of Silver* chapter 6.]

I have encountered no reference to maple sap in this country. The sap which flows from poles cut in late winter may be weaker than that of the Canadian *Acer saccharum*, but I have drunk it with appreciation, and thoughts of maple beer and syrup have crossed my mind.

Modern ecology

Woods, wood-pastures, and hedges

All three species are palatable trees which occur in woods and hedges rather than wood-pasture. The fallow deer of Hayley Wood are particularly fond of ash and very effectively prevent its regrowth (Fig. 12.16); after ash they prefer hazel and then maple. Horses can be very destructive of hazel.

The decline of hazel in uncompartmented wood-pasture is widely recorded (pp. 241, 294). The same presumably happened with ash and maple, although a pollen record is lacking. In some places they were preserved by pollarding. In Havering Park (Essex) in 1565, which had been a park for at least 350 years, there were maples 'lopped & shredd for browze'.[460] In Hatfield Forest there are still pollard ashes and maples in the plains, as there were in 1639.[458] When grazing has declined, ash sometimes returns; it forms secondary woodland on clay soils in Hainault Forest and Enfield Chase. [See also Fig. 31.5 and p. 513.]

It is possible that maple, being slightly less palatable than ash or hazel, is favoured under the intermittent protection from grazing provided by compartmented wood-pasture. It is unusually and significantly abundant in the coppices of those few Forests that are on calcareous soils: those of Hatfield Forest, Rockingham Forest (both in 1564–5 (Table 13.1) and in what remains of them now),[100] and the remains of Wychwood Forest (Oxon) and of Neroche Forest (Somerset).[125]

All three trees are common in hedges, even in areas such as the Chiltern plateau where the local woods may lack them. Ash grows in hedges of all ages and in much of the east Midlands is the commonest hedgerow tree. It makes an excellent pollard, but in enclosure-act hedges is usually a timber tree, although so treated it is seldom successful; it illustrates the triumph of fashion over experience. Maple and hazel are usually in ancient hedges: maple in hedges with not less than three other tree and shrub species, and hazel in medieval hedges with at least five other species.

Shade, competition, and *Armillaria*

Ash is a lightly-shading and light-demanding tree. Maple casts a shade nearly as heavy as hornbeam or beech, and is relatively tolerant of shade. Hazel casts rather less shade than maple, and is itself nearly as sensitive to shading as ash.

The three species coppice equally well, but there can be no doubt that coppicing, particularly on a short rotation, favours hazel. Hazel can flower and fruit within a shorter coppice cycle than either of its competitors; even five years would be just sufficient. If shaded by taller neighbours, its growth-rate is much reduced and flowering stops. [The stools, however, can live on almost unchanged for many decades (pp. 379–85).]

The shade-sensitivity of hazel is connected with the honey-fungus (*Armillaria mellea* and related species). This is a well-known and dreaded parasite of gardens and plantations; it colonizes stumps and buried wood and spreads through the soil by bootlace-like strands called ***rhizomorphs*** to attack and kill trees.[823] *Armillaria* is probably present throughout every ancient wood. Any log left lying around for a couple of years is almost certain to be invaded by rhizomorphs from the soil beneath. Native woodland has lived with *Armillaria* for thousands of years, and under normal management it is harmless. In the first or second autumn after coppicing it often produces toadstools in great abundance, presumably on sustenance derived from redundant roots. Toadstools may even grow on the stools themselves, but have no appreciable effect on their vigour of regrowth. This co-existence can be upset by any change of management, especially by replanting,[684] but also by neglect. In a wood left uncoppiced, toadstools tend to be produced at the bases of hazel stools that have been overtopped and are declining. In the Bradfield Woods, for instance, this was particularly noticeable in 1973 in a panel last coppiced in 1945. This panel was eventually coppiced in 1975–6, but many of the hazels did not recover.

The obvious explanation is that all hazels have *Armillaria* forever gnawing at their roots, but shaded hazels photosynthesize less and make insufficient material to repair the damage. Whether or not this simple hypothesis can be sustained, the interaction illustrates the principle that relatively trivial problems for a tree can be aggravated by shade. We shall see other examples in Chapter 17. Coppicing enables more stools of hazel to co-exist with other trees, including ash or maple, than would otherwise be possible. In uncoppiced parts of Hayley Wood, hazel was still strong in 1965, some sixty years after the last coppicing, but the stools have become much less vigorous since then.

This process does not apply to woods in which hazel has only other hazels to compete with. Coppicing has not created hazel-woods, which have existed throughout pre-history, but it has enabled hazel to be commoner in mixtures than it would otherwise be.

In a neglected wood the ash underwood often overtops and kills the standard oak trees. Maple occasionally does the same; I have no record of hazel overtopping oak, although in wind-exposed parts of the west it might well do so. Ash and maple co-exist with each other; the ash often grows taller but the maple withstands its shade.

Reproduction and longevity

Ash

The longevity of ash depends on site and treatment. In Madingley Wood (Cambs), which is a good ash site, *standard* trees collapse in a decisive manner at about 180 years [pp. 379–85]. In Hayley Wood, where ash grows slowly, small standard trees, with microscopic annual rings, are over 200 years old and are evidently capable of struggling on much longer.

Ash *stools*, on the other hand, are capable of living indefinitely. Most of the Hayley standards are promoted from stools, which are presumably at least 300 years old. Even small stools can be of considerable age: I have counted rings back to 1775 in a stool only 16 in. diameter in Hayley, which (allowing for the hollow centre) cannot be younger than the year 1700. Most ancient woods have ash stools at least 5 ft (1.5 m) across, and I have several records of diameters over 10 ft [Plate 9, Fig. 3.0b].

In Hayley Wood the stools range evenly in diameter from about 8 in. to 7 ft, the smallest – cut only once, at the last coppicing – being the most numerous and the frequency declining to the largest size (Fig. 13.2). This suggests a continuous turnover over the last 500 years. At each coppicing some new ashes were established from seed, being cut for the first time at the next coppicing. The most likely cause of death is shading by timber trees, which would strike at random regardless of age, so that a few stools are much larger, and presumably older, than average. At Bradfield the turnover is apparently slower. Many ash stools are very large; peculiarities of growth-habit and of the pigmentation of coppice shoots prove that they are genetic individuals and are not formed by the amalgamation of several separate trees. Bradfield has the largest ash stool of all, 18½ ft (5.6 m) across; although on a quite good ash site, it can hardly be less than 1,000 years old; it shows no sign of declining vigour.

Ash fruits erratically, but the good and bad years are not synchronous as are those of other trees; in any season some trees fruit and others rest. Most seed lies dormant for two or more winters before germinating.[161] Seedlings appear in most years but in variable numbers. Ashlings are quite resistant to shade and can wait many years until a felling gives them the chance to get away. Ash therefore has little difficulty in reproducing by seed in existing woods. Seedlings, however, cannot get through a dense stand of dog's-mercury (p. 95) and in well-drained woods the regeneration of ash may depend on coppicing to break up the mercury carpet. Saplings are eaten by deer but seldom killed: Hayley Wood is full of maimed ashlings [for whose fate see pp. 490–1, 513].

Maple

Large maples are seldom felled and their annual rings are difficult to count. E. W. Jones quotes a maple at least 300 years old in the New Forest,[756] and I suspect that many pollards, such as those in Hatfield Forest, are of at least this age.

Most stands of maple, as of ash, contain stools of all ages from 300 years or more down to the time of the

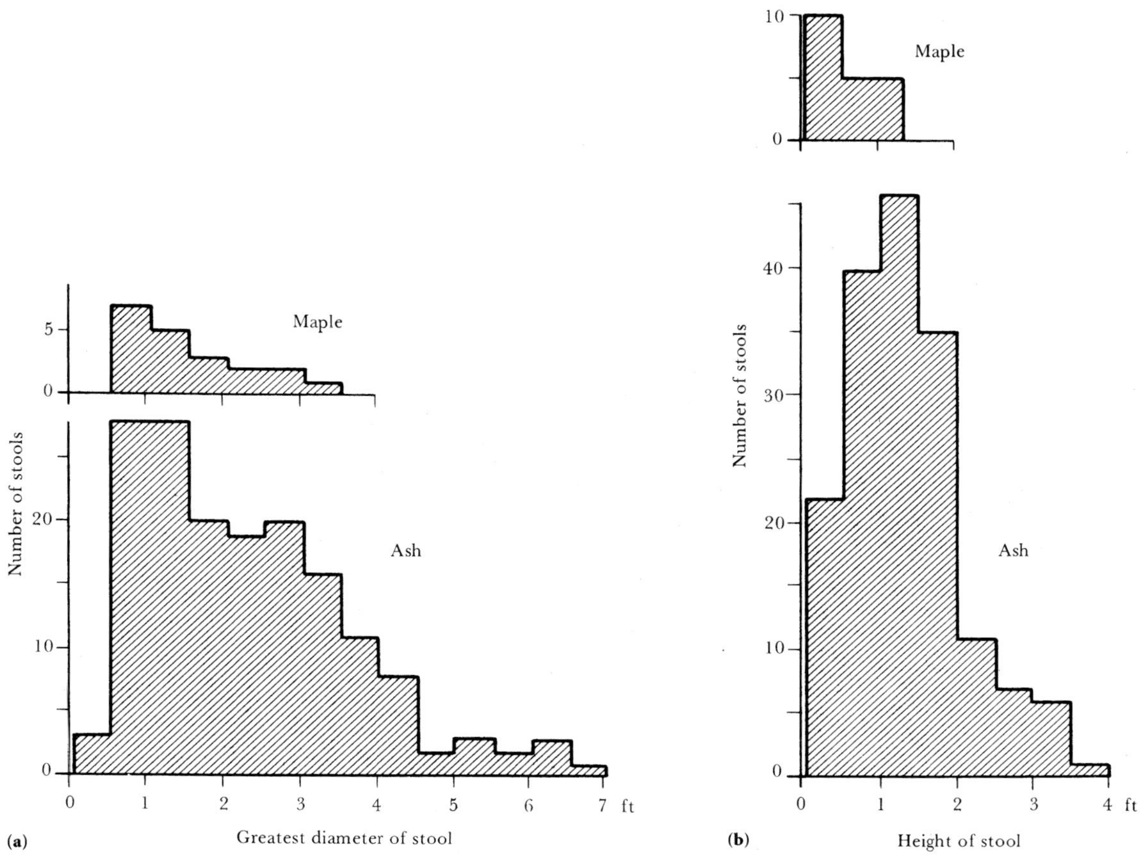

Fig. 13.2 Size-distributions of ash and maple stools in Hayley Wood. Compiled by measuring all the stools of these species on a one-acre plot.[120] (**a**) Stools classified by greatest diameter. (**b**) Stools classified by height above ground at which last coppiced.

last coppicing. In Hayley Wood the maple stools are, on average, considerably smaller than those of ash (Fig. 13.2), which suggests that they are shorter-lived, even though maple is less easily killed by shade and is rarely seen dead. Although giant maple stools are less common than those of ash, the very largest are of similar size. There was one 14 ft (4.3 m) in diameter, probably now destroyed, in Lumpit Wood (Glemsford, W. Suffolk), a wood recorded in 1251;[270] there are at least two over 13 ft across in the woods of Hatfield Forest.

Maple is near its climatic limit and fruits erratically; 1977, preceded by two very hot summers, was a good year. Many trees become male in resting years.[756] The seed usually waits till the second spring before germinating. Maple seedlings are less abundant than those of ash or sycamore. [Maple reproduction, which seemed in the 1970s to be declining, has revived since (especially where woods are coppiced or elms have died) and is now probably adequate.]

Hazel

Unlike most ash and maple stools a hazel stool is usually underground. Neglected stools often have a 'self-coppicing' mechanism: stems die after thirty to fifty years and are replaced by new shoots. It is thus very difficult to tell the age of a hazel. The stools often reach 6 ft (1.8 m) in diameter but rarely much more. By analogy with other species this should represent an age of at least 300 years. It is possible that they cease to grow beyond a certain size, and they may even get smaller by underground decay.[120]

What has happened to the regeneration of hazel? In past centuries the nuts were a frequent but irregular crop, qualified, like acorns (p. 155), by the phrase *cum acciderint*, 'when they happen'. The ***plashing*** of hazel – bending shoots down from the stool and pegging them to the ground to take root – is occasionally recommended as a means of multiplying stools, but I have no records to show that it was generally found necessary. Until the early twentieth century hazel reproduced effectively by seed; it got into attached secondary woods such as the Hayley Triangle (Fig. 5.2). But in my experience a ripe hazel-nut is almost a thing of the past. Nobody steals nuts any more because there are so few. Fewer nuts are produced because many hazels are shaded, and predators take the entire crop while still green. The proliferation of grey squirrels and possibly of woodpigeons[803] are the most likely causes. Because the nuts, unlike acorns (Chapter 17), are taken while still green, any that are dropped or buried do not grow. There were young hazels in the Bradfield Woods, where the parent hazels are not shaded and where squirrels used to be kept down, but it is my impression generally that hazels younger than 1960 are now rare. Bearing in mind the parallel case of oak, I hesitate to counsel alarm without having studied the problem in depth, but appearances suggest that reproduction in hazel is even more problematical than in other heavy-seeded trees.

Soils

Writers on these trees have associated them with fertile, calcareous, usually well-drained soils. My studies in Eastern England to some extent confirm these attributions but extend the range of the three trees, all of which can grow on quite strongly acid soils.

Ash, maple, and hazel are abundant in the Calcareous Province on moderately calcareous soils (pH 5.0–7.0) with a moderately high clay content mixed with some loess and sand. Often they fall within the Soil Survey's Hanslope series.[739] They extend outside this soil range to different degrees (Fig. 13.3), hazel being the commonest on the most acid soils (pH <4.0). Maple has a distinct preference for the heaviest soils (>30% clay, <20% sand) and hazel a weaker preference for the more sandy soils.

All three species usually generate mull humus but can form mor on their most acidic sites (Table 4.1); ash does so in Brooklands (Weeley-hall) Wood, hazel in Soane Wood, maple in Boxted Great Wood (all three in N.E. Essex).

[The three trees can be affected by drainage, ash being abundant on waterlogged sites, hazel intermediate, and maple avoiding them (pp. 488–92, Fig. 31.7).] Poor drainage can favour ash by preventing dog's-mercury from competing with its seedlings (p. 95). Timber ash-trees grow slowly on ill-drained sites (p. 208),[759] though coppiced or pollarded ash grows normally.

Where ash, maple, and hazel are rare, as in the more extreme hornbeam, chestnut, or oak woods, they tend to occur in places of increased fertility, in dells and valleys and around springs and on woodbanks, where nutrients are accumulated by downwash or where London Clay or Boulder-clay comes near the surface or has been brought up by embanking. They are accompanied by herbs such as dog's-mercury and primrose and form pockets of a more fertile type of woodland. For instance, in Dodnash Wood (E. Suffolk), a map of 1629 specially mentions 'Two great ashes';[501] there are still two great ash trees – not the same ones, of course – on exactly the same spot, the one place where ash grows well in this otherwise acid and infertile wood. In the Writtle area, maple and hazel are confined to boundary banks (cf. p. 35). Maple has also been reported from Germany as a wood-margin tree.[91]

Types of ash–maple–hazel woodland in Eastern England [see also Chapter 31]

To subdivide this large and heterogeneous class of woodland involves continuous variation at its most difficult. We can estimate with reasonable certainty the relative proportions of ash and maple in a wood. Hazel has a different growth-form and to compare it with ash or maple is unavoidably less exact and objective; moreover it is often difficult to know whether a scarcity of hazel is due to an unsuitable environment or to neglect of coppicing. For this reason the relative proportions in Fig. 13.1 must be treated as approximate.

In many woods, as well as the 'first-order' mosaic of tree communities – ash–maple–hazel versus lime, hornbeam, etc. – careful inspection shows a smaller-scale mosaic of patches of different composition within the ash–maple–hazel community. Some of this 'second-order mosaic' has an ecological meaning, being associated with changes in soil or ground vegetation, but this cannot always be separated from random aggregations of stools. A maple–hazel wood may have a small patch of pure hazel on a sand-lens, a site unsuitable for maple; another patch of pure hazel may result from a chance gap in the scatter of maple stools. Either kind of hazel group becomes more prominent if the wood is neglected, because the rest of the hazel stools, dispersed singly among maple, become overshadowed and may die out. Without detailed study it is not always possible to distinguish the two kinds of group.

For simplicity I have characterized each wood as a whole by its ratio of ash: maple: hazel, passing over – for the moment – internal variation and the second-order mosaic. The ash–maple–hazel stand in each wood has been further characterized in terms of the other tree communities (if any) which abut on or accompany it and of the ground vegetation growing under it (Chapter 6). The tree ratios of Fig. 13.1 have been divided into classes whose boundaries are chosen to correspond, as far as possible, to differences in the associated trees or in the ground vegetation. The resulting classification may not be definitive, but is workable and comprehensible within the limits of the data at hand and of the space which can be devoted to this corner of woodland ecology. Like all classifications of continuous variables, it is rough-and-ready and discourteous to border-line cases.

(i) Pure hazel-woods [Fig. 13.10]

These are defined, roughly, as stands whose underwood is more than three-quarters hazel. They are widely

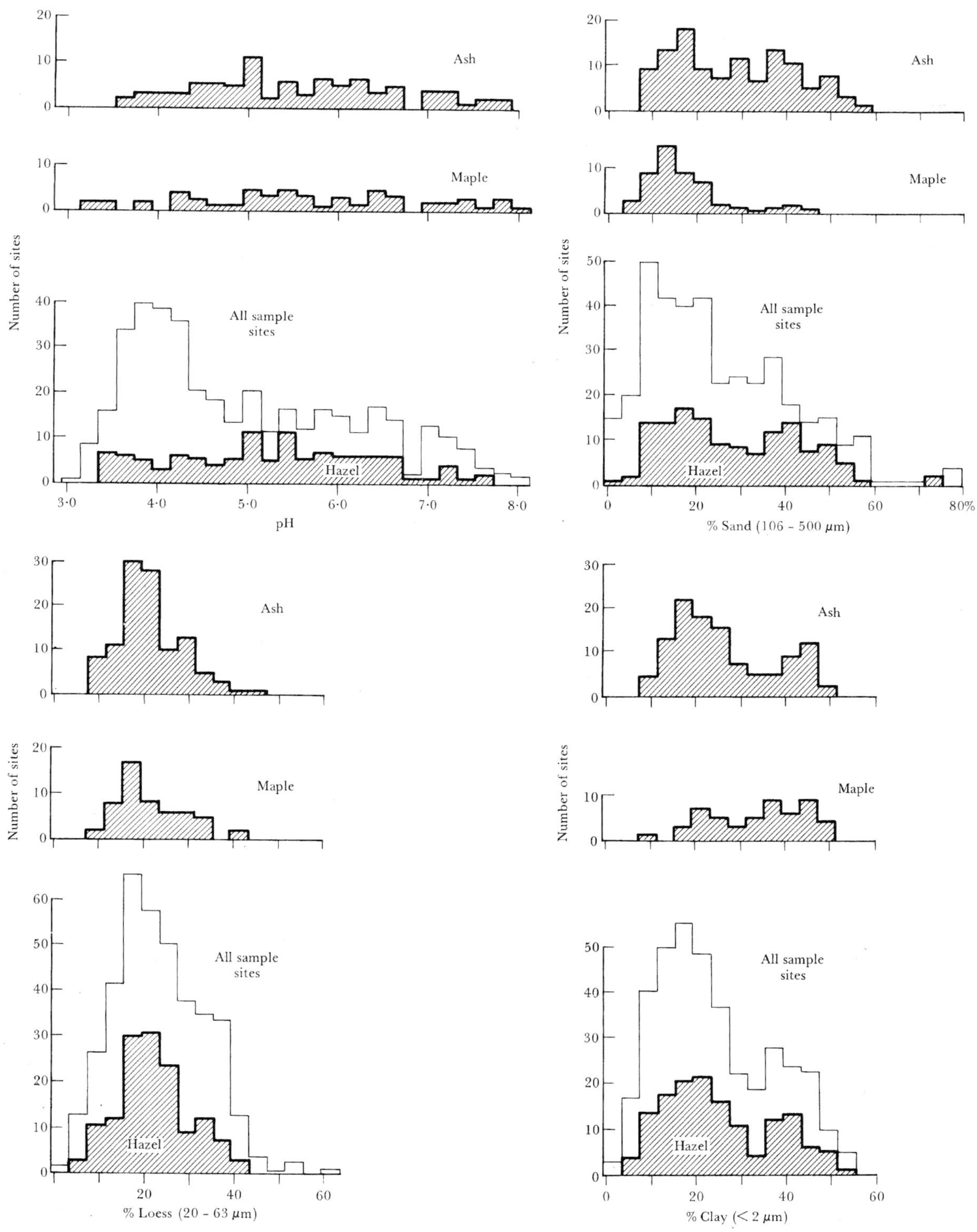

Fig. 13.3 Distribution of topsoil acidity and composition under ash, maple, and hazel in the ancient woods of Eastern England. For comparison the distribution of soil characteristics in all the woodlands sampled is shown by thin outlines. For further details see caption to Fig. 7.5.

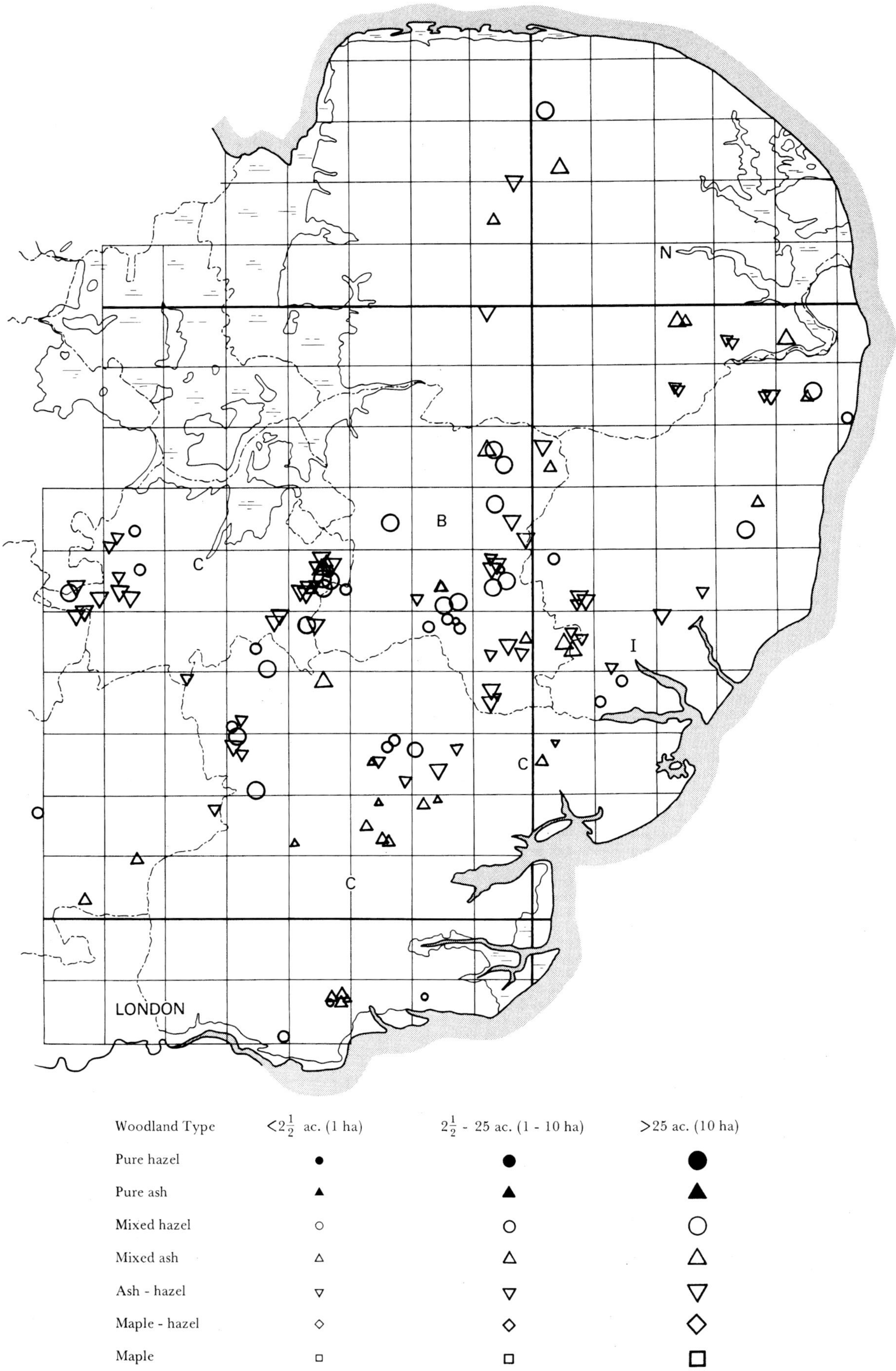
N
B
C
C
I
C
C
LONDON
Woodland Type
<2½ ac. (1 ha)
2½ - 25 ac. (1 - 10 ha)
>25 ac. (10 ha)
Pure hazel
Pure ash
Mixed hazel
Mixed ash
Ash - hazel
Maple - hazel
Maple

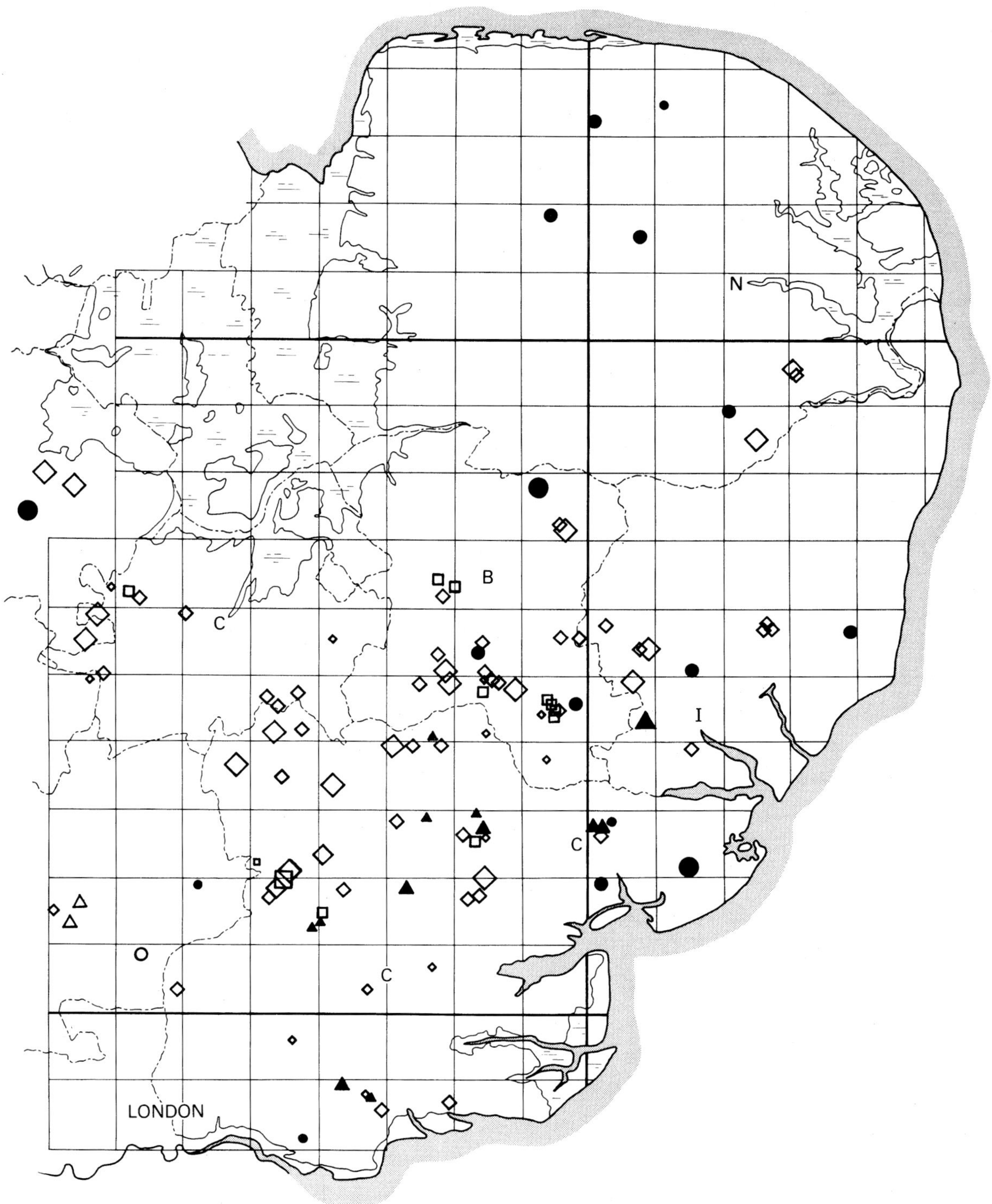

Fig. 13.4 Distribution of the seven types of ash–maple–hazel woodland in Eastern England. Woods are classified according to which type predominates. The size of the symbol is determined by the total area of ash–maple–hazel woodland in the wood in question.

scattered (Fig. 13.4) mainly in the Acid Province (Fig. 4.10). They are typically the most acidic of all the ash–maple–hazel woods; pHs in five woods range from 3.4 to 3.9. This is borne out by the ground vegetation (Table 6.3) with its predominance of brambles, bluebell and bracken (the dog's-mercury results from the inclusion of some border-line cases which would belong better with the mixed hazel-woods). Pure hazel-woods often adjoin even more acidic woodland dominated by hornbeam, oak, birch, or chestnut (Table 6.2).

Pure stands of hazel are usually on infertile, very acid sites with a high proportion of sand or loess. A typical example, occupying a slightly less infertile pocket in what is otherwise an oakwood, is described under Iken Wood (Suffolk) (pp. 289–90).

(ii) Pure ashwoods [Fig. 13.8]

Woods in which ash forms more than three-quarters of the underwood are often also very acidic: pH measurements average 4.1. They are thinly scattered, mainly in Essex. They are associated particularly with hornbeam and lime and their ground vegetation is dominated most often by brambles. They are usually damper than the pure hazel-woods, and the occurrence of primrose, nettle, and occasionally elder suggests some degree of fertility.

Acid ashwoods may be unfamiliar to many readers; they are characteristic of those unusual soils that are acidic, fertile, and well-drained. A good example is Coombe Wood, Langdon Hills (Fig. 1.4), on the steep sides of a gravel-capped hill overlying London Clay, with mixing and downwash of nutrients. The slopes and valleys have well-grown, thinly-spaced ash-trees over a magnificent carpet of bluebells.

(iii) Mixed hazel-woods

These are defined roughly as those in which hazel outweighs ash and maple but is less than 75% of the total underwood canopy. They are widely scattered but mainly in Suffolk. Typically they are acidic but less extreme than the pure hazel-woods (pH 4.0–5.4); the classification has, however, included some calcareous woods (e.g. Hardwick, Cambs) which belong better with the maple–hazel type. The associated plants include chestnut and bracken indicators of acid soils, but there are also some calcicoles such as meadowsweet and ivy. These woods involve the more acid part of the soil range of oxlip, including the large populations in Bull's Wood (Cockfield, Suffolk), and Alpheton Wood (Suffolk).

Mixed hazel-woods are intermediate between pure hazel-woods and those that involve maple. They are most often on a thin layer of sand, or sand and loess, overlying Boulder-clay.

A special kind of hazel-wood fringes some alder valleys (Chapter 18) in acid woods of hornbeam, lime, or chestnut. Good examples, highly calcareous (pH 7.2), occur in Chalkney Wood (Fig. 15.7) where London Clay comes near the surface and springs flow from it. In Dodnash Wood a similar narrow hazel zone results apparently from a calcareous outcrop of Red Crag beneath gravel.

(iv) Mixed ashwoods

These are woods with a ratio of about four parts ash to one maple and one hazel. They are mainly in the Acid Province of Essex and Norfolk, and are moderately acidic, apart from some calcareous examples such as Hempstead Wood (Essex). Their outstanding association is with hornbeam. The ground vegetation is like that of mixed hazel-woods but with more bluebell and bramble; they lie mainly outside the geographical range of oxlip. This is the commonest transition between ash–maple–hazel woodland and hornbeam.

(v) Ash–hazel woods [Fig. 13.9]

This type comprises woods with roughly equal ash and hazel but with less than a fifth of maple. It includes most of the Boulder-clay woods of East and West Cambridgeshire and many, such as part of the Bradfield Woods, in West Suffolk.

Ash–hazel woods range, often within the same wood, from moderately acid to calcareous; they usually have at least surface acidification and some, as in parts of Groton Wood and the Bradfield Woods, have sufficient loess or sand to be strongly acidic. They are typically the wettest of all the variants, as shown by the prevalence of aspen and occasional occurrence of plateau alder.

(vi) Maple–hazel woods

These are woods in which maple and hazel are equally prominent and which are less than half ash. They are mainly in West Suffolk and N.W. Essex, particularly in and around Hatfield Forest. They are typically calcareous but with some surface acidification; the mean pH is 6.0. Calcicolous shrubs, such as dogwood and spindle, although present in many ash–hazel woods, are commoner in this variant. These woods are particularly prone to invasion by elm (Chapter 16) and sometimes have much hawthorn, especially *Crataegus laevigata*. Mercury predominates in the ground vegetation, but bluebells (of the calcicolous Cambridgeshire kind), primrose, and oxlip are frequent.

Maple–hazel woods appear to be on heavier and more calcareous soils than ash–hazel or mixed hazel, but are often better-drained. They are the typical woodland of heavy Boulder-clay on sloping ground.

(vii) Maple-woods [Fig. 13.10]

Woods in which maple forms more than half the underwood are chiefly confined to Hatfield Forest and to the Milden Thicks area of Suffolk. They are a more extreme variant of the maple–hazel woods: mercury is even more predominant, and calcifuge plants even rarer. Where flooding occurs it is indicated by *Deschampsia caespitosa* rather than by oxlip. Soil pH (mean 5.9) and associated trees differ little from those of maple–hazel woods.

Examples of variation within woods

Milden Thicks (Fig. 13.5)

This group of woods, in Brent Eleigh, Little Waldingfield, Milden, Edwardstone, and Groton, West Suffolk, illustrates the interrelation of types of ash–maple–hazel woodland. The topography is flat or (Camps Wood) gently sloping, a Boulder-clay plateau variably overlain by loess and sand. There are many small ancient woods (e.g. Walding Wood, which may be anciently connected with the naming of the two Waldingfield parishes). Some of these increased in size after the Middle Ages (cf. Groton Wood nearby, Fig. 15.9); Bull's Cross Wood, for instance, probably results from the amalgamation of at least three separate groves. Some woodland has been grubbed out in the last 200 years.

The first-order mosaic of tree communities is exceedingly complex, including hornbeam, lime, chestnut, aspen, and various elms as well as ash–maple–hazel. The ash–maple–hazel portions of these woods can be divided into areas dominated by ash and those dominated by maple (Fig. 13.5). Ash woodland tends to be acidic, abutting on hornbeam, lime, and chestnut, with brambles for its ground vegetation; maple woodland is more calcareous, more often adjoins elms and has mercury and primrose. To some extent, however, hornbeam and lime cross the ash–maple boundary to abut on maple, a matter to which we shall return in Chapters 14 and 15. In this group of woods, the maple variant is replaced by ash when the clay content of the topsoil falls below about 25%; when the clay content falls below 18%, as on a sand-lens in Camps Wood, we get acid hazel-wood.

Bradfield Woods

Here it is impossible to draw sharp boundaries between ash–hazel woodland and birchwood (Chapter 19) or plateau alder-wood (Chapter 18). Some ash or hazel are present almost everywhere. Maple, however, is only locally abundant, as we should expect since the topsoil usually has less than 25% clay. In Figure 13.6 the ash, maple, and hazel at each of 84 points are assigned (regardless of the other trees present) to their variant woodland types. Maple is associated with the more clayey parts of the wood and pure hazel (together with birch) with the least clayey and most acidic places; ash–hazel mixtures are intermediate.

In the ordination analysis for Bradfield (Chapter 3), maple is correlated with the second most important axis of variation in the underwood and the third axis in the ground vegetation. Both axes link it to a group of plants, including hawthorn (both species), blackthorn, oxlip, wood-anemone, *Rubus caesius, Geum rivale, Carex sylvatica, Arum maculatum, Tamus communis*, and *Brachypodium sylvaticum*, associated with the peripheral parts of the wood, with periodically-waterlogged Boulder-clay soils. The analysis sets these in opposition to alder, oak as underwood, *Dryopteris* spp., *Lysimachia nemorum, Holcus mollis*, etc., plants of sandy soils, sometimes flooded by moving water, in the wood interior.

An ashwood on chalk: Watt's Wood, Aveley, South Essex

By a freak geological fold an outlier of the North Downs intrudes into the extreme south of Essex and provides the only ancient wood in Eastern England which grows directly on a chalk outcrop not masked by surface deposits. It establishes a link between East Anglian ashwoods and the classic 'hard-rock' ashwoods described on thin limestone soils elsewhere.

'Jack Watts Wood' is first recorded in 1532–3[273] and appears on a seventeenth-century map.[323] About half of it has been lost to agriculture and roadworks, but the remainder, though surrounded by a lunar landscape of vast chalk-pits, is in good condition. The wood occupies a north-facing scarp and extends on to a plateau on the south side. The plateau portion is acidic owing to sand and gravel masking the chalk. Calcareous woodland is confined to the scarp, which has a blackish well-drained soil much contaminated by sand.

The scarp woodland is dominated by ash and hazel with much hawthorn; there are patches of hornbeam, aspen, and cherry woodland, and elm invasions (Fig. 13.7). The ground is carpeted by ivy. The flora is quite rich and includes the full range of calcicolous shrubs: privet, wayfaring-tree (*Viburnum lantana*), dogwood, spindle, *Clematis*.

Despite the very different soil texture, this wood closely resembles the better-drained Boulder-clay woods of North Essex or Cambridgeshire. Although it is a good medieval wood, with sinuous outline and strong woodbanks, the ivy carpet and absence of dog's-mercury indicate that it may not be primary; it does however have wood-spurge (*Euphorbia amygdaloides*), an ancient woodland plant. The abundant evidence of Roman agriculture in the area[664] suggests that this may be a post-Roman secondary wood.

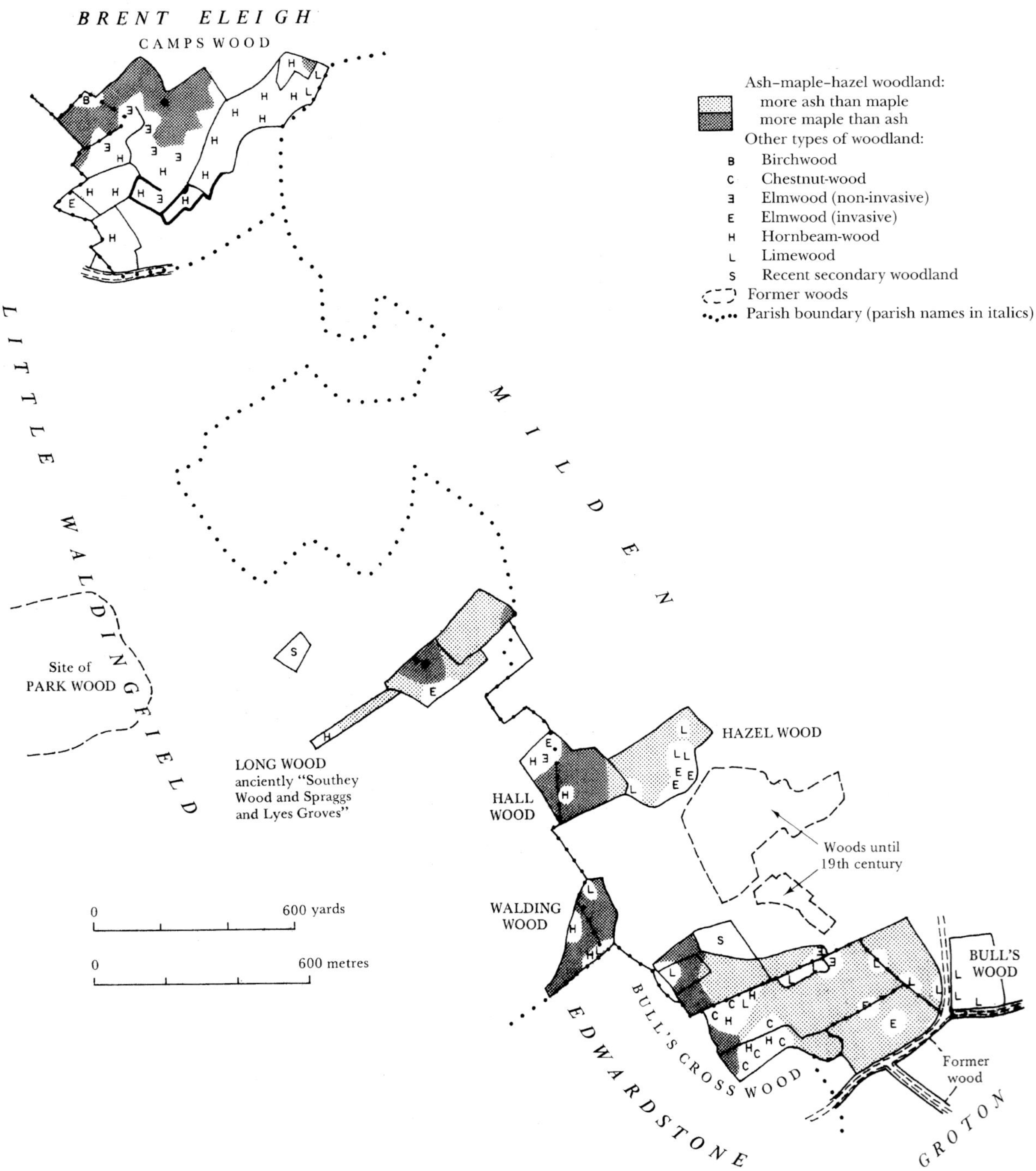

Fig. 13.5 Tree communities of the Milden Thicks group of woods. Internal earthworks are shown in a simplified form.

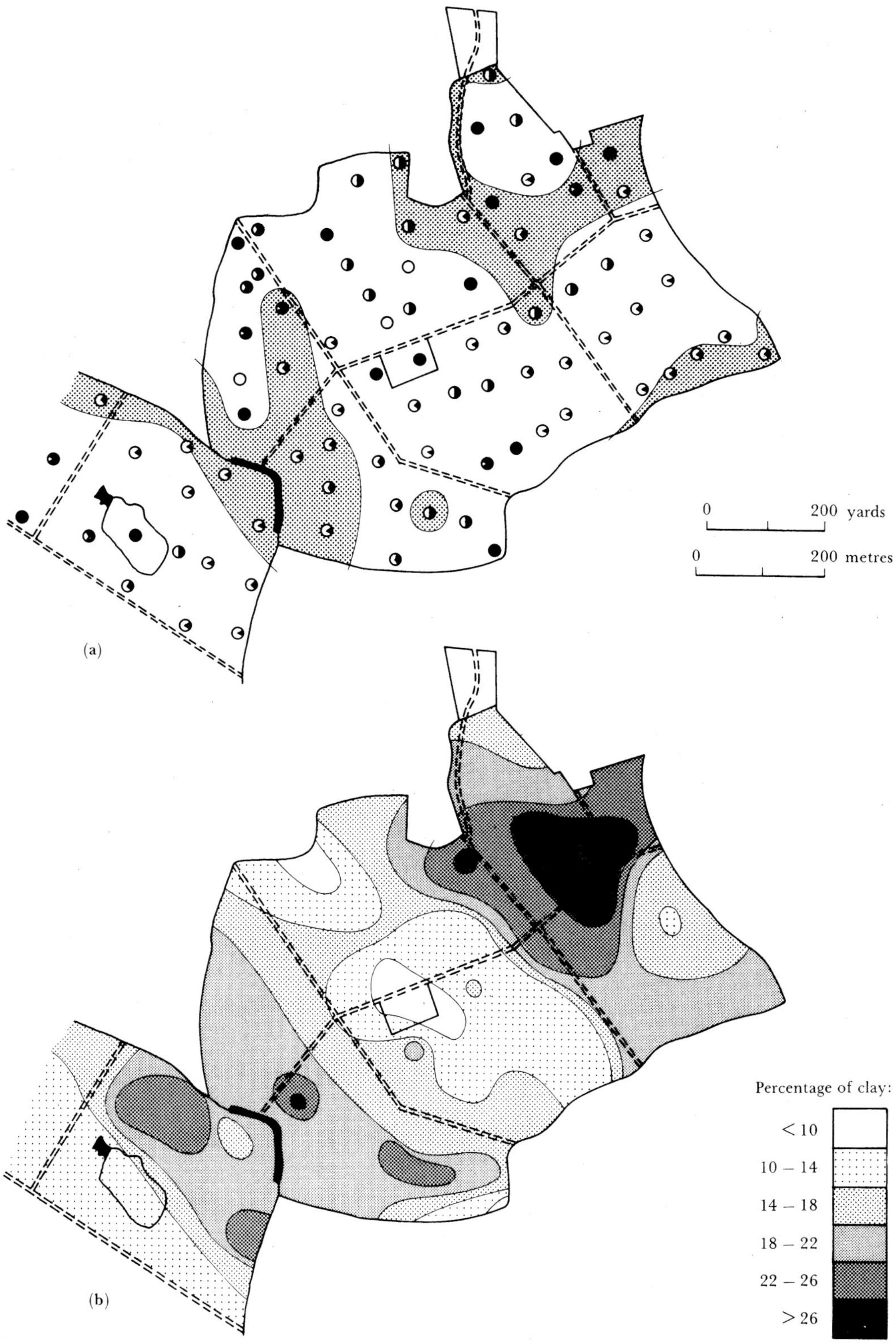

Fig. 13.6 The Bradfield Woods. (**a**) Distribution of ash, maple, and hazel. The points indicate the ratio of ash (white) to hazel (black) irrespective of the presence of other trees. Maple is frequent in the shaded areas. (**b**) Distribution of clay (particle size < 2 μm) in the topsoil (cf. Fig. 3.4).

Flora and effects of coppicing

Ash–maple–hazel woods have more species of flowering plants and ferns than any other woodland of Eastern England. Most of the woods celebrated for rich floras either have a high proportion of these types (e.g. Bradfield, Foxley Park (Norfolk), Hayley, Buff) or a wide range of other woodland types (e.g. Swanton Novers (Norfolk), Chalkney). The longest species lists are usually for ash–hazel woods on heavy, moderately calcareous, poorly drained soils. The other outstandingly rich woods of Britain, namely limestone ashwoods[106, 801] and the woodland mosaic of Bedford Purlieus,[129] are closely related to ash–hazel woods and also combine basic soils with only moderate shade.

The effects of coppicing have been discussed in Chapter 7, much of which is based on evidence from woods of this type. In the wetter parts of Hayley and Buff Woods the coppicing response is usually very strong, particularly by oxlips, primroses, bluebells, *Ajuga reptans*, violets (*Viola riviniana* and *V. reichenbachiana*), wood-anemones, and *Centaurium erythraea*. In summer the vegetation takes on a fen-like character, with abundant meadowsweet, *Lythrum salicaria*, *Cirsium palustre*, and often *Carex acutiformis* and *C. riparia*; wet hollows contain *Galium palustre* and *Ranunculus flammula*. Most of these plants also respond at Bradfield, where in addition *Geum rivale* and, in more acid areas, *Euphorbia amygdaloides* are very abundant in some seasons.

In ash–hazel woods less of the flora is strictly dependent on coppicing than in more densely-shading woodland; many species can persist, in reduced numbers, under thin places in the canopy or in woodland grassland. In Hayley Wood fewer than twenty species are recorded as wholly confined to coppiced areas, but this is probably unusual. In woods such as Buff Wood with a lower proportion of the less densely-shading ash, with fewer rides and glades and less well-developed margins, and with better drainage and more extensive mercury, more of the flora depends on coppicing.

Relations with woods elsewhere in Britain

Woods of these types are widespread but are unevenly covered in the literature and are often confused with oakwoods. There are, for instance, woods of ash, ash–hazel, hazel, and maple on clays and shales in the Neroche area of Somerset;[125] maple-woods on Clay-with-Flints and ash–hazel woods on chalk on the Grovely Ridge of Wiltshire (p. 185); maple–hazel woods on the scarp of the North Downs; and maple–thorn woods in Northamptonshire (Table 13.1).

Maple-woods, although widespread, seem never to have been described. Hazel-woods are familiar because of the specialized hazel crafts. The Forestry Commission census of 1947–9 reckoned that there were at least 114,000 acres of hazel coppice, a tenth of all broadleaved woodland and plantation in England;[61] although this actual figure is hardly credible – I suspect over-recording by people brought up to expect underwood to be hazel – hazel-woods are still very extensive in Lowland England. They have been neglected by ecologists, partly because of the unsubstantiated tradition that they are all planted. Pockets of hazel-wood in Ireland and in the Highlands of Scotland have been given more attention.[614, 753–4]

Ashwoods have been widely described as a calcareous woodland type on chalk or limestone soils, as in the

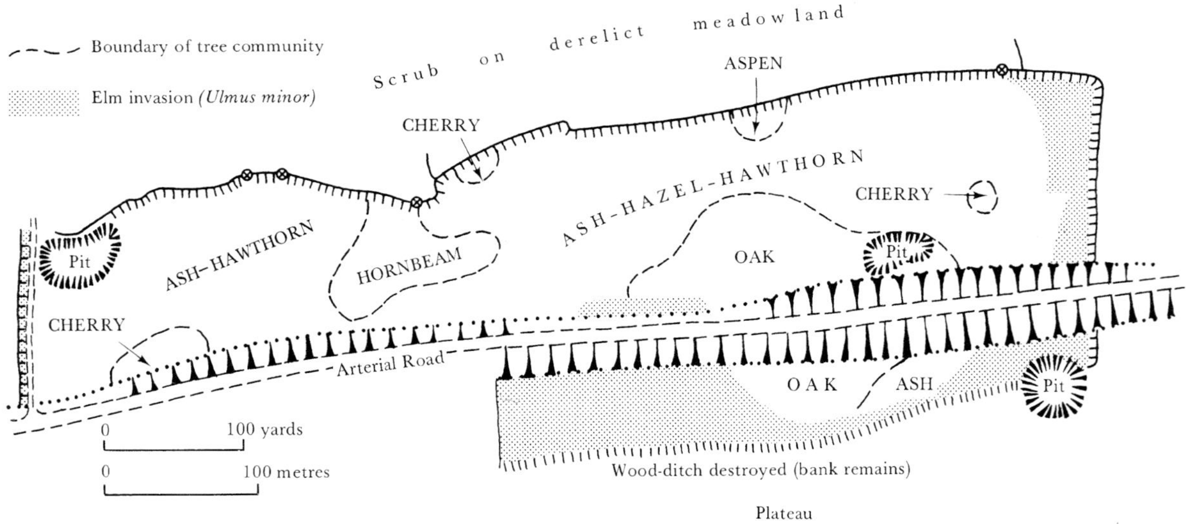

Fig. 13.7 Watt's Wood, Aveley. Topography and tree communities.

Mendips,[800] Derbyshire,[106, 801] the Pennines,[150] and the Western Highlands.[780, 850] Limestone ashwoods, even in the Scottish Highlands, are more closely related to ash–hazel woods and mixed hazel-woods than to the purer, acidic, ashwoods of Eastern England. Some of them are secondary woodland, and even in ancient woods ash has often not long been dominant. The Mendip limestone 'ash woods', for instance, are really hazel-woods (and limewoods) in the process of turning into ashwoods. Most of the ash is no older than the last coppicing but one; among the older stools hazel greatly outnumbers ash. Asham Wood, though officially a 'Mendip ashwood', still has much more hazel than ash; it closely resembles the less acidic mixed hazel-woods of East Anglia. The reasons for this ash invasion, which I have observed also in Shropshire 'ashwoods', are not clear.

Relations with Continental woodland

Ashwoods are not prominent in Continental literature, and woods of maple or hazel are rarely heard of at all. Maple is said to be frequent in the early stages of beech regeneration in the Forêt de Fontainebleau (p. 303) on *lessivé* soils over limestone;[13] this is very different from its more permanent function in English woods.

Several variants of ashwood have been described under the name of *chênaies-frênaies* (oak–ashwoods) from the Ile-de-France.[758] They are on chalk, limestone, or calcareous clays; they are usually well-drained; they include many plants of warmer climates.

Our less acidic ash–hazel woods resemble members of the alliance Alno-Fraxinion, described particularly from north Switzerland[52] and S.W. Germany.[809] Within this alliance, the associations which most closely correspond to our woods are the Aceri-Fraxinetum (named after *Acer pseudoplatanus*, not *A. campestre*) and the Carici remotae-Fraxinetum. The former has among its defining species anemone, *Carex pendula*, *C. sylvatica*, *Circaea lutetiana*, *Dryopteris filix-mas*, *Galeobdolon luteum*, dog's-mercury, *Oxalis*, *Paris quadrifolia*, and *Stachys sylvatica*; it approximates to the better-drained facies of our ash–hazel woods (e.g. the slopes of Hayley Wood, p. 37). The latter association is defined by alder, *Carex pendula* and *C. remota*, *Deschampsia caespitosa*, *Primula elatior*, *Ranunculus ficaria*, and *Veronica montana*; it approximates to the worst-drained facies of woods such as Hayley or Bradfield.

These European parallels cover little of the variation of English ash–maple–hazel woods, and the parallelism should not be pressed too far. Despite the many species in common, the Swiss woods are topographically very different from their East Anglian counterparts. Aceri-Fraxinetum, although on gleyed sites like our woods, is a woodland type of valleys rather than of plateaux or slopes. Carici remotae-Fraxinetum forms a narrow fringe to streams and does not extend over many acres as do our wet ashwoods.

General conclusions

Ash–maple–hazel woods are the common woodland of the heavier and more calcareous soils of Eastern England; some types extend well outside this soil range. Woods of ash and hazel and to a lesser extent maple are widely scattered throughout the British Isles. All the types appear to be much less prominent on the Continent, and the acidic woods and maple-woods may not be known there.

The historic record indicates that some of these woods have existed, with recognizably similar proportions of species, for at least 1,000 years. Hazel-woods have been widely regarded as a very artificial variant, but the evidence from pollen and archaeology proves that this is not so: almost throughout Britain there have been hazel-woods continuously since the pre-Neolithic – and neither the alleged planting of hazel nor its unintended encouragement by coppicing have had any large effect on its abundance. Some ashwoods may result from human activity, as an indirect effect of Neolithic agriculture, but others could have arisen from ash-rich types of wildwood. The origin of maple-woods is unknown; compartmented wood-pasture may have encouraged them, but they are not confined to such sites.

Conservation

Ash–maple–hazel woodland has shared the fortunes of ancient woodland in general: at least a third of that in Eastern England has been destroyed since 1945 (Fig. 6.1). As a whole these woods are still quite abundant: but because of their complexity and beauty and their richness in plant species they deserve protection on a large scale which shall encompass the many different combinations of tree and ground-vegetation communities. They appear to be a particular responsibility of the British Isles: our oak-woods and hornbeam-woods are outliers of Continental vegetation, but ashwoods carpeted with bluebells or hazel-woods with primroses are not so easily found overseas. Hazel, as one of the two or three trees that have most influenced the history of our particular civilization, deserves to be better studied and treated with respect.

Ash–hazel and mixed hazel-woods are represented in reserves such as Hayley and Buff Woods (Cambs), the Bradfield Woods and Wolve's Wood (Suffolk), Monks' Wood (Hunts), and Wayland Wood (Norfolk), besides others elsewhere in Britain. For further nature reserves preference ought perhaps to be given to variants that are strongly acid or contain much maple.

The floras of ash–maple–hazel woods depend to some extent on coppicing for their maintenance, although neglect seldom results in irreversible losses: in Hayley Wood, where there was no coppicing for 42 years,[120] there is only one recorded extinction attributable to this cause (Table 5.4). These woods have benefited from the recent revival of conservation and commercial coppicing: in several woods such as Monks' Wood, Buff, and Hayley, and in Hatfield Forest over ten acres are in rotation. Ash is usually the more valuable commercial underwood.

The most serious problems concern hazel, which is difficult to use commercially because of the decline of the faggot trade. There is a strong demand for wattle hurdles (for garden and motorway fencing) and thatching-wood – indeed it is often difficult to get underwood suitable for making them – but such specialized crafts did not use up all the hazel in the past and cannot be expected to do so now. Much of a hazel crop, particularly if neglected, is too large, too small, or too crooked for specialized use yet too small for pulpwood or logs. This is not a new problem – it is another reason for doubting the story that most hazel-woods were planted – but some modern substitute for the laborious making of faggots would be a great advantage.

Hazel is threatened by apparent failure of reproduction and establishment combined with competition from oak, ash, and other taller trees. In the last thirty years the number of individuals has declined from natural causes as well as grubbing, and this is likely to continue. Hazcl is probably already a relict; it is the most threatened of common trees other than elms.

Fig. 13.8 Pure Ashwood. The flooding in a very wet winter is significant (Chapter 31). Hayley Wood. February 2001

Fig.13.9 Ash–Hazel-wood. The ash and accompanying aspen are not yet in leaf; the hazel and accompanying hawthorn form a leafy understory. The standard oaks are not distinctive of this woodland type. Hayley Wood. April 1967

Fig. 13.10 Pure Hazel-wood. Hazel grows tall and is the dominant tree; only in this state does it produce significant amounts of pollen (p. 101). Hatfield Forest. February 1981

Fig. 13.11 Maple-wood. Maple is a tree which is easily uprooted and often survives (Chapter 28). Barton Leys, Barton Bendish, Norfolk. November 1995

14

The hornbeam-woods

Hornbeam (*Carpinus betulus*) is local in Britain but being the commonest woodland tree around London it used to be relatively well studied, notably by E. J. Salisbury[136–7] and M. Christy[21] in the 1910s and 1920s. On the Continent it is very widespread and in much of Germany and France is one of the three commonest woodland trees; it is not now a forester's tree but is well known to phytosociologists.

Present distribution

Hornbeam, as an apparently native tree, is confined to particular areas of southern and eastern England, where it is abundant in wood-pasture and (rarely) ancient hedges. The biggest such area is in Essex, Hertfordshire, and Middlesex (Fig. 14.1). In South Essex and S.E. Hertfordshire hornbeam occupies more than half of most ancient woods and wood-pastures. Outwards from this heartland it diminishes in every direction and becomes rare in the Chilterns and West Cambridgeshire. A second heartland of abundant hornbeam, again surrounded by an outer zone of scattered occurrence, is centred on Harleston on the Norfolk–Suffolk border. In the Ipswich area, midway between the heartlands, hornbeam is uncommon.

Outside Eastern England there is a large hornbeam area in Kent and Sussex, and small areas of apparently native hornbeam occur as far west as the Bristol area and the lower Wye.[21] Hornbeam is scattered as a plantation tree over most of the British Isles; native and planted occurrences have often been confused.

Prehistory and history

The pollen record

Hornbeam was abundant in earlier interglacial periods; it is specially characteristic of the later part of each interglacial (p. 103). Its prehistory in the present interglacial is not well known owing to the apparent lack of suitable deposits in areas where it is now abundant. Apart from an uncertain record at Hockham (Norfolk) in Zone VI it is first known in the Early Neolithic.[710] Since it is a good pollen producer and has distinctive fruits, it is unlikely – despite the deficiencies of the record – that its presence in earlier periods could have been overlooked had it been as abundant as it is now. It is just possible that the tree reached this country by human agency, although deliberate introduction is unlikely because it has no known specific uses.

From the Neolithic onwards small amounts of pollen and occasional finds of charcoal and wood are known from as far north as Norfolk and possibly Lancashire and as far west as Somerset.[710] Hornbeam charcoal reported from Roman Wroxeter (Salop)[21] would be important if correct, but depends on an early and perhaps uncertain identification. This evidence suggests that hornbeam expanded rapidly in the Neolithic and came to be rather more widespread but less abundant than it is now. Further evidence for the late attainment of its present abundance comes from two pollen diagrams from within the present heartland. At Hampstead Heath[701] the deposit extends well after the Elm Decline without containing any hornbeam. In Epping Forest[8] the rise of hornbeam is carbon-dated as late as the Anglo-Saxon period.

Place-names

Hornbeam is the least documented of common trees. As a woodland tree, it has rarely been noticed except by people concerned with woods; being very gregarious, it would often have been too commonplace to be worthy of record. It is a poor timber tree; it produces no nuts, no fibre, no fodder except for deer; it does nothing that other species will not do as well; and even, as Gerarde remarks in his Herbal,[340] 'This tree is not used in medicine'. It is difficult to identify and hence useless as a landmark. We confuse it with beech, but our ancestors, who were less familiar with beech, mistook it for hazel or elm; the name 'wych-hazel', formerly applied to both hornbeam and elm, sums up both confusions.

Apart from one unhelpful Anglo-Saxon citation, the earliest probable allusion to hornbeam appears to be the place-name *Herinbeme*gatestret in Essendon, S.E. Hertfordshire in 1367.[717] There are three similar medieval hornbeam place-names in Hertfordshire and Middlesex.[719]

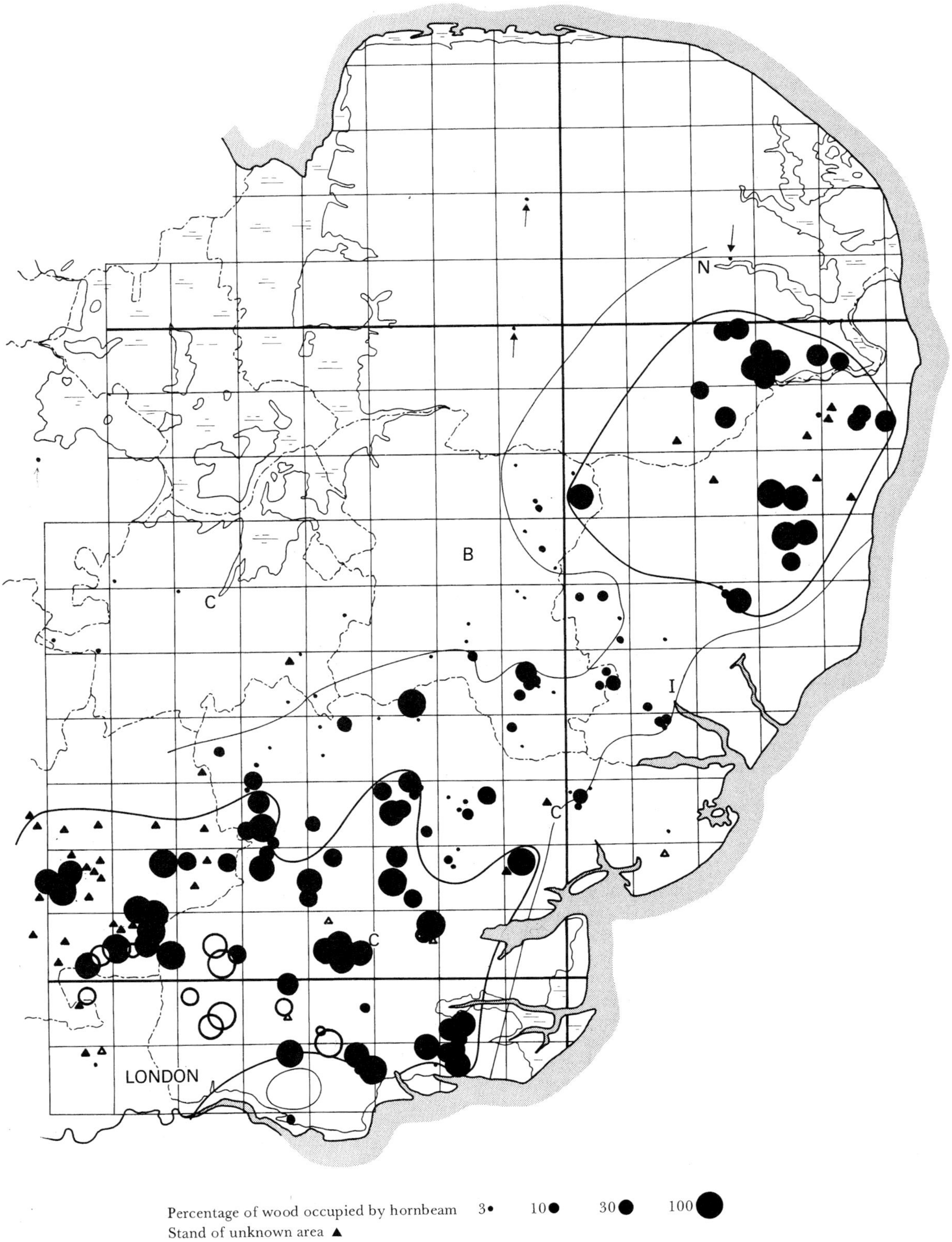

Fig. 14.1 Relative abundance of hornbeam in ancient woods. (●) hornbeam in woodland; (○) hornbeam in wood-pasture. The thick lines define the two 'heartlands' in which hornbeam is the commonest woodland tree. The thin lines define an outer zone in which some hornbeam was found in every ancient wood visited. Arrows draw attention to outlying points.

Surveys

Hornbeam, alias 'hardbeam', is first recorded on a large scale in sixteenth-century surveys which detail species of pollards and underwood. At Redgrave (Suffolk) in 1540 part of the *ci-devant* Abbot of Bury's park comprised:

> 30 acres thyn sett with pollyng [pollard] okes and hardebeme growing by parcelles . . . the wood ys old and groweth by parcelles in the parke . . . which once fallen shall never by any wood agayne.[220]

In 1565 a survey of the parks on the Crown estate at New Hall in Boreham (Essex) reported, *inter alia*:[460]

> Bulles Wood set with underwood of sapling oak of 30, 36 or 40 years growth and of hornbeam maple ash of like age 8 acres 3 roods
> Hawkes Wood set with underwood of hornbeam of 16 years growth and staddled with sapling oaks of 40 or 50 years growth 7 ac. 3 r.
> Creke Coppice set with beeches maples and hornbeam of 16 years growth well staddled with oak like 60 or 80 years growth 9 ac. 2 r.
>
> . . . .
>
> LITTLE PARK. There is growing dispersedly . . . divers oaks ashes and hornbeams commonly used to be shredd [p. 5] for browse for the deer . . . 8 ac.

The latter survey included also the parks and accompanying woods at Little Easton and Havering Park (Essex). Hornbeam ocurred in all the nine woods for which the underwood was specified, and also in wood-pasture. In Easton and Havering Parks it was pollarded; at New Hall and Havering it was shredded and provided browse for the deer.

None of these places survives intact: for a comparison with modern vegetation we turn to a survey of Hainault Forest (S.W. Essex) by G. Maxey and W. Mildmay in 1544.[352] The Forest was uncompartmented, but was divided into parcels for the purpose of the survey, for example:

> Furste, in a certen Comen . . . one hill called Greate Hoghill parte Hornbeame Woode well sett with Oke for Husbandrye, very moche verte of blake Thorne, part lately lopped cont. 63 Acr' one roode at 13*s* 4*d* the Acre . . .
>
> Ravensokehill cont. 67½ Acres valued at 40*s* the Acre well sett with husbandez of Oke and hardbeame . . .
>
> Beche hill sett with straglynge Trees of Oke and hornebeame cont. by estimacion 82½ acres at 18*s* the Acre . . .

The trees are specified in eleven of the parcels as follows:

Hornbeam in 10 parcels	Blackthorn in 2 parcels
Oak in 9 parcels	Birch in 1 parcel

In five parcels the oaks were described as 'husbands', i.e. pollards.[919]

Hainault Forest was reduced to one-twelfth of its area after 1851. The surviving fragments have changed remarkably little in vegetation since 1544, though they have been neither grazed nor pollarded for at least half a century. There is now rather less blackthorn and oak and more hornbeam and birch, and there is some holly which was not listed in 1544.

There are many references to the hornbeams of Epping Forest from the sixteenth century onwards. In Enfield Chase (Middx) the 'hornbeam and other woode' was valued in 1650 at 30*s* an acre, excluding timber.[41]

Gerarde in 1597[340] says that the tree 'groweth plentifully in Northamptonshire' – which is no longer so: there are only a few outlying sites where it may be native. He also refers to it in Kent. Another early record in an area where it is now rare is by Ray (1660) for Abington in Cambridgeshire.[466] Evelyn in *Sylva*[335] says it is 'no where more abounding in the South, than in the Woods of *Hartfordshire*; very few Westward'. The Swedish traveller Pehr Kalm refers to old hornbeam pollards on Northaw Common (Herts) (p. 226) in 1753–6.[21]

Historical conclusions

The 'natural' limits of hornbeam appear to be south and east of the line Weymouth–Hereford–Norwich. It achieved such a distribution by Roman times or earlier, and still grows in large or small quantities in native woods over much of this region. Its rise to its present abundance over a more limited area took place too late to appear on most pollen diagrams, although written records show that where hornbeam is now abundant it has been so for at least 400 years. The Essex–Hertfordshire heartland was established by A.D. 1500 at the latest; wherever there survives a survey which specifies the underwood, hornbeam is consistently the commonest species, both in woodland and wood-pasture. The Redgrave survey, recording trees that were already old and declining, suggests that the Harleston heartland had become established by 1400 or earlier.

There is some evidence for a decline of hornbeam outside the heartlands. The finds in Wessex and the Wye valley suggest that in prehistoric and Roman times it was not as rare as it is now, and Gerarde's record suggests a more recent decline in Northamptonshire. Although much of the hornbeam in these outlying counties has been planted, there may be some relict stands as well.

The management of hornbeam

Hornbeam is seldom heard of as a timber tree. It is hard and difficult to work; it rarely comes in large sizes because most trees have fluted trunks and inclusions of bark. It is said to have been used for pulley-sheaves, gear-teeth, the yokes of oxen and milkmaids, and the works of pianos, where hardness and resistance to wear are all-important; but there are alternatives for these purposes and only trivial amounts can have been so used.

A few timber sales are recorded for South Weald (S. Essex). In 1804 hornbeam bollings fetched 1*s* 3*d* per cubic foot (compared with ash bollings, 1*s* 4*d*, and oak bollings, 2*s* 10*d*).[321] In 1868 hornbeams, evidently timber trees, still sold for a little less than ash.[322]

As wood, hornbeam is brittle, crooked, and non-durable, and not very suitable for poles or wattle, but it has a supreme reputation as fuel. Presumably hornbeam, with beech, was the chief provider of the billets and charcoal which, together with coal, formed the fuel of medieval and Tudor London.

The growth of coppiced or pollarded hornbeam is rather slow in the first few years. We might expect it to be cut on a long rotation for billets and logs rather than faggots. The statutory sizes for London billets (p. 143) would take at least fifteen years to grow, and there is some direct evidence for the practice in the Middle Ages. Tindall Wood in Ditchingham (E. Norfolk), now about 80% hornbeam, was described in 1270 as 'Underwood. 4 score acres of which 5 acres can be sold annually at £4 10*s*'.[447] This sixteen-year rotation is unusually long for that period, and the income was about one and a half times the average – though this may result from the general scarcity of wood in Norfolk. Logs are specifically mentioned (p. 142). On the other hand coppice cycles in other woodland surveys in the Harleston hornbeam area – e.g. five and a third years at Kelsale in 1270,[447] five years at Sibton in 1325,[261] four years at Pulham in 1251[270] – are no longer than usual.

By the sixteenth century most hornbeam was being grown for big firewood. In the South Essex surveys most of the hornbeam is said to be of at least sixteen, and once as much as forty, years' growth. In Basildon (S. Essex) in 1558–9 estate accounts record the sale of 115,000 'Bylletts et talwood' (p. 142) for nearly £70, as well as logs (*ligni focal' voc' Loggs*).[367] At Sotterley in the Harleston hornbeam area, large sales of 'le Billetts' are recorded for 1598–1602.[366] In the eighteenth and nineteenth centuries the numerous coppice cycles recorded for Writtle Forest[315] and other South Essex hornbeam woods average around fifteen years.

It is possible that the present abundance of hornbeam has been influenced by the local preference of past woodmen or their customers for logs and big underwood. As we shall see, a long coppice rotation might be expected to increase the proportion of hornbeam against other trees. Unfortunately we have not quite enough information to explore this hypothesis.

The timber trees in hornbeam woods are normally oak, although some of the Harleston group of woods have many ash standards. Although hornbeam is very densely shading there seems until recently to have been no difficulty in replacing the oaks; the stools grow so slowly at first that an oakling ought to be able to keep up with them.

Modern ecology

Hornbeam is a gregarious tree which tends to form pure stands rather than to be scattered through a wood; sometimes the stands continue into an adjacent wood. In some places, however, pure stands of hornbeam are the result of neglect of coppicing which allows it to suppress other species.

Hornbeam in woods, wood-pasture, and hedges

Hornbeam is almost equally a woodland and a wood-pasture tree. Since at least the sixteenth century it has occurred as coppice-stools, wood-boundary stubs or pollards, and free-standing pollards. In Hatfield Forest (Essex), hornbeam areas in the coppices are continued as tracts of pollards in the adjacent plains (Fig. 14.2), although hornbeam forms a higher proportion of the pollards than it does of the coppice stools. Despite the historic records of feeding hornbeam to deer, presumably as iron rations, they do not enjoy it; I find that they browse it less than any other common tree except aspen.

Hornbeam has the reputation of rarely being a standard tree; as Christy remarks, 'a mature wild-grown example in its natural condition is very seldom seen'. This is no longer true; I have noted standard trees in 17 out of 115 woods containing more than five acres of hornbeam. Occasionally they form a quarter of all the timber trees. The beautiful hornbeams of Buff Wood are familiar to generations of Cambridge botanists, and there are some in Hatfield Forest as big as very large oaks. Possibly in recent decades, as standard oaks became difficult to replace, woodmen took to promoting hornbeam as a substitute, even though it is such an unsuitable tree for timber. Standard trees are strikingly variable, particularly in habit: a very elegant genotype has a fan-shaped crown of slender straight branches radiating from a shortish trunk.

In a few places hornbeam grows in ancient hedges, particularly in the Harleston hornbeam area, where some of the gaps in the distribution caused by absence of woodland can be filled by hedgerow hornbeams.

Reproduction and longevity

Hornbeam sets abundant seed in some years; this germinates freely in the second spring. Seedlings appear to be rather light-demanding and seldom live beyond a year even under the shade of other and less dense trees; but severe disturbance and sometimes ordinary coppicing allow new hornbeams to be established. Hatfield Forest contains some good examples.

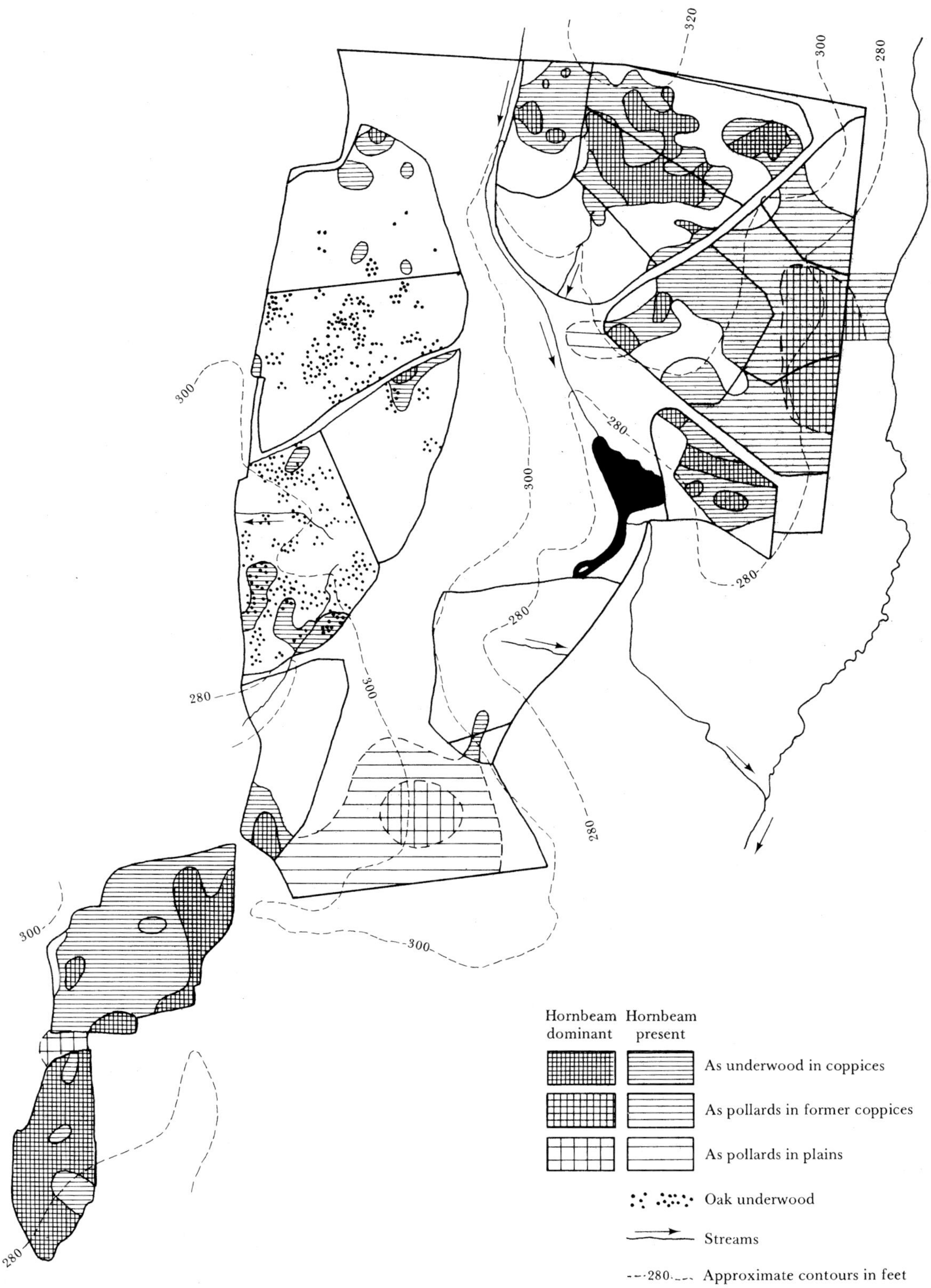

Fig. 14.2 Distribution of hornbeam in the coppices and plains of Hatfield Forest, Essex (cf. Fig. 12.6). Oak coppice is also shown; the dots indicate its general distribution, not individual stools.

The longevity of hornbeam is difficult to determine. The annual rings are faint, contorted, and difficult to count; coppice stools are of very irregular shapes and it is difficult to tell individuals apart. Pollards live to a considerable age; the north-eastern coppices of Hatfield Forest were converted to pollards around 1700, and many of the pollards then made still flourish, some of them in pairs and threes arising from the original stool. An average age for a big hornbeam pollard is likely to be about 300 years. Coppice stools, although they seldom reach the imposing size of lime or ash, often exceed 7 ft (2 m) across and are likely to be of similar age [Fig. 14.7].

The survival of hornbeam depends partly on management. After coppicing, some stools usually die, but are replaced by new saplings provided that some trees are left uncut for long enough to produce seed. If the coppice rotation is less than about fifteen years and there are no standard hornbeams, the lack of seed places the species at a disadvantage compared with hazel, which fruits on a shorter coppice cycle, or with lime, whose stools rarely die. Hornbeam is thus favoured by long-rotation coppicing. At present it appears to be in general equilibrium with other species, although there are instances of local advance or retreat.

Hornbeam in secondary woodland

Hornbeam is rarely a first invader of non-woodland sites. An abandoned common or field next to any kind of hornbeam wood is invaded by oak, birch, or hawthorn; only within a few yards of the wood does hornbeam invade. This was observed by Salisbury in the 1910s in Hertfordshire,[138] and by Adamson in the 1920s in the Danbury area of Essex;[2] it can still be seen in both counties. Hornbeam generally appears after the first felling of the new wood; most older secondary woods adjoining ancient hornbeam woods are themselves hornbeam-dominated. The complete process can take at least 100 years. Northaw Great Wood, for instance, is on the site of an ancient Hertfordshire wood-pasture common, most of which was destroyed in the last century leaving only a small area of hornbeam pollards. Since then it has reverted to semi-natural woodland, but little of it is hornbeam as yet.

Besides these secondary woods naturally colonized by hornbeam, there are many others where it has certainly or probably been planted, either outside the tree's distribution in ancient woodland (as with nineteenth-century hornbeam groves in Cambridgeshire

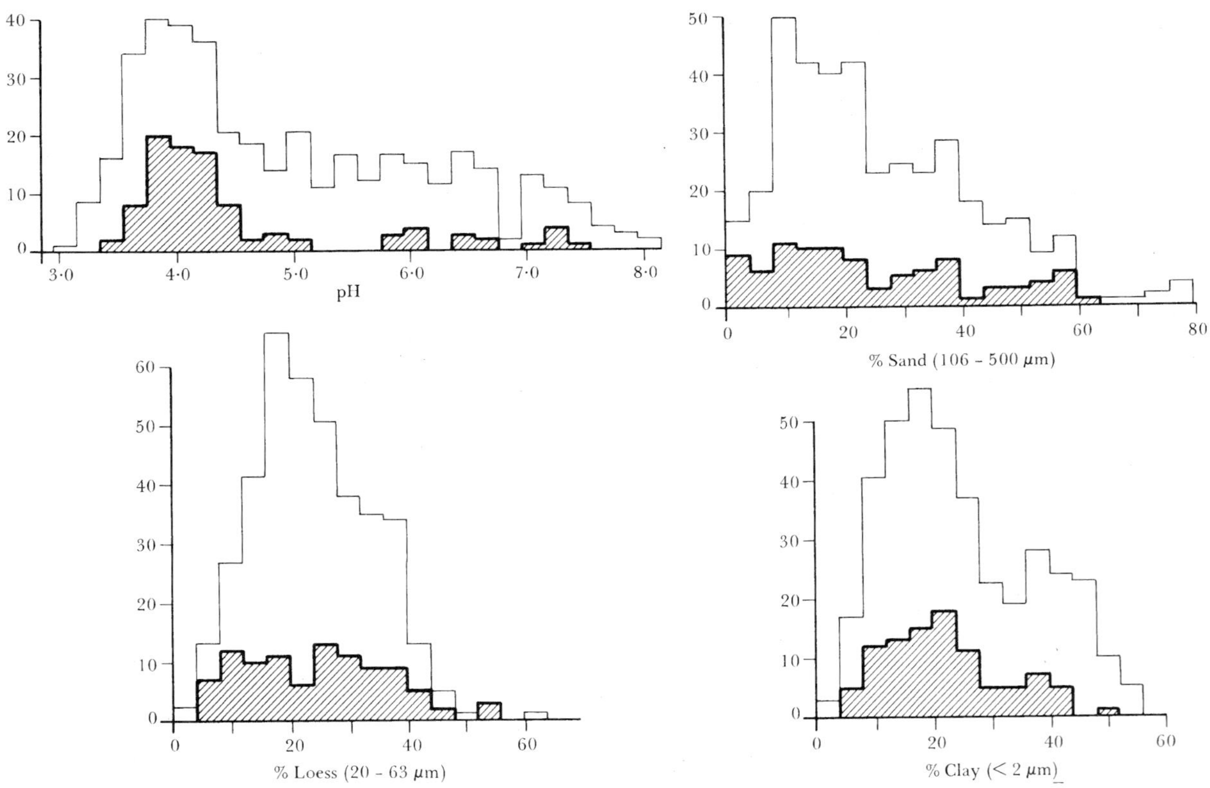

Fig. 14.3 Distribution of topsoil acidity and composition under hornbeam in the ancient woods of Eastern England. For comparison, the distribution of soil characteristics in all the woods sampled is shown by thin outlines. For further details see caption to Fig. 7.5.

and Huntingdonshire) or within a hornbeam area but remote from older woods (e.g. the eighteenth-century Blake's and Ladies' Groves in Redenhall, S. Norfolk). Hornbeam was popular with silvicultural writers either for underwood or as a nurse for timber trees. In the Chilterns, where native hornbeam is uncommon, the beechwoods often have hornbeam boundary-hedges; it is the only hedge-plant that withstands the shade of beech. Around Beaconsfield (Bucks) hornbeam trees are associated with internal banks running through the beechwoods and are probably descended from hornbeam hedges planted along property boundaries. Apart from these wood-hedges I know of no evidence that it was ever planted in an existing wood.

The historical significance of hornbeam varies. In areas of extensive recent woodland, such as Langdon Hills (pp. 8–10), its presence picks out the ancient woods; conversely, away from the main distributions of hornbeam, it gives rise to suspicions of planting.

Soils

Hornbeam grows mainly in the Acid Soil Province of Eastern England, but is slightly less calcifuge than lime; some large stands (e.g. Hempstead Wood (N.W. Essex), Westhall Wood (Rickinghall Inferior, Suffolk)) are on calcareous soils. Under it the pH (Fig. 14.3) usually ranges from 3.6 to 4.6 but can be as high as 7.6. The commonest humus type is a thin mor.

The topsoils are either high or low in sand or loess and of moderate clay content (Fig. 14.3). Those of the Essex Hertfordshire heartland, typically clayey loess or clay-loess, differ from the clayey sands of the Harleston area. Hornbeam generally avoids soils very high in clay (Cambs, N.W. Essex) or very low in clay (e.g. the outcrops of chalk and gravel in S. Essex).

Hornbeam plant communities

Salisbury[136–7] described two kinds of hornbeam-wood in Hertfordshire: the '*Quercus robur-Carpinus*' woods and the '*Quercus sessiliflora-Carpinus*' woods. These were differentiated by whether the timber trees growing with the hornbeam were *Quercus robur* or what we now call *Q. petraea*: a distinction strongly correlated with differences of woodland structure, of surface geology and soil, of associated trees and shrubs, and of ground vegetation. Some of Salisbury's woods are still extant; his two types extend almost throughout South Essex as well as Hertfordshire; but further north most hornbeam-woods are different from either.

Having observed 198 woods containing hornbeam in Eastern England, I propose four types of hornbeam woodland which I shall call maple–hornbeam, hornbeam–ash, pure hornbeam, and oak–hornbeam. The last two correspond closely to Salisbury's '*robur-Carpinus*' and '*sessiliflora-Carpinus*' woods; the first two lie almost wholly outside his study area. They have a definite geographical distribution (Fig. 14.4); although intermediate and mosaic stands occur, it is usually possible to assign the hornbeam in any one wood to one of the four types. The structures and soil ranges are set out in Table 14.1; the trees adjoining hornbeam and the ground vegetation beneath it are analysed in Tables 6.2 and 6.3.

(i) Maple–hornbeam woods [Fig. 14.8]

Woods in which there is at least as much *Acer* as *Fraxinus* in the vicinity of *Carpinus* are mainly on the north-west edge of the range of hornbeam; nearly half the area is in Hatfield Forest. The stands are usually small, never more than thirty acres; in half of them hornbeam forms less than 4% of the wood in which it occurs. After maple, the commonest trees adjoining hornbeam are hazel and ash, then elms. The ground vegetation is most commonly dominated by dog's-mercury, followed by *Deschampsia caespitosa*, bluebells, and primroses.

Maple–hornbeam stands are usually set amid the maple or maple–hazel woodland of the Boulder-clay. This is the most calcareous of the hornbeam woodland types, though pHs are often below 5. Hornbeam tends to occupy flat ill-drained hilltops as in Hatfield Forest (Fig. 14.2): whence the *Deschampsia caespitosa*, primroses, and occasionally oxlip on sites too winter-wet for mercury (p. 37). The soils are heavier and more calcareous than those of other hornbeam-woods; the pHs below 5 may result from greater acidification on ill-drained sites, from hornbeam's tendency to promote such acidification, or from its tendency (as in Buff Wood) to occupy small pockets of more silty soil.

(ii) Hornbeam–ash woods

These are the most numerous hornbeam-woods, especially in Norfolk, Suffolk, and North Essex. The stands vary in size from a few stools up to 100 acres; half of them occupy a quarter or more of their woods. Ash and hazel are the commonest adjacent trees, followed by lime – a very significant association – and elms. In some woods aspen is prominent. Most woods of this type are definitely acidic, with pHs usually below 5 and often a thin layer of mor. Mercury is still the commonest ground dominant but is followed by the more acid-tolerant brambles and bluebells.

Hornbeam–ash stands are rather heterogeneous. In the north-west they merge with maple–hornbeam woodland and in the south with pure hornbeam. Soil textures are variable but usually lighter than those under maple–hornbeam. In the big hornbeam-woods of the Harleston area (see Sexton Wood later) the soils are at least half sand; in North Essex they contain much loess. In both districts hornbeam tends to grow in places of intermediate drainage. In Essex it occupies a position

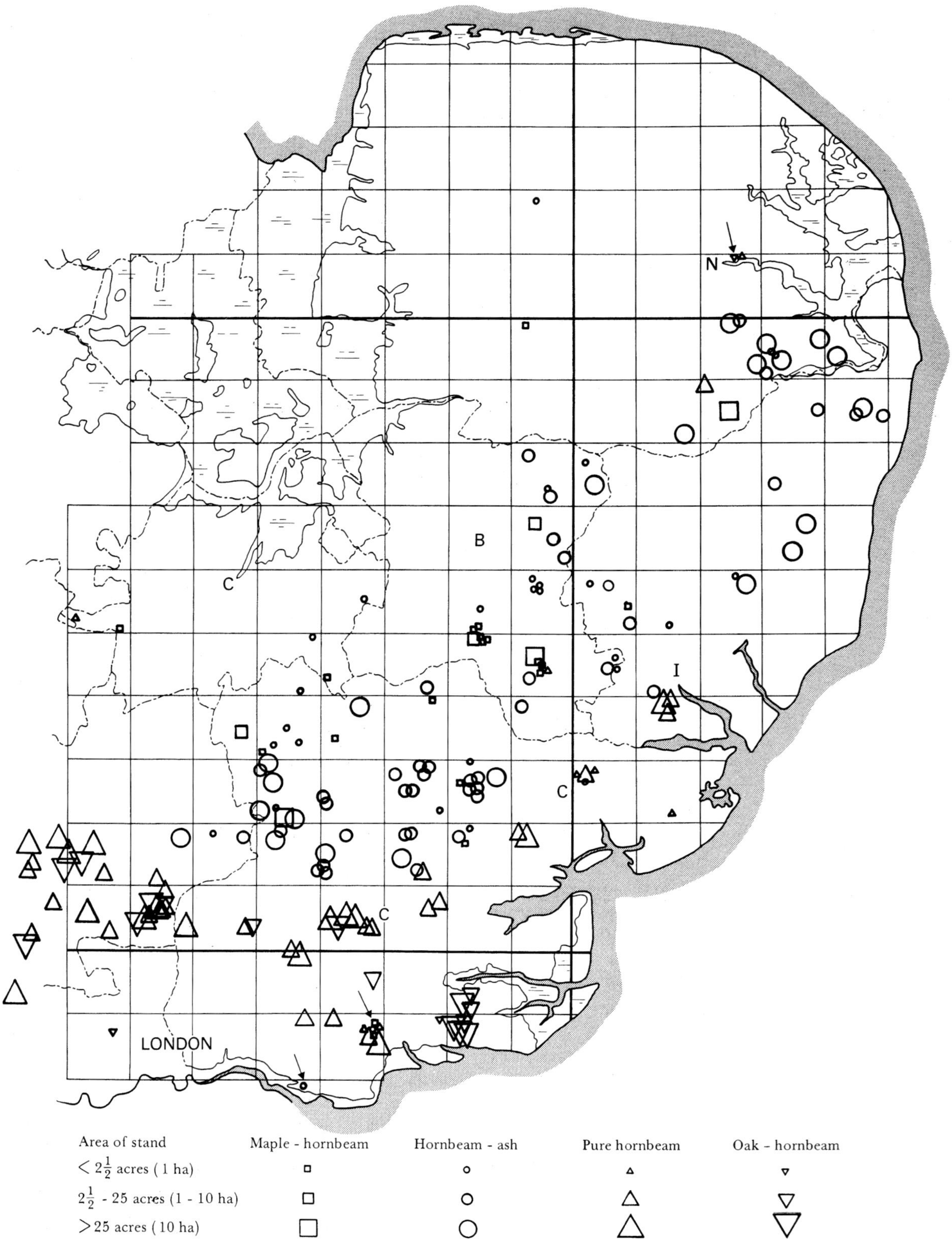

Fig. 14.4 Distribution of the four types of hornbeam woodland. Woods are classified according to which type predominates. Arrows draw attention to outlying occurrences.

Table 14.1 Types of hornbeam woodland in ancient coppices.

	Maple–hornbeam	Hornbeam–ash	Pure hornbeam	Oak–hornbeam
Number of woods seen	33	97	41	17
Average (median) area of hornbeam per wood, acres (ha)	2(0.8)	5(2.0)	35(14)	30(12)
Average (median) ratio of hornbeam to total area of wood	4%	25%	60%	55%
Typical woodland structure	Coppice with standards	Coppice with standards	Coppice with standards	Standards with sparse coppice
Species of oak	*robur*	*robur*	*robur*	*petraea* or mixture
Soil humus type	Mull, rarely mor	Mull or mor	Mor, rarely mull	Mor
pH of mineral soil	(4.1)4.9–7.5	(3.6–)3.8–4.9(–7.3)	(3.4–)3.5–4.4(–4.7)	3.5–4.0
Percentage weight of Sand (212–500 μm)	2–7(–11)	6–32(–46)	(0–)2–10(–46)	1–10
Silt (20–63 μm)	16–32	6–34(–42)	(8–)28–45(–55)	(18–)30–39
Clay (< 2 μm)	21–42	(6–)10–36(–42)	7–22(–26)	(7–)11–19(–22)
Commonest soil unit as mapped by the Soil Survey[637, 739, 889, 895]	Hanslope (calcareous surface-water gley)	Beccles, Hornbeam, Oak (non-calcareous surface-water gleys of varying texture)	Wickham, Bursledon, Essendon (non-calcareous surface-water gleys of varying origin	Not yet mapped

between lime on the ill-drained hilltops and elm or ash–hazel on the steepest slopes (e.g. Chalkney Wood, pp. 248–9); in the Harleston area it is replaced on the worst-drained terrain – which here is in shallow valleys – by variants of ash–maple–hazel.

(iii) Pure hornbeam-woods

These predominate in South Essex and Hertfordshire. They are defined as stands without extensive *Mercurialis* or other relatively calcicolous plants, but with little or no *Quercus petraea*. They are fewer than ash–hornbeam woods but much larger: an entire wood may contain little but hornbeam. The commonest associated trees are birch and chestnut. Ash, maple, and hazel are much less common and often indicate patches of more calcareous vegetation; elms and aspen are still relatively frequent. An uncommon but important abuttal is with alder in valley bottoms. In the ground vegetation, bracken is almost as common as brambles; bluebells are often abundant, but calcicole plants are almost absent.

Soils under pure hornbeam are strongly acid, although – despite the great differences in vegetation – there is much overlap with those under hornbeam–ash. This is the commonest woodland type on soils with a large silt content. In mid Hertfordshire it is the typical woodland of 'loess-with-flints' – a concrete-hard silty variant of Clay-with-Flints, often so thin as to be ignored by the Geological Survey, so that one finds this very acid woodland on what is officially mapped as Upper Chalk.

(iv) Oak–hornbeam woods

These are also largely confined to South Essex and Hertfordshire. Although few they usually have a high proportion of hornbeam, and include some very large woods such as Wormley Wood near Cheshunt. This woodland type, unusually, is distinguished mainly by its timber trees and structure rather than by its underwood. The oaks are largely *Quercus petraea*; all woods with more than 30% of definite *petraea* are here assigned to this type. Oaks are much more numerous and often smaller than those in the other woodland types, generally forming an almost complete canopy beneath which there is a correspondingly sparse and weak understorey of hornbeam. The vegetation is even more calcifuge than that of pure hornbeam-woods. Birch is less common and chestnut very common; aspen is more frequent than in any other kind of hornbeam-wood; in some woods there is oak coppice; service and alder buckthorn (*Frangula alnus*), though rare, are very typical of these woods. The ground vegetation is most commonly dominated by bracken, followed by brambles; bluebells are uncommon. These differences from pure hornbeam-woods are broadly similar to those recorded by Salisbury, although there are discrepancies of detail, partly because he worked in Hertfordshire in which, for instance, chestnut is less common than in Essex, and partly because his '*robur-Carpinus*' woods included a few areas of what is here distinguished as ash–hornbeam.

Oak–hornbeam woodland tends to be on slightly more acid soils than pure hornbeam, but it is difficult to find any consistent soil distinction between the two types. Salisbury claimed that the *sessiliflora* woods were on the more sandy soils and the *robur* woods on those that were at least half silt and clay, and that these differences were related to the underlying geology. However, if we include measurements in Essex it becomes impossible to separate oak–hornbeam from pure hornbeam woods on soil texture. Even in Hertfordshire, on the evidence of the present Geological Survey, the correlation with geology may not be as strong as Salisbury supposed; there is no geological formation on which sessile oak definitely predominates.

How did the distinction between oak–hornbeam and pure hornbeam woods arise? Why should their differences of structure, which reflect the decisions of woodland owners mainly in the last 200 years, be correlated with differences of flora and vegetation which appear to be independent of management? The two types are geographically intermingled, and their four characteristics – structure, species of oak, other trees, ground vegetation – are very well correlated throughout their range. Salisbury pointed out that the oak–hornbeam woods are larger and are often in areas with a stronger forestry interest, but the distinction is not related to particular estates; moreover their characteristic oak, *Q. petraea*, is the species which early foresters tried to discourage when they first became capable of distinguishing it (p. 299).

A probable explanation is that oak–hornbeam woods form a natural transition to oakwoods (Chapter 17). Under normal coppicing, oak would be a major part of their underwood – indeed oak coppice is often present even now – and would be *petraea*, the characteristic oak of oakwoods. In 'pure' hornbeam woodland, on the other hand, oak – *Quercus robur* – has always been a minority tree, and has no more ecological significance than the oak standards in any other woodland.

On this hypothesis, both types of hornbeam-wood were probably normal coppice-with-standards in earlier centuries; the *petraea* woods would have had oak standards and oak plus hornbeam coppice. When timber and bark became more highly valued than underwood, many woodland owners would have been reluctant to continue coppicing their oaks. In *petraea* woods, where there was already a lot of oak, this change would automatically increase the number of standard trees, especially if there were one or two years like 1977 in which *petraea* but not *robur* grew abundantly from seed (pp. 296–7). A nineteenth-century map of what is now Hadleigh Great Wood (S.E. Essex) has the note: 'The land is better here but the Timber is too thick for the Underwood.'[301] Oak–hornbeam woods, like oakwoods, are not on good sites for the *commercial* growing of oak. Their oaks are very slow-growing – often they have hardly changed since Salisbury's time – and not of much value; but the men who promoted them in the nineteenth century might not have known that this would be the outcome.

We therefore expect to find oak–hornbeam woods on sites which are almost too poor for hornbeam, on the fringe of those very acid and infertile soils on which only oak (or beech) will grow. Thundersley West Wood (pp. 234–5) is an example. The differences in soil texture are as yet inconclusive and it is possible that the depth of the surface deposits is critical. Where the roots can reach only sand, gravel, or silt the wood is likely to be oak or oak–hornbeam. Where there is chalk or clay within reach enough nutrients can be brought up from below to support pure hornbeam woodland. Where nutrients are more abundant – the surface deposits being thinner or more fertile – we have hornbeam–ash. These correspondences are not easily quantifiable and are unlikely to be exact, since they will be influenced by waterlogging and rooting depth and by the historical caprices of oak reproduction in relation to the felling of particular areas.

Both oak–hornbeam and pure hornbeam woodland are poor in flowering plants: few species can withstand the heavy shade, acidity, and summer drought. Many woods have quite long species lists, but most of the herbs belong to valley bottoms and the neighbourhood of springs, where clay comes near the surface. These more fertile and often less shaded pockets were described by Salisbury as the '*Ficaria verna* [i.e. *Ranunculus ficaria*] Society'; other species include *Ranunculus auricomus*, *Cardamine flexuosa*, and *Lysimachia nemorum*, and occasionally *Hottonia palustris* in waterholes. They are really islands of a different plant community which do not belong to the surrounding hornbeam woodland.

Effects of coppicing

The coppicing flora of hornbeam-woods is often very striking and because of the slow regrowth may persist for several years. The range of temporary plant communities is illustrated by Sexton, Tindall, and Hedenham Woods in south Norfolk, in which the commoner species

Table 14.2 Coppice plants in Sexton, Tindall, and Hedenham Woods. Summary of thc commoner plants on sixteen recently-felled areas, recorded summer 1975.

Species	Number of areas on which:			
	Sole dominant	Co-dominant	Abundant	Frequent
Epilobium hirsutum	2	2	—	—
Juncus effusus	1	3	2	1
Holcus mollis	1	1	—	—
Cirsium palustre	—	2	1	2
Lychnis flos-cuculi	—	1	7	1
Hypericum hirsutum	—	1	1	—
Rubus fruticosus agg.	—	1	1	—
Epilobium montanum and *adenocaulon*	—	1	1	—
Juncus conglomeratus	—	1	—	—
Poa trivialis	—	1	—	—
Lotus uliginosus	—	—	2	2
Primula vulgaris	—	—	2	2
Hypericum tetrapterum	—	—	1	2
Pulicaria dysenterica	—	—	1	1
Carex remota	—	—	1	—
Circaea lutetiana	—	—	1	—
Hypericum perforatum	—	—	1	—
Luzula multiflora	—	—	1	—
Poa pratensis	—	—	1	—
Vicia tetrasperma	—	—	1	—

from fourteen small coppice panels, felled between two and a half and six and a half years before being recorded, and from two recently-made glades are summarized in Table 14.2. Much of the vegetation is of a wet-land kind, despite the apparently dry appearance of the woods; it varies greatly even between two panels cut in the same year. Only three of the twenty-one commonest plants – *Poa trivialis*, *Primula*, *Circaea* – are likely to have been growing in the fully-shaded wood before coppicing; this illustrates the special importance in hornbeam-woods of species from buried seed or from other coppiced areas within the wood [Chapter 26].

In the Harleston hornbeam area, summer-flowering perennials predominate after coppicing; in other areas, particularly mid Essex, brambles may be so vigorous as to suppress the herbs and even to interfere with the underwood. In Hertfordshire, Salisbury observed that in the more acid '*sessiliflora-Carpinus*' woods coppicing had less effect, particularly on spring-flowering herbs, than in the '*robur-Carpinus*' woods.[139] This is still broadly true, although in a very acid wood in Broxbourne, coppiced in winter 1972, I have seen a coppicing community – involving *Anthoxanthum odoratum*, *Rumex acetosella*, and *Digitalis purpurea* – as distinctive as any of those in the more familiar neutral to calcareous woods. Broom (cf. Frontispiece, Fig. 26.7c) frequently appears in the S.E. Essex woods. In all cases a rich coppice flora appears to depend on adequate rainfall in the spring after felling.

Hornbeam in wood-pasture

Hornbeam is abundant in the Forests of Epping, Hainault, and Enfield, and in the plains of Hatfield Forest, and occurs on wooded commons such as Woodham Walter (Essex) and Northaw. Most of the notable great hornbeams described by Christy were in ancient parks, notably Skreens and Writtle near Chelmsford, since destroyed. Most wood-pasture hornbeam is in the form of old pollards, interspersed, since the decline of grazing, with younger trees, often birches [Plate 13e]. It is not possible to identify wood-pasture parallels to the four types of hornbeam woodland because wood-pasture usually lacks the differential tree species and ground vegetation.

Sexton Wood, Hedenham

The traditional management of hornbeam survives best in the Harleston area, on both the Norfolk and Suffolk sides. Four great medieval woods in S.E. Norfolk – Gawdy Hall Wood in Redenhall, Sexton Wood, Hedenham Wood, and Tindall Wood in Ditchingham – are almost unaltered and are still coppiced. Gawdy Hall Wood has an excellent flora (with nineteenth-century records by F. W. Galpin[690]), earthworks (including two medieval moats), and ancient standard trees; but for an illustration I shall take Sexton Wood. All these woods are private.

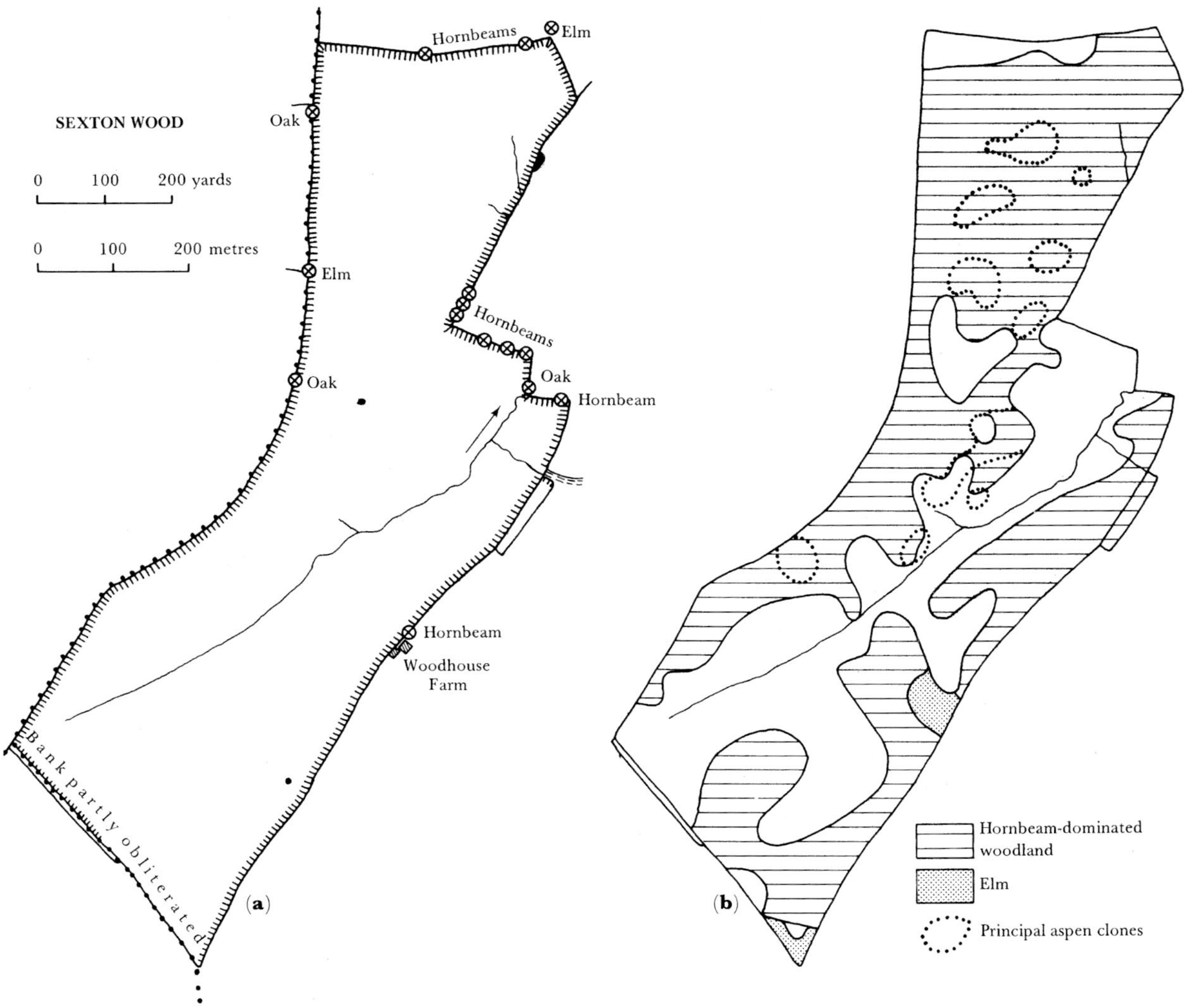

Fig. 14.5 Sexton Wood (Hedenham, Norfolk). (**a**) Topography. (**b**) Tree communities: unmarked areas are chiefly mixed ashwood and mixed hazel-wood, both with some hornbeam.

Topography

Sexton Wood (Fig. 14.5) lies on a plateau and is traversed by a shallow internal valley. The site is mapped as Boulder-clay but the typical topsoil is more than half sand (0.1–0.5 mm), with about 12% silt and 15% clay. There are lenses of deep and almost pure sand. The sandy topsoil varies in depth and is often waterlogged in winter. The same topography and soils are repeated in the other three big woods; they are good examples of a site remaining woodland because difficult to cultivate.

History and archaeology

Hugo le Bygot, one of the bold and haughty Bigods, Earls of Norfolk, died in 1266. His lands, parks, and woods were seized by the Crown, and the estate rolls found their way into the Public Record Offfice. A survey of Ditchingham manor in 1270 records two great woods called 'le Tyndhae' and 'le Sexting'; their areas of 80 and 86½ acres agree reasonably well (given the medieval tendency to under-estimate the size of woods) with the modern Tindall (105 acres) and Sexton (100 acres) Woods.[447]

There is no reason to suspect any change of outline in Sexton or Tindall Woods since 1270. Both are completely surrounded by strong banks which follow their irregular perimeters. A fine map of 1617 explains the more complex history of Hedenham Wood, including a moated site by then already deserted;[435] it also proves the antiquity of two small groves, one overlying yet another deserted settlement. (The 'moat-in-a-wood' is a frequent kind of medieval settlement in Norfolk.)

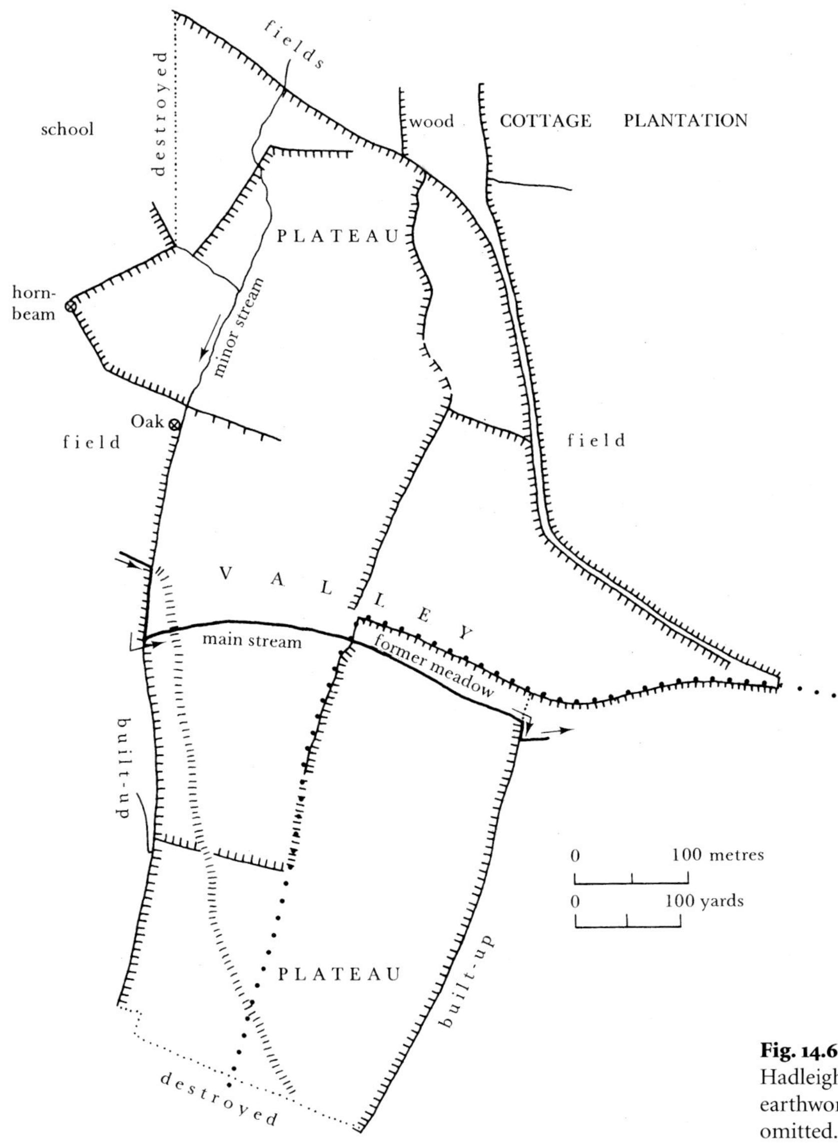

Fig. 14.6 West Wood (Thundersley and Hadleigh, S. Essex). Topography and earthworks. The many footpaths are omitted.

Tindall and Sexton Woods were normally coppiced on an unusually long 16-year rotation. Henry III had little reason to preserve Bigod interests, and in 1271 he sold off 42¼ acres of underwood in Tindall – half the wood – and 14 acres more in the next year.[462] A note in 1271 implies that the underwood poles were cut into logs – the earliest known instance of the word – and their branches made into faggots (p. 142), a practice particularly suitable for big hornbeam. There are also many notes of oaks felled for repairs and new buildings on the estate and in Bungay castle.

Sexton Wood had some damp grassy glades. In 1272 the *plassiz in le Sexting* ('plash' = a wet place) yielded 2*s* 6*d* worth of 'herbagium' – equivalent to about one acre of hay – besides feeding six foals for six weeks in autumn.

Vegetation

About 70% of Sexton Wood is covered by hornbeam. As in the other Harleston woods the tree is less gregarious than elsewhere, and in only about 15% of the wood is the hornbeam pure. Hornbeam occupies mainly the plateau, merging into an intricate mosaic of ash, hazel, sallow, and maple in the central valley. There are large bracken glades on a sand-lens. The aspen variant of hornbeam woodland is well represented on the plateau in the north and middle. There are two small marginal areas of elm. The wood has the normal scatter of timber oaks.

The soils are uniformly acid, with pHs from 4.0 to 4.3; in other woods in the area I have recorded a range of 3.9 to 6.2. Surprisingly, apart from a few species including *Digitalis purpurea* (foxglove), *Teucrium scorodonia* (wood sage), and the moss *Polytrichum formosum*, the flora is not particularly calcifuge and the humus is mainly mull.

The shaded ground vegetation is a large-scale mosaic of areas dominated by dog's-mercury, primrose, brambles, and bracken, not closely related to the topography or the trees. The frequency of mercury on sloping ground and near the wood-edges is remarkable for an acid and winter-wet wood. The central valley has a swampy strip with *Filipendula ulmaria* and *Carex acutiformis*. The wood is coppiced in a multitude of small panels of different ages, with a varied and often colourful vegetation (Table 14.2) which includes some annuals characteristic of wet acid sandy places, such as *Isolepis setacea* and (in Tindall) *Peplis portula*.

Each of the three other woods has its special character: Gawdy Hall has as much maple as ash; Hedenham is more sloping and less acid; Tindall has more hornbeam and more bramble. In each wood hornbeam tends to avoid the central hollow.

Conclusions

Hornbeam is here at the edge of its world distribution but is still the commonest tree. Its less-gregarious behaviour may be the result of continued coppicing, which enables poorly-competing trees such as sallow to co-exist with it and may also restrain hornbeam's power to build up mor and to acidify the soil. The flora is surprisingly rich for an acid wood; this may be due not wholly to coppicing but also to slightly greater fertility than usual: for instance, there are several nettle areas.

This wood is apparently unchanged for at least 700 years. It exemplifies the common relation between hornbeam and other species in the heyday of coppicing. Without continuity of management the balances between hornbeam and other trees, between hornbeam and the ground vegetation, and between calcifuges and non-calcifuges would immediately be upset and it would lose much of its remarkable diversity.

West Wood, Hadleigh and Thundersley (S. Essex)

[see also Rackham (1986) *Woods of S.E. Essex*]

This wood has a physical and social environment very different from that of Sexton: it lies in the middle of the Southend conurbation; half its boundary adjoins built-up areas, and it is a very public place; but it is in similar condition and is actively coppiced.

The wood (Fig. 14.6) is bisected by a pronounced valley, sloping from each end down to a stream. The geology is typical of South Essex, with sandy Bagshot Beds on high ground at both ends and London Clay in the valley. These are thickly blanketed by loess-like surface deposits and the soils consist largely of silt (32–55%) and fine sand.

The many *-ley* parish-names (pp. 127–8) suggest that this was one of the last extensive woodland areas in Essex, and the name *Thunders*ley summons up the ghosts of heathen gods. Domesday Book has only small swine-entries in the area. West Wood is named in 1554;[851] in 1717 it belonged to the Dean and Chapter of St Paul's.[325] In 1777 Chapman and André's atlas of Essex shows it at the middle of a large tract of almost contiguous woods, much of which disappeared shortly after.[250] A mid-eighteenth-century map[294] shows West Wood as covering 81 acres, with almost exactly its present outline.

The wood-boundaries are mostly smooth curves and, although embanked and set with oak stubs, may not be of great antiquity. Inside the wood are several massive much-eroded banks which represent some earlier phase of wood-embanking. The parish boundary which divides the wood, already obsolete in the eighteenth century, follows these banks in part. Where the valley is flat-bottomed it formed a salient of meadow-land within the wood which became overgrown only in recent decades.

To the south of the stream there is oak–hornbeam woodland of the classic Salisbury type. The standard oak trees, small and slow-grown, cover 50–60% of the ground; between them is quite dense underwood of hornbeam and service, with some chestnut and aspen. The oaks are nearly all *Quercus petraea*, with some *Q. robur* near the stream. North of the stream the timber trees are represented by stumps of about sixty years' decay, and the underwood – a mosaic of hornbeam, oak, and chestnut – is predominant. The oak stools, some of them 8 ft (2½ m) across, are most abundant on the higher ground; they, too, are chiefly *petraea*.

The stream-side and the old meadow have a narrow strip of hazel, maple, and ash. Much of the flora of the wood is confined to this area. Elsewhere there is a mosaic of areas of brambles, bracken, and bluebells; in the north, under the oak coppice, strong calcifuges such as heather (*Calluna*), *Galium saxatile*, and *Deschampsia flexuosa* give a heathland character to the vegetation. Typical of ancient woods in South Essex are patches of *Melica uniflora* on level ground (elsewhere it is chiefly on woodbanks) and of *Asperula odorata*.

The wood has one of the largest concentrations in England of service, which is the fourth commonest tree, forming about 15% of the underwood. Alder-buckthorn is another typical associate of oak–hornbeam.

The soils are very acid, ranging from pH 3.6 to 4.0. Although West and Sexton Woods differ by less than half a pH unit, this comes at a critical part of the pH range and the woods differ almost totally in vegetation. In West Wood, the humus is almost wholly mor and much of the flora – all but the calcifuges – is confined to the valley bottom; mercury and primrose, abundant in Sexton, are absent from West.

West Wood is the nearest approach to a real example of the kind of ecological catena that appears to underlie the South Essex and Hertfordshire hornbeam-woods, though usually disturbed by irregularities of topography or management. On the topmost very infertile soils overlying Claygate and Bagshot Beds we have oak woodland, represented by oak coppice (in other places beech), associated with heathland plants. In the valley bottom, whether because of downwash or the greater accessibility of London Clay, there is a narrow strip of ash–maple–hazel woodland with its characteristic rich flora. Oak–hornbeam and pure hornbeam woodland form zones of increasing fertility between these extremes.

The urban surroundings of West Wood are not detrimental to its management. Most of it is within a coppice rotation. Not only does the underwood grow well, but there are oaks, hornbeams, services, etc. of all ages including saplings; it is one of those rare British woods in which all the trees regenerate freely from seed. In dense shade near the entrances, the vegetation has been worn away by the treading of many feet; but elsewhere the brambles and bracken are sufficient to keep visitors to the paths.

Conservation

From 1945 to 1980 hornbeam fared consistently worse than ancient woodland in general (Fig. 6.1). My recorded losses for Eastern England – which contains much of the total hornbeam in Britain – amount to 37% of the area; allowing for stands destroyed without record, nearly half the hornbeam in ancient woods is likely to have been grubbed or poisoned. It has fared better in wood-pasture, though it has been much persecuted in Epping Forest.[126]

The ecosystems associated with hornbeam are particularly dependent on coppicing, although the effects of the tree's extreme shade may be mitigated if there are standard trees or other underwood species (p. 79). Fortunately I have noted coppicing – continuing or revived – in over 50 out of 200 hornbeam woods visited. The many public hornbeam-woods in South Essex are often well managed: a strong woodmanship tradition has been reinforced by urbanization and a demand for logs. In Hadleigh Great Wood ('Belfairs Nature Reserve') there is the oldest example of conservation coppicing in England; it has run since 1938.[875] As in West Wood, such management is compatible with quite severe use by the public. In the Harleston hornbeam area many woods are on estates with a strong shooting interest: young underwood provides cover for pheasants. Owners are often proud of their woods and manage them as well as any conservation body could hope to do.

[The Hertfordshire woods where Salisbury worked were less well protected and attracted modern forestry. Since 1980 they have fared much better, especially owing to the Woodland Trust.]

General conclusions

English hornbeam woods are an extension of those on the Continent: they correspond roughly to the Querco-Carpinetum which is widespread in France, Germany, and Poland. The range of soils in Europe is broadly similar, though none of the phytosociological variants so far described corresponds in detail to our four types of hornbeam wood.[809, 891]

On the Continent, hornbeam is often regarded as a kind of substitute for beech. The two trees grow in much the same range of soils and climate. Both became abundant late in post-glacial history; there is some pollen evidence that both expanded into places where agriculture had been interrupted by events such as the Thirty Years' War.[710, 913] Coppicing and wood-pasture are said to cause hornbeam to become dominant on land that would otherwise be occupied by beech.

In England hornbeam is much less closely connected with beech. Their native ranges are broadly similar, but in detail they seldom overlap (cf. Frithsden Beeches, pp. 325–6) and it appears that the main expansion of hornbeam was later than that of beech. In Eastern England hornbeam is a substitute, not for beech, but for lime. Their ecological preferences and associations are so similar as strongly to suggest that hornbeam is a replacement for the lime of the Atlantic wildwood.

The rise of hornbeam was probably connected in some way with human affairs, but how it happened can only be conjectured. Since lime is more useful than hornbeam its replacement can hardly have been deliberate. England escaped the Continental cataclysms of famine and sword which, in any case, would hardly have affected the uncultivable lands on which much of our hornbeam grows. There is no evidence that hornbeam is particularly connected with secondary woodland. But it is resistant to browsing, and if lime finally declined through the rise of wood-pasture (pp. 253–4), hornbeam might well have replaced it. The hornbeam woods may be a monument to the pre-conservation phase in the development of woodland management.

Added in 2003 edition

Hornbeam is still a historically, archaeologically, and palynologically under-recorded tree. It figures largely in the books on South-East Essex (Rackham 1986) and the Blean, N.E. Kent (Holmes & Wheaten 2002). Outlying hornbeam areas, with small groups of hornbeam-woods, occur as far away as south-east Wales, and seem to be genuine: there is even a Welsh name for the tree, *oestrwydden*, apparently from *ostrya*, one of the Latin names for hornbeams.

The non-invasive behaviour of the tree in England contrasts with its contrary reputation in France and its colonization of abandoned fields and plantations in Poland.

Fig. 14.7 Ancient stool of hornbeam, Thornden Wood, Blean (Kt). On the Blean (unlike other areas) hornbeam often forms well-conditioned giant stools and rings, up to 24 feet in diameter. February 2003

Fig. 14.8 Maple–Hornbeam wood with dog's-mercury. Wall Wood, Hatfield Forest. May 1979

Fig. 14.9 Pure Hornbeam wood with bluebell. Hornbeam is a very gregarious tree. Meepshole Wood, Billericay, S. Essex. May 1978

Fig. 14.10 Oak–Hornbeam wood with bramble. Tile Wood, Hadleigh, S.Essex. April 1980

equally historic example is *Lynderswood* in Black Notley, Essex. The name first appears as *boscus de lindris* in 1250,[851] but its etymology from *linde* and the Anglo-Saxon *hris*, underwood, implies that lime was already being coppiced before the Conquest. The wood partly survives, now called Paul's Wood (Fig. 15.2), and still contains lime as underwood.

Lime rarely occurs in Anglo-Saxon charters, which deal mainly in non-woodland trees, but there are two cases in Worcestershire[722] which is still a lime area.

In Eastern England there are three Anglo-Saxon villages with lime-tree names: *Bast*wick and Wood*bast*-wick in Norfolk and *Lind*sell in Essex. Around the Fens there are four lime names, two of them of Anglo-Saxon form: *Bass*enhally (*Bastenhale* 1250 'at the lime[-tree] corner', cf. Ffelsham*halle* (p. 26)) in Whittlesey and *Barst*on (*Baston* 1319)[852] in Swaffham Prior. Another name of similar form and probably *linde* derivation is *Lyndenehalle*feld in Takeley, Essex, in 1331.[851]

Medieval and other pre-1700 records

Medieval records are widely scattered in those districts where native lime still exists. Examples are valuations of lime bark in Needwood (Staffs) in 1297,[234] protection of lime by Sherwood Forest by-laws,[43] and *linden* stolen at Goathland (N.E. Yorks) in 1407–8.[39] Then as now, lime was a local tree of disjunct distribution, as is confirmed by early naturalists: Gerarde (1597) knew the limes of Northamptonshire,[340] and Aubrey (1695) those of Bedfordshire and the very few in Cranborne Chase (Dorset).[769]

To look in more detail at Eastern England (Fig. 15.3), there was a *Lyndeland* in Kelvedon (Essex) in 1356 and a *Lyndherst* (= lime-grove) in Felsted (Essex) in 1357.[851] A personal name *de Lyndhold* (= lime-grove) appears in 1279[345] in Groton (Suffolk), next to Groton Wood (see later), and there is a similar connection in Little Bentley, N.E. Essex, where the local wood also has native lime.

Turner's *Herball* (1568) says of lime:

> It groweth very plenteously in Essekes in a parke within two miles of Coltchestir in the possession of one Maister Bogges.[505]

The place is probably Welshwood Park, which still had lime in the 1970s. Tusser (1573) alludes to 'prie',[506] and Ray a century later mentions the Essex limewoods;[468] both naturalists were born within four miles of *boscus de lindris*.

These and other Suffolk and Essex records exemplify what is probably general in England: that lime contracted to little more than its present range more than a thousand years ago and has since suffered only from the general erosion of primary woodland. It has held on to its range, and often on to identifiable woods, with remarkable tenacity. The stability of the distribution is strikingly confirmed by the one *modern* record in South Essex, a single stool in Northlands Wood, Corringham (discovered by A. Griffiths in 1974). This is only one and a half miles away from the only *medieval* record in South Essex, *Lyndewud* in Langdon Hills 1248,[851] and is the last remnant of a small detached lime area.

For the Norfolk lime area there is a sale of 'lym bark' in 1610 from a wood at Melton Constable, close to Swanton Novers where the tree is still abundant.[370] The Hindolveston accounts of 1361–2 record the purchase of '8 cord' de bast'.[415] The scarcity of references to lime results from the generally poorer state of place-name studies and woodland documentation in Norfolk.

The place-names show one important change: the disappearance of a former fen-margin distribution of lime. The limes round the Fens and the Norfolk Broads, so prominent in the pollen record, persisted late enough to give rise to place-names, even though forest clearance was early in both areas and by Domesday Book there was hardly any woodland at all. At Lingwood in March (*boscus de Lindwod* 1230) there was still either a wood or a field with many trees in 1650.[393, 852] There is little prospect of re-finding the native lime of the Fens proper; the last of the ancient woods of the Isle of Ely was destroyed, almost unrecorded, in 1942. It may yet survive in the fens of the north-east Breckland, where I have found a lime-grove, too small to be readily traced in documents, in a valley at Great Hockham. Possibly some such local survival accounts for the persistence of lime right to the top of the pollen deposit at Old Buckenham Mere not far away. In Lincolnshire there is a fen-margin limewood at Potterhanworth.[98]

Successions away from lime

The disappearance of lime from many upland areas cannot be explained, as it can from the fen edge, by the destruction of all native woodland. It happened so long ago that we can hardly hope for historical records of the disappearance. A hint is given by evidence of succession in one particular habitat in three widely-separated places.

One of the few lime place-names in southern England is *Lynd*hurst – 'lime-grove' – in the New Forest. Evidently *Tilia* survived into the Anglo-Saxon period. It disappeared as part of a general impoverishment of the flora, known both from documents and pollen, involving the loss also of hazel and, more recently, the decline of oak and rise of beech.[156] In the Forêt de Fontainebleau south of Paris (p. 303), on acid sandy soils not unlike those of the New Forest, there is clear evidence of identical changes. These are well exemplified by a stand of beeches, some of them 250 years old, with a few magnificent ancient oaks from its earlier history, called La Tillaie. This place-name – *tilietum*, the equivalent of Lyndhurst – is widespread especially in the northern third of France[652] and clearly implies an earlier limewood phase. There are still a few native limes in Fontainebleau. In Epping Forest (p. 187) a peat-bog has yielded evidence of a lime-dominated phase until the middle Anglo-Saxon period;[8, 848] this again has been followed by a tendency for oak to be displaced by beech.

All these sites are on infertile sands or gravels and are Forests; the change from lime to oak to beech could be due either to loss of nutrients from the soil or to some effect of wood-pasture. At Epping lime declined in two stages: a sudden fall to about a third of the pollen frequency, followed after an interval by a gradual decline to extinction. In view of the medieval history of the Forest (p. 188) it is tempting to interpret the first 'clearance' as the pollarding of the lime-trees round the bog, which would reduce their pollen output, and the second as the eventual death of these trees without replacement. It would be unwise to extend this explanation to the disappearance of lime from more fertile soils or from sites that were not wood-pasture.

Management of limewoods

The lime-tree produces timber, bast, and wood. There are occasional medieval references to lime timber, chiefly for furniture and panelling.[477] More recently it is said to be a favourite timber in small quantities for sculpture and the works of pianos. Bast ropes were used, among other purposes, for lashing scaffolding-poles; some of the records (e.g. for Calais in 1441) suggest long-distance transport.[477]

In general, however, lime seems to have been coppiced in the same way as other trees. For instance, Groton Wood (p. 251) was surveyed in 1544 when Henry VIII, who had confiscated it from Bury St Edmund's Abbey, granted it to Adam Winthrop I (ancestor of the Winthrops of New England). It was then coppiced on an irregular rotation of about fourteen years and contained about five young oaks to the acre:[455]

> Growton woode conteyneth xxxvij acres,
> howe wood conteyneth iiij acres . . .
> Wherof x acres of iij yeres growth x acres of vij yeres growith xv acres of x yeres growthe and vj acres resydue of xiij yeres growthe . . .
> And in the seyd woodes be growinge CC sapling okes of xxx and xl yeres growthe wherof lxxx reseruyd for tymber for the ffermor* to repayre the howses . . . of the seyd Mannor and Cxx resydewe valluid at iijd the tree . . .

There is some evidence that lime was slightly more valued than other underwood. In Chalkney Wood (see later) it is specially mentioned; there were sales of bast there and at Groton[471] in the 1660s. At Markshall (mid Essex) the limewoods were coppiced at fifteen years' growth in the eighteenth century, yielding hop-poles and other products.[290–1]

* 'Farmer', i.e. sitting tenant of the manor.

In the nineteenth century lime from the great wood at Shrawley (Worcs) was used for 'poling' copper, the practice of stirring the molten metal with green poles which, as they char, reduce the cuprous oxide which contaminates the copper.[671, 833] There seems to be no special virtue in lime for this purpose.

Some charcoal-burners are said to prefer lime, others to disapprove of it because it tends to reignite when the stacks are opened.[108, 748]

Limewoods normally contain a full complement of oak-trees. Pry might be expected to compete severely with young oaks because of its vigorous regrowth, spreading habit when young, and dense shade; but in practice the oaks seem to have been replaced without special difficulty (see Chalkney and Markshall later).

Modern ecology and recent history

Lime is a densely-shading gregarious tree, like beech, hornbeam, and Lineage elm, and even more than these is confined to woods. It seldom grows in hedges and then is usually a relict of former woodland (as with the 600-yard long pry hedge at Shelley (Suffolk), the ghost of Withers Wood). It is rare in wood-pasture. In woodland it tends to form pure stands with sharply-defined edges.

Lime is usually treated as underwood; timber trees are infrequent, but it is sometimes a wood-boundary pollard. The vigorous young coppice shoots grow out sideways at first and later mysteriously become erect. Alone among native trees, it is not obliged to form an annual ring every year: cross-sections of poles often show a curious pattern of annual rings formed on only

Fig. 15.4 Section through a 18-year-old pole of lime, Groton Wood, showing incomplete annual rings. On parts of the circumference only 11 rings can be discerned.

part of the circumference (Fig. 15.4) and suppressed shoots can live many years without forming a ring. Ring-counts thus often underestimate a tree's age. Another peculiarity is that timber and underwood can grow on the same stool: if one pole on a stool is promoted to a standard tree (as was occasionally done by modern foresters) the stool retains its vigour and continues to coppice normally.

Reproduction

In prehistory lime presumably reproduced by seed, being dispersed by its winged clusters of nuts, as still happens in central Europe. Even at that time it spread rather slowly through Britain (Fig. 8.1). Successful establishment from seed is now rare in England; in the days before pollen analysis the supposed lack of good seed was often quoted as evidence that *Tilia* was not indigenous.

There must have been at least one or two good establishment years since the Middle Ages to account for the occasional trees in secondary woodland and hedges near ancient limewoods and for the smallish stools which occur, together with ancient ones, in most lime stands. With these exceptions, lime behaves as a relict tree, maintaining itself in its old localities but unable to colonize new ground.

Among plant geographers lime has a reputation for being a warmth-loving tree, but this has been overstated. In the post-glacial it reached Britain no later than oak; although it took longer to reach its maximum abundance, this is as readily explained by oak's well-known efficiency at dispersal and colonization as by the supposition that lime was waiting for the climate to improve. Lime extends further north than oak into Finland[750] and I have seen it ascending consistently higher than oak in many Alpine valleys, e.g. in South Tyrol.

At its northern native limit, in the Lake District, C. D. Pigott and J. P. Huntley have found *Tilia cordata* in 150 places, at most of which there are only a few trees, often of great age, in rocky and relatively inaccessible sites. At only three localities has there been any establishment from seed for at least a century. There is good meteorological and plant-physiological evidence that the cool summers of this latitude are the limiting factor, even the exceptionally hot summers of 1975–6 produced very little fertile seed.[108]

Summer temperatures are unlikely to explain why lime behaves as a relict in the south of its British distribution. Pigott and Huntley show that in some years in the Midlands 30–50% of fruits contain fertile seed. In Eastern England, I noted successful germination after the 1975–76 summers. Like most other trees with medium-sized fruits, lime waits two or three years before germinating. I first saw pry seedlings, with their remarkable palmate cotyledons, in 1977 in Groton Wood. In 1978 more appeared there and in several other woods. [With increasingly frequent hot summers after 1985, lime seedlings have come to appear almost every year, though not in every limewood (Fig. 15.13).] Seedlings are liable to many hazards including shade, competition of tall herbs in glades, and being unable to produce sufficient root to penetrate the mor humus. Successful establishment requires an unusual combination of circumstances in addition to a good seed year; but for so long-lived a tree as lime, once in a hundred years may be more than adequate.

Coppicing reduces the chance of seed production because the regrowth of lime takes longer to flower than that of any other tree except perhaps beech. At Markshall some pry stools flower in the eighth year, but fifteen years is more usual. With the short coppice rotations of the Middle Ages flowering would have been prevented almost completely. Coppicing would have increased the tendency of lime to behave as a relict: it would have prevented new stands from arising but would have preserved the existing stands by rejuvenating the stools.

Longevity and variation

Both species of lime are notoriously long-lived. There are many famous ancient trees on the Continent and a few in this country: the Pitchford Lime, Shropshire, must be well over 300 years old.[724] Lime coppice-stools are at least as long-lived. Most stands have a high proportion of giant stools; stools over 10 ft (3 m) diameter are probably commoner in this than in any other species except wych-elm. Attempts to date stools accurately are frustrated by the tree's irregular growth-pattern and by the missing of growth-rings, but they certainly take several centuries to reach this size. Nor do such single stools represent the limit of the tree's life-span; rings of lime stools of even larger size can often be recognized as coming from a common origin by some peculiarity of growth habit or leaf shape or colour (cf. ash, p. 208) [Fig. 15.10]. In Swanton Novers Great Wood, for instance, such an aggregate stool measures 27 ft (8.3 m) across. These clonal groups must be treated with caution, for some individuals can spread by suckers or even form new plants by the stems bending over and taking root like brambles. The capacity to do this, however, is unusual in the lime populations of Eastern England, and there is no evidence of it in the individuals forming aggregate stools.

The giant stools strongly suggest that there is little turnover among these populations of lime. Many stools are centuries old and some may even date from the first encoppicement of the woods. Under coppicing we should expect lime to be extremely long-lived, for its tolerance of shade enables it to survive when it happens to be overshadowed by a timber tree, which is probably the commonest cause of death among species such as ash (p. 208). Some of the largest stools are isolated relicts on the edges of the tree's geographical range. The single individual in the Leaden Roding woods (Essex), for instance, is a ring over 19 ft in diameter.

Lime as a tree of ancient woods

Almost all the *Tilia cordata* in Eastern England is in woods which there is strong reason to regard as medieval or earlier on the evidence of earthworks or written evidence or both. C. D. Pigott and G. F. Peterken discuss this characteristic of lime in Derbyshire and Lincolnshire and its correlation with other plants of ancient woodland;[98, 106] the most consistent of such plants to accompany lime in Eastern England is service.

The few exceptions confirm that the ability of *Tilia cordata* to colonize new sites is very limited. Groton Wood (Fig. 15.9b) illustrates the 'halo' of scattered colonization which occasionally surrounds a big stand of lime in an ancient wood.

Lime as a planted tree

There are many stories of introduced or planted *Tilia cordata*. At Chantilly, J. L. Reed alleged that lime was introduced by the Condé family and overran the Forest at the expense of the native hornbeam.[853] The limewood at Shrawley (Worcs), known since the 1830s as probably the largest stand of *Tilia cordata* in England, is said to have been planted; Elwes & Henry stated that the stools are in rows.[65, 671] The *Flora of Norfolk* regarded lime as introduced in Hockering and Swanton Novers Woods,[831] and there are similar claims about some limewoods in Essex.[62]

These allegations are not backed up by quotations from contemporary documents, and there are usually grounds for disbelief. At Chantilly, lime is certainly not now invasive; it is, if anything, losing ground to hornbeam; and the nearby place-names Les Tilles and Le Thillay testify to its presence in past centuries. The great wood of Hockering, with its imposing boundary pollards of lime, is the largest single limewood in Eastern England (220 acres until recently); anciently called Swinnow Wood, it is documented back to 1317;[213, 432] and there is no suggestion as to how, when, or why any previous underwood should have been converted to pry. The same argument applies to Shrawley Wood, documented to 1558.[724]

All the genuinely planted limewoods that I have seen are of the modern hybrid. At Wandlebury near Cambridge, for instance, plantations of beech and ash with *Tilia vulgaris* underwood were made in the early nineteenth century on what had been chalk downland. As the 1976 drought showed, hybrid lime is probably the ideal tree for this arid spot. In Little Bentley Hall Wood (N.E. Essex) the main ride is lined with stools of *T. vulgaris*, resulting from the felling of an ornamental avenue and clearly distinguishable from the clusters of native lime (*T. cordata* and a few natural hybrids) elsewhere in the wood. Until recently *T. cordata* was difficult to procure in bulk and was usually planted only as a specimen tree.

Most of the claims for planted pry-woods appear to be rationalizations: *Tilia cordata*, with its habit of growing in pure stands and its reluctance to reproduce by seed, does not fit most people's preconceptions of how a native tree ought to behave. [Shrawley Wood (Fig. 15.11) is a normal limewood, in which I find the stools to be everywhere of uneven age and not in rows.]

Although it is possible that *Tilia cordata* has occasionally been encouraged in woods, it is most unlikely that this has had any appreciable effect on its distribution, which is not related to particular ownerships or to recent management. The presence of native woodland lime may indeed have influenced the planting of non-woodland lime rather than vice versa. In the neighbourhood of the Suffolk limewoods there are old lime-trees of indigenous genotypes in the churchyards of Lavenham, Groton, and Lindsey, by the lane to Great Waldingfield church, and in the ancient avenue of Kentwell;[122] they strongly suggest that seventeenth- and eighteenth-century gardeners and churchwardens went to the local woods for their limes.

Soils

Lime grows on a great variety of soils, from the Carboniferous Limestone of N.W. England to the sands of Chantilly. The following analysis applies to Eastern England and should not hastily be extrapolated to other regions.

The two lime areas straddle the boundary between Acid and Calcareous soil provinces, but lime is predominantly a tree of acid soils with pHs between 3.6 and 4.9 (Fig. 15.5). Like hornbeam it occasionally grows on soils up to pH 7.1; but most calcareous stands of lime are very small, sometimes only a single stool. Mull and mor are equally common humus types in limewoods, the transitional pH being 4.1 (Table 4.1). In Groton Wood (p. 251) fallen leaves collect in slight hollows inhabited by earthworms and are turned into mull; the ridges between, with little worm activity, have a thin skin of mor.

Lime is associated with soils rich in loess. The two lime areas of Fig. 15.1 agree with the two areas of Fig. 4.8 in which 20–35% of the soil comes in the particle-size range 20–63 μm. The remainder of the soil consists of sand and clay, roughly equal in the southern lime area, but with more sand than clay in Norfolk. Most limewoods are officially mapped as Boulder-clay, but only under some of the smaller peripheral stands is the Boulder-clay sufficiently near the surface to contribute to the topsoil.

Most lime, especially big stands, is on level hilltops with evidence of poor drainage and gleying. Where lime is abundant on a slope, as in Colchester High Woods, there is evidence of water seepage from underlying clay.

The typical pry site thus has a close-textured acid

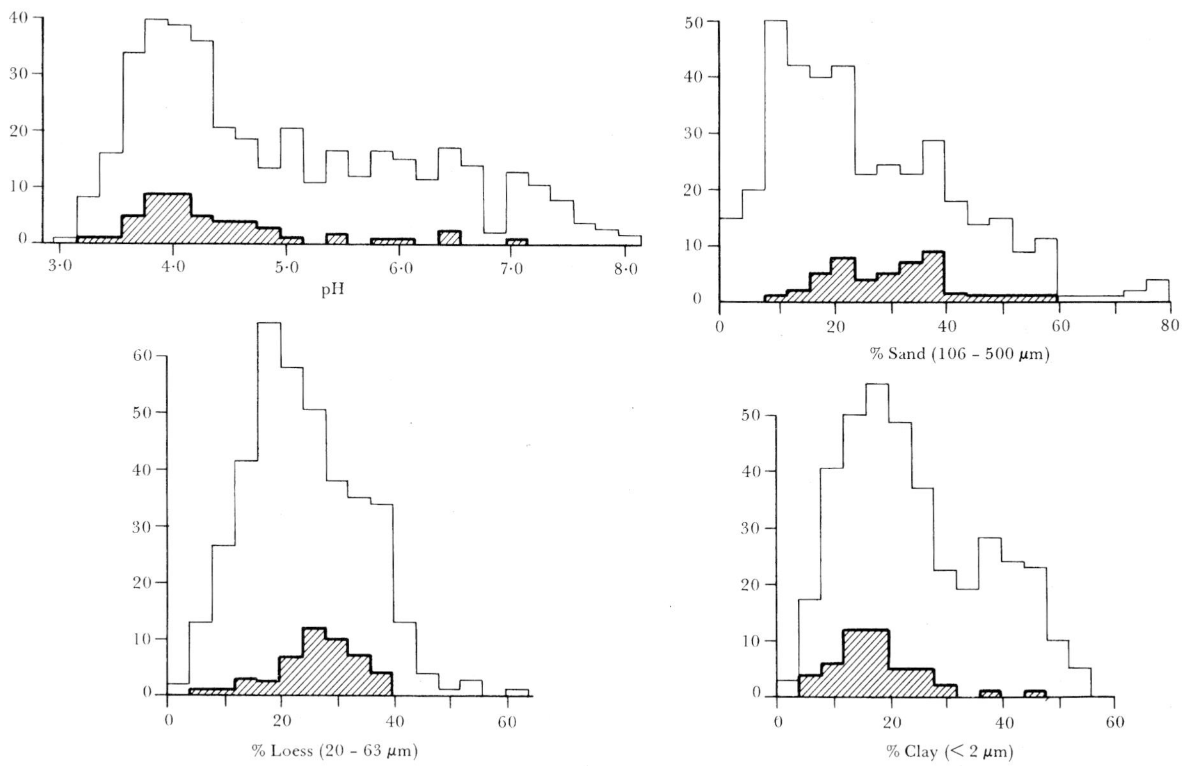

Fig. 15.5 Distribution of topsoil acidity and composition under *Tilia cordata* in the ancient woods of Eastern England. For comparison, the distribution of soil characteristics in all the woods sampled is shown by thin outlines. For further details see caption to Fig. 7.5.

soil overlying clay on a plateau, often with water-filled hollows. A common soil profile is that of the Oak Series, the ill-drained surface-water gleys characteristic of loess over Boulder-clay.[895] The connection probably involves some regeneration process which can no longer be observed; adult pry trees on non-typical soils appear to grow and compete no less successfully than those on typical soils.

Associations with other trees

The boundaries of stands of *Tilia cordata* are usually abrupt but sinuous, not coinciding with management boundaries. The abuttals on other tree communities have been analysed for 63 woods in Norfolk, Suffolk, and Essex; they vary with the size of the lime stand (Table 6.2).

Limewood is, to some degree, the central woodland type in the ecology of Eastern England. The larger stands tend to adjoin moderately acidic woodland of ash or hornbeam; less often they abut on very acid oak or chestnut woodland. The smaller stands are more associated with maple and Lineage elm, trees of more basic and more fertile soils. The frequent association with aspen illustrates the tendency of lime to grow on gleyed soils. The association with plateau alder-wood, apparently on flushed soils, is discussed in Chapter 18.

There are three small and widely-separated stands of a combination of lime and sessile oak in Swanton Novers Great Wood (Norfolk), Bovingdon Wood (Bocking, Essex), and White Wood (Gamlingay, W. Cambs). These are all on unusually acid soils; their structure is remarkably like that of the parallel woods of hornbeam and sessile oak, with close-set oaks and correspondingly sparse underwood. They adjoin normal limewood and evidently form a transition between it and oakwood.

Ground vegetation

Large stands of pry have a poor range of ground vegetation (Table 6.3) with only five communities. Brambles are the commonest dominant on mor and transitional soils; on mull soils pry overlaps the more acidic part of the range of dog's-mercury. Bracken sometimes occurs although the heavy shade and often waterlogged soils are unfavourable to it. Smaller stands have more varied ground vegetation, in which plants of wet sites

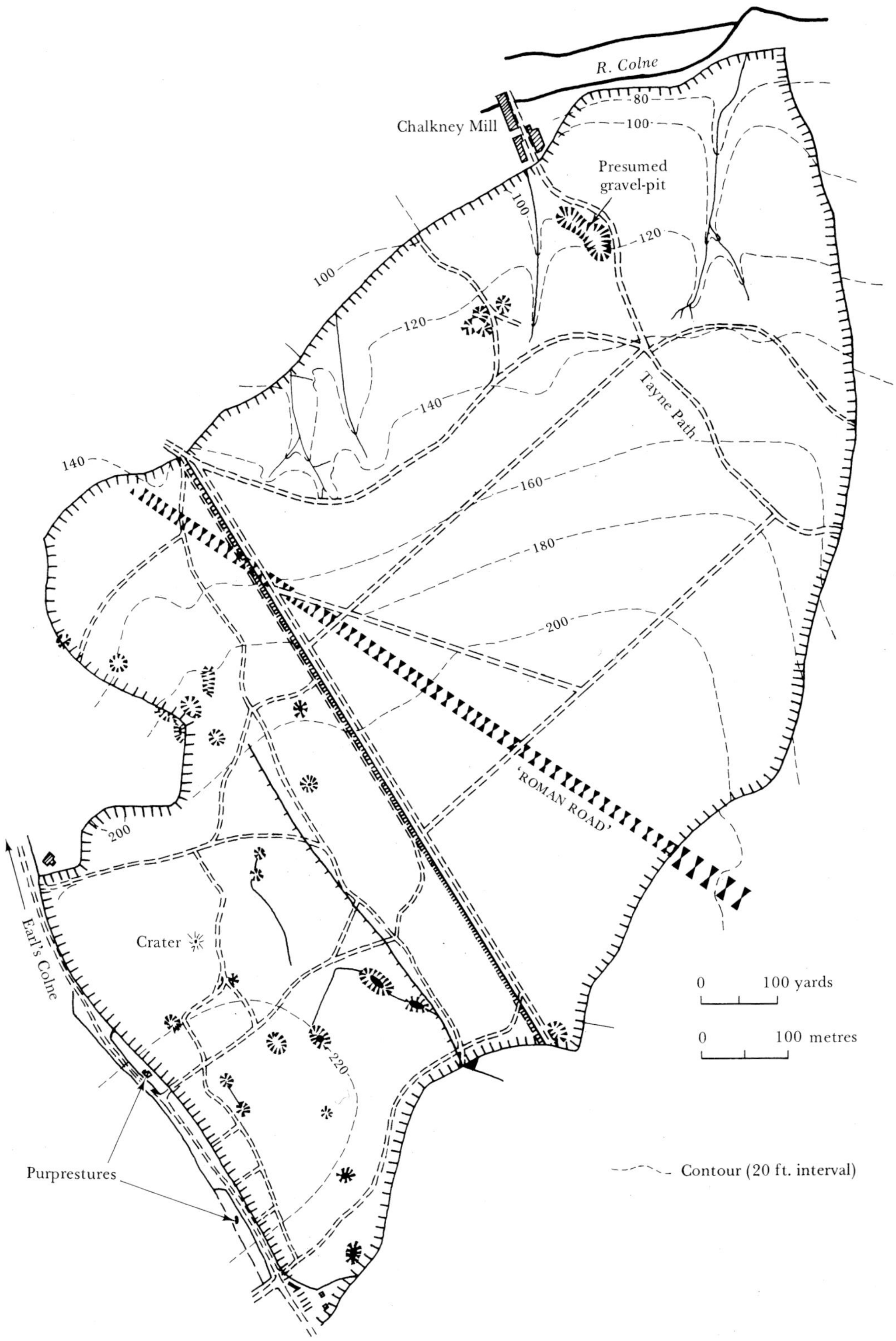

Fig. 15.6 Chalkney Wood (Earl's Colne, Essex). Topography and earthworks, with approximate contours. Dells and ponds exist in the N.E. two-thirds of the wood but were mainly inaccessible at the time of mapping.

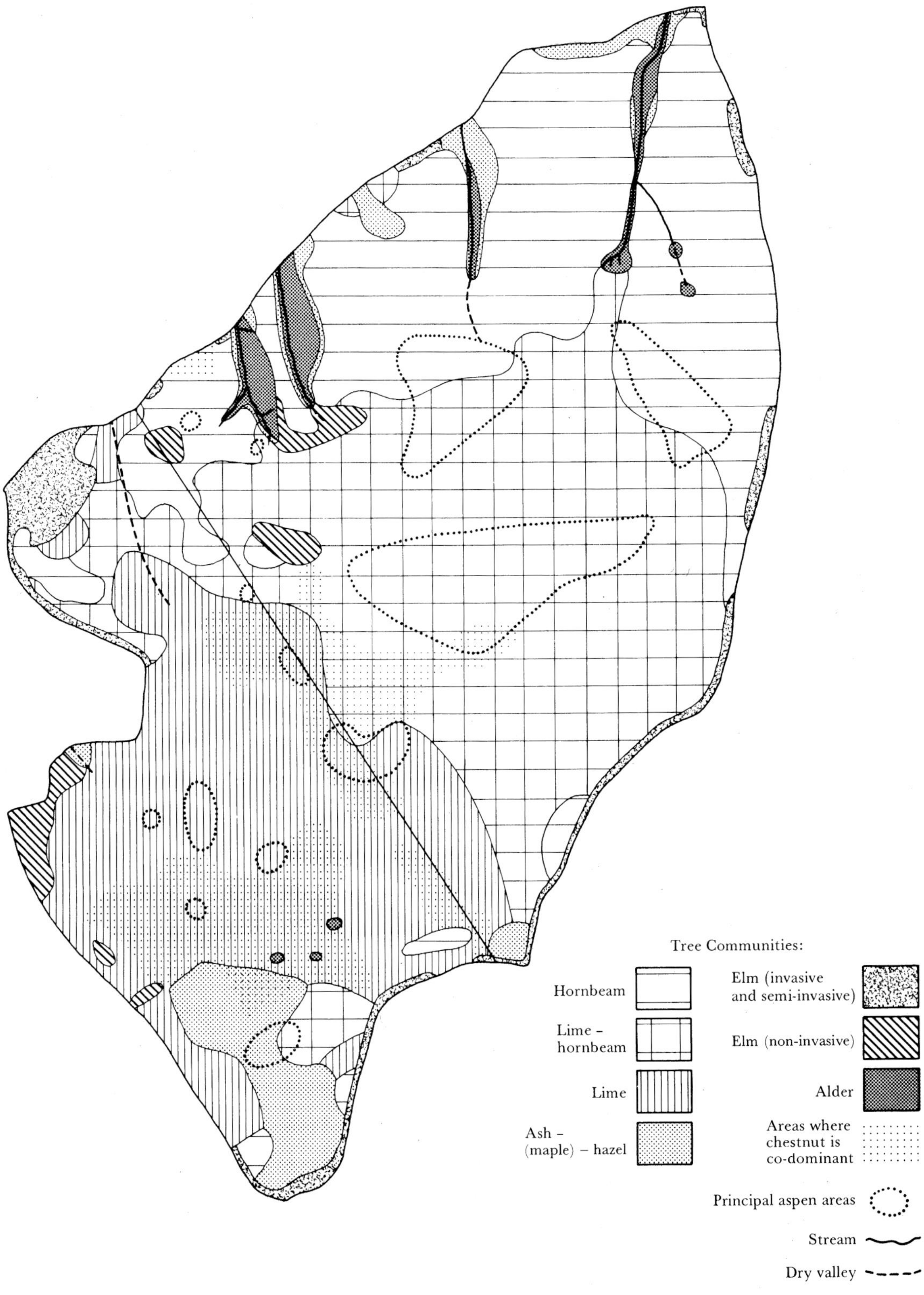

Fig. 15.7 Chalkney Wood: tree communities. In the south-western third of the wood the native vegetation is intact and has been mapped in detail. In the remainder of the wood the native vegetation was partly destroyed and partly inaccessible; except in the alder valleys some details are uncertain.

(*Deschampsia caespitosa*, *Geum rivale*) and of relatively high fertility (*Silene dioica*, *Digitalis purpurea*) are to be noted; but nettles are rare, and where lime abuts on elm the associated 'elm plants' (p. 96) normally stop at the edge of the elm. The frequency of ivy, normally associated with secondary woodland (p. 95), is surprising; the stands of lime containing it are small and are near the edges of woods or in woods with complex histories. Primroses are commoner under lime (whatever the size of stand) than in other types of woodland, perhaps because of the combination of relatively high fertility and poor drainage.

Under the dense shade of lime, especially in the middle stages of regrowth, the ground vegetation is very sparse. The effects of coppicing are strong and diverse. Existing plants that respond include bluebell, primrose, wood-anemone, and *Potentilla sterilis*; bracken under lime presumably relies on coppicing for its survival. Plants presumed to come from buried seed include *Centaurium erythraea*, *Euphorbia amygdaloides*, *Hypericum humifusum*, and *Rubus idaeus* (raspberry). *Poa trivialis* is sometimes abundant. *Juncus conglomeratus* may become dominant after a wet spring.

Taking trees and herbaceous plants together, lime stands divide themselves naturally into three types:

(1) lime–ash woods: often small areas of lime, on weakly acid soils, with mercury, primrose, etc.;
(2) pure limewoods: usually large areas of lime, on strongly acid soils, with brambles, bracken, or bluebell;
(3) limewoods with sessile oak.

These are analogous to hornbeam–ash, pure hornbeam, and oak–hornbeam woods. The lime counterparts of maple–hornbeam woods are too small and indistinct to count as a separate type. Although weakly-acid and strongly-acid limewood are very different, one having mull humus and the other mor, they are more difficult to separate and more closely intermingled than are the parallel hornbeam woods.

Outside Eastern England lime–ash woods are more abundant. They are, for instance, a characteristic woodland type of ancient woods in the Mendips, e.g. Cheddar Wood.

Wood-pasture and non-woodland lime

Pry may once have been somewhat more frequent as a hedgerow and wood-pasture tree than it is now. After the Anglo-Saxon charters, the earliest named hedgerow tree in English literature is a 'linde' in the twelfth-century *The Owl and the Nightingale*. Tusser's reference to pollarding:

> Lop popler and sallow, elme, maple, and prie . . .[506]

suggests that he knew it as a hedgerow tree; and in the north of his native Rivenhall the ancient hedges still contain a few pry stools along with sallow, elm, and maple, though black poplar no longer grows there.

Lime rarely appears in parks. In 1433 the Earl of Oxford made a forty-year lease of 'bast . . . issuing from certain trees called Lyndes' in Earl's Colne Park (Essex).[334] In Woodbury Park (W. Cambs) there are still a few gigantic lime pollards close to the woodland limes of White Wood.

On the common at Dedham (Essex) pollard limes were specially protected by two by-laws (codified *c.* 1575):

> If any maner of parson within the Towne of Dedham doth fell a tree, called Lynde Trees vpon Deham heath, by the grounde, shall forfaite . . . 3*s* 4*d*.
> It is lawfull for ye Tenantets of Dedham to Croppe the saide Linde trees with all other softe woode vpon the heath . . . without forfite . . . *so that they kille not**.[317]

Dedham Heath has long been enclosed but Mr D. Chesterfield tells me that there are still a few lime stools in hedges on the site.

Some Suffolk and Essex pry-woods

Chalkney Wood, Earl's Colne

The big medieval wood of Chalkney (*Chealtenheia* – derivation unknown) was part of the ancestral estates of the Earls of Oxford. Edward de Vere, seventeenth earl, sold up his lands to spite his father-in-law, and his steward, Roger Harlackenden, bought Earl's Colne and became lord of it in his stead. Harlackenden caused a great map of Earl's Colne to be made in 1598, which shows the outline of Chalkney Wood exactly as it is now together with many of the surrounding lanes, hedges, cottages, etc.[122, 318, 333]

The wood and its surroundings remained almost unaltered until the 1950s. Two-thirds were then felled, poisoned, and coniferized [but are now rehabilitated (pp. 427–32, 521–3)]; the most interesting parts are relatively unharmed. The remainder, still in its medieval state and still actively coppiced, belongs to Essex County Council and is open to the public. Chalkney still gives one of the best impressions of a medieval wood. The south-west side, with the lane adjoining and the little house in a long narrow garden taken out of the width of the lane (Fig. 15.6), has hardly changed in 400 years. The garden with the predecessor of the house are already there on the 1598 map and are now bounded by a six-species hedge; they are independent of the wood, for the woodbank passes behind them.

Topography and vegetation

The wood is of some 200 acres, sloping down from a plateau to the edge of the River Colne meadows (Figs. 15.6, 15.8). The slope is dissected by four small steep valleys. The site is mapped as Boulder-clay overlying London Clay, but neither contributes much to the soils.

* Italicized words are an addition in the original hand.

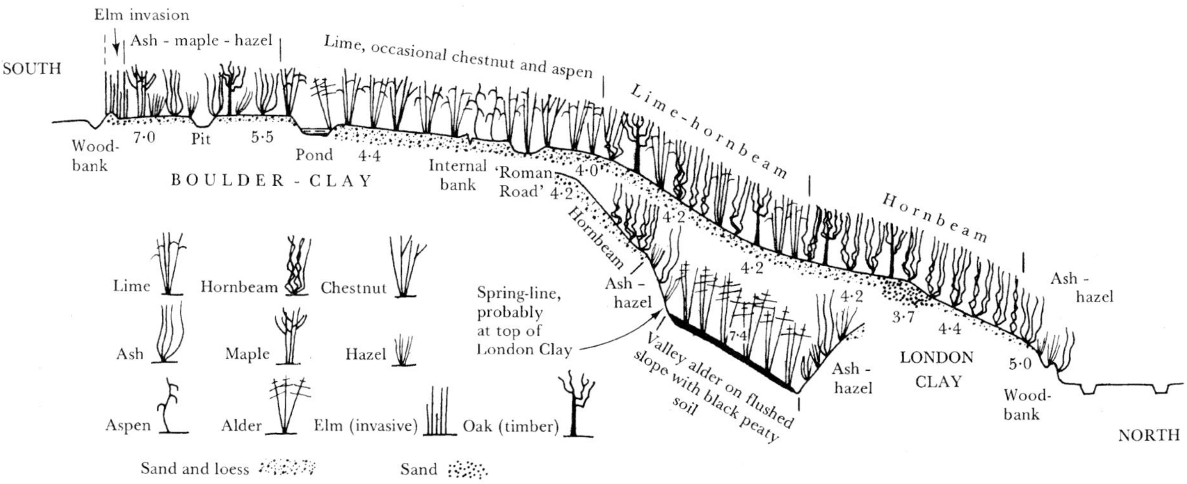

Fig. 15.8 Schematic section through Chalkney Wood, roughly from south to north, illustrating topography, soils, and tree communities. The lower profile is a transverse section (east to west) of one of the small alder-valleys. The numbers are typical figures for the pH of topsoil. Approximately ten-fold vertical exaggeration.

The typical topsoils of the plateau and slope contain 30–50% sand and 25–40% loess; only in the valleys is there more than 20% clay (Fig. 4.5). Despite the sand the plateau is ill-drained in wet seasons. The valleys (p. 308) are fed by powerful calcareous springs. There are at least 22 apparently natural ponds in the 63 acres of wood in which they can be observed, plus others hidden among the conifers.

Lime and hornbeam woodland form a mosaic with lime most abundant on the plateau, hornbeam on the slope, and a long transitional zone between (Figs. 15.7, 15.8). The chief associated trees are standard oaks (*Quercus robur*), often killed by the overgrowing of the underwood; frequent patches of aspen; an admixture of chestnut on the plateau; and a very thin scatter of single stools of wych-elm. There are three small clones of service. A third element in the mosaic is non-invasive or weakly invasive elm, which forms less extensive sharp-edged patches, mostly on the steeper slopes. A fourth element is ash–maple–hazel woodland, forming diffuse-edged patches on the plateau. The valleys are zoned with alder-wood (Chapter 18) in the bottom and ash–hazel on the sides. There is a marginal elm invasion so extensive and so narrow as to suggest suckering from elms planted as a perimeter hedge.

Topsoils under both pry and hornbeam are in the pH range 3.8–4.9; although quite narrow this variation includes both mull and mor humus types. The ground vegetation is dominated by bluebells or more locally by bracken, brambles, or primroses. Non-invasive elm has mull soils which, although only slightly less acid (pH up to 4.4) are very different in their vegetation, with mercury, *Silene dioica*, *Moehringia trinervia*, *Galium aparine*, and *Poa trivialis*. Ash–maple–hazel areas have much less acid soils (pH up to 7.1) with abundant mercury, primroses, and other normal Boulder-clay wood plants. Although their topsoil is little different in parent materials from that elsewhere on the plateau (Fig. 4.5), we must suppose that the Boulder-clay comes sufficiently near the surface (Fig. 15.8) to influence the vegetation, perhaps through minerals taken up by the deeper tree-roots and falling with the leaf-litter.

Archaeology

The oldest feature is a holloway (Fig. 8.5, Fig. 26.18a) which cuts across the wood and can just be traced in the fields outside; its dead-straight alignment is taken up by a nearby parish boundary. It is independent of the medieval wood outline and of all recent features. It is probably a Romano-British road; the most likely candidate is the road from Cambridge to Colchester, recently shown to be a pre-Roman trackway partly modernized in Roman times.[655] It is bordered by the faint remains of what may be the oldest woodbanks so far recognized.

The wood is still surrounded by a medieval bank some three miles long, except at the south corner where a cottage has been built. In many places the woodbank stands at the top of a little cliff where several feet of soil have disappeared from the surrounding fields through centuries of cultivation (Fig. 4.1).

Chalkney was the last large wood in Eastern England to retain the medieval system of tracks winding about among the stools. The winding tracks, though partly replaced by straight rides in the northern part, can still be seen in the County Council portion.

Management history

In the Middle Ages Chalkney Wood was put to a curious use. Attached to the Harlackenden map is the legend:

> This wood in tymes paste was empaled: And the Erles of Oxenforde in former tymes (for their pleasure) bredd and maintayned wilde Swyne in the same untill the Reigne of Kinge Hary the Eight. About wch tyme they were destroied by John (then Erle of Oxenford) for yt he understode, that the Inhabitaunts thereabouts sustained by them very greate losse and damage.

The De Veres had a particular attachment to the wild boar: it was their rebus, used as a crest and seal. They im agined a link between the family name and the Latin *verres*, a boar. Genuine wild swine had probably become extinct in Essex in Anglo-Saxon times or earlier; for other swine-parks see p. 188. The rootling of wild swine is supposed to be important for the tree regeneration and ground vegetation of European forests[107] but we can no longer tell what effects it may have had at Chalkney.

The account-book of the Harlackendens[332] has some unusually instructive entries relating to the wood.

[Punctuation added]

[1] 5 Jan. 1603 [i.e. 1604]. Sould vnto nicolas Cowlings of tarling the bast of 2 akers of prye wood standing together in Chalkney wood for 3*li.* 15*s.*

[2] 28 Feb. 1603/4. Sould vnto Richard Horewell of Tarling . . . 2 akers of wood . . . reserving my Stadles* . . . & 2C [i.e. 240 – see item 5] of hoppoles for 4*li.* 16*s.* 8*d.*

[3] Ffeb. 1605/6. Sould . . . 4 Loades of prye wood. Viz 2 loades, to be layd vp in boughes & to be [illegible] by ye woodfeller & carter, to be deliuered him . . . between this & easter; & the other two loades to be cut without shredding† about 7 foote long moer or lysse, & the loppes‡ to be put into the fagotts & [illegible] by my wood feller & carters . . .

[4] 25.2.1605/6. Sould . . . 6 akers of wood. To begin at ye hither end of tayne path, ** & to go on to a staddle* of hardbeam†† there marked toward the sandpitt in the bottome in breadth, so along tayne path to take his 6 akers together. Reserving 600 [i.e. 720] of good ashen poles, yt is of euery akre a hundreth, & all the ould staddles and 16 young staddles of euery akre. To have all his wood, except some tufts [?] of prye wood, by Maye day next taken out of ye wood, & those tufts to be had of [off] by ye latter end of may. For this he is to paye 20*li* . . .

[5] 22 Feb. 1606. Sould . . . 10 akers of my woods . . . To begin at ye lower end close to the gravell pitte, 20 rodds in breadth, & so upward all together till his 10 akers be cut. Allowing me 20 hundreth – vj [score] to ye hundred – of the best ashe & salowe poles; I to appoint one to fell them, & he to paye for felling of them. Reserving all the olde stadles, and 16 newe Stadles of every aker. He is to hewe of [off] all his wood by the latter end of Maye next, except his prye wood, & yt he is to hewe of by the xiiijth of June. For this he is to paye 3*li.* 10*s.* ye aker . . .

[6] 2.4.1606 Rec[eived] . . . in part for 2 Loads of boughes of prye wood 25*s.*

[7] 10.1.1609/10. Sould vnto Robt Rooke . . . 3 akers of vnderwood in Chalkney wood . . . Leading from the cartway to the mill along a sand pitt . . . Reserving all the ould staddles . . . & 30 more of euery aker . . . The wood to be all caried of betwixt this & the first of June next . . . He is to have the refusing of this whole bargayne till monday next by eyght of the clocke in the morning, & then yf he like of it to give me security for this money . . .

[8] 25 March 1612. [Sale of] 3 bundles of long asshe poles . . . at chalkney wood . . .

* Young timber trees promoted in coppicing.
† Cutting off the lower branches.
‡ Upper branches.
** The path to Great Tey through the north of the wood, still a public right-of-way.
†† Hornbeam.

Harlackenden knew his wood well and drove a shrewd bargain. Some he sold to distant purchasers: Terling (items 1 and 2) is twelve miles away. Although he habitually sold wood late in the season he insisted on it being taken away before the regrowth could be damaged, and was particular about the arrangements for felling and carting (items 4, 5, 7). He reserved the best poles for himself, probably for use as hop-poles (item 2). He was concerned to maintain the succession of timber trees, promoting a remarkably large number of staddles (item 7) – perhaps because he wanted to grow more timber, or else because he did not expect many staddles to survive. The prices that he got for the remaining wood, even if it was as much as twenty years old, seem to be well above average. He arranged for payment by instalments.

Pry poles yielded bast, which was worth not much less than the wood itself (items 1 and 2). They had to be carefully handled and cut into long lengths (item 3), doubtless to avoid severing the bast fibres. They could be felled some weeks later than the other underwood (items 4 and 5), presumably because in late spring the bast could more easily be stripped and split into its constituent layers. (Lime stools seem not to be harmed by late cutting.)

In the 1600s some parts of Chalkney Wood consisted entirely of pry ('2 akers . . . standing together', item 1); some were partly pry and partly something else (items 4 and 5), and others (item 7) have no mention of pry. *Tilia cordata*, therefore, was irregularly distributed within the wood in much the same general way as it is now. Three sites can be identified (items 4, 5, and 7), on the northern slope by 'Tayne path' and the big pit; the woodland in this area – to judge by what remains of it – was dominated in modern times by hornbeam, with only scattered groups of pry and patches of ash.

Hornbeam, having no special use, is mentioned only casually (item 4); the word 'staddle' implies that the tree was intended to grow on as timber. Ash, however, appears to have been more abundant in Harlackenden's time than it would have been in 1945, for he expected at least 120 good poles to the acre.

Conclusions

The tree communities in Chalkney Wood appear to have been much the same over at least four centuries. The changes include small-scale elm invasion, a probable slight retreat of ash, and the introduction of chestnut. The last tree would surely have been mentioned by Harlackenden had it been there, since it makes more durable poles than ash; and as none of the stools is very large Chalkney cannot be counted as an ancient *Castanea* site.

Many Essex limewoods have the same four main woodland types: lime on the level ill-drained plateau, hornbeam on slopes, ash–hazel or mixed ashwood in parts of the plateau with more calcareous soil, and non-invasive elm in places that receive downwash at the bottoms of slopes. Bovingdon and Parkhall Woods, seven miles west of Chalkney, are in an area mapped by the Soil Survey (unpublished). There is a good correlation of pry with acidic surface-water gleys of the Oak soil series, of hornbeam with less-gleyed acid soils of the Hornbeam series, and of ash with the gleyed and more calcareous soils of the Hanslope series. At Bovingdon there is a small patch of sessile-oak–lime wood; this could have occurred at Chalkney on a sand-lens but the trees have been destroyed.

Groton Wood

Groton Wood (Fig. 15.9), near Hadleigh, Suffolk (Suffolk Trust for Nature Conservation), falls into two parts. The northern third is the medieval 'Growton woode'. Originally it extended further to the north.[122] The southern two-thirds is secondary woodland of the sixteenth or seventeenth century on former farmland. The written evidence is supported by the massive woodbank of the medieval wood, the straight and slighter earthwork representing the truncation of its north side, and the tangle of small banks and ditches which pervade the secondary woodland.

The wood is on an acid, very loessy soil on a plateau. The ancient part of the wood is almost entirely dominated by pry, apart from tracts of non-invasive elm in damp hollows. Many of the lime and elm stools are at least 7 ft across. The secondary part of the wood also consists of lime up to twenty yards outside the old woodbank. The rest of the secondary wood consists of small irregular scattered stools of ash, hazel, etc., with only a few lime stools, most of which are on banks.

Besides these woodland occurrences there is a thin scatter of pry stools in the surrounding mixed hedges. Some of these are relicts from woodland, e.g. from the northern part of Groton Wood and from Brook Wood which disappeared in the nineteenth century. Others, however, as on the earthworks of a medieval castle, must represent colonization. The hedgerow stools flourish and there is clearly no functional reason why pry should not be a hedge shrub. There are also groves entirely of secondary woodland which do not contain it at all. Several other ancient woods within three miles, e.g. Bull's Cross Wood (Fig. 13.5), have histories like Groton Wood and similar distributions of lime.

By the Middle Ages woodland in the area had been reduced to roughly the extent which it occupies now. Pry was evidently abundant in this primary woodland. Most of the hedges, to judge from their composition, are medieval. Later there was an increase in the wooded area, followed in the nineteenth century by a further decline. Lime has been presented with many opportunities for colonizing secondary woodland and hedges, but has made little use of them. Only a few trees have become established and their number falls off rapidly with distance from the source of lime. In secondary woodland a distance of as little as twenty yards largely prevents colonization: most of the trees outside this limit probably started life in hedges before the secondary wood existed. In hedges there has been occasional colonization up to half a mile from the wood; but of the many millions of lime fruits trapped by the hedges around Groton Wood over the centuries only a handful have produced trees.

The Markshall Woods

These ten contiguous woods, three miles from Chalkney, until recently covered some 400 acres, more than half of it lime – one of the biggest areas of *Tilia cordata* in England. Most of it was bequeathed for the benefit of the nation by the late owner, Mr Thomas Phillips Price. This portion has since been largely destroyed by replanting [but is now being rehabilitated]. In May one can still walk through a mile of lime along the lanes between the woods, and admire the delicate variation from stool to stool in the shape, colour, and texture of the unfolding leaves. Great Monk Wood, still privately owned, is actively coppiced [Fig. 15.12].

The site is almost level and very wet in spring. The vegetation corresponds chiefly to the lime and ash–hazel areas of Chalkney; there is some hornbeam on sloping margins. As in Chalkney there are traces of plateau alder.

The history of the woods includes some unusual vicissitudes. Great and Little Monk Woods formed part of an estate bestowed on Coggeshall Abbey by Queen Maud in 1142. The monks made a park of their woods in 1203.[406] The two woods appear in Dissolution surveys but we are told nothing of their composition.

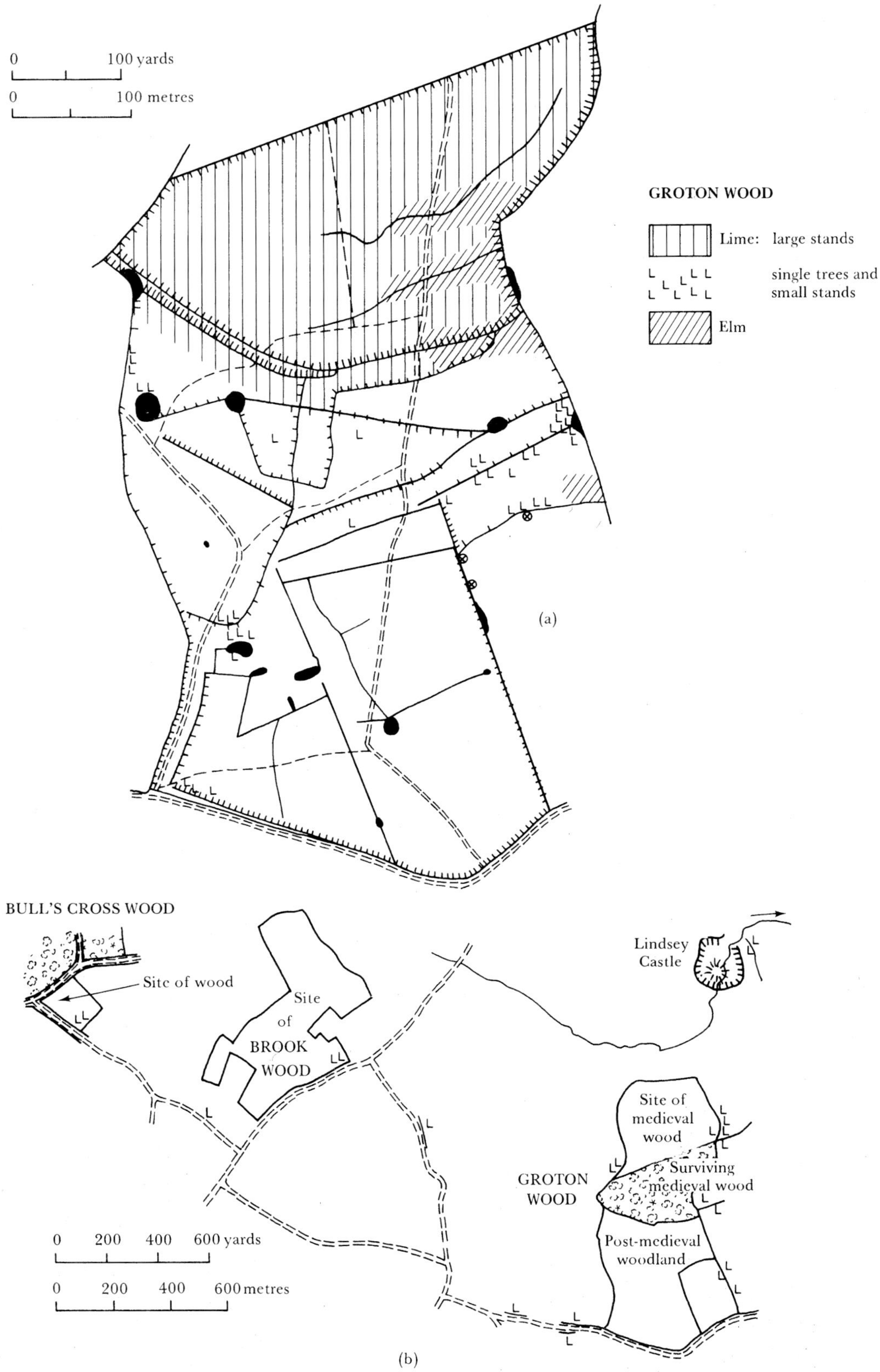

Fig. 15.9 (**a**) Groton Wood (W. Suffolk): earthworks and other surface features, with extent of *Tilia cordata*. (**b**) Surroundings of Groton Wood showing isolated stools of *Tilia* in hedges. Some of these survive from former woods, others result from occasional colonization.

To the other woods only scattered medieval references are known. Nunty Wood was *Noteheye* (nut-enclosure) in 1285,[851] suggesting that hazel was even then uncommon enough in this area for a wood to be named after it.

In 1571 the Monk Woods were found to have been badly mismanaged by a former lessee, who had felled too much timber and underwood and had neglected to protect their regrowth from 'byting of cattaile', so that

> 'within . . . great Moncke Woodde, there is twentie acres, And in . . . lytle Moncke Woodde is Tenne acres, the Springe whereof is greatly Wasted, and in a manner utterly spoyled, and very unlyke to be recovered agayne for increase of woodde.'[452]

The opposite problem arose 200 years later through an eccentric provision in the will of General Philip Honywood, the owner. He allowed his heirs to fell timber only for repairs on the estates; they might sell wood, but if they sold timber they forfeited the inheritance. The heirs were unable to devise sufficient repairs to keep up with the growth of oaks, 'great part whereof' by 1788 'are now decaying and others are at their full growth'. Eventually a special Act of Parliament had to be passed to resolve the problem.[284] Probably because of this 'overgrowth of timber', the eighteenth-century sales of wood average only 8*d* to 20*d* per acre per year of growth.[290–1] They include hop-poles, 'coopers' poles' (presumably rods for making barrel-hoops), and small quantities of birch and 'poplers' (presumably aspen); but the largest sums are for firewood. Such an episode would, if anything, encourage the dominance of lime at the expense of less shade-bearing underwood. Much of Great Monk Wood is again full of oaks; it demonstrates the remarkable ability of lime to survive and grow under a complete canopy of oak.

Conservation

Since 1945 the limewoods of Eastern England have fared slightly better than ancient woodland in general (Fig. 6.1). As usual, it is the large woods that have come off worst; the four largest concentrations of lime were all partly converted to plantations. The remaining stands are in good condition and in more than a quarter of them (including nine of the twenty-one largest stands) there is active coppicing, particularly important for the flora and fauna of such a densely-shading tree.

The prospects for conservation of native lime are relatively good: it is excellent as underwood, is in demand for brush-backs and pulp-wood, and resists silvicultural poisoning [Fig. 33.11]. So interesting and important a tree is still under-represented in nature reserves: in Eastern England one reserve, Groton Wood, was founded partly for its protection, and it occurs in Swanton Novers Great Wood (Nature Conservancy Council) and the Bradfield Woods, as well as under Essex County Council protection in Chalkney and Garnett's Woods.

Conclusions

The limewoods of Eastern England are closely related to the hornbeam-woods; to some extent the trees are interchangeable, though their geographical distributions are very different and their soil characteristics are not identical (compare Figs. 15.5 and 14.3).

In Continental phytosociology, lime is rather neglected: most woods are placed in one or other of the sub-associations of the Querco–Carpinetum types. Although no specifically lime-containing woodlands in western Europe appear to have achieved the respectability of a phytosociological Latin name, there are accounts of several variants of *chênaies–charmaies–tillaies* in Valois (near Chantilly),[758] and *Traubeneichen–Winterlinden–Hainbuchenwälder* in N.W. Germany.[873] These mosaics of oak, hornbeam, and lime are of the same general kind as the mid Essex woods; the German ones, although very different in their ground vegetation, are said, like ours, to be on fertile ground and to have 'given way more and more to farmland in the course of the centuries'. The forest of Białowieża, often supposed to be the most nearly natural lowland forest in Europe, consists in large part of mixtures and mosaics of lime, hornbeam, *Quercus robur*, and *Ulmus glabra*.[107] The English wood most nearly approximating to this composition is Chalkney.

The discontinuous distribution of lime in modern England cannot adequately be explained by the tree's preferences for soil and climate, which are wide and do not appear to constrain it except at its northern limit. We cannot believe that there should be many suitable habitats in the north of Essex but practically none in the south. The distribution must depend mainly on historical events whose effects are irreversible, since lime can no longer recover lost ground. The Lime Decline came to an end about 1,200 years ago, since when the distribution – even, as far as we can tell, within existing woods – has been remarkably stable: lime has lost further ground by the destruction of woodland in general but has not been replaced by other trees.

While any further argument is bound to be conjectural, the most plausible reason for the end of the Lime Decline is the extension of woodland conservation and coppicing. Lime, as we have seen, tends to disappear from wood-pastures; one of the few on which it survives is Dedham Heath, where it was specifically preserved. In counties with little woodland and much population, e.g. Lincolnshire, Norfolk, and Suffolk, the woods were encoppiced while there was still some lime left. In Hertfordshire and most of southern England the woods were much larger, less intensively used, and less effectively protected against grazing until after lime had become extinct; the chief exception was Devon, with its many small private woods in Domesday Book (Table 9.1), and it is noteworthy that most of the surviving lime south of the Thames is in that county. In South Essex the many medieval parks (Fig. 12.10) and large wooded commons would have been unfavourable for lime; the Epping Forest story might well have been widely repeated.

Added in 2003 edition

A few outlying sites of lime have been discovered, notably by Simon Leatherdale, who has found a handful of stools in Ditton Park Wood, east Cambridgeshire.

Limewoods are faring very well, because lime (more than any other tree) resisted foresters' attempts to destroy it in the 1950s and 1960s, and now plays a central part in the rehabilitation of ancient woodland (pp. 521–3, Fig. 33.11). The coppice shoots also have some resistance to browsing by deer.

Fig. 15.10 The last surviving tree of the wildwood? The only lime stool in Silk Wood, Westonbirt (Gloucs) is a ring nearly 50 feet in diameter. A few limes have the property of branches bending over and taking root, which makes the stools younger than their diameter would indicate. This does not appear to be such an individual: its age is thus in thousands rather than hundreds of years. May 1987

Fig. 15.11 Pure Limewood with bluebell, showing the gregariousness of lime. Shrawley Wood, Worcestershire. May 1985

Fig. 15.12 Pure Limewood, coppiced in the ancient manner with edge tools. This wood probably supplied the oak timber for the Coggeshall Barn (Fig. 10.8). Great Monk Wood, Coggeshall. March 1980

Fig. 15.13 One- and two-year lime seedlings (p. 243). Note the five-fingered cotyledons. Lime seedlings, following the hot summers of recent decades, are no longer rare, but seldom get beyond this stage. Chalkney Wood, Essex. June 1993

16

The elmwoods

Elms are the most difficult genus of British trees to analyse: they have two sources of complexity which are peculiarly their own. They come in a remarkable range of forms – there are arguably more different kinds of elm than of all other British trees put together – and are influenced by several important diseases. Evolution and pathology are more obvious factors in the ecology of elmwoods than of other native woodland.

Elms are among the commonest trees outside woods. Many writers assume them (apart from *Ulmus glabra*) to be almost exclusively non-woodland. Even Tansley largely passed over the existence of woodland elms, no complete account of which has ever been published. An account of elms in general could easily fill a book; in this chapter I limit myself to elms in woods, and to aspects of taxonomy, pathology, and history which are relevant to this theme.

The different elms

The elms as a 'critical' genus

One species, wych-elm (*Ulmus glabra*), reproduces by seed in the conventional way; it is variable, and narrow-leaved forms are named subspecies *montana*, but presents no particular difficulty. Most other elms reproduce almost exclusively by suckers which arise from the root-system to form a *clone* (p. 1) of genetically identical trees, all of which are, in effect, parts of the same individual. Once established a clone can spread indefinitely and lives for ever unless destroyed.

Cloning occurs in some other trees (aspen, cherry, sometimes service) and in many herbs (e.g. bracken (p. 85), dog's-mercury (p. 95)). The complexities of elms arise from cloning combined with unusual genetic variability and with the rarity of other means of reproduction. Contrary to some popular belief, most elms set seed in most years (though it is often sterile); seedlings are not particularly rare but are delicate and very edible. Elm occasionally gets established from seed – as is shown by trees on railway embankments and in other places where they could not have arisen otherwise – but this is so infrequent, particularly in a wood, that individual clones can be counted and mapped.

Elms are one of the 'critical genera' of taxonomically difficult plants that have largely abandoned sex as a means of reproduction. These include brambles (*Rubus*) and dandelions (*Taraxacum*) and, among British trees, part of the genus *Sorbus*, although the critical *Sorbus* species are not important woodland trees. Each of these genera consists of a multitude of forms maintained by asexual reproduction. When sexual reproduction does occur it is liable to generate new forms which maintain themselves in the same way. In critical genera other than *Ulmus*, taxonomists have described a large number of 'microspecies' which are given Latin names and grouped into sections; for instance *Flora Europaea* lists some 2,300 species of *Taraxacum*. The details may be disputed but the general procedure is well recognized.

Ulmus is the most difficult critical genus in the British flora: it is unique in being the subject of two systems of taxonomic research which fail to agree over the principles as well as details of classification. Elms have many distinguishing characters, but few that can precisely be expressed in words or figures; the trees cannot be preserved in herbaria; the leaf characters vary from one part of the tree to another, and careful sampling is needed. There is the problem of how many kinds of elms to recognize and what to call them. There has been enough sexual reproduction to generate an unmanageable number of distinguishable clones, some of which have been widely planted as hedgerow trees. Pteleologists (students of elms) are reluctant to bestow a Latin name on what they suspect to be the dispersed fragments of a single individual; but without a system of formal naming it is diffficult to identify any particular elm.

Classifications of elms

The common ground among British and Continental pteleologists is that elms can be divided into three groups on the lines of the sections of other critical genera. These are:

(1) *Ulmus glabra*, wych-elm. Non-suckering; coppicing when felled; tree spreading, often with diverging branches and twigs; leaves large, rough, with stalks less than 6% of the leaf-length, with a slender point (often three points at the leaf apex on fast-growing shoots).

(2) The *Ulmus procera*, 'English' elm, section. Suckering;

non-coppicing; trees large, erect, with heavy masses of dark foliage; leaves broad (at least two-thirds as wide as long), rough, appearing early in the year and staying late, usually attacked by the leaf-gall mite *Eriophyes ulmicola*; very susceptible to the current form of Dutch Elm Disease.

(3) The *Ulmus minor* (= *carpinifolia*), 'smooth-leaved' elm, section. Suckering; rarely coppicing; habit various; leaves smooth at top of tree, less than two-thirds as wide as long, usually appearing late and falling early very seldom attacked by *Eriophyes*.

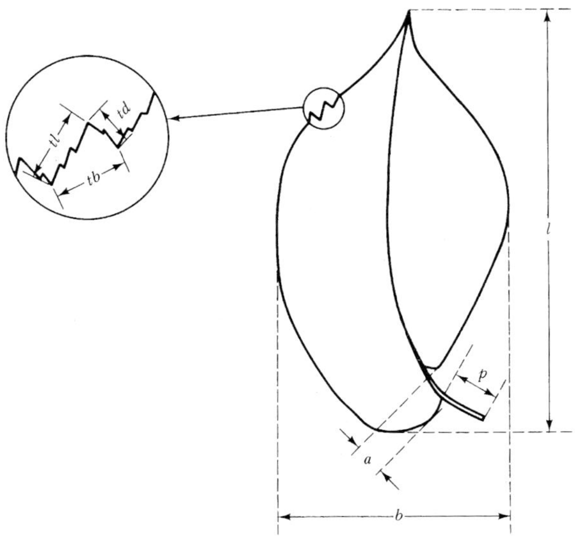

Fig. 16.1 Diagram of an elm leaf, showing the conventions for measuring length *l*, relative breadth *b/l*, relative petiole length *p/l*, relative asymmetry *a/l*, and tooth length, breadth, and depth (*tl*, *tb*, *td*). These last are measured on a representative *main* tooth; tooth number is the total number of secondary as well as of main teeth.

Many elms are intermediate between sections and are supposed to be hybrids.

In Suffolk and Essex there are innumerable forms of *minor* elms as well as the less variable *procera* and *glabra*. Northwards and westwards the elms gradually become simpler. *Procera* is the common elm of most of the Midlands and of western and southern England, and *glabra* of the Highland Zone. Other forms of *minor* appear in Cornwall as well as in France and Belgium.

Dr R. Melville divided *minor* elms into four species, namely *minor* itself, *coritana*, *angustifolia*, and *plotii*. He also recognized eleven hybrids, some of which are claimed to have three or four parent species, making a total of seventeen kinds.[789–92a] These are defined by characters of the tree and of leaf shape and colour as well as of leaf measurement.

Dr R. H. Richens described elms almost exclusively in terms of their leaves. He had a standard procedure for recording ten leaf characteristics – eight measurements (Fig. 16.1), whether rough or smooth, and whether *Eriophyes* is present. These are collated to produce groups of elm clones (or of different occurrences of the same clone) named after places where they occur. In a systematic analysis of elms associated with ancient village closes in the counties of Cambridge, Huntingdon, Bedford, Hertford, Essex, and in the Fens[854–60] he recognized some 35 groups of *minor* elms, 4 of *procera*, and a few intermediate groups. This survey has been extended to France.[862] Elms with similar leaf characters have been found in widely separated places. Richens claimed that this resulted from artificial introduction on many separate occasions: since the Iron Age, and especially in Roman times, people imported their favourite elms – either by way of immigration or of trade – and established them around settlements, where the elms have propagated themselves ever since.

I shall not try to reconcile the systems of these two learned men. The difference appears to be that in the Melville system diversity of elms results chiefly from hybridization within this country, whereas in the Richens system the variants evolved mainly overseas, hybridization in Britain playing only a small part. The evidence for both is circumstantial. Prehistoric remains of elms cannot be identified as to species, so that we cannot tell directly what elms are indigenous. We can hardly hope to verify the hybridization theory by experiment, least of all the supposed triple and quadruple hybrids. Too little is yet known of early international relations to corroborate in detail the importation theory. The reader of Melville's papers will not find it easy to ascertain how it is decided which elms are to be species and which to be hybrids. The reader of Richens may ask whether eight leaf-measurements – not all of which can vary independently – are sufficient to establish that two elms in different parts of Europe are really the same elm, still less that one has been imported from the other. In the great avenue of Wimpole (Cambs) I had occasion to compare two elms – one belonging to Richens's Boxworth group, the other undescribed – which though very different in other respects happened to have very similar leaf characters (Fig 16.2).

While intending no disparagement to the theoretical basis of the Melville system, I shall adopt that of Richens as a more practical means of specifying elms. The seventeen Melville categories are too few adequately to describe the British elm flora; to categorize a particular tree is difficult and two observers cannot be relied upon to get the same answer. Richens's forty-odd categories, although limited to the elms of one habitat, cover a larger proportion of the total range; by following the rules even an inexperienced pteleologist can decide with confidence whether a randomly chosen tree fits (as far as its leaves are concerned) into a Richens category or is different from all of them.

Woodland elms

We might expect clues to the differentiation of elms to lie in the elms of ancient woods rather than those of more artificial habitats. Woodland trees are more difficult to study than free-standing elms and have been neglected. The form of the tree is often indeterminate when it is hemmed in by other trees. Most elms produce six to seven different kinds of leaves, of which the only ones suitable for identification are those on short-shoots exposed to full sunlight, which are difficult to reach in a wood. Unless one can get identifiable leaves at the wood edge, or from high branches by means of a specially-trained monkey[638] or by courtesy of a summer storm, one may have to fall back on recognizing short-shoot leaves at the general leaf-fall in autumn. A useful character is the time of leaf-opening or of leaf-fall, which varies by several weeks and can often be used to delimit the boundaries of otherwise similar clones.

The most important ecological characteristic of a woodland elm is whether or not it suckers. Elms which sucker usually do not coppice, and I call these *invasive*. Elms which do not sucker (or which sucker weakly) form coppice stools, and I call them *non-invasive*.

Invasive elms

Suckering elms in woods belong to both the *minor* and the *procera* sections or occasionally are intermediate between them. Many, but by no means all, are obviously related to, or identical with, the elms of the local hedges and villages.

Non-invasive elms

Wych-elm is a common woodland tree in the north and west. In Eastern England it is much less abundant, but there is a peculiar and hitherto undescribed group of woodland elms often mistaken for it. These have the coppicing, non-suckering behaviour of *Ulmus glabra* and often its spreading habit and divergent twigs, but their leaves are usually smooth, with long stalks and more asymmetrical bases. Most such elms are intermediate between *glabra* and members of the *minor* (or occasionally *procera*) sections, and by the Melville canon should be regarded as hybrids, although there is no proof that this is so. They are gregarious – unlike *glabra*, which occurs as single stools – and appear to form clonal patches, despite the absence of obvious suckering. From a Richens-type analysis of such elms from some 25 woods (Fig. 16.2 and Table 16.1) I conclude that they range continuously from trees almost indistinguishable from *glabra* to those which would be regarded as *minor* had they the power of suckering. Different *glabra* and *minor* characters are combined almost at random; some of these elms resemble non-woodland intermediates between the sections, such as Richens's Boxted group of elms,[860] but as a whole they are heterogeneous. In order to have a name for them, I shall use the term Lineage Elms, after their chief locality, for all non-invasive woodland elms with the exception of *glabra* (and of rare introductions into woods of cultivated varieties such as the Huntingdon Elm).

The diseases of elms

Elm diseases in general

The commonest disease of elms is bacterial wet-wood, from which probably all woodland and most non-woodland elms suffer. This is responsible for the white incrustations and black tarry seepages which exude from wounds and fissures in elm trunks, for the water-soaked appearance and sour smell of elm heartwood, and for the gradual dying-back of the crowns particularly of *minor* elms. It occurs less commonly in many other trees. It was first described nearly 200 years ago[902] but only in the 1970s was it recognized as a definite disease.[864] It is attributed to bacteria, especially '*Erwinia nimipressuralis*', which invade the heartwood through wounds or through the roots, and which can live without oxygen by turning wood into methane. The methane can generate enough gas pressure to split open the trunk [Fig. 16.12]. This is a possible explanation for the curious property, for which *Ulmus procera* is well known, of branches dropping off without apparent cause. As I can vouch on several occasions, branches fall, not in gales or under the load of heavy rain, but on calm summer days [Fig. 16.13]. The pressures generated by *Erwinia* are a conceivable agent of the internal disruption which undoubtedly takes place.

Elms are attacked probably by more wood-rotting fungi than any other tree: these include many Polyporaceae and species of *Pleurotus*, and some, such as *Lyophyllum* (= *Pleurotus*) *ulmarium* and *Fomes ulmarius*, that are peculiar to elm. Most of these are wound-parasites that rot the tree internally without affecting its vitality. Elms survive, not by resisting damage, but by repairing its consequences and by regenerating missing parts. The loss of over half the crown of a tree, by disease or storm, may be difficult to detect thirty years later. Old free-standing elms often 'self-pollard'; they break off leaving a tall stump which sprouts new branches, as happened long ago to many of the 'pseudo-Boxworth' elms at Wimpole.

Elms are also liable to damage by horses and pigs eating the bark, to defoliation by caterpillars when the leaves emerge, and to severe drought. Apart from Dutch Elm Disease, horse or pig damage appears to be the only common cause of dead elms.

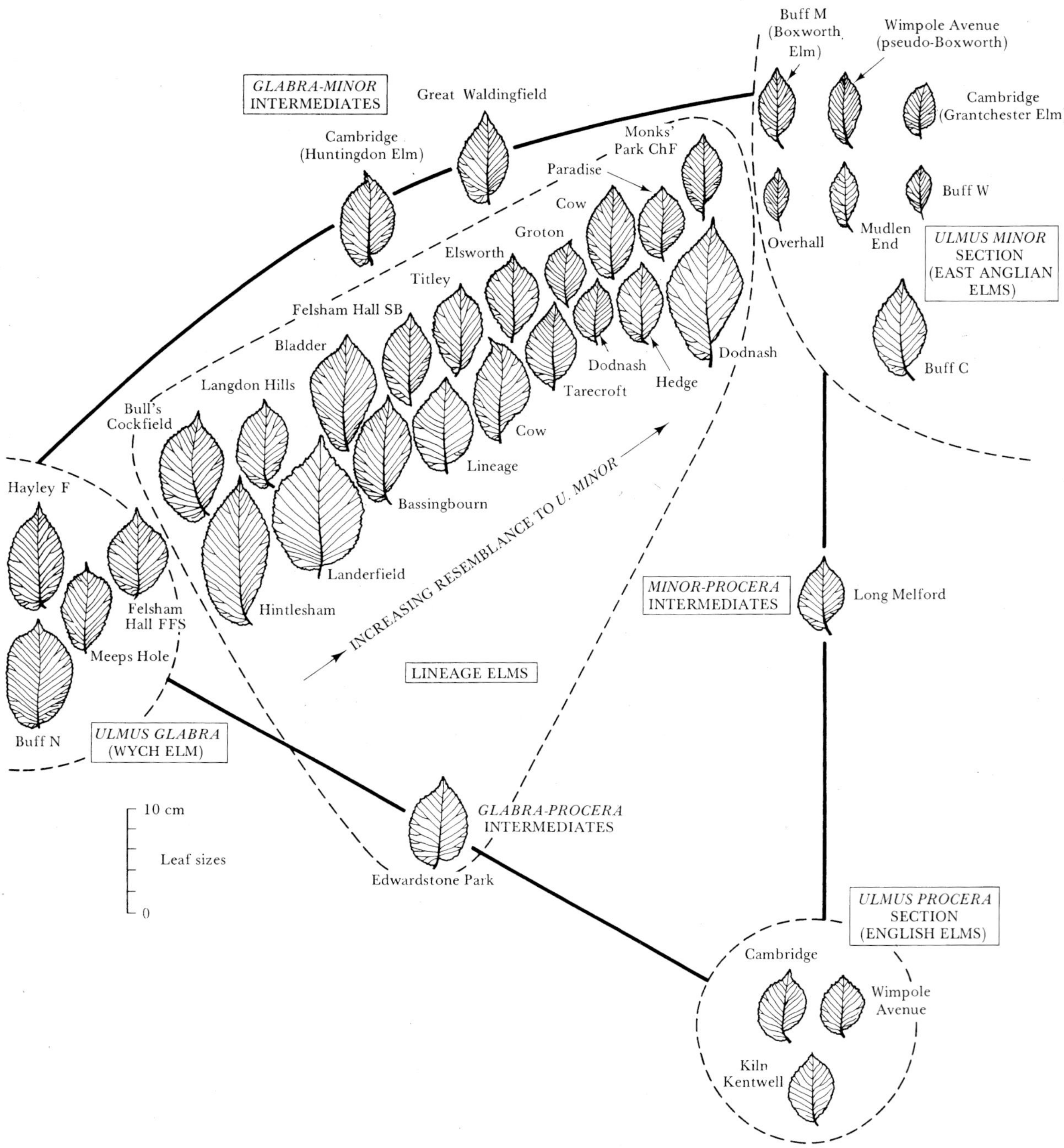

Fig. 16.2 Typical leaves of a number of Lineage elm populations [named after Lineage Wood in Long Melford] arranged to illustrate their resemblances to other kinds of elm.

Leaves from populations belonging to the three recognized British sections of *Ulmus*, namely *U. glabra* and the *minor* and *procera* sections, are grouped at the corners of an equilateral triangle. Twenty Lineage-type elms – i.e. weakly-suckering or non-suckering woodland elms other than *glabra* – are illustrated. Nineteen of these are intermediate in leaf characters between *glabra* and *minor* and are arranged roughly in order of their resemblance to these two sections. Note the usually smaller size, longer stalks and greater asymmetry of the leaves placed nearer *minor*. The remaining Lineage-type elm is placed between *glabra* and *procera* as being intermediate in leaf characters between those sections.

Dutch Elm Disease

General behaviour

This most-publicized of tree diseases is the work of an ascomycete fungus, *Ceratocystis* (= *Ceratostomella*, *Graphium* (whence the French name *graphiose* for the disease)) *ulmi*. Its general characteristics are described in many books and articles.[693, 822–3] The fungus inhabits the wood-vessels of the current year's growth. It damages the tree, partly by blocking the conduction of water, and partly by interfering with the tree's hormones (whence the bending into curves of twigs, and even of branches several years old, that is a characteristic symptom).

Ceratocystis gets from tree to tree mainly by the two elm bark-beetles, *Scolytus scolytus* (= *destructor*) and *S. multistriatus*. The female bark-beetle lays eggs in a gallery which she excavates between the bark and wood of recently dead elm; the larvae excavate galleries of their own, at the ends of which they eventually pupate. *Ceratocystis* fructifies in these galleries, so that the emerging beetles are contaminated with spores. Young beetles fly off to living elms and feed by nibbling the bark and wood of the crotches of twigs. In many elm trees a large proportion of the crotches bear the scars of bites. These bites do no appreciable damage but are liable to introduce spores into the vessels of a healthy elm, from which the fungus may spread downwards to involve the branch and eventually the whole tree. Beetles emerge, to start new infections, between May and October; in winter the larvae lie dormant in the bark. The effects of beetle infection range from no appreciable damage to death of the whole tree within a few weeks. The earlier the infection the more likely it is to be severe. Trees not killed in one season sometimes recover, though often the disease continues in the following year.

If the fungus reaches the roots it may be sucked up directly into the wood of other trees of the clone. Trees infected via the roots usually die rapidly and all at once; those infected by beetles die branch by branch.

The current epidemic

After many years of quiescence *Ceratocystis* reappeared as a serious pest from about 1965. It spread as an epidemic starting from foci near Gloucester, Southampton, Bristol, London, and Ipswich, and within 13 years had killed some 60% of the non-woodland elms over 20 ft high in England and Wales.[617, 694, 700]

This epidemic is associated with a change in the characteristics of *Ceratocystis*; the new form, called the 'aggressive strain', kills trees more quickly than that previously known, and is more likely to continue into the following year, so that recovery from a slight infection is less common than it used to be.[696–7, 699] It spreads more readily from tree to tree by the roots. It can be recognized in culture.

The present epidemic is particularly deadly towards *procera* elms, as is apparent at all levels from the country as a whole[694] to the fate of individual trees. At the time of writing (early 1978) the last intact areas of *procera* in Wiltshire and Oxfordshire have almost disappeared; as an upstanding tree the English Elm survives chiefly in East Sussex, where the local authority has been particularly diligent in protecting it.[618] *Minor*

Also shown are two non-woodland elms intermediate between *glabra* and *minor*: the Huntingdon Elm, a common non-suckering variety not found outside cultivation; and the Great Waldingfield elm, a suckering clone with extremely pendulous branches. The Long Melford elm exemplifies a non-woodland clone intermediate between *procera* and *minor*.

The diagram shows most of the range of variation in Lineage elms, but in the other sections, especially *minor*, only a few leaf-shapes can be illustrated. The *minor* elm from Cambridge is an example of Richens's Grantchester group; Buff M is very close to Richens's Boxworth group of elms. The other populations illustrated here cannot with certainty be referred to any of the named groups of village elms. The *minor* elm from Wimpole Avenue is what I have called the 'pseudo-Boxworth' clone (p. 261). Broken lines indicate the boundaries of the *glabra*, *minor*, *procera*, and Lineage sections.

Provenances:
Bassingbourn Wood in Bocking, mid Essex
Bladder Wood in Wheathampstead, Herts
BuffWood, W. Cambs (four elms, Fig. 16.8)
Bull's Wood in Cockfield, W. Suffolk
Cambridge: ancient elm on Christ's Pieces (*minor*); elm planted c. 1750 on Trinity College Piece (*procera*); Huntingdon Elm on Parker's Piece
Cow Wood in Panfield, mid Essex (two elms)
Dodnash Wood, S.E. Suffolk (two elms)
Edwardstone Park Wood, W. Suffolk
Elsworth Wood, W. Cambs
Felsham Hall Wood, Bradfield Woods, W. Suffolk: elms from Front Fell and Strawberry Bank (Fig. 3.1)
Great Waldingfield, W. Suffolk: great elm by church tower
Groton Wood, W. Suffolk
Hayley Wood, W. Cambs: elm F (Fig. 16.4)
Hedge Wood, Bradfield St Clare, W. Suffolk
Hintlesham, S.E. Suffolk: elm at Wood Lodge
Kiln Wood, Kentwell in Long Melford, W. Suffolk
Landerfield Wood in Rivenhall, mid Essex
Langdon Hills, S. Essex: grove in Salisbury Avenue (Fig. 1.4)
Lineage Wood in Long Melford (Fig. 16.10)
Long Melford: three great elms on the Green, survivors of a former grove
Meeps Hole Wood, Ramsden Crays, S.E. Essex
Monks' Park, Bradfield Woods, W. Suffolk: Cherry-tree Fell
Mudlen End, Felsham, W. Suffolk
Overhall Grove in Boxworth, W. Cambs
Paradise Wood in Long Melford (Fig. 16.10)
Tarecroft Wood in Rivenhall, mid Essex
Titley Grove in Barking, mid Suffolk
Wimpole Avenue (p. 261), *procera* and *minor* elms planted c. 1718

Table 16.1 Leaf characteristics of certain elms.

Category or provenance	Length (mm)	Relative breadth	Relative petiole length	Relative asymmetry	Number of teeth	Tooth length (mm)	Tooth breadth (mm)	Tooth depth (mm)	Roughness	*Eriophyes*
Typical *glabra* (after Richens)[860]	90–115	0.45–0.60	0.04	0.04–0.08	150–210	5.5–6.5	5.0–6.0	2.0–3.0	+ + +	—
Glabra-like Lineage-type (Bull's Wood, Cockfield)	94	0.62	0.08	0.04	118	4.7	4.9	2.2	—	—
Intermediate Lineage-type (Titley Grove)	77	0.64	0.06	0.02	99	5.9	5.5	3.0	—	—
Minor-like Lineage-type (Monks' Park)	76	0.52	0.13	0.12	113	4.3	4.0	2.7	—	—
Boxworth-type *minor* (after Richens)[855]	45–55	0.45–0.55	0.08–0.16	0.04–0.08	70–100	4.0–5.0	3.0–4.5	1.5–2.5	—	—
Chrishall-type *minor* (after Richens)[860]	50–60	0.60–0.65	0.18–0.20	0.14–0.16	80–100	4.5–5.5	5.0–5.5	1.5–2.5	—	—
Procera-like Lineage-type (Foxhunters' Fell, Felsham Hall Wood)	58	0.78	0.04	0.01	111	5.5	4.8	3.7	+ + +	?
Typical procera (after Richens)[858]	55–60	0.75–0.85	0.08–0.10	0.06–0.12	60–80	5.5–6.5	5.5–6.0	2.5–3.5	+ + +	+ + +

Figures for woodland elm are the means from a number of typical leaves. For provenances see Fig. 16.1

Table 16.2 Genotype and date of death of elms in Wimpole South Avenue.

	Ulmus procera	*U. minor* (chiefly pseudo-Boxworth)	Uncertain genotype	Total
Died before 1973	6	0	1	7
Died in 1973	10	1	2	13
Died in 1974	15	0	4	19
Died in 1975	48	2	7	57
Died in 1976	50	22	1	73
Still alive, late 1976	0	50	0	50
Totals	129	75	15	219

elms, although their resistance varies, are seldom as badly affected as *procera*; in much of Eastern England, even close to Ipswich, the disease has affected chiefly pockets of *procera* elms in what is mainly *minor* country. Essex was one of the earliest- and worst-affected counties, losing vast numbers of *procera* in the south; yet in North Essex there are still some areas full of *minor* elms with very little disease. In Cambridge city it is chiefly *procera* elms that have gone, although *glabra* often succumbed in the drought year 1976.

What amounts to an experiment on the susceptibility of different elms took place in the great avenue at Wimpole (Cambs), planted some 250 years ago – the annual rings suggest 1718. The four rows of original elms, most of which were still there in 1970, were a random mixture of a *procera* clone and *minor* (chiefly the 'pseudo-Boxworth' clone). In 1972 they began to die, and in 1976, before the northern third of the avenue was destroyed, I scored 219 original trees for genotype and date of death (Table 16.2). Although identical in age and exposure, the *procera* elms died well before the *minor*. It was not until 1976, when they were bombarded with vast numbers of beetles emerging from the dead *procera*, that the *minor* were seriously affected; two-thirds of them were still alive after the last *procera* had died. Nor, until 1976, was the disease prevalent among the *minor* elms of the surrounding fields, despite the nearness of the Avenue as a source of beetles. *Minor* trees showed innumerable beetle bites, and it would appear, not that *Scolytus* avoids *minor* trees for feeding, but that it takes more bites to infect a *minor* tree than a *procera*.

Elm suckers less than 12 ft high are much less affected than big trees. In parts of Gloucestershire and South Essex, several years after the death of the last big tree, the hedges are full of healthy *procera* suckers. There is little danger of elms, even *procera*, becoming extinct.

Elms in woods are less affected than hedgerow trees.[700] Marginal elms may be attacked, and narrow belts of elms may be reduced to suckers; in Cambridgeshire *glabra* elms are sought out and killed, and in Hayley Wood the largest elm clone has, exceptionally, been severely attacked by a combination of *Ceratocystis*, *Scolytus*, and drought. In a compact wood, however, even *procera* often survives, and in parts of Gloucestershire and South Essex the only big elms remaining are in woods. What aspect of the woodland environment is responsible is not known. It may be the habits of *Scolytus*, which is seldom abundant in dead elms in a wood. It may be woodpeckers and other birds, which in a wood strip off the bark of dead elms and often peck around the entrance-holes of breeding beetles. Or it may be competition within the dead tree between *Ceratocystis* and some other fungus, notably *Flammulina* (= *Collybia*) *velutipes* which in the damp environment of a wood invades dead elms with remarkable speed and often occupies the entire trunk by winter before the disease has had an opportunity to be transmitted.

Elms that are damaged, e.g. by passing vehicles brushing the twigs, or that are growing fast after pollarding, are peculiarly liable to Elm Disease.

There are at least four similar epidemics in Europe: one, starting *c.* 1964, within a 120-mile radius of Paris; one around Geneva; another in the Innsbruck area, where elms are rare but are found and killed with remarkable efficiency; and a fourth around Reggio (Emilia), devastating the pollard elms on which the Italians, as in the days of Columella and Vergil, train their vines. I have seen the disease in the southernmost elms in Europe, at Piazza Armerina (Sicily). Another epidemic is in progress in the N.E. United States and in Canada, and the disease also exists in western Asia.[695]

Recent history

This is not the first epidemic of Dutch Elm Disease. It was first noticed in France in 1918 and in the ensuing years almost throughout Europe. It was most severe, and most extensively studied, in Holland, whence the name of the disease. The elms now being killed in Emilia are replacements for those that perished in the 1930s.[618] In England it was first reported in 1927, and its behaviour thereafter was recorded in detail by T. R. Peace.[822]

The epidemic of the 1930s had much in common with that of the 1970s. Attempts to control it were soon abandoned, partly because (as now) of lack of co-operation by landowners and public authorities, partly because of doubts about their effectiveness. It was widely predicted that elms would become extinct. The disease reached a peak around 1936 and then slowly declined; new infections were less common and trees more often recovered. By the late 1950s the dead elms had been replaced by suckering and the epidemic had been forgotten. Peace estimated that between 10% and 20% of the full-grown elms in Britain were killed; in some areas over half the trees died.

This story is corroborated, in general, by evidence in the annual rings of existing trees. A tree that recovers from Elm Disease leaves a record in the wood formed in the year of infection; this is highly distinctive and unlike the discolorations produced by other diseases. The affected wood-vessels are densely stained with a black or dark-brown pigment which slowly diffuses in a radial direction [Fig. 16.12d]. They are blocked by ***tyloses***, balloon-like structures whereby the tree seals off damaged sections of vessel, which are visible to the naked eye as white specks. These affect varying fractions of the circumference of the tree; it is sometimes possible to decide whether the infection was early or late in the season. Extensive infections are usually accompanied by some reduction in the width of the subsequent annual rings;[122] by following the infection along the length of the tree it is sometimes possible to trace it to the death of one or more major branches, long since rotted away and replaced by new growth. Infected vessels contain dormant *Ceratocystis*, and I have cultured the fungus from annual rings up to 25 years old. It is unlikely that it will be possible to recover older *Ceratocystis* in this way, because old rings are invaded by wet-wood which, although it may not obliterate the markings, appears to kill the fungus.

Whether the 1930s epidemic was caused by the same strain of *Ceratocystis* as that active now is uncertain. Contemporary accounts show that the fungus varied in cultural characteristics and in virulence.[822] The ecological evidence, although inadequate, suggests a different pattern from that of the 1970s. Peace's highest death-rates were in Cambridgeshire and North Essex, where the elms are likely to have been *minor*; predominantly *procera* areas, except in Sussex, were infected but got off lightly. My own tree-ring observations suggest that non-fatal attacks were commoner in woodland than in non-woodland elms and probably commoner in *minor* than in *procera*.

Why the 1930s epidemic declined is a mystery. It was not through running out of susceptible elms; nor has any sufficient change in climate or in human activities ever been proposed. Similar spontaneous declines, leaving many elms unattacked, were reported from Holland, Austria, Poland, etc.[694, 736]

Earlier history

Most writers on Dutch Elm Disease assume that it was not present in England before 1927 or in Europe before 1918, but this view is based on no stronger evidence than sup posed failure to observe it earlier.

Evidence in old annual rings proves that *Ceratocystis* was widespread in England well before it was first noticed: for instance it occurred in the 1912 ring of a tree at Kettering.[822] My own observations include many from before this date, the oldest being in the 1867 ring of a tree in Buff Wood.[120] Earlier evidence is difficult to get owing to the rarity of large clean sections with many annual rings, but Elm Disease streaks should be looked for especially in furniture: they are sometimes treated as decorative [Fig. 16.12].

In the first half of the nineteenth century there are many reports of epidemic deaths of elms, often with symptoms strongly suggesting *Ceratocystis*. For instance, in 1823 it was said of the elms in St James's Park, London:

> In spring we see the leaves sprout forth from the venerable trunks in all the luxuriance of vegetation, when of a sudden they are blasted as if by lightning, the bark falls from the stem, and long ere winter the finest tree perhaps in the park is only fit for fire-wood . . .

Scarcely two trees had been attacked in 1819, but

> . . . now every elm is in some degree infected, and every week we may observe that a tree has perished.[260]

In 1864, W. Menzies, describing the manner of death of different trees in Windsor Great Park, remarks:

> In an elm a great limb dies all at once from the point right into the trunk, while all the rest keeps green; then another limb goes, and so on until the whole tree is dead within a few weeks . . .[90]

The epidemic apparently lasted from 1819 to 1864. Deaths were reported particularly in and around London, Oxford, and Cambridge in the 1820s[254, 262, 391] and again in London in the 1840s.[339, 438] After a third outbreak in the London area, an editorial in *The Times* in 1862 predicted that 'elms will be extinct in England before another century has elapsed'.[497] The elms of north France, Belgium, and Holland were ravaged in the 1830s and 1840s.[339, 343, 482, 497] For forty years correspondents debated whether bark-beetles were the cause or the effect; other alleged causes included wet-wood, too much drainage, too little drainage, excavations for gas-mains, escapes of gas, vandalism, and 'old age and the want of nourishment'. Recommendations were made for felling or lopping infected trees and for controlling beetles, and attention was drawn to the danger of leaving felled logs lying near standing elms. Many of the credulous in England and France adopted the 'remedy' of removing part of the lower bark of threatened trees.[355, 497]

The 1819–64 epidemic affected no trees other than elm. Of the agents considered at the time only *Scolytus* is sufficiently specific to elm to have been a possible cause. Some contemporary observers believed that the beetles themselves could damage living trees by breeding in them; a belief which still lingers among aged woodmen. Such damage certainly did occur in the great drought of 1976. In August and September of that year I noticed attempts by *S. scolytus* to make egg-laying galleries in the living trunks of various species of elm in Cambridge and West Cambridgeshire [Fig. 16.12f]. Most of the galleries were flooded and the insects drowned by a copious flow of sap; in Hatley Park and Hayley Wood the sap attracted many wasps and other insects, a phenomenon last reported by Guérin-Méneville near Paris in 1846.[342–3] The only certain successful breeding in living trees was in the avenue at Wimpole. In and around Oxfordshire similar attacks were reported from July onwards by J. N. Gibbs and B. J. W. Greig; in some instances, as at Blenheim Palace, breeding was successful.[698]

In very hot weather a mother *Scolytus* can evidently mistake a droughted elm for a dead one. Usually this results only in egg-laying galleries which – unless *Ceratocystis* is introduced by the mother beetle – do only trivial damage to the tree. If the elm is very dehydrated it fails to exude sap, in which case the larvae survive and make numerous horizontal galleries which cut up the cambium and severely, perhaps mortally, injure the tree. This clearly does not happen in every hot summer.* For a living elm to be attractive to *Scolytus*, let alone to be capable of supporting larvae, requires a degree of dehydration unlikely to arise more than twice in a century. In 1976 the mean July temperature in central England was 18.4°C and the rainfall from June to August was 35% of average, a combination of heat and drought not recorded for at least 300 years and preceded by an almost equally severe summer in 1975. Attempts at breeding (conspicuous because of the dribbling sap) were not reported in 1975 nor in the three months with mean temperatures over 18.0°C – July 1934, August 1947, August 1955 – which fell in the period of Peace's study. Nor are they commonly reported from countries, such as middle France, where the mean temperature of a *normal* July reaches 18°C; this suggests that breeding in living elms required not only desiccation but also an excessive beetle population, built up the previous year in elms killed by disease.

No drought in the nineteenth century was as severe as that of 1975–6. Some of the early reports of elm death and damage were in hot summers; for instance in June 1846 (the year of Guérin-Méneville's observations in France) the monthly temperature reached 18.2°C, and in 1826 the temperatures were within ½° of those in 1976 and the rainfall little greater.[767, 782] But the epidemic in general was not dependent on the weather. In the London parks it was first noticed in the rather hot summer of 1819 and increased during the cold summers of 1820–4. The outbreaks of the early 1840s and 1860s built up in years of average to cool summers.

*It was rarely seen in the great summers of 1989, 1990, 1995, or 1997.

Direct attack by breeding *Scolytus* probably occurred in 1826 and 1846 but could not have been the main cause of the epidemic; it was controversial precisely because it was a relatively rare and non-repeatable event. Most careful observers were emphatic that *Scolytus* did not damage healthy trees: for instance S. Hibberd in 1863, after showing that experimental borings simulating breeding galleries healed in a few days, concluded: 'To Scolytus has been assigned the task of eating up *dying* elm-trees.'[346] The descriptions agree with death from *Ceratocystis* rather than from *Scolytus*. Elms died year after year regardless of weather. The 1823 account shows that they died week after week, not merely during exceptional heat-waves when they might have supported *Scolytus* larvae. The 1865 account agrees exactly with a tree stricken by beetle-borne Elm Disease. Great trees succumbed and not merely the small- and middle-sized elms which were the chief victims of *Scolytus* in 1976. As far as we can ever diagnose a historical disease, the cause appears to have been unrecognized *Ceratocystis*. Healthy elms were attacked by egg-laying *Scolytus* only when an exceptional drought coincided, as in 1976, with an unusually high beetle population. By 1868 the epidemic had declined; there were few recently-dead elms to produce mother beetles; despite the unusual drought of that summer (July temperature 18.3°C) T. A. Chapman, writing in 1869, could flatly deny that *Scolytus* attacked healthy trees.[251]

An earlier epidemic is suggested by the remark of J. C. Fabricius, the German entomologist, in 1781 that '*Bostrichus* [i.e. *Scolytus*] *scolytus*... lives under the bark of elm in England, which it sadly destroys'; he got this information from an Oxford man named Lee.[676] No date is given; although the summer of 1780 was dry and fairly hot (August 17.6°C) there had not been a combination of exceptional heat and drought since 1714, so I suspect *Ceratocystis* as the real cause. M. Olivier, the French entomologist who named the beetle *Scolytus destructor*, probably knew of this report but gives the habitat merely as 'decayed wood'.[437]

Some hints have come down from earlier periods. Does not Poins, horse-playing in a tap-room, address Falstaff as 'thou dead Elme'?[480] So specific a term of opprobrium suggests that elms were particularly often dead in 1598; and what could have killed them, in the notoriously cold summers of those years, but *Ceratocystis*? Why, in November 1743, should Mrs L. Barnston of Condover (Salop) have ordered her gardener to plant 'Elm trees, in lieu of all yt died, which were all insur'd?[385] What are we to make of the small dead and half-dead trees, looking like young elms smitten with Elm Disease, which form the sinister background to many of the Madonnas and New Testament scenes of Giovanni Bellini and other Venetian painters of *c.* 1500? Mrs Hilary Belcher draws my attention to an observation by Sir Thomas Brown in 1658 that 'in Elmes set in hedges... if one dieth the neighbouring Tree prospereth not long after'.[216a]

In a house in S. E. Suffolk the annual rings of a fifteenth-century elm beam display cycles of sudden drops in ring-width, followed by gradual recovery, identical with those produced in recent decades by severe but not mortal *Ceratocystis* attack (Fig. 16.3). The beam is over 11 ft long and quite sound, which rules out pollarding as an alternative explanation.

Conclusions

The appearance of Dutch Elm Disease in the 1920s is often attributed to the introduction of *Ceratocystis* from central Asia; this is an unfounded conjecture, for there is apparently no evidence that it is native there. The evidence strongly suggests that it is an ancient, probably indigenous, inhabitant of Europe and Britain. Normally it exists in mild forms which do little damage, but from time to time virulent strains appear which cause epidemics. At least six epidemics are in progress now and there is historical evidence of others. The detection of *Ceratocystis* as late as 1918 results, not from a change in its distribution, but from the development of techniques for identifying and culturing micro-fungi. When it had last been a serious pest, in 1864, mycologists had recognized only the more conspicuous pathogenic fungi and could hardly have detected *Ceratocystis*.

The appearance of virulent strains is readily explained by genetic change – mutation or rare recombination – of a kind familiar in animal and plant pathology. It is widely supposed that the virulent strain now current in England was introduced from North America. The evidence, though circumstantial, is strong: elm logs, with bark attached, have been imported from infected areas of Canada; beetles carrying what appears to be this strain of the fungus have been found in the bark; most of the foci of the epidemic are near ports.[617, 695–6] Americans universally believe that their Elm Disease, together with *Scolytus multistriatus*, was imported in a similar way from Europe in the 1920s. (The unsophisticated reader may well think it irrational to spend money on sending elm timber – let alone elm bark – in both directions across the Atlantic; but rationality is not a strong feature of intercontinental trade, and other examples of 'sending coals to Newcastle' will be noted elsewhere in this book.) The balance of evidence is that the British Elm Disease of the 1970s is not identical in behaviour to that of the 1930s, so a genetic change probably took place during its sojourn in America. In countries not thus connected with Canada the virulent strains are more likely to be of local origin.

The chief unsolved problem of Elm Disease is why the epidemics should decline, as has been well substantiated

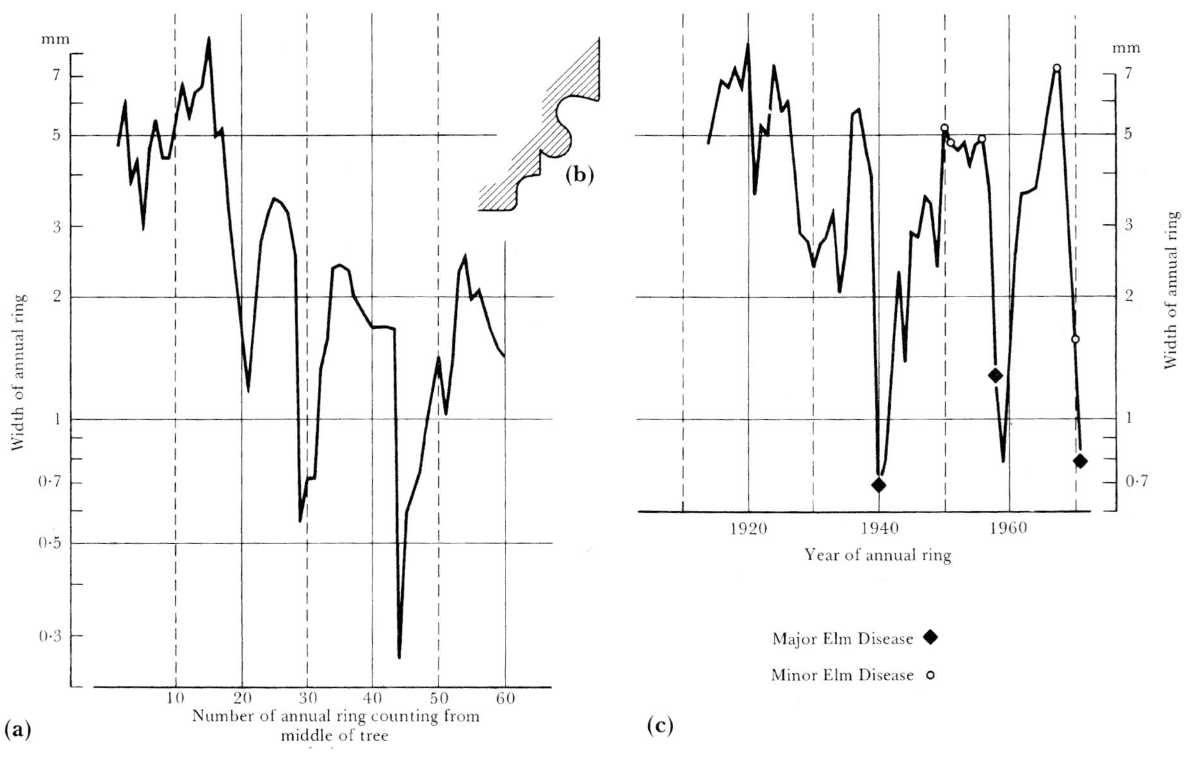

Fig. 16.3 (**a**) Widths of annual rings in elm beam forming chimney bressumer, Valley Farm, Flatford, S.E. Suffolk. (**b**) Profile of moulding on this beam, characteristic of the late fifteenth century.[734, 868] (**c**) Ring-widths in section of woodland elm, showing two cycles of slow growth and recovery following severe *Ceratocystis* attack. A third attack killed the tree. Hayley Wood.

on several independent occasions. None of the obvious explanations, such as running out of susceptible trees, fits the facts. Plants, having no immunological system, cannot apparently develop resistance of the kind that limits the spread of epidemics in man. Possibly the genes for virulence somehow become lost or dispersed through hybridization with local populations of non-virulent *Ceratocystis*. A parallel change has occurred in the epidemic of chestnut blight occasioned by the fungus *Endothia parasitica* in Italy, which is now much less damaging than it was in the early years of the epidemic.[796] This has been traced to the spread of a virus infection which cripples the fungus.[603a]

In the twentieth century, Elm Disease epidemics have been getting more frequent and more destructive, partly because of the increasing habit of transporting timber and bark, which disperses virulent strains. The warnings for other tree diseases – and not only diseases of trees – are plain. On previous experience the present epidemic should eventually decline, but we cannot tell how soon.

An ecological parallel is the decline in chestnut (*Castanea dentata*) in North America following the introduction of *Endothia* in 1904.[823] Chestnut has not been exterminated but has been changed from a major dominant species to a small tree of the understorey. The progress and ecological effects of the disease have been extensively recorded.[620] Similar records should be kept of the consequences of Elm Disease in this country [Chapter 28]. The greatest effect is likely to be on *Ulmus glabra*, which is sometimes killed outright and does not easily return. With suckering elms only the tall trees are killed; the suckers remain alive and can, if necessary, wait indefinitely for a chance to grow up again. In the long term clones are at greater risk from human activities, such as destroying the suckers in order to plant other species as replacements, than from the disease itself.

Elms in prehistory

The early post-glacial and Atlantic Period

Elm arrived in Britain in the middle stage of post-glacial recolonization. By the Atlantic Period it had become the commonest or second commonest tree over most of Ireland and locally in Great Britain, often associated with hazel.

The species of elm have never been fully identified from British material. It is usually conjectured that *Ulmus glabra* was the commonest elm, especially in the Highland Zone; some authorities suppose it to have been the only elm.

The Elm Decline [see also p. 451]

The decline in elm, which is used to define the end of the Atlantic Period (Chapter 8), is the most rapid vegetational change in post-glacial history.[710] Elm pollen suddenly falls, typically to about half its former frequency,[710] and either remains scarce or slowly and incompletely recovers. Radiocarbon dates for Britain place the Decline between 3600 and 3950 B.C.,[881] and the span for Europe as a whole is little if any wider.[707] It is almost universal in N. W. Europe, though absent from North America, and is highly specific to elm. In 500 years, or possibly much less, half the elm vanished from Europe without affecting other trees.

Many possible explanations have been proposed.[151] A deterioration of climate is inadequate to explain so sudden, universal, and specific a change. Had the climate become less favourable for elm, this would not have caused a general decline in elm and elm alone; it would have wiped out elm in areas where the climate had been marginal for it, but would not have affected elm at the middle of its climatic range unless the change was so great as to affect other species also. A climatic change universal in Europe ought to have had some effect on North American elms. By similar arguments we can dismiss as general explanations theories of deterioration in soils or soil moisture.

The strong association of the Elm Decline with the first records of farming and of farmland weeds suggests the widely held theory that elm decreased through being exploited by Neolithic men.[73, 898] The argument runs that the first farmers spread rapidly through Northern Europe, bringing with them livestock for which there was at first no pasture because of the abundance of trees. Instead of grass they took to feeding stalled animals on leafy branches shredded or pollarded from trees, of which elm was the favourite. I have seen such a practice in the remoter parts of the Alps and it is widely reported from Kashmir;[70] it is occasionally mentioned in non-woodland tree management in Britain,[335] for instance by Tusser in the sixteenth century;[506] there is archaeological evidence for it in Switzerland.[898] The pollarded elms would not have died – indeed their lives would have been prolonged – but their pollen output would have been reduced even though elm flowers again relatively quickly after lopping.

This theory explains the absence of an elm decline in America, where the history of domestic animals is different. It may in part account for the archaeological connection, although recent work indicates that the Decline is not as simply related to the Mesolithic–Neolithic transition as used to be thought.[615] In quantitative terms it is less satisfactory. If Neolithic farmers used most of the elm in Ireland, where elm was abundant, they ought to have run out of elm and to have turned to other species in parts of Great Britain where elm was less common. Modern Alpine farmers use ash as well as elm for feeding stock, and there is some indication of the use of hazel in Neolithic Somerset (p. 107). The Elm Decline, however, affects only elm regardless of how common or rare it was.

In about a quarter of the British Isles, chiefly in Ireland, elm was very common: at a rough estimate it formed at least a third of the Atlantic dry-land wildwood. Over a further two-thirds of the British Isles it was less common; on average it apparently formed about a fifteenth of the wildwood. (This takes into account the pollen productivity of elm.) These figures, multiplied by the appropriate land areas, add up to a total area of elm, just before the Elm Decline, of some ten million acres or about an eighth of the British Isles: an area roughly twice as large as all woods and plantations of the present day and at least three times the total area of coppicing and pollarding at any time in recorded history. For Neolithic men to have pollarded this gigantic area of elm so effectively as to halve its pollen production requires a population much larger and more elm-centred than any archaeologist has hitherto proposed. Even if a man or woman with stone tools could maintain as much as twenty acres of elm within a pollarding cycle, this implies half a million adults spending all the summer pollarding elms, and a total population at least ten-fold too large for the Early Neolithic.

This leads us to disease as the only agent sufficiently powerful and specific to have had such an impact on the elms. If, as I have argued, *Ceratocystis* caused epidemics in the nineteenth century there is no reason why it should not have done so in the Neolithic. Recent observations suggest how early agriculture might have been linked to the spread of the disease, for *Ceratocystis* (or its vector) is particularly attracted to pollard elms, especially those recently cut, and to free-standing rather than woodland elms.

I propose that a combination of agriculture and disease could have had more impact on the elms than either operating by itself. The earliest farmers pollarded elms and other trees on a small scale and grubbed out small areas of wildwood. The pollard and free-standing elms thereby formed were a habitat attractive to beetles and thus favourable to an aggressive strain of *Ceratocystis*. That such a strain should have arisen at approximately that time is no great coincidence: recent experience shows *Ceratocystis* to be constantly present in woodland elms and frequently changing in virulence. When the first elms to be pollarded had died they were replaced by pollarding others which died in turn. The ground occupied by the dead elms would have been used as grassland or arable. Such a process, with civilization helping the spread of the disease and the disease helping the spread of civilization, could enable a much smaller human population to get through most of the elms in N. W. Europe in a few centuries or even decades.

It has recently been shown that hemlock (*Tsuga*) suddenly declined in North America much as elm did in Europe. The Hemlock Decline is dated 2800 b.c. and has no archaeological connection. There can be little doubt that it was due to a wholly natural epidemic; a species of looper-moth which can mortally defoliate hemlock-trees has been proposed as a cause.[653]

Elm in Eastern England

The prehistory of elm in the region is very like that of most of the British Isles outside the elm-dominated part of Ireland. Elm usually formed between 1% and 10% of the wildwood, but often exceeded 20% in mid Norfolk (Fig. 8.2). Probably it occurred in patches much as non-invasive elm does now, although before the Elm Decline it was considerably more abundant than non-invasive elm now is in ancient woods.

Elm in the historical period

Anglo-Saxon evidence

The Anglo-Saxon words *wice* and *elm* both mean elm. *Elm* is very common in place-names as far north as Yorkshire, *wice* slightly less common; examples are the villages of *Witch*ford and *Elm* in the Isle of Ely.[852] In charters *wice* is uncommon and *elm* seems not to occur. The inference is that, apart from woodland, elms were predominantly trees of the neighbourhood of villages; free-standing elms did grow on estate boundaries, away from villages, but were nowhere near so prominent in hedges as they are now.

The two words may well be an attempt to discriminate between species, but we should not rashly equate *wice* with the modern *wych*-elm. Early botanists such as Gerarde[340] were confused about elm taxonomy; the distinction between *U. glabra* and other elms was not firmly established until the seventeenth century, and it is not to be assumed without further evidence that the Anglo-Saxons were consistent about it.

Welsh *llwyfen* and Gaelic *leamhan* establish the early presence of elm in Wales and the Scottish Highlands. There seems to be no parallel Cornish word; the elms of Cornwall may be a relatively late introduction.

Documentation, archaeology, and management

The historical record of elm is very copious but must be treated with caution. Most references are to timber trees or pollards in hedges. Elms in woods are less well documented. The traditional management of woodland elm is as coppice or suckers treated as underwood, with standard trees of elm or oak. As with other species, documents usually specify only the timber trees and are thus liable to under-record woodland elm; small areas of elm, and the less competitive sorts of elm amid which it was possible to maintain oaks as standard trees, usually escape being mentioned.

The many records of hedgerow elm show that by the end of the Middle Ages it was as widespread and nearly as abundant as it is now. Examples are the elms around the garden of Sir Henry de Hadham at Witham (Essex) *c.* 1320;[337] the two elms among eight hedgerow trees at

Polstead (Suffolk) in 1407;[216] and the 'elme wood, wherwith most part of al Somersetshire ys yn hegge rowys enclosid' noted by Leland in 1542.[386] Many other instances are to be found in Richens's papers.

The existence of woodland elm on a large scale is shown by a dispute concerning Sheerhatch Wood (Willington, Beds; now replanted) in 1366: it was claimed that 6,000 elms, 6,000 ashes, 6,000 hazels, and 3,000 hawthorns had been felled.[858] At Gamlingay in 1359–60 a timber elm was felled in the wood to make planks for a door.[401] As we shall see there is some evidence that the remarkable stands of elm in the woods of Long Melford (Suffolk) go back at least to the Middle Ages.

From the seventeenth century onwards references to woodland elm become more frequent: for instance a few elms are mentioned among the timber trees in woods at Aveley (S. Essex) in 1656,[297] Langley (Norfolk) in 1679,[426] and Hatfield Peverel (Essex) in *c.* 1700.[298] This may mean that elm was getting commoner in woods or merely that it was more often treated as timber.

For two N.W. Essex woods we can compare the proportion of elm among the timber trees in 1801 with the proportion of the wood now occupied by elm (timber or underwood). In both woods there has been a considerable apparent increase (Table 16.3).

Elm is the second commonest timber in medieval buildings. This results from a definite choice, for ash is the commonest species (other than oak) in records of timber trees; indeed elm is sometimes used where we should expect oak to have been readily available. Examples are given on pp. 145, 459, 462–3. Elm tends to be used for unusually long or thick timbers in buildings and for floor-boards of unusual width. Growing to larger sizes than oak, it was used for the keelsons of ships up to the nineteenth century. It appears in underground and underwater work such as causeways (it is represented in the Early Neolithic Sweet Track in Somerset),[25] the piles of bridges (dating back to Roman times), water-pipes, and coffins. Because of its high tensile strength at right angles to the grain it has many specialized uses such as the naves of wheels, the seats of chairs, and the heads of mallets (for which purpose a specially tough elm was supposed to be got from the neighbourhood of Dovercourt (N.E. Essex)[258, 506]).

In the eighteenth and nineteenth centuries elm-trees usually fetched between half and three-quarters the price of oaks per cubic foot of timber. From the grower's point of view much of the difference would have been made up by the faster growth of elm: its chief disadvantage was the lack of a use for the bark.

I know of no specific uses for elm underwood other than for longbows. Contrary to some modern belief, it makes excellent firewood if dry.

Conclusions

For over five centuries elm has been almost as ubiquitous a non-woodland tree as it is now, and has been present but probably uncommon in woods. Neither archaeology nor written evidence tells us much about the past distribution of different elms. Sometimes, as at Gloucester (p. 145), enough of the shape of the tree is visible in a timber to identify it as *U. procera*, but elm species cannot yet be reliably determined from small samples of timber. We usually have to fall back on the argument that the elm now present in a medieval site is the same elm that was there in the Middle Ages. Because of the persistence of suckers this is a plausible assumption, but elm clones could conceivably disappear through competition with other elms or through past Elm Disease, and confirmation is needed.

Modern ecology: invasive elms in woods

Elmwoods are among the more familiar kinds of woodland. In Eastern England elm covers about 7% of the area of ancient woodland – much less than ash, hazel, or hornbeam – but this is divided among several hundred woods; I have recorded some elm in about three woods out of four. Two-thirds of the elm is of suckering kinds, the remainder being chiefly Lineage (Table 6.1). Elm invasion appears to be commonest in Eastern England, but I have seen it in the east Midlands, Somerset, Kent, and northern France.

Table 16.3 Elm timber trees in two Essex woods, 1801.

	Timber trees, 1801		Elms, 1973	
	Total	Elm	Species	Approximate percentage of wood occupied
Shadwell Wood, Ashdon[300]	520	4 (0.8%)	*minor* or Lineage	8%
Dunmow High Wood[299]	3,326	49 (1.5%)	*minor* and *procera*	4%

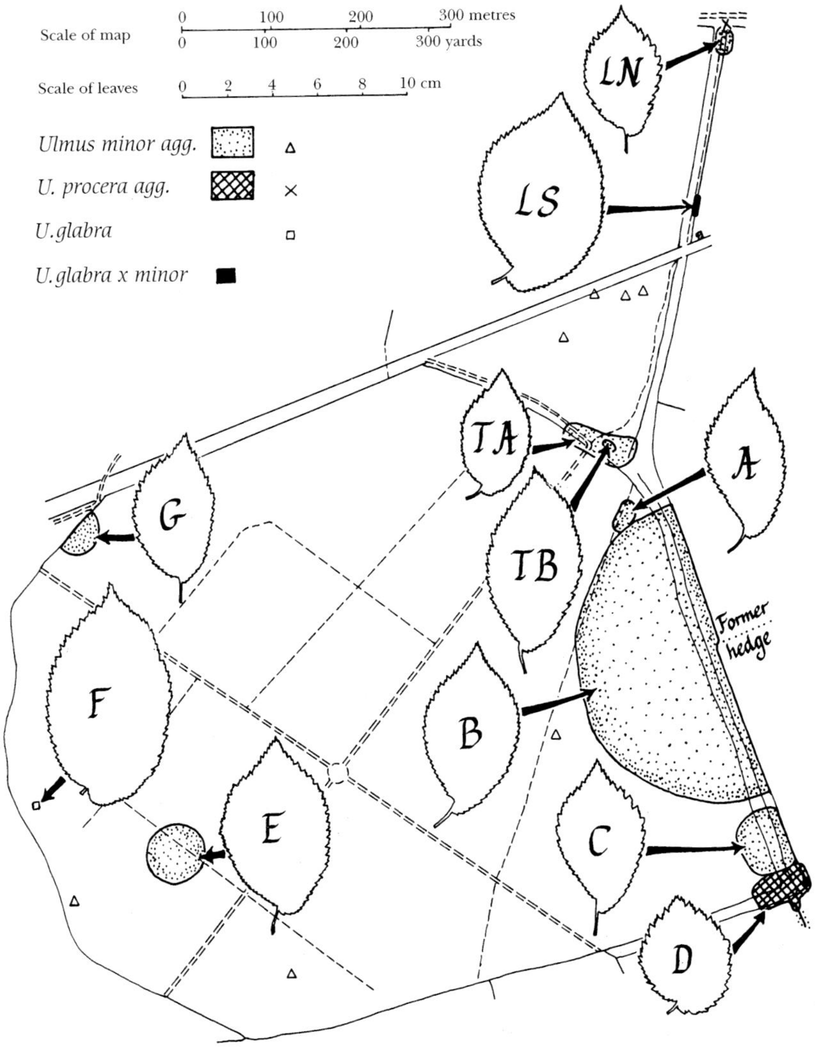

Fig. 16.4 The elms of Hayley Wood. The map shows the area occupied by each elm clone, together with the outline of a typical representative leaf. Isolated elm trees are shown by small symbols.

Elm in secondary woodland

Because of their suckering habit, *minor* and *procera* elms are among the commonest trees to form secondary woodland. An elm hedge, given the chance, develops into an elm belt; a field, abandoned for a few years, may turn into an elm-grove. There are innumerable examples in West Cambridgeshire and wherever elm hedges are common. Often the site of a deserted village such as Little Gidding (Hunts) (p. 96) is occupied by an elmwood. In Cornwall the plateau of the Lizard Peninsula is dotted with elm-groves on and around the sites of medieval hamlets and farms; one such clings to the 70° slopes of the collapsed sea-cave of the Devil's Frying-pan at Cadgwith. Secondary elmwoods have been formed at all times since the Middle Ages if not before. They may be of interest as ancient woodland (e.g. Boxworth Grange (Cambs) (Fig. 5.1)), as covering archaeological sites, or as perpetuating clones of elm which originally formed part of the homestead.

The mechanism of elm invasion

The taking-over by elm of a wood originally of some other tree is a common and obvious process, but has been recognized only recently as a result of air photography.[117] Before 1970 it appears to have been unknown to the ecological literature apart from a mention in a little-known paper in Germany.[91] Some typical examples are to be found in Hayley Wood.

On the east side of the wood there is a patch of *minor* elms which, seen from the air, is a suspiciously perfect semi-circle (Elm B, Fig. 16.4). The elms are *minor*, genetically identical, and form a clone. The inner part of the semi-circle has a mixture of old elms, up to 200 years old, and younger trees, the results of former management as elm timber over elm underwood. The outer zone has only younger elms. The elm semi-circle abuts on ash–maple–hazel woodland with standard oaks; some of these four trees stand scattered among the elms but have been surrounded and overtopped and are in various stages of decline, death, and decay. Outside the elm semi-circle, in a zone 50 yards wide outside its curved margin, there are numerous elm suckers prevented by shade from growing more than a few inches high.

There can be no doubt that this is a succession to elm woodland. Elm roots advance into the wood and send up suckers. At the next coppicing the suckers are released and grow into trees; they compete successfully with the existing underwood and even with oaks and send out suckers of their own. The process differs only in scale from the familiar concentric spread of rhizomatous plants such as bracken (p. 85) and dog's-mercury. In this instance the semi-circle is centred at a point where an elm hedge, dating probably from *c.* 1650,[120] used formerly to abut on the wood-margin lane. The radius of the semi-circle (including the outer zone of small suckers) is 230 yards(210 m) giving a rate of spread of 2.1 ft (0.65 m) a year.

The second largest elm clone in Hayley (E, Fig. 16.4) is a perfect circle evidently spreading outward from a single tree established in the interior of the wood. This tree has disappeared and its oldest successors are about 150 years old; this clone has spread more slowly than Elm B. Such internal invasions are presumably started by rare seedlings; in Hayley there are three isolated *minor* elms, dating from about 1920, which have not yet given rise to clones.

Most elm invasions start from the edges of woods; some can be related, as in Hayley, to hedges abutting on the wood, but many can only have started from seedlings, for which, presumably, the variable shade and moisture of the boundary ditch provide a more favourable habitat than the level ground of the wood interior. Elm clones can be centred on internal as well as external boundaries. Woods can also increase in size to incorporate what had previously been hedgerow or settlement elms; moats and the sites of farmsteads are often foci of elm invasion, as with the site of Man Hall in Little Chesterford (N.W. Essex), now partly overgrown by an extension of E*manuel* Wood.

The planting of elms, much talked about from the seventeenth century, is not an important source of woodland elm. Elm clones have the circular shapes of territorial expansion rather than rectangular outlines imposed by silviculture. Also they are of the wrong sorts: with a few exceptions the elms which were successively fashionable for planting purposes – *U.-procera* (in areas where it is not the traditional elm), the Dutch, Huntingdon, and Wheatley cultivars – are rare in woods.

Taxonomic and ecological variation in invasive elms

In Eastern England I have records of suckering elm in 227 woods. These comprise some 504 invasions by elms of the *minor* group and some 100 invasions by *procera* elms. (The former figure includes fifteen clones intermediate between *glabra* and *minor* but possessing the suckering habit of *minor*; the latter figure includes twelve intermediates between *procera* and *minor*.) The distribution (Figs. 16.5, 16.6) is very uneven and is poorly correlated with the distribution of hedgerow elm. Where woodland elms are most common, in West Cambridgeshire, Huntingdonshire, and N.W. Essex, elm is also abundant in hedges; but hedgerow elms are even more abundant in S.E. Essex and East Suffolk, where there is little invasion of woods, and are common to the S.W. of Chelmsford where the woods have no elm.

The distribution of *procera* versus *minor* elms in woods to some extent reflects other evidence for their history. *Procera* elms occur in woods in and near those areas – the Bedfordshire–Cambridgeshire border and South Essex – where *procera* appears to be the historic elm of settlements (Fig. 16.6). In the rest of Eastern England *procera* appears to be a post-1700 introduction and has rarely got into woods. The correspondence is not exact and there are several anomalies.

Within the *minor* and *procera* sections woodland elms vary widely. Some correspond in leaf measurements and other characters to the local non-woodland elms, others do not, and many cannot be exactly assigned to any Richens group. This supports the theory that some elm clones are derived vegetatively from, and are thus identical with, non-woodland elms, while others come from seedlings. Every seedling differs genetically from any existing clone, especially if it results from outbreeding.

Elm invasions vary from a fraction of an acre to the 100 acres of Holland Wood (Abbot's Ripton, Hunts), a pre-Conquest wood (p. 131) now largely taken over by what appears to be a single clone of *minor* elm. They vary in density: many West Cambridgeshire elm clones (as in Papworth Wood) are very aggressive and have eliminated all other trees; some elms in and around Hatfield Forest are weakly competitive and are thinly scattered in a mixture with other species.

The progress of an elm invasion depends on many factors. Fast expansion, as in Hayley Wood B, presupposes a system of shallow roots spreading horizontally for a distance exceeding the height of the tree and sending up suckers well in advance of the elm front. The competitive power of the suckers depends on their numbers, tolerance of shade, and ability to grow up as emergents between existing trees. The different behaviour of elm clones in the same wood shows that the paramount factors are genetic: the differences between one *minor* elm and another are not merely of interest to specialized pteleologists but result in very great differences in the ability of clones to take over a wood. Differences in soil (particularly as affecting root and sucker production), in the other trees present, and probably in the frequency of coppicing must also be taken into account.

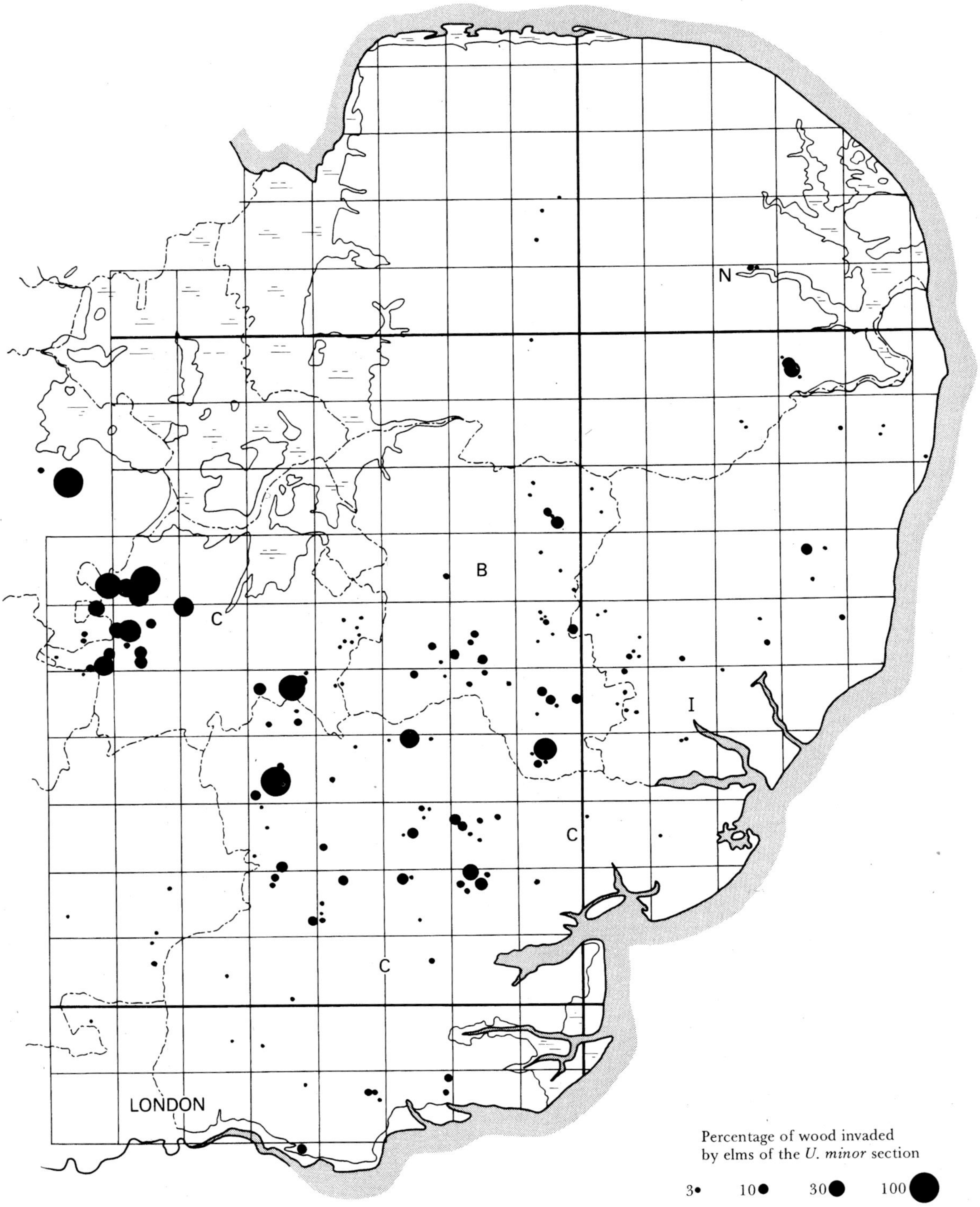

Fig. 16.5 Relative abundance of East Anglian elms (i.e. elms of the *minor* section) in ancient woodland.

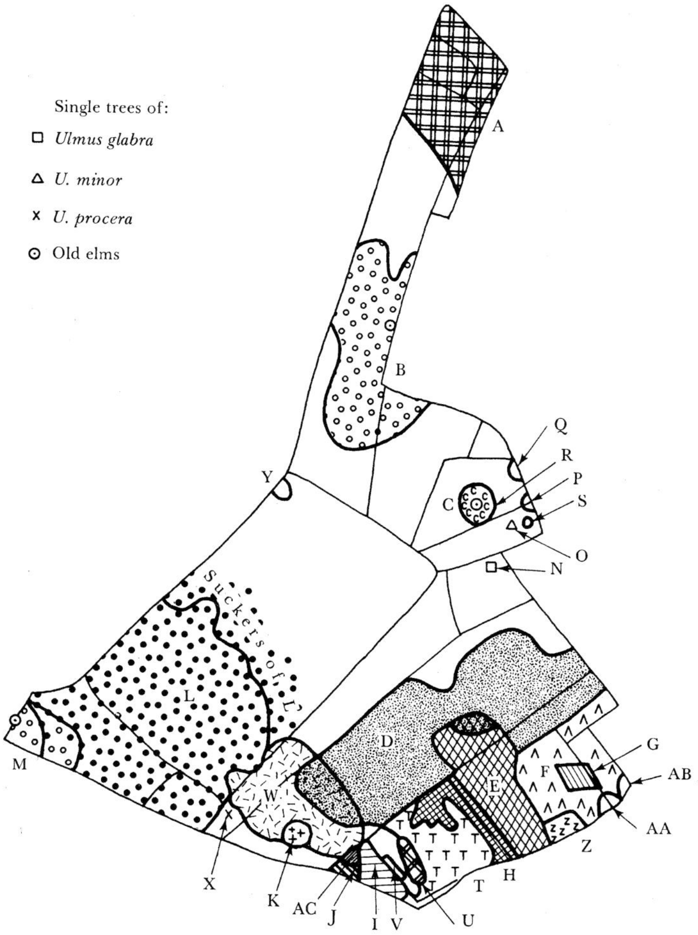

Fig. 16.8 Buff Wood, West Cambridgeshire. (**a**) Earthworks and relation to East Hatley village. (**b**) Distribution of hornbeam, nettle, and ivy (cf. Chapter 7). (**c**) Elms. Each letter represents a separate elm invasion. Clones of *Ulmus procera* and *procera* x *minor* are shown by different kinds of double-hatching; a single tree by x. *U. glabra* and hybrids are shown by single-hatching; a single tree (N) by a square. *U. minor* clones are shown by various kinds of stippling; small clones are left blank; a single tree (O) is shown by a triangle.

village elms. This diversity of elms is unusual but is not surprising since the village elms of East Hatley and its surroundings are also very heterogeneous.

The elms vary in ecology. Clone L is dense and aggressive; it has almost wholly suppressed the trees that it has overrun and has sent out suckers well ahead of the advancing front. Clone B, although extensive, is thinly scattered among other trees. When two clones meet they may intermingle (D and W), or stop along a line of demarcation (D and F), or one may invade the other (L invading M). Many clones are accompanied by elm plants such as *Poa trivialis*, but the matter is complicated by variations in soil fertility resulting from the diverse history of the wood.

Dutch Elm Disease has been in Buff Wood for over 100 years (p. 262). The present epidemic, first noticed in 1971, has sought out, with curious precision, the elms with *procera* genes. By autumn 1977 it had killed 139 out of about 163 large and middle-sized elms in clones A, E, H, and U. In 1977 there was also an attack on *glabra* elms and hybrids; but out of some thousands of *minor* elms only 71 had been killed. [For later report see p. 455.]

Conclusions

Elm invasion can start almost anywhere but progresses only on favourable soils and with certain genetic variants of elm. It is associated chiefly with clayey soils of unusual fertility for woodland, but how far the fertility is the cause or the effect of the invasion is uncertain. It is assisted by coppicing, which provides more frequent opportunities for elm suckers to grow into trees than would have been available in the wildwood. Elm invasion and birch invasion (Chapter 19), the two great successions now going on in woods, are complementary and seldom happen in the same wood.

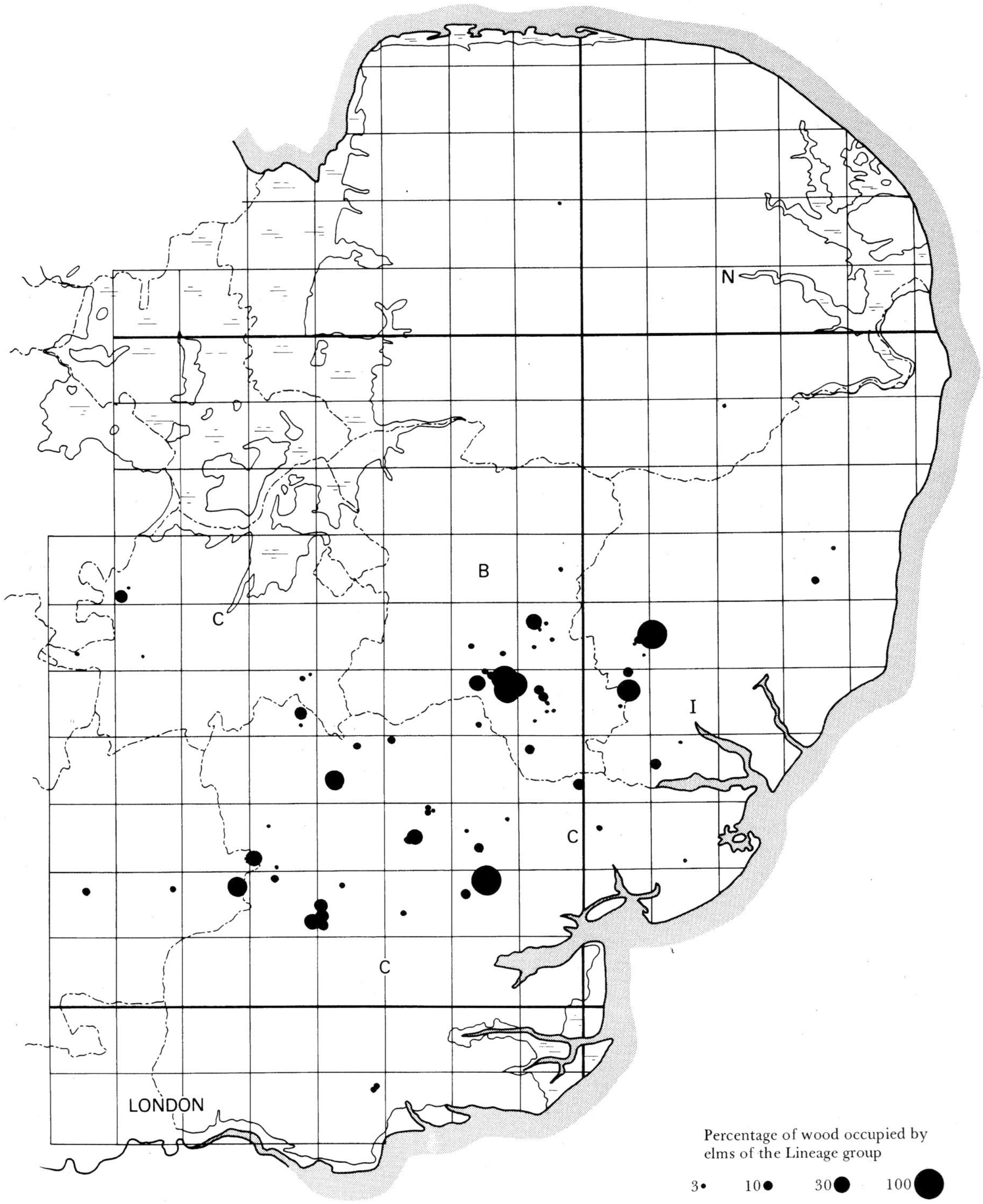

Fig. 16.9 Relative abundance of Lineage elms in the ancient woods of Eastern England.

Different *minor* elms vary in invasiveness, but there is no evidence that *minor* as a whole differs from *procera*. The average size of a *minor* clone is 1.3 acres and of a *procera* clone 1.0 acres, but much of the *procera* elm in Eastern England is on unfavourable soils.

Modern ecology: the Lineage or non-invasive elms

These elms are intermediate in leaf and other characters between *Ulmus glabra* and *U. minor* (or less often *U. procera*); they have the coppicing habit of *glabra* and are not to be confused with those *glabra* x *minor* hybrids, including Dutch elm (a cultivar much planted in the early eighteenth century), which have the suckering habit of *minor*. Suckering hybrids are relatively rare in woods.

Lineage elms are gregarious, unlike *glabra*; they form pure stands varying from a fraction of an acre to nearly 100 acres. They differ genetically from stand to stand and are never in contexts which suggest planting. Usually all the elms of a stand are identical in leaf and habit, although sometimes there appears to be more than one genotype in a stand. As far as I am aware these elms are peculiar to Eastern England and may be confined to woods. They are in almost every ancient wood from Bishop's Stortford to Stowmarket (Fig. 16.9); outside this area they are thinly but widely scattered as far as West Cambridgeshire and Norfolk.

Giant stools, up to 8 ft in diameter, are frequent, but in many stands of Lineage elm the stools are no bigger than 3 ft.

Soils and associated vegetation

Lineage elms grow on the middle range of soils, with moderate amounts of clay, loess, and sand (Fig. 16.7). The pH typically ranges from 4.0 to 6.5 but occasionally is low enough to form mor. Many of the smaller stands are in shallow valleys or depressions, suggesting a preference for damper soils but not standing water.

Large and small Lineage elm stands have the same associated vegetation and are all included in Tables 6.2 and 6.3. Both trees and herbs have a weaker calcicolous bias than those that go with *U. minor* or *procera*. Hornbeam, lime, and chestnut are more often found with Lineage elms, as are bramble and primrose. Nettles and 'elm plants' are distinctly less common in non-invasive than in invasive elm stands.

Lineage elms are ecologically distinct from *minor* and *procera*. They are much less associated with calcareous soils, clays, or high fertility. Nor are they associated with the edges of woods, with internal boundaries, or with ancient earthworks.

The elms of the Long Melford woods

The heart of the distribution of non-invasive elms is at Long Melford (Suffolk), the country seat of the medieval abbots of Bury, whose woods of Lineage and Spelthorne (Fig. 16.10) were, until recently, among the largest elmwoods in England. Both have unfortunately been coniferized, but substantial remains of their ancient vegetation survive. They are private.

'Boscus de Lenynge' and 'le Spelterne' are documented at intervals back to 1386, when they were coppiced on a six-year rotation.[397, 819] They appear on a map dated 1580[221] and are surrounded by strong banks. The Abbots had nearby a park which had been made out of a wood called *Elme*sete, the scene of a famous incident in the twelfth century when Abbot Samson had ingeniously cheated the Bishop of Ely out of some timber which he had not dared to refuse him.[376] Elm was thus connected with the immediate vicinity of Lineage Wood at least 850 years ago; indeed, since Long Melford was a Romano-British town,[879] we are tempted to see in *Lin*eage or *Len*yng itself the rare survival of a wood-name from the Roman countryside involving the Celtic root *lem*, elm. (It happens that the third largest intact stand of non-invasive elm is in another Suffolk wood called *Elm*sett Park.)

The dominant native tree over some 80% of Lineage and Spelthorne Woods was a coppicing elm with large smooth leaves, very unlike wych-elm. There are similar elms in many other nearby woods; their distribution is unrelated to ownership or management.

Lineage and Spelthorne are slightly acidic woods in loess country. Besides elm, they contain maple–hazel woodland and lime; there are small elm invasions at the margins. Elms, unusually, occupy the plateau, other trees being mainly on slopes and valleys. The ground vegetation involves mercury, brambles, primroses, and small areas of bracken; nettles and 'elm plants' are not abundant.

Modern ecology: wych-elm

Wych-elm in general

Ulmus glabra is not normally a gregarious tree. Throughout Britain it is scattered through many types of ancient woodland, usually on the more calcareous soils and on steep slopes; it is associated with ash and hazel rather than with oak. It occurs in ashwoods in Mull[754] and in hazel-woods along Loch Carron (Wester Ross). In the Derbyshire Dales it grows with lime in ancient woods and with ash in secondary woodland.[106] It is common in the Lincolnshire limewoods. On the limestone scarpwoods of the Cotswolds it occurs with ash and less often with beech.

In most of these places wych-elm occurs as single stools or small groups. I have seen it as a dominant tree

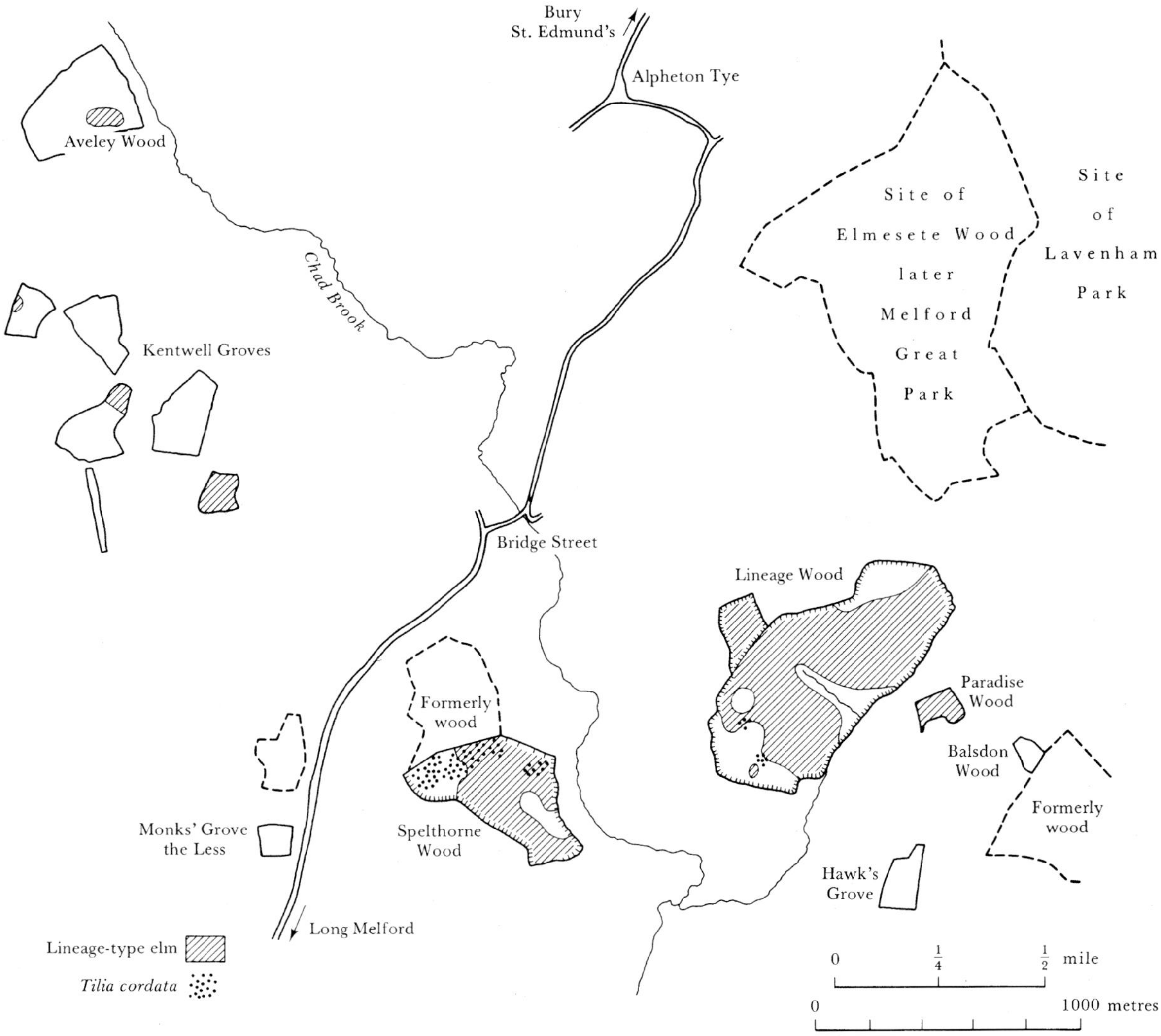

Fig. 16.10 Lineage and Spelthorne woods, together with other medieval woods in their neighbourhood and the sites of medieval woods now destroyed. Woodland dominated by Lineage-type elm is hatched; lime woodland is stippled. Woodbanks are shown only for Lineage and Spelthorne Woods.

in Bunny Old Wood (Notts) and parts of Launde Park Wood (Leics) and Thurlbeare Wood (Somerset); in each case it shares a scarp of soft limestone with ash–hazel woodland and tends to grow on the steepest slopes.

Eastern England

In Eastern England genuine *Ulmus glabra* is quite rare. It is recorded for about one wood in four (Fig. 16.11) but usually in very small quantities, often only one stool per wood. Only in Meep's Hole (Ramsden Crays, S. Essex) have I recorded as much as one and a half acres of continuous wych-elm. It is doubtfully native in Cambridgeshire.

Wych-elm often suffers from drought in Eastern England, and this may be the cause of its rarity, although it withstands hotter summers on the Continent. In the 1830s it was planted as underwood in secondary woodland (e.g. in wood-closes at Hardwick Wood, Cambs) and has prospered; it has sometimes invaded adjacent ancient woods by seed. However, many of the stools are clearly native relicts of great size – the one stool in Cow Wood (Panfield, Essex) is 24 ft across – with no descendants.

Wych-elm resembles Lineage elm in distribution and ecology. It occurs in the same tract of country and often in the same woods, though seldom in direct contact. The associated trees and herbs (Tables 6.2, 6.3)

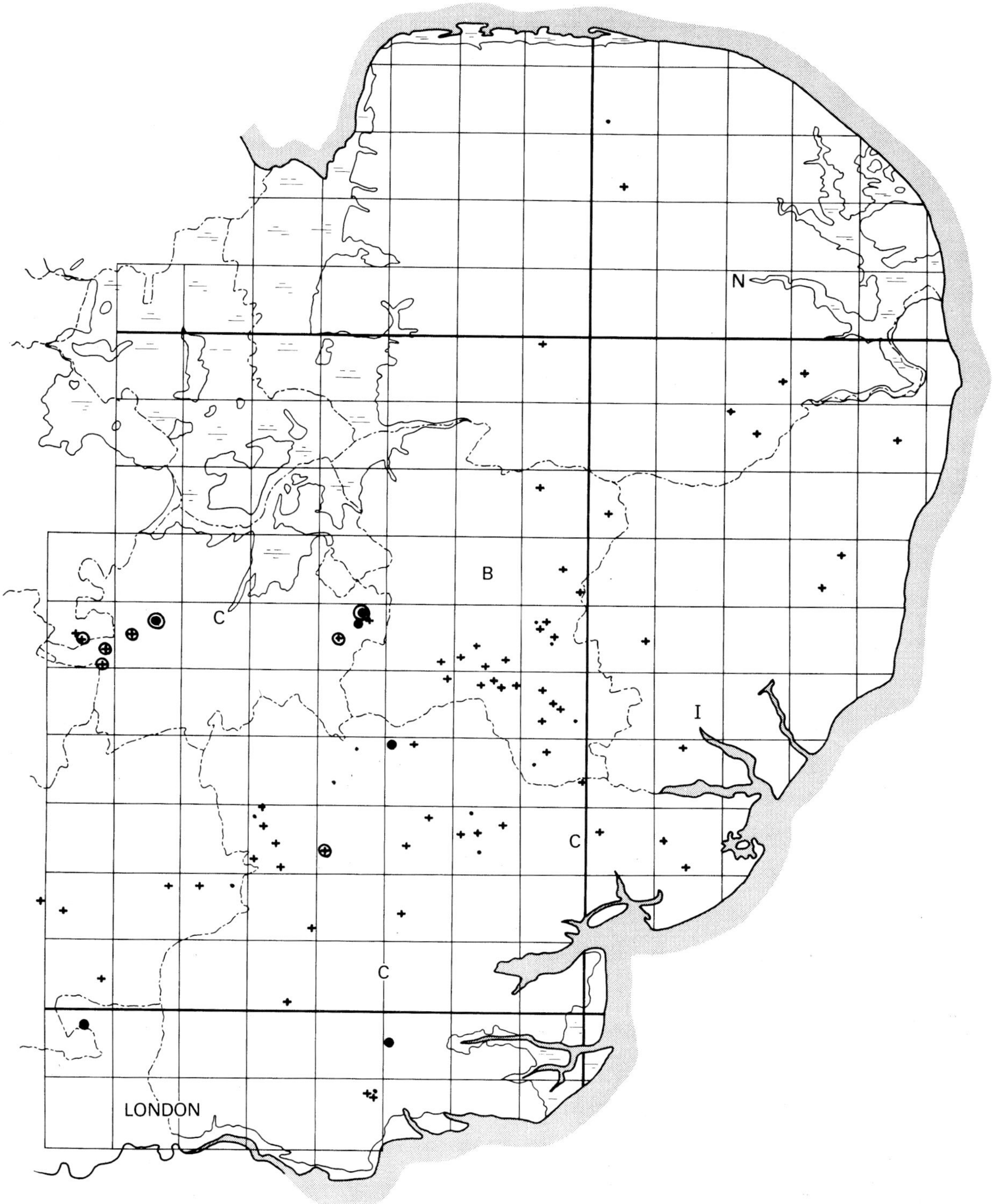

One or a few stools of *Ulmus glabra* per wood +
At least $\frac{1}{4}$ acre (0·1 ha) of *U. glabra* • At least 1 acre (0·4 ha) ●
Instances of known or suspected planting are shown by rings round symbols

Fig. 16.11 Occurrence of wych-elm in the ancient woods of Eastern England.

are almost identical to those of Lineage elm. The soil evidence (Fig. 16.7), although meagre, suggests a similar range of textures but more calcareous pHs. In Eastern England wych-elm is not strongly associated with very calcareous and well-drained soils as it is in the rest of Britain.

General conclusions

British and Continental elmwoods

European phytosociological literature treats elm very differently from my account of it in Britain. It is regarded as chiefly a fen-wood tree, a constituent of the 'hardwood fen' (*Hartholzau*), elm–ash woods which together with 'softwood fens' of willow and poplar are supposed to be the natural vegetation of the flood-plains of great rivers. The species of elm is given as *glabra* in the Ulmo-Fraxinetum of Switzerland,[52] as *minor* in the Fraxino-Ulmetum of south Germany,[809] and as '*campestris*' (? = *procera*) in the Ficario-Ulmetum campestris of Poland.[891] This habitat for elm is unrepresented in Britain, which has had no native flood-plain woodland for at least a thousand years.

On the Continent, as here, *Ulmus glabra* is thinly scattered through many of the more acidic upland woodland types. *Minor* and *procera* elms are widespread in hedges and scrub, though rarely as abundant as in Britain. Elm invasions exist in France and Germany, but almost unrecognized and probably on a small scale; I am unaware of any exact Continental parallel to our scarp wych-elm woods or of anything remotely like the Lineage elmwoods.

The origins of our elms

Without positive evidence about what elms were in Britain in prehistory, argument about the origins of the present range of elms is bound to be speculative. It is probable that Melville's hybridization and Richens's importation have both played a part, but the problem has too many variables to be soluble on circumstantial evidence alone. It is often claimed that *minor* and especially *procera* elms are not indigenous on the grounds that they do not reproduce by seed and do not enter into natural vegetation. For *minor* elms neither premise is true but even for *procera* the argument is not conclusive. With the behaviour of *Tilia cordata* in mind, we dare not claim that failure to observe a tree producing seedlings is proof that it has never done so.

Although direct proof is lacking, we can hardly doubt that the river gravels of Britain once had 'hardwood fens' like those of the Continent and were a chief habitat for elm; they could well have had *minor* and *procera* as well as *glabra*. The general abundance of elm pollen, even in places such as mid-Norfolk remote from flood-plains makes it certain that elms grew in upland habitats as well, and we must look for traces of this distribution in surviving woods.

Most elm invasions are artefacts to the extent that they are derived, directly or indirectly, from hedgerow or village elms and have been assisted by coppicing. But they are of varied ages and there is no reason why some of the larger or slower invasions should not have begun in prehistory. Coppicing is not essential: if *minor* or *procera* elms were present in flood-plains, we might expect their more aggressive variants to have begun slowly to colonize the upland wildwood. Elms in small valleys in existing woods (e.g. Bedford Purlieus near Peterborough)[99] have been claimed as relicts of this stage.

The woodland elms for which there is the strongest historical evidence are the Lineage section. This depends not only on written evidence (Long Melford and Gamlingay) but also on their apparently clonal nature despite their lack of overt suckering. For a stand of Lineage elm to arise by vegetative spread would take very much longer than a *minor* clone of the same size, and the age of the big stands is probably to be reckoned in millennia. If, as is probable, the Lineage elms are hybrids, this implies that *minor* and *procera* as well as *glabra* were widespread in Eastern England before they began.

The argument that all village elms are imported is not compelling. Some, at least, may have come out of the local woods and may have been influenced by the natural pattern of elm varieties. This may account for the existence of similar elms in distant parts of Europe. If Iron Age settlers in Flanders and Brittany each had a range of elms from which to choose in what was left of the local fen-woods, it is to be expected that they should sometimes have chosen genetically similar elms. The reader may think this more plausible than the importation hypothesis that the settlers in Flanders, disdaining the local elms or not having any, sent to Brittany for elm suckers.

The evidence that our present *minor* elms are, at least in part, indigenous is stronger than for *procera*. *Procera* is less variable than *minor*; indeed most of the vast number of 'English' elms appear to be of a single clone. It enters less easily into native vegetation than does *minor*, perhaps because it more rarely sets good seed. It is possible that indigenous *procera* disappeared with the Elm Decline or the destruction of the fen-woods – except in so far as its genes survive in some Lineage elms – and that the present *procera* results, in accordance with Richens's theory, from a Roman or earlier reintroduction. This hypothesis awaits a detailed study of woodland elms in a *procera* region of England.

Evolution in elms

The woods of Eastern England are the scene of very active elm evolution. Different elms are brought together and their genes reshuffled. New variants are emerging more rapidly than in any other tree genus. As

Buff Wood shows, natural selection at present favours strongly-suckering clones. A similar phase of evolution in the past, at least partly in this country, gave rise to the multitude of village elms. Here, too, suckering would have been favoured, for a non-suckering elm is unlikely to be dug up and propagated. It may well be that prehistoric *minor* and *procera* elms suckered less than their modern descendants.

Lineage elms probably have their origin in an earlier period of evolution, in Roman times or before, when *minor* and *procera* of the now-vanished flood-plain woods met the *glabra* of the uplands. On this occasion the selection pressures were different; the elms that survived were those that suckered weakly and could cope with less calcareous soils, on which they have ultimately prospered better than the wych-elm parent and have generated their own type of woodland.

The conservation of woodland elms

With regard to Dutch Elm Disease there is little to be done for woodland elms. Fortunately they are less at risk than hedgerow trees. Pollarded or coppiced elms, however, lose this protection: the owner of an elmwood should leave it strictly alone while the present crisis lasts, apart from destroying the bark of dead trees (an operation less important for woodland than for non-woodland elms because they produce fewer bark-beetles). Should the elms die their suckers will probably remain alive and there is no urgent need to do anything about replacement. Invasive elms are well protected in nature reserves, of which there are seven in West Cambridgeshire, not seriously affected by disease.

Lineage elmwoods are in a more precarious state than any other type of woodland. Between 1945 and 1975 at least 45% by area fell victim to poison and bulldozer. Now there is *Ceratocystis*, to which Lineage elms, although relatively resistant, are vulnerable because they hardly sucker. The largest surviving stand, in Sampford West Wood, belongs to Essex Naturalists' Trust, but is in a poor state from the effects of an earlier attempted replanting which prepared the way for disease. The future of this peculiar class of elms and of their special woodland type should be a matter for concern.

Added in 2003 edition

The further effects and progress of Elm Disease are discussed and mapped in *The History of the Countryside*, Chapter 11. For the subsequent fate of elmwoods see this book, Chapter 28. For 50 years of changes in an elmwood apart from Elm Disease see pp. 376–85. More data on elm, as the second commonest timber in ancient buildings, appear in Chapter 29.

Fig. 16.12 (a–f) Diseases of elms.

(**a**) East Anglian elm affected by wet-wood: note the flange, down which a brown exudation dribbles and dries to a white crust. This condition is very common on elms throughout Europe and in America and Japan, less common on oak and other trees. Buff Wood. October 1969

(**b**) Section of such an elm, with brown water-soaked core communicating with the outside by a crack splitting the flange (top). Buff Wood. March 1969

(**c**) Flame of fire spurting from a hole bored into such a crack when the escaping methane is ignited. Buff Wood. October 1969

Fig. 16.12 (cont)

(**d**) Section of East Anglian elm, showing wetwood (brown core) and repeated attacks of Elm Disease (dark dots in early-wood of annual rings) and the interaction between them. Buff Wood. February 1974

(**e**) Elm Disease streaks treated as decorative. The last attack killed the tree.

(**f**) Attempts by bark beetles to breed in living but very droughted elm. Exuding sap drowned the eggs or grubs. Hardwick Wood. October 1976

Fig 16.13 English Elm surviving in its Sussex enclave, showing the shape of the tree and its characteristic habit of shedding big branches on hot still days when least expected. University of Sussex. August 1980

Fig. 16.14 Invasive Elmwood of East Anglian elm (Chapter 16). Note lack of effect of Elm Disease, although the 1970s epidemic reached the wood fourteen years previously. Overhall Grove, Cambridgeshire. May 1991

Fig. 16.15 Non-invasive Elmwood (Chapter 16): a stool of Lineage Elm on a great woodbank. Grimsditch Wood, Saffron Walden. May 1979

Fig. 16.16 Elms associated with deserted village: Boxworth Elm at Little Gidding, Huntingdonshire. November 1989

17

Oakwoods and the general history of oak

In Chapter 2 we saw that there is an almost embarrassing wealth of historical information about oak. In Chapters 10 and 11 this was analysed in terms of the part that oak has played in human affairs. This chapter considers the biology and natural ecology of the tree and the part that human affairs have played in the history of oak.

Oak is not a tree of dull ubiquity, the universal dominant of a vaguely-inclusive 'oakwood'. It grows in a uniquely wide range of habitats but behaves differently in each; the habitats need to be differentiated carefully.

(*i*) Woods in which oak occurs as underwood, with or without oak standards. These are the most typical oakwoods, in which oak is so abundant that some or all of it has been coppiced despite the value of oak timber, and in which oak competes with oak rather than with other species.

(*ii*) Semi-natural 'high forest' oakwoods, consisting of oak timber trees with little or no underwood. For instance Ken Wood (Highgate, London), with its variable and undoubtedly native population of great oaks of 250 years old and upward, is a normal medieval wood except that it has not been coppiced for at least two centuries. Woods of this kind will also be counted as ancient oakwoods; they are rare in Eastern England but may be commoner elsewhere, and include many of the western and northern oakwoods described by Tansley.[150]

(*iii*) Woods of other species of underwood with oak only as timber trees. Even where the oaks are unusually numerous (e.g. Hayley Wood)[120] these are readily distinguished from genuine oakwoods in which oak forms the underwood as well.

(*iv*) Secondary woodland with oak as a pioneer tree, e.g. on Hampstead Heath outside Ken Wood.

(*v*) Wood-pasture with oak as timber trees or pollards, e.g. parts of the New and Epping Forests.

(*vi*) Hedges and fields with oak as timber trees or pollards (or sometimes hedgerow underwood).

(*vii*) Plantations containing oak. Where these occupy the sites of ancient woods they may be confused with category (*ii*). Part of Hardwick Wood (Cambs), for instance, is a stand of close-set oak planted *c.* 1840; the records and remains of underwood show that it had been a wood very like Hayley; although it superficially resembles Ken Wood it is not an ancient oakwood. Such woods may be abundant in well-wooded areas (e.g. Herefordshire) and may outnumber genuine examples of (*ii*).

Oakwoods – categories (*i*) and (*ii*) – form only part of the history of oak; oak in other habitats, namely (*iii*) to (*vii*), is better documented and is arguably more important.

The two oaks and their variation

The two native species of oak are *Quercus robur* and *Q. petraea*, called pedunculate and sessile oaks after their former Botanical Latin names. They are differentiated by such features as the long 'peduncle' or fruit-stalk and the auricles at the base of the leaf of the former, contrasted with the tapering leaf-base and almost sessile acorns of the latter.[626, 631] The differences are clear, although difficult to express convincingly by measurement (whence, in part, the trouble that learned taxonomists have got into with oaks). But they are rather inconspicuous and sometimes blurred by hybridization, and the existence of two species remained unnoticed until the French botanist Dalechamps drew attention to it in 1586–7.[642] Early British botanists got the two oaks badly confused, and it was not until the 1790s that people concerned with woods became aware of the distinction.[691] (The word 'durmast' is often used as a book-name for *Q. petraea*, but its meaning is unclear, and it is unlikely to be a genuine vernacular name.)[691, 816]

Quercus robur will be the common oak to nearly all my readers. *Q. petraea*, though locally more abundant, tends to occur in woods and away from habitations and is less familiar to the public.

Apart from the existence of two species and hybrids, oak – especially *Q. robur* – is very variable in such features as whether the trunk is straight, curved, or corkscrewed; whether it is smooth or burred; whether the branches and twigs are spreading or erect; and at what time the leaves fall. It is often possible to distinguish wild oaks, which are variable in such features, from planted populations which are often genetically uniform and selected for modern ideas of timber quality.[120, 122]

Although our forefathers failed to notice the two species, they did observe these other variations, which were sometimes used to identify individual oaks as landmarks. The name Hatfield Broad-oak (*Hatfeld Brodehoke* 1121 x 1136)[851] reminds us of one genetic variant. The 'Red lyved ooke' of a Somerset perambulation of 1567,[493] and possibly the 'read leafe treow' of a Hampshire perambulation dated 901,[208] remind us of that rare and striking form of *Quercus robur* that produces bright scarlet lammas shoots every August.

Oak in the wildwood

Oak first appeared in the Early Boreal period (Zone V) and spread rapidly (Fig. 8.1). In the fully-developed wildwood (Zone VIIa) it was present throughout Britain except in the far north but was unevenly distributed. In northern England, S.E. Scotland, parts of Wales and Somerset, and in a belt from N.E. to S.W. Ireland it forms 20–40% (rarely more) of the tree pollen including hazel. Allowing for the copious pollen production of oak and for the diluting effect of local sources of alder pollen, this means that oak and hazel were the commonest trees in those regions. In the rest of the British Isles oak was less abundant, rarely reaching 20% of the tree pollen.

The distribution of oak in Great Britain in 4000 B.C. was remarkably like its distribution in ancient woods today. Then as now, oakwoods were chiefly in the Highland Zone of England, Wales and southern Scotland. In the Lowland Zone oaks were less abundant; they may have been thinly scattered through the forest as a whole (like our present standard trees) or concentrated on special soils (like the present lowland oakwoods). In the Scottish Highlands oak was locally abundant, then as now, as far north as Sutherland.

In Eastern England, taking pollen productivity into account, oak was often the second commonest dry-land tree, but in many places was quite rare (Fig. 8.3); there was evidently both a general scatter and local concentrations. One such concentration is revealed in more detail by the bog oaks of the Fens (p. 103).

During and after the Neolithic the general distribution of oak changed very little, but in Lowland England it often increased slightly relative to other trees. Early farmers probably avoided sites with many oaks, and also gave the tree opportunities to form secondary woodland in abandoned clearings.

Oak was much used in early carpentry, usually as timber, for instance in the cleft planks of the Sweet Track (p. 106).

Several pollen diagrams show oak increasing relative to other trees well into the historical period. For instance, at Barton Turf (Norfolk) oak comprises 11% of the tree pollen (excluding hazel) in Zone VII but 45% at the top of the deposit;[768] at Old Buckenham Mere the figures are 20 and 27%. A detailed calculation would not be worthwhile because too many deposits are truncated, but in many areas oak now possibly forms a higher proportion of the total native tree pollen than at any time in the past.

Oakwoods in the Highland Zone and S.W. England

Most accounts of British woodlands seriously overestimate the extent of oakwoods by including all woodland in which any oak occurs. This over-estimation is greater in the Lowland Zone, with its many woods containing oak only as a timber tree. In the Highland Zone the majority of 'oakwoods' still satisfy the more rigorous definition adopted here.

Oakwood vegetation

Oak coppice, oakwoods without underwood, and oak 'scrub' are – or were before the Forestry Commission – often the predominant woodland in regions of Palaeozoic geology in the Highlands of Scotland, the Lake District, the Pennines, Wales, S.W. England, and apparently Ireland.

Many variants of Highland oakwoods have been described.[86, 146, 150, 850] Some of the variation is connected with the presence of other trees, but much of it is due to the remarkable capacity of oak for generating different kinds of woodland by changes of woodland structure rather than of composition. These include the overgrown oak coppices around Loch Lomond; the widely-spaced standard oaks, without underwood, in some Pennine woods and the closer-set standard oaks in North Wales; the low and extremely wind-pruned oak groves of high altitudes on Dartmoor; and oakwoods with a holly understorey, widespread in the far west and especially in S.W. Ireland. Each of these has its characteristic flora; some are extremely rich in bryophytes. Occasionally different structural variants can be compared in the same wood: Lowland examples are Nap Wood (Sussex) and Brooklands or Weeley-Hall Wood (N.E. Essex). The parts played by climate, soil, and management history in determining these variants have not been studied on a large scale. As well as coppicing an important factor has been grazing: in the Highland Zone the distinction between woodland and wood-pasture is often poorly developed and many woods have recently had the function of sheltering stock.

Quercus petraea is the commoner, sometimes the only, oak in most Highland oakwoods. Both oak underwood and *Q. petraea* are found on a wider range of soils than in Lowland England, occasionally on quite calcareous soils. *Q. robur* occurs irregularly, often on low ground or in valley bottoms; it is the commoner or only species in parts of the far north (e.g. parts of Ross and Cromarty) and the south-west (Lizard Peninsula); it is the only oak in Wistman's Wood and other groves at the altitudinal extreme of Dartmoor.

History

Some oakwoods in S.W. England are reasonably well documented. Around the Helford River in Cornwall, for instance, the fine oakwoods until very recently corresponded closely to the woods of Domesday Book [Fig. 31.1]. The Dartmoor groves, although not recorded for so long, have been objects of wonder for at least three centuries.[143, 915]

In Scotland the heyday of woodmanship came much later than in England,[122] sufficiently late to be the subject of a textbook by E. Monteath.[405] For the Loch Lomond oakwoods, R. M. Tittensor has been able to compare the textbook practice with what actually happened.[152] There is a general review by J. M. Lindsay.[84] Coppicing is seldom recorded before 1650, but this may be partly due to a lack of detailed early records: Lindsay quotes one instance in 1550. By the eighteenth century oak coppices existed in most parts of mainland Scotland, especially Perthshire and Argyll.[84a]

The coppices of Scotland were worked mainly for bark (p. 154); wood and timber were by-products. The planting of oak coppices was recommended and occasionally carried out, but most coppices were derived from existing woods consisting mainly of oak. Around Loch Lomond these woods had earlier been used for fuelling ironworks. In Knapdale (Argyll) the iron and bark trades were combined with other woodland industries.[135] The coppice rotation was usually between 21 and 30 years; Monteath thought that a 24-year cycle gave the best yield of bark. Oak was grown for bark at least as far south as Cumberland,[22] in the Welsh *spring-goed* woods,[68] and in the Belgian *taillis à écorce*.[47]

The bark trade was the effect, and not the cause, of the Scottish oakwoods, but it may have increased the proportion of oak in them. On some highly-organized estates attempts seem to have been made to replace 'barren wood' – trees not bearing saleable bark – with oak; Monteath has a chapter 'Of extirpating barren wood from oak coppices'. We cannot tell how widespread or successful these attempts were.

Ancient oakwoods in the Lowland Zone

The literature on Lowland 'oakwoods' is almost entirely concerned with oak trees in other kinds of woodland, with wood-pasture, or with oak plantations. Genuine oakwoods are comparatively rare (although most counties probably have one or two) and have never been systematically described.

Eastern England, other than Hatfield Forest

This is an account of some twenty woods or parts of woods that have oak as underwood, plus five 'high forest' woods – ancient stands of oak timber trees lacking underwood. (I include as 'oak underwood' only that produced by regular coppicing, not casual regrowth from stumps of timber trees.) These woods are thinly scattered (Fig. 17.1), mainly in the Acid Soil Province. Oak underwood is gregarious, forming pure stands with well-defined boundaries; the largest stand, at Swanton Novers (N. Norfolk), covers fifty acres.

Soils and vegetation

Oakwoods are an extreme woodland type, very sharply defined in terms of soil. They are the most acidic of all woodland; no pH above 4.0 has been recorded (Fig. 17.3). They are on well-drained sandy or gravelly hilltops with sandy or loessy soils extremely low in clay. The humus is always mor, up to 20 cm deep in hollows, with a tendency to podzolization on ridges and hummocks.

There is a strong tendency for the oak of oakwoods to be, at least in part, *Quercus petraea*; in Eastern England this is by far the rarer of the two oaks and seems not hitherto to have been definitely recorded as indigenous in Norfolk or Suffolk. The connection is evident from comparing Figs. 17.1 and 17.2, and is analysed in Table 17.1. In Norfolk, for instance, the five known oakwoods coincide with the five sites for indigenous *petraea*. In Suffolk the only modern record of native *petraea* – there is a medieval representation of it[726] – is in Dodnash Wood, one of four oak coppice sites. In Essex, of fourteen oakwoods, nine contain *petraea*, and all but one of the others are in the anomalous Forest of Hatfield. Even within a wood, *petraea* tends to occur in areas of oak coppice and *robur* in the rest of the wood: Soane Wood (see later) is one of eight examples. The association between the rare woodland type (under 2% by area of all ancient woods) and the rare oak is highly significant: almost all the sessile oak in Eastern England is in oakwood or in its transitions to hornbeam, lime, or chestnut woodland (pp. 229–30, 248, 332).

The trees which adjoin stands of oak are shown in Table 6.2. Oak underwood keeps company with the trees of poor soils – birch, hornbeam, and sweet chestnut. It is often intermingled with holly and rowan. It seldom or never abuts on species of relatively fertile soils – maple, ash, or elms.

The ground vegetation beneath oak coppice (Table 6.3) is dominated chiefly by bracken, less often by brambles. The less abundant species, e.g. *Deschampsia flexuosa*, *Melampyrum pratense*, *Luzula sylvatica*, are also typical of the most acid and least fertile soils. Even honeysuckle and bluebell are uncommon, and plants of moderately fertile woods, such as mercury and primrose, are absent. A characteristic moss of Norfolk oakwoods is *Leucobryum glaucum*, a *Sphagnum*-like plant of very acid soils (as also in some Chiltern beechwoods) which contributes to the mor humus.

Oakwoods without coppice form a distinct sub-type: although the sites and soils are similar, the commonest associated tree is holly, while the ground vegetation is

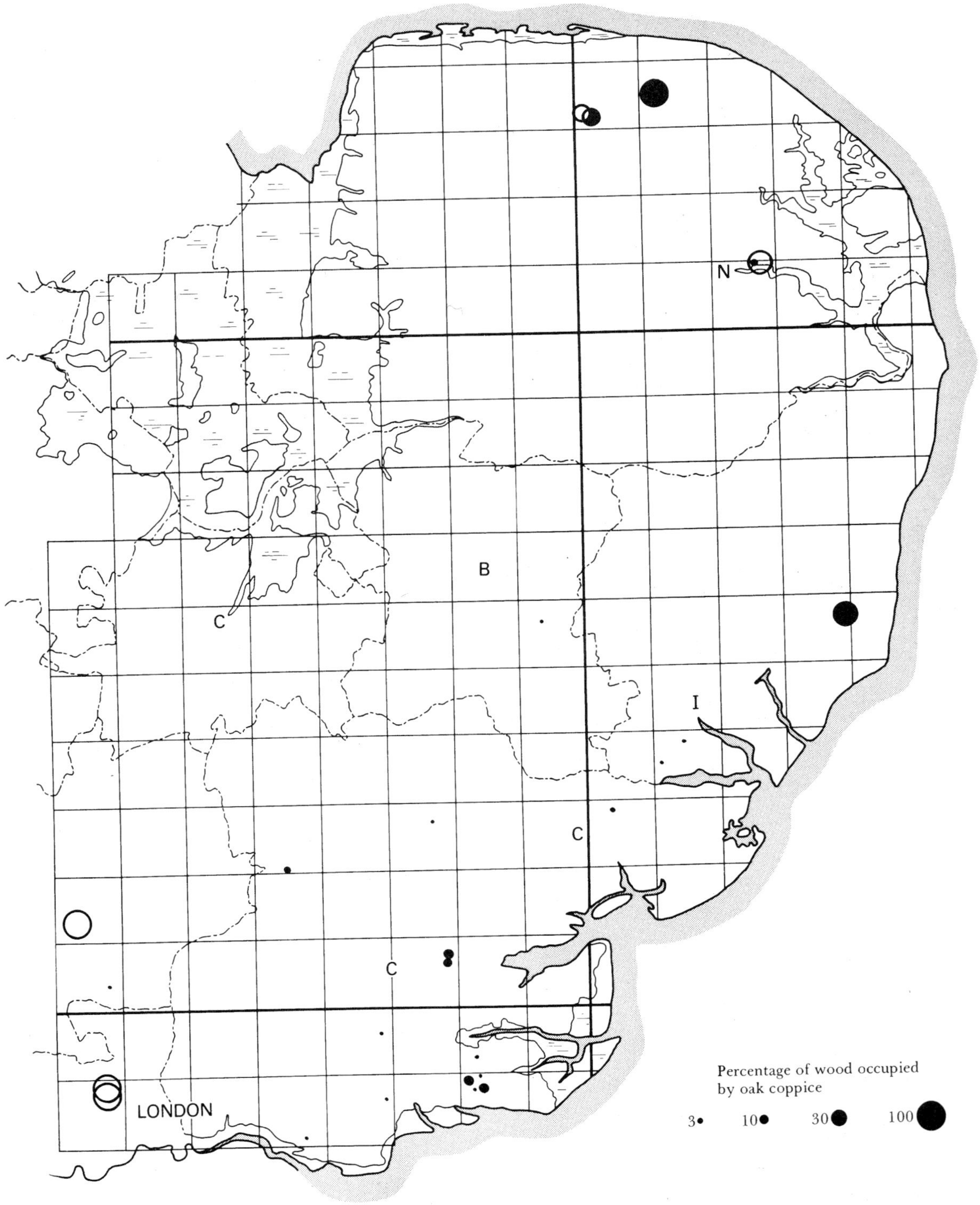

Fig. 17.1 Relative abundance of oakwoods in Eastern England. (o) shows the relative abundance of oakwood of the non-coppice type.

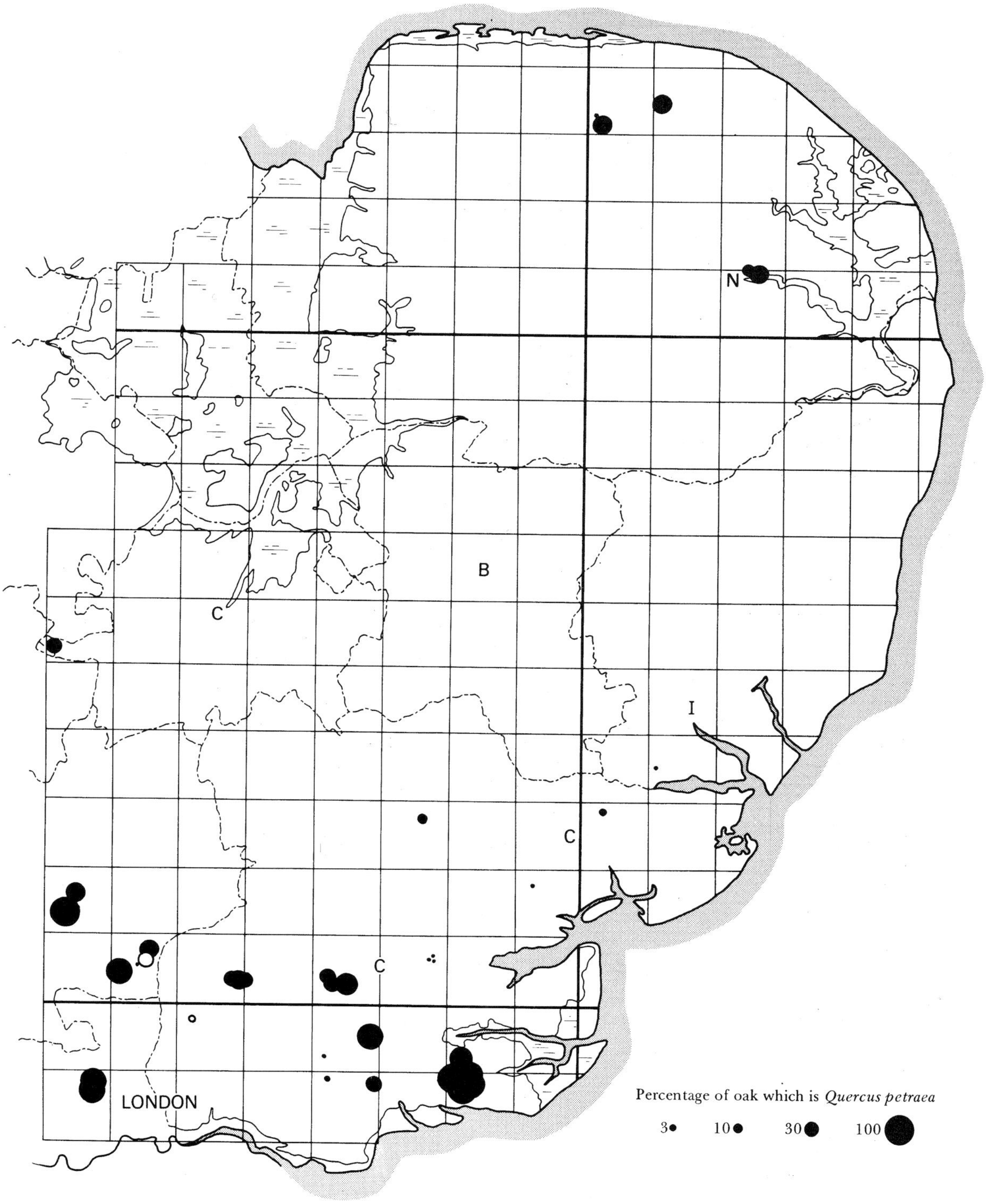

Fig. 17.2 Occurrence of sessile oak in Eastern England, with a rough indication of the proportion of *petraea* in the oak population. No account is taken of occasional *petraea* genes in predominantly *robur* populations, nor of sites with evidence of planting. White points indicate wood-pasture.

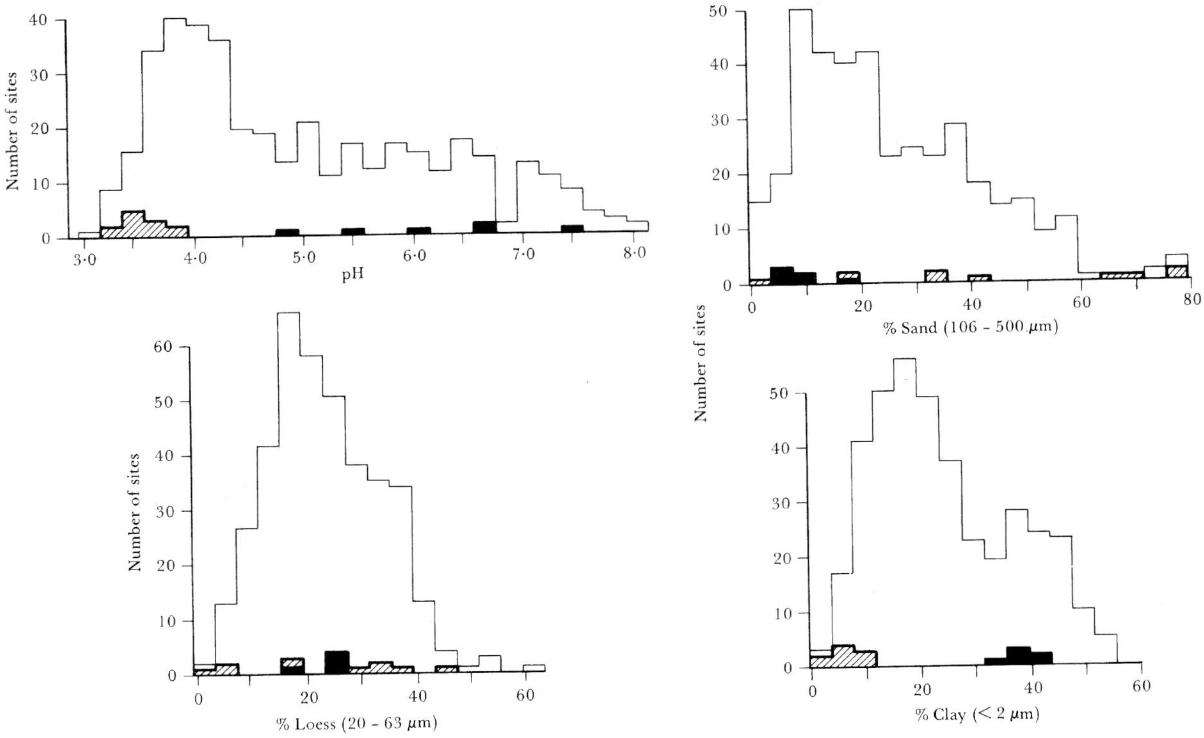

Fig. 17.3 Distribution of topsoil characteristics under oak coppice (or other ancient oakwood) in Hatfield Forest (black) and in other ancient woodland in Eastern England (hatched). The thin upper line gives, for comparison, the characteristics of all woodland topsoils sampled. For further details see caption to Fig. 7.5.

Table 17.1 Oakwoods and *Quercus petraea* habitats in Eastern England. This table includes only sites known to the author and takes no account of *petraea* records in the literature.

	Total oakwoods	Oakwoods with only *robur*	Oakwoods with *petraea*	Transitional woods with *petraea*: oak–hornbeam	oak–lime	chestnut–oak	Wood-pasture with *petraea*	Total *petraea* sites
Norfolk	5	—	5	—	1	—	—	5 †
Suffolk	4	3	1	—	—	—	—	1
Essex	14	5 *	9	10	1	4	4	28
Cambridgeshire	—	—	—	—	1	—	—	1
Hertfordshire	—	—	1	14	—	1	3	18 †
Middlesex	2	—	2	1	—	—	—	3
Total	25	8	18	25	3	5	7	56

*Including four in Hatfield Forest, see later. †One wood appears under two headings.

very limited indeed. They are transitional to the oakwoods of western and Highland Britain, many of which have a history of grazing.

Heather (*Calluna vulgaris*) and *Galium saxatile* are characteristic coppicing plants of oakwood. Heather, which has arisen in four *petraea* woods – none of which adjoins heathland – after recent felling, is killed by shade and presumably spends much of the coppice cycle as buried seed. (Heather was regarded as a serious woodland weed in eighteenth-century France, and coppice rotations of at least nine years were recommended in order to suppress it.)[269]

History

All the oak stands are in ancient woodland, including such historic woods as Edgefield Wood, Norfolk (Fig. 9.4) and Norsey Wood, Essex (p. 335). Many of the oaks themselves are of obvious antiquity, moots of over 6 ft (2 m) diameter being common.

An early piece of evidence for oak woodland in Norfolk is a document dated 1236 setting out the respective rights of the Bishop and the Cathedral Priory of Norwich in 'the part of Thorpe Wood which was covered with oaks'.[495] Both the surviving fragments of Thorpe Wood are oak woodland (and both have sessile oak).

With this exception, references to oak woodland are difficult to separate from the vastly more numerous references to oak in general. Oak faggots are specified at Little Bentley (N.E. Essex) in 1386,[233] and oak underwood is apparently mentioned at Dunton (S. Essex) in 1566[313] and at St Osyth (N.E. Essex) in 1845.[283] These allusions are sufficiently rare to suggest that it was no commoner in the past than it is now, and that it was not treated differently from other underwood: it is reasonably certain that oakwoods were not the subject of a special bark trade as in Scotland.

Iken Wood, E. Suffolk

The wood of the lonely parish of Iken stands between the heaths and plantations of the Suffolk Sandlings and the formerly-reclaimed tidal marshes of the River Alde. Already in Domesday Book the area stands out as almost woodless (Fig. 9.5). The continuity of Iken Wood is well documented back to 1600–1, when it appears on a map of the Stanhope estates by John Norden.[371] The original boundary touched salt water. Successive grubbings have reduced it to about a third of its 38 acres (Fig. 17.4, Fig. 6.7). The wood is private.

Iken Wood is that great rarity in England, a wood on blown sand (Fig. 4.4). Sand still blows in the surrounding

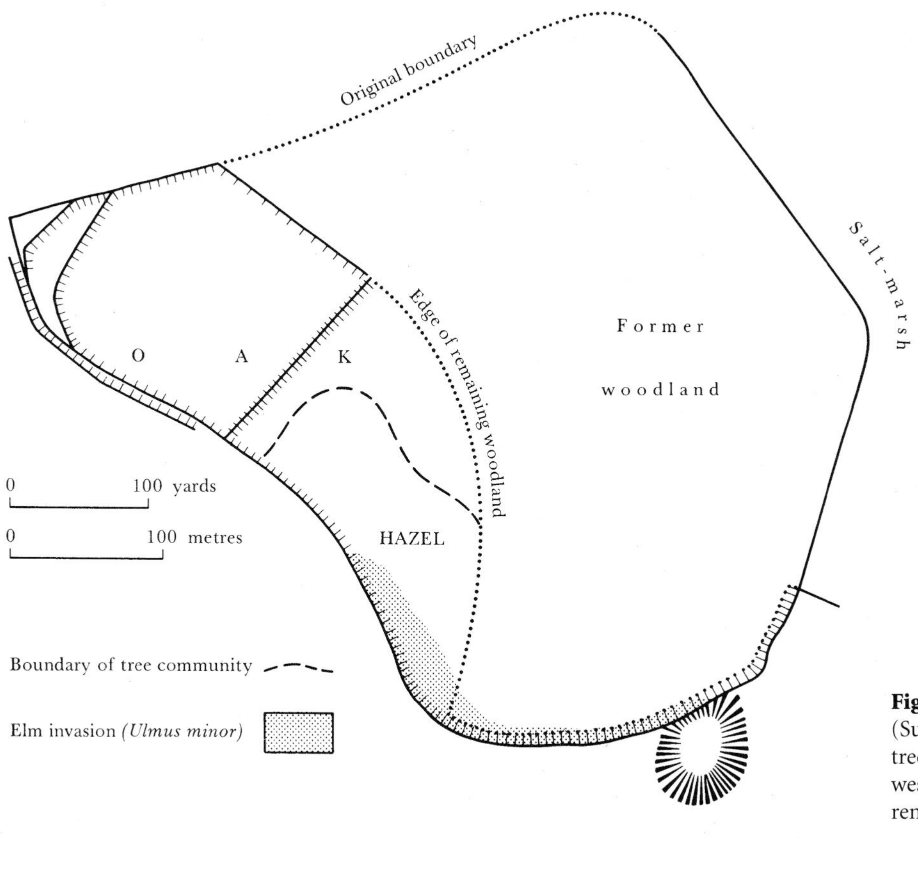

Fig. 17.4 Iken Wood (Suffolk): topography and tree communities. Only the western third of the wood remains.

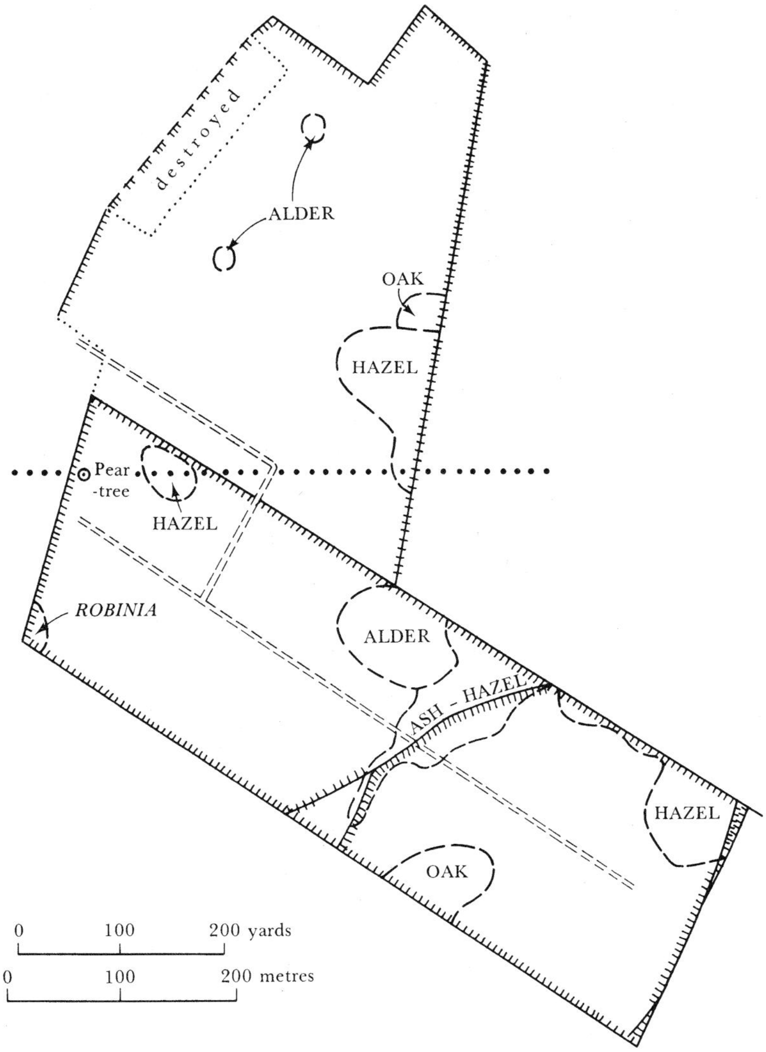

Fig. 17.5 Soane *alias* Bullock Wood, Colchester and Ardleigh: topography and tree communities. Unlabelled parts of the wood are chestnut and birch woodland with occasional aspen clones and single stools of oak and alder.

In the eighteenth century the wood extended well beyond its present limits in all directions.

fields, and this instability probably explains the multiplication of ancient banks at its western end.

This is a most impressive oakwood, with widely-spaced moots up to 9 ft (2.8 m) across and with large spreading standard trees, some branched almost from ground level. It was last coppiced about a century ago. All the oaks are *Q. robur*. Other trees include hollies (some of exceptional size), birches, and the occasional rowan. On the lower slope there is a sudden transition to hazel-wood, which in turn is invaded by elm. The soils are everywhere very acid (pH 3.4–3.8) and well drained. Oak forms mor humus with weak podzolization. Hazel, here at its limit of acidity, also forms mor; but elm, even at pH 3.7, contrives to form mull.

Iken is a glorious bluebell wood, with bracken and occasional brambles. The flora is distinctive, including butcher's broom (*Ruscus aculeatus*) and the white calcifuge fumitory *Corydalis claviculata*. The hazel-wood has the same ground vegetation as the oaks. The elms, although on so acid a soil, are accompanied by the 'elm plants' *Poa trivialis*, *Galium aparine*, and *Glechoma hederacea*; the expected *Anthriscus sylvestris* is accompanied by *A. neglecta*.

A survey of 1710[365] says that 'the underwood is felled for sale and tenants firing' – there is no mention of a bark trade.

Soane or Bullock Wood, Colchester and Ardleigh

The antiquity of this wood is concealed by early nineteenth-century encroachments which have reduced its boundaries to straight lines (Fig. 17.5); but on one interpretation of the evidence it may be the earliest known artificial wood, a partial anticipation of modern forestry not to be repeated for 300 years.

Soane Wood can be traced back at intervals to 1312,

when John Unwyne was fined for not maintaining his ditch alongside it.[375] The name is spelt Sowenwode and was thought at the time to mean 'sown wood', for it appears in Latin as *boscus seminatus*. It belonged to the Benedictine abbey of St John, Colchester. In 1330 there was a lawsuit settling a dispute, said to date back to 1242, about whether there were common rights in it. J. L. Fisher has proposed[337] that, at some time before 1242, the monks had enclosed and planted the site and thereby had offended those who had previously had common on it. Other explanations are possible – something other than trees might have been 'sown' in or near the wood, or the etymology might be wholly mistaken – but this remains perhaps the most likely interpretation. Sowing of acorns, etc., was the normal method of forming a plantation in the seventeenth and eighteenth centuries.

Soane Wood is on an almost level plateau with very acid loess-derived soils (pH 3.5). Various banks and an unmarked parish boundary run through the wood, suggesting that it has a more complex history than the available records show. The flora is moderately poor; the absence of species such as lime, characteristic of other ancient woods around Colchester, corroborates the possibly secondary origin of this wood.

Most of the woodland is of chestnut and birch, with smaller areas of oak, hazel, plateau alder, and aspen woodland. In one corner there is a patch of invading *Robinia pseudacacia* – a northernmost outlier of a type of woodland that in France is as common as elm invasion in England. The chestnut includes some giant stools. The humus is uniformly mor: this is another place where even hazel forms mor. Most of the wood is carpeted by brambles; bluebells are remarkably uncommon.

Besides areas of oak coppice, forming a small part of the wood, there are single oak stools thinly scattered throughout the wood. Alder and aspen grow nearby, showing that the site is less well-drained than most oakwoods. Patches of bracken grow under the oak coppice.

Both species of oak are present; *Q. petraea* comprises roughly half the coppice stools but only a sixth of the standard oaks. I have no other record of *petraea* from the Colchester woods but would expect it to be indigenous in some of the other woods nearby on very poor soils.

Other Lowland oakwoods

The ecology of oakwoods in Eastern England, as an uncommon and extreme woodland type, is repeated in many other Lowland areas. Some typical examples are compared in Table 17.2. They occur on a wide range of topographies but always on the most acid and least fertile of the available soils, except at Ellenden where beech underwood is even more extreme. The place-name Acrise, not far from Ellenden, apparently from Anglo-Saxon *ac + hris* 'oak underwood', reminds us of the antiquity of this type of woodland.

The peculiar oakwoods of Hatfield Forest

In a small part of the coppices of Hatfield Forest (Fig. 14.2) there is oak underwood not conforming to the rule; it is the only ancient calcareous oakwood which I have seen. The oak moots, up to 9 ft across, clearly result from a long history of coppicing. They occur in patches mixed with other trees (Fig. 14.2); they are all *Q. robur*. The soils are derived from Chalky Boulder-clay with a small admixture of silt (clay fraction 34–42%); they are calcareous (pH mostly between 6.0 and 7.0, range 4.8–7.5); the humus is always mull. The associated trees (Table 6.2) are ash, maple, hazel, elm, and hornbeam, with some recent birch invasion; chestnut is conspicuously absent. The ground vegetation (Table 6.3) is dominated by *Mercurialis* or by *Deschampsia caespitosa*, plants of well-drained and poorly-drained calcareous clays respectively; there are no calcifuges.

Why should we get oakwood where we should normally expect only standard oaks scattered in woodland of ash, maple, or hazel? The answer is to be sought in the history of Hatfield as a compartmented Forest. Evidently something happened which increased the proportion of oaks to such an extent that it became worth-while to coppice them. A temporary grazing episode could have destroyed the regrowth of the previous trees, and thereby have enabled oak to make use of its power to colonize vacant ground (cf. p. 293) as a pioneer tree. This might have happened in the remote past before the coppices were demarcated; but the Forest records show that the system of intermittent enclosures was not always effective in keeping stock away from young underwood. For instance, in 1612 it was alleged that

> 'the Springs that come after of the Stumps of the Trees are bitten with the deer and Cattle that they dye and never come to any great profit'.[276]

Such an event, if it coincided with a good acorn year, might well produce the irregular patches of unusually dense oak that we see today.

Oak in secondary woodland

Quercus robur is one of the four common pioneer trees that colonize abandoned farmland, heathland, railways, etc. Practically every common in the Home Counties has at least partly declined to oakwood in the last hundred years. There is a popular notion that oakwood is the end-product of a succession that begins with colonization by some other tree such as birch or hawthorn. Although this sometimes happens, it is more common for all species to be roughly contemporary; the oaks, being slower-growing when young, give the illusion of being later colonizers when they eventually overtake the other trees. Oak often colonizes on its own.

Recent oakwoods are not related to soils or geography

Table 17.2 Synopsis of some other Lowland oakwoods.

	Grovely Forest, Ridgeley Wood, Stockton Wood, Great Ridge	King's Wood and Oaken Grove	Ellenden Wood	Sutton Coldfield Park	Bois du Mont-Mal
Location	West of Salisbury, Wilts	North Downs near Dorking, Surrey	The Blean near Canterbury, Kent	Greater Birmingham	Le Bec-Hellouin, Eure, Normandy
Topography	Chalk ridge capped by Clay-with Flints	Chalk scarp capped by Clay-with-Flints	Eocene gravel hills over London Clay	Triassic sandstone and gravel	Limestone plateau
Oakwood	*Q. robur* coppice; giant moots (to 16 ft); no other trees	*Q. robur* coppice with areas of *petraea*	Coppice mainly *petraea*; alder-buckthorn and service present	Mainly *Q. robur*; little coppice structure remains; holly abundant	Coppice of *Q. petraea*, beech, chestnut; alder-buckthorn present
Oakwood soils	Derived from thick loess; pH 3.5–4.5; mainly mor	Derived from thick loess; very acid; mor	Derived from loess and gravel; very acid; mor	Very acid; derived probably from solid geology; mor	Derived from thick loess (30% in range 20–63 μm); pH 4.4
Oakwood ground vegetation	Bracken, brambles, bluebell, *Luzula sylvatica*, goldenrod (*Solidago virgaurea*)	Bluebell, bracken, bilberry, *Holcus mollis*, *Deschampsia flexuosa*	Bracken, *Melampyrum pratense, Luzula sylvatica, Deschampsia flexuosa*	Bracken, bluebell, *Deschampsia flexuosa*, *Holcus mollis*	Heather, bilberry, *Deschampsia flexuosa*, *Molinia caerulea*
Adjacent woodland types	Maple–hazel on Clay-with-Flints exposure (sometimes with standard beech, p. 321); ashwood on chalk exposure	Maple–hazel with occasional beech on Clay-with-Flints exposure; much secondary woodland on plateau	Oakwood forms mosaic with chestnut-wood; ancient beech coppice on hilltops	Holly-wood; nearby name Lindridge suggests history of *Tilia* (p. 241)	Hornbeam zone on edge of plateau; calcareous woodland of many species including *Q. robur*, *Tilia cordata* and *T. platyphyllos* on scarp soils below
Historic land-use	Most of oakwood is ancient secondary woodland (Iron Age and Romano-British settlement remains). Woodland area increased between 1086 and 1500. Medieval compartmented wood-pasture in Grovely Forest (p. 185) and the three woods. Survey of 1566 mentions 'divers crooked oaks to get firewood from' (*diverse curve quercus pro Fyerwood inde habendo*)[493]	Ancient woodland (rare in Surrey)	Presumed ancient woodland	Large medieval park with embanked coppices (Seven Hays) and large plain[613, 793]	Medieval wood (Abbey of Bec)[43a] with perimeter wall on massive woodbank
Present condition	Well-preserved in Stockton and Great Ridge; otherwise replanted	Well-preserved in places	Well-preserved and still coppiced	Well-preserved though long uncoppiced	Poorly preserved (part coniferized)

as are ancient oakwoods. Oak will colonize even the peat of Wicken Fen, the boulder-strewn slopes around the edges of Wistman's Wood, or the Norman masonry of Colchester Castle, besides all 'ordinary' soils. The most important determining factor is the distance to the nearest existing oak-tree. Acorns are carried, and either dropped or buried, by jays, rooks, pigeons, and other animals; the distribution of oaklings is random up to at least 200 m from the parent tree.[787]

Quercus petraea much less readily forms secondary woodland. For example, at Belfairs Wood (Hadleigh, Essex – not to be confused with Belfairs Nature Reserve) an ancient wood adjoins, on the same topography, secondary woodland of forty years' growth; the oaks of the ancient wood are 98% *petraea* and of the secondary wood about 70% *robur*. It has been suggested that the greater colonizing power of pedunculate oak is due to its dispersal by birds; the peduncle provides a handle whereby jays and crows break off the almost-ripe acorn and fly away with it.[726] This, however, hardly applies to pigeons or to squirrels, which are dispersal agents of at least equal importance.[787]

Oak in wood-pasture

Oak is, or was, the predominant tree in most wood-pastures: in Forests such as the New Forest, Dean, Sherwood, Wyre, and Fontainebleau, and in innumerable ancient parks and commons. To some extent wood-pastures occupy soils on which few trees other than oak will grow; but the evidence that they used to have a wider range of trees (p. 199) suggests that some aspects of wood-pasture management favour oak, presumably at the seedling or sapling stage.

Moderate grazing is less harmful to oaklings than to other trees because they are full of tannins and taste nasty, and are difficult to kill: the uniquely enormous tap-root – which can comprise over three-quarters of the weight of the plant – stores material which can be used to replace a bitten-off leading shoot.[140] Wood-pasture also favours oak because, almost by definition, it contains grassland and grassland edges in which oak can use its colonizing ability and can become established more easily than in existing woodland. Even if grazing is quite severe, new oaks can grow up in the protection of thorn or holly scrub (p. 173). In several Forests there was heavy regeneration of oak in the reign of Charles II (p. 187); we are now seeing it again in many wood-pastures, e.g. the plains of Epping Forest (p. 202).

An uncompartmented wood-pasture resembles a mosaic of secondary woodlands of different ages and is thus a favourable habitat for *Q. robur*. Sessile oak is not so favoured and tends to be less abundant than in woodland; it is uncommon in places such as Epping and Windsor Forests on soils where we might expect it to be the commoner species. It is notable that the Forests of Wyre and Dean, in which *petraea* is or was the common oak, have a strong coppicing tradition.

Staverton Park (Wantisden and Eyke, E. Suffolk)

This is an awesome place. Oaks of unknown age, surrealistic shapes and improbable girth moulder in the dim shade of yet mightier hollies or rise out of a sea of tall bracken. Half-fallen trees lean against other trees. There is the largest known holly in the kingdom,[97] and the fallen trunk of almost the largest recorded birch. Big hollies and birches are rooted high in the crotches of oaks. The atmosphere of timeless decay – a combination of M. R. James and J. R. R. Tolkien – and the nearness of Rendlesham, seat of the East Anglian kings, have invested Staverton with many legends. The antiquarian believes it to be an unaltered remnant of prehistoric wildwood, and the death-place of the martyred King Edmund. In factual history, it is one of the best-preserved uncompartmented medieval parks. This account is based on the researches of G. F. Peterken,[97] supplemented by my recent finding of the thirteenth-century papers of the lost manor of Staverton. Staverton Park is private.

The park boundary (Fig. 17.6) has a typical 'economical' shape with rounded corners (p. 193). Although an early park, it extends into two parishes, Wantisden and Eyke; there was somewhere a third parish, Lyonswell, which has disappeared.[447]

Staverton is the wood-pasture equivalent of Iken Wood, on the same very acid blown sand. Half its 370

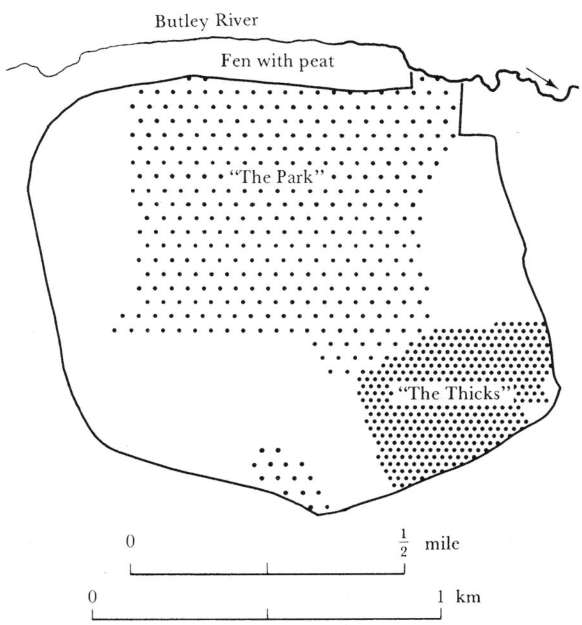

Fig. 17.6 Staverton Park, Suffolk. The perimeter is that of the original park; dotted areas are surviving wood-pasture.

acres is arable, formerly heathland, with a few oaks in places. Of the remainder, the greater part, called The Park [Plate 14a, Figs 32.7a, 32.9], is set with ancient pollard oaks and a few old hollies, so spaced that their crowns cover about half the ground area, amid dense bracken. The lesser part, The Thicks [Plate 14b, Figs 23.3, 32.7b], has rather closer-spaced oaks, pollarded unusually high; the gaps between them are filled with hollies; there are also a few giant birches, and some rowans and hawthorns. The hazel which is a feature of Iken Wood is absent.

The ancient oaks, to the number of about 4,000, are almost all pollards. Ring-counts suggest that they vary in age from about 220 to well over 400 years; many have the combination of a massive trunk and a small crown that characterizes oaks of medieval date. They appear to have been last pollarded in the late eighteenth century. Despite their age they are in good health – save for those that have been overtopped by holly – and change little from year to year. There are few younger oaks. All the oaks are *Q. robur*. The hollies vary continuously in age but many are over 200 years old.

Staverton, like most ancient wood-pastures, is poor in flowering plants. But the oaks and hollies are rich in lichens, including several species characteristic of ancient wood-pasture trees (e.g. *Haematomma elatinum*, *Lecanora cinnabarina*, *Thelotrema lepadinum*, *Phlyctis aegalea*). On these grounds F. Rose regards Staverton as derived from primary woodland.[97]

Staverton Park, a deer-park of the Bigods (p. 232), is first referred to in the 1260s. The manor, whose name now survives only in the Park, was then a flourishing estate, deriving about a quarter of its income from peat-cutting in the fen to the north of the Park; there must be a lost village somewhere. A survey in 1270 estimates the park at twenty acres, worth 13*d* per acre per annum, the same value as for enclosed pasture.[447] The accounts for the financial year 1268–9 include 51*s* 10*d* for herbage sold in the park, 12*s* for bracken 'sold in the wood', plus small sums for the bark of felled oaks and for pannage. In 1273–4 the park brought in 56*s* 10*d* in sales of herbage and 14*s* in bracken, and more timber was felled.[462] In 1362 the agistment – letting of grazing – was valued at 26*s* per annum.[450]

There was evidently a biggish park in Staverton by 1268: it may already have been obsolete, since no deer are mentioned; and it was sometimes called a wood, as in the 1268–9 accounts (two of the witnesses swearing to the 1270 survey were surnamed de Bosco). The 1270 acreage seems much too small, and we suspect a mistake: a numeral such as *viiij*^{xx} (= 180) in the original draft might have been miscopied as *xx* (= 20) in the surviving fair copy. The returns of 63*s* 10*d* and 70*s* 10*d* for grass and bracken show that the park was equivalent to at least sixty acres of pasture at 13*d* per acre, besides the timber, wood, or deer which it produced.

No earlier reference to the Park is known. Domesday Book records a wood 'for 30 swine' at Staverton, one of the very few woods in the Suffolk Sandlings in 1086. There are many records after 1270. The monks of Butley Priory, who owned Staverton briefly before the Dissolution, entertained the Queen of France there in 1528 with a fox-hunting party, a picnic, and fun and games (*joco et ludo*) under the oaks.[263] The Stanhope Atlas by John Norden (1600–1) shows the park boundary with something like the present distribution of trees and plains within it.[371]

Staverton Park is still a place of mystery but much of its history is clear. It was founded between 1086 and *c.* 1250. An existing wood probably formed its nucleus. The absence of a podzol suggests that the site has never been under heather for any length of time (p. 36). Apart from the evidence of the lichens, it is difficult to tell how far the Park is derived from wildwood and how far from early secondary woodland of *Quercus robur*. For centuries it was intensively grazed and cut for bracken. The existing trees show that it was intensively used as a source of wood for at least four centuries. The present 'wildwood' appearance is largely the result of the decline in these land-uses in the last 200 years. The distinct vegetation of The Thicks is partly due to the exclusion of sheep from this area from *c.* 1820 onwards, although the difference in pollarding heights shows that there must have been some difference in management between The Thicks and The Park at a much earlier period.

The decline of grazing was followed by a great increase of holly and birch, relatively sensitive trees. But oak, which had regenerated moderately freely under grazing, ceased to do so after grazing ended.

In Norfolk a number of Staverton-like wood-pastures survived into the nineteenth century.[341] The former common at Thursford near Fakenham still remains (and cf. Felbrigg Beeches, p. 326).

Reproduction

A common topic of conversation among naturalists is the supposed failure of oaks to establish themselves from seed. Many people concerned with the conservation of woods take it upon themselves to plant oaks in the hope of replacing the missing natural regeneration. Sometimes, as in parts of Hatfield Forest, a wood was bulldozed away in order to replant oaks on the site. Acorns and oaklings have been the subject of much research, which has not solved the main problem, though it has made the issues clearer, both for oak and for the three other large-seeded trees – beech, hazel, and sweet-chestnut – which share some of the apparent disadvantages of oak.

The extent of the problem

In most habitats other than woods oak regenerates more than adequately and, given half a chance, rapidly forms secondary woodland. The much lamented lack of new oaks in hedges is often more apparent than real: the oaks are there – especially in mixed hedges – but get cut by hedge-trimmers. Oak regenerates embarrassingly well in the less-wooded parts of most wood-pastures. Staverton Park is an apparent exception: but that part of it which has not reverted to dense woodland (The Thicks) is now covered by tall bracken (The Park), an almost equally unpromising environment for oaklings (p. 85). [See also p. 499.]

The extent of the problem is thus reduced to woods and the wooded parts of wood-pastures. In the great majority both of oakwoods and of woods of other species, there is indeed a scarcity of oaks between two and fifty or more years of age. This is often thought to be an anomaly calling for explanation and remedy.

This view is based on the preconception that a healthy oak population should be an intimate mixture of all ages of trees. This is usually thought to be self-evident, but is sometimes justified by the theories that oak should be the climax dominant tree, and that a climax tree ought, as in North America,[908] to be able to regenerate in its own shade.

M. W. Shaw[141] shows that oak in practice is not biologically fitted to regenerate in its own shade. Continental foresters growing oak for timber sometimes, it is true, contrive to have all the commercial ages of oak side by side in a small area, but they do so by judiciously creating clearings after good acorn years – a highly-developed artificial technique seldom, if ever, applied to oak in Britain. D. T. Streeter[149] points out that, for reasons of management history, most of our woods lack the old oaks whose impending deaths will provide gaps wherein their successors can arise. Both authors reject the notion that the present state of regeneration is anomalous.

This may be true if we consider only the natural element in woodland. In wildwood, as we must suppose, the degeneration and death of certain areas of oaks or of other species created clearings in which new oaks became established. (This cannot, however, be demonstrated for oak in the modern semi-wildwood of Białowieża (p. 253).) There is a case, as Streeter proposes, for setting aside certain oakwood reserves to recover the degeneration phase in the life-cycle which is the necessary precursor to natural regeneration. But this is not how our woods have been managed in the historic past; for centuries natural death seldom played any large part.

The history of oak reproduction in woods

In woodland other than oakwoods, there can be no doubt that oak regenerated in the past more freely than it does now. Medieval carpentry presupposes an abundant supply of small oaks, with a rapid turnover in just that age-class, of less than fifty years' growth, which is now deficient. Numbers of oaks were allowed to fluctuate widely without any suggestion that they were difficult to replace. In later centuries the number of oak staddles to be promoted was often well above the statutory minimum of twelve to the acre. There is no record that any action or expense was necessary to ensure the succession.

By the eighteenth century there are possible hints of trouble in the occasional leases which allow other species to be promoted if there are insufficient oaks, or allow a deficiency of staddles on one acre to be made up by promoting more on another acre. In one particular wood (Fig. 10.9c) a 'modern' age-structure, with a lack of young oaks, already existed by *c.* 1700. The problems of maintaining oaks in a coppice-wood are well analysed in this report, dated 1792, on the copses of Whittlewood Forest:

> if . . . it is not a Year for Acorns, then there are few or no Saplings, and by a Copse going to Sale Twice or Thrice in a scarce Year, the Succession of Oaks is entirely lost. There are a few Copses of this Description, as well as some where the young Oaks stand, in particular Spots, as thick as possible (too thick even to grow Twenty Years without injuring one another). I am informed these particular Spots are Places where the Keepers have had Skirmishes with poor People, who make a Practice of collecting Acorns to sell, and have cut their Bags, by which many of the Acorns have been trod into the Ground.[350]

On a very few estates we find records of planting or sowing oaks, as at Bedford Purlieus (Peterborough) from 1760 onwards.[128] Nevertheless, up to the mid-nineteenth century there is rarely any record of failure to maintain or increase the numbers of oaks in all types of woodland, even in limewoods with their excessive shade. As late as 1835 it was complained at Saham Toney (Norfolk) that 'where saplings have been left they stand considerably too thick'.[434]

I have argued elsewhere,[118] partly on archaeological evidence, that much of the regeneration of oaks may have been by coppicing rather than by seed. This would be highly practical for the rapid turnover of small oaks in the Middle Ages, and less so for the slower turnover of bigger trees in later centuries. Most of the present oaks in woods appear to have originated from seed, but in Eastern England some of them have come from stumps in about one wood out of three. In East Cambridgeshire and S.E. Hertfordshire stool-grown oaks locally outnumber those coming from seed.

For oak in oakwoods we do not have the same documentation, but the age-structure of the stands tells a similar story. Ancient moots are widespread in the Lowland Zone but are rarely a large proportion of the total. In most woods the moots vary widely in size, suggesting active turnover and replacement continuing until some time in the last century.

This historical evidence largely vindicates the popular view of what the 'normal' age-structure of an oak population ought to be. The behaviour attributed to oak in the wildwood of the past or in the 'non-intervention' nature reserves of the future differs from its behaviour in managed woodland. In historic times the moots of oakwoods and the standard oaks of other woods both formed populations of mixed age, with a rapid turnover much of which was by seed. Since about 1850 something has happened to prevent this turnover, but without affecting the ability of oak to reproduce outside woodland. By the 1910s this was a widely-recognized problem, the subject of a classic study by A. S. Watt.[162]

Oak reproduction in woods now

Oak regeneration – the production of oaklings which survive to form timber trees – ended at different times in different woods, and in a few woods has not ended. I have recorded some oaks of between three and forty years' growth in about a fifth of the woods of Eastern England. In most of these there are merely occasional young oaks, usually along rides. Only about 7% of the woods have anywhere near as many staddles as would ensure normal replacement.

Woods in which oaks still regenerate adequately are widely scattered, with a concentration in mid Suffolk. They tend to have been coppiced within the last few decades and not to be dominated by lime, hornbeam, or chestnut. In the south, for instance, oak regeneration is largely limited to woods (e.g. Ken Wood (p. 57) and Thundersley West Wood (p. 234)) in which hornbeam is less oppressive than usual. Oak establishment occurs chiefly on soils of the middle range, avoiding heavy clays or sands.

The Bradfield Woods are exceptional in that oak regenerates fully as it did in the historic past. Most parts of the woods, on a variety of soils, have a full complement of oak staddles [Plate 8]. As recently as 1967 coppicing was followed by the establishment of more than enough new oaks to produce the highest historic density of timber trees. The Bradfield Woods are in the middle of the Suffolk oak regeneration area and satisfy the conditions of coppicing, composition, and soil mentioned above.

The causes of failure of oak regeneration

We need to look for some factor which changed in the nineteenth century, is strictly limited to woodland, and does not operate in Bradfield and a few other woods. The second condition is stringent; there are many places where oak regeneration begins only a few feet outside a wood boundary. The factor applies both to oakwoods and to other kinds of woodland and to both species of oak.

Seed production

A decline in the acorn supply cannot be the cause. Fluctuations in the acorn crop are recorded throughout the last thousand years (p. 155), and mast years, if anything, have become more frequent. Except in the worst years, enormously more acorns are produced than are needed to maintain the oaks. Acorns, especially of *Q. petraea*, can be killed by drought, frost, or fungal attack,[162, 757] but the slightest protection keeps them alive and they germinate very easily and almost at once.

Perils of the acorn

Many studies have concentrated on the consumption of acorns by animals. In most years and in most woods the bulk of the crop disappears with remarkable speed after being shed. Acorn-eaters vary from wood to wood;[141] they include woodpigeons, which greatly increased in the nineteenth century,[803] grey squirrels [and deer], which are a new influence, and pheasants, which have become more numerous on some estates. Watt argued that the rise of gamekeeping, by reducing the numbers of beasts and birds of prey, allowed rodents and other acorn eaters to multiply. This seems not to have been tested, although it is known that mice and voles are sometimes the chief eaters of acorns.[140]

This hypothesis may be a partial answer. Although there is some gamekeeping in some of the woods where oaks still regenerate, I have not recorded adequate regeneration in any wood with pheasant pens, keepers' gibbets, or other instruments of intensive preservation. At Bradfield pigeons, squirrels, and pheasants are less numerous than in most woods. However, the influence of predators ought not to stop at the edge of a wood; nor need the destruction of 99.9% of the acorns make any difference to the regeneration of oak. What matters is the difference between the survival to maturity of one acorn in 100,000 (in which case oaks will take over the world) and one acorn in 10,000,000 (which is roughly what happens now). Predators drop or bury some of the acorns taken; predation is not necessarily a disadvantage and without it there would be no dispersal.[141, 787]

In most woods some acorns do survive these perils. Oak, unlike beech, produces seedlings after moderate as well as good mast years. On average they usually exceed the number – roughly one every four acres annually – needed to maintain the population.

The diversity of factors involved in the survival of acorns is illustrated by the events of 1976–7 in Eastern England. Both species of oak fruited very heavily after the exceptional summer of 1976 and often covered the ground with acorns. The acorns of *Q. robur*, although unusually large, disappeared from view in all types of woodland (on both mull and mor soils) with almost their usual rapidity. In the following year *robur* oaklings were appreciably more common than usual. The acorns of *petraea*, however, remained lying on the surface or thinly covered with litter, and despite their reputed perishability germinated very freely. This includes one wood where pheasants are preserved. In the following spring in the Norfolk, Essex, and Hertfordshire sessile oakwoods there was the amazing sight of a shimmering carpet of countless oaklings, most of which were still alive a year later. I estimated that seven million oaklings survived into 1978 in 220 acres of Sherrard's Park Wood, Welwyn Garden City. Watt records a similar abundance of oaklings in some years before 1918.

Perils of the oakling

Even in normal years enough acorns survive to germination: the critical factor is their fate during, or soon after, their first summer. Their prospects are worse since the decline of woodland management, especially of coppicing, which has deprived oaklings of opportunities to escape the effects of shade. This factor accounts for the regeneration of oak outside woods and at Bradfield, which is still coppiced; but the correlation between coppicing and regeneration is not as good as we might expect. When Watt wrote, coppicing was still widespread; and in Hayley Wood, for example, oak regeneration virtually ceased in about 1840, fifty years before the decline of coppicing.[120]

Garden experiments show that healthy oaklings (most of the work has been done on *petraea*) grow under about 10% of full daylight and reach their maximum growth rate at only 30% of full daylight.[76] They ought therefore to survive even if quite heavily shaded either by oak or by other trees. In practice this does not happen; oaks in woodland need at least 30% daylight to survive. M. W. Shaw[141] attributes the discrepancy to caterpillars which happen to fall off while feeding on the overhanging trees. The lucky caterpillar that lands on an oakling continues to feed and partly defoliates its new host; this is a fatal setback for a seedling in shade, which needs all its leaf area to manufacture enough reserves to keep it alive.

Shaw's theory explains why oak should not regenerate in its own shade. Big oaks not only shade oaklings but also drop hungry caterpillars on them. The theory does not immediately explain why oak should not regenerate under other trees: it ought not to be defoliated by caterpillars specific to, say, ash or hornbeam. But the principle is more general. Oaklings growing in the open are difficult to kill and recover from severe damage (p. 293); but slight damage of any kind endangers a seedling that has shade to contend with as well.

Any agent of damage, therefore, makes oak less shade-tolerant than it would be if healthy. In 1908 Europe was suddenly overrun by a new agent of damage, the oak-mildew fungus (*Microsphaera alphitoides*). With Dutch Elm Disease in mind, we must be cautious about claims of 'new' parasitic fungi, but this fungus is very conspicuous and there is little doubt that it had not been in Europe before. Pre-1908 editions of plant-pathology textbooks describe many obscure species of *Microsphaera*, but regard what we now call *alphitoides* as peculiar to North America.[338a, 483–4] Oak mildew is a relatively trivial disease in the open but may be death to a shaded oakling.

In the Bradfield Woods we see how coppicing enables oaks to regenerate. Oaklings arising in the season after coppicing, or remaining alive from the previous season, are freed from shade (and perhaps caterpillars) and enabled to make normal growth. As has been shown experimentally at Monks' Wood (Hunts) oaks grown *in situ* from the acorn can just keep up with the regrowth of underwood.[147] At Bradfield oaklings germinating one, two or even more years after coppicing can struggle upwards, though somewhat shaded, until a future coppicing releases them. The oaklings, therefore, are not exactly synchronized with the underwood and do not necessarily fail if the year of coppicing is a bad acorn year.

This non-synchronization may explain, in part, why the youngest oaks in many woods are older than the date of the last coppicing. Oaks which fail to keep up with the underwood – for instance because they start late – often stay alive till released at the next coppicing. If the next coppicing is delayed or never comes they die. For this reason, unless the oaklings of the last coppicing got off to a good start, the youngest surviving oaks may well be those of the last coppicing but one – or even of the last coppicing but two, if the last rotation was abnormally long.

Conclusions

The oak regeneration problem depends on many factors. Several changes unfavourable to woodland oak have happened in the last 150 years: not all of them have happened everywhere, and a few places, such as Bradfield, have apparently escaped all the changes apart from the ubiquitous oak mildew.

It is unlikely that oak ever regenerated freely in its own shade or in the dense shade of other trees. The interaction between shade and damage appears to be more severe in oakwoods than in other kinds of woodland; this may be offset to some extent by the reputedly greater inherent shade-tolerance of *Q. petraea* – the oak of oakwoods – than of *Q. robur* (see below). The historic regeneration pattern of oak is largely the product of coppicing; the cessation of coppicing is the chief factor in its decline, though not always a sufficient cause by itself. [See also pp. 499–503.]

Several predators of acorns have increased. This is unlikely to be a critical factor – indeed it may assist dispersal – but it may reduce the number of oaklings and hence the surplus available to meet losses later in life.

The arrival of oak mildew probably made oaklings succumb to a degree of shade which they would formerly have survived. The same applies to attacks on oaklings by animals: the increasing access by sheep to some Highland woods and the proliferation of deer in the Lowlands are often sufficient in themselves to prevent oak regeneration. Rabbits are seldom a sufficient cause: their destruction by myxomatosis was not followed by any general establishment of oak.

Table 17.3 Summary of the habitats of oak.

Habitat	Page reference	Species of oak	Present distribution of habitat	Soil	Increase or decrease, A.D.. 1500–1930: in extent of habitat	in abundance of oak within habitat	Present state of oak regeneration
Highland-zone oakwoods	284–5	Mainly *petraea* (except far north and Dartmoor groves)	Widespread	Mainly acid	Little change?	Probable slight increase	Usually poor or none
Lowland-zone oakwoods	285–92	Mainly *petraea* (exceptions include Iken Wood and Grovely Ridge)	Rare	Very acid sands and silts	Probable decline	Probably stable	Poor or none
Oakwoods of Hatfield Forest	291	*Q. robur*	Hatfield Forest only	Calcareous silty clay	Stable?	Stable?	Has occurred after felling
Oak–hornbeam and chestnut–oak woods	229–30, 332	Mainly *petraea*	Locally abundant	Acid clayey silt	Little change	Unknown	Poor or none
Other woods	285	Almost all *robur*	Widespread	Variable	Decline	Moderate increase	Usually none
Wood-pasture	293–4, 499–503	Mainly *robur*	Uncommon	Variable, mainly acid	Severe decline	Usually stable	Usually good (except Staverton)
Secondary woodland	291–3	Almost all *robur*	Widespread	Variable	Increase	—	Good outside existing woodland
Hedges	—	Almost all *robur*	Widespread	Variable	Increase then decline	Decline	Usually good
Plantations	299	Usually *robur* *petraea* fashionable at present)	Widespread	Variable	Increase	—	—

The two oaks reconsidered

Habitats and physiology

The correlation between sessile oak and oak woodland is of very general application. Throughout Great Britain, *Q. petraea* is the typical oak of oakwoods (and of oak–hornbeam woods) and *Q. robur* of all other woodland and of all other habitats (Table 17.3). There are some systematic exceptions, in that *robur* tends to occur within oakwoods in valleys and on moister soils, and also in the extreme climates of the far north and high altitudes; other exceptions (e.g. Iken and Stockton Woods) do not fit any obvious pattern. These exceptions show that the general relationship between *petraea* and oakwoods is not due to some simple factor such as an inability of *robur* to coppice.

These very striking differences in behaviour must spring from some strong physiological difference between the two oaks. The fact that both oaks can grow very well on the 'wrong' kinds of site rules out the simple explanation that *robur* cannot cope with the poor soils that carry oakwood, or *petraea* cannot cope with the more calcareous soils that carry other kinds of woodland (although I. G. Simmons has claimed a differentiation by soils in the extreme climate of Dartmoor[143]). It is more likely to be some subtle difference that makes *petraea* a more gregarious tree than *robur*: *petraea* is the oak that grows where it has oak (or hornbeam) to compete with, whereas *robur* is the oak that competes better with other tree species or with herbaceous vegetation. The difference probably operates on the seedling or young tree. As Shaw's experiments show, the older trees may exercise their influence not so much by direct shading or root competition, as by the insects and other animals that they attract.

Oaks make poor experimental material. Their extreme variability makes it necessary to use large numbers to get representative results, and this is difficult to arrange because of the space needed by their root systems. Although the bibliography of oak physiology is very great,[774] few studies are of much help in interpreting the oaks' native ecology, and remarkably few have compared the two oaks under the same conditions. E. W. Jones[757] has made the important suggestion, supported by French and German measurements, that *robur* oaklings are less tolerant of shade than *petraea*. Less easily applicable to actual woods is the finding by R. M. Newnham and A. Carlisle[807] that first-year *robur* oaklings, grown in a glasshouse, needed three times as much phosphate but only half as much nitrate as *petraea* for optimum growth. The subject badly needs further study.

Are both oaks native?

Ever since the two species were distinguished, botanists have speculated that one or the other is not indigenous. Latterly it has been widely supposed that *robur* has become much more abundant and widespread, at the expense of *petraea*, as a result of tree-planting. The late Professor M. L. Anderson, an extreme exponent of this view, even claimed[604] that *robur* was not native but had been introduced centuries ago, probably by the tree-planting which he attributed to Cistercian monks.[7] Anderson seems not to have published any primary evidence in support of any stage in this argument, which was apparently based merely on the supposedly poorer performance of *robur* as a timber tree in Britain.

The matter cannot be settled, as it can with the two limes (pp. 237–9), from fossil evidence; for the pollen grains cannot be distinguished and fragments of the tree appear never to be suffficiently complete to be identified with certainty. It has been claimed in Germany that the microscopic structure of the timber is distinctive;[747] the method has recently been applied in Britain[903a] but not yet on a wide enough range of material to establish its consistency.

The notion that *robur* has been introduced in the last 800 years can be disposed of by the fact that the great majority of very old living oaks and almost all the oak leaves and acorns in medieval sculpture[726] are *robur*. Long before the first recorded extensive tree-planting, *robur* must have been common, at least in wood-pastures (where it was likely to live long) and in hedges (where it was likely to be noticed by sculptors).

From 1790 to 1840 sessile oak was strongly disapproved of by forestry writers and nurserymen,[691] and there is some evidence that this had a practical effect; for instance, in the Forest of Dean, intensively replanted at this time, the oak population is said to have been changed from predominantly *petraea* to predominantly *robur*.[863] It is often argued that planters of oak before 1790, even though they did not recognize *robur* as a distinct species, unwittingly selected in its favour. This may be partly true, if only because *petraea* tends to grow away from settlements, and the first oak-tree that an acorn-collector comes to is likely to be *robur*. Acorns were occasionally transported long distances and even from England to Scotland;[757] these are likely to have been predominantly *robur* (despite its greater weight per acorn) and may have introduced this species to what had been *petraea* areas. We should not exaggerate the effects of this preference. Anderson, collecting data in the New Forest from which to argue against *robur*, found that inclosures planted between 1700 and 1808, and between 1843 and 1870, contained at least as high a proportion of *petraea* as there was in the ancient unenclosed wood-pasture; only in plantations made between 1809 and 1829, when *petraea* was very unfashionable, was it rarer than in the rest of the Forest.[605]

Human activities have favoured *robur* in various ways. Sometimes it has been preferred for new plantations. Occasionally the native *petraea* of an existing wood may have been destroyed and replaced by *robur* – though in nearly all ancient woods where the oaks appear to be of nursery origin (p. 283) any surviving trees from the original wood are *robur* also. To suppose that either process had much effect before 1750 is to go well beyond the evidence. There appears to be no evidence that the Cistercians planted woods – I have searched their historical journal *Cîteaux* – still less that they preferred *robur*. Soane Wood, Colchester, the one wood which may have been planted by monks (p. 291), in fact contains some *petraea*, which is rare in the district. In so far as *robur* has been helped by civilization, it is almost certainly by the more subtle effects – by the formation of hedges, scrub, and wood-pasture which enable *robur* to use its greater colonizing ability – rather than by the temporary consequences of tree-planting fashions.

There is no reason to suppose that civilization has affected the broad distribution of the two oaks. *Q. robur* occurs in particular environments – though we know little of why it should – rather than in particular landownerships. It grows in many places, such as Wistman's Wood, isolated from direct human intervention; it is commoner than *petraea* in the relict woods of Ross and Cromarty. I have seen hybrids, with at least half *robur* characteristics, in remote gorges below Sgùrr na Coinnich on Skye. There is no need for ingenious schemes to explain away these occurrences: *robur* extends further north than *petraea* in Scandinavia, Finland, and Russia,[682, 757] and it should withstand our extreme climates too. The two oaks have roughly the same geographic range, in Britain as in most of Europe, and there is no reason to doubt that both reached their present limits in prehistoric times.

Hybridization

The hybridization of oaks has been the subject of several studies.[915] The greater degree and apparently longer history of hybridization in Scotland than in England has been attributed[839] to more extensive mixing of the two species by planting. This is unlikely since in England the two oaks have been in contact for at least three times as long as there has been oak-planting in Scotland. A more probable hypothesis is that in the north the flowering times of the oaks overlap more and give more opportunities for crossing.[639]

A historical summary

Despite the complications of all the interrelations between oaks and men, there can be little doubt that in the present distribution of oaks we have the fading remains of a pattern set up in the wildwood over 6,000 years ago. The extensive oakwoods of the Highland Zone, perpetuated by the bark trade, are derived from the oakwoods of that part of Britain in the Atlantic Period. Oak, growing probably on the poorer soils, has survived more often than the hazel then associated with it. The majority of the Highland oak was probably *petraea*, perhaps with a local preponderance of *robur* on the better soils or in the worst climates.

In the Lowland Zone the present oakwoods are almost all on the most acid and least fertile soils; usually they are on high ground, but where the low ground happens to be less fertile than the high (as in the Forêt de Fontainebleau, p. 303) the oaks occupy the former. Oak, especially *petraea*, is the dominant tree in places where few other native trees will grow: its chief rival is beech, but we can only rarely (as at Ellenden, p. 292) compare them side by side on equal management terms. This is a consistent and apparently natural vegetation pattern, and probably goes back to prehistoric times. In phytosociological terms it is parallelled by the Belgian Luzulo-Quercetum,[47] the leucobryetosum variant of which strongly recalls the Norfolk oakwoods (p. 285).

The second aspect of Lowland oak, the trees scattered throughout almost all kinds of woodland, appears also to be a natural feature, as is suggested by the general availability of oak for prehistoric artefacts and the general occurrence of its pollen. *Quercus robur* is thinly scattered amid groups of hornbeam, lime, etc. in the wildwood-like Forest of Białowieża (p. 253). The felling, by prehistoric men, of wildwood having this composition and structure would lead easily and naturally to the formation of coppice-with-standards woodland. In Britain there is no foundation for the myth, often repeated especially by archaeological writers, that oak is particularly a tree of the claylands; it grows well on clay but is, if anything, less abundant than on lighter soils.

The march of civilization has favoured oak more than other trees, and has favoured *robur* more than *petraea*. Forest clearances tended to destroy the trees of more fertile soils and to leave the oaks. Woodland management encouraged oak, in balance with other species, by treating it as a timber tree and by providing clearings and coppiced areas in which it could reproduce. Wood-pasture encouraged oak by eliminating other species more sensitive to grazing and by providing glades and scrub areas which *Q. robur* could colonize.

By the Middle Ages the larger remaining wood-pastures (e.g. Windsor Forest and Thorpe Wood (p. 134)) were usually on poor soils, and were dominated chiefly by oak and to a lesser extent beech – the trees of the bad lands. Wood-pasture, favouring long-lived oaks and regeneration in glades, perpetuated, in a modified form, the slow cycle of areas of middle age, degeneration, death, and re-establishment that we must suppose had been the regeneration pattern of oak in the wildwood.

Coppice-woods were on a wider range of soils; some were derived from oak-dominated wildwood and some from other kinds. Although the presence of oak probably

18

The alder-woods

Of all familiar native trees alder (*Alnus glutinosa*) is the most obviously restricted to particular habitats. We see it most often as a non-woodland tree, fringing streams and rivers and penetrating to the heart of cities on rotting river-walls; it is a good indicator of land liable to flooding. Alder is abundant almost throughout Britain, but is rather less common in the far north of Scotland and in mid-Ireland; it is curiously rare in the Fens.

There are three more or less distinct types of alder woodland:

(1) ***Fen alder-woods*** on low, level ground in the flood-plains of rivers and streams, usually away from other kinds of woodland. These are extensive and well known.[150, 777]
(2) ***Valley alder-woods***, forming narrow fringes to streams, often within woodland of other types. Sometimes they climb up flushed slopes, especially in western Britain.[85]
(3) ***Plateau alder-woods***, in which alder is a normal constituent of the mosaic of tree communities on level uplands.

The types are very distinct though connected by intermediates; (2) and (3) are of great interest though small in area.

Alder readily colonizes new sites: its seeds are dispersed efficiently by water and to some extent by wind.[777] Most fen alder-woods are of recent origin. It coppices very easily; unless otherwise stated it will be assumed that alder-woods have been coppiced.

The history of alder

The prehistoric record

Alder recolonized this country comparatively slowly, not reaching its full extent until the early Atlantic Period. By the end of this period it accounts for over half the total pollen sampled in many districts.[12] This, of course, reflects the tree's habit of growing in wet places – even around quite small basins – where its pollen is likely to be preserved. Alder grew around bogs, fens, and lakes almost throughout Great Britain; then as now it was slightly less common in Ireland and much less common in the far north.[710]

During and after the Neolithic the abundance and distribution of alder, relative to other trees, remained remarkably steady; it has neither profited nor suffered from human activities. It frequently appears in archaeological structures back to the Neolithic period.

Place-names and charters

Alder is not the most striking of trees and is little noticed by literary writers. It makes a good place-name element, for it has specific uses and does not grow everywhere. Names involving *alder*, the Anglo-Saxon *aler*, Old Norse *elri*, Welsh and Cornish *gwernen*, or Gaelic *fearna* sprinkle every sheet of the Ordnance Survey.

In Anglo-Saxon charters alder, although rare, is useful because of its ecological limitations. For instance, in a perambulation at Stockton (Wiltshire), A.D. 901,[207] there is an unexpected *alercum*, 'alder-valley', in a seemingly waterless chalk landscape; when I went over the ground with Mr Michael Stratton, he was able to point out from local knowledge the one place where winter flooding occurs and so to fix the spot with confidence, though the alders have long since gone.

There is a specific word, ***carr***, for woodland composed of alder. Nowadays all kinds of fen woodland and scrub are loosely so called, but in medieval documents the word 'ker' appears to be the exact equivalent of *alnetum*. A few alder-woods are specified in Domesday Book.

Medieval uses and management

Alder is not a useful tree for most general purposes. It rots easily, burns badly, and is usually too small to be timber. But it has the qualities of lightness, straightness, and ease of sawing for which we now value conifers. In the Middle Ages, when coniferous softwoods were harder to come by, alder was valued for temporary carpentry. It was the chief tree for scaffold poles;[477] for instance, the stores at Westminster in 1324 included 400 alders 38 ft long – a great length for an alder-tree. (For imported scaffold poles see p. 151.) Alder was sometimes used for piles (which, if under water, would not rot), levers (*boturs*) – for which lightness would be an advantage – and furniture.[477] In 1257 and 1260 alders were sent from Havering (Essex) to the maker (*attiliator*) of the king's crossbows in the Tower of London.[235] These uses imply that alder was managed as large coppice or small timber.

In documents *alnetum* – the same word is used for the woodland and the tree – is regularly distinguished from other kinds of wood. Small carrs, rarely more than ten acres, are recorded in many fens. They varied in value from rather more to much less than the average for woodland; it seems that many of them were secondary woodland arising on former meadows and pastures. For instance, the *alnetum* at Ditchingham (E. Norfolk) was felled in 1272 (cf. p. 233) and the wood sold for 6*s* an acre;[447, 462] at Hadleigh (Suffolk) in 1305 there was a six-acre *alnetum* called Muchelfen, only partly wooded and worth 4*s* a year in underwood and 8*s* in pasture.[330]

The manorial accounts for Hindolveston (Norfolk) (p. 157) mention alder in nearly half the years.[415] There were several small carrs, some of them belonging to tenants of the manor, and scattered alders in other places, e.g. in 1262 by a pond below the manor-house. Eastwood and Westwood both contained a small proportion of alder [as Eastwood still does], and there was also an *alnetum* immediately outside one of the woods. Evidently a plateau alder-wood sloped gently down to an adjoining fen carr; a similar topography still survives nearby at Swanton Novers. Sales of alder from the woods in 1311–12 realized £6 6*s* 8*d*. Sales of *mundura in alneto* in 1261–2 and of *parings Alneti in Westwode* in 1327–8 suggest that management included pruning (p. 159). But the lessee of Puttokesker (? 'hawk's carr') in 1376 was allowed to fell it twice in eight years, which would have been too short an interval to exploit alder for its specific uses. When the Priory felled Grenesker ('Green's carr') in 1387 it yielded 3,300 splints worth 27*s* 6*d*, 2,400 faggots worth £3, and eight loads of thorns worth 8*s*; the felling (one man for 36 days, excluding making up the faggots) cost 12*s*.

We conclude that alder was locally common in the Middle Ages; some of it was grown on the rather long rotations necessary to produce softwood poles and small timber; but much of it was treated as any other underwood. Fen alder-woods occupied very valuable land – the alternative land-use was meadow – and were of small extent and apparently impermanent.

Post-medieval history

Alder was the preferred tree for charcoal for making gunpowder, and coppices, some of which still remain, were planted near the works. It was also preferred for making clogs (which when in fashion are now often made of other trees) and is used for tool-handles and brush-backs.

The manufacture of gunpowder reached its peak during the Napoleonic Wars. The Royal Gunpowder Factory at Waltham Abbey (Essex) produced an average of 855 tons a year from 1809 to 1815.[804] Powder was then about 15% charcoal, so that it took nearly a ton of wood to make a ton of powder. Since an alder coppice ought to yield about two tons per acre per annum, the Factory could have been supported at this wartime rate by about 400 acres of alder-wood. This may seem surprisingly little to fuel a world war, but the weaponry of those days used explosives mainly for propulsion and was relatively economical.

There were many complaints of difficulty in getting supplies of alder.[518] In 1789 Waltham bought poplar and 'Black Birch, provided it should be found upon experiment to make as good coal as Alder-wood'. Probably, as with naval oak, this was due to parsimony rather than to scarcity. In 1788 Waltham paid a mere 15*s*–16*s* an 'Essex cord', roughly 1.4*d* a cubic foot, for alder. In Napoleonic times all the charcoal was brought from Surrey and Sussex.[48] In the 1830s an 'Alder bed', shown on the Ordnance Survey of 1844 as about 31 acres, enough to keep the Factory going in peacetime, was established at Waltham.

Trade in alder in Essex and Suffolk was not dominated, even in wartime, by the gunpowder industry. Alder was relatively cheap. In Bruisyard Wood (E. Suffolk) in 1829 it was sold as timber for £2 a load, the lowest value of any tree in the wood except aspen.[363] At South Weald (S. Essex) in 1804 large alder poles 'Average measure . . . 22 ft long by 4¼ in. square' were worth 2*s* 4*d* each, i.e. 14*d* a cubic foot.[321] Both figures are equivalent to about 9*d* a cubic foot in the money of 1788. Other prices suggest that poles were usually smaller. Alder was generally about a third of the value per cubic foot of the smallest oak, but this was more than offset by its greater productivity, and it could yield a considerable income: the few acres in Norsey Wood (p. 335) produced 2,000 alder poles, worth £60, in 1806.[308] Except around powder-mills, few attempts were made to encourage alder: most of it was there by accident rather than intention.

Fen alder-woods

The written evidence establishes the antiquity of alder in all its habitats. Fen alder-woods, however, have not had the stability of other kinds of woodland, and the great majority of them are recent. The carrs of the Norfolk Broadland, now among the most extensive in Britain, are chiefly on abandoned meadow and fen: Donald and Milne's map of 1795 shows most of the area as fen with scattered trees,[265] and on the Ordnance Survey of 1838 it is largely treeless. Future research may identify a few ancient fen carrs, but for alder-woods with historical continuity we must look to the other two types.

Valley alder-woods

Woodland streamsides are fringed with alder in many parts of Britain. Alder valleys in Eastern England are

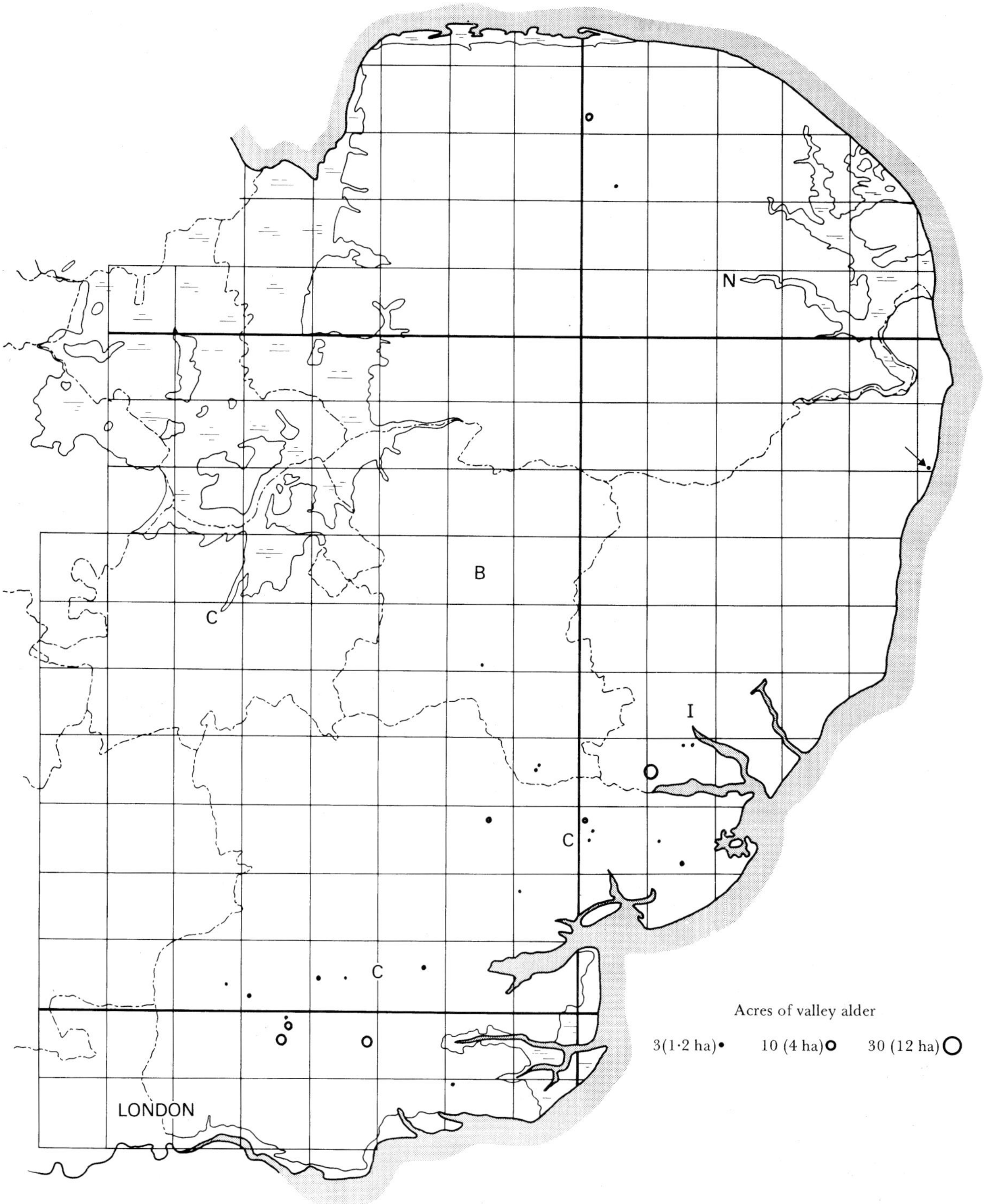

Fig. 18.1 Distribution by area of valley alder-wood within ancient woods in Eastern England. Arrows draw attention to outlying sites.

uncommon and of small extent (Fig. 18.1), but are a very distinctive plant community repeated in other parts of England. Valley alder is always associated with springs and hence occurs most often in woods in which, for instance, gravel overlies London Clay. Mere surface run-off from Boulder-clay will not do.

The presence and amount of alder may vary from valley to valley within the same wood, as in Norsey Wood (Fig. 21.4). A typical alder 'slade' begins at a permanent spring within the wood, surrounded by a steep-sided hollow; from this there runs a valley, narrow and steep-sided in places, broadening here and there into peat-filled basins. The stream is augmented by seepages from the valley sides; where these are strong the alders may climb the slopes. Alder valleys are often very asymmetric one side only being flushed (Fig. 15.8).

Alder often grows on its own, but some slades have a small proportion of crack willow (*Salix fragilis*) – probably the only situation in which the big willows enter into native woodland. Some slades in Writtle Forest have willow without alder. Alder is sometimes mixed with ash or blackthorn (cf. medieval Hindolveston).

Most Essex alder slades are in woods consisting chiefly of chestnut and hornbeam. The alders may abut directly on these trees (Table 6.2) but many alder valleys are separated from the rest of the wood by a narrow fringe of ash or hazel (p. 214, Fig. 15.7). Alder valleys are sometimes very acidic but are often the only calcareous feature in an otherwise acid wood. The broader valleys accumulate a distinctive soft black non-fibrous peat, often with shells of freshwater mussels and other molluscs.

Alder valleys have several characteristic plant communities. The delicate herbs *Chrysosplenium oppositifolium* (occasionally *C. alternifolium*), *Cardamine flexuosa*, and *Adoxa moschatellina*, and the liverwort *Conocephalum conicum* are confined to streamsides and soft peat. On firmer ground a common dominant species is *Carex pendula*, associated with *Humulus lupulus*, *Solanum dulcamara*, *Calystegia sepium*, and other tall herbs. Nettles and foxgloves often indicate enhanced fertility. *Dryopteris dilatata* may grow on the alder stools. Flushed slopes may be acid enough for *Sphagnum* (as in Norsey Wood); *Allium ursinum* and *Equisetum telmateja* may grow on moderately acid slopes.

Our valley alder-woods are small outliers of the extensive and varied alder-woods of the Continent, called by the alliance name Alno-Fraxinion *alias* Alno-Padion. Several associations within this alliance resemble different alder slades in Eastern England.[809]

Plateau alder-woods

As well as its association with watercourses, alder has a curious habit of turning up on the highest ground. There is an alder-wood on very nearly the highest point of Norfolk at Swanton Novers. Another in the Bradfield Woods crowns the watershed between the three principal river-basins of Suffolk. There are a few acres of alder on the highest point of Hatfield Forest in Essex. These and other examples (Fig. 18.2) constitute plateau alder-wood, which is typically on level ground, sometimes with slight depressions, and often on a watershed.

Alder is less gregarious here than in its other habitats; it is usually mixed with other species, and areas of plateau alder-wood merge gradually into other types of woodland. The trees associated with plateau alder (Table 6.2) are very different from those that are mixed with, or abut on, valley alder: the commonest is lime and the second commonest is birch; chestnut and hornbeam are both uncommon with plateau alder.

The ground vegetation beneath plateau alder (Table 6.3) is somewhat like that adjacent to valley alder: brambles and bracken are both abundant, though bluebell is remarkably rare. Some of the species beneath valley alder – *Carex riparia*, *Allium ursinum*, *Filipendula ulmaria* – occasionally grow under plateau alder also, but the more exacting species of streamsides and flushes do not.

Plateau alder-woods have no exact parallel on the Continent. They have many species in common with a Fraxino-Alnetum described from broad valleys in Poland.[891]

Alder in the Bradfield Woods

Alder is the third commonest tree in the Bradfield Woods: it is co-dominant over about 100 acres (40 ha), which is by far the largest plateau alder-wood. The antiquity of alder is attested by local place-names such as *Car*gate (recorded in the fourteenth century) and *Carr* Fell. Many of the stools are of great age, often over 10 ft diameter, larger than in other alder-woods. The old stools expand into a ring of living stems and roots surrounding a mound of mouldering wood and debris; this is peculiar to Bradfield alders.

Alder at Bradfield grows over the whole range of soils from pH 3.3 to 7.3. The soils, with their varying thicknesses of sand and silt overlying Boulder-clay (pp. 47–50), are winter-wet; they are flooded at the surface only for short periods, but there is evidently much seepage beneath the surface, and in places there are small surface streams in spring. In summer the woods dry out, but are markedly less liable to drought than the surrounding fields.

Alder grows in several different assemblages of trees; commonly with ash, hazel, and birch; less frequently with non-invasive elm and lime. Ordination analysis (pp. 28–31) shows that alder defines the second most important axis of variation in the underwood, being positively associated with sallow and elder, and avoiding the neighbourhood of hawthorn, maple, and blackthorn.

The Bradfield Woods also have the largest area in Suffolk of *Allium ursinum*, which is strongly associated with alder (p. 95). Alder ground vegetation also includes

may have been blown from a distant source. Only occasionally, in the Breckland and the Fens, is there sufficient pollen (Fig. 8.3) to suggest a substantial local presence.

Birch forms many place-names, for instance the parish of Birch (Domesday *Bricce*, 'at the birch') near Colchester. As well as the Birchet woods there are Birch woods, fields, etc. These are shown, together with references to the existence or felling of birch, in Fig. 19.1. Allowing for the fact that birch is a tree particularly likely to be mentioned by name, they suggest that up to 1800 it was rather local, about as common as native lime is now; it grew in south and east Essex, especially round Colchester, extending to S.E. Suffolk, with an outlier in N.E. Norfolk. It is unlikely to be native to Cambridgeshire; Ray in 1660 says it grew only 'About Sir Francis Russells house at Chippenham', which sounds like a garden plantation.[466]

East Anglian birch has been used on a small scale for turnery: coppice poles from Bradfield were made into rake-handles and scythe-sticks, being light, strong, and free from shivers; larger poles were used for brush-backs. Historic references, beginning with a sale of 2*s* 8*d* worth of 'Birches' from Bacton Wood (Norfolk) in 1415–16,[411] are particularly concerned with ***brushwood***, the fine twigs, derived either from very short-rotation coppice or from the *spray* of larger underwood, and used for birch brooms. This use is occasionally specified in wood-leases; for instance in 1736 the lessee of woods in Redgrave (Suffolk) was 'to have liberty of cutting Birch for Brooms at any Time in the Year'.[369] Birch had a scarcity value: Susannah Hornby paid £3 15s per acre, increased in 1764 to £6 6*s* per acre, to 'gather birch' in Hintlesham Woods (Suffolk).[361] In Glebe Grove, Felsham (Suffolk) it was apparently coppiced in the 1800s on a special two-year rotation.[224]

Ordinary sales of birch as poles and faggots are recorded at Haveringland (Norfolk) from 1775 to 1822.[408] Birch extended into the Weald and was one of the commonest fuels for seventeenth-century ironworks there.[888] The only price for timber that I have seen, at Haveringland in 1820, is 1*s* 6*d* a cubic foot, about half the value of oak.

Finally there is the use of birch rods as a teaching aid. Norwich Grammar School bought 7*d* worth of 'byrche for ye Schollers' in 1571.[479]

Modern ecology

Highland birchwoods

Birchwoods are the commonest native woodland of Scotland. Often *Betula pubescens* grows by itself, but *B. pendula* may also be present, and there may be an admixture of rowan (*Sorbus aucuparia*). The ground vegetation is varied but includes few specifically woodland plants. D. N. McVean and D. A. Ratcliffe distinguish two classes: '*Vaccinium*-rich birchwoods' usually with abundant blaeberry (*Vaccinium myrtillus*) and 'herb-rich birchwoods' often with a grassy floor.[780] Mosses and liverworts are luxuriant and form many interesting sub-communities on the ground, fallen logs, and boulders, and in gorges.[614] Birchwoods can adjoin and intermingle with woods of oak, hazel, or pine.

Highland birchwoods usually adjoin moorland without any definite boundary. They seldom show any sign of management but since the tree is short-lived we would hardly expect to find any. Birchwoods are usually of only one or two ages of tree, most commonly of old or declining trees with no sign of regeneration; the seedlings die in infancy. This has been widely attributed to sheep which take shelter in the woods, but birch has also been thought incapable of regenerating within birchwoods because it is intolerant of shade or root competition.[780] Since 1960 regeneration has become more common, probably through the decline of sheep-grazing and the spread of deer-fencing; in Ross-shire one often sees young stands of birch, or old stands developing a young generation in gaps, in places from which sheep and deer have been excluded. Probably these will ultimately develop into a patchwork of different ages.

McVean and Ratcliffe regard most birchwoods as secondary, replacing either pine or oak. This may be largely true, but pollen evidence shows that all parts of Scotland have had some birch throughout the post-glacial, and some birchwoods may be relics from Pre-Boreal times. H. H. Birks's remarkable pollen diagram from Loch Maree, for instance, shows that there have been pinewoods, birchwoods, and oakwoods round the loch for 9,000 years; the proportion of birch pollen has varied little in that period.[11]

Lowland birchwoods

Birch is very common as a pioneer tree forming secondary woodland on all kinds of derelict land. On fenland the tree is reverting to one of its prehistoric habitats. Invasion by birch is one of the chief causes of the disappearance of heathland, notably in Surrey; this results from the decline in grazing and in the cutting of heather, furze, and bracken, the traditional uses of heathland. Birch occurs in almost any secondary wood, but because of its powers of dispersal it can form pure birchwoods in places distant from any existing trees.

Birkland in Sherwood Forest (Notts)

With its Viking birch-name, this is the kind of place where the tree might have survived the lean millennia before its recent return. The site is peculiarly dry and infertile, a plateau overlying Bunter Sandstone, from which its very sandy soils are said to be derived.[743] The

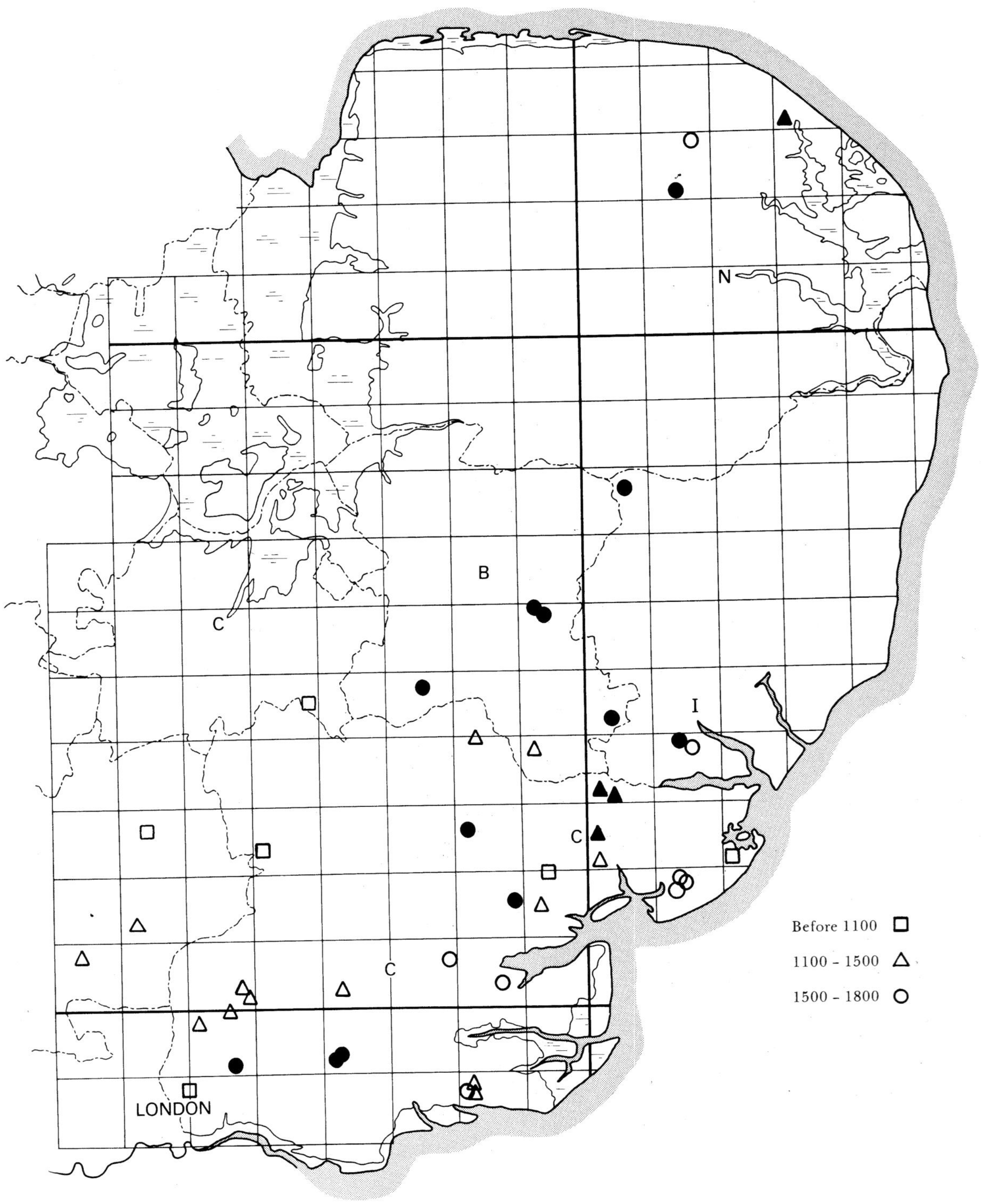

Fig. 19.1 Pre-1800 evidence for the occurrence of birch. White symbols: records which indicate only the presence of birch (e.g. place-name Birch Wood). Black symbols: records which indicate that birch was abundant (e.g. series of sales; place-name Birchet Wood).

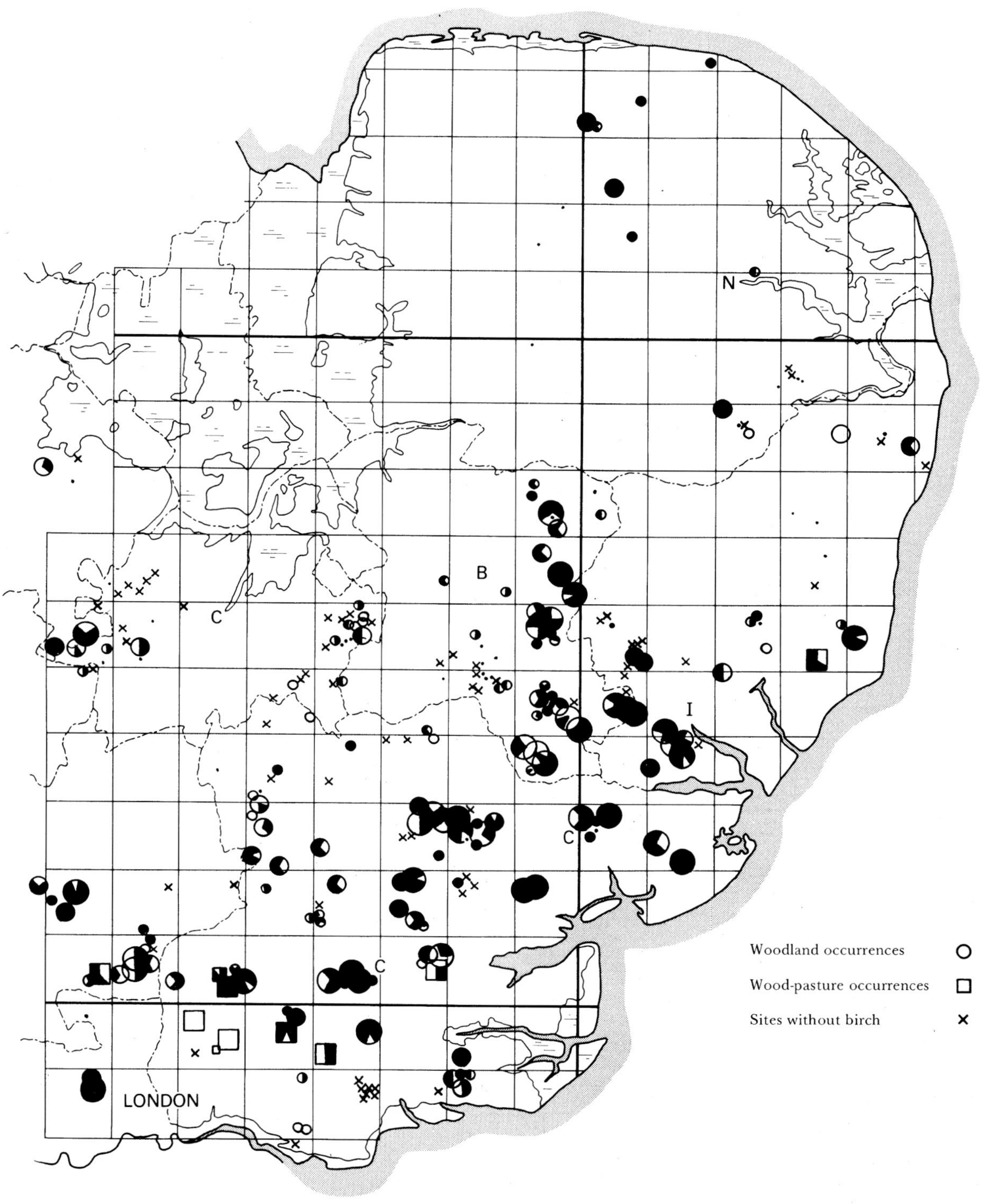

Fig. 19.2 Approximate relative abundance of birch within ancient woods in Eastern England. The size of each circle and square is roughly proportional to the fraction of the woodland area occupied by birch. Black and white sectors are a rough guide to the relative abundance of *Betula pubescens* (black) and *B. pendula* (white).

flora is extremely poor; oak and birch are almost the only woody plants.

Birkland – now a Country Park – is famous for its several hundred ancient oaks, of both species, scattered over a wide area (Fig. 17.7). They appear to date from the later Middle Ages. They are almost all dead in the top – sometimes more than half dead, and about one in four dead altogether – as a result of some forgotten catastrophe. This presumably happened before 1906, when it was said that 'decay has set in from the top downwards'[43] and conceivably as long ago as 1793 when the oaks were already described as 'very antient Trees', 'the far greater Part . . . in a state of Decay'. Even in 1609 nearly half the oaks of Birkland were recorded as 'not Tymber' through decay.[351] They are not, as is sometimes stated, dying trees, for they have not declined further since this one event; they survived unharmed the great droughts of 1975–6. This landscape of stag-headed oaks is a place of surrealist beauty; their dead limbs are stripped of bark and sapwood, bleached, drooping, and eroded to sharp points. With its superabundance of dead wood, it is famous for beetles.[627] There is probably nothing quite like it elsewhere, and it is doubly precious since recent events in the Forêt de Fontainebleau (pp. 303–4). Birkland does not, as sometimes stated, lack oak regeneration; there is a thin scatter of most of the younger ages.

The birches of Birkland – both species are present – form a mosaic of mainly even-aged patches, ranging from saplings to dying trees. They grow chiefly in areas where there are few or no oaks.

The ground vegetation is dominated by bracken or the calcifuge grasses *Deschampsia flexuosa* and *Holcus mollis*. *Deschampsia* occurs mainly in dry valleys and forms extensive grassy launds without trees.

At first sight this seems to be a nearly natural system, with a very slow turnover of slow-growing and long-lived oaks – for the site is almost too infertile even for oak – and a more rapid turnover of birch, perhaps in a cyclical succession of birch-groves and lawns, as suggested by Tansley.[150] We might suppose that it has gone on since Viking times with little change. But there can be little doubt that the system has been much altered by human activity. Much of the younger birch grows in areas disturbed by military manoeuvres. In the longer term, although the widely-spaced oaks give the impression of wood-pasture, they are, on closer inspection, relics of a wood. They are timber trees (some have been 'giraffe-pollarded' p. 5) and do not have the broad crowns of oaks that have grown up in the open. Their tall growth and narrow crowns are witnesses to the former existence of other trees, oaks or birches, which once filled the gaps between and restricted their sideways growth; these disappeared so long ago that the stumps have vanished. Earlier documents[214] refer to Birkland as a wood, differentiated from the heathland of the Forest. The 1609 survey states that there were about five oaks to the acre, considerably more than there are now. The story is complex and invites further study.

Eastern England

Birch forms extensive secondary woods in such places as Holme Fen (Hunts) and Mousehold Heath (Norwich). As elsewhere in Lowland England, the conservation of heathland and fens is often a matter of fighting against birch.

Birch is one of the commonest trees of ancient woodland. I have recorded some birch in 236 out of 323 woods examined – 73% – but in most of them it is clearly a recent arrival. There is some correlation between the modern distribution of birch (Fig. 19.2) and the pre-1800 records: birch is most abundant in areas from which there are early records and is still absent from some more remote districts.

It is reputed to be a tree of light soils. To some extent this is true of Eastern England: birch is more frequent on soils with over 35% sand and less than 20% clay (Fig. 19.3). This applies to most big birch stands and to patches of birch occupying sand-lenses in other types of woodland. But birch is becoming common even on heavy soils [pp. 362–73]. Probably the soil preference is expressed by the seedling. On a favourable soil seedlings become established almost anywhere and in any season; on an unfavourable soil they may need more luck with the weather or the micro-habitat to survive, but once started they grow no less well than on favourable soils.

There is no detectable correlation between soil pH and the occurrence of birch (Fig. 19.3). Since it tends to grow on soils that would normally be acid, this supports the theory that birch is a deacidifying plant, its fallen leaves being particularly rich in calcium brought up by the roots.[657]

The ecology of established birchwoods

Because of the short life of birch it is not always possible to be sure whether it is a recent invader. In an attempt to assess its traditional ecology I have selected thirty woods in which birch has either been regularly coppiced, or is represented by pre-1800 records, or (at Bradfield) has a pollen record. An analysis of the trees and herbs associated with birch in such woods (Tables 6.2, 6.3) confirms their relation to other types of woodland on coarse-textured acid soils. Birch is particularly strongly associated with chestnut and with the herbs that go with chestnut, even though the dense shade and heavy leaf-litter of chestnut ought to make it a poor companion for birch. To a lesser degree birchwoods are related to pure hornbeam woods and the more acidic ash and hazel woods. The more calcicolous trees (e.g. maple and elms) and herbs (e.g. oxlip and dog's-mercury) are rare in established birchwoods, as are lime and bluebell for less obvious reasons.

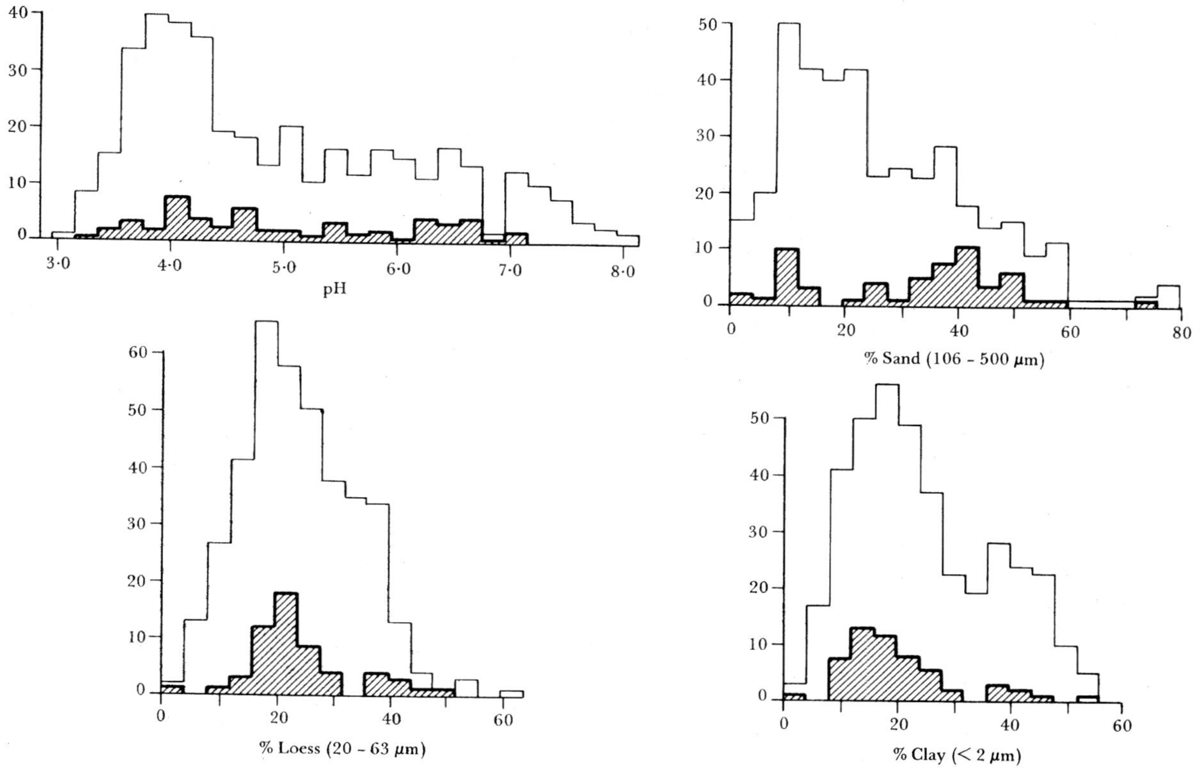

Fig. 19.3 Distribution of topsoil characteristics under birch in ancient woods in Eastern England. The thin upper line gives, for comparison, the characteristics of all woodland topsoils sampled. For further details see caption to Fig. 7.5.

Birch invasion

Many large stands of birch have sprung up after unusual fellings in recent decades. A good example is Birch Wood in Little Baddow (Essex), formerly an oak–hornbeam wood having a high density of standard trees (cf. Fig. 10.10b). These were felled all at once, probably in World War II, and have been replaced by birches which now dominate the wood. (The name, of course, is much older than these events.)

Birch invasion also results from replanting. It may get in in the process of destroying the existing woodland, or if the new crop fails or when it is ultimately felled; in each case birch eventually possesses the site. There are many examples throughout Britain, for instance in Colchester High Woods, where a century of coniferization has converted a mixed limewood into even-aged stands of birch with residual pines.

Most large birchwoods on ancient sites have a history of drastic disturbance: the previous underwood has been eliminated by grubbing or shade, leaving nothing to cover the ground once the timber trees disappear. But birch is now entering woods, even on the heaviest soils, through normal felling or coppicing: it inserts itself between stools or takes the place of stools or timber trees that have disappeared.

The two birches

In ancient woods *B. pubescens* is the commoner birch. The following are the proportions in 243 woods in which I have recorded the species:

All or nearly all *pubescens*	92 woods
More *pubescens* than *pendula*	51 woods
Roughly equal	53 woods
More *pendula* than *pubescens*	15 woods
All or nearly all *pendula*	32 woods

I have detected no ecological difference between the species, although it is often held that in other environments *pubescens* is the birch of wetter soils.[77] There may have been a difference in the past. Of the 30 long-established birch*woods*, 26 are mainly *pubescens* and none has a preponderance of *pendula*. Epping and Hainault *Forests*, however, both of which are ancient birch sites – the tree is recorded in 1498 and 1544 respectively[124] – have much more *pendula* than *pubescens*. Possibly *pubescens* may have been the birch of woodland and *pendula* that of wood-pasture.

The proportion of the two birches varies between different groups of woods according to no obvious pattern (Fig. 19.2). Where there are two generations of birch the species may differ: for instance in Holme Fen the old birches are almost all *pendula* and the young ones almost all *pubescens*. This suggests that the species are now determined more by accidents of colonization and the weather of particular seasons than by any systematic ecological preference.

Conclusions

According to classical succession theory[150] birch is a primary colonizer, occupying the ground for less than one generation and being displaced by a 'climax' tree, such as oak or beech, growing up and eventually overtopping it. This can still be seen, for instance, in neglected wood-pasture in Epping Forest, where former glades and the gaps created by the collapse of single ex-pollard beeches are colonized by birch, beneath which saplings of oak or beech become established. However, these circumstances – a small gap surrounded by existing trees – especially favour colonization by oak and beech; in practice it is more common for birch to be replaced by more birch.

Throughout the history of birch its supreme colonizing ability has been balanced against the greater competitive ability and longer life of other trees. The decline of birch in Mesolithic times was due to the arrival of more competitive trees such as oak, hazel, and lime; once the wildwood had settled down, colonizing ability was of little advantage save in the peculiar circumstances of some fen-woods. From the Neolithic onwards, human activities provided vacant ground and led to a partial recovery of birch; but it remained a relatively local tree, mainly on light soils, and there is no evidence that it increased in abundance in the historical period. Sometimes it was permanent, sometimes not: of our Suffolk examples the Hintlesham woods still have plenty of birch, but it has largely disappeared from Glebe Grove (Felsham).

In the last hundred years circumstances have shifted greatly in favour of birch. The breakdown of the traditional management of heaths, fens, and railways has provided it with ground to colonize outside woods. Within woods, the encouragement of oak and the planting of conifers were both, ultimately, to provide gaps from which birch could profit. At the same time the competitive ability of other trees has declined; oak, in particular, does not easily become established in shade, even that of birch (Chapter 17).

The resulting increase of birch was at first mainly in the neighbourhood of existing birchwoods and on the soils which birch traditionally favours. More recently the tree has spread to other areas and to less favourable soils. The process is self-catalysing, for every new birch tree is a source of seed for further birches; the steady fall-out of birch seed ensures that the tree instantly occupies any suitable space and stands some chance of establishment even on unfavourable soils. Birch is first recorded in West Cambridgeshire, which it had probably colonized from Bedfordshire, in the nineteenth century on the sands of Gamlingay,[200a] where it is now very abundant in both ancient and secondary woodland [Fig. 25.5]. From that bridgehead it has invaded the heavy clays. A few trees became established in Hayley Wood, probably after a felling in the 1920s; it is abundant in Eversden Wood after a great felling in 1941; and further birches have colonized Hayley in some of the panels coppiced since 1964. There are still some pockets of country which birch invasion has not yet reached. For example, the Langdon Hills (pp. 8–10), despite having gravel soils and extensive secondary woodland, are still almost free of birch.

The hypothesis that birch will some day be replaced by oak or some other tree may have been valid in the 1920s, but its credibility declines with every decade that passes without its fulfilment. Many birchwoods, even those that have some standard oak trees, are well into their second generation of birch without any sign of a new generation of oak. The reproductive ability of birch is so great as to outweigh even the disability of its short life-span. The classical birch-to-oak succession is now more often an oak-to-birch succession; not that birch overtops and kills oak – although even that can happen – but that when the oaks die or are felled their places will be filled for the foreseeable future by birch.

The birches have come to stay and are likely to increase further. It is a pity that so little use should be made of a beautiful and potentially valuable tree which grows whether we want it or not and costs nothing. In woodland conservation birch, although not the arch-enemy that it is of heaths and fens, is generally unwelcome as it dilutes and supplants more interesting plant communities. The best we can do about it is to avoid giving birch a foothold; to cherish the existing stools, knowing that any that die are likely to be replaced by birch; and to be careful where bonfires are sited. Attempts to get rid of birch are difficult and expensive and often counter-productive. Above all we should think twice about planting trees in ancient woods, for trees of almost any species, planted in an existing wood, have a curious tendency to turn into birches sooner or later.

appear always to be planted; as far as I know they never occur in areas where beech is indigenous. Beech is unpopular as a hedgerow standard tree, even in beech areas, doubtless because it kills the hedge beneath.

Beech in wood-pasture

Most of the early records of beech are from wood-pasture. This is not wholly explained by the over-representation of Forests in the available documentation: in Eastern England, for which the written record is more even, the relatively small area of wood-pasture accounts for almost all the beech, and the relationship is undoubtedly genuine.

In some wood-pastures beech seems to have been only a timber tree, but in many places it was pollarded. Shredding (p. 5) is recorded in the Forest of Dean although it would hardly work well with beech, which does not produce strong epicormic shoots. In Epping Forest pollarding of beech continued until 1878; written evidence and annual rings show that the cycle averaged thirteen years in the eighteenth and nineteenth centuries.

The beeches of Writtle (mid Essex)

Wood-pasture beech management is described in the court rolls of Writtle for five years between 1396 and 1426.[311–12, 314] Writtle was a large estate containing two parks and a wooded common called Highwood which was part of Writtle Forest (Fig. 12.8), besides many groves and hedges. The beeches grew in Writtle Park and Highwood. Both of these are on very acid soils overlying Eocene sands and gravels; they also produced small amounts of coppice.

Beechwood was generally sold in terms of *lopp' fagorum* or *capita fagorum* (literally 'heads' or 'ends' of beeches). A typical entry reads:

> To John Howchin in Heywode for five *capita fagorum* 15*d*.

Lopp' and *capita*, which are not used together and are distinguished from the *cropp'* of trees felled for timber, must both mean the products of pollarding of beeches. 119 beeches were pollarded in 1397–8, realizing £2 16*s* 6*d*, and smaller numbers in other years. Those in the Park averaged 5.4*d* per tree but those in Highwood only 2.5*d* per tree. The Park beeches were evidently big trees pollarded on a long rotation, for underwood in the Park sold for 13*s* 4*d* an acre, equivalent to thirty beeches.

An entry in 1396–7 shows how pollarding was organized and confirms that the pollard wood was of large size. One John Bachelor had bought eight lops and was suing John Borell, a haulage contractor, for not turning up to transport them. Borell brought a counter-claim for 3*s* 4*d* in lost time, alleging that Bachelor

> should have faggoted up the topmost branches of the aforesaid lops and should have split with wedges (*faculasset*) all the great underwood ready to load on the cart according to contract, which was not duly done; so that the aforesaid John Borell took 3 days longer to carry the said wood than if it had been faggoted and split . . .

Other entries relate to the *defrondacio* of beeches. When this item appears in the woodsales at 4*d* a tree it evidently has its normal meaning of 'shredding'. The sale of areas of *defrondacio* for the large sum of 16*s* an acre possibly refers to some kind of pruning or thinning operation on a dense even-aged stand of beech.

Pollarding continued at least into the seventeenth century. In 1564–70 we find sales of 'loppes' of unspecified trees, at prices ranging from 2*s* to 8*s* per lop;[307] the difference cannot all be due to rising prices, and suggests that by then the pollards were even bigger trees. The last reference to 'lopinge of beach in the parke' is in 1653–4.[305] Although much of the site still survives (Fig. 12.8) there is now no evidence of pollard beech; the few beeches appear all to have been planted.

Beech as industrial fuel

Beech had a specific use as fuel for the glass industry, especially in the West Sussex Weald in the sixteenth and seventeenth centuries.[762] A large Elizabethan glasshouse used as much as a medium-sized iron furnace. The industry continued around Kirdford for at least 200 years and thus would appear to have conserved its fuel. The furnaces burnt beech billets; shredding is mentioned as a source of supply, but timber may also have been split into billets. Potash came from the ashes of beech and bracken. Beech was not essential, for glass was also made in non-beech areas such as Staffordshire.

Beech as timber

Medieval sources rarely refer to beech as timber. In 1269 Henry III, affected by the poverty of the nuns of Bromhall (Berks), gave the Prioress a retrospective felling licence to cut down some beeches in the legal Forest of Windsor for repairs after a fire.[233] This was exceptional; nearly all the grants of beech in the Close Rolls are for fuel, and its only use in the Forest of Dean appears to have been to feed iron furnaces. L. F. Salzman[477] refers to beech timber in the Middle Ages, chiefly for making the king's kitchen tables and other fittings; the frequent mention of beech laths is surprising for a timber which is not easily worked by cleaving.

I have seen beech used as structural timber in France, but in England it was never popular; even in places such as Penn and Wendover, in the heart of the Chiltern beechwoods, the buildings are framed in oak. About 2% of the timber used by naval dockyards in the 1780s and 1790s was beech.[353]

In recent centuries beech has been treated as a timber

tree to such an extent that survivals of its earlier coppicing and pollarding are now rare. The monotonous, almost pure stands of beech, so characteristic of the Chilterns, were formed in the late eighteenth century out of what had previously been a more diverse system of coppices and wood-pasture; as late as 1794 the Chiltern woods were fetching high prices for firewood.[392] They are now the most extensive imitation in this country of the 'selection system' tradition in Continental forestry, whereby single trees are taken out on reaching commercial maturity, leaving small gaps wherein new trees arise. The reasons for the change are not clear. It is popularly associated with the rise of the High Wycombe furniture industry and in particular with the 'Windsor' chair,[885] but as far as I know there has been no study of whether the industry commanded all the Chiltern woods or whether its expansion was anticipated by the growers of beech. Beech is eminently suitable for lathes and other woodworking machinery but is not essential. Many of the earliest Windsor-type chairs, which have stood the test of time, contain no beech, whereas the seat of a chair – the largest component – can only be satisfactorily made of elm.

The price of beech timber trees for the last 200 years has been generally about two-thirds that of oak, but this would have been offset by the reputation of oak for slower growth.

Types of beechwood and their relation to other woodlands

A. S. Watt recognizes three series of beechwoods in England. Table 20.1 is a brief summary of his descriptions with some added particulars. Although these woods are, in the main, products of recent succession or of nineteenth-century forestry, the three series result from fundamental differences of site which can be observed also with ancient beeches and which resemble the main categories of beechwood recognized on the Continent.

The colonization and regeneration of beech are influenced by its erratic seed production at this extreme edge of its geographical range. Beech sets a little good seed in many years, but, as Watt points out, these seeds rarely give rise to established trees. At long intervals of years there is a massive and successful crop of seed; this requires favourable weather at several successive critical times. By concentrating seed production into infrequent mast years, beech in Britain – rather like such tropical plants as the 31-year bamboo (*Chusquea abietifolia*)[675] – surfeits its predators while still leaving enough seeds to grow.

Watt described the successions by which beechwoods can arise from nuts dropped by birds and mammals on abandoned farmland or commons. Beech, unlike oak, does not colonize open ground but grows up only in

Table 20.1 Types of beechwood in England. Summarized mainly from Watt[163, 164, 167] and Tansley.[150]

	'Fagetum ericetosum'	'Fagetum rubosum'	'Fagetum calcicolum'
Soil type	Strongly acid, tends to podzolization and gleying	Neutral to moderately acid brown earth	Thin calcareous soil (rendzina)
Underlying material	Gravels, sands, loess	Clay-with-Flints, often mixed with loess	Chalk or limestone
Humus type	Mor	Mull or thin mor	Mull
pH of mineral soil	< 4.2	4.0–7.5	> 7.0
Name of commonest soil series in Chilterns[765]	Batcombe	Winchester	Icknield
Height of beeches	< 70 ft (21 m)	70–110 ft (21–33 m) maximum at pH 5)	< 75 ft (23 m)
Ground vegetation dominants	*Deschampsia flexuosa* or *Pteridium*; *Leucobyum* (dense shade); *Calluna* (glades)	*Rubus fruticosus* and *Corylfolii* agg.; *Oxalis acetosella* and *Melica uniflora; Asperula odorata* and *Galeobdolon* (on more calcareous sites)	(*a*) *Sanicula* (on drier more calcareous sites) (*b*) *Mercurialis* (on sites with deeper soil) (*c*) *Allium ursinum* (on Cotswold limestone)
Alternative trees	*Quercus petraea, Q. robur*, birch	*Quercus robur*, ash; less commonly hazel, maple, hornbeam	(*a*) and (*b*) ash (*c*) ash, *Ulmus glabra*
Approximate equivalent in Continental phytosociology[809]	Luzulo-Fagetum	Melico-Fagetum	(*a*) and (*b*) Fagetum calcareum (*c*) Fagetum calcareum allietosum
History	Most ancient coppices and wood-pastures belong here (e.g. Ellenden, Epping, Burnham)	Partly on ancient beechwood sites, but because beech grows good timber they have been transformed by 19th-century forestry and survive in their very rarely earlier state	Small areas, often on former downland; Westridge is an ancient coppice of subtype (*c*)

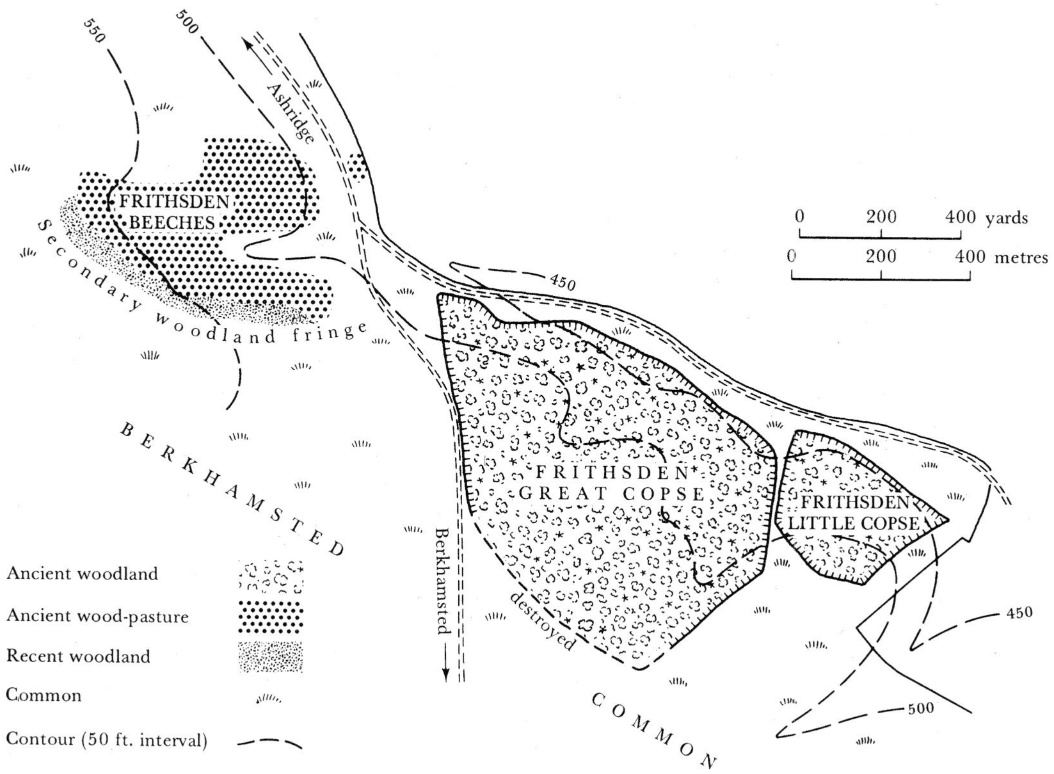

Fig. 20.3 Frithsden Copses and Beeches in Berkhamstead, Herts. This map takes no account of the destruction of much of the Common and of the Great Copse in 1950–70. Much of the remaining Common is now secondary woodland, but for simplicity this is shown only where described in the text.

the shelter of bushes and trees. On heathland a birch succession can lead, sometimes via an oak stage, to 'ericetosum' beechwood. On Clay-with-Flints grassland, gorse or hawthorn scrub can lead via oak or ash to 'rubosum' beech. Chalk grassland is colonized by juniper or hawthorn, giving rise, sometimes via ash, to 'calcicolum' beech. These successions were visible in many places in the 1920s, since the hot summers of 1911 and 1921 resulted in exceptional crops of mast at a time of agricultural decline when there was much land in a suitable state for colonization. There has been no mast year on this scale since, although seedlings were abundant in some places two years after the summers of 1959 and 1976.

Within existing beech stands, new trees may grow up directly in the gaps formed by removing just one tree, as is supposed to happen in selection forestry; indeed if the beech canopy is not quite closed there may already be an understorey of beech saplings waiting their opportunity. Larger clearings are colonized by birch or ash, in whose shelter beech saplings become established at the next mast year and eventually take over. These expectations may not be realized in practice. Some gaps in Chiltern plateau beechwoods have been occupied by ash for many decades. Whether or not beech grows in a particular place depends not so much on whether the site is good for beech as on whether there happens to be a mast year at a time when a suitable gap is available. It sometimes regenerates well from planted trees in Aberdeenshire, far outside its natural range.[166]

Frithsden Beeches and Copses (Berkhamsted, Herts) (Fig. 20.3)

These groves, a rare survival of the medieval Chiltern landscape, illustrate the extreme importance of management history in the behaviour of beech. They belong to the National Trust.

The two Copses and the Beeches are on the steep slopes of a dry valley on the dip-slope of the Chilterns. The soils are virtually identical, based on Clay-with-Flints with a large admixture of loess. The woods run on to the plateau at the top of the slope and there abut on Berkhamsted Common. The Copses are old embanked coppice woods; the Beeches are a tract of wood-pasture not demarcated from the Common. Most of the Great Copse fell victim to a replanting commemorating the Queen's accession; the Little Copse is intact though neglected.

The Little Copse, and the Great Copse as reconstructed, have a mixture of underwood: hornbeam, cherry, chestnut, and maple, with hazel at the foot of the slope. Patches of aspen and sallow indicate water seepages. The soil pH is mainly around 4.2; there is thin mor in places. The standard trees are few and mainly oak, including some sessile oak on the plateau edge. Some of the standard trees are beech, and about half the stubs of the old boundary hedge on the woodbank, but none of the other underwood. The ground vegetation is predominantly bracken with some bluebells.

Frithsden Beeches are a magnificent stand of ancient pollard beeches, with bollings up to 5 ft thick. They were last pollarded between 1820 and 1850, and have since developed crowns up to 120 ft (35 m) in diameter. On the plateau mor humus has accumulated up to 15 cm thick, with a mineral soil pH down to 3.95. Gaps are usually colonized by birch, but apart from this and a little holly there are practically no trees other than beech. There are at least three generations of beeches younger than the pollards, growing in what were probably grassland glades in the wood-pasture days. The ground vegetation consists mainly of bracken on the plateau and *Holcus mollis* on the slopes, with occasional brambles.

Towards Berkhamsted Common the Beeches are bordered by a secondary woodland fringe of almost pure oak of thirty to forty years' growth, though oaks are almost absent among the beeches themselves. This fringe is separated from the remaining open Common by an outer zone of birch. There appears to be no succession to beech.

The whole area – Common, Beeches, and Copses – is presumably derived from the 'wood for 1,000 swine' in Berkhamsted in Domesday. By the thirteenth century, Berkhamsted Frith was a wooded common of 800 acres, probably the largest in the Chilterns.[131] The trees later disappeared from the plateau, remaining on the remoter slopes (cf. Thorpe Wood near Norwich).[122] This remaining woodland was demarcated into coppices and a wood-pasture portion. The former have developed into almost normal hornbeam woodland; apart from the abundant cherry, they could be almost anywhere in Hertfordshire. The only beeches are boundary stubs and a few timber trees. The wood-pasture, in contrast, has become almost pure beech. Although beech maintains itself in gaps in the wood-pasture neither it nor hornbeam has recolonized the common, which – if the succession continues – will turn into oak or birch woodland. The soil differences between Beeches and Copses reflect the greater ability of beech to form mor.

Felbrigg Beeches

Despite its name, Felbrigg Great Wood (N. Norfolk) is a series of plantations established by the Windham family from the 1670s onwards.[764] These are among the earliest and best-documented surviving plantations and would repay study by a historian of modern forestry. They belong to the National Trust.

Embedded in the plantations are five groups of ancient beech pollards which date from an earlier period. They include one of the largest beeches in England (bolling girth 26 ft 10 in. = diameter 2.18 m). Their annual rings, though microscopic, suggest that they were last pollarded in the eighteenth century; they probably survive from a wood-pasture common in Aylmerton parish later emparked by the Windhams. The presence of beech nearby is attested by many references to 'beaches' as standards over underwood in Edgefield Great Wood (now no longer extant) from 1676 onwards.[223, 419]

The Felbrigg Beeches are the northernmost known stand of native beech in Britain. The soil is very acid and infertile – hence the slow growth and longevity of the trees – with glacial gravels reaching the surface. The ground vegetation consists mainly of brambles and bracken, placing these woods at the most acid extreme of the 'rubosum' series, though the abundance of the fern *Dryopteris dilatata* in tree-fall gaps suggests an affinity with the German Fagetum dryopteridetosum.[670]

Conservation

Beechwoods in general are less threatened than other native woods. Like other large woods, they tend to be coniferized, and selection management, which demands too much skilled attention to detail to be attractive to twentieth-century forestry, has declined; but there are still large areas left, many of which belong to conservation bodies. The chief problems are those of ensuring continued regeneration and of identifying areas, particularly of the orchid-rich 'calcicolum' woods, for special treatment.

The growing of beech as a timber tree resulted in woods which, though attractive to the public, are comparatively monotonous in species and structure. The greatest scientific and historical interest is in coppices and wood-pastures that escaped this transformation, and which are important for their old trees and rotten wood, and for their mor humus and acid soil profiles.[45] Most of them happen to be in public or semi-public ownership, though that has not of itself guaranteed continuity, as the 1971 proposals for the New Forest (p. 304), which would have sacrificed many ancient beeches, demonstrate. Beech more than other trees demonstrates the disastrous effects of ceasing to coppice and pollard, not only on the other vegetation but ultimately on the beeches themselves; every gale brings a few down, and the fall of one tree weakens its neighbours. Without specific action to maintain them (p. 202), beech wood-pastures, especially Epping Forest,[124] are in danger of losing their distinctive character and turning into just another Chiltern-type beechwood.

General conclusions

Within its native range beech can grow on practically any well-drained soil, from limestone to gravel, and on some of the less heavy clays. Its distribution in space and time is erratic and it is not indigenous in many apparently suitable places. It has been in Epping Forest for at least 4,000 years. In Hainault Forest – a topographical replica of Epping, only four miles away – there is no record of beech apart from an uncertain place-name,[124] and even when introduced it fails to spread. In Middlesex the beeches of Enfield Chase are indigenous; those in Ken Wood, Highgate, a very similar site, are evidently planted, for a nearby pollen diagram shows very little beech pollen right to the surface.[701] In Grovely Forest beech has been present on the clay for at least 300 years, but the adjoining chalk, which might be thought a more suitable habitat, remains under ash and maple.

It is sometimes supposed that beech eventually fails to maintain itself because it forms mor humus which the seedlings cannot penetrate. The forestry practice of 'screefing', a mechanical version of rootling by swine, breaks up the mor and allows the seedlings to root. The place-names of east Germany and Poland indicate wide areas from which beech has now disappeared;[670] but in England the larger stands of beech are permanent.

The delayed expansion of beech in prehistory, both in Britain and on the Continent, has been variously ascribed to climate (the Sub-Atlantic Period) and human activity.[710] Beech is supposed to be limited by several different aspects of climate. In Britain, the most plausible is summer drought. In the Cambridge area, it seldom regenerates naturally, probably because of competition for moisture between seedlings and large trees, and many full-grown beeches died in 1976. Beech on chalk is shallow-rooted and unable to reach moisture deep in the ground, and it is significant that there are no historical records of beech on the chalklands north-east of Luton, which have a lower rainfall than the Chilterns proper.

Beech, however, is much more sensitive to weather than to climate. The mast year of 1922, coming at a time when much land was out of cultivation, had a greater effect than many normal seasons. Similar combinations of events may have happened from time to time in prehistory, but cannot be inferred from general climatic trends. Such fortuitous circumstances may explain some of the anomalies. The admission of beech to Epping Forest and its exclusion from Hainault could depend on some very slight difference of land-use history which we can hardly hope to specify in detail.

Human activities which might favour beech include wood-pasture and the abandonment of farmland. Many beechwoods have not always been woodland: the evidence ranges from Iron Age hill-forts to medieval lynchets, place-names like Little-boys Heath (a wood in Great Hampden, Bucks), and early maps. Any such site, if abandoned at the right time in relation to a mast year, might become beechwood by one or other of the classic successions. Wood-pasture might also provide such opportunities at times when the fluctuations of grazing permitted trees to return to previously open areas. Once well established, beech tends – unless coppiced – to invade surrounding land. On the gravelly heights of Epping Forest it apparently supplanted lime (p. 242). For centuries it co-existed with oak, but since the abandonment of pollarding it has overtopped and killed most of the oaks, and is now replacing hornbeam on the lower slopes. Similar increases of beech in other Forests are described on p. 241.

Added in 2003 edition

The prehistory of beech still gives rise to controversy, as shown by correspondence in *Tree News* in 1997: it has even been alleged that it is not native. Although no wood or charcoal has been identified before the Neolithic, pollen is found in the Mesolithic in quantities sufficient to prove the local presence of the tree: for instance at Wareham (Dorset) in *c.* 6000 BC it accounts for over 2% of tree pollen. (As Godwin showed, beech is an under-producer of pollen, which is unlikely to be transported far by wind, so that even a sparse pollen record indicates that the tree was there.)

The earliest definite records are from *c.* 7000 BC, long before people moved trees around the world. Beech thus got to Britain at about the time it became an island; it may not have had to cross the sea, though it did to reach Corsica, which never had a land connexion. It showed the same behaviour in previous interglacial cycles, in which it was a late arrival. The difference in the present interglacial is that beech went on, later still, to become locally dominant.

Beech pollen in prehistory is known from scattered parts of England and Wales. For example the famous pollen diagram from Diss Mere, Norfolk shows small amounts of beech in the limewoods back to the beginning of the Neolithic. If we believe the further testimony of odd grains (omitted from Fig. 20.4) the tree grew generally up to the Scottish border and even in Ireland, as it certainly did in previous interglacials. Beech went on to become a common tree in certain areas but to disappear from most of the country, for example round Diss Mere, until the planting period. In one of these strongholds, in S.E. Wales, it occurs at high altitudes and even, at the Punch-Bowl near Abergavenny, forms the altitudinal tree-limit at 1400 feet, as it does in Slovenia.

The famous remark by Julius Caesar, that in Britain 'there is timber of all kinds, as in Gaul, except beech and fir', does not, of course, mean that beech was absent, but that it did not occur as timber: he uses the special word *materia* by which the Romans distinguished timber from wood. It is perfectly possible that all the beeches Caesar saw in 40 BC were pollards or coppice stools.

Beech is an opportunist tree: it comes and goes in response to unusual events. An example of spontaneous decline (albeit in an unusual environment) is in Lady Park Wood, in the Wye gorge on the Welsh border. This limestone ex-coppice wood of many species, including elm, beech, and lime, has been observed, and undisturbed, since 1944. Beech fared well after the end of coppicing, and became increasingly dominant until the 1970s. Then outside impacts began: first the severe impact of Elm Disease; then the 1976 drought, which particularly hit the beeches. Many beeches died of drought; others have been blown down or have fallen over cliffs. By the 1980s ash and lime appeared to be benefiting from the decline of elm and beech (Peterken and Jones 1987).

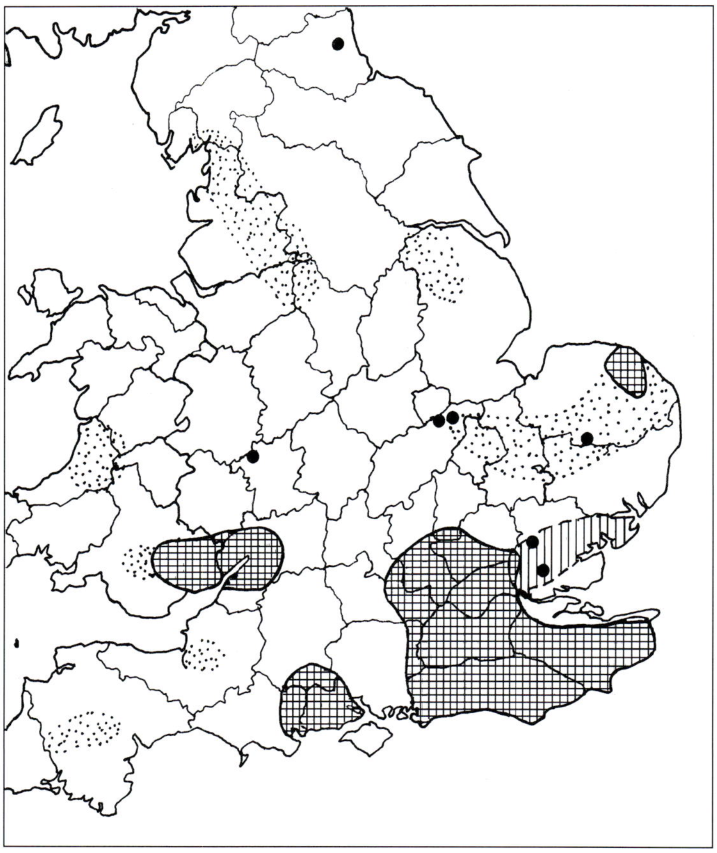

Fig. 20.4 Native distribution of beech, as far as is known. Double-hatched: areas where it survives as native. Black spots: outlying surviving localities. Single-hatched: extinct since middle ages. Dotted areas: prehistoric records only (excluding odd grains whose evidence is uncertain).

Fig. 20.5 Ancient beechwood (Chapter 20). Note the big coppice stools. This grows on limestone scree (thus partly on air) but has wild garlic for ground vegetation: a rare if not unique woodland type. Westridge Wood, Wotton-under-Edge, Gloucestershire. April 1977

21

The Chestnut-woods

The chestnut, chess, or sweet-chestnut (*Castanea sativa*) appears in this book as an 'honorary native' tree. It has almost certainly been artificially introduced from overseas, but is a historic member of our flora and enters into native vegetation; until the invention of pollen analysis there was no means of proving that it was not indigenous.

Chestnut has been spread widely by people who eat the nuts, and its range as a native tree is controversial. *Flora Europaea* takes a 'moderate' view in regarding it as indigenous in S.E. Europe west to Italy and north to Hungary. Despite the eighteenth-century name Spanish chestnut it may not be native to Spain. (Horse-chestnut (*Aesculus hippocastanum*) is of course an unrelated tree, a much later introduction, much planted but hardly naturalized, and poisonous.)

The chestnut controversy

The earlier writers, including Evelyn,[335] apparently had no idea that chestnut might not be native. Ray, who was less familiar with it than Evelyn, was uncertain whether it was indigenous.[468] The hypothesis that it was exotic was first seriously proposed by Daines Barrington, the correspondent of Gilbert White, in 1769;[9] this led to a controversy involving, for the first time, the combined application of field, written, and archaeological evidence to a problem in historical ecology.

Barrington claimed that chestnut did not fulfil four conditions which, *a priori*, he proposed that a native species ought to satisfy:

1. They must grow in large masses, and cover considerable tracts of ground; nor must such woods end abruptly, by a sudden change to other trees, except the situation and strata become totally different.
2. If the tree grows kindly* in copses, and shoots from the stool, it must for ever continue in such a wood, unless grubbed up with the greatest care . . .
3. The seed of such tree must ripen kindly:* nature never plants but where a succession may be easily continued, and in the greatest profusion.

Lastly; Many places . . . must receive their appellation from indigenous trees which grow there . . .

*i.e. naturally

A reply was made by E. Hasted, the Kentish antiquary, with A. C. Ducarel and J. Thorpe.[46] They demonstrated, with examples, that chestnut did sometimes fulfil Barrington's four postulates; they also argued against postulates 1, 2 and 3 on the grounds that some undoubtedly indigenous trees failed to meet them. They stated that chestnut grew freely from seed and was not, as Barrington had claimed, usually to be found in regular planting rows; the stools were commonly not all of the same age; and it sometimes grew 'intermixed with other trees'. They also produced positive evidence of its antiquity in England: quotations from ancient documents; place-names supposed to be derived from it; ancient buildings in which, as they claimed, its timber had been identified – not only in England but also in Normandy, where the timber was supposed to have been imported from England; and ancient chestnut trees still alive in 1772 or mentioned in earlier works.

A further reply by Hasted[732] gives us an insight into Kentish woods at the time. The locality is south-west of Sittingbourne; little of the woods now remains.

> *Milton.* In the western part of this parish there are several hundred acres of coppice-wood, which are adjoining to a much larger tract of the like sort, extending southward . . . for the space of near five miles. These woods, especially those in and near this parish, are noted for the great plenty of chesnut stubs interspersed promiscuously throughout them, which, from the quick and strait growth of this kind of wood, makes them very valuable. These are so numerous . . . as to give name to most of these woods near Milton, which besides their particular names to each of them, are usually called by the general name of *Chesnut-woods*. And in the . . . customs of the manor of Milton in 1575, it is mentioned, that the occupiers of the three mills . . . should gather yearly for the lord of it nine bushels of chestenottes, in Chestnott wood, or pay eighteen-pence by the year to the queen, who then had the manor . . . and was possessed of three hundred acres of chesnut wood . . .
>
> These chesnuts are undoubtedly the indigenous growth of Britain, planted by the hand of nature. They are interspersed throughout the whole tract, without any form or regularity, and are many of them, by their appearance, of great age; and by numbers of them, which now seem almost worn out and perishing, being made use of as *the termini* or *boundaries*, as well of

> private property as of parishes, it is plain they were first pitched upon, in preference to others, for that purpose, as being the largest and most antient ones of any then existing; and as these are hardly ever cut down or altered, they must have stood sacred to this use from the first introduction of private property into this kingdom, and the first division of it into parishes.

The arguments of Ducarel and Hasted are sound, even if many of their examples do not stand up to modern scrutiny: they establish *Castanea* as an ancient member of the British flora. In logic, Barrington had the worst of the debate, but his views, despite the lack of good evidence, gained credence. Eventually it even came to be believed that *Castanea* was not indigenous anywhere in Europe, a notion based partly on a misinterpretation of Pliny and partly on a supposed derivation of the name from Kastania in Asia Minor. In recent years, Barrington has been vindicated by fresh evidence, though not in the sense of medieval or sixteenth-century introduction in which he originally wrote.

The history of chestnut

Pollen evidence

Castanea is almost absent from the British pollen record; finds are very few and are attributed by most pollen analysts to contamination with modern pollen. The grains are small and are not very distinctive and might easily be overlooked; but their small size should make for good dispersal, and they are recorded in quantity in some southern European deposits. It is thus as certain as negative evidence can be that chestnut was not here in prehistory.

Archaeological evidence

There is no certain identification of chestnut in Britain before the Roman period. Wood and charcoal have been found on six Roman sites in southern England and Essex.[710] (Records of nuts are discounted because they could have been imported.)

Chestnut timbers in medieval buildings, one of the pillars of Ducarel's argument, turn out to be an illusion. In the days of Evelyn and Barrington it was supposed that many early timber frames were made of chestnut and for this reason were not frequented by spiders, a belief still occasionally current today. The visitor to the Château de Sully near Orleans is told that the roof, a marvel of fourteenth-century carpentry, is made of chestnut, 'like those of Westminster Hall and King's College Chapel, Cambridge'. In truth these three mighty roofs, although they have little else in common, are all of oak. The mistake is easy to make. Chestnut timber is very like oak but lacks its conspicuous medullary rays. Oak furniture and wainscot are often cut in a radial plane to display the rays as a decorative feature. Medieval structural timbers, being made usually from whole trees squared up (p. 145), display tangential faces in which the rays are much harder to make out; anyone knowing oak only in furniture might suppose they were chestnut.

There is no reason why chestnut timber, of which there are some medieval records and a charcoal find for Hertfordshire,[916] should not have been used for buildings. But I have only once seen it myself – at the Palace of Fontainebleau, in sixteenth-century wainscot with 'medullary rays' cunningly painted on to make it look like oak! – and I do not know of any identification by anyone else who is aware of the difficulty. Chestnut in ancient buildings, like 'Irish bog oak' and 'timber from old ships', remains a legend, not wholly implausible but lacking confirmation.

Place-names

The Anglo-Saxon for the tree is *cyst* or *cisten*, several times given as a gloss for *castanea* and evidently a familiar word. It is a survival from Classical Latin; *castanea* became *cisten* (pronounced 'chisten') and later *chesteine* much as *castrum* became Chester.

As a place-name element, chestnut is easily confused with others such as *cisel* 'gravel', and many of Ducarel's examples are doubtful. Hasted's Chesnut-woods by Sittingbourne – the name survives as Chestnut Street – are genuine and go back at least to the thirteenth century, being called *bosci de castanar'* in 1255[236] and *boscus de Chastynners* in 1256;[236] In 1207 one Ralph de Chastaneslad was a witness in a case at Powick near Worcester.[257] Other examples are Chest Wood near Colchester (*Cystewde* 1272[851]), Chesteyns in Little Bentley (N.E. Essex) in 1471[278] and Chisbon Heath in St Osyth (N.E. Essex) (*Chesbenheth* 1539, from Anglo-Saxon *cystbeam* 'chestnut-tree'[851]).

Written records (Fig. 21.1)

The earliest localized record is in the Forest of Dean, where (as Ducarel points out) Henry II granted the tithe of chestnuts to Flaxley Abbey. Chestnut was well established by the mid-twelfth century, but was only in one place: in 1282 only 34 out of 12,648 stumps in the Forest were identified as chestnut.[69] There are references throughout the Middle Ages, and there is still chestnut in Chestnuts [Fig. 21.7].

In Kent, besides the Chestnut Woods by Sittingbourne, there are records for the woods of Lessness Abbey (Greenwich) and in sixteenth-century herbals. In the New Forest there was a *boscus de castaneariis* in the mid-fourteenth century.[36] The tree is recorded for Ashdown Forest (Sussex) in 1633[79] and in Stour Wood (N.E. Essex) – still one of its strongholds – in 1682.[228]

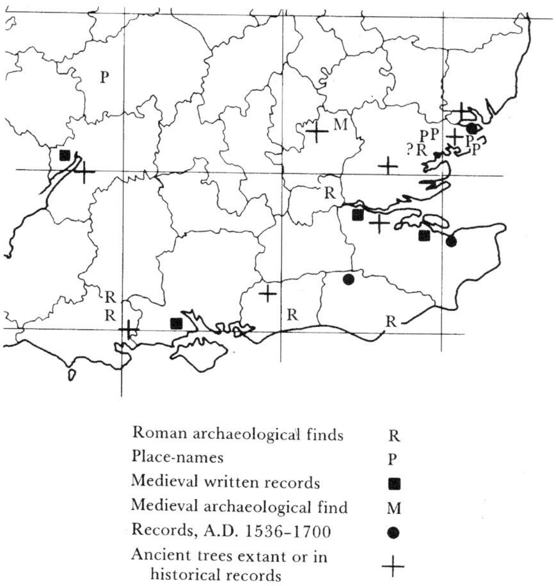

Fig. 21.1 Records of chestnut, A.D. 1–1700, excluding planted trees. Principal sources[710] plus others given in the text.

Old trees

Although fast-growing, chestnut is a long-lived tree with a very prolonged old age. The Tortworth Chestnut (Glos) was already described in 1706 as a tree of legendary antiquity.[336] It is free-standing and has propagated itself by the sprawling of its lower limbs: the original trunk is now surrounded by seventeen secondary trunks. How old it was in 1706 can hardly be conjectured: the original trunk has not altered much in appearance, and in 1977 measured 36 ft 1 in. in girth below the lowest branch, whereas eighteenth-century figures vary from 44 to 57 ft![389] This one tree [Fig. 21.8] begins to constitute a wood, for under it grow several clones of dog's-mercury (p. 95) together with bluebells, lesser celandine (*Ranunculus ficaria*), and a patch of garlic (*Allium ursinum*).

According to Ducarel and other eighteenth-century writers, there were chestnuts of similar size at Frating and Writtle (Essex), Wymondley (Herts), and other places. These must all have dated from well back into the Middle Ages. As we shall see, stools in some woods are larger still.

Ancient specimens overseas include the Tortworth-like Hundred-Horse Chestnut (*Castagna di Cento Cavalli*)[677] and others on Mount Etna, and the gigantic stools in the meadows of *Casta*segna in Val Bregaglia, Switzerland (Mrs J. Evans).

Management

As timber, chestnut has a poor modern reputation because of its spiral grain and tendency to split. As underwood it is more durable than any other species, outlasts oak in the ground, and is easily cleft; it is particularly suitable for stakes, hop-poles, and latterly for pale-and-wire fencing; but it is little valued for firewood. The nuts are now curiously unpopular, and some authors even deny that they are produced in Britain; in fact they are abundant in some years, are of better flavour (especially when frosted) than imported chestnuts, and are a welcome addition to a winter picnic in the Essex woods.

Medieval sources mention nuts and timber but seldom underwood. In Dean chestnut was not supposed to be felled for firewood or charcoal. The place where it grew was coppiced in the early fourteenth century and was embanked in 1325.[59] Timber from the Sittingbourne chestnuts is mentioned in 1255 and 1278.[233] Also in 1278, 100 *robora* of chestnut, probably pollard bollings (p. 182), were sent from there to Dover Castle for building works. Thorpe in 1769 refers to 'very large chestnut pollards' in this area;[46] but nowadays chestnut is remarkably rare as a pollard.

Later references are mainly to wood, though timber and nuts are sometimes mentioned. I can find little evidence to support the commonly-held view that it was particularly valued for its qualities as underwood in the eighteenth and early nineteenth centuries. Had this been so, one would expect chestnut to command a higher price than other species, especially since its durability would reduce the opportunity of selling replacements in the future. Records of woodsales in south Essex (pp. 166–8) show no systematic difference in the income per acre per year between chestnut woods and those of other species, despite the faster growth of chestnut. Where poles are sold by number, those of chestnut are not separated from birch, alder, etc. Hop-poles of ash are recorded at least as often as those of chestnut. In Kent, although I have no details of actual sales, the Board of Agriculture Report of 1798 says that there was no appreciable difference in price between chestnut poles and ash, willow, or maple.[215]

From 1850 onwards chestnut did not share in the decline of the underwood trades; it was still used in large quantities for hop-poles and later for pale-and-wire fencing. It was never adopted for telegraph poles as it is in Italy and Greece. It was probably only at this time that a difference developed in value between chestnut and other underwood.

Planting chestnut

It is often supposed that all chestnut woods are plantations. The arguments of Hasted and Ducarel against this view apply not only in Kent but also to most of the larger Essex and Suffolk stands: the stools are variable in size and age, some of them very large; they are 'promiscuously' arranged; and they merge irregularly and some times gradually into other kinds of woodland. On the other hand some stands of chestnut are definite plantations, with small stools all of the same size regularly arranged in areas with abrupt boundaries; sometimes these are obvious additions to the area of an ancient wood of other species. The contrast appears in Nap Wood (E. Sussex), one part of which is an obvious plantation of dense small chestnut stools which stop abruptly at a boundary earthwork and are very different from the sparse big stools, interspersed with other species, elsewhere in the wood.

Records of planting chestnut are surprisingly few. At Felbrigg (N. Norfolk) William Windham I in 1676 sowed 1,500 chestnuts, with other tree seeds, in a nursery,[419] the first of many such enterprises by himself and his successors. These chestnuts or others from this period are still to be seen in the form of stools up to 7 ft across in the Great Wood (p. 326). Even at Felbrigg chestnuts were only a small part of the total planted.

Most of the obvious plantations of chestnut appear to date from after 1850, when, despite the general decline, first-class underwood occasionally commanded fancy prices (e.g. £6 per acre-year in Kent in 1875).[40] Planting chestnut continued to be recommended in forestry textbooks; in Essex I have even seen some post-1945 examples. Recent plantations of chestnut are easily distinguished from the uneven-aged stands of which the records tell us little except that some of them may be more than 750 years old.

Modern ecology

The tree occurs in plantations and parks almost throughout Britain; 'quasi-native' woods are concentrated in S. E. England and Essex, with outliers elsewhere. England is remarkably far north for this mainly sub-Mediterranean tree. It is common in Italy and in southern France, and is extensively coppiced; the many thousand acres of active chestnut coppice in Calabria are a reminder of what parts of England used to be like.

Its distribution in Eastern England, as a tree of ancient woodland, is shown in Fig. 21.2. Chestnut is abundant in east Essex and S.E. Suffolk, growing in almost every ancient wood and widely dominant. Elsewhere it is very thinly scattered and usually recent. It is mostly in woods and is almost absent from Forests, commons, and hedges. Chestnut is gregarious, often in pure stands; it casts a dense shade and forms a heavy, very persistent leaf-litter. Despite its poor reputation as timber most woods have a few standard trees.

Soils

Chestnut is reputed to be a tree of acid soils almost throughout Europe. This is true of Eastern England, where it is almost as calcifuge as oak coppice; pHs under it are usually below 4.0 (Fig. 21.3). Humus is almost always mor, sometimes accumulating to 20 cm depth. The tree is typical of sandy or silty soils with no more than 20% clay.

Although it discourages worms and tends to acidify the soil, chestnut is evidently strongly constrained by the soil parent material. Single trees, however, flourish well outside the soil range of chestnut-woods: for instance the Tortworth Chestnut grows on a calcareous, strongly mull-forming soil.

Plant communities

The larger stands of chestnut are closely related to the acid hornbeam-woods and oakwoods. Hornbeam and birch are the commonest associated trees (Table 6.2); oak coppice is well represented considering its rarity. Chestnut-woods also occur with the more acidic hazel and lime woods. The ground vegetation is typical of strongly acid soils. Brambles, bracken, and bluebells are the commonest dominants; *Holcus mollis* is less common; dog's-mercury and primrose are rare. The more extreme stands of chestnut, like those of hornbeam, have *Quercus petraea* among the standard trees. The smaller stands are distinctly less acidic, with less birch and more ash, maple, and lime. There is much more mercury and primrose and less bracken and bluebell.

By analogy with hornbeam and lime woods (pp. 227, 248) we should divide chestnut-woods into three variants:

(1) ***Chestnut–lime*** woods, the least acid type, usually small areas of chestnut associated with lime or ash and growing over mercury or primrose.
(2) ***Chestnut–hornbeam*** woods, larger stands of chestnut associated with hornbeam and birch and lacking calcicolous herbs.
(3) ***Chestnut–oak*** woods, in which chestnut is associated with sessile oak and oak coppice.

These correspond to the hornbeam–ash, pure hornbeam, and oak–hornbeam woods, but are less well differentiated; chestnut–oak woods do not have a special structure like those of oak–hornbeam. It is doubtful whether any of them have Continental parallels.

Coppicing

Chestnut underwood grows fast and can be very productive. A particular Kentish wood has been analysed by E. D. Ford and J. P. Newbould[59] in as much detail as is possible in a three-year study. About two years' production was lost after coppicing while the canopy was re-established. The standing crop then put on weight at about 1.7 tons per acre-year (4.2 tons per ha-year); by the eighteenth winter there were 35 tons of stems per acre (88 tons per ha). Chestnut produces an

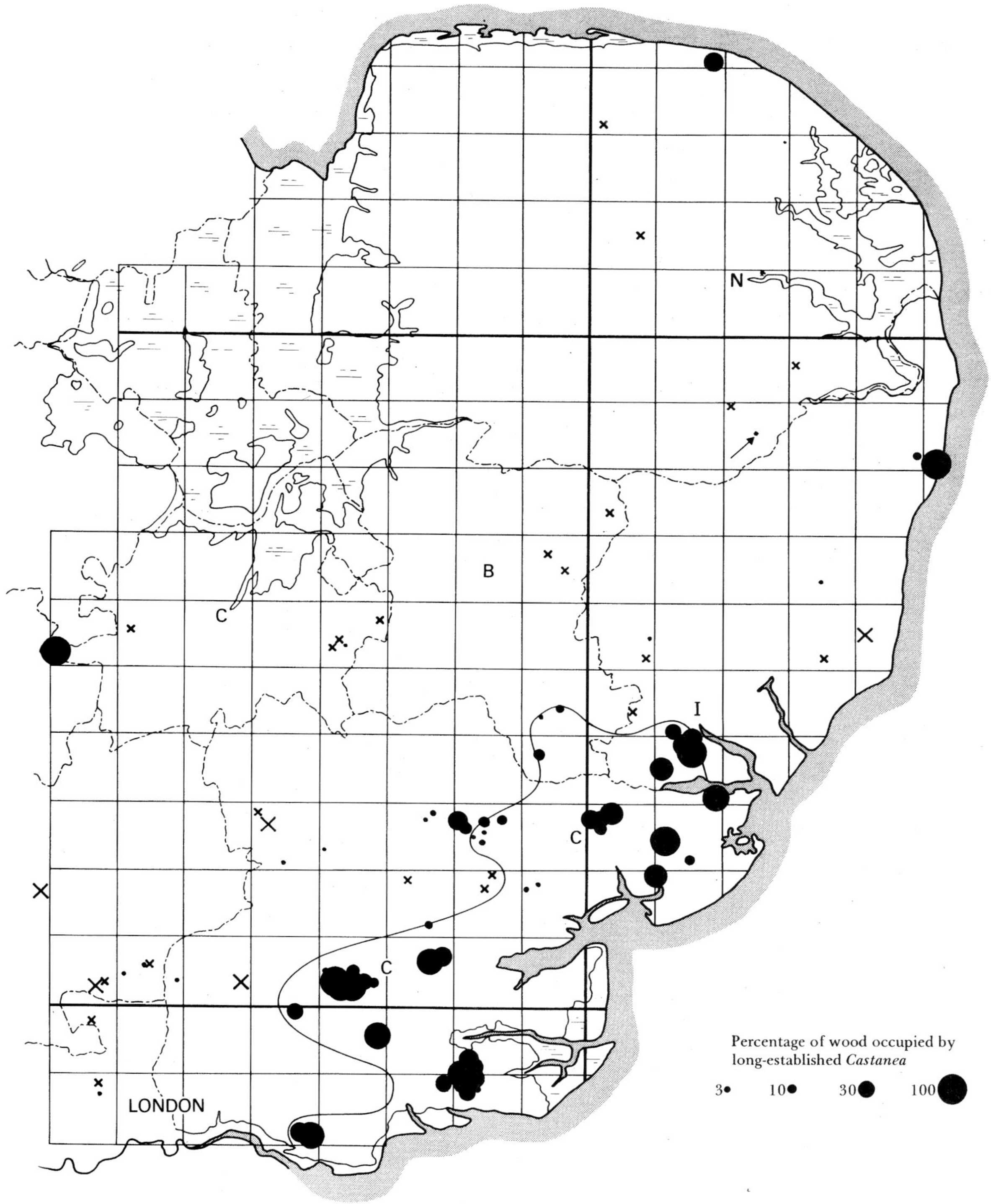

Fig. 21.2 Relative abundance of chestnut in the ancient woods of Eastern England. Black circles indicate long-standing occurrences of the tree (the spot in N. Norfolk represents the early plantations of Felbrigg). Post-1850 introductions of chestnut into, or adjacent to, ancient woods are shown by large crosses (for extensive stands) or small crosses (for one or a few trees). Recent plantations on previously unwooded sites are ignored. S.E. of the sinuous line chestnut was found in every ancient wood examined.

enormous excess of new shoots: on average each stool began by producing 122 sprouts, of which nearly three-quarters died in the first three years; at eighteen years' growth there were fewer than seven poles remaining alive on a stool. The dead stems are killed by the competition of their fellows; their weights are not included in the figures I have quoted, though some of them form part of the usable crop. This wood was apparently on clay and contained from 21 to 35 timber trees per acre, so is unlikely to have been an ideal chestnut site.

A further study[60] shows that the leaf area index (acres of leaf produced by each acre of underwood) was 1.0 at the end of the first season and reached a maximum of about 5 in ten seasons. A single thickness of leaf transmits only about 2% of total light and less than 1% of the wavelengths more useful in photosynthesis, so it is not surprising that little will grow beneath the denser stands of chestnut.

The ground vegetation after coppicing is usually less varied than in other woodland. The acidity, good drainage, and prolonged heavy shade do not encourage a rich flora. Brambles or bracken, often present in shade, may take over the site in the first year. I have seen responses by primrose and *Holcus mollis*, and less often by *Viola* spp., *Centaurium erythraea*, and *Euphorbia amygdaloides*. Heather (*Calluna vulgaris*), *Melampyrum pratense*, and *Galium saxatile* may give a heath-like appearance to chestnut–oak woodland after coppicing (cf. p. 289).

Regeneration

Chestnut, a big-seeded tree far to the north of its native range, might be expected to be at a reproductive disadvantage in Britain. In practice it often does better than beech, hazel, or oak. At least in Essex and Kent, chestnut is capable of perpetuating itself indefinitely and probably of invading woodland of other species. Its rapid regrowth gives it an advantage particularly over hornbeam, its chief competitor. Occasionally it overtops standard oak trees. Nuts are produced at least as often as acorns and are less eaten (except by the author); they lie about throughout the winter and germinate copiously. The tree will not regenerate in its own shade, but young chestnuts are often seen in gaps or under other species. The seed is sometimes dispersed for long distances, presumably by rooks; saplings, although not common in secondary woodland, occasionally appear in remote

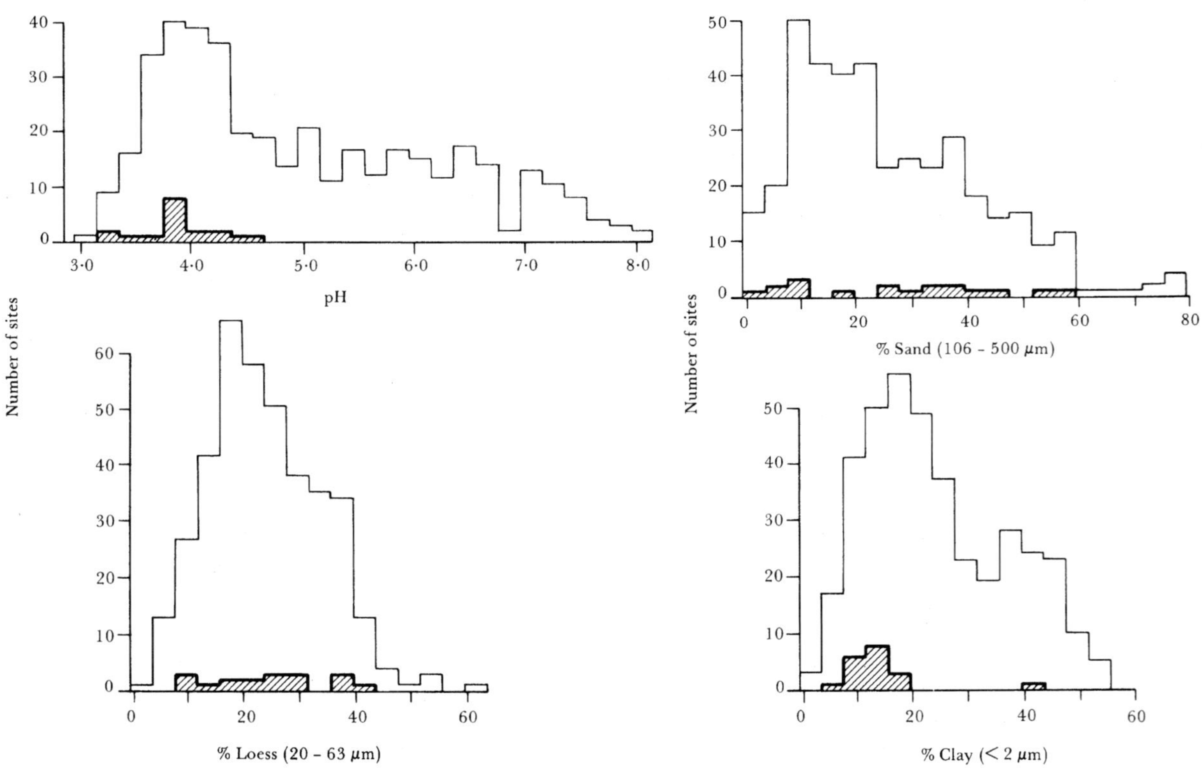

Fig. 21.3 Distribution of topsoil pH and composition beneath long-established chestnut in the woods of Eastern England. The thin upper line gives, for comparison, the characteristics of all woodland topsoils sampled. For further details see caption to Fig. 7.5.

places. Single stools and small groups, when not accompanied by other exotic trees, probably result from spontaneous colonization.

In other parts of England this may not be so. At Chestnuts in the Forest of Dean the chestnuts partly disappeared between 1565 and 1686, being replaced by hazel;[69] this was attributed to mismanagement, but it is difficult to see what mismanagement could have produced this change, and it is possible that the poor summers of much of this period[767] interrupted seed production.

Norsey Wood, Billericay (S. Essex)

Topography and soils

This is a typical Essex chestnut-wood [Fig. 21.6]. It consists of a plateau sloping down to the north and dissected in the south by a system of steep-sided valleys (Fig. 21.4). It is close to the middle of Billericay town and on the north-west is surrounded and in part invaded by houses. It has long been a public place.

The plateau is composed of Eocene and other sands and gravels, overlying London Clay which crops out in the valleys. There is a strong admixture of loess, comprising 25–40% of the plateau soils; much of the remainder is fine sand in the unusual 63–100 μm range; clay seldom exceeds 14%. The soils are strongly acid, with mor humus; only in the valleys has a pH above 4.0 been recorded.

Most of the wood is relatively well-drained. The valleys are fed by powerful springs and in places broaden into swamps with deep soft peat. In places springs and flushes break out of the valley sides. There is another group of springs in the north of the wood.

Earthworks and archaeology

Norsey is one of the few medieval woods to show abundant evidence of earlier periods of activity; it is even scheduled as an Ancient Monument. There has been little proper excavation and most of the finds are casual. There are two Bronze Age barrows. From the Iron Age there is evidence of settlements, especially in the west of the wood. From the Roman period, when Billericay was a small town, the many finds in the wood include burials and kilns for smelting lead and making pottery.[35]

Until recently the whole wood was surrounded by a substantial earthwork known as the Deerbank, much of which survives. It follows a sinuous course and consists of a bank with a well-marked external ditch and a faint internal ditch. On part of the south side it splits into three sub-parallel banks and ditches. From careful measurements I deduce that the Deerbank represents three successive embankments, which are usually superimposed but part company on the south side. Deerbank I, the oldest, has an internal ditch. Banks II and III have external ditches, III being more acute in profile than II. The documentation (see later) suggests that banks I and II are older than 1593 but does not support the local tradition that the Deerbank is an Iron Age encampment.

There is also a huge internal bank with ditches both sides, some 70 ft in total width, whose origin and function are a mystery. There are many small gravel-pits, especially around the highest point, Great Fox Hill, where they cover about five acres.

Flora and vegetation

There are five types of woodland. Sweet-chestnut coppice of the chestnut–oak type covers most of the plateau and the ridges between the valleys. Hornbeam is dominant along the east and south margins and among the central gravel-pits, and birch around the northern springs. The valleys are excellent examples of valley alder-wood, with occasional willow (*Salix fragilis*) and ash; they are not fringed by hazel as in less acidic woods (p. 214). There is a very little oak coppice. The four dominant trees are almost pure in some areas but elsewhere are mixed with aspen, rowan, and other species. Boundaries between the woodland types are irregular; alder stops abruptly above the spring-line but the others intergrade.

The coppice structure is well preserved; felling was regular until the 1940s and sporadic after. There is a thin scatter of standard oaks and chestnuts. The oaks have a large proportion of *Quercus petraea*.

The ground vegetation is dominated by bluebells, bracken, brambles, anemones, and *Holcus mollis*, forming an irregular mosaic not correlated with the trees. The valleys have a more complex vegetation including *Chrysosplenium oppositifolium* and *Sphagnum* spp. The more interesting plants of the plateau include *Convallaria majalis*, *Blechnum spicant*, *Ruscus aculeatus*, and *Luzula sylvatica*. These are rare, and a map left by the late Dr Doris Crofts shows that *Convallaria* and probably others much decreased under dense chestnut after coppicing declined.

Written records

There are many references to the wood at intervals as far back as 1250.[851] It belonged to Stratford-Langthorne Abbey. The early spellings are Nossesheye or Notesheye: the latter appears to mean 'nut-enclosure', but whether hazel (now rare) or chestnut is meant cannot be determined. In 1323 it is described as a park. There is a plausible but unconfirmed tradition that a branch of the Peasants' Revolt came to a bad end in Norsey in 1381.

A somewhat diagrammatic map dated 1593[327] shows the wood occupying exactly the same area as when it began to be encroached upon in the 1930s. It was already divided into six compartments by straight rides – the oldest known woodland rides – which still exist.

Fig. 21.4 Norsey Wood in Billericay, S. Essex: earthworks, streams, and tree communities. Dominant trees: a alder, B birch, C chestnut, H (oak–)hornbeam. The sixteenth-century rides are shown but not the many modern rides and paths. The grey areas have been wholly or partly built upon in the twentieth century – hence the gaps in the boundary bank.

On the south the boundary splits into two, apparently corresponding to Deerbanks I and II.

The earliest management record is a Forest Law felling licence of 1280 to fell 'wood to the value of £10' in 'Nossessheygh' (equivalent to at least forty acres of underwood in the values of the time).[236]

In later centuries the wood belonged to the Petre family. A lease of 1617[310] deals with coppicing. The whole wood might be felled within the first seven years of the lease; thereafter it was to be cut on a rotation of not less than twelve years. The lessee was required to promote seventy new timber trees to the acre as well as those promoted at previous coppicings – an unusually large number (but cf. Chalkney Wood, p. 250) which would have been detrimental to the underwood. Underwood in the valleys and swamps was not highly regarded: the lessee was allowed 'to cutt digg and stubb upp any of the voyde watrye Moorye or wast places of ground . . . to sett and plant the same with hopps or Orsyers'. It is just possible that 'Orsyers' (osiers) are in fact the tree-willows now in the valleys.

Detailed records survive for most years between 1699

and 1863.[315a] At first the old method of irregular panels was followed. After 1760 the wood was set out in twenty regular fells, but because two were sometimes taken together the average rotation was eighteen years. The prices followed the changing value of wood in general: there was a slow rise (in real terms) up to 1845, followed by a rapid fall. In the nineteenth century there are signs of declining management. Larches were planted sporadically from 1825 until about 1930, but not in sufficient numbers to interrupt coppicing; a few still remain.

Historical summary

Without further excavation we cannot say with confidence what Norsey was before the Middle Ages. Some of the evidence suggests that part of it was not woodland in the Roman period; but the kilns, spanning several centuries, strongly indicate that part of the site or its immediate neighbourhood was woodland affording a permanent wood supply.

By the Middle Ages Norsey was woodland. Its use as a park is attested by the written record, by the earliest boundary bank with a ditch on the inside, and by the name Outwood – a wood excluded from a park – given to the adjacent common. The park did not last long, although its memory lingers in the name Deerbank. It was apparently uncompartmented but is unlikely seriously to have interrupted the continuity of the wood. Deerbanks II and III are re-embankings of Norsey after it had reverted to being an ordinary wood.

Whether Norsey has a lime phase in its history awaits pollen analysis. The present native woodland types – oak, hornbeam, alder – represent either primary or post-Roman secondary woodland. Birch is probably also an ancient inhabitant of the site, although its present abundance may be more recent.

How or when did chestnut come to Norsey Wood? There is a local tradition of planting in the late nineteenth century. This may well be true: there are tracts of small stools all of the same size, which probably represent the planting-up of gaps. Chestnuts were planted in Bishops Wood, another Petre wood, in 1829, and in 1813 there is the enigmatic record '2,440 Layers put down in Norsey'. But most of the chestnut consists of stools of various sizes, some several feet across, dominating an area that merges gradually and irregularly into other types of woodland. Had there ever been a massive replanting, we would expect to find some mention of the operation itself, of the consequent disruption of coppicing, or of increased value once the new underwood had begun to yield. The invasion of chestnut into what would otherwise be an oak and hornbeam wood is almost certainly a semi-natural process continuing unnoticed over a long period and still not complete. On the evidence of stool sizes it began not later than the eighteenth century; it could go back to the deer-park period or even – in a wood on a Roman site – to the first importation of the tree.

Holbrook Park, E. Suffolk

This singular wood lies on a low loess-covered plateau near Ipswich. The soils are relatively uniform, with a very high silt content (32–53%), most of the remainder being sand. The site is mapped as 'glacial sands and gravels'; although almost flat, it is well-drained, probably because the surface silt is thin enough to let water through. The soils are acid, leached, and mor-covered; pH ranges from 3.6 to 4.2. The wood is private.

Vegetation

Much of the wood is dominated by chestnut, which grows rather sparsely and is mingled with birch and interspersed with glades. In two areas the chestnut stools are of colossal size, many exceeding 10 ft in diameter and one being no less than 16 ft (5 m) across. They are among the largest chestnuts recorded in Britain and are bigger than the original trunk of the Tortworth Chestnut.

Chestnut woodland intergrades into a mixture of hornbeam and birch. Elsewhere there is a small area of coppice oak (*Quercus robur*). The trees are very diverse and include small numbers of service, rowan, holly, lime, cherry, aspen, and at least three different elms. Holbrook Park is one of the grandest of all bluebell woods. Even without coppicing, shade is relatively light and the bluebells flower in unusual abundance. Bracken and brambles are abundant in places, sometimes over bluebells; there are small areas of anemone.

History and archaeology

About a third of Holbrook Park was grubbed out in the eighteenth and nineteenth centuries – hence its straight northern and eastern boundaries. The original outline, roughly rectangular (Fig. 21.5), is preserved by a parish boundary which surrounds almost the entire perimeter; the one surviving corner has been squared off but the boundary-bank shows that it was originally rounded as usual for early parks. The ancient part of the perimeter has a broad massive bank with an external ditch only; it continues unchanged past the small woods that adjoin. Another bank zigzags through the interior and suggests either compartmentation of the park or the boundary of a pre-existing wood.

The site is poorly documented. The park was evidently formed in the eleventh or twelfth centuries when parish boundaries were still flexible. It is first mentioned in a thirteenth-century charter[230] and appears briefly in various later documents. The small adjoining woods are first listed in 1617;[359] the name Birch Wood shows that this tree was then already in the area.

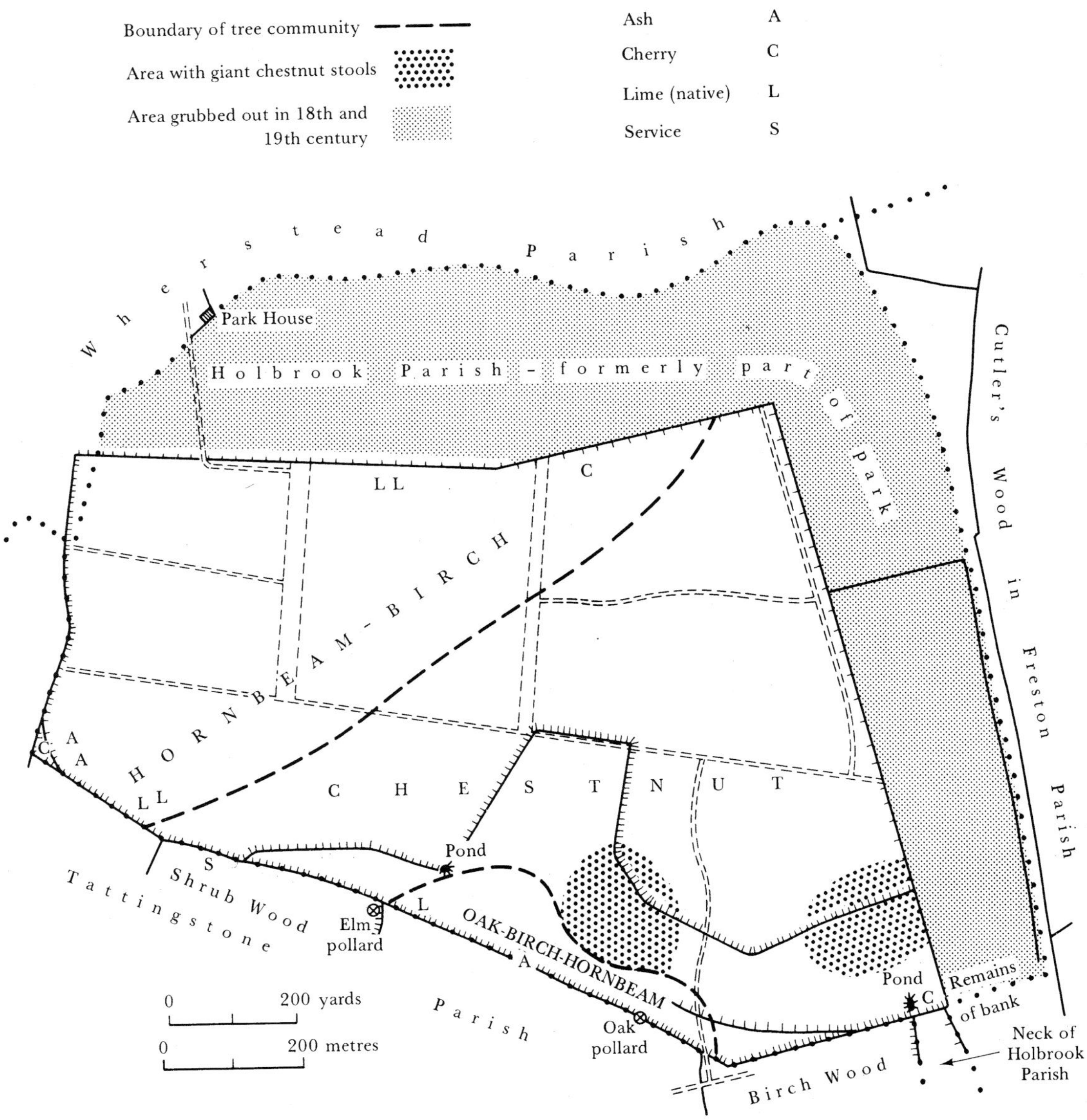

Fig. 21.5 Holbrook Park, S.E. Suffolk: earthworks and tree communities.

Conclusions

The derivation of Holbrook Park from primary woodland is attested by the presence of lime and service, but the nature of the park and its degree of continuity are not known. Like Iken Wood (pp. 289–90) Holbrook is a sparse wood with many glades and gaps not easily colonized by trees; probably the bluebells and bracken in both woods (and in several others with these plants) are so dense as to overcome the tree seedlings.

The giant stools of the Park, of at least medieval antiquity, must be added to our list of ancient chestnuts. Either they were introduced for some reason connected with the park or they are derived from a yet earlier land-use.

Conservation

Chestnut is the most prosperous of all underwoods; it is extensively coppiced in Kent and on a smaller scale in Essex and elsewhere [but see p. 518]. Stakes, hop-poles, and especially pale-and-wire fencing are the products. Ecologically it is relatively poor; much of the biological value of chestnut-woods is in plants other than chestnut.

Chestnut is usually not a high priority for conservation but some thought should be given to protecting special and historic woods. Norsey Wood now belongs to Basildon District Council, who have begun systematically to reconcile the conservation and public appreciation of the wood with heavy public use. In 1980 coppicing was being restored and paths reorganized to divert attention away from the valleys where the vegetation is most easily damaged.

General conclusions

Although it is still possible that its remains may be identified from some earlier period, the evidence is very strong that chestnut arrived here in Roman times, and the inference is that it was deliberately introduced.

Evidence that it persisted through the Dark Ages comes from the Anglo-Saxons' knowledge of the tree and from the nature and distribution of medieval records. By the thirteenth century or soon after, chestnut had acquired much of its present geographical distribution: the records are clustered especially in the two areas, Kent and East Essex (plus S.E. Suffolk), where chestnut-woods are still abundant.

Some of the early evidence and some ancient individuals may result from growing chestnut in gardens and orchards. But many early records specifically mention it in *woods*, and moreover in woods well away from habitation. Already in the thirteenth century the tree had a definite ecological context. Both in Dean and at Sittingbourne the records state that it was accompanied by oak and beech, trees known also to have been present in the New Forest and on the type of site which chestnut occupied in Essex (Fig. 20.1). In Ellenden Wood near Canterbury (Table 17.2), also an old chestnut site with giant stools, all three can be seen together. This association of chestnut with what were then the typical trees of very acid soils shows that it had developed a natural ecology and did not depend on where the whims of growers had put it.

We may contrast chestnut with walnut, that other southern nut-bearing tree, also grown by the Romans, but which is much shorter-lived and does not grow in woods. People have grown walnut in gardens almost everywhere, regardless of the soil preferences attributed to it; but it does not last long, nor become established in native woods, and it has vanished from the hedges in which it was often planted in former centuries. Walnut could not have persisted through the Dark Ages except possibly in gardens.

Chestnut appears to be a replacement for both hornbeam and beech, which in turn replace lime. The beginning of the process can be seen in Chalkney Wood (pp. 248–51), where chestnut is a fairly recent arrival and much lime remains; the middle in Holbrook Park, where only a few lime stools are left; a late stage in Norsey and Ellenden Woods, where chestnut predominates but some hornbeam or beech remains.

Many ecologists regard chestnut-woods as too artificial to be worth studying: Tansley hardly mentions the tree. Such a judgement is mistaken. For many centuries after its original introduction it behaved as if it were indigenous. In recent times it has been widely planted in plantations and to a lesser extent in existing woods, but this has not wholly concealed its historic distribution. It grows in a definite ecological niche which it had already found when first recorded after the Dark Ages; its occurrence does not, as does much of the modern distribution of beech, result from eighteenth- or nineteenth-century beliefs about the kind of site which it ought to occupy.

Fig. 21.6 Ancient chestnut-wood (note big stools). Norsey Wood, S. Essex. May 1978

Fig. 21.7 Chestnut in its oldest documented locality – twelfth century – in England. Stools are up to 8 feet across. The area is full of Roman activity, but so is all the Forest of Dean. Chestnuts, Forest of Dean. October 1993

Fig. 21.8 The Tortworth Chestnut, Gloucestershire: already a famous ancient tree in 1700. It is anomalously situated on limestone soil outside a churchyard, and may be the relic of an orchard.

Fig. 21.9 Ancient chestnut stool in Crete. In Crete, as in England, chestnut is an ancient introduction, but more for nuts than wood. Alygoi, Kissamou, Crete. August 1981

22

Aspen

The historic poplars

The largest and most distinctive poplar in Britain is the black poplar (*Populus nigra*). The word *popeler* in medieval documents, for a very large non-woodland tree, can only be this species; the identification is confirmed by finds of its distinctive rugged boughs used for medieval cruck-frames.[122, 729] It is one of our most interesting historic trees – in Eastern England it was once one of the commonest farmland trees – but it never grows in woods and is thus outside the scope of this book.

White poplar or abele (*P. alba*), though usually supposed to have been introduced in the seventeenth century, is recorded in thirteenth- and fourteenth-century documents under the name *abel*, a large tree resembling, but not the same as, the *popeler*; it is therefore either native or anciently introduced. It was quite common in the Breckland and elsewhere in Suffolk,[226, 373] but was also a non-woodland tree.

Aspen (*P. tremula*), *asp* in medieval documents, is the only native woodland poplar. It grows throughout the British Isles in ancient woods, in wood-pasture and secondary woods and rarely in hedges. It is clonal, spreading by suckers to form circular patches all the trees of which are either male or female. Aspen is very variable: clones differ in pigmentation, hairiness, etc. and some people claim to be able to distinguish the sexes when not in flower. The only variant likely to be of ecological interest is a 'giant aspen', half as large again as an ordinary aspen in all its parts, which I have noted in a few Suffolk and Essex woods.

All the other poplars, nowadays more familiar than the native species, are hybrids and cultivars. The only one that occasionally comes the way of the historian of woods is the grey poplar (*P. canescens*) now known to be a hybrid between white poplar and aspen.[786] Because of the much greater popularity of cultivar poplars aspen is almost always a wild, not a planted, tree.

The history of aspen

Aspen has a respectable historical record. Poplar pollen does not always survive and is not identifiable as to species, but enough has been recorded to show that aspen, which is almost as arctic a tree as birch, was one of the first trees to enter Britain in the Late-Glacial. Being weakly competitive it was apparently uncommon in the Atlantic wildwood.

Aspen appears occasionally in charters and place-names (Table 2.1), e.g. *Asp*ley Guise (Beds), Stonham *Asp*all (Suffolk). Field-names (e.g. *Apes*field in Leaden Roding (Essex) 1439[288]) suggest that it was formerly more common outside woods than it is now.

Although nowadays ignored as a timber tree, aspen is often so described in the past. Presumably, like alder (p. 304) and black poplar, it had a special value as one of the few non-coniferous softwoods. At Hatfield Broadoak (Essex) in 1442 two 'aspes' were among the 72 trees felled in the Forest and Park for making a new windmill.[295] From 1564 to 1571 there were biggish sales from a wood at Ingatestone (Essex), at from 4*s* 8*d* to 7*s* 4*d* the load[307] – about a third the value of oak. In 1769 somebody there was induced to pay 12*s* for 'an Asp full of woodpec[k]e'd holes & dead at Top, being one half rotten'.[306a] Aspen makes a poor building timber but I have found it in a late timber-framed house at Great Waldingfield (Suffolk). It is mentioned as underwood at Little Easton (Essex) in 1565.[460] [See pp. 464–5.]

Aspen had two specialized uses, the making of clogs and of arrow-shafts. The earliest statute concerning timber, dated 1416, concerns competition between these trades:

> . . . That the Patenmakers in the Realm of England from henceforth shall make no Patens nor Clogs of Timber called Aspe, upon Pain to pay to the King a Hundred Shillings . . . so that the Fletchers . . . shall sell their Arrows at a more easy and reasonable Price.[485]

In 1464 the statute was repealed on the grounds that turners, carpenters, woodmongers, and 'colemakers' used aspen without restraint, and that

> very much Asp Timber there is, which will in no wise serve the Fletchers to make thereof Shafts, which is . . . able . . . to be made in Pattens and Clogs.[486]

Modern ecology

Aspen occurs in about half the ancient woods of Eastern England (Fig. 22.1). Most clones consist of only

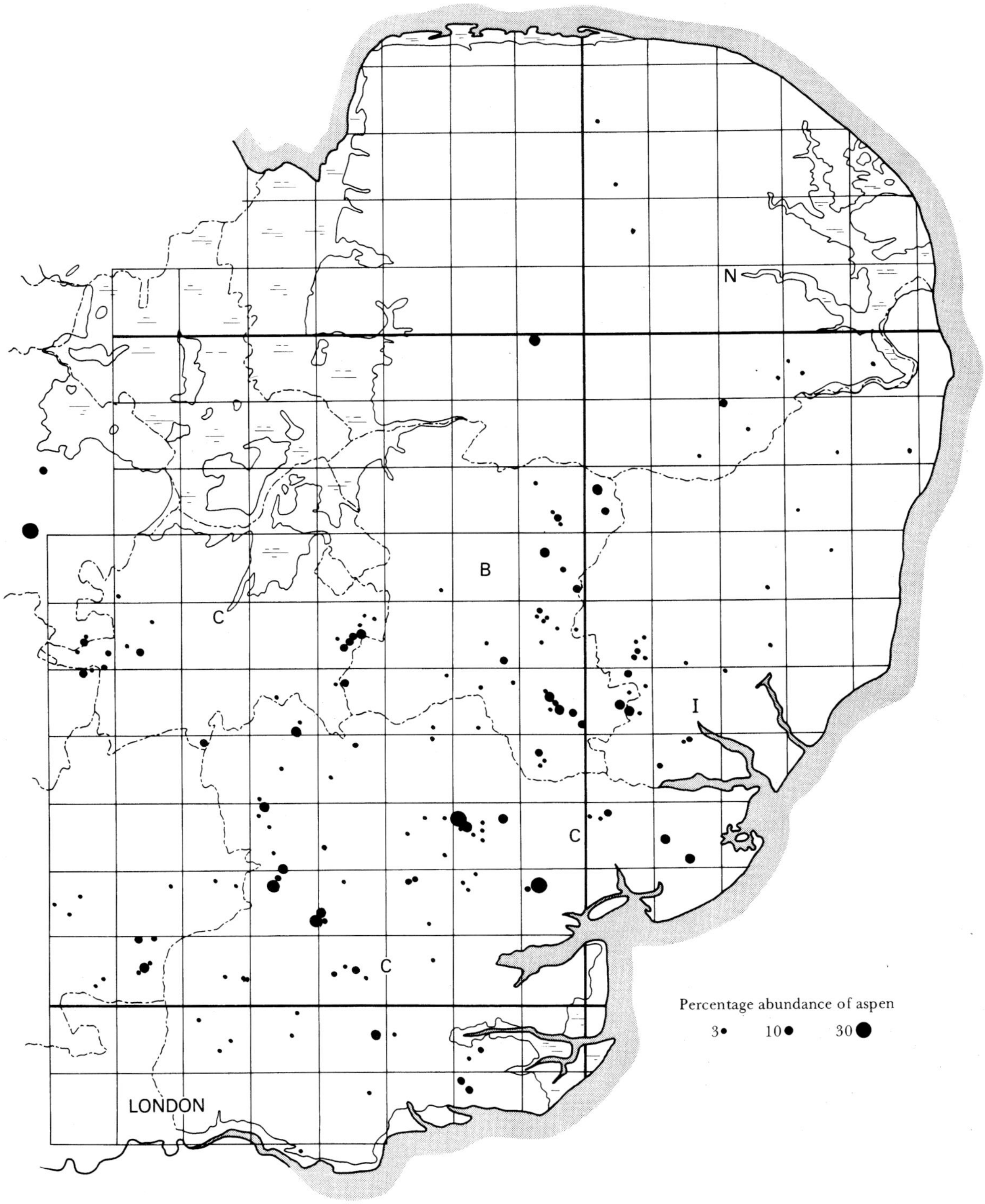

Fig. 22.1 Relative abundance of aspen in the ancient woods of Eastern England. The size of each dot is proportional to the percentage contribution of aspen to the tree communities of the wood. Wood-pasture occurrences are insignificant and are not differentiated from woodland.

a few trees, but sometimes they are extensive, forming aspen variants of several woodland types. In a few woods, such as Hayley and those at Leaden Roding and Stisted (Essex), there are areas of up to ten acres of aspen-dominated woodland. It is predominantly a tree of seasonally wet plateau woods. It occurs (Table 6.2) chiefly in woods of hazel, maple, hornbeam, and lime; it is rare with elm, chestnut, oak, alder, or birch. The ground vegetation often involves oxlip, primrose, *Deschampsia caespitosa*, brambles, or *Carex pendula*; less often mercury, and rarely bracken.

The behaviour of aspen in the field and the contexts in which it occurs suggest that it is influenced by shade, waterlogging, and grazing. It is weakly competitive and lives no more than about fifty years.[120] The suckers which would perpetuate it are not formed in dense shade, and unless regularly coppiced the clones are less permanent than those of elm. Overgrown woods of hornbeam, lime, or maple often have the remains of dead aspen clones which have died or been killed by shade and have not regenerated.

Most aspen in Eastern England is on level ground, on soils with a high content of either clay or loess (the Hanslope and Oak series)[739, 895] which are strongly gleyed and wet in spring. It tends to avoid the company of plateau or valley alder which indicate moving water (Chapter 18). It is almost indifferent to soil acidity and is equally characteristic of the oak–hornbeam woods of S.E. Hertfordshire and the ash–hazel woods of West Cambridgeshire. It goes with those herbs that can tolerate poor drainage. The grown tree does not particularly require moisture – as the events of 1975–6 showed, it is more drought-resistant than ash or birch – but the seedling is very exacting. Dr A. S. Watt told me that seed is produced possibly every year; unlike most tree seed, it has to germinate within a week if at all; the seedling is small and for a long time is very vulnerable to drought.[120] To establish aspen from seed requires several weeks of unbroken wetness from May onwards, a relatively rare event which seldom happens except on particular types of soil.

Aspen has a very bitter taste and is the tree least preferred by fallow deer. In Hayley Wood aspen is rapidly increasing on this account.

Conclusions

Aspen, like birch, is particularly a tree of cold climates. Although present throughout the post-glacial, it was probably rarer in the wildwood than it is now. It too has exploited the habitats provided by agriculture and woodmanship; but its expansion, unlike that of birch, has been hindered by its poor ability to colonize new sites. It is likely to benefit from the present increasing numbers of deer combined with the revival of coppicing.

The aspens of other northern countries are a valued crop, but those of Britain are now almost entirely unused. The tree is worth encouraging for pulpwood; it may produce less cellulose than a well-tended cultivar poplar, but it needs no planting or other attention.

Added in 2003 edition

Aspen has markedly declined in many woods, as is documented in detail for Gamlingay Wood (pp. 364–72). In Hayley Wood it appears to last 60–80 years since the last coppicing; the old stems then fall down and die, and no suckers are produced. In replanted woods it often flourished for a time, since its vital parts were underground and were inaccessible to poison, but then died out from competition, either from the planted trees or from resurgent native trees. Only in coppiced woods does it persist, indeed flourish if deer eat its competitors.

Although aspen is very perishable, its timber and wood both occur surprisingly often in medieval buildings (Chapter 29), which testifies to the all-prevalence of coppicing in the woods whence the material came.

Fig. 22.2 Aspen joist and black poplar floorboards, 16th-century floor inserted into medieval building, Harleston, Norfolk. (Acknowledgement to John Bloomfield.)

Fig. 22.3 Aspen benefiting from coppicing and deer. The dense shoots in the foreground are aspen suckers of 1½ years' growth, which fallow deer will not eat (though they fray them with their antlers). Behind are ash pollards whose regrowth they have devoured within reach, leaving a browse-line (cf Fig. 12.16). They have exterminated all other underwood. Hayley Wood. July 1976

23

Holly

Holly (*Ilex aquifolium*) is distributed almost throughout the British Isles but is less common in Eastern England and East Scotland. It is a tree of woodland and particularly of wood-pasture; it is locally common in hedges but only in parts of England and Wales where the majority of hedges are older than 1700.[837]

Its ancient association with Christmas is only one of the links between holly and mankind. It used to be widely coppiced and pollarded as fodder for sheep and deer.[832] The bark was one of the sources of bird-lime for catching birds. The timber had many small uses for the cogs of machinery and for carving and turning, but these were general to all close-grained trees. Holly still brings bad luck if cut down and for that reason is now the commonest hedgerow tree remaining in prairie-farming parts of East Anglia.

History

Holly is a moderate pollen producer although insect-pollinated. It is first recorded in Zone VI and rapidly became widespread, especially in Ireland where it was apparently locally dominant. The present distribution – abundant in the west, less common in the east – goes back well into prehistory.

The tree has many names: Anglo-Saxon *holegn*, Middle English *holin*, later *holm* and *hulver*, Medieval Latin *hussetum*, Welsh *celynen*. In place-names it is often difficult to distinguish from irrelevant elements such as *holm* (= island), *hole*, *holy*, etc.; it is often mistranslated 'holm-oak', a tree not present in Anglo-Saxon England. Genuine holly-names, such as the various *Holling*tons, are scattered over England, predominantly in the west. Although a conspicuous tree it is surprisingly rare in Anglo-Saxon charters.

The particular association of holly with wood-pasture can be traced back to the Middle Ages. It was specially protected by some Forest authorities, perhaps because it was supposed to feed the deer. In 1249 Robert de Northampton was granted felling or extraction licences for 160 holly trees (*fusta de Husso*, *ligna de Husseto* – the words imply timber) in a wood at 'Ginge Joyberd' (? in Mountnessing) in the Forest jurisdiction of Essex.[233] This is by far the largest-scale record of holly in Eastern England. In Epping Forest, where holly is now abundant, only two trees of it were mentioned in Great Monk Wood in 1582.[509] It appears as part of the underwood on the wood-pasture common at Lingwood in Little Baddow (Essex) in 1560.[286] In a park at Hundon (Suffolk) in 1611 one of the compartments was called 'The hollyus quarter'.[370a]

Much evidence for the history of holly has been collected by G. F. Peterken and the late P. S. Lloyd. In the New Forest, a stronghold of holly, its antiquity is attested by *Holms*ley Copse, which, apart from the Anglo-Saxon form of the name, was recorded as consisting of very old hollies in 1609.[832] At Dungeness, on a shingle ridge called *Holm*stone, there is a famous and well documented holly-wood, the only wood of any kind on this substratum in Britain; it is apparently documented in the eighth century and has certainly been known as a curiosity since before 1617.[104] Many nineteenth-century writers, in various parts of Britain, claimed that holly had formerly been more common.[832]

Modern ecology

Holly has a western and southern distribution in Europe; its eastern limit appears to be set by winter cold.[751] Its preference for Western Britain and its rarity in Cambridgeshire have been ascribed to its avoidance of either severe frost or severe drought; but trees planted around Cambridge survived, though in a sorry state, the exceptional winter of 1963 and the exceptional summer of 1976.

The tree coppices and pollards freely and is very difficult to kill;[104] it suckers weakly. As we all discover at Christmas, it fruits very erratically but heavily in some years. The seed waits two to three years before germinating; the seedling and sapling are sensitive to drought but otherwise not exacting. Hollies vary widely in growth-rate; slow-growing trees often bear nineteenth-century graffiti. The tree is long-lived and almost certainly can much exceed the greatest recorded age of 254 years.[832]

Holly occurs in many kinds of woodland throughout Britain.[832] It has a preference for oakwoods and for acid soils (cf. Table 17.2), although it is also reported from limestone ashwoods. Usually it is an understorey tree. Holly-woods are widespread in the New Forest, where they are sometimes a stage in succession to oak or beech; the few other published instances of holly as

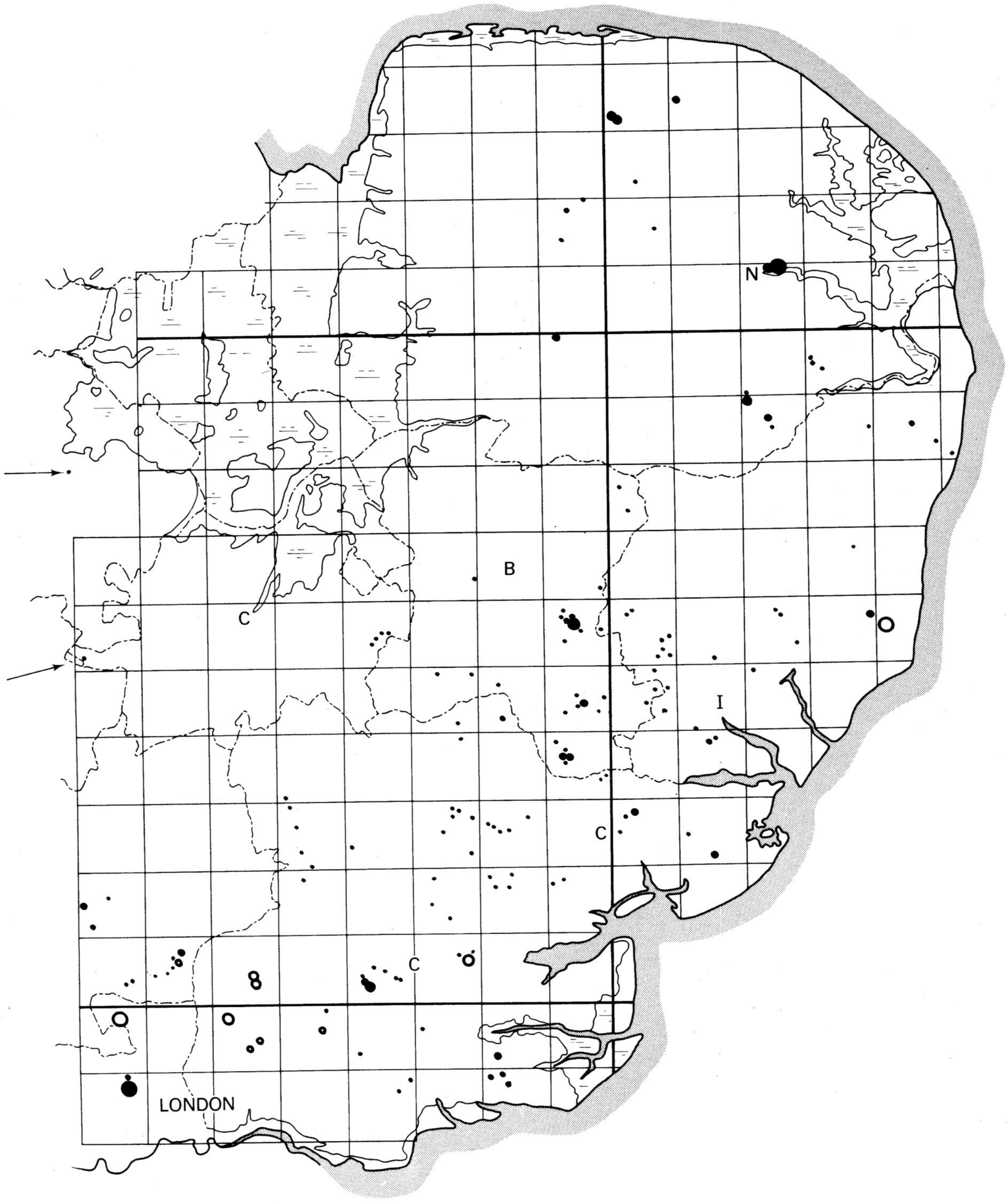

Fig. 23.1 Abundance of holly in ancient woods (●) and wood-pasture (○) in Eastern England. The size of each dot is a very approximate guide to the relative abundance of holly in the site.

a dominant tree include the holly-wood of Dungeness and a pollard holly-grove on the Stiperstones (Salop). Holly casts (and tolerates) a very dense shade and few flowering-plants will grow beneath it, although holly-woods are sometimes rich in bryophytes.

In Eastern England holly is predominantly a tree of wood-pasture. I have recorded it in every Forest and wooded common. It forms extensive thickets in Epping Forest and Enfield Chase. The grandest stand of holly in Britain is in Staverton Park (Suffolk), where in the Thicks (p. 293) it has become dominant, overtopping and often killing the ancient oaks. Peterken found one of these hollies to measure 74 ft high by 7 ft 2 in. girth, which appears to be the biggest in the kingdom.[97] Holly occurs in wood-pasture on most soils: it is often on very acid sands and gravels, as at Staverton, but in Epping and Wintry Forests (and in the New Forest) it extends on to clays.

This abundance of wood-pasture holly apparently follows a decline of grazing. In Epping Forest the tree has been recorded for at least 400 years and may have been abundant as grazed-down bushes, but it has become prominent chiefly in the last 150 years; being exceedingly tolerant of shade it is the only tree to have profited from the termination of woodcutting in 1878.[124] The hollies of Staverton Thicks, large as they are, have grown up mainly since sheep ceased to be admitted *c.* 1820. Holly was relatively insignificant when the trees were still managed, although at Staverton some hollies show signs of giraffe-pollarding.

As a woodland tree holly is widespread in Eastern England (Fig. 23.1); it occurs in about half the woods outside Cambridgeshire. In oakwoods it is common and characteristic, as in Sherrard's Park Wood (Welwyn Garden City) where some of the hollies are almost as large as those of Staverton. In all other woodland types it is rare (Table 6.2). Often it is confined to woodbanks, where it may persist even if the wood expands beyond the bank (a peculiarity which I have observed elsewhere, e.g. on the Grovely Ridge (Wilts)). At Bradfield and in some other woods holly occurs as saplings, which may be many years old: they linger in shade but do not grow appreciably even when released by coppicing.

Holly is well known for its strong tendency to form mull humus, and apparently can even de-podzolize heathland soils.[45] In Eastern England, however, it often grows on extremely acid soils ($pH < 3.5$) on which, so far, it can only form mor.

Conclusions

The fortunes of holly have fluctuated down the centuries. In the last 150 years it has increased, as in Eastern England, in the New Forest since 1850,[832] and in Sutton Coldfield Park (Warwicks) where parts of the former 'hursts' or coppices are now holly-woods. Most of the increase has been in wood-pasture, and it is reasonable to attribute it to a general decline of grazing. Holly is still increasing: in Staverton young hollies are growing up in gaps in the canopy [deer permitting] and in most years there are abundant seedlings.

There is much evidence that holly had earlier phases of abundance, when it was more numerous and more often of timber size than it was before the present increase. Peterken and Lloyd quote instances of great holly-woods said to have disappeared, apparently around 1800, from Scotland, Ireland, and northern England. We have seen a medieval example in Essex. Holly existed in quantity in the Roman New Forest, according to an archaeological identification of charcoal.[890a] Whether the increases and decreases of holly were contemporaneous throughout Britain, and whether they are due to fluctuations of grazing or of weather, remain to be seen.

Holly-woods are apparently a speciality of the British Isles. Along with the woods of strawberry-tree (*Arbutus unedo*) in S.W. Ireland, they are among the world's rare examples of broad-leaved evergreen forest extending into cool-temperate latitudes. They are a plant community which we have a particular duty to preserve, especially such historic holly-woods as the one on Dungeness.

Fig. 23.2 Holly Hurst, Sutton Coldfield Park. Despite this name, most of the hursts of this compartmented park are now dominated by holly. June 1998

Fig. 23.3 Giant holly, Staverton Thicks. About a hundred years ago it overtopped and killed a tall 'giraffe-pollard' oak. Hollies here tend to grow ajdacent to oaks, as they do in the New Forest and (with *Ilex cassine* and *Quercus virginiana*) in Georgia (America). July 1983

Fig. 23.4 Great holly on the edge of the North York Moors, the browse-line and lack of ground vegetation are due to sheep. Note the holly and oak growing very close together, as at Staverton. Birk Hagg, Bilsdale. April 1985

24

The rosaceous trees

Trees of the family Rosaceae – cherries, thorns, apples, services, etc. – are well represented in history. They were valued and documented for a variety of utilitarian, social, culinary, or supernatural qualities. It is sometimes difficult to distinguish records of the wild species from 'feral' trees derived from cultivation. The written record is extended by finds of pips or stones and of charcoal in archaeological deposits from the Neolithic onwards; but, being insect-pollinated, rosaceous trees produce very little pollen, so their behaviour in the wildwood is poorly understood.

Except for the suckering species of *Prunus*, rosaceous trees are non-gregarious; they occur as single individuals mixed with other species. This is evident in such common species as crab [Fig. 24.7] and even hawthorn, but is particularly noticeable with the rarer service and pear.

Cherry

Wild cherry (*Prunus avium*) is a tree of great beauty and distinction: a cherry-wood in blossom [Fig. 24.5], or a single giant and aged tree covered in white flowers from top to bottom, are things to be remembered. Cherry can grow at least 80 ft (25 m) high: in the Chilterns it keeps up with well-grown beech. It is one of the few trees to grow freely both from suckers and seed. It grows fast; at about 100 years it enters on a venerable old age, when the characteristic smooth bark, banded with outsize lenticels, breaks up into furrows. It yields small edible fruit.

Cherry occurs almost throughout Britain but has a strangely patchy distribution: it is common chiefly in S.E. England and in the agricultural country of east Scotland. In Eastern England it is almost exclusively a woodland tree, although elsewhere it grows in hedges.

The tree is also called *merry-tree* (cf. French *merisier*), *gean* (pronounced as 'green' without the *r*[816]) and *bird-cherry* (a name which it shares with *Prunus padus*). These names distinguish wild from cultivated cherries.

History and uses

The prehistoric record of the tree is limited to finds of charcoal and stones from the Neolithic onwards.[710] These suffice to rebut the old theory that it was introduced by the Romans.

The historical record is surprisingly meagre for an easily-recognized tree with specific uses. It is exceedingly rare as a place-name element, although the Anglo-Saxon *ciris* or *cyrs* 'cherry' might be overlooked through confusion with the common element *cirice*, *cyrice* 'church'. There is one allusion to a *cirscumb* 'cherry-combe' in a charter of Meon (Hants) dated 956.[211] Other written references begin with the sixteenth-century herbalists.

Merries are said to have been an important peasant foodstuff in France and Switzerland[80, 389] and would presumably have been eaten in Britain as well. From at least the eighteenth century the timber was used in cabinet-making, sometimes to counterfeit mahogany.[389]

From Eastern England I have a few records of timber sales: for instance from Felbrigg (Norfolk) in 1780 – including some big trees up to 28 ft in usable length and 32 in. in average girth[418] – and from Dodnash Wood (S.E. Suffolk) in 1809.[500] Cherry fetched 6*d* a cubic foot in 1780 and 2*s* 7½*d* in 1809, well below the price of oak (Fig. 11.2), so it was not the grower who benefited from its value as a furniture timber.

Modern ecology: Eastern England

Merry is abundant in the woods of south Suffolk and in small areas of N.W. and South Essex (Fig. 24.1). Elsewhere it is thinly scattered; it is absent from nearly all Cambridgeshire and from much of south Norfolk and N.E. Suffolk. This may be a long-standing distribution. In 1807 Thomas Martyn wrote: 'In Suffolk it abounds about Polstead and is commonly called the Polstead Cherry';[404] it is still abundant in just this area.

Being a suckering tree, cherry is gregarious, forming small clones like those of elm or aspen. It is often treated as timber, although it grows well as underwood. Occasionally it is the dominant or co-dominant tree over several acres; examples are Arger-fen Wood (W. Suffolk), Alsa Wood (N.W. Essex), and Hall Wood (Langdon Hills).

Cherry has a strong tendency to form secondary woodland. A famous example is Lime-kiln Close, Cherry Hinton (Cambridge) where it has been known for centuries.[395] The chief other Cambridgeshire site, Rivey Wood, Linton, is also a secondary wood.[244] In Groton

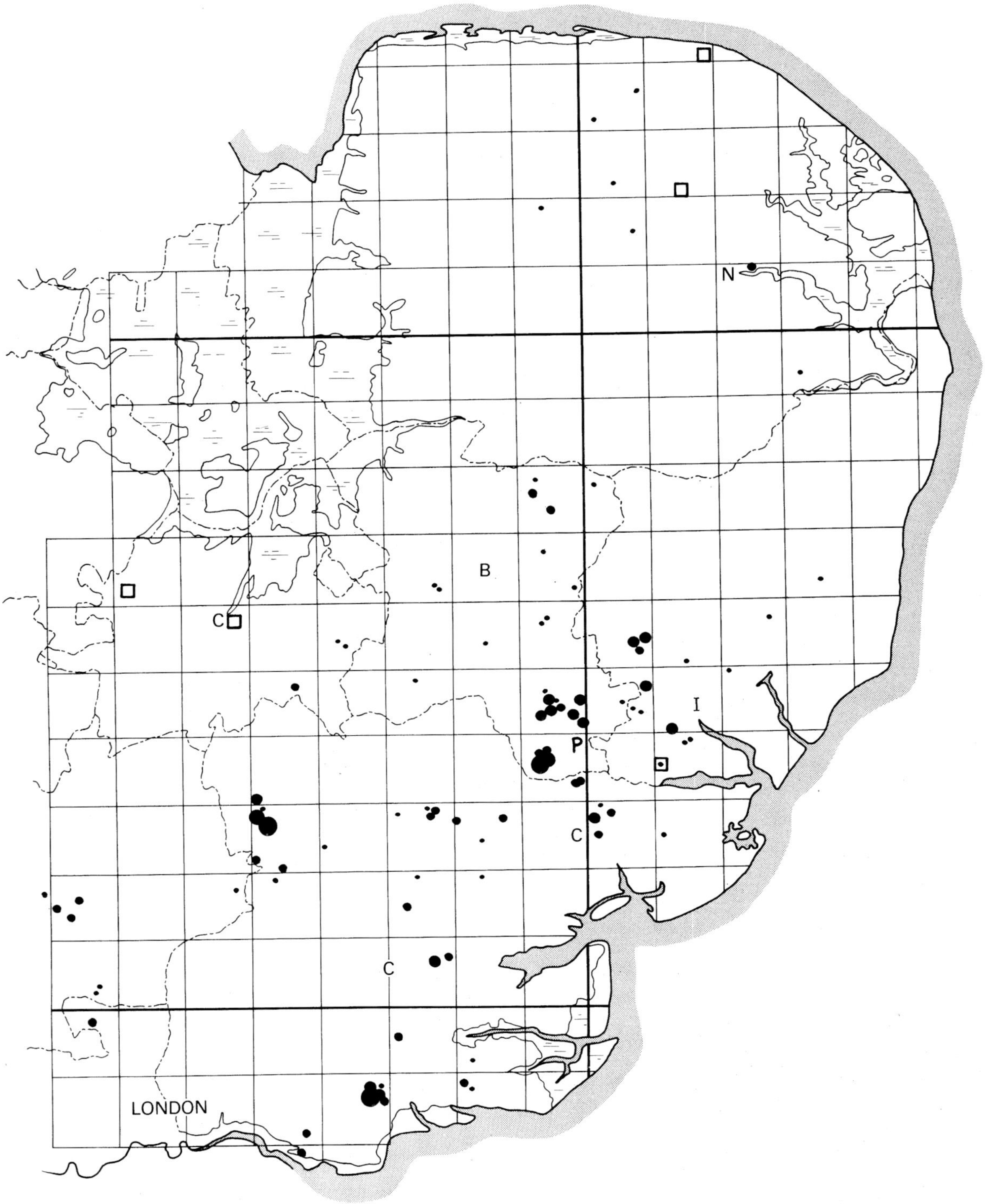

Fig. 24.1 Occurrence of wild cherry (*Prunus avium*) in the ancient woods of Eastern England. The size of each spot is a rough indication of the proportion of each wood which is occupied by cherry. □: historic records. P: Polstead.

Wood (Fig. 15.9) most of the cherry is in additions to the original wood. There are many similar instances. However the tree is well established in some woods of unquestionable antiquity, such as Alsa Wood[118] and Priestley Wood, Barking (Suffolk).[120] In ancient woods it is usually on or near the wood margin: in the Bradfield Woods the cherries are all on woodbanks. In blossom-time the woods around Polstead look from outside like cherry-woods, but this is partly an illusion, for most of the cherry is marginal. It can be weakly invasive.

Cherry is most often found in conjunction with the more acidic ash and hazel woods (Table 6.2). It appears to favour light, well-drained, weakly to moderately acid, not particularly fertile soils. The commonest dominant herb is bluebell, followed by dog's-mercury. On woodbanks it can occur on a wider range of soil types.

Outside Eastern England the best-defined merry habitat is the Clay-with-Flints variant of the Chilterns beechwoods (Chapter 20), in which the tree occurs singly. The soils here, although heavier, are moderately acid and moderately well-drained.

Conclusions

There can be little doubt that merry is a native tree which has benefited from human activities. The poor documentation compared to other rosaceous trees strongly suggests that it was much less common in Anglo-Saxon times, and even in the Middle Ages, than it is now. In wildwood it may have been capable of competing with other species – especially the heavily-shading lime and hornbeam – only on a narrow range of soils. Arger-fen Wood and Hall Wood, where large stands of cherry occur twice on an unusual topography, could well be relics of its natural habitat: both woods climb steep scarps of gravel overlying London Clay with springs breaking out halfway up.

Cherry has been favoured by the formation of secondary woodland; by the making of woodbanks which enable it to colonize soils which would otherwise be too ill-drained or too acid; by the decline of lime which may have been its chief competitor; and probably by coppicing which reduces competition. It is often said to have been planted but of this I have only one record. It is possible that some cherry may be derived by bird-sown seed from cultivated trees.

The expansion of merry has probably been slow, and is likely to continue. Although many stands, including Arger-fen Wood, have been coniferized, the tree is not easy to kill and much of it has survived. Merry is favoured by some timber-growers because it fetches high prices as a furniture timber, and its preservation should be encouraged on these grounds; unfortunately many owners are unaware of its short life-cycle and forget to fell it before it goes rotten!

Bird-cherry, *Prunus padus*

This small non-suckering uneatable relative of merry has a remarkable distribution. It is a Highland Zone tree, widespread in Scotland, Wales, and northern England, but almost absent from Lowland England except for curious outliers in Norfolk and in Chippenham Fen (Cambs). It is more a tree of fens and water-courses than of woods.

Prunus padus has a good subfossil record, chiefly from stones, which are known throughout the post-glacial.[710] The find-spots include not only Scotland and Norfolk, which are still strongholds of the tree, but also Ireland and Nottinghamshire, where it is now very rare.

The historical record of the tree is meagre but suggests that it was once more widespread. Gerarde, the herbalist, wrote in 1597: 'The Birds Cherry-tree . . . groweth in the wilde woods of Kent . . . very plentifully in the North of England'. His text-figure unmistakably shows *P. padus*.[340] T. Martyn in 1807 knew of it 'about Watton and Dereham' in Norfolk and also quotes a locality in Leyton (S.W. Essex).[404] In Suffolk, where it may be extinct as a native, Dr John Birks has identified its pollen from the Bradfield Woods. (Table 5.4).

In ancient woods, which are part of its range of habitats in Norfolk, *Prunus padus* usually occurs as underwood, sometimes in abundance and replacing part of the hazel in damp, weakly calcareous ash–hazel woodland. This plant community is best developed in Wayland Wood, Watton, one of the historically most distinguished woods in England (p. 131). It also occurs in the Swanton Novers woods, extending into lime and plateau alder woodland, and elsewhere.

The subfossil and written evidence strongly indicate that this tree has rapidly retreated towards the north in recent centuries. It is still retreating in Ireland, where its pre-1930 records greatly outnumber those made since 1930.[830] In the light of this evidence we should reconsider those scattered occurrences in southern England which are generally regarded as garden-escapes: for instance, the reported find in Norsey Wood (S. Essex)[755] and my own discovery of a stool in Hadleigh Great Wood (S. Essex). Both of these, in ancient woodland, could well be relicts.

Why *P. padus* should decline is not obvious. Although it extends far into the Arctic it flourishes in central Europe and is not limited to high altitudes.

Blackthorn and other *Prunus* Species

Blackthorn or sloe (*Prunus spinosa*) is a small tree abundant in woods and hedges throughout Britain except the Scottish Highlands. It is strongly suckering and forms wickedly spiny thickets through which nobody larger than a rabbit can pass. Our ancestors contrived to eat the fruits, which are also used in home brewing and dyeing and were once 'said to enter largely into the manufacture of the cheaper kinds of port wine'.[389] Although unpleasant to handle – the spines have a reputation for causing septic wounds – blackthorn was a favourite wood for faggots for heating ovens.

Charcoal and stones of blackthorn have been reported from Mesolithic and later sites; in the Iron Age sloes were evidently gathered for large-scale use.[710]

The written record is poor because blackthorn was not always distinguished from hawthorn. The word is usually said to be medieval, but I have come across a *blace þyrne* in a perambulation, dated 958, at Ducklington (Oxon).[212] From the fifteenth century onwards the two thorns are often separated, as in the 1544 survey of Hainault Forest (Essex) (p. 223).

Blackthorn nowadays commonly forms secondary woodland, especially near an existing wood or hedge. It sometimes invades ancient woods, particularly on the site of overgrown rides or where the soil has been badly rutted during an unusual felling of timber. Despite its suckering habit it is not persistent, being easily overtopped and killed by other trees; timber fellings of the 1920s are sometimes now marked, as in Hatfield Forest, by tracts of dying blackthorn. It is a permanent inhabitant of woodland margins and ride-sides. In the wildwood it presumably found opportunities to colonize glades and gaps.

Bullace (*Prunus domestica* spp. *insititia*) is a larger and more hairy kind of blackthorn producing a more edible fruit. It is usually in hedges and is regarded as a relic of cultivation, although its stones have been found as far back as the Iron Age.

Cherry-plum (*P. cerasifera*) is another blackthorn-like tree; its twigs are glabrous and green rather than blackish, and its flowers appear with the leaves and earlier than those of blackthorn. It was introduced from the Near East and is now widely naturalized. It has probably been under-recorded because in shade it becomes difficult to distinguish from *P. spinosa*.

Hawthorn

The species of hawthorn

As well as the familiar hedgerow hawthorn or whitethorn (*Crataegus monogyna*), which also grows in woods, there is a second species, the woodland hawthorn (*Crataegus laevigata* (= *oxyacanthoides*)), which is strongly associated with ancient woods (Chapter 5) and seldom grows in hedges, scrub, wood-pasture, or secondary woodland. Hedgerow hawthorn is a tree – I have seen it drawn up to a height of 50 ft (15 m) by the competition of lime – with angular, deeply divided leaves, one style to the flower and one pip to the fruit. Woodland hawthorn is a multi-stemmed bush of floppy habit, with rounded, shallowly-lobed leaves, two styles and two pips; it flowers readily in shade and the flowers open at least a week earlier. Both species are very variable; they hybridize freely when they meet.[14] The distinction between the hawthorns was first recognized in France in 1790[897] and is not reflected in vernacular names.

C. monogyna occurs almost throughout Britain; *C. laevigata*, unfortunately named Midland Hawthorn by learned authors, is restricted to the south and east, hardly occurring north of Lincolnshire or west of Gloucestershire and Sussex.

History and prehistory

Remains of hawthorn, described as *C. monogyna*, are abundantly recorded from the Early Boreal onwards. It undoubtedly formed part of the wildwood, though its pollen is too scanty to be often noticed.

The historical record is very copious. Thorn is more noticed than any other tree (Table 2.1). As the Anglo-Saxon *Runic Poem* reminds us,[817] people remember it because it hurts; it is also a workaday tree of hedges and firewood, and a symbolic and ceremonial tree. Hawthorn is the tree of May-day celebrations (before they altered the calendar in 1752), the tree of the Hethel Thorn or Glastonbury Thorn, and the tree after which the Anglo-Saxon rune **þ** is named.

Thorn and ash are the trees which most often appear in place-names. In general, names involving *þorn* (or Danish *þyrne* or Welsh *draenen*) are so ubiquitous as to tell us merely that thorns grew almost everywhere. Usually they do not differentiate blackthorn from whitethorn, although Gaelic has separate words (*droigheann, sgitheach*) for these species[812] and some English place-names (e.g. *Hather*leigh, Devon) are derived specifically from hawthorn (Anglo-Saxon *hagaþorn*).

Thorn (occasionally *hagaþorn* is specified) is by far the commonest tree named in Anglo-Saxon charters. Individual trees are often specified in terms such as 'old thorn', 'hoar thorn', 'pigeon's thorn', 'Heaðebolde's thorn', 'gate thorn', and 'pollard thorn' (*loppede þorn*, Ducklington (Oxon), 958).[212] There were evidently many isolated thorn-trees and standard thorns in hedges, some of which had permanent identities and proper names. Hawthorn hedges (*þornræwe* 'thorn-row') are often mentioned.

Thorn is also by far the commonest *woodland* tree specified in charters. The usual expression is *þorngræf* 'thorngrove', equivalent to the Medieval Latin *spinetum* (a place of thorns (*spine*)) and the modern 'spinney'. A parallel place-name is Thornets (Surrey), from *þorn* + *-ett*, a stand of thorns. There were evidently many groves of thorns. An identifiable example is in a Saxo-Cornish perambulation of 977, which gives the name *cruc draenoc* 'thorny barrow' to the Dry Tree barrow on the Goonhilly Downs, an otherwise treeless moorland, from which the parish boundaries of the Lizard Peninsula radiate.[259] A few spinneys are mentioned in Domesday Book.

Thorn is very common in medieval documents. Many allusions are to thorns in hedges and to casual scrub on commons, in corners of fields, etc., all of which were cut from time to time and sold for small sums. But thorns were also important woodland trees and could form much of the underwood in established woods:

> There is a wood of thorns called Contassetayl in which there is no pasture because of the thickness of the thorns. Nothing can be sold from those thorns for the next 15 years; but after each 15 years those thorns can be sold for 1 mark per acre so that they are worth 10*s* a year.
>
> *Kimbolton (Hunts) 1336*[449]

The wood-name in *-tayl* (from Norman-French *tailz*, a coppice (p. 5)) confirms that this was an established coppice-wood. The figures imply that the wood covered 11¼ acres and brought in 10.7*d* per acre-year, which is above the average return from woodland at the time (Fig. 11.6). Other examples, as at Writtle and Little Baddow (Essex) in 1336,[449] show thorns as a commercial crop, though seldom as valuable as at Kimbolton. The tenants' labour services at Abbot's Ripton (Hunts) in 1252 included collecting and transporting the lord's thorns from Haulunde, now Holland, Wood.[247]

Surveys and byelaws of the sixteenth century show thorns to have been important underwood especially in wood-pasture. In Rockingham Forest (Northants) in 1565 thorn was the commonest underwood recorded; it was mentioned, often with maple, in almost every one of more than a hundred coppices (Table 13.1). Examples from uncompartmented wood-pasture are Monk Wood (part of Epping Forest), where the felling of 86 modern acres in 1582 involved '618 crabtrees and hawthornes'[509] and Tiptree Heath (Essex), where thorns might be cut at any time of year (p. 175). Thorns were now declining in value; sometimes they are stated to be 'of little worth', and only a third of the underwood in Rockingham had been cut within the previous twenty years.[100] Hawthorn underwood is rarely considered worthy of mention in later centuries.

Thorns were used for fencing, before the invention of barbed wire (as the spiny bushes *Paliurus spina-Christi* and *Calicotome villosa* are still used in Yugoslavia and Greece), and were faggotted for fuel. I have no record of hawthorn as timber. Woods were a source of live thorn plants for hedging, as at Gamlingay in 1333–4 (p. 157); at Thorndon (Essex) in 1652, 21,060 'quicke set' were 'pulled . . . for ye use of the gardner'.[304] It is probably for this reason that woodland hawthorn occasionally turns up in hedges. An eleventh-century recipe for ink uses hawthorn bark as a substitute for oak galls (then imported).[499]

Many early forestry writers recommend hawthorn as a nurse tree when sowing a new plantation.

Modern ecology: secondary woodland

Crataegus monogyna is readily dispersed by seed and is one of the commonest trees to form secondary woodland. It was the subject of some of the classic studies in succession, summarized by Tansley,[150] of which Watt's hawthorn–beech succession (Chapter 20) is an example.

Hawthorn invasion is still very active and is one of the chief threats to semi-natural grassland; much steep chalk downland has become 'bushed-over' since the decline of rabbits. In ecological theory hawthorn should be a temporary phase in the establishment of some other woodland, a view supported by the many 'spinneys' on the map which are now composed of some other tree (although this may often have been planted). In practice thorn-groves can be unexpectedly permanent. In the 1930s R. Ross described a number of fields on the Boulder-clay near Hayley Wood which had been abandoned at various times in the previous fifty years. They had been colonized by a variety of shrubs of which hawthorn had eventually got the upper hand, killing its competitors and forming a dense dark canopy with little ground vegetation.[150] Two of these spinneys are still extant and have changed surprisingly little in the forty years since Ross wrote. Hawthorn is almost the only tree except for patches of ash and elm near hedges. The canopy, some 20–25 ft (6–8 m) high, shows no sign of instability. The ground vegetation is scanty, *Brachypodium sylvaticum* being the commonest species; there are no plants specific to woodland. These isolated secondary woods contrast with contemporary extensions to existing woods, such as the Hayley Wood Triangle (Fig. 5.2), which have become partly assimilated to the ancient woodland.

Modern ecology: ancient woods of Eastern England

Hawthorn is present in almost every ancient wood (Fig. 24.2). It is non-gregarious and is thinly scattered through many tree communities; it avoids the most acid soils and in many limewoods, hornbeam-woods, oakwoods, and chestnut-woods is confined to the woodbank. Hawthorn is abundant chiefly in ash–maple–hazel woods and is a characteristic member of the maple communities on the heaviest soils (Table 6.2).

Hawthorn populations in ancient woods can range from pure *monogyna* to almost pure *laevigata*; often there are many apparent hybrids and it may be difficult to find typical *laevigata*. The ratio of woodland to hedgerow hawthorns varies irregularly but tends to be highest on heavy soils in Huntingdonshire, Cambridgeshire, N.W. Essex, and S.W. Suffolk (Fig. 24.2), especially in those woods that have much total hawthorn. A good example are the Rivenhall woods (Fig. 2.4), on an outlying area of clay soils in mid Essex, in which hawthorn is unusually abundant and contains some of the best *laevigata* populations in Britain.

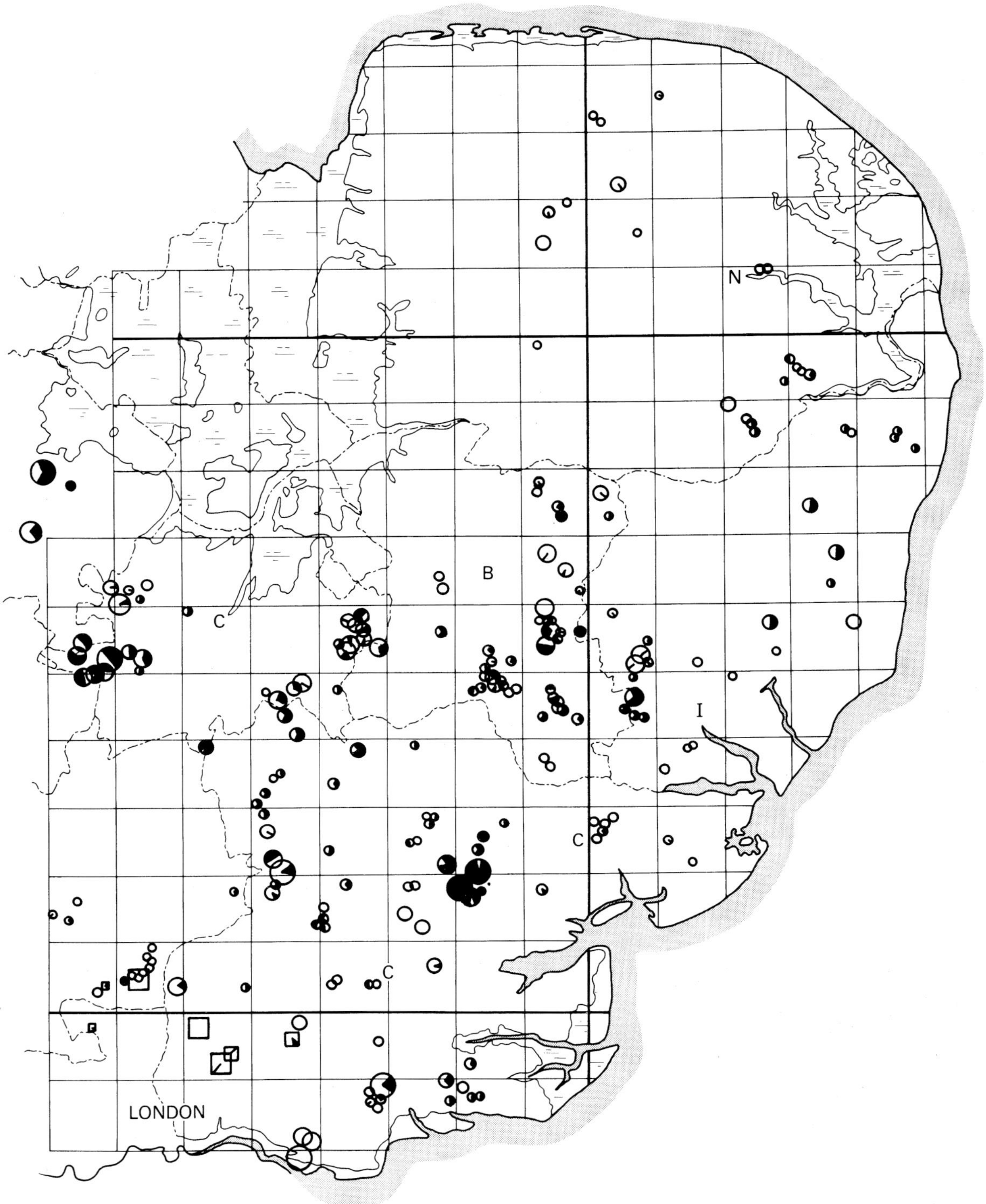

Fig. 24.2 Approximate relative abundance of hawthorn within ancient woods in Eastern England. (O) woodland occurences. The size of each circle is roughly proportional to the fraction of the woodland area occupied by hawthorn. Black and white sectors are a rough guide to the relative abundance of *Crataegus laevigata* (black) and *C. monogyna* (white). (□) wood-pasture occurrences similarly expressed.

Woodland hawthorn is usually a regular member of the underwood, forming massive stools, whereas hedgerow hawthorn is more usually a scrubby single-stemmed tree.[120] Most *monogyna* hawthorns appear to be relatively young, having been coppiced only once if at all. Both species are easily overtopped by other trees. Woodland hawthorn is one of the most shade-resistant of trees; hedgerow hawthorn is killed by the heaviest shade but can survive the shade of ash and probably maple indefinitely.

Modern ecology: wood-pasture

Young hawthorn, especially spring, is highly palatable to deer and other livestock, but only for a few weeks before the spines harden. The tree in general is resistant to grazing; hedgerow hawthorn is abundant in Forests and on lightly-grazed commons. Patches of thorn scrub, arising during times of slack grazing, protect young timber trees when grazing returns and are an essential part of the renewal cycle of wood-pasture (p. 173). Ancient thorn-trees, at least 300 years old, occur in Forests such as Hatfield and parks such as Heveningham (Suffolk); the Hethel Thorn, which still flourishes in Hethel (Norfolk), has been famous as an ancient tree since before 1765.[389] These, like thorns in Anglo-Saxon charters, are sometimes 'hoar' with lichens; they are among the few wild trees on which mistletoe regularly grows.

Hawthorn is particularly common in the coppices of some compartmented wood-pastures, such as Hatfield Forest, where there are extensive scrubs, mainly of hedgerow hawthorn, inside as well as outside the coppices. Probably the compartmentation system was not wholly successful in preventing cattle from damaging the normal underwood (cf. pp. 185–7, 291) and thorn arose as a replacement. In sixteenth-century Rockingham Forest a high proportion of thorn underwood is associated with evidence, from long coppice cycles, that the compartmentation was not being regularly looked after.

Conclusions

Crataegus monogyna is so familiar as a pioneer tree that ecologists often assume that this is the only function of hawthorn, even though *monogyna* is well recorded in established woodland and *laevigata* is seldom found anywhere else.

Hawthorn has been common in woods since the Mesolithic period. Most of the prehistoric evidence is for *monogyna*, though *laevigata* may have been overlooked through poor identification. Although the presence of *monogyna* is therefore by no means wholly artificial, human activities of various kinds have given it innumerable opportunities to extend its range and increase its abundance. Most of these involve the ability of *monogyna* to act as a pioneer and thus do not apply to *laevigata*, a relict species with a more nearly natural distribution.

How much of the hawthorn in woods in the Middle Ages was *laevigata* we cannot tell. Field observation suggests that *monogyna* has increased recently. It is possible that the species were less intermingled than they are now: *monogyna* was predominantly the hawthorn of woods on lighter, and *laevigata* on heavier, soils. Hybridization probably dates back many centuries, but the invasion of *laevigata* woods by large numbers of *monogyna* may be the work of the last 150 years, when unstable woodland management coincided with a vast proliferation of *monogyna* in enclosure-act hedges and later in scrubland. The preservation of good populations of woodland hawthorn deserves attention.

Crab

Wild apple or crabtree (*Malus sylvestris* ssp. *sylvestris*) anciently called *wilding* and in Medieval Latin *pomerium silvestre*, in a tree of woods, wood-pasture, and hedges. It differs from cultivated and feral apples (ssp. *mitis*) in its smaller, glabrous, more pointed leaves, glabrous inflorescences, and small sour fruit. There is seldom any doubt as to which subspecies a tree belongs to.

Crab occurs throughout most of the British Isles. Being very non-gregarious it is the least abundant of common trees: it seldom occurs more than singly. In Eastern England it is scattered through almost all types of woodland at roughly one crabtree to every ten acres; many small woods thus lack crab or have only one individual. It is not known why crab, like several of its relatives, should be so few in numbers yet should lack any evident habitat preference.

Archaeological finds of *Malus* are common from the Neolithic onwards but many may be of cultivated apple.[710]

Crab has similar human associations to hawthorn and is well documented. Place-names from Anglo-Saxon *apuldor* or *æppeltrēow* 'apple-tree' or from Old Norse *apaldr* or Welsh *afallen* are common but do not distinguish between wild and cultivated apples. *Crabbe* names are recorded at *Crab*adon and *Crab*tree (Dorset), and in Sussex there is even a Crabbet which implies a wood (*-ett*) of crabtrees.[882] Hedgerow crabs are implied by such field-names as Crabbebushfeld in Offton (Suffolk) *c.* 1290.[451] I know of no *wilding* place-names, but the element would be hard to distinguish from *wild*.

The third commonest tree in Anglo-Saxon charters is *apuldor*, often described as 'hoar' or 'old'. Many were in remote places and unlikely to be cultivated apples.

Crabtrees attract attention in the records for their timber – supposed, like pear and service, to be specially resistant to abrasion and used for such purposes as the gear teeth of mills – and for their fruit. In 1464 somebody was fined for damaging *arbores voc' crabtres* in Gamlingay Wood.[408] In 1814 there was a sale of crab timber at Haveringland (Norfolk).[408] The courts of Forests gavc particular protection to crabtrees, apparently because they were thought to provide food for deer (for instancc in 1307 John Miller lost 6*s* 7*d* worth of cart and horses for taking a load *de pomeriis silvestribus* by night in Epping Forest).[95a] Whether the deer benefited is doubtful; crabs came at a season when there was much else to eat, and could be a danger: the casualties among deer in Hainault Forest in 1498 included a hart 'choked with a doildyng [mistranscription of *wildyng*]' and a stag (i.e. a young hart) 'choked with a crabbe'.[509]

In general the abundance and behaviour of crab have not greatly changed throughout history. In some places it has declined. In Epping Forest sixteenth- and seventeenth-century records show that crab was much more abundant than it is now: the decline is attributable to increasing shade since 1878 (pp. 201–2).[124]

Pear

In Hayley Wood there used to stand a large tree with a massive unbranched trunk, broad rounded crown, and small rounded crab-like leaves. It never fruited and was assumed to be a crabtree (despite its size) until in 1972 Mr W. H. Palmer and I examined it with field-glasses and identified it as a pear. It differs from feral pear-trees, also found in woods and having a tall pyramidal habit and ovate curled leaves, to much the same degree as does crab from cultivated apple. Its taxonomy has not been fully investigated, but it was recognized as a possible survivor of the wild pear-trees which are abundantly recorded in history. It proved very difficult to propagate by cuttings or grafts. In 1974 the top of the tree fell off; the annual rings showed it to be 150–200 years old. Its exceptionally dense timber, which only just floats in water, was sold to a maker of harpsichords (one of the traditional uses of rosaceous trees). Both the stump and the roots have sprouted vigorously.

Four similar pear-trees (one now destroyed) are known in Eastern England (Figs 24.3 and 24.4), all solitary and all in medieval woods.

The charcoal of pear (*Pyrus pyraster* = *P. communis*) is widely recorded from the Neolithic onwards, mainly in southern England.[710]

Pear (Anglo-Saxon *pirige*) is abundantly represented in place-names and is one of the six commonest trees in the charters. Some place-names are of villages, where pear might have been cultivated, but others, such as Peryegrove, a wood in Eastwood (S.E. Essex) in 1589,[292] link pear with woodland. Most of the pears in charters appear to be hedgerow or free-standing trees well away from settlements or probable cultivation; occasionally they are related to woodland (e.g. *pirgraf*, pear-grove, in Kingsclere (Hants) in 943).[209] Wild pear is rare in medieval documents, though it continues to appear in field-names. It reappears with the herbalists. Gerarde in 1597 says that pears

> grow of themselves . . . in most places, as woods, or in the borders of fields, and neere to high waies . . . [they are] not to be eaten, because their nourishment is little and bad.[340]

Most Floras are undecided on whether to count pear as indigenous. The historical evidence strongly suggests that there is a native pear, whose fruit is rarely produced and uneatable. In Anglo-Saxon times it was not much less common than crab, but in recent centuries it has declined and has become increasingly confused with feral pears. If correctly equated with the Hayley pear it is now one of the rarest British plants.

Rowan

This tree, *Sorbus aucuparia*, the commonest member of a large genus, is also known as *rountree*, *quicken*, and *mountain-ash*. It is particularly a tree of the Highland Zone and is rather local in the lowlands.

Rowan is a relatively arctic tree; its seed, charcoal, or pollen are recorded from Zone IV onwards and possibly as early as Zone II.[710]

In modern times rowan has been much used and cultivated for fruit or ornament or to frustrate witches, but its historical record is poorer than that of other rosaceous trees. It appears in the place-names *Wicken*low (Lancs) and *Quick*stavers (W. Yorks), both from Anglo-Saxon *cwicen*;[882] the Gaelic *caorann* is common in place-names of the Scottish Highlands. Gerarde in 1597 says it was common *inter alia* in Cheshire and the Weald.[340]

Rowan occurs in many Highland Zone woods, notably in the birchwoods of Scotland in which it is the second commonest tree; isolated rowans grow wherever rock outcrops and gorges afford protection from grazing and encroaching blanket-peat.

In Eastern England rowan is very local and confined to acid woods on very poor soils (Fig. 24.3). It is characteristic of oakwoods (Table 6.2) in which it is sometimes a regular part of the underwood, and of the wood-pastures of South Essex; a few trees grow in chestnut-woods, hornbeam-woods, and acid hazel-woods.

The apparently poor historical record of rowan indicates that in the past it was limited, perhaps more strictly than now, to the Highland Zone for which early documentation, other than place-names, is scanty. Rowans in gardens grow abundantly from seed and it is possible that some of the Lowland rowan is naturalized.

Other *Sorbus* species

Apart from service, the genus includes whitebeam (*Sorbus aria*) and many apomictic micro-species (cf.

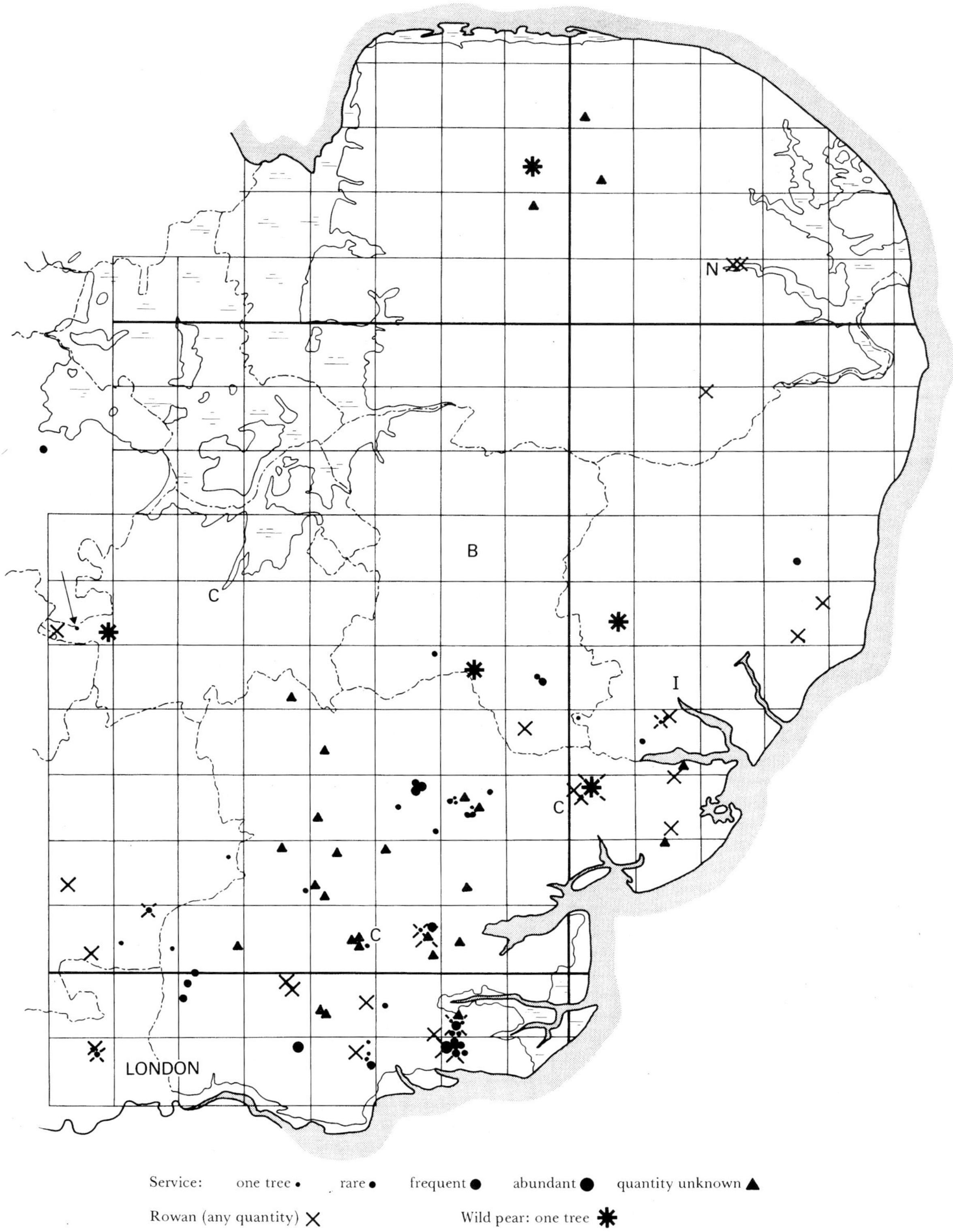

Fig. 24.3 Occurrence of service, rowan, and wild pear in ancient woods in Eastern England. Arrow indicates outlying occurrence.

Fig. 24.4 Wild pear-tree in Oxenholt (now Lumpit) Wood in Glemsford, Suffolk, one of five known in Eastern England. Now destroyed.

p. 255) often confined to small areas. Whitebeam is widespread in woodland, mainly in southern England, but the others are chiefly in scrub and on limestone cliffs.

Whitebeam is a tree chiefly of secondary woodland and of the edges of woods. It is mainly on chalk and limestone and is important in the calcareous beechwood successions (Chapter 20); in the Chilterns it sometimes extends on to acid soils. In Eastern England it is rare and may not be native.

Service

The remaining *Sorbus* species are *S. torminalis*, the service or chequer-tree, widespread but uncommon, and *S. domestica*, the whitty pear, the rarest wild tree in Britain. Books call them the 'wild' and 'true' service.

Service is thinly scattered through England as far north as the Lake District in woods and wood-pastures and occasionally in hedges in their immediate vicinity. It has attracted attention owing to its reputation as an indicator of ancient woodland;[169] although it is inconspicuous its distribution is reasonably well known. Like crab and pear it is strictly non-gregarious; many woods have only one service-tree or group of suckers. It is most easily found by looking for its fallen leaves, which persist through the winter; they are brightly coloured and have an unmistakable shape with triangular lobes.

Service can be as big as a large oak; there are some fine trees near Ken Wood (Middlesex; the best recently destroyed) and in Thorley Wood (Herts) and Meeps Hole Wood (Ramsden Crays, Essex). It is very variable in leaf and fruit characters. Many individuals are weakly suckering. Saplings are uncommon.

History

Charcoal has been positively identified as service from the late Iron Age in Dorset.[710]

Service is well documented. It probably attracted more attention as a rare curiosity than for any specific uses. The fruits are said to be just edible if allowed to go sleepy like medlars, and to be used in home-brewing (whence a false etymology of 'service' from *cerevisia*, beer); the timber has a similar reputation to crab.

The Anglo-Saxon original of 'service' is *syrfe*, which is not known as a place-name element but is mentioned in several charters, especially in Worcestershire. Among medieval references, at Felsted (Essex) in 1390 a *sorftre* was felled in Alwenhey Wood (no longer extant) and carted to a mill, presumably for use in the machinery, at a cost of 8*d*,[319] which implies a big tree. In Epping Forest the crabtrees stolen in 1307 were accompanied by *lignis seriis* (mistranscription of *seruis*). 'Servis' is mentioned again in the Forest in 1656[56] and still grows there in small numbers. In Dodnash Wood (Bentley, E. Suffolk) a map of 1629 depicts a 'seruis tree'[501]; the exact spot is now coniferized and no service can be seen, but it still grows elsewhere in the wood.

Modern ecology

Service is known from about a third of the ancient woods of Essex (Fig. 24.3); it is also widespread in S.E. England. In South Essex it is frequent, and West Wood, Thundersley (pp. 234–5), is our nearest approach to a service-wood. Further north it rapidly becomes rarer: in Cambridgeshire there is only one service-tree, a celebrated individual in Gamlingay Wood.

The records for Eastern England fully confirm the tree's association with ancient woodland. Sometimes it occurs in hedges or (as at Langdon Hills) plotland just outside an ancient wood, which shows that it can occasionally be dispersed by seed, but its powers of colonization are no better than those of lime. Sometimes, as in Dodnash Wood, it grows in a wood-hedge in such a position as to suggest that somebody has transferred a sucker from the wood's interior.

Service has some preference for acid woods; the South Essex woods where it is common are dominated by oak–hornbeam, hornbeam, or chestnut.

Whitty pear

Only one individual of *Sorbus domestica* has ever been recorded; it grew in the middle of Wyre Forest (Worcs) until vandalized in 1862. It was kept alive in cultivation and has been replaced on the original site.[71] This one tree had its own vernacular name and a respectable history, being first described in 1678,[445] when the name *S. pyriformis* was invented for it.

Sorbus domestica is ignored by most British Floras. It is a tree of southern Europe, but in Brittany extends not so very far from its English outlier. It is not commonly cultivated; the theory that the whitty pear is an escape from cultivation seems unlikely from its antiquity and remote site. Whether it is a chance introduction by a migratory bird or a relict of a once larger population may never be known. In its isolation it is an extreme example of the behaviour of many rosaceous trees.

Added in 2003 edition

The researches of Dr B. Juniper show that crab is not the wild ancestor of the orchard apple, which originated independently in Asia.

Service is thinly scattered in ancient woodland, often oakwoods, through southern and middle England and Wales, and indeed as far as north Greece, but only in S.E. Essex is it common. I have found it at the cliff edges of the seaside woods of the Helford River in Cornwall. It is weakly clonal, especially on acid soils.

Dr David Morfitt draws my attention to the remarkable history of whitty pear. The seventh-century *Historia Brittonum* ('Nennius') reports:

> By the river which is called Guoy [Wye], apples are found on an ashtree on the declivity of the wood which is near the mouth of the river.

As Morfitt asks, 'What can this be but *Sorbus domestica*?' This, probably the earliest written record of any British plant, is of one of the rarest British plants.

Whitty pear is not recorded again until its discovery in Wyre Forest a thousand years later. It passed into three centuries' more oblivion until Marc Hampton found it in Glamorgan in 1983. Several localities are now known on limestone cliffs, including one 'declivity' near the mouth of the Wye, and some of the trees are ancient.

Fig. 24.5 Clonal patch of cherry. Hall Wood, Langdon Hills, S.Essex. April 1975

Fig. 24.6 Ancient pollard hawthorn, Hatfield Forest. Although now embedded within a spinney, it was originally free-standing in a grassy plain, and in the 1930s became hemmed in by its children (cf. infilled savannas, p. 497). February 1989

Fig. 24.7 Crabtree left standing in a coppice-wood. As usual, there is only one crab. Hatfield Forest. April 1993

Fig. 24.8 Pollard rowan. The habitat, on boulders not soil, is common in mountain areas. Llanfoist, Monmouthshire. June 1999

25

Woodland Vegetation: Stability or Change?

The almost total absence of Birch trees and Bracken . . . is attributable to the heavy soil.

Hatfield Forest, 1925[1]

[Birch is now the fifth commonest tree in the Forest, but bracken is still almost absent.]

Where have all the flowers gone?

Peter Seeger, singer, 1961, and Keith Kirby, ecologist, 2001

The modern science of ecology is now over a century old. Although a hundred years is not a long time in the life of a wood, it begins to be possible to use early ecological records as a historical source. Such records – treated with appropriate caution[2] – provide a check on assertions made about the effects of recent events such as acid rain, global warming, replanting, and increase of deer.

The investigations reported here were started for various purposes, some of them no longer fashionable. Their function has become that of finding out whether the vegetation of woods, especially the herbaceous plants, has the stability (on which coppice cycles are superimposed) that is often supposed. They are not intended to have a consistent theme, still less to verify a theory.

The sites

Most of the sites are in the west Cambridgeshire boulder-clay woods (Hayley Wood and its neighbours, Fig. 25.1). They are referred to many times in the original book, but here I give a summary of their environment and ecology.

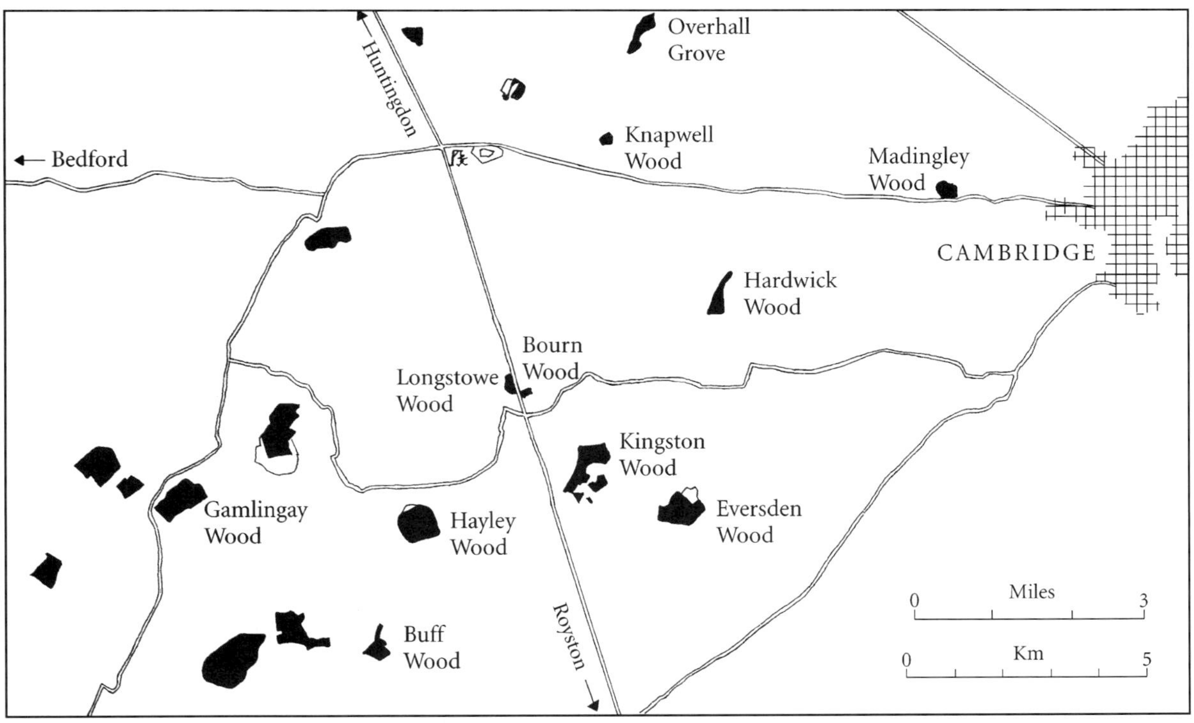

Fig. 25.1 Woods chiefly dealt with in this chapter.

1 *Essex Naturalist*, **21**, (1927) 89.

2 Kirby, K. (2001). Where have all the flowers gone? are our woodland flowers disappearing? *Biologist*, **48**, 182–6.

The woods belong to the Ash-Maple-Hazel group of woodland types, with the exception of clonal patches of suckering elm. Timber trees are mostly oak. The soils have a high clay content with a small but definite proportion of loess; there is one well-defined sand-lens, in Gamlingay Wood. Long before this book was originally written, my predecessors' research, beginning with Dr Alex Watt, had defined the herbaceous plant communities (Table 25.1, Plate 6, p. xxv), and to a large extent explained how they functioned (Chapter 7).

Plants lower in the table were known to be more competitive but to require better drainage, because in waterlogged soil they are less tolerant of poisoning by iron in the ferrous state. Oxlip, being resistant to ferrous iron, is tolerant (up to a point) of waterlogging. It grows perfectly well in the mercury zone provided that mercury is prevented from competing with it. Bluebell grows on faint earthworks and other raised areas in the oxlip zone; primrose grows in hollows in the mercury zone.

Boulder-clay woods get waterlogged because the high clay content of the soils renders them impermeable. Subsurface drainage is limited to cracks and old root holes. The clay shrinks and swells on an annual cycle of drying and wetting; in parts of Hayley Wood it forms a regular pattern of polygonal hummocks known by the Russian name of *gilgai*. Over the summer the woods lose moisture by transpiration faster than they gain it by rainfall, reaching their driest usually in late summer. In autumn and winter they gradually regain moisture, both through accumulating rainfall and also, it seems, because the subsurface cracks gradually close as the clay swells. In a wet spring the plateau parts of the woods have too little slope to carry away the rainfall, which is ponded up on the surface by slight irregularities (Plate 6h, p. xxvi). An analysis of 33 years of flooding and rainfall shows that rain in April is the most significant, followed by May and March.

Fallow deer (*Dama dama*) are not an ancient feature of these woods; they arrived at Hayley in the 1930s and have since increased and spread to other woods. Some woods are severely browsed, such as Hayley before it was fenced, where their numbers fluctuated between about 30 and 70 head, which is a lot of deer for a wood of 100 acres. Muntjac deer (*Muntiacus reevesi*), a more recent arrival, smaller and less numerous, occur in all the woods. In Hayley they get into all the fallow-deer exclosures except the small 1968 one.

It might be thought that the vegetation zones, depending as they do on the micro-topography, would be very stable. Their particulars should be affected by variations of shade (e.g. coppicing) or by browsing animals, but the zones should still be recognizable at least for decades – short of artificial drainage operations or a change of climate. Is this so?

Gamlingay Wood over Ninety Years

This, the next ancient wood to Hayley Wood, is remarkable in several respects.[3] It is a prime source for medieval woodland management: on present knowledge it is the best documented wood in England. In 1911 R. S. Adamson wrote an account[4] which was one of the first ecological descriptions of a natural wood in England; his article was among those which introduced the American idea of plant-associations to Britain.

Gamlingay Wood is a very wet boulder-clay wood. It has the full suite of vegetation zones, ranging from those dominated by big sedges in the wettest parts, to mixtures and mosaics of meadowsweet, oxlip, and *Deschampsia caespitosa* in most of the wood, through

Table 25.1 Plant communities in the West Cambridgeshire boulder-clay woods, in their shade phase (between coppicings)

	Dominant plants	Situation	Degree of drainage
Zone 1	*Carex acutiformis* and *riparia*	Hollows and pools in plateau	Water stands much of the year
Zone 2	Meadowsweet, oxlip, anemone, *Deschampsia caespitosa*	Plateau	Frequently flooded in spring
Zone 3	Oxlip, primrose (in woods that have it), anemone, bluebell	Fringes of plateau, hollows on slopes	Occasionally flooded in spring
Zone 4	Bluebell	Gentle slopes (<1°), raised areas on plateau	Rarely flooded
Zone 5	Bluebell + dog's-mercury	Moderate slopes (0.5–1.5°)	Well drained
Zone 6a	Dog's-mercury with occasional bluebell	Steeper slopes	Very well drained (as boulder-clay goes)
Zone 6	Dog's-mercury	Steeper slopes (>1°) and banks	Very well drained

3 Rackham, O. (1992). Gamlingay Wood. *Nature in Cambridgeshire*, **34**, 3–14.
4 Adamson, R. S. (1912). An ecological study of a Cambridgeshire woodland. *J. Linn. Soc. Bot.*, **40**, 339–87, Pl. 12–17.

bluebell in dryish areas, to dog's-mercury in the best-drained parts. Adamson partly understood their relation to the degree of waterlogging in spring. This wood has an additional source of variation, a large sand-lens (Adamson's 'Loam Area'), giving rise to a patch of acidic sandy soils.

The area of the wood has not changed since before 1268 (though the earthworks embody evidence for earlier increases and decreases). One-third of the wood was given to Merton College, Oxford by Walter de Merton in 1268. The college bought Avenel's manor, and with it the remaining two-thirds of the wood, in 1599, and two years later commissioned a great atlas of maps including the wood and its surroundings (Fig. 25.2). The college sold Gamlingay in the 1950s, and the wood was bought by the Wildlife Trust for Bedfordshire & Cambridgeshire in 1991.

A woodbank surrounds the perimeter, and another bank and ditch marks the pre-1599 boundary between the Mertonage and Avenel's parts.[5] A ring-shaped earthwork, now inside the wood, is probably prehistoric; the original woodbank excludes it, showing that at some time (too early to be recorded in writing) this feature stood outside the wood (Fig. 25.3). The wood was a well-known botanical locality from the 1830s until the 1950s, when attention moved to Buff and Hayley Woods.

In Adamson's time the wood was still coppiced, though not regularly; he did not regard coppicing as the dominating influence on its vegetation. In 1938 Harry Godwin wrote: 'many changes, such as felling and burning, have affected it since Adamson described it', but alas gives no more details. The allusion to fire is one of the very few in English woodland: presumably it was dry bracken on the sand-lens that burnt.

Coppicing probably ceased in the 1930s. From 1949 to 1963 the occupiers of the wood cut down about two-thirds of it and replanted these areas with various conifers, oak, ash, and hybrid poplar in various combinations and usually in alternating rows (Fig. 25.4). Gamlingay Wood therefore offers a rare opportunity to measure what a replanting episode actually did to the trees and ground vegetation.

Adamson's account includes vegetation maps of the trees and shrubs and the 'field layer' (i.e. ground vegetation) in a rectangular area comprising about one-third of the wood (Fig. 25.5a, 25.6a). He recognized the perimeter bank as giving rise to a separate plant community, but was unaware of any difference between the Mertonage and Avenell's parts.

In 1991 I mapped the entire wood, recording the principal trees and ground vegetation at and around 849 points (Tables 25.1, 25.2, Fig. 25.5–6). Each record corresponds (on average) to one-seventh of an acre, or roughly to a square 24 x 24 metres, of vegetation. From these records it should be possible to determine the effects on boulder-clay vegetation of lapse of time, and of the various types of replanting. The sand-lens was wholly replanted, so it is not possible to separate the two factors on the acid soil.

Changes over eighty years: intact areas

The part of the wood mapped by Adamson was recorded in 1991 at a slightly greater density than the rest, giving 468 records. About 30% of Adamson's area (130 records'-worth) remained intact; a small part (8 records) was planted with poplars; the rest was replanted with various conifers combined with oak and ash.

Differences in the intact part of Adamson's area between 1911 and 1991 should record the effects of lapse of time not complicated by replanting. (I include the 'poplarized' area since, as we shall see, the poplars have not much altered the existing ecosystem.)

Adamson's map shows hazel the commonest tree, followed by oak and ash, with somewhat less aspen, throughout the area in question; maple comes well behind and is patchy. In Table 25.4 I try to quantify this and compare it with the 1991 survey. The figures can only be approximate, since Adamson gave no details of his survey method, but there can be little doubt that the changes are real.

Oak declined by more than half. Many standard oaks were felled in the intervening years, and although there was some recruitment this did not make up for the losses. This fits the general pattern of non-replacement of oak in existing woods in the 20th century (p. 296f).

Among underwood trees, ash changed little; its apparent rise in proportion is accounted for by the subtraction of oak. Hazel declined by one-third. Grey squirrels arrived in the area *c.* 1932, since when few or no new hazels have arisen (pp. 209–10), so that hazel stools that die from time to time are no longer being replaced. Maple, aspen, and sallow increased. Elm (mentioned but not mapped by Adamson) is unlikely to have increased much since 1911.[6] A clonal patch of service, long famous as the only one in Cambridgeshire, is still there (Fig. 25.7); there are two other clones (found by Charles Turner and Mark Powell) which could have been overlooked by Adamson.

The most dramatic change in wild trees is the increase of birch (Fig. 25.5b). In Adamson's time this was confined (except for a single tree) to the sand-lens, but it is now the sixth commonest tree in the non-replanted part of the wood. This fits the general increase of birch in the 20th century and its spread on to soils, such as boulder-clay here, formerly thought unsuitable for it (Chapter 19).

5 For the mysterious Hazelcroft see: Turner, C. (1993). A note on Hazelcroft in Gamlingay Wood. *Nature in Cambridgeshire* **35**, 77–8.
6 Elm is recorded in Mertonage Wood in 1368, presumably one of the two clones still extant.

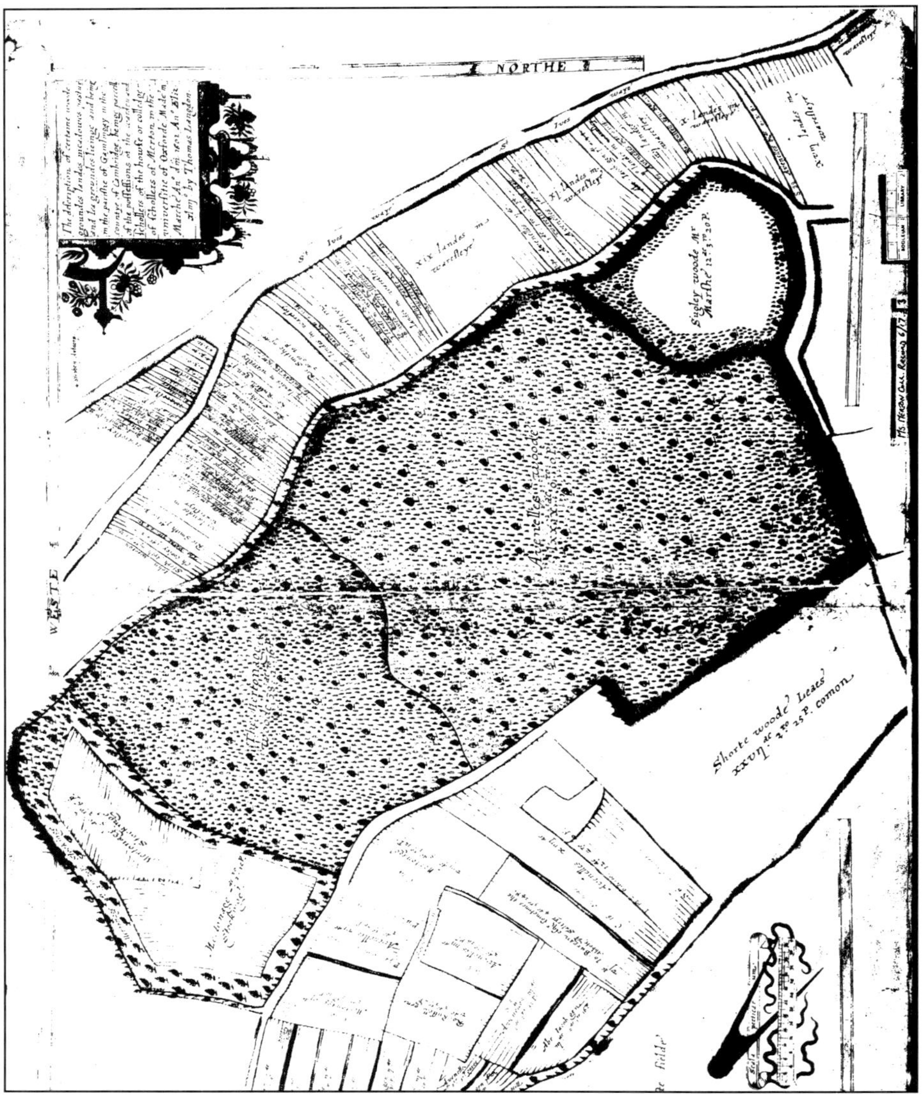

Fig. 25.2 Gamlingay Wood in 1601. From a map made by Merton College, Oxford, and published by kind permission of the Warden & Scholars [Merton College Record 6/17]. Note:
(a) surrounding strip-cultivation of arable land – each strip is labelled with the name of its owner;
(b) the 'Mertonage Stocking' field at the S.W., grubbed out from the wood in the 12th century, surrounded with a hedge in the 14th (p. 157), and by 1601 partly overgrown by the expansion of the hedge;
(c) the sinuous boundary, made in the 12th century to divide the wood into two ownerships later called Mertonage (to the west) and Avenell's, and made obsolete in 1599 by re-amalgamation of the ownerships.

Among herbaceous plants, Adamson mapped nearly all the present non-replanted area as dominated by meadowsweet, with *Deschampsia caespitosa* co-dominant with it over about 70% of the area (Fig. 25.6a). This corresponds to Zone 2. Oxlip, characteristic of that zone, was 'abundant' in Adamson's time, especially in newly-coppiced areas, but not mapped by him. Eighty years on, *Deschampsia* was almost unaltered. Meadowsweet had much declined, being present at only 25 of the 138 points in the intact part of Adamson's area in 1991 (Fig. 25.6b). This is most unexpected: the plant is still abundant in Zone 2 in the other woods, and there is no obvious reason for Gamlingay being different. Oxlip is now only locally abundant.

In Adamson's time dog's-mercury was 'confined to small areas of the wood, all at or near the edges', especially on the woodbank. He mapped it only in a part later to be replanted. Bluebell, which he did not map, was mainly associated with mercury. There has been a modest increase of both, especially along the Mertonage-Avenell's woodbank, where Adamson did not notice them.

The rushes mapped locally by Adamson were probably temporary relics of coppicing.

Changes in replanted areas

Replanting was of five kinds, in descending order of area: oak + conifers; oak + ash + conifers; conifers; poplars; poplars + conifers (Fig. 25.4). The sand-lens was planted with conifers and patches of oak. The conifers were various mixtures of Scots and Corsican Pine, 'Norway' Spruce, Douglas Fir, and larch. The poplars are a then-fashionable hybrid black poplar, probably of American origin.

The existing trees were felled but probably not poisoned. Whatever attempts were made to exterminate them were given up after a few years. Thinning was neglected. Forty years on, the plantation has been part-successful in that many of the planted trees are still

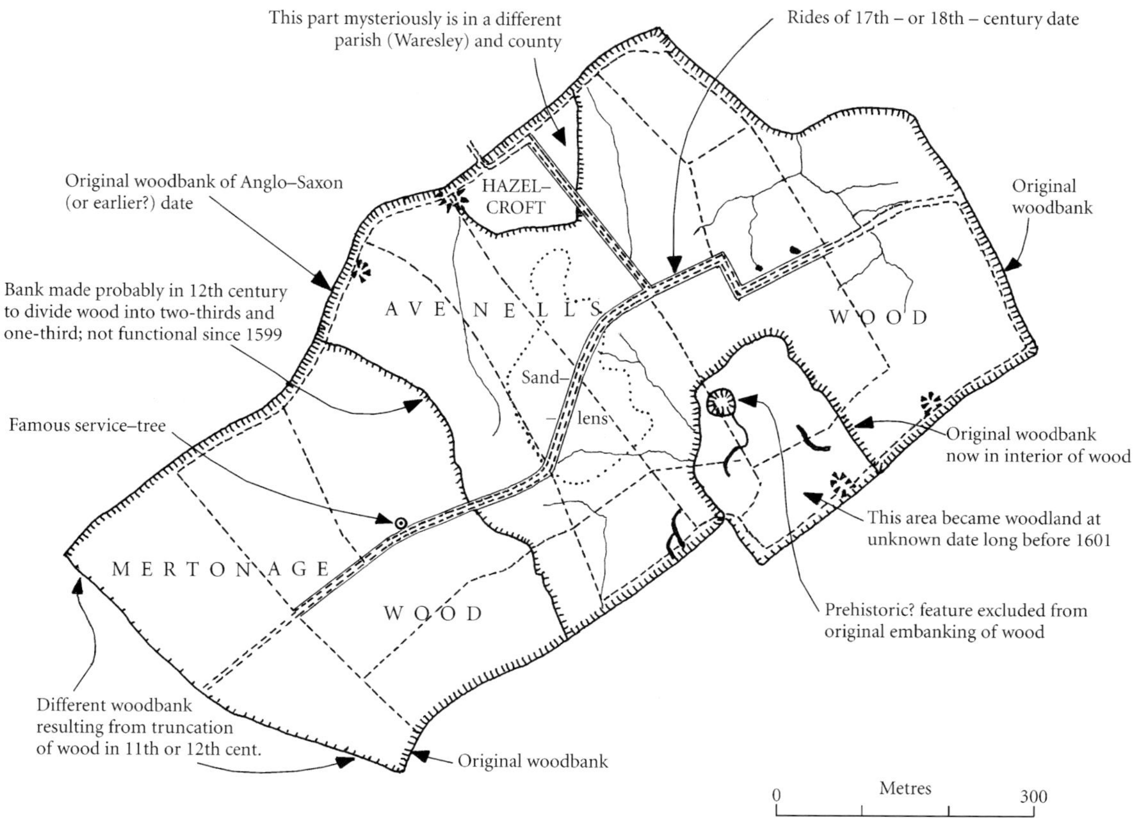

Fig. 25.3 Earthworks and topography of Gamlingay Wood, mapped by the author in 1991.

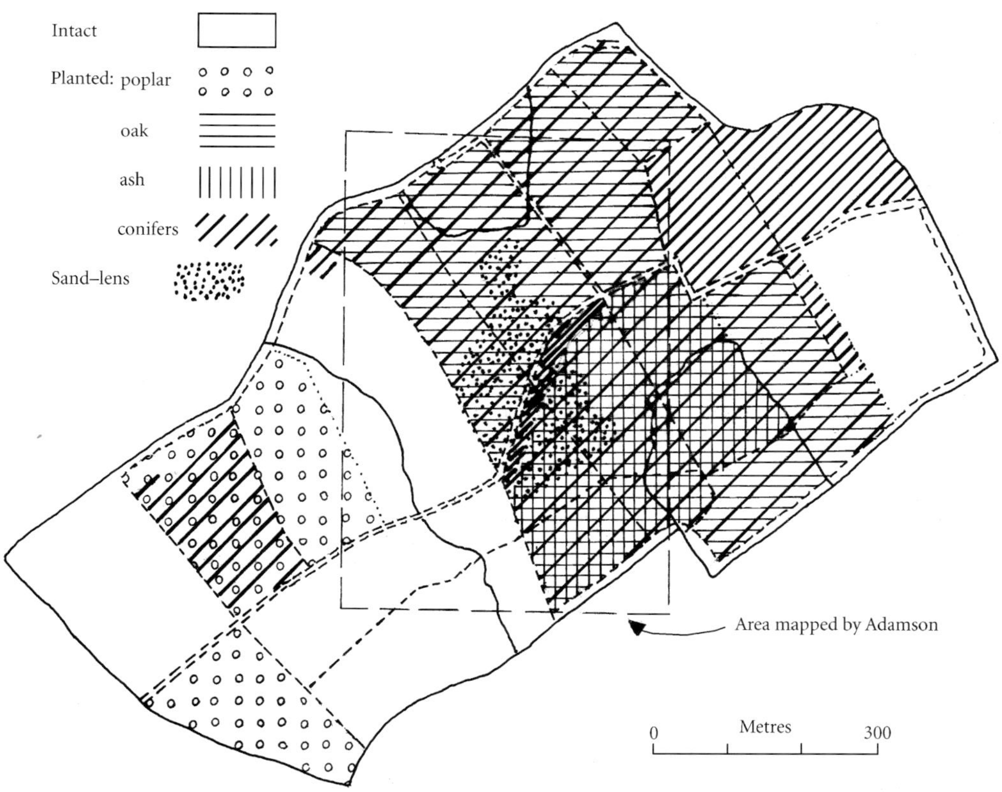

Fig. 25.4 Gamlingay Wood, 1991, showing intact and planted areas.

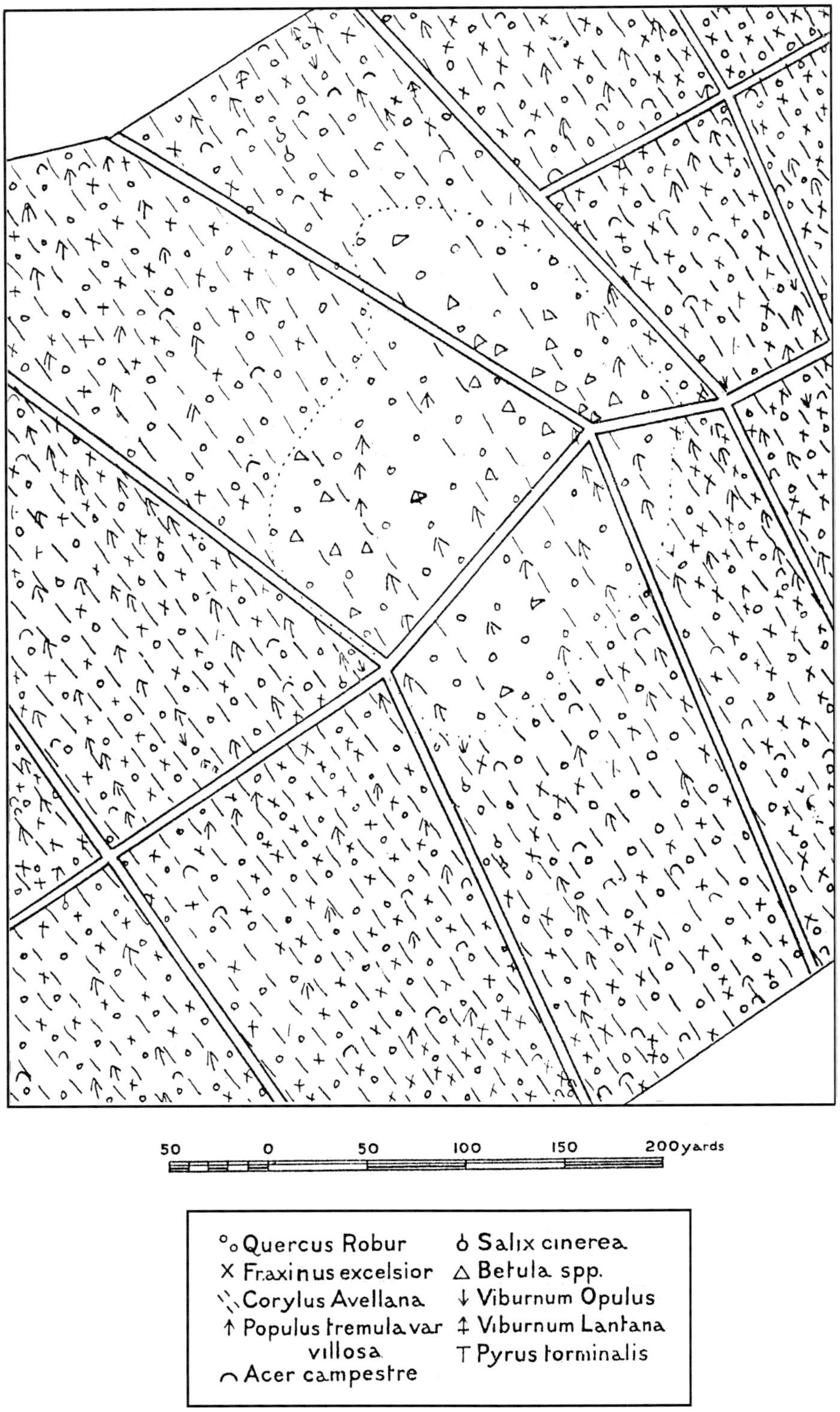

Fig. 25.5 **(a)** Adamson's map of trees of Gamlingay Wood in 1911 (by kind permission of the Linnean Society of London). **(b)** Birch in Gamlingay Wood, 1911 and 1991, and elm (hatched), 1991. In this and similar figures the 1911 information covers only the central rectangle of the wood, and is derived from Adamson's map, corrected to fit the true topgraphy. The dotted outline represents the sand-lens or 'loam area', which differs slightly in Adamson's and Rackham's estimations. The dots for 1991 are intended to give a general impression of the density of trees; they do not represent individual trees, nor do they correspond numerically to Adamson's symbols.
(c) Aspen in Gamlingay Wood, 1911 and 1991, on the same basis as birch.

Table 25.3 Mean abundance of some dominant herbs under various treatments in the whole of Gamlingay Wood, 1991
Recorded on a scale ranging from 0 (absent) to 6 (pure stand).

	Intact	Planted poplars	Planted poplars + conifers	Planted oak + ash + conifers	Planted oak + conifers	Planted conifers	Sand-lens (planted oak + conifers)	Whole wood
No. of points	258	59	24	156	222	64	66	849
Mean abundance of:								
Oxlip	0.81	0.66	0.42	0.18	0.41	0.53	0.09	0.49
Meadow-sweet	0.42	0.03	0	0.06	0.05	0.26	0	0.18
Desch-ampsia	1.89	1.71	0.17	1.14	0.83	0.28	1.14	1.24
Bluebell	1.06	0.93	0.71	1.16	1.27	1.34	1.39	1.16
Mercury	1.22	1.73	2.54	1.82	2.06	1.52	0.13	1.56
Bracken	0	0	0	0	0	0	1.25	0.10

Table 25.4 Relative abundance of trees in the part of Gamlingay Wood mapped by Adamson in 1911 and re-surveyed in 1991, under four treatments applied in the 1950s.

	Intact (and planted poplar)			Planted oak + ash + conifers			Planted oak + conifers (and conifers only)			Sand-lens (planted oak + conifers)		
	138 points			108 points			152 points			66 points		
	1911	1991	change	1911	1991	change	1911	1991	change	1911	1991	change
Oak	25.4	11.7	– –	25.6	17.9	insig.	28.7	13.8	–	40.0	13.3	– – –
Ash	21.9	26.2	insig.	23.3	13.2	–	17.7	10.2	–	–	6.7	+++
Hazel	38.7	24.8	–	37.5	15.7	– –	40.2	16.5	– –	26.4	9.3	– – –
Maple	3.9	7.5	+	6.1	1.6	– –	5.1	2.1	– –	–	0.1	insig.
Aspen	9.0	17.7	++	6.1	0.8	– – –	6.7	1.8	– – –	15.7	0.8	– – –
Sallow	0.4	1.7	++	0.8	3.6	+++	0.4	0.8	+	–	1.9	++
Elm	–	3.9	insig.	–	0.5	insig.	–	0.9	insig.	–	–	
Birch	–	5.9	++	–	16.1	+++	–	3.8	++	17.9	7.4	– –

Table 25.5 Herbaceous plants in the part of Gamlingay Wood mapped by Adamson in 1911 and re-surveyed in 1991, under four treatments applied in the 1950s.
Numbers for 1911 indicate the percentage area (where available) assigned to the plant by Adamson. Pairs of numbers for 1991 indicate the percentage of points where the plant was (i) present, (ii) abundant.

	Intact (and planted poplar)			Planted oak + ash + conifers			Planted oak + conifers (and conifers only)			Sand-lens (planted oak + conifers)		
	138 points			108 points			152 points			66 points		
	1911	1991	change	1911	1991	change	1911	1991	change	1911	1991	change
Oxlip	abund.	25/12	– –	abund.	15/1	– – –	abund.	12/6	– – –	0	5/0	insig.
Meadow-sweet	100	19/14	– – –	90	2/12	– – –	*c.* 70	3/1	– – –	0	0	0
Desch-ampsia	*c.* 70	69/63	insig.	*c.* 65	29/27	– –	*c.* 22	22/22	0	occ.	29/27	doubtful
Bluebell	rare	18/14	+	*c.* 5	36/30	++	rare	37/27	+++	0	39/27	+++
Straw-berry	freq.	5/2	–	3	3/0	insig.	*c.* 22	3/2	– –	marg.	2/1	insig.
Mercury	0	13/12	++	7	38/30	+++	rare	40/35	+++	0	5/2	insig.
Holcus	0	2/3	insig.	0	2/0	insig.	0	1/1	insig.	35	15/14	– –
Bracken	0	0	0	0	0	0	0	0	++	70	44/24	– –

reaching the ground. Compared with deciduous trees, conifers reduce the effective winter rainfall and increase the effective drainage; this works in favour of bluebell and mercury and against oxlip and meadowsweet. This confirms the widely-held belief that coniferization 'lowers the water-table', although (strictly speaking) the clay subsoils here do not have an identifiable water-table.

On and around the (replanted) sand-lens, bracken was still widespread, though usually sparse because of dense shade. *Holcus mollis*, an important grass in 1911, was insignificant by 1991.

The ground vegetation in planted parts of the wood often involved nettle, ground-ivy, archangel, and brambles. These increased since Adamson's time, being still uncommon in the unplanted parts. I suspect that planted trees, especially pines, acidify the soil; they also accelerate the general increase in fertility which affects woods surrounded by arable land.

Changes in the last eleven years

After many centuries of stable management, Gamlingay Wood got caught by a twist in human values which favoured replanting (Chapter 33). Its state in 1991, when it became a nature reserve, was a monument to the defeat of those values. Coppicing was resumed almost at once, and has been extended over about one-third of the then 'intact' area, plus a small part of the 'poplarized' area. More slowly, conifers have been removed from some replanted areas, and in other replanted areas have largely died out. Such areas do not quite revert to native woodland: oak (mostly planted with the conifers) survives and is dominant, as it would not have been in the historic wood.

This was the situation when I re-surveyed the whole wood in 2002. The survey was limited to ground vegetation, there being little change in trees except those noted. (Elms changed little between 1991 and 2002.)

Table 25.6 is based on 562 survey points. It being impracticable to re-locate all the points surveyed in 1991, I have compared each point with the one or two points nearest to it in the earlier survey. To avoid having too many treatments based on small amounts of data, I have aggregated some of the treatments.

Oxlip has further declined throughout the wood and under all treatments. The distribution is much as it was in 1991, but with less than half the number of plants. Former areas of high density (more than 1 plant per square metre) are still concentrations of oxlip, but at a much lower density. The scattered plants which survived replanting are now more thinly scattered, even where the conifers have failed or been removed. Coppicing has not reversed the decline.

Meadowsweet has further declined, despite coppicing and deconiferization, and is now largely confined to rides. *Deschampsia*, too, has mostly declined further, except where it has benefited from deconiferization.

Bluebell has further increased under all treatments except in the sand-lens. The bluebell area has both extended and become more continuous.

Mercury has decreased, losing some of the ground that it gained before 1991. There has been a general retreat towards the edges of the wood (the Adamson state) and a greater decline under some treatments, especially coppicing and conifers (with or without poplar).

Bracken, which is very dependent on reduced shade, has increased in deconiferized parts of the sand-lens. *Holcus mollis* has returned to abundance in fringe parts of the sand-lens where conifers have died out.

Conclusions

In ninety years the intact parts of Gamlingay Wood, although still recognizable from Adamson's description, show some changes that fit a general pattern, such as decline of natural oak, decline of hazel, and increase of birch. Others – decline of oxlip, increase of bluebell, increase followed by decline of mercury – are not so easily explained. Loss of meadowsweet is a peculiarity of this wood.

The replanting was of near-average intensity, neither perfunctory nor persevering. It encountered the usual difficulties which anyone experiences who tries to plant trees where there are trees already. The planted trees mostly stayed alive, but probably have not fulfilled the ambitions of the people who planted them. The 'hard facts of economics,' which inspired the Forestry Commission and its imitators in the 1950s, were defeated by changing economics and the harder facts of ecology. Many of the original trees stayed alive, and others have sprung up spontaneously.

Planting has favoured birch and sallow, and disfavoured hazel, maple, and especially aspen. Gamlingay is a good instance of the principle that whatever trees you plant you will get birch.

In 1911 birch was confined to the sand-lens, and ash to the boulder-clay parts of the wood. These distinctions have broken down: each tree has invaded the other's territory, previously thought unsuitable for it.

As far as I know this is the first attempt to describe the detailed effects of a replanting. In the first 40–50 years planting was bad for oxlip and good for bluebell and dog's-mercury, as well as creating its own plant communities of relatively fertile and well-drained soil. It bore out the claim that replanting a wood damages its individuality and promotes commonplace plant communities at the expense of rare ones. The apparent increase of drainage is a previously little-known way for this to happen.

However, the survival of even a fraction of the original wood is due to this being, in forestry terms, an unsuccessful replanting. Had it been successful, in the sense of producing a pure stand of oak or pine

Table 25.6 Some herbaceous plants in Gamlingay Wood, mapped in 1991 and re-surveyed in 2002.
Recorded on a scale ranging from 0 (absent) to 6 (pure stand). The figures are the mean value per species and treatment.

	Intact (and planted poplar)			Coppiced			Planted: Oak + failed conifers			Deconiferized leaving planted oak		
	158 points			66 points			89 points			49 points		
	1991	2002	change	1991	2002	change	1991	2002	change	1991	2002	change
Oxlip	0.62	0.42	– –	1.02	0.61	– –	0.28	0.13	– – –	0.56	0.27	– – –
Deschampsia	1.66	1.63	insig.	1.93	1.00	– –	0.51	0.60	insig.	0.15	1.33	+++++
Bluebell	0.94	2.02	++++	1.54	1.93	+	1.18	2.36	+++	1.74	2.10	+
Mercury	1.75	1.20	– –	1.16	0.23	– – – –	2.06	1.67	–	2.31	1.80	–
Bracken	0	0	0	0	0	0	0	0	0	0	0	0

	Planted: Oak + conifers and Oak + ash + conifers			Planted: Conifers and Poplar + conifers			Sand-lens deconiferized and Failed conifers			Sand-lens planted oak + conifers		
	113 points			36 points			18 points			33 points		
	1991	2002	change	1991	2002	change	1991	2002	change	1991	2002	change
Oxlip	0.26	0.16	– –	0.53	0.28	– –	0	0		0	0	
Deschampsia	1.28	0.54	– – –	0.11	0.69	+++++	0.61	0.33	– –	1.06	0.27	– – – –
Bluebell	1.04	1.77	++	1.50	2.11	+	2.08	2.28	(+)	1.09	0.48	– – –
Mercury	1.89	1.77	insig.	1.56	0.50	– – – –	0	0.06	insig.	0	0	
Bracken	0	0		0	0		0.94	1.61	++	1.32	0.82	– –

yielding a reasonable timber crop, little of the ground vegetation, let alone the native trees, would have remained – as happened, for example, at Borley Wood in Linton, S.E. Cambridgeshire.

Here the decline of oxlip is not, for the most part, due to replacement by something else. In the wetter parts of the wood, where oxlip, meadowsweet, and *Deschampsia* were abundant in 1911, all three have gone, often to be replaced by a carpet of mosses (especially *Thuidium tamariscinum* and *Eurhynchium swartzii*). *Arum maculatum* and *Carex sylvatica* have become the characteristic flowering-plants of Zone 2, but seldom cover more than 5% of the ground. An important factor here may be the increase of deer. In 1991 the wood was still almost free, but since then muntjac have become abundant. In 2002 Gamlingay Wood has a distinctly deer-bitten appearance, being (for example) full of small, repeatedly browsed ashes, though not yet to the extent of Hayley Wood.

Recent changes in bluebell and dog's-mercury may have to do with unusual weather since 1991. At first, lack of wet springs allowed bluebell to spread into what had been Zone 2 areas and mercury into Zone 4. Then the very wet spring of 2000 and the phenomenal wetness of 2001 were a greater setback to mercury than to bluebell. Mercury, however, survives as low-density areas of stunted stems, as well as on earthworks, and will easily return when the weather favours it.

Ground Vegetation Zones over Fifty Years: Hayley Wood and Buff Wood compared with other woods

In 1948 the young botanist B. A. Abeywickrama made detailed maps and descriptions of the ground vegetation of Hayley Wood and Buff Wood under the direction of Alex Watt, the great Cambridge plant ecologist.[7] He never returned – he had a distinguished career in Colombo University – but the present writer has repeated his mapping from 1966 to 2002.

The object of the following comparison is to ask whether the vegetation zones, determined by seasonal waterlogging, have changed since Abeywickrama's time.

Hayley Wood

The middle and north of the wood are Zone 2 (oxlip, meadowsweet, *Deschampsia caespitosa*). Towards the east, south, and west there succeed zones 3 (oxlip-bluebell), 4 (bluebell), 5 (bluebell-mercury), and 6 (mercury)

7 Abeywickrama, B. A. (1949). *A study of the variations in the field layer vegetation of two Cambridgeshire woods*. Ph.D. thesis, Cambridge.

(Fig. 25.8). The 1966 state was very similar to 1948. Since then the communities have changed in composition: oxlip in particular has become uncommon except where protected from deer. But there has been no general shift, and even some details are unaltered. Strips of bluebell, corresponding to faint, probably prehistoric, earthworks, still cross the north and east quarters of the wood.

There are several minor changes. In the south and west of the wood, dog's-mercury has retreated, and bluebell or *Deschampsia* have advanced (Fig. 25.9). The vegetation zones are less sharply-defined than they were 36 years ago; the once dense stands of bluebell and mercury are now gappy, with patches of *Deschampsia*. A possible cause is the general lack of wet winters in the 1990s allowing bluebell and mercury to spread into areas which had been too wet for them, followed by setbacks in the two very wet seasons 2001–2.

The south-east of the wood tells a different story. What had been a regular succession of bluebell and mercury zones is now largely occupied by an impoverished form of Zone 2, often reduced to patches of *Deschampsia*. Relicts of bluebell and mercury sometimes remain as rings of stems round the bases of trees, which tend to be slightly raised and better drained than the surroundings (Fig. 25.10). This phenomenon, noted also elsewhere in Hayley and other woods, points to increased waterlogging as the cause. The changes appear to be gradual; a survey in 1974 shows an intermediate state. South-eastern Hayley Wood has two peculiar factors. A large and a small clone of elm in 1975–6 died without regeneration, and for several years this part of the wood became wetter. Deer activity has greatly increased, as fallow deer have been excluded by fences from other parts of the wood. Although they do not eat much bluebell or mercury, their trampling may have been so severe as to affect the hydrology through soil compaction.

Buff Wood

This is a smaller and much more complex wood (Fig. 16.8), full of banks and ditches and with two moats and four areas of ridge-and-furrow (Fig. 31.7) resulting from medieval cultivation when the wood was smaller. With two small exceptions it has all been woodland since *c.* 1700 and probably since the late middle ages.

Abeywickrama's maps reveals a situation rather like Hayley Wood, with a small area of oxlip-meadowsweet (Zone 2) in the worst-drained part of the plateau. Primrose was abundant and marked an extensive area corresponding to Hayley Zone 3 (Fig. 25.22). Bluebell and mercury were dominant in the comparatively well-drained south of the wood, and also along the earthworks and on ridges of the ridge-and-furrow.

The fate of oxlip and primrose will be followed later. Bluebell somewhat increased down to 1981, and has since very slightly retreated (Fig. 25.11). Mercury has increased, especially in the SW of the wood, but has

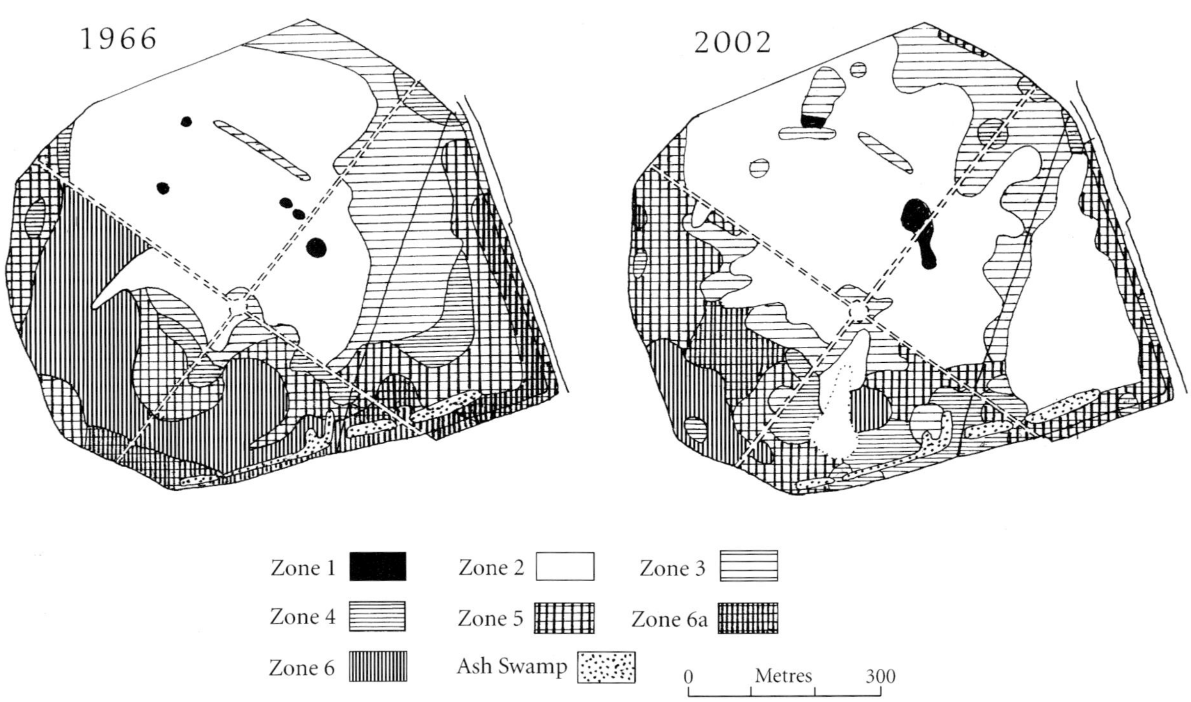

Fig. 25.8 Vegetation zones of Hayley Wood in 1966 (cf Fig. 4.2) and 2002. The dotted outline in the south quarter is the grassy glade made in 1968.

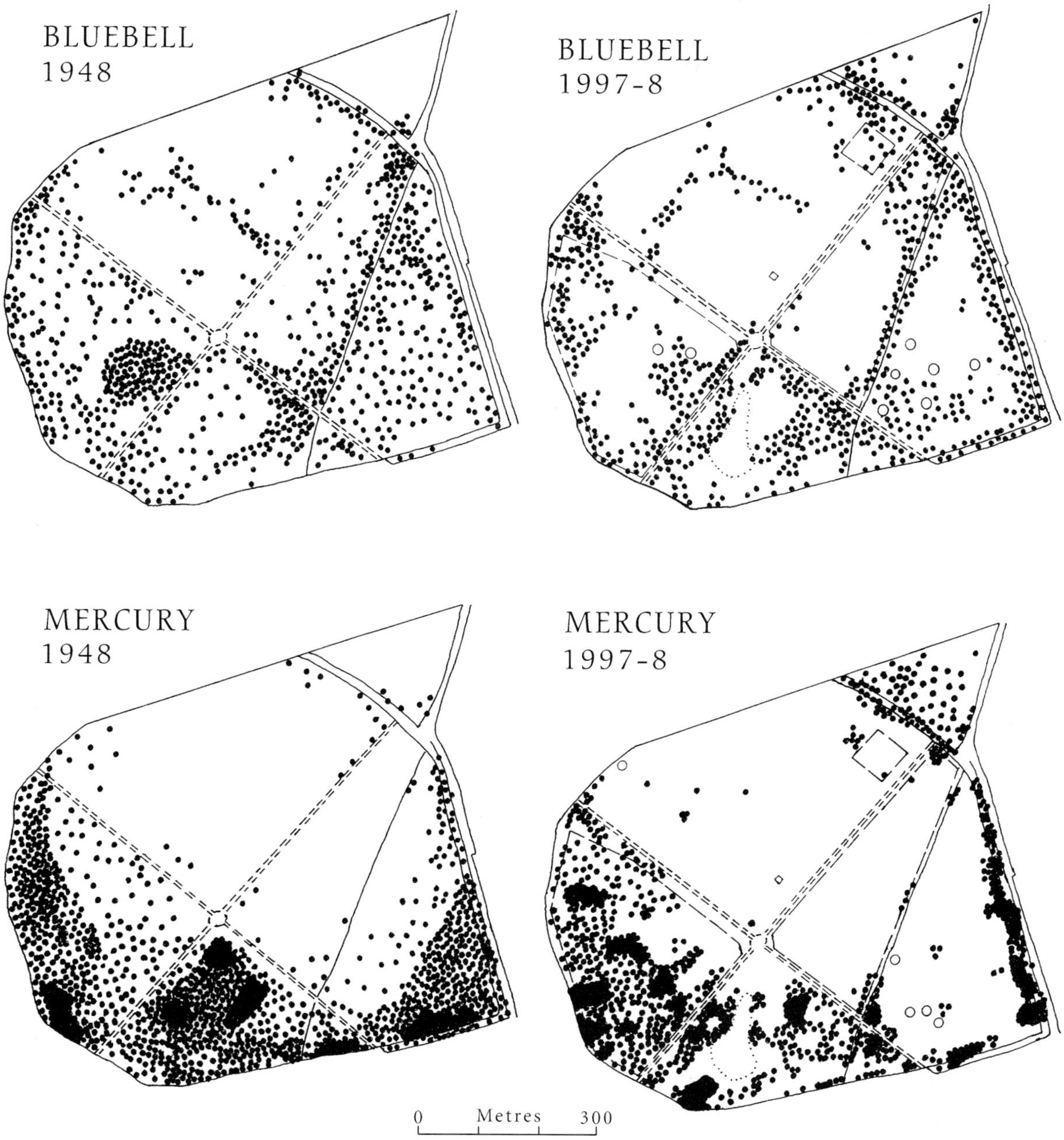

Fig. 25.9 Distribution of bluebell and dog's-mercury in Hayley Wood, 1948 (after Abeywickrama) and 1997–8. Broken lines indicate fences. Circles indicate bluebell or mercury confined to bases of trees (which was commoner in 2002).

retreated or become sparser elsewhere. The south-western increase has been gradual, but the other changes have been more marked in the last twenty years.

Other woods

Results for Hayley and Buff Woods can be compared with maps of the zones of Gamlingay Wood (already mentioned). I have gathered data at various dates for Knapwell Wood (a miniature of Hayley, Fig. 25.20) and Hardwick Wood. These are summarized in Table 25.7.

Conclusions

The five woods are curiously inconsistent. Mercury has spread in Knapwell Wood much more than in Hayley. In Hayley much of the former dense mercury stand has been invaded by bluebell; but the dense bluebell stands have become less dense.

In general the drier zones (4, 5, 6) have increased at the expense of the wetter zones (2 and 3) most strongly in Gamlingay (coniferized), to a lesser extent in Knapwell, Hardwick, Buff and and Gamlingay (intact),

Fig.25.10 Rings of bluebell round the bases of trees, a sign of the retreat of bluebell from areas where it was once more continuous. Hayley Wood. May 1997

and least in Hayley Wood apart from the south-east. In the south-east of Hayley the reverse has happened.

The strong discrepancy within Gamlingay Wood is clearly an effect of replanting, mainly via reduced waterlogging.

Without replanting, increase of the drier zones could be due to increased drainage on the surrounding farmland. It is true that some of the boundary ditches of woods have been deepened in the relevant period, but on impermeable soils this should not much affect the interior of the wood. The effect, it will be noted, is greater in small or narrow woods (Knapwell, Hardwick) and least in big compact woods (Gamlingay (intact), Hayley).

A more likely cause is a decline in spring rainfall, leading to rarer waterlogging. I have kept observations of flooding in Hayley Wood since 1964. Up to 2000, the season with the greatest degree of flooding was 1983, followed by 1964, 1969, and 1975, then by 1970, 1978, 1988, and 1994, and with a modest degree of flooding in 1972, 1979, and 1989. Out of 11 flood seasons in 37 years, there was only one in the 1990s. However, lest this be taken as a general trend, 2001 produced an even greater (though brief) flooding than 1983, and 2002 was also a wet spring. The balance, however, has not yet been restored: mercury is set back by flooding, but it takes more than two wet seasons to kill an established clone.

Some of the apparent discrepancies may have to do with year-to-year fluctuations, with comparing (let us say) bluebell in a wood in a year of temporary setback with its performance in another wood in a year of temporary advance. The year-to-year recording of plots (pp. 403, 417ff) shows that such changes may be great enough to have a measurable effect. The results might have been more consistent had it been possible to record all the woods in the same years.

Fifty Years of Photographs of Individual Trees: Madingley Wood

In 1950 David Coombe was devising methods to record the canopy of trees and to measure the light transmitted by them. In a first attempt he pointed a quarter-plate camera in 40 different directions, from the ground to directly overhead, and stuck the resulting prints together to form an approximately hemispherical mosaic image. In 1951 he made use of a camera with a fish-eye lens, invented by Robin Hill the biochemist, to take an entire hemisphere at once. The original purpose of these images was to measure shade, as described on pp. 77ff, but they have since become historical documents for the development of woodland. They were to be repeated at intervals by Coombe and his associates and students, Clifford Evans, Margaret Anderson, Paul Freeman, Gerald Stanhill, Jonathan Hodge, and myself. From this mass of data, much of it unpublished, I pick out for comparison with Coombe's originals the repetition in 1976, in which I took part (Fig. 25.12), and the set which Freeman and I took in 2001, fifty years after the original almost to the day. We have used later models of fish-eye lens, mounted in 35-mm film cameras, which are easier to use than the original but take less detailed pictures and have a slightly different projection.

The pictures were taken at four sites in Madingley Wood (Fig. 25.13), marked in later years by permanent 'cradles' constructed to receive the camera and to help

Table 25.7 Approximate areas of vegetation zones in five West Cambridgeshire woods at different dates. Percentage of the area of each wood, or at Gamlingay of the area mapped by Adamson.

		Gamlingay intact + poplarized	Gamlingay coniferized (except sand-lens)	Hayley	Buff	Hardwick	Knapwell
Zone 1	1911	1	0.3	—	—	—	—
	1948	—	—	?0.5	0.3	—	—
	1966–9	?	—	0.5	0.3	0	0
	1973–4	—	—	0.5	—	—	—
	1981	—	—	—	0.3	—	—
	1991–8	3	0	0.6	0.3	0	0
	2002	3	0	0.6	0.4	0	—
Zone 2	1911	90	80	—	—	—	—
	1948	—	—	36	9	—	—
	1966–9	43	—	37	11	2	17
	1973–4	—	—	38	—	—	—
	1981	—	—	—	15	—	—
	1991–8	68	17	42	12	3	14
	2002	62	13	48	12	5	—
Zone 3	1911	9	16	—	—	—	—
	1948	—	—	12	44	—	—
	1966–9	38	—	16	21	20	20
	1973–4	—	—	15	—	—	—
	1981	—	—	—	17	—	—
	1991–8	14	14	13	19	9	3
	2002	10	14	16	19	10	—
Zone 4	1911	0	?2	—	—	—	—
	1948	—	—	13	2	—	—
	1966–9	18	—	5	11	27	6
	1973–4	—	—	10	—	—	—
	1981	—	—	—	16	—	—
	1991–8	12	26	16	14	24	3
	2002	20	34	7	14	24	—
Zone 5	1911	0	2	—	—	—	—
	1948	—	—	24	18	—	—
	1966–9	1	—	16	40	35	21
	1973–4	—	—	17	—	—	—
	1981	—	—	—	32	—	—
	1991–9	1	20	18	35	39	16
	2002	1	18	17	15	39	—
Zone 6a and 6	1911	0	0	—	—	—	—
	1948	—	—	15	26	—	—
	1966–9	1	—	25	12	9	35
	1973–4	—	—	20	—	—	—
	1981	—	—	—	14	—	—
	1991–9	3	23	10	15	24	63
	2002	3	20	8	15	22	—

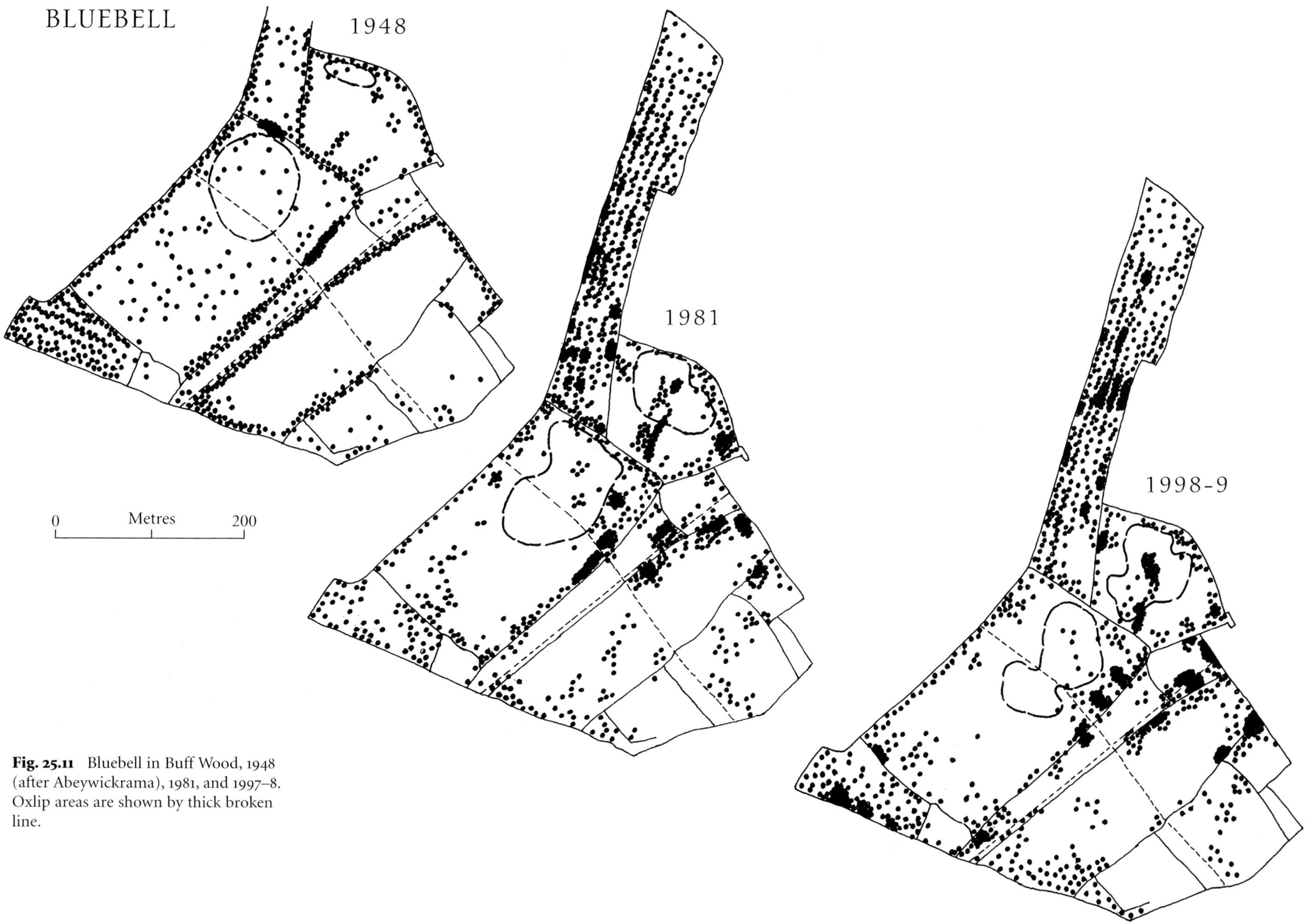

Fig. 25.11 Bluebell in Buff Wood, 1948 (after Abeywickrama), 1981, and 1997–8. Oxlip areas are shown by thick broken line.

with levelling and orientation.[8] The first three are in a part of the wood dominated by the peculiar Madingley Wood elm, the largest elm clone in the wood (thought to have begun from a single elm in the seventeenth century) and the one least affected by Elm Disease. This area is a neglected coppice. It was felled down to the late nineteenth century – there is a sale advertisement for underwood in 1882 – but was of at least 50 years' growth when Coombe began.[9] Some of the standard trees are oaks and some elms; it is still possible to distinguish the original timber elms from suckers that grew up since the last coppicing.

The 'Photosite', scene of the original set of shots in 1950, was surrounded by elms and one standard oak, but looked beyond the elms to an area now dominated by ash. The 'Oak Site', beginning in 1951, corresponded originally to a small canopy gap; it is on the edge of the elm clone and sees several oaks, ashes, and maples. The 'Hazel Site', also beginning in 1951, was densely shaded by a hazel under the elms. The 'Large Clearing', beginning in 1957, is well outside the elm area; the trees included large ashes and maples as well as oaks, and a few spruces, relics of a planting in the 1870s.

The three sites in the elm area in Madingley Wood have been remarkably stable, especially the Oak Site (Fig. 25.14). The elms have grown considerably taller, filling in the canopy gap and encroaching on the oaks. The oak after which the site is named was declining in 1951, with many dead lower branches. It died in the 1980s, and has lost its younger boughs, but in other respects it is still little changed: boughs which were long-dead in 1951 are still there 50 years later. Other oaks are almost unaltered apart from a general increase in height.

The Hazel Site, too, is almost unaltered. A remarkable detail is the hazel itself, suppressed and seemingly declining in 1951, and little altered in 2001; even some individual hazel stems are still there.

The Photosite shows rather more change, recorded not only in the hemispherical photographs but also in Coombe's original forty shots of 1950, which I repeated in 2001. Some elms have disappeared (Fig. 25.15). Two pollard-like elms in 1950, which possibly had lost their tops to Elm Disease in *c.* 1940, vanished, one between 1958 and 1976, the other after 1977. The Great Storm of 1987 brought down other elms, creating canopy gaps which subsequent growth has not yet filled. Suppressed elms can be extraordinarily stable. Coombe photographed a small elm with a curious twisted trunk in 1950 and 1987; it had hardly changed at all. Soon after, a big elm fell on it. By 2001 the squashed elm had recovered and was filling the gap left by its neighbour, but still retains the twist (Fig. 25.16).

A big oak next the site, declining in 1950, has grown a new and taller canopy, but still retains most of the dead branches of 1950 (Fig. 25.17) and others that have died since. Another oak has fared less well from competition, as well as losing a big bough *c.* 1980. Hazels, again, have been remarkably stable over 50 years. Maples, however, can die and rot away suddenly; one suppressed maple was alive in 1983, but by 1986 Coombe could not find a vestige of it. Such ashes as can be seen from the site have grown much bigger.

Most of the big trees have noticeably increased in thickness, but not the oaks. The Photosite oak had a girth at breast height of 2.159 m in 1957 and 2.347 m in 2002. Its increment from 1957 to 1976 was equivalent to a mean annual ring-width of 0.67 mm; from 1976 to 1985, following the great drought, the mean ring-width fell to only 0.35 mm; from 1985 to 1995, after the fall of two neighbouring elms but despite further droughts, it rose to 0.85 mm; it continued at 0.82 mm until 2002.

The Large Clearing, in contrast, has an unstable history. Only here have any new trees arisen. Six conifers, relics of a planting in 1873, were visible in 1957. Twenty years later, only two remained, and these have died since (though their fallen remains are still there). Two great ashes had fallen by 1977, in each case splitting at a narrow fork and falling one half at a time (p. 443). Two oaks have been felled, but others remain, even to dead branches. An oak that was dead in the top in 1957 has since grown a new, higher crown. To the west the canopy has been reduced by coppicing in 1994. Despite these subtractions of trees, the growth of surrounding ashes and maples has made the canopy gap smaller than in 1957. It was becoming smaller still due to the fast growth of a new ash tree, which had got away by 1977 and was a sizeable tree by 2001, when it was removed between two photographs.

Sny – an intercontinental question

By one of those strokes of fortune which happen in historical ecology, Madingley Wood illustrates a rare and curious problem. In the elm clone most of the trees are neither straight nor crooked but grow in a regular curve, leaning from the base and bending over in a great arc. The elms do not lean in any one direction; some of the ashes growing with them are sny too.

This gives the wood an American appearance. In the eastern United States 'sny' trees (as they are called[10]) are too commonplace to call for an explanation; most

8 Evans, G. C., Freeman, P. and Rackham, O. (1975) 'Developments in hemispherical photography' *Light as an Ecological Factor II*, ed. G. C. Evans, R. Bainbridge, O. Rackham, Blackwell Scientific Publications, Oxford 549–57.

9 Coombe, D. E., and Rackham, O. (1996). Madingley Wood. *Nature in Cambridgeshire*, **38**, 27–54.

10 The word is probably derived from Old Norse *snúa* 'to turn'; it is used of the curves of ships' ribs and of certain types of human nose – *Oxford English Dictionary*.

Fig. 25.12 The author (supine) re-finding one of the sites of hemispherical photographs in Madingley Wood, 1976. Photo. D. E. Coombe.

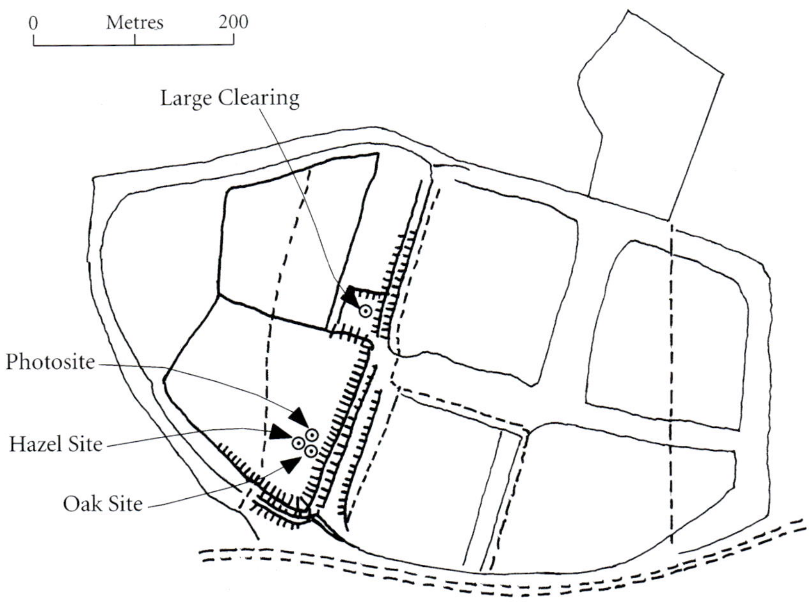

Fig. 25.13 The sites in Madingley Wood. Topographical details are given in full only near the sites.

Fig. 25.14 Successive hemispherical photographs at four sites in Madingley Wood.

O: oak. Ø: dead oak. E: elm (East Anglian). A: ash. M: maple. h: hazel. th: hawthorn. S: spruce. Large, medium, and small letters indicate standard, canopy (ex-underwood), and sub-canopy trees; the size of these on the print depends, of course, on how near they are to the camera. Trees are marked in earlier photos only if they disappear or become unrecognizable in later photos.

North is at the top; east (contrary to intuition) to the left. North and south markers are visible on some photos. The black disk on a cane that appears in some photographs marks the position of the sun.

(see a–d on following pages)

botanists assume that this is how trees grow. If pressed for an explanation, they sometimes mention the load of ice during a glazed frost (p. 495). Sny trees are also to be found in Japan.

Madingley Wood is one of fewer than a dozen areas of sny trees known to me in all Europe (I have recently found another on Athos, the Holy Mountain in Greece).

Comparing successive photographs, the oaks remain rigid (apart from the tendency of branches, living and dead, to sag over the years) but the elms move to a remarkable degree (Fig. 25.18). The elms were already sny in 1950, but the degree of sny has gradually increased. Sny cannot be solely due to a one-off event like an ice-storm. Since it involves ashes as well as elms

PHOTOSITE

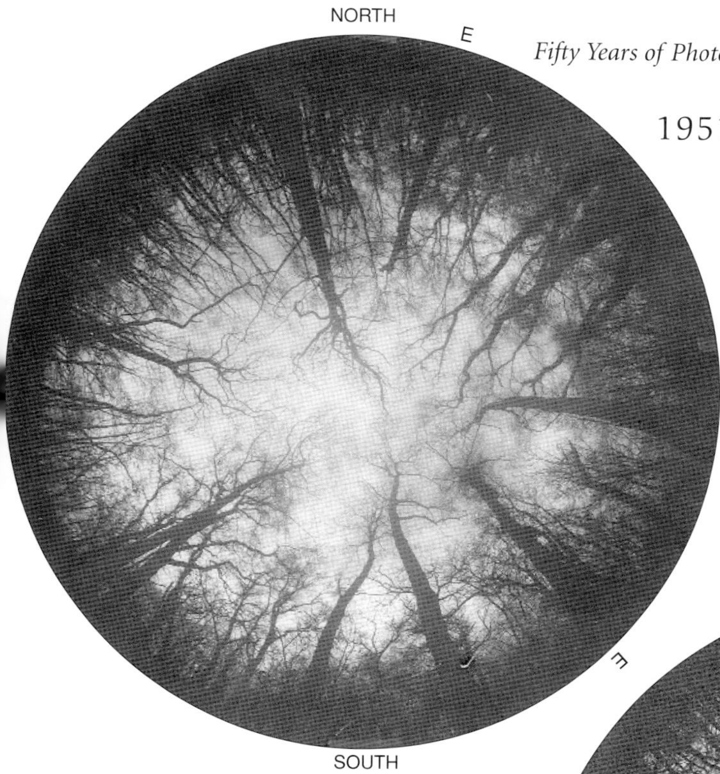

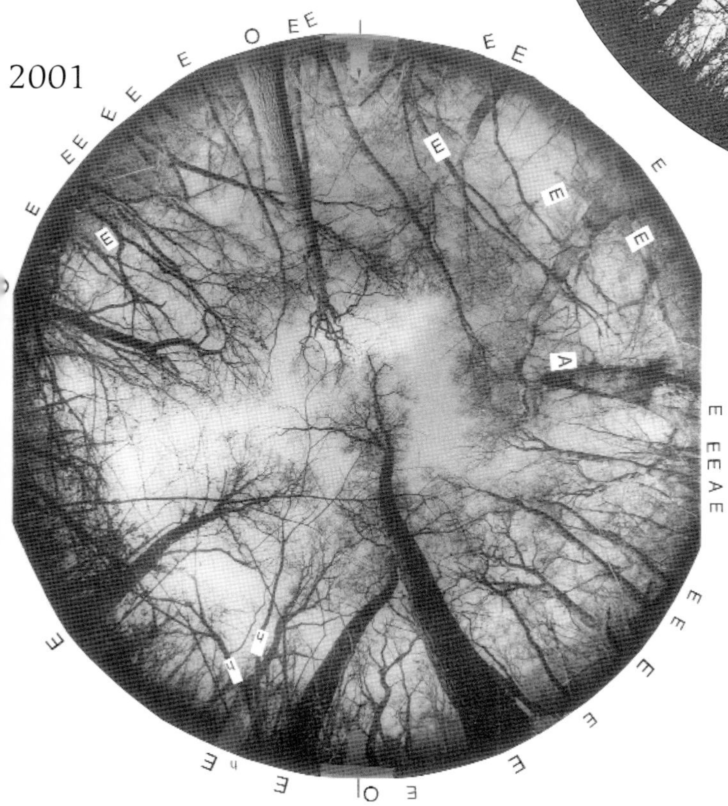

(a) Photosite in 1951 and 1977 (by D. E. Coombe) and 2001 (by P. Freeman and the author). North is marked in later photographs by a white arrow.

OAK SITE

1951

1977

2001

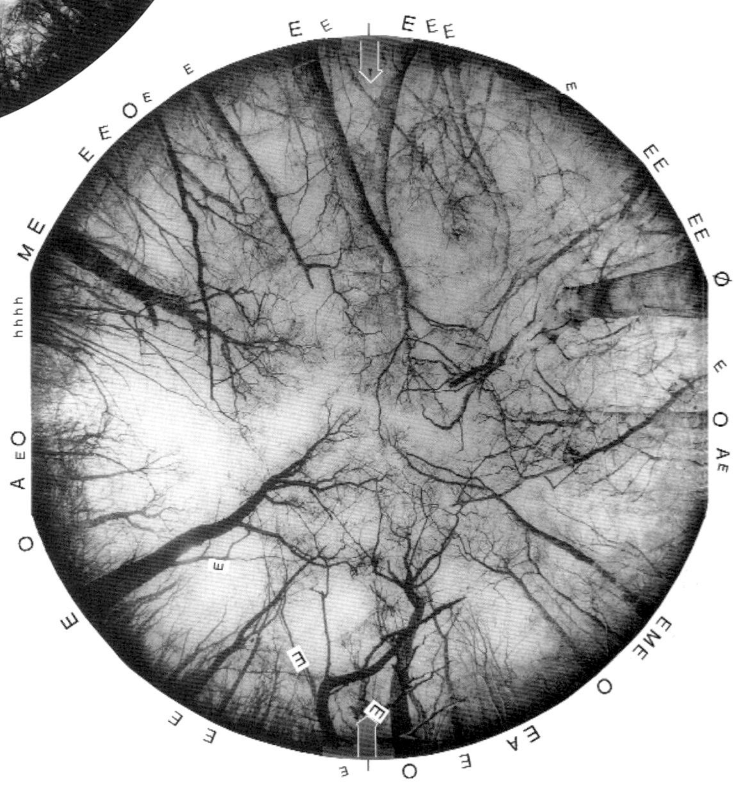

(**b**) Oak Site in 1951, 1977, and 2001.

HAZEL SITE

1951

1977

(c) Hazel Site in 1951, 1977, and 2001, and the hazel that appears in the photographs (in the very wet April of 2001).

2001

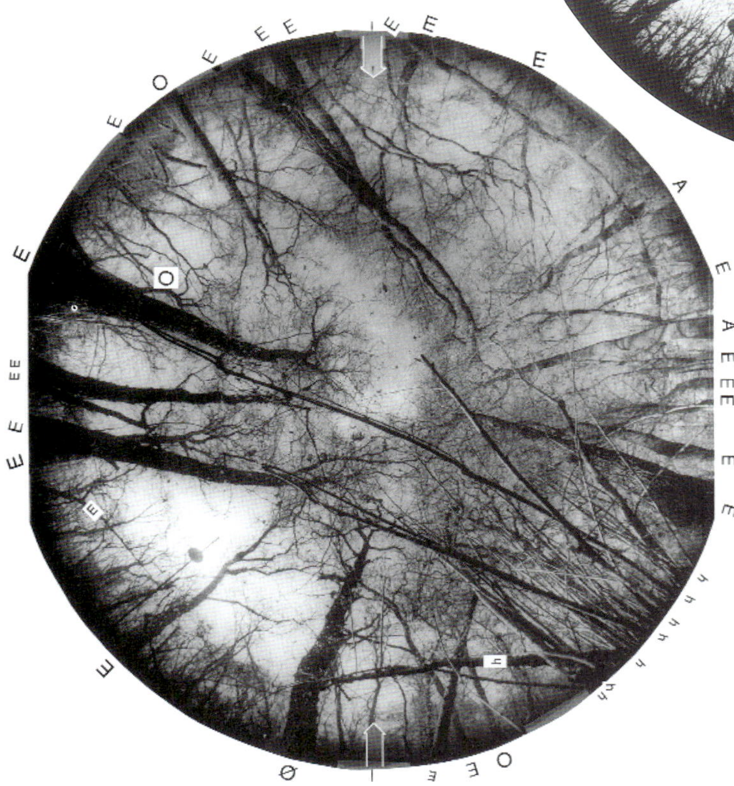

LARGE CLEARING

1957

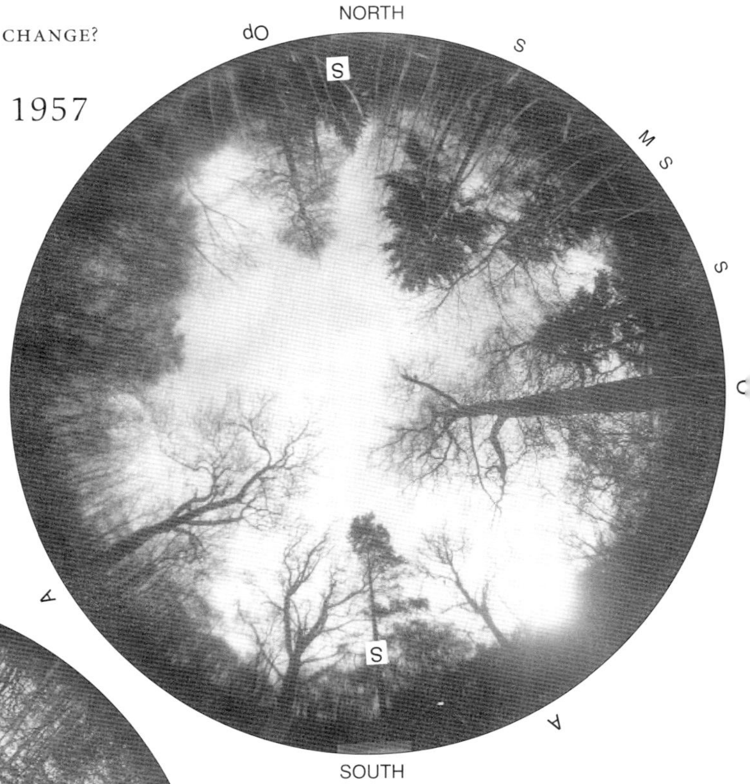

1977

2001*a*

(d) Large Clearing in 1957, 1977, and 2001 (on two occasions an hour or so apart). dO: oak showing dieback (recovering in later photos).

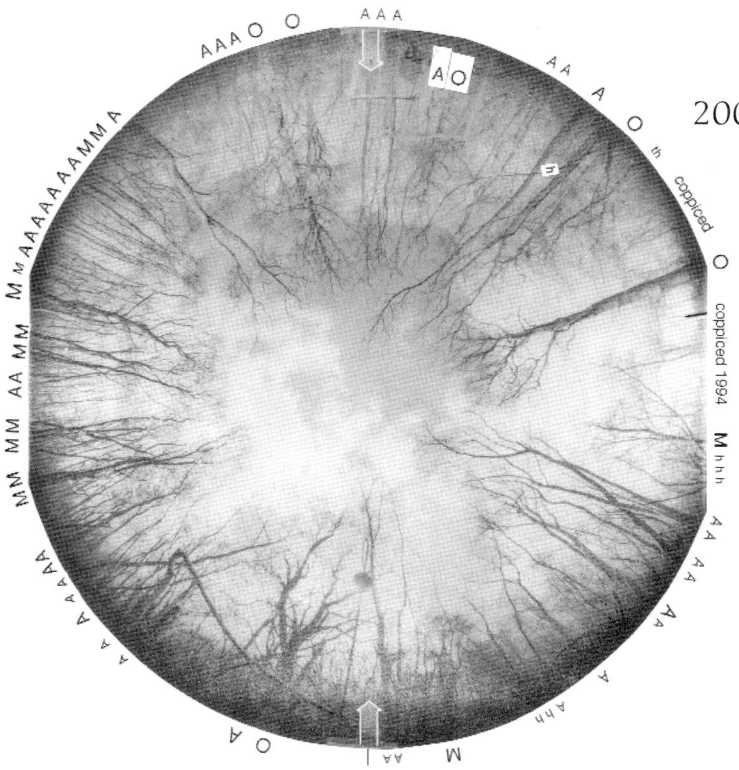

2001b

the cause must be at least partly environmental, not wholly due to the genetic peculiarities that make every elm clone unique.

Apart from the sny phenomenon, Madingley Wood illustrates a common fate of woods in the twentieth century. Abandonment of coppicing was followed by long decades of little change, interrupted by brief catastrophes due to felling, storms, Elm Disease, etc. It also illustrates the great stability of dead oaks and dead oak branches, compared to other trees. Although muntjac deer have become common, there is little for them to eat under shade, and the ground vegetation is no sparser than it was half a century ago.

Table 25.8 Summary of changes in trees in Madingley Wood photographs.

Elm	Increased curvature; increased thickness; increased height of standard trees; a few large suppressed trees disappear; some uprooting and boughbreaking in 1987 storm; small suppressed trees unchanged unless released by fall of neighbours
Oak	Decline especially where overtopped by elm; some trees escape or recover from decline and grow new, higher crowns; dead boughs lose bark and sapwood in 20 years, but heartwood persists for well over 50 years
Ash	Increased height of existing trees; big trees split, fall down, and disappear; new trees only in large clearing
Maple	Canopy trees get bigger; suppressed tree vanished
Hazel	Stable

1950

Fig. 25.15 A view from the Photosite, 1950 (by D. E. Coombe) and 2001. Trees nearly all elm, except for oak just visible at extreme left; ground vegetation dog's-mercury with scattered nettle. One elm has fallen, but scene is otherwise little changed. Beyond the elm stump is the Hazel Site (with camera cradle in 2001) and its hazel.

2001

1950

1987

2002

Fig. 25.16 A suppressed elm near the Photosite in 1950 and 1987 (by D. E. Coombe) and 2002. Note also the hazel (left background).

1950 2001

Fig. 25.17 Oak near the Photosite, 1950 (by D. E. Coombe) and 2001. The apparent loss of height is due to the fall of a bough which in 1950 (arrowed) had overhung the camera. Arrows in 2001 mark five dead branches which were already long-dead in 1950.

Fig. 25.18 Changing scene near the Photosite: 1950 (by D. E. Coombe) and 2001. The pollard-like elm in the middle has vanished. The sny elms have become much more sny, as compared with the oak and its dead boughs (arrowed) which serve as reference points.

A Hundred Years of Oxlip and Primrose

Hayley Wood 31.7.[19]44.
15 x 1 ft. strip in Oxlip type — Mer[cury] type 15′ x 1′
No. of individuals — Mer. per (shoots) 192
Oxlip . . . 70 — Oxlip 17

Copy of page of notebook in Alex Watt's hand, in Hayley Wood archives

[This works out at 50 oxlip plants per sq.m in the oxlip zone, 12 per sq.m in the mercury zone. 5 per sq.m is now an exceptional density, even in the oxlip zone.]

One of the earliest systematic ecological researches concerned oxlip and primrose. Primrose occurs almost throughout Britain and Ireland, with certain gaps in London and other conurbations, which are traditionally supposed to be because city-dwellers persecute primroses (though not convincingly, p. 92). Oxlip, in contrast, has a very restricted distribution, but is often very abundant in those woods where it occurs (Fig. 25.19).

Outside Britain, primrose is an 'Atlantic' species, common in parts of north-west Europe with wet, cool summers. About as far inland as Paris it is a plant of the general countryside. It extends into southern Europe – even reaching dry Crete – as a specialized plant of wet flushes and streamsides. Oxlip, however, is a 'Continental' plant, widespread in parts of Central Europe with hotter, if usually wetter, summers than England.

In 1897 Miller Christy read a paper on oxlip and primrose in eastern England.[11] His pioneer conclusions, which have stood the test of a century, are these. Within two limited areas, one west of Cambridge, the other east (Fig. 7.8), most ancient woods contain oxlip; some woods contain primrose as well; a few contain primrose but not oxlip. [An outlier has since been discovered in Buckinghamshire.] Oxlip is still in exactly those woods where he found it; it is strongly associated with ancient woodland; it responds strongly to coppicing; and it forms hybrid swarms with primrose in woods that contain both.

11 Christy, M. (1897). *Primula elatior* in Britain: its distribution, hybrids, and allies. *J. Linn. Soc. Bot.*, **33**, 172–201.

PRIMROSE

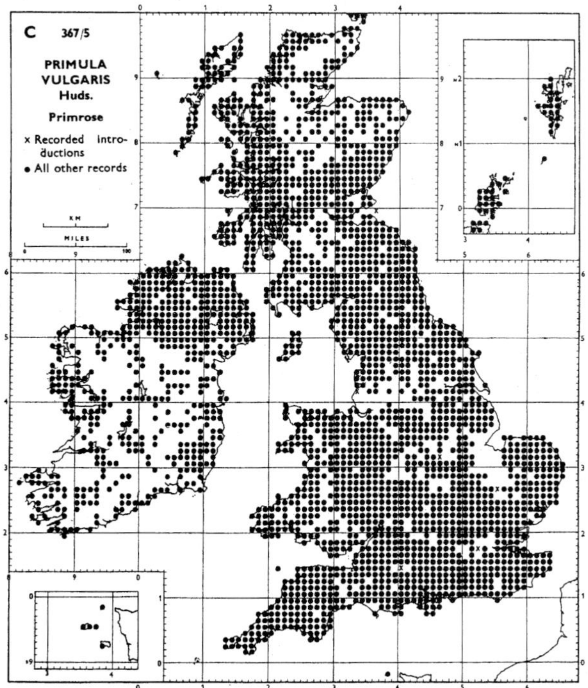

OXLIP

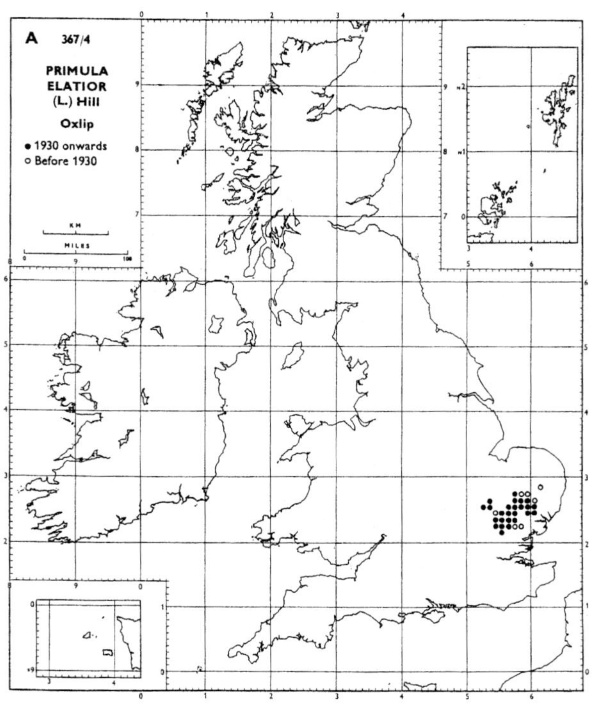

BLUEBELL

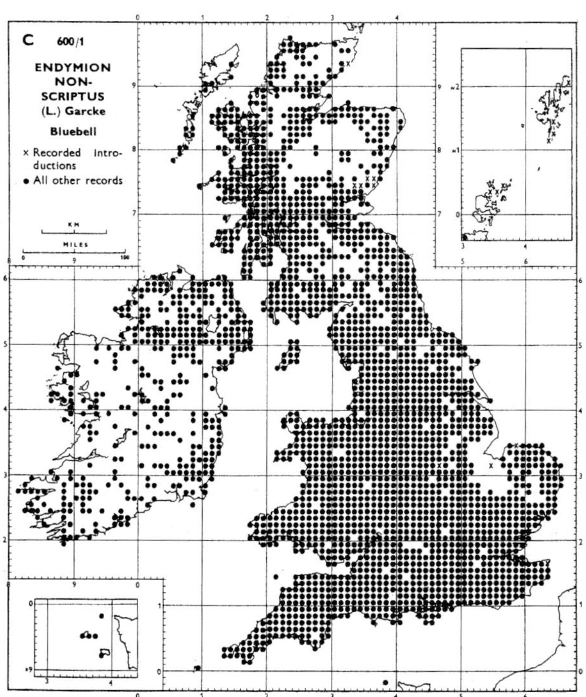

Fig. 25.19 Distribution of primrose, oxlip, and bluebell, from *Atlas of the British Flora*, 1962 (by kind permission of the Botanical Society of the British Isles).

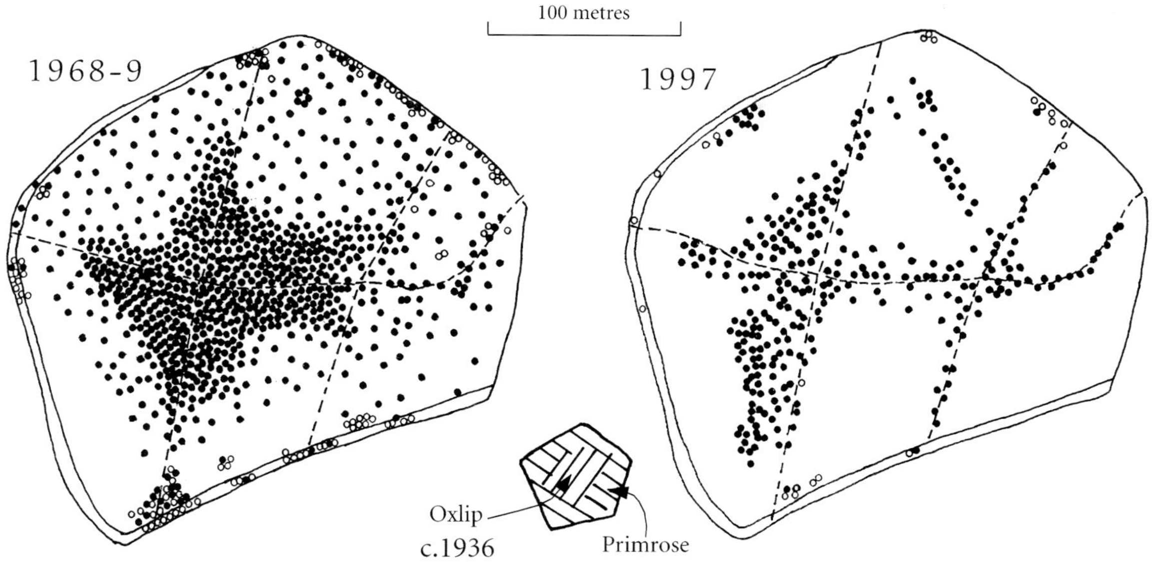

Fig. 25.20 Knapwell Wood: oxlip (black dots) and primrose (white dots) in *c.* 1936, 1967–69, and 1997. The reader is warned not to try to count the dots, which are intended to show the general distribution, not individual plants. Hybrids are not mapped separately: a mixture of black and white dots means that both species and usually their hybrids are present. The *c.* 1936 map is enlarged from a tiny original by Meyer & Meyer.

Christy proposed that oxlip, the rarer species in Britain, was a relict of prehistoric times, gradually being 'hybridized out of existence' by primrose, a commoner, 'aggressive and extending species'. Has primrose indeed increased at the expense of oxlip in the hundred years since the prediction?

The data continue with small maps made by Doris and Harry Meyer and David Valentine in the 1930s,[12] and with Abeywickrama's large-scale maps of Buff and Hayley Woods in the 1940s. I have mapped the distribution of oxlip, primrose and hybrids within west Cambridgeshire woods at various times from the 1960s onwards, and can compare the present state with that of 30 years ago and with earlier records by others back to Miller Christy.[13] From successive photographs of the same scenes year by year, going back sometimes to the 1960s, and from permanently marked plots, the local distribution and sometimes the fate of individual plants can be worked out.

Changes in woods with oxlip and primrose

Knapwell Wood (Fig. 25.20)

A test example should be this small ancient wood with both species, where oxlip has been known since 1860. There is little deer activity. In the 1930s the Meyers and Valentine found primroses round the edges and a much large number of oxlips in the middle. On Miller Christy's hypothesis primrose should have been spreading into the interior of the wood and should by now have eliminated some or all the oxlip.

In reality, when the Meyers returned in 1947 they found that 'primrose had decreased round the edges of the wood, leaving the margins without either species' (as Harry Meyer told me in 1969). In 1966–67 I was unable to find any pure primroses at all. In 1969 I looked more carefully, mapping every primrose and hybrid plant, as well as the general distribution of oxlip; I found 221 hybrid and 144 primrose plants, mostly on the massive ancient bank round the perimeter of the wood.

In 1997 I tried to refind these plants and could find only 10 hybrids and 18 primroses. The summary is as follows:

	1969	1997	1997 as % of 1969
Oxlip plants	*c.* 10,000	*c.* 4,000	*c.* 40%
Hybrid plants	221	10	5%
Hybrid inflorescences	462	29	6%
Primrose plants	144	18	12%

Knapwell Wood thus shows the opposite of Miller Christy's prediction: the oxlip majority has somewhat declined, but primrose is nearly extinct.

12 Meyer, H. & Meyer, D. (1951). The distribution of *Primula elatior* (L.)Hill. In: *the study of the distribution of British plants*, ed. J. E. Lousley, 80–81. Botanical Society of the British Isles.

13 Rackham, O. (1999). The woods 30 years on: where have the Primroses gone? *Nature in Cambridgeshire*, **41**, 73–87.

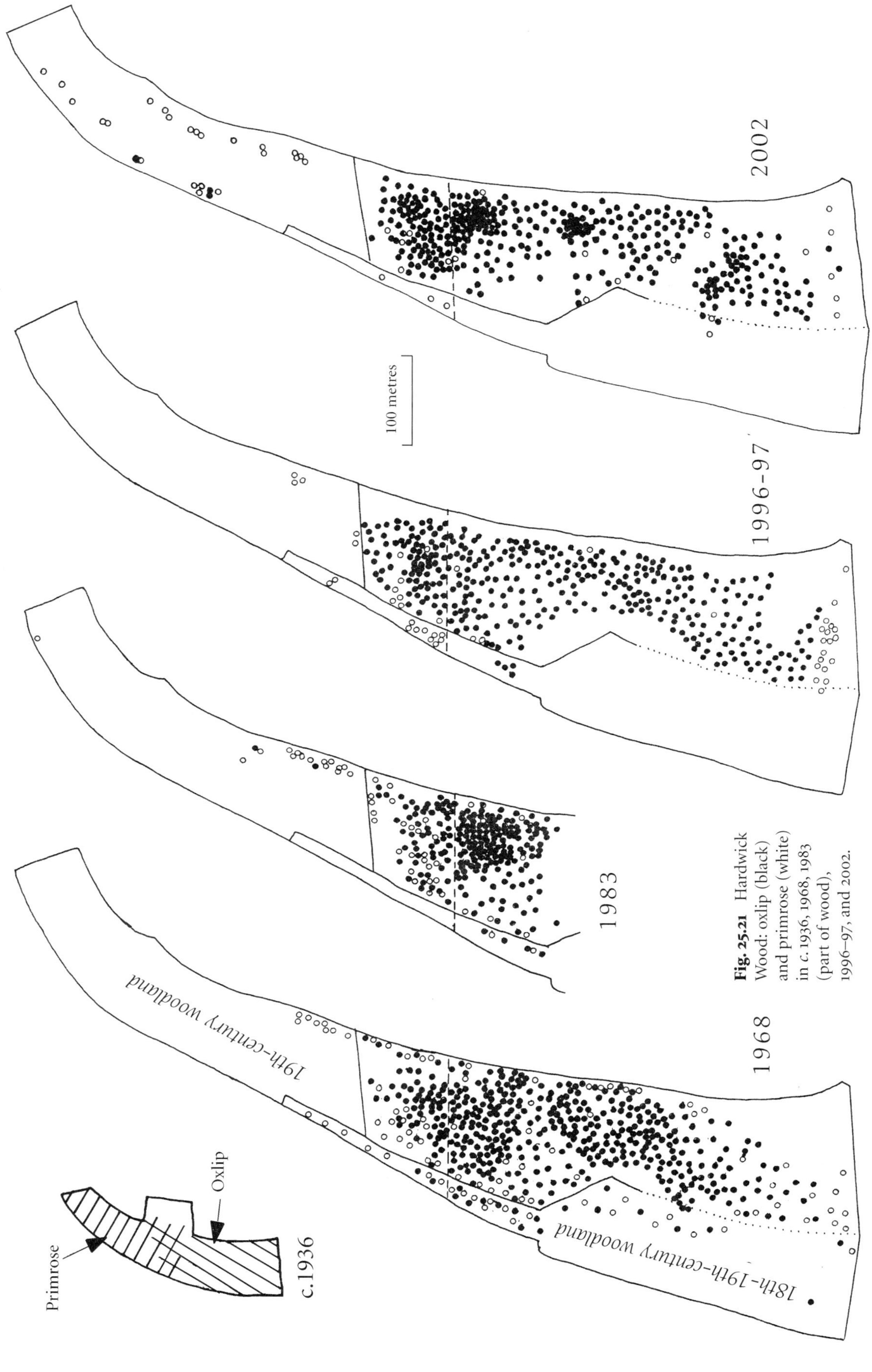

Fig. 25.21 Hardwick Wood: oxlip (black) and primrose (white) in *c.* 1936, 1968, 1983 (part of wood), 1996–97, and 2002.

Hardwick Wood (Fig. 25.21)

This is another oxlip-majority wood; there are some muntjac deer. Miller Christy remarked in 1897 that the boundary between primrose and oxlip ran through the wood. The Meyers in the 1930s mapped the southern part (now known to be ancient woodland) as oxlip and the northern, recent part as primrose, with a zone of overlap.

In 1968 I mapped a large oxlip population in the old wood, with a scatter of primroses and hybrids round the edges; primrose had largely disappeared from the northern part. Remapping the middle of the wood – the Meyers' overlap zone – in 1983, after resumption of coppicing, I found little change or a slight increase in both. In 1996–7 I remapped the whole wood and found a modest decline in oxlip and a considerable decline in primrose. A further re-mapping in 2002 showed a revival of oxlip, now more abundant than at any time I have known. Primrose has further declined, but shows some tendency to spread into the recent woodland in the north of the wood.

Madingley Wood

Oxlip and primrose both used to occur. Here in 1660 was one of the two first records of oxlip in Britain (p. 94). It had disappeared by the eighteenth century, probably owing to the grubbing-out of part of the wood.[14] The Meyers in the 1930s mapped primrose throughout the wood. It was still widely scattered in the 1960s, but in 1998 I could find only 16 plants on one of the rides. These have been further reduced by a scheme to 'open out the rides', which would have helped in conserving the light-demanding flora (p. 83) had it not been carried out in the depths of a very wet winter.

Gamlingay Wood

This wood has more oxlip than primrose. Adamson in 1910 described oxlip as 'abundant' and primrose as 'locally abundant'. In the 1930s primrose was mainly on the north-west side. When I knew the wood in 1968 this was still so, but with some indication of an increase in primrose.

By 1991 oxlip had declined, especially in coniferized areas (p. 370ff). Primrose had almost disappeared, except around the sand-lens in the middle of the wood. By 2002 oxlip has further declined, and primrose less so.

Buff Wood (Fig. 25.22)

This is probably the best primrose wood in Cambridgeshire, with an oxlip minority. The Meyers in the 1930s found oxlip in the interior, primrose round the edges, and neither in the northern 'panhandle'. In 1948 Abeywickrama found a central patch of oxlip with a 'halo' of hybrids; primrose extended, at least as a scattering, throughout the rest of the wood.

When I mapped the wood in 1967 oxlip had increased and a second oxlip area had appeared; primrose had somewhat declined. By 1981 the second oxlip area had somewhat increased, and primrose had partly recovered. In 1999 oxlip had slightly diminished; primrose had become much sparser, especially in the outer fringes of the wood, and was barely still in the majority. In 2002 there were slight signs of further decline in oxlip and recovery in primrose.

Bradfield Woods

The Bradfield Woods in west Suffolk are a classic coppicing site (pp. 24–32). When I first knew them in 1969 oxlip was widely distributed, though seldom at the densities then usual in Hayley Wood. Primrose was less common, mainly on acid soils. Both responded strongly to coppicing.

Both species have gradually declined to something like one-tenth of their former abundance.

Changes in oxlip-only woods

Hayley Wood (Fig. 25.23)

Hayley was the second best oxlip wood in England when the then Cambridgeshire & Isle of Ely Naturalists' Trust acquired it in 1962. It never had primrose. Abeywickrama's map of 1948 showed oxlip throughout the old wood; it was abundant, sometimes dominant, over about two-thirds of the wood. I estimated that there were then about four million plants. In 1966 I mapped it again: there were only minor changes in distribution, although the plants were being thinned out by the depredations of fallow deer. Exclosures set up in 1968 and 1971–2 (Chapter 26) established that these animals were the predators.

In 1976 I noticed a population crash of oxlip, put down to the combined effects of two hot summers and predation by deer. After this the Trust established two large deer-fenced exclosures. The 1997–8 remapping showed that oxlip had recovered much of its former abundance in the fenced areas, and sometimes along rides where the deer are deterred from feeding. Outside fenced areas it had largely disappeared from the north quarter (once the densest area) and east quarter; it had slightly increased in the south quarter, which was partly isolated by fences and less frequented by deer. It was often replaced by dense meadowsweet.

The Triangle is the north-east corner, a field with the ridge-and-furrow of seventeenth-century cultivation,

14 Rackham & Coombe (n.6).

Fig. 25.22 Buff Wood: oxlip (black) and primrose (white) in *c.*1936, 1948, 1967, 1981, 1998–99, and 2002. 1948 map is redrawn after Abeywickrama.

2002

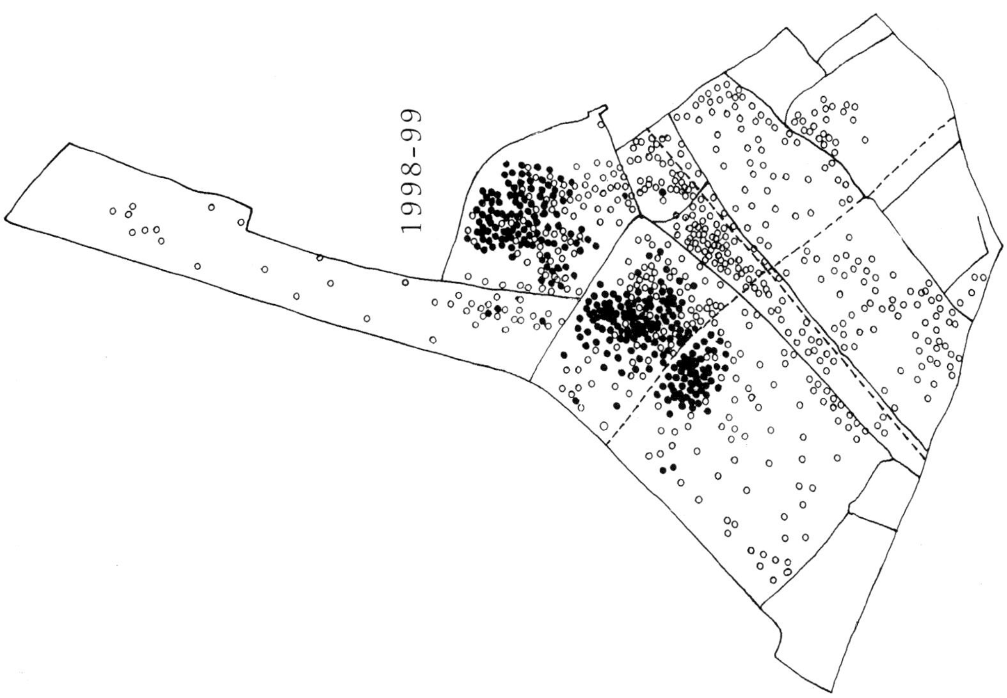
1998–99

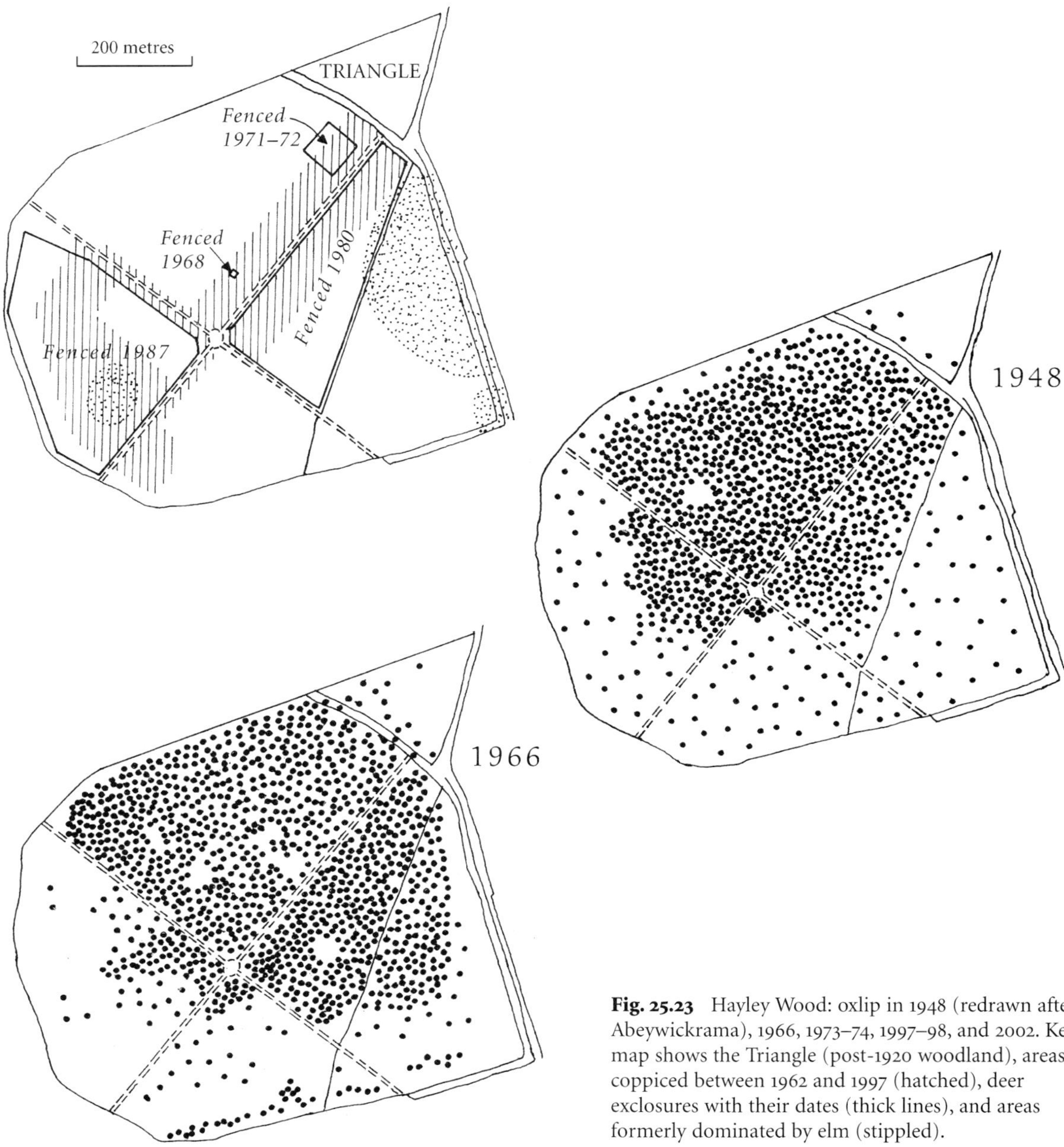

Fig. 25.23 Hayley Wood: oxlip in 1948 (redrawn after Abeywickrama), 1966, 1973–74, 1997–98, and 2002. Key map shows the Triangle (post-1920 woodland), areas coppiced between 1962 and 1997 (hatched), deer exclosures with their dates (thick lines), and areas formerly dominated by elm (stippled).

became woodland in the 1920s. It was a classic area for measuring the rate of spread of oxlip and other plants into 'attached' recent woodland. Up to 1973 it spread out from the original wood at about 1 m per year (Fig. 5.2). A re-mapping in 1987 indicated a slight acceleration (Fig. 25.25). But by 1997 I found that oxlip had almost vanished from the Triangle, where deer activity had noticeably increased in the intervening years. The Triangle, like the rest of the wood, was deer-fenced in 2001, and already in 2002, after two wet years, there are signs of recovery.

Kingston Wood (Fig. 25.26)

Ray recorded oxlip 'abundantly' in this wood in 1660. By the 1960s it was still abundant in parts of the wood not dominated by dog's-mercury, and elsewhere was on rides. By 2000 it was very much reduced. In the interval coppicing has declined and fallow deer have appeared: they now browse Kingston at least as severely as Hayley Wood.

Longstowe and Bourn Woods (Fig. 25.27)

These woods, either side of the road from London to Huntingdon, are famous as the scene of a murder by highwaymen in *c.* 1280, in consequence of which the landowners on either side were required to grub out a strip or 'trench' on either side of the road. These strips

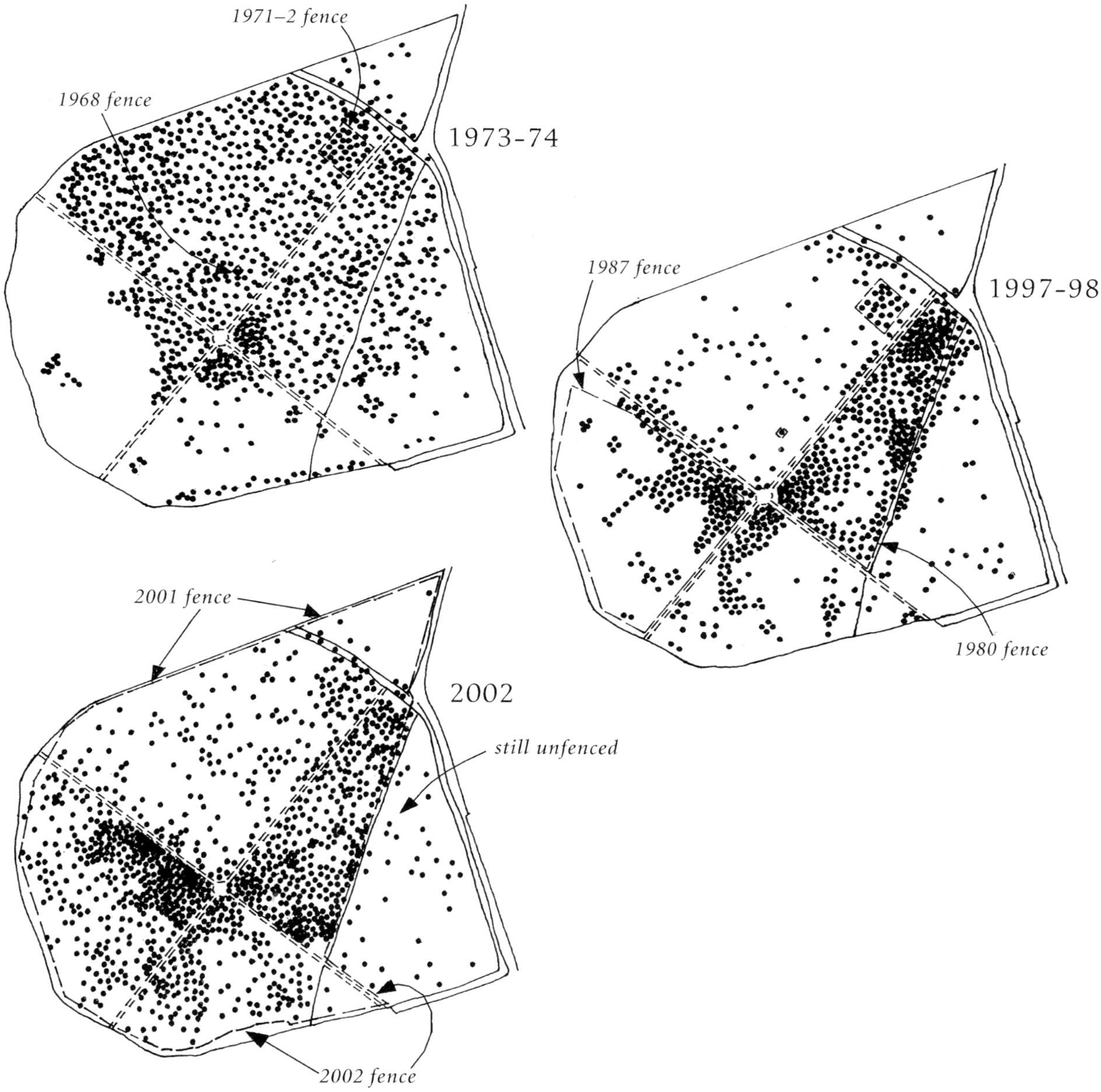

Fig. 25.24 Flooding in Hayley Wood: ridge-and-furrow in the Triangle in the wettest spring for at least 40 years. April 2001

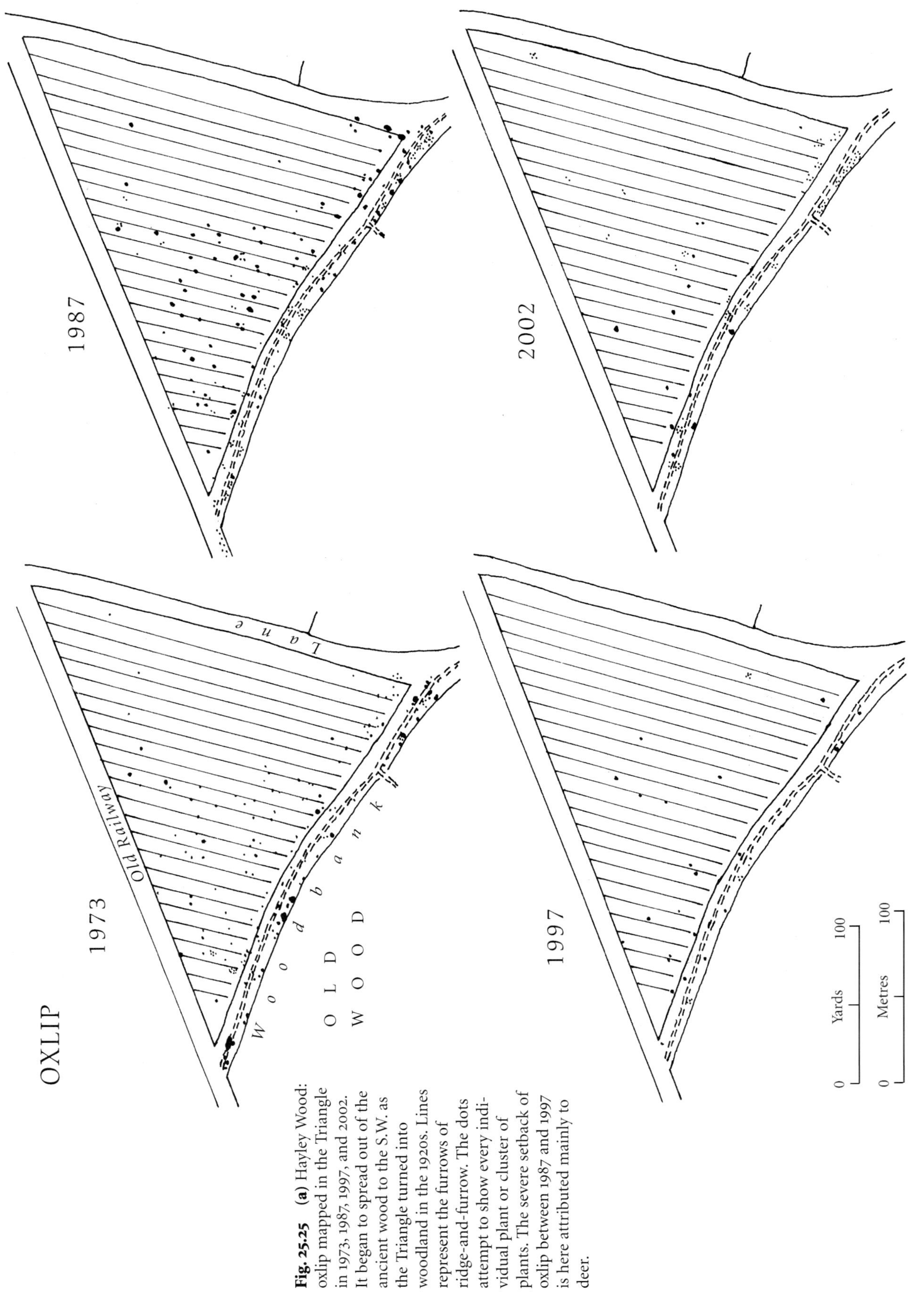

Fig. 25.25 (a) Hayley Wood: oxlip mapped in the Triangle in 1973, 1987, 1997, and 2002. It began to spread out of the ancient wood to the S.W. as the Triangle turned into woodland in the 1920s. Lines represent the furrows of ridge-and-furrow. The dots attempt to show every individual plant or cluster of plants. The severe setback of oxlip between 1987 and 1997 is here attributed mainly to deer.

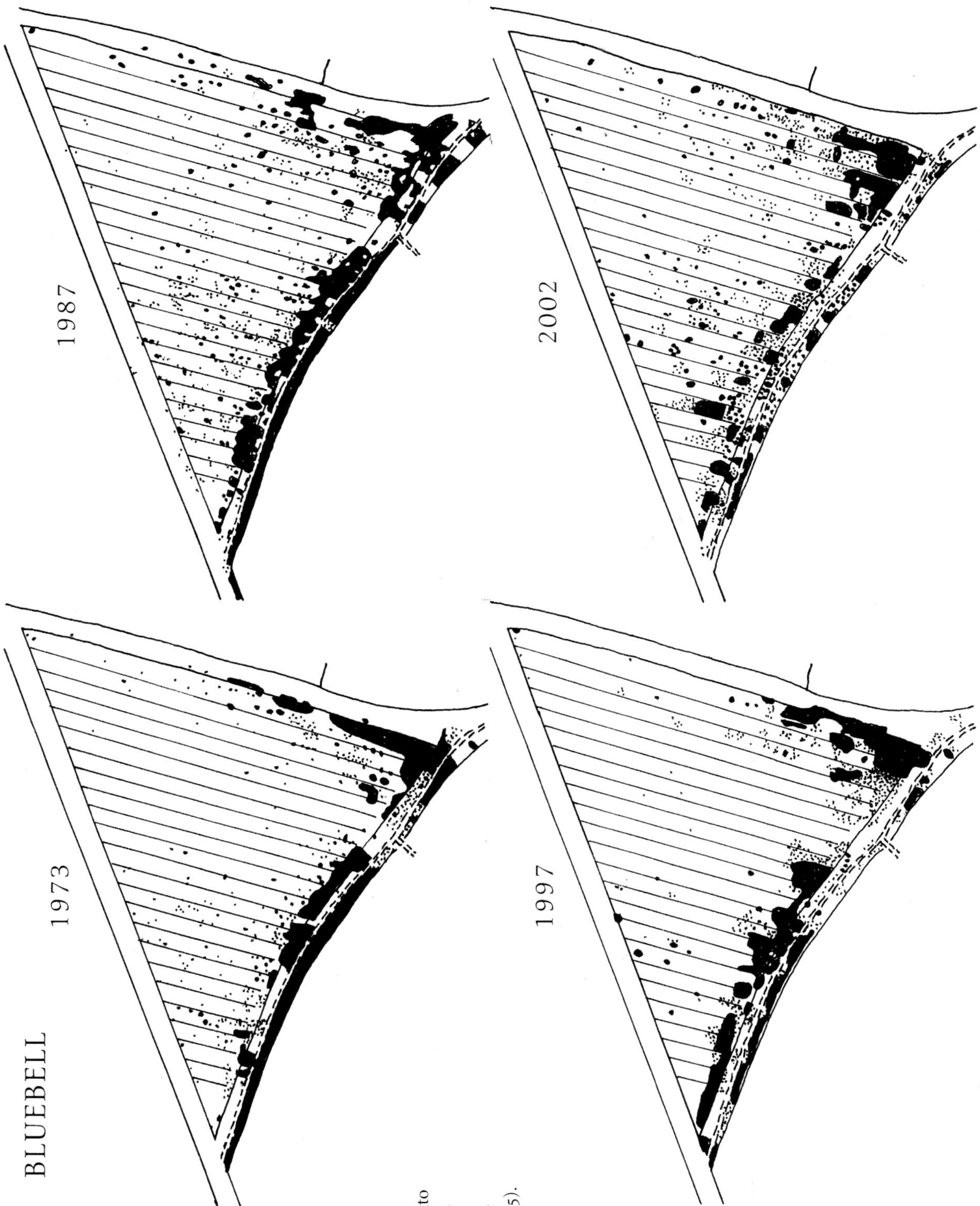

(b) Spread of bluebell into the Triangle. The setback between 1987 and 1997 is attributed to three severe summers (1989, 1990, 1995).

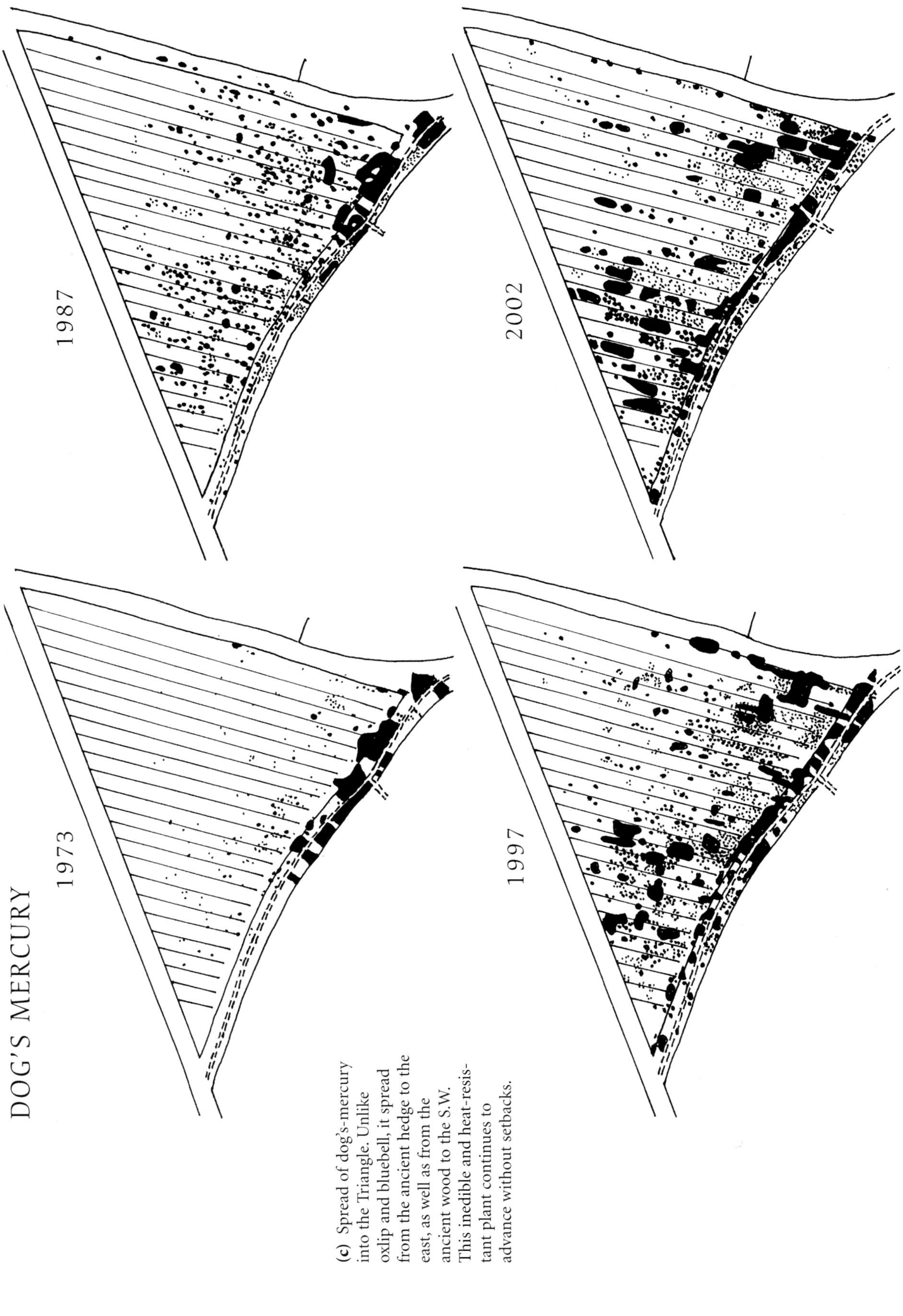

(c) Spread of dog's-mercury into the Triangle. Unlike oxlip and bluebell, it spread from the ancient hedge to the east, as well as from the ancient wood to the S.W. This inedible and heat-resistant plant continues to advance without setbacks.

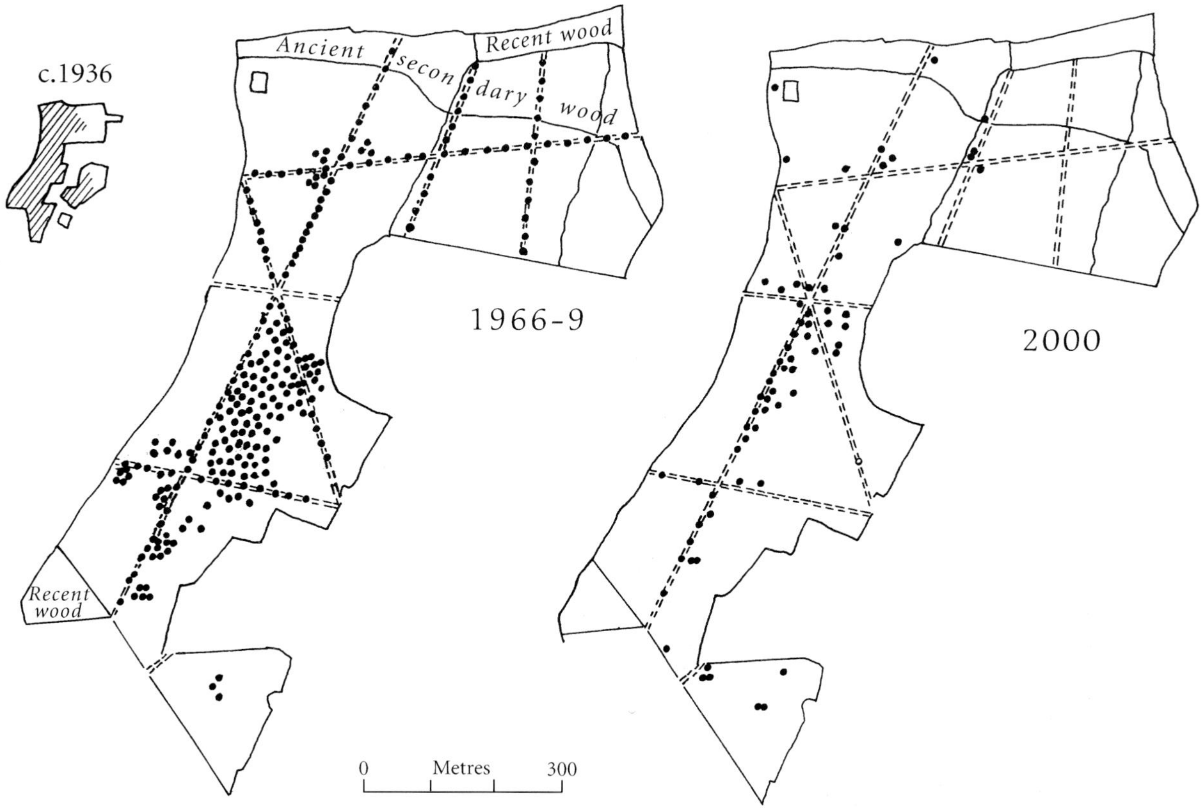

Fig. 25.26 Kingston Wood: oxlip in *c.* 1936, 1966–9, and 2000 (with the help of Peter Reynolds).

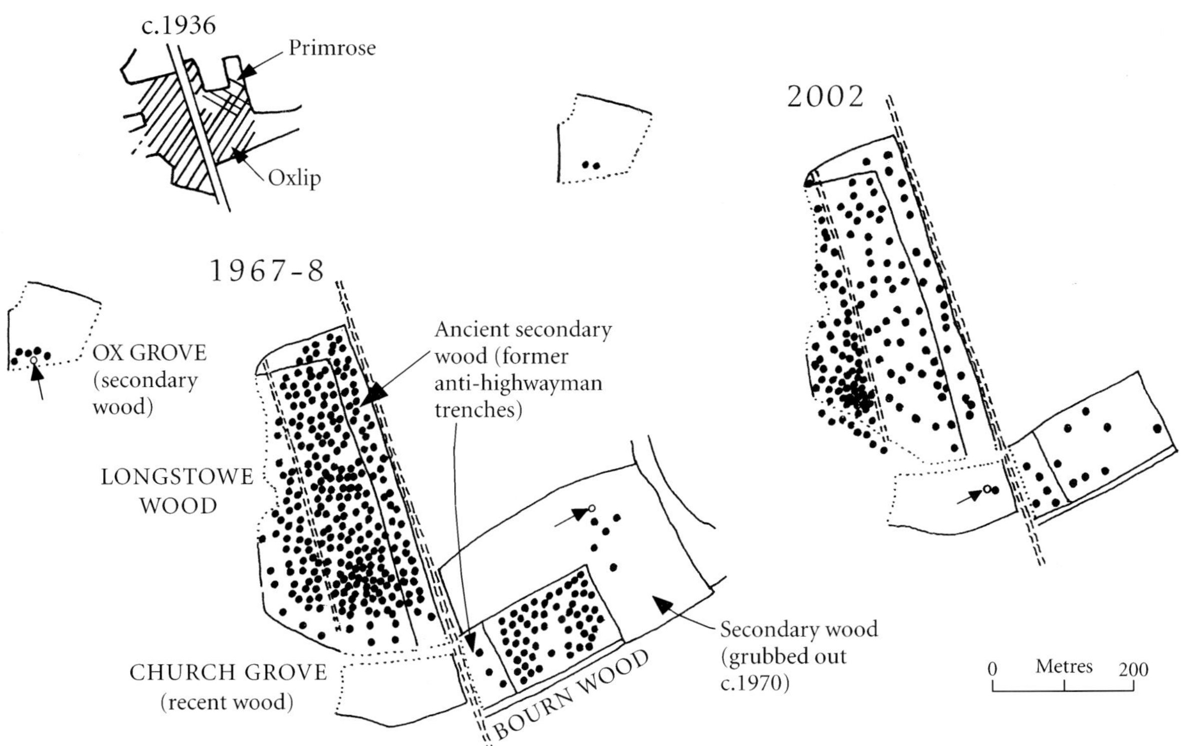

Fig. 25.27 Longstowe and Bourn Woods: oxlip (black) and primrose (white) in *c.* 1936, 1967–8, and 2002.

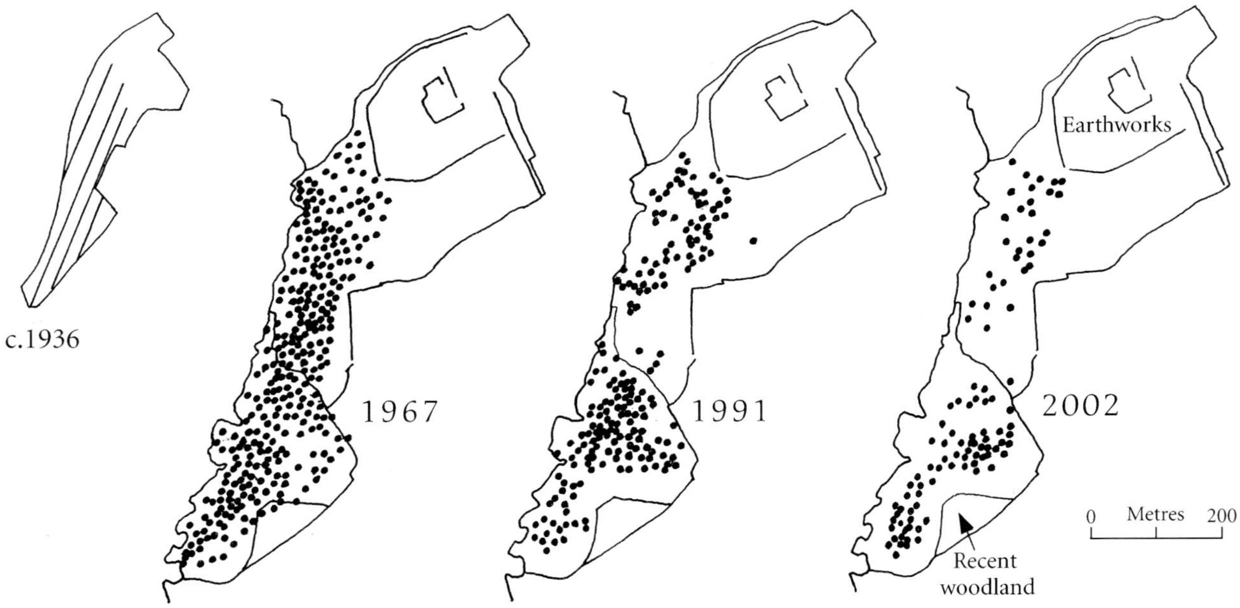

Fig. 25.28 Overhall Grove: oxlip in *c.* 1936, 1967, 1991, and 2002.

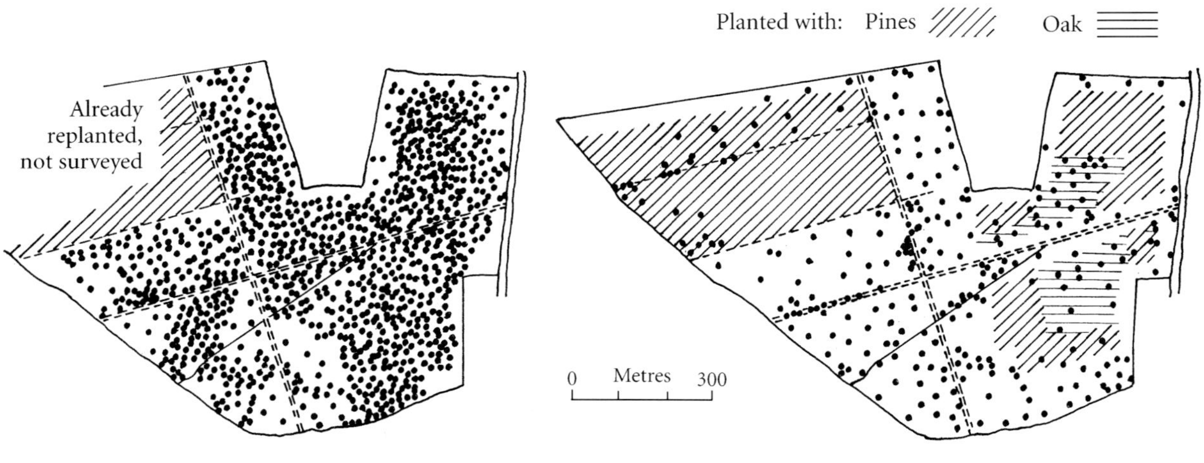

Fig. 25.29 Hempstead Wood: oxlip in 1971–5 and 2002.

are again woodland, but the new woodbanks then made are still there.[15]

The Meyers in the 1930s recorded oxlip generally, but primrose in extensions to Bourn Wood since grubbed out. In 1967–8 both woods had dense stands of oxlip, which was limited to the old woods and was very sparse or absent in later additions. Oxlips, however, were abundant in the trench of Longstowe Wood but not of Bourn Wood. In Bourn Wood they were still abundant in the 1980s and flourished after the death of the dominant elms.

In 2002 oxlips had declined by about 80% in Longstowe and 90% in Bourn Woods. Both woods have large numbers of muntjac deer. In addition they have been extensively replanted, combined with periodic cutting of the vegetation between the planted trees.

Overhall Grove, Boxworth (Fig. 25.28)

This wood, most of which is medieval secondary woodland dominated by elm (Fig. 5.1), has only oxlip. In the 1930s and in 1967 oxlip was abundant over the

15 *The History of the Countryside* 268–71.

whole lower half of the wood. By 1991 it had declined and become more patchy, but in one area was as dense as ever. A slow decline continued through the 1990s, except in the extreme south of the wood, where oxlip has increased. A feature of this area is that elms, killed to the ground by Elm Disease in the 1980s, have recovered and now form a dense shade (Fig. 28.3).

Hempstead Wood (Fig. 25.29)

This N.W. Essex wood was probably the greatest oxlip wood in England. When I first mapped it in 1971–5, the density of plants was less than in Hayley, but they were spread over three-quarters of the 204-acre wood. Most of the remainder of the wood had been killed and planted with Corsican Pine in 1963–4. As in Hayley, the oxlip zone occupied the flat, wet plateau, with dog's-mercury dominant on the sloping fringes and in valleys. Bluebell was much scarcer than at Hayley, confined to part of the woodbank and the wood adjacent.

Oxlip now occupies nearly the whole of its former area but at a much lower density: for every twenty plants present in 1972 there is only one in 2002. (Ray Tabor estimates that there are now about 30,000 oxlips.[16])

At Hempstead an exceptional number of factors conspire against oxlip. More of the wood was replanted with Corsican Pine, oak etc. from 1971 to 1975. There are red deer, fallow, roe, muntjac, and possibly Japanese; Tabor's exclosure experiments confirm their drastic effects on oxlip. Deer were active by 1975 but have greatly increased since; they ate much of the Corsican Pine. And there is *Carex pendula*, a big tufted sedge, which is competitive and particularly helped by deer (none of the deer eat it) and by replanting. Oak-planted areas are often a dense mass of this sedge. Coppicing was resumed in 1987 after a lapse of about 60 years, but the regrowth has struggled against deer, while sedge has thrived, and here and there the occasional oxlip is to be seen. The importance of deer has been confirmed by Tabor in exclosure experiments.

In successfully coniferized areas oxlip disappeared as soon as the conifer canopy closed in. In the part of the wood replanted in 1963–4 oxlips were conspicuously absent already by 1972, although a few have come back in patches where hornbeam and maple refused to die and the pine canopy did not close. They have declined in oak-planted areas, in coppiced areas, and in intact areas, under both the dense shade of hornbeam and the lighter shade of other trees. There are signs of a slight return where pines have been removed in the last few years. Records from intermediate years show that except under conifers the decline was continuous decade by decade. Coppicing has failed to arrest it.

Dog's-mercury has changed little since 1972, except in the N.E. of the wood where (as in Gamlingay Wood) it greatly increased after coniferization. (However, it is possible that 2002 was a temporary bad year for mercury, because it had been set back by exceptional waterlogging in spring and autumn 2001.) Bluebell occupies the same fringe area as in 1972.

The fact that oxlip has declined under all treatments – including no treatment – indicates that deer are largely responsible: they are active in all parts of the wood except under dense pines. Although it has declined even without competition, another factor must be the spread of *Carex pendula*. For some reason this giant sedge is particularly aggressive in Hempstead and some other N.W. Essex woods: it takes over felled areas. It can hardly have taken over the wood every time it was felled in past centuries. (Although it is a garden plant it has been known in Essex for 300 years, and there is no other reason to suspect it is an introduction.) In Hayley Wood, where *Carex pendula* was probably accidentally introduced in the 1970s, it has slowly increased, but only as single tufts here and there.

Observations on individual plants and small areas

Since 1972 I have kept records each spring of oxlip and other plants at twenty marked locations (circles of 1 m radius) in Hayley Wood. The plots are in the oxlip and oxlip-bluebell zones, and were originally chosen as having particular densities of these plants. Ten plots were accessible to fallow deer (up to 2001) and ten were within the one-acre deer exclosure (Fig. 25.23). Together with the original 1968 exclosure and its two control plots, this makes 11 unbrowsed and 12 browsed plots. Browsing affects oxlip not only directly but by retarding the recovery of the underwood canopy after coppicing, and thus by encouraging species that compete with oxlip.

Leaf cover indicates trends in the survival of plants over the years. It is not a good indicator, for it develops around the time that the plots are recorded, and it thus liable to be underestimated in late seasons. There is much inconsistency from plot to plot under the same treatment. In fenced plots leafage tends to vary with the coppice cycle, being greatest in the later years as competitors are shaded out and oxlip adapts to increasing shade by spreading its leaves more thinly.

Oxlip has declined over the years, both in fenced and unfenced plots. In 1977–8 six of the twelve unfenced plots showed a consistent decline, only one of which later recovered; seven of the eleven fenced plots also declined and two recovered. There was another decline around 1990, in which oxlip died out

16 Tabor, R. C. (2002). Notes on Essex specialities. 7: The distribution of the Oxlip . . . in Essex – 2002. *Essex Naturalist*, **19**, 113–34.

altogether from three plots, all unfenced. 1996 was another consistently bad year, usually followed by recovery, although oxlip died out in one fenced plot.

These declines follow extreme summers. The two great summers of 1975–6 were followed by a noticeable decline in oxlip throughout Hayley Wood. The other bad years are associated with the pair of hot dry summers of 1989–90 and the great summer of 1995. These five summers were among the eight severest of the twentieth century.

Although oxlip plants are long-lived, there is some turnover. Seedlings are not uncommon, and were recorded in some of these plots. In one of the plots in which oxlip died out in 1990 it re-colonized in 1997. However, for seedlings to be produced there must be seed. In 1974 I estimated that deer were taking about nine-tenths of the then much larger numbers of oxlip flowers.

Eight plots were originally chosen because they contained bluebell as well as oxlip. Thirty years on, they all have bluebell still, though in seven it has declined, sometimes almost to extinction. Six more plots have been colonized by bluebell since 1972, though it has persisted in only four. Of the hot summers, 1989–90 were a bad time for bluebell; 1975–6 and 1995 less clearly so. Bluebell colonized new plots in the years 1979–85.

Fig. 25.30 (a–c) Oxlip plants inside deer exclosure, Hayley Wood:

(a) on 4 May 1969,

(b) on 15 April 1976,

(c) on 17 April 2001. Many of the plants are the same, although in 2001 their leaves are less advanced.

Fig. 25.31 (a–b) Primrose plants (and primrose-oxlip hybrids) at the same spot in Buff Wood:

(a) on 6 May 1985 (2 years after coppicing),

(b) on 8 April 2000. Many of the plants have persisted through what would be a whole normal coppice cycle.

Although the plots lie well outside dog's-mercury territory, mercury was recorded in four of the 23. In each case there were only a few weak stems, which have not spread into a clonal patch and have seldom flowered. In one plot a mercury clone appeared as a couple of stems in 1980 and lasted for 21 years, but never with more than five stems, and with two gaps, when for two and three years it was not recorded at all.

Interpretations

Miller Christy was wrong about oxlip being 'hybridized out of existence'. On the contrary, primrose and hybrids have vastly declined since he wrote, whereas oxlip has declined to a lesser extent. Hybrids remain where there are both parents: they have not increased at the expense of either parent. This is generally true of oxlip in Cambridgeshire woods, and in Suffolk and Essex as well. Although most of the non-woodland populations of oxlip, in hedges and grassland, have been lost by destruction of habitat, Christy's woodland populations nearly all remain unless the wood itself has been grubbed out.[17] Oxlip still exists in broadly the same part of each wood, but at a lower density.

Primrose and oxlip are both perennials, but are not strongly clonal. Are they mortal? Seedlings are not uncommon. Photographs of the same scene in two successive coppice cycles generally show different patterns of plants, suggesting that some of those seedlings become adults and replace others. Tracing the fate of individual plants in small-scale photographs is not straightforward, because they vary in size and leafage from year to year.

In 1982 I marked two large oxlips in Hayley Wood and then photographed them every year. One plant died after 14 years, the other after 15, in both cases after several years of decline. But some of the oxlips which I photographed in the first deer exclosure in Hayley in 1968–69 are still there 33 years later (Fig. 25.30). In scenes in Buff Wood which I photographed in 1983–5 and 1998, 26 out of 28 primroses seemed to have survived, and many small plants had been recruited (Fig. 25.31). From such rather meagre data I infer that the half-life of oxlip and primrose in a favourable environment is about 50 years. Their long-term survival depends on at least occasional seed production, germination and establishment (unlike, for example, wood anemone, which is clonal).

17 Preston, C. D. (1993). The distribution of the Oxlip . . . in Cambridgeshire. *Nature in Cambridgeshire*, **35**, 29–60.

1969

1981

Fig. 25.32 Primroses one year after coppicing in Buff Wood, 5 May 1969 and 7 April 1981. The prodigious effect of the 1968 coppicing was not repeated on so spectacular a scale.

Oxlip is weakly competitive, easily squeezed out by stronger-growing neighbours (pp. 92–5). Its decline could be due to factors favourable to its competitors, especially bluebell, dog's-mercury, or *Carex pendula*, rather than unfavourable to oxlip itself. It typically comes into leaf in mid-March and blooms in April; the leaves may wither in June or persist into October, depending on summer weather. Primrose is a slightly stronger competitor; it has a much longer leafing and flowering season; in mild winters it is evergreen. Where oxlip or primrose have gone, the site may be occupied by a competitor, such as mercury in Knapwell Wood or meadowsweet in Hayley. Competition cannot, however, be a factor in Gamlingay Wood or much of the north of Hayley, where ex-oxlip sites are usually now bare ground or at most bryophytes.

Oxlip and primrose are stimulated to flower by coppicing: flowering reaches a peak usually in the second or third summer after the wood is cut. The magnitude of the coppicing effect is influenced by several other factors (Chapter 26).

Woods have changed less than the rest of the landscape, and the changes have not all been unfavourable to oxlip or primrose. Some changes, such as renewed coppicing and perhaps the death of elms, might be expected to be favourable; others, such as increasing deer or eutrophication (fertilisers blowing off adjacent fields and encouraging nettle etc.) might be adverse.

Weather: dry summers

The Cambridge area is the driest part of Britain, with annual rainfall averaging about 500 mm, in some years less than 400. An Atlantic plant should be getting towards the limit of its drought tolerance. Primrose in wetter regions grows in grassland and hedges; around Cambridge it occurs only in woods; in Breckland, with its dry soils, it is absent. In Cambridge gardens it tends to die in dry summers.

Probably the most brilliant display of primroses in the area in living memory happened in a part of Buff Wood felled in winter 1968 (Fig. 25.32). Primrose came into bloom in November 1968 and was spectacular for the next 18 months. This was repeated, but not on quite the same scale, in 1981 after the same area was felled in 1980. 1968 was a phenomenally wet summer, with June–September rainfall twice the average. 1980 had rather more than average summer rainfall. 1983 was

Fig. 25.33 Oxlip bitten by fallow deer. Hayley Wood. April 1968

another excellent primrose-coppicing season, following the wet summer of 1982.[18]

The log-books of coppicing plots show that oxlip is set back by dry summers. The most brilliant display of oxlips in living memory was in 1987 in the part of Hayley Wood felled in 1986 (Plate 7b, p. xxvii); summer 1986 had been nearly 30% wetter than average. The small deer exclosure set up in 1968 came up for felling in 1976, the year of the great summer, whose effects on vegetation (by drought as well as heat) were unrivalled in the twentieth century. There was no coppicing response at all. The next time the area was felled, in 1992, was followed by a summer over 30% wetter than average, and a response inside the exclosure (in 1993) almost on the scale of 1987 (p. 418, Fig. 26.3).

Dry or hot summers shorten the leafing season of oxlip. Leaves wither in early summer and do not make the substance which goes into extra leaves and flowers in the following season. In newly coppiced areas the soil can dry out early in a hot summer, and high temperatures develop near the ground between the stools,[19] which in summers like 1976 cancels the advantages of extra light.

Bluebell, one of oxlip's chief competitors, has an Atlantic distribution like primrose, but extends a little less far into Europe than primrose. Like primrose, around Cambridge it avoids hedges and is confined to ancient woods. It is much less browsed than oxlip. It has not shared in the decline of primrose. In none of the woods has it fared badly during the time of recording, although very dense stands have become less dense and some of their boundaries have shifted. Any adverse effect of hot summers is perhaps compensated by its being able to advance into Zone 2 in years without spring flooding.

Deer and other animals

Oxlip is at the top of the menu for fallow deer, which bite out the middle of the plant, leaves, flowers and all, and swallow it (Fig. 25.33). In Hayley Wood, in every exclosure from 1968 onwards, oxlip has become more abundant than outside it. Muntjac appear not to eat much oxlip or primrose leafage, but preliminary results from muntjac exclosures in Hayley Wood show that they eat flowers, as well as reducing competition from bramble. This confirms exclosure experiments in Shadwell Wood, Ashdon, N.W. Essex.[20]

Something other than deer bites off the flowers of oxlip and either swallows or drops them, in some years accounting for well over half the flowers (p. 418).

By 1974 fallow deer were known to be eating most of the flowers in Hayley Wood outside exclosures and, by eating the leaves, were causing fewer flowers to be produced. Oxlip flowering in the wood was reduced by at least 90%; such flowers as escaped the deer were often eaten by other animals (p. 92). But worse was to come. In 1968, when the first exclosure was set up, two unfenced plots had been selected to be as similar as possible to the fenced plot in numbers of oxlip. Up to spring 1976 they continued to have a high density of plants, albeit stunted. After that year – the summer of the century – the number of plants in the control plots crashed and did not recover. Many plants in the exclosure survived and recovered, going on to a mass flowering after the 1992 coppicing (Fig. 26.3).

The twenty small plots told a similar story. Oxlip declined after 1975–6, and then recovered in enclosed plots but not in most of those accessible to deer. There were similar observations after the hot summers of 1989–90 and 1995 (p. 418ff).

18 Clarke, J. W. (1960 ff). Weather notes for Cambridgeshire. *Nature in Cambridgeshire*, all volumes. [The station, at Swaffham Prior, escapes the 'heat island effect' which complicates urban weather stations.]
19 Rackham, O. (1975). Temperatures of plant communities as measured by pyrometric and other methods. In: *Light as an Ecological Factor II* (*see* 50), 423–49.
20 Tabor, R. C. C. (1997). The effects of Muntjac deer . . . and Fallow deer . . . on the Oxlip . . . *Deer* **11**, 14–9.

Table 25.9 Summary of changes in woods

Wood	Change in Oxlip	Change in Primrose & Hybrid	Change in Bluebell	Coppicing	Death of Elms	Replanting	Deer	Competition	Eutrophication
Knapwell	60% decline since 1969	decline 1935–69; 90% decline since 1969	*c.* 50% decline since 1969	++	++	+	+	++ mercury	+
Hardwick	small net increase, 1968–2002	substantial decline 1935–68; *c.* 90% decline since 1968	small decline since 1968	++	+	– –	+	–	– –
Madingley	long extinct	almost extinct since 1960	?	++	+	– –	+	++ mercury?	– –
Gamlingay	stable 1911–68?; *c.* 50% decline 1968–91; *c.* 50% further decline 1991–2002	stable 1911–68?; *c.* 70% decline 1968–91; *c.* 10% further decline 1991–2002	increase	– –	– –	++	++ (muntjac)	–	– –
Buff	increase 1948–68, then nearly stable	fluctuations, then *c.* 50% decline since 1981	decreases slightly outweigh increases	+++	++	– –	++	+ mercury	+
Hayley (unfenced)	slight decline 1948–76; *c.* 70% decline since 1976	absent	modest decreases outweigh increases	+++	++	– –	++++	–	+
Hayley (fenced)	decline followed by partial recovery	absent	fluctuates	++++	+	– –	+ (muntjac)	–	+
Longstowe	80% decline 1967–2002	absent	decline	– –	++	+++	+++ (muntjac)	+++ (*Deschampsia*)	–
Bourn	90% decline 1982–2002	absent	decline?	–	+++	+++	++ (muntjac)	+++ (*Deschampsia*)	–
Overhall	c 50% decline since 1967	absent	constant?	+	++++	– –	– –	–	– –

Wood	Change in Oxlip	Change in Primrose & Hybrid	Change in Bluebell	Coppicing	Death of Elms	Re-planting	Deer	Competition	Eutrophication
Bradfield	*c.* 90% decline since 1969	*c.* 90% decline since 1969	constant	+++	+	– –	++ (roe)	– –	– –
Hempstead	*c.* 95% decline since 1972, spread over 3 decades	absent	slight decline	+++	+	++++	++++	++++ *Carex pendula*	–

By 1977 oxlip (and coppice regrowth) were faring so badly in Hayley as a whole that the Trust decided to set up large-scale exclosures for conservation: one was finished in 1980, another in 1987. Oxlip has recovered inside the fences, but seldom to quite the density that it had before 1976. The fences, enclosing about 40% of the wood, shifted the pattern of deer activity in the remainder. Deer used the South Quarter less, and here too oxlip recovered. There was much more activity in the Triangle, where the invading oxlip population crashed after 1987 (Fig. 25.23).

The Trust has just fenced the whole of Hayley Wood to exclude fallow deer, except for half the east quarter. Already by spring 2002, oxlip showed a distinct revival both in the old exclosures and in the north quarter of the wood, where the fence had been effective for only a few months. Oxlip continued to decline in the east of the wood, still much frequented by fallow deer.

Changes in tree canopy

Besides the local effects of resumption of coppicing, there are two other changes. Replanting in Gamlingay Wood, as we have seen, has reduced the density of

Fig. 25.34 (a–b) *Helleborus viridis* at the same point in Buff Wood,

(a) March 1974 and

(b) March 2002. The plants have hardly altered at all.

oxlip compared to areas that escaped planting; loss of primrose is not related to replanting. In Knapwell Wood, small replanted areas tend to behave like coppiced areas, with local increases of oxlip.

Where areas of elm have died of Elm Disease, the ground is taken over more or less rapidly either by elm suckers or by other trees. The Elm Disease area in the east of Hayley Wood is a favourite hideout of fallow deer, and has largely lost both oxlip and bluebell. Oxlip will have been eaten by the deer, and waterlogging seems to have increased so as to overcome the bluebell.

In Overhall Grove, in contrast, areas of dead elm were often taken over for a few years by coarse grasses and nettles, highly competitive plants which may be responsible for the decline of oxlip. Places where oxlip remains abundant tend to be either avoided by nettle, or where the tree canopy remains intact, or coppiced areas under electricity cables.

Increased fertility

Nutrient-poor places, such as ancient woods, are becoming rare and beleaguered. Surrounding farmland is drenched in fertilizer, which migrates into the woods either by drift or via bird-droppings. This may not be bad for primroses and oxlips directly, but it encourages competitors with a high demand for phosphate or nitrate, especially nettle, *Galium aparine* and ground-ivy *Glechoma hederacea*.

These plants have indeed increased in many ancient woods. In Hayley they are codominant in a band round the north and part of the west side. In the 1971–72 exclosure and its control plots, ground-ivy became prevalent from the mid-1980s onwards; it doubtless helps that deer never eat it (Table 25.9).

General Conclusions

The twentieth century has seen a number of historically unique or unusual events. Proliferation of deer has never happened before, nor has replanting in this group of woods. Many woods, even where not replanted, are more shady than they have historically been. The Elm Disease episode of the 1970s was more severe than any other known, but its effects were multiplied by deer eating the suckers after the big trees had died. Such a combination of new and drastic events has probably not happened in any previous century in historic times. There have been Great Storms before, rivalling that of 1987, but when woods were regularly coppiced their effects would be subdued and would last only one coppice cycle.

The exceptional run of hot dry summers in the last thirty years is probably without precedent at least since the medieval warm period of the twelfth to thirteenth centuries. The most severe in its effects on vegetation was 1976 (which killed many beech trees in Cambridgeshire and other places where beech is not native). The 1997 summer, although roughly as hot, was wet and did less damage. In descending order of severity were 1995, 1975, 1989, 1990, 1970 and 1983. In the previous 70 years there were probably only three comparable summers – 1959, 1921 and 1911 – and two in the nineteenth century – 1826 and 1846. It is impossible to say whether the declining frequency of wet springs is quite so exceptional.

The dynamics of trees may seem different from those of herbaceous plants. But trees are not necessarily longer-lived than herbs: it is not known whether a birch outlives an oxlip individual, or whether an oak can outlive a mercury clone. However, the distribution of trees seems to be determined by conditions prevailing in their first few years. If unusual circumstances conspire to allow a birch to get started, it will survive even in a generally unsuitable place. One might therefore expect the tree population to reflect conditions from decades or centuries in the past, whereas herbs are more responsive to the drought or deer of the recent past.

This may be counteracted by constraints of dispersal. Bluebell, oxlip, and dog's-mercury do not easily colonize new sites. Bluebell and especially mercury might take many years to occupy ground made available to them by a run of dry springs. However, the small-scale observations reveal a surprisingly dynamic situation. Oxlip areas are being forever colonized by bluebell and mercury, which can persist in a very attenuated state – even invisibly in the case of mercury – and could respond rapidly if conditions changed in their favour.

Stability

Although woods turn out to be unexpectedly dynamic, not all aspects are in a state of flux. The patch of Green Hellebore *Helleborus viridis* in Buff Wood, which I have known for 40 years, is almost unaltered: photographs from 1974 to 1993 show individual plants unchanged in every detail (Fig. 25.34). (But the similar patch in Kingston Wood has declined.) Orpine *Sedum telephium* in Hayley Wood occurs as two patches, probably clonal, which have not altered since before 1964. The rare Atlantic liverwort *Nowellia curvifolia*, discovered in 1962 on long-fallen dead oaks under the eastern elms in Hayley, still grows on those same oaks, even after the death of the elms has exposed it to the heat of six great summers.

The Madingley Wood photographs illustrate the stability of woods that happen to escape catastrophes. At three of the sites not much happened in 50 years; even small maples and suppressed elms are still there. The extreme stability of oaks, especially dead oaks and parts of oaks, is confirmed elsewhere. In *Hayley Wood* (1975) I reported that stumps and tops of oaks felled in the 1920s were still very visible, though reduced to heartwood. Nearly thirty years on, they are still visible, and photographs show that they have not much changed. Oak logs and stumps therefore last at least a hundred years, unlike elm which persists for about 40 years, and maple which disappears in less than ten.

Stag-head

Stability is important in relation to the 'stag-head' question. In some areas, especially Sherwood Forest (p. 316) and hedges in Norfolk farmland, many oaks are dead at the top, with branches that have lost their bark and sapwood. These have sometimes been thought to be 'dying trees' due to air pollution, ploughing damaging their roots, etc. Whatever the cause, the dead boughs are not necessarily recent.

Why should stag-head be thought abnormal? When I visited Australia, the first thing botanists told me was that eucalypts respond to great droughts by boughs dying, reducing the leafage, and growing new boughs when the rains return. Is this not part of the normal behaviour of oaks too (there is an example in Fig. 25.14d)? I suspect that many stag-headed oaks date from the great drought of 1921. 1975–6 was followed by a dieback, not of oaks, but of hedgerow ashes. Such ashes as survived have grown new leafage; their dead branches have rotted away by now, and will not persist to create illusions of acid-rain damage in the twenty-first century. Stag-head is not specially common in oak, but attracts more attention because dead boughs of oak are very persistent (Fig. 25.17).

The oxlip-primrose problem

This is more complex than at first appeared. The original hypothesis (hybridization) turns out to be insignificant. Instead six factors appear to be involved – hot summers, wet springs, deer, coppicing, replanting, contamination with fertilizer – and they interact. Oxlip could withstand hot summers and survive deer browsing, but the two together are deadly, especially when the hot summer follows coppicing.

The pattern of severe summers fits the decline of primrose, an Atlantic plant in the least Atlantic part of England, which only just withstands ordinary summers. The 'Cambridge hole' in its distribution is getting bigger. I have no reports of primrose declining in western England, well within its climatic tolerance. Competition probably plays a part: in Knapwell Wood the few remaining primroses mostly contend with vigorous mercury, and anything that encourages mercury, such as several years without a wet spring, puts them in jeopardy. (Probably my 1969 mapping of Knapwell Wood, coming after the drenched summer of 1968, recorded an unusually favourable state of primrose, a temporary remission in the long decline.)

Those who believe in Global Warming will conclude that its first victim is primrose, not bluebell as is often predicted. Bluebell, although also a species of Atlantic distribution, has been less affected. Its onward march into the Hayley Triangle was reversed between 1987 and 1997 (but less severely than that of oxlip), and has since resumed (Fig. 25.25). Established bluebell populations have declined in hot summers, but more easily recover than primrose. Some fluctuations can be ascribed to the year-to-year incidence of waterlogging and competition by mercury or to increasing competition from high-fertility plants. Is the absence of primrose from conurbations (which bluebell does not share) really because great concentrations of buildings make summers hotter – the 'urban heat island' effect?

Oxlip is less simple. From its Continental distribution it might be expected to benefit from hot summers. In reality it is set back by hot summers, which kill some of the plants, especially in Hayley Wood. (Beech has a similar European distribution and a similar behaviour.) Ordinarily the dead oxlips are replaced by seed set by the remaining plants. In unbrowsed woods a single drought has little long-term effect, but the five severe summers between 1975 and 1995 took their toll in most woods. If drought happens during the shade phase of a coppice cycle, replacement will be slow because the surviving plants will not flower immediately. In browsed areas there may never be replacement, because any plants that have survived both browsing and drought will be prevented from flowering. Other effects, such as lack of waterlogging in spring, or loss of tree canopy and thus increased growth of competing herbs, contribute in some woods.

Exposure to full sunlight for two or three years, as with normal coppicing, is beneficial to oxlip as to many woodland herbs, but prolonged exposure is a different story. Light-demanding competitors take over the site and suppress the oxlip. This can happen in various ways. Deer (as in Hayley) not only eat oxlips, but prevent or delay the underwood from growing again and encourage browsing-resistant competitors. Replanting delays the closure of the canopy – for planted trees grow slowly at first, even if the deer spare them. This may also happen where elms are killed and fail to sucker (cf Overhall Grove). The combination of replanting and deer is particularly bad for ground vegetation (Hempstead).

Aggressive, browsing-resistant competitors have increased in recent decades. These include *Deschampsia*, *Carex pendula*, and *Calamagrostis epigejos* (the 'Forestry Commission grass'). They are beginning to cause the trouble in English woods that aggressive, usually introduced, 'elephant-grasses' do in tropical forests: they take over felled areas and prevent recovery.

Hayley Wood was set up as a nature reserve in 1962 specifically to conserve oxlip. There are few woods in which oxlip has failed so badly. This is more to do with bad luck than bad management, but one should ask whether oxlip would have been worse off under sympathetic private management. Conservation organizations are very reluctant to kill deer because they think (often wrongly) that their members would object. A private owner might have tried to control the deer, although whether this would have worked is doubtful.

Fig. 25.35 Oxlips in shade phase of coppice cycle. Such a density of plants, once unremarkable, now survives only where deer have not reached. Buff Wood. April 1998

Fig. 25.36 Successful replanting, Gamlingay Wood: the original ground vegetation as well as the trees have been annihilated, and locally there is nothing to show that this was an ancient wood. Destruction, however, has seldom been so thoroughgoing as this. April 2002

26

On Coppicing Plants

> [*Melampyrum pratense* grows] only in the copses of one year's growth, which are hedged round; the seeds . . . must lie dormant in the soil fifteen or sixteen years, until, by some of the wonderful works of Nature, the earth is prepared to cause vegetation [enough to fatten pheasants; also valerian, which is an article of commerce].
>
> *Cranborne Chase, Dorset and Wiltshire, 1818*[1]
>
> [I found this plant in a part of Holne Chase, Devon, felled for the first time in 125 years]

The woodland flora tends to be concentrated in three kinds of place: margins and permanent openings; wet places; and recently-felled areas. Many woodland plants come and go in relation to the coppice cycle. Usually they increase after each felling: typically about one-third of the flora of a wood consists of 'buried-seed' plants that are not visible every year. 'Coppicing plants' that appear or increase after coppicing are often characteristic of a particular wood, distinguishing it from other woods. This makes it less useful to describe a wood merely in terms of the species visible.

The original account of coppicing plants (pp. 79–82) can now be extended by 22 years of further data, following coppiced areas through two or three cycles. Buried-seed plants are now better known through information published by A. H. F. Brown, J. P.Grime, and their colleagues.

The data

My field observations extend over many woods, not all of them discussed here. In general the data are from whole areas cut in any one year, not from samples of areas. In Chalkney Wood, Essex County Council has continued the preceding coppicing (and restored it where it had lapsed) since it acquired one-third of the wood in 1973; the first cycle under the present regime has been completed and a second cycle begun. The rest of Chalkney, belonging to the Forestry Commission, was replanted in the 1950s; by way of comparison with normal coppicing I give observations made after conifers were removed, beginning in 1988.

In the Bradfield Woods, Suffolk, the data include (among others) the very long list (101 species) made after a two-acre fell was cut in 1970, which was re-recorded after a second felling in 1980 and a third felling (103 species) in 2001.[2]

In Hayley Wood there are four experiments in particular.

The Seven One-Acre Plots. Fourteen coppice plots, each of one acre (64 x 64 m) were cut year by year from 1964 to 1977 (cf Fig. 25.23). The first seven were exposed to deer until 1980, when they were enclosed within a fence which keeps out fallow deer but not muntjac. The fourteen plots were then re-coppiced from 1980 to 1993, and are now on their third cycle (1994 to 2007). Plots 1 to 7, therefore, were felled in 1964 to 1970, 1980 to 1986, and 1994 to 2000. After fencing, coppice growth was normal but was sometimes delayed for one year by muntjac. Plots 3 to 6, on which fallow deer killed most of the original underwood after the first felling, became infilled with ash from seed. I have estimated the numbers of oxlip and other flowers year by year within each acre, as well as keeping more general records of coppicing plants from 1964 onwards.

The Little Exclosure. In winter 1968, with the help of Geoffrey McBride, I built the first fallow-deer exclosure in Hayley in what was to be plot 12 of the series. It was a little bigger than the permanent quadrat of 14 x 14 feet (4.3 x 4.3 m) which it enclosed. Two nearby quadrats (controls I and II), as nearly identical as possible in their vegetation and tree cover, were marked but not fenced. They had last been coppiced probably in 1924. They came up for coppicing (but the ash-trees were pollarded, p. 202) in 1976 and again in 1992. All three had been browsed by fallow deer for many years before the experiment started. The two control plots continued to be browsed until 2001. There is no sign that muntjac have forced their way into the exclosure. Records and

1 Chafin, W. (1818). *The Anecdotes and History of Cranbourn Chase*, 2nd ed. Nichols & Bentley, London, p. 57ff.

2 I acknowledge the help of Ann Hart in 1970 and 2001.

photographs follow the fate of the enclosed oxlip plants since 1968.

The One-Acre Exclosure. In 1971–2 a one-acre fence was built, comprising half of plot 8, coppiced in 1971 (for the first time since 1898), and half of plot 9, coppiced in 1972 (previously 1899). Twenty permanent markers were set up, five in each of the two half-acres inside and the two outside, to include a range of densities of oxlip (p. 403). These define twenty circular plots of radius 1 metre, area 3.14 sq.m. each, ten browsed by fallow deer and ten not. Early records of oxlip from this experiment were shown in Fig. 7.3. I have recorded all species year by year from each of the twenty plots, continuing through the re-coppicings of 1987 and 1988 and of 2001 and 2002. This and the previous experiment were modified in 2001, when fallow deer were excluded from nearly the whole wood.

The Deer-fence Corridor. In late winter 2001, in order to erect a deer-fence, a narrow strip, about 15 feet wide and 800 yards long, was felled along the north side of Hayley Wood. This formed, in effect, a linear transect through three kinds of terrain: (1) an area last felled in 1914, and thus of 87 years' growth, which is an unusually long interval between coppicings; (2) an area of 57 years' growth; (3) the part of the wood known as the Triangle, which developed out of grassland in the 1920s (p. 51ff) and had never been felled. The first year's observations of what appeared are included in this chapter. (They should not be influenced by edge effects, because this edge of the wood dates only from when the wood was truncated in 1862; previously areas (1) and (2) had been in the interior.)

Kinds of coppicing plant

As in the original book, I divide coppicing plants into:

1. *Spring-flowering persistent perennials*, e.g. oxlip, bluebell.
2. *Summer-flowering persistent perennials*, e.g. meadowsweet.
3. *Seed-bank plants* that germinate from seed buried after the previous coppicing, e.g. wood-spurge. (This is now known to be the biggest category.)
4. *Mobile plants* that move around the wood from one coppiced area to another, e.g. willowherbs and thistles.
5. *Casual species*, crops and weeds, that come in sporradically from outside and are not sustainable within the wood, e.g. borage.
6. *Species that do not respond* to coppicing, or that decline, e.g. herb paris.

I have a further category of *aquatics* (principally the coppicing plants of woodland ponds).

Discriminating between categories is not always straightforward. *Deschampsia caespitosa* can persist through a coppice cycle if the shade is not too dense; it is also reported to have a seed-bank, and probably is dispersed in animals' fur. The seed-bank category best reflects its behaviour from my long-term observations in Hayley. Evening primrose (*Oenothera* sp.) has turned up as a casual in the Bradfield Woods, but could easily establish itself as a permanent inhabitant, just as its relative, the American *Chamae(ne)rion angustifolium*, did some 80 years ago.[3]

Tree Seedlings

Coppicing gives an opportunity for new trees to get started, either through seeds germinating along with the coppicing herbs, or by stimulating the 'advance regeneration' of young trees which germinated in previous years and languished in shade. New trees presuppose that there shall be space between the existing stools, which most often happens if some of the stools have been destroyed either by deer browsing or by an attempt at replanting. In the past gaps would have been provided by the felling of standard trees along with the underwood.

Most British trees have short-lived seed, which germinates either immediately (e.g. oak) or in the second or third year (ash, lime, hawthorn etc.) and does not persist as a seed-bank. Brown and Warr, however, report germinating birch from woodland soil samples.[4]

The trees that now behave as coppicing plants are ash and birch, both of which increased in the twentieth century (pp. 219, 318). Birch comes up in its legions in many coppiced woods, but only a few individuals survive the competition of existing stools to become permanent inhabitants of the wood. Ash is often the tree encouraged by intermittent deer-browsing. In Hayley, the 'maimed ashlings' mentioned in this book in 1980 (p. 208) were bitten for many years. When enclosed by a deer-fence they shot up to fill the gaps which deer had made in the underwood, leaving their gnarled base as a witness to their stunted youth. Hawthorn can behave similarly.

The connexion of lime seedlings with hot summers, reviewed on p. 243, has been corroborated in the last twenty years. A series of extreme summers, combined with lime's propensity to germinate in the second or third year after the summer in which the seeds were produced, has resulted in seedlings in some limewoods

3 *The History of the Countryside* p. 57ff.
4 Brown, A. H. F., and Warr, S. P. (1992). The effects of changing management on seed banks in ancient coppices. Buckley (1992) pp. 147–66.

in most years. In 1978 I estimated that there were nearly 800,000 lime seedlings in 12 acres of Chalkney Wood just felled (Fig. 15.13). As far as I know not one grew into a tree, the area being crammed with lime stools already.

Coppicing presumably gave oak an opportunity to grow from seed, which it must have done freely to produce the many millions of small oaks used in medieval buildings (p. 146; see also p. 460). It no longer does so (p. 296f.); I occasionally record oaklings in coppiced areas, but only in the Bradfield Woods is there still a steady turnover of young oaks. Similarly I have very rarely seen new hazels in coppiced areas (p. 210).

Spring Perennials: the Hayley Wood Oxlip Experiments

Spring-flowering perennials are the best-known feature of coppice woods. The species are few: for example anemone, bluebell, lesser celandine, primrose, oxlip, archangel, pignut, and several orchids (Fig. 26.1, Table 26.1). They typically occur in great numbers; they flower in shade, but after the shade has been removed they flower much more, and the flowering season is often prolonged. Primrose and violets (the latter classed as summer perennials) can flower continuously for a year and a half after coppicing.

Fig. 26.1 (a–c) Coppicing plants of the spring-perennial group, in each case one year after felling.

(a) Oxlip. Note prodigious number of stems per plant and of flowers per stem; the plant itself lasts through several coppice cycles. Bradfield Woods. April 1982

(b) Anemone. There is a considerable response, even though the leafing season of anemone is short and most of it happens before the trees come into leaf. Groton Wood. April 1998

(c) Early Purple Orchid. Bradfield Woods. May 1979

Table 26.1 Plants which appeared in the 2001 deer-fence corridor, Hayley Wood.

	Last felled 1914 (87 years)	Last felled 1944 (57 years)	Triangle (new (woodland)
Tree seedlings			
Ash	++	++	+++
Spring perennials			
Anemone nemorosa			(+)
Endymion (Scilla) non-scriptus			+
Primula elatior			(+)
Summer perennials			
Agrostis stolonifera			+
Brachypodium sylvaticum		++	
Sanicula europaea			(+)
Solanum dulcamara		(+)	
Viola riviniana			++?
Seed-bank			
Ajuga reptans		+	
Carex remota			(+)
C. sylvatica	+	+	
Cerastium vulgatum	(+)		
Deschampsia caespitosa		(+)	
Dipsacus sylvestris		+	
Fragaria vesca		+	++
Galium aparine			(+)
G. palustre	++++	++++	
Geranium robertianum		+	+
Glechoma hederacea	+		
Hypericum hirsutum	++	++	+
H. tetrapterum		+	
Juncus bufonius		(+)	
J. conglomeratus		?+	
Lychnis flos-cuculi	+	+	
Myosotis arvensis		(+)	(+)
Plantago major		(+)	
Poa annua	(+)		
P. trivialis		+	
Potentilla sterilis		(+)	
P. reptans			++
Prunella vulgaris	+	+	(+)
Ranunculus ficaria		+	
R. repens		+	(+)
Rubus caesius		+	
R. Corylifolii		+	
R. fruticosus			(+)
Rumex crispus		+	+
R. sanguineus		+	
Scrophularia aquatica	+++	+	
S. nodosa	++	+++	
Veronica chamaedrys			(+)
V. serpyllifolia	+	+	++
Mobile			
Arctium minus			(+)
Circaea lutetiana		+	++
Cirsium palustre		+	(+)

	1914	1944	Triangle
C. vulgare		+	
Epilobium adenocaulon		(+)	
E. adnatum		(+)	(+)
E. parviflorum		(+)?	
Geum urbanum	+		+++
Picris echioides		+	
Aquatic			
Ranunculus flammula	(+)		
Casual			
Arrhenatherum elatius		(+)	
Geranium ?parviflorum		(+)	
Taraxacum sp.			(+)
Veronica arvensis		(+)	
Unresponsive			
Arum maculatum			+
Mercurialis perennis			++

Oxlip shall stand as a representative of these plants, being much the most studied.

Little Exclosure

The number of oxlip flowers produced year by year before coppicing and through one coppice cycle and two-thirds of another is shown in Fig. 26.2. (These numbers include an estimate for flowers eaten or broken off by predators.)

Flower production varies widely from year to year, and good and bad years tend to be the same for the exclosure and the control plots. However, within a few years after fencing, plants in the browsed control plots had declined, producing a fraction of the flowers of the fenced plot. This was correlated with reduced leafage: in the 1980s and 1990s oxlip leaves covered 4–10% of the ground in the fenced plot, but usually less than 2% of the browsed plots.

Bad years tend to follow extreme summers. The first

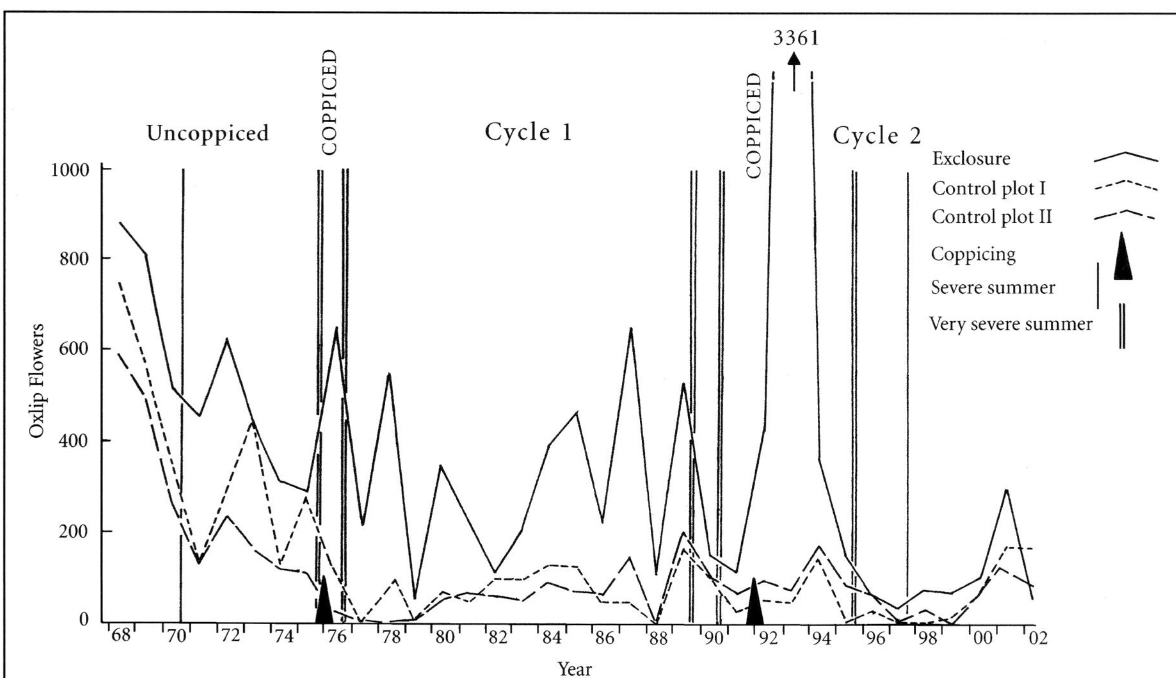

Fig. 26.2 Numbers of oxlip flowers produced year by year in the Little Exclosure and its control plots, Hayley Wood, following the fencing of the exclosure in 1968. Numbers include an estimate for flowers eaten or bitten off.

coppicing came between the phenomenal hot summer of 1975 and the even hotter summer of 1976 – these two being the most severe, in their effects on vegetation, of the twentieth century (p. 409). As fate had it, the experimental plots came up for coppicing in winter 1976. In the fenced plot there was somewhat of a coppicing response in spring 1976 itself: this is paradoxical but, as we shall see, not unique. The plants, then suddenly exposed to the heat of the summer of the century, withered early and did not make the material needed for increased flowering in 1977.

The pair of severe summers (hot and dry) in 1989 and 1990, and the severe summer of 1995, were also followed by years of poor flowering. As we have seen (Chapter 25), oxlip is susceptible to heat and drought, although it extends into the interior of Europe where ordinary summers are hotter than ours.

The next coppicing, in 1992, produced a phenomenal response in 1993 in the exclosure (Fig. 26.3). The number of flowers went up roughly tenfold from previous years – made up of five times the number of flowering stems and twice the flowers per stem. This was then followed by a marked depression in flowering, as the trees grew again and the shade was restored, though the oxlip leafage remained much the same.

Fig. 26.3 Oxlips in the Little Exclosure, Hayley Wood, fenced for 25 years, one year after it was felled for the second time. Note pollarded ashes inside and outsided the fence. April 1993

Flowers are eaten by fallow deer and muntjac outside the exclosure, and also by creatures that can get into the exclosure: some swallow the entire umbel (often before the flowers open); some eat only the flowers; others bite off the umbel and drop it. Such damage, often accounting for more than half the flowers, occurred in the fenced and unfenced plots. Probably the greater concentration of flowers inside the fence attracts such predators. However, in some years there was no predation inside the fence: in the phenomenal year 1993 and the good year 1985 no flowers were eaten, and very few in the good year 1987.

Although seedlings were often recorded, oxlip plants are long-lived: most of the individuals on photographs taken inside the fence in 1968–9 are still recognizable in later photographs including 2002 (Fig. 25.30).

Differences between the fenced plot and the two controls are not due only to the direct influence of browsing. Outside the fence, the plants never fully recovered from the 1975–6 summers. But as time went on, the environment grew less shaded than inside the fence, because deer prevented most of the underwood from growing. In consequence the plants outside maintained a steady low level of flowering, on which the 1992 coppicing had little effect. In 2002, for the first time, more flowers were produced by the control plants than in the exclosure. This is presumably the result of the expulsion of fallow deer in 2001 from outside as well as inside, combined with the greater shade inside the fence.

One-Acre Exclosure

The mean number of oxlip flowers per square metre, for two whole coppice cycles, is shown in Fig. 26.4. As expected, there was a great rise in flowering in the fenced plots in the years after coppicing. The half-acre felled in 1971 reached its peak flowering in 1972; the 1972 fell had an even higher peak one year later than expected. (There is no obvious peculiarity of weather to account for the delay.) After this flowering very drastically fell, doubtless due to the 1975–6 summers, and then slowly increased in the latter part of the cycle. Further peaks of flowering occurred one year after the coppicings of 1987 and 1988. This was followed by a rapid decline, attributable to the severe summers of the 1990s. In 1999 a fallow doe broke in and could not get out for some days; she ate nearly all the oxlips and much else. This explains why there was not much of a peak in 2002.

As in other experiments, the coppicing effect was both an increase in number of flowering stems and an increase in flowers per inflorescence. Leafage fluctuated in no systematic way. In the plot felled in 1971 leaf area

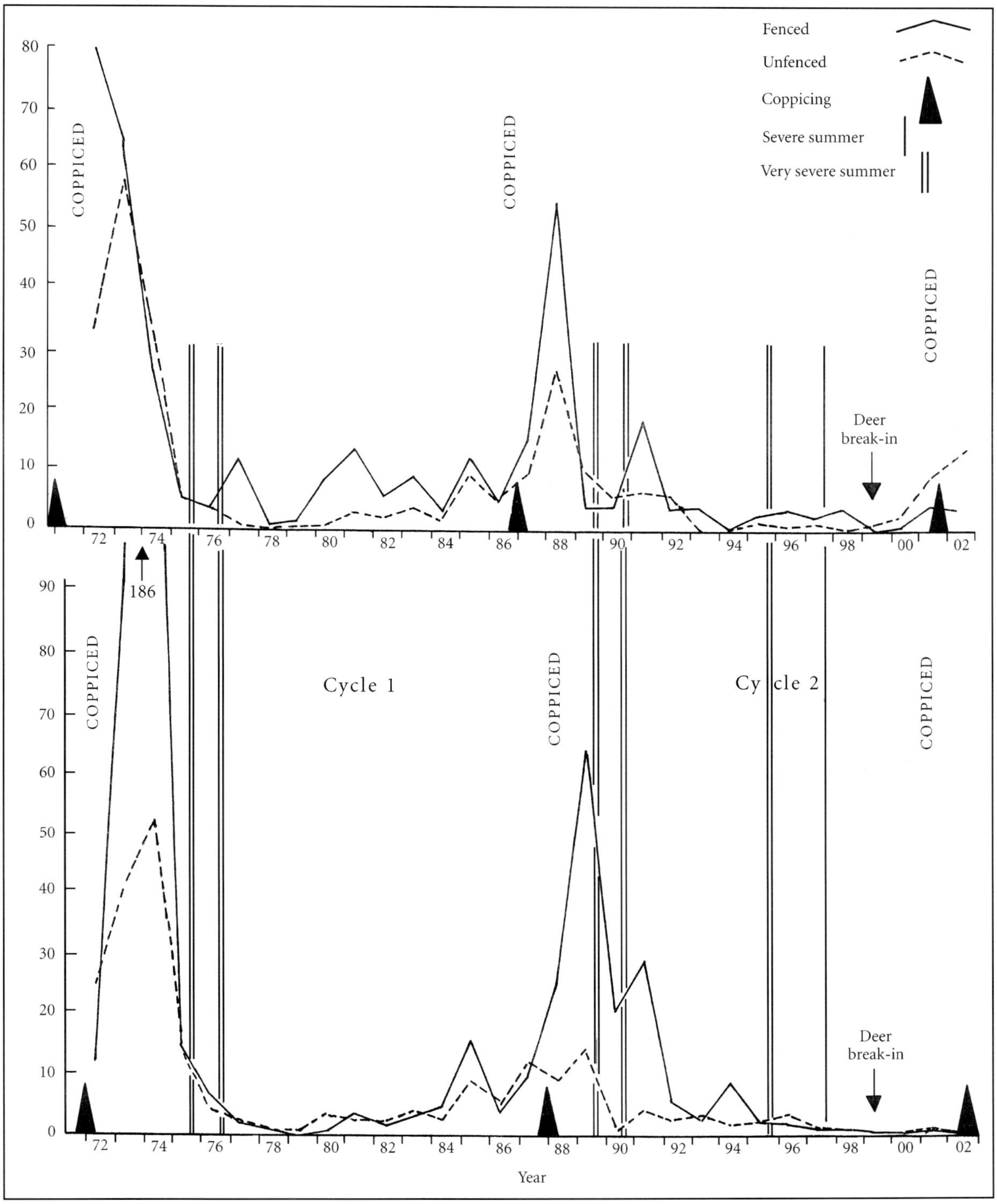

Fig. 26.4 Numbers of oxlip flowers per square metre produced year by year in the two halves of the One-Acre Exclosure and its unfenced control areas, coppiced in successive years. Each count is the mean count on of five permanent 1-metre circles.

increased markedly in the middle of the cycle: oxlip, like other shade-adapted plants, produces large thin leaves in dense shade.

Oxlips in the browsed plots, too, responded to the first round of coppicing. Thereafter they suffered severely from the 1975–6 drought and did not easily recover. In some quadrats the underwood was browsed and shade was not restored; this was of direct benefit to the oxlips, but also encouraged the persistence of *Deschampsia* and rushes which competed with them. In general oxlips fared worse than in the fenced plots. The second round of coppicing had little effect on them, since in many of the plots there was little shade to remove.

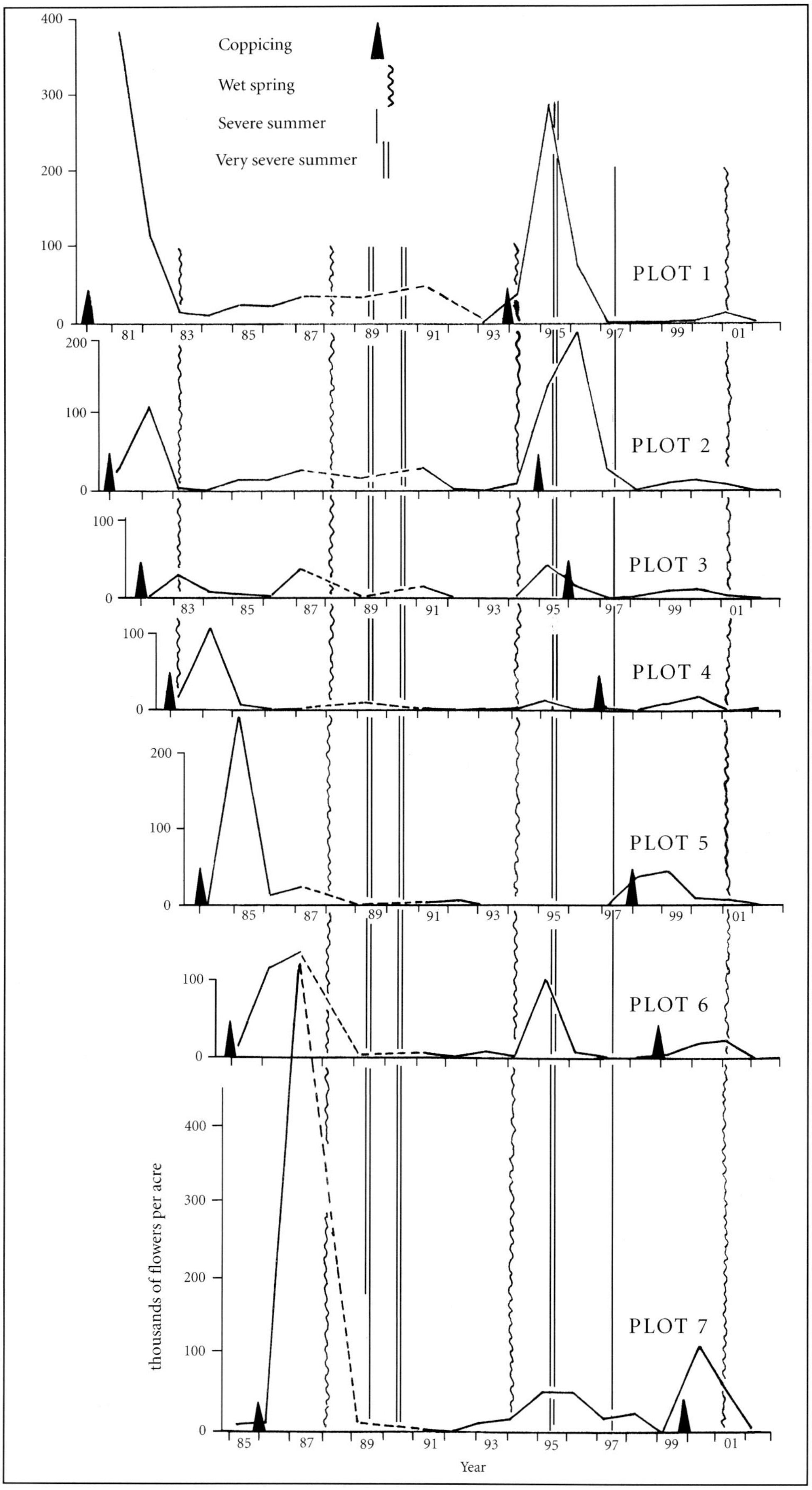

Fig. 26.5 Estimated numbers of oxlip flowers surviving year by year in the Seven One-Acre Plots, fenced against fallow deer and coppiced year after year. 100,000 flowers per acre = 25 per sq.metre.

The Seven One-Acre Plots

In Fig. 26.5 I roughly estimate numbers of oxlip flowers for the whole of each one-acre plot over one whole cycle and a fraction. Fallow deer were absent. Oxlip plants are not uniformly distributed, being densest in plots 7 and 1, and sparsest in 3 and 4. The coppice-response pattern was observed every time except following the severe summers of 1995 and 1997. However, there are other fluctuations which affect most plots at whatever stage of the cycle: for example 1995 was a good year nearly throughout (although this was not observable in the other experiments).

Peak flowering came usually in the second year after felling, sometimes in the third (plot 6, both cycles). However on a few occasions there was a marked rise in the first year, rarely even a first-year peak (plot 7, second cycle). This seems paradoxical, since the flowers should have been laid down in embryo the previous summer, and there would not be time, after a subsequent felling, to generate more for the following spring. However, it is possible that oxlip, like many other plants, develops more flower primordia than it would normally need and aborts the unused ones. It would thus have a reserve of extra flowers to develop should conditions be unexpectedly favourable.

Plot 7, felled in 1986, produced in 1987 what is probably the most spectacular display of oxlips that any living eye has seen. On one acre there were some 600,000 flowers (Plate 7b, p. xxvii). This was generally a good year (Fig. 26.2), and there were almost comparable densities of oxlips in other parts of Hayley Wood at similar stages of coppicing. The previous felling, in 1970, had been followed in 1972 (a year delayed) by a display of about 400,000 oxlip flowers. On both occasions there were unusually many flowers per stem as well as stems per plant. However, the 1986 felling also encouraged *Deschampsia caespitosa*, which became dominant and severely competed with oxlip (Plate 7c, p. xxviii; Plate 7p, p. xxxi). Oxlip flowers fell to a few thousand in 1991–2, and after the 2000 felling the display was nowhere near as dense. But on carefully studying the 1987 photographs, I find that some 60% of the oxlip plants are still there.

Conclusions

The oxlip story turns out to be surprisingly complex. Coppicing, although the main influence, interacts with deer, weather, and competition. Prolific flowering calls for a combination of previous coppicing, a previous cool and wettish summer, and no deer; but even these can be overruled by insufficient shade in the previous cycle leading to a strong growth of *Deschampsia*.

Summer Perennials

Summer perennials, such as water-avens, are shade-resisters rather than shade-evaders (Fig. 26.6). They should be more responsive to coppicing because they

Fig. 26.6 (a–b) Coppicing plants of the summer-perennial group, one year after felling.

(a) Violet (*Viola riviniana*), Bradfield Woods. May 1975

(b) Water-avens (*Geum rivale*), Bradfield Woods. June 1976 do most of their photosynthesis when the trees are in leaf and when coppicing makes a greater difference to light reaching the ground (p. 79). However, this is often not obvious: meadowsweet continues to flower even in moderate shade.

Seed-bank Plants

Among the plants in the remarkably rich two-acre 1970 fell at the north end of the Bradfield Woods was the tiny sedge *Isolepis setacea* (Fig. 26.7a) I had never seen it in a wood before, and seldom since. It lasted for a year and then disappeared. Thirty years and two coppicings later, it reappeared on exactly the same spot. Since its seeds have been reported in woodland soil samples, there can be little doubt that it survived between coppicings as buried seed. At the other end of the scale, foxglove (*Digitalis purpurea*) is very gregarious, confined to acid-soil woods, and reappears every time such a wood is felled. In 1993 a big area of Wentwood, the huge Monmouthshire wood, was felled of conifers: several million foxgloves appeared from seed laid down fifty years earlier when the previous trees had been destroyed (Fig. 26.7b). The seeds of both plants, like many long-lived seeds, are very small.

Seed-bank plants are the biggest category of coppicing plants: well over 100 species have been germinated from samples of woodland soil.[5] Where sufficiently studied they form at least one-fifth of the entire flora of a wood, rising to one-third in very shady woods like Chalkney with its lime and hornbeam. They are laid down *in situ*, not transported from nearby rides or open areas, as shown by the fact that seeds in soil samples are not specially abundant in the vicinity of rides;[6] in any case few seed-bank plants occur much in woodland grassland.

I include among seed-bank plants those with some of the following features: occurring frequently or in large quantities after felling; having no visible means of dispersal; known to have persistent seed, or in the same genus as a plant that does; and dying out in the course of a coppice cycle.

Two of the earliest recorded coppicing plants are buried-seed species: broom in Benninck's fifteenth-century picture of a limewood (Frontispiece), and Ray's *Chenopodium polyspermum* in the 1650s (p. 79). The latter is now more common as a farmland weed, but was recorded by Ray only as a coppicing plant.

Records year by year in the 1-metre-radius circles of Hayley Wood show that many seed-bank plants appear in the first or second summer after felling – occasionally later if the weather is unfavourable – and last one to four years. This happens, for example, with ragged robin (*Lychnis flos-cuculi*) and marsh bedstraw (*Galium palustre*). *Hypericum hirsutum* behaves similarly, as does *H. tetrapterum* and other St John's-worts in other woods. Among these is the little creeping *H. humifusum*, common especially in limewoods where it appears in the second and persists into the third year. The big St John's-Wort *Hypericum androsæmum* appeared in 1980 in a 1-year fell in Chalkney Wood, its only recent Essex record; it has since been reported in similar circumstances in Hatfield Forest.

Some seed-bank plants are dominant, like the various brambles and rushes: they can determine the course of the vegetation during the whole coppice cycle, and even (if they shed copious seed) during the next cycle. Others, like figwort (*Scrophularia nodosa*), are common but seldom abundant, appearing in the first or second summer and lasting 1½ years. *S. aquatica* appeared in Hayley Wood in the 2001 deer-fence corridor. It had never before been recorded for this wood or (with one exception) in any other of the West Cambridgeshire woods. It was one of a number of plants that had apparently been lying dormant for 87 years since the area had last been felled. Many others had been dormant for 57 years (Table 26.1).

Wood-spurges are characteristic seed-bank plants. The relatively common *Euphorbia amygdaloides* is especially characteristic of the Bradfield Woods (Fig. 26.7f), germinating in the first summer, persisting over the winter, flowering next spring, and dying out over several years as the canopy closes in. It is very gregarious, coming up in thousands on certain moderately acidic soils, but entirely absent from the rest of the wood. The three rare wood-spurges, *E. hyberna*, *pilosa*, and *serrulata* (*stricta*), are thought to have disappeared from record owing to lack of felling in the woods where they occur. In 1985 I visited Coed Wen (Penhow, Monmouthshire), which had been felled five years before owing to Elm Disease. An odd set of coppicing plants resulted, including *Malva moschata*, *Hypericum perforatum*, *Aethusa cynapium*, and many thousand plants of *Euphorbia serrulata*, which had not been known in the area before. By 1985 they were declining; in 1999 I found the wood fully grown up and only three straggly *E. serrulata* left.

Seed-bank plants sometimes germinate, for unknown reasons, later in the coppice cycle. They may persist throughout the cycle if there is not too much shade. Bugle (*Ajuga reptans*) and ground-ivy (*Glechoma hederacea*) in the Hayley plots sometimes persist, sometimes not. If the underwood is not dense enough or the cycle too short, *Deschampsia caespitosa* tussocks may survive to become dominant in the next cycle.

5 Grime, J. P., Hodgson, J. G. and Hunt, R. (1988). *Comparative Plant Ecology*. Unwin Hyman, London.
6 Brown, A. H. F., and Oosterhuis, L. (1981). The role of buried seed in coppicewoods. *Biological Conservation*, **21**, 19–38.

Fig. 26.7 (a–h) Buried-seed plants, one year after felling.

(a) *Isolepis setacea*, Bradfield Woods. September 2001

(b) Foxglove arising from 50-year-old buried seed, Wentwood. June 1999

(c) Broom (cf Frontispiece), Whitehall Wood, Aveley (S. Essex). May 1980

(d) *Chenopodium polyspermum*, Bradfield Woods. September 1980

(e) Tutsan (*Hypericum androsaemum*), Chalkney Wood. July 1980

(f) Wood-spurge (*Euphorbia amygdaloides*); the white flowers are wild garlic (*Allium ursinum*), an unresponsive plant. Bradfield Woods. May 1987

(g) Red campion and wild raspberry, Chalkney Wood (of which wood they are characteristic). May 1979

(h) Hound's-tongue (*Cynoglossum officinale*), Hatfield Forest (of which it used to be characteristic). June 1994

How do seed-bank plants know when to germinate?

Plants like red campion, raspberry, and wood-spurge tend to be exactly confined to newly-felled areas. In Chalkney Wood, for example, raspberry seedlings extend undiminished up to the edge of a new fell and decline to zero within 15 feet or so into the surrounding old underwood; this is about half the canopy height, and does not vary noticeably according to whether the edge faces the sun. Buried-seed plants were set off by the uprooting even of single stools in the 1987 storm.

In the nature of things, buried seeds can hardly see the increased light directly. They might be brought to the surface by disturbance, and some such plants, such as *Gnaphalium uliginosum*, do seem to go with tracks and wheel-ruts in coppiced areas; but many common coppice plants come up everywhere regardless of disturbance.

Coppiced areas tend to be several degrees warmer than the uncut canopy, especially where the growing stools give shelter and in the lee of an edge. They are warmer still compared to the ground in the wood before coppicing.[7] But if germination is stimulated by temperature, buried-seed plants ought to be set off even in shade by very hot summers like 1976, or especially by summers that are both hot and wet, like 1989. This I have not observed to happen.

Another hypothesis is that a proportion of the seed-bank germinates every year, but if the seedlings emerge into shade they are damped off by fungi or eaten by something (let it be slugs) before anyone notices them. Exposure to light keeps off the predators and allows the seedlings to grow rapidly past the vulnerable stage.

I leave it to readers to investigate this intriguing little problem. The observation that some coppicing plants do reappear in later years of the cycle, even if they fail to flower, would favour the last hypothesis.

Mobile Plants

These are typically biennial species or short-lived perennials, dispersed by wind (thistles, willowherbs), which germinate in the first year, form a rosette, flower in the second summer (Fig. 26.8), and leave their dead remains in the third year.

Unresponsive Plants

A few woodland plants probably require continuous shade, such as filmy-ferns and delicate bryophytes such as *Hookeria lucens*. These, obviously, do not occur in coppice-woods unless long uncut or in ravines and other special places.

Dog's mercury is set back by removal of shade; indeed coppicing may benefit other plants, not only directly, but also by reducing competition from mercury (Fig. 26.11a). (N. J. Hunter, however, tells me of a positive response in Bunny Old Wood, Notts.) Herb paris seems to suffer a temporary setback in a coppiced area. Bracken benefits from coppicing, but other ferns are set back, at least in dry eastern England.

In the Bradfield Woods the dense stands of wild garlic (*Allium ursinum*) sometimes wither early and loses their flowers, except in a circular patch under each standard tree (Fig. 26.11b). The patch is directly under the canopy of the tree and is not displaced to the north, so it cannot be due to shade. This effect was strong in the dry spring of 1974: did the leafless oaks comb moisture out of fog or driving rain and drip it beneath their canopies, thus adding to the effective rainfall to the benefit of the garlic underneath?

Coppicing Plants and the Identity of Woods

Coppicing plants are difficult to include in the inventory of a wood's flora. It is a matter of chance which of them happen to be visible in any one year. I have known surveyors include them in data for the *National Vegetation Classification*, which had the curious effect that adjacent fells were assigned to different plant communities according to which stage of the cycle they had reached at the time of recording.

Coppice plants, as we have seen, are very subject to weather and other variables at the time of recording, but they do not occur at random. When 101 species were recorded in a fell of the Bradfield Woods cut in 1970, and 103 after it was cut again in 2000, 73 species were common to both lists. Seed-bank plants come up again and again in the same 1-metre-radius circles in Hayley Wood.

Each wood has a characteristic suite of coppicing plants. In Chalkney Wood, red campion and wild raspberry appear again and again whenever any part of the wood is felled, a combination which I have not seen elsewhere even in nearby limewoods. In the generally acidic woods of S.E Essex broom, heather, and cow-wheat (*Melapyrum pratense*) are characteristic. In the Bradfield Woods there is a series of assemblages: oxlip and rushes in wet calcareous areas; water-avens (*Geum rivale*) and violets; wood-spurge (*Euphorbia amygdaloides*) in intermediate areas; brambles; and bracken and cow-wheat on sand-lenses. Hayley Wood has oxlip

7 Rackham, O. (1975). Temperatures of plant communities as measured by pyrometric and other methods. In: *Light as an Ecological Factor II* (*see original reference* 50), 423–49.

Fig. 26.8 Mobile coppicing plant: marsh thistle (*Cirsium palustre*) in the second summer after coppicing. Buff Wood. August 1969

Fig. 26.9 Aquatic coppicing plant: water violet (*Hottonia palustris*) in a woodland pond in the second season after coppicing. Chalkney Wood. September 2000

Fig. 26.10 Casual coppicing plant: borage, a cultivated plant which often escapes into felled woods from farmers' fields. Chalkney Wood. September 1999

Fig. 26.11 (a–b) Unresponsive (or, in these instances, counter-responsive) coppicing plants.

(a) Dog's-mercury scorched to a crisp in a great summer. Chalkney Wood. September 1990

(b) A carpet of wild garlic (*Allium ursinum*) in the first spring after felling. It has been temporarily set back, and this year's flowers withered, except for near-normal patches under the drip – not shade – of each oak. Bradfield Woods. May 1974

and ragged robin. Buff Wood has primrose. Hempstead Wood (before its decline) had forgetmenot (*Myosotis sylvatica*) and oxlip. In Hatfield Forest the characteristic coppicing plant is historically hound's-tongue (*Cynoglossum officinale*), which has the great advantage in a wood-pasture that nothing will eat it. *Cirsium palustre* is reported as prevalent in Dutch ash coppices.[8]

In Table 26.2 I have grouped the various classes of coppicing plants according to their occurrence in particular woods. They form assemblages – if I had more data I might call them plant communities – parallel to those formed by the permanently-visible plants. Seed-bank plants tend to be the most distinctive category and mobile species the least.

New woodland

Table 26.1 lists the plants which responded to felling in the Hayley Wood Triangle, woodland 70 years old which had never been cut before. Coppicing plants were generally much less copious than in the old wood. They included the occasional perennials, such as oxlip and dog's-mercury, which had invaded gradually from the old wood (Fig. 25.25). Seed-bank plants were few, and mostly of the kind that occur in woodland grassland and at the edges of woods (e.g. *Fragaria, Potentilla reptans*); probably the seed had been laid down in the early stages of the wood arising. Seventy years is much too short a time for a new wood to acquire a full suite of coppicing plants.

Deconiferization

Table 26.2 includes two examples of deconiferization, the removal of conifers planted in replacement of wild trees, as discussed further in Chapter 33. In each case a set of plants followed, analogous to coppicing plants. In Chalkney Wood this was more than an analogy, for deconiferization plants reproduced the characteristic coppicing plants of this wood. The correspondence was not exact: most of the spring and summer perennials had perished in the long years of evergreen shade. Moreover the part of the wood which was replanted, and then unreplanted, has more gravelly soils than the south where coppicing persisted (p. 249). Deconiferization, however, produced red campion (*Silene dioica*) and raspberry (*Rubus idaeus*), the 'trademark' coppicing plants of Chalkney Wood, while adding species of acid gravels such as *Rumex tenuifolius*.

8 Pons, T. L. and During, H. J. (1987). Biennial behaviour of *Cirsium palustre* in ash coppice. *Holarctic Ecology* **10**, 40–4.

Table 26.2 Summary of coppicing plants recorded in certain woods

This does not include the entire coppicing flora of each wood, but only the species recorded on the occasions analyzed in this chapter.

Abundance is roughly indicated, ranging from +++++ (dominant) to (+) (rare).

The data are arranged so as to illustrate resemblances and differences between the coppicing floras of the woods, and to compare the floras resulting from removal of conifers with normal coppicing. The woods are arranged from predominantly dry, acidic (left) to seasonally wet, calcareous (right).

Hockley Woods: data from Rackham, *The Woods of South-East Essex* (1986), with further observations since.

Wood	Arger-Fen Wood (Suffolk) deconiferized	Hockley Woods (Essex)	Chalkney Wood (Essex) deconiferized	Chalkney Wood (Essex)	Bradfield Woods (Suffolk)	Hayley Wood (Cambs)	Buff Wood (Cambs)	Hempstead Wood (Essex)
Tree and shrub seedlings								
Birch		+++	++	+++	+	(+)		
Alder			+		+			
Hornbeam		+++		++			++	
Chestnut		+	+	+++				
Lime			++	+++				
Ash			++	(+)	+++			
Cherry				++				
Elder				++				
Holly				++				
Sallow				+		(+)		
Maple	+			(+)		++		
Hazel					(+)			
Oak	(+)		+	+	(+)	(+)		
Honeysuckle				+	++	+++		
Ivy					(+)	(+)		
Guelder-Rose						(+)		
Briar (*Rosa arvensis*)						+++		
Hawthorn						+++		
Privet						+		
Number of species	2	3	6	12	7	10	1	0
Spring perennials								
Endymion nonscriptus	+++	+++		++++	++	++++	+++	
Stellaria holostea		(+)						
Galeobdolon luteum	+	++			++	+		
Conopodium majus	+				++	++		
Anemone nemorosa			(+)	++++	++++	++++	+++	
Primula vulgaris		(+)		++	++		+++++	
Listera ovata						++		
Orchis mascula						(+)		
Primula elatior					+++	++++	+++	++++
Number of species	3	4	1	3	6	7	4	1
Summer perennials								
Pteridium aquilinum		+++						
Luzula sylvatica		++						
Deschampsia flexuosa		+						
Chaerophyllum temulum		(+)						
Melica uniflora		+		(+)				
Holcus mollis		+++	+	+++	++			
Ribes sylvestre				+				
Epipactis helleborine				(+)				
Agrostis stolonifera		+		++		+		(+)
Brachypodium sylvaticum				++	+	++		
Heracleum sphondylium		+		(+)	(+)			

Wood	Arger-Fen Wood	Hockley Woods	Chalkney Wood deconif.	Chalkney Wood	Bradfield Woods	Hayley Wood	Buff Wood	Hemp-stead Wood
Summer perennials (cont.)								
Solanum dulcamara		++		+++	++	++	(+)	
Viola riviniana			+++	+++	++++	++	++	
Viola reichenbachiana				++	+++	++	+	
Zerna ramosa				(+)	(+)	(+)		
Stachys officinalis					(+)			
Succisa pratensis					(+)			
Geum rivale					+++			
Tamus communis					++	(+)		
Carex pendula			+++	++	+++	(+)		+++++
Filipendula ulmaria					(+)	++++	+++	
Orchis fuchsii					+	++		
Sanicula europaea						+++		++
Agropyron repens								++
Number of species	0	9	3	12	14	11	4	4
Seed-bank plants								
Corydalis claviculata	+++							
Digitalis purpurea	+++++	++	+++	+++				
Rumex tenuifolius	+++	(+)	+++++	++				
Sarothamnus scoparius		++++	+					
Agrostis canina		+++						
Calluna vulgaris		+++						
Carex pilulifera		+						
Galium saxatile		+						
Pulicaria dysenterica		+						
Teurium scorodonia		+						
Hypericum pulchrum		(+)						
Potentilla erecta		(+)						
Ulex europaeus		(+)						
Luzula campestris			(+)					
Melampyrum pratense		+++			+			
Rubus idaeus		+++	+++++	+++++				
Silene dioica		++	++++	+++++				
Galeopsis tetrahit		++	+++	++	(+)			
Chenopodium polyspermum			++++	++				
Silene alba			+++	++				
Cardamine flexuosa			+++	+	(+)			
Senecio viscosus			++	+				
Chenopodium rubrum			++		(+)			
Carex remota		(+)	+++	+++	(+)	+	++	
Polygonum hydropiper			+	++				
Polygonum lapathifolium			+++	++	++			
Polygonum persicaria			+++	++	++		(+)	
Gnaphalium uliginosum			++	+++	++			
Hypericum humifusum			++	+++	++			
Veronica officinalis		(+)	+	+++	(+)			
Veronica montana		(+)		+++				
Carex strigosa				++				
Reseda luteola				++				
Lotus corniculatus				+				
Ranunculus auricomus				(+)				
Veronica serpyllifolia	+	(+)		+++	++			
Holcus lanatus		++	+	(+)	+++	+		
Cardamine pratensis		+		+++	++			
Rumex obtusifolius		(+)		++	+			
Hypericum perforatum		+		(+)	++			
Chenopodium album			(+)	(+)	+			
Capsella bursa-pastoris				++	+			

Wood	Arger-Fen Wood	Hockley Woods	Chalkney Wood deconif.	Chalkney Wood	Bradfield Woods	Hayley Wood	Buff Wood	Hemp-stead Wood
Seed-bank plants (cont.)								
Lapsana communis				++	+			
Sagina procumbens				++	+			
Stellaria media				++	+	(+)		
Polygonum convolvulus			++	++	+++			
Rumex crispus		(+)	+	+	++			
Senecio vulgaris			(+)	+++	++	(+)		
Senecio erucifolius	+	(+)		++	++	(+)		
Poa annua	+	(+)		+++	+++			
Lysimachia nemorum			(+)	++	++			
Galium aparine		(+)		(+)	++			
Rubus Corylifolii		++++		+++	+++	++	+++	+
Juncus conglomeratus	+	++	++++	++++	++	++++	++++	++
Hypericum hirsutum		++	++	+++	+	+++	++	
Veronica chamaedrys				+++	++	++		
Carex sylvatica			+++	+	++	+++	+++	
Solanum nigrum			+++	+			(+)	
Luzula pilosa	+	(+)	++	+++	++	++	+++	
Rubus fruticosus		++	++++	++++	++++	+++	+++	++
Juncus effusus			+++	++++	++	++	++++	++
Moehringia trinervia		+	+++	++++	+			+
Angelica sylvestris		++			+	+	+	
Urtica dioica	+	(+)		++	+			++
Polygonum aviculare				+	++			
Senecio sylvaticus		(+)		++	++	(+)		
Scrophularia aquatica			+++					++
Scrophularia nodosa	+	(+)	++	+++	++	+++		+
Plantago major		(+)		+++	++	++		
Rumex sanguineus	+			+++	+	++		++
Prunella vugaris	+			+	++	++		
Euphorbia amygdaloides		+			+++++			
Lotus uliginosus		+			+++			
Carex pallescens					++			
Isolepis setacea					+			
Luzula multiflora		(+)			+			
Mentha aquatica					+			
Carex flacca					(+)			
Galium erectum					(+)			
Malva moschata					(+)			
Myosotis arvensis				++	+	++		
Dactylis glomerata				++	(+)	++		
Cerastium vulgatum				(+)	++	+		
Potentilla reptans					(+)	(+)		
Lychnis flos-cuculi		(+)		+	++	+++		
Centaurium erythraea				(+)	++	(+)	++	
Fragaria vesca			(+)	++	++	+++	+++	
Galium palustre		(+)		++	++	+++	++	(+)
Hypericum tetrapterum				++	+++	++	+++	(+)
Juncus bufonius		+	+	++	++		+++	
Lysimachia nummularia				+	(+)		++	
Deschampsia caespitosa		++			++	+++	+++	++
Ajuga reptans		(+)			+++	+++		++
Ranunculus ficaria			+	++	(+)	+++	++++	
Ranunculus repens	+	(+)		++	+	+	++	++
Milium effusum		(+)		+	+	+++	++	
Potentilla sterilis			+	(+)	++	+++	+++	
Poa trivialis		(+)		+++	+++	+++	+++	+++
Lythrum salicaria						+		
Rubus caesius						+++	++++	

Wood	Arger-Fen Wood	Hockley Woods	Chalkney Wood deconif.	Chalkney Wood	Bradfield Woods	Hayley Wood	Buff Wood	Hemp-stead Wood
Seed-bank plants (cont.)								
Glechoma hederacea		+		++		++++	++	+++
Juncus articulatus					++	+	+++	
Carex otrubae						(+)	(+)	
Carex acutiformis							+	
Juncus inflexus		+					(+)	
Poa nemoralis							(+)	
Dipsacus sylvestris				(+)			(+)	++
Barbarea vulgaris					+		++	++
Myosotis sylvatica				(+)				+++++
Number of species	13	52	39	73	73	40	32	19
Mobile species								
Hieracium perpropinquum		(+)						
Cham(ae)nerion angustifolium		++++	++++	++++	++	+++		
Calamagrostis epigejos				(+)				
Epilobium roseum				+	+			
Picris echioides			++	+	(+)		+	
Sonchus asper			++	++	++	(+)		
Circaea lutetiana			+++	+++	++	+++	++	
Sonchus arvensis				++	(+)	+	(+)	
Arctium minus				++	+++	++	+	
Cirsium arvense		(+)		++	++	++	+	
Sonchus oleraceus				(+)	++		(+)	
Epilobium montanum				+	+	+++		
Epilobium hirsutum		+		+	++	++	+++	
Cirsium palustre		+++		+++	++	++++	+++	++
Stachys sylvatica		+		++	++	(+)	++	++
Geum urbanum	+	(+)		+	+	+++	+++	+
Cirsium vulgare				+++	++	+	++	++
Epilobium adenocaulon				+	++	++	++	+
Epilobium adnatum		(+)			+	(+)	(+)	
Epilobium parviflorum				(+)	++	++		+
Number of species	1	8	4	18	18	15	13	6
Aquatics								
Chrysosplenium oppositifolium			+					
Callitriche stagnalis			++	++		(+)		
Hottonia palustris				++				
Lemna minor				++				
Alisma plantago-aquatica				(+)				
Ranunculus flammula				+++		++		
Veronica beccabunga			++		(+)		+	
Number of species	0	0	3	5	1	2	1	0
Casuals								
Artemisia vulgaris		(+)						
Buddleja davidii		(+)						
Medicago lupulina		(+)						
Ranunculus acris		(+)						
Vulpia bromoides		(+)						
Lactuca virosa			++					
Anthoxanthum odoratum		+	+					
Pisum sativum			(+)					
Verbascum thapsus			(+)					
Crepis taraxacifolia		(+)			(+)			
Borago officinalis			++	++				
Anagallis arvensis			+		(+)	(+)		

Wood	Arger-Fen Wood	Hockley Woods	Chalkney Wood deconif.	Chalkney Wood	Bradfield Woods	Hayley Wood	Buff Wood	Hemp-stead Wood
Casuals (cont.)								
Atriplex patula			(+)		(+)			
Hypochaeris radicata				++				
Conium maculatum				+				
Rumex acetosa				+				
Sagina nodosa				+				
Vicia tetrasperma				+				
Alliaria petiolata				(+)				
Bromus mollis				(+)				
Bryonia dioica (cretica)				(+)				
Geranium dissectum				(+)				
Impatiens glandulifera				(+)				
Onopordon acanthium				(+)				
Papavaver somniferum				(+)				
Plantago lanceolata				(+)				
Setaria viridis				(+)				
Sisymbrium officinale				(+)				
Urtica urens				(+)				
Arrhenatherum elatius				(+)	(+)			
Erigeron canadense				(+)	(+)			
Leontodon autumnalis				(+)	(+)			
Taraxacum spp.				+	+	(+)	+	
Avena fatua					+			
Centaurea nigra					(+)			
Lactuca serriola					(+)			
Lolium perenne					(+)			
Medicago sativa					(+)			
Oenothera sp.					(+)			
Phleum pratense					(+)			
Potentilla anserina					(+)			
Sinapis arvensis					(+)			
Veronica arvensis					(+)			
Vicia cracca					(+)			
Torilis japonica					(+)			
Triticum aestivum					+	(+)		
Tussilago farfara					(+)	(+)		
Matricaria maritima					+		(+)	
Ranunculus acris						(+)		
Alopecurus myosuroides							(+)	
Festuca gigantea								+
Number of species	0	7	7	21	22	5	3	1
Unresponsive								
Adoxa moschatellina			+					
Anthriscus sylvestris		(+)		++				
Arum maculatum				++	(+)	+++		
Athyrium filix-foemina					(+)			
Dryopteris borreri				+				
Dryopteris dilatata				++	(+)	(+)	(+)	
Dryopteris filix-mas				+++				
Allium ursinum					++++			
Mercurialis perennis				++	+++	++	++++	+++
Ophioglossum vulgatum						(+)		
Paris quadrifolia								++
Number of species	0	1	1	6	5	4	2	2
Total species	19	84	64	150	146	94	60	33
Total excluding trees and unresponsive herbs	17	80	57	132	134	80	57	31

Coppicing Plants in Other Countries

Sweden

On the Baltic island of Øland Dr Tommy Knutsson kindly showed me a group of woods which would not be out of place in East Anglia. They would fall into our Ash–Hazel subcategory, with standard oaks, patches of suckering elm, aspen clones, and birch invasion. Soils are weakly acidic, derived from glacial till with granite boulders, overlying limestone. Unfamiliar trees include *Ulmus laevis*, *Acer platanoides*, and *Sorbus intermedia*. Here too, deer are troublesome – here it is elk, a deer as big as a horse.

Some of the woods are ancient, some secondary, others developed out of *lövangar* wood-pastures. Much of the ground vegetation comprises familiar plants such as anemone, meadowsweet, twayblade, lily-of-the-valley, *Paris*, and *Ranunculus auricomus*; there are also Central European species such as *Hepatica nobilis*.

Woods that are still coppiced produce a well-developed coppice vegetation. Oaklings are very abundant in places, as they must formerly have been in England. All the classes of English coppicing plants are represented, and many common species are the same: for example strawberry, water-avens, sanicle, cow-wheat, and *Veronica chamaedrys*. Others are less familiar, such as the Central European *Campanula persicifolia*.

However, Øland has coppicing plants which do not behave in this way in England. The two most conspicuous spring flowers are cowslip and dandelion (Fig. 26.12). In England cowslip does not flourish in woodland and gradually dies out. In Øland it regularly lives in shade and flowers in vast abundance after felling, taking on the classic role of English oxlip. The dandelion, probably *Taraxacum latissimum* (which is said to be introduced where it occurs in England), is a big gregarious species, vastly abundant in the second year. Dandelions occur in English coppice, but only as sporadic casuals.

Greece

In the middle altitudes of the Pindus Mountains, N.W. Greece, are coppice-woods on a grand scale, going on for tens of miles. They are of deciduous oak (mainly *Quercus frainetto* and *pubescens*); other trees – hornbeam, hazel, service, elm – are rare; the soils are acid, on sandstones and serpentines. The woods are very slow-growing – the growing season is only two months – and are cut on cycles of 30–70 years. The flora is generally Central European, not Mediterranean, but with many peculiar Balkan species.

Fig. 26.12 Cowslip and dandelion as coppicing plants, Øland, Sweden. June 1995

Fig. 26.13 Coppiced oakwood of 1 year's growth, Pindos Mountains, Greece, with *Geranium asphodeloides*. May 1988

Here too is a conspicuous coppicing flora. A few species are coppicing plants in England, either widespread there (strawberry, *Veronica chamaedrys*, *Myosotis arvensis*) or very local (oxlip, *Melittis melissophyllum*, *Lithospermum purpureocaeruleum*). Others are found in England but not as coppicing plants: daisy, white clover, *Lathyrus nissolia* and *L. aphaca*. The most common coppicing plant, *Geranium asphodeloides* (Fig. 26.13), is south-east European. Accompanying it is *Euphorbia amygdaloides*, in a miniature form very unlike the wood-spurge of England. The many other unfamiliar plants include *Symphytum ottomanum*, *Vicia grandiflora*, and *Ranunculus constantinopolitanus*.

Compared with English woods there is a larger proportion of spring and summer perennials. Most of those mentioned, including *Geranium*, appear to persist in the not very dense shade of the grown-up wood. Buried-seed plants appear to be few: even *Euphorbia amygdaloides* is, at least partly, a spring perennial.

Japan

Japan has its own coppicing tradition independent of Europe. All the tree species are different, although many of them are of European genera. There are many kinds of coppice-woods on a vast scale: deciduous oakwoods, evergreen woods, and mixed deciduous woods. They contain giant stools and other features of ancient woodland. Although woodland and plantation cover more than half of Japan, all forms of timber- and woodcutting are much in decline.

From what I have seen, coppicing plants in Japan are less well developed than in England. This may be due to the crowded and rapid regrowth, which within a year can generate a closed, dark thicket that shades out herbaceous plants. A specially Japanese factor are the dwarf bamboos which carpet many woods and suppress other ground vegetation, more vigorously than dog's-mercury does in England.

The coppicing plants that I have seen are strong-growing grasses such as *Miscanthus sinensis*. The *koshida* fern (*Gleichenia*) and the Japanese form of bracken are persistent perennials. There are also ericaceous shrubs such as *Pieris japonica* and *Rhododendron obtusum* (Fig. 26.14) which flourish in felled areas and may flower in the first year: some of these may come from buried seed, like heather in England.

North America

Coppicing has a much shorter history in North America. American Indians seem to have got by without it. It was introduced by settlers and became widespread among

Fig. 26.14 Coppiced evergreen oakwood of 1 year's growth, near Kyoto, Japan, with *Rhododendron obtusum*. October 1998

Fig. 26.15 Coppice stool of *Acer rubrum*, Harvard Forest, Massachusetts. May 1981

trees mostly of the same genera, but different species, as in Europe. Biggish stools of red maple (*Acer rubrum*) and other trees, up to nearly 3 feet diameter (Fig. 26.15), occur in the wood-lots of New England, where there were some 250 years of coppicing before the countryside became depopulated. Later-settled regions have shorter coppicing histories, as far west as Texas. It can be difficult to distinguish coppicing from self-coppicing (p. 495) and (in this flammable continent) from regrowth after successive fires.

In 1981 I was shown a small experimental coppiced area in Hopkins Forest, Massachusetts. After two years there was strong regrowth from sprouts of red maple, suckers of aspen (*Populus tremuloides*), and other trees, despite deer browsing. America, unlike Europe, has a seed-bank tree, fire-cherry (*Prunus pensylvanica*), which despite its name comes up after felling as well as fire. Spring perennials – *Maianthemum*, *Trientalis*, *Oxalis* species – increased after felling. There are also buried-seed plants like those of Europe, such as *Carex pensylvanica* (recalling *C. sylvatica*), species of *Luzula*, and a *Rubus* corresponding to *R. caesius*.

In Mexico, a rare precursor of maize, *Zea diploperennis*, is threatened by the decline of slash-and-burn cultivation. This fire-promoting grass was probably originally adapted to fires in the native forest, but has more recently been maintained by felling as a substitute for fire.[9]

Australia

Australia is a miniature planet: its ecosystems work on different principles from the rest of the globe. Most trees (outside rainforest) are species of the vast genus *Eucalyptus*; they cast a very light shade; they are distasteful, except to koala bears; and fire does the recycling job that fungi do elsewhere. Most eucalypts sprout from the base or the trunk or branches; some grow very readily from seed.

Australian Aborigines did not go in for coppicing. Woodcutting, introduced by settlers, developed into a huge logging industry that now supplies Japan with wood (instead of using Japanese woodland), and has attracted the wrath of conservationists. Part of it, however, has more in common with coppicing than with modern forestry.

Daniel Lunney introduced me to an area at Merimbula, south-east New South Wales, that had been cut for the third time. The trees are mainly silvertop ash (*Eucalyptus sieberiana*). In this region it is the practice to leave any rotten trees that are not worth taking, and any trees along watercourses. After cutting and removing the usable trees, the fell is burnt, in order to preempt what might be a fiercer fire later. This confusion of charred logs and scorched (but surviving) trees soon develops into a thicket (Fig. 26.16). Seedling silvertop ash and sprouts of other eucalypts, exhibiting their colourful and paradoxical juvenile leaves, proliferate among shrubs, tall herbs, climbers, and grasses, species of *Bursaria*, *Goodenia*, *Pimelea*, *Solanum*, and *Senecio*, with bracken the sole reminder of Europe. I was assured that these are not universal tropical weeds but native species.

In three rotations of felling and regrowth a eucalyptus forest has thus turned into something like a coppice-wood, complete with coppicing flora. The illusion is completed by the big eucalyptus stools in later stages of regrowth. It may not be particularly good as an animal habitat because around ten years' growth it passes through a densely shading phase, which

Fig. 26.16 Area of 2 years' growth in logged eucalyptus forest, with 'coppicing' plants, Merimbula, New South Wales. November 1996

9 Sánchez-Velásquez, S. and 4 others (2002). Population dynamics of *Zea diploperennis*, an endangered perennial herb: effect of slash and burn practices. *J. Ecol.* **90**, 684–92.

is unnatural for eucalyptus woodland. Did English coppices pass through a stage like this in their prehistoric evolution from wildwood?

Where Did Coppicing Plants Come From?

Are coppicing plants merely a consequence of human woodmanship, or did they have antecedents in wildwood? The origins of coppicing itself are discussed in Chapter 32, where I argue that the ability to coppice evolved long before people cut down trees, possibly as an adaptation to elephants in the wildwood of previous interglacials. Coppicing plants might have arisen in the same conditions.

Coppicing plants are unlikely to have any one origin. On the one hand, they merge into ordinary weeds, like docks and thistles, some of which came from the Mediterranean origins of agriculture. They will have been augmented down the centuries by later introductions (Fig. 26.17) such as rosebay willowherb.[10] (Conversely, some weeds may have originated as coppicing plants.) But many coppicing plants are either mainly in woods (*Cirsium palustre*) or have no other habitat (*Euphorbia amygdaloides*): they are as much woodland plants as dog's-mercury or herb paris.

Fig. 26.17 A new coppicing plant: Himalayan Balsam (*Impatiens glandulifera*) in Kingcombe Coppice, Dorset, where it behaves as a mobile species. September 2002

Although there is some overlap of categories, coppicing plants are not the same as the plants of woodland grassland, that is of permanent open areas in a wood (p. 83f); nor are they the pasture component of wood-pasture (Chapters 12, 32); nor the 'circumboscal plants' of woodland edges (p. 84f); nor are they the successional plants arising in 'scrub' (that is, young woodland developing out of grassland or heath).

Coppicing plants would not be expected to have much of a pollen record: they would grow inevitably in confined spaces, so that their pollen would not travel to sites of deposit, and many are insect-pollinated. Nevertheless, at least ten species have a pre-Neolithic pollen record (Table 8.1, p. 108).[11]

Vera's reconstruction of wildwood as wood-pasture (Chapter 32) seems to leave little room for coppicing plants. After the loss of elephants, two main presursors of coppicing come to mind, windblow and fire. But there are others. In the northern Appennines in Italy, every few decades, whole hillsides of chestnuts and other trees are plucked out of the ground by an ice-storm (p. 495). A yet more awesome natural phenomenon, perhaps a closer analogy of coppicing, was described to me by Dr Hermann Margl on the Danube below Vienna: a sudden thaw causes an ice-dam on the river to collapse, which releases great islands of ice-floes to race across the flooded flood-plain, shearing off everything in their path at a metre or two high.

What about fire, on the pattern of *Zea diploperennis*? Flammable countries like Australia and North America have a profusion of fire-adapted herbs, many of whose seeds need to be heated or smoked before they will germinate. In the *maquis* of Southern Europe, which burns every 5 to 50 years, each fire is followed by a profusion of herbs, irresistibly recalling the plants of a coppice cycle.[12] A study on the Greek island of Kythera shows that the greatest number of species is to be found in areas burnt one or two years previously.[13] Even in England a profusion of oxeye daisy and other plants follows fires in furze or heath, especially on Cornish cliffs. However, these parallels will not work for English *woodland*, in which there is seldom anything combustible at all, let alone fuel to support the fierce tree-killing fire which would be needed. The only

10 *The History of the Countryside* p. 57f.
11 *Chamae[ne]rion angustifolium* should be omitted, as it represents the native mountain form of this plant, not the woodland ecotype which is an introduction.
12 *Nature of Mediterranean Europe* chapter 13.
13 O. Rackham & J. A. Moody, unpublished.

scope for fire, and then only rarely, is when there is enough bracken (or possibly heather) to sustain a fire in the first year or two *after* felling.

Windblow was a nebulous influence until the hurricane of 1987 (Chapter 27). It somewhat resembled coppicing. Shade was reduced, or rather redistributed, but the trees remained alive and restored the canopy within a few years. Coppicing plants (like the red campion of Chalkney Wood) were stimulated by uprooting just one tree. However, it may be argued that (in the present climate) windblow on any one spot is too rare an event for the flora, especially buried-seed plants, to wait for it to happen.

Coppicing is an ecological factor in its own right, and need not be a close copy of any natural process: the processes which it resembles occur at long and irregular influences. In various parts of the world it has operated long enough to create its own ecosystems; the American and Australian examples suggest that these may be initiated in surprisingly few cycles of felling and regrowth. Probably, as in many ecosystems of the unstable Pleistocene-Holocene period in which we live, these plant communities are composed of species which previously were doing something else: species which are not adapted to their present environment but which are making the best of the environment into which an accident of history has thrust them.

However, some of the species have short enough life-cycles to be susceptible to natural selection over the centuries for which coppicing has operated. Mechanisms for withstanding intervals of shade, or for prolonged dormancy of seed, could have been favoured. It is thus, maybe, that the Øland cowslips and dandelions have taken up the role which is played in England by oxlips and willowherbs. It may even be that individual woods have been isolated for long enough for evolutionary differences to contribute to the different coppicing floras of apparently similar woods – for the red campion of Chalkney Wood *versus* the forgetmenot of Hempstead Wood.

Fig. 26.18 (a–b)

(a) The 'Roman Road' in Chalkney Wood. The three men mark the middle of the (probably Iron Age) holloway and the faint banks (the earliest known woodbanks?) on either side. March 2002

(b) Nearly the same scene 14 months later. Underwood of lime and hornbeam. Coppicing plants include spring perennials (bluebell, in foreground), seed-bank plants (red campion), and mobile species (marsh thistle). May 2003

Fig. 27.1 Are trees necessarily meant to be upright? A flourishing horizontal hornbeam, overturned in 1987. Hatfield Forest. April 2003

Fig. 27.2 The remembrance of a storm long ago. Horizontal oak, Iken Wood (Suffolk). May 1975

27

Windblow and the Great Storms

And þe south-weste wynde on a Saturday at euene

. . . . .

Pere-trees and plum-trees were poffed to þe erthe

. . . . .

Beches and brode okes were blowe to þe grounde

And turned vpward here [their] tayl in tokenynge of drede.

Piers Plowman on the Great Storm of 1362[1]

It is not given to every human generation to experience a new ecological factor, or to re-experience a forgotten one. The Great Storms of 16 October 1987 and 25 January 1990 created a new body of knowledge about how trees and woods respond to windblow. Before 1987 I, like other ecologists, assumed that hurricanes were a factor in other countries, and that the tracks of historic storms could be followed in New England, for example, but not in Old England. In October 1987 I had the great good fortune that Professor Henry Art, of Massachusetts, expert on the effect of hurricanes, was in Cambridge, and we were able to abandon whatever else we were doing and study its immediate effects. (What greater honour can one do a visiting scholar than put on a hurricane for his especial entertainment?)

History shows that sudden events, such as great storms and earthquakes, soon get forgotten, their precise consequences not put on record, and their lessons not learnt.[2] (Even as I write, the 1987 'destruction' of most of the 'mature' trees in southern England is being cited as responsible for the decline of the hawfinch!) It is inherent in human nature and in scientific method to pay more attention to gradual, repetitive processes. Although in the nature of things a formal quantitative study of the 1987 and 1990 storms is hardly possible, I here make some record of what did, or did not, happen at the time, and of what the consequences were.

The 1987 storm was an unusual one in England south-east of a line from Southampton to Great Yarmouth. North and west the intensity quickly diminished. Damage was patchy. Some of the greatest was in places on the edge of the storm area (e.g. Kew, Newmarket); conversely, many areas of Suffolk and Sussex were hardly affected. Damage was often greater on south-facing slopes or at the top of such. Because it happened at night there were few eye-witnesses, but some described the storm as 'a bundle of tornadoes'. This is confirmed by the fallen trees lying higgledy-piggledy but with a majority towards the north-east.

The 1990 storm was also southern but more western, especially in Cornwall. However it did greater damage than 1987 in some outlying spots, notably Ely Cathedral and Staverton Park. There have been two comparable storms since in France. On 27 October 2002 I witnessed a storm in Hayley Wood which, locally, had the same effect as that of fifteen years before: it is a rare privilege to have oak boughs tumbling about one's ears.

How did the Great Storms compare with previous storms?

Exact comparisons are impossible. Instrumental readings are unsatisfactory because anemometers, designed for ordinary winds, misrecord gusts or are blown off scale. Intensities vary regionally and locally: an event that would be called a Great Storm at Cambridge might be little more than routine at Land's End. The effect on trees of a given intensity of wind varies with the time of year and with changes in the tree population. The best measure of comparison is probably structural damage to buildings. Compared with previous great storms, those of 1987 and 1990 were remarkable for the great

1 C text, V.116f.

2 For a four-year survey see: Whitbread, A. M. (ed.) (1991), *Research on the ecological effects on woodland of the 1987 storm*. Nature Conservancy Council: *Research and survey in nature conservation* **40**.

damage to trees, the small loss of human life, and very small loss by shipwreck.

One might expect storms to behave like other catastrophic events, for example floods or Australian bush-fires. The greatest event in a thousand years should be much greater than the greatest in a hundred years.

Great storms are recorded from about 1100 onwards. In relation to the total quantity of surviving archives, the thirteenth and fourteenth centuries (before and shortly after the first phase of the Little Ice Age) were remarkably stormy. Presumably such storms would have had less effect then than now, because of the rarity of plantations in the middle ages and scarcity of the big, young, crowded trees which are the most vulnerable. However, a regular aspect of storms was the disposal of windfallen wood, called *cablish* (Latin *cablicium*), which was often someone's perquisite. (I cannot say whether the medievals believed that fallen trees were killed.)

Probably the greatest storm in English history came from the south-west in the evening of Saturday 15 January 1362. It blew down the spire of Norwich Cathedral and many others: Gavin Simpson tells me that spires were being rebuilt in the 1360s all over England. A rival storm in December 1222 had kept the sellers of the king's cablish, as well as his carpenters and masons, busy over much of England;[3] there had been another in 1211. In 1360 a post-mortem inquiry made the curious claim that a wood in Gussage St Michael (Dorset) contained no underwood because it all blew down the year before the death of the owner – but was this a pretext to cover some suspicious dealing by the executors?

Another storm of greater magnitude than 1987 or 1990 was that of 26 November 1703. By this time the country was full of chimney-stacks, many thousands of which collapsed, including one that killed the Bishop of Bath & Wells in his bed.

More recently, a hurricane struck Cornwall on 9 March 1891. The great storm of 31 January 1953, which did vast damage by flooding and shipwreck in Holland and eastern England, plucked out wide areas of plantations in Scotland. Another hurricane had similar effects in south-west Scotland in January 1968.

A storm equivalent to 1987 can be expected in any one place at least once in a hundred years. (There have been periods, such as 1400 to 1550, apparently lacking in such storms.) The particularly high ratio of tree to building damage in 1987 was partly due to this storm coming when the trees are in leaf (most great storms are between November and March), preceded by heavy rain which weakened the ground. However, there may also be a demographic effect, of more of the tree population being vulnerable than on previous occasions.

Great Storms are only one aspect of windblow. In a wood such as Hayley a few trees fall every year, mostly oaks and other big trees killed or weakened by their neighbours overtopping them or honey-fungus gnawing their roots; this will have been less prevalent in the past when woods were more intensively managed. Tornadoes and other locally intense storms result in windblow not corresponding to great gales, for example at Helmingham (E. Suffolk) in 1870. Trees may rarely be broken or uprooted by the weight of very intense rain on a still summer day, or by an accumulation of ice in freezing rain (p. 495).

Immediate effects on trees

A tree can fall in four distinct ways:

1. Bough-breakage.
2. Top-breakage – all or most of the crown is lost but at least part of the trunk remains standing.
3. Base-breakage – the trunk fails at ground level and takes little or none of the roots with it.
4. Uprooting.

Situation: free-standing trees versus *woods and plantations*

Other things being equal, free-standing trees were much less often uprooted than trees in woods and plantations, although they were more exposed to wind. (This was also true of the Massachusetts hurricane in 1938.) This is presumably because free-standing trees, having no competition from neighbours, develop more substantial root-systems which grasp a greater weight of soil to act as a counter-weight to the wind.

Trees at the edges of woods and plantations, *including the windward edges*, were much less often uprooted than trees in the interior. (Among many examples noted by Art and myself, in a beech plantation on the road from Newmarket to Bury St Edmund's, almost every tree in the middle was uprooted but those on the edges escaped except where internal trees fell on them.) Trees on the edges develop half their root-systems unrestricted by competition.

The above applies to uprooting. But bough-breakage and top-breakage, too, were distinctly less common in free-standing or marginal trees than among trees in the interiors of woods and plantations. (An extreme example was in Rendlesham Forest, E. Suffolk, where almost every tree in the interior of several square miles of fifty-year-old Corsican and Scots Pine was top-broken or uprooted, but the marginal row, including the windward edge, was intact (Fig. 27.3).) Trees in the interior, sheltered from ordinary winds, evidently produce weaker wood. Professor Art refers to experiments in New England, in which trees were tethered by

3 *Rotuli Litterarum Clausarum*, 1, 533ff.

Fig. 27.3 Plantation of Corsican pine, about 50 years old, after the Storm. Note the upright trees on the edge in the distance. Rendlesham Forest, E. Suffolk. March 1988

cables so that they could not sway in normal winds; the wood laid down by such trees was weaker than by those allowed to sway.[4]

Inside woods there was often a windrow effect where lines of trees toppled, apparently because one tree knocked over a neighbour, which in turn knocked over a third, and so on.

In Cornwall in 1990 most of the uprooting was in places sheltered from ordinary winds. Big middle-aged beeches and giant young Monterey pines (*Pinus radiata*) toppled in deep valleys, whereas most trees on the edge of moorland proved invulnerable.

Planted versus *wild trees*

Uprooting was much commoner in plantations than in natural woods. Foresters by tradition plant trees close together and expect to thin them later. The original plan tends to be forgotten or postponed, and the thinning is left undone or unfinished. Root competition is therefore very severe, and the root systems have little resistance to wind. (It is the foresters' business to grow stems, not roots, and they trade off the greater yield of stems against the risk of loss to windblow.)

Planted trees in general were more often uprooted than wild. This is specially true of oaks, in which most uprooted trees had been planted; wild oaks escaped with bough-breakage. Arboreta and botanic gardens fared particularly badly. Does the act of transplanting, especially to a site on which the tree would not normally grow wild, cause life-long alteration to a tree's root system?

Effects of age

The greatest proportion of casualties (in all modes except perhaps base-breakage) was among young trees that had recently reached full size. (A well-publicized example was the Seven Oaks of Sevenoaks, said to have been planted in 1902, and 85 years old at the time of the Great Storm.) Most species of tree reach nearly their maximum size, and therefore maximum windage, early in life. Thereafter the tree becomes better able to withstand wind through adding new annual rings to its boughs, trunk, and roots.

After this vulnerable age had passed, age had no observable effect for a long time.

The least affected group were ancient trees (Fig. 27.4, 27.6). The ecological importance of 'veteran' trees was newly recognized in 1987, and lichenologists in particular were dismayed at the prospect of losing many trees that were specific habitats for rare species. This fear was nourished by the canard that the effects of the storm had been aggravated because England was full of 'senile' trees owing to lack of recent planting. As reports came in, it emerged that quite the contrary had happened, and ancient trees in general had withstood even the worst of the storm. Among many examples, the 4000 ancient oaks of Staverton Park, surrounded on all sides by the devastated Rendlesham Forest and by wrecked buildings, mostly lost not a twig. The ancient hornbeams of Merstham-Hatch Park, Kent, survived not only the storm but also having a plantation of big, young poplars collapse on top of them.

Effects of species and genetics

Differences between species were not great, with some exceptions. Wild oaks were specially liable to bough-breakage (unlike planted oaks, which uprooted). I have often noted that oaks which lose boughs tend to lose more than one bough, either in the same storm (Fig. 27.5) or in successive storms, for example in Table 27.1 overleaf.

Are brittle boughs a survival mechanism, appropriate to a long-lived tree? Shallow-rooted beech on chalk and chestnut on clay were specially liable to uprooting. Wellingtonia (*Sequoiadendron giganteum*) was very

4 Wilson, B. F. (1970). *The Growing Tree*. University of Massachusetts Press, Amherst. (Chapters 9, 10.)

Fig. 27.4 Oak, about 500 years old, after the 1987 storm. Staverton Park, surrounded by Rendlesham Forest. March 1988

Fig. 27.5 Free-standing oak surrounded by a litter of broken boughs. Hatfield Forest. October 1987

Table 27.1 Loss of boughs among about 1000 oaks, Hayley Wood, 2002 storm.

Number of boughs broken per tree	1	2	3	4	5
Number of trees observed	36	5	3	1	1
Number of trees expected on the basis that breakage was random	60	1.9	0.04	0.0007	0.0000

Instances where a bough could have been broken by another bough falling on it are counted as single breakages.

seldom damaged; this giant tree was introduced in 1851 and has not yet reached the vulnerable age.

The most vulnerable species, apart from cricket-bat willow, was Monterey pine in 1990. Taken from arid California to the wet climate of Cornwall, this tree became a super-fast grower, reaching 70 ft high and 4 ft in diameter in 50 years, and then toppling because it had put all its substance into the trunk and left little for the roots.

Effects of condition

In 1987 there was an English tradition, built into legal custom and the profession of tree surgery, that trees fell because they were 'unsound': they suffered from recognizable 'defects', of which decay and especially hollowness was the chief. Defective trees were supposed to be recognizable in advance of falling, and their owners were liable for damages if they fell on cars or people. Much of the business of tree surgeons in England was in identifying and removing or 'making safe' supposedly defective trees. This seems not to have been based on much evidence: I have never encountered any statistics of casualties, lawsuits, or damages, or of whether trees that fell were more defective than trees in general. Still less does anyone seem to have done the experiment of identifying and marking a group of defective trees (in an unfrequented place) and seeing what happened to them over the next thirty years.

These preconceptions were disconfirmed by the 1987 storm. The great majority of bough-broken, top-broken, or uprooted trees were perfectly sound. Trees which, before the storm, would have been classed as rotten or 'dangerous' were no more often broken or uprooted than those apparently sound (Fig. 27.6).

Base-breakage – an uncommon mode of failure in this storm – was often associated with butt-rot. A white-rot fungus such as *Inonotus* (*Polyporus*) *dryadeus* gets in via the roots and reduces a conical part inside the base of the trunk to the texture of Brie cheese, though still with the annual rings of oak. Usually this could not have been detected in advance.

These events are in line with the American researches of Alex L. Shigo, which show that decay is not a disease which spreads and spreads through a tree until it falls down.[5] Trees do not have an immune system like that of vertebrate animals, but they have mechanisms of damage control and compensatory growth which respond to wounds and defects. When a tree loses a branch it sets up a 'reaction zone' within the wood which walls off a pocket of tissue. Wood-rotting fungi and insects invade the walled-off tissue and consume the wood until they reach this predetermined boundary. The size and shape of the rot-pocket are determined by the size of the injury and not by subsequent treatment. Although European trees behave in this way just as American trees do, the works of Shigo are still not easily accessible in Britain, although there is now a critical and well-informed textbook involving his work.[6]

If the injury is sufficiently extensive, as with pollards, coppice stools, and most old trees, the trunk becomes hollow. When the core has finished rotting out, it leaves a compartment boundary which forms a hard, stable, almost bark-like lining to the inside of the tree. A hollow tree has, in effect, got rid of the wood no longer needed to hold up the tree, and has recycled the minerals in that wood.

This said, 1987 and later storms confirmed the reality of an unconventional defect that I had suspected for many years, namely narrow forks. Where two limbs diverge at a narrow angle a fold of bark is liable to get trapped as the limbs increase in diameter, creating a permanent weakness. Many narrow forks split in 1987 as on other occasions before or since (Fig. 27.7).

Dead trees were seldom blown down: for example at Box Hill, the Surrey chalkland site, most of the surviving big beeches were those that had been killed by the 1976 drought.

Root systems

Root systems revealed by uprooting turned out to be remarkably shallow: seldom more than two feet, and often less than a foot. A remarkable sight was a massive beech on chalk, or a giant chestnut stool on clay, where

Fig. 27.6 Beechwood after the 1987 storm. It is not an ancient wood but an infilled wood-pasture (p. 497). The trees that remain upright are the old pollards, dating from before it became a wood. Toys Hill, Kent. October 1989

Fig. 27.7 Youngish horse-chestnut, otherwise sound, which split at five narrow forks. Hyde Park, London. October 1987

5 Shigo, A. L. (1983). *Tree Defects: a photo guide.* United States Department of Agriculture, Forest Service, Washington.
6 Lonsdale, D. (1999). *Principles of tree hazard assessment and management.* Forestry Commission (HMSO).

Fig. 27.8 Great beech, showing shallow root-plate. Box Hill, Surrey. March 1988

Fig. 27.9 Shallow root-plate of chestnut stool. Hockley Woods, S.E. Essex. November 1987

a stem several feet in diameter was supported by a root-plate only a few inches thick (Fig. 27.8. 27.9).

It may be that deep roots are seldom seen because it is the shallow-rooted trees that get uprooted. (In Greece, where there is plenty of bulldozing, one can often see root systems sliced through by road-cuts.) However, the storm failed to confirm – for England – several widespread beliefs about roots: that they are an appreciable fraction of the height of the tree; that they are necessarily deeper than the roots of grasses and other herbs; or that trees have tap-roots. In England, as in Greece, deciduous oaks are generally shallow-rooted: I have encountered a few respectable reports of oaks with tap-roots, but these are evidently rare.

Short-term consequences

The proportion of trees killed by the storm was much less than expected. Top-broken and bough-broken broadleaved trees nearly always survived, however badly shattered. For these, wind-breakage was equivalent to pollarding. As with pollarding, survival was less universal, though still common, among conifers.

A new and unsuspected feature revealed by the storm was that large and ragged wounds stimulated sprouting, especially in species such as beech that sprout from a callus formed by the cambium. Arboriculturalists' preference for small tidy wounds is counter-productive in this respect.

Base-breakage, where it occurred, usually killed the tree, unless it was of a species which coppices or suckers freely when old: lime thus generally sprouted from the base, but not beech.

The wet summer of 1988 favoured the survival of root-damaged trees. One year on, a large majority of uprooted broad-leaved trees (in some places nearly 100%), were still alive; a majority were in apparently normal health; many appeared to flourish in their new orientation (Fig. 27.10). Most species remained alive if one-sixth of the original root-system remained in the ground, and flourished if they retained more than one-quarter. In general uprooted chestnuts, willows and small-leaved lime came off best; beeches came off worst, although even these were usually alive. Larch, being deciduous, survived nearly as well as broadleaved trees. Evergreen conifers, being liable to dry out immediately after uprooting, came off worse still, apart from cedar (a Mediterranean conifer used to droughts) which survives uprooting very well.

Here too, there is a new principle to be learnt. In the British climate, the amount of root needed to hold up a tree is much greater than the amount needed to supply it with water and minerals. Trees can suffer the loss of more than half their roots and still survive a moderate summer. This explains why so many trees survive honey-fungus attacks, transplanting, or cable-layers digging up the road. Butt-rot is walled off by the tree leaving enough roots to supply the tree and hold it up against ordinary, though not always exceptional, winds.

People's reactions to the storm did much more damage than the storm itself. Unexpected events bring out the worst in human tidy-mindedness. All through the very wet winter machines galumphed through woods tearing up and destroying fallen trees, as if they had been mutinous soldiers lying down on parade (Fig. 27.11). This dangerous work caused casualties among the workmen. (Where it was not done, public activities quickly resumed: people soon found ways over, under, or round toppled trees.) Millions of young 'replacement' trees were produced from somewhere and stuck into the ground. Fortunately the task was too vast to be completed; a year later there were complaints that 'time was running out'.

However, the Forestry Commission did a notably efficient job in removing the fallen trees of Rendlesham Forest. They had a purpose: the timber was saleable if not left too long. They reorganized their felling programme all over the country in order to winkle out the logs, keep them wet (to delay the progress of blue-stain fungi) and find markets for them.

The effect on ground vegetation was often similar to a coppicing. Buried-seed plants, in particular, were awakened and flourished until the canopy closed in again.

The next fifteen years

Bough- and top-broken trees continued to recover. Hedgerow trees with vigorous new growth became as familiar in parts of south and east England as they were in south-east Texas after the Galveston hurricane of 1961.

The hot dry summers of 1989, 1990, and 1995 were particularly unkind to trees that had not re-established a complete root system. But they favoured top-broken trees: on drought-prone sites the only oaks to flourish in those summers were those whose leafage had been reduced in 1987.

In the longer term uprooted trees died more from shade than drought. A single overturned tree finds its leaves in the shade of its neighbours, and is at a severe disadvantage. It is more likely to live if is tolerant of shade, such as lime, beech, or holly.

Fig. 27.10 Overturned beech one year after the Storm. The Blean. August 1988

Fig. 27.11 Clearing-up operations turned the 1990 Storm into a battlefield. Cornwall. February 1990

A surviving tree gradually comes to terms with the new direction of gravity. It sprouts from the upper side of the trunk and branches, and often also from the base as in coppicing. Strips of new wood maintain a link from the sprouts along the top of the fallen trunk and through the root-plate to those roots that remain in the ground (Fig. 27.12a, 27.13).

Where a single tree has fallen among upright neighbours (Fig. 27.12b), these basal sprouts take over. The tree will live if the sprouts reach the canopy gap before it has been filled by the sideways expansion of the neighbours. Years later, after redundant wood has rotted away, the result is a very characteristic lop-sided tree, of which one recognizes examples from previous great storms (Figs. 27.14, 27.15). Dr Jim Dickson points out that the woods around Glasgow are full of living oaks, larches, and (in one place) ancient yews overturned in the hurricane of 1968.

Table 27.2 summarizes my observations of the fate of the commonest uprooted trees on successive visits to the woods of The Blean, north of Canterbury. Of these three species, more than half are still alive after 10–15 years. The survival rate varies considerably between woods. The survival of beech is remarkable, for this is a drought-sensitive but shade-tolerant tree. Nearly all overturned beeches – including some big trees – are still alive after ten years (ten years in which many upright beeches succumbed to drought), beech being more tolerant of shade than oak or chestnut (Fig. 27.16).

Holly is also shade-tolerant. Many of the giant hollies of Staverton Park (p. 293) toppled in the great storm of 1990 or in lesser storms since. Although hollies of this size were already an anomaly in this dry part of England, they all flourish – except that deer have eaten the foliage which has come within their reach.

The woods have returned to something like normal. Where coppicing was in progress, as in Chalkney Wood (p. 248ff), the overturned stools were cut when their turn came and sprouted, resulting in a coppice-wood in which some of the stools seem to be lying on their sides. In some places there are areas of horizontal, flourishing trees.

Windrow effects and 'impenetrable forest'

If a whole windrow or swathe of trees has been uprooted, so that they no longer compete with upright neighbours, they nearly all live. They sprout both from the base and along the trunk, producing a coppice-like thicket of pole-sized stems (Fig. 27.12c). This has happened, for example, with areas of maples in Hatfield Forest and hazel in Groton Wood.

In Hockley Woods, S.E. Essex, great numbers of chestnuts, birches, and oaks were uprooted in the 1987 storm. Where reached by later coppicing operations they went back into their holes and are now 'normal' but askew. In areas that have not been coppiced since, the death-rate for *single* uprooted trees has been about 90% for birch, 70% for oak, and 40% for chestnut. However, *windrows* of fallen chestnut are surreal places of horizontal, living trees, with the occasional upright tree, now pollard-like, that was smashed by other trees falling on it (Fig. 27.17). The same can be seen in Colchester High Woods – an impenetrable place close to the middle of a large and busy town.

Table 27.2 Observations on the fate of uprooted trees, Blean woods.

Nearly all are attributed to the 1987 hurricane.
f: 'flourishing' or 'healthy' a: alive d: dead

Date of visit	Wood	Beech			Oak			Chestnut		
		f	a	d	f	a	d	f	a	d
Aug. 1988	Church, Grimshill, North Bishopsden	most	few		all			all		
Feb. 1990	Bossenden, N.Bishopsden	21	—	1	19	1	3	1	—	—
Feb. 1992	Thornden				20	8	—			
Feb. 1994	Ellenden	2	3	2	5	—	—	2	—	—
Feb. 1995	Church	1	—	1	15	3	7	3	—	1
Mar. 1997	Thornden				1	—	1			
Mar. 1998	Ellenden	7	7	4	9	4	7	24	10	9
Feb. 1999	Church, Grimshill	4	9	—	1	1	5	8	5	2
Feb. 2002	East Blean				10	11	22	0	1	5
Feb. 2002	North Bishopsden	6	0	1	5	8	3	9	7	17
Survival after 5 years			67% (but numbers small)			87%			83%	
Survival after 10 years			86%			57%			66%	

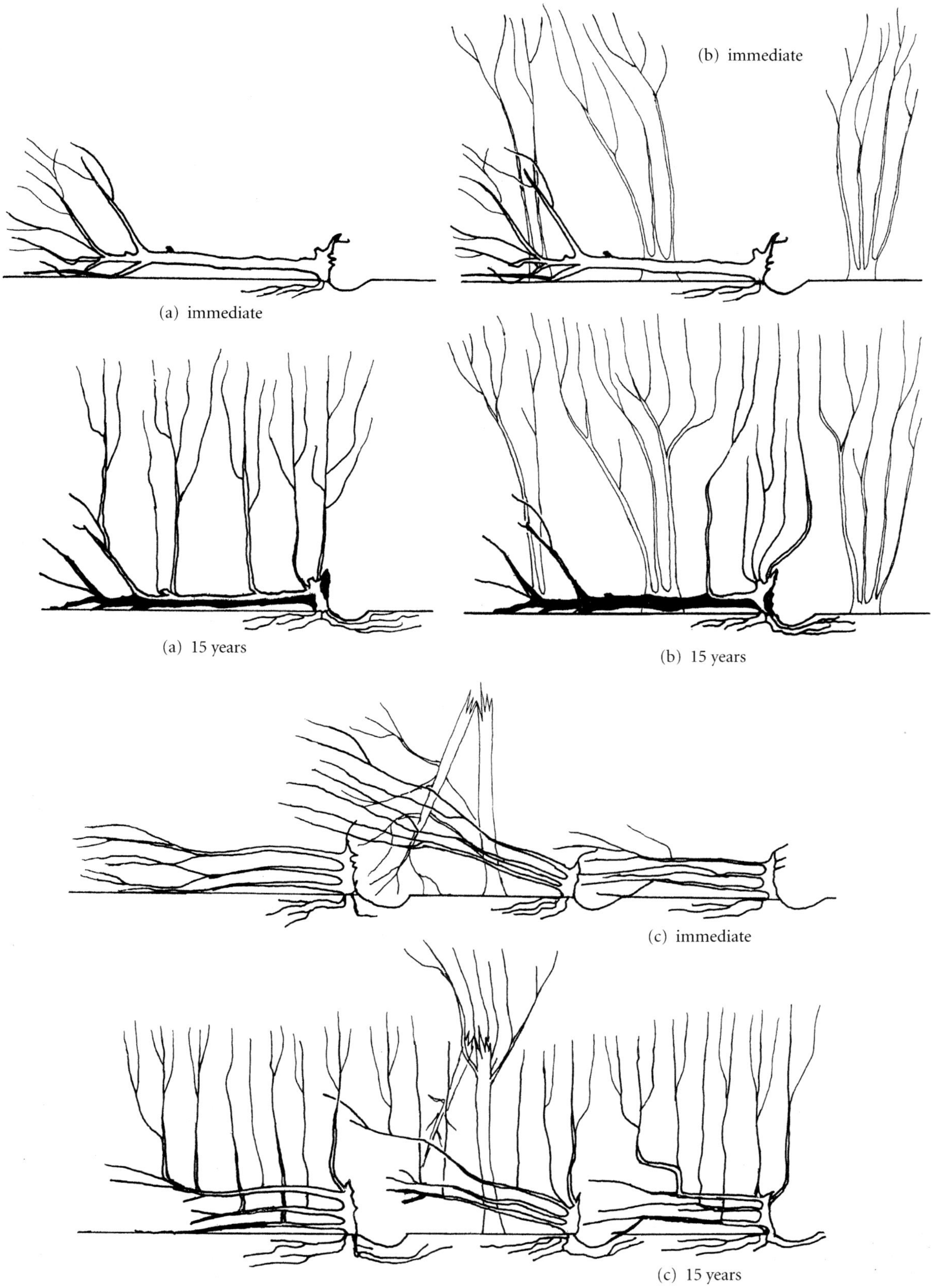

Fig. 27.12 Effects of uprooting trees, each shown immediately after falling and 15 years after falling.
(a) Single tree in the open or in a large clearing.
(b) Single tree surrounded by other trees.
(c) Windrow of uprooted trees in a wood.

Fig. 27.13 An oak which was uprooted into a wood, survived fourteen years of shade, and is now exposed by coppicing. The Blean. February 2002

Fig. 27.14 A lime stool uprooted, creating a biggish gap, which is flourishing after fourteen years. Groton Wood. March 2002

Fig. 27.15 The characteristic shape of a tree (a lime) uprooted in some long-forgotten hurricane, which has come to terms with the new direction of gravity. Piles Coppice, Warwickshire. March 1990

Fig. 27.16 A great beech, uprooted into a wood, still flourishing fourteen years on. The Blean. February 2002

Fig. 27.17 (a–b)

(a) Windrow of chestnuts and birches uprooted. Hockley Woods, S.E. Essex. November 1987

(b) Almost the same scene, fifteen years on: an 'impenetrable forest'?

Conclusions

The Great Storms were not unique, but their consequences were. Previous events had set up a population of trees ripe for maximum damage. Vast numbers of young trees, the result of decades of planting, had reached the vulnerable age. Ancient woods were crowded with overstood coppice stools as a result of decades of neglect. (Are the millions of trees planted as replacements setting the scene for another Great Windblow in *c.* 2060?)

Except in formal gardens or plantings (and not always even there?) the Great Storms were in no way a tragedy or a disaster. As far as I know they destroyed no woodland, and seldom destroyed any irreplaceable trees – although clearing-up operations often destroyed both.

The storms were excellent for wildlife. A horizontal tree, dead or alive, is at least as good a habitat as an upright one. Hundreds of woods, uniformly shady since the last time they were felled, now had gaps in which woodland flora and fauna could flourish. These gaps are closing in, either with regrowth or with new seedlings that boost the increase of ash and birch characteristic of the twentieth century. The only adverse effect that I can think of is that areas of fallen trees may have encouraged more deer than if the trees had remained standing, as they are said to have done in France after the 1999 hurricane.

The storms, although they formed the pretext for a last fling of replanting in a few ancient woods, may have hastened the discrediting of plantation forestry. Although foresters regard windblow as a normal hazard of business, the idea has made headway that planting a uniform stand of trees close together and forgetting to thin them is asking for trouble. (The same point was made in France in 2000.[7])

Fallen trees are objects of curiosity and wonder, a relief from thousands of boring, upright, unclimbable trees. They will delight generations yet unborn (Fig. 27.18).

7 *La Lettre des Sylves*, **36** (2000) 3–7. (I am grateful to Alain Desbrosse for supplying this reference.)

Fig. 27.18 The horizontal tree is the most popular tree. Loch Lomond. May 1991

Fig. 27.19 Tip-up mounds, Alleghany National Forest, Pennsylvania. April 1999

New insights arising from the Storms

The storms enlarged the horizons of knowledge about what trees are and how they behave. They showed that windblow was a normal but rare ecological factor; that instability was impossible to predict in advance, but the prime factors for promoting it were youth, crowding, and narrow forks, not age and decay; that trees in general are shallow-rooted; and that trees generally survive uprooting. These discoveries have still to be fully assimilated into ecological thought. Scientists, by training, do not welcome new data that gate-crash unexpectedly into their research, without a pre-existing body of theory to fit them into.

Tip-up mounds

Is there evidence of past Great Storms? An uprooted tree leaves a very distinctive hollow, where the roots were, with a mound beside it, which persists long after the tree has died and disappeared. Such mounds, resulting from the accumulated disturbance of centuries of hurricanes and tornadoes, are common in American woods, as in Massachusetts. In the Alleghany National Forest they distinguish the original forest from areas that have been through a phase as farmland (Fig. 27.19). Why do English woods seldom contain tip-up mounds?

Tip-up pits, buried and preserved by the later accumulation of sediment, have occasionally been reported by archaeologists in England from sites now outside woodland, for example the Neolithic phase of Sutton Hoo, Suffolk.[8] They seem to be very rare in ancient woods. Evidently the state in 1987, with many crowded young trees and overstood coppice stems waiting to be uprooted, is historically anomalous: for most of the last centuries the underwood was not allowed to get big enough to blow over. However, one might expect at least faint traces of windblow dating from before coppicing was established. These I have never seen, even in Hayley Wood where periodic flooding should make it possible to detect mounds worn down to only an inch or so high.

A final thought

The storm called in question the assumption that the normal state of a tree is upright. Was wildwood full of horizontal living trees? Does a distant memory of that state still linger in the cliché phrase 'impenetrable forest'?

8 Carver, M. (1998). *Sutton Hoo: burial ground of kings?* British Museum Press, London (p. 94).

28

Elmwoods: What has become of them?

In the 1980s much was written about elms. R. H. Richens distilled a lifetime's study of elms into a great book, a compendium of the taxonomy, archaeology, place-names, history, uses, mycology, entomology, and especially portraiture of elms in Britain and nearby Europe.[1] In 1986 I included a chapter on elms in *The History of the Countryside*, among other matters dissenting from Dr Richens's theory of the dissemination of elms from Europe by prehistoric gardeners. Interest in elms then declined, probably in the belief that they no longer exist or at least are a lost cause. However, in 1997 the Conservation Foundation set up a Native Elm Programme which gathers information on surviving big trees.

Elm Disease and the Elm Decline

Some of the gaps in the inferred relation between Elm Disease and the Elm Decline of the early Neolithic have been filled in. At least one of the bark beetles is known to go back so far, although whether it increased at the time of the Decline is not yet known.[2] A detailed study in Denmark, pushing radiocarbon dating to its limit of precision, reveals four elm declines over 1100 years in the Neolithic,[3] which is what we would expect given the recurrent behaviour of Elm Disease in historic times – a behaviour now confirmed from the isolated elm population at Bergen, Norway.[4]

At one exceptional pollen site, Diss Mere (Norfolk), the sediment contains annual layers (varves) which made it possible for Sylvia Peglar to follow the Elm Decline year by year. The results are dramatic. Elms were common, comprising about 10% of the wildwood. In their heyday they produced varying amounts of pollen according to good and bad years. This ended with one very good year, following which all the years were bad. The Elm Decline here either happened from one year to the next, or at most in only three or four years. The only other tree affected was hazel, which increased its pollen production, probably because it was released from shade. What else, other than Elm Disease, could have produced so sudden a change?[5]

Hans Heybroek, long-standing supporter of the hypothesis that the Decline was due to people making excessive use of elm, has lately re-asserted it. He claims that people were cutting elms and stripping their bark on such a scale as to generate an epidemic of bark-beetles which killed most of the elms without the assistance of Elm Disease.[6] This ingenious idea hardly explains why the Decline should have been so sudden, or so limited to elm, at a time when there were still very few people in relation to the number of elms. Moreover, Professor Heybroek continues to assume that Elm Disease is only a twentieth-century phenomenon, without responding to the earlier evidence for it (this book, p. 262f).

Elm Disease since 1979

In the original book I reported on the spread of the late-20th-century epidemic of Elm Disease (since re-christened *Ceratocystis novi-ulmi*) down to 1979. Its further progress is reported and mapped in *The History of the Countryside*. Since 1985 the disease has spread more slowly, partly through running out of susceptible elms. Outside woods, in most parts of England, a live big elm is now a rarity. Only occasionally can one see a whole landscape of living elms: as in Huntingdonshire,

1 Richens, R. H. (1983). *Elm*. Cambridge University Press.
2 Girling, M. A. and Greig, J. R. A. (1985). 'A first fossil record for *Scolytus scolytus* . . . : its occurrence in elm decline deposits from London and the implications for Neolithic Elm Desease.' *Journal of Archaeological Science* **12**, 347–52.
3 Andersen, S. T. and Rasmussen, K. L. (1993). Radiocarbon wiggle-dating of elm declines in northwest Denmark and their significance. *Vegetation History & Archaeobotany* **2**, 125–35.
4 Moe, D. and Rackham, O. (1992). Pollarding and a possible explanation of the neolithic elmfall. *Vegetation History & Archaeobotany* **1**, 63–8.
5 Peglar, S. (1993). The mid-Holocene Ulmus decline at Diss Mere . . . : a year-by-year pollen stratigraphy from annual laminations. *Holocene* **3**, 1–13.
6 Heybroek, H. M. (2002). Ulmen in Geschichte und Kultur. *Mitteilungen der deutschen dendrologischen Gesellschaft* **87**, 147–61.

due to a combination of the relatively resistant 'Boxworth' group of elms and a vigorous reaction by at least one of the big landowners. The only urban elms commonly left alive are of the 'Huntingdon' and 'Wheatley' clones.

The current epidemic is not radically different from its predecessors, but is undoubtedly more severe, being helped by modern communications. Elm Disease has ravaged throughout Europe except for remote outliers of elm, as in Norway and Crete. In America its progress has been patchy: it has ravaged New England and as far as distant Colorado; but there are still plenty of great elms in Pennsylvania, and the Texas Elm, looking like a drought-resistant East Anglian elm, is unscathed. In Japan the disease is apparently unknown (despite its reputed Asian origin). In Tasmania there survives intact a curious landscape of suckering elms – an odd selection from the East Anglian group – initiated by English colonial gentry.

The loss of big elms has consequences for the creatures that live on or in them. The bark and wood characteristics of elms, and their alkaline character (especially when infected by wetwood, p. 257), are not easily replicated by other trees. The long-lived polypore fungus *Fomes ulmarius* used to be characteristic of the insides of hollow elms; it still occasionally sprouts from the roots of long-dead elms. The beautiful gill-fungus *Rhodotus palmatus* grows on standing dead elm. The White-Letter Hairstreak butterfly and at least six lichen species are at risk from the loss of big elms.[7]

However, elms are not a lost cause. Trees are usually killed only down to the ground: the roots survive and send up suckers. Elm Disease by itself rarely destroys a whole clone of elms: deer or people have to intervene as well. In some areas of East Anglian elms, as in parts of Essex and Huntingdonshire, elms are gaining on the disease. Even the common form of English Elm, which is very susceptible – I have not seen a single live big tree of it for nearly 20 years, except in its Edinburgh form and its East Sussex outlier – repeatedly re-suckers, although the disease smoulders on and seldom lets the suckers reach flowering stature. Wych-elm might be thought to be at a disadvantage because it does not sucker, although the disease often stops short of the base of a big stool, which then sprouts. However, wych-elm easily grows from seed and produces more seed when only 15 years old or so, so its survival is not in doubt: indeed in some areas it is spreading.

Death of woodland elm clones

The eleven-acre semicircle of elms in Hayley Wood (Fig. 16.4, p. 268) was attacked by Elm Disease in the 1970s. The great summer of 1976 stimulated a huge population of bark-beetles to attack elms on their own account. Every tree succumbed to a combination of Elm Disease, drought, and bark-beetle attack. Suckers were produced only at the edge of the clone, and deer devoured them. The dead trees, some of them huge, snapped off over the next eight years, creating an elm graveyard (Fig. 28.1, 28.2). Elm snags and logs still moulder, 26 years on, much as in the 1960s there were remains of great elms thought to have been killed by the 1930s epidemic.

The immediate effect was like a normal coppicing (Chapter 26), although delayed for three or four years. Oxlip flourished for a year or two; buried-seed plants such as *Lychnis flos-cuculi* and *Carex remota* appeared; and aquatic coppicing plants such as *Callitriche* spp and *Ranunculus flammula* were stimulated in the many wet hollows. As the site collapsed into a chaos of giant fallen logs and tall snags it became very attractive to deer. Grasses such as *Deschampsia caespitosa*, *Poa trivialis*, and *Agrostis stolonifera* became abundant, possibly stimulated by minerals released from rotting logs and elm roots.

No elms survive from this clone, except a very few suckers inside a deer-fence. But despite the deer, trees have returned. Pre-existing oaks and hazels have recovered from years of shade by the taller elms. The new generation of trees are ash (already present as suppressed saplings, which quickly got away above deer height) and maple (which is somewhat resistant to deer browsing).

It was very unusual for such a large area of elm to succumb almost without trace. More commonly elm suckers grow up among the fallen trunks, or trees that had intermingled with the elms fill some of the gaps. Hazels which had been languishing in the shade of the elms suddenly produce abundant catkins, recalling the burst of hazel pollen at Diss Mere.

Surviving elmwoods

As I reported in 1980, elms much more often survive in woods than outside. Many big elms hide among other trees, and several large clones still retain big trees. These include the biggest elm clones in Madingley and Buff Woods (each of about 4 acres of elm) and two in Gamlingay Wood (Fig. 25.5b).

The biggest area of elm in England known to me is the 42-acre Overhall Grove west of Cambridge. It is almost entirely an ancient secondary wood, at least 350 and probably over 600 years old, on complex medieval earthworks (Fig. 5.1). Although there are signs that it was once an ash-maple wood, completely lacking hazel, it has been invaded and taken over from end to end, by

7 Watson, M. F., Hawksworth, D. L., and Rose, F. (1988). Lichens on elms in the British Isles and the effect of Dutch Elm Disease on their status. *Lichenologist* **20**, 327–52.

elms mostly of the Boxworth sub-group of East Anglian elm. It was managed as an elm coppice – the elms suckered after each felling – with elm standard trees. After coppicing ceased *c.* 1930 it developed into a dark and eerie place of crowded slender towering elms, of fallen logs and mysterious hollows and iron-bearing springs buried in ear-high nettles, of bats and badgers, with an unexpectedly magnificent display of oxlips every spring: a unique site which escaped from the *National Vegetation Classification*.

Overhall Grove became a nature reserve of the then Cambridgeshire & Isle of Ely Naturalists' Trust in 1971. Elm Disease was first noticed in 1977, and at once the Trust took a pessimistic view of the wood's future. The next year it contemplated a recommendation from the County Council Planning Department to try to replace the Grove by an oak plantation. ('The nature of the ground, its status as a nature reserve leads to one tree Pedunculate Oak' – so ran the minds of well-meaning advisers 25 years ago!) Had this been acted upon, the most likely outcome would have been that Overhall Grove would have joined all the other failed plantations on the site of ancient woods.

The contrary view was that Overhall was a unique wood. It was impossible to predict the course or the consequences of Elm Disease, which in any case was a normal (if intermittent) part of the functioning of elmwoods. A conservation trust ought not to despise dead trees. The effects of work done in reaction to the disease could not be predicted: there were no precedents elsewhere as there were no comparable woods. There was very little room for manoeuvre. It was pointless to draw up a management plan without awaiting developments.

In the event, little was done beyond felling some areas of (mostly dead) elm, partly to avoid dead trees falling on people's heads, partly for the timber value of the bigger dead trees.

Through the 1980s, Elm Disease spread through the wood, eating up the elms at the rather slow rate of about 7% of the remaining elms per year. By 1991 it had killed about 60% of all the elms. Since then it has almost stopped killing trees: nearly all the elms alive in 1991 are still alive in 2002 (Fig. 28.3). (Outside the wood, nearly all the ancient pollard elms that marked the streets and closes of the shrunken village of Knapwell have, alas, succumbed.)

Why did this happen? It is not that out of every three elms one survived. In 2002, about one-fifth of the wood has no big elms at all. One-quarter is still a dark and eerie place of crowded slender towering elms, of fallen logs and mysterious hollows and iron-bearing springs buried in ear-high nettles. In most of the remainder the trees have sprouted either from the roots

Fig. 28.1 Elm graveyard, Hayley Wood, four years after the death of the elms. It is characteristic of dead elms to snap off several feet above ground – the French have a word for such trees (*volis*). April 1980

Fig. 28.2 Huge dead elm attacked by the fungus *Lyophyllum ulmarium*, Hayley Wood. June 1981

Fig. 28.3 Overhall Grove, Cambridgeshire.
(a) March of Elm Disease (black areas) and recovery (dotted), 1973–1990.
(b) The situation in 2002.
(c) Elm clones (of the *Ulmus minor* group), as detectable from visible characteristics.

or the trunk. The distinctions can be very abrupt, as in the north-east of the wood, where two intact areas have been separated for more than ten years by a tract with no surviving elms at all. As in other woods, it is clear that the disease has taken out some clones but not others. The elms of Overhall are less diverse than in other elm-woods: before the disease I recognized eleven mostly rather similar clones. The pattern of survival strongly suggests that nearly indistinguishable elms can differ widely in susceptibility: in other words, Elm Disease is better at distinguishing clones than I am.

Resistance in elms might take many forms. The tree might be inhospitable to grubs of the bark-beetle vector, or might attract creatures which eat it; or resistant elms might not produce the smell that attracts the beetle; or the fungus spores might be prevented from germinating on injection; or the tree's defences might stop the disease at various stages of invasion. In Overhall, as in other woods, resistant elms certainly get attacked: branches, and occasionally a whole tree, can succumb. Although the ecology of bark-beetles and their predators probably plays some part, much of the survival of living clones seems to lie in the tree's damage-limitation mechanism, which walls off the parasite before it gets far down the tree.

What are the consequences? The degree of recovery varies (Fig. 28.4). Some patches lack elm altogether: they are open glades, with scattered ashes and maples from before the elms invaded, and occasional maple and ash saplings. Recolonization by seedling trees is slow, probably because the very fertile site promotes competition from grasses and nettles. At the other extreme, some areas are full of pollard-like elms in which the top has disappeared and branches sprout from the trunk. These evidently represent clones whose damage-control got ahead of the fungus before it reached the base of the trunk. More common are areas of more or less vigorous suckers: some parts, where in 1991 not an elm remained standing, have returned to dense elmwood. Like a coppice cycle, this has encouraged the vigour of oxlip (p. 393).

The future

The Overhall Grove story is repeated in many other woodland elm clones, which vary from complete survival to complete disappearance. The western elms of Hayley Wood took much longer to die, and a few survive in a pollard-like state. In Buff Wood (Fig. 16.8, p. 275) clones L, M, T, and AB still have big trees, and nearly all the others are represented by suckers.

Weakly invasive elms tend to disappear, their places

Fig. 28.4 (a–d) State of different elm clones, Overhall Grove. (**a**) Graveyard. April 1991

(**b**) Intact. July 1998

(c) Suckers, with probable muntjac browse-line. May 1991.

(d) Recovery by sprouting from the trunks, some 5 years after disease attack. April 2002

being filled by expansion of neighbouring trees. Stronger clones that have failed to sucker are replaced by maple or ash from seed. Elm Disease, like great storms, is not altogether a tragedy for woodland. In one respect, producing great quantities of dead wood, it has been beneficial.

But the effects of Elm Disease, like many other influences on woodland, are compounded by browsing. Elm suckers are very palatable indeed. It was as much deer as disease that eliminated the eastern elms of Hayley Wood. In south Wales wych-elm has often been eliminated, not by disease, but by sheep: disease killed the tree nearly to the ground and brought the regrowth within a sheep's reach.

Where the soil is not too acid, the fate of elm suckers is a good index of the health of a wood. They are the first plants to succumb to browsing or perverse management.

29

Trees and Ancient Buildings

> In times past men were contented to dwell in houses, builded of sallow, willow, plumtree, hardbeame [hornbeam] and elme . . . but now all these are reiected, and nothing but oke anie whit regarded . . . when our houses were builded of willow, then had we oken men; but now that our houses are come to be made of oke, our men are not onlie become willow, but a great manie . . . altogither of straw . . .
>
> *John Harrison in Holinshed's Chronicle, 1577*[1]

In the original *Ancient Woodland* I sought to identify the actual timber trees and underwood of medieval woods in contemporary buildings, and to listen to what they had to say about woodland management at the time (pp. 144–7).

Since then, knowledge has accumulated, especially in the field of dendrochronology. This is the science of dating oaken artefacts by the sequence of wide and narrow annual rings corresponding to years of favourable and unfavourable weather. Although it has been very useful in dating medieval structures in general, I shall not make much use of it here, since many medieval buildings contain too few annual rings to give a date.

Timber

Why build in timber?

Why did people choose to build in timber, stone, brick, mud, etc.? Not out of mere practicality. Timber-framed buildings occur in some parts of the country but not others. Nobody seems to have drawn a map, but it is clear that their occurrence is related neither to the occurrence of woodland nor to lack of other materials. In Cambridge people built houses with timber brought from a distance, rather than using the cheap and easily-worked local stone. But churches and colleges, even such a humble college as my own (Corpus Christi, Cambridge), had to use stone or brick for their outer walls. Not until after Henry VIII had set a precedent with Nonsuch Palace did the President of Queens' College, Cambridge commit the solecism of building himself a grand timber-framed lodge.

Ordinary timber buildings occur in the Weald, with superabundant woodland; in Essex, with a moderate amount; in Suffolk, with less than average; and in the Breckland, with none. Where there was not much timber building, it was a mark of urban status. In Devon timber buildings are confined to Exeter, Tavistock, Totnes, and Dartmouth. In west Norfolk the holy city of Little Walsingham marked itself out from its neighbours by terraces of stylish timber-framed houses, as if it were Norwich or King's Lynn. The pattern repeats itself in Scotland and (formerly) Ireland.

Timber could be a high-status material. Canterbury (another holy city) is full of huge, grand, often disguised timber houses and inns. The burghers of Norwich built themselves houses with brick and flint side-walls and a visible timber façade, a pattern repeated in Hull, Southampton, and Fowey: all places without much access to woodland.

Which timber?

Strength and rigidity were seldom critical requirements for building timbers. Many a medieval house has lost two-thirds of its timbers by decay or alteration and still stands up. Innumerable leaning walls and sagging floors, which often developed in the first few years of a house's life, show that no great importance was attached to rigidity. Timber was an impressive architectural feature, an expression of the Age of Chivalry, even quite low in the social scale.

Oak was the commonest timber, the most expensive of ordinary timbers, and the most durable. It is over-represented in extant buildings: individual timbers or whole buildings of other species are less likely to survive. I have hardly ever encountered any other timber in a church. Until recently most timber structures studied were churches, great barns, and upper-class houses.

1 1807 edition, I. 356.

Fig. 29.1 Timber-framed house of *c.* 1400: Valley Farm, Flatford.

Fig. 29.2 Interior of great hall, Valley Farm, Flatford. Each rafter is a small oak; several of the wall timbers are elm.

Scholars thus thought elm and other species were indicators of late date, and refrained from looking for them.

Middle- and lower-class buildings have now been recognized and investigated in greater numbers. Upper-class dwellings were all oak. Relatively poor people used other timbers, but tried to include some oak as well: it would generate what must have been the respectable smell of a new timber-framed house. In between, then as now, were people building a little beyond their means, who wanted the appearance of grandeur without paying for the substance. They would use cheaper cuts of oak, or would set the timbers closer at the front of the house than the rear.

There is something to be said for Harrison's remarks at the head of the chapter, although he exaggerates: I have never seen plum or hornbeam used in a house. As we shall see, oak probably got more plentiful in the sixteenth century, but the price was going up (Fig. 11.3), and the 1570s do not mark any great change in the pattern of use. Whether the men of oak were turning into men of straw I leave to more eminent historians to judge.

Valley Farm, Flatford

I have spent about a year of my life teaching for the Field Studies Council at Flatford Mill, east Suffolk, and living in what is now called Valley Farm, a hall-house of *c.* 1400 painted by Constable. This is a middle-class house: there are still many both bigger and smaller in the parish of East Bergholt (Fig. 29.1). It has the standard pattern of a central hall, soot-blackened from the chimneyless hearth, and two-storeyed 'ends' with their own stairs. The roof is held up by the usual oak poles, each rafter a single tree (*quercus de cheveron*, p. 145) (Fig. 29.2). The bark was left on (probably because the oaks were felled at the wrong time of year to strip and sell it) and gradually curled up and fell off; some of it lasted until after the central hearth was given up, and left curious light-coloured patches where the soot had failed to penetrate under the bark.

I once hoped to calculate the number of trees that went into Valley Farm, as outlined on p. 145–6. The builder's economies prevent this. Many of the wall studs are in two pieces, interrupted by a horizontal rail, and are short logs with many knots: they are not whole trees but are the top ends from trees whose bottom lengths went into a more expensive structure. This is a feature of many buildings, including even such a grand one as the great barn of Widdington (Essex). Any carpenter's workshop (including my own) accumulates a pile of oddments, too short to use but too long to burn, waiting for structures like these to give them a home. Next there are reused oak timbers, recognizable from the mortices and peg-holes which did duty in their previous incarnation. In Valley Farm these appear in the service rooms, the lower-class end of the house. About one-tenth of the timber is elm and ash. These too are mainly in the service rooms and (with one exception) in places not exposed to the weather. But elm also occurs in the bigger timbers of the internal partitions of the great hall. Here its different appearance would not have mattered, for all the timbers were originally painted red under the soot. The floorboards are oak and elm. The original stairs – a very rare survival, still in daily use – are solid baulks of oak and elm, triangular in section; the stair-cage is of poplar boards.

Eagle Inn, Cambridge

From a later period (*c.* 1590), this is an example of a lower-class building in a town with almost no local timber (Fig. 29.3). It was built as an inn, of four storeys with garrets and cellars. The timber content (excluding boards) originally added up to about 218 trees, only about 70 of which were felled for the purpose. The commonest timber in the Eagle is reused oak, some of which can be recognized as components of medieval buildings dating from the 13th to the 15th century. Some of these were sawn lengthwise into two reused timbers. This shows that recycling timber was a definite process, not merely a matter of scavenging usable fragments from the previous building on the site. New oak, where used, often consisted of offcuts, the oddments left over after sawing a square timber out of a round log.

Most of the bigger timbers are elm, small crooked trees generally left round. Aspen poles enter into the roof. The next commonest timber is pine, which must have come from Scandinavia. There are a few pine timbers in the frame, and the occasional recycled medieval pine. Most of the pine, however, is boards: broad, often machine-sawn, and left rough on the underside in the manner of pine boards of the period.

These rough and miscellaneous materials called for great skill on the part of the carpenter and interior decorator. Rough undersides of floors and reused joists were covered by newly fashionable ceilings, here laid on reeds instead of the more expensive laths. Projecting into each corner of the principal upstair rooms was an elm trunk, with the bark left on and painted green.

Oak

The foregoing will show that there is little purpose in investigating what proportion of ancient timbers are oak. Of the medieval timbers I have seen about 95% are oak, but that is biased by the greater durability of oak and its preponderance in churches and other very visible structures. Most people, as Harrison says, lived in the sort of house that is not all oak; and even those who dwelt in oak would have had outbuildings of

Fig. 29.3 Eagle Inn, Cambridge, built as an inn, *c.* 1590; the galleries are later.

Table 29.1 Summary of the timber components of the Eagle Inn, Cambridge.

New oak	81
New oak offcuts	51
Oak reused	105
Elm	28
Ash	3
Aspen	9
Pine	4 + all the floorboards (and a number of smaller parts)
Total (in terms of trees)	218 + boards

Fig. 29.4 Roof of Poor Priests' Hospital, Canterbury.

Fig. 29.5 Little Barn, Faversham, Kent: forked post, made from a tree that was not quite big enough.

cheaper or reused timbers. In reality new oak might have comprised only half of building timbers or even less.

Later researches amply confirm the tendency for timbers (with rare exceptions such as those listed on p. 153) to comprise the whole of the smallest tree that will do the job: often less than 4 inches in diameter. In the middle ages the woodland economy was geared to producing a rapid turnover of small oaks.

This is not confined to parts of the country with little woodland. There are equally good examples in and around Canterbury, which was surrounded by a great ring of woods. The roof (13th century?) of the guest-hall of St Augustine's Abbey and the series of medieval roofs of the Poor Priests' Hospital (Fig. 29.4) are each made of small, not quite straight oaks. It was difficult to get even moderately big trees. The giant barn of Littlebourne, originally 200 by 39 feet, was built from at least a thousand small, sinuous oaks; but its principal posts (16 of the original 22 survive), between 14 and 20 inches in diameter, are even more crooked and waney (that is, rounded at the corners where they reach the outside of the tree). St Augustine's, its builders, owned at least 800 acres of woodland, but even this did not guarantee a supply of straight trees for an imposing building. 'The timbers of this barn are like snakes!' as Alexander Wheaten put it.[2]

The two barns of Faversham Abbey – the Great Barn dendrochronologically dated *c.* 1426, the Little Barn *c.* 1475[3] – are each built of some 650 oaks, most of them less than 10 inches in diameter. The Great Barn involves two batches of oaks, one straighter than the other, used in different stages of the framing. The Little Barn is rather more heavily timbered. Here too the great posts are anomalous. They come from trees some 2 feet in diameter at the base – middle-sized by modern standards. Like most barn posts they are set upside-down. They taper markedly towards the top of the tree, and three of the surviving 29 posts fork at the base (that is, the top as the tree grew) (Fig. 29.5).

2 Rackham, O. (2002). The Blean woods and timber-framed buildings. *The Blean: the woodlands of a cathedral city*, ed. W. Holmes and A. Wheaten, Blean Research Group, Canterbury, 77–82.

3 Nottingham Dendrochronology Laboratory, *Vernacular Architecture* **30** (1999) 93f. The first date is of the latest tree-ring represented in 11 timbers including great posts; there is an uncomfortably large amount of variation between different timbers. The Little Barn date is based on only five timbers, mostly common rafters. Coppicing could be a disturbing factor, not mentioned in the publication.

Fig. 29.6 Barley Barn, Cressing Temple, Essex: the biggest structure that could be built from ordinary oaks.

Owning at least 1100 acres of woodland did not guarantee to Faversham Abbey two sets of sixteen respectable barn posts.

The famous barns of the Knights Templars at Cressing Temple, Essex – the Barley Barn of *c.* 1210 and the Wheat Barn of *c.* 1270 – are also built of trees mostly less than 10 inches diameter, about 480 oaks per barn (Fig. 29.6). The Knights had 110 acres of woodland, which might have yielded one barn's worth of oaks every five years. The principal posts, twelve per barn, were less of a constraint than in Kent. The Barley Barn needed oaks each 2 feet in diameter, the Wheat Barn somewhat smaller. They seem to have been hedgerow trees. The posts are straight, but some of them come from very waney trees which were rotten before they were felled; these were put in dark corners where they would not detract from the architecture.[4]

The oak-tree population evidently changed in the later middle ages. The amount of timber in successive buildings of the same size increased: close-set studs in the fifteenth century often contrast with the wide panels of the fourteenth. The small, crooked oaks used in fourteenth-century Corpus Christi College contrast with the massive close timbering of fifteenth-century Queens' and sixteenth-century Jesus College.

Big oaks got bigger. In a comparative study of Essex barns, I found the biggest trees in the Rookwood Hall barn, dendrochronologically dated to 1539, where each great post was one-quarter of an oak log 3 feet in diameter, by medieval standards a giant tree. In upper-class houses ceiling-timbers got heavier and more decorative. If a particular house moved up in the social scale, a massive ornate floor would be inserted into a plain, lightly-timbered hall. It often happens that the biggest timber in a medieval house is a later insertion (Corpus Christi has a good example). The increasing practice, from the late sixteenth century onwards, of sawing oaks lengthwise, must be related to the increasing size of trees, as well as the increasing amount of building.

It looks as though felling had got somewhat ahead of regrowth in the densely-populated decades before 1350. After the Black Death the population, reduced by plague, was not felling quite enough oak to keep up with the growth of trees, which therefore got bigger. Small oaks, however, remained obtainable well into the eighteenth century.

What should be very clear, in the context of recent concern about growing high-quality oak timber (p. 524f), is that nearly all ancient buildings, from cathedrals to cottages, used what would now be the worst quality, 'fencing-grade', oak, or what estate foresters call 'rubbish'. This is a diagnostic feature distinguishing genuine medieval buildings. The timbers of nineteenth- or twenty-first-century reproductions are sawn out of

4 Rackham, O. (1993). Medieval timber economy as illustrated by the Cressing Temple barns. *Cressing Temple: a Templar and Hospitaller manor in Essex*, ed. D. D. Andrews, Essex County Council.

big oaks, eschewing crooked rafters and waney edges; they therefore use trees less efficiently, needing a bigger tree for the same size of beam.

Baltic oak

All the above applies to English oak. Baltic oak (p. 151, Fig. 29.11) was, in effect, a different timber. Oak boards came via Danzig (Gdánsk), Riga, Königsberg (Kaliningrad), and Hamburg; the excavated Gdánsk W5 ship was carrying a cargo of oak planks.[5,6]

Baltic oak came from either *Quercus robur* or *Q. petraea* – nobody seems to know which – but not from such oaks as England afforded. Boards identified as Baltic are conspicuously straight-grained and free from knots, with annual rings typically of only 1 mm, cut in an exact radial direction (not quarter-sawn) from huge, columnar, centuries-old trees. They were mass-produced by specialists, were not expensive and were widely used. They came in various thicknesses and were often made to special profiles, with tongue-and-groove, keels, mouldings imitating door-battens, and even false joins so that an expensive wide board looks like two cheap narrow ones.[7]

The trade began in the early thirteenth century or before. John Harrison remarked in 1577 on 'the wainscot that is brought out of Danske, for our wainscot is not made in England',[8] but by then time was running out. Among the last Baltic boards are those that the writer sits on in his stall in his college chapel, dating from about 1590.

Baltic boards make the painted panels of church screens, contrasting with the crooked, fast-grown, small 'local' oaks used for the frame of the screen. They are extremely stable: the join between the boards can be almost invisible after 500 years of damp and heat and rough treatment. Baltic oak, slow-grown and therefore soft, is the usual medium for carved tracery and other delicate work. It is used in church doors and furniture, and in about one-third of linenfold panelling. All these are uses in which stability was important. Making and seasoning boards, especially from English oak, was a special skill which the ordinary carpenter did not have. Another advantage of boards from an East European factory would be that the long voyage would show up any tendency to warp or split. However, I find that floorboards are always English oak or elm: Baltic oak was perhaps thought too soft and liable to abrasion. Portraits are sometimes on Baltic boards; but artists were strangely indifferent to the quality of their substrate, and more often used English oak, whose warping was to make jobs for picture restorers in later centuries.

One might expect to find Baltic oak beams as well as boards, but they seem not to have been identified, even by dendrochronologists who claim to infer the source of oak as well as its date from annual rings.

Elm

Elm comprises about half the non-oak timber in medieval buildings. It is reported from all over England, especially from regions with little oak, like the Vale of White Horse.[9] In Worcestershire it is so abundant that dendrochronologists have constructed a 'Droitwich elm chronology'.[10] But well-wooded regions like Kent have it too.[11] The medieval house from North Cray (Kent), now in the Weald & Downland Museum, is mainly of elm, except at the service end which was the side towards the street. Elm had many specialized uses, such as water-pipes, naves of wheels, headstocks of bells, and coffins.

I have seen elm in houses of all dates from the thirteenth century onwards. It is in roughly constant proportion until it increases in the eighteenth century, especially in barns. Elm is generally a mark of low or middle status, but I noted it in the roof of the great barn at Frocester (Gloucs), and it is recorded in the early-sixteenth-century great gates of Chepstow Castle (Monmouthshire).[12] Elm enters into repairs and replacements in the Cressing Temple barns from the fifteenth century onwards.

Most common are houses with some elm, like Valley Farm, Flatford (above), or Grundle House, Stanton (p. 145) – the latter being an upper-middle-class house at the limit of the status of elm. Elm tends to be used for particularly long components, in inconspicuous places, and where protected from the weather. It is often used for chimney-beams, perhaps because of its reputation for not burning easily.

I know some all-elm houses (e.g. at East Hatley, p. 145). John Blair tells me of an all-elm cruck house of the 13th or 14th century at Waterstock (Oxfordshire). In East Bergholt, the same parish as Valley Farm, is a small hall-house, now the Carrier's Arms inn. This is almost

5 Tossavainen, J. (1996). 'The collapse of Danzig's export in the first half of the 17th century – a case of ill-considered forest exploitation'. *News of Forest History* 23/2/3.
6 Hutchinson, G. (1994). *Medieval ships and shipping*. Leicester University Press.
7 Rackham, O. (1982). The growing and transport of timber and underwood. *Woodworking techniques before A.D. 1500*, ed. S. McGrail, *British Archaeological Reports International Series* **129** 199–218.
8 *Holinshed's Chronicle* **1**. 357 (1807 edition).
9 Currie, C. (1992). *Vernacular Architecture Group Newsletter* **22**, 9.
10 *Vernacular Architecture* **20** (1989) 44, 47.
11 Pearson, S. (1997). Tree-ring dating: a review. *Vernacular Architecture* **28**, 26.
12 *Vernacular Architecture* **29** (1998) 127.

Fig. 29.7 Pine timbers of *c.* 1320 in the Great Guest-Hall, Ely.

all built of pole-sized East Anglian elms, complete with bark-beetle galleries (p. 259). It would have been a lower-class house, but in the sixteenth century it came up in the world and was given an inserted floor of oak. (The converse is more usual.)

Elms in buildings, where enough of the tree survives to be identifiable, tend to be of similar groups (East Anglian or English) as those in the local hedges now. The timber consists of poles or small standard trees, of similar sizes to oaks, or occasionally of floorboards or clapboards sawn from much bigger trees.

The middle ages, therefore, had a copious production of small sizes of elm timber, more than one would expect from the rather small known extent of elm in woods. One of the elm clones in Gamlingay Wood, still going strong, seems to be recorded in 1359 (p. 267), but most woodland elm is probably the result of post-medieval invasion (p. 268f). The commonest source in the middle ages was probably elm hedges.

Poplar

The next commonest surviving medieval timber is probably black poplar. In crucks and other great timbers its distinctive knobbly surface and rugged bark draw attention to it; in boards and scappled timbers it is recognizable by its yellow colour and 'woolly' texture.

I know of no all-poplar house, but internal walls and floors of middle- and lower-class dwellings are often framed in it. Great curved poplars were often used for crucks in Worcestershire and Warwickshire. Poplar, as the only large native softwood tree, was much used for floorboards; although soft, it has a reputation for resisting abrasion. Another characteristic use is in the lids of church chests. A particular style of chest, of unknown date, has a pine body and a half-cylinder lid dug out of a poplar log: examples are in Hadleigh and East Bergholt churches, Suffolk, and in the Poor Priests' Hospital, Canterbury.

Considering its poor durability, black poplar may in its time have been the third commonest timber. This is confirmed by numerous mentions of poplar trees and poplar artefacts in medieval documents. A higher proportion of poplar than of elm and oak comes from big trees. Seeing that black poplar, then as now, never grew in a wood, this confirms the great importance of hedgerow and meadow trees in the medieval supply of timber. I have yet to recognize any *abel* or white poplar (p. 341).

Pine

The only reference I have ever seen to pine growing in medieval England is in 1243, when the trees inventoried in a garden at Bures (Suffolk) include three *pini.*[13] Pine was not the normal word for the timber, which was called 'fir' or Latin *abies*. The most likely identification is *Pinus pinea*, the stone-pine of the Mediterranean, grown for its edible seed. Had a pilgrim pocketed one of the huge cones from some Italian beach or Cretan garden? Stone-pine does surprisingly well in England and even produces cones.[14]

Pine timber was, of course, always imported: even Scotland got most of its pine from Norway rather than the Highlands.[15] The well-documented Baltic trade, parallel to that in oak boards, at first centred on King's Lynn. Pine occurs in all sizes. Some of its surviving examples are in upper-class contexts, but it was also used for scaffold poles.

At Ely, pine timbers – probably re-used scaffolding

13 Harper-Bill, R.. and Mortimer, R. (1982), *Stoke-by-Clare Cartulary*, Boydell & Brewer, Woodbridge, §397.
14 *HF* p. 214f.
15 e.g. Smout, C. (1997). Highland land-use before 1800: misconception, evidence and realities. Smout (ed.), *Scottish Woodland History*, 5–24.

Fig. 29.8 Wattle in medieval house, Lavenham. The bark has been stripped off the rods because they are of lime, whose bast fibre was saleable (p. 242). Lime still grows in the local woods (Fig. 15.1).

Fig. 29.9 Wattle-and-daub in a house at Wickhambrook, Suffolk. The sallow rods have contemporary lichens on their bark.

from the Cathedral – occur in the thirteenth-century 'Three Blackbirds', an early and experimental brick building. Larger pine beams form much of the huge roof (*c.* 1320) of the Great Guest-Hall, now the Bishop's palace (Fig. 29.7); oak is used for principal timbers and curves. Pine boards, with tongue-and-groove like Baltic oak, form thirteenth-century doors at York Minster and Lakenheath church. Pine then appears in humbler contexts at Swavesey (Cambs) and Cambridge. It is also to be found in chests and strong-boxes.

The trade grew vastly in the post-medieval period. In Bene't Street, Cambridge, a mid-sixteenth-century house of oak had an extra storey added in pine. By *c.* 1600 pine boards as well as timbers had become commonplace.

Ash

Ash was a specialized material for tools, rakes, weapons, etc. Much of this would have been coppice poles. Ash as a timber tree was uncommon and valuable as a specific timber for felloes of wheels. But it also occurs as a building timber in low-status contexts.

I have about 14 records of ash in houses from the thirteenth to the seventeenth century, mainly in Suffolk. It never forms a whole house. The commonest use is floor-joists, where its reputation for springiness might be an advantage. Exceptionally, it forms much of the roof of a rather large sixteenth-century house at Stradbroke (Suffolk). The trees, like elm, are large poles, with a few standard trees.

Aspen

I have seen aspen in eight houses, from the thirteenth century onwards (the latest being the Eagle Inn, above). Finds by other observers are probably hidden under the term 'poplar'. It too is a minority timber in low-status contexts; but its lack of durability means that at the time it would have been quite common.

Chestnut

Chestnut is still a phantom timber (p. 330). Rumours of chestnut roofs and other artefacts never cease; but they remain factoids until verified, which I have never succeeded in doing. (It is not that I am unable to recognize chestnut, which is a common and familiar timber in Portugal, Tuscany, and Crete.)

Underwood

Wattle-and-daub (p. 144) was the commonest infill between the timbers of frame buildings (Fig. 29.8). Usually it was carefully constructed to expose both faces of the timbers, but there is a lower-class variant (commoner in later periods) which covers one side of the timbers and exposes the other side. There were several alternatives. Vertical oak laths might be tied to the horizontal splints between the timbers, being sprung at their ends into grooves cut in the top and bottom rails. This slightly grander form of wattle-and-daub is to be found, for example, in Corpus Christi College, Cambridge. Broad thin oak laths interwoven are characteristic of the West Country with its square panels. Brick was an upper-class infill in the middle ages, descending the social scale from the seventeenth century onwards. In Normandy the infill is either stone or mud without the wattle.

Wattle rods are usually of 7–8 years' growth, fast-grown by modern standards, and free from the bite of deer or cattle. They bear the marks of a sharp but notched bill or axe. Sometimes the thin crusts of medieval lichens can be discerned on their bark (Fig. 29.9), which confirms that the poor growth of lichens on underwood today is due to acid rain and not a dry climate.

Wattle-and daub was a minor use of underwood: wattle rods formed a smaller proportion of all underwood than building timbers did of all timber. The samples which I have identified, dating probably from the fourteenth to the seventeenth century, are listed in Table 29.2.

For wattle the species did not matter much, for at least ten trees were admissible. However, wattlers evidently had some preference, at least to the extent of not mixing species within the same panel.

Compared to the composition of woodland, sallow and aspen seem over-represented, especially as they are among the least durable species. Medieval short-rotation coppicing undoubtedly favoured these trees: as we have seen, aspen occurs among timber as well.

Why choose sallow and aspen? Presumably the rods were not grown for the purpose but picked out of a mixture of general underwood. Wattle has to be stout enough to resist the assaults of children and burglars. If a wood was being cut at only 8 years' growth the biggest rods, $1\frac{1}{2}$–2 in. thick, would be preferred. Sallow and aspen, the fastest-growing species, would be the ones most likely to reach a suitable size within the short rotation.

Table 29.2 Analysis of 46 samples of wattle, comprising 416 rods, from East Anglia and Essex.

Second column: number of samples in which each species occurred.
Third column: number of samples in which all the rods were of the species.
Fourth column: percentage composition of all the material together.

	Species occurred in:	Species occurred alone in:	Percentage
Sallow	19	7	29
Hazel	13	7	22
Ash	12	6	18
Aspen	8	3	11
Elm	5	1	6
Maple	6	0	3
Oak	0	2	4
Lime	2	1	3
Birch	1	1	2
Willow	1	0	1
			100

Fig. 29.10 In the middle ages this would have been a phenomenally large oak and might have ended in the tower of a distant cathedral, being used up to the insertion of the higher bough on the left. Gawdy Hall Wood, Norfolk. May 1974

Fig. 29.11 (a–c)
(a) 12th-century church door, the planks sawn (not split) from a crooked, fast-grown 'local' oak. Stillingfleet, Yorkshire.

(b) Church door of *c.*1200 (cut down to fit later-medieval arch), planks of straight-grained, slow-grown, tongue-and-grooved Baltic oak. Elmsett, Suffolk.

(c) 15th-century church door, planks and tracery of Baltic oak, radially cut so that the 'medullary' rays form a pretty pattern. Blythburgh, Suffolk.

30

Species and Area: are small woods impoverished?

There is a sentiment among conservationists that nature reserves are too small, and effort should be put into extending and linking them. For over thirty years the size, shape, and surroundings of reserves have been debated at conferences (although I have never heard of a proposed woodland reserve actually being rejected because it was too small or the wrong shape). There is a general consensus that large reserves are a good thing, that a hundred-acre site has more species than 10 ten-acre sites, and that this applies to woods as well as to grassland, heath, or fen. One Wildlife Trust appealed for funds – and got them swiftly – to construct 'corridors' between existing woods, along which species would supposedly travel from wood to wood, as though this was self-evidently a good objective.

It is claimed that woods are 'fragmented', implying that they are reduced from once continuous tracts of woodland, and that this has impoverished their wildlife. To construct an example, if someone grubs out three-quarters of a 200-acre wood, this results not only in the loss of species that were confined to the part of the wood destroyed, but also in a further loss of species which cannot be sustained permanently on only 50 acres of habitat. More species still will be lost (it is claimed) if those remaining 50 acres are in two separate lots rather than one. The objective of the enlargers, however, goes beyond restoring parts of woods that are known to have been grubbed out in the 1960s or 1860s.

Whatever may be said of other habitats, is the fragmentation story true of woodland? It is a matter of record that most surviving fens, heaths, and old grassland are small fragments of what not long ago were much vaster extents.[1] This is not so for all habitats: churchyards – however small – are not fragments of what was once a wide continuum of Churchyard. Nor is it a verifiable matter of history in the case of woodland. Most woodland nature reserves are entire woods or large fragments, and have been islanded among farmland for a thousand years or more. Isolation is part of the historical process that converted wildwood (or prehistoric farmland) to woodland, not something imposed recently.

Large woods have a greater variety of habitats within them, and afford modest economies of scale in matters such as deer-fencing. They have fewer edge effects, such as contamination by fertilizer – although edge effects are not among the foremost problems in woodland conservation. But are there other advantages of size?

Floras of Woods of Different Sizes

On pp. 58–62 I discussed the relation between the area of a wood and the number of plant species in it. Large ancient woods tend to have more species than small; ten times the size of the wood typically doubles the number of species. This is a statistical relationship overlain by a great deal of random variation, partly because recording is dependent both on the time of year and on the state of the coppicing (especially with buried-seed plants). It does not in itself prove that, on average, a wood of 100 acres has more species than ten woods of 10 acres: to demonstrate this would require a much bigger data-base.

The analogy of island biogeography

Species-area relations derive from the analogy of island biogeography. Long ago a double-logarithmic relation was reported between the number of species of reptiles, insects, etc. on each of a group of islands and the area of the island. This was explained in terms of a balance between species dying out on individual islands and recolonizing from neighbouring islands.[2] On a modest body of original data was built an inverted pyramid of theory; extinction and recolonization were represented

1 *The History of the Countryside* chapters 13, 15, 17.
2 MacArthur, R. H. and Wilson, E. O. (1967). *The Theory of Island Biogeography*. Princeton University Press.

by mathematical models worthy of a hard science like astronomy or particle physics. This is still popular among theoreticians. It is supposed to extend to woods as 'islands' among farmland.

Island biogeography is a zoologists' theory, and I shall begin by showing that it can apply to plants and real islands. There is a quite good fit (on a double-logarithmic scale) between the sizes of islands in the South Aegean and the number of flowering-plant species (Fig. 30.1). The relation is steeper than for most groups of woods: five times the area of an island doubles the number of species. (An Aegean islet of 0.4 sq.km (100 acres) typically has about 30 species of plant, one-quarter of the number in an English wood of the same size.)

But there are complications. As one discovers on visiting the remoter islets, the number of species depends on the effort put by botanists into listing them. (This problem must be more severe for zoologists: how do they cope with it?) The range of sizes covers nearly six orders of magnitude (0.013 to 8,000 sq.km), whereas ancient woods cover $2\frac{1}{2}$ orders (1 to 300 acres). Part of the reason for big islands having more species is that they have more habitats. Much of the flora of Crete is confined to high mountains (the different mountain ranges themselves acting as islands-within-an-island). Kárpathos, that jagged and soaring splinter of land, does its best to have an alpine flora, but no smaller island has a chance of any.

Island zoogeography theory does not transfer smoothly to plants, nor to woods as imitation islands. Some annual plants, like most animals, have to reproduce sexually every year, and die out if they miss a year. But most island and woodland plants are perennial, and many extend their lives by cloning, coppicing, or long-lived seed. Even though they may consist of very few individuals, they are not in danger of dying out at random. If they die out this is from some general environmental change, such as islets getting drier, or woods getting more shady (p. 59).

Further data

I have now investigated the relationship for flowering-plants and ferns in other groups of woods, some of which are illustrated in Fig. 30.2, supplementing Fig. 5.4.

To summarize the findings:

1. The number of species, S, is correlated with the area of the wood, A, according to the formula
$$\log S = \log a + b \log A$$
which is the 'island biogeography' model. The relationship holds good – subject to statistical fluctuation – wherever it has been tested on a sufficiently wide range of sizes of ancient woods.
2. The value of the parameter b (Table 30.1) varies for different groups of woods between 0.19 (double the number of species in 40 times the area of wood) and 0.40 (double the species in 5–6 times the area). Despite the earlier claim by Max Hooper that lower figures result from a lesser degree of separation between the woods of a group (as island biogeography theory would require), I find it difficult to relate higher values of b to woods known to have been separated for a longer time or by a greater distance.
3. The value of b for trees and shrubs is always less than for the flora as a whole, typically about two-thirds. Trees and shrubs are therefore less affected by the size of the wood than herbaceous plants; to put it another way, in a large wood about one-fifth of the flora is woody, in a small wood nearly half.

Table 30.1 Values of the parameter b, which measures the extent to which large woods have more species than small.

Group of woods	Number of woods	Separation, km	b for all flowering-plants and ferns	b for trees & shrubs	b for bryophytes
Rockingham Forest, Northants (after Hooper)	—	—	0.19	—	—
S.E. Essex	38	0.5	0.22	0.15	—
Long Melford, Suffolk	9	0.1	0.32	0.22	—
Milden Thicks, Suffolk	7	0.3	0.35	0.18	—
Harleston hornbeam area, S.E Norfolk and N.E. Suffolk	32	3	0.35	0.19	—
West Cambridgeshire	21	4	0.40	0.21	0.28
Helford River, Cornwall	14	0.8	0.40	0.25	—

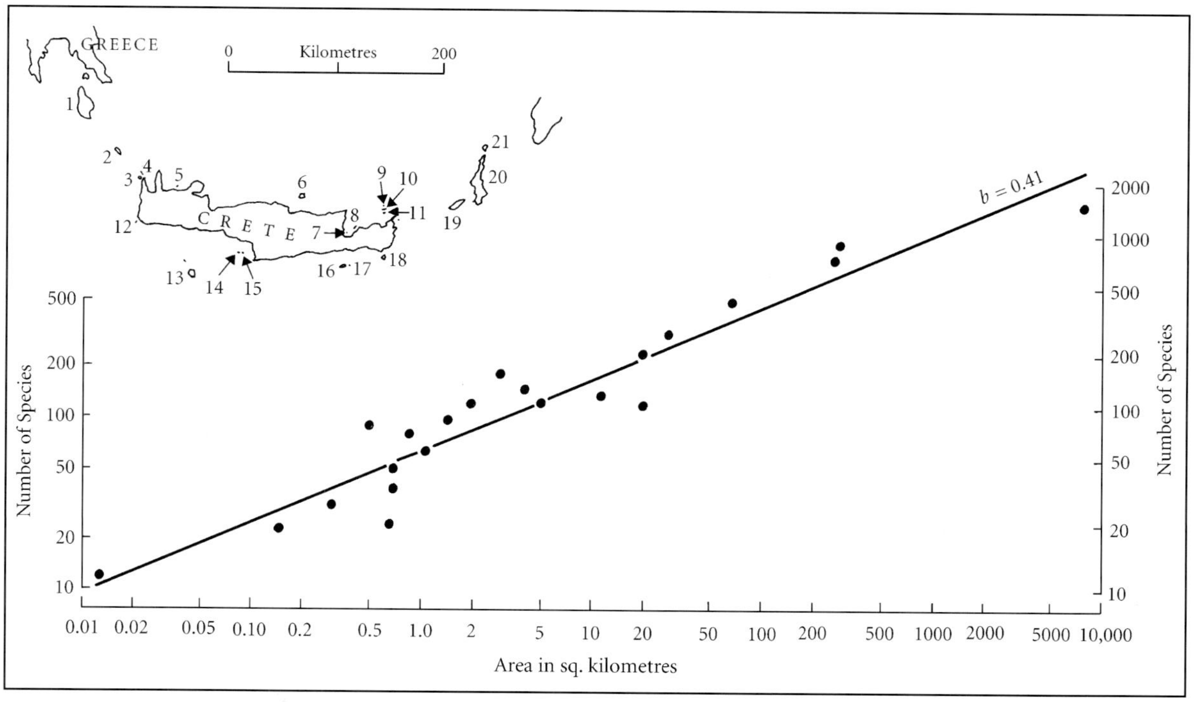

Fig. 30.1 Relation between number of species and area for flowering-plants and ferns on South Aegean islands. Both scales are logarithmic. Data from various published sources plus fieldwork by the author and Dr J. A. Moody. Correlation coefficient = 0.959; $\log S = 1.796 + 0.409 \log A$.

4. The value of *b* for plants characteristic of ancient woodland is the same as for the flora as a whole (whether calculated on the basis of the simple number of species, or of species weighted according to their degree of affinity with ancient woodland). Ancient-woodland plants, therefore do not specially tend to occur in the larger (or smaller) woods.
5. Small woods close to big woods do not systematically have a richer flora than would be expected from their size, although island biogeography would predict that they should have.
6. Individual woods widely separated from the rest of the group do not systematically have a poorer flora than would be expected from their size. This, too, is contrary to island biogeography theory.

It is seldom possible to get consistent enough information to do this with other groups of plants, but Fig. 30.3 attempts to show the relation with bryophytes.[3] The number of bryophyte species, too, is related to the size of the wood, less strongly than with herbaceous plants but more strongly than with trees and shrubs. Bryophytes, even more than flowering-plants, are related to special habitats – ruins, an old railway, a chalk-pit – unconnected with the size of the wood.

Which Species are Confined to Bigger Woods?

This field has been much influenced by a study by N. W. Moore and M. D. Hooper three decades ago. They found that most woodland birds rarely occur in woods below a certain size. This can hardly be a matter of island biogeography, for birds are better able than any other creatures to move from wood to wood. Their study covered a much wider range of sizes than is possible here; their smallest 'woods' were of only 1/1000 hectare, or one biggish bush, whereas ancient woods are difficult to find smaller than 1 hectare. Nevertheless, some of their birds, such as nightjar or lesser spotted woodpecker, seldom occurred in woods smaller than 100 ha.[4]

Is there a group of plant species confined to the bigger woods? If island biogeography were the underlying cause, smaller woods would not be big enough to

3 I doubt whether the fungus floras of woods will ever be completely enough known for such a comparison to be meaningful. I have studied agarics and other 'visible' fungi in Brandon Park (Breckland) almost every autumn since 1959. The list has reached 450 species, and on average 8 species have been added to it every year for the last ten years. Brandon Park is not an ancient wood, but experience in Hayley, Buff, and Bradfield Woods is similar.

4 Moore, N. W. and Hooper, M. D. (1975). 'On the number of bird species in British woods'. *Biological Conservation* **8**, 239–50.

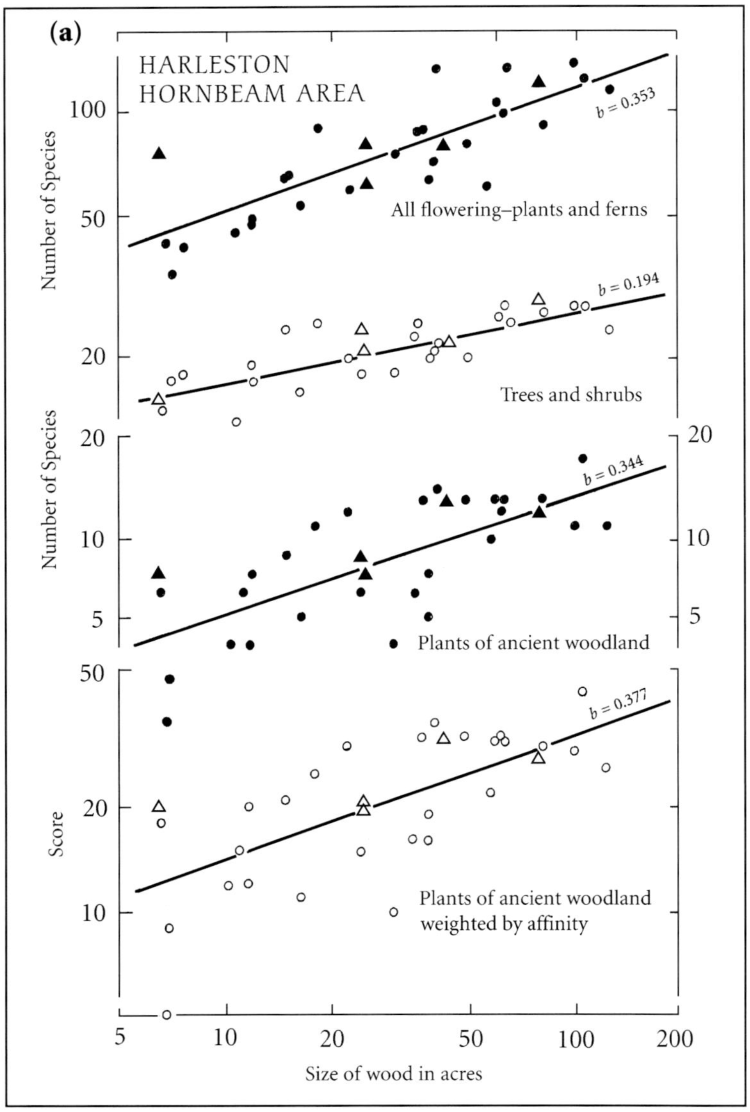

Fig. 30.2 Relation between number of species and area for various groups of ancient woods:
(a) Harleston hornbeam area (S.E. Suffolk and N.E. Norfolk, Fig. 14.1;
(b) Helford River (W. Cornwall);
(c) S.E. Essex.
Triangles: specially isolated woods. Circled points: woods close to bigger woods. Small points: woods of doubtful antiquity (which are not counted in calculating the regression lines).

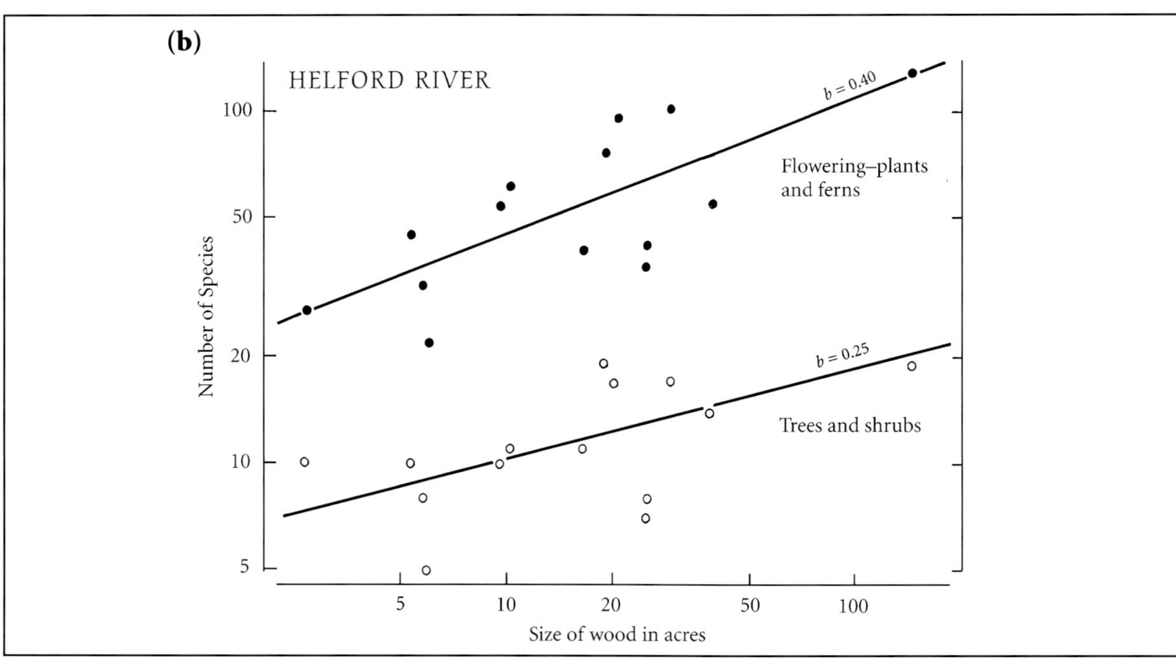

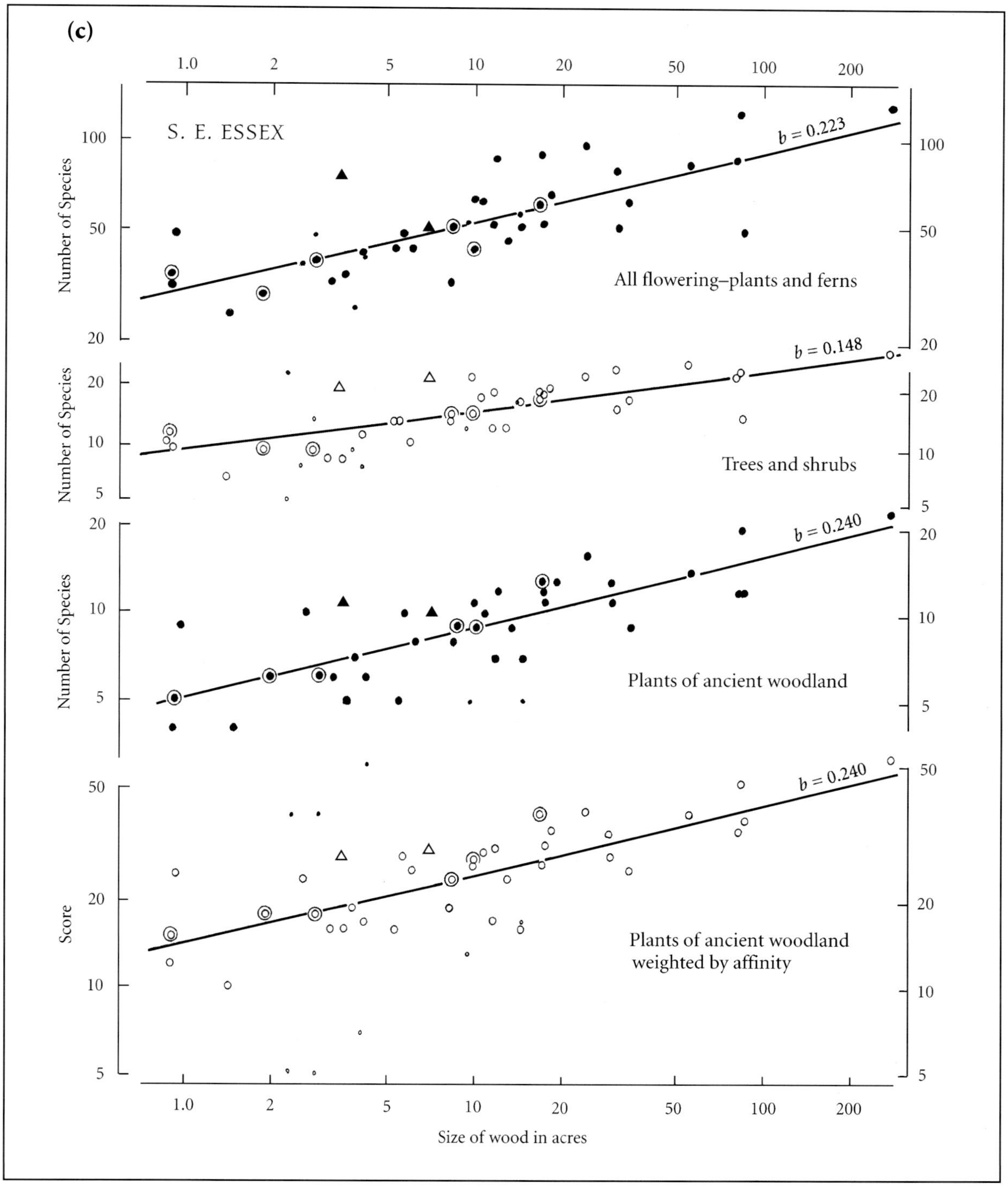

sustain permanent populations of such species: they would have died out over the centuries for lack of sufficient numbers. These species should be of the type that does not easily recolonize; that is, they should be characteristic of ancient woodland.

To test the theory calls for a large data-base. As a first attempt, I have collated species lists from 151 woods in Norfolk and Suffolk, ranging from 1.34 to 303 acres. (Two or more contiguous woods count as one.) These are divided into seven size-classes on a logarithmic scale, each being $\sqrt[3]{10}$ (a little more than twice) the area of the next below:

class I	1.00 to 2.15 acres
II	2.15 to 4.64
III	4.64 to 10.0
IV	10.0 to 21.5
V	21.5 to 46.4
VI	46.4 to 100
VII	more than 100

To illustrate the handling of the data I take the crab-tree, *Malus sylvestris*, as an example. Table 30.2 shows the calculation of the percentages of woods in each size-class in which crab occurs. These percentages are

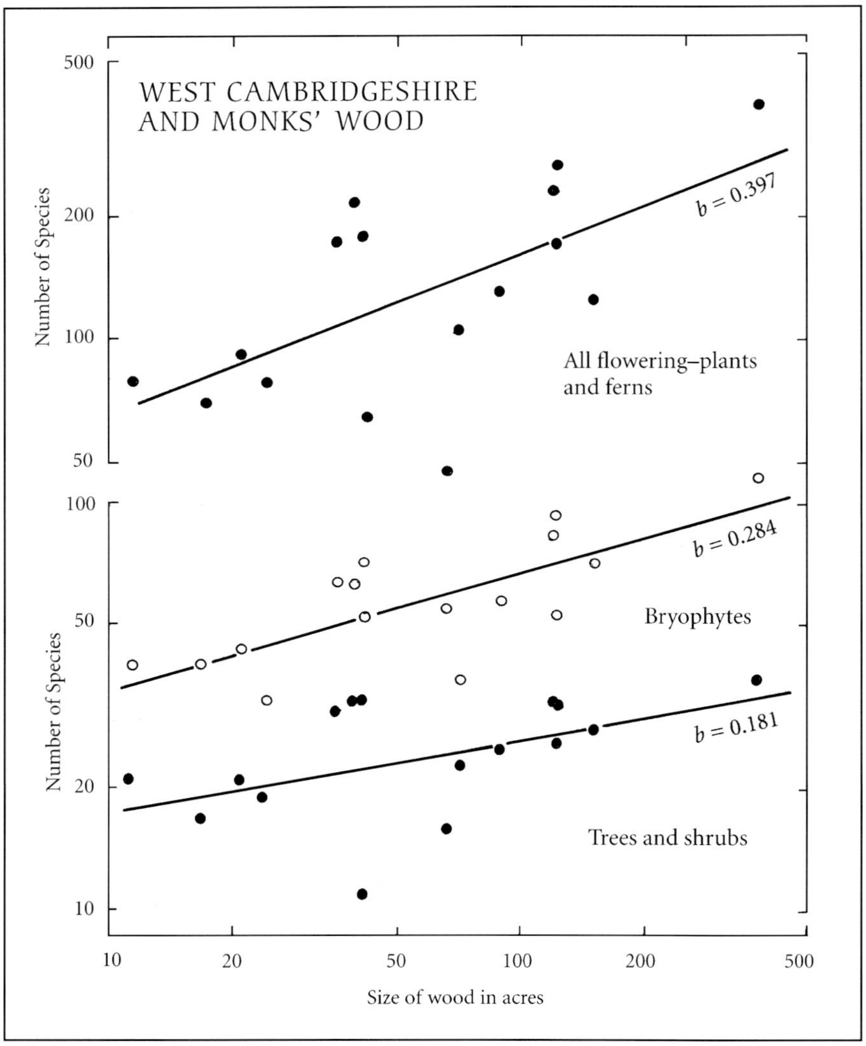

Fig. 30.3 Relation between species and area for flowering-plants and ferns, and for bryophytes, in the West Cambridgeshire group of woods. Monks' Wood, Huntingdon, has been included to extend the range of sizes. (Bryophyte records were mostly accumulated over many years by the Cambridge Bryophyte Group; I am indebted to Dr Chris Preston for supplying them.)

Table 30.2 Occurrence of crab, *Malus sylvestris*, in woods of different sizes.

Size-class Acres	I 1–2.15	II 2.15–4.64	III 4.64–10	IV 10–21.5	V 21.5–46.4	VI 46.4–100	VII > 100	TOTAL
Number of woods with crab	4	5	13	21	16	23	5	87
Total number of woods	7	9	24	38	29	29	15	151
Percentage in which crab occurs	57	55	54	55	55	79	33	53

expressed as a graph in the first diagram of Fig. 30.4.

Crab, which is conspicuously anti-gregarious (two individual trees are very rarely close together), clearly occurs in ancient woods of all sizes down to the smallest. Indeed, in terms of trees per acre it is undoubtedly commoner in small woods.

Fig. 30.4 gives similar graphs for other significant species. Those displayed are neither so common that they occur in almost every wood, nor so rare that the numbers are statistically non-significant.

Why should a species occur more often in bigger woods? Part of the reason for Moore & Hooper's finding with birds is that birds require territories of above a minimum size, which has no analogy among plants. Three other possibilities come to mind.

(1) Any plant occurring as randomly scattered individuals or scattered clones may be missing by chance from any small area. For instance, a plant that grows once every 10 acres has a 0.1 probability of

occurring in a 1-acre wood, a 0.5 probability of occurring in a 10-acre wood, and a 0.999 probability of occurring in a 100-acre wood (Fig. 30.4, end). The same could happen with a plant needing a special habitat that is randomly scattered, as may be so with sand-lenses. If either were the predominant reason, a hundred-acre wood should have as many species as ten 10-acre woods.

(2) Some plants need specialized habitats, which may occur less often in small woods for some systematic reason (rides, waterlogged areas). If this were the reason, a big wood should have more species than the equivalent area in small woods. This, presumably, also applies to Moore & Hooper's birds.

(3) Plants may need a minimum population to avoid dying out, as in island biogeography. Here, a big wood should have more species than the same area of small woods.

Trees vary from the anti-gregarious crab, which prefers smaller woods, to aspen, which fits theory (1) very well. Aspen occurs as scattered clones on average about every 20 acres, is almost certain to ocur in woods bigger than 100 acres, and is absent from woods smaller than 5 acres. (But it is associated with waterlogged areas, perhaps less likely to occur in small woods surrounded by artificially drained farmland.)

Among shade-bearing herbs, a plant conforming to island biogeography theory ought to be *Moehringia*, associated with ancient woodland. Being an annual, it should have plenty of opportunities of dying out if the population is too small. It does indeed fail to occur in woods smaller than 5 acres; above that size it occurs in about 40% of all woods regardless of area. *Circaea*, a perennial, occurs in about 60% of woods bigger than 5 acres. Herb paris, a rather rare clonal plant, is associated with big woods.

Most spring perennials, such as primrose, have a rather weak association with bigger woods. Oxlip, however, extends into even the smallest ancient woods. Anemone is clonal, with a distribution rather like aspen.

Summer perennials are not much affected by the size of the wood, with the notable exception of *Deschampsia cespitosa*, which mysteriously prefers big woods.

Most strongly associated with big woods are *Succisa pratensis*, *Potentilla anserina*, and *Plantago major*. These are non-shade-bearing species of rides and woodland grassland, habitats seldom developed in woods smaller than 20 acres. *Succisa* is a woodland-grassland plant with a pollen record from wildwood. The others are not specially woodland plants at all.

Buried-seed plants, which are seldom clonal, tend to be associated with bigger woods, perhaps because coppicing is less common in small woods.

Associations with big woods are particularly common among plants of woodland grassland, mobile species, and aquatics (*Callitriche*). Rides and newly-felled areas occur in most big woods but are less common in small woods.

Woodland-edge plants, *Euonymus europaeus* and *Melica uniflora*, weakly favour small woods, which have more edge in relation to their area. *Ulmus minor* is clonal and tends to start from edges; it is independent of area except for the smallest woods.

There may be other plants that more strongly favour big woods. I suspect that parasitic orchids (*Neottia* and *Epipactis* species) may do so, but have not enough evidence on these secretive and mysterious plants which live off fungi. Plants of ancient woodland, on the whole, show no such bias. Among the plants that most strongly favour big woods are commonplace species of open ground, such as plantain and silverweed. The specialized-habitat effect would seem to explain most of the bias.

Metapopulations

Woodland conservationists often link species-area theory to the doctrine of metapopulations. A metapopulation of some creature consists of a number of local populations inhabitating patches or islands of suitable habitat within a region. The local populations have their ups and downs and sometimes go extinct, whether because their numbers get too small to be viable or because their patch of habitat disappears. They are renewed by migration from surviving populations not too far off.

Metapopulations are characteristic of certain butterflies. The Silver-spotted Skipper, for example, is confined to heavily-grazed chalk grassland. In the twentieth century this habitat, formerly continuous, became fragmented. The butterfly has much declined; it tends to persist *either* in big patches or in small patches close enough to other patches to allow migration.[5]

Do any woodland plants behave in this way? A patchy population is not necessarily a metapopulation: three further conditions have to be fulfilled. (1) Even the largest local populations (or all but the very largest one) must have a measurable rate of extinction. (2) Patches must not be too isolated to prevent recolonization after local extinction. (3) Local populations must not have synchronous dynamics.[6]

Metapopulations could occur within a large wood.

5 Thomas, C. D. and Jones, T. M. (1993). 'Partial recovery of a skipper butterfly (*Hesperia comma*) from population refuges: lessons for conservation in a fragmented landscape'. *Journal of Animal Ecology* **62**, 472–81.

6 Freckleton, R. P. and Watkinson, A. R. (2002). 'Large-scale spatial dynamics of plants: metapopulations, regional ensembles and patchy populations.' *Journal of Ecology* **90**, 419–34.

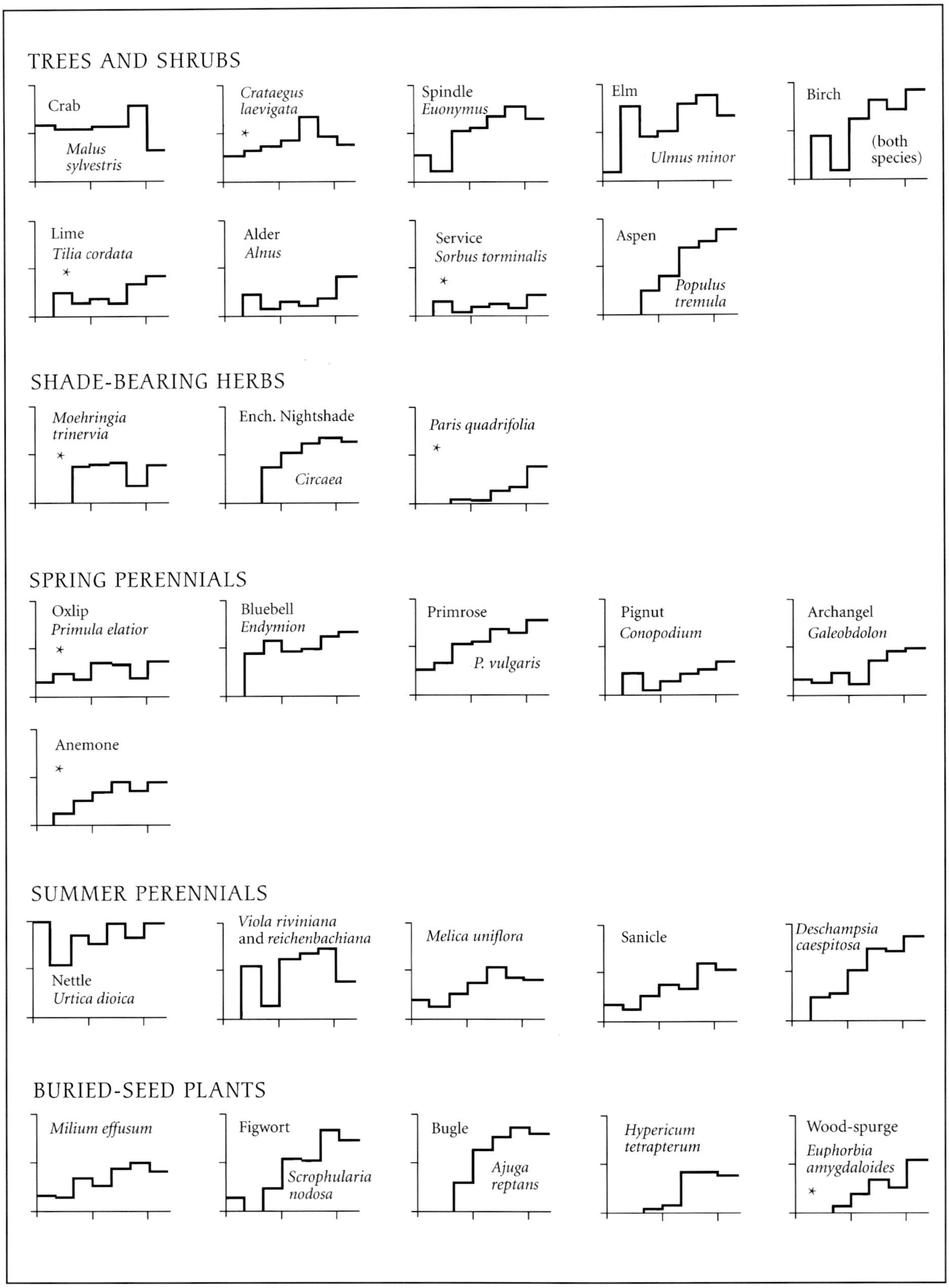

Fig. 30.4 Species-area relationships for single species, based on woods in Norfolk and Suffolk. The probability of occurrence of each species is shown as a function of the size of the wood, plotted on a logarithmic scale of area. Plants are grouped according to their ecological characteristics, and within each group are arranged in ascending order of association with big woods. * = associated with ancient woodland. The last graph shows the theoretical function for a plant that occurs at random as one individual (or clone) every ten acres.

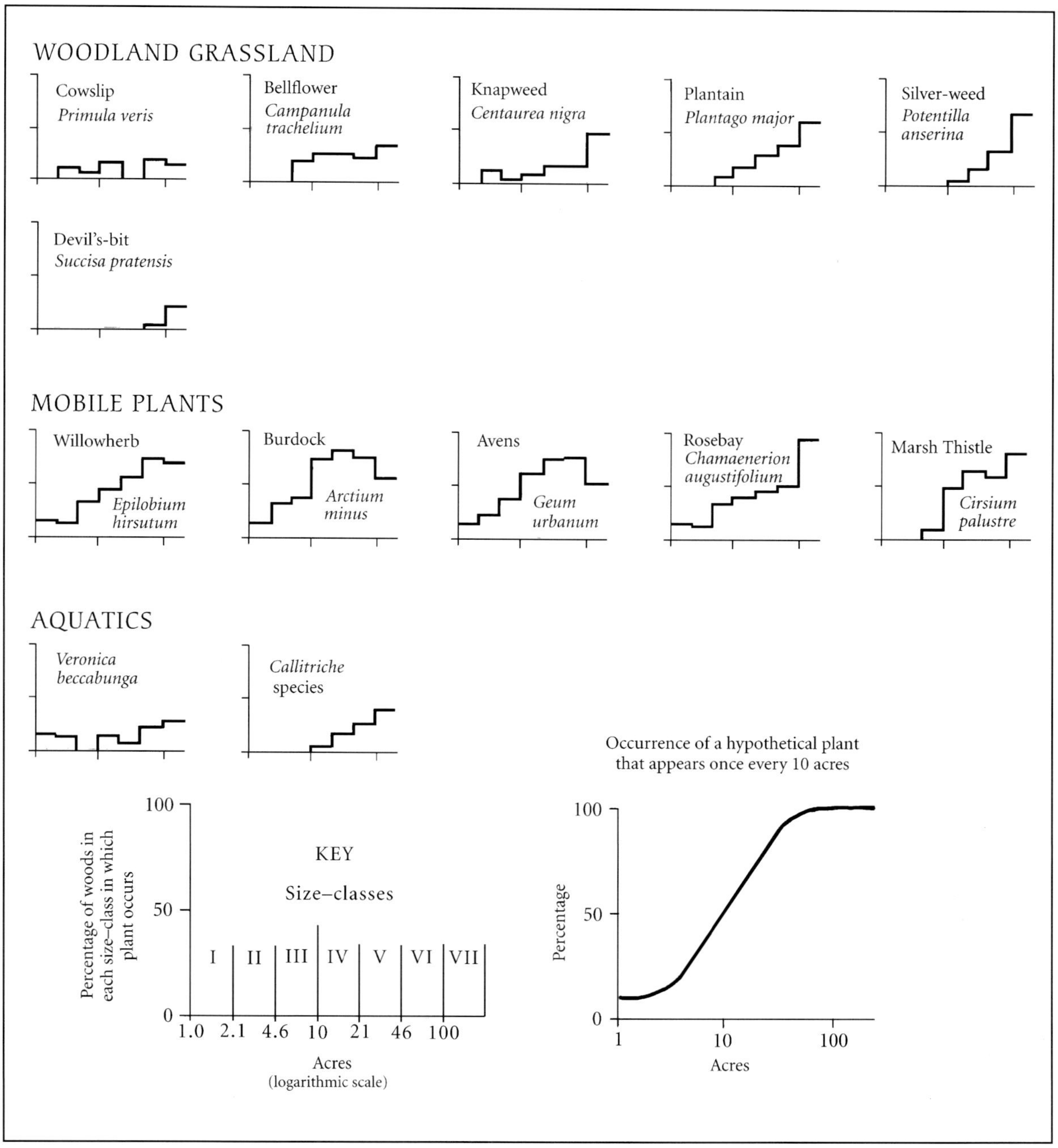

Teresa Valverde and Jonathan Silvertown presented primrose as a plant of this kind, claiming that it colonized canopy gaps as they arose and died out as they filled in.[7] In my experience the model that they constructed is not really applicable to primrose, in which plants persist through many years of shade and respond to coppicing mainly by increase of existing plants rather than establishment of new ones (cf Buff Wood, p. 404). A more promising group of candidates for within-wood metapopulations are the 'mobile' group of coppicing plants that chase newly-felled areas round the wood, and might disappear if coppicing were interrupted: thistles and willowherbs, among others. However, remarkably few species are limited to this kind of behaviour: most of them either have alternative habitats outside the wood, or have buried seed as well. Seed-bank behaviour or tolerance of shade are much commoner among woodland plants than metapopulation behaviour.

The present discussion, however, is more concerned

7 Valverde, T. and Silvertown, J. (1997). 'A metapopulation model for *Primula vulgaris*, a temperate forest understorey herb.' *Journal of Ecology* **85**, 193–210.

with between-wood metapopulations, in which whole woods constitute the patches. Not many plants, however, meet the three conditions. As we have seen (pp. 56–59), plants that have a measurable rate of extinction (condition (1)) tend to go extinct for reasons that apply to all woods irrespective of size; that is to say, dynamics are synchronous and condition (3) is not fulfilled. A study of 81 wood-lots in south Sweden also failed to identify clear examples of metapopulation behaviour among plants.[8]

A plant with between-wood metapopulation behaviour must not be clonal nor have long-lived seed (which would defeat condition (1)), nor be characteristic of ancient woodland (condition (2)), nor liable to die out with the general increase of shade (condition (3)). Maybe there are species that fulfil all these conditions: I leave the reader to think of them.

Conclusions

A close plant equivalent to the nightjar and lesser spotted woodpecker, creatures characteristic of big woods, has yet to be found. Relations between species and area are complex, and vary from one species to another. It is dangerous to treat them as though species all behaved much the same, or to apply 'laws' extrapolated from very different situations. Some plants characteristic of ancient woodland tend to go with bigger woods, others not. A few plants apparently prefer small woods.

The most significant factor is that large woods have more habitats than small, especially unshaded habitats. Some of the plants which for that reason occur more often in big woods are generalized farmland species such as *Potentilla anserina* and *Plantago major*. Others, such as *Succisa*, are specialized woodland-grassland plants. The random effect is common, especially among clonal plants.

Although the species-area statistics conform to the island biogeography model, attempts to identify the island biogeography process have so far failed.

Trees and shrubs are less sensitive to the size of the wood than herbs are, perhaps because few call for special habitats: there is no equivalent among trees to the woodland-grassland herbs.

Lessons for nature reserves

As I concluded in 1980 (p. 56ff), plants do die out from woods, but not at random. If primrose dies out from global warming in Madingley Wood (p. 391), it is unlikely to be restored by linking that wood to Hardwick Wood, where primrose is also in decline. Betony will be saved in Hayley Wood by combating increasing shade; enlarging the wood is irrelevant.

It is not obviously an advantage for species to move from one wood to another. *Campanula trachelium* has nearly died out in Hayley Wood. Are we to suppose that establishing a link to Gamlingay Wood (where it is still common) will bring it back? Or will whatever prevented it from being common in Hayley spread along the corridor and eat it up in Gamlingay? (I concede, in favour of the linkage argument, that a skilled magician can be hired to transform the fields between the woods into an effective corridor, into woodland such as would have existed had the woods always been joined.)[9]

Enlarging and joining woods, and encouraging species to pass between them, carries the implication that differences between woods are somehow bad. Should conservationists be promoting homogenization? What is wrong with apparently similar woods behaving in different ways, for reasons as yet unknown? One has only to transfer the idea to real islands to turn it into fallacy: would the conservation of the rare plants of the Aegean be served by translocating the endemics of Crete to Kárpathos and *vice versa*?

Epilogue: Does a hundred-acre wood really have more plant species than 10 ten-acre woods?

This may be one of those 'truths which are too well known to need demonstration', but let us try to demonstrate it nevertheless. Table 30.3 presents seven examples, in each of which the combined floras for ten small ancient woods in a region are compared with the flora for one big wood of roughly the same area as the ten put together.

On each of the seven occasions the big wood turns out, on average, to have *fewer* species than ten small woods of equivalent area. Woods being highly variable, it is possible for an individual big wood to have more species than ten small woods, but this is rather unusual. There are, no doubt, reasons for this. Ten separate woods may well cover a wider range of natural environments than is likely in a single site. It is difficult to find big woods that have not been drastically disturbed by modern forestry or deer. And (despite precautions taken) small woods may have been more fully recorded than big ones.

A rigorous disproof of the fragmentation theory – that small woods are fragmentary habitats and of less

8 Dupré, C. and Ehrlén, J. (2002). 'Habitat configuration, species traits and plant distributions'. *Journal of Ecology* **90**, 796–805.

9 On hedges as corridors in America see: Corbit, M., Marks, P. L., and Gardescu, S. (1999) 'Hedgerows as habitat corridors for forest herbs in central New York, USA.' *Journal of Ecology* **87**, 220–32. Their findings somewhat contrast with those in England, where hedges, almost by definition, do not form habitat corridors for the more exacting woodland herbs.

Table 30.3 Combined species list of ten small woods, compared with the number of species expected in one wood of the same total area.

The fifth column gives the number of species expected in a wood of the equivalent total area, from the species-area relationship of the region (e.g. from Fig. 30.2). The last column gives the range of numbers of species actually recorded in big woods of similar area, adjusted to the exact area required using the species-area relation. Woods that are recent or partly grubbed out are excluded from the data.

Region	Range of sizes of ten woods, acres	Total area of ten woods, acres	Total number of species found in ten woods	Number of species expected in a single wood of the same area	Range of numbers actually encountered in one wood of the same area
S.E. Essex	0.93–5.7	28.4	118	68	51–102
E. Suffolk	2.7–12.9	78.0	130	115	57–182
Mid Suffolk	5.8–11.9	86.5	152	119	70–210
W. Suffolk	6.9–14.5	100.9	152	100	52–129
S.E. Essex	7.9–24.3	135.6	157	101	90–115
Mid Suffolk	12.0–22.8	171.3	202	160	102–240
E. Suffolk	14.8–24.9	200.6	167	115	57–182

value than big woods – would call for a much more ambitious research project. However, even on this limited set of data the theory has been tested seven times, and each time the result has been the opposite of that predicted. It should no longer be taken for granted that big woods have a special conservation value disproportionate to their area. Some do, like the Bradfield Woods; others do not.

Fig. 30.5 Buff Wood, although of modest size, has a variety of habitats and a richer flora than many big woods. April 1984

Fig. 31.1 (a–c)

(a) Ancient woodland rarely meets the sea. Here a Cornish sessile-oakwood adjoins a drowned estuary. The oaks (with an occasional service in the last row) hang over the cliff, and hook seaweed in their boughs at high spring tides. Oaks dislike salt at their roots but their leaves do not mind the occasional dip.

(b) The same type of oakwood can exist in giant form in a sheltered ravine –

(c) – or, close by, in dwarf form on a wind-exposed ridge.

All from the Helford River. 1987–93

31

Types of Ancient Woodland: can any advance be made?

Critics of the original book occasionally claimed that it was limited to East Anglia, which they supposed to include Essex. Since 1980 I have studied many more woods outside this region, but without adding greatly to the woodland types encountered. Woods in Somerset and Dorset, for instance, can usually be understood in terms of types already published here. Wales (to be the subject of another book) is different: indeed even the distinction between woods and fields, which English ecologists take for granted, is not the same in Wales. In Scotland there are both woods which are extensions of English woodland types and the peculiar Highland birchwoods and pinewoods. These latter are different again, for they 'do shift their stances' as an eighteenth-century Scots writer put it, and do not have fixed boundaries.

Peterken's Stand Types

In 1981 George Peterken published *Woodland Conservation and Management*,[1] which classified 'ancient, semi-natural woodland' into 58 stand-types and subdivisions. This was based on tree communities subdivided by ground vegetation, roughly parallel to the method in *Ancient Woodland*. Its geographical coverage is wider, extending throughout Great Britain. It was formalized by the recording of plots, mostly 30 x 30 m. Plantations were expressly rejected. Peterken and *Ancient Woodland* together yield a total of 67 stand-types.

In the second edition of 1993, Peterken proposed adding chestnut-woods as a separate stand group, and redefining the characters discriminating different kinds of oakwood.

The National Vegetation Classification

In 1992 there appeared the woodland volume of the *National Vegetation Classification*;[2] it too covers the whole of Great Britain. This is an admirably thorough study, based on many years of fieldwork, especially in Scotland, and includes a number of new communities not previously described. The material, however, is an ill-defined mixture of ancient woodland, recent natural woodland, plantations on former woodland, wood-pasture, plantations on former non-woodland sites, osier-beds – no attempt being made to treat these separately – together with 'scrub' (young woodland) and 'underscrub' (brambles etc.): much as if the companion volume on grassland were to include cornfields and football-pitches along with ancient pasture and meadow, and not say which was which.

For reasons that were never explained, the *NVC* at once became the most widely used woodland classification, especially in official circles. This *floristic* scheme was taken up as a *general-purpose* classification, without anyone asking whether it was really suitable for this. There was no debate on the merits of the three schemes, on their suitability for different purposes, or on whether a synthesis could be created incorporating the best features of each.

In the whole of Great Britain the *NVC* has only 19 'communities' (so-called) for 'woodland' and six more for 'scrub' and underscrub. The woodland 'communities' are divided into a total of 58 'subcommunities'; only 34 of these are part of ancient woodland, the others being short-lived stages in succession. Having only half the number of divisions (34 against 67), the classification is less detailed or comprehensive than those in this book or in *Woodland Conservation and Management*. A later classification ought to have more, not fewer, categories

1 Peterken, G. F. (1981, 2nd ed. 1993). *Woodland Conservation and Management*. Chapman& Hall, London.

2 Rodwell, J. S., Pigott, C. D.., Ratcliffe, D. A., Malloch, A. J. C., Birks, H. J. B, Proctor, M. C. F., Shimwell, D. W., Huntley, J. P., Radford, E., Wigginton, M. J., and Wilkins, P. (1991). *British Plant Communities: woodlands and scrub*. Cambridge University Press.

than an earlier one: it should include all (or nearly all) the types described by the earlier authors, plus extra ones appearing as new distinctions are recognized, or rare types discovered, which the earlier authors missed.

The *NVC*'s method is very different from that used here. It is a rigorously floristic approach, defining woodland types by the plant species present in sample areas, and paying little attention to other characteristics. It thus suffers from the same kind of incompleteness as, for example, a historical work that is based solely on written documents and takes no account of archaeology. A floristic scheme is particularly defective for ancient woodland, in which one-third of the plants can easily be dormant in the seed-bank and escape detection (Chapter 26).

The *NVC* copes well with the oakwoods of Wales, northern England, and Scotland, and the pinewoods of the Scottish Highlands. Here it pays particular attention to bryophytes, and adds to the stock of recognized plant communities. It gives a convincing account of the relation between woodland types and topography in regions where soils depend strongly on the solid geology.

At the other extreme it does not adequately subdivide the central core of English ancient woodland types. This is a difficult problem because variation is continuous, and a divisive system can at best be only an approximation to the reality. However, the *NVC* gives the impression that most ancient woods, despite their infinite variety and the numerous stand types already published, can be crammed into the categories **W8** and **W10** which include much recent woodland as well. My own garden keys out at **W8**, as does Hayley Wood, which cannot be right.

Any classification of woodland has to reckon with the trees and shrubs not being closely correlated with the herbs and undershrubs. As Chapters 6 and 7 of this book show, there is a statistical relation, but it is not strong enough to justify treating trees and ground vegetation together. The authors of the *NVC* dealt with this by classifying mainly the ground vegetation (including ground bryophytes) and playing down the trees. They treated the trees as if they were a relatively artificial component of the wood. If one part of a wood is dominated by lime, another by hornbeam, and a third by hazel, this is supposed to have little phytosociological significance: it depends on the whim of past woodmen in favouring these trees. This theory is of course often true for recent woods and plantations, which form the greater part of the 'woodland' area of Britain. However, the *NVC* offers no evidence for extrapolating this claim to ancient woodland, nor does it suggest when, how, why, or with what success the woodmen are supposed to have made these changes.[3]

The *NVC*'s attempts to relate the trees and ground vegetation led to the pessimistic conclusion that

> variation in the woody component of the community has been dislocated to some extent [by sylvicultural treatment] from differences in the herbaceous element. This can be seen very clearly where the same field and ground layers occur under very different canopies derived by diverse manipulations of the same basic assortment of trees and shrubs. The *Primula-Glechoma* herbs and bryophytes, for example, can be found beneath coppiced underwood of *Corylus*, *Acer campestre* or *Fraxinus*, or various combinations of these . . . where similar treatment has been applied to stands of different sub-communities, it has often evened out any natural variation among the woody species ao that virtually identical canopies survive over different field and ground layers . . . (p. 139)

The implication is that in the olden days (whenever that was) the composition of woods followed the natural variation of climate and soil; the ground vegetation still does so, but the trees have been separated from that variation by differences of silvicultural treatment. No evidence of any kind is offered to support this assertion, and I have failed to find any. Whatever created the 'variation in the woody component', it was not 'diverse manipulations'. It is too much to be told that (to concoct an illustration) Merton College favoured maple in their part of Gamlingay Wood (Fig. 25.2), the Avenells favoured ash in the other part, and the Bishop of Ely favoured hazel in Hayley Wood. That is not how woods work: the Bishop's woods in Cambridgeshire and Suffolk resemble the woods of neighbouring owners in Cambridgeshire and Suffolk, and do not follow a general pattern of Ely bishopric woods. The only relevant treatment – down to the 20th century – was coppicing, promoting any oaks to be timber trees. This was applied in all the woods. Variations in canopy survive despite, not because of, centuries of coppicing.

Most information on woodland history, whether documents, archaeology, fieldwork, or palynology, inevitably relates to trees. The history of ground vegetation is far less well known. As the years advance, data on the stability or change of ground vegetation begin to unfold, and it becomes possible to see the effects of deer or Global Warming. I presented some of these in Chapter 25; but I hardly expect to live long enough to get far in this pursuit. Concentrating on ground vegetation loses nearly all the time dimension of the past and allows little hope of anticipating the future.

The *NVC* has two further shortcomings. It lacks rare vegetation types: one looks askance at a classification in which no sub-community occurs in fewer than four 10-km squares on the distribution map. It does not tell

3 Woodmen may have had more of this kind of influence in Scotland: see Worrell, R. and Mackenzie, W. (2003). The ecological impact of using the woods. T. C. Smout (ed.) (see supplementary Bibliography), 195–213.

the reader how to recognize additional communities and sub-communities, present or future, not encountered by the authors. These are not too difficult to find, for example the curious elm-groves with ground vegetation of alexanders (*Smyrnium olusatrum*) on the sandy sea-cliffs of East Anglia. (Peterken acknowledged that there were other stand-types which he had not fully investigated.)

The *National Vegetation Classification*, therefore, is not an alternative to, nor does it supersede, the classification used in this book. Its objectives are different, and it has no time-depth: it offers an account of British woodland, wood-pasture and plantation at one moment in time, the 1980s. It does not set out to find the *genius loci* of a wood, to define what makes that wood special and different from other woods, which is all-important in setting out priorities for conservation. As a reviewer put it: 'Heaven forbid that *British Plant Communities* in its present form should be used for the identification of rare or unusual types of vegetation for conservation purposes'.

To take an extreme example, Staverton Park (p. 293) works out as '**W10** *Quercus robur – Pteridium aquilinum – Rubus fruticosus* woodland', which is a common type, and Staverton is a species-poor example of it. This is true but trivial: Staverton (although it has two distinctive plants not mentioned in the *NVC*) is not memorable for its flora. What makes it special is its huge concentration of ancient pollard oaks and giant hollies, its long freedom from disturbance and its well-recorded history. It is not really woodland at all but wood-pasture; its parallels are with the wood-pastures of southern Europe and the savannas of other continents. To characterize it as woodland in floristic terms is to miss the point.

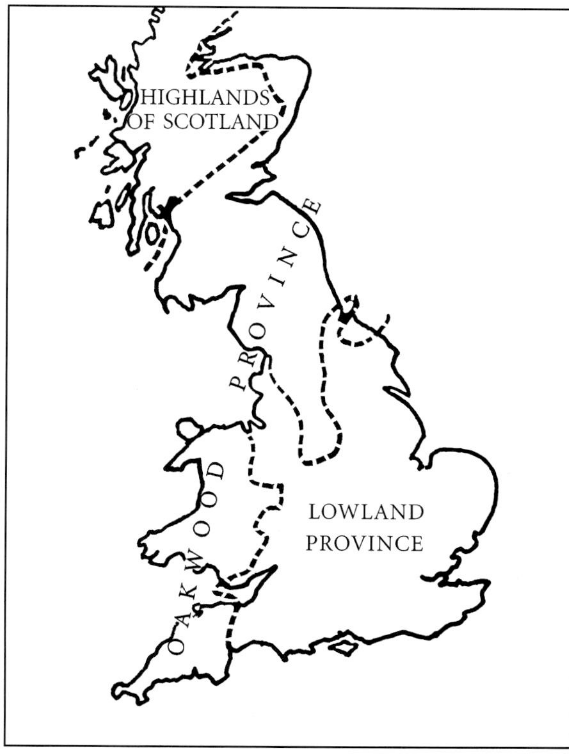

Fig. 31.2 Provinces of Great Britain, as used in defining the distribution of woodland types. These fundamental divisions go back into wildwood times (p. 99).

Table 31.1 Combined classification of ancient woodland.
I omit wood-pasture, and also omit the many types and subtypes of the *NVC* not known in ancient woodland.

Mainly in the LOWLAND PROVINCE (Fig. 31.2)
(Lowland England excluding Devon and Cornwall)

	Peterken	Rackham	National Vegetation Classification	Geographical range
Ash – Wych-elm Woods				
1	1Aa Chalk and lowland limestone	not represented	**W8e** *Fraxinus excelsior – Acer campestre – Mercurialis perennis* woodland, *Geranium robertianum* sub-community (part)	S. England, Midlands
2	not separated	not represented	**W8f** *Fraxinus excelsior – Acer campestre – Mercurialis perennis* woodland, *Allium ursinum* sub-community	Mendips, Cotswolds; also S.W. England, Wales
3	1Ba Wet clayey	Mixed Ashwood (part)	not separated	Midlands, rare in E.Anglia
4	1Bb Wet sandy	Mixed Ashwood (part)	not separated	rare, E. England
5	1Ca Limestone, eastern	Mixed Ashwood (part)	not separated	Bedford Purlieus (Peterborough) & S.W. Lincs

Peterken	Rackham	National Vegetation Classification	Geographical range
Ash – Maple Woods			
6 2Aa Ash – Maple on wet clay (part)	Ash – Hazel-wood (part)	approx. **W8a** *Fraxinus excelsior – Acer campestre – Mercurialis perennis* woodland, *Primula vulgaris – Glechoma hederacea* sub-community (part)	England except north & S.W.
7 2Aa Ash – Maple on wet clay (part)	Mixed Ashwood (aspen variant)	approx. **W8c** *Fraxinus excelsior – Acer campestre – Mercurialis perennis* woodland, *Deschampsia cespitosa* sub-community	E. and middle England
8 not represented	not separated	**W1** *Salix cinerea – Galium palustre* woodland	in ancient woodland, confined to tiny patches within the two previous types
9 2Ab Maple on wet clay (part)	Maplewood	not separated	E. and S.E. England and in Forests elsewhere
10 2Ab Maple on wet clay (part)	Maple – Hazel-wood	not separated	E. England, Midland Forests
11 not represented	Aspen-wood	not represented	widespread in middle and E. England
12 not represented	Hatfield Forest oakwood	not represented	Hatfield Forest, Essex
13 2Ba Ash – Maple on wet light soils	Ash –Hazel-wood (part)	not separated	mainly Norfolk & N.E. Midlands
14 2Bb Ash – Maple on dry light soils	not represented	not separated	3 sites in Lincs & Surrey
15 2C Ash – Maple on dry heavy soils	Mixed Hazel-wood (part)	not separated	especially Mendips & Somerset
Hazel – Ashwoods			
16 3Aa Heavy acid soils, with *Quercus robur*	Mixed Hazel-wood (hawthorn – bramble variant)	partly **W10c** *Quercus robur – Pteridium aquilinum – Rubus fruticosus* woodland, *Hedera helix* sub-community	England, Wales, S. Scotland (common); Ireland
17 3Ab Light acid soils, with *Quercus robur*	Mixed Hazelwood (part)	not separated	S., middle, E. England (rare); Ireland (rare)
18 3B Southern calcareous	Mixed Hazelwood (part)	partly **W8d** *Fraxinus excelsior – Acer campestre – Mercurialis perennis* woodland, *Hedera helix* sub-community	mainly S. and middle England
19 not represented	Pure Ashwood (acidic)	not represented	as ancient woodland confined to Essex?
Ash – Limewoods			
20 4A Acidic, with birch	Lime – Ash-wood (part)	not separated	E. and middle England
21 4Ba With maple, eastern	Lime – Ash-wood (part)	not separated	Norfolk, Lincs
22 4Bb With maple, western	Lime – Ash-wood (part)	not separated	Mendips, S.E. Wales

Peterken	Rackham	National Vegetation Classification	Geographical range
Oak – Limewoods			
23 5A With *Quercus robur*	Pure Limewoods	not separated	E.England, Midlands
Chestnut-woods			
24 not represented	Chestnut – Lime	not separated	rare, S.E. Suffolk, N.E. Essex, N.E. Kent
25 not represented	Chestnut – Hornbeam	**W10b** *Quercus robur – Pteridium aquilinum – Rubus fruticosus* woodland, *Anemone nemorosa* sub-community	S.E. England, E.Essex, S.E. Suffolk
26 not represented	Chestnut – Oak (*Q. petraea*)	not separated	S.E. England, S.E. Essex
Birch – Oakwoods			
27 6Cb With *Q. petraea*, lowland	Oakwood	not separated	Lowland England (sparse)
28 6Cc With *Q. petraea* and hazel, lowland	Oakwood (part)	not separated	Lowland England (sparse)
29 [6Cd] With *Q. petraea*, calcareous	not represented	not represented	Darenth Wood, Kent (?due to recent changes)
30 6Db With *Q. robur*, lowland	Oakwood (part)	**W10a** *Quercus robur – Pteridium aquilinum – Rubus fruticosus* woodland	Lowland England (rare in ancient woodland)
31 6Dc With *Q. robur* and hazel, lowland	Oakwood (part), Pure Hazelwood	not separated	Lowland England (often not ancient woodland)
32 not represented	Holly-wood	not represented	widespread but rare, esp. in ex-wood-pastures
Alderwoods (omitting Sump Alderwood, **7Ba**, as never ancient)			
33 7Ab Neutral – calcareous valleys	Valley Alderwood (part)	not separated	widely scattered; also in Wales & Lake District
34 7Bb Calcareous springlines	Valley Alderwood (part)	not separated	N., E., S.E., W.England; rare in Scotland
35 not separated	Valley Alderwood (nettle variant)	**W7a** *Alnus glutinosa – Fraxinus excelsior – Lysimachia nemorum* woodland, *Urtica dioica* sub-community	especially N.W. Lowland England
36 7C Plateau Alderwood	Plateau Alderwood	not represented	mainly E.England (rare)
37 7E With *Prunus padus*, lowland	Valley or Plateau Alderwood	not represented	Norfolk

	Peterken	Rackham	National Vegetation Classification	Geographical range
Beechwoods				
38	8A Acid, with *Q. petraea*	not represented	approx. **W15b** *Fagus sylvatica – Deschampsia flexuosa* woodland, *Deschampsia* sub-community	S.England; also S.E. Wales
39	not separated	not represented	approx. **W15b** *Fagus sylvatica – Deschampsia flexuosa* woodland, *Vaccinium myrtillus* sub-community	S.England, not often in ancient woodland
40	not separated	not represented	approx. **W15b** *Fagus sylvatica – Deschampsia flexuosa* woodland, *Calluna vulgaris* sub-community	S.England, scarce and usually in wood-pasture?
41	8B Acid, with *Q. robur*	acid beechwood	approx. **W14** *Fagus sylvatica – Rubus fruticosus* woodland	S.England, Essex, Forest of Dean (often wood-pasture)
42	8Ca Dry calcareous, with *Q. robur*, ash, wych-elm	not represented	approx. **W12b** *Fagus sylvatica – Mercurialis perennis* woodland, *Mercurialis* sub-community	S.England, Chiltern scarp, S.E. Wales
43	8Cb Damp calcareous, with ash, wych-elm	not represented	not separated	mid-S. England, Gloucs (often not ancient)
44	8Cc Damp calcareous, with ash, maple	not represented	approx. **W12a** *Fagus sylvatica – Mercurialis perennis* woodland, *Sanicula europæa* sub-community	mid-S. England, Gloucs
45	8D Acid, with ash and *Q. robur*	not represented	not separated	Chilterns, Hants
Hornbeam-woods				
46	9Aa With birch, hazel, *Q. robur*	Pure Hornbeam-wood (and its hazel variant)	not separated	E. and S.E. England, E. Midlands
47	9Ab With ash, maple (part)	Hornbeam – Ashwood	approx. **W8b** *Fraxinus excelsior – Acer campestre – Mercurialis perennis* woodland, *Primula vulgaris – Glechoma hederacea* sub-community (part)	E. and S.E. England
48	9Ab With ash, maple (part)	Maple –Horn-beam-wood	not represented	mainly Essex
49	9Ba Acid, with *Q. petraea*	Oak – Horn-beam-wood	not separated	mainly E. Chilterns
50	9Bb Calcareous, with *Q. petraea*	not represented	not represented	N. Kent
Elmwoods				
51	10A Invasive	Elm Invasion (part)	not represented	throughout lowland England; extends into Highland Zone, Wales, Scotland
52	10B Valley elmwood	Elm Invasion (part)	not represented	Bedford Purlieus (Peterborough)
53	not represented	Lineage Elmwood	not represented	mainly Suffolk and N.Essex

OAKWOOD PROVINCE
(Cornwall, Devon, Pennines, Lake District, North York Moors, plus Wales, south and middle Scotland)

Peterken	Rackham	National Vegetation Classification	Geographical range
Ash – Wych-elm Woods			
54 1Ab Limestone, 'upland'	not represented	not separated	N. and S.W. England, Wales & Border, S. Scotland; often not ancient
55 1Cb Clay on limestone, with *Quercus petraea*	not represented	not represented	Wenlock Edge and Herefordshire
56 1D Western valley	not represented	not separated	Wales, N.W. half of England
Hazel – Ashwoods			
56a 3Aa Heavy acid soils, with *Quercus robur*	Mixed Hazel-wood (hawthorn – bramble variant)	not separated	England, Wales, S. Scotland (common)
57 3C Northern calcareous, with *Quercus petraea*	not represented	**W9a** *Fraxinus excelsior – Sorbus aucuparia – Mercurialis* woodland	N. England, W. Wales, W. Scotland
58 3D Acidic, with *Quercus petraea*	not represented	not separated	mainly Wales, W. England, S.W. Scotland
59 not separated	not represented	**3Ab** *Fraxinus excelsior – Sorbus aucuparia – Crepis paludosa* sub-community	Pennines, W. Scotland
Ash – Limewoods			
60 4C With *Quercus petraea*	not represented	**W8e** *Fraxinus excelsior – Acer campestre – Mercurialis perennis* woodland, *Geranium robertianum* sub-community (part)	N. and S.W. England, England, Welsh Border, Scotland
61 not separated	not represented	**W8g** *Fraxinus excelsior – Acer campestre – Mercurialis perennis* woodland, *Teucrium scorodonia* sub-community (part)	Derbyshire Dales (rare and distinctive type)
Oak – Limewoods			
62 5B With *Q. petraea*	Oak – Limewood	not separated	Lake District, Wales, E. & middle England (rare)
Birch – Oakwoods			
63 6Ab With *Q. petraea*, 'upland'	not represented	**W16** *Quercus* spp – *Betula* – spp – *Deschampsia flexuosa* woodland	Wales, Highland England, W. Scotland (common); also Ireland; in Lowland England rarely ancient

	Peterken	Rackham	National Vegetation Classification	Geographical range
64	not separated	not represented	**W17a** *Quercus petraea – Betula pubescens – Dicranum majus* woodland, *Isothecium myosuroides – Diplophyllum albicans* sub-community	N. Wales, Lake District; also Ireland
65	not separated	not represented	**W17b** *Quercus petraea – Betula pubescens – Dicranum majus* woodland	N. Wales, Lake District; also Ireland?
66	not separated	not represented	**W17c** *Quercus petraea – Betula pubescens – Dicranum majus* woodland, *Anthoxanthum odoratum – Agrostis capillaris* sub-community	Wales, Dartmoor, N. England (doubtfully ancient)
67	6Ac With *Q. petraea* and hazel, 'upland'	not represented	**W11a** *Quercus petraea – Betula pubescens – Oxalis acetosella* woodland, *Dryopteris dilatata* sub-community	Wales, Highland England, W. Scotland (on less infertile soils)
68	6Bb With *Q. robur*, 'upland'	not represented	not separated	Wales, Highland England, Scotland (often not ancient)
69	6Bc With *Q. robur* and hazel, 'upland'	not represented	not separated	widely scattered
Alderwoods				
70	7Aa Acid valleys	Valley Alderwood (part)	approx. **W7c** *Alnus glutinosa – Fraxinus excelsior – Lysimachia nemorum* woodland, *Deschampsia caespitosa* sub-community	ravines in Wales and Highland England (common); also in Scotland and lowland England
71	7Bc Acid springlines	Valley Alderwood (part)	partly **W7b** *Alnus glutinosa – Fraxinus excelsior – Lysimachia memorum* woodland, *Carex remota – Cirsium palustre* sub-community	Wales, S.W. and N.W. England, W. Scotland (also S.E. and E. England)
72	7C Slope alderwood	not represented	not separated	S. and middle Scotland (rare)
73	7Ea With *Prunus padus*, 'upland'	not represented	not separated	scattered over Wales, Highland England, S. and mid Scotland
Beechwoods (within the limited native range of beech)				
74	8Ea Acid, with ash and *Q. petraea*	not represented	not separated	S.E. Wales and Welsh Border
75	8Eb Calcareous, with ash & *Q. petraea*	not represented	not separated	Wye Gorge

Mainly in the HIGHLANDS OF SCOTLAND

Peterken	Rackham	National Vegetation Classification	Geographical range
Oakwoods			
76 not separated	not represented	**W11b** *Quercus petraea – Betula pubescens – Oxalis acetosella* woodland, *Blechnum spicant* sub-community	Western Scottish Highlands
77 not separated	not represented	**W11c** *Quercus petraea – Betula pubescens – Oxalis acetosella* woodland, *Anemone nemorosa* sub-community	Eastern Scottish Highlands
78 not separated	not represented	**W11d** *Quercus petraea – Betula pubescens – Oxalis acetosella* woodland, *Stellaria holostea – Hypericum pulchrum* sub-community	Eastern Scottish Highlands
Pinewoods			
79 11A Acid birch – pinewoods (part)	not represented	**W18b** *Pinus sylvestris – Hylocomium splendens* woodland, *Vaccinium myrtillus – V. vitis-idaea* sub-community	N.E. Scottish Highlands
80 11A Acid birch – pinewoods (part)	not represented	**W18c** *Pinus sylvestris – Hylocomium splendens* woodland, *Luzula pilosa* sub-community	middle Scottish Highlands
81 11A Acid birch – pinewoods (part)	not represented	**W18d** *Pinus sylvestris – Hylocomium splendens* woodland, *Sphagnum capilliforme – Erica tetralix* sub-community	W. Scottish Highlands
82 11A Acid birch – pinewoods (part)	not represented	**W18e** *Pinus sylvestris –Hylocomium splendens* woodland, *Scapania gracilis* sub-community	Wester Ross (local)
Birchwoods			
83 12A Rowan – birchwoods	not represented	**W17d** *Quercus petraea – Betula pubescens – Dicranum majus* woodland, *Rhytidiadelphus triquetrus* sub-community	S. and mid Scottish Highlands; doubtfully ancient
Total number of types			
83 58	**31**	**34**	

A Synthesis of Types of Ancient Woodland in Great Britain

Table 31.1 is the skeleton of a combined classification of ancient woodland, combining the types published in the three schemes. The total appears to come to 83 woodland types, including only those recognized by the respective authors at the time of their publication. I have no doubt that rare types recently discovered and subdivisions more recently recognized would bring the total over 100, which would be in line with classifications published for comparable areas of continental Europe.

Ash, Maple, and Hazel: do trees form communities related to the ground vegetation?

Most books on woodland ecology presuppose some degree of integration between trees and herbaceous plants: for the *National Vegetation Classification* this should be so in theory, even if it is often broken in practice. This book originally set out to investigate how far it was so. I concluded that the relation is statistical rather than absolute, and is not strong (see especially Table 6.3). Peterken held much the same view (*Woodland Conservation and Management*, 2nd ed., p. 320). At best one can say that some woodland types tend to have particular kinds of ground vegetation more often than other kinds.

Understanding ash–maple–hazel woods is the central problem in English woodland ecology. Woods dominated by one or other of these trees (and usually with standard oaks) account for more than one-third of the total area of ancient woodland. The trees are not gregarious and can coexist in any proportion. Ash–maple–hazel woods combine great diversity with a lack of sharp boundaries between types. They are a test of the relation between tree communities and ground vegetation. Almost any kind of ground vegetation can be found (if one looks far enough) under one or other variant of ash–maple–hazel woodland, which goes against the theory that trees and ground vegetation interlock to form one series of plant communities.

The *NVC* avoids this difficult task. Ash–maple–hazel woods, along with many hornbeam-woods, limewoods and much else, form '**W8**: *Fraxinus excelsior-Acer campestre-Mercurialis perennis* woodland', that great dump or catch-all of ancient woodland, divided into seven 'sub-communities', of which two (*Primula vulgaris-Glechoma hederacea* and *Deschampsia caespitosa*) are relevant here.

The analysis in the original book (Chapter 13) was based, for the most part, on some 250 woods each treated as a whole, which were assigned to one or other of the seven sub-categories of ash–maple–hazelwood on the proportions of these trees in the entire wood. In many woods such as Hayley, all three trees occur throughout the wood, and it is not obvious that they are correlated at all with the environment or ground vegetation of different parts of the wood. Nevertheless, even taking each wood as a whole, it was clear that there is some large-scale correlation between, for example, dog's-mercury and maple, or oxlip and hazel (Table 6.3).

Buff Wood

A first step in taking the matter further came with an observation in Buff Wood. The northern 'panhandle' of the wood is ancient secondary woodland on pronounced ridge-and-furrow, which has two obvious ground-vegetation communities. Bluebell and mercury grow on the better-drained ridges, and primrose and *Deschampsia caespitosa* in the furrows where water accumulates – a familiar and well-known pattern (Fig. 31.6).

The trees here are ash, maple, and suckering elm. What is not so obvious is that the ashes (including big stools evidently dating from the early years of the site as woodland) are mainly in the furrows, and the maples on the ridges. A ready explanation comes to mind: mercury, being clonal and very competitive, suppresses the growth of other plants including ash seedlings (p. 95), but maple seedlings compete better with it.

By any standard of comparison these are two different plant communities, ashwood and maple-wood, growing in different environments, each with its own ground vegetation, and with an explanation for the difference based on physiological research. (The *NVC* fails to separate them.) However, there is the unhappy thought that they would not be detectable by conventional plant sociology. Each community occurs as a strip 5–6 m wide, and even a 10 x 10 m quadrat (the smallest sample size used in woodland) would include both. If there were not the ridge-and-furrow to draw attention to the pattern, they would almost certainly be overlooked.

Hayley Wood

Hayley Wood as a whole is Ash–Hazelwood with frequent maple and hawthorn, and with clonal patches of aspen and suckering elm (now largely in abeyance, Chapter 28). A cursory survey reveals that, as in other woods, aspen clones are almost confined to Zone 2 (Oxlip–Meadowsweet).

In 1997 I recorded trees and ground vegetation at and around 537 points, each corresponding (on average) to about one-fifth acre of woodland, or a 29 x 29 m square. Of these points, 512 could be assigned to one of the vegetation zones of Table 25.1, or to a border between zones.

With this amount of data it is clear that aspen is not the only tree to show a relation to ground vegetation. Ash is about 1½ times as abundant in the more waterlogged zones (Fig. 31.3 compared with 25.8; Plate 13.8, p. 220). Maple is more than four times as abundant in the drier zones (Table 31.2). Hazel shows a slight but definite preference for the middle zones. Elm seems to be associated with Zone 5: although this is probably a real effect, confirmed from other woods, it is partly a consequence of elm occurring as a few big clones, each containing many points, which happen to be in a particular zone. Hawthorn as a whole shows no consistent association with particular zones; among the two hawthorns the hedgerow species favours the drier zones and the woodland species the wetter zones (Fig. 31.4).

On comparing the abundance of trees (Fig. 31.3)

32

Wildwood and the Origins of Woodland, Wood-Pasture, and Savanna

What is Coppicing For? Did it Occur in Wildwood?

Trees are wildlife, not environment; they are not part of the scenery of the theatre of landscape: they are actors in the play, and they perform different roles.

As the original book began by saying (p. 1ff), the consequences of cutting down a tree depend on the tree (Plate 1, p. xxiii). A pine dies. A lime or ash sprouts from the stump: dormant buds, already present, awaken and bore their way out through the bark, giving rise to coppice shoots, each of which can grow into a full-sized trunk. A European beech achieves the same effect differently: a callus forms at the junction of bark and wood, within which the new shoots develop. Most elms sucker: new shoots form from the roots, giving rise to a clone, a circular patch of genetically-identical elms. Anyone investigating the woods of an unfamiliar country must begin by learning these properties.

Coppicing and suckering occur the world over, but in no obvious pattern. They do not follow particular branches of the evolutionary tree: they cut across families and even genera. Usually trees coppice or sucker but not both. Europe, North America, and Japan have, broadly, the same genera of trees, but all the species are different. They each have a coppicing species of elm and several suckering species. They each have suckering species of poplar, like our aspen, and non-suckering species corresponding to our black poplar. However, European and Japanese beeches coppice, whereas the American *Fagus grandifolia*, looking very like our *F. sylvatica*, suckers, which makes it ecologically very different (Fig. 32.1). Most conifers die when felled and do not coppice, but there are exceptions. Californian redwood coppices very vigorously. In Bix Bottom, Oxfordshire, there is a small patch of coppiced yew-wood. In Australia, many species of *Eucalyptus* coppice, having a built-in underground 'lignotuber' which begins like a wooden radish and can grow into a giant coppice-like stool (Fig. 32.2). The related genus *Melaleuca* goes in for suckering. Many of the non-eucalypt Australian rainforest trees are usually seen as coppice stools.

Most trees that coppice or sucker will also respond to pollarding. Some trees that do not coppice, such as pines and firs, can be pollarded.

Fig. 32.1 American beech (*Fagus grandifolia*) surrounded by its suckers. Warren Woods, Michigan. May 1981

Fig. 32.2 Giant lignotuber of jarrah (*Eucalyptus marginata*), the result of centuries of burning and regrowth. Avon Valley National Park, S.W. Australia. December 1996

Coppicing before people?

Now that evolution is once again a fashionable subject to study, let us ask: Why do trees coppice? What did trees do with this property before people came and invented axes? In response to what stimulus or environmental demand did it evolve? What is there in common among the trees that have it?[1]

Coppicing is not a fundamental consequence of being a tree, for many trees lack it. It has arisen several times by different and independent means.

Is it an evolutionary response to woodmanship? The time-scale seems too short: there have not been enough generations of trees since the invention of the axe for such an intrinsic property to arise where it did not exist before. We might surmise that woodcutting would favour strongly-sprouting varieties of trees such as elms, and eliminate trees such as pines which refused to sprout. However, even in Europe, where people have been coppicing woods for at least 6000 years, there are still some non-sprouting trees. Sprouting behaviour is no less prevalent in Japan, where coppice management probably has a shorter history, or in North America, where it goes back for only 350 years. Human activity is therefore not the chief factor in the evolution of coppiceability.

Is fire the reason? Every visitor to the Mediterranean knows how evergreen oaks and strawberry-trees are burnt to the ground and vigorously sprout again. In the woods of Texas there are stools of oak which are far too big to result from 150 years of European settlement: they go back to a time when prairie fires, set by Plains Indians as part of their land management, licked into the woods and burnt some of the trees. Combustibility is in general an adaptation, not a misfortune. Trees burn because they make flammable chemicals: it is the business of strawberry-trees to catch fire from time to time (by lightning if necessary, Fig. 32.3) and burn up their non-fire-adapted neighbours. Other fire

Fig. 32.3 Isolated burnt patch on dead elm. In flammable countries this is how fires start: lightning ignites dry debris under loose bark of standing dead trees, which then drops off into flammable leaf-litter. This fire got no further because (as usual in Britain) the surrounding vegetation was not flammable. Chalkney Wood. April 1996

1 For an American perspective see: Del Tredici, P. (2001). Sprouting in temperate trees: a morphological and ecological review. *Botanical Review* **67**, 121–40.

adaptations are a loose, persistent leaf-litter which does not pack down, and a light shade which allows fire-promoting kinds of undershrub to build up fuel beneath the trees. These are familiar to anyone who has been to the Mediterranean or Australia, but English native trees are not like this. Their dead leaves, even those of hazel which has been claimed as fire-adapted (p. 104), have rotted into a soggy mass by the time the fire season comes round in March.

Among the world's fire-promoting trees – pines, tree-heathers, eucalypts, palms – the ability to coppice or sucker is no more prominent than among incombustible trees such as elms, beeches, and poplars. Scots Pine is the only fire-promoting native tree in Britain, and is the only tree that neither coppices nor suckers: it responds to fire by germinating freely from seed.

What about beavers? They gnaw down smallish trees of various species, but seem not to harvest the sprouts to generate regular coppice stools (although my experience is limited to places which have not had them long). This might provide an explanation for palatable aquatic trees, which will not burn.

What about windblow? As the 1987 and 1990 storms showed, trees seldom break at the base; uprooting is much more common. Uprooted trees usually stay alive and sprout along the top of the fallen trunk (Fig. 27.10). Species that coppice strongly tend to concentrate the sprouts at the base of the trunk; they can then re-occupy the gap left by the fall of the parent tree.

What about snow and ice? Ice-storms – when rain falls into a freezing atmosphere, and turns bough and twig into weighty cylinders of ice – break down trees as well as plucking them out of the ground. I have seen the mayhem created by such a *galaverna* among the chestnut-woods of the northern Appennines, and noted traces of the mayhem left by the previous one. Avalanches, when a steep mountainside sheds its load of snow in a sudden thaw, can roar down far into the deciduous forest zone. Like fire, ice-storms and avalanches tend to recur on the same spot. I have just visited an immense avalanche in the unlikely location of Mount Athos in the Aegean, and noted signs of others in earlier years; they favoured coppicing and especially suckering trees. In one ancient wood in Britain avalanches are an ecological factor, the Punchbowl on the slopes of Mount Blorenge, Abergavenny. However, it is hard to imagine that even in a Pleistocene climate ice-storms or avalanches can have been widespread enough to account for such commonplace behaviour as coppicing and suckering.

Did coppicing occur in wildwood independently of people? *Tilia americana*, American lime ('basswood'), occurs in the supposed wildwood of the Great Smoky Mountains as great rings of tall stems, which if they occurred in an English wood would unhesitatingly be attributed to centuries of coppicing. The tree grows for hundreds of years, rots at the base, and falls down, having previously sent up shoots from the base which form its successors (Fig. 32.4). The same 'self-coppicing' behaviour is found in both species of Japanese lime (Fig. 32.5), and I bet it occurred also in English *T. cordata*. Self-coppicing occurs in one of the Japanese beeches, in both Japanese and American magnolias, and in at least one American ash (*Fraxinus americana*). It is also how European hazels renew themselves: a hazel sends up new shoots from the base which can replace the old stems.

Perhaps coppicing cannot be explained in terms of processes that still operate. Was it an adaptation to recovering from elephant attack? In Pleistocene times all continents had elephants – even Australia had a marsupial 'elephant'. By elephants I do not mean the puny monsters that we ride at the Zoo: I mean the West Runton elephant, from the Cromer Interglacial, the size of a double-decker bus, displayed in Norwich Castle. 'His kin that live still in latter days are but memories of his girth and majesty', as Tolkien said. Wildwood could not have been the same when there were beasts who could break down and eat a big tree. Did they induce coppicing and pollarding? Exterminating elephants and rhinoceroses may have been the earliest effect of humanity on woodland. Was the profoundest impact so far of the human species on woodland the extermination, by Palaeolithic people, of these living bulldozers?

Coppicing and suckering are among the ways in which trees and other plants are profoundly different from people and animals, and fit awkwardly into conventional, zoology-based habits of thought on evolution. Most animals, and annual plants, are short-lived and are supposed to adapt gradually to changes in the environment through generations of sexual reproduction. Many plants, in contrast, have at least partly abandoned sex, and with it most of the ability to respond to environmental change by genetic adaptation. Trees, especially, are too long-lived to be able to keep up with the rapid changes of climate characteristic of the last two million years. Many trees, even the very long-lived lime and redwood, have yet further extended their generation time by coppicing and suckering. For them, the ability to hold on to a site once established, avoiding the hazards of starting again from seed, outweighs the ability to adapt to an unstable environment. This may explain the obvious mismatches between the environments in which trees occur naturally and those in which they flourish. Beech, for instance, grows at least as well where introduced in Aberdeenshire as in southern England where it is native.

Origins of Wood-Pasture

Wood-pasture in Europe has had a bad press; despised by foresters as not being proper forest, and neglected by

Fig. 32.4 Basswood (*Tilia americana*) self-coppicing: **(a)** a big tree has fallen, having sent up stems from around the base. Jay Cooke Park, Duluth, Minnesota. December 1984

(b) original trunk has disappeared, leaving a ring of gigantic stems. Jakes Gap, Great Smoky Mountain. May 1981

Fig. 32.5 *Tilia japonica*, big tree surrounded by self-coppicing sprouts. Mount Odaigahara, Japan. October 1998

grassland specialists as not being proper grassland. In the *National Vegetation Classification* it skulks through the pages of the woodland volume, not even meriting an index entry, let alone its own volume.

Wood-pasture results (p. 173) from the fact that cows and sheep cannot climb. Even modern cattle, after hundreds of generations of being bred as grassland animals, still hanker after tree leaves (Fig. 32.6). Woodland herbs are insubstantial, poisonous, or inedible. Cattle, sheep, or deer in a wood soon eat up everything edible within reach, creating a browse-line, and it does not grow again. When livestock are reported as grazing in 'forests', the term cannot mean what a modern forester would call a forest: it has to have a grassland or heath component as well as trees.

Grassland with trees has a very respectable history; it still covers vast areas in Portugal, Spain, Sardinia, and Greece, and formerly in France, Germany, Italy, and even Sweden. Disapproval of wood-pasture originated in the land-use philosophy of the eighteenth-century Enlightenment, that trees and pasturage do not mix. Trees, the savants said, ought to grow crowded into forests, mainly organized by the state on the model of either French or German 'rational' forestry (depending on which state); agriculture should be carried on by private owners in rectangular fields. The Enlightenment especially disapproved of the communal land-uses and pollarding which often went with wood-pasture. In the

Fig. 32.6 Cattle eating leaves and bark of willow, a rare treat brought to them by a summer storm. Cambridge. July 2000

following century these ideas captured the minds of governments. The degree of survival of wood-pasture thus reflects, inversely, the degree of Enlightenment of particular states and their success in enforcing it.[2] In England, bursts of Enlightenment converted many Forests and wood-pasture commons into marginal arable land, but not to the degree that prevailed in Italy or Sweden.

It was easy to suppose that the normal state of wildwood was trees growing close together with nice straight untapered trunks, provided by a beneficent Providence for the north European timber trade. The historic state of Epping Forest, like a Portuguese *montado* or a Cretan scree landscape, was what my south European colleagues still insist on calling a 'degraded forest', meaning a forest from which some trees have been subtracted. This view was reinforced by the observation that wood-pastures turn into continuous woodland when grazing ceases: the spaces between the trees infill, either with the same species or with another species (spectacularly with hollies between oaks in Staverton Park, Fig. 32.7). It seemed finally to be confirmed by early pollen analysts, who always found tree pollen dominating pre-Neolithic samples.

That was the position that I accepted in the original *Ancient Woodland*: that coppice-woods and wood-pastures were both semi-natural, derived from wildwood in different directions, and diverging through different human treatments from prehistory onwards.

Wood-pasture and savanna

In all continents except Europe, tree'd grassland is accepted as a natural phenomenon partly or wholly independent of human activity. It appears under various names, but generally as *savanna*, an American-Indian word applied at first to various kinds of North American and Caribbean vegetation, and later to the tree'd grasslands of Africa. Why should Europe be the only non-savanna continent? Why is it that even in Britain so very many birds – blackbird, robin, sparrowhawk, buzzard, rook, etc. etc. – are not really woodland nor grassland species but flourish best with combinations of grassland and trees?

It used to be thought that the savannas of Africa and America were very different from the wood-pastures of southern Europe: they were due to the rainfall being too little for forests but sufficient for individual trees. The roots of scattered trees can extend well beyond the canopy of the tree, and thus capture rain falling between the trees as well as on them (Fig. 32.8). However, it is now clear that drought is partly responsible for south European savannas: if not grazed they may infill, but the young trees are held back by drought. Moreover, human activity is partly responsible for tropical savannas. Much of the 'primaeval forest' of West Africa, for example, is shown by James Fairhead and Melissa Leach (1998) to be infilled from former savanna, whose human population was carried off or murdered by slavers.

Savanna happens at junctions between forest and steppe or desert, where whatever factor limits the forest may allow individual trees to outlie in an extensive transitional zone beyond the limit of continuous forest. That factor may be drought, as in the interior of Australia; or cold, as at the alpine limit in parts of the Alps; or fire, as in Tasmania or the 'oak openings' of the state of Michigan; or domestic livestock, as in the wetter parts of Spain or in Epping Forest. There is a seamless transition between 'natural' drought savannas and 'cultural' wood-pastures. Moreover, limiting factors interact. Australian and American savannas were greatly influenced, often created, by Aboriginal and Native American land management by burning. Where the

2 Grove & Rackham, *The Nature of Mediterranean Europe* chapter 12.

Fig. 32.7 (a–b) Staverton Park:

(a) Scattered ancient pollard oaks. March 2002

(b) The Thicks: younger hollies infilling spaces between ancient oaks, and often overtopping and killing them. June 1986

Fig. 32.8 (a–b)

(a) Savanna of grassland with scattered trees. Davis Mountains, W. Texas. March 1999

(b) Savanna live-oak, Davis Mountains. The roots (exposed in the road-cut) extend at least as far from the tree as the man. March 1999

Fig. 32.9 Youngish dead oak in gap between ancient oaks, Staverton Park. This tree probably began in the late 18th century, was pollarded in the early 19th, and died in the early 20th. September 1995

rainfall is only just enough for forest, it takes less browsing to maintain savanna than where there is plenty of rain.

In general English wood-pastures are maintained by browsing. The annual rainfall in the driest parts, some 500 mm, is well below the amount needed to sustain forest by Mediterranean or tropical standards, but in a land of cool summers trees need less moisture. However, a drought influence may explain an enigma of Staverton Park (p. 293f.). Staverton has a century's accumulation of dead trees. In the part known as 'The Park', which is not much infilled, the most numerous dead trees are not the huge ancient pollards which are presumably the oldest: they are the smallest and presumably *youngest* generation of trees, dating from the mid to late eighteenth century, which have been pollarded only once (Fig. 32.9). This is in the driest part of England, a landscape of blown sand. The effects of drought are magnified because the sand retains little moisture. It may be that (despite the apparently open tree cover) there is no room for any more oaks. New trees may establish and grow for a century or two, but they never acquire enough root-space to withstand a drought like that of 1921. Within the same site is 'The Thicks', infilled with giant and flourishing hollies (Fig. 32.7b), which (being an oceanic, drought-sensitive tree) might be thought to disprove this explanation. However, there is a patch of clay beneath the surface which retains moisture long after The Park has dried up.

Savanna in prehistory

Herbs of shaded woodland have a poor pollen record, being insect-pollinated and flowering near the ground, but there are a few exceptions (Table 8.1).

In *Ancient Woodland* (p. 108f) and *The History of the Countryside* (p. 331) I pointed out that numerous plants which do not flower in shade have a prehistoric record from pollen grains or other remains. Some of these now grow in meadow or pasture, but others are associated either with coppicing (e.g. ragged robin, *Lychnis flos-cuculi*) or with permanent glades and open areas (devil's-bit, *Succisa pratensis*). Since these, too, are meagre pollen producers even a scanty record must be taken seriously. One might attribute them to the browsing of wild beasts, either alone or in conjunction with land management, for Mesolithic people, like their historic counterparts in America and Australia, presumably manipulated the landscape to favour the wild animals on which they preyed.

This raises the most difficult questions in prehistoric ecology: what was the density of deer and wild oxen? what did they eat? what effect did they have on the vegetation? Since they cannot climb, one would hardly expect them in continuous forest. They might have congregated at high altitudes, in fens, and perhaps in very dry places where tree growth was difficult. But did they also maintain permanent openings? The pollen record suggests that they did.

The wildwood of earlier interglacials contained a wider range of grassland plants. Something then was more effective at maintaining wood-pasture. Were Boxgrove Man and his descendants more skilled at this than *Homo sapiens*? Or was it the living bulldozers?

That was the position in 1996, when I gave the opening speech on 'Savanna in Europe' at the International Conference on Advances in Woodland and Forest History (Rackham 1998).

The Vera theory of wildwood

In 2000 this interpretation of wildwood was further developed in an extraordinary book by Franciscus Vera, *Grazing Ecology and Forest History*.[4] This, at long last, seeks to assign a function to wild beasts in the

4 See supplementary bibliography.

pre-Neolithic wildwood. Vera's claim is that wildwood was not a forester's forest, but a mosaic of patches of woodland, scrubs, and savanna, on the lines of the present New Forest. Grazing did not destroy wildwood, but was a necessary part of its functioning, continuing down the millennia into cultural wood-pasture as beeves and steeds took over from aurochsen and wild horses, until the foresters and conservationists of the Enlightenment rationalized it away.

As I understand the theory, wildwood was subject to a cyclical succession. Patches of hawthorn, blackthorn, and holly would start in grassland. Light-demanding trees, especially oak and hazel, would grow up in the protection of these thorny bushes (as in Watt's beechwood succession, p. 324f). There would thus arise a 'grove' of trees, each lasting for one generation of oaks, followed by more shade-tolerant species, especially beech. A fully-developed grove would be some tens of hectares in extent, typically round in shape, with a 'fringe' of coarse herbs slowly advancing into the grassland, a 'mantle' of thorns and hazel, an outer zone of oak, and an inner zone of beech, lime, and ash. The final death of beeches and other trees would prepare the way for a grassy opening to re-start the cycle. The author regards grazing as essential for the replacement of oaks: 'Without horse and ox oak will not survive', as the title of an article of his puts it.

This book, written with panache and imagination, addresses a number of peculiarities, such as the pre-Neolithic abundance of oak (which now does not easily grow from seed inside existing woods) and hazel (which is difficult to fit into 'climax' wildwood, owing to its supposedly low stature and not producing pollen in shade). It offers an explanation for such unsolved questions as how people could have made farmland without exhausting their energies on digging up trees (answer: they began in the grassland areas and left the groves till last). There are gaps in the argument: most obviously in the lack of information about numbers of browsing animals, and the effects of particular degrees of browsing. But in a pioneering work one hardly expects an author to get everything right first time. Although I cannot agree with everything in the book, I accept with gratitude many of its insights.

The book is mainly synthesized from other people's researches, which Vera has read with prodigious diligence: he refers to some 1200 publications. This will have involved great labour in reconciling contradictory interpretations, but there is a risk in using so many data that have passed through other hands and may perpetuate others' misinterpretations. (I know from experience!) Vera does not often cite his own data, either from reading original documents or from his own fieldwork – even to the extent of visiting a site to decide who is right about some point.

Some of Vera's methods will not appeal to everyone. He makes much of arguments from the same or similar words in Low and High German, Dutch, and English, e.g. *Holz*, *hout*, *holt*, but without fully investigating what they mean and how they change from one language to another. Meanings of words are not constant: Australians use 'woodland' to mean savanna, and 'bush' for tropical rain-forest; English 'sapling' changed in the last century from a pole-sized tree to a pencil-sized tree. In English 'underwood' does not mean shrubs as he supposes, and is not the same as 'brushwood' (twigs small enough to make brushes from). But Vera makes curiously little of the names of woods: he discusses at length the New Forest and the Forêt de Fontainebleau without noticing the evidence for lime from place-names (*La Tillaie*, a place of limes, and *Lyndhurst*, lime-grove).

Vera makes the present author say some surprising things. For example, to support his thesis that 'pedunculate and sessile oak no longer regenerate in woods in England when grazing stops' he combines my statement that between 1850 and 1919 oaks stopped regenerating within woods (this book, p. 296) with the claim, attributed to me, that 'the grazing in virtually all the "commons" came to an end at about this time as a result of the abolition of grazing rights' (his p. 155 n.). What I actually say (p. 6) is that 'Forests and commons . . . were destroyed . . . between 1770 and 1860': I mean the *destruction* of commons, not abolishing the grazing rights. Woods and commons are different places: there was grazing in commons but not in woods; and the destruction of Forests and commons did not affect the woods. I will not labour the point – I could give other examples – but I hope Vera has been less hasty in citing other people's work that I have not been able to check. (George Peterken makes a similar complaint about Vera's interpretation of his work in the New Forest.[5])

Does the Vera theory apply to England?

Vera's book is mainly about the Netherlands and Germany, but with frequent references to other countries – especially England, because of the quantity of English historical archives. Unfortunately, instead of going through the evidence country by country (as, for example, Fairhead & Leach do), he combines evidence from over half Europe: fieldwork from Germany can be used to interpret records from England. It is as well to recollect that England is not a mere extension of the Continent but has its own peculiarities, just as Wales and Scotland are not mere extensions of England.

Not many large herbivores survived the last glaciation, and England had a meagre set of them. In this interglacial there has been no horse (other than feral domestic horses) or bison. Elk and probably bear died

5 Review, *British Wildlife*, Feb. 2001, 225–6.

out in the Mesolithic; aurochs – more of a fen than a forest animal[6] – in the Bronze Age. This left red and roe deer, wild swine, and beaver, and even these were not common by historic times. Were they enough to maintain the very large quantities of oak and hazel which the pollen record implies, especially in the Highland Zone?

Nor are the trees quite the same. In early historic England beech was a local tree, mainly south-eastern, not distributed over the countryside but concentrated in wood-pastures. (Lime, to which Vera assigns a similar role to beech, avoids places with a browsing history.) Holly and hazel are much more prominent than in Continental vegetation. Lime was restricted to certain areas, and is a relict tree which does not spread.

England was apparently much more densely populated than most of the Continent. It ceased to be half wildwood by the Iron Age at latest. Anglo-Saxon documents make it perfectly clear that by then there was no wilderness: every inch of England had an owner. Woods were normally private property. There may be other relevant social differences: for example in England the 'peasant' class, if it ever existed, disappeared early, and English history is a story of uppish commoners and downtrodden, institutional, or absentee lords unable to control the common-lands. Common-land regulations were generated by the commoners themselves.

The situation envisaged by Vera in Central Europe, with large areas of wilderness out of which parks and coppices could be carved, does not transfer to England. He may be right that in Germany and Poland the 'waste' out of which medieval cultural landscapes were being created was indeed the last phase of primaeval wildwood – although even here I would like to be assured that that assumption is based on something more than lack of archaeological knowledge of earlier human activity. In England the formative stages of the landscape were very much earlier: long unwritten centuries of the Roman period and later prehistory lay between the times of elk and aurochs and the period of written records. Most of the big wooded areas of medieval England, and many ordinary wood-lots, did not emerge straight out of wildwood: they contain earthworks of settlement and property division from earlier periods.

Relations between people and deer were not the same. Vera envisages medieval kings and lords as spending their time running after plentiful wild deer and swine. On the Continent some certainly did: Alfonso XI, King of Spain 1312–50, wrote a wonderful *Book of Hunting* full of reminiscences of pig-sticking and bear-smiting in arbutus maquis, live-oak savannas, and piney sierras.[7] But here too England was different. Our only convincing account of a royal hunt as a real adventure – King Edmund the Magnificent was rescued from falling into Cheddar Gorge by the miraculous intervention of St Dunstan – is from the tenth century.[8] By the middle ages kings' and lords' venison was reared in a park – like a modern deer-farm – or caught in a Forest by professional hunters (Chapter 12). English writers produced wistful editions of French books on the courtly ritual of hunting, or set their adventures in a half-remembered world of Arthurian romance.[9] In the real world there was the occasional foxhunt in a park (p. 294), but hunting cannot be claimed as an activity that shaped whole landscapes. As I have related elsewhere, Henry VIII made fashionable the hunting of deer in parks, in a form almost as stylized as a modern Spanish bullfight, but that is too late to be relevant.[10] Deer and wild sows roaming the countryside at large are a twentieth-century development.

Vera and pollen analysis

Vera's thesis might be confirmed or disconfirmed by palynology. Although he cites a few pollen diagrams he pays little attention to the small print. He is probably right that free-standing trees produce at least as much pollen as forest trees: but he then makes the remarkable assertion that lime is really a wind-pollinated tree, and that therefore evidence that it is not a prolific pollen producer can be dismissed (p. 93). He makes the contrary assumption that hawthorn is so entirely insect-pollinated that the absence of its pollen from most pollen records is immaterial.

Vera misses most of the pollen record of grassland and woodland-grassland plants abovementioned, which would have supported his thesis. He may be right in saying that grasses themselves are under-represented in pollen diagrams because animals had eaten the flowering tops. I see this happening in Hatfield Forest – but I note that the amount of grazing needed to achieve it also halts the dynamics: it eliminates the 'fringe' vegetation from the edges of the scrubs, and prevents the expansion of the 'mantle' of the scrubs themselves. (I fail to find *Artemisia*, which he claims among 'fringe' vegetation, his p. 90.)

Hawthorn and blackthorn, central to Vera's thesis, are more problematic. They were present and were a favourite firewood, as their charcoal demonstrates in many archaeological sites. Their pollens are not very distinctive, and they are insect-pollinated, but they are not negligible pollen producers. As I write, close to Old

6 Rackham, O. (2002). *Treasures of Silver at Corpus Christi College, Cambridge*. Cambridge University Press, chapter 4.
7 Alfonso XI *Libro de la Monteria* . . . ed. D. P. Seniff (1983) Hispanic Seminary of Medieval Studies, Madison.
8 Stubbs, W. 1874 *Memorials of Saint Dunstan Archbishop of Canterbury* Longman & Trübner, London.
9 Cummins, J. (1988). *The Hound and the Hawk*, Weidenfeld & Nicholson.
10 *Trees & Woodland*, 2nd ed. p. 158f.

May Day, the local hawthorns are white with blossom – more flowers than leaves – and are not proportionately visited by insects. Even if they require a correction factor of 20 relative to oak (as against 8 for lime) there ought to be a regular pollen record if they occurred in the quantities that Vera requires. As it is, seldom more than the odd grain of '*Prunus*-type' pollen is reported, and even less for *Cratægus*. (As I have remarked, there are similar problems for maple and hornbeam.)

If Vera is right in inferring a dynamic cycle, from grassland to beechwood and back to grassland in 300–400 years, it should be detectable as fluctuations in favourable pollen diagrams. I leave it to other investigators to find this out.

In *The Nature of Mediterranean Europe* I pointed out the need for palynological criteria for distinguishing forest from savanna (or coppice). So far, European pollen analysts have not paid much attention to this question, assuming that trees must have been in forest. The study of beetle remains might also be of use. So far, those found in pre-Neolithic deposits are predominantly of wood- and tree-living species rather than dung-beetles and other grassland indicators.[11] This seems to support the forest model of wildwood; but supporters of the savanna model might argue that the surviving samples were biased towards the forest component of the landscape.

Vera and the properties of trees

Vera, very commendably, has gathered experimental data on the shade-tolerance of various trees. Mysteriously he says nothing about American oak mildew, although he must have read about it (this book p. 297). Is the introduction of this fungus, as I conjectured in 1980, the reason why oak is now more light-demanding than it used to be? Data are badly needed on the comparative shade tolerance of pedunculate *versus* sessile oak, and of each with and without mildew.

The non-reproduction of hazel may indeed be parallel to that of oak, as Vera quotes me as saying. It too is the result of contact with America, in this case through the grey squirrel. However, hazel is not particularly a species of 'mantle' scrubs, for example at Hatfield Forest, even the older ones that arose before the grey squirrel came.

Another omission is the suckering behaviour of trees. He mentions blackthorn's clonal behaviour, but otherwise concentrates on the establishment of trees from seed: for example cherry (his p. 340), in which suckers are much commoner than seedlings. He does, however, attribute suckering to hazel (his p. 337), which I have never seen.

Palatability is a serious omission. The distinction between grazing and browsing animals is not absolute. Even modern cattle eat tree leaves whenever they can get them. However animals do not attack trees indiscriminately. One would expect the preferences of most animals to work against elm and hawthorn, which are tasty, and in favour of the unpalatable aspen and alder. Is this so?

Fire plays little part in Vera's arguments, but has been proposed as an alternative means of maintaining open areas.[12] In England it is less plausible than on the Continent, because of the lack of fire-promoting trees after the decline of pine. Fire could conceivably have maintained open areas of heath, bracken, or moorland, which involve combustible plants, but these would have a pollen record, and on present knowledge were poorly developed before the Neolithic. Where the open areas were grassland, as they would have to have been over most of England, fire is only just possible, and implies too few grazing animals to eat the grass and reduce the fuel. If grasses and other plants of open ground were left sufficiently uneaten to support a fire, they should have a much more copious pollen record than they do.

Is Vera right (as regards England) about oak needing grazing for replacement?

In English wood-pastures there is indeed some correlation between oak regeneration and grazing. I referred to this as a feature of Hatfield Forest, where cattle have from time to time broken into the woods within the Forest and destroyed the stools, preparing the way (or so I argued) for a new generation of oaks. I used this argument to explain the anomalous occurrence of oak coppice in some of the woods (p. 291). Vera might properly claim that the post-1920 generation of oaks within Hatfield Forest woods was the result of felling combined with not maintaining the fences. In the Avon Gorge (Bristol), an original limewood turned under wood-pasture into a savanna of pollard oaks, even though the limestone soil would not normally favour oak.[13] After grazing ceased, the oaks were infilled, not with lime (which does not recover lost ground), but with wych-elm and ash. However, grazing is not a sufficient condition. Staverton Park is again grazed by large numbers of fallow and red deer, but this has not yet created a new generation of oaks.

However, oaks flourished in woodland as well as

11 Robinson, M. A. (2000). 'Coleoptera evidence for the Elm Decline, Neolithic activity in woodland, clearance and the use of the landscape' in *Plants in Neolithic Britain and beyond*, ed. A. S. Fairbairn, Oxbow, Oxford, 27–36.

12 Bradshaw, R. H. W. (2002) [Review of Vera's book.] *Forest Ecology & Management*, **165**, 327–9.

13 Rackham, O. (1981). The Avon Gorge and Leigh Woods. *Archaeological aspects of woodland ecology*, ed. M. Bell and S. Limbrey, British Archaeological Reports International Series **146**, 171–6.

Fig. 32.10 Hatfield Forest, a Vera-esque wood-pasture? The grassy plain is encroached upon by a 'mantle' of scrub, preceded by a poorly-differentiated 'fringe' of taller herbs. In the background is a coppice-wood (in Vera's terms a 'forest'). This landscape is not very dynamic: the Forest Lodge probably dates from the 15th century, and its site presupposes the same distribution of woods that there is now. For another example see Fig. 12.7. February 1981

wood-pasture, and here I find no relation between lack of grazing and lack of oaks. The recent proliferation of deer has not set off a new oak generation. The last generation of oaks in Hayley Wood is of about 1840; grazing had stopped centuries before. Between 1970 and 2001 the wood was more grazed (by fallow deer) than at any time for at least 700 years, yet this did not bring back the oaks. Oaks, however, still come from seed in the more acid parts of the Bradfield Woods, where deer have largely been excluded. In the Blean Woods (Canterbury) there are occasional thickets of sessile oak, the product of the great mast year of 1976 and similar events, although these woods have not yet been reached by deer.

A study which has continued for 25 years, is by Daniel Kelly in Tomies Wood, Killarney, S.W. Ireland. He found that oaklings were affected by browsing by Japanese deer, by shade, and to a lesser extent by competition of herbs and other young trees; he was unable to demonstrate an effect of mildew.[14]

An aspect missing from Vera's work is the study of medieval timbers. The house-builders of medieval England every year consumed millions of oaks less than 70 years old. Little of this can have come from wood-pasture, especially in eastern England where there was not much wood-pasture. Most of the oaks came from islands of woodland, usually surrounded by farmland and heavily fenced to exclude livestock. Whatever favoured the replacement of oaks at this time, it was not grazing. Oak grew freely from seed in medieval woods, as birch has done since oak lost that property.

Dynamics

Vera's dynamics are not altogether persuasive. If the end-product of the succession from grassland is beech or ash, these are trees with a well-defined life-span, and their death could complete the cycle. But what if it is lime, a very long-lived tree which prolongs its life-span still further by self-coppicing, and survives uprooting? Has Vera ever seen a dead lime? What about elm, with its prolific (but very palatable) suckers, which enable it to hold on to a site indefinitely? Or hazel – does it die from any cause other than shade?

I incline to the view that, at least where beech does not play a part, the landscape was less dynamic than Vera supposes. There is another factor here. Where a landscape consists of a mixture of trees and grassland, the tree'd areas are not at random, as they should be if the dynamics had been frozen at a moment in time. They are in particular kinds of place. In surviving wood-pastures the woods tend to be on hilltops and the pastures in valleys, even on the gentlest topography. This can be seen in Hatfield Forest, and on a larger scale in Wychwood Forest (Oxfordshire), where the 'copses' are on plateaux and the 'lights' in dry valleys, and similarly in Savernake Forest (Wilts). On a world scale, trees tend to be on rocky ground and grassland where there is soil. I have seen this in southern Europe[15] and in many other places from west Texas to Japan. Bradgate Park (Leics) is a good example, and there are many in Wales. Whatever the reason for these patterns, they do not offer much room for manoeuvre in cyclically interchanging tree'd areas and plains.

Conclusion: Comparing Wildwood with Ancient Woodland

Vera's is a notable achievement. He develops the counter-arguments to the traditional thesis that England was once covered with trees, trees, and trees

14 Kelly, D. (2002). The regeneration of *Quercus petraea* . . . in southwest Ireland: a 25-year experimental study. *Forest Ecology and Management* **166**, 207–26.
15 *Nature of Mediterranean Europe* pp. 57, 59, 193.

from coast to coast and from the Fens to the top of Skiddaw. He provides an explanation of what grassland and heath were doing in the first half of the Holocene.

In Lowland England, on present evidence, in the pre-Neolithic dry-land wildwood lime was the commonest tree (adjusting its pollen production by a factor of 8 relative to oak), with hazel next, followed by oak and elm. Fig. 32.11 is an updated version of Fig. 8.3, including new sites in Norfolk with evidence of abundant ash, which in one place is dominant. These are from small meres in the south Norfolk boulder-clay, and afford a closer link with the sort of place where ancient woodland still survives.

In Somerset it is possible to compare wildwood from pollen evidence both with wood used by Neolithic people and with ancient woods as they are now (Table 32.1). The pollen and prehistoric wood are from sites in the Somerset Levels (p. 106); the present woods are on the south slope of the Mendip Hills overlooking the Levels.

Table 32.1 Comparison of wildwood and present ancient woodland, Somerset

All figures are percentages. Alder and other wetland trees are omitted. Pollen percentages are translated into tree percentages using the coefficients set out on p. 101. Proportions of trees in the present woods were estimated on a visit in 1979.

	Hazel	Ash	Lime	Oak	Elm	Pine	Maple	Hornbeam	Holly	Crab
Wildwood just before Elm Decline (from pollen)	19	2	35	17	26	2	—	—	—	—
Neolithic woodland just after Elm Decline (from pollen)	34	4	25	24	12	1	—	—	—	—
Neolithic trees used in Sweet Track	41	13	4	22	7	—	—	rare	12	0.4
Ancient woods as they are now:										
Hale Coppice (pollards & stools)	86	5*	2	2**	1	—	4	—	rare	rare
Rose Wood (stools)	40	—*	55	1**	—	—	4	—	rare	—
King's Wood (stools & pollards)	34	30*	34	—**	2	—	1	—	rare	—
Mascall's Wood (stools)	20	45*	35	—**	—	—	rare	—	rare	—
Cheddar Wood (stools, Fig. 32.12)	25	30*	40	5	rare	—	—	—	rare	—

* figure excludes maiden trees arising since last coppicing. ** figure excludes standard trees.
Sources: Westhay,[16] Tollgate House,[17] Meare Pool,[18] Glastonbury Lake Village,[18] Drake's Drove;[18] Sweet Track.[25, 26]

16 Clapham, A. R. and Godwin, H. (1948). Studies of the post-glacial history of British vegetation. VIII, IX. . . . Somerset Levels. *Phil. Trans. roy. Soc. Lond.*, **B 233**, 233–73.

17 Godwin, H. (1960). Prehistoric wooden trackways of the Somerset Levels: their construction, age and relation to climatic change. *Proc. prehist. Soc.*, **26**, 1–36.

18 Godwin, H. (1956). Studies of the post-glacial history of British vegetation. XIII: the Meare Pool region of the Somerset Levels. *Phil. Trans. roy. Soc. Lond.*, **B 239**, 161–90.

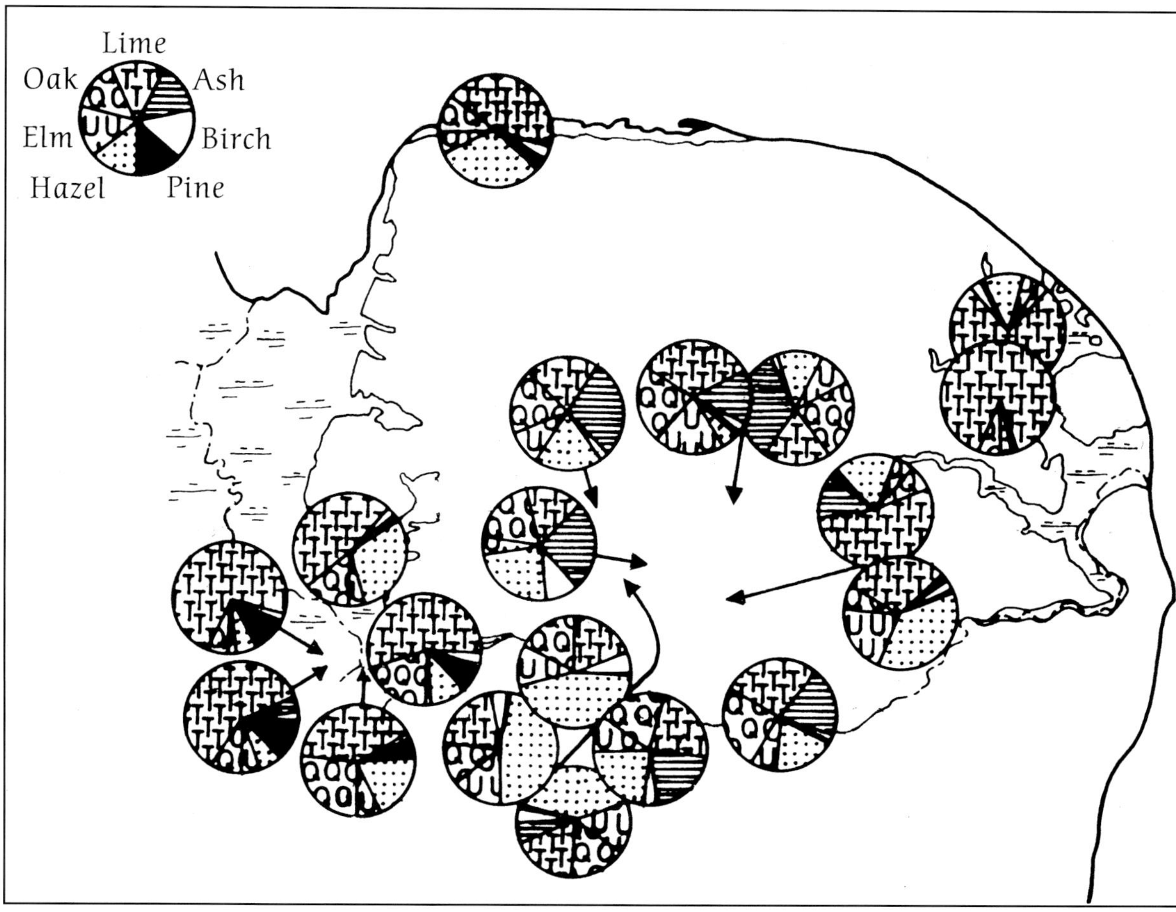

Fig. 32.11 Proportions of trees in dry-land wildwood, plotted on the same basis as Fig. 8.3. After Rackham (1986c, bibliography p. 549), where sources are listed.

The Norfolk evidence indicates that the landscape included limewoods and hazel-woods, and oak-, elm-, and ashwoods, although these last three could have been combined.

In Somerset the dry-land wildwood, just before the Elm Decline, varies similarly. Of the five pollen sites used in the table, lime was the commonest tree at three, hazel at one, and oak and elm jointly at the fifth; the second commonest tree was either hazel or elm. After the coming of Neolithic settlers, elm had declined by more than half and lime by a third; the contribution of hazel was nearly doubled, and there were lesser apparent increases in oak and ash. In the Sweet Track, a work of quite elaborate carpentry, hazel was the predominant species used, followed by oak. Lime is under-represented compared to the pollen record, but there is a surprisingly frequent choice of ash. Holly is also frequent, but being a poor producer it might have escaped representation in the pollen record. The Somerset evidence strongly points to the specific exploitation of a local hazel-ashwood different from the limewoods. Compared to surviving woodland, there is now much more ash and much less elm. Oak is about equally prominent, but most of the oaks are timber trees resulting from the encouragement of oak in the nineteenth century. One of the smaller woods, Hale Coppice, mainly hazel with a little ash, is very similar in composition to the somewhat later hurdle-work tracks of the Levels (p. 106f).

In both Norfolk and Somerset, at least the makings of the present diversity of woodland types existed by the Neolithic. (The reader is reminded not to expect any exact correspondence in their proportions, because pollen deposits, preserved trackways, and surviving woods represent different samples of wildwood.) It is more than probable that browsing animals were among the factors determining their distribution.

In comparison with Vera's hypothesis there seems to be too much evidence for hazel in wildwood, and not enough for hawthorn. I can believe that there was a rough kind of compartmentation corresponding, though informally, to the plains, scrubs, and coppices of historic Hatfield Forest. Lime would have been dominant in the most wooded parts of the landscape, where there was little for deer and aurochsen to eat and where they seldom went. In the London area and the Norfolk Broads, indeed, such dense, shady woods were probably the norm (Fig. 8.3). The details of what grew

Fig. 32.12 A Mendip wood: a lime-dominated part of Cheddar Wood. February 1979

where, how compartment boundaries were defined and determined, and whether they changed over time must await further investigation. Some details, depending on the behaviour patterns of lost beasts, may forever be obscure.

Did any of the compartmentation survive to influence the historic landscape? If it was not very dynamic this cannot be ruled out. Prehistoric farmers would have preferred the grassland plains for making their first fields, as early colonists in America did. It would be nice to think that some of Vera's 'groves' in primaeval wood-pasture turned ultimately into the coppices of medieval and modern England. Where a wood adjoins a common, as with Wall Wood and Monk Wood abutting on Woodside Green outside Hatfield Forest, one is tempted to imagine the lord and the commoners doing a deal: the lord took the more wooded part of a wood-pasture as his absolute property, in return for relinquishing his rights in the rest. It may even be that woods with rounded outlines, such as Hayley or Knapwell Wood, derive from groves in a prehistoric landscape and are thus 'the oldest boundaries of coppice wood', older than angular or zigzag woods like Gamlingay or Eversden which were defined against arable land. But (contrary to what Vera asserts, his p. 161) I cannot tell which is the older: it is seldom possible to date woodbanks. There is a huge gulf of time between early settlements and the first evidence for individual woods.

Vera's conjecture that parks developed out of the '*haye* for catching roedeer' in Domesday Book (his p. 160f) can hardly be sustained, with the possible exception of Ongar Great Park (this book, p. 191).[19] The many examples that he quotes from me in support of this notion are all from Eastern England, far from the Welsh Border where most references to *haye* are, and from a part of the country which had few if any wild deer. They are a mixture of different things: parks, coppices in Forests, and woods; one (Bottisham Park) I expressly state to be a new eighteenth-century park incorporating a deserted village.[20] Most parks were about farming exotic deer, not trapping wild ones. A landowner would buy up land to make a site, surround it with a deer-proof pale, and get some fallow deer from the king or another park-owner to put in it. The shape (often a rectangle with rounded corners, or at Staverton a pentagon with rounded corners) was chosen for economy in fencing; it was different from the shapes of woods.

However, Vera's book arouses many thoughts. Lime was certainly ubiquitous in prehistoric Lowland England. Why does it survive in abundance in every ancient wood in some areas, but rarely if at all in other groups of ancient woods with similar histories (p. 237)? Is it that Cambridgeshire, for example, passed through a type of wood-pasture management in the Bronze or Iron Age that wiped out lime, whereas in south Suffolk, north Essex, and the Mendips a different transition from wildwood to managed woodland conserved it?

Vera rightly points to the great importance of conserving wood-pasture and its shrubs and ancient trees. (I would add conserving the grassland component, which seldom survives in good condition.) The relation between different aspects of wildwood and the woods or wood-pastures of medieval England may be closer than I then thought when writing the original *Ancient Woodland*.

19 For a recent re-assessment of this point see: Liddiard, R. (2003). The deer parks of Domesday Book. *Landscapes*, **4**, 4–23.
20 *The History of the Countryside*, p. 128.

33

Conservation and the Future

The original *Ancient Woodland* had no chapter on conservation. It was written at a gloomy time, when farming and forestry between them had destroyed (or so it seemed) nearly half the ancient woodland of England in thirty years: the most rapid destruction known in historic times. Woodland conservation in 1980 seemed to have simple objectives: preventing any more crude destruction by farmers and foresters seeking a little more land; and restoring coppicing and other practices in surviving woods and wood-pastures, on which many ecosystems depended. There was little to add to what I had written four years before in *Trees & Woodland in the British Landscape*.

But 'the years that the locust hath eaten' were coming to an end. Within five years farming and forestry were themselves in trouble and ceased to be a significant threat to ancient woodland. Woodland was to grasp the attention of the public, bureaucrats, and protesters alike. The new Woodland Trust grew into one of the biggest conservation bodies in the country. Not that threats of crude destruction have entirely gone away: developers still occasionally have designs on woodland, but many such projects are instantly publicized by the Woodland Trust, and some are successfully opposed. A *cause célèbre* of the 1990s was Oxleas Wood (Greenwich), where a plan not to destroy an ancient wood but to bisect it by a main road was defeated, even though the road had nowhere else to go. To attack woodland invites conflict, delay, and expense, and the wise developer goes elsewhere.

Ancient woods are still so numerous that one can scarcely expect an attrition rate of zero: no human will can ever eliminate the occasional mistake, corruption, or hard case. But the dynamics of ancient woodland have reverted from the unchallenged and almost unnoticed destruction of the Locust Years – roughly one-seventieth of the remaining ancient woodland each year for 25 years – to the near-equilibrium of ordinary decades in past centuries.

I now review the scene as it appears in 2002. Woodland is faring better than it has for a hundred years; it seldom lacks funds or goodwill – though the funds are not always put in the right place, and the goodwill does not yet extend to 'scrub', that is young woodland. The new problems are beyond the reach of politics or even money.

What is conservation?

Conservation in the English (not American) sense means 'preservation from destructive influences, natural decay, or waste' (*Oxford English Dictionary*). In English woodland, conservationists are continuing centuries of previous conservation and stable management. They do not normally have to decide that such-and-such is the ideal period in a wood's history and try to perpetuate it forever. (This kind of argument used to be used in designed landscapes to justify the practice of destroying and replanting historic avenues: a *perpetually young* avenue, it was asserted, was what the eighteenth-century design called for.) Woodmanship, unlike modern forestry, has not always been a creature of fashion. Many woods in 1950 were still in recognizably the same state that they had been in 1250: there were differences (bigger oaks, longer coppice cycles) but there had not been a radical discontinuity.

Opposing twentieth-century changes in woods is more than vaguely objecting to changes in general. A few changes may have added to conservation value. The spread of birch (Chapter 19) is arguably a gain: it brings a new suite of species, such as the mycorrhizal fungi of birch, and (up to a point) seems not to displace anything else. Other changes are within what I shall call the ***normal dynamics*** of landscape. It would be foolish to object to droughts or great storms (or in Mediterranean countries to erosion), which are normal if rare events. Elm Disease and hot summers are on the fringes of normal dynamics. But most twentieth-century changes were one-way, outwith normal dynamics: grubbing woods out, replanting, and the coming of oak mildew, grey squirrels, and deer. Each of these subtracted features from a wood without adding features: acid rain took away rare lichens and favoured common ones. They diminished the conservation value. It would be perverse to argue that the influence of deer on Hayley Wood since 1962 has been other than subtractive.

An under-appreciated aspect of conservation is the

maintenance of local values. It should be obvious from this book that ancient woods are all uniquely different. Most twentieth-century changes are in the direction of homogenization. A wood successfully replanted with Corsican Pine or ravaged by deer looks much the same as any other wood so treated.

A wise conservation philosophy begins by asking: What are the special features of each wood, the *genius loci*, that make it different from other woods? Are they conservable, or are they merely an aspect of a particular passing phase? What are the normal dynamics of the site? Are the apparent threats within or outside those dynamics? As we shall see, the minds of conservationists, especially professionals, too seldom run on these lines. They love to fit woods into predetermined categories, to emphasize the commonplace features of a wood in which it resembles other woods, and overlook rare or unexpected features. In recent years they take their categories out of the few provided ready-made by the *National Vegetation Classification*, and thus go further down the road towards homogenization. They divorce biological conservation from the historic and social values which ancient woodland also embodies.

Conservation, as a long-term human activity, risks being subverted by fashion much as modern forestry has been. Alston Chase recounts the comic history of Yellowstone National Park under successive 'preservation' regimes.[1] English conservationists have never been able to play God on such a glorious scale, but any long-standing nature reserve or public place has been through a succssion of fashions: the first 'do nothing' phase, the 'pollards are unnatural' phase, the 'plant trees everywhere' phase, the thinning phase, the second 'do nothing' phase, and the 'turn part of the site into a car-park' phase. Each of these subtracts something from the historic character of a site. Steady attrition results from the human urge to tidy up, and from the conflicts between the interests of a site and the interests (or more often the supposed interests) of visitors. Even the National Trust, with its insistence that 'preservation . . . must always take precedence over public access', is not immune, as the histories of Wicken Fen and Hatfield Forest show.[2, 3]

Conservation is more than applying a few simple rules. Very properly, conservationists strenuously cut down trees in England, and strenuously oppose cutting down trees in the Borneo rain-forest. They conserve deer in Hatfield Forest but seek to eliminate them from other woods in north-west Essex. Each of these decisions should be based on historical knowledge of the particular ecosystem, and of whether the factor in question is, or is not, part of its normal dynamics.

Woodland and the modern conservation movement

The modern conservation movement in England began when the Commons, Footpaths, and Open Spaces Preservation Society was formed after the destruction of most of Hainault Forest in the 1850s. Its first big success was in 1878 with the Epping Forest Act, which frustrated plans similarly to destroy Epping Forest; but although the site was preserved the Forest lost much of its character through changes in management and their unforeseen effects (p. 201f).[4] The National Trust was founded in 1894, but did not acquire much woodland until it was given Hatfield Forest in 1924.

The next stage was in 1912–14, when Nathaniel Charles Rothschild founded what is now the Royal Society for Nature Conservation. He listed 182 sites which he proposed should be acquired as National Nature Reserves. Of these, 26 included what would now be called ancient woodland or wood-pasture. They are a curious selection, illustrating mainly how little was known about woodland at the time. The only one which appears prominently in this book is Staverton Park.[5] Gamlingay Wood was not listed, although it should have been known about. Of the 26, only five were to become National Nature Reserves many years later, and five others now have some sort of conservation status. None of the 26 woods has disappeared completely, but eight have been badly damaged (mostly by replanting) and four show significant damage (over and above the usual increase of shade and depredations of deer).

The Waning of 'the Years that the Locust hath Eaten'

Will the Locust Years ever recur? By the 1960s farmers' need for more land was being undercut by the success of plant and animal breeders in making it possible to grow more food on the existing land. A few people, such as Max Walters and Colin Ranson, already realized this. If 2½ tons of wheat now grow where 1 ton grew before, what is to happen to the land on which the extra 1½ tons used to grow? This is likely to be a permanent change: matters can only get worse as eastern Europe's

1 Chase, A. (*c.* 1986). *Playing God in Yellowstone: the destruction of America's first National Park*. Atlantic Monthly Press, Boston (Mass.).
2 Friday, L. E. (1997). *Wicken Fen: the making of a wetland nature reserve*, Harley Books, Great Horkesley.
3 *The Last Forest* chapter 6.
4 Although the Forest authorities now appreciate the problem, many of the changes, such as lack of pollarding, went too far to be easily reversible.
5 Rothschild, M. and Marren, P. (1997). *Rothschild's Reserves: time and fragile nature*. Harley Books, Great Horkesley.

Fig. 33.1 Attempt to destroy Ditton Park Wood, Cambridgeshire, by poison and replace it by forestry: a grimly familiar sight during the 'locust years'. August 1971

agriculture, having at its disposal much of the world's best land, recovers from Communism.

Forestry fell on hard times for different reasons. The Forestry Commission was founded in 1919. For thirty years its business was to establish new plantations on open land: cheap arable land, heath, and moorland. Although in South Wales some of this had been woodland only fifty years before, the young Commission seldom meddled with existing woodland: its clashes with conservation interests are not relevant to this book. Only after World War II did the Commission begin to acquire existing woods to treat as in effect vacant land, replacing them by plantations, and to encourage and subsidize private landowners (and even the National Trust) to do the same.

During the Locust Years official foresters had a mysterious obsession with fast-growing trees. They justified this by financial predictions, on the premise that planting trees was an alternative investment, something that people did instead of buying stocks and shares. They would solemnly calculate the cost of buying the land, destroying the existing wood, planting and maintaining the trees, to be offset against future income from sales of thinnings and the final crop. Present costs would be weighed against future income by a process called Net Discounted Revenue, the object being to predict the final profit. They would cite such a computation as showing that it was rational, indeed the only rational use of the land, to poison an ancient wood (Fig. 33.1) and replace it with Norway or Sitka Spruce. The more conservation-minded among them might 'compromise' by leaving a width of one chain's-length (20 m) intact round the roadside edge, or even by planting some oak (possibly, on occasion, to be poisoned in its turn when a new boss took over).

This procedure now seems comically inappropriate, especially since, as Jonathan Spencer points out, whatever the Commission might have said in public, their real concern was with finance, not profit. Why did it ever gain acceptance? It was always predictive, and never verified by working out the actual profit or loss of past plantations. Foresters in practice care little about whether a particular plantation did, in fact, make a profit – they seldom care enough to keep the archives needed to compute the profitability of a plantation at the end. (W. E. Hiley, who introduced the method to Britain, was unable to illustrate it from British examples: he had to fall back on the experience of the Nilambur Teak Plantations in India.[6])

When I put the question to foresters, I get three kinds of answer. (1) The procedure was foisted on a reluctant Forestry Commission by a hard-headed and stupid Treasury. (2) Any calculation, however unsound, is better than no calculation. (3) The answer will be revealed when So-and-So writes his memoirs. Some foresters, however, did have faith in the Net Discounted Revenue calculation. Peter Marren recalls (as I do) the curious lack of shame with which some professional foresters of the old school wrecked Sites of Special Scientific Interest in the later Locust Years, while speaking the language of 'integration' and 'multi-purpose use'.[7]

Opposition from conservationists was lukewarm. The calculation immediately took on that mystical authority which attaches to all *financial* computations, whether or not their data are good or their logic sound. It became a knock-down argument against opponents who seldom had the knowledge to pick holes in the arithmetic: their reaction took the form 'it's a pity they have to do this, but . . .'. Some conservationists even took up the practice. Cambridgeshire Naturalists' Trust listened to, but rejected, a proposal to replant part of Hayley Wood. The National Trust replaced Frithsden

6 Hiley, W. E. (1930). *The Economics of Forestry*. Oxford.
7 Marren, *Nature Conservation* (supplementary bibliography), p. 159.

Great Copse (p. 325) and other historic woods by plantations; at Hatfield Forest they thought they had done a good deal with the Commission by persuading them to replace the historic coppices by oak plantations rather than conifers.

At length I timidly pointed out that the weak spot in Net Discounted Revenue was the discount rate: the exponential number used to balance the pounds spent on poison in 1970 against the pounds expected from timber sales in 2010. The calculation stood or fell by small variations in this number (p. 169). But the discount rate was not a quantity ascertainable by measurement or observation: it had been conjured up from whatever lay between the ears of some long-dead accountant. This alone should have discredited the whole operation, but bigger holes in the fabric soon appeared. It was based on three gambles: that the planted trees would grow; that the cost of tending them would rise no faster than inflation; and that they would sell themselves once grown. All three proved to be losers.

Afforesting woodland was evidently thought to be much the same as afforesting moorland. But there were two important differences: there were trees already, and woodland comes in small areas often remote from Commission bases. The original trees often refused to die, and the new trees refused to prosper. The budget for weeding and thinning ran out as workmen demanded higher wages, or could not be found at all. The great summers of 1975, 1976 and later dried out Sitka Spruce, *Thuja*, and other oceanic species; the Great Storm of 1987 plucked out multitudes of overcrowded planted trees; native trees recovered from the poison and reasserted themselves.

But worse was to come. When the time came the surviving planted trees had to be got out: I know of two sites that had become inaccessible because the roads would not take Juggernaut lorries. The trees had to be sold in competition with Britain's traditional, well-organized suppliers of ordinary coniferous timber in the Baltic and elsewhere. (Were foresters so fond of fast-growing trees because they wanted them to reach saleable size while there was still a market? If so, they were to be disappointed.) Even growers of ordinary pine or spruce on ex-farmland, despite economies of scale and avoidance of the extra problems of woodland, complain that the low price makes it hardly worthwhile to fell the trees. This is not only a British problem: I was given a similar explanation for the decline of felling among the mountain plantations of Japan.

Selling trees is not impossible, but it is a skilled art in which many foresters are not trained, and it can be more a matter of cutting losses than of making profits. Never again (at least among people with common sense) will growing trees, or allowing trees to grow, be presented in merely economic terms. This is not to say that woodland economics are unimportant, but they are unpredictable, indeed unquantifiable. I was once rebuked in a letter to *The Times* on the grounds that contemporary forestry ought to be growing trees to supply the industries of today – but it is inherent in the nature of plantation forestry to be growing trees for the industries of forty years ago.

In the 1980s the Forestry Commission fell on desperate and depressing days. Conservationists might have killed it by a serious campaign of opposition. In my view they were right to desist and instead encourage it to reform. It has diversified out of the single-minded business of growing ordinary coniferous timber, and has taken up conservation and public amenity. This seems to be a genuine change of ethos, not merely a response to outside forces which may reverse at the next round of a boom-and-bust cycle. A new generation of foresters has arisen with other things to do with their lives than grow millions of identical trees.

The planting mentality – 'for every tree we cut down, we plant six' – lingered on. The Forestry Commission used officiously to make replanting a condition of granting licences to other people to fell their woods. However, this too gradually died out: my lecture slide of chestnuts planted in a perfectly good chestnut coppice (Fig. 33.2) dated from 1991. (But I have now replaced it with a similar picture taken in 2002 – from a nature reserve!)

Fig. 33.2 The planting mentality: chestnut trees planted in a coppice-wood already crammed with chestnut trees. Essex. October 1991

The Ancient Woodland Inventory

The greatest institutional advance is the listing of ancient woodland: a formidable task which I thought impossible in 1980. Within ten years, the Nature Conservancy Council (predecessor of English Nature) had compiled a provisional Inventory of Ancient Woodland. Athough, as with the register of Listed Buildings, it will need revision for many years, it enables the concept of ancient woodland to enter the planning process.

This improves on the older system of Sites of Special Scientific Interest. In the 1960s and 1970s, when ancient woods were being destroyed weekly, the then Nature Conservancy had the dreadful task of being a Chooser of the Slain. They had to decide which woods had just enough scientific interest, or not quite enough, to qualify as an SSSI, in the knowledge that posterity would almost certainly discover aspects of scientific interest which were not known about at the time of listing. Now, at least, it is possible in principle to know whether a wood existed in the year 1600 or not.

Deer *versus* Conservation

> I am . . . tired of landowners not living up to their promises to address the deer problem.
>
> *Specialist woodman, 2000*

With the threat of crude destruction reduced to something like its historic proportions, the chief threat to ancient woodland is browsing. In Wales and Scotland this is browsing by sheep (or sometimes feral goats). In England the twentieth century has been very kind to deer; there are now more head of deer running round England than there have been for a thousand years, and more species than there have ever been.

In the first edition I wrote about red, fallow, and roe deer; since 1980 others have proliferated. Muntjac, introduced from south China in *c.* 1900, are now probably the commonest deer in England. They are deer of non-woodland as well as woodland, extending almost to the middle of Cambridge. Japanese Deer (commonly called Sika, from a mispronunciation of the Japanese word for 'deer') are abundant in scattered areas such as east Dorset. Chinese Water Deer are still largely confined to fenland areas of eastern England.[8]

These will not be the last deer to be established in Britain. Anyone visiting a deer park should admire the oriental deer, and should speculate on which will be the next species to escape when a tree falls on the boundary fence. (And not only oriental deer: the white-tailed deer of North America is yet to come.)

Red, Japanese, and fallow deer and muntjac are not really woodland animals. They feed on most plant material, from brambles to heather, but (like goats) have their likes and dislikes. They shelter in woods, where they eat all the palatable leafage within reach, up to a browse-line which varies with the height of the animal. When that is gone they feed on surrounding fields or grassland. In time past they would go hungry in hard winters, but no longer: with the dominance of autumn-sown cereals since 1970, there is always plenty to eat outside the wood. Roe, more of a woodland animal than other deer, are reputed particularly to eat brambles. But deer in general are losing their association with woods: I find people in Suffolk, miles from any wood, whose gardens are ravaged by roe.

Deer may often be beneficial to grassland, including grassland in wood-pasture; like sheep or rabbits, they prevent it from being overrun by trees or taken over by coarse grasses.[9] Whether wildwood was adapted to browsing depends on how much of the Vera model (p. 499ff) one accepts, on whether it was already differentiated into 'woodland' and 'wood-pasture' zones. But there is no doubt that woods, as they have existed in historic times separately from Forests and parks, are not adapted to the numbers of big herbivores that have suddenly irrupted into them.

The first question to ask in an unfamiliar wood is 'What deer are there?'. Besides looking for tracks, one crouches down to below the height of a deer's head, and if there is much deer damage one can suddenly see a long way. Deer subtract the shrubs and low leafage between the browse-line and the ground (Fig. 33.3, 33.15). Browse-lines are easily observed on palatable species such as ivy and holly. One looks for missing bramble leaflets, and young ashes 'crippled' by having their tops repeatedly bitten off. Coppice shoots are useful in establishing an order of preference. All deer love elm and hawthorn. Ash is preferred by fallow deer, hazel by roe and muntjac. Most deer hate aspen and chestnut, although they fray the bases of aspens with their antlers. (Sheep will eat aspen.)

There is now a *more than ideal habitat* for deer, a mosaic of woodland and winter-sown crops. Farmers are surprisingly tolerant. Unlike rabbits, which emerge from a gap in a fence and eat an ever-widening semicircle of crop flat to the ground, deer wander through the fields and take a mouthful here and a mouthful there, and the damage to the crop is made good by the greater growth of neighbouring plants.

Numbers of deer are not easy to define. From 1978 to

8 For deer in general see: Jones, M., Robertson, I. D., and McCarthy, A. J. (eds) (1996) *Deer or the New Woodlands? Journal of Practical Ecology & Conservation, Special Publication* **1**.

9 Virtanen, R., Edwards, G. R., and Grawley, M. J. (2002). Red deer management and vegetation on the Isle of Rum. *Journal of Applied Ecology* **39**, 572–83.

Fig. 33.3 (a–d) Effects of fallow deer.

(a) Wood protected from fallow deer. The tree canopy extends to ground level, and there are plenty of young trees and ground vegetation (invisible in this winter picture). The young ash-trees are a legacy from the sudden termination of browsing twenty years before (Fig. 31.5). Hayley Wood. February 2002

(b) The other side of the fence. The tree canopy ends 124 cm, 4ft 1in., above ground; no low cover and very little ground vegetation. Hayley Wood. February 2002

(c) Wood reduced to trees plus grassland by a combination of coppicing and fallow deer. N.W. Essex. March 1999

(d) Shady, deer-infested limewood reduced (in spring) to little more than trees plus mud by concentrated trampling and browsing. Grange Wood, Coggeshall, Essex. April 2001

2000 a deer count was held every November in Hayley Wood and the surrounding country; it became a popular event with local naturalists. The fallow deer found fluctuated between 23 and 75 head. This was a lot of deer for a wood of 120 acres, but they spent much of their time in other woods and in the fields. It was never possible to be sure that a low count was real: even such a large animal is easily missed in a hollow of a big field. Moreover, many areas of England have a continuum of deer, in which it is unrealistic to assign particular individuals to any one wood or group of woods. Muntjac ranged up to 15 head, but this is almost certain to be an underestimate with such a secretive animal.[10]

Historic numbers of deer

Red and roe deer were abundant in Neolithic times: the flint miners of Grime's Graves (Norfolk) got through many thousands of hartshorn picks. By Anglo-Saxon times they were very local. In the twelfth century came the introduction of fallow deer and a renewed interest in deer husbandry. In the middle ages deer were confined to parks and Forests and did not roam the countryside. Outside parks, the numbers were not large.

How did the medievals keep numbers of deer down, when the twentieth century failed? Henry III, even allowing generously for unrecorded orders, took fewer than a thousand head per year from all England (p. 181). He was much less of a predator than the motor-car is today. His consumption of Forest deer would be in equilibrium with a population of only 3000–4000 animals, which is absurdly few for nearly a million acres of physical Forest.

Records of 'trespasses against the venison' before Forest courts are remarkable for the delay in prosecution, the small numbers of animals, the lenient penalties, and the status of the defendants, mainly gentry, nobility, and clergy (cf p. 180). The ordinary individual, snaring a deer for the pot, rarely came before the courts, and when he did was usually pardoned. The authorities made no sustained effort to prevent poaching: why should they? Their business was to raise a little revenue from fines. Only if there was an organized poaching gang, like the one organized by the Precentor of St Paul's Cathedral in Hatfield Forest in 1273, was it worth serious prosecution and a deterrent fine.[11] I have to suppose that numbers were kept down by a great deal of unpoliced deer-stealing.

Modern effects of deer

Deer regularly make woodland management impossible by eating coppice shoots. Even a slight degree of browsing can spoil high-value underwood. Deer are particularly destructive to ancient ash stools, often the oldest trees in a wood and an important habitat.

They influence tree composition by subtracting palatable species, whether in the form of seedlings or coppice shoots. In Hayley Wood fallow deer have converted an ash-dominated to an aspen-dominated area within one round of coppicing. Deer seem also to encourage maple, a characteristic tree of wooded Forests (p. 207). Intermittent browsing may favour a generation of ash. Ashlings, although crippled by repeated attack, are not easily killed, and get away if there is a lull in the browsing (Fig. 31.5). In the long run, deer can reduce a wood to grassland, as probably happened in many parks. There seem not to be any figures on how many deer are needed to achieve this.

In Chapters 25 and 26 I explored the part played by deer in the decline of various woodland herbs. Many other such studies are reported.[12, 13] Deer eat the foliage of many specifically woodland herbs and shrubs, doing damage which is not easily repaired in shade. Others are avoided as distasteful. They also eat flowers, which for long-lived and especially clonal species matters less. Fallow deer eat oxlip leaves and flowers, whereas muntjac eat mainly the flowers.[14] Deer encourage coarse grasses, *Carex pendula*, and bracken, which compete adversely with more delicate woodland herbs. Their only beneficial effect may be in reducing palatable competitors such as bramble. The seeds of many flowering-plants are known to survive passing through a deer's gut; but these include no trees, and very few ancient-woodland herbs.[15]

Deer affect other animals through changes in woodland structure (Fig. 33.3): 'eating out the bottom' of an uncoppiced wood, or delaying coppice regrowth or making it patchy. They are particularly harmful to birds that nest in thick low cover, such as nightingales and warblers. They threaten rodents such as dormice

10 For these numbers I am indebted to Ray Symonds.
11 *The Last Forest* chapter 4.
12 Kirby, K. J. (2001). The impact of deer on the ground flora of British broadleaved woodland. *Forestry*, **74** (2001), 219–29.
13 Morecroft, M. D., Taylor, M. E., Ellwood, S. A., and Quinn, S. A. (2001). Impacts of deer herbivory on ground vegetation at Wytham Woods, central England. *Forestry*, **74** (2001), 251–7.
14 Tabor, R. C. C. (1997). The effects of Muntjac deer . . . and Fallow deer . . . on the Oxlip. *Deer*, **11**, 14–9.
15 Gill, R. M. A. (2001). The impact of deer on woodlands: the effects of browsing and seed dispersal on vegetation structure and composition. *Forestry*, **74** (2001), 209–18.

Fig. 33.4 Coppicing in Hatfield Forest. The sparse regrowth and abundant grasses are characteristic of coppices in Forests. Spittlemoor Coppice. September 1994

and yellow-necked mice, and even the owls that prey on them.[16, 17, 18, 19, 20]

Browsing in woods such as Hayley, though severe, is not extreme. Monks' Wood, Huntingdon has long had an exceptional density of muntjac (at least one to 2½ acres). (Is this because it is the seat of the Institute of Terrestrial Ecology? or because it is a very big wood?) Exclosures have demonstrated what they can do. Muntjac devour obvious species such as privet, ivy, ash, and bramble, and go on to swallow poisonous and distasteful plants: bluebell, dog's-mercury, and even arum. (These latter usually escape in other woods: early observations on muntjac exclosures in Hayley indicate little effect.) Plants that they favour are ground-ivy, whose rank flavour even a hungry muntjac cannot stomach, and grasses and tussock-sedges that are adapted to grazing.[21] Muntjac in the 1990s did more damage to the wood than the felling in the 1910s which had left more than half of it 'a desert of grey ashes'.

Hatfield Forest illustrates long-continued browsing by deer and other livestock in woodland (Fig. 33.4). The woods were supposed to be fenced after each felling, but only for six years, and not always effectively. The abundance of grass in the coppices, presumably *Deschampsia caespitosa*, was noted as early as 1612 (p. 94f). The Forest still has a rich coppicing flora, strongly biased towards distasteful species such as hound's-tongue (Fig. 26.7h). Although it is within the geographical range of oxlip, there are now only a handful of plants left.

Objections to the effects of deer in English woodland are not merely general objections to novelty. Nearly all the effects are anti-conservation: they subtract features from woodland without adding features. Like replanting, deer create a simplified, homogenized ecosystem composed of those plants and animals that happen to be resistant. They are usually a new factor, like grey squirrels, and are not part of the normal dynamics.

That said, there are a handful of sites where deer *are* part of the normal dynamics. Hatfield Forest has had fallow deer for 900 years. Deer damage is part of the consequences of being a Forest, and should be tolerated to a higher level than in woodland (Best 1998). Even here, however, numbers are now greater than in most of the Forest's history.

Some will argue that deer and other large beasts were a normal feature of wildwood and should again be tolerated. However, ancient woodland is not wildwood and should not be treated as if it were. It is the product of centuries of human cultural activity, which did not involve deer (except in compartmented Forests and parks). Ancient woodland ecosystems are not adapted to deer and are easily damaged by them. There are now *artificially large numbers* and *exotic species* of deer. To keep the numbers constant one must kill at least one-quarter of the stock each year. The only effective predator, the motor-car, does its best but fails to achieve the body-count required.

Where browsing is reported to favour woodland birds or invertebrates, this mostly concerns moderate degrees of browsing. The effect in Hatfield Forest, for example, is to delay coppice regrowth. Woodmen dislike slow growth, especially for high-value produce, but

16 Stewart, A. J. A. (2001). The impact of deer on lowland woodland invertebrates: a review of the evidence and priorities for future research. *Forestry*, **74** (2001), 259–70.

17 Feber, R. E., Brereton, T. M., Warren, M. S. and Oates, M. (2001). The impacts of deer on woodland butterflies: the good, the bad and the complex. *Forestry*, **74** (2001), 271–6.

18 Flowerdew, J. R. and Ellwood, S. A. (2001). Impacts of woodland deer on small mammal ecology. *Forestry*, **74** (2001), 277–87.

19 Fuller, R. J. (2001). Responses of woodland birds to increasing numbers of deer: a review of evidence and mechanisms. *Forestry*, **74** (2001), 298–98.

20 Perrins, C. M. and Overall, R. (2001). Effect of increasing numbers of deer on bird populations in Wytham Woods . . . *Forestry*, **74** (2001), 299–309.

21 Cooke, A. S. and Farrell, L. T. Impact of muntjac deer . . . at Monks Wood . . . *Forestry*, **74** (2001), 242–50.

in prolonging the useful early stages of the habitat there is something to be said for it. However, fine control of browsing – enough to delay regrowth but not enough to prevent it – cannot be legislated for. Deer will not do as they are told.

Deer control

If deer were confined to woodland they would be few and not much of a problem. Trouble arises because they are fed and supported from outside the wood. The increasing tendency for woods to be owned by someone different from the surrounding farmer makes it more difficult to control deer. In the writer's experience, neighbouring landowners seldom agree together on anything more complex than keeping down rabbits. With deer, the parties have conflicting priorities. Woodmen want to prevent damage. Sporting shooters want fine masculine heads on their walls. Farmers have no great interest in keeping down numbers: damage to crops is assuaged by a carcase in the freezer.

Deer control involves shooting or fencing. Shooting is difficult: it does not do to loose off a rifle at random in a level and densely-populated country. Skilled marksmen, though not difficult to find, often cannot shoot enough deer to keep the numbers constant. Anything less is not effective. Even if one kills half the deer in the wood, the survivors may spend twice as much time doing the same amount of damage.

If there is to be an acceptable balance between deer and woodland, then (except in Forests) it must be at a low density of deer. This is difficult to achieve and maintain, year in, year out. Keeping a constant low density will be hard and unproductive work: long hours in a chilly high seat waiting for deer that miss their date with death.

Marketing deer needs attention. Meat from wild deer ought to appeal to anyone pernickety about animal welfare. But all deer meat is usually labelled just 'venison', as if a butcher were to sell sheep and goat together and not say which was which. (Muntjac are especially tasty.)

Fencing, as shown by 34 years' experience in Hayley Wood, is effective against fallow deer, and presumably other middle-sized and large species. A substantial fence is needed – the animals are stronger than pigs and more agile than goats – but the outlay is not vast, spread over the 40 years that a deer-fence should last. The fence needs watching and maintaining, for trees will fall on it. Getting deer out at the start, and removing any that find their way in, is not too difficult provided one watches their habits and closes the fence when the deer are out feeding in the fields.

In England there is seldom the complication of rare and lumbering birds blundering into a fence and breaking their necks. In Scotland, however, the conservation of black grouse and capercaillie is at odds with that of the Caledonian pinewoods which are their habitat. Fences may also be buried by snowdrifts (when did we last see a snowdrift in England?) and allow deer to walk in.

In the Bradfield Woods there began the practice of fencing newly-felled areas with 'dead hedges' about 6 feet high made from the waste lop-and-top of underwood, stakes roughly entwined with ethers (Fig. 33.5). This is labour-intensive: for many years two ladies put endless hours of work into the fences. Against roe-deer (as at Bradfield) it works surprisingly well: they could easily break in but seem to lack perseverance. The fences last about three years, and then their work is done.

Individual stools can be protected with lop-and-top piled over them: this has some success in saving big old stools of ash and other palatable species. The pollarding experiment in Hayley Wood (p. 201) continues, though deer-fencing has now made it redundant. However, pollarding is much more laborious than coppicing, and neither of these methods protects the ground vegetation.

Fencing against muntjac is problematic. I have seen them jump 6 feet high; they can get through a hole 8 inches in diameter, and are strong enough to force such a hole in a pig-wire fence. Any gap that badgers get through will also admit muntjac. Whether fencing out fallow deer may increase numbers of muntjac is still an open question. In Hayley Wood the large fallow-deer exclosures show muntjac activity, but damage is tolerable. Muntjac are anti-social animals and do not form herds as fallow do. Severe muntjac damage seems to be a special problem at Monks' Wood.

People and dogs may be a minor deterrent. Fallow deer ravaged the Markshall woods (p. 251ff), and twenty years ago began to invade Chalkney Wood two miles away. Why has this not progressed? Possibly because Chalkney has been increasingly used by people and dogs. Elsewhere, as in Hayley Wood, deer tend to avoid areas near a path. Dogs bring their own problem from what comes out of them, but they keep away deer – at least until deer come to appreciate that dogs, for all their sound and fury, are as harmless as chainsaws.

'Bring back the wolf'? Almost nothing is known about what predators did to deer in wildwood times, and whether they did keep deer down to what would now be an acceptable level. A famous parallel is with the moose of Isle Royale in Lake Superior, which for decades had been eating themselves out of a home, until one hard winter a pack of wolves trotted across the ice and began eating the moose.[22] Whatever the

22 Allen, D. L. (1979). *Wolves of Minong: their vital role in a wild community*. Houghton Mifflin, Boston. (I am indebted to Dr J. A. Moody for bringing this to my attention.)

Fig. 33.5 (a–b) 'Dead hedge', effective against roe-deer:

(a) during construction;

(b) after one season. Bradfield Woods. March and September 1990

outcome, a thousand moose and a few dozen wolves imprisoned on an uncultivated island a little bigger than the Isle of Wight is not a scenario easily transferable to England.

Deer elsewhere

Deer are an unsolved problem where anthropology, zoology, and botany intersect. On finding a solution (by contraception?) depends the future of English woodland. This is not only an English problem. In the Highlands of Scotland, also, there have been too many red deer for seventy years. In France, it is claimed, there were 10–100 times more red and roe deer per square kilometre in 1999 than in Palaeolithic times, and yet more in 2000 because the hurricane favoured them (p. 449); whether this is good or bad depends on whether one is a *chasseur* or a *sylviculteur*.[23] Deer fare only too well in much of the Northern Hemisphere, and where introduced into Australia and New Zealand.

Americans, surprisingly, have not repeated Britain's mistake of letting loose oriental deer, but their own deer have increased, and deer problems are not unlike ours.[24] Moose have regained much of the territory in New England that they lost after the time of the Pilgrim Fathers. On my friends' ranch in Texas the appearing of a white-tailed deer is not the event that it was twenty years ago – but very recently deer have been overtaken by feral pigs.

American attitudes are different. The Alleghany National Forest is an area of about 800 square miles (as big as Leicestershire), now dominated largely by black cherry, which it has not always been. I was told that in aboriginal times there had been 2–3 head of white-tailed deer per square mile. Since the 1920s there have been 50–60 per square mile, and it shows. Every tree of hemlock (*Tsuga canadensis*) has a strong browse-line, and there are none younger than 70 years (Fig. 33.6). The only trees to get away are species like black cherry at the bottom of the menu. There is a lack of the spectacular

23 Roucher, F. (2000). Les cervidés après la tempête: nécessité d'une gestion intégrée forêt-gibier. *La Lettre des Sylves* **36**, 10. (A. Desbrosse brought this to my attention.)

24 Rooney, T. E. (2001). Deer impacts on forest ecosystems: a North American perspective. *Forestry*, **74** (2001), 201–8.

Fig. 33.6 Browse-line of white-tailed deer on the youngest trees of hemlock (*Tsuga canadensis*) in the Alleghany National Forest. Note the lack of ground vegetation. April 1999

Fig. 33.7 Effect of Japanese deer on the rather rare conifer *Abies homolepis*. Mount Odaigahara, Japan. October 1998

spring flowers – trilliums, *Maianthemum canadense*, etc. – which one expects in an eastern North American wood. But I am assured that people say there are still not enough deer. Every December, they take to the woods with anything that will shoot, and are disappointed that even now an unaimed shot is not sure of hitting something.[25]

Anyone who thinks they have a deer problem should go to Japan. Deer are sacred in the Shinto religion, and wander round certain holy cities. The Monarch of the Glen (shaped like a red deer, but a little smaller than a fallow buck) greets the pilgrim, and if one does not feed him he puts his head in one's pocket or prods one with a horn. Killing a deer is a capital crime (or used to be), but I got the impression of a rough balance between births and road-kills.

In the Japanese countryside most woods are happily free of browsing, but there is an amazing exception. Odaigahara is a mountain towering above the Pacific coast, clothed with a zonation of different tree communities. Its top is a graveyard of standing dead trees. It seems that since 1970 the population of deer residing on this particular mountain has exploded, eating its way through an ever-expanding circle which (in 1998) was some 7 km in radius. Any tree of *Abies homolepis*, the dominant tree at the top of the mountain, is instantly killed by deer prising off the bark with their antlers and eating it (Fig. 33.7). When those are gone they work their way through the other conifers. Their main sustenance is probably the dwarf bamboos which form carpets or thickets in Japanese woods. At a pinch they eat almost anything; even rhododendrons show a browse-line.[26]

The world's deer populations are getting mixed up, to nobody's benefit. Three species of Chinese deer eat up eastern England; red deer and Himalayan Tahr (*Hemitragus jemlahicus*) devour New Zealand: Japanese deer hybridize away the distinctive features of the historic red deer population of S.W. Ireland. All too often the first consequence of conservation is unnaturally large populations of deer. In England, conservation trusts dare not shoot deer for fear of what

25 Information from Stephen Wingate.
26 I owe this visit to the kindness of Professor Toru Nakashizuka and Dr Hiroshi Tanaka.

their members might think; in America, game conservers want plenty of easy targets. In either event the ecosystem, adapted to at most one-tenth of the amount of browsing, is devastated.

Coppicing

Commercial coppicing[26]

In 2002 'conservation coppicing' fares very well (subject to the vagaries of deer), but traditional commercial coppicing has taken a downturn for reasons not anticipated in 1980.

Contrary to popular belief, there is little difficulty in marketing the specialized products of coppice crafts. Good hazel underwood, which deer have not nibbled, commands fancy prices in the thatching trade. There is a national shortage of thatching spars, and a thriving market for wattle hurdles. Markets in the civil-engineering aspect of the business (e.g. sea defences, Fig. 10.6) need developing. The problem is selling ordinary bulk underwood – firewood, stakes, charcoal, pulpwood – which provides most of the income from the average coppice.

Coppicing, I assure the reader, is a hard, wet, muddy, and bloody job. Making specialized products calls for dexterity and hard-earned skill. But coppicing is not much better organized or paid than in the 1920s, when Helen Fitzrandolph and Doriel Hay, two Oxford dons, did their remarkable investigation of the underwood trades (p. 168). Long ago it retreated from northern England and Wales, where there was then plenty of money from coal-mining, but where it might now provide much-needed employment. Its stronghold, unfortunately, is now in south-east England, where it competes in the labour market with well-paid indoor jobs. Anyone wishing to enter the craft has the formidable task of finding somewhere to live within reach of a wood. Coppice workers find it difficult to get woodland owners to give them security of supply; their raw material is increasingly attacked by deer; and because their craft happens to be classed as industry rather than agriculture they meet with petty obstruction from planners and bureaucrats.

In 1989 the Sittingbourne paper-mill took to recycling paper instead of subsisting on the chestnut-woods. Conservationists thereby scored a famous 'own goal', said to have put 2000 woodcutters out of a job. Kentish underwood is now sent to the remaining mill in Monmouthshire; big orders for pale fencing and other chestnut products can be difficult to carry out because woodcutters have found other occupations.

Underwood products now compete, not so much with plastic and metal, but against wood products from countries with cheaper labour than Kent or Sussex: either underwood from Europe where coppicing still flourishes, or charcoal from other continents (some of which is reputed to come from wildwood). It is small consolation to know that plantation forestry also finds ordinary produce difficult to sell, and that most farming is kept going by subsidies. The economics of both coppicing and forestry depend on cultivating markets for poorer-quality produce.

Conservation coppicing

Maintaining coppicing as a deliberate conservation activity probably began in 1936, when Southend Borough Council was persuaded – by distinctly rough methods – to acquire Hadleigh Woods as a nature reserve.[27] It expanded especially in the 1970s, as county wildlife trusts acquired many woods and almost automatically resumed coppicing. The Suffolk Trust made coppicing into a considerable business, building on the work of the Bradfield Woods Management Committee in continuing the ancient coppicing in that reserve. In the 1990s the Forest Authority, in its new function as protector of woodland, favoured coppicing, with subsidies in parts of south England, the lower Wye Valley, and the limestone Lake District in order to encourage butterflies. Coppicing has even been initiated in new woods which have never been cut before (Fig. 33.8).

Amenity bodies such as the National Trust, Woodland Trust, and the public amenity departments of county councils also maintain coppicing on a large scale. However, it is still unusual for coppicing to extend to a whole wood, as in the Bradfield Woods (other than small designated non-intervention areas) and Chalkney Wood, where Essex County Council has completed a long coppice cycle since acquiring one-third of the wood in 1973.

Most conservation coppicing is done by contractors, who often need supervision, especially when using vehicles in unsuitable weather. A common fault is leaving too many trees standing, which weakens the regrowth (Fig. 33.9). Conservationists are rightly reluctant to cut down oaks, which have become difficult to replace (p. 296f). It adds variety to have some standard ashes, maples, hornbeams, or limes, but there is no need to promote too many.

Length of the coppice cycle

Dense, early stages of regrowth are favourable to warblers and nightingales, with a peak around 3 to 6 years.

26 Much of this is derived from a conference in February 2002 organized by J. Edward Milner of ACACIA Environment. I am particularly indebted to Debbie Bartlett and David Maylam, and to comments on another occasion by Mark Powell.

27 *Woods of South-East Essex* p. 34f.

Fig. 33.8 A 50-year-old secondary wood in plotland (p. 8) coppiced for the first time. This is of the greatest interest for the study of coppicing vegetation; it happens too rarely to be a significant threat to creatures sensitive to disturbance. Rayleigh, Essex. April 1986

Fig. 33.9 A 'conservation' coppice-wood with too many trees left standing. Hadleigh Great Wood. May 1977

Older underwood is favourable to robins, tits, and other birds which are not so dependent on woodland.[28] Small mammals also benefit from young underwood. The dormouse is reputedly a creature of young ages of hazel, although it benefits from having older hazel as well;[29] dormice, however, occur in other habitats, such as thickets at the edges of expanding woods. The six species of butterflies dependent on coppicing – five fritillaries and Wood White – depend on the food plants, especially perennial violets and buried-seed cow-wheat, that flourish in the first few years.

For plants there is no definite indication that any one coppice cycle is better than another. If the cycle is too short or if deer delay regrowth, brambles and *Deschampsia* may not be shaded out, and may become dominant early in the next cycle and interfere with the growth of weaker species (Plate 7, p. xxvii). If the cycle is too long, buried seeds may die, but this seems to take at least 50 years to become noticeable.

Present knowledge does not justify laying down an ideal length of coppice cycle. Short cycles, like those of the middle ages, are often impractical in a deer-ridden world. Commercial considerations often favour longish cycles, to produce logs and stakes. On conservation grounds there is little to be said against this, provided that some coppicing is done every year to maintain the succession. There is much to be said, if the wood is big enough and not harried by deer, for having two cycles, as in the Bradfield Woods: a cycle of 10–12 years for thatching wood and high-value hazel products, and a long cycle of 25 years.

Woodland conservationists need to compromise over the details of length of cycle and season of cutting and carting, which can be an insuperable obstacle to specialist woodcutters. As one of the latter told me, 'it is no use telling a spar or hurdle maker that a plot is available to cut Nov.–March but it will have to be extracted when the rides are dry in summer', because cut hazel is perishable and will not last until then.

Although woodmen may have been tidy-minded in

28 Fuller, R. J. (1992). Effects of coppice management on woodland breeding birds. Buckley (see supplementary bibliography) 169–92.
29 Gurnell, J., Hicks, M., and Whitbread S. (1992). The effects of coppice management on small mammal populations. Buckley (supplementary bibliography) 213–32.

the past (especially when there was a photographer around), is important not to be tidy now. Old, hollow, and dead trees, and especially boundary pollards and big dead logs, should always be kept.[30] Care should be taken to preserve ancient stools, both as historic features and as a habitat. Where dormice are present it is as well to remember that they are not down-to-earth animals; overhanging hazels should be left to form bridges across rides, so that they can get from one newly-coppiced area to another without leaving the trees.

Too much coppicing?

In the mid-1990s one met the argument that there was too much coppicing, which had advanced (it was said) to the point at which it was encroaching on the habitats of animals, especially insects, that would not tolerate disturbance. Scholars such as Clive Hambler and Martin R. Speight urged that woodland conservation ought to be dominated by the objective of re-creating wildwood. The early Holocene was assumed to be the ideal period of woodland history, to the extent that conservationists were in duty bound to drop whatever else they were doing and turn all their efforts to make existing woods conform to the 1990s' reconstruction of that period. Human activities, it was claimed, are not an influence integral to the historic landscape, but are 'the damage our ancestors wrought on our landscape' whose evil effects must somehow be unpicked.[31] This amounted, in practice, to a plea for doing nothing to woodland. (What was to happen to the deer was not explained.)

The fact is that in Britain, of all countries, human influence is pervasive and not always negative; it has destroyed species and habitats, but has also created new species and habitats. The cultural landscape, formed by the interaction between mankind and the natural world, is all the landscape that we fully know about. Many aspects of it are of value in their own right as biological habitats, such as meadows, chalkpits, and medieval churches. Coppice-woods do not claim to be wildwood and are not just an inferior substitute for it.

Indeed, many of the creatures intolerant of disturbance are dependent on ancient and hollow trees, which are usually semi-artefacts (e.g. pollards) rather than wholly natural features. Their conservation and perpetuation are not necessarily achieved by doing nothing. Often these trees did not originate in woodland, and are threatened by the shade of younger neighbours.

The first problem in re-creating wildwood is defining it. In Britain 'primaeval forest' is one of those phantoms, like 'primitive man', that haunt popular understanding of the past. Wildwood, if it existed during the Holocene, lasted for a relatively brief period in the Mesolithic, and even then had lost some wildwood features, such as elephants. Nobody knows for certain what it looked like, let alone how it would have changed over the last 6000 years had it been spared. In North America and Australia, human activities have determined whole continents throughout the post-glacial period. By Columbus's time, there were not many forests on earth (other than on remote islands) that had never been altered by people's activities. The obsession of some conservationists with untouched wildwood has been steadily undermined by archaeological research.

Was wildwood forest or savanna? Is it to be re-created on Sir Arthur Tansley's model of climax forest, as it might have been in 4500 BC? Or on Vera's model of wood-pasture in 4500 BC? Or as either might have developed by 2000 AD had it never been encoppiced? These cannot be re-created either by doing nothing or by management. Environment, plants, and animals are all different now. An abandoned coppice-wood will not turn into either wildwood as it once was or the wildwood that would have been by now. For a start, it does not regain lime, once the dominant tree. New woods on former farmland suffer from over-fertility: wildwood was not sodden with phosphate as ex-arable woods are.

However, the distinctions between historic managed woodland and wildwood are not so absolute as was thought ten years ago. Coppicing is an inherent feature of trees and is more than just a response to management (Chapter 32). Wildwood contained permanent open spaces, if not wide open areas, corresponding to the rides and glades of ancient woodland today.

The recent comeback of coppicing has nearly always been in woods with a previous history of coppicing, from which (by definition) all intolerant non-mobile species disappeared long ago. It has not encroached on ancient woods that have never been coppiced. The balance between coppiced and non-coppiced woods has yet to reach the point at which it could fairly be claimed that there is too much coppicing. Let us say that one-tenth of the area of ancient woodland is now coppiced (problems of definition make an exact figure meaningless). The most strenuous efforts of conservationists might, at most, increase this to one-quarter. Hambler and Speight's objectives can be achieved, if at all, on the remaining 75%. Conservationists are already doing most of what they recommend.

However, it is well to be reminded that doing nothing in ancient woodland has its uses. During the Locust Years conservationists were apologetic about acquiring tracts of land and then, apparently, neglecting them. The doctrine that every inch of land ought to look as if it was doing something 'useful' is now dead,

30 Kirby, K. (1992). Accumulation of dead wood – a missing ingredient in coppicing? Buckley (supplementary bibliography) 99–112.
31 Hambler, C. and Speight, M. R. (1995). Biodiversity conservation in Britain: science replacing tradition. *British Wildlife* **6**, 137–47.

but it is still useful to have a respectable reason for non-intervention. But there is no need to apply this principle to all woodland.

Hambler and Speight's philosophy implied that biological conservationists should overrule all other kinds of conservation; should 'clarify' and 'make explicit the aims of woodland management'; and that 'suspect management' should not be 'condoned'. In effect they invited conservationists to make up their minds what constitutes sound conservation management and apply it to nearly all woodland that they could get their hands on. This invites disaster: it leaves little room for manoeuvre if further experience shows it not to be good conservation management after all. Foresters made exactly this mistake when they sought to apply to all woods what they thought were 'the principles of sound forestry' in the 1950s. Clear and narrowly-defined objectives will soon go out of fashion and be superseded by fresh evidence. Varied styles of management are needed, even if some are less fashionable than others.

Each country should specialize in the conservation of whatever is best represented in it. In Britain this means (among other things) coppice-woods, old trees, heath and moorland. It would be splendid if there were real wildwood to conserve, but history has assigned this responsibility to others. Britain should not be ashamed of doing nothing to many woods, but should not put all conservation effort into trying to reconstruct the might-have-been wildwood. Scotland should be Scotland, and not try to turn into a second Norway.

Counter-indications to coppicing

Coppicing is no longer the automatic choice for a new woodland reserve. Priorities need to be set. Continuing existing coppicing is a top priority: resuming long-abandoned coppicing is no longer as important as it was in the 1970s. Doing nothing is a good second-best option for ancient woodland. (A belief used to be current that coppice stools will not sprout if they were last felled more than 40 years ago, but many counter-examples disprove this.)

Deer are an obvious counter-indication to resumed coppicing. Where coppicing is long-established it should be continued, even if this means taking drastic action to prevent deer from gaining a hold. However, non-intervention makes more sense for woods that have already gone some way down that road. There is no purpose in re-coppicing if deer will kill the stools.

I commend two reserves of the Royal Society for the Protection of Birds west of Ipswich. Wolve's Wood has been a reserve for some thirty years: a splendid wet coppice-wood, much appreciated by the public and (perhaps for that reason) not much appreciated by deer. Across a busy road is Ramsey Wood, a recent acquisition, overrun with deer but for half a century little visited by people. The intention is that Ramsey shall remain a secretive place of non-intervention. Woodland conservation needs to have this diversity of treatments, and to record their effects.

Deconiferization: Back from the Dead

In the Locust Years I used to deplore the one-third or so of ancient woodland that had been replaced by plantations. Like most ecologists, I accepted the foresters' assurances that they had killed off the original woodland, and wrote off some 40% (by area) of ancient woods as lost. Twenty years on, what has become of them? Replanted ancient woods are now in one of three states (Fig. 33.10).

(A) Planted trees have fared well and few or none of the native trees survive (see also Fig. 25.36). This is the fate, for example, of some of the coppices of the compartmented Black-moor Forest or Cranborne Chase, Dorset. It is the most likely outcome on reasonably well-drained sites, on acid soils, where the previous underwood was oak, or where the planted trees were Corsican Pine or oak.

(B) Planted trees have fared badly and the native trees have recovered. This tends to happen on wet, flat, and clayey sites, where beech or *Thuja* were planted, or where the native tree is lime, which resists 2,4,5-T poison. Examples are Shrawley Wood and much of Tiddesley Wood, Worcestershire.

(C) Native trees have died, planted trees have died, and the site has been taken over by self-sown ash, sallow, or birch. This can be the fate of replanted ash-maple-hazel woods, like Reydon Wood (near Southwold), Suffolk.

In the 1980s I gave several field study courses for Forestry Commission personnel. The question was emerging of what was to happen to ancient woods that had been replanted unsuccessfully. In 1989 we were discussing the fate of the north-eastern two-thirds of Chalkney Wood, replanted in the 1950s with a variety of trees, mainly conifers. This was a wood in State B, an outlying property of the Commission that had fallen into neglect. Determined attempts had been made to kill the native trees, especially by assaulting them with a *jimjam* (a sort of poisoned axe). Some of the planted trees had soon died; others had grown for a time but were losing ground to the inroads of dry summers and the reurgence of native trees. Many of them were still saleable, provided one had the skill to find markets.[32]

The whole wood was a Site of Scientific Interest: at one stage I had written to the Nature Conservancy

32 The art of *higgling*, according to Simon Leatherdale, an expert at it.

Fig. 33.10 (a–c) Replanted woods.

(a) State A. Plantation successful; original trees and ground vegetation gone; very little remains (except woodbanks) to show that this was once an ancient wood. Borley Wood, Linton, Cambridgeshire. October 1999

(b) State B. Some of the planted trees are still alive, but they will never achieve their purpose, and are losing ground to the recovery of the original trees. Potton Wood, Bedfordshire. November 1990

(c) State C. The original trees have died, and most of the planted trees have perished too. A new generation of wild trees has taken over the site. Reydon-by-Southwold Wood, Suffolk. September 1988

Council to support a plea by the Commission not to de-schedule their part of the wood. (I argued, successfully, that the Commission's attempts to destroy its scientific interest had failed.) I now took the view that replanting had done all the damage it was likely to do, and there was no particular hurry to reverse it: the conifers should be removed as opportunities for sale appeared.

Opportunities did appear, and twelve years on the conifers have all gone except for part of a block of Corsican Pine, the most successful species. Most of the ground vegetation has come back, especially the buried-seed plants. In most parts enough of the original trees survived to form a canopy. Many of the limes bear the characteristic 'needle's-eye' scars of jimjam attack (Fig. 33.11). Although hornbeam is less resistant to poison, surprisingly many have emerged from the wreckage of the plantations.

Chalkney is once again a magnificent limewood, something of a show-place of Forest Enterprise in its new role of protector of woodland. Both parts of the wood are public places, and I detect some friendly

Fig. 33.11 (a–b) The unreplanting of the Forestry Commission part of Chalkney Wood.

(a) Once again a beautiful limewood. August 1997

(b) Needle's-eye lime-tree, recovered from jimjam attack. April 1994

'I'm the man that tried to poison the lime in Shrawley Wood. We sprayed it with gallons and gallons of 2, 4, S–T: we couldn't kill the b—— stuff.' *Anon., 1999*

rivalry between the foresters and Essex County Council.

Chalkney was relatively easy, with its high proportion of lime and many surviving trees. Replanting had done little permanent damage. Felling the conifers awoke buried-seed and other plants very like the coppicing plants in the County Council part of the wood (Table 26.2): there is, however, an indication that coniferization somewhat increased the acidity.

De-coniferization of ancient woods is now widely practised by the Forestry Commission, applying among others to most of its plantations in the east Midlands. As Simon Leatherdale has shown, it works with woods in a distinctly worse state (in terms of surviving native trees) than Chalkney. It is not just the ethos of a new generation of foresters; it is also an economic response, cutting their losses in the face of falling world prices for this kind of timber. As I write, Jonathan Spencer has published a survey report on the extent of surviving ancient woodland on the Commission's estate in England. Out of some 35,000 ha of woods and plantations on ancient woodland sites, some 12% were more than half composed of native (rather than planted) trees and 18% were between one-fifth and one-half of native trees.[33] These correspond roughly to States B plus C above.

Some years ago I was criticized for supporting the argument that most ancient woods that were Sites of Special Scientific Interest should be de-coniferized. My critic held that successful plantations ought not to be sacrificed to conservation interests. (I cannot say whether he would still hold this now that the economics have changed.) My reply was that woods normally remained SSSIs precisely because they had not succeeded as plantations. De-coniferizing woods in State A should normally be the third priority, after the methods have been tested on B and C.

Ancient Trees

In the original *Ancient Woodland* (pp. 199ff, 301ff) I pointed out that ancient trees are rarely found in ancient woodland (except in the form of coppice stools or as boundary pollards), but in sites with a wood-pasture or farmland history. The great majority are pollards. Ancient trees are not only objects of beauty, wonder, and delight; they are historical monuments and witnesses to the past activities of plants, animals, and people; and they are the specific habitat of a large proportion of the animals and plants that depend on trees.

33 Spencer, J. (2002). *Ancient Woodland on the Forestry Commission Estate in England.* Forest Enterprise.

The English have loved them at least since the time of Shakespeare, but they became unfashionable, especially among foresters, in the 1920s. They were referred to in anthropomorphic terms like 'senile' and 'geriatric' by writers who had lost their respect for their human elders and imagined that trees behaved in a similar way. Twenty years ago the researches of Francis Rose and Keith Alexander had brought ancient trees to the attention of specialists on lichens and invertebrates, but they were not particularly well known to a wider public.

A change came in 1991, when a meeting was called by the Corporation of London, which is responsible for many ancient trees at Burnham Beeches and Epping Forest. Several hundred people came and started the Veteran Trees Initiative. English Nature has made 'veteran trees' one of its main objectives. Among the many publications are *Pollard and Veteran Tree Management*, the report of the 1991 meeting; *Veteran Trees: a guide to good management*; and *Moccas: an English deer park*, a book on a site which has been famous for ancient trees for more than a century. Studies include not only well-known trees such as ancient churchyard yews and non-churchyard yews, but have sought out less familiar kinds, such as the ancient pollard hawthorns of Hatfield and Savernake Forests (Plate 13, pp. xxxiv).

Because foresters disapproved of ancient trees and would not study them, there was little scientific basis for understanding how they function. Recently, more has been discovered about damage limitation mechanisms, and the function of the decay fungi on which so much of their interest depends. Much more is known, especially from experiments at Hatfield Forest and Burnham Beeches, about whether and how to re-pollard. Re-pollarding is more likely to be successful if the tree is an individual that develops epicormic twigs, and if some of the original leafage is left on.

Ancient trees of the future need to be provided for – especially the critical stage when a middle-aged tree starts to be called 'decrepit' or 'unsafe' and is liable to be removed before it has a chance to become ancient. A notable start was made in Hatfield Forest in the 1990s when the National Trust started new pollards. Pollarding not only prolongs the life of a tree but makes it unsuitable for timber, and thus reminds a future generation not to cut it down.

Estate Forestry

Conferences on woodland management tend to be dominated by a particular kind of big or middle-sized estate, putting forward a compromise between modern forestry, amenity, and nature conservation. Often their owners are enthusiastic and claim to have found the key to the future maintenance of woodland. (I say 'owners', but some land agents are trained in this philosophy too.) What they actually do is determined by the forestry aspects, growing timber (rather than other tree products), and especially what is called 'quality timber', meaning the sort that is now fashionable and commands fancy prices. They are not wholly reliant on tree-planting; they are interested in natural regeneration and in selection systems, continuous cover, and other forms of Continental (especially French) modern forestry. They boast of their success in combining timber production with amenity and nature conservation. To understand the philosophy one should read *Woodland Heritage Journal*, which puts the arguments for what I shall call 'estate forestry'. A learned account has been written of the effects on wildlife of what amounts to this form of modern forestry.[34]

As far as the records reveal, the growth of modern forestry before World War I was mainly in the hands of big or middle-sized landowners. They varied widely in what they tried to do, with what degree of perseverance, how far their activities affected existing woods, and what the outcome was. Estate forestry, in the form that I have just outlined, which has now come to the fore with the decline of official forestry, would be well worth a historical study in its own right. It can be traced to the writings of John Claudius Loudon in the 1830s, combining landscape design with land-use; it goes back through Uvedale Price in the 18th century, probably to John Evelyn and the beginnings of modern forestry. As a non-enthusiast has written of the 18th-century estate forestry of Fonthill in Wiltshire:

> Those dull woods that [William Beckford] spent so much energy in planting round the Abbey up on the hills to the west were conventional products of the Gardenesque: timber for profit with flowering shrubs for camouflage and quick growth. Predictably, J. C. Loudon admired them: they were the Victorians' park ideal, long before their time. They inspired no writing and they have left little trace beyond mere commonplace forestry plantations.[35]

This branch of modern forestry, however, is a welcome contrast to what was the dominant branch for most of the 20th century. An emphasis on quality is better than the fast growth and early harvesting that used to obsess official foresters. 'Estate forestry' has many achievements, especially when starting with non-woodland sites. For example the Coke family of Norfolk created Weasenham Woods (north of Swaffham), the plantation in England probably most acclaimed among dendrologists. This did not encroach on ancient woodland, and although one regrets that Weasenham Heath no longer exists, it would almost certainly have been destroyed for arable land had the tree-planters not got there first.

34 Harris, E., and Harris J. (1991). *Wildlife Conservation in Managed Woodlands and Forests*. Blackwell, Oxford.
35 Mowl, T. (2002). Inside Beckford's landscape of the mind. *Country Life*, Feb. 7, 60–3.

'Estate forestry' (here I try to summarize a very varied set of practices) is often a labour of love. It tends to be linked with farming and other rural activities. Owners often see it as part of their hereditary duty of maintaining a historic estate through the booms and busts of the world outside; they find good uses for the income. Moreover, estate foresters often inherit a situation and an ethos which they did not themselves create, and sometimes have to make the best of a less-than-ideal position. This is why I shall now depart from my usual practice of identifying specific sites. It would be invidious to hold individual owners responsible for their grandfathers' activities.

Estate foresters tend to be proud of their achievements in the direction of amenity and ecology. Modern forestry inevitably conflicts with amenity, because trees develop timber value early in life, whereas amenity value comes with age: foresters make their living by felling trees before they develop individual character. But (at its best) the practice of estate forestry gets away from the tradition of growing thousands of identical trees and felling them all at once. Some conifers at least are allowed to grow to an impressive size, if not to a respectable age. Estate plantations can be popular places; many of the Forestry Commission's more visited sites are those that approximate to the estate forestry tradition or that inherit the estate forestry of previous owners.

Estate forestry claims to preserve, indeed enhance, the ecology of a site. These claims are usually generalized, and sometimes startlingly misinformed, even when they appear in print:

> . . . the quality of the outputted timber should be the central core of all management systems. We have long held the belief that blue tits and bumble bees live just as happily in a tree of excellent form, as they do in a 'twister'.

However, estate plantations are at least more favourable to many forms of wildlife than even-aged plantations. They tend to be less densely and evenly shading. In theory, estate forestry should work against homogenization, as different estates adopt different ideas.

The economics of growing 'quality' timber are not as straightforward as its enthusiasts suppose. Like the official forestry of the 1950s, it speculates on future prices. It is assumed that trees matching the high-quality trees being sold today will fetch similar prices one generation into the future. There are various reasons why this may not be so.

(1) Definitions of quality change. A high-quality oak now – to be used for veneer or other decorative purposes – is straight-grained, knot-free, and rather fast-grown. Our successors (like the Victorians) may take a dislike to it as bland and lacking the proper character of oak. The wheel of fashion will not be forever stuck in the year 2003.

(2) If everybody grows 'quality' timber it ceases to be high-quality, becomes ordinary, and sells at the price of ordinary timber.

(3) As with ordinary timber, other countries play this game on a much larger scale. 'Quality' timber is a new product in which England has never specialized before. In the middle ages high-quality oak came from the Baltic. (It was, of course, different from high-quality oak today, p. 461f). The Baltic countries, having economies of scale and probably cheaper labour, could produce it cheaply, so that even with the cost of medieval transport it was not expensive. Even in the 1920s oak for making barrels came from Russia.[36] The high-quality oaks now being grown will be sold at prices determined by competition with France and America, which have greater experience and work on a larger scale. Anyone who planted cherry in the 1970s, in the hope that it would still be a costly furniture timber in the 2010s, must look apprehensively at the Alleghany National Forest (p. 516), one of the world's biggest concentrations of cherry.

(4) Britain is at a particular disadvantage for growing high-quality timber because of grey squirrels. This special purpose is frustrated by even slight squirrel damage to oak, ash, and beech. Competing countries do not have this problem, and it is not a matter for international research: grey squirrels are absent from Europe (or were until recently), and somehow they behave themselves in America. Hence the impotent rage which is the response of estate foresters in Britain.

Growing trees for specific purposes is the game of the moving goalposts. Is not the countryside full of trees that were planted to provide the battleships and pit-props and matches of the 1990s?

Estate forestry and ancient woods

Estate forestry is mainly concerned with plantations, not woods, and it is a matter of chance whether they are on the sites of ancient woods or not. As with Commission-type forestry, its impact on an ancient wood depends on the degree of perseverance with which it is pursued. Ancient woods on estates which fared badly in the twentieth century are often not very different from other surviving ancient woods, but tend to have a group of features, relics of an 'estate management' phase in their history. These often include a scatter of conifers (now often dead), especially *Abies grandis* whose towering, ragged tops make a distinctive skyline; abundance of birches, successors to other planted trees; snowberry, cherry-laurel, box, and

36 Fitzrandolph & Hay (original bibliography ref. 57), pp. 42, 46.

Fig. 33.12 Gamekeeper's gibbet, Dorset. May 1998

other 'gamekeepers' plants' introduced as shelter and food for pheasants; oaks with straight trunks and a small but constant scatter of epicormic shoots, the Victorian ideal of a high-quality tree; and one or two yews, horsechestnuts, or rhododendrons at eye-eatching points.

However, where an ancient wood has been for several generations on a well-run estate it can be a great disappointment. Estate foresters, for all their interest in amenity and *nature* conservation, seldom display a interest in the characteristics of ancient woodland, least of all in the individual character of woods and how this should affect management. For many of them an ancient wood is merely another piece of land to do what they fancy with.

Well-run estate forestry very effectively drains out the meaning of an ancient wood – even, in one instance which I shall not name, where it has been owned by a distinguished family of archaeologists. Old and distinctive trees and coppice stools disappear; compartment boundaries (should the site once have been a Forest) vanish from the map. What replaces them are the usual straight close-set trees of 20th-century forestry – uneven-aged and sometimes of magnificent size, but they could be anywhere. The visitor may be reminded that the site is Barchester Forest, but there is nothing to show for it: apart, perhaps, from compartment banks wandering forgotten through the plantations, it is difficult to find any feature older than one generation of timber trees.

Even if the third Duke of Barset spared parts of the site, later owners and agents encroach on these so that ultimately little can be expected to survive. Some of the ground vegetation persists under this treatment; how much will never be known, for there was not the pre-treatment survey, *à la* Gamlingay (p. 362f), to record what was there before. Without hollow trees, wild-type oaks and old coppice stools much of the habitat of ancient woodland has been lost. The habitat value of oak is not in foresters' oaks but in crooked oaks, corkscrew oaks, and oaks with holes. Anyone doubting this should go to the west country and observe the ferns and epiphytes that grow specifically on big horizontal branches of oak (the nearest thing in temperate countries to the massive 'fern-gardens' that grow high on trees in tropical rain-forests).

I wish good luck to the practitioners of estate forestry. They are going to need it: they need to be cultivating markets for their produce. I do not necessarily call for Barchester Forest to be restored to what it was before the third Duke took it in hand: it is now a feature in its own right, and too little is known about the original to be the basis of a restoration. There is something to be said (with reservations about the economics) for making estate forestry the model for new plantations on non-woodland sites, including National Forests, or the sites of former plantations. However, I am not persuaded that the general future of woodland lies down this road. High-quality timber can easily become an obsession, as fast growth was in the 1960s. The more there is of it, the less valuable it becomes. No more ancient woodland should be eroded in the pursuit of an ideal whose fruition is not assured.

Gamekeeping

In the past, the 'preservation' of pheasants generally favoured the conservation of woods. It saw many woods through the Locust Years when every wood had to look as if it was doing something 'useful'. Game-keepers took their toll of carnivores such as ravens, buzzards, and polecats; but the stoats and weasels, and latterly grey squirrels, that were their chief prey were well able to withstand such predation, and their gibbeted bodies, swinging and sun-drying like pirates', developed a curious ecosystem which delighted entomologists (Fig. 33.12). Above all, gamekeepers promoted coppicing to provide food and shelter. Pheasants prefer hazel at three years' growth and hornbeam at six.[37]

Gamekeepers also like open areas within woods as

37 C. E. Bealey & P. A. Robertson 'Coppice management for pheasants' Buckley (supplementary bibliography), 192–210.

providing fields of fire and making it easier to persuade birds to fly towards the guns. (There is an obvious evolutionary selection pressure in favour of birds programmed not to fly.) Up to a point this too is a gain to conservation: it is precisely the plants of permanent open areas in woodland that have declined.

Unfortunately, a motorized fashion for 'cutting back the undergrowth' has begun to spread to the game-keeping world. Every year a tractor with mower or swipe is sent to rampage over felled areas, chopping off the regrowth except for a scatter of remaining or planted trees. The results are disastrous to the trees and in the long term to the survival of the wood. Nor are they any help to the flora of permanent open areas, for the practice encourages the spread of tussock species like *Carex pendula* and *Deschampsia caespitosa* which crowd out everything else. Areas so treated are peculiarly attractive to deer. I do not know whether this is a common practice, but it is a misuse of ancient woodland and should be discouraged.

Conservation and the Sizes of Woods

The examples discussed in Chapters 25 and 30 do not support the theory that big woods are more worth conserving, or easier to conserve. In the recent past, big woods have attracted modern foresters: most woods of more than 100 acres present problems of rehabilitation. In regard to browsing, it is not the middle-sized woods – Buff Wood, Overhall Grove – that are in trouble but the big ones. Hardwick Wood is only 40 acres (one-third of which is recent woodland) and an awkward shape: yet it is one of the few woods where sensitive plants like oxlip and elms have increased since I have known it. The interior of a large (100-acre) wood such as Hayley or Gamlingay is, if anything, in a worse state than the edges. Monks' Wood, over three times the size of Hayley, is a muntjac slum with the most severe of all browsing damage. Indeed in this group of woods there is a negative correlation between the size of the wood and either the damage done by deer or the effort put into preventing damage (Table 33.1). I will not press this point, although it is statistically significant, but it is another corrective to the doctrine that bigger woods are necesssarily better. Even expanding a woodland reserve to the size of an entire English county would not alleviate the deer problem, as Alleghany National Forest illustrates.

Table 33.1 Woods of various sizes in relation to deer damage

Name	Size, acres	Deer	Deer control	Degree of damage
Knapwell	11	muntjac?	none?	nil?
Hardwick	40	muntjac	none	+
Buff	40	muntjac	weak, fencing	++
Overhall	42	muntjac	none	+
Madingley	45	muntjac	none	+
Hayley	120	fallow, muntjac	partial, fencing	++++
Gamlingay	123	muntjac	weak, fencing	+++
Bradfield	150	roe	fencing, shooting	++
Monks'	377	muntjac	partial fencing, shooting	+++++
Alleghany National Forest	513,000	white-tailed	much shooting	++++

Woodland and Conservation in General

Conservation is, or should be, a continuum of many things, from the conservation of the Amazon rain-forests to the conservation of Benjamin Britten's manuscripts in the Fitzwilliam Museum, Cambridge. The conservation of timber-framed buildings (including their wattle-and-daub) has an obvious bearing on woodland history, as does that of waterlogged peat and the structures embedded in it. But conservationists in different fields, although they have much to learn from each other's methods, have a tradition of not talking to each other, even when warring against the same foe. (The Locust Years were quite as destructive to archaeology as to ecology.)

In 1994 I visited Welshbury, a splendid hillfort situated in an ancient limewood, one of the ring of limewoods that surrounds the Forest of Dean. Forest Enterprise had been converting the limes from their traditional state of coppice to timber trees. My companions and I agreed that this was not an ideal treatment either for the wood or the hillfort: the archaeology would be at risk both from uprooting of the big trees in storms and from machinery used when they were eventually harvested. However, it was claimed that (the wood being very prominent) the public would not tolerate the changes in appearance brought about by

Fig. 33.13 Iron Age earthworks, in limewood, Welshbury, Gloucestershire. October 1994

renewed coppicing. I was reminded that the archaeological authorities might have recommended that the trees be destroyed, as they did in the 1950s to the wood on Llanmelin hillfort not far away. I mused on what might then have happened if the limes had withstood attempts to destroy them, as in Chalkney Wood.

Archaeologists in Britain traditionally dislike trees, believing that trees promote erosion and their roots disrupt buried features. This can be a useful corrective to the doctrine, common in other countries, that trees – and not other vegetation – protect against erosion. However, the Welshbury limewood, while coppiced, has preserved the visible remains unusually well (Fig. 33.13). Any damage by its roots will have been completed long ago. Moreover, the trees are an integral part of the story of the hillfort. Some of the limes are huge clonal patches which sprout through the ramparts in a way which suggests that the limes were already there when the fort was built.

Invasion of grassland or heathland earthworks by trees damages the archaeology and the ecology, and both kinds of conservationist should oppose it. However, long-established trees, like the elms of Buff Wood and Overhall Grove, are part of the archaeology. At Llanmelin nobody can ever find out what the relation was between the trees and the hillfort, because archaeologists destroyed half the story.

In 1990 the Institute of Field Archaeologists held a conference on relationships between the conservation of archaeological remains (visible and hidden), ecology, and the landscape generally. I recommend its proceedings, although they deal less with practicalities than with philosophy (e.g. what is meant by 'landscape') and bureaucracy (laws, schedules, plans).[38] It is a pity that it has not had more effect.

Research

> There are plenty of intellectual tasks to be undertaken which are twenty years in the working and if a man or a woman cannot look forward with confidence to that kind of time-span, it will be impossible to undertake such tasks.
>
> *Editorial,* Cambridge Review, *March 1986*

For the foreseeable future, ancient woods in England are more threatened by deer than by people. The future of ecology is less assured. Political 'ecology' has become a force at which Prime Ministers shudder a little. Ecology as a science has fared less well, especially at Cambridge which for so long was its capital. The world contains many more professors of ecology than thirty years ago; the number of ecological journals has increased, as well as the output of old-established journals like the *Journal of Ecology*. But the expertise is now thinly spread over the whole world; not much of it is on woodland; and much of it has been diverted to theory, or to the links between ecology and fashionable sciences such as evolution or microbiology.

This is mainly for anthropological reasons. Ecology has been forced into a mould determined by other sciences, dragged into a world of full-time research, careers, expensive apparatus, short-term experiments, grant applications, research assessments, and Ph.Ds to be completed within three years, none of which is particularly suited to the study of processes taking place over a longer period. A scientist must investigate a specific question, and is now expected to know the approximate answer before seeking a research grant. This encourages reductionism: attempts to explain the whole in terms of only one or two of its parts: for example to treat an ancient wood as if it were no more

38 Macinnes, L. & Wickham-Jones, C. R. (1992). *All Natural Things: archaeology and the green debate*. Oxbow Monograph 21, Oxford.

than a collection of woodland plants (much as if a picture were to be explained in terms of the chemical nature of its pigments). In a society obsessed with spending money it becomes a disgrace, not a virtue, to prolong one's Ph.D. studies in order to gather more data. Anything long-term, or cheap, or low-technology, or unexpected, or difficult to express in numbers gets neglected.

Events like Great Storms need to be studied by people who are able to abandon whatever else they are doing, go out and discover what happened before the evidence disappears, and spend a few days each year over the next twenty years recording the effects. Without such studies scientists will inevitably be biased towards the sort of explanation that can be fitted into a modern research programme, and will not appreciate the importance of sudden events.

Long-term ecological studies

These studies are a philosophical as well as an anthropological anomaly. Ordinary scientists formulate questions and then design experiments and observations to answer them. Their ultimate object is to formulate a theory, which develops into a law of nature, from which the behaviour of particular instances of the natural world can be predicted in top-down fashion: for example the law of gravitation predicts, to a very high degree of precision, the movement of objects ranging in size from an apple to a galaxy, and anyone claiming exceptions will find it difficult to get them published.

The long-term ecologist cannot do this. Biological laws of nature characteristically have exceptions.[39] Attempts to find universal laws of ecology, such as the species-area theory, have not got far, and it will probably always remain a bottom-up science in which data are paramount. The questions may not emerge until long after the observations have begun. By the time a problem has been noticed and the questions formulated it is too late to re-start the observations. We have to make do with data which we in our youth, or our predecessors, gathered for some different purpose which by now, maybe, has gone out of fashion. Much of the material in these supplementary chapters was gathered either to record coppice cycles or to investigate the relation between vegetation and waterlogging. I lament the observations which I would have begun if I had known in the 1960s what were to be the ecological problems of the 1990s. But without the baselines set up by Miller Christy, Adamson, the Meyers, and Abeywickrama, working to agendas of yet longer ago, I could not identify the problems of the 1990s: there would not be enough data to distinguish temporary fluctuations from long-term trends.

Observations need to be simple and cheap: photographing from fixed points, setting up exclosure fences, recording permanently marked plots or transects, or following the fate of marked individual plants. Such observations need to continue over decades and human lifetimes without depending on grants, objectives, and people's careers. ***They should be written into the management plans of sites.*** Without them it will hardly be known even what questions to ask in woodland ecology. Comparing Gamlingay Wood in 1911 and 1991, it might have been expected that birch would have greatly increased (see Chapter 19), but who could have foreseen that meadowsweet, then the commonest plant, should have largely disappeared, although it is still common in most other woods in the area?

Research, conservation, and restoration

Universities, geared to PhDs, research grants, departmental ratings, and to following trends and fashions in research, cannot be expected to gather unglamorous data for which there is no immediate chance of publication. Conservation trusts need to be more active in long-term research, experimentation and maintaining archives, as the Cambridgeshire Trust was in the 1960s. Without such data there will be only the vaguest evidence of whether conservation is working, let alone of what to do about it.

There has never been much interest in recording the results of conservation action. Even in those fondly-remembered days when conservationists wielded their own axes and saws, it was much easier to get people to cut down trees than to persuade them to return and record the consequences. Despite all the effort put by wildlife trusts into education, their members remain strangely indifferent to what the trust actually does or whether it succeeds in its objectives.

Lack of long-term recording opens the way to attacks on ancient woodland in the guise of 'restoration'. A developer pleads to be allowed to destroy a wood on condition of creating an equivalent wood elsewhere. 'Eurotunnel Moves Ancient Wood', as an ecological journal put it. As a research experiment this might yield valuable evidence on how ancient woods work and what differentiates them from recent woods. It is not a substitute for conservation, since ancient woods contain features, such as big coppice stools, that result from a particular historical sequence that cannot be repeated. 'Restoration' raises various questions. Is the wood to be established on the new site intended as a copy of the wood destroyed on the old site, or a reconstruction of the wood that might have existed on the new site had it remained as woodland? Can a development company promise to remain in existence long enough to follow

39 For example white clover arose by polyploidization, and is an exception to the law of evolution.

the project through the decades or centuries needed to find out whether it has worked? Maybe such observations are properly provided for and published in the United States and the Netherlands, where restoration ecology is a big industry. In this country restorations have seldom been followed for more than ten years, though even that is often enough to show that they have failed.

The twentieth century was the great age of tree-planting, and not only by the Forestry Commission. Almost every conservation body committed itself to planting trees, occasionally in surprisingly unsuitable places. The public is very generous in subscribing for 'new woodland': but will the result really be like the pretty bluebell woods shown on the appeal leaflets? I doubt it, but nobody knows. Where are the follow-up studies? What happened to the millions of trees planted in the 'Plant a Tree in '73' campaign? What studies are there of the development of similar plantations from previous centuries?

People have been persuaded to plant tens of millions of trees without knowing whether those trees will replicate the values – ecological, social, and historic – attached to existing wild trees and woods. In one respect, ancient pollards, the answer is definitely No. Ancient trees are the result of a particular combination of genetics and management history which needs to be studied and deliberately copied. The best way to secure the ancient trees of the future is not to cut down the elderly trees of today.

Ecological archives

Here I make a plea for a proper archive of ecological records. Scientists tend to believe that the original data can be thrown away when the research is published, or at least when the investigator dies. This may be so in fields such as physics or microbiology, where circumstances do not change and observations can readily be repeated, but not in sciences where observations are time-dependent. One cannot go back to Hayley Wood before deer arrived, or to the week after the Great Storm, or to the behaviour of oak in the nineteenth century.

As most pages in this book show, data can become significant long after the original purpose of collecting them has been forgotten. Ecologists seldom publish all their data, but only those that seemed at the time to be relevant to the purpose of the publication: editors and referees would not have it otherwise. Indeed, as time passes and theories harden into laws of nature, it becomes more difficult to publish evidence that seems not to fit the theory.

But the data can easily be of more lasting value than the theory derived from them. When repeating the Gamlingay observations, it would have been far better to have had Adamson's field notes than having to make do with his published version. (He did not confine his observations to the one-third of the wood that he mapped.) What would I give for a sight of the notebooks and photographs of Sir Arthur Tansley? Ecological records are part of the archives of local history, and should be treated with the respect that is given to tithe apportionments, churchwardens' accounts, and court rolls.

Records, especially the notebooks and photographs of deceased ecologists, need to be properly housed and catalogued like any other archives. (Electronic 'storage' is not a solution: many archives from the 1980s are already unreadable, because either the discs or tapes have decayed or the machines to read them are obsolete.)

I invite readers to let me know of other material bearing on the past vegetation of particular woods, especially maps and photographs of known locations. I urge any reader who comes across any observations or photographs more than thirty years old to repeat them from the exact spot (Fig. 25.12) and find out what has happened. The results may be surprising.

Management Plans and Reductionism

Between the two editions of this book there was an enthusiasm for management plans; conservationists devoted time and effort to drawing one up for every woodland reserve in the kingdom. Management plans have the important function of preserving continuity against changes of fashion, and against the tendency for conservationists to pursue professional careers which take them away from a site as soon as they have begun to know it. They have the lesser function of forming the basis of a *concordat* which removes the need to get English Nature's licence every time a tree is cut down. The first function often failed: management plans were drawn up according to a prearranged format which made them unreadable and seldom read; and conservationists were ordered to update them every five years, which destroyed the continuity.

Management plans were often written by outside professionals who had not the time or enthusiasm to get to know the site. This reinforces the insidious tendency to describe a site, not in terms of what makes it special, but of how it resembles other sites. Every ancient wood differs from every other ancient wood, just as every medieval church differs from every other. As these chapters have shown, even woods that appear to be similar often behave differently over time. Conservation should be about seeking out what is rare and wonderful and has meaning. Resemblances are the stuff of research, but differences are the stuff of conservation.

The *National Vegetation Classification* made matters worse by its coarse-grained but rigid categorization. An unfamiliar wood can be assigned to the category **W8** in half an hour, without taking the trouble to investigate further and define what makes it different from all the other woods which are also **W8** (indeed, without realizing that **W8** is the 'dump' category to which any wood is assigned that fails to key out to something else).

This plays into the hands of anti-conservationists. One can hardly get up at a public inquiry and swear: 'This site should not be developed because it is a good example of **W10**: *Quercus robur–Pteridium aquilinum–Rubus fruticosus* woodland'. It invites the riposte (if counsel for the developer is worth his fee) that there are thousands of **W10** woods, and one more or less does not matter.

When they are being acquired, nature reserves are usually presented to the public as being special and exceptional. Once taken into the management system, their generic features are emphasized. What the appeal leaflet called a 'unique ancient wood' appears in its management plan as an example of **W10** to be treated the same as other **W10**s. This saves a lot of trouble, but hardly does justice to the site or to the people who subscribed to 'save' it.

Where a wood has been a nature reserve or Site of Special Scientific Interest for some decades, it is instructive to go back to the original description or citation of what were thought to be its significant features. As time has marched on and knowledge has accrued, some of these seem oddly commonplace ('a fine example of an Oak-Ash wood'), but the wood usually turns out to be significant in other ways not thought of at the time: rare woodland types, earthworks, ancient trees, bryophytes, fungi, freedom from deer. I have rarely heard it said that it was a mistake to make a wood a nature reserve, even if the original reason no longer exists or is known to be fallacious.

The existence of past investigations is part of the scientific value of a site, and should be written into the management plan of a nature reserve or the citation of a Site of Special Scientific Interest. This is true whether or not the investigations seem to be going on at the moment. One of the obstacles to finding out how woods function is that research areas, even if specifically designated for long-term studies, tend to fall victim to new management practices introduced at random.

'The Rise of Conservationists and the Slow Death of Natural History'

> Botanical surveys are often done by students or relatively inexperienced workers, because field work may be considered to be a low-grade activity.
>
> *Keith Kirby, 2001*

As Peter Marren points out, since 1980 nature conservation has grown to be a middle-sized industry, spending eight- and nine-figure sums, especially public money from the Heritage Lottery and Landfill (that is, Rubbish) Tax. The original enthusiasm, clear objectives ('save Hayley Wood' in 1962), and successes against what seemed to be heavy odds, achieved by an alliance of amateurs and professional ecologists, have given way to an ethos of bland triumphalism against no well-defined enemy. With large amounts of money to find a use for, objectives have become vague and inclusive, such as creating 'nature reserves' on random pieces of land that developers happen not to want. Amateur naturalists and professional ecologists are somewhat marginalized, except for their subscriptions. The staff are professional conservationists with degrees in environmental management, which is not the same as ecological science.

It is easy to raise funds for the start of a specific project, or to devise a project on which to spend the landfillers' bounty. It is less easy to finance the 'core activities' of a trust: the day-to-day footsoldiering work in field and office, the continuing of projects started long ago. Conservationists are not paid enough to make them stay many years in one place and accumulate experience. Some of them still do so for love of place or of knowledge – if any read these words I hope they will recognize themselves – but this is not the way to a successful career in conservation. Enthusiasm, delight in discovery, and wonder at the unexpected seldom survive in a world in which bureaucracy, procedures, plans, guidelines, safety regulations (in contrast to practical safety), fund-raising, and committees eat up the hours. Getting to know sites, marking out work, getting contractors to finish on time, and mending fences get pushed down the pile, and recording the results comes right at the bottom. As Matt Ridley points out, 'Most conservationists can and do talk for hours to each other without mentioning an animal or plant'. I too have seen them do it many times.

Woodland conservation is difficult. It involves thousands of unique sites, which at best can be dealt with only at a *National Vegetation Classification* level. But conservation stands or falls by attention to detail. I have known a scheme, admirable in itself, melt into disaster because the contractor was allowed to postpone it until the ground had become too wet. (As often, the pretext given was 'foot-and-mouth restrictions', even though the site was miles from any livestock and fifty miles from any disease.)

If conservation is an industry, it is becoming overextended, and one looks forward with apprehension to what will happen when, like all industries, it comes to a recession. Wildlife trusts have an agenda which commits them to remaining in existence for hundreds of years, like Cambridge colleges; but they too often regard themselves as upstart companies, and think they are doing excessively well if they have as much as one year's reserve funds in hand.

As far as I dare predict, woodland is likely to increase in quantity but get worse in quality. New community forests will appear, designed on standard 'havens for wildlife' principles, as though wildlife were some single entity that would come when called and do what its masters want and yet remain wildlife. No doubt they will be appreciated and enjoyed by those who never knew the delights of the real thing. Meanwhile the ancient woods will remain on the map. A very few will be strenuously protected. More may escape through isolation or small size. The rest will have the guts eaten out of them by deer or sheep.

Fig. 33.14 A 1960s failure of conservation: grubbed-out ancient wood which by 1985 had become a thistle-field. The remaining part of the wood is now a National Nature Reserve.

Fig. 33.15 The shape of things to come? Ancient wood with browse-line, devoured by Japanese deer. Povington Wood, Dorset. September 1999

Bibliography and References to 1980 Edition

The arrangement of these references is intended (*i*) to give the reader a list – necessarily incomplete – of what has been written about ancient woods and their workings, separated from the much larger mass of publications on subjects peripheral to this theme; (*ii*) to identify the primary historical documentation on which the book is based. The references are thus classified into three lists:

I. Books and articles on the history, prehistory, ecology, physiology, and uses of native woodland and wood-pasture (references 0 to 173).
II. Primary historical documents, whether published or MS, and books and articles used as historical documents (references 200 to 519).
III. Other publications used in this book; these include works on trees, general ecology, plant pathology, modern forestry, pollen analysis, and legal history which are not specially concerned with woodland (references 600 to 919).

The boundaries between these categories are inevitably somewhat ill-defined but doubtful instances have been cross-referenced.

I. Bibliography and Author Index on Ancient Woodland and Wood-pasture

0 Abeywickrama, B. A. (1949). *A study of the variations in the field layer vegetation of two Cambridgeshire woods.* Ph.D. thesis, Cambridge. 77–8, 92

Adam, H. *see* 16.

1 Adamson, R. S. (1912). An ecological study of a Cambridgeshire woodland. *J. Linn. Soc. Bot.*, **40**, 339–87, Pl. 12–17. 42, 80, 92

2 Adamson, R. S. (1932). Notes on the natural regeneration of woodland in Essex. *J. Ecol.*, **20**, 152–6. 226

3 Albion, R. G. (1926). *Forests and Sea Power. The Timber Problem of the Royal Navy 1652–1862.* Harvard. 154

4 Andersen, S. T. (1970). *The Relative Pollen Productiviy and Pollen Representation of North European Trees, and Correction Factors for Tree Pollen Spectra.* Danmarks Geologiske Undersøgelse, København. 101, 204

5 Anderson, M. C. (1964). Studies of the woodland light climate. I. The photographic computation of light conditions. *J. Ecol.*, **52**, 27–41. 77–8

6 Anderson, M. C. (1964). Studies of the woodland light climate. II. Seasonal variation in the light climate. *J. Ecol.*, **52**, 643–63. 77–8

7 Anderson, M. L. (1954). The ecological status of Wistman's Wood, Devonshire. *Trans. bot. Soc. Edin.*, **36**, 195–206. 299

Anderson, M. L. *see also* 604–5.

Aubrey, J. *see* 200. 241, 321

Babington, C. C. *see* 200a. 56

8 Baker, C. A., Moxey, P. A. and Oxford, P. M. (1978). Woodland continuity and change in Epping Forest. *Fld Stud.*, **4**, 645–69. 101, 221, 242, 321

9 Barrington, D. (1769). A Letter . . . on the Trees which are supposed to be indigenous in *Great Britain. Phil. Trans. roy. Soc. Lond.*, **59**, 23–38. 329–30

Beda *see* 202. 133

10 Beevor, H. E. (1924). Norfolk woodlands, from the evidence of contemporary chronicles. *Trans. Norf. Norw. Nat. Soc.*, **11** 488–508. 147

11 Birks, H. H. (1972). A radiocarbon-dated pollen diagram from Loch Maree, Ross and Cromarty. *New Phytol.*, **71**, 731–54. 99, 313

12 Birks, H. J. B., Deacon, J. and Peglar, S. (1975). Pollen maps for the British Isles 5,000 years ago. *Proc. roy. Soc. Lond.*, **B189**, 87–105. 99, 203, 305, 312

Birks, H. J. B. *see also* 614 *and pp.* 28, 56, 237, 351.

13 Bouchon, J., Faille, A., Lemée, G., Robin, A.-M. and Schmitt, A. (1973). *Notice sur les cartes des sols, du peuplement forestier et des groupements végétaux de la réserve biologique de la Tillaie en forêt de Fontainebleau.* Orsay. 219

Boulton, H. E. *see* 214.

14 Bradshaw, A. D. (1953). Human influence on hybridization in *Crataegus. The Changing Flora of Britain* (ed. J. E. Lousley) 181–3. Bot. Soc. Br. Isl., London. 352

15 Bradshaw, R. (1978). *Modern pollen representation factors and recent woodland history in S.E. England.* Ph.D. thesis, Cambridge. 101

Brandon, P. *see* 616. 124–5

16 Brenchley, W. E. and Adam, H. (1915). Recolonisation of cultivated land allowed to revert to natural conditions. *J. Ecol.*, **3**, 193–210. 7, 95

Brown, T. *see* 216a. 263

17 Bunce, R. G. H. (1969). [Classification of British woodlands.] *Merlewood Research Station Report 1967–69*, 12–15. 23

17a Bunce, R. G. H. and Jeffers, J. N. (eds) (1977). *Native Pinewoods of Scotland.* Institute of Terrestrial Ecology. 65

Carlisle, A. *see* 148, 626, 807 *and* p. 299.

18 Chalmers-Hunt, J. (1969). Insect conservation in mixed woodland and ancient parkland. *Entomologist's Rec. J. Var.*, **81**, 156–63. 202, 303

Chapman, J. and André, P. *see* 250. Fig. 12.9, 234

Chapman, T. A. *see* 251. 263

19 Christy, M. (1897). *Primula elatior* in Britain: its distribution, hybrids, and allies. *J. Linn. Soc. Bot.*, **33**, 172–201. 51, 93–4

20 Christy, M. (1922; 1924). *Primula elatior* Jacquin: its distribution in Britain. *J. Ecol.*, **10**, 200–10; **12**, 314–16. 93–4

21 Christy, M. (1924). The hornbeam (*Carpinus betulus* L.) in Britain. *J. Ecol.*, **12**, 39–94. 221, 223, 231

22 Clarkson, L. A. (1974). The English bark trade 1660–1830. *Agric. Hist. Rev.*, **22**, 136–52. 154, 285

23 Cleere, H. (1974). The Roman iron industry of the Weald and its connexions with the *Classis Britannica*. *Archaeol. J.*, **131**, 170–99. 108–9

24 Cleere, H. (1976). Some operating parameters for Roman ironworks. *Bull. Inst. Archaeol.*, **13**, 233–46. 108, 239, 319

25 Coles, J. M., Hibbert, F. A. and Orme, B. J. (1973). Prehistoric roads and tracks in Somerset: 3. The Sweet Track. *Proc. prehist. Soc.*, **39**, 256–93. 106, 239, 267

26 Coles, J. M. and Orme, B. J. (1976). The Sweet Track, Railway Site. *Somerset Levels Papers*, **2**, 34–65. 106

27 Coles, J. M. and Orme, B. J. (1976). A Neolithic hurdle from the Somerset Levels. *Antiquity*, **50**, 57–61. 106

28 Coles, J. M. and Orme, B. J. (1977). Neolithic hurdles from Walton Heath, Somerset. *Somerset Levels Papers*, **3**, 6–29. 106

29 Coles, J. M. and Orme, B. J. (1977). Rowland's hurdle trackway. *Somerset Levels Papers*, **3**, 39–51. 106

30 Coles, J. M. and Orme, B. J. (1977). Garvin's Tracks. *Somerset Levels Papers*, **3**, 73–81. 106

31 Coles, J. M. and Orme, B. J. (1978). The Abbot's Way. *Somerset Levels Papers*, **4**, 7–20. 106

32 Coles, J. M., Orme, B. J. and Hibbert, F. A. (1974). The Eclipse Track. *Somerset Levels Papers*, **1**, 20–8. 106

Coles, J. M. *see also* 634.

33 Coombe, D. E. (1957). The spectral composition of shade light in woodlands. *J. Ecol.*, **45**, 823–30. 79

34 Coombe, D. E. (1966). The seasonal light climate and plant growth in a Cambridgeshire wood. *Light as an Ecological Factor* (eds R. Bainbridge, G. C. Evans and O. Rackham) 148–66. Blackwell, Oxford. 77

Coombe, D. E. *see also* 54, 635–6 *and* pp. 35, 84

35 Couchman, G. (1975). Norsey Wood, Billericay. Archaeological evidence presented at a Public Inquiry. 335

36 Cox, J. C. (1905). *The Royal Forests of England*. London. 330

37 Cox, J. C. (1907). *Forestry. Victoria County History – Berks*, **2**, 341–53. 3, 303

38 Cox, J. C. (1907). Forestry. *Victoria County History – Oxfordshire*, **2**, 293–302. 187

39 Cox, J. C. (1907). Forestry. *Victoria County History – Yorks*, **1**, 501–23. 152, 241

40 Cox,J. C. (1908). Forestry. *Victoria County History – Kent*, **1**, 471–8. 332

41 Cox, J. C. (1911), Forestry. *Victoria County History – Middlesex*, **2**, 223–52. 223

42 Cox, J. C. and Greswell, W. H. P. (1911). Forestry. *Victoria County History – Somerset*, **2**, 547–72. 177, 180

43 Cox, J. C. and Whitworth, R. A. (1906). Forestry. *Victoria County History – Notts*, **1**, 365–81. 152, 180, 241, 316

Cross, J. R. *see* 639a.

Dalechamps, J. *see* 642. 283

Darby, H. C. *see* 643–50. 111–12

Deacon, J. *see* 12.

43a Devèze, M. (1961). *La vie de la forêt française au XVIe siècle*. S.E.V. P.E.N. 292, 303

44 Dimbleby, G. W. (1971). The Ancient and Ornamental woods of the New Forest. *Ecologist*, **1**, 16–18. 304

45 Dimbleby, G. W. and Gill, J. M. (1955). The occurrence of podzols under deciduous woodland in the New Forest. *Forestry*, **28**, 95–106. 35–6, 326, 347

Dimbleby, G. W. *see also* 657–9.

Donald, T. and Milne T. *see* 265. 306

46 Ducarel, A. C., Hasted, E. and Thorpe, J. (1772). A Letter . . . concerning Chesnut Trees. *Phil. Trans. roy. Soc. Lond.*, **61**, 136–69. 329–31

Duhamel du Monceau *see* 269. 12

47 Dumont, J.-M. (1975). Les anciens taillis à écorce de la région du Plateau des Tailles (Haute-Ardenne belge). *Colloques phytosociologiques III: la végétation des forêts caducifoliées acidiphiles*, 89–106. Cramer, Vaduz. 285

48 Dymond, T. S. (1907). Charcoal-burning. *Victoria County History – Essex*, **2**, 447–51. 306

Earl, D. E. *see* 666. 168

49 Edlin, H. L. (1973). *Woodland Crafts in Britain*, 2nd edition. David and Charles, Newton Abbot. 142, 206–7

50 Edwards, D. P. and Evans, G. C. (1975). Problems involved in the design of apparatus for measuring the spectral composition of daylight in the field. *Light as an Ecological Factor II* (eds G. C. Evans, R. Bainbridge and O. Rackham) 161–87. Blackwell, Oxford. 77

Ehrhart, J. F. *see* 668. 311

51 Ellenberg, H. (1939). Über Zusammensetzung, Standort und Stoffproduktion bodenfeuchter Eichen- und Buchen-Mischwaldgesellschaften Nordwestdeutschlands. *Jahresber. naturhist. Ges. Hannover*, **Beiheft 4**. 67

52 Ellenberg, H. and Klötzli, F. (1972). Waldgesellschaften und Waldstandorte der Schweiz. *Forstl. Versuchsw.*, **48**, 589–930. 65, 219, 280

53 Evans, G. C. (1956). An area survey method of investigating the distribution of light intensity in woodlands, with particular reference to sun-flecks. *J. Ecol.*, **44**, 391–428. 77

54 Evans, G. C. and Coombe, D. E. (1959). Hemispherical and woodland canopy photography and the light climate. *J. Ecol.*, **47**, 103–13. 77, 82

55 Evans, G. C. and Hughes, A. P. (1961). Plant growth and the aerial environment. I. Effect of artificial shading on *Impatiens parviflora*. *New Phytol.*, **60**, 150–80. 79

Evans, G. C. *see also* 50, 675.

Evelyn, J. *see* 335–6. 12, 16, 161, 223, 329–30

Fabricius, J. C. *see* 676. 263

Faille, A. *see* 13.

Fisher, J. L. *see* 337. 291

56 Fisher, W. R. (1897). *The Forest of Essex*. Butterworth, London. 321, 358

57 Fitzrandolph, H. E. and Hay, M. D. (1926). *The Rural Industries of England and Wales. I. Timber and Underwood Industries and Some Village Workshops*. Oxford. 142, 168

Fitzstephen, W. *see* 338. 123

Fletcher, J. M. *see* 680–1.

58 Flinn, M. W. (1959). Timber and the advance of technology: a reconsideration. *Ann. Sci.*, **15**, 109–20. 153

59 Ford, E. D. and Newbould, P. J. (1970). Stand structure and dry weight production through the sweet chestnut (*Castanea sativa* Mill.) coppice cycle. *J. Ecol.*, **58**, 275–96. 332

60 Ford, E. D. and Newbould, P. J. (1971). The leaf canopy of a coppiced deciduous woodland. I. Development and structure. *J. Ecol.*, **59**, 843–62. 332

61 Forestry Commission (1956). Utilization of hazel coppice. Bull. **27**. H.M.S.O., London. 218

Forestry Commission *see also* 684–6.

62 French, J. (1908). Notes on some Essex woods. *Essex Nat.*, **15**, 24–30. 244

Galpin, F. W. *see* 690. 231

Gerarde, J. *see* 340. 221, 223, 241, 266, 351, 356

Gibbs, J. N. *see* 693–700. 263

Gill, J. M. *see* 45.

Godwin, H. *see* 603, 704–14, 905.

Gonner, E. C. K. *see* 715. 132

63 Grant, R. (1959). Royal Forests. *Victoria County History – Wiltshire*, **4**, 391–457. 117, 133, 179

Greig, B. J. W. *see* 698. 263

Greswell, W. H. P. *see* 42.

Grigor, J. *see* 341.

Grundy, G. B. *see* 722–3. 111

Guérin-Méneville, M. F. E. *see* 343. 263

64 *Guide de sentiers de promenades du massif forestier de Fontainebleau* (1975), 3e édition. Société des amis de la Forêt de Fontainebleau. 303

65 Hadfield, M. (1963). Shrawley Wood. *Quart. J. For.*, **57**, 35–43. 244

Hadfield, M. *see also* 724–6.

66 Hammersley, G. (1957). The Crown woods and their exploitation in the sixteenth and seventeenth centuries. *Bull. Inst. hist. Res.*, **30**, 136–61. 185

67 Hammersley, G. (1973). The charcoal iron industry and its fuel. *Econ. Hist. Rev.*, **2nd ser. 26**, 593–613. 109, 153

Harding, P. T. *see* 102, 103.

68 Harris, M. C. (1974). When the sap was rising: the spring-goed. *Country Life* (1974), 870–1. 285

69 Hart, G. E. (1966). *Royal Forest. A History of Dean's Woods as Producers of Timber*. Clarendon Press, Oxford. 93, 135, 152–3, 180, 185, 319, 330–1, 335

Hasted, E. *see* 46.

Hay, M. D. *see* 57.

70 Heybroek, H. M. (1963). Disease and lopping for fodder as possible causes of a prehistoric decline of *Ulmus*. *Act. bot. neerl.*, **12**, 1–11. 107, 265

Hibberd, S. *see* 346. 263

Hibbert, F. A. *see* 25, 32.

71 Hickin, N. E. (1971). *The Natural History of an English Forest: the Wild Life of Wyre*. Hutchinson, London. 359

72 Hooper, M. D. (1973). History. *Monks Wood: a Nature Reserve Record* (eds R. C. Steele and R. C. Welch) 22–35. Nature Conservancy. 115, 149, 155

Hooper, M. D. *see also* 93, 837 *and* pp. 60–2.

Hoppus, E. *see* 744.

Hubbard, J. C. E. *see* 104.

Hughes, A. P. *see* 55.

Huntley, J. P. *see* 108.

73 Iversen, J. (1941). *Landnam i Danmarks Stenalder: Land Occupation in Denmark's Stone Age*. Reitzel, København. 104, 265

74 Iversen, J. (1956). Forest clearance in the Stone Age. *Sci. Amer.*, **194**, 36–41. 104

75 Iversen, J. (1964). Retrogressive vegetational succession in the post-glacial. *J. Ecol.*, **52 suppl.** (Jubilee Symposium), 59–70. 36, 237

James, P. W. *see* 133.

76 Jarvis, P. G. (1964). The adaptability to light intensity of seedlings of *Quercus petraea* . . . *J. Ecol.* **52**, 545–71. 78, 297

Jeffers J. N. *see* 17a, 862.

Johnson, T. *see* 337. 56

Jones, E. W. *see* 756–7 *and* pp. 208, 299.

Jovet, P. *see* 758. 65

77 Kinnaird, J. W. (1968). Ecology of birch woods. *Proc. bot. Soc. Br. Isl.*, **7**, 181–2. 317

Klötzli, F. *see* 52.

78 Knight, G. H. (1964). Some factors affecting the distribution of *Endymion nonscriptus* (L.) Garcke in Warwickshire woods. *J. Ecol.*, **52**, 405–21. 77

79 Legge, W. H. (1907). Forestry. *Victoria County History – Sussex*, **2**, 291–325. 125, 152, 188, 319, 330

80 *Leitfaden für die Bearbeitung von Regionalwaldgeschichten, Reviergeschichten und Bestandesgeschichten* (1973). International Union of Forest Res. Organizations, Zürich. 349

Leland, J. *see* 386. 267

81 Lemée, G. (1966). Sur l'intérêt écologique des réserves biologiques de la forêt de Fontainebleau. *Bull. Soc. bot. France*, **113**, 305–23. 304

Lemée, G. *see also* 13.

82 Lennard, R. (1945). The destruction of woodland in the eastern counties under William the Conqueror. *Econ. Hist. Rev.*, **15**, 36–43. 120

83 Le Sueur, A. D. C. (1972). *Burnham Beeches and the Manor of Allerds-in-Burnham*, 2nd edition. Corporation of London. 174, 320

84 Lindsay, J. M. (1975). The history of oak coppice in Scotland. *Scot. For.*, **29**, 87–93. 285

84a Lindsay, J. M. (1975). Charcoal iron smelting and its fuel supply: the erxample of Lorn furnace, Argyllshire, 1753–1876. *J. hist. Geog.*, **1**, 283–98. 285

Lloyd, P. S. *see* 832. 345, 347

85 McVean, D. N. (1956). Ecology of *Alnus glutinosa* . . . V. Notes on some British alder populations. *J. Ecol.*, **44**, 321–30. 305

86 McVean, D. N. (1964). Woodland and scrub. *The Vegetation of Scotland* (ed. J. H. Burnett) 144–67. Oliver and Boyd, Edinburgh. 65, 284

McVean, D. N. *see also* 777–80 *and* p. 313.

Maitland, F. W. *see* 781. 111, 113

87 Martin, M. H. (1968). Conditions affecting the distribution of *Mercurialis perennis* L. in certain Cambridgeshire woodlands. *J. Ecol.*, **56**, 777–93. 37, 92

88 Martin, M. H. and Pigott, C. D. (1975). Soils. In: *Hayley Wood* (*see* 120), 61–71. 37, 38, 49

Martyn, T. *see* 396. 349, 351

89 Mellars, P. (1976). Fire ecology, animal populations and man: a study of some ecological relationships in prehistory. *Proc. prehist. Soc.*, **42**, 15–45. 103

Mellars, P. *see also* 753a.

Melville, R. *see* 789–792a. 256–7, 280

90 Menzies, W. (1864). *The History of Windsor Great Park and Windsor Forest*. Longman, London. 3, 193, 262, 303

91 Meusel, H. (1954). Uber die Wälder der mitteleuropäischen Löss-Ackerlandschaften. *Wiss. Z. Univ. Halle, Math.-Nat.*, **4**, 21–35. 210, 268

92 Meyer, H. and Meyer, D. (1951). The distribution of *Primula elatior* (L.) Hill. *The Study of the Distribution of British Plants* (ed. J. E. Lousley), 80–1. Bot. Soc. Brit. Isl. London. 94

Monteath, R. *see* 405. 285, 312

93 Moore, N. W. and Hooper, M. D. (1975). On the number of bird species in British woods. *Biol. Conserv.*, **8**, 239–50. 62

94 Morris, M. G. (1974). Oak as a habitat for insect life. *The British Oak: Its History and Natural History* (eds M. G. Morris and F. H. Perring), 274–97. Classey, Faringdon.

Moxey, P. A. *see* 8. 301

Newbould, P. J. *see* 59, 60.

Newnham. R. M. *see* 807. 299

95 Nicholls, P. H. (1972). On the evolution of a forest landscape. *Trans. Inst. Brit. Geog.*, **56**, 57–76. 185

95a Nisbet, J. (1907). Forestry. *Victoria County History – Essex*, **2**, 615–28. 356

Olivier, M. *see* 437.

Orme, B. J. *see* 25–32.

96 Ovington, J. D. (1953). A study of invasion by *Holcus mollis* L. *J. Ecol.*, **41**, 35–52. 88

Oxford, P. M. *see* 8.

Paul, C. R. C. *see* 821.

Peace, T. R. *see* 822. 261

Peglar, S. *see* 12.

Pennington, W. *see* 824. 97, 104

97 Peterken, G. F. (1969). Development of vegetation in Staverton Park, Suffolk. *Fld Stud.*, **3**, 1–39. 36, 293–4, 347

98 Peterken, G. F. (1974). A method for assessing woodland flora for conservation using indicator species. *Biol. Conserv.*, **6**, 239–45. 52, 54, 237, 241, 244

99 Peterken, G. F. (1975). Trees and shrubs. In: *Bedford Purlieus* (*see* 105), 85–112. 280

100 Peterken, G. F. (1976). Long-term changes in the woodlands of Rockingham Forest and other areas. *J. Ecol.*, **64**, 123–46. 206–7, 353

101 Peterken, G. F. (1977). Habitat conservation priorities in British and European woodlands. *Biol. Conserv.*, **11**, 223–36 ix

102 Peterken, G. F. and Harding, P. T. (1974). Recent changes in the conservation value of woodlands in Rockingham Forest. *Forestry*, **47**, 109–28. 117–18

103 Peterken, G. F. and Harding, P. T. (1975). Woodland conservation in Eastern England: comparing the effects of changes in three study areas since 1946. *Biol. Conserv.*, **8**, 279–98. 118

104 Peterken, G. F. and Hubbard, J. C. E. (1972). The shingle vegetation of southern England: the holly wood on Holmstone Beach, Dungeness. *J. Ecol.*, **60**, 547–72. 51, 345

105 Peterken, G. F. and Welch, R. C. (1975). *Bedford Purlieus: Its History, Ecology and Management*. Institute of Terrestrial Ecology, Monks Wood. 27, 218

Peterken, G. F. *see also* 129, 832 *and* pp. 115, 237, 345, 347.

106 Pigott, C. D. (1969). The status of *Tilia cordata* and *T. platyphyllos* on the Derbyshire limestone. *J. Ecol.*, **57**, 491–504. 52, 204, 218–19, 237, 244, 277

107 Pigott, C. D. (1975). Natural regeneration of *Tilia cordata* in relation to forest-structure in the forest of Białowieża, Poland. *Phil. Trans. roy. Soc. Lond.*, **B270**, 151–79. 250, 253

108 Pigott, C. D. and Huntley, J. P. (1978). Factors controlling the distribution of *Tilia cordata* at the northern limit of its geographical range. I. Distribution in north-west England. *New Phytol.*, **81**, 429–41. 237, 242–3

109 Pigott, C. D. and Taylor, K. (1964). The distribution of some woodland herbs in relation to the supply of nitrogen and phosphorus in the soil. *J. Ecol.*, **52 suppl.**, 175–86. 95

110 Pigott, C. D. and Walters, S. M. (1953). Is the box-tree a native of England? *The Changing Flora of Britain* (ed. J. E. Lousley), 184–7. Bot. Soc. Br. Isl. 51, 63

Pigott, C. D. *see also* 88, 834–5 *and* p. 82.

111 Pollard, E. (1973). Hedges. VII. Woodland relic hedges in Huntingdon and Peterborough. *J. Ecol.* **61**, 343–52. 51

112 Prince, H. C. (1958). Parkland in the English landscape. *Amat. Hist.*, **3**, 332–49. 197

113 Rackham, O. (1966). The restoration of old coppice. *Handbook of the Soc. for the Promotion of Nature Reserves.* 168

114 Rackham, O. (1967). The history and effects of coppicing as a woodland practice. *The Biotic Effects of Public Pressures on the Environment* (ed. E. Duffey), *Monks Wood E.xperimental Station Symposium*, **3**, 82–93. 38, 140

115 Rackham, O. (1969). Knapwell Wood. *Nature in Cambs*, **12**, 25–31. 51–94

116 Rackham, O. (1971). Ancient woods of East Anglia. *Country L.ife*, **150**, 1062–6. 27

117 Rackham, O. (1971). Historical studies and woodland conservation. *The Scientific Management of Animal and Plant Communities for Conservation* (eds E. Duffey and A. S. Watt), 563–80. Blackwell, Oxford. 60, 268

118 Rackham, O. (1974). The oak tree in historic times. In: *The British Oak* (*see* 94), 62–79. 147, 162, 295, 351

119 Rackham, O. (1975). Temperatures of plant communities as measured by pyrometric and other methods. In: *Light as an Ecological Factor II* (*see* 50), 423–49. 78, 81

120 Rackham, O. (1975). *Hayley Wood: its History and Ecology*. Cambs and Isle of Ely Naturalists' Trust. vii, 12–13, 18,37, 51, 53, 57–8, 77–8, 80–1, 92, 95, 137, 142, 151, 170, 174, 201, 209, 219, 262, 269, 283, 297, 343, 351, 355

121 Rackham, O. (1976). The Hayley Wood deer count. *Nature in Cambs*, **19**, 32–4. 177, 201

122 Rackham, O. (1976). *Trees and Woodland in the British Landscape*. Dent, London. vii, ix, 13, 17–18, 52, 121, 123, 133–4, 137, 153, 155–6, 162, 168, 174, 187, 189, 195, 197, 244, 248, 251, 262, 283, 285, 326, 341

123 Rackham, O. (1977). Neolithic woodland management in the Somerset Levels: Garvin's, Walton Heath, and Rowland's Tracks. *Somerset Levels Papers*, **3**, 65–71. 106–7, 312

124 Rackham, O. (1978). Archaeology and land-use history. *Epping Forest – The Natural Aspect?* (ed. D. Corke). *Essex Nat.*, **N.S. 2**, 16–57. 121, 130, 185, 188, 202, 321, 327

124a Rackham, O. (1979). Neolithic woodland management in the Somerset Levels: Sweet Track I. *Somerset Levels Papers*, **5**, 59, 61. 106

125 Rackham, O. (1988). The Forest of Neroche and the fuel supply of the Donyatt kilns. *Excavations in the Donyatt Potteries, Somerset* (eds R. Coleman-Smith and T. Pearson), Phillimore, 3–8. 115, 128, 180, 207, 218

Rackham, O. *see also* 844–7.

126 Ranson, C. E. (1978). Nature conservation in Epping Forest. *Epping Forest – The Natural Aspect?* (ed. D. Corke). *Essex Nat.*, **N.S. 2**, 58–79. 202, 235

Ratcliffe, D. A. *see* 780, 850 *and* p. 313.

127 Rawitscher, F. (1945). The hazel period in the post-glacial development of forests. *Nature, Lond.*, **156**, 302–3. 104

Ray, J. *see* 466–8. 56, 79, 94, 223, 241, 313, 321, 329

Reed, J. L. *see* 853. 244

Richens, R. H. *see* 854–62. 256–7, 260, 267, 269, 271, 280

128 Rixon, P. (1975). History and former woodland management. In: *Bedford Purlieus* (*see* 105), 14–42. 118, 156, 295, 319

129 Rixon, P. and Peterken, G. F. (1975). Vascular plants. In: *Bedford Purlieus* (*see* 105), 101–8. 27, 218

130 Robbins, R. W. (1915). The flora of Epping Forest. *Trans. Lond. Nat. Hist. Soc.* (1915), 44–8. 90

Robin, A.-M. *see* 13.

131 Roden, D. (1968). Woodland and its management in the medieval Chilterns. *Forestry*, **41**, 59–71. 319, 321, 326

132 Rose, F. (1974). The epiphytes of oak. In: *The British Oak* (*see* 94), 250–73. 199, 200

133 Rose, F. and James, P. W. (1974). The corticolous and lignicolous [lichen] species of the New Forest, Hampshire. *Lichenologist*, **6**, 1–72. 200–1

Ross, R. *see* 150 (pp. 480–4). 353

134 Round, J. H. (1897). The Forest of Essex. *J. Brit Archaeol. Ass.*, **N.S. 3**, 36–42. 180

Round, J. H. *see also* 867. 120

135 Rymer, L. (1977). The exploitation of woodlands in the parish of North Knapdale, Argyllshire. *Scot. For.*, **31**, 244–50. 285

136 Salisbury, E. J. (1916). The oak–hornbeam woods of Hertfordshire. I and II. *J. Ecol.*, **4**, 83–117. 80, 221, 227

137 Salisbury, E. J. (1918). The oak–hornbeam woods of Hertfordshire. III and IV. *J. Ecol.*, **6**, 14–52. 80, 90, 221, 227

138 Salisbury, E. J. (1918). The ecology of scrub in Hertfordshire: a study in colonization. *Trans. Herts Nat. Hist. Soc.*, **17**, 53–64. 226

139 Salisbury, E. J. (1924). The effects of coppicing as illustrated by the woods of Hertfordshire. *Trans. Herts Nat. Hist. Soc.*, **18**, 1–21. 80–1, 231

Salzman, L. F. *see* 477. 323
Schmitt, A. *see* 13.
Schofield, J. M. *see* 147.

140 Shaw, M. W. (1968). Factors affecting the natural regeneration of sessile oak (*Quercus petraea*) in North Wales. I. A preliminary study of acorn production, viability and losses. *J. Ecol.*, **56**, 565–83. 293, 296

141 Shaw, M. W. (1974). The reproductive characteristics of oak. In: *The British Oak* (*see* 94), 162–181. 295–7

142 Shirley, E. P. (1867). *Some Account of English Deer Parks.* Murray, London. 191, 193

143 Simmons, I. G. (1964). The Dartmoor oak copses: observations and speculations. *Fld Stud.*, **2**, 225–35. 285, 299

Simmons, I. G. *see also* 887a.

144 Smith, A. G. (1970). The influence of Mesolithic and Neolithic man on British vegetation. *Studies in the Vegetational History of the British Isles* (eds D. Walker and R. G. West), 81–96. Cambridge. 104

145 Steane, J. M. (1975). The medieval parks of Northamptonshire. *Northants Past and Present*, **5**, 211–34. 191

146 Steele, R. C. (1974). Variation in oakwoods in Britain. In: *The British Oak* (*see* 94), 130–140. 284

147 Steele, R. C. and Schofield, J. M. (1973). Conservation and management. *Monks Wood: a Nature Reserve Record* (eds R. C. Steele and R. C. Welch), 296–335. Nature Conservancy. 297, 301

148 Steven, H. M. and Carlisle, A. (1959). *The Native Pinewoods of Scotland.* Edinburgh. 65

149 Streeter, D. T. (1974). Ecological aspects of oak woodland conservation. In: *The British Oak* (*see* 94), 341–354. 295, 304

150 Tansley, A. G. (1939). *The British Islands and Their Vegetation.* Cambridge. 8, 22, 36, 63, 83, 203, 219, 237, 255, 283–4, 305, 316, 318–19, 339

Taylor, C. S. *see* 893. 111
Taylor, K. *see* 109.

151 Ten Hove, H. A. (1968). The *Ulmus* fall at the transition Atlanticum-Subboreal in pollen diagrams. *Palaeogeog., Palaeoclimatol., Palaeoecol.*, **5**, 359–69. 265

Tennyson, A. *see* 496. 311
Thorpe, J. *see* 46, 331. 331

152 Tittensor, R. M. (1970). History of the Loch Lomond oakwoods. *Scot. For.*, **24**, 100–18. 136, 285

153 Tittensor, A. and Tittensor, R. (1977). *Natural History of The Mens, Sussex.* Horsham Nat. Hist. Soc. 175, 321

154 Troup, R. S. (1928). *Silvicultural Systems.* Clarendon Press, Oxford.

155 Tubbs, C. R. (1964). Early encoppicements in the New Forest. *Forestry*, **37**, 95–105. 136

156 Tubbs, C. R. (1968). The New Forest: an Ecological History. David and Charles, Newton Abbot. 174, 177, 180, 187, 241, 319

157 Turner, J. (1962). The *Tilia* decline: an anthropogenic interpretation. *New Phytol.*, **61**, 328–41. 105, 239

158 Turner, J. (1965). A contribution to the history of forest clearance. *Proc. roy. Soc. Lond.*, **B161**, 343–54. 106

Turner, W. *see* 505. 92, 241
Tusser, T. *see* 506. 174, 241, 248, 265

159 Valentine, D. H. (1948). Studies in British Primulas. II. Ecology and taxonomy of primrose and oxlip (*Primula vulgaris* Huds. and *P. elatior* Schreb.). *New Phytol.*, **47**, 111–30. 94

160 Valentine, D. H. (1951). Studies in British Primulas. III. Hybridization between *Primula elatior* (L.) Hill and *P. veris* L. *New Phytol*, **50**, 383–99. 92, 94

Vancouver, C. *see* 507. 185
Waller, W. C. *see* 509.
Walters, S. M. *see* 110, 829, 830, 904.

161 Wardle, P. (1959). The regeneration of *Fraxinus excelsior* in woods with a field layer of *Mercurialis perennis. J. Ecol.*, **47**, 483–97. 95, 208

162 Watt, A. S. (1919). On the causes of failure of natural regeneration in British oakwoods. *J. Ecol.*, **7**, 173–203. 296

163 Watt, A. S. (1923). On the ecology of the British beechwoods with special reference to their regeneration. I. The causes of failure of natural regeneration of the beech (*Fagus silvatica* L.). *J. Ecol.*, **11**, 1–48. 324

164 Watt, A. S. (1925). On the ecology of the British beechwoods . . . II. The development and structure of beech communities on the South Downs. *J. Ecol.*, **12**, 145–204; **13**, 27–73. 324

165 Watt, A. S. (1926). Yew communities of the South Downs. *J. Ecol.*, **14**, 282–316. 63

166 Watt, A. S. (1931). Preliminary observations on Scottish beechwoods. *J. Ecol.*, **19**, 137–57, 321–59. 325

167 Watt, A. S. (1934). The vegetation of the Chiltern Hills, with special reference to the beechwoods and their seral relationships. *J. Ecol.*, **22**, 230–70, 445–507. 36, 327

Watt, A. S. *see also* 907.

168 Welch, R. C. (1972). *Windsor Forest Study. Wildlfe Conservation Report.* Crown Estate Commission and Nature Conservancy. 200, 303

Welch, R. C. *see also* 105.
West, R. G. *see* 912–13. 97, 103
Whitworth, R. A. *see* 43.

169 Willmot, A. (1977). *Sorbus torminalis* . . . in Derbyshire. *Watsonia*, **11**, 339–44. 358

170 Witney, K. P. (1976). *The Jutish Forest.* Athlone Press, London. 124, 155

171 Woodell, S. R. J. (1969). Natural hybridization in Britain between *Primula vulgaris* . . . and *P. elatior* . . . *Watsonia*, **7**, 115–27. 93–4

172 Woodhead, T. W. (1906). Ecology of woodland plants in the neighbourhood of Huddersfield. *J. Linn. Soc. Bot.*, **37**, 333–406. 79, 85

173 Woodruffe-Peacock, E. A. (1918). A fox-covert study. *J. Ecol.*, **6**, 110–25. 51

II. Primary Historical Sources

200 Aubrey, J. (1691). *The Natural History of Wiltshire* (ed. J. Britton. David and Charles, Newton Abbot, 1969).

200a Babington, C. C. (1860). *Flora of Cambridgeshire.* London. [I have used copies in Cambridge University Botany School Library annotated by the author and others.]

201 Bates, E. H. (1899). *Two Cartularies of the Benedictine Abbeys of Muchelney and Athelney . . . Somerset*, 35–6. London.

202 Beda (*c.* 720). *Vita Sancti Cuthberti* (ed. B. Colgrave: *Two 'Lives' of Saint Cuthbert*, 160–2. Cambridge, 1940).

203 Beda (731). *Historia ecclesiastica gentis Anglorum* (ed. C. Plummer. Clarendon Press, Oxford, 1896).

204 Bennett, R. and Elton, J. (1899). *History of Corn Milling. II. Watermills and Windmills.* Simpkin and Marshall, London.

205 Bibliothèque Nationale, Paris. MS Latina 5650 [copy in Essex Record Office, Acc. 2062].

206 Birch, W. de G. (1885–93). *Cartularium Saxonicum.* 3 vols, London. [Contains the texts of most Anglo-Saxon charters including some not in Kemble.] No. 513.

207 Idem, No. 595.

208 Idem, No. 596.

209 Idem, No. 787.

210 Idem, No. 898.

211 Idem, No. 982.

212 Idem, No. 1036.
213 Blomefield, J. (1739–1775). *History of .Norfolk.* Fersfield and Norwich.
214 Boulton, H. E. (1965). *The Sherwood Forest Book.* Thoroton Soc., Nottingham.
215 Boys, J. (1794). *General View of the Agriculture of the County of Kent* . . . Brentford.
216 British Library *alias* British Museum. Add. Roll 27687.
216a Brown, T. (1658). *The Garden of Cyrus.*
217 Suffolk Record Office (Bury). 269.
218 Suffolk Record Office (Bury). 468/2/53/1.
219 Suffolk Record Office (Bury). 553/73.
220 Suffolk Record Office (Bury). 1066.
221 Suffolk Record Office (Bury). 2130/1.
222 Suffolk Record Office (Bury). 2503.
223 Suffolk Record Office (Bury). 2753/3/23.
224 Suffolk Record Office (Bury). 2776/5.
225 Suffolk Record Office (Bury). 2413/120.
226 Suffolk Record Office (Bury). E2/9/1.
227 Suffolk Record Office (Bury). E2/30/2.
228 Suffolk Record Office (Bury). E2/43/1.
229 Suffolk Record Office (Bury). EXY4/W2/166.
230 Suffolk Record Office (Bury). Redgrave 1066.
231 Suffolk Record Office (Bury).Tithe Map, Bradfield St Clare (1843).
232 *Calendar of Charter Rolls*, **2**, 313.
233 *Calendar of Close Rolls.* [Entries in this and the three following published Calendars are too numerous to list separately. They are specified in the text by place and year and can be found by using the index to the volume covering the year in question.]
234 *Calendar of Inquisitions Post Mortem.*
235 *Calendar of Liberate Rolls.*
236 *Calendar of Patent Rolls.*
237 Cambridge Natural History Society. Card-index of plant records. [In Cambridge University Botany School Herbarium.]
238 Cambridge Record Office. Q/R Dc19.
239 Cambridge Record Office. R52.12.4.11–12.
240 Cambridge University Library. Doc 1446.
241 Cambridge University Library. Gg 4.4.
242 Cambridge University Library. Maps 53.85.12.
243 Cambridge University Library. Mm 4.19.
244 Cambridge University Library. MS Plans a.4.
245 Cambridge University Library. MS Plans 550R.
246 Cambridge University Library. MS Plans 558.
247 *Cartularium monasterii de Rameseia* (Ramsey Cartulary, eds W. H. Hart and P. A. Lyons, 1884–93).
248 *Cartularium monasterii Sancti Johannis Baptiste de Colecestria* (Colchester Cartulary, ed. S. A. Moore. Chiswick, London, 1897).
249 Chapman, J. (1776). *Nottinghamshire, Survey'd in 1774.* London.
250 Chapman, J. and André, P. (1777). *A Map of the County of Essex.* London [reprinted by Essex County Council 1970].
251 Chapman, T.A. (1869). Observations on the oeconomy of the British species of *Scolytus. Entom. mon. Mag.*, **6**, 126–31.
252 Chicago University Library. Bacon Collection – Brandon Compotus Rolls 653–63. Microfilm in Suffolk Record Office (Bury). [Kindly communicated to me by the late Rev. J. T. Munday.]
253 Columella (*c.* 60). *Res rustica.* (Loeb Classical Library. Heinemann, London, 1941.)
253a Commissioners appointed to enquire into the Woods, Forests and Land Revenues of the Crown. *Reports.* See *House of Commons Journal* (*see* 348–52).
254 Constant Reader (1826). On a disease which has attacked certain elm trees in Camberwell Grove, Surrey. *Loudon's Gard. Mag.*, **1**, 378–84.
255 Copinger, W. A. (1905–11). *The Manors of Suffolk: Notes on their History and Devolution.* Vol. **4**, 283. London.
256 Corpus Christi College, Cambridge. MS 169, item 5, p. 501.
257 *Curia Regis Rolls.* See note to ref. 233.
258 Dale, S. (1730). *The History and Antiquities of Harwich and Dovercourt.* London.
259 Davidson, J. B. (1883). On some Anglo-Saxon charters at Exeter. *J.* [*Brit.*] *Arch. Ass.*, **39**, 259–303.
260 Dendrophilus (1823). Discovery of the secret Destroyers of the Trees in St James's Park. *Phil. Mag.*, **62**, 252–4.
261 Denney, A. H. (1960). *The Sibton Abbey Estates. Select Documents 1325–1509.* Cowell, Ipswich.
262 Denson, J. (1831). Scolytus destructor not a destroyer of healthy trees. *Ann. Mag. Nat. Hist.*, **4**, 152–7.
263 Dickens, A. G. (1951). *The Register or Chronicle of Butley Priory, Suffolk, 1510–1535.* Wykeham, Winchester.
264 Dodwell, B. (1958). *Feet of Fines for the County of Suffolk, for the Reign of King John, 1199–1214.* Pipe Roll Soc., London.
265 Donald, T. and Milne, T. (1797). *A Topographical Map of the County of Norfolk. Surveyed and Measured in the Years 1790, 91, 92, 93 and 94.* Faden, London.
266 Douglas, D. C. (1932). *Feudal Documents from the Abbey of Bury St Edmund's.* Oxford.
267 Downing College, Cambridge. *Downing Estate Atlas*, 1750.
268 Duchars, A. [1976]. *Thorndon Country Park.* Essex County Council.
269 Duhamel du Monceau, H.-L. (1764). *De l'exploitation des bois.* Guerin et Delatour, Paris.
270 *Ely Coucher Book* (1251). Unpublished; three medieval copies are British Museum Cott. Claud. C xi, Gonville & Caius College (Cambridge) MS 489/485, Ely Diocesan Registry (in Cambridge University Library) G/3/27.
271 Ely Diocesan Registry (in Cambridge University Library). H1/1–9.
272 Emmison, F. G. (1947). *Catalogue of Maps in the Essex Record Office, 1566–1855.* Essex County Council.
273 Essex Record Office. D/DAc 291.
274 Essex Record Office. D/DAc 347.
275 Essex Record Office. D/DAc 359.
276 Essex Record Office. D/DB L1/9/4.
277 Essex Record Office. D/DB L1/10.27.
278 Essex Record Office. D/DB M122.
278a Essex Record Office. D/DB P37.
279 Essex Record Offce. D/DB T16/4.
280 Essex Record Office. D/DBa M10, 11, 27.
281 Essex Record Office. D/Dc 2/46.
282 Essex Record Office. D/DCm Z18/7.
283 Essex Record Offce. D/DCr A19.
284 Essex Record Office. D/DE E2.
285 Essex Record Office. D/DFg 1/1–25.
286 Essex Record Offce. D/DGe M136.
287 Essex Record Offce. D/DH X65.
288 Essex Record Office. D/DHf M19.
289 Essex Record Offce. D/DHg L14.
290 Essex Record Offce. D/DHt A4.
291 Essex Record Offce. D/DHt E13.
292 Essex Record Office. D/DHt M42.
293 Essex Record Offce- D/DHt M145.
294 Essex Record Office D/DHt P51.
295 Essex Record Office. D/DK M1.
296 Essex Record Offce. D/DL E9.
297 Essex Record Offce. D/DL T1/779.
298 Essex Record Office. D/DLm T1.
299 Essex Record Offce. D/DMg E3/2, nos 2 and 3.
300 Essex Record Office. D/DMg E3/2, no. 11.

301 Essex Record Offce. D/DMq E7.
302 Essex Record Office. D/DP 18/3/74.
303 Essex Record Offce. D/DP 87.
304 Essex Record Office. D/DP A43.
305 Essex Record Office. D/DP A44.
306 Essex Record Office. D/DP A58/1–27.
306a Essex Record Office. D/DP A68/7.
307 Essex Record Office. D/DP A83–86.
308 Essex Record Office. D/DP A91.
309 Essex Record Office. D/DP E20/1.
310 Essex Record Office. D/DP E/25.
311 Essex Record Office. D/DP M200–1.
312 Essex Record Office. D/DP M210.
313 Essex Record Oflice. D/DP M1325.
314 Essex Record Offce. D/DP M1422.
315 Essex Record Office. D/DP P71–74.
315a Essex Record Office. D/DP passim.
316 Essex Record Office. D/DQ 18.
317 Essex Record Offce. D/DQ 23/3.
317a Essex Record Office. D/DRa E7.
318 Essex Record Office. D/DSm.
319 Essex Record Office. D/DSp M37.
320 Essex Record Office. D/DSp M40.
321 Essex Record Offce. D/DTw E2/6.
322 Essex Record Office. D/DTw E8.
323 Essex Record Office. D/DU 15.
324 Essex Record Oflice. D/DU 268/4.
325 Essex Record Office. D/DU 560/14.
326 Essex Record Office. L1/12/4.
327 Essex Record Offce. Ph 1/105.
328 Essex Record Offce. T/A 262/4, 5.
329 Essex Record Offce. T/A 262/14/1.
330 Essex Record Office. T/A 262/37.
331 Essex Record Offce. T/M 5.
332 Essex Record Office. Temp. Access. 897.
333 Essex Record Office. Temp. Access. 898.
334 Essex Record Office. Earl's Colne Court Rolls [kindly communicated to me by Professor A. Macfarlane].
335 Evelyn, J. (1664). *Sylva, or a Discourse of Forest-trees*, 1st edition. London.
336 Evelyn, J. (1706). *Sylva, or a Discourse of Forest-trees*, 4th edition. London.
337 Fisher, J. L. (1951). The Leger Book of St John's Abbey, Colchester. *Trans. Essex Arch. Soc.*, **N.S. 24** 77ff.
338 Fitzstephen, W. (*c.* 1180). *Vita Sancti Thomae Cantuariensis Archiepiscopi* (ed. J. Sparke. Bowyer, London, 1723).
338a Frank, A. B. (1896). *Die pilzparasitären Krankheiten der Pflanzen*, 2. Aufl. Breslau.
339 *Gardeners' Chronicle* (1848). [Editorial, p. 283, on elm disease and its 'treatment'].
340 Gerarde, J. (1597). *The Herball or Generall Historie of Plantes*. London.
341 Grigor, J. (1841). *Eastern Arboretum*. London.
342 Guérin-Meneville (1846). *Ann. Soc. Entom. France*, **2e sér. 4**, lxix–lxxi.
343 Guérin-Meneville, M. F. E. (1846). Observations sur les moeurs et l'anatomie des Scolytes des ormes ... *Rev. zool.*, **9**, 289–98.
344 Hart, C. R. (1966). *The Early Charters of Eastern England*. Leicester.
345 Hervey, Lord F. (1925). *The Pinchbeck Register*. Brighton.
346 Hibberd, S. (1863). The elm and its insect enemies. *Intellectual Observer*, **2**, 191–4.
347 Hockey, S. F. (1975). *The Account-book of Beaulieu Abbey*. Roy. Hist. Soc., London.
348 *House of Commons Journal*, **13**, (1701), 533.
349 *House of Commons Reports*, **3**, (1771), 15–52.
350 *Houseof Commons Journal*, **47**, (1792), 159.
351 *House of Commons Journal*, **48**, (1793), 467–511.
352 *House of Commons Journal*, **48**, (1793), 512–22.
353 *House of Commons Journal*, **57**, (1802), 960–1.
354 *House of Commons Journal*, **78**, (1823), 623.
355 Humphreys, H. N. (1863). Insects injurious to the elm. *Intellectual Observer*, **2**, 28–35.
356 Huntingdon Record Office. The Plott or Description of Boxworth in Cambridgesheire ... anno Domini 1650.
357 *Ickworth Survey Boocke Ano 1665* (ed. T. Hervev). Ipswich.
358 *Inquisitio Comilatus Cantabrigiensis . . . subjicitur Inquisitio Eliensis* (ed. N.E.S.A. Hamilton. Murray, London, 1876).
359 Suffolk Record Office (Ipswich). 50/1/204.
360 Suffolk Record Office (Ipswich). B1/38/1b.
361 Suffolk Record Office (Ipswich). FB62/N1/1.
362 Suffolk Record Office (Ipswich). HA1/BD3/1.
363 Suffolk Record Office (Ipswich). HA11/C41/3/1.
364 Suffolk Record Office (Ipswich). HA49 (331) Box 6.
365 Suffolk Record Office (Ipswich). HA49 (337) Box 6.
366 Suffolk Record Office (Ipswich). HA53/359/637.
367 Suffolk Record Office (Ipswich). HA68/484/751.
368 Suffolk Record Office (Ipswich). HA93/722/220.
369 Suffolk Record Office (Ipswich). HA240/2508/1263.
370 Suffolk Record Office (Ipswich). HA240/2508/1267.
370a Suffolk Record Office (Ipswich). HD417/14.
371 Suffolk Record Office (Ipswich). V5/22/1.
372 Suffolk Record Office (Ipswich). X6/1/1.
373 Iveagh muniments (Eleveden Hall, Suffolk). Suffolk MS 148 (Brandon court roll 1386–7). [Kindly communicated to me by the late Rev. J. T. Munday.]
374 James, M. R. (1912). The earliest inventory of Corpus Christi College. *Proc. Cambridge Antiq. Soc.*, **16**, 88–114.
375 Jeayes, I. H. and Benham, W. G. (1921). *Court Rolls of the Borough of Colchester. I. 1310–52*. Colchester.
376 Jocelyn of Brakelond (*c.* 1205). *The Chronicle of Jocelyn of Brakelond, containing the Acts of Samson, Abbot of the Monastery of St Edmund* (ed. H. E. Butler. Nelson, London, 1949).
377 Johnson, T. (1629). *Ericetum Hamstedianum, sive plantarum ibi crescentium observatio habita* (appendix to *Iter plantarum ... in agrum Cantianum*; translated in *Thomas Johnson: Botanical Journeys in Kent and Hampstead*, ed. J. S. L. Gilmour, Pittsburgh, 1972).
378 Kemble, J. M. (1839–48). *Codex diplomaticus aevi Saxonici*. 6 vols, London. [Contains the texts of most Anglo-Saxon charters.] **2**, 65.
379 Idem, **3**, 77.
380 Idem, **3**, 381.
381 Idem, **5**, 194.
382 Idem, **5**, 221.
383 Idem, **4**, 97.
384 *Laxton's Builders' Price Book*. 14th edition (1840) and later editions. London.
385 Leighton correspondence at Urchfont Manor, Wilts. [Kindly communicated to me by Mr A. Slee.]
386 Leland, J. (1542). *Itinerary*, Part II (ed. L. T. Smith. London, 1907).
387 *Letters and Papers Foreign and Domestic, Henry VIII*, **20**, (1), item 465 (14).
388 Lindley, J. and Crosley, W. (1793). *Map of the County of Surrey*. Islington.
389 Loudon, J. C. (1838). *Arboretum et fruticetum britannicum*. Longmans, London.
390 Lyte, H. (1578). *A niewe herball, or historie of plants*. Antwerp.
391 Macleay, W. S. (1824). Abstract of a report on the state of the elm trees in St James's and Hyde Parks. *Edinb. Philos. J.*, **11**, 123–9.

392 Malcolm, J. and James, W. (1794) *General View of the Agriculture of the County of Buckingham* . . . London.

393 March District Council. 17th-century map of Doddington.

394 Marshall, J. (1834). *A Digest of all the Accounts Relating to the Population, Productions, . . . Shipping, . . . in . . . Great Britain and Ireland*. London.

395 Martyn, J. (1727). *Methodus plantarum circa Cantabrigiam nascentium*. London. [A copy in Cambridge University Botany School Library contains notes by T. Martyn, which I have used.]

396 Martyn, T. (1763). *Plantae Cantabrigienses*. London.

397 *Melford Cartulary*. [Original in Long Melford Hall; extracts have been published (*see* 819).]

398 Merton College, Oxford, Records 5357, 5361.

399 Merton College, Oxford Records 5385–90.

400 Merton College, Oxford. Record 5409.

401 Merton College, Oxford. Record 5410.

402 Merton College, Oxford. Record 5478.

403 Mettingham College and Castle, 1562. *Proc. Suffolk Inst. Archaeol.*, **11** (1903), 315–19.

404 Miller, P. and Martyn, T. (1807). *The Gardener's and Botanist's Dictionary . . . Corrected and Newly Arranged*. London.

405 Monteath, R. (1836). *The Forester's Guide and Profitable Planter*, 3rd edition. Tegg, London.

406 Morant, P. (1768). *The History and Antiquities of the County of Essex*. London.

407 Nicholson, P. (1823). *The Practice Builder and Workman's Companion*.

408 Norfolk Record Office. 19B3 7701–5.

409 Norfolk Record Office. 30D5 12554.

410 Norfolk Record Office. 30E1 MS 12058.

411 Norfolk Record Office. 34E7 MS 21094.

412 Norfolk Record Office. 44D1 15451.

413 Norfolk Record Office. Bradfer-Lawrence 71.

414 Norfolk Record Office. Dean and Chapter. Church Commission Map 11917.

415 Norfolk Record Office. Dean and Chapter. Rolls 4739–4793 [Hindolveston accounts for 1255–1405, one roll per year].

416 Norfolk Record Office. Dean and Chapter. Roll 4814.

417 Norfolk Record Office. Dean and Chapter. Roll 4899.

418 Norfolk Record Office. Felbrigg miscellaneous papers.

419 Norfolk Record Office. Felbrigg muniments. W. Windham's Green Book.

420 Norfolk Record Office. HOW 612/4.

421 Norfolk Record Office. MR 108 241 x 4 (too fragile to be read).

422 Norfolk Record Office. MR 235 242 x 1.

423 Norfolk Record Office. MS 419 L8182.

424 Norfolk Record Office. MS 21498/3 (361 x 4).

425 Norfolk Record Office. NRS 1120 10B3.

426 Norfolk Record Office. NRS 1126 25E5.

427 Norfolk Record Office. NRS 4105 119/4.

428 Norfolk Record Office. NRS 8409.

429 Norfolk Record Office. NRS 18275 33B1.

430 Norfolk Record Office. NRS 20888 (47A3).

431 Norfolk Record Office. NRS 21400 Hav. Box 9.

432 Norfolk Record Office. NRS 21428 Box F.

433 Norfolk Record Office. NRS A6 18260.

434 Norfolk Record Office. NRS HET 63 169 x 2.

435 Norfolk Record Office. P150B.

436 Norfolk Record Office. *Suffolk Deer Parks* [articles by E. Farrar], 1923.

437 Olivier, M. (1795). *Entomologie, ou histoire naturelle des insectes*. **IV**. Paris.

438 Ormerod, E. A. (1848). *The Manual of Injurious Insects and Methods of prevention* [quoted in *Yearb. Intern. Dendrol. Soc.*, 1972, 48–50].

439 *Parliamentary Accounts and Papers*, **33** (1844), **36** (1846), **60** (1853).

440 Pearsall, D. and Salter, E. (1973). *Landscapes and Seasons in the Medieval World*. Paul Elek, London.

441 Pembroke College, Cambridge. Hardwick muniments A4.

442 Pembroke College, Cambridge. Hardwick muniments A9.

443 Pembroke College, Cambridge. Hardwick muniments I2.

444 *Pipe Rolls* [*The Great Roll of the Pipe*, pub. Pipe Roll Soc.].

445 Pitt, E. (1678). Concerning the *Sorbus pyriformis*. *Phil. Trans. roy. Soc. Lond*, **11**, 978–9.

446 Public Record Office. C132/15(4).

446a Public Record Office. C132/18.

447 Public Record Office. C132/38(17).

448 Public Record Office. C135/28(19).

449 Public Record Office. C135/48(2).

450 Public Record Office. C135/162.

451 Public Record Office. DL43/9/8.

452 Public Record Office. DL44/329.

453 Public Record Office. E134 (5 Jas I Hil. 26).

454 Public Record Office. E134 (21 Chas II Mich. 7). [I am indebted to Mr D. P. Dymond for transcribing this document.]

455 Public Record Office. E318/1271.

456 Public Record Office. E143/9/2.

457 Public Record Office. E178/4564.

458 Public Record Office. E178/5297.

459 Public Record Office. E318/11/477.

459a Public Record Office. E318/1271.

460 Public Record Office. LRRO 5/39. [I am indebted to Dr. J. Sheail for the transcription.]

461 Public Record Office. Ministers' Accounts.

462 Public Record Office. SC6/933/21–2.

463 Public Record Office. SC6/1005/7–8.

464 Public Record Office. SP14/42.

465 Public Record Office. SP16/64.

466 Ray, J. (1660). *Catalogus plantarum circa Cantabrigiam nascentium*. Cambridge. [A copy in Cambridge University Botany School Library contains notes by J. Martyn, which I have used.]

467 Ray, J. (1660). *Index plantarum agro Cantabrigiensi*. Cambridge.

468 Ray, J. (1690). *Synopsis methodica stirpium britannicarum*. London.

Ray, J. *see also* 769.

469 Rendall, G. H. (1937). *Dedham in History*. Colchester.

470 Ribbans, R. (1829). *Effusions of Genius* p. 34. Ipswich [published posthumously].

471 Robinson, G. W. (1929). *The Winthrop Papers*. **I**. p. 125. Boston, Mass.

472 Rocque, J. (1746). *An Exact Survey of the City's of London . . . and the Country Near Ten Miles Round*. London.

473 Rocque, J. [1754]. *A Topographical Map of the County of Middlesex*. London.

474 *Rotuli hundredorum temp. Hen. III & Edw. I in Turr' Lond' et in curia receptae Saccarij Westm. asservati*. H.M.S.O., London, 1818.

475 *Rotuli litterarum clausarum*. See note to ref. 233.

476 *Sacrist rolls of Ely* (ed. F. R. Chapman. Cambridge, 1907).

477 Salzman, L. F. (1952). *Building in England down to 1540*. Clarendon Press, Oxford.

478 Saunders, H. W. (1930). *An Introduction to the Obedientiary and Manor Rolls of Norwich Cathedral Priory*. Jarrold, Norwich.

479 Saunders, H. W. (1932). *A History of the Norwich Grammar School*. Norwich.

480 Shakespeare, W. (1600). *The Second Part of Henrie the Fourth* . . . Wise and Aspley, London.

481 Shakespeare, W. (1600). *A Midsommer Nights Dreame.* Fisher, London.
482 Spierenburg, D. (1929). Eenige oude gegevens over ziekten in boomen (voornamelijk in iepen). *Tijdskr. Plantenziekten*, **35**, 289–309.
483 Sorauer, P. (1896). *Handbuch der Pflanzenkrankheiten II. Die parasitären Krankheiten.* 2. Auflage. Parey, Berlin.
484 Sorauer, P. (1908). *Handbuch der Pflanzenkrankheiten II Die pflanzlichen Parasiten.* 3. Auflage. Parey. Berlin.
485 *Statutes of the Realm* 4 Hen. V Stat. 2 c. 3.
486 Idem, 4 Ed. IV c. 9.
487 Idem, 34–5 Hen. VIII c. 3.
488 Idem, 35 Hen. VIII c. 17.
489 Idem, 7 Ed. VI c. 7.
490 Idem, 9 Wm III c. 33.
491 Idem, 6 Geo. III c. 41.
492 Idem, 41–2 Vict. c. 213.
493 Straton, C. R. (ed.) (1909). *Survey of the Lands of William, First Earl of Pembroke.* Roxburghe Club, London.
Suffolk Record Office *see* 217–31 *and* 359–72.
494 *Sunday Telegraph*, 23 April 1978. The Queen gives seven deer to start a herd in Nova Scotia.
495 Supple, W. R., (1917). *A History of Thorpe-next-Norwich.* Jarrold, Norwich.
496 Tennyson, A. (*c.* 1830). *A Dirge.*
497 *The Times*, 30 Jan. 1862. [Editorial, p. 8, on elm disease, followed by correspondence in later issues.]
498 *The Times*, 5 Oct. 1976.
499 Theophilus (pre-1100). *De diversis artibus* (ed. C. R. Dodwell. London, 1961).
499a Thorpe, B. (1865). *Diplomatarium anglicanum aevi Saxonici.* Macmillan, London, p. 429.
500 Tollemache muniments (in Helmingham Hall, Suffolk). B4(a)/8/2.
501 Tollemache muniments. Map of 'Dodnish Farm', Bentley, 1629. [A similar map, dated 1635, is Suffolk Record Office (Ipswich) B1/11 Shelf 19.]
502 *Trans. Suffolk Naturalists' Soc.*, **1** (1931), xvii.
503 *Trans. Suffolk Naturalists' Soc.*, **3** (1937), xli.
504 Turner, G. J. (1901). *Select Pleas of the Forest.* Selden Soc., London.
505 Turner, W. (1568). *The Herbal.* Birkman, Koln.
506 Tusser, T. (1573). *Five Hundred Pointes of Good Husbandrie* (ed. W. Payne and S. J. Herrtage. Trübner, 1878).
507 Vancouver, C. (*c.* 1810). *General View of the Agriculture of Hampshire, Including the Isle of Wight.* London.
508 Wade-Evans, H. W. (1909). *Welsh Medieval Law, Being a Text of the Laws of Howel the Good.* Oxford.
509 Waller, W. C. (1891). Monk Wood in Loughton: A fragment of Forest History. *Essex Nat.*, **5**, 174–8.
510 Walsingham muniments [seen in Norfolk Record Office] IV/6.
511 Walsingham muniments XXXV/1 418 x 7.
512 Walsingham muniments LVI/15.
513 Walsingham muniments LXVII/2 433 x 1.
514 Walsingham muniments LXVII/4 433 x 1.
515 Watson, C. E. (1932). The Minchinhampton custumal and its place in the story of the manor. *Trans. Bristol Gloucs Arch. Soc.*, **54**, 203–385.
516 Whitelock, D. (1930). *Anglo-Saxon Wills*, p. 82. Cambridge.
517 Wiltshire Record Office. Grovely Forest: copy of sixteenth-century map.
518 Winters, W. (1887). *Centenary Memorial of the Royal Gunpowder Factory, Waltham Abbey.* Waltham Abbey.
519 Worlidge, J. (1675). *Systema Agriculturae Being the Mystery of Husbandry Discovered and layd Open.* London.

III. Other References

600 Adams, K. J. (1974). The county. *Flora of Essex* (by S. Jermyn), 23–41. Essex Naturalists' Trust.
601 Aitken, M. J. (1974). *Physics and Archaeology.* 2nd edition. Clarendon Press, Oxford.
603 Allison, J., Godwin, H. and Warren, S. H. (1952). Late-Glacial deposits at Nazeing in the Lea Valley, North London. *Phil. Trans. roy. Soc. Lond.*, **B236**, 169–240.
603a Anagnostakis, S. L. (1978). The American chestnut: new hope for a fallen giant. *Bull. Connecticut Agric. Exp. Station, New Haven*, **777**.
604 Anderson, M. L. (1950). *The Selection of Tree Species.* Edinburgh.
605 Anderson, M. L. (1951). Distribution of the sessile oak in the New Forest, Hampshire. *Forestry*, **24**, 79–113.
605a Atherden, M. A. (1976). Late Quaternary vegetation history of the North York Moors. III. Fen Bogs. *J. Biogeog.*, **3**, 115–24.
605b Atherden, M. A. (1976). The impact of late prehistoric cultures on the vegetation of the North York Moors. *Trans. Inst. Brit. Geog.*, **N.S.1**, 284–300.
606 Asser (c. 890). *Life of King Alfred* (ed. W. H. Stevenson. Oxford, 1939).
608 Avery, B. W. (1973). Soil classification in the soil survey of England and Wales. *J. Soil Sci.*, **24**, 324–38.
609 Avery, B. W. and Bascomb, C. L. *Soil Survey Laboratory Methods.* Soil Survey, Rothamsted.
610 Baldry, G. (1939). *The Rabbit Skin Cap.* Collins, London.
611 Barkman, J. J. (1958). *Photosociology and Ecology of Cryptogamic Epiphytes.* Assen.
612 Bazeley, M. L. (1921). The extent of the English forest in the thirteenth century. *Trans. roy. hist. Soc.*, **4th ser. 4**, 140–72.
613 Beresford, M. (1957). *History on the Ground.* Methuen, London.
614 Birks, H. J. B. (1973). *Past and Present Vegetation of the Isle of Skye: a Palaeoecological Study.*Cambridge.
615 Bradley, R. (1978). *The Prehistoric Settlement of Britain.* Routledge and Kegan Paul, London.
616 Brandon, P. (1974). *The Sussex Landscape.* Hodder and Stoughton, London.
617 Brasier, C. M. and Gibbs, J. N. (1973). Origin of the Dutch elm disease epidemic in Britain. *Nature, Lond.*, **242**, 607–9.
618 Brasier, C. M. and Gibbs, J. N. (1978). Origin and development of the current Dutch elm disease epidemic. *Plant Disease Epidemiology* (eds. P. R. Scott and A. Bainbridge) 31–9. Blackwell, Oxford.
619 Brasier, C. M. and Strouts, R. G. (1976). New records of Phytophthora on trees in Britain. I. Phytophthora root rot and Bleeding canker of Horse chestnut . . . *Eur. J. For. Path.*, **6**, 129–36.
620 Braun, E. L. (1950). *Deciduous Forests of Eastern North America.* Blakiston, Toronto.
621 Braun-Blanquet, J. (1964). *Pflanzensoziologie.*, 3. Auflage. Springer, Wien.
622 Bray, J. R. and Curtis, J. T. (1957). An ordination of the upland forest communities of southern Wisconsin. *Ecol. Monog.*, **27**, 325–49.
623 Brodribb, A. C. C., Hands, A. R. and Walker, D. R. (1968–73). *Excavations at Shakenoak* (privately published).
624 Brown, E. H. and Hopkins, S. V. (1956). Seven centuries of the prices of consumables, compared with builders' wage-rates. *Economica*, **23**, 296–313.
625 Bulleid, A. and Gray, H. St G. (1911). *The Glastonbury Lake Village.* Glastonbury.

626 Carlisle, A. and Brown, A. H. F. (1965). The assessment of the taxonomic status of mixed oak (*Quercus* spp.) populations. *Watsonia*, **6**, 120–7.
627 Carr, J. W. (1906). Insects. *Victoria County History – Notts*, **1**, 79–130.
628 Chapman, D. I. (1977). Deer of Essex. *Essex Nat.*, **N.S. 1**, 4–50.
629 Chapman, D. I. and Chapman, N. (1975). *Fallow Deer: Their History, Distribution and Biology*. Dalton, Lavenham.
630 Clapham, A. R., Tutin, T. G. and Warburg, E. F. (1952). *Flora of the British Isles*, 1st edition. Cambridge.
631 Clapham, A. R., Tutin, T. G. and Warburg, E. F. (1962). *Flora of the British Isles*, 2nd edition. Cambridge.
632 Clapham, A. R., Tutin, T. G. and Warburg, E. F. (1968). *Excursion Flora of the British Isles*, 2nd edition. Cambridge.
633 Clark, J. G. D. and Godwin, H. (1962). The Neolithic in the Cambridgeshire Fens. *Antiquity*, **36**, 10–23.
634 Coles, J. M. (1973). *Archaeology by Experiment*. Hutchinson, London.
635 Coombe, D. E. (1977). Air photography and plant ecology. *The Uses of Air Photography* (ed. J. K. S. St Joseph), 2nd edition, 86–102. Baker, London.
636 Coombe, D. E., Frost, L. C., Le Bas, M. and Watters, W. (1956). The nature and origin of the soils over the Cornish serpentine. *J. Ecol.*, **44**, 605–15.
637 Corbett, W. M. and Tatler, W. (1970). *Soils in Norfolk: Sheet TM 49 (Beccles North)*. Soil Survey, Harpenden.
638 Corner, E. J. H. (1955). Botanical collecting with monkeys. *Proc. roy. Instn*, **36**, 1–16.
639 Cousens, J. E. (1965). The status of the pedunculate and sessile oaks in Britain. *Watsonia*, **6**, 161–176.
639a Cross, J. R. (1975). Biological Flora of the British Isles: *Rhododendron ponticum* L. *J. Ecol.*, **63**, 345–64.
640 Curtis, L. F., Courtney, F. M. and Trudgill, S. T. (1976). *Soils in the British Isles*. Longman, London.
641 Dahl, E. (1956). *Rondane: Mountain Vegetation in South Norway and Its Relation to the Environment*. Aschehoug, Oslo.
642 Dalechamps, J. (1586–7). *Historia generalis plantarum*. Lyon.
643 Darby, H. C. (1971). *The Domesday Geography of Eastern England*, 3rd edition. Cambridge.
644 Darby, H. C. (1973). The Anglo-Scandinavian foundations. *A New Historical Geography of England* (ed. H. C. Darby) 1–38. Cambridge.
645 Darby, H. C. (1977). *Domesday England*. Cambridge.
646 Darby, H. C. and Campbell, E. M. J. (1962). *The Domesday Geography of South-East England*. Cambridge.
647 Darby, H. C. and Finn, R. W. (1967). *The Domesday Geography of South-West England*. Cambridge.
648 Darby, H. C. and Maxwell, I. S. (1962). *The Domesday Geography of .Northern England*. Cambridge.
649 Darby, H. C. and Terrett, I. B. (1971). *The Domesday Geography of Midland England*, 2nd edition. Cambridge.
650 Darby, H. C. and Versey, G. R. (1975). *Domesday Gazetteer*. Cambridge.
651 Darwin, C. (1881). *The Formation of Vegetable Mould Through the Action of Worms*. Murray, London.
652 Dauzat, A. and Rostaing, C. (1963). *Dictionnaire étymologique de noms de lieux en France*. Larousse, Paris.
653 Davis, M. B. (1979). Outbreaks of forest pathogens in Quaternary history. *Proc. 4th Int. Palynolog. Conference, Lucknow*.
654 Davis, R. (1962). *The Rise of the English Shipping Industry in the Seventeenth and Eighteenth Centuries*. David and Charles, Newton Abbot.
655 Dewhurst, P. C. (1963). Wool Street. *Proc. Camb. Antiq. Soc.*, **66**, 42–60.
656 *Dictionary of Medieval Latin from British sources. I. A–B.* (1975). British Academy, London.
657 Dimbleby, G. W. (1952). Soil regeneration on the North-East Yorkshire moors. *J. Ecol.*, **40**, 331–41.
658 Dimbleby, G. W. (1952). The historical status of moorland in North-East Yorkshire. *New Phytol.*, **51**, 349–54.
659 Dimbleby, G. W. (1962). *The Development of British Heathlands and Their Soils*. Clarendon Press, Oxford.
660 Dodgson, J . McN. (1970). *The Place-names of Cheshire, Part I*. Cambridge.
661 Donk, M. A. (1974). *Check List of European Polypores*. North-Holland, Amsterdam.
662 Dony, J. G. (1967). *Flora of Hertfordshire*. Urban District Council, Hitchin.
663 Drayton, M. (1613–22). *Poly-Olbion. Or a Chorographicall Description . . . of Great Britaine . . . Digested in a Poem*. London.
664 Drury, P. J. and Rodwell, W. J. (1979). Belgic and Romano-British small town and rural settlement in Essex. *Archaeology in Essex* (ed. D. Buckley). Council for British Archaeol.
665 Duffey, E. (1974). Changes in the British spider fauna. *The Changing Flora and Fauna of Britain* (ed. D. L. Hawksworth), 323–69. Academic Press, London.
666 Earl, D. E. (1975). *Forest Energy and Economic Development*. Clarendon Press, Oxford.
667 Edwards, C. A. and Lofty, J. R. (1972). *Biology of Earthworms*. Chapman and Hall, London.
668 Ehrhart, J. F. (1791). *Beiträge zur Naturkunde*. Band **VI** p. 98. Hannover.
669 Ekwall, E. (1960). *The Concise Oxford Dictionary of English Place-names*. Clarendon Press, Oxford.
670 Ellenberg, H. (1963). *Vegetation Mitteleuropas mit den Alpen*. Ulmer, Stuttgart.
671 Elwes, H. J. and Henry, A. (1913). *The Trees of Great Britain and Ireland*. VII. Edinburgh.
672 Emery, F. (1974). *The Oxfordshire Landscape*. Hodder and Stoughton, London.
673 Emmison, F. G. (1970). *Elizabethan Life: Disorder. Mainly from Essex sessions and assize records*, p. 31. Essex County Council, Chelmsford.
674 Emmison, F. G. (1976). *Elizabethan Life: Home, Work and Land. From Essex wills and sessions and manorial records*, pp. 255–9. Essex County Council, Chelmsford.
675 Evans, G. C. (1976). A sack of uncut diamonds: the study of ecosystems and the future of resources of mankind. *J. Ecol.*, **64**, 1–40.
676 Fabricius, J. C. (1781). *Species insectorum*. Hamburg and Kiel.
677 Figuier, L. (1865). *Histoire des plantes*. Paris.
678 Finberg, H. P. R. (1961). *The Early Charters of the West Midlands*. Leicester Univ. Press, Leicester.
679 Finberg, H. P. R. (1964). *The Early Charters of Wessex*. Leicester Univ. Press, Leicester.
680 Fletcher, J. M. (1974). Annual rings in modern and medieval times. In: *The British Oak* (*see* 94), 80–97.
681 Fletcher, J. M. (1977). Tree-ring chronologies for the sixth to sixteenth centuries for oaks of southern and eastern England. *J. Archaeol. Sci.*, **4**, 335–52.
682 *Flora Europaea* (1964). Vol. I. *Lycopodiaceae to Platanaceae*. Cambridge.
683 Ford, W. J. (1976). Some settlement patterns in the central region of the Warwickshire Avon. *Medieval Settlement, Continuity and Change* (ed. P. H. Sawyer), 274–94. Edward Arnold, London.
684 Forestry Commission (1958). *Forestry Practice*. Bull. **14**, 1958 edition. H.M.S.O., London.

685 Forestry Commission (1949). *Census of Woodlands I. Woods of five acres and over, 1947–9*. H.M.S.O., London.

686 Forestry Commission (1970). *Census of Woodlands 1965–67*. H.M.S.O., London.

687 Fowler, G. (1933–4). Fenland waterways, past and present. South Level District. *Proc. Cambridge Antiq. Soc.*, **33**, 108–28; **34**, 17–33.

688 Fox, L. and Russell, P. (1948). *Leicester Forest*. Backus, Leicester.

690 Galpin, F. W. (1888). *An Account of the Flowering Plants, Ferns and Allies of Harleston*. Cann, Harleston.

691 Gardiner, A. S. (1974). A history of the taxonomy and distribution of the native oak species. In: *The British Oak* (*see* 94), 13–26.

692 Gelling, M. (1973–6). *The Place-names of Berkshire*. English Place-name Society.

693 Gibbs, J. N. (1974). *Biology of Dutch Elm Disease*. Forestry Comm. Forest Record **94**.

694 Gibbs, J. N. (1978). Dutch elm disease in southern England, 1971–6. *Ann. appl. Biol.*, **88**, 219–28.

695 Gibbs, J. N. (1978). Intercontinental epidemiology of Dutch Elm Disease. *Ann. Rev. Phytopathol.*, **16**, 287–307.

696 Gibbs, J. N. and Brasier, C. M. (1973). Correlation between cultural characters and pathogcnicity in *Ceratocystis ulmi* from Britain, Europe and America. *Nature, Lond.*, **241**, 381–3.

697 Gibbs,J. N., Brasier, C. M., NcNabb, H. S. and Heybroek, H. M. (1975). Further studies on pathogenicity in *Ceratocystis ulmi*. *Eur. J.. For. Path.*, **5**, 161–74.

698 Gibbs, J. N. and Greig, B. J. W. (1977). Some consequences of the 1975–1976 drought for Dutch Elm Disease in southern England. *Forestry*, **50**, 145–54.

699 Gibbs, J. N., Heybroek, H. M. and Holmes, F. W. (1972). Aggressive strain of *Ceratocystis ulmi* in Britain. *Nature, Lond.*, **236**, 121–2.

700 Gibbs, J. N. and Howell, R. S. (1972). *Dutch Elm Disease Survey 1971*. (With supplementary leaflets for later years). Forestry Comm. Forest Record **82**.

701 Girling, M. and Greig, J. (1977). Palaeoecological investigations of a site at Hampstead Heath, London. *Nature, Lond.*, **268**, 45–7.

702 Glasscock, R. E. (1973). England *circa* 1334. *A New Historical Geography of England* (ed. H. C. Darby), 136–85. Cambridge.

703 Glover, J. (1976). *The Place-names of Kent*. Batsford, London.

705 Godwin, H. (1941). Studies in the post-glacial history of British vegetation. III. Fenland pollen diagrams. *Phil. Trans. roy. Soc. Lond.*, **B230**, 239–85.

706 Godwin, H. (1944). Age and origin of the 'Breckland' heaths of East Anglia. *Nature, Lond.*, **154**, 6–7.

707 Godwin, H. (1961). Radiocarbon dating and Quaternary history in Britain. *Proc. roy. Soc. Lond.*, **B153**, 287–320.

708 Godwin, H. (1966). Pollen-analytic evidence for the cultivation of Cannabis in England. *Rev. Palaeobot. Palynol.*, **4**, 71–80.

709 Godwin, H. (1968). Studies in the post-glacial history of British vegetation. XV. Organic deposits of Old Buckenham Mere, Norfolk. *New Phytol.*, **67**, 95–107.

710 Godwin, H. (1975). *History of the British Flora*, 2nd edition. Cambridge.

711 Godwin, H. (1978). *Fenland: Its Ancient Past and Uncertain Future*. Cambridge.

712 Godwin, H. and Godwin, M. E. (1960). Pollen analysis of peats at Scolt Head Island, Norfolk. *Scolt Head Island* (ed. J. A. Steers), 73–84. Heffer, Cambridge.

713 Godwin, H. and Tallantire, P. A. (1951). Studies in the post-glacial history of British vegetation. XII. Hockham Mere, Norfolk. *J. Ecol.*, **39**, 285–307.

714 Godwin, H. and Vishnu-Mittre (1975). Studies of the post-glacial history of British vegetation. XVI. Flandrian deposits of the Fenland margin at Holme Fen and Whittlesey Mere, Hunts. *Phil. Trans. roy. Soc. Lond.*, **B270**, 562–604.

715 Gonner, E. C. K. (1912). *Common Land and Enclosure*. Macmillan, London.

716 Gover, J. E. B., Mawer, A. and Stenton, F. M. (1936). *The Place-names of Warwickshire*. Cambridge.

717 Gover, J. E. B., Mawer, A. and Stenton, F. M. (1938). *The Place-names of Hertfordshire*. Cambridge.

718 Gover, J. E. B., Mawer, A. and Stenton, F. M. (1939). *The Place-names of Wiltshire*. Cambridge.

719 Gover, J. E. B., Mawer, A., Stenton, F. M. and Madge, S. J. (1942). *The Place-names of Middlesex*. Cambridge.

720 Gower, J. C. (1966). Some distance properties of latent root and vector methods used in multivariate analysis. *Biometrika*, **53**, 325–38.

721 Greenhalgh, G. N. (1975). Society autumn foray, Cambridge. *Bull. Brit. myc. Soc.*, **9**, 59–66, 107.

722 Grundy, G. B. (1931). *Saxon Charters of Worcestershire*. Birmingham Arch. Soc.

723 Grundy, G. B. (1939). The ancient woodland of Wiltshire. *Wilts Arch. Nat. Hist. Mag.*, **48**, 530–98.

724 Hadfield, M. (1961). Notes on lime trees in Britain (I). *Quart. J. For.*, **55**, 303–12.

725 Hadfield, M. (1967). *Landscape with trees*. Country Life, London.

726 Hadfield, M. (1974). The oak and its legends. In: *The British Oak* (*see* 94), 123–9.

727 Hammond, P. M. (1974). Changes in the British coleopterous fauna. *The Changing Flora and Fauna of Britain* (ed. D. L. Hawksworth), 323–69. Academic Press, London.

728 Hardcastle, E. J. B. (1976). The forester saga: a story of forest economics in retrospect. *Quart. J. For.*, **70**, 148–53.

729 Harris, R. (1974). Poplar crucks in Worcestershire and Herefordshire. *Vernac. Archit.*, **5**, 24–5.

730 Hassall, W. O. (1957). Shotover. *Victoria County History – Oxford* **5**, 275–81.

731 Hassall, W. O. and Dickinson, J. G. (1957). Stowood. *Victoria County History – Oxford*, **5**, 293–5.

732 Hasted, E. (1798). *The History and Topographical Survey of the County of Kent*. Vol. VI. Canterbury.

733 Hawksworth, D. L., Coppins, B. J. and Rose, F. (1974). Changes in the British lichen-flora. *The Changing Flora and Fauna of Britain* (ed. D. L. Hawksworth), 47–78. Academic Press, London.

734 Hewett, C. A. (1969). *The Development of Carpentry, 1200–1700: an Essex Study*. David and Charles, Newton Abbot.

735 Hewett, C. A. (1974). *English Cathedral Carpentry*. Wayland, London.

736 Heybroek, H. M. (1967). The Dutch elm disease in the Old World. *Referate, XIV IUFRO Kongress, München*, **5**, 447–54.

737 Hiley, W. E. (1954). *Woodland Management*, 2nd edition. Faber, London.

738 Hind, W. M. and Babington, C. (1889). *The Flora of Suffolk*. Gurney and Jackson, London.

739 Hodge, C. A. H. and Seale, R. S. (1966). *The Soils of the District Around Cambridge*. Agricultural Research Council, Harpenden.

740 Holt, J. C. (1965). *Magna Carta*. Cambridge.

741 Holt, J. C. (1961). *The Northerners*. Clarendon Press, Oxford.

742 Hooper, M. D. (1971). The size and surroundings of nature reserves. *The Scientific Management of Animal and Plant Communities for Conservation* (eds E. Duffey and

A. S. Watt), 555–61. Blackwell, Oxford.
743 Hopkinson, J. W. (1927). Studies on the vegetation of Nottinghamshire. I. The ecology of the Bunter Sandstone. *J. Ecol.*, **15**, 130–71.
744 Hoppus, E. (1736). *Practical Measuring Made Easy to the Meanest Capacity*. London.
745 Horrill, A. D. (1972). Biological Flora of the British Isles: *Melampyrum cristatum* L. *J. Ecol.*, **60**, 235–44.
746 Hubbard, C. E. (1954). *Grasses*. Penguin, Harmondsworth.
747 Huber, B., Holdheide, W. and Raack, K. (1941). Zur Frage der Unterscheidbarkeit des Holzes von Stiel- und Traubeneiche. *Holz*, **4**, 373–80.
748 Hughes, G. B. (1953). *Living Crafts*. Lutterworth, London.
749 Hull, M. R. (1963). Roman gazetteer. *Victoria County History – Essex*, **3**, 35–204.
750 Hultén, E. (1950). *Atlas över växternas utbredning i norden*. Kartografiska institutet, Stockholm.
751 Iversen, J. (1944). *Viscum*, *Hedera* and *Ilex* as climatic indicators. *Geol. Fören. Stockh. Förh.*, **66**, 463ff.
752 Iversen, J. (1967). *Danmarks Natur* (trans. as *The Development of Denmark's Nature Since the Last Glacial*. 1973). Reitzel Copenhagen.
753 Ivimey-Cook, R. B. and Proctor, M. C. F. (1966). The plant communities of the Burren, Co. Clare. *Proc. roy. Ir. Acad*, **64**, 211–301.
753a Jacobi, R. M., Tallis,J. H. and Mellars, P. A. (1976). The southern Pennine Mesolithic and the ecological record. *J. Arch. Sci.* **3**, 307–20.
754 Jermy, A. C., James, P. W. and Eddy, A. (1978). Terrestrial ecosystems. *The Island of Mull: a Survey of Its Flora and Environment* (eds A. C. Jermy and J. A. Crabbe), 10.1–10.77. British Museum, London.
755 Jermyn, S. T. (1974). *Flora of Essex*. Essex Naturalists' Trust.
756 Jones, E. W. (1945). Biological Flora of the British Isles: *Acer* L. *J. Ecol.*, **32**, 215–52.
757 Jones, E. W. (1959). Biological Flora of the British Isles: *Quercus* L. *J. Ecol.*, **47**, 169–222.
758 Jovet, P. (1949). *Le Valois: phytosociologie et phytogéographie*. Société d'Édition d'Enseignement Supérieur, Paris.
759 Kassas, M. (1951). Studies in the ecology of Chippenham Fen. II. *J. Ecol.*, **39**, 19–32.
760 Kelly, M. R. and Osborne, P. J. (1965). Two faunas and floras from the alluvium at Shustoke, Warwickshire. *Proc. Linn. Soc. Lond.*, **176**, 37–65.
761 Kent, D. H. (1975). *The Historical Flora of Middlesex*. Ray Soc., London.
762 Kenyon, G. H. (1967). *The Glass Industry of the Weald*. Leicester Univ. Press, Leicester.
763 Kerridge, E. (1953). The movement of rent, 1540–1640. *Econ. Hist. Rev.*, **2nd ser. 6**, 16–34.
764 Ketton-Cremer, R. W. (1962). *Felbrigg: the Story of a House*. Hart-Davis, London.
765 King, D. W. (1969). *Soils of the Luton and Bedford District*. Soil Survey, Harpenden.
766 Kubiëna, W. L. (1953). *The Soils of Europe: Illustrated Diagnosis and Systematics*. Murby, London.
767 Lamb, H. H. (1972; 1977). *Climate Present, Past and Future*. Vols **I**; **II**. Methuen, London.
768 Lambert, J. M., Jennings, J. N., Smith, C. T., Green, C. and Hutchinson, J. N. (1960). *The Making of the Broads*. Roy. Geog. Soc., London.
769 Lankester, E. (1848). *The Correspondence of John Ray*. Ray Soc., London.
770 Latham, B. (1957). *Timber: Its Development and Distribution*. Harrap, London.
771 Leathart, P. S. (1965). A forestry tour in France. *Quart. J. For.*, **59**, 16–35.
772 Lebrun, J., Noirfalaise, A., Heinemann, P. and Vanden Berghen, C. (1949). Les associations végétales de Belgique. *Bull. Soc. roy. Bot. Belg.*, **82**, 105–207.
773 Liebermann, F. (1906). *Die Gesetze der Angelsachsen*. **2**. Band. Halle.
774 Longman, K. A. and Coutts, M. P. (1974). Physiology of the oak tree. In: *The British Oak* (*see* 94), 194–221.
775 Lowday, J. E. and Wells, T. C. E. (1977). *The Management of Grassland and Heathland in Country Parks*. Countryside Commission.
776 Macgregor, J. J. (1959). The preparation of pricc index numbers for forestry products. *Forestry*, **32**, 30–51.
777 McVean, D. N. (1953). Biological Flora of the British Isles: *Alnus glutinosa*. *J. Ecol.*, **41**, 447–66.
778 McVean, D. N. (1956). Ecology of *Alnus glutinosa* . . . III. Seedling establishment. *J. Ecol.*, **44**, 195–218.
779 McVean, D. N. (1956). Ecology of *Alnus glutinosa* . . . IV. Root system. *J. Ecol.*, **44**, 219–25.
780 McVean, D. N. and Ratcliffe, D. A. (1962). *Plant Communities of the Scottish Highlands*. H.M.S.O., London.
781 Maitland, F. W. (1897). *Domesday Book and Beyond*. Cambridge. [Reprinted (Fontana, London) 1960 and later.]
782 Manley, G. (1974). Central England temperatures: monthly means 1659 to 1973. *Quart. J. roy. met. Soc.*, **100**, 389–405.
783 Matthews, B. (1971). *Soils in Yorkshire I: Sheet SE 65 (York East)*. Soil Survey Record **6**.
784 Maycock, A. L. (1963). *Nicholas Ferrar of Little Gidding*. S.P.C.K., London.
785 Mayhew, A. (1973). *Rural Settlement and Farming in Germany*. Batsford, London.
786 Meikle, R. D. (1975). *Populus* L. *Hybridization and the Flora of the British Isles* (ed. C. A. Stace), p. 303. Academic Press, London.
787 Mellanby, K. (1968). The effect of some mammals and birds on regeneration of oak. *J. appl. Ecol.*, **5**, 359–66.
788 Mellanby, K. (1971). *The Mole*. Collins, London.
789 Melville, R. (1939). Contributions to the study of British elms. II. The East Anglian elm. *J. Bot., Lond.*, **77**, 138–45.
790 Melville, R. (1940). Contributions to the study of British elms III. The Plot elm, *Ulmus plotii* Druce. *J. Bot., Lond.*, **78**, 181–92.
791 Melville, R., (1955). Morphological characters in the discrimination of hybrids and species. *Species Studies in the British Flora* (ed. J. E. Lousley), 55–64. Bot. Soc. Br. Isl., London.
792 Melville, R. (1975). *Ulmus* L. *Hybridization and the Flora of the British Isles* (ed. C. A. Stace), 292–9. Academic Press, London.
792a Melville, R. (1978). On the discrimination of species in hybrid swarms with special reference to *Ulmus* and the nomenclature of *U. minor* Mill. and *U. carpinifolia* Gled. *Taxon*, **27**, 345–51.
793 Midgley, M. M. (1947). The borough of Sutton Coldfield. *Victoria County History – Warwick*, **4**, 230–45.
794 Miller, S. H. and Skertchly, S. B. J. (1878). *The Fenland Past and Present*. Wisbech.
795 Mingay, G. E. (1956). The agricultural depression, 1730–1750. *Econ. Hist. Rev.*, **2nd ser. 8**, 323–38.
796 Mittempergher, L. and Raddi, P. (1975). Considerazioni sullo stato attuale del 'cancro della corteccia' in Italia. *Ann. Accad. ital. Sci. for.*, **24**, 15–28.
797 Mittre, V. (1971). Fossil pollen of *Tilia* from the East Anglian fenland. *New Phytol.*, **70**, 693–7.
798 Mollat, M. (1971). *Histoire de l'Ile-de-France et de Paris*. Toulouse.
799 Moore, H. I. and Burr, S. (1948). The control of rushes on newly reseeded land in Yorkshire. *J. Brit. Grassl. Soc.*, **3**,

283–90.
800 Moss, C. E. (1907). *Geographical Distribution of Vegetation in Somerset: Bath and Bridgwater District.* Roy. Geog. Soc., London.
801 Moss, C. E. (1913). *Vegetation of the Peak District.* Cambridge.
802 Munby, L. M. (1977). *The Hertfordshire Landscape.* Hodder and Stoughton, London.
803 Murton, R. K. (1965). *The Woodpigeon.* Collins, London.
804 Nathan, F. L. (1907). Making of gunpowder. *Victoria County History – Essex,* **2**, 451–5.
805 Nef, J. U. (1932). *The Rise of the British Coal Industry.* Routledge and Kegan Paul, London.
806 Neilson, N. (1949). The Forests. *The English Government at Work, 1327–1336* (eds J. F. Willard and W. A. Morris), 394–467. Cambridge (Mass.).
807 Newnham, R. M. and Carlisle, A. (1969). The nitrogen and phosphorus nutrition of seedlings of *Quercus robur* L. and *Q. petraea* (Mattuschka) Liebl. *J. Ecol.,* **57**, 271–84.
808 Newton, K. C. (1970). *The Manor of Writtle.* Phillimore, London.
809 Oberdorfer, E. (1957). *Süddeutsche Pflanzengesellschaften.* Fischer, Jena.
810 Oinonen, E. (1967). The correlation between the size of Finnish bracken (*Pteridium aquilinum* . . .) clones and certain periods of site history. *Acta forest. Fennica,* **83**, 97–144.
811 Ordnance Survey (1966). *Map of Britain in the Dark Ages,* 2nd edition. Southampton.
812 Ordnance Survey (1973). *Place Names on Maps of Scotland and Wales.* Southampton.
813 Orloci, L. (1967). An agglomerative method for classification of plant communities. *J. Ecol.,* **55**, 193–206.
814 Orwin, C. S. and Orwin, C. S. (1938). *The Open Fields.* Oxford.
815 *Oxford Dictionary of Quotations* (1953). 2nd edition. Oxford.
816 *Oxford English Dictionary* (1884–1928). Oxford.
817 Page, R. I. (1973). *An Introduction to English Runes.* Cambridge.
817a Paris, M. (*c.* 1250) and Walsingham, T. (*c.* 1395). *Gesta abbatum monasterii S. Albani.* (ed. H. T. Riley. Longmans, London, 1867.)
818 Parker, V. (1971). *The Making of Kings Lynn.* Phillimore, London.
819 Parker, W. (1873). *The History of Long Melford.* London.
820 Parsons, J. L. (1882). The Sussex ironworks. *Sussex Arch. Coll.,* **32**, 19–32.
821 Paul, C. R. C. (1975). Molluscs. In: *Hayley Wood* (see 120), 183–5.
822 Peace, T. R. (1960). *The status and development of elm disease in Britain.* Forestry Comm. Bull., **33**.
823 Peace, T. R. (1962). *Pathology of Trees and Shrubs.* Clarendon Press, Oxford.
824 Pennington, W. (1969). *The History of British Vegetation.* English Universities Press, London.
825 Pennington, W. (1970). Vegetation history in the northwest of England: a regional synthesis. *Studies in the Vegetational History of the British Isles* (eds D. Walker and R. G. West), 41–79. Cambridge.
826 Perrin, R. M. S. (1956). Nature of 'Chalk Heath' soils. *Nature, Lond.,* **178**, 31–2.
827 Perrin, R. M. S. (1977). Air photography and soil science. *The Uses of Air Photography* (ed. J. K. S. St Joseph), 2nd edition, 66–85. Baker, London.
828 Perrin, R. M. S., Davies, H. and Fysh, M. D. (1974). Distribution of late Pleistocene aeolian deposits in eastern and southern England. *Nature, Lond.,* **248**, 320–3.
829 Perring, F. H., Sell, P. D., Walters, S. M. and Whitehouse, H. L. K. (1964). *A Flora of Cambridgeshire.* Cambridge.
830 Perring, F. H. and Walters, S. M. (1962). *Atlas of the British Flora.* Bot. Soc. Brit. Isl., London.
831 Petch, C. and Swann, E. L. (1968). *Flora of Norfolk.* Jarrold, Norwich.
832 Peterken, G. F. and Lloyd, P. S. (1967). Biological Flora of the British Isles: *Ilex aquifolium* L. *J. Ecol.,* **55**, 841–58.
833 Peters, E. D. (1907). *The Principles of Copper Smelting.* New York.
834 Pigott, C. D. (1962). Soil formation and development on the Carboniferous Limestone of Derbyshire. I. Parent materials. *J. Ecol.,* **50**, 145–56.
835 Pigott, C. D. (1977). The scientific basis of practical conservation: aims and methods of conservation. *Proc. roy. Soc. Lond.,* **B197**, 59–68.
835a Pinto, E. M. (1949). *Treen or Small Woodware throughout the Ages.* Batsford, London.
836 Poel, L. W. (1961). Soil aeration as a limiting factor in the growth of *Pteridium aquilinum* . . . *J. Ecol.,* **49**, 107–11.
837 Pollard, E., Hooper, M. D. and Moore, N. W. (1974). *Hedges.* Collins, London.
838 Poore, M. E. D. (1956). The use of phytosociological methods in ecological investigations. IV. General discussion of phytosociological problems. *J. Ecol.,* **44**, 28–50.
839 Postan, M. M. (1972). *The Medieval Economy and Society.* Weidenfeld and Nicholson, London.
840 Power, E. and Postan, M. M. (1933). *Studies in English Trade in the Fifteenth Century.* Routledge, London.
841 Preston, F. W. (1962). The canonical distribution of commonness and rarity. *Ecology,* **43**, 182–215, 410–32.
842 Prince, H. C. (1964). The origin of pits and depressions in Norfolk. *Geography,* **49**, 15–32.
843 Pritchard, N. M. and Anderson, A. J. B. (1971). Observations on the use of cluster analysis in botany with an ecological example. *J. Ecol.,* **59**, 727–47.
844 Rackham, O. (1972). The vegetation of the Myrtos region. *Myrtos: an Early Bronze Age Settlement in Crete* (by P. M. Warren) 283–98. Thames and Hudson, London.
845 Rackham, O. (1972). Grundle House: on the quantities of timber in certain East Anglian buildings in relation to local supplies. *Vernac. Archit.,* **3**, 3–8.
846 Rackham, O. (1977). Hedgerow trees: their history, conservation, and renewal. *Arboric. J.,* **3**, 169–77.
847 Rackham, O., Blair, W. J. and Munby, J. T. (1978). The thirteenth-century roofs and floor of the Blackfriars Monastery at Gloucester. *Medieval Arch.,* **22**, 105–22.
848 *Radiocarbon* (1975) **17**, 260–1; (1976) **18**, 257.
849 Raftis, J. A. (1974). *Assart Data and Land Values: Two Studies in the East Midlands.* Toronto.
850 Ratcliffe, D. A. (1977). *A Nature Conservation Review.* Cambridge.
851 Reaney, P. H. (1935). *Place-names of Essex.* Cambridge.
852 Reaney, P. H. (1943). *Place-names of Cambridgeshire and the Isle of Ely.* Cambridge.
853 Reed, J. L. (1954). *Forests of France.* Faber, London.
854 Richens, R. H. (1955). Studies on *Ulmus.* I. The range of variation of East Anglian elms. *Watsonia,* **3**, 138.
855 Richens, R. H. (1958). Studies on *Ulmus.* II. The village elms of southern Cambridgeshire. *Forestry,* **31**, 131–49.
856 Richens, R. H. (1959). Studies on *Ulmus.* III. The village elms of Hertfordshire. *Forestry,* **32**, 138–54.
857 Richens, R. H. (1961). Studies on *Ulmus.* IV. The village elms of Huntingdonshire and a new method for exploring taxonomic discontinuity. *Forestry,* **34**, 47–64.
858 Richens, R. H. (1961). Studies on *Ulmus.* V. The village elms of Bedfordshire. *Forestry,* **34**, 181–200.
859 Richens, R. H. (1965). Studies on *Ulmus.* VI. Fenland elms. *Forestry,* **38**, 224–35.
860 Richens, R. H. (1967). Studies on *Ulmus.* VII. Essex elms.

Forestry, **40**, 184–206.

861 Richens, R. H. 'Reapers' by Stubbs. *The Times*, 10 Aug. 1977.

862 Richens, R. H. and Jeffers, J. N. R. (1975). Multivariate analysis of the elms of Northern France. I. Variation within France. *Silvae Genetica*, **24**, 141–9.

863 Riddelsdell, H. J., Hedley, G. W. and Price, W. R. (1948). *Flora of Gloucestershire*. Cotteswold Naturalists' Field Club, Cheltenham.

864 Rishbeth, J. (1973). Slime flux and wetwood. *Newsl. Ass. Brit. Tree Surg. Arborists*, Aug. 1973, 6–8.

865 Rodwell, W. and Rowley, T. (1975). *The 'small towns' of Roman Britain*. Brit. Archaeol. Rep., Oxford.

866 Rogers, J. E. T. (1882; 1887). *A History of Agriculture and Prices in England. III. 1401–1582. VI. 1583–1702*. Clarendon Press, Oxford.

866a Rook, T. (1978). The development and operation of Roman hypocausted baths. *J. Arch. Sci*, **5**, 269–82.

867 Round, J. H. (1903). Introduction to the Essex Domesday. *Victoria County History – Essex*, **1**, 333–426.

868 Royal Commission on Historical Monuments (1959). *City of Cambridge*. H.M.S.O., London.

869 Royal Commission on Historical Monuments (1968). *West Cambridgeshire*. H.M.S.O., London.

870 Royal Commission on Historical Monuments (1972). *East Cambridgeshire*. H.M.S.O., London.

871 Salway, P., Hallam, S. J. and Bromwich, J. I. (1970). *The Fenland in Roman Times*. Roy. Geog. Soc., London.

872 Schlich, W. (1895). *A Manual of Forestry. III. Forest Management*. Bradbury and Agnew, London.

873 Schmidt, G. (1969). *Vegetationsgeographie auf ökologisch-soziologische Grundlage*. Leipzig.

874 Sheail, J. (1971). *Rabbits and Their History*. David and Charles, Newton Abbot.

875 Sheail, J. (1976). *Nature in Trust: the History of Nature Conservation in Britain*. Blackie, Glasgow.

876 Shimwell, D. W. (1971). *The Description and Classification of Vegetation*. Sidgwick and Jackson, London.

877 Simmons, I. G. (1964). Pollen diagrams from Dartmoor. *New Phytol.*, **63**, 165–80.

878 Sims, R. E. (1972). The anthropogenic factor in East Anglian vegetational history: an approach using A[bsolute] P[ollen] F[requency] techniques. *Quaternary Plant Ecology* (eds H. J. B. Birks and R. G. West), 223–36. Blackwell, Oxford.

879 Smedley, N. (1960). Roman Long Melford. *Proc. Suffolk Inst. Archaeol.*, **28**, 272–89.

880 Smedley, N. (1977). *East Anglian Crafts*. Batsford, London.

881 Smith, A. G. and Pilcher, J. R. (1973). Radiocarbon dates and vegetational history of thc British Isles. *New Phytol.*, **72**, 903–14.

882 Smith, A. H. (1956). *English Place-name Elements*. Cambridge.

883 Smith, A. H. (1961–3). *The Place-names of the West Riding of Yorkshire*. Cambridge.

884 South, A. (1974). Changes in composition of the terrestrial mollusc fauna. *The Changing Flora and Fauna of Britain*, (ed. D. L. Hawksworth), 255–74. Academic Press, London.

885 Sparkes, I. G. (1973). *The English Country Chair: an Illustrated History of Chairs and Chairmaking*. Spurbooks, Bourne End.

886 Sparks, B. W. and West, R. G. (1972). *The Ice Age in Britain*. Methuen, London.

887 Spevack, M. (1973). *The Harvard Concordance to Shakespeare*. Harvard.

887a Spratt, D. A. and Simmons, I. G. (1976). Prehistoric activity and environment on the North York Moors. *J. Arch. Sci.*, **3**, 193–210.

888 Straker, E. (1931). *Wealden Iron*. Bell.

889 Sturdy, R. G. (1971). *Soils in Essex I: Sheet TQ 59 (Harold Hill*. Soil Survey, Harpenden.

890 Suess, H. E. (1970). Bristlecone pine calibration of the radiocarbon time-scale 5200 B.C. to the present. *Radiocarbon Variations and Absolute Chronology*, (ed. I. V. Olsson), 303–313. Almqvist and Wiksell, Stockholm.

890a Sumner, H. (1926). Geography and prehistoric earthworks in the New Forest district. *Geogrl J.*, **67**, 244–8.

891 Szafer, W. (1966). *The Vegetation of Poland*. (Trans. W. H. Paryski.). Warszawa.

892 Taylor, C. C. (1970). *The Dorset Landscape*. Hodder and Stoughton, London.

893 Taylor, C. S. (1889). *An Analysis of the Domesday Survey of Gloucestershire*. Jefferies, Bristol.

894 *Thaxted Guildhall: a consultative document for renovation* [*c*. 1973]. Essex County Council (County Architect and County Planner).

895 Thomasson, A. J. (1969). *Soils of the Saffron Walden District*. Agric. Res. Council, Harpenden.

896 Thompson, E. P. (1975). *Whigs and Hunters: the Origin of the Black Act*. Allen Lane. London.

897 Thuillier, J. L. (1790). *La Flore des Environs de Paris*. Paris.

898 Troels-Smith, J. (1960). *Ivy, Mistletoe and Elm: Climate Indicators – Fodder Plants*. Reitzel, København.

899 Turner, J. (1970). Post-neolithic disturbance of British vegetation. *Studies in the Vegetational History of the British Isles* (eds D. Walker and R. G. West), 97–116. Cambridge.

900 Tutin, T. G. (1953). Natural factors contributing to a change in our flora. *The Changing Flora of Britain* (ed. J. E. Lousley), 19–25. Bot. Soc. Br. Isl., London.

901 Tutin, T. G. (1957). Biological Flora of the British Isles: *Allium ursinum* L. *J. Ecol.*, **45**, 1003–10.

902 Vauquelin (An VII, i.e. 1799). Observations sur une maladie des arbres, et spécialement de l'orme (*ulmus campestris Lin.*), analogue à un ulcère. *Mém. Inst. nat. Sci. math. phys.*, **2**, 23–30.

903 Vinter, C. H. S., Waller, A. P. and Bishop Whittingham (1937). *The Lepidoptera of Suffolk*. Mem. Suffolk Naturalists' Soc.

903a Walker, F. S. (1978). Pedunculate and sessile oaks: species determination from differences between their wood. *Dendrochronology in Europe* (ed. J. Fletcher), 329–38. Nat. Marit. Mus., Greenwich.

904 Walters, S. M. (1968). *Betula* L. in Britain. *Proc. bot. Soc. Br. Isl.*, **7**, 179–80.

905 Warren, S. H., Clark, J. G. D., Godwin, M. E. and Macfadyen, W. A. (1934). An Early Mesolithic site at Broxbourne sealed under Boreal peat. *J. roy. Anthropol. Inst.*, **64**, 101–28.

906 Watson, W. C. R. (1958). *Handbook of the Rubi of Great Britain and Ireland*. Cambridge.

907 Watt, A. S. (1964). Some factors affecting bracken in Breckland. *J. Ecol.*, **52**, 63–77.

908 Weaver, J. E. and Clemcnts, F. E. (1929). *Plant Ecology*. McGraw-Hill, New York.

909 Wells, H. B. (1953). *Doddington. Victoria County History – Cambs*, **4**, 111.

910 West, R. G. (1956). The Quaternary deposits at Hoxne, Suffolk. *Phil. Trans. roy. Soc. Lond.*, **B239**, 265–356.

911 West, R. G. (1961). Interglacial and interstadial vegetation in England. *Proc. Linn. Soc. Lond.*, **172**, 81–9.

912 West, R. G. (1968). *Pleistocene Geology and Biology*. Longmans, London.

913 Wiermann, R. (1965). Moorkundliche und vegetationsgeschichtliche Betrachtungen zum Aussendeichsmoor bei Sehestadt (Jadebusen). *Ber. dt bot. Ges.*, **78**, 269–78.

914 Wightman, W. R. (1968). The pattern of vegctation in the Vale of Pickering area c. 1300 A.D. *Trans. Inst. Brit. Geog.*, **45**, 125–42.

915 Wigston, D. L. (1974). Cytology and genetics of oaks. In: *The British Oak* (*see* 94), 27–50.

916 Williams, A. (1946). A homestead moat at Nuthampstead, Hertfordshire. *Antiq. J.*, **26**, 138ff.

917 Wilson, D. G. (1975). Plant remains from the Graveney Boat and the early history of *Humulus lupulus* L. in W. Europe. *New Phytol.*, **75**, 627–48.

918 Woodell, S. R. J. (1965). Primula elatior in Norfolk: immigrant or relic? *Proc. bot. Soc. Br. Isl.*, **6**, 37–9.

919 Wright, J. (1898–1905). *English Dialect Dictionary*. Frowde, London.

Bibliography to 2003 Edition

Actes du Symposium International d'Histoire Forestière (1982). École Nationale du Génie Rural, des Eaux, et des Forêts, Nancy.

Atherden, M. A. and Butlin, R. [1999]. *Woodland in the Landscape: past and future perspectives*. Leeds University Press.

Best, J. A. (1998). Persistent outcomes of coppice grazing in Rockingham Forest . . . Kirby & Watkins (below) 63–72.

Birks, H. N. and H. J. B., Kaland, P. E., and Moe, D. (1988). *The Cultural Landscape: Past, Present and Future*. Cambridge University Press.

Bridge, M. C., Hibbert, A., and Rackham, O. (1986). 'Effects of coppicing on the growth of oak timber trees in the Bradfield Woods, Suffolk'. *Journal of Ecology*, **74**, 1095–1102.

Broad, J. and Hoyle, R. (eds) (1997). *Bernwood [Oxfordshire]: the life and afterlife of a Forest*. University of Central Lancashire.

Buckley, G. P. (ed.) (1992). *Ecology and Management of Coppice Woodlands*. Chapman & Hall, London.

Cannell, M. G. R., Malcolm, D. C., and Robertson, P. A. (1992). *The Ecology of Mixed-Species Stands of Trees*. Blackwell Scientific Publications, Oxford.

Clément, V. (2002). *De la Marche-Frontière au Pays-des-Bois. Forêts, sociétés paysannes et territoires en Vieille-Castile (XIe–XXe siècles)*. Casa de Velásquez, Madrid.

Coombe, D. E. and Rackham, O. (1996). 'Madingley Wood'. *Nature in Cambridgeshire*, **38**, 27–54.

Dargavel, J. (1995). *Fashioning Australia's Forests*. Oxford University Press.

Dargavel, J. (ed.) (1997). *Australia's Ever-Changing Forests III*. National Conference on Australian Forest History, Canberra.

Dargavel, J. and Libbis, B. (eds) (1997). *Australia's Ever-Changing Forests IV*. National Conference on Australian Forest History, Canberra.

Fairhead, J. & Leach, M. (1998). *Reframing Deforestation*. Routledge, London. [Deals with West Africa.]

Grove, A. T. and Rackham, O. (2001). *The Nature of Mediterranean Europe: an ecological history*. Yale University Press.

Gulliver, R. (1995). 'Woodland history and plant indicator species in north-east Yorkshire'. *Ecological Relations in Historic Times: human impact and adaptation*, ed. R. A. Butlin and N. Roberts, Blackwell, Oxford, 169–89.

Gulliver, R. (1998). 'What were woods like in the seventeenth century? Examples from the Helmsley Estate, northeast Yorkshire'. Kirby & Watkins (see below), 135–54.

Harding, P. T. and Wall, T. (eds) (1999). *Moccas: an English deer park*. English Nature.

Hart, C. (1983). *Coleford: the history of a West Gloucestershire Forest town*. Alan Sutton, Gloucester.

Hepple, L. W. and Doggett, A. M. (1992). *The Chilterns*. Chichester Press.

Holmes, W. and Wheaten, A. (2002). *The Blean: the woodlands of a cathedral city*. Blean Research Group, University of Kent.

Hunter, J. M. (1985). *Land into Landscape*. Goodwin, London.

Huntley, B. and Birks, H. J. B. (1983). *An atlas of past and present pollen maps for Europe: 0–1300 [C14] years ago*. Cambridge University Press.

Kirby, K. J. and 3 others (1998). The Ancient Woodland Inventory in England and its uses. Kirby & Watkins (below) 323–36.

Kirby, K. J. and Watkins, C. (1998). *The Ecological History of European Forests*. CAB International, Wallingford.

Linnard, W. (1982, 2nd ed. 2000). *Welsh Woods and Forests: a history*. Gomer, Llandysul.

Marren, P. (2002). *Nature Conservation: a review of the conservation of wildlife in Britain 1950–2001*. Harper Collins, London.

Moe, D. and Rackham, O. (1992). 'Pollarding and a possible explanation of the neolithic elmfall'. *Vegetation History and Archaeobotany*, **1**, 63–8.

Moreno, D. (ed.) (1986). *Boschi: Storia e Archeologia 2. Quaderni Storici*, **n.s. 62**, 435–537.

Moreno, D., Piussi, P., e Rackham, O. (eds) (1982). *Boschi: Storia e Archeologia. Quaderni Storici*, **49**, 7–216.

Nakashizuka, T. and Matsumoto, Y. (eds) (2002). *Diversity and Interaction in a Temperate Forest Community: Ogawa Forest Reserve of Japan*, Springer, Tokyo. (Especially W. Suzuki, 'Forest vegetation in and around Ogawa Forest Reserve in relation to human impact', pp. 27–42.)

Peglar, S. M., Fritz, S. C., and Birks, H. J. B. (1989). Vegetation and land-use history at Diss, Norfolk . . . *Journal of Ecology*, **77**, 203–22.

Peterken, G. F. and Jones, E. W. (1987). Forty years of change in Lady Park Wood [Hereford]: the old-growth stands. *Journal of Ecology*, **75**, 477–512.

Peterken, G. F. (1993). *Woodland Conservation and Management*. 2nd ed. Chapman & Hall, London.

Peterken, G. F. (1996). *Natural Woodlands: ecology and conservation in north temperate regions*. Cambridge University Press.

Pilcher, J. R. and Mac an tSaoir, S. (eds) (1995). *Woods, Trees and Forests in Ireland*. Royal Irish Academy, Dublin.

Pott, R. (1981). Anthropogene Einflüsse auf Kalkbuchenwälder am Beispiel der Niederholzwirtschaft und anderer extensiver Bewirtschaftungsformen. *Allgemeine Forstzeitschrift*, **23**, 569–71. [Pollarding in Germany.]

Rackham, O. (1981). 'The Avon Gorge and Leigh Woods' in M. Bell and S. Limbrey, *Archaeological aspects of woodland ecology*. British Archaeological Reports International Series, **146**, 171–6.

Rackham, O. (1982). 'The growing and transport of timber and underwood' in *Woodworking techniques before* A.D. *1500*, ed. S. McGrail, *British Archaeological Reports International Series*, **129**, 199–218.

Rackham, O. (1984). 'The Forest: woodland and wood-pasture in medieval England', in *Archaeological Approaches to Medieval Europe*, ed. K. Biddick. Western Michigan University, Kalamazoo, 70–104.

Rackham, O. (1985). 'Ancient woodland and hedges in England', in *The English Landscape – past, present, and future* [being the Wolfson College Lectures for 1983], ed. S. R. J. Woodell. Oxford, 48–67.

Rackham, O. (1986a). *History of the [British and Irish] countryside*. Dent, London.

Rackham, O. (1986b). *Ancient woodland of England: the woods of South-East Essex*. Rochford District Council.

Rackham, O. (1986c). 'The ancient woods of Norfolk'. *Transactions of Norfolk & Norwich Naturalists' Society*, **27**, 161–77.

Rackham, O. (1987). 'The countryside: history and pseudo-history'. *The Historian*, **14**, 13–17.

Rackham, O. (1988). 'Trees and woodland in a crowded landscape – the cultural landscape of the British Isles', in *The Cultural Landscape: Past, Present and Future*, ed. H. H. Birks and others, Cambridge, 53–78.

Rackham, O. (1989). *The Last Forest: the story of Hatfield Forest [Essex]*. Dent, London.

Rackham, O. (1990). *Trees and woodland in the British landscape*, revised edition. Dent, London.

Rackham, O. (1991). 'Landscape and the conservation of meaning' [being the Reflection Riding Memorial Lecture for 1990]. *Royal Society of Arts Journal*, **139**, 903–15.

Rackham, O. (1992a). 'Mixtures, mosaics and clones: the distribution of trees within European woods and forests', being the introductory review to Cannell, *The Ecology of Mixed-Species Stands of Trees*, above, 1–20.

Rackham, O. (1992b). 'Gamlingay Wood'. *Nature in Cambridgeshire*, **34**, 3–14.

Rackham, O. (1992c). 'Woodland ecology in recent and historic aerial photographs'. *Photogrammetric Record*, **14**, 227–39.

Rackham, O. (1994). *The Illustrated History of the Countryside*. Weidenfeld & Nicolson, London.

Rackham, O. (1998a). 'The Abbey woods'. *Bury St Edmunds: medieval art, architecture, archaeology and economy*, ed. A. Gransden, British Archaeological Association, London. 139–60, Plates XXXIII–XXXIV.

Rackham, O. (1998b). 'Savanna in Europe'. Kirby and Watkins, (above), 1–24.

Rackham, O. (1999). 'The woods 30 years on: where have the Primroses gone?' *Nature in Cambridgeshire*, **41**, 73–87.

Rackham, O. (2000a). 'Prospects for landscape history and historical ecology'. *Landscapes*, **2**, 3–15, Plates 1–3.

Rackham, O. (2000b). 'Woodland in the Ely Coucher Book'. *Nature in Cambridgeshire*, **42**, 37–44, 61–7.

Read, H. (ed.) (1992). *Pollard and Veteran Tree Management*. City of London Corporation.

Read, H. (ed.) (2000). *Veteran Trees: a guide to good management*. English Nature.

Roberts, G. (1999). *Woodlands of Kent*. Geerings, Ashford.

Rodwell, J. S. (ed.) (1991). *British Plant Communities: woodlands and scrub*. Cambridge University Press.

Smout, T. C. (ed.) (1997). *Scottish Woodland History*. Scottish Cultural Press, Edinburgh.

Smout, T. C. (ed.) (2003). *People and Woods in Scotland: a history*. Edinburgh University Press.

Spooner, B. M. and Bowdrey, J. P. (1988). *Hadleigh Great Wood: the wildlife and history of Belfairs Nature Reserve [S.E. Essex]*. South Essex Natural History Society.

Steel, D. (1984). *Shotover: the natural history of a royal Forest*. Pisces, Oxford.

Tack, G., van den Bremt, P. and Hermy (1993). *Bossen van Vlaanderen*. Davidsfonds, Leuven.

Vera, F. W. M. (2000). *Grazing Ecology and Forest History*. CABI, Wallingford.

Wager, S. J. (1998). *Woods, Wolds and Groves: the woodland of medieval Warwickshire*.

Williams, M. (1989). *Americans and their Forests: a historical geography*. Cambridge University Press.

Index and Glossary

Words here given a definition are printed in ***bold italic***. Cross-references to other defined words are given in *italic*. Further definitions or explanations are to be found on pages numbered in ***bold italic***. Page-numbers in **bold** are main references under a subject.

Languages are identified thus:

C	Cornish	Mod E	Modern English
EME	Early Modern English	NF	Norman-French
Ga	Gaelic	OE	Old English (i.e. Anglo-Saxon)
G	German	ON	Old Norse
ME	Middle English	W	Welsh
ML	Medieval Latin		

Main entries for names of plants are in English or Latin according to whichever is used in the text (see p. xiii). '*Quercus robur*' is thus cross-referenced to 'Oak' but 'Cow-wheat' is cross-referenced to '*Melampyrum*'.

CODA

A stray from the age of Eric Bloodaxe
and King Edmund the Magnificent (p. 201)?

Don't forget the non-woodland trees. Thomas Hardy wrote in 1891 of 'the hollow-trunked trees that shade so many of its pastures' in the Vale of Blackmoor. He thought them to be relics of woodland, but this has always been a field tree. Such a pollard oak with an immense trunk and small head of branches can be over a thousand years old; but it will not be 'in Domesday Book', which never mentions trees.

Middlemarsh, Dorset, April 2003

English Nature

Ancient semi-natural woods are irreplaceable, and must be protected and managed so as to maintain and enhance their special character. In ancient woods that are now coniferous plantations restoration of their native tree and shrub communities should be encouraged as the first step in the rehabilitation of their rich woodland ecosystems.

English Nature
Northminster House, Peterborough, PE1 1UA
Tel: +44(0)1733 455000 Fax: +44(0)1733 568834
E-mail: enquiries@english-nature.org.uk Website: www.english-nature.org.uk

Forestry Commission
England

The Forestry Commission's mission is to protect and expand Britain's forests and woodlands and increase their value to society and the environment.

Forestry Commission England
Great Eastern House
Tenison Road, Cambridge, CB1 2DU
Tel: 01223 314546 Fax: 01223 460699
Website: www.forestry.gov.uk/england

International Tree Foundation

The ITF aims to create a world richer in trees, by planting, preserving and educating about the value of trees worldwide. In the UK, ITF county groups work in their local communities and on a global scale the world's poorest environments and societies are helped through tree planting grants.

International Tree Foundation
National office: Sandy Lane, Crawley Down, West Sussex, RH10 4HS, UK
Tel: 01342-712536 & 01342 717300 Fax: 01342 718282
E-mail: info@internationaltreefoundation.org Website: www.internationaltreefoundation.org

Publisher's End Note

The publisher takes the liberty of intruding into print to record his considerable indebtedness to all those who made the book possible. He trusts the reader will indulge, and indeed forgive, his need to name names. Jon and Sue Atkins of Summerfield Books Ltd. suggested reprinting the original text, and pointed him in the geographical direction of the author (i.e. draw a line around Cambridge, Crete and Texas). Of course, without Oliver's responsiveness, his unbounding enthusiasm, and prodigious writing efforts, the book would not be here in this greatly expanded edition. The end result is testimony to his immense, Cantabrian scholarship.

Many people have given, apparently willingly, of their time and expertise – usually on the mere strength of a pleading phone call. George Peterken's support for the author and publisher should not be merely confined to a footnote. At English Nature, Keith Kirby, Dave Storey and the Terrestrial Wildlife Team have been exceptionally supportive. We gratefully acknowledge the analytical contribution to the book by Dr Andrew Brown. This equally applies to Forestry Commission England, with Lord Clark's incisive text having great merit. Rod Leslie's initial enthusiasm for the book and Simon Pryor's eloquently expressed knowledge of conservation issues were vital, as were his consultations on the proof sheets with many Forestry Commission staff. The financial support of English Nature, Forestry Commission England and the International Tree Foundation has been critical in offsetting the costs of producing such a large book with so many colour illustrations. The one substantive criticism of the first edition in 1980 concerned its price hindering it reaching a wide readership. By rights, the £50 cost in 1980 would be around £140 at today's prices. Our sponsors hoped the book could be sold at a price which allowed broad dissemination of this text, and we thank them for their contributions towards achieving this aim.

We are grateful to the trustees and officials of The Tree Council, The Woodland Trust, The Arboricultural Association and the British Ecological Society. We very much appreciate the written contributions by Caroline Davis MBE of the Tree Council, Mike Townsend OBE of the Woodland Trust, and Peter Rapson of the International Tree Foundation who all wrote, most eloquently and pointedly, at extremely short notice.

Living with the minutae of the text for two years has given the publisher – very much a non-scientist – a partial insight into what *Ancient Woodland* is all about. It has made him look at trees, all trees, differently. This insight was enhanced at the Sheffield Conference on Ancient Woodland, May 2003. Ian Rotherham, Paul Howden-Leach, and Keith and Diane Harrison of Sheffield Hallam University shared their knowledge and energy as did Steve Woodley and Sue Pendlebury with their very practical perspectives on trees. Many Sheffield Conference delegates were brave enough to be named 'subscribers', and we accord them, and those who did not wish to be named, our thanks for their faith in the book.

Dr Keith N. A. Alexander, Pam Bailey, Dr Nicola R. Bannister, The Rev. Nigel Cooper, Miss Debbie Court, Dr Joan Dixon, Mr Jay Doyle, Miss C. M. Groves, Mr Gary Haley, Mrs Ann Hill, Dr Della Hooke, Neil Hunter, Mr M. B. Jeeves, Professor Melvyn Jones, Dr John Knight, Dr David Morfitt, Professor B. K. Roberts, Ms Rebecca Roseff, Mr Philip Sansum, A. Shepley, Ms Angela Simco, Mr Jonathan Spencer, Dr Hilary Thomas, Mr E. M. Thorpe, F. C. P. Wolferstan.

Certain aspects of the text took on a life of their own, which will no doubt continue long after publication. As a single example the following exchange is cited, between the author and a final proofs 'reader' (a very select sub-species, to whom the task of 'seeing what was said about.' was given). There were others.

Reader: 'page 510, para 1, 3rd sentence: This is not quite true as the discount rate used was directly transferred from the rate of return that Treasury demanded (and usually got) from all public investments. That is, it was empirically set and ascertainable by observation. The big leap in rationale was directly transfering this discount rate from conventional short-term commercial investments to ones with a 50–150 year life. It might be worth pointing out that NDR was probably only the dominant factor in the 1960s and 1970s. Before and after this period it was the reliance on imports that drove most foresters and owners, either the strategic reserve argument post-war or subsequently the belief (some would say laudable, others – including Treasury – misguided) that we should not rely on other countries to grow more than 90% of the timber we use.'

Author: 'I don't agree. This merely transfers the mystery from the FC to the Treasury, according to theory (3) of three paragraphs above. Had the discount rate been based on measurement, it would have gone up and down with fluctuations in the performance of investments, and probably also with the vagaries of inflation. It was ascertainable by observation only in the anthropological sense that an outsider could have observed that this was how the Treasury went about its business, rather as his colleague might be observing the details of the initiation ceremonies of the Trobriand Islanders.'

By this time the page proofs were die-cast, so the anecdote rests on this last page. It deserves better.

Casting the die was the responsibility of Lesley Beaney and Janet Dunn. The publisher wishes to state – categorically, emphatically and indisputably – that without them this book would not have happened. They brought their wealth of experience, knowledge and skill to bear on the author's mountain of material, and the publisher's mountain of optimism, instilling reality at every flight of fancy by author and publisher. Only years of hard-wrought experience could have produced this book, and their dedication, patience and pride in their work is reflected in the style and quality of the layout. It is also reflected in the standard of the typography. Both author and publisher are in their debt; especially the publisher, who also needs to thank LSS, SFJS and SMES for putting up with him while *Ancient Woodland* took over his life.

JS, Kirkcudbrightshire, 1st August 2003.

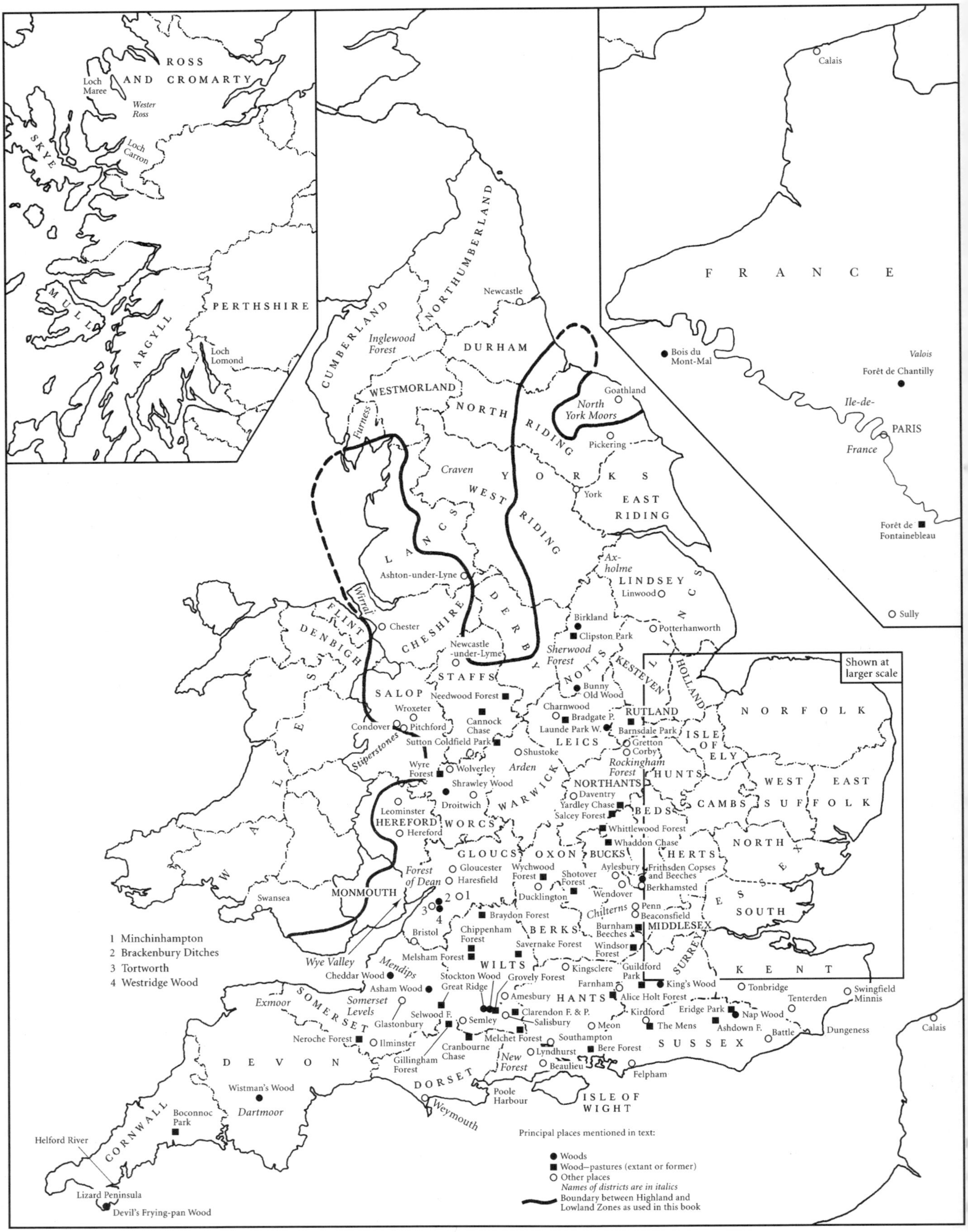
ROSS AND CROMARTY
Loch Maree
Wester Ross
SKYE
Loch Carron
MULL
ARGYLL
PERTHSHIRE
Loch Lomond
Calais
FRANCE
Bois du Mont-Mal
Valois
Forêt de Chantilly
Ile-de-France
PARIS
Forêt de Fontainebleau
Sully
NORTHUMBERLAND
Newcastle
CUMBERLAND
Inglewood Forest
DURHAM
WESTMORLAND
Furness
NORTH RIDING
Goathland
North York Moors
Pickering
Craven
YORKS
WEST RIDING
York
EAST RIDING
LANCS
Ashton-under-Lyne
Axholme
LINDSEY
Linwood
LINCS
Wirral
FLINT
Chester
DENBIGH
CHESHIRE
DERBY
Birkland
Clipston Park
Potterhanworth
Newcastle-under-Lyme
Sherwood Forest
NOTTS
KESTEVEN
HOLLAND
Shown at larger scale
STAFFS
Bunny Old Wood
SALOP
Needwood Forest
Charnwood
Bradgate P.
RUTLAND
NORFOLK
Wroxeter
Cannock Chase
Launde Park W.
Barnsdale Park
Condover
Pitchford
Sutton Coldfield Park
LEICS
Gretton
Corby
ISLE OF ELY
Stiperstones
Shustoke
Rockingham Forest
WALES
Wyre Forest
Wolverley
Arden
HUNTS
Shrawley Wood
NORTHANTS
WEST SUFFOLK
EAST SUFFOLK
Daventry
Leominster
Droitwich
WARWICK
Yardley Chase
CAMBS
HEREFORD
WORCS
Salcey Forest
BEDS
Hereford
Whittlewood Forest
NORTH ESSEX
Whaddon Chase
GLOUCS
OXON
BUCKS
HERTS
Forest of Dean
Gloucester
Wychwood Forest
Shotover Forest
Aylesbury
Frithsden Copses and Beeches
Haresfield
Berkhamsted
MONMOUTH
Ducklington
Wendover
Swansea
2
1
Penn
SOUTH ESSEX
3
4
Chilterns
Beaconsfield
Braydon Forest
Burnham Beeches
MIDDLESEX
1 Minchinhampton
2 Brackenbury Ditches
3 Tortworth
4 Westridge Wood
Bristol
Chippenham Forest
BERKS
Savernake Forest
Windsor Forest
SURREY
Melsham Forest
WILTS
Guildford Park
KENT
Wye Valley
Mendips
Cheddar Wood
Stockton Wood
Grovely Forest
Kingsclere
Farnham
King's Wood
Tonbridge
Swingfield Minnis
Asham Wood
Great Ridge
Amesbury
HANTS
Alice Holt Forest
Tenterden
Exmoor
SOMERSET
Somerset Levels
Glastonbury
Selwood F.
Semley
Clarendon F. & P.
Salisbury
Kirdford
Eridge Park
Nap Wood
Calais
Meon
The Mens
Ashdown F.
Battle
Dungeness
Neroche Forest
Ilminster
Melchet Forest
Southampton
Cranbourne Chase
Lyndhurst
Bere Forest
SUSSEX
Gillingham Forest
New Forest
Beaulieu
DEVON
Felpham
DORSET
Poole Harbour
Wistman's Wood
ISLE OF WIGHT
Dartmoor
Weymouth
Boconnoc Park
CORNWALL
Principal places mentioned in text:
Helford River
Woods
Wood–pastures (extant or former)
Other places
Names of districts are in italics
Boundary between Highland and Lowland Zones as used in this book
Lizard Peninsula
Devil's Frying-pan Wood